BUTTERWORTHS RULES C

CIVIL COURT PRACTICE

BUTTERWORTHS RULES OF COURT

CIVIL COURT PRACTICE

Editor
District Judge R Greenslade

Foreword by Lord Woolf

Text preparation
Henrietta Chapman, BA (Hons)
Annette Charak, BA, LLB, Solicitor

Rules of the Supreme Court
County Court Rules

BUTTERWORTHS
LONDON, DUBLIN, EDINBURGH
1994

United Kingdom	Butterworth & Co (Publishers) Ltd, Halsbury House, 35 Chancery Lane, LONDON WC2A 1EL and 4 Hill Street, EDINBURGH EH2 3JZ
Australia	Butterworths, SYDNEY, MELBOURNE, BRISBANE, ADELAIDE, PERTH, CANBERRA and HOBART
Canada	Butterworth Canada Ltd, TORONTO and VANCOUVER
Ireland	Butterworth (Ireland) Ltd, DUBLIN
Malaysia	Malayan Law Journal Sdn Bhd, KUALA LUMPUR
New Zealand	Butterworths of New Zealand Ltd, WELLINGTON and AUCKLAND
Puerto Rico	Butterworth of Puerto Rico, Inc, SAN JUAN
Singapore	Butterworths Asia, SINGAPORE
South Africa	Butterworths Publishers (Pty) Ltd, DURBAN
USA	Butterworth Legal Publishers, CARLSBAD, California; SALEM, New Hampshire

A CIP catalogue record for this book is available from the British Library.

ISBN 0 406 04930 0

ISBN Complete Series 0 406 04929 7

Printed and bound in Great Britain by Mackays of Chatham plc, Kent

∞ This text paper meets the requirements of ISO 9706/1994. Information and Documentation—paper for documents—requirements for permanence.

Foreword

I am writing this foreword shortly after being asked by the Lord Chancellor to conduct an inquiry into Access to Justice. Its objective is to simplify civil procedure. The daunting nature of this task is underlined by the fact that as is pointed out in the Introduction to this book, since 1851 there have been some 58 reports on civil procedure and the organisation of the civil and criminal courts. Many of the recommendations contained in those reports have been implemented. In addition, over the years without waiting for yet another report sensible improvements have been made to individual County and High Court rules. An immense amount of effort has been devoted to trying to make our civil procedure as efficient as possible. However, despite all this effort our civil procedure remains highly technical and extremely complex and above all expensive.

The strength of this book is that it manages to explain this complex subject in remarkably succinct terms. The text is clear and readily understandable. Anyone making use of this book will appreciate why I am grateful to the Lord Chancellor for making Judge Greenslade one of the assessors to my inquiry.

I am sure that anyone who is involved in litigation, whether in the county court or in the High Court and whether the litigation is a small claims arbitration or a heavy High Court action, will find this book a source of considerable assistance. In many situations it will provide the answer which is needed. In others it will provide a useful guide as to where to look in the County Court or Supreme Court Practice for the more detailed information if this is required.

Unless you have, I am not sure whether it is the good fortune or misfortune to be an extremely experienced litigator, this book will rapidly become a trusted and valued friend.

Lord Woolf
June 1994

Contents

CONCISE SUBJECT GUIDE TO PRINCIPAL RULES

	RSC	CCR
DAMAGES		
assessment	**37**, 1–6	**22**, 6
interim	**29**, 9–18	**13**, 12 and as RSC
provisional	**37**, 7–10	**22**, 6A
DISCONTINUANCE		
costs	**62**, 5(3)	**18**, 2
effect of	**21**, 4	**18**, 2
leave	**21**, 3	—
without leave	**21**, 2	**18**, 1
DISCOVERY		
affidavit	**24**, 5	**14**, 1
automatic	**24**, 2; **25**, 8	**17**, 11(3)(a)
copy documents	**24**, 11A	**14**, 5A
disclosure	**24**, 11	**14**, 5
documents referred to in pleadings	**24**, 10	**14**, 4
enforcement	**24**, 16	**14**, 10
further and better	**24**, 3	**14**, 2
inspection	**24**, 9, 10	**14**, 3
lists	**24**, 5	**14**, 1
'necessary'	**24**, 8, 13	**14**, 8
pre-action and third party	**24**, 7A; **62**, 6(9)	as RSC (**13**, 7)
specific	**24**, 7	**14**, 2
ENFORCEMENT		
attachment of earnings	—	**27**
charging order	**50**	**31**
partnership	**81**, 10	—
committal	**45**, 5; **52**	**29**
equitable execution	**51**	**32**
execution against goods	**47**	**26**, 1–15
garnishee	**49**	**30**
oral examination	**48**, 1	**25**, 3, 4
receiver	**51**	**32**
recovery of goods	**45**, 4	**26**, 16
recovery of land	**45**, 3	**26**, 17
sequestration	**45**, 5, **46**, 5	—
EVIDENCE		
admissions	**27**, 1	**20**, 1
affidavit	**41**	**20**, 6, 7
court expert	**40**	—
expert	**25**, 8; **38**, 35–44	**20**, 27, 28; **17**, 11
hearsay	**38**, 21–34	**20**, 14–26
notice to admit documents	**27**, 5; **62**, 6(8)	**20**, 3
notice to admit facts	**27**, 2; **62**, 6(7)	**20**, 2

INTRODUCTION

RULES OF COURT

There are two sets of rules, namely the Rules of the Supreme Court 1965 (RSC) which control procedure in the High Court, and the County Court Rules 1981 (CCR) which govern procedure in the county courts. These rules are often virtually or actually identical, but in many cases they differ, and the detailed nature of the differences can cause confusion. This complexity, and also the apparently ever-increasing bulk of the rules, is subject to continual criticism in the area of civil justice. When they were first made the extent of the RSC was 382 pages; and that of the CCR was 190 pages: both have increased substantially since then.

The rules however, only reflect the practice of the two court systems, which has evolved over the years, adapting to meet changes not only in society and law but in technology. The rules have been altered to indicate and encourage changes in practice. They have been changed following criticism in the courts when omissions and defects have been revealed. They have been subject to constant scrutiny by the courts and much case law has evolved over the years. When criticism is made of the bulk of the rules reference is made usually not to the rules themselves but to the two practice books, the *Supreme Court Practice* ('The White Book') and the *County Court Practice* ('The Green Book'), the former published biennially and the latter annually. The bulk of these two practitioner's works is due not to the rules themselves but by the need for a commentary on them which takes account of the rapidly developing case law that they have brought about. In parentheses it is worth mentioning that the current edition of the *County Court Practice* comprises 2,099 pages, the 1937 edition comprised 3,358, although it is fair to say that the content of the latter was much increased by the inclusion of the Workmen's Compensation Acts occupying approximately 380 pages.

The main problem lies in the complexities of procedures within the High Court and county court. The Report of the Civil Justice Review records that—

> 'since 1851 there have been some 58 reports on civil procedure and on the organisation of the civil and criminal courts. Two of these made a wide-scale and lasting impact. The first, in 1869, was the first report of the Royal Commission on the Judicature which proposed and achieved the consolidation into one Supreme Court the (seven) re-existing separate courts ... the second report to achieve major change on a similar scale was not published till 100 years later in 1969 ... the Beeching Report ... the results of the remaining 56 reports fell into three broad categories: worthwhile improvements within a limited frame; one or two particular achievements mainly of a procedural nature; and (in many cases) early or ultimate futility'.

The Report of the Civil Justice Review itself made many detailed recommendations for improving the work of the civil courts. It failed to recommend the establishment of a single civil court on the model of the Crown Court established as a result of the Beeching Report. The Beeching Report did seek to re-open the issue of a single court 'but reluctantly concluded that it did not have the resources with which to work up proposals to establish a single civil court or to keep two courts and have a single point of entry.'

The Report of the Civil Justice Review, while not upholding the case for a single court, made some movement towards the selective introduction of a single point of entry at county court level. This recommendation has, as yet, only been applied to personal injury cases not exceeding £50,000. This means that large numbers of very small debt claims are commenced in the High Court, actions which often, if commenced in the county court and defended, would be heard by county court arbitration within a few weeks of the issue of proceedings.

The Report also recommended that there should be a common core of rules between the High Court and the county court. Though many of the recommendations of the Civil Justice Review have now been implemented, this one has not.

A combined working party of the Bar Council and the Law Society produced a report in June 1993 entitled 'Civil Justice on Trial — the Case for Change' (The Heilbron/Hodge Report). The report falls short of recommending a single Civil Court, but suggests an amalgamation of the Queen's Bench and Chancery Divisions of the High Court and the organisation of the High Court Judges of those Divisions into specialist lists. It recommends that procedural rules in the High Court should be standardised and simplified and all unnecessary distinctions removed, and further that there should be a 'uniform Rule Book for the High Court and county court'.

In response to the recommendations in the Report of the Civil Justice Review and, no doubt, in part, to those of the Heilbron/Hodge report, the Lord Chancellor has recently announced the establishment of a review team under Lord Woolf with the aim of producing a combined set of rules for the High Court and county court and to review civil procedure generally. This team is expected to report within two years.

THE RULES

As stated above, the present rules are the Rules of the Supreme Court 1965 (RSC) and the County Court Rules 1981 (CCR). Both sets of rules are made by Rules Committees. In the case of the RSC the Rule Committee was set up under the Supreme Court Act 1981, ss 84, 85, 87, and in the case of the county court under the County Courts Act 1984, s 75. In the case of the Supreme Court the statutory powers are exercisable by the Lord Chancellor and any four or more members of the Committee. The work of the Rule Committee is in practice informed by recommendations of the Supreme Court Procedure Committee, a semi-official body representing the judiciary and court users. In the case of the county court the rules are made by the committee but are subject to the approval of the Lord Chancellor. Both rules take effect when made as statutory instruments.

There are many differences between the two sets of rules in terms of wording as well as substance. As an example of the latter the rules relating to irregularity can be cited (an example given to me by Michael Kron of the Lord Chancellor's Department).

The High Court rule is as follows—

'ORDER 2
EFFECT OF NON-COMPLIANCE

Order 2, r 1 Non-compliance with rules

(1) Where, in beginning or purporting to begin any proceedings or at any stage in the course of or in connection with any proceedings, there has, by reason of any thing done or left undone, been a failure to comply with the requirements of these rules, whether in respect of time, place, manner, form or content or in any other respect, the failure shall be treated as an irregularity and shall not nullify the proceedings, any step taken in the proceedings, or any document, judgment or order therein.

(2) Subject to paragraph (3), the Court may, on the ground that there has been such a failure as is mentioned in paragraph (1), and on such terms as to costs or otherwise as it thinks just, set aside either wholly or in part the proceedings in which the failure occurred, any step taken in those proceedings or any document, judgment or order therein or exercise its powers under these rules to allow such amendments (if any) to be made and to make such order (if any) dealing with the proceedings generally as it thinks fit.

(3) The Court shall not wholly set aside any proceedings or the writ or other originating process by which they were begun on the ground that the proceedings were required by any of these rules to be begun by an originating process other than the one employed.

Order 2, r 2 Application to set aside for irregularity

(1) An application to set aside for irregularity any proceedings, any step taken in any proceedings or any document, judgment or order therein shall not be allowed unless it is made within a reasonable time and before the party applying has taken any fresh step after becoming aware of the irregularity.

(2) An application under this rule may be made by summons or motion and the grounds of objection must be stated in the summons or notice of motion.'

In the county court the same situation is met by CCR Order 37, r 5, viz,—

Order 37 r 5 Non-compliance with rules

(1) Where there has been a failure to comply with requirement of the rules, the failure shall be treated as an irregularity and shall not nullify the proceedings, but the court may set aside the proceedings wholly or in part or exercise its powers under these rules to allow any such amendments and to give any such directions as it thinks fit.

(2) No application to set aside any proceedings for irregularity shall be granted unless made within a reasonable time, nor if the party applying has taken step in the proceedings after knowledge of the irregularity.

(3) Where any such application is made, the grounds of objection shall be stated in the notice.

(4) The expression 'proceedings' in paragraph (1), and where it first occurs in paragraph (2), includes any step taken in the proceedings and any document, judgment or order therein.'

Both examples may be compared with Order LIX of the 1873 Rules of the (then recently combined) Supreme Court, viz—

'Non-compliance with any of these Rules shall not render the proceedings in any action void unless the Court or a Judge shall so direct, but any such proceedings may be set aside either wholly or in part as irregular, or amended, or otherwise dealt with in such manner and upon such terms as the Court or Judge shall think fit'

While the county court rule, in this case, has advantages of brevity and (dare one say) elegance over the High Court rule, one may ask whether either rule has any advantage over the shorter rule of 1873.

There are differences in logic between the two sets of rules. For example all matters relating to partnerships are dealt with in the High Court by RSC Order 81. In the county court provisions relating to partnerships are dealt with under subject matter, eg, proceedings in the name of a firm and disclosure of partners names (CCR Order 5, r 9), service (CCR Order 7, r 13), and enforcement (CCR Order 25, r 9). Is it better to deal with all matters relating to service in one rule, or all matters relating to partnerships in one rule?

There is clearly a need for a common set of rules dealing with procedures for the bulk of general litigation with additional specialist 'bolt on' rules where required. Such rules should so far as possible be self-sufficient and should be phrased as simply and directly as possible with the use of few (if any) terms of art. It may well be important that the rules should include an overriding principle of interpretation to provide a sense of uniformity of purpose, similar to that provided by the statutory objective for the provision of legal services in the Courts and Legal Services Act 1990, s 17.

ALTERNATIVE DISPUTE RESOLUTION

Another relatively new factor in England and Wales, though well known in other common law jurisdictions, is the gradual growth of alternative dispute resolution in the form of mediation. While, save for county court arbitration, there is no formal provision in the RSC for either arbitration or mediation as part of, or ancillary to, the court process, the role of alternative dispute resolution has been recognised in commercial disputes and in family law. The county court arbitration system — often misleadingly referred to as 'the small claims court' — provides the only form of alternative dispute resolution within the court structure and now deals reasonably quickly and cheaply with approaching (if not exceeding) 100,000 cases a year. A number of experiments in the use of pre-trial reviews as a form of 'settlement conference' have been made but unfortunately none have been properly monitored so that the advantages cannot be proved.

There is a clear need to consider the interface between court procedures and alternative dispute resolution. Should such forms of dispute resolution be provided by the court or as ancillary to the court process? Should there be information about 'referring out' suitable cases for mediation or arbitration, and encouragement to the courts to do so? Much can be learned from a study of the place of arbitration and mediation in other common law systems, particularly that of Australia.

TOPICAL GUIDE TO THE RULES

The following guide is not intended to be a comprehensive guide to the Civil Rules but merely a broad outline of the effect of certain of the main core rules dealing primarily with the conduct of an action prior to trial. It is intended to point out some of the differences between the High Court and the county court procedures.

JURISDICTION

The jurisdiction of the High Court is unlimited subject to a number of specific instances in which Statute has given the county court an exclusive jurisdiction. The principal instances of the county court's exclusive jurisdiction are—

    (1) Actions for personal injury not exceeding £50,000 (High Court and County Court Jurisdiction Order 1991, art 5).

    (2) Actions for possession of premises protected by the Rent Act 1977 (Rent Act 1977, s 141).

    (3) An application to reopen an extortionate regulated credit agreement or a fixed-sum credit or running credit account (Consumer Credit Act 1974, s 139(5)).

    (4) Actions to enforce a regulated agreement, any security relating to it or to enforce any linked transaction against the debtor or hirer or his relative (Consumer Credit Act 1974, s 141(1)).

Although the High Court has jurisdiction, a plaintiff commencing proceedings in the High Court will not be entitled to his costs in the following circumstances—

    (1) Actions for possession of secure tenancies under the Housing Act 1985 (Housing Act 1985, s 110(3)).

    (2) Actions for possession of premises let under an assured tenancy under the Housing Act 1988 (Housing Act 1988, s 40(4) (costs limited to those which would have been recoverable in the county court)).

Where an action is wrongly brought in the High Court it may be transferred to the county court. However where the action was wrongly so brought and the court is satisfied that the plaintiff knew or ought to have known of that requirement it *may* order the proceedings to be struck out. (NB this power is permissive and not mandatory, see *Restick v Crickmore* [1994] 2 All ER 112, [1994] 1 WLR 420, CA). Furthermore the court may impose a costs sanction under the Supreme Court Act 1981, s 51(8)–(12) although there is no reported instance of this power having been exercised.

The jurisdiction of the county court is created by Statute and was severely restricted until 1991. However, as a result of amendments made by the Courts and Legal Services Act 1990 the *common law* jurisdiction of the county court is, in theory at least, unlimited subject to specific exceptions in the County Courts Act 1984, s 15, namely—

(1) any action in which the title to any toll, fair, market or franchise is in question, and

(2) any action for libel or slander.

This theoretically unlimited jurisdiction is in practice significantly curtailed by the provisions of the High Court and County Court Jurisdiction Order 1991, which provides for a general presumption that where the 'value' of an action exceeds £50,000 it shall be transferred to, and tried by, the High Court.

The *Equity* jurisdiction of the county court is far more restricted. The detailed provisions are to be found in the County Courts Act 1984, ss 23–25, 32, 33 and in the Schedule to the High Court and County Court Jurisdiction Order 1991. In general the county court jurisdiction is limited to cases where the value does not exceed £35,000, although there is unlimited jurisdiction under the Inheritance (Provision for Family and Dependants) Act 1975 and under certain sections of the Law of Property Act 1925, primarily s 30. In certain equity proceedings it may be possible to consent to the county court having jurisdiction beyond the £35,000 limit (County Courts Act 1984, s 24).

In addition, there are certain restrictions on the power of the county court (other than in family proceedings) to make a *Mareva* injunction or an *Anton Piller* order (County Court Remedies Regulations 1991)). There are also some restrictions on the enforcement of High Court judgments of less than £2,000 by execution against goods (High Court and County Court Jurisdiction Order 1991, art 8) and less than £5,000 by charging order (Charging Orders Act 1979, s 1(2)). Such enforcement must take place in the county court. On the other hand where there is a county court judgment exceeding £5,000 it may only be enforced by execution against goods in the High Court (High Court and County Court Jurisdiction Order 1991, art 8).

Finally, within its statutory jurisdiction, a county court has all the powers of the High Court (except the power to make a *Mareva* or an *Anton Piller* order). Thus it is now possible to issue proceedings for an injunction without seeking other relief.

TIME

The rules of both the High Court and the county court make provision for various time limits, and orders of either court may also require acts to be done within particular times. The rules deal with the computation of time and for applications to extend time before or after that time has elapsed.

In the High Court RSC Order 3 deals with time, with r 2 being probably the most important rule as to the computation of time. Rule 2(2) and (3) apply where the order (or rule) requires an act to be done within a particular period before or after a particular date. The rules exclude that date from the computation of time. Where the rule or order requires an act to be done a number of 'clear days' before or after a specified date, both that date and the date of performance are excluded (r 2(4)).

In any order or rule requiring an act to be done within a period of less than seven days, Saturdays, Sundays, Good Friday, Christmas Day and Bank Holidays are excluded (r 2(5)).

If any act has to be done at a court office and the period expires on a day when the court office is not open the time is extended to the next day on which the court office is open (RSC Order 3, r 4).

The county court rules (CCR Order 1, r 9) are simpler but unfortunately do not always have the same effect. Where an order is made for an act to be done within a period after or before a certain date, the date before or after which the act is to be done and the date of performance are both excluded in all cases whether or not the words 'clear days' are used. If a period expires on any day on which the court office is not open and *for that reason* the act cannot be performed, time is extended until the next day.

The most significant difference however, is that it is only where a period of three days or less is allowed or ordered that days on which the court office is not open are excluded. This can make significant differences which are most obvious in situations where a summary possession order is sought. The effect of the very short notice required for a hearing will often be different in the High Court and the county court.

The rules as to extension of time (RSC Order 3, r 5, CCR Order 13, r 5) differ in detail but both allow the court in a proper case to extend any time limit even though the time has already expired. The county court rule has advantages of brevity but it is subject to any other provision which prevents extension of time. Thus, in the county court, where one year has elapsed from the date of service of the summons and either no defence, admission etc has been served and judgment has not been entered, or an admission has been delivered and no notice of acceptance or non-acceptance has been received by the court, an action is automatically struck out under CCR Order 9, r 10. In such a case time may not be extended as CCR Order 13, r 4 is specifically excluded. On the other hand it has been held that time for applying for a date to be fixed for trial under CCR Order 17, r 11(9) may be extended (and the action restored) even though the action has been 'automatically struck out' pursuant to that rule: *Rastin v British Steel* [1994] 144 NLJ 425, Times 18 February, CA.

Though time may be extended after a period has expired such an extension is in the discretion of the court. Clear guidelines were laid down in *Rastin v British Steel* (above) as to the manner in which the power to extend time for applying for a date to be fixed in the county court after automatic striking out should be exercised. In *Samuels v Linzi Dresses Ltd* [1981] 1 QB 115, [1980] 1 All ER 803, CA it was said that while the court had power to extend time for compliance with an 'unless order' after it had expired, this power was to be exercised cautiously and with due regard to the principle that orders were made to be obeyed.

PARTIES

Both RSC and CCR make detailed provisions relating to parties, as to joinder, nonjoinder, capacity, service and enforcement.

These include provisions as to the joinder of parties and the effect of misjoinder or nonjoinder (RSC Order 15, rr 4, 6, CCR Order 5, rr 2, 4), and provision for amendment of pleadings (inter alia) to join parties (RSC Order 20, CCR Order 15, r 11). Provision is also made for joinder of causes of actions (RSC Order 15, r 1, CCR Order 5, r 1) and for consolidation of separate actions (RSC Order 4, r 9, CCR Order 13, r 9). Where the joinder of separate causes of actions or parties causes embarrassment provision is made for separate trials (RSC 15, r 5,

CCR Order 5, r 3). The rules also enable notice to be given to non-parties of actions which concern them and enable them to become parties. This is particularly the case with regard to possession proceedings (RSC Order 15, r 10, Order 45, r 3, Order 113, r 5; CCR Order 7, r 15A, Order 15, r 3, Order 24, r 4, Order 26, r 17). Where it appears to the court that a deceased person had an interest in the proceedings RSC Order 15, r 15 (CCR Order 5, r 7) makes provision for the court to appoint a representative of the estate for the purpose of the proceedings.

The rules also include various provisions relating to proceedings against estates including the ability to sue 'the personal representatives' or to appoint a person to represent the estate (RSC Order 15, rr 6A–9, CCR Order 5, rr 7, 8, 11, 12).

In addition the rules make provision for partnerships, their capacity to sue and to be sued in the firm name (RSC Order 81, r 1, CCR Order 5, r 9), for service of proceedings upon them (RSC Order 81, r 3, CCR Order 7, r 13) and for the enforcement of judgments against them (RSC Order 81, rr 5, 7, 10, CCR Order 25, r 9 and Order 30, r 4).

Proceedings by or against persons under a disability (minors or mental patients) will require the appointment of a 'next friend' (for a plaintiff) or a 'guardian ad litem' (for any other party). There are also special provisions relating to the need to approve and compromise by a person under disability (RSC Order 80, CCR Order 10).

Finally the county court (only) has a useful provision for service of a summons on a limited company not only on its registered office but 'at any place of business of the company which has some real connection with the cause or matter' (CCR Order 7, r 14). This often overlooked rule is useful in avoiding, or at least delaying, potentially harmful consequences of the automatic transfer provisions.

ORIGINATING PROCESS

It is in the area of originating process that the rules of the High Court and the county court differ most dramatically.

In the High Court the majority of proceedings are commenced by the issue of a writ of summons or originating summons. In the county court the normal originating process is either a summons or originating application. There are relatively few differences between originating summonses and applications but many more between the writ of summons and the county court summons.

In the High Court the writ of summons (RSC Order 6) is a document prepared and served by the plaintiff, although before it has any effect it must be sealed by the court. It need not be — though it frequently is — accompanied by or incorporate a statement of claim. Its initial purpose is to require the filing of an acknowledgment of service indicating whether or not the action is to be defended. Failure to serve an acknowledgment giving notice of intention to defend can result in summary judgment upon proof of service (RSC Order 13). If a statement of claim is incorporated in or accompanies the writ, and notice of intention to defend has been given, a defence must be served within the time prescribed by RSC Order 19.

In the county court the basic procedure under CCR Order 3, r 3 is for the summons to be prepared by the court upon information provided by the plaintiff in a request for issue of a summons. The particulars of claim (equivalent to the statement of claim in the High Court) is attached to the summons which is then served by the court which will give notice to the plaintiff of the date of service. The county court has no 'acknowledgment of service' stage; the defendant being required to file his defence within 14 days of the deemed date of service of the summons. Failure to do so may result in a default judgment.

In fact the county court procedure is more varied as a result of relatively recent rule changes. It is now common for a combined form of request and summons (N 202) to be completed by the plaintiff for sealing by the court (CCR Order 3, r 3(1A), (1B)) and this document frequently incorporates brief particulars of claim. While postal service by the court applies in the majority of cases, provision is made for the plaintiff to effect postal service of the summons in personal injury cases.

Both the High Court rules and the county court rules make provision for proceedings to be commenced by petition, and the county court also makes provision for appeals against certain decisions of statutory authorities.

In the county court recent rule changes have instituted a new 'accelerated procedure' for certain Housing Act assured tenancies. Such proceedings are commenced by an application to which the normal rules relating to summonses and originating applications do not apply. The application incorporates an affidavit by the plaintiff.

Any originating process is initially valid for a period of four months (or, in the case of a writ for which leave to serve out of the jurisdiction is required, six months) (RSC Order 6, r 8, CCR Order 8, r 20). Such period may be extended by the court (RSC Order 6, r 8(2), (2A), CCR Order 8, r 20(2), (3)). However the courts have taken a very restrictive view of the circumstances in which the validity of a writ may be extended. The principal authorities are *Kleinwort Benson Ltd v Barbrak Ltd,* (The Myrto No 3) [1987] 1 AC 576, [1987] 2 All ER 289, [1987] 1 WLR 1053, [1987] 2 Lloyd's Rep 1, HL and *Waddon v Whitecroft Scovell Ltd* [1988] 1 All ER 996, [1988] 1 WLR 309, HL. These cases stressed the duty of the plaintiff to serve the writ promptly and the requirement that there must always be 'good reason' for the extension. Furthermore the application for extension must be made while the writ is valid (including any extension of its validity) or within four or six months (as the case may be) of the date on which its validity expired. Two or more extensions may not be granted: *Chappell v Cooper* [1980] 2 All ER 463, [1980] 1 WLR 958, CA.

While the principles laid down in *Kleinwort Benson* are clearly reasonable in the High Court, where the plaintiff has the responsibility of serving the writ, they are less easy to apply in the county court where it is normally the court which will have failed to serve the summons timeously. None the less the same principles apply: *Singh (Joginder) v Duport Harper Foundries Ltd* (1993) Times, 15 November, CA. However in exceptional circumstances, at least where it is the court that fails to serve timeously, an application may be made under CCR Order 13, r 4 for an extension of time and under CCR Order 37, r 5 for the irregularity to be waived as was done in *Ward-Lee v Lineham* [1993] 2 All ER 1006, [1993] 1 WLR 754, CA.

Application for an extension of the validity of the writ or summons, whether in the High Court or the county court, is normally made ex parte by affidavit showing the 'good reasons' or, where appropriate, that it is the court which has delayed in serving the summons without fault by the plaintiff. Any order made ex parte may be challenged by an application on notice to set aside the order and the service of the writ or summons as irregular.

POINT OF ISSUE, TRANSFER, CONSOLIDATION

Point of issue

The High Court is a single court and the majority of proceedings can be issued in the Central Office or in any district registry. The main exceptions to this rule are probate proceedings, which cannot be issued out of a district registry, (RSC Order 76, r 2) and a number of Chancery proceedings (primarily those commenced by originating summons), which may only be issued in the Central Office or in one of the 'Chancery District Registries' at Birmingham, Bristol, Cardiff, Leeds, Liverpool, Manchester, Newcastle-upon-Tyne and Preston.

Strictly speaking there is no single county court but a number of county courts with local jurisdictions. In the past there were strict rules as to the court in which particular proceedings could be commenced but default actions may now be brought in any county court. Other actions may be brought in the court for the district in which a defendant resides or in which the cause of action arose (CCR Order 4, r 2). There are specific provisions for venue in the case of proceedings relating to land (CCR Order 4, r 3), proceedings under the Settled Land Act 1925, the Trustee Act 1925 and for the administration of the estate of a deceased person (r 4), for partnership proceedings (r 5) and for proceedings for wrongful interference with goods (r 6). Originating applications may be issued in the court in whose district one of the respondents resides or carries on business or where the subject matter of the proceedings is situated. If there is no respondent then the proceedings may be issued in the court in which the applicant (or one of them) resides or carries on business (CCR Order 4, r 8).

Transfer

Although in the majority of cases a plaintiff may select the forum in which he commences proceedings, both sets of rules make provision for a (more or less) automatic right of transfer to a more appropriate venue.

If a writ is issued out of a district registry it should be indorsed with a statement that the cause of action arose wholly or in part in a place in the district of that registry (RSC Order 6, r 4). A defendant not residing or carrying on business in the district of that registry may apply in his acknowledgment of service for an order that the action be transferred to some other district registry or to the Royal Courts of Justice. Where such application is made notice is given by the court to the plaintiff, who has eight days in which to object. If the plaintiff objects the court will fix an appointment to consider transfer (RSC Order 4, r 5(3)). If no objections are fixed, the action is automatically transferred.

A similar procedure applies when a writ issued in a Chancery district registry is not indorsed with a statement that the cause of action arose in the circuit in which the Chancery registry is situated (RSC Order 6, r 5, Order 4, r 5(3A)).

In addition to these powers of transfer there is a general power to apply to transfer from one district registry (or the Central Office) to another district registry or the Central Office (RSC Order 4, r 5 (4)–(6)) or to a county court (RSC Order 107, r 2, CCR Order 16, r 6). A county court action may be transferred to another county court (CCR Order 16, r 1) or to the High Court (CCR Order 16, r 9; see also RSC Order 78).

Consolidation

Both the RSC (Order 4, r 9) and CCR (Order 13, r 11) make provision for the consolidation of two or more actions where—

(1) some common question of law or fact arises,

(2) the rights to relief are in respect of or arose out of the same transaction or series of transactions,

(3) that for some other reason it is desirable to consolidate.

In the county court the order may be made of the court's own motion but generally one party will apply by summons or notice of application to consolidate. It is clearly desirable that such an application is made as early as possible. Appropriate directions will be given if the actions are consolidated. In the High Court the power to consolidate is limited to actions in the same division and in the county court it is limited to actions in the same court. In the county court where two actions proceed in different courts it may therefore be necessary to apply first to transfer one or more actions to another court so that all are in the same court.

SERVICE

This is an area where the rules are complex although the majority of court documents are now served through the post. There are differences between the rules relating to service of originating process and other documents. Service of originating process in the county court is commonly effected by the court; service out of the jurisdiction may in many cases now be effected without leave, but where service is to be effected in a non-convention country leave may be required. Furthermore recent rule changes have taken into account Document Exchange systems and the use of FAX.

There is an essential difference between the High Court and the county court so far as service of originating process is concerned. In the county court, with the exception of personal injury cases (CCR Order 7, r 10A), postal service can only be effected by the court, and this is normal practice unless the plaintiff specifically asks to serve personally. In the High Court postal service is by the plaintiff.

Personal service of any document is effected by leaving a copy of the document with the person to be served (RSC Order 65, r 2) or delivering it to such person (CCR Order 7, r 1(1), r 10(1)). These provisions do not apply where 'provision is ... otherwise made by any enactment' — in particular service upon a company where the provisions of the Companies Act 1985, s 725 apply.

Postal service is effected in the High Court by the plaintiff posting a sealed copy of the originating process together with acknowledgment of service by pre-paid first class post or by placing them through the letter box (RSC Order 10, r 1(2)). Service is deemed to be effected on the seventh day after posting or placing the documents through the letter box. This time covers both the time taken in the post and also a reasonable time for the writ to come to the attention of the defendant. Service must be at an address at which the defendant has some continuing presence. It is not sufficient to serve on an address with which he has a direct and immediate connection if he may never be present there: *Willowgreen Ltd v Smithers* [1994] 2 All ER 533, CA. Though service is deemed to be effected on the seventh day the plaintiff can substitute an earlier date for service if he is able to show that the writ (or summons) came to the defendant's attention on an earlier date: *Hodgson v Hart District Council* [1986] 1 All ER 400, [1986] 1 WLR 317, CA.

No evidence of service is required where the defendant files an acknowledgment of service. In other cases the plaintiff seeking a default judgment will need to prove service by an affidavit. The affidavit must, in addition to proving the means of service, contain a statement that in the opinion of the deponent the writ or other originating process will have come to the attention of the defendant within seven days after posting or placing the originating process through the letter box and in the case of postal service that the writ has not been returned undelivered (RSC Order 10, r 1 (3)(b)).

In the county court the same general principles apply although there is no provision for service through the letter box. Service is by an officer of the court and is proved by a certificate of that officer under the County Courts Act 1984, s 133. The evidence of service in the county court is less satisfactory than that in the High Court in that there is no requirement for evidence that the summons will have come to the defendant's attention within seven days of the date of posting, merely that the court staff have posted the summons to the address for service provided by the plaintiff. However, judgments may be set aside somewhat more easily in the county court and a defendant could rely on *Willowgreen Ltd v Smithers* (above) if service was at an address other than his place of residence or business.

In neither the High Court or the county court may service of originating process be effected by FAX at present. However it might be possible to obtain an order for substituted service by FAX.

Both the High Court (RSC Order 10, r 4) and the county court (CCR Order 7, r 15) make special provision for service of possession proceedings when the prescribed method is not practicable.

If there has been pre-issue correspondence with a solicitor acting for the defendant who is prepared to accept service of the originating process, service may be proved in the High Court by the solicitor indorsing a statement on the writ that he accepts service on behalf of the defendant, and service is deemed to be effected on the date the indorsement is made. (RSC Order 10, r 1 (4)). In the county court the procedure differs slightly in that the solicitor is required to give a certificate and to give an address for service (CCR Order 7, r 11). There is no reason why the 'certificate' should not be indorsed on the summons.

Service out of jurisdiction

As a general rule service of a writ or summons may only be effected outside England and Wales where leave is given. This is subject to the substantial exception that where the defendant is resident in a 'convention' country service may in many cases be effected abroad (including Scotland and Northern Ireland) without leave. This is provided that the request for issue of a summons (in the case of the county court), or the writ or summons, (in the case of both the High Court and the county court), is indorsed with a statement that the claim is one which by virtue of the Civil Jurisdiction and Judgments Act 1982 the court has power to hear and determine (RSC Order 6, r 7(1)(b), CCR Order 3, r 3 (5)–(8)). In such cases the restrictions on entering judgment in default should be noted (RSC Order 13, r 7B, CCR Order 9, r 7(4).

Where leave is required to serve out of the jurisdiction an application should be made ex parte by affidavit showing that the conditions of RSC Order 11, r 1 or CCR Order 8, r 2, as the case may be, are met.

Companies

Service on a company is to be effected in accordance with the Companies Act 1985, s 287, at the registered office of the company. In the county court special provision is made enabling a summons to be served on the company at 'any place of business of the company which has some real connection with the cause or matter in issue' (CCR Order 7, r 14).

Partnerships

Service on a partnership is provided for in similar terms by RSC Order 81, r 3 and CCR Order 7, r 13. Despite the somewhat restrictive wording of the rule it has been decided that service on a person other than a partner or a person having control or management of the business but having the direct authority of a partner to accept service is good service: *Kenneth Allison Ltd v A E Limehouse and Co (a firm)* [1991] 2 AC 105, [1991] 4 All ER 500, [1991] 3 WLR 671, HL.

Service of other documents

The rules relating to service of other documents are contained in RSC Order 65 and CCR Order 7, Part 1. The detailed wording of RSC Order 65, r 5 and CCR Order 7, r 1 differs but the effect is generally similar. Service is to be effected by the party serving the document sending the same by first class post to any solicitor on the record or in the county court. There is no provision for service by the county court though this may in practice be done. If there is no solicitor on the record the document should be sent to the address given for service by the party to be served, or to—

    (1) in the case of an individual, the 'usual or last address' (High Court), or 'his last known residence' (county court),

    (2) in the case of a firm, its 'principal or last known place of business ... within the jurisdiction' (High Court) or 'last known place of business' (county court),

    (3) in the case of a body corporate in the High Court, 'the registered or principal office of the body' (there is no express provision in the county court).

Provision is made for service of documents *other* than originating process by document exchange—

    (a) in the High Court—

        (i) where the address for service includes a numbered box in a document exchange, or

        (ii) where a party in person or a solicitor has 'inscribed' on his writing paper a document exchange box number *and* the party or solicitor has not indicated in writing an unwillingness to accept service through a document exchange.

> (b) in the county court—
>
>> (i) only where a solicitor's address for service includes such a box number.

In both cases service is deemed to be effected on the second day after the day on which the document is left.

In the High Court (only) RSC Order 65, r 5(2B) makes provision for service by FAX where both parties are represented by solicitors and the recipient's solicitor has indicated that he is prepared to accept service by FAX. He is deemed to have done so if his notepaper includes a FAX number and he has not indicated in writing an unpreparedness to accept service by FAX.

There is no corresponding provision in the county court but it would appear that service by FAX can be effected in the county court upon the terms laid down in *Hastie & Jenkerson (a firm) v McMahon* [1991] 1 All ER 255, [1990] 1 WLR 1575, CA, namely that it must be proved that the document had been received in a complete and legible state by the person on whom service was to be effected.

DEFAULT JUDGMENT

Judicial statistics show that only a small percentage of actions commenced in both the High Court and the county court come to trial. Many are settled but the majority are disposed of by default judgments.

In the High Court judgment may be entered in default of notice of intention to defend an action commenced by writ (RSC Order 13), or in default of defence. In the county court default judgment may only be entered in default of defence.

High Court

In the High Court a defendant served in England and Wales has 14 days in which to give notice of intention to defend. A longer period may be allowed where service is outside the jurisdiction (RSC Order 12, r 5). Judgment in default of notice of intention to defend may be entered once the due time for giving notice of intention to defend has expired where the writ was indorsed with or accompanied by a statement of claim in the following circumstances—

> (1) where the writ is indorsed with a claim for a liquidated sum (RSC Order 13, r 1) or for unliquidated damages (RSC Order 13, r 2),
>
> (2) where the writ is indorsed with a claim for detention of goods (RSC Order 13, r 3),
>
> (3) where the writ is indorsed with a claim for possession of land (RSC Order 13, r 4),
>
> (4) where the writ is indorsed with one or more of the above claims (RSC Order 13, r 5).

Where the writ is indorsed with one or more of the above claims but also with a claim for some other form of relief the plaintiff may elect to abandon the claim(s) for which default judgment is not available and enter default judgment on the remaining claims: *Morley London Developments Ltd v Rightside Properties Ltd* (1973) 231 EG 235, CA.

As the acknowledgment of service is filed at the appropriate office of the High Court it is only necessary to prove service of the writ, unless leave is required. This will normally be done (in the absence of an indorsement showing that the defendant's solicitor has accepted service) by filing an affidavit proving service (RSC Order 13, r 7). In the case of postal service (or service through a letter box) the affidavit must state that it is the deponent's belief that the writ will have come to the attention of the defendant within seven days of service (RSC Order 10, r 1(3)(b)).

Leave is required to enter a default judgment in a number of circumstances. These include—

(1) service out of the jurisdiction where leave is not required or writ served in England and Wales on a defendant domiciled in a convention country (RSC Order 13, r 7B),

(2) where the claim is for possession of a dwellinghouse and the plaintiff cannot certify that the rateable value or the rent payable in respect of the property exceeds the Rent Act limits (RSC Order 13, r 4),

(3) action against the Crown (RSC Order 77, r 9),

(4) once notice has been served under the Consumer Credit Act 1974 (RSC Order 83, r 3),

(5) proceedings in tort between husband and wife (RSC Order 89, r 2(3)),

(6) proceedings against a foreign state (RSC Order 13, r 7A).

Where a default judgment is sought it will be a final judgment in the case of an action for a liquidated debt or for possession of land, and an interlocutory judgment in other cases (or mixed where the writ is indorsed with more than one claim for which default judgment is available).

If notice of intention to defend has been given but a defence has not been served within the 14 days allowed by the rules — or any extension of such time that may be agreed or ordered by the court — the plaintiff may enter default judgment (RSC Order 19, rr 2–7). As the defence does not have to be filed with the High Court the plaintiff will need to certify that the time allowed for service of the defence has elapsed and that no such defence has been served.

The same requirements for leave prior to entering judgment in default of defence and the same provisions as to the nature of such a judgment apply as on failure to give notice of intention to defend. However a plaintiff may apply by summons for judgment in default of defence to be entered in any claim in respect of which the rules require service of a defence in cases not covered by RSC Order 19, rr 2–6. On such a summons the court is to give such judgment as the plaintiff is entitled to on his statement of claim (RSC Order 19, r 7).

In the High Court (only) judgment may be entered in default of defence to a counterclaim (RSC Order 19, r 8, which applies rr 2–7 to this situation as if the defendant were the plaintiff and vice versa).

Judgment may not be entered against a person under a disability until a guardian ad litem is appointed (RSC Order 80, r 6).

Judgment in default may be entered for interest up to the date of judgment provided that the writ is indorsed with a claim for such interest.

County court

The situation differs in many respects in the county court. Judgment may only be entered in default of defence and there is no provision to enter judgment in default of a defence to counterclaim. Judgment may be entered in default of defence in any default action (CCR Order 9, r 6). In the case of a fixed date action the plaintiff may, in the absence of a defence, apply on notice for judgment and the court may give judgment or such directions on the application as it thinks fit (CCR Order 9, r 4A). Where the plaintiff is able to seek default judgment on a default summons he is required to certify that the defendant has not sent to him any reply to the summons. This provision was introduced to deal with 'admissions direct'. However it has the side-effect of preventing a plaintiff from entering a default judgment where the defendant has failed to file any form of defence with the court, but has none the less sent direct to the plaintiff or his solicitor—

(1) a defence,

(2) a counterclaim,

(3) an admission of the whole of the plaintiff's claim accompanied by a counterclaim or request for time to pay,

(4) an admission of part of the plaintiff's claim, or 'any other written reply of a similar kind'.

(CCR Order 9, r 6(1A))

Thus any letter indicating an intention to defend or making an offer to pay by instalments would prevent a default judgment (unless in the latter case the offer were accepted).

However judgment may not be entered in default of defence where the defendant, although not filing a defence — or even if he files an admission — files a third party notice under CCR Order 12 (CCR Order 12, r 1(7)).

Judgment may not be entered in default without leave—

(1) where the summons has been served without leave out of jurisdiction or served on a defendant in the jurisdiction but domiciled in Scotland or Northern Ireland or any other convention country (CCR Order 9, r 6(4)),

(2) in proceedings against a foreign state (CCR Order 9, r 6(3)),

(3) against the Crown (CCR Order 42, r 5(3)),

(4) where the defendant is a minor or a mental patient prior to the appointment of a guardian ad litem (CCR Order 10, r 6).

In the county court special provisions are made enabling defendants to admit the whole or part of a claim and to make a request for time to pay, commonly by instalments. Where such a request is made the plaintiff may not enter a default judgment unless he accepts the amount admitted (if the whole is not admitted) and the offer to pay. If the amount admitted is accepted but not the proposal for payment the plaintiff has the opportunity to make a counter-proposal. The offer is considered by the 'proper officer', in practice a member of the court staff, who determines the method of payment and enters judgment. If either party disagrees with that determination application can be made for the determination to be reviewed by a district judge (CCR Order 9, r 3).

SUMMARY JUDGMENT

Both the High Court and the county court provide a swift and comparatively cheap method of obtaining an early judgment where there is no genuine defence to the claim (or counterclaim as the case may be): *Home and Overseas Insurance Co Ltd v Mentor Insurance Co (UK) Ltd (in liquidation)* [1989] 3 All ER 74, [1989] 1 WLR 153, CA. The county court rules (CCR Order 9, r 14) are modelled upon or incorporate RSC Order 14.

The procedure is the same in the High Court and the county court subject to the limited differences mentioned below.

In the High Court an application for summary judgment may be and indeed normally is made before the service of a defence. The sole requirement is that notice of intention to defend has been given. In the county court the application may only be made after the filing of a defence.

In the High Court RSC Order 14A makes specific provision for the disposal of a case on a point of law. As yet RSC Order 14A has not been applied to the county court. The precise extent by which this limits the county court to determine a point of law on the application for summary judgment is not clear. It may be that in the county court it will prove difficult to do other than give leave to defend where the defendant shows a triable issue on a point of law rather than, as in the High Court, utilise RSC Order 14A to proceed to determine that point. However, a strong case can be made for saying that RSC Order 14A merely makes statutory provision for what had previously been held to be the law under RSC Order 14 (see for example *Cow v Casey* [1949] 1 KB 474, [1949]1 All ER 197, 152 EG 482, CA and *European Asian Bank AG v Punjab & Sind Bank (No 2)* [1983] 2 All ER 508, [1983] 1 WLR 642). What is clear is that whereas the High Court can proceed to determine a point of law in favour of the defendant and dismiss the action, the county court can do no more than dismiss the application for summary judgment unless there is a cross application to strike out the particulars of claim as disclosing no reasonable cause of action (CCR Order 13, r 5(1)). An application under Order 14A in the High Court is not restricted to Order 14 proceedings but may be made at any stage of the proceedings.

The summary judgment procedure does not apply to—

(1) actions where the plaintiff makes a claim for libel, slander, malicious prosecution or false imprisonment (RSC Order 14, r 1, CCR Order 9, r 14 (1)(c)),

(2) Admiralty actions in rem (county court only — CCR Order 9, r 14(1)(e)),

(3) an action for possession of land or in which title to land is in dispute (county court only — CCR Order 9, r 14(1)(b)),

(3) an action referred to arbitration under CCR Order 19, r 3 (county court only — CCR Order 9, r 14(1)(a)).

The application is to be made by summons (notice of application in the county court) which must be served on the defendant not less than 10 clear days in the High Court and seven clear days in the county court before the return date and is to be accompanied by an affidavit in support. The application will be heard in the High Court by a master or district judge unless it includes an application for an injunction, in which case it will be heard by a judge in chambers. In the county court the district judge will hear the application and may grant an injunction if the action falls within his trial jurisdiction under CCR Order 21, r 5.

The affidavit in support must—

    (a) verify the facts on which the claim (or that part of the claim to which the application relates) is based, and

    (b) state that in the deponent's belief in the High Court there is no defence to the claim or that part or, in the county court that, notwithstanding the delivery of a 'defence', there is no defence to the claim (or that part of the claim to which the application relates).

As in the county court a defence will have been served if it appears that the short form of affidavit used in the High Court is not appropriate and that the affidavit, in addition to dealing with the formal matters as required by the rule, must deal with the matters raised in the defence. If this is not done the deponent is not able to depose that there is no defence.

In both the High Court and county court the affidavit in support may contain statements of information and belief with the sources and grounds for such belief (RSC Order 14, r 2(2), CCR Order 20, r 10 (4), (5)) unless the court otherwise orders. If the affidavit is not made by the plaintiff the deponent should state that he is duly authorised by the plaintiff to make the affidavit (*Chirgwin v Russell* (1910) 27 TLR 21, CA). The affidavit should be made by a responsible person: *Hallett v Andrews* (1897) 42 SJ 68 and *Pathe Freres Cinemas Ltd v United Electric Theatres Ltd* [1914] 3 KB 1253, CA. Defects or omissions in the statement of claim cannot be cured by the affidavit: *Gold Ores Reduction Co v Parr* [1892] 2 QB 14.

If the defendant attends there will be no need to prove service formally. If he does not attend and unless clear oral evidence can be given of service it is common practice to make such order as is made conditional upon the filing of an affidavit of service.

Unless the court dismisses the application on some technical point or where it is clearly unjustified, the practical effect of the provisions of Order 14 (incorporated into the county court rules by CCR Order 9, r 14) is to place the responsibility of satisfying the court that there is an issue or question in dispute which should be tried — or that there ought for some other reason to be a trial —upon the defendant. The defendant is to show cause 'by affidavit or otherwise'. However the practice is to require an affidavit except where objection is taken on some technical ground when no affidavit is required: *Bradley v Chamberlyn* [1893] 1 QB 439. Discretion might be exercised in the special circumstances of the case, eg to take into account a letter from a defendant unable to attend court.

The normal rules as to service apply but there is no provision as to any minimum period prior to the hearing date before which any affidavit in reply is to be served. The plaintiff may well be faced with an affidavit served on him on the morning of the hearing. Where this is the case an adjournment may well be granted but the court will usually wish to consider whether the defendant's affidavit sufficiently satisfies the onus on him to show cause. If so leave to defend could be given without any adjournment.

Upon hearing an application for summary judgment the court may—

    (a) dismiss the application,

    (b) give unconditional leave to defend,

    (c) give conditional leave to defend, or

    (d) grant summary judgment.

Application dismissed

Such an order will normally be made only where there is some technical reason for dismissal. Whenever a decision is made on the merits the most appropriate course is to give unconditional leave to defend rather than dismiss the application.

Unconditional leave to defend

An application under Order 14 is not to be a trial of the action upon affidavits. In *Jones v Stone* [1894] AC 122 it was said that summary judgment should only be given in cases 'where there is no reasonable doubt that a plaintiff is entitled to judgment'. In *Home and Overseas Insurance Co Ltd v Mentor Insurance Co (UK) Ltd* (above) the purpose was said to be 'to enable a plaintiff to obtain a quick judgment where there is plainly no defence to the action', in *British and Commonwealth Holdings plc v Quadrex Holdings Inc* [1989] 1 QB 842, [1989] 3 All ER 492, [1989] 3 WLR 723 the court was said to be entitled to give summary judgment in cases where 'the defendant is unable to show that he has a real defence'. The test to be applied has been variously described but 'semantic dissection' of decisions of the courts is likely to be of little assistance. If the defendant is able to point to evidence of what the court must recognise as an arguable defence he is entitled to be given leave to defend.

The position where the defendant seeks to set up a set off or counterclaim was analysed in *United Overseas Ltd v Peter Robinson Ltd (trading as Top Shop)* 26 March, 1991, [1991] CA Transcript 297.

Conditional leave to defend

A problem arises where the defendant advances a defence which is regarded as 'improbable' or 'shadowy' — in what circumstances can the court go behind the sworn statement of the defendant? At first instance in *Paclantic Financing Co Inc v Moscow Narodny Bank Ltd* [1983] 1 WLR 1063 it was said—

> 'I can reject any evidence in Mr Wong's affidavit only if that evidence is inherently unreliable because it is self-contradictory or if it is inadmissible, or if it is irrelevant but I should not reject the defendant's evidence if, merely because of its inherent implausibility or its inconsistency with other evidence I find it incredible, or almost incredible.' The judge gave leave to defend upon payment in. An appeal was dismissed — it was submitted that the defence was 'shadowy' and the case was 'a classic case where leave to defend should be made conditional upon a payment into court, if not of the entire sum at stake, then at least of a substantial part'.

However while desisting from expressing any concluded view the court expressed its reservations about a statement 'which seeks to categorise, in exclusive terms, the circumstances in which such affidavit evidence can be rejected'. In *Famous Ltd v Ge Inn Ex Italia SRL* (1987) Times 3 August, CA the court said that it did not have to treat every Order 14 affidavit as truthful and at face value when every probability and circumstance might point to the contrary.

In *M V Yorke Motors (a firm) v Edwards* [1982] 1 WLR 444, HL the House of Lords upheld a decision of the Court of Appeal granting conditional leave to defend where it regarded the defence as 'shadowy' and had doubts as to its bona fides. It indicated that the dicta in *Jacobs v Booth's Distillery Co* (1901) 85 LT 262, HL were no longer of great value as an authority against giving conditional leave to defend. In *Yorke Motors* consideration was given to the amount of any payment in. It was accepted that to require a sum to be paid in as a condition of granting leave to defend which the defendant would never be able to pay would be a wrongful exercise of discretion because it would be tantamount to giving the plaintiff summary judgment when the court had decided that there was an issue to be tried. The mere fact that the defendant was in receipt of legal aid with a nil contribution was not of itself decisive that no such condition could be made. The court must look at the evidence before it and if on that evidence it appeared that the defendant could, even with difficulty, raise a particular sum of money it would be proper to make leave to defend conditional upon payment in. The court approved submissions by the plaintiff that where a defendant seeks to avoid or limit a financial condition by reason of his own impecuniosity the onus is upon him to put sufficient and proper evidence before the court — 'He should make full and frank disclosure'.

Relationship with interim damages

The relationship between the standard required to grant leave to defend and that for making an order for interim damages was considered in *British and Commonwealth Holdings plc v Quadrex Holdings Inc* [1989] QB 842, [1989] 3 All ER 492, CA. Where unconditional leave to defend is given the court cannot be satisfied that substantial damages will be recovered and it will not be proper to make an order for interim damages. Where conditional leave is given such an order may be made and leave may be conditional upon paying interim damages as assessed: *Andrews v Schooling* [1991] 3 All ER 723, CA.

Costs

Where an application for summary judgment is dismissed because it was not properly made or it is clear that the plaintiff knew prior to issue of the application that there was a triable issue the defendant will normally be entitled to his costs and these may be ordered to be paid forthwith (RSC Order 14, r 7).

If a part judgment or unconditional leave to defend is given, costs will normally be in the cause. If conditional leave is given costs will normally be in the cause if the condition is satisfied but the plaintiff's if not.

Where summary judgment is entered for the full amount claimed the plaintiff will be entitled to costs. Both the High Court and the county court rules make provision for fixed costs on an application for summary judgment. These will normally apply only where there is no significant opposition and the application is dealt with on the first hearing. In other cases it is more common for an order to be made for costs to be taxed, or for them to be fixed as a gross sum or assessed by the master or district judge.

Directions

Whenever leave to defend is given in the High Court the master or district judge will need to consider—

(a) whether the action should be transferred to the county court, and

(b) if not, what directions should be given.

If it is decided to transfer and no defence has been served it may be helpful to give directions for the service of a defence as the county court automatic directions will normally apply on transfer and pleadings are deemed to be closed 14 days after the date of transfer (CCR Order 16, r 6(1A)).

In the county court a defence will have been filed and in the majority of cases automatic directions will apply, indeed the timetable will already have started to run. Nevertheless this may be a good opportunity to consider whether the timetable is appropriate and make any variations that may be required.

PLEADINGS

A noteworthy difference between the RSC and CCR is that while the latter has no rule specifically relating to pleadings RSC Order 18 provides a reasonably comprehensive code not only on the procedural aspects but also on the drafting of pleadings. There is, eg, no CCR equivalent to RSC Order 18, r 7. While a number of the rules in RSC Order 18 have their equivalents in various places in the CCR the county court regime, tailored as it is to some extent to the litigant in person, avoids undue emphasis on rules of pleading. There is no provision in the CCR for service of a reply. What is sought in practice is a sufficient statement of facts to show that there is a claim in law and, in the defence, a sufficient statement of facts to show a genuine dispute. In more substantial cases (and the county court now has a formally unlimited common law jurisdiction) this is arguably not sufficient. However in practical terms the pleading of more substantial cases tends to follow the High Court rules and practice. What is required is that all material facts are pleaded, that only material facts are pleaded and that facts and not law or evidence are pleaded. Most of these propositions come not simply from RSC Order 18, r 7 but from many decisions of the courts. They are well established principles and they apply to the county court as well as to the High Court. Sadly much pleading in both courts falls well short of these principles both from the point of view of prolix and over complicated pleadings and from that of omission.

Both sets of rules make provision for a party to seek further particulars of his opponent's pleadings. In the past such applications frequently strayed beyond the true area of pleadings. The recent introduction of the principle of 'cards on the table' litigation (rather than 'trial by ambush'), particularly in the form of the ability to seek interrogatories without order and the general requirement for service of witness statements from non experts and reports from experts, should hopefully limit applications for further particulars to appropriate cases where material facts are not adequately pleaded.

THIRD PARTY PROCEEDINGS

Both sets of rules provide for third and subsequent parties to the action to be joined. The broad outline of the rules is similar but there are a number of specific differences, largely arising from the different procedures in each court.

Third party proceedings may be issued where a defendant—

(a) claims against a person not already a party to the action a contribution or indemnity or any other relief or remedy connected with the subject matter of the action and substantially the same as claimed by the plaintiff, or

(b) requires any question or issue related to the original action to be determined not only between plaintiff and defendant but also as between either of them and a person not already a party to the action.

(RSC Order 16, r 1, CCR Order 12, r 1).

In the High Court leave is always required although the application may be made, initially at least, ex parte by affidavit giving the information set out in RSC Order 16, r 2.

In the county court leave is only required—

(1) in a fixed date action,

(2) in a default action in which a date for the pre-trial review or trial has been fixed, or when pleadings are deemed to be closed for the purposes of Order 17, r 11 (CCR Order 12, r 1(2)), and

(3) where the third party proceedings are issued against the Crown (CCR Order 42, r 11).

Leave is not required to issue third party proceedings against a person who is already a party (CCR Order 12, r 5).

Where leave is required application is on notice. An important feature of county court procedure is that if the defendant issues a third party notice but does not defend (or even files an admission), judgment in default of defence may not be entered against him (CCR Order 12, r 1(7)).

Detailed provisions as to what is to be served on the third party are contained in RSC Order 16, r 3 and in CCR Order 12, r 1(6). In the county court service is by the court office which will appoint a pre-trial review for all parties where the third party notice was issued without leave and, in practice, in other cases (CCR Order 12, r 1(5)). In the High Court the third party is required to file a notice of intention to defend. If he does so the defendant is required to issue a summons for directions to be served on all parties to the action. RSC Order 16, r 4(3) makes specific provision as to the power of the court on making third party directions. There is no direct equivalent in the county court but the High Court powers would appear to be within the powers of the district judge on a pre-trial review (RSC Order 17, rr 1–10).

RSC Order 16, r 5 deals with the situation where no notice of intention to defend is served. There is no equivalent provision in the county court but in practical terms an application can be made by the defendant if the third party does not file a third party defence (or comply with other directions) for an order that the third party be debarred from defending the proceedings — such order could follow the wording of RSC Order 16, r 5(1) as appropriate in the particular case.

In the High Court and the county court similar provisions apply with regard to the introduction of fourth or subsequent parties into the proceedings (RSC Order 16, r 9, CCR Order 12, r 6).

The payment into court procedure is not available to third and subsequent parties but RSC Order 16, r 10 and CCR Order 12, r 7 provide for an offer of contribution to be made.

The role to be played by the third party in any trial will normally be defined by directions subject always to the overriding discretion of the trial judge.

AUTOMATIC DIRECTIONS

Both the High Court and the county court rules make provision for automatic directions in similar terms but with two noteworthy differences. The High Court rule applies only to certain personal injury actions (RSC Order 25, r 8) taking the place of a summons for directions in such actions. However in the county court automatic directions apply to the vast majority of county court actions (the exceptions are listed in CCR Order 17, r 11(1)). In the second place while there is no direct sanction for failure to comply with the High Court directions, failure in the county court to apply to set down within 15 months of the deemed close of pleadings or within nine months of the expiration of any extended time for so doing will lead to 'automatic striking out'.

Other than 'automatic striking out' the only sanction for failure to comply with the directions is to apply for an 'unless' order.

The timetables have similar periods, save in the question of striking out, running from "close of pleadings"—

	High Court	*County Court*
Discovery	14 days	28 days
Inspection	7 days	7 days
Expert reports	14 weeks	70 days
Witness statements	14 weeks	70 days
'set down'	6 months	6 months
Strike out	—	15 months or 9 months from any extended period for 'setting down'

Automatic directions will by their nature not apply to all circumstances and there will be many actions for which longer time limits are required. The sensible and proper approach to such a situation is to seek to agree an amended timetable and apply to the court, by consent if appropriate, for a revised timetable. Many county courts will deal with such an application by letter although it will be wise to give full reasons why the automatic timetable is not appropriate and explain the reason for any very lengthy extension of time sought, particularly as to the 'setting down' date.

Doubts as to whether an action could be restored after having been automatically struck out under CCR Order 17, r 11(9) have now been resolved by the Court of Appeal's decision in *Rastin v British Steel* (1994)(above). The powers given by Order 13, r 4 to extend time apply. However the purpose of the rule in preventing delay is to be observed and a plaintiff seeking to restore such an action must as a threshold requirement show that he had been otherwise diligent in proceeding with the action. Once the threshold test had been met such issues as prejudice the defendant could be taken into account in deciding whether or not to extend time and restore the action.

DISCOVERY

Discovery is the process of disclosing the existence of relevant documents in the possession or power of a party. 'Document' includes any artefact recording information and can include a computer database (*Derby & Co Ltd v Weldon (No 9)* [1991] 2 All ER 901, [1991] 1 WLR 652) or audio tapes (*Grant v Southwestern and County Properties Ltd* [1975] Ch 185, [1974] 2 All ER 465, [1974] 3 WLR 221, 232 EG 333). The locus classicus for the test of relevance is in *Compagnie Financiere et Commerciale du Pacifique v Peruvian Guano Co* (1882) 11 QBD 55, but more recently it has been suggested that the practical test is whether a document might or could reasonably be expected to provoke a line of inquiry which would be of assistance to a party: *The Captain Gregos* (1990) Times 21 December, CA. However the overriding rule of discovery is contained in RSC Order 24, r 6 (CCR Order 14, r 8); namely that the court should refuse to make an order for discovery if it is of the opinion that discovery is 'not necessary either for disposing fairly of the action or matter or for saving costs'.

Discovery is normally commenced by the preparation by each party of a list of relevant documents in the possession or power of that party. In the High Court such lists are required to be served within 14 days of the deemed close of pleadings (RSC Order 24, r 2). Either party may apply for an order and if the other party has failed to comply with Order 24, r 2 the order may be for the list to be verified by affidavit (Order 24, r 3). Where an order is sought the court should consider whether such discovery is necessary and may limit discovery to specific documents or classes of documents (ibid). There are limitations on the extent of discovery in road accident cases.

In the county court discovery will normally take place under the automatic directions within 28 days of 'close of pleadings' but in other cases an order may be sought (CCR Order 17, r 11(3), Order 14, r 1). The same general principles that apply in the High Court also apply in the county court.

In addition to general discovery by lists provision is made for discovery of particular documents (RSC Order 24, r 7, CCR Order 14, r 2). Application is on notice accompanied by an affidavit stating that the other party has or has had in his possession, custody or power the document or class of document of which discovery is sought. It will normally be important to show how such documents are relevant and 'necessary'. On hearing the application the court may order the party concerned to make an affidavit stating whether or not such documents are in his possession, power or control or have been so, and if so what has become of them.

Following discovery by list or affidavit the next step is inspection which should normally be allowed within seven days (RSC Order 24, r 9, CCR Order 14, r 3). Where appropriate a party may require the other party to provide copies of documents included in the list upon undertaking to pay the reasonable copying charges (RSC Order 24, r 11A, CCR Order 14, r 5A).

A party may claim privilege for documents but must list the documents and give reasons for that claim. The other party may challenge the privilege and on any dispute the court may inspect the document(s) to decide whether the claim for privilege is appropriate (RSC Order 24, r 13, CCR Order 14, r 6). There has been considerable case law on this issue.

Finally, where documents are referred to in any pleading or affidavit filed or served in the proceedings, the other party may serve notice requiring the production of those documents (RSC Order 24, r 10, CCR Order 14, r 4).

Discovery, while essential in many actions, can in many others be a cause of delay and expense out of proportion to the benefit achieved and there have been arguments for a more restricted form of automatic discovery (see eg the Heilbron/Hodge report) leaving it to the parties to seek more specific discovery where appropriate.

INTERROGATORIES

The Rules of Court (RSC Order 26, CCR Order 14, r 11) have for a long time provided for the making of an order for the delivery of interrogatories 'relating to any matter in question between the applicant and the other party'. However the rule has tended to be regarded as more restrictive than was intended because of the required test that the information sought must be 'necessary either (a) for disposing fairly of the cause or matter, or (b) for saving costs'. The 'necessary' test seems to have been regarded quite differently with regard to discovery than with regard to interrogatories. Considerable case law developed which tended to restrict the use of interrogatories. Though the basic principle has not changed the modern principle of 'cards on the table' litigation has been recognised by providing for interrogatories without order (save on the Crown). Since then the use of interrogatories as an alternative to what were in many cases improper applications for further particulars seems to have substantially increased. A party may serve interrogatories 'without order' no more than twice. The recipient has 14 days to apply to the court for the interrogatories to be varied or withdrawn, but failing that is expected to comply with the request. Indeed it is at least arguable that on failure to comply within a reasonable time limit the party administering the interrogatories should be entitled to an 'unless' order.

WITNESS STATEMENTS

Following the practice of the Commercial Court, first the High Court and subsequently the county court made provision for an order that each party should serve on the other written statements of each witness whose evidence he proposed to adduce. Such an order is not a breach of legal professional privilege as it is a condition of calling the witness rather than a direct order for disclosure. Experience with such orders seemed to be fairly satisfactory though limited and the rules (RSC Order 38, r 2A, Order 25, r 8, CCR Order 20, rr 12A and Order 17, r 11(3)(b)(iii)) now require disclosure unless some other order is made. The rules make provision for the statements to be signed and dated and to be exchanged simultaneously. Where it is impractical to obtain a statement from a witness, the court may order that a statement of the nature of the evidence be given by that witness and his name and address be given to the other party.

The precise purpose of disclosure is not altogether clear. In part it is an aspect of the 'cards on the table' approach and to that extent the important factor is the disclosure of the evidence to the other party in the hope that this may prevent hopeless cases from going to court and in other cases to encourage early settlements. In part however the intention is to save time in court by permitting the trial judge to direct that the statement stand as evidence in chief of that witness. Experience to date shows a reluctance to prevent the advocate from at least enlarging on the statement in adducing evidence in chief.

EXPERT WITNESSES

The rules have for a long time provided that expert witnesses' evidence should be disclosed in the form of a written report as a prerequisite to the calling of the expert to give oral evidence. RSC Order 38, r 38, applied to the county court by CCR Order 20, r 28, also enables the court to order a meeting of experts. While this procedure seems to have some success with surveyor and engineer witnesses it appears to be less effective with medical witnesses. Undoubtedly the costs and delays caused by a growing multiplicity of experts in modern litigation is a matter requiring attention.

APPLICATIONS IN THE COURSE OF PROCEEDINGS

Although the intention of automatic directions, particularly in the county court, is to avoid applications to the court before the trial wherever possible, there will frequently be need for applications to be made. Applications for summary judgment have already been considered. Other common types of application are for specific directions, for interim payments, for security for costs and for an interlocutory injunction.

Applications are made in a similar manner in the High Court and the county court although in the High Court applications are by way of summons and in the county court by way of notice of application. Applications by summons are dealt with by RSC Order 32 and county court applications by CCR Order 13, r 1. In both cases the summons or application has to be issued and sealed by the appropriate court office and must be served at least two (clear) days before the hearing. Delays in giving hearing dates on such applications are such that normally much longer notice is given. The application should state clearly the order sought and it will be helpful to state brief grounds unless the application is accompanied by an affidavit in support. Such an affidavit is not required in the generality of applications for specific directions but certain rules make specific requirements for evidence in support of the application.

In both the High Court and the county court such applications are commonly heard in chambers and the majority are heard, at least in the first instance, by a master or district judge.

Interim payments

An application for such an order may be made in either the High Court or the county court. Subject to the various minor changes set out in CCR Order 13, r 12 the provisions of RSC Order 29 rr 9–17 apply to both the High Court and the county court.

RSC Order 29, r 11 sets out the conditions to be satisfied on an application for interim damages and r 12 sets out the conditions where the claim relates to a payment other than damages.

Any application must be accompanied by an affidavit setting out the factual circumstances. Where the claim is for damages and there has been no admission of liability or interlocutory judgment full details of the basis upon which the plaintiff alleges that he will recover 'substantial damages' will be required. It is not necessary for the plaintiff to show a specific need for the money (*Schott Kem Ltd v Bentley* [1990] 1 QB 61, [1990] 3 All ER 850, [1990] 3 WLR 397, CA) although evidence of need will always assist the court in deciding whether to make an order for such payment and more particularly how much should be paid.

Security for costs

While the courts generally impose no restriction on the ability of a plaintiff to take proceedings it may be possible for a defendant to obtain an order relating to security for costs. The main instances in which such an order may be obtained are where the plaintiff is an insolvent company (Companies Act 1985, s 726(1)), where the plaintiff is ordinarily resident outside the jurisdiction (RSC Order 23, r 1(1)(a), CCR Order 13, r 8) and, in the High Court, on the other grounds set out in RSC Order 23, r 1(1). An application should be supported by an affidavit setting out the facts on which the defendant relies in order to justify the making of such an order. Even where the technical grounds are made out, the court has a jurisdiction whether or not to make an order, and it will be advisable to consider the judgment in *Sir Lindsay Parkinson & Co Ltd v Triplan Ltd* [1973] 1 QB 609, [1973] 2 All ER 273, [1973] 2 WLR 632, 226 EG 1393, CA in which the circumstances to be considered are set out. However, although the prospects of success are one of those factors, warnings against a trial by affidavits save in the clearest of cases were given in *Porzelack KG v Porzelack (UK) Ltd* [1987] 1 All ER 1074, [1987] 1 WLR 420. The affidavit should state — preferably by reference to an exhibited draft bill — the amount of costs incurred to date and to be incurred in the future if the action continues to trial. On hearing the application the master or district judge will first wish to consider whether the jurisdiction to make the order has been established and, if it has, to go on to consider whether or not he should exercise his discretion to make it. If an order is made it is usually for security to be provided in the form of a payment into court of a stated amount, the action being stayed until such payment is made.

Interim injunction

Both the High Court and the county court have power to make an interim injunction and in a proper case an ex parte injunction. However the county court's power is limited by the County Court Remedies Regulations 1991 in that it may not make a *Mareva* injunction or an *Anton Piller* order save in the limited circumstances set out in reg 3(2), primarily in a patents county court, in family proceedings, an order for the preservation, custody or detention of property the subject of proceedings and an injunction in aid of execution.

The procedure on an application for an interim injunction is set out in RSC Order 29, r 1 and CCR Order 13, r 6. Applications in the High Court will be to a judge; in the county court the application may be to a district judge if the action is within his trial jurisdiction (CCR Order 21, r 5).

PAYMENT INTO COURT

Both the High Court (RSC Order 22, r 1) and the county court (CCR Order 11, r 1) make similar provisions for a defendant in any action for debt or damages to pay into court a sum of money in satisfaction of the cause of action or one or more of the causes of action. The main differences relate to the giving of notice of such payment in and to time limits for giving notice accepting such payment.

In the High Court the defendant is required to give notice to the plaintiff and every other defendant of such payment in (RSC Order 22, r 1(2)). In the county court the defendant is required in certain circumstances to accompany the payment in with a notice but it is the task of the proper officer 'if time permits' to send to every other party to the action notice of payment in (CCR Order 11, r 1(1)). This is not a satisfactory process and it is good practice for the party paying in to give a notice, similar to that given in the High Court, to all other parties.

The plaintiff(s) must then decide whether or not to accept in satisfaction the payment in. Both the High Court and the county court allow 21 days for acceptance. In the High Court this time limit is abridged by a requirement that the notice of acceptance must be given before the trial begins; in the county court it must be given not less than three days before the trial begins. If money is paid in (or a payment in increased) after the trial has commenced, the plaintiff(s) may accept such payment in within two days of receipt of notice (RSC Order 22, r 3(2) or in the county court 14 days (CCR Order 11 r 3(2)) but in any case before the judge commences to give judgment.

If notice is given within these time limits then unless leave is required the effect is to stay the action or the cause(s) of action to which the payment in relates (RSC Order 22, r 3(4), CCR Order 11, r 3(3)). Notice may be given outside these time limits (provided that the judge has not commenced giving judgment) but in the absence of consent to payment out the plaintiff(s) must apply to the court for leave to take the money out of court (RSC Order 22, r 5(1), CCR Order 11, r 5).

The plaintiff is entitled to his costs up to the expiry of 21 days from the date of notice of payment in (RSC Order 62, r 5(4), (5), CCR Order 11, r 3(5)). Any application for leave to accept the payment in out of time could be met by an attempt to vary the normal provision as to costs. Leave is required in certain cases — these cases are set out in RSC Order 22, r 4 and CCR Order 11, r 4.

Both sets of rules require non-disclosure to the trial judge of the payment in until he has decided the issues other than costs. There is an exception relating to actions for damages (RSC Order 82, r 4(2)) and reference to a payment in may be made on an application for interim damages: *Fryer v London Transport Executive* (1982) Times 4 December, CA.

"Calderbank" letters

There will be instances in which a simple payment into court will not resolve the dispute, eg because there may be an application for an injunction, for a declaration, for specific performance etc. In such circumstances it is now possible to serve what is commonly known as a "Calderbank" letter. This is a letter offering terms to settle an action (or for that matter an application within an action). The letter is written 'without prejudice' but the right is reserved to bring the letter to the court's attention once the action (or application) is decided solely as to the issue of costs.

Such letters are contemplated by RSC Order 22, r 14 and CCR Order 11, r 10. Any such letter should be taken into account by the court in exercising its discretion as to the award of costs provided that the defendant could not have protected his position by a payment into court (RSC Order 62, r 9(1)(d), CCR Order 11 r 10 (2)). A "Calderbank" letter does not generally have the same effect as a successful payment into court. In the latter case if the eventual judgment equals or is less than the payment in, the general approach is that the defendant is to be regarded as the successful party from the date of such payment in and will normally be entitled to his costs from that date. The court's discretion is wider where the terms offered in the "Calderbank" letter are not 'beaten'.

There is an exception to the rule that a "Calderbank" offer will have no effect if the defendant could have protected his position by a payment in. This is in personal injury cases where the defendant has applied for but not received a certificate of total benefit under the Social Security Administration Act 1992, s 95 (RSC Order 22, r 14, CCR Order 11, r 10(3)).

DISCONTINUANCE

Both the High Court (RSC Order 21) and the county court (CCR Order 18) enable a plaintiff to discontinue an action and make provision for the defendant to receive the costs of the action up to the date of discontinuance (RSC Order 62, r 5(3) (where discontinuance is effected without leave), CCR Order, r 2).

It is important to note that the court cannot order discontinuance. This is an action taken by the plaintiff subject only to the requirement in the High Court in certain circumstances to obtain leave. In the High Court leave may be granted to discontinue where required, and in both the High Court and the county court the court may make some order relating to the costs of discontinuance other than that the plaintiff should pay the defendant's costs. On considering an application relating to costs following discontinuance the general rule is that the plaintiff should pay the defendant's costs: *J T Stratford & Son Ltd v Lindley (No 2)* [1969] 3 All ER 1122, [1969] 1 WLR 1547, CA. The court may make some other order such as no order for costs where the proceedings were discontinued because the matter became purely academic (see eg *Barretts & Baird (Wholesale) Ltd v IPCS* [1987] 1 FTLR 121, [1988] NLJR 357. However, except where the defendant has been guilty of misconduct there should be no order against the defendant: *Richard Roberts Holdings Ltd v Douglas Smith Stimson Partnership* (1988), 47 Build LR 113, 22 Con LR 94.

In the High Court an action may be discontinued without leave at any time up to 14 days after service of defence (in the case of two or more defendants the last defence served commences the period), provided that no interim payment has been made (RSC Order 21, r 2). In all other cases leave must be sought unless the defendant consents (RSC Order 21, r 2(4)). The High Court may impose terms on giving leave to discontinue — these normally deal with costs and state that no other action may be brought on the same subject matter.

The regime in the county court is more straightforward. No leave is required to discontinue and the court will normally only be involved if the plaintiff seeks some other order as to costs than that provided by the rule.

SUMMONS FOR DIRECTIONS/PRE-TRIAL REVIEW

The High Court summons for directions and the pre-trial review in the county court have much the same purpose, namely to ensure that an action is ready for trial and that appropriate steps are taken to shorten the trial and save costs generally by way of discovery and disclosure of evidence. The origin of both procedures lies in the Evershed Report recommending a thorough stocktaking of actions after completion of discovery and inspection of documents. Neither procedure at present lives up to the objectives set out in that Report.

The county court pre-trial review suffered from being made at a rather early stage in proceedings when frequently neither party was in a position to assist the court in its task of narrowing and defining issues and making appropriate directions. The practice grew of simply seeking, often by letter, the 'usual orders'. This led to the court having standard forms of directions and, increasingly, issuing such directions as a matter of course without the formality of a hearing. This practice was effectively sanctioned by the Civil Justice Review which recommended a standard form of automatic directions, a recommendation which was put into effect by rule changes in 1991. These largely did away with the pre-trial review in county court actions save those listed in Order 17, r 11(1). These were on the one hand actions which could normally be disposed of at a pre-trial review and on the other hand more complex actions in which it was thought that 'tailor-made directions' would be required. Order 17, r 11 preserves the right of the district judge to direct a pre-trial review in cases to which the automatic directions would otherwise apply. The rules applying to pre-trial reviews are to be found in CCR Order 17, rr 1–10.

In the High Court the plaintiff is required to issue a summons for directions in the majority of actions commenced by writ within one month after close of pleadings. While observance of time limits is often poor there can be few which are more seldom observed. While this may have the advantage that at the hearing of the summons the issues should be clear — though this is unfortunately not always the case — it has the disadvantage of leaving any real effort at court control until a date which is in reality very late in the proceedings. The High Court rules make provision for automatic directions in some personal injury cases (RSC Order 25, r 8) which obviate the summons for directions. These directions are seldom fully observed.

Arguments have raged, and will continue to rage, over the desirability or otherwise, and the extent, of court control. In the High Court control should be exercised by proper use of the summons for directions and an effective use of the powers — indeed the duty — of the court under Order 25, r 2 to consider all matters relating to the trial. This needs both a robust attitude on the part of the court and the provision of the fullest assistance and information by the parties. It may well be that the way ahead is to deal with the small and medium size cases by automatic directions both in the High Court and the county court — including a provision for 'automatic striking out' on failure to set down within set time limits — but to provide a more tailor-made system in larger cases where an early appointment could lead to the setting of a suitable time-table and control remaining with the master or district judge throughout the course of the action. The use of information technology may assist in permitting the court to adopt a more proactive role in ensuring that actions are brought on for hearing at an early stage. Consideration may need to be given to the adoption of the system applied in the Liverpool and Central London County Courts of 'deadline listing' whereby a 'trial week' is allocated in the filing of a defence, detailed listing is then made at about six weeks prior to that 'trial week'.

SETTING DOWN

The theoretical procedure for obtaining a date for trial differs considerably between the High Court and the county court. In the High Court the parties have control (save in limited circumstances) whereas in the county court it is the court which has to fix the date, either on issue (fixed date summons (CCR Order 3, r 3(3), (4)) or at the pre-trial review (CCR Order 17, r 9). However, even in the county court this position has been substantially altered by the introduction of automatic directions for the majority of actions which leave the application for a date to be fixed in the hands of the plaintiff (though imposing a striking out sanction in the case of delay). This reflects the reality of the position except in those few areas which have followed the Liverpool system of 'deadline listing' whereby a date, or at least a 'trial week', is fixed on the filing of a defence.

In the High Court the order for directions will fix the period within which the action is to be set down (although this period is largely ignored in practice). The time limit in the county court is fixed by the automatic directions, and the imposition of a striking out sanction where there is significant delay beyond this date has introduced some discipline into this area.

The procedure for setting down in the High Court is laid down by Order 34. A bundle of pleadings is required in view of the fact that there is no 'court file' in High Court cases. In the county court practice may vary locally but generally application is by letter — preferably supported by a time estimate — and perhaps a certificate of readiness by the proposed advocate.

In both the High Court and the county court further provision is made for a bundle of witness statements, expert reports etc to be lodged shortly before the trial date (RSC Order 34, r 10, CCR Order 17, r 12).

TRIAL

The High Court and county court both rely heavily on oral evidence although in this area there has been some progress by the requirement for the service of witness statements which may stand as evidence in chief. In addition provision is made for evidence to be given by affidavit (RSC Order 38, r 2, CCR Order 20, rr 6, 7) in limited circumstances and for depositions (RSC Order 39, r 1, CCR Order 20, r 13) to be taken. There is encouragement for expert reports to be agreed and for there to be a meeting of experts for this purpose (RSC Order 38, r 38, applied to the county court by CCR Order 20, r 28). Furthermore oral argument may now be limited to a degree by the increasing practice of preparing a summary of each party's case.

The rules enable the judge to direct the procedure at the trial (RSC Order 35, r 7, CCR Order 21, r 5A) but proposals for a power to limit the length have not as yet been adopted. In the absence of any particular directions the order of the trial is as set out in RSC Order 35, r 7. In general the party which opens is that on whom the onus of proving the substantive issue rests.

Jury trial is provided for in a limited number of cases including defamation (in the High Court only), fraud, malicious prosecution or false imprisonment. Efforts to extend the cases in which juries will be allowed have been resisted by the judiciary.

ENFORCEMENT

Enforcement of judgments for payment of money may be effected by various means depending on the defendant's financial position — and the plaintiff's knowledge of this. In both the High Court and the county court the judgment debtor may be examined in order to discover information to assist in the process of execution (RSC Order 48, CCR Order 25, rr 3, 4).

The available methods of enforcing a money judgment are—

(1) execution against goods (RSC Order 47, CCR Order 26),

(2) garnishee proceedings (RSC Order 49, CCR Order 30),

(3) charging order (RSC Order 50, CCR Order 31),

(4) appointment of a receiver (RSC Order 51, CCR Order 32),

(5) attachment of earnings order (CCR Order 27),

(6) judgment summons (CCR Order 28).

As the county court tends to deal more especially with individual debtors and cases of multiple debt there is extensive provision to suspend warrants upon payment of the judgment debt by instalments. In addition, though primarily as an aid to the debtor in cases of multiple debt, the county court can make an administration order.

Where the order is for possession of land the procedure for the issue of a writ or warrant of possession is laid down by RSC Order 45, r 3 and CCR Order 26, r 17. To enforce an order for delivery of goods a writ or warrant of delivery may be obtained (RSC Order 54, r 4, CCR Order 26, r 16). In either case enforcement may also be by writ of sequestration or committal in the High Court and by committal in the county court.

Where the court's order is for a party to do or abstain from doing an act, enforcement may be obtained by a writ of sequestration and/or committal in the High Court (RSC Order 46, r 5 and Order 52) or committal in the county court (CCR Order 29 r 1).

The procedures in the High Court and the county court are generally similar. The main points of difference relate to the fact that enforcement by execution in the High Court is carried out by bailiffs acting under the under-sheriff for the county. In the county court the work is carried out by county court bailiffs. Another significant difference is the need to obtain leave to issue a writ of possession in the High Court (see RSC Order 45, r 3) where judgment was by default. There is no such procedure in the county court.

COSTS

The provisions of RSC Order 62 and CCR Order 38 are in many ways similar, indeed much of Order 62, Part 2 is incorporated into Order 38. The similarity is increased by the fact that county court costs on scale 2 (ie where the judgment was for £3,000 or more) are to be taxed in accordance with the provisions of Order 62, Appendix 2.

The main difference between the provisions in the RSC and the CCR relates to costs on scale 1, namely those where the judgment exceeded £100 but did not exceed £3,000. Such costs are to be taxed in accordance with a detailed scale of costs. Unlike other costs provisions for non-legally-aided cases the scale provides maximum amounts to be allowed unless the taxing officer decides to exercise discretion to exceed the scale. The scale also provides for an allowance to be made for "mechanical items", ie work normally done by a non-fee-earner in physically preparing or copying documents. Counsel's fees are laid down and provision is made for the costs of a successful party to be assessed within amounts laid down by the scale if he so applies. This provision has some similarities to the High Court procedure applied to county court costs on scale 2 for fixing costs as a gross sum (RSC Order 62, r 7(4)). It is thought that the procedure for fixing costs does not apply to county court scale 1 costs.

Costs may be awarded on either the "standard" or "indemnity" basis. The essential difference is that on the standard basis the onus of showing reasonableness is on the taxing party, whereas on the indemnity basis costs are deemed to be reasonable unless the paying party is able to satisfy the taxing officer that the work done or the amount charged is unreasonable. The indemnity basis is therefore more generous to the taxing party. An order on this basis is to be regarded as exceptional. Typical cases relate to costs against a contemnor, costs of an innocent third party, eg in *Mareva* proceedings, and costs of a test case.

Except on scale 1 in the county court and where costs of the solicitor for a legally assisted person are prescribed by Legal Aid regulations, the general principles of taxation are that a reasonable amount should be allowed for work reasonably required to be done in the course of litigation. The amount allowed is to be determined in general by deciding on the reasonable time spent by the successful party's solicitor and applying to that time an appropriate expense rate. The expense rate is to be determined by averaging such information that is available to the taxing officer as to the expense rates of solicitors in the particular area. The assessment of such rates has been assisted by Expense Rate surveys conducted by Local Law Societies. To the amount so calculated is added an uplift for "Care and Conduct". This varies — 35% being commonly allowed for attending court or conference with counsel, and 50% for general preparatory work, though discretion can be exercised to increase the uplift in more complex cases. No uplift is allowed on waiting and travelling time.

In the High Court the taxing officer is the Taxing Master of the Supreme Court Taxing Officer, a taxing officer of the same office for smaller bills up to £25,000 and, in the provinces, the district judge in respect of work carried out in his registry and appeals from that registry. In the county court the taxing officer is the district judge of the court although there is power for the Lord Chancellor to appoint senior members of staff to tax certain bills (a power which has not as yet been exercised).

The process of taxation is similar in the High Court and county court although provisional taxation, ie taxation of a bill without attendance subject to the right of the taxing party or solicitor to ask for a full taxation, is more common in the county court.

Rules of the Supreme Court
(Revision) 1965

RULES OF THE SUPREME COURT (REVISION) 1965

(SI 1965/1776)

Amendments References to "district judge", "assistant district judge" and "deputy district judge" substituted by virtue of the Courts and Legal Services Act 1990, s 74, throughout these Rules.
Modification References to solicitors etc modified to include references to bodies recognised under the Administration of Justice Act 1985, s 9, by the Solicitors' Incorporated Practices Order 1991, SI 1991/2684, arts 4, 5, Sch 1, throughout these Rules.
Forms References to form by number alone are to the form so numbered in Appendix A to these Rules. References to forms with the prefix PF are to Practice Forms and with the prefix ChPF are to Chancery Masters' Practice Forms.

1.—(1) The rules set out in Schedule 1 hereto are hereby made.

(2) The enactments specified in columns 1 and 2 of Schedule 2 hereto (being enactments relating to matters with respect to which the rules specified in column 4 of that Schedule are hereby made) are hereby repealed to the extent specified in column 3 of that Schedule.

(3) The Rules and Orders specified in Schedule 3 hereto are hereby revoked, but subject to the provision in relation thereto made at the end of that Schedule.

Commencement 1 October 1966

2. The Interpretation Act 1889 applies in relation to this instrument and in relation to the revocations and repeals effected by it as if this instrument, the rules and orders revoked by it and any rules and orders revoked by the rules and orders so revoked were Acts of Parliament, and as if each revocation were a repeal.

Commencement 1 October 1966

3. This instrument may be cited as the Rules of the Supreme Court (Revision) 1965 and shall come into operation on 1st October 1966.

Commencement 1 October 1966

SCHEDULE 1
RULES OF THE SUPREME COURT 1965

ARRANGEMENT OF ORDERS

PRELIMINARY

COMMENCEMENT AND PROGRESS OF PROCEEDINGS

Order 32 Applications and proceedings in chambers

TRIAL

Order 33 Place and mode of trial

Order 38 [Evidence]

JUDGMENTS, ORDERS, ACCOUNTS AND INQUIRIES

Order 42　Judgments and orders

Order 43　Accounts and inquiries

[Order 44　Proceedings under judgments and orders: Chancery Division]

ENFORCEMENT OF JUDGMENTS AND ORDERS

Order 50 Charging orders, stop orders, etc

Order 51 Receivers: equitable execution

Order 52 Committal

DIVISIONAL COURTS, COURT OF APPEAL, ETC

[Order 53 Applications for judicial review]

Costs

GENERAL AND ADMINISTRATIVE PROVISIONS

Order 63 [Offices]

Order 64 Sittings, vacations and office hours

SPECIAL PROVISIONS AS TO PARTICULAR PROCEEDINGS

Order 72 Commercial actions . . .

Order 73 Arbitration proceedings

SPECIAL PROVISIONS AS TO PARTICULAR PROCEEDINGS

Order 89 Proceedings between husband and wife

[*Order 90* . . . (revoked)]

[Order [91] Revenue Proceedings . . .]

Order 92 Lodgment, investment, etc of funds in court: Chancery Division

Order 93 Applications and appeals to High Court under various Acts: Chancery Division

Order 94　Applications and appeals to High Court under various Acts: Queen's Bench Division

Order 95　The Bills of Sale Acts 1878 and 1882 [and the Industrial and Provident Societies Act 1967]

Order 96　The [Mines (Working Facilities and Support) Act 1966], etc

Order 106 Proceedings relating to solicitors: the Solicitors Act [1974]

Order 107 [The County Courts Act 1984]

Order 108 Proceedings relating to charities: the Charities Act 1960

Order 109 The Administration of Justice Act 1960

PRELIMINARY

ORDER 1
CITATION, APPLICATION, INTERPRETATION AND FORMS

Order 1, r 1 Citation

These rules may be cited as the Rules of the Supreme Court 1965.

Commencement 1 October 1966.

Order 1, r 2 Application

(1) Subject to [paragraph (2)], these rules shall have effect in relation to all proceedings in [the High Court and the civil division of the Court of Appeal].

(2) These rules shall not have effect in relation to proceedings of the kinds specified in the first column of the following Table (being proceedings in respect of which rules may be made under the enactments specified in the second column of that Table):—

TABLE

Proceedings	*Enactments*
[1. Insolvency Proceedings	Insolvency Act 1986, ss 411 and 412.]
2. Proceedings relating to the winding-up of companies.	Companies Act 1948, section 365.
3. Non-contentious or common form probate proceedings.	[Supreme Court Act 1981, section 127.]
4. Proceedings in the High Court when acting as a Prize Court.	Prize Courts Act 1894, section 3.
5. Proceedings before the judge within the meaning of [Part VII of the Mental Health Act 1983].	[Mental Health Act 1983, section 106].
[6. Family Proceedings Rules.	Matrimonial and Family Proceedings Act 1984, section 40.]

[(3) Nothing in this rule shall be taken as affecting any statutory provision whereby the Rules of the Supreme Court 1965, or any provisions of them, are applied to proceedings other than those to which they are applied by this rule.]

Commencement 1 October 1989 (para (3)); 1 October 1966 (remainder).
Amendments Para (1): words "paragraph (2)" and words from "the High Court" to "Court of Appeal" substituted by SI 1989/1307, r 8(a).
Para (2): item 1 of the Table substituted by SI 1986/2001, art 2, Schedule; in item 3 of the Table words "Supreme Court Act 1981, section 127" substituted by SI 1982/1111, r 115, Schedule; in item 5 of the Table words "Part VII of the Mental Health Act 1983" and "Mental Health Act 1983, section 106" substituted by SI 1983/1181, r 36, Schedule; item 6 of the Table originally added by SI 1968/1244, r 3(1), substituted by SI 1991/1884, r 2.
Para (3): substituted for existing paras (3), (4) by SI 1989/1307, r 8(b) (original para (3) revoked and original paras (4), (5) renumbered as paras (3), (4) by SI 1968/1244, r 3(2)).
Cross references See CCR Order 1, r 2.

Order 1, r 3 Application of Interpretation Act

[The Interpretation Act 1978] shall apply for the interpretation of these rules as it applies [to subordinate legislation made after the commencement of that Act].

Commencement 1 October 1966.
Amendments Words in square brackets substituted by SI 1982/1111, r 115, Schedule.

Order 1, r 4 Definitions

(1)   In these rules, unless the context otherwise requires, the following expressions have the meanings hereby respectively assigned to them, namely—

"the Act" means the [Supreme Court Act 1981];

["an action for personal injuries" means an action in which there is a claim for damages in respect of personal injuries to the plaintiff or any other person or in respect of a person's death, and "personal injuries" includes any disease and any impairment of a person's physical or mental condition;]

"cause book" means the book [or other record] kept in the Central Office, [Chancery Chambers,] [the principal registry of the Family Division], the [Admiralty and Commercial Registry] and every district registry in which the letter and number of, and other details relating to, a cause or matter are entered;

"Central Office" means the central office of the Supreme Court;

["Chancery Chambers" means the offices of the Chancery Division;

"Chancery district registries" means the district registries of Birmingham, Bristol, Cardiff, Leeds, Liverpool, Manchester, Newcastle upon Tyne and Preston;]

"chief master" means the [Chief Chancery Master];

["circuit" means one of the six areas into which England and Wales are divided for the purposes of the conduct of judicial business;]

"Crown Office" means the Crown Office and Associates' Department of the Central Office;

["FAX" means the making of a facsimile copy of a document by the transmission of electronic signals;]

"folio" means 72 words, each figure being counted as one word;

[. . .]

"master" means a master of the Supreme Court other than a [taxing master];

[. . .]

. . .

[. . .]

["notice of intention to defend" means an acknowledgment of service containing a statement to the effect that the person by whom or on whose behalf it is signed intends to contest the proceedings to which the acknowledgment relates;]

["official referee" means a [person] nominated under section 68(1)(a) of the Act;]

"official solicitor" means the official solicitor to the Supreme Court;

"officer" means an officer of the Supreme Court;

"originating summons" means every summons other than a summons in a pending cause or matter;

"pleading" does not include a petition, summons or [Part One of a] preliminary act;

"probate action" has the meaning assigned to it by Order 76;

"receiver" includes a manager or consignee;

. . .

"senior master" means [the Senior Master of the Queen's Bench Division];

["statement of the value of the action" means a statement showing—

(a) whether the value of the action (or, as the case may be, of the counterclaim) exceeds the sum for the time being specified in article 7(3) of the High Court and County Courts Jurisdiction Order 1991 or, as the case may be, that it has no quantifiable value, and

(b) if it does not exceed that sum or if it has no quantifiable value, that by reason of one or more of the criteria mentioned in article 7(5) of the said Order the action is suitable for determination in the High Court;]

["vacation" means the interval between the end of any of the sittings mentioned in Order 64, rule 1, and the beginning of the next sittings;]

["value", in relation to an action, means the value as defined by articles 9 and 10 of the High Court and County Courts Jurisdiction Order 1991;]

"writ" means a writ of summons.

(2)   In these rules, unless the context otherwise requires, "the Court" means the High Court or any one or more judges thereof, whether sitting in court or in chambers or any master, [the Admiralty Registrar or any [district judge] of the Family Division], or [district judge] of a district registry; but the foregoing provision shall not be taken as affecting any provision of these rules and, in particular, Order 32, rules 11, 14 and 23, by virtue of which the authority and jurisdiction of a master or any such [district judge] is defined and regulated.

[(3)   In these rules, unless the context otherwise requires, any reference to acknowledging service of a document or giving notice of intention to defend any proceedings is a reference to lodging in the appropriate court office an acknowledgment of service of that document or, as the case may be, a notice of intention to defend those proceedings.]

Commencement   3 June 1980 (para (3)); 1 October 1966 (remainder).

Amendments   Para (1): in definitions "the Act", "chief master" and "senior master" words in square brackets substituted by SI 1982/1111, r 115, Schedule; definition "an action for personal injuries" inserted by SI 1974/295, r 2; in definition "cause book" words "or other record" inserted by SI 1980/629, r 2, words "Chancery Chambers," inserted by SI 1982/1111, r 4(1), words "the principal registry of the Family Division" substituted by SI 1971/1269, r 38(b), Schedule, words "Admiralty and Commercial Registry" substituted by SI 1987/1423, r 2; definitions "Chancery Chambers", "Chancery district registries" and "circuit" inserted by SI 1982/1111, r 4(2), (3); definition "FAX" inserted by SI 1990/2599, r 2; first definition omitted originally inserted by SI 1971/1955, r 2, subsequently revoked by SI 1976/1196, r 3(1); in definition "master" words "taxing master" substituted by SI 1986/632, r 2; second definition omitted originally inserted by SI 1968/1244, r 3(4), revoked by SI 1991/1884, r 3; third definition omitted revoked by SI 1976/1196, r 3(2); fourth definition omitted originally inserted by SI 1976/1196, r 3(1), revoked by SI 1982/1111, r 4(4); definition "notice of intention to defend" inserted by SI 1979/1716, r 2(1); definition "official referee" inserted by SI 1982/1111, r 98, word "person" substituted by SI 1982/1786, r 2; in definition "pleading" words "Part One of a" added by SI 1990/1689, r 2; final definition omitted revoked by SI 1980/629, r 23; definitions "statement of the value of the action" and "value" inserted by SI 1991/1329, rr 2, 3; definition "vacation" inserted by SI 1972/1194, r 2.

Para (2): words "the Admiralty Registrar or any district judge of the Family Division" substituted by SI 1971/1269, r 2(1).

Para (3): inserted by SI 1979/1716, r 2(2) (para (3) originally added by SI 1970/1208, r 2, subsequently revoked by SI 1976/337, r 2).

Cross references   See CCR Order 1, r 3.

[Order 1, r 4A Construction of references to proceedings in Queen's Bench Division, etc

In these Rules, unless the context otherwise requires—

(a) any reference to proceedings in the Queen's Bench Division shall be construed as including a reference to proceedings in the Commercial Court but not to proceedings in the Admiralty Court; and

(b) any reference to a master, if it relates only to a master of the Queen's Bench Division, shall in relation to any Admiralty cause or matter be construed as including the Admiralty Registrar.]

Commencement 1 October 1971.
Amendments This rule was inserted by SI 1971/1269, r 2(2).

Order 1, r 5 Construction of references to Orders, rules, etc

(1)   Unless the context otherwise requires, any reference in these rules to a specified Order, rule or Appendix is a reference to that Order or rule of, or that Appendix to, these rules and any reference to a specified rule, paragraph or sub-paragraph is a reference to that rule of the Order, that paragraph of the rule, or that sub-paragraph of the paragraph, in which the reference occurs.

(2)   Any reference in these rules to anything done under a rule of these rules includes a reference to the same thing done before the commencement of that rule under any corresponding rule of court ceasing to have effect on the commencement of that rule.

(3)   Except where the context otherwise requires, any reference in these rules to any enactment shall be construed as a reference to that enactment as amended, extended or applied by or under any other enactment.

Commencement 1 October 1966.
Cross references See CCR Order 1, rr 4, 7.

Order 1, r 6 Construction of references to action, etc for possession of land

Except where the context otherwise requires, references in these rules to an action or claim for the possession of land shall be construed as including references to proceedings against the Crown for an order declaring that the plaintiff is entitled as against the Crown to the land or to the possession thereof.

Commencement 1 October 1966.

Order 1, r 7 Construction of references to Lord Chancellor and Lord Chief Justice

. . . for references in these rules to the Lord Chief Justice there shall, in relation to any period for which the office of Lord Chief Justice is vacant, be substituted references to the Lord Chancellor.

Commencement 1 October 1966.
Amendments Words omitted revoked by SI 1980/1908, r 19.

Order 1, r 8 *(revoked by SI 1980/629)*

Order 1, r 9 Forms

[(1)] The forms in the Appendices shall be used where applicable with such variations as the circumstances of the particular case require.

[(2) A form marked with the words "(Royal Arms)" shall have printed, or embossed by an officer of the Court, at the head of the first page a replica of the Royal Arms.]

Commencement 2 June 1981 (para (2)); 1 October 1966 (remainder).
Amendments Para (1): numbered as such by SI 1980/2000, r 15(1).
Para (2): added by SI 1980/2000, r 15(2).

[Order 1, r 10 Rules not to exclude conduct of business by post

Nothing in these rules shall prejudice any power to regulate the practice of the Court by giving directions enabling any business or class of business to be conducted by post.]

Commencement 1 January 1971.
Amendments This rule was added by SI 1970/1861, r 2.
Cross references See CCR Order 2, r 5.

ORDER 2
EFFECT OF NON-COMPLIANCE

Order 2, r 1 Non-compliance with rules

(1)   Where, in beginning or purporting to begin any proceedings or at any stage in the course of or in connection with any proceedings, there has, by reason of any thing done or left undone, been a failure to comply with the requirements of these rules, whether in respect of time, place, manner, form or content or in any other respect, the failure shall be treated as an irregularity and shall not nullify the proceedings, any step taken in the proceedings, or any document, judgment or order therein.

(2)   Subject to paragraph (3), the Court may, on the ground that there has been such a failure as is mentioned in paragraph (1), and on such terms as to costs or otherwise as it thinks just, set aside either wholly or in part the proceedings in which the failure occurred, any step taken in those proceedings or any document, judgment or order therein or exercise its powers under these rules to allow such amendments (if any) to be made and to make such order (if any) dealing with the proceedings generally as it thinks fit.

(3)   The Court shall not wholly set aside any proceedings or the writ or other originating process by which they were begun on the ground that the proceedings were required by any of these rules to be begun by an originating process other than the one employed.

Commencement   1 October 1966.
Cross references   See CCR Order 37, r 5.

Order 2, r 2 Application to set aside for irregularity

(1)   An application to set aside for irregularity any proceedings, any step taken in any proceedings or any document, judgment or order therein shall not be allowed unless it is made within a reasonable time and before the party applying has taken any fresh step after becoming aware of the irregularity.

(2)   An application under this rule may be made by summons or motion and the grounds of objection must be stated in the summons or notice of motion.

Commencement   1 October 1966.
Cross references   See CCR Order 37, r 5.

ORDER 3
TIME

Order 3, r 1 "Month" means calendar month

Without prejudice to [section 5 of the Interpretation Act 1978] in its application to these rules, the word "month", where it occurs in any judgment, order, direction or other document forming part of any proceedings in the Supreme Court, means a calendar month unless the context otherwise requires.

Commencement 1 October 1966.
Amendments Words "section 5 of the Interpretation Act 1978" substituted by SI 1982/1111, r 115, Schedule.

Order 3, r 2 Reckoning periods of time

(1) Any period of time fixed by these rules or by any judgment, order or direction for doing any act shall be reckoned in accordance with the following provisions of this rule.

(2) Where the act is required to be done within a specified period after or from a specified date, the period begins immediately after that date.

(3) Where the act is required to be done within or not less than a specified period before a specified date, the period ends immediately before that date.

(4) Where the act is required to be done a specified number of clear days before or after a specified date, at least that number of days must intervene between the day on which the act is done and that date.

(5) Where, apart from this paragraph, the period in question, being a period of 7 days or less, would include a Saturday, Sunday or bank holiday, Christmas Day or Good Friday, that day shall be excluded.

In this paragraph "bank holiday" means a day which is, or is to be observed as, a bank holiday, or a holiday, under the [Banking and Financial Dealings Act 1971], in England and Wales.

Commencement 1 October 1966.
Amendments Para (5): words "Banking and Financial Dealings Act 1971" substituted by SI 1979/1542, r 9(1), Schedule.
Cross references See CCR Order 1, r 9(1)–(4).

Order 3, r 3 *(revoked by SI 1990/1689)*

Order 3, r 4 Time expires on Sunday, etc

Where the time prescribed by these rules, or by any judgment, order or direction, for doing any act at an office of the Supreme Court expires on a Sunday or other day on which that office is closed, and by reason thereof that act cannot be done on that day, the act shall be in time if done on the next day on which that office is open.

Commencement 1 October 1966.
Cross references See CCR Order 1, r 9(5).

Order 3, r 5 Extension, etc, of time

(1)   The Court may, on such terms as it thinks just, by order extend or abridge the period within which a person is required or authorised by these rules, or by any judgment, order or direction, to do any act in any proceedings.

(2)   The Court may extend any such period as is referred to in paragraph (1) although the application for extension is not made until after the expiration of that period.

(3)   The period within which a person is required by these rules, or by any order or direction, to serve, file or amend any pleading or other document may be extended by consent (given in writing) without an order of the Court being made for that purpose.

(4)   In this rule references to the Court shall be construed as including references to the Court of Appeal[, a single judge of that Court and the registrar of civil appeals].

Commencement 1 October 1966.
Amendments   Para (4): words ", a single judge of that Court and the registrar of civil appeals" added by SI 1981/1734, r 2.
Cross references See CCR Order 13, r 4.
Forms Summons for time (PF1).
Order for time (PF2).

Order 3, r 6 Notice of intention to proceed after year's delay

Where a year or more has elapsed since the last proceeding in a cause or matter, the party who desires to proceed must give to every other party not less than one month's notice of his intention to proceed.

A summons on which no order was made is not a proceeding for the purpose of this rule.

Commencement 1 October 1966.

COMMENCEMENT AND PROGRESS OF PROCEEDINGS

ORDER 4
ASSIGNMENT, TRANSFER AND CONSOLIDATION OF PROCEEDINGS

Order 4, r 1 Assignment to masters of actions . . .

(1) Every action proceeding in [the Chancery Division or] the Queen's Bench Division, other than an action which is proceeding in a district registry, shall be assigned to a master at the time of issue or the first summons in the action, and after the action is assigned to a master by virtue of this paragraph—

　(a) all proceedings therein which by these rules are to be dealt with by a master shall, subject to rules 7 and 9, be dealt with by the master to whom the action is assigned, and

　(b) all summonses in the action shall be marked with his name.

(2) Paragraph (1) shall not apply to an action which is entered in the commercial list under Order 72, rule 4(1), unless and until it is ordered to be removed from that list, and shall cease to apply to an action on its transfer to that list or on its being referred to an official referee.

(3) Where an action in the commercial list is ordered to be removed from that list, paragraph (1) shall apply to that action subject to the modification that for the reference to the first summons in the action there shall be substituted a reference to the first summons in the action after the making of the order for removal of the action from the commercial list.

Commencement 1 October 1966.
Amendments Rule heading: originally r 2, renumbered as r 1 and words omitted revoked by SI 1982/1111, r 5(1).
Para (1): words "the Chancery Division or" added by SI 1982/1111, r 5(1).

Order 4, r 2 [Companies]

. . .

Where an order has been made by the Court for the winding-up of a company, all proceedings in chambers in any action against that company at the instance or on behalf of debenture holders shall be dealt with by an officer of the High Court who is a registrar within the meaning of any rules for the time being in force relating to the winding-up of companies.

. . .

Commencement 1 October 1966.
Amendments Originally r 1, renumbered as r 2 and words omitted revoked by SI 1982/1111, r 5(2).

Order 4, r 3 Transfer between Divisions

A cause or matter may, at any stage of the proceedings therein, be transferred from one Division to another by order of the Court made in the Division in which the cause or matter is proceeding.

. . .

Commencement 1 October 1966.
Amendments Words omitted revoked by SI 1982/1111, r 6.

Order 4, r [4] Transfer of proceedings after making of order for administration of estate

Where an order for the administration under the direction of the Court of the estate of a deceased person is made in the Chancery Division, then, notwithstanding anything in rule 3 . . . , a judge of [that Division] may by order [transfer to that Division] any pending cause or matter brought by or against the executors or administrators of that person and assigned to some other Division . . . .

Commencement 1 October 1966.
Amendments Originally r 5, renumbered as r 4 and original r 4 revoked by SI 1982/1111, r 11.
Words omitted revoked and words "that Division" and "transfer to that Division" substituted by SI 1982/1111, r 8.

Order 4, r [5] Transfer between district registries and between such registries and London

(1)   Where a writ or originating summons is issued out of the Central Office, [Chancery Chambers,] [the principal registry of the Family Division] or the [Admiralty and Commercial Registry], the cause or matter shall proceed in the Royal Courts of Justice, unless it is transferred to a district registry under this rule or to a county court or some other court.

(2)   Where a writ or originating summons is issued out of a district registry, the cause or matter shall proceed in the district registry, unless . . . it is transferred to the Royal Courts of Justice under this rule or any other rule or to a county court or some other court.

[(3)   [Subject to paragraph (5A), where]—
    (a)   a sole defendant or one of the defendants to an action begun by writ which is proceeding in a district registry does not reside or carry on business in the district of the registry or, being a body corporate, does not have a registered office or carry on business in that district, and
    (b)   the writ is not indorsed with a statement that a cause of action in respect of which relief is claimed arose wholly or in part in a place in that district,

that defendant may, on acknowledging service of the writ, include in his acknowledgment a statement to the effect that he applies for an order transferring the action to some other district registry or to the Royal Courts of Justice, and in that case, unless the plaintiff within 8 days after the defendant's acknowledging service gives notice to the [district judge] of the district registry that he objects to the making of such an order, the [district judge] shall make an order accordingly.

If the plaintiff gives notice of objection within the time aforesaid, the [district judge] shall fix a time and place for the hearing of the defendant's application and give notice thereof to every party to the proceedings.

(3A) In relation to a writ in the Chancery Division which is issued out of [one of the Chancery district registries], paragraph (3) shall have effect as if for the references to the district of that registry there were substituted references to the [circuit within which that registry is situate, and the Northern and North Eastern Circuits shall be treated for this purpose as one circuit].]

[(4) [Subject to paragraph (5A), without] prejudice to paragraph (3) where a cause or matter (whether begun by writ, originating summons or otherwise) is proceeding in a district registry or in the Royal Courts of Justice, the Court may, on the application of a party to the cause or matter or of its own motion, make an order transferring the cause or matter, or any summons or other application therein, from that registry to some other district registry or to the Royal Courts of Justice or, as the case may be, from the Royal Courts of Justice to a district registry, and the Court may make an order accordingly on such terms, if any, as may be just.

. . .]

(5) [Without prejudice to paragraph (4)] where an originating summons by which a cause or matter assigned to the Chancery Division is begun is issued out of a district registry, then, if—

(a) the cause or matter is not one with respect to which specific provision is made by these rules for the issue of the summons out of any district registry, or

(b) the summons ought to have been issued out of some other district registry,

the Court shall, either of its own motion or on the application of a party to the cause or matter, by order transfer the cause or matter to the Royal Courts of Justice or, as the case may be, to that other district registry on such terms, if any, as to costs as it thinks just.

[(5A) A probate cause or matter may only be transferred under this rule to Chancery Chambers or to one of the Chancery district registries.]

(6) An application for an order under this rule may not be made to a [district judge] except where the application relates to a cause or matter which is proceeding in a district registry, in which case it must be made to the [district judge] of that registry.

Commencement 1 October 1993 (para (5A)); 14 October 1991 (para (4)); 3 June 1980 (paras (3), (3A)); 1 October 1966 (remainder).

Amendments Originally r 6, renumbered as r 5 by SI 1982/1111, r 11.
Para (1): words "Chancery Chambers," inserted by SI 1982/1111, r 9(1); words "the principal registry of the Family Division" substituted by SI 1971/1269, r 38(b), Schedule; words "Admiralty and Commercial Registry" substituted by SI 1987/1423, r 2.
Para (2): words omitted revoked by SI 1979/1716, r 3(1).
Para (3): substituted, together with para (3A), for para (3) as originally enacted, by SI 1979/1716, r 3(2); words "Subject to paragraph (5A), where" substituted by SI 1993/2133, r 3(1).
Para (3A): substituted, together with para (3), for para (3) as originally enacted, by SI 1979/1716, r 3(2); words "one of the Chancery district registries" and words from "circuit within which" to "as one circuit" substituted by SI 1982/1111, r 9(2).
Para (4): substituted by SI 1991/1884, r 27; words "Subject to paragraph (5A), without" substituted by SI 1993/2133, r 3(2); words omitted revoked by SI 1992/1907, r 2.
Para (5): words "Without prejudice to paragraph (4)" inserted by SI 1971/1955, r 3(3).
Para (5A): inserted by SI 1993/2133, r 3(3).
Forms Notice by district judge of time to hear application to transfer (PF199).
Order on transfer (PF198).

Order 4, r [6] Transfer between masters

[The chief master in the Chancery Division and the senior master in the Queen's Bench Division may transfer an action from the master to whom it has been assigned to some other master in the same Division.]

Commencement 1 October 1982.
Amendments Originally r 7, renumbered as r 6 by SI 1982/1111, r 11.
This rule was substituted by SI 1982/1111, r 10.

Order 4, r [7] Exercise of one judge's jurisdiction by another

(1)   A judge who consents to do so may, if the Lord Chancellor so directs, hear and dispose of an application in a cause or matter which has been assigned to a Division of which he is not a judge or to some other judge.

(2)   Where, by virtue of . . . any of these rules, any application ought to be made to, or any jurisdiction exercised by, the judge by whom a cause or matter has been tried, then, if that judge dies or ceases to be a judge of the High Court, or if for any other reason it is impossible or inconvenient for that judge to act in the cause or matter, the President of the Division to which the cause or matter is assigned may, either by a special order in any cause or matter, or by a general order applicable to any class of causes or matters, nominate some other judge to whom the application may be made or by whom the jurisdiction may be exercised.

Commencement   1 October 1966.
Amendments   Originally r 8, renumbered as r 7 by SI 1982/1111, r 11.
Para (2): words omitted revoked by SI 1982/1111, r 115, Schedule.

Order 4, r [8] Exercise of one master's or registrar's [district judge]'s jurisdiction by another

(1)   A master may hear and dispose of an application in a cause or matter on behalf of any other master of the same Division by whom the application would otherwise have been heard, if that other master so requests or an application in that behalf is made by a party to that cause or matter; and where the circumstances require it, the master shall, without the need for any such request or application, hear and dispose of the application.

[(2)   Paragraph (1) shall apply in relation to [district judges] of the Family Division, and as between masters of the Queen's Bench Division and the Admiralty Registrar, as it applies in relation to masters.]

Commencement   1 October 1971 (para (2)); 1 October 1966 (remainder).
Amendments   Originally r 9, renumbered as r 8 by SI 1982/1111, r 11.
Para (2): substituted by SI 1971/1269, r 3.

Order 4, r [9] Consolidation, etc, of causes or matters

(1)   Where two or more causes or matters are pending in the same Division and it appears to the Court—
  (a)   that some common question of law or fact arises in both or all of them, or
  (b)   that the rights to relief claimed therein are in respect of or arise out of the same transaction or series of transactions, or
  (c)   that for some other reason it is desirable to make an order under this paragraph,

the Court may order those causes or matters to be consolidated on such terms as it thinks just or may order them to be tried at the same time or one immediately after another or may order any of them to be stayed until after the determination of any other of them.

(2)   Where the Court makes an order under paragraph (1) that two or more causes or matters are to be tried at the same time but no order is made for those causes or matters to be consolidated, then, a party to one of those causes or matters may be treated as if he were a party to any other of those causes or matters for the purpose of making an order for costs against him or in his favour.]

Commencement   28 April 1986.
Amendments   Originally r 10, renumbered as r 9 by SI 1982/1111, r 11.
This rule was substituted by SI 1986/632, r 3.
Cross references   See CCR Order 13, r 9.

ORDER 5
MODE OF BEGINNING CIVIL PROCEEDINGS IN HIGH COURT

Order 5, r 1 Mode of beginning civil proceedings

Subject to the provisions of any Act and of these rules, civil proceedings in the High Court may be begun by writ, originating summons, originating motion or petition.

Commencement 1 October 1966.
Cross references See CCR Order 3.

Order 5, r 2 Proceedings which must be begun by writ

Subject to any provision of an Act, or of these rules, by virtue of which any proceedings are expressly required to be begun otherwise than by writ, the following proceedings must, notwithstanding anything in rule 4, be begun by writ, that is to say, proceedings—

(a) in which a claim is made by the plaintiff for any relief or remedy for any tort, other than trespass to land;

(b) in which a claim made by the plaintiff is based on an allegation of fraud;

(c) in which a claim is made by the plaintiff for damages for breach of duty (whether the duty exists by virtue of a contract or of a provision made by or under an Act or independently of any contract or any such provision), where the damages claimed consist of or include damages in respect of the death of any person or in respect of personal injuries to any person or in respect of damage to any property;

[(d)] . . .

. . .

Commencement 1 October 1966.
Amendments   Original para (d) revoked, para (e) renumbered as para (d), and final words omitted revoked, by SI 1975/911, r 2; existing para (d) revoked by SI 1978/579, r 8.
Cross references See CCR Order 3, r 1.

Order 5, r 3 Proceedings which must be begun by originating summons

Proceedings by which an application is to be made to the High Court or a judge thereof under any Act must be begun by originating summons except where by these rules or by or under any Act the application in question is expressly required or authorised to be made by some other means.

This rule does not apply to an application made in pending proceedings.

Commencement 1 October 1966.
Cross references See CCR Order 3, r 4.

Order 5, r 4 Proceedings which may be begun by writ or originating summons

(1) Except in the case of proceedings which by these rules or by or under any Act are required to be begun by writ or originating summons or are required or authorised to be begun by originating motion or petition, proceedings may be begun either by writ or by originating summons as the plaintiff considers appropriate.

(2)   Proceedings—
  (a)   in which the sole or principal question at issue is, or is likely to be, one of the
        construction of an Act or of any instrument made under an Act, or of any
        deed, will, contract or other document, or some other question of law, or
  (b)   in which there is unlikely to be any substantial dispute of fact,

are appropriate to be begun by originating summons unless the plaintiff intends in
those proceedings to apply for judgment under Order 14 or Order 86 or for any
other reason considers the proceedings more appropriate to be begun by writ.

Commencement 1 October 1966.
Cross references See CCR Order 3, rr 2, 4.

Order 5, r 5 Proceedings to be begun by motion or petition

Proceedings may be begun by originating motion or petition if, but only if, by these
rules or by or under any Act the proceedings in question are required or authorised to
be so begun.

Commencement 1 October 1966.
Cross references See CCR Order 3, r 5.

Order 5, r 6 Right to sue in person

(1)   Subject to paragraph (2) and to Order 80, rule 2, any person (whether or not
he sues as a trustee or personal representative or in any other representative capacity)
may begin and carry on proceedings in the High Court by a solicitor or in person.

(2)   Except as expressly provided by or under any enactment, a body corporate may
not begin or carry on any such proceedings otherwise than by a solicitor.

Commencement 1 October 1966.

ORDER 6
Writs of Summons: General Prov.

Order 6, r 1 Form of writ

Every writ must be in Form No 1, . . . in Appendix A, . . .

Commencement 1 October 1966.
Amendments Words omitted revoked by SI 1979/1716, r 4(1).

Order 6, r 2 Indorsement of claim

(1) Before a writ is issued it must be indorsed—
  (a) with a statement of claim or, if the statement of claim is not indorsed on the writ, with a concise statement of the nature of the claim made or the relief or remedy required in the action begun thereby;
  (b) where the claim made by the plaintiff is for a debt or liquidated demand only, with a statement of the amount claimed in respect of the debt or demand and for costs and also with a statement that further proceedings will be stayed if, within the time limited for [acknowledging service], the defendant . . . , pays the amount so claimed to the plaintiff, his solicitor or agent; . . .
  [(c) where the claim made by the plaintiff is for possession of land, with a statement showing—
    (i) whether the claim relates to a dwelling-house; and
    [(ii) if it does, whether the rateable value of the premises on every day specified by [section 4(2) of the Rent Act 1977] in relation to the premises exceeds the sum so specified [or whether the rent for the time being payable in respect of the premises exceeds the sum specified in section 4(4)(b) of the Rent Act 1977]][and
    (iii) in a case where the plaintiff knows of any person entitled to claim relief against forfeiture as underlessee (including a mortgagee) under section 146(4) of the Law of Property Act 1925 or in accordance with section 38 of the Supreme Court Act 1981, the name and address of that person.]]
  [(d) where the action is brought to enforce a right to recover possession of goods, with a statement showing the value of the goods.]
  [(e) where the action relates to a consumer credit agreement, with a certificate that the action is not one to which section 141 of the Consumer Credit Act 1974 applies.]
  [(f) where the action is an action for personal injuries, with a statement that the action is not one which by virtue of article 5 of the High Court and County Courts Jurisdiction Order 1991 must be commenced in a county court.]

[(2) Where particulars are given pursuant to paragraph (1)(c)(iii), the plaintiff shall send a copy of the writ to the person named.]

(3) . . .

Commencement 1 October 1986 (para (2)); 1 October 1966 (remainder).
Amendments Para (1): in sub-para (b) words "acknowledging service" substituted by SI 1979/1716, r 48, Schedule, Pt 1, words omitted revoked by SI 1979/1725, r 3(1); sub-para (c) added by SI 1966/1514, r 2; sub-para (c)(ii) substituted by SI 1973/1384, r 2, words "section 4(2) of the Rent Act 1977" substituted by SI 1979/1542, r 9(1), Schedule, words from "or whether the rent" to "the Rent Act 1977" inserted by SI 1990/492, r 2(1); sub-para (c)(iii) added by SI 1986/1187, r 2; sub-para (d) added by SI 1970/1208, r 3;

sub-para (e) inserted by SI 1989/177, r 2; sub-para (f) inserted by SI 1991/1329, r 4.
Para (2): substituted by SI 1986/1187, r 3.
Para (3): revoked by SI 1980/1908, r 19.
Cross references See CCR Order 3, r 3, Order 6, r 8.

Order 6, r 3 Indorsement as to capacity

(1)   Before a writ is issued it must be indorsed—
    (a)   where the plaintiff sues in a representative capacity, with a statement of the capacity in which he sues;
    (b)   where a defendant is sued in a representative capacity, with a statement of the capacity in which he is sued.

(2)   ...

Commencement 1 October 1966.
Amendments Para (2): revoked by SI 1980/1908, r 19.

Order 6, r 4 Indorsement as to place where cause of action arose

Where a writ is to be issued out of a district registry and any cause of action in respect of which relief is claimed by the writ wholly or in part arose in a place in the district of that registry [. . .], the writ may be indorsed with a statement to that effect before it is issued.

[In relation to a writ in the Chancery Division which is to be issued out of [one of the Chancery district registries] this rule shall have effect as if for the reference to the district of that registry there were substituted a reference to the [area of the circuit within which that registry is situate, and the Northern and North Eastern circuits shall be treated for this purpose as one circuit.]]

Commencement 1 October 1966.
Amendments Words omitted originally inserted by SI 1971/1955, r 4, revoked by SI 1976/1196, r 4; first words in square brackets added by SI 1976/1196, r 4, words from "area of the circuit" to "as one circuit" and "one of the Chancery district registries" substituted by SI 1982/1111, r 12.

Order 6, r 5 Indorsement as to solicitor and address

(1)   Before a writ is issued it must be indorsed—
    (a)   where the plaintiff sues by a solicitor, with the plaintiff's address and the solicitor's name or firm and a business address of his within the jurisdiction and also (if the solicitor is the agent of another) the name or firm and business address of his principal;
    (b)   where the plaintiff sues in person, with . . . the address of his place of residence and, if his place of residence is not within the jurisdiction or if he has no place of residence, the address of a place within the jurisdiction at or to which documents for him may be delivered or sent, ...

(2)   The address for service of a plaintiff shall be—
    (a)   where he sues by a solicitor, the business address [(to which may be added a numbered box at a document exchange)] of the solicitor indorsed on the writ or, where there are two such addresses so indorsed, the business address of the solicitor who is acting as agent for the other;
    (b)   where he sues in person, the address within the jurisdiction indorsed on the writ.

(3)   Where a solicitor's name is indorsed on a writ, he must, if any defendant who has been served with or who has [acknowledged service of the writ] requests him in writing so to do, declare in writing whether the writ was issued by him or with his authority or privity.

(4)   If a solicitor whose name is indorsed on a writ declares in writing that the writ was not issued by him or with his authority or privity, the Court may on the application of any defendant who has been served with or who has [acknowledged service of the writ], stay all proceedings in the action begun by the writ.

Commencement   1 October 1966.
Amendments   Para (1): words omitted revoked by SI 1979/1716, r 4(2).
Para (2): in sub-para (a) words "(to which may be added a numbered box at a document exchange)" inserted by SI 1986/632, r 12.
Para (3): words "acknowledged service of the writ" substituted by SI 1980/1908, r 20.
Para (4): words "acknowledged service of the writ" substituted by SI 1979/1716, r 48, Schedule, Pt 1.

Order 6, r 6 Concurrent writ

(1)   One or more concurrent writs may, at the request of the plaintiff, be issued at the time when the original writ is issued or at any time thereafter before the original writ ceases to be valid.

(2)   Without prejudice to the generality of paragraph (1), a writ for service within the jurisdiction may be issued as a concurrent writ with one which . . . is to be served out of the jurisdiction and a writ which . . . is to be served out of the jurisdiction may be issued as a concurrent writ with one for service within the jurisdiction.

(3) A concurrent writ is a true copy of the original writ with such differences only (if any) as are necessary having regard to the purpose for which the writ is issued.

Commencement   1 October 1966.
Amendments   Para (2): words omitted revoked by SI 1980/2000, r 21.
Forms   Praecipe for concurrent writ (PF4).

Order 6, r 7 Issue of writ

[(1) No writ which is to be served out of the jurisdiction shall be issued without the leave of the court unless it complies with the following conditions, that is to say—
  (a)   each claim made by the writ is either—
    (i)   one which by virtue of the Civil Jurisdiction and Judgments Act 1982 the Court has power to hear and determine, or
    (ii)   one which by virtue of any other enactment the Court has power to hear and determine notwithstanding that the person against whom the claim is made is not within the jurisdiction of the Court or that the wrongful act, neglect or default giving rise to the claim did not take place within its jurisdiction; and
  (b)   where a claim made by the writ is one which the Court has power to hear and determine by virtue of the Civil Jurisdiction and Judgments Act 1982, the writ is indorsed before it is issued with a statement that the Court has power under that Act to hear and determine the claim, and that no proceedings involving the same cause of action are pending between the parties in Scotland, Northern Ireland or another Convention territory.]

(2)   Except where otherwise expressly provided by these rules, a writ may be issued [out of—

(a) the Central Office if it relates to proceedings intended to be conducted in the Queen's Bench Division; or

[(b) the Admiralty and Commercial Registry if it relates to proceedings intended to be conducted in the Admiralty Court or the Commercial Court; or]

[(c)] Chancery Chambers if it relates to proceedings intended to be conducted in the Chancery Division; or

[(d)] a district registry.]

(3) [Subject to rule 7A] issue of a writ takes place upon its being sealed by an officer of the office out of which it is issued.

(4) The officer by whom a concurrent writ is sealed must mark it as a concurrent writ with an official stamp.

(5) No writ shall be sealed unless at the time of the tender thereof for sealing the person tendering it leaves at the office at which it is tendered a copy thereof signed, where the plaintiff sues in person, by him or, where he does not so sue, by or on behalf of his solicitor [. . .].

[(6) For the purposes of this rule, "Convention territory" means the territory or territories of any Contracting State, as defined by section 1(3) of that Act, to which [the Brussels Conventions or the Lugano Convention as defined] in section 1(1) of that Act apply.]

Commencement 1 January 1987 (paras (1), (6)); 1 October 1966 (remainder).
Amendments Para (1): substituted by SI 1983/1181, r 3.
Para (2): first words in square brackets substituted by SI 1982/1111, r 13; sub-para (b) inserted and original sub-paras (b), (c) renumbered as sub-paras (c), (d) by SI 1987/1423, r 3.
Para (3): words "Subject to rule 7A" inserted by SI 1990/2599, r 3.
Para (5): words omitted, originally added by SI 1979/1716, r 4(3), revoked by SI 1982/1111, r 106.
Para (6): added by SI 1983/1181, r 4; words "the Brussels Conventions or the Lugano Convention as defined" substituted by SI 1992/1907, r 12.
Cross references See CCR Order 3, r 3(5)–(8) as to para (1).
Forms Order for service out of jurisdiction (PF6).

[Order 6, r 7A Issue of Writ out of Admiralty and Commercial Registry when that Registry is closed

(1) When the Admiralty and Commercial Registry (in this rule referred to as "the Registry") is closed to the public, a writ may be issued out of the Registry in accordance with the provisions of this rule.

(2) A writ issued under this rule must—
(a) be signed by a solicitor acting on behalf of the plaintiff, and
(b) not require the leave of the court to be issued, unless such leave has already been given.

(3) A solicitor causing a writ to be issued under this rule (in this rule referred to as "the issuing solicitor") shall:
(a) endorse on the writ to be issued an endorsement in accordance with Form No 2C in Appendix B and sign the same; and
(b) transmit a copy of the writ, including the said endorsement, to the Registry by FAX for issue under this rule; and
(c) when he has received a transmission report stating that the transmission of the writ to the Registry was completed in full and the time and date of transmission, complete and sign the certificate in Form No 2C in

Appendix B with the date and time that, according to the transmission report, the FAX was transmitted to the Registry.

(4) Subject to paragraph (7) of this rule, the issue of a writ under this rule takes place when the FAX under paragraph (3)(b) is recorded at the Registry as having been received, and the writ bearing an endorsement under paragraph (3)(a) shall have the same effect for all purposes as a writ issued under rule 7 of this Order.

(5) When the Registry is next open to the public after the issue of a writ in accordance with this rule, the issuing solicitor or his agent shall:
- (a) attend and deliver to the Registry—
  - (i) the document which was transmitted by FAX, or, if the same has been served, a true copy thereof (including the endorsement and certificate referred to in paragraph (3)(a) and (c) above) endorsed by the issuing solicitor with the words "true copy of writ served on day of 19 ", for sealing in accordance with paragraph 5(b); together with as many copies thereof as are required by these rules;
  - (ii) the transmission report.
- (b) upon receipt of the documents under sub-paragraph (a) and evidence that the proper fee for issue of the writ has been paid, and upon satisfying himself that the document delivered fully accords with the document received by the Registry under paragraph 3(b), the proper officer shall allocate a folio number to the action, seal as the writ with the seal of the Registry the document delivered, stamp the same with the time and date when the writ was issued under paragraph (4), mark the same "original" and stamp the copies referred to in sub-paragraph (a)(i).

(6) Unless otherwise ordered by the Court, the sealed writ retained by the Court shall be conclusive proof that the writ was issued at the time and on the date stated.

(7) Notwithstanding Order 2, rule 1, if the issuing solicitor does not comply with the provisions of paragraphs (2) and (3) or if the document delivered under paragraph (5)(a)(i) is not sealed under paragraph (5)(b), the writ shall be deemed never to have been issued.

(8) As soon as practicable after the sealing of a writ under paragraph (5) the issuing solicitor shall inform any person served with the unsealed writ of the folio number of the action and, on request, serve any such person with a copy of the sealed writ at such address in England and Wales as he may request; and any such person may, without paying a fee, inspect and take copies of the documents lodged at the Registry under paragraphs (3) and (5).]

Commencement 1 February 1991.
Amendments This rule was inserted by SI 1990/2599, r 4.

Order 6, r 8 Duration and renewal of writ

[(1) For the purposes of service, a writ (other than a concurrent writ) is valid in the first instance—
- (a) if an Admiralty writ in rem, for 12 months;
- (b) where leave to serve the writ out of the jurisdiction is required under Order 11, for 6 months;
- (c) in any other case, for 4 months

beginning with the date of its issue.]

[(1A) A concurrent writ is valid in the first instance for the period of validity of the original writ which is unexpired at the date of issue of the concurrent writ.]

[(2) Subject to paragraph (2A), where a writ has not been served on a defendant, the Court may by order extend the validity of the writ from time to time for such period, not exceeding 4 months at any one time, beginning with the day next following that on which it would otherwise expire, as may be specified in the order, if an application for extension is made to the Court before that day or such later day (if any) as the Court may allow.

(2A) Where the Court is satisfied on an application under paragraph (2) that, despite the making of all reasonable efforts, it may not be possible to serve the writ within 4 months, the Court may, if it thinks fit, extend the validity of the writ for such period, not exceeding 12 months, as the Court may specify.]

(3) Before a writ, the validity of which has been extended under this rule, is served, it must be marked with an official stamp showing the period for which the validity of the writ has been so extended.

(4) Where the validity of a writ is extended by order made under this rule, the order shall operate in relation to any other writ (whether original or concurrent) issued in the same action which has not been served so as to extend the validity of that other writ until the expiration of the period specified in the order.

Commencement 1 October 1993 (para (1)); 4 June 1990 (paras (1A), (2), (2A)); 1 October 1966 (remainder).
Amendments Para (1): substituted, together with para (1A), for para (1) as originally enacted, by SI 1989/2427, r 2; further substituted by SI 1993/2133, r 4.
Para (1A): substituted, together with para (1), for para (1) as originally enacted, by SI 1989/2427, r 2.
Paras (2), (2A): substituted for para (2) as originally enacted by SI 1989/2427, r 3.
Cross references See CCR Order 7, r 20.
Forms Praecipe for renewal of writ (PF3).

ORDER 7
ORIGINATING SUMMONSES: GENERAL PROVISIONS

Order 7, r 1 Application

The provisions of this Order apply to all originating summonses subject, in the case of originating summonses of any particular class, to any special provisions relating to originating summonses of that class made by these rules or by or under any Act.

Commencement 1 October 1966.
Cross references See CCR Order 3, r 4.

Order 7, r 2 Form of summons, etc

[(1)   Every originating summons (other than an ex parte summons) shall be in Form No 8 or, if so authorised or required, in Form No 10 in Appendix A, and every ex parte originating summons shall be in Form No 11 in Appendix A.]

(2)   The party taking out an originating summons (other than an ex parte summons) shall be described as a plaintiff, and the other parties shall be described as defendants.

Commencement 3 June 1980 (para (1)); 1 October 1966 (remainder).
Amendments Para (1): substituted by SI 1979/1716, r 5.
Cross references See CCR Order 3, r 4.

Order 7, r 3 Contents of summons

(1)   Every originating summons must include a statement of the questions on which the plaintiff seeks the determination or direction of the High Court or, as the case may be, a concise statement of the relief or remedy claimed in the proceedings begun by the originating summons with sufficient particulars to identify the cause or causes of action in respect of which the plaintiff claims that relief or remedy.

(2)   Order 6, rules 3 and 5, shall apply in relation to an originating summons as they apply in relation to a writ.

Commencement 1 October 1966.
Cross references See CCR Order 3, r 4(2).

Order 7, r 4 Concurrent summons

Order 6, rule 6, shall apply in relation to an originating summons as it applies in relation to a writ.

Commencement 1 October 1966.

Order 7, r 5 Issue of summons

(1)   An originating summons by which proceedings intended to be assigned to the Queen's Bench Division are begun may be issued [out of the Central Office or out of the Admiralty and Commercial Registry] or out of a district registry.

(2)   An originating summons by which proceedings intended to be assigned to the Chancery Division are begun may be issued either out of [Chancery Chambers or

out of one of the Chancery district registries], but may be issued out of any other district registry only in the cases specifically provided for by these rules.

(3)   Order 6, rule 7 (except paragraph (2)), shall apply in relation to an originating summons as it applies in relation to a writ.

Commencement 1 October 1966.
Amendments Para (1): words "out of the Central Office or out of the Admiralty and Commercial Registry" substituted by SI 1987/1423, r 4.
Para (2): words "Chancery Chambers or out of one of the Chancery district registries" substituted by SI 1982/1111, r 14.
Cross references See CCR Order 3, r 4(4).

Order 7, r 6 Duration and renewal of summons

Order 6, rule 8, shall apply in relation to an originating summons as it applies in relation to a writ.

Commencement 1 October 1966.
Cross references See CCR Order 3, r 4(6), Order 7, r 20.

Order 7, r 7 Ex parte originating summonses

(1)   Rules 2(1), 3(1) and 5(1) and (2) shall, so far as applicable, apply to ex parte originating summonses; but, save as aforesaid, the foregoing rules of this Order shall not apply to ex parte originating summonses.

(2)   Order 6, rule 7(3) and (5), shall, with the necessary modifications, apply in relation to an ex parte originating summons as they apply in relation to a writ.

Commencement 1 October 1966.

ORDER 8
ORIGINATING AND OTHER MOTIONS: GENERAL PROVISIONS

Order 8, r 1 Application

The provisions of this Order apply to all motions subject, in the case of originating motions of any particular class, to any special provisions relating to motions of that class made by these rules or by or under any Act.

Commencement 1 October 1966.

Order 8, r 2 Notice of motion

(1)   Except where an application by motion may properly be made ex parte, no motion shall be made without previous notice to the parties affected thereby, by the Court, if satisfied that the delay caused by proceeding in the ordinary way would or might entail irreparable or serious mischief may make an order ex parte on such terms as to costs or otherwise, and subject to such undertaking, if any, as it thinks just; and any party affected by such order may apply to the Court to set it aside.

(2)   Unless the Court gives leave to the contrary, there must be at least 2 clear days between the service of notice of a motion and the day named in the notice for hearing the motion.

Commencement 1 October 1966.

Order 8, r 3 Form and issue of notice of motion

(1)   The notice of an originating motion must be in Form No 13 in Appendix A and the notice of any other motion in Form No 38 in that Appendix.

Where leave has been given under rule 2(2) to serve short notice of motion, that fact must be stated in the notice.

(2)   The notice of a motion must include a concise statement of the nature of the claim made or the relief or remedy required.

(3)   Order 6, rule 5, shall, with the necessary modifications, apply in relation to notice of an originating motion as it applies in relation to a writ.

[(4)   [Subject to Order 75, rule 33A, the notice] of an originating motion by which proceedings assigned to the Queen's Bench Division are begun [may be issued out of the Central Office or out of the Admiralty and Commercial Registry] [. . .].

(5)   The notice of an originating motion by which proceedings assigned to the Chancery Division are begun may be issued either out of [Chancery Chambers or out of one of the Chancery district registries].

(6)   Issue of the notice of an originating motion takes place upon its being sealed by an officer of the office out of which it is issued.]

Commencement 1 January 1972 (paras (4)–(6)); 1 October 1966 (remainder).
Amendments Para (4): substituted, together with paras (5), (6), for para (4) as originally enacted, by SI 1971/1955, r 6; words "Subject to Order 75, rule 33A, the notice" substituted by SI 1984/1051, r 16; words "may be issued out of the Central Office or out of the Admiralty and Commercial Registry" substituted by SI 1987/1423, r 5; words omitted originally inserted by SI 1975/911, r 3, subsequently revoked by SI 1984/1051, r 16.

Para (5): substituted, together with paras (4), (6), for para (4) as originally enacted, by SI 1971/1955, r 6; words "Chancery Chambers or out of one of the Chancery district registries" substituted by SI 1982/1111, r 14.
Para (6): substituted, together with paras (4), (5), for para (4) as originally enacted, by SI 1971/1955, r 6.

Order 8, r 4 Service of notice of motion with writ, etc

Notice of a motion to be made in an action may be served by the plaintiff on the defendant with the writ of summons or originating summons or at any time after service of such writ or summons, whether or not the defendant has [acknowledged service in the action].

Commencement 1 October 1966.
Amendments Words "acknowledged service in the action" substituted by SI 1982/1111, r 115, Schedule.

Order 8, r 5 Adjournment of hearing

The hearing of any motion may be adjourned from time to time on such terms, if any, as the Court thinks fit.

Commencement 1 October 1966.

ORDER 9
PETITIONS: GENERAL PROVISIONS

Order 9, r 1 Application

Rules 2 to 4 apply to petitions by which civil proceedings in the High Court are begun, subject, in the case of petitions of any particular class, to any special provisions relating to petitions of that class made by these rules or by or under any Act.

Commencement 1 October 1966.

Order 9, r 2 Contents of petition

(1)   Every petition must [have printed or embossed by an officer of the Court, at the head of the first page a replica of the Royal Arms and must] include a concise statement of the nature of the claim made or the relief or remedy required in the proceedings begun thereby.

(2)   Every petition must include at the end thereof a statement of the names of the persons, if any, required to be served therewith or, if no person is required to be served, a statement to that effect.

(3)   Order 6, rule 5, shall, with the necessary modifications, apply in relation to a petition as it applies in relation to a writ.

Commencement 1 October 1966.
Amendments Para (1): words from "have printed" to "and must" inserted by SI 1980/2000, r 16.
Cross references See CCR Order 3, rr 4(2), 5.

Order 9, r 3 Presentation of petition

(1)   A petition may be presented in [one of the Chancery district registries].

(2)   Subject to paragraph (1), a petition must be presented by leaving it at [Chancery Chambers].

Commencement 1 October 1966.
Amendments Para (1): words "one of the Chancery district registries" substituted by SI 1982/1111, r 15(1).
Para (2): words "Chancery Chambers" substituted by SI 1982/1111, r 15(2).
Cross references See CCR Order 3, rr 4(3), 5.

Order 9, r 4 Fixing time for hearing petition

(1)   A day and time for the hearing of a petition which is required to be heard shall be fixed—
  (a)   in the case of a petition presented in a district registry, by the [district judge] of that registry, and
  (b)   in any other case, by the [proper officer in Chancery Chambers].

(2)   Unless the Court otherwise directs, a petition which is required to be served on any person must be served on him not less than 7 days before the day fixed for the hearing of the petition.

Commencement 1 October 1966.
Amendments Para (1): in sub-para (b) words "proper officer in Chancery Chambers" substituted by SI 1982/1111, r 16.
Cross references See CCR Order 3, rr 4(5), 5.

Order 9, r 5 Certain applications not to be made by petition

No application in any cause or matter may be made by petition.

Commencement 1 October 1966.

ORDER 10
SERVICE OF ORIGINATING PROCESS: GENERAL PROVISIONS

Order 10, r 1 General provisions

(1)   . . . a writ must be served personally on each defendant by the plaintiff or his agent.

[(2)   A writ for service on a defendant within the jurisdiction may, instead of being served personally on him, be served—
  (a) by sending a copy of the writ by ordinary first-class post to the defendant at his usual or last known address, or
  (b) if there is a letter box for that address, by inserting through the letter box a copy of the writ enclosed in a sealed envelope addressed to the defendant.
        In sub-paragraph (a) 'first-class post' means first-class post which has been pre-paid or in respect of which prepayment is not required.

(3)   Where a writ is served in accordance with paragraph (2)—
  (a) the date of service shall, unless the contrary is shown, be deemed to be the seventh day (ignoring Order 3, rule 2(5)) after the date on which the copy was sent to or, as the case may be, inserted through the letter box for the address in question;
  (b) any affidavit proving due service of the writ must contain a statement to the effect that—
      (i) in the opinion of the deponent (or, if the deponent is the plaintiff's solicitor or an employee of that solicitor, in the opinion of the plaintiff) the copy of the writ, if sent to, or, as the case may be, inserted through the letter box for, the address in question, will have come to the knowledge of the defendant within 7 days thereafter; and
      (ii) in the case of service by post, the copy of the writ has not been returned to the plaintiff through the post undelivered to the addressee.]

[(4)] Where a defendant's solicitor indorses on the writ a statement that he accepts service of the writ on behalf of that defendant, the writ shall be deemed to have been duly served on that defendant and to have been so served on the date on which the indorsement was made.

[(5) Subject to Order 12, rule 7, where a writ is not duly served on a defendant but he acknowledges service of it, the writ shall be deemed, unless the contrary is shown, to have been duly served on him and to have been so served on the date on which he acknowledges service.

(6)   Every copy of a writ for service on a defendant shall be sealed with the seal of the office of the Supreme Court out of which the writ was issued and shall be accompanied by a form of acknowledgment of service in Form No 14 in Appendix A [in which the title of the action and its number have been entered].]

[[(7)] This rule shall have effect subject to the provisions of any Act and these rules and in particular to any enactment which provides for the manner in which documents may be served on bodies corporate.]

Commencement   3 June 1980 (paras (5), (6)); 24 April 1979 (paras (2), (3), (7)); 1 October 1966 (remainder).
Amendments   Para (1): words omitted revoked by SI 1979/402, r 2(1).
Paras (2), (3): inserted by SI 1979/402, r 2(2).
Para (4): originally para (2), renumbered as para (4), and original para (4) revoked, by SI 1979/402, r 2(3).
Para (5): originally para (3), renumbered as para (5) by SI 1979/402, r 2(3); substituted, together with para (6), for existing para (5), by SI 1979/1716, r 6(1).

Para (6): substituted, together with para (5), for existing para (5), by SI 1979/1716, r 6(1); words "in which the title of the action and its number have been entered" added by SI 1982/1111, r 107.
Para (7): added as para (6) by SI 1979/402, r 2(4)); renumbered as para (7) by SI 1979/1716, r 6(2).
Cross references See CCR Order 7, rr 9, 10, 10A, 11, 12.

Order 10, r 2 Service of writ on agent of overseas principal

(1)   Where the court is satisfied on an ex parte application that—

(a)   a contract has been entered into within the jurisdiction with or through an agent who is either an individual residing or carrying on business within the jurisdiction or a body corporate having a registered office or a place of business within the jurisdiction, and

(b)   the principal for whom the agent was acting was at the time the contract was entered into and is at the time of the application neither such an individual nor such a body corporate, and

(c)   at the time of the application either the agent's authority has not been determined or he is still in business relations with his principal,

the Court may authorise service of a writ beginning an action relating to the contract to be effected on the agent instead of the principal.

(2)   An order under this rule authorising service of a writ on a defendant's agent must limit a time within which the defendant must [acknowledge service].

(3)   Where an order is made under this rule authorising service of a writ on a defendant's agent, a copy of the order and of the writ must be sent by post to the defendant at his address out of the jurisdiction.

Commencement 1 October 1966.
Amendments Para (2): words "acknowledge service" substituted by SI 1979/1716, r 48, Schedule, Pt 1.

Order 10, r 3 Service of writ in pursuance of contract

(1)   Where—

(a)   a contract contains a term to the effect that the High Court shall have jurisdiction to hear and determine any action in respect of a contract or, apart from any such term, the High Court has jurisdiction to hear and determine any such action, and

(b)   the contract provides that, in the event of any action in respect of the contract being begun, the process by which it is begun may be served on the defendant, or on such other person on his behalf as may be specified in the contract, in such manner, or at such place (whether within or out of the jurisdiction), as may be so specified,

then, if an action in respect of the contract is begun in the High Court and the writ by which it is begun is served in accordance with the contract, the writ shall, subject to paragraph (2), be deemed to have been duly served on the defendant.

(2)   A writ which is served out of the jurisdiction in accordance with a contract shall not be deemed to have been duly served on the defendant by virtue of paragraph (1) unless leave to serve the writ . . . out of the jurisdiction [has been granted under Order 11, rule 1(1) or service of the writ is permitted without leave under Order 11, rule 1(2)].

[(3)   Where a contract contains an agreement conferring jurisdiction to which [Article 17 of Schedule 1, 3C or 4] to the Civil Jurisdiction and Judgments Act 1982 applies and the writ is served under Order 11, rule 1(2) the writ shall be deemed to have been duly served on the defendant.]

Commencement 1 January 1987 (para (3)); 1 October 1966 (remainder).
Amendments Para (2): words omitted revoked by SI 1980/2000, r 21; words from "has been granted" to "Order 11, rule 1(2)" substituted by SI 1983/1181, r 5.
Para (3): added by SI 1983/1181, r 6; words "Article 17 of Schedule 1, 3C or 4" substituted by SI 1992/1907, r 13.

Order 10, r 4 Service of writ in certain actions for possession of land

Where a writ is indorsed with a claim for the possession of land, the Court may—
  (a) if satisfied on an ex parte application that no person appears to be in possession of the land and that service cannot be otherwise effected on any defendant, authorise service on that defendant to be effected by affixing a copy of the writ to some conspicuous part of the land;
  (b) if satisfied on such an application that no person appears to be in possession of the land and that service could not otherwise have been effected on any defendant, order that service already effected by affixing a copy of the writ to some conspicuous part of the land shall be treated as good service on that defendant.

Commencement 1 October 1966.
Cross references See CCR Order 7, r 15.
Forms Order (PF5).

[Order 10, r 5 Service of originating summons, notice of motion or petition

(1)   The foregoing rules of this Order shall apply, with any necessary modifications, in relation to an originating summons (other than ex parte originating summons or an originating summons under Order 113) as they apply in relation to a writ, except that an acknowledgment of service of an originating summons shall be in Form No 15 in Appendix A.

(2)   Rule 1(1), (2), (3) and (4) shall apply, with any necessary modifications, in relation to a notice of an originating motion and a petition as they apply in relation to a writ.]

Commencement 3 June 1980.
Amendments This rule was substituted by SI 1979/1716, r 7.
Cross references See CCR Order 7, rr 9, 10.
Forms Affidavit of service of originating summons (PF131).

ORDER 11
SERVICE OF PROCESS, ETC, OUT OF THE JURISDICTION

[Order 11, r 1 Principal cases in which service of writ out of jurisdiction is permissible

(1)   Provided that the writ does not contain any claim mentioned in Order 75, rule 2(1) and is not a writ to which paragraph (2) of this rule applies, service of a writ out of the jurisdiction is permissible with the leave of the Court if in the action begun by the writ—

- (a)   relief is sought against a person domiciled within the jurisdiction;
- (b)   an injunction is sought ordering the defendant to do or refrain from doing anything within the jurisdiction (whether or not damages are also claimed in respect of a failure to do or the doing of that thing);
- (c)   the claim is brought against a person duly served within or out of the jurisdiction and a person out of the jurisdiction is a necessary or proper party thereto;
- (d)   the claim is brought to enforce, rescind, dissolve, annul or otherwise affect a contract, or to recover damages or obtain other relief in respect of the breach of a contract, being (in either case) a contract which—
  - (i)   was made within the jurisdiction, or
  - (ii)   was made by or through an agent trading or residing within the jurisdiction on behalf of a principal trading or residing out of the jurisdiction, or
  - (iii)   is by its terms, or by implication, governed by English law, or
  - (iv)   contains a term to the effect that the High Court shall have jurisdiction to hear and determine any action in respect of the contract;
- (e)   the claim is brought in respect of a breach committed within the jurisdiction of a contract made within or out of the jurisdiction, and irrespective of the fact, if such be the case, that the breach was preceded or accompanied by a breach committed out of the jurisdiction that rendered impossible the performance of so much of the contract as ought to have been performed within the jurisdiction;
- (f)   the claim is founded on a tort and the damage was sustained, or resulted from an act committed, within the jurisdiction;
- (g)   the whole subject-matter of the action is land situate within the jurisdiction (with or without rents or profits) or the perpetuation of testimony relating to land so situate;
- (h)   the claim is brought to construe, rectify, set aside or enforce an act, deed, will, contract, obligation or liability affecting land situate within the jurisdiction;
- (i)   the claim is made for a debt secured on immovable property or is made to assert, declare or determine proprietary or possessory rights, or rights of security, in or over movable property, or to obtain authority to dispose of movable property, situate within the jurisdiction;
- (j)   the claim is brought to execute the trusts of a written instrument being trusts that ought to be executed according to English law and of which the person to be served with the writ is a trustee, or for any relief or remedy which might be obtained in any such action;
- (k)   the claim is made for the administration of the estate of a person who died domiciled within the jurisdiction or for any relief or remedy which might be obtained in any such action;

(l)   the claim is brought in a probate action within the meaning of Order 76;

(m)   the claim is brought to enforce any judgment or arbitral award;

(n)   the claim is brought against a defendant not domiciled in Scotland or Northern Ireland in respect of a claim by the Commissioners of Inland Revenue for or in relation to any of the duties or taxes which have been, or are for the time being, placed under their care and management;

(o)   the claim is brought under the Nuclear Installations Act 1965 or in respect of contributions under the Social Security Act 1975;

(p)   the claim is made for a sum to which the Directive of the Council of the European Communities dated 15th March 1976 No 76/308/EEC applies, and service is to be effected in a country which is a member State of the European Economic Community;

[(q)   the claim is made under the Drug Trafficking Offences Act 1986;]

[(r)   the claim is made under [the Financial Services Act 1986 or] the Banking Act 1987;]

[(s)   the claim is made under Part VI of the Criminal Justice Act 1988.]

[(t)   the claim is brought for money had and received or for an account or other relief against the defendant as constructive trustee, and the defendant's alleged liability arises out of acts committed, whether by him or otherwise, within the jurisdiction.]

[(u)   the claim is made under the Immigration (Carriers' Liability) Act 1987.]

(2)   Service of a writ out of the jurisdiction is permissible without the leave of the Court provided that each claim made by the writ is either:—

(a)   a claim which by virtue of the Civil Jurisdiction and Judgments Act 1982 the Court has power to hear and determine, made in proceedings to which the following conditions apply—

    (i)   no proceedings between the parties concerning the same cause of action are pending in the courts of any other part of the United Kingdom or of any other Convention territory, and

    (ii) either—

        the defendant is domiciled in any part of the United Kingdom or in any other Convention territory, or

        the proceedings begun by the writ are proceedings to which Article 16 [of Schedule 1, 3C or 4] refers, or

        the defendant is a party to an agreement conferring jurisdiction to which Article 17 [of Schedule 1, 3C or 4] to that Act applies,

    or

(b)   a claim which by virtue of any other enactment the High Court has power to hear and determine notwithstanding that the person against whom the claim is made is not within the jurisdiction of the Court or that the wrongful act, neglect or default giving rise to the claim did not take place within its jurisdiction.

(3)   Where a writ is to be served out of the jurisdiction under paragraph (2), the time to be inserted in the writ within which the defendant served therewith must acknowledge service shall be—

(a)   21 days where the writ is to be served out of the jurisdiction under paragraph (2)(a) in Scotland, Northern Ireland or in the European territory of another Contracting State, or

(b)   31 days where the writ is to be served under paragraph (2)(a) in any other territory of a Contracting State, or

(c) limited in accordance with the practice adopted under rule 4(4) where the writ is to be served under paragraph (2)(a) in a country not referred to in sub-paragraphs (a) or (b) or under paragraph (2)(b).

(4) For the purposes of this rule, and of rule 9 of this Order, domicile is to be determined in accordance with the provisions of sections 41 to 46 of the Civil Jurisdiction and Judgments Act 1982 and "Convention territory" means the territory or territories of any Contracting State, as defined by section 1(3) of that Act, to which [the Brussels Conventions or the Lugano Convention] as defined in section 1(1) of that Act apply.]

Commencement 1 January 1987.
Amendments This rule was substituted by SI 1983/1181, r 7.
Para (1): sub-para (q) added by SI 1986/2289, r 16; sub-para (r) added by SI 1988/298, r 10, words "the Financial Services Act 1986 or" inserted by SI 1990/2599, r 7; sub-para (s) added by SI 1989/386, r 3; sub-para (t) added by SI 1990/1689, r 12; sub-para (u) inserted by SI 1993/2760, r 3.
Para (2): words "of Schedule 1, 3C or 4", in both places where they occur, substituted by SI 1992/1907, r 14.
Para (4): words "the Brussels Conventions or the Lugano Convention" substituted by SI 1992/1907, r 15.
Cross references See CCR Order 8, rr 1, 2.

Order 11, rr 2, 3 *(revoked by SI 1980/2000)*

Order 11, r 4 Application for, and grant of, leave to serve writ out of jurisdiction

[(1) An application for the grant of leave under rule 1(1) must be supported by an affidavit stating—
(a) the grounds on which the application is made,
(b) that in the deponent's belief the plaintiff has a good cause of action,
(c) in what place or country the defendant is, or probably may be found, and
(d) where the application is made under rule 1(1)(c), the grounds for the deponent's belief that there is between the plaintiff and the person on whom a writ has been served a real issue which the plaintiff may reasonably ask the Court to try.]

(2) No such leave shall be granted unless it shall be made sufficiently to appear to the Court that the case is a proper one for service out of the jurisdiction under this Order.

(3) Where the application is for the grant of leave under rule 1 to serve a writ in Scotland or Northern Ireland, if it appears to the Court that there may be a concurrent remedy there, the Court, in deciding whether to grant leave, shall have regard to the comparative cost and convenience of proceeding there or in England, and (where that is relevant) to the powers and jurisdiction of the [sheriff court] in Scotland or the county courts or courts of summary jurisdiction in Northern Ireland.

(4) An order granting under rule 1 . . . leave to serve a writ . . . out of the jurisdiction must limit a time within which the defendant to be served must [acknowledge service].

Commencement 1 January 1987 (para (1)); 1 October 1966 (remainder).
Amendments Para (1): substituted by SI 1983/1181, r 9(1).
Para (3): words "sheriff court" substituted by SI 1982/375, r 2.
Para (4): first words omitted revoked by SI 1983/1181, r 9(2); second words omitted revoked by SI 1980/2000, r 21; words "acknowledge service" substituted by SI 1979/1716, r 48, Schedule, Pt 1.
Cross references See CCR Order 8, rr 5, 6.
Forms Order (PF6).

Order 11, r 5 Service of writ ... abroad: general

(1)   Subject to the following provisions of this rule, [Order 10, rule 1(1), (4), (5) and (6)] and Order 65, rule 4, shall apply in relation to the service of a writ ... notwithstanding that the writ ... is to be served out of the jurisdiction[, save that the accompanying form of acknowledgment of service shall be modified in such manner as may be appropriate].

(2)   Nothing in this rule or in any order or direction of the Court made by virtue of it shall authorise or require the doing of anything in a country in which service is to be effected which is contrary to the law of that country.

(3)   A writ ... which is to be served out of the jurisdiction—
   (a)   need not be served personally on the person required to be served so long as it is served on him in accordance with the law of the country in which service is effected; and
   (b)   need not be served by the plaintiff or his agent if it is served by a method provided for by rule 6 or rule 7.

(4)   ...

(5)   An official certificate stating that ... a writ, as regards which rule 6 has been complied with, has been served on a person personally, or in accordance with the law of the country in which service was effected, on a specified date, being a certificate—
   (a)   by a British consular authority in that country, or
   (b)   by the government or judicial authorities of that country, [or
   (c)   by any other authority designated in respect of that country under the Hague Convention.]
shall be evidence of the facts so stated.

(6)   An official certificate by the Secretary of State stating that ... a writ has been duly served on a specified date in accordance with a request made under rule 7 shall be evidence of that fact.

(7)   A document purporting to be such a certificate as is mentioned in paragraph (5) or (6) shall, until the contrary is proved, be deemed to be such a certificate.

[(8)   In this rule and rule 6 "the Hague Convention" means the Convention on the service abroad of judicial and extra-judicial documents in civil or commercial matters signed at The Hague on 15th November 1965.]

Commencement   1 September 1968 (para (8)); 1 October 1966 (remainder).
Amendments   Rule heading: words omitted revoked by SI 1980/2000, r 21.
Para (1): words "Order 10, rule 1(1), (4), (5) and (6)" substituted, words omitted revoked, words from ", save that" to "as may be appropriate" inserted, by SI 1980/2000, r 18.
Para (3): words omitted revoked by SI 1980/2000, r 21.
Para (4): revoked by SI 1979/402, r 4(2).
Para (5): words omitted revoked by SI 1980/2000, r 21; in sub-para (b) word "or" and sub-para (c) inserted by SI 1968/1244, r 15(1).
Para (6): words omitted revoked by SI 1980/2000, r 21.
Para (8): added by SI 1968/1244, r 15(2).
Cross references   See CCR Order 8, rr 8, 9.

Order 11, r 6 Service of ... writ abroad through foreign governments, judicial authorities and British consuls

(1)   [Save where ... a writ is to be served pursuant to paragraph (2A),] this rule does not apply to service in—

(a) Scotland, Northern Ireland, the Isle of Man or the Channel Islands;
[(b) any independent Commonwealth country;]
[(c) any associated state;
(d) any colony;
(e) the Republic of Ireland.]

(2) Where in accordance with these rules . . . a writ is to be served on a defendant in any country with respect to which there subsists a Civil Procedure Convention [(other than the Hague Convention)] providing for service in that country of process of the High Court, the [writ] may be served—
   (a) through the judicial authorities of that country; or
   (b) through a British consular authority in that country (subject to any provision of the Convention as to the nationality of persons who may be so served).

[(2A) Where, in accordance with these rules, . . . a writ is to be served on a defendant in any country which is a party to the Hague Convention, the [writ] may be served—
   (a) through the authority designated under the Convention in respect of that country; or
   (b) if the law of that country permits—
      (i) through the judicial authorities of that country, or
      (ii) through a British consular authority in that country.]

(3) Where in accordance with these rules . . . a writ is to be served on a defendant in any country with respect to which there does not subsist a Civil Procedure Convention providing for service in that country of process of the High Court, the [writ] may be served—
   (a) through the government of that country, where that government is willing to effect service; or
   (b) through a British consular authority in that country, except where service through such an authority is contrary to the law of that country.

(4) [A person who wishes to serve . . . a writ by a method specified in paragraph (2), (2A) or (3)] must lodge in the Central Office a request for service of . . . the writ by that method, together with a copy of the [writ] and an additional copy thereof for each person to be served.

(5) Every copy of a [writ] lodged under paragraph (4) must be accompanied by a translation of the [writ] in the official language of the country in which service is to be effected or, if there is more than one official language of that country, in any one of those languages which is appropriate to the place in that country where service is to be effected:

Provided that this paragraph shall not apply in relation to a copy of a [writ] which is to be served in a country the official language of which is, or the official languages of which include, English, or is to be served in any country by a British consular authority on a British subject, unless the service is to be effected under paragraph (2) and the Civil Procedure Convention with respect to that country expressly requires the copy to be accompanied by a translation.

(6) Every translation lodged under paragraph (5) must be certified by the person making it to be a correct translation; and the certificate must contain a statement of that person's full name, of his address and of his qualifications for making the translation.

(7)   Documents duly lodged under paragraph (4) shall be sent by the senior master to the Parliamentary Under-Secretary of State to the Foreign Office with a request that he arrange for . . . the writ to be served by the method indicated in the request lodged under paragraph (4) or, where alternative methods are so indicated, by such one of those methods as is most convenient.

Commencement   1 September 1968 (para (2A)); 1 October 1966 (remainder).
Amendments   Rule heading: words omitted revoked by SI 1980/2000, r 21.
Para (1): first words in square brackets inserted by SI 1980/629, r 5(1); words omitted therein revoked by SI 1980/2000, r 21; sub-para (b) substituted by SI 1976/337, r 3(1); sub-paras (c)–(e) substituted by SI 1980/629, r 5(1).
Para (2): words omitted revoked and word "writ" substituted by SI 1980/2000, rr 21, 22(a); words "(other than the Hague Convention)" inserted by SI 1968/1244, r 15(3).
Para (2A): inserted by SI 1968/1244, r 15(4); words omitted revoked by SI 1982/1111, r 115, Schedule; word "writ" substituted by SI 1980/2000, r 22(a).
Para (3): words omitted revoked and word "writ" substituted by SI 1980/2000, rr 21, 22(a).
Para (4): first words in square brackets substituted by SI 1968/1244, r 5(5); second word in square brackets substituted, and words omitted revoked, by SI 1980/2000, r 21, 22(a).
Para (5): word "writ" wherever it occurs substituted by SI 1980/2000, r 22(b).
Para (7): words omitted revoked by SI 1980/2000, r 21.
Cross references   See CCR Order 8, r 10.
Forms   Request for service abroad (PF7).

Order 11, r 7 Service of . . . writ in certain actions under certain Acts

[(1)   Subject to paragraph (4), where a person to whom leave has been granted under Rule 1 to serve . . . a writ on a State, as defined in section 14 of the State Immunity Act 1978, wishes to have the [writ] served on that State, he must lodge in the Central Office—

    (a)   a request for service to be arranged by the Secretary of State; and

    (b)   a copy of the [writ]; and

    (c)   except where the official language of the State is, or the official languages of the State include, English, a translation of the [writ] in the official language or one of the official languages of that State.

(2)   Rule 6(6) shall apply in relation to a translation lodged under paragraph (1) of this Rule as it applies in relation to a translation lodged under paragraph (5) of that Rule.

(3)   Documents duly lodged under this Rule shall be sent by the senior master to the Secretary of State with a request that the Secretary of State should arrange for the [writ] to be served.

(4)   Where section 12(6) of the State Immunity Act 1978 applies and the State has agreed to a method of service other than that provided by the preceding paragraphs, the writ . . . may be served either by the method agreed or in accordance with the preceding paragraphs of this rule.]

Commencement   3 June 1980.
Amendments   This rule was substituted by SI 1980/629, r 5(2).
Rule heading: words omitted revoked by SI 1980/2000, r 21.
Paras (1), (3), (4): words omitted revoked, and words "writ" in square brackets substituted, by SI 1980/2000, rr 21, 22(c), (d).

Order 11, r 8 Undertaking to pay expenses of service by Secretary of State

Every request lodged under rule 6(4) or rule 7 must contain an undertaking by the person making the request to be responsible personally for all expenses incurred by the Secretary of State in respect of the service requested and, on receiving due notification of the amount of those expenses, to pay that amount to the Finance Officer of the office of the Secretary of State and to produce a receipt for the payment to the proper officer of the High Court.

Commencement 1 October 1966.

Order 11, r 9 Service of originating summons, petition, notice of motion, etc

[(1)   Subject to Order 73, rule 7, rule 1 of this Order shall apply to the service out of the jurisdiction of an originating summons, notice of motion or petition as it applies to service of a writ.]

(2), (3) . . .

(4)   Subject to Order 73, rule 7, service out of the jurisdiction of any summons, notice or order issued, given or made in any proceedings is permissible with the leave of the Court[, but leave shall not be required for such service in any proceedings in which the writ, originating summons, motion or petition may by these rules or under any Act be served out of the jurisdiction without leave].

(5)   Rule 4(1), (2) and (3) shall, so far as applicable, apply in relation to an application for the grant of leave under this rule as they apply in relation to an application for the grant of leave under rule 1 . . . .

(6)   An order granting under this rule leave to serve out of the jurisdiction an originating summons . . . must limit a time within which the defendant to be served with the summons must [acknowledge service].

(7)   Rules 5, 6 and 8 shall apply in relation to any document for the service of which out of the jurisdiction leave has been granted under this rule as they apply in relation to . . . a writ.

[(8)   . . .]

Commencement   1 January 1987 (para (1)); 3 June 1980 (para (8)); 1 October 1966 (remainder).
Amendments   Para (1): substituted by SI 1983/1181, r 10.
Paras (2), (3): revoked by SI 1983/1181, r 11(1).
Para (4): words from ", but leave shall not be required" to "jurisdiction without leave" inserted by SI 1983/1181, r 11(2).
Para (5): words omitted revoked by SI 1983/1181, r 11(3).
Para (6): words omitted revoked and words "acknowledge service" substituted by SI 1979/1716, r 48, Schedule, Pts 1, 2.
Para (7): words omitted revoked by SI 1980/2000, r 21.
Para (8): added by SI 1980/629, r 29; revoked by SI 1980/2000, r 19.
Cross references   See CCR Order 8, rr 8–10.

[Order 11, r 10 Service abroad of county court process

Rule 6(7) shall apply, with the necessary modifications, to any county court documents sent to the senior master for service abroad in accordance with the County Court Rules, and every certificate or declaration of service received by the senior master in respect of such service shall be transmitted by him to the [district judge] of the county court concerned.]

Commencement   3 June 1980.
Amendments   This rule was added by SI 1980/629, r 5(3).
Cross references   See CCR Order 8, rr 8–10.

ORDER 12
[Acknowledgment of Service of] Writ or Originating Summons

Amendments   Words "Acknowledgment of Service of" substituted by SI 1979/1716, r 48, Schedule, Pt 1.

[Order 12, r 1 Mode of acknowledging service

(1)   Subject to paragraph (2) and to Order 80, rule 2, a defendant to an action begun by writ may (whether or not he is sued as a trustee or personal representative or in any other representative capacity) acknowledge service of the writ and defend the action by a solicitor or in person.

(2)   The defendant to such an action who is a body corporate may acknowledge service of the writ and give notice of intention to defend the action either by a solicitor or by a person duly authorised to act on the defendant's behalf but, except as aforesaid or as expressly provided by any enactment, such a defendant may not take any step in the action otherwise than by a solicitor.

(3)   Service of a writ may be acknowledged by properly completing an acknowledgment of service, as defined by rule 3, and handing it in at, or sending it by post to, the appropriate office, that is to say, if the writ was issued out of [an office of the Supreme Court at the Royal Courts of Justice], that office, or if the writ was issued out of a district registry, that registry.

(4)   If two or more defendants to an action acknowledge service by the same solicitor and at the same time, only one acknowledgment of service need be completed and delivered for those defendants.

(5)   The date on which service is acknowledged is the date on which the acknowledgment of service is received at the appropriate office.]

Commencement   3 June 1980.
Amendments   This rule was substituted by SI 1979/1716, r 9.
Para (3): words "an office of the Supreme Court at the Royal Courts of Justice" substituted by SI 1982/1111, r 17.

Order 12, r 2   (*revoked by SI 1979/1716*)

[Order 12, r 3 Acknowledgment of service

(1)   An acknowledgment of service must be in Form No 14 or 15 in Appendix A, whichever is appropriate, and, except as provided in rule 1(2), must be signed by the solicitor acting for the defendant specified in the acknowledgment or, if the defendant is acting in person, by the defendant.

(2)   An acknowledgment of service must specify—
   (a)   in the case of a defendant acknowledging service in person, the address of his place of residence and, if his place of residence is not within the jurisdiction or if he has no place of residence, the address of a place within the jurisdiction at or to which documents for him may be delivered or sent, and
   (b)   in the case of a defendant acknowledging service by a solicitor, a business address [(to which may be added a numbered box at a document exchange)] of his solicitor's within the jurisdiction;

and where the defendant acknowledges service in person, the address within the jurisdiction specified under sub-paragraph (a) shall be his address for service, but otherwise his solicitor's business address shall be his address for service.

In relation to a body corporate the references in sub-paragraph (a) to the defendant's place of residence shall be construed as references to the defendant's registered or principal office.

(3) Where the defendant acknowledges service by a solicitor who is acting as agent for another solicitor having a place of business within the jurisdiction, the acknowledgment of service must state that the first-named solicitor so acts and must also state the name and address of that other solicitor.

(4) If an acknowledgment of service does not specify the defendant's address for service or the Court is satisfied that any address specified in the acknowledgment of service is not genuine, the Court may on application by the plaintiff set aside the acknowledgment or order the defendant to give an address or, as the case may be, a genuine address for service and may in any case direct that the acknowledgment shall nevertheless have effect for the purposes of Order 10, rule 1(5), and Order 65, rule 9.]

Commencement 3 June 1980.
Amendments This rule was substituted by SI 1979/1716, r 10.
Para (2): in sub-para (b) words "(to which may be added a numbered box at a document exchange)" inserted by SI 1986 No 632, r 13.

[Order 12, r 4 Procedure on receipt of acknowledgment of service

On receiving an acknowledgment of service an officer of the appropriate office must—
- (a) affix to the acknowledgment an official stamp showing the date on which he received it;
- (b) enter the acknowledgment in the cause book with a note showing, if it be the case, that the defendant has indicated in the acknowledgment an intention to contest the proceedings or to apply for a stay of execution in respect of any judgment obtained against him in the proceedings;
- (c) make [a copy] of the acknowledgment, . . . having affixed to it an official stamp showing the date on which he received the acknowledgment, and send [it] by post to the plaintiff or, as the case may be, his solicitor at the plaintiff's address for service . . .].

Commencement 3 June 1980.
Amendments This rule was substituted by SI 1979/1716, r 11.
Words "a copy" and "it" substituted and words omitted revoked by SI 1982/1111, r 108.

Order 12, r 5 Time limited for [acknowledging service]

References in these rules to the time limited for [acknowledging service] are references—
- (a) in the case of a writ served within the jurisdiction, to [14 days] after service of the writ (including the day of service) or, where that time has been extended by or by virtue of these rules, to that time as so extended; and
- (b) in the case of a writ . . . served out of the jurisdiction, to the time limited under Order 10, rule 2(2), Order 11, rule 1(3), or Order 11, rule 4(4), or, where that time has been extended as aforesaid, to that time as so extended.

Commencement 1 October 1966.
Amendments Rule heading: words "acknowledging service" substituted by SI 1979/1716, r 48, Schedule, Pt 1.
Words "acknowledging service" substituted by SI 1979 No 1716, r 48, Schedule, Part 1; words "14 days" substituted by SI 1970/1861, r 3; words omitted revoked by SI 1982/1111, r 115, Schedule.
Cross references See CCR Order 8, r 7 as to service out of jurisdiction.

[Order 12, r 6 Late acknowledgment of service

(1)   Except with the leave of the Court, a defendant may not give notice of intention to defend in an action after judgment has been obtained therein.

(2)   Except as provided by paragraph (1), nothing in these rules or any writ or order thereunder shall be construed as precluding a defendant from acknowledging service in an action after the time limited for so doing, but if a defendant acknowledges service after that time, he shall not, unless the Court otherwise orders, be entitled to serve a defence or do any other act later than if he had acknowledged service within that time.]

Commencement   3 June 1980.
Amendments   This rule was substituted by SI 1979/1716, r 12.
Cross references   This rule is applied to business list actions in the central London county court by CCR Order 48C, r 8(4).
Forms   Acknowledgment of service by leave (PF8).

[Order 12, r 7 Acknowledgment not to constitute waiver

The acknowledgment by a defendant of service of a writ . . . shall not be treated as a waiver by him of any irregularity in the writ . . . or service thereof or in any order giving leave to serve the writ out of the jurisdiction or extending the validity of the writ for the purpose of service.]

Commencement   3 June 1980.
Amendments   This rule was substituted by SI 1979/1716, r 13.
Words omitted revoked by SI 1982/1111, r 115, Schedule.
Cross references   See CCR Order 9, r 13.
This rule is applied to business list actions in the central London county court by CCR Order 48C, r 8(4).

[Order 12, r 8 Dispute as to jurisdiction

(1)   A defendant who wishes to dispute the jurisdiction of the court in the proceedings by reason of any such irregularity as is mentioned in rule 7 or on any other ground shall give notice of intention to defend the proceedings and shall, [within the time limited for service of a defence], apply to the Court for—
- (a)   an order setting aside the writ or service of the writ . . . on him, or
- (b)   an order declaring that the writ . . . has not been duly served on him, or
- (c)   the discharge of any order giving leave to serve the writ . . . on him out of the jurisdiction, or
- (d)   the discharge of any order extending the validity of the writ for the purpose of service, or
- (e)   the protection or release of any property of the defendant seized or threatened with seizure in the proceedings, or
- (f)   the discharge of any order made to prevent any dealing with any property of the defendant, or
- (g)   a declaration that in the circumstances of the case the court has no jurisdiction over the defendant in respect of the subject matter of the claim or the relief or remedy sought in the action, or
- (h)   such other relief as may be appropriate.

(2)   . . .

(3)   An application under paragraph (1) must be made—
- (a)   in an Admiralty action in rem, by motion;

(b)   in any other action in the Queen's Bench Division, by summons;

(c)   in any other action, by summons or motion,

and the notice of motion or summons must state the grounds of the application.

(4)   An application under paragraph (1) must be supported by an affidavit verifying the facts on which the application is based and a copy of the affidavit must be served with the notice of motion or summons by which the application is made.

(5)   Upon hearing an application under paragraph (1), the Court, if it does not dispose of the matter in dispute, may give such directions for its disposal as may be appropriate, including directions for the trial thereof as a preliminary issue.

[(6)   A defendant who makes an application under paragraph (1) shall not be treated as having submitted to the jurisdiction of the Court by reason of his having given notice of intention to defend the action; and if the Court makes no order on the application or dismisses it, the notice shall cease to have effect, but the defendant may, subject to rule 6(1), lodge a further acknowledgement of service within 14 days or such other period as the Court may direct and in that case paragraph (7) shall apply as if the defendant had not made any such application.]

(7)   Except where the defendant makes an application in accordance with paragraph (1), the acknowledgment by a defendant of service of a writ . . . shall, unless the acknowledgment is withdrawn by leave of the Court under Order 21, rule 1, be treated as a submission by the defendant to the jurisdiction of the Court in the proceedings.]

Commencement 1 October 1991 (para (6)); 3 June 1980 (remainder).
Amendments This rule was substituted by SI 1979/1716, r 13.
Para (1): words "within the time limited for service of a defence" substituted by SI 1983/1181, r 12; in sub-paras (a)–(c) words omitted revoked by SI 1980/2000, r 21.
Para (2): revoked by SI 1983/1181, r 12.
Para (6): substituted by SI 1991/1884, r 28.
Para (7): words omitted revoked by SI 1980/2000, r 21.
Cross references This rule is applied to business list actions in the central London county court by CCR Order 48C, r 8(4).

[Order 12, r 8A Application by defendant where writ not served

(1)   Any person named as a defendant in a writ which has not been served on him may serve on the plaintiff a notice requiring him within a specified period not less than 14 days after service of the notice either to serve the writ on the defendant or to discontinue the action as against him.

(2)   Where the plaintiff fails to comply with a notice under paragraph (1) within the time specified the Court may, on the application of the defendant by summons, order the action to be dismissed or make such other order as it thinks fit.

(3)   A summons under paragraph (2) shall be supported by an affidavit verifying the facts on which the application is based and stating that the defendant intends to contest the proceedings and a copy of the affidavit must be served with the summons.

(4)   Where the plaintiff serves the writ in compliance with a notice under paragraph (1) or with an order under paragraph (2) the defendant must acknowledge service within the time limited for so doing.]

Commencement 1 October 1987.
Amendments This rule was inserted as r 12A by SI 1987/1423, r 32; it was renumbered as rule 8A by SI 1988/298, r 2.
Cross references This rule is applied to business list actions in the central London county court by CCR Order 48C, r 8(4).

[Order 12, r 9 Acknowledgment of service of originating summons

(1)   Each defendant named in and served with an originating summons (other than an ex parte originating summons or an originating summons under Order 113) must acknowledge service of the summons as if it were a writ.

(2)   Where an originating summons is issued out of principal registry of the Family Division, the appropriate office for acknowledging service is that registry.

(3)   The foregoing rules of this Order shall apply in relation to an originating summons (other than an ex parte originating summons or an originating summons under Order 113) as they apply to a writ except that after the word "extended", wherever it occurs in rule 5(a), there shall be inserted the words "or abridged" and for the reference in rule 5(b) to Order 11, rules 1(3) and 4(4), there shall be substituted a reference to Order 11, rule 9(6).]

Commencement   3 June 1980.
Amendments   This rule was substituted, together with r 10, for r 9 as originally enacted, by SI 1979/ 1716, r 14.

[Order 12, r 10 Acknowledgment of service to be treated as entry of appearance

For the purpose of any enactment referring expressly or impliedly to the entry of appearance as a procedure provided by rules of court for responding to a writ or other process issuing out of the High Court, or of any rule of law, the acknowledgment of service of the writ or other process in accordance with these rules shall be treated as the entry of an appearance to it, and related expressions shall be construed accordingly.]

Commencement   3 June 1980.
Amendments   See the note to Order 12, r 9.

ORDER 13
[Failure to Give Notice of Intention to Defend]

Amendments Words "Failure to Give Notice of Intention to Defend" substituted by SI 1979/1716, r 48, Schedule, Pt 1.

Order 13, r 1 Claim for liquidated demand

(1)   Where a writ is indorsed with a claim against a defendant for a liquidated demand only, then, if that defendant fails to [give notice of intention to defend], the plaintiff may, after [the prescribed time], enter final judgment against that defendant for a sum not exceeding that claimed by the writ in respect of the demand and for costs, and proceed with the action against the other defendants, if any.

(2)   A claim shall not be prevented from being treated for the purposes of this rule as a claim for a liquidated demand by reason only that part of [the claim is for interest under section 35A of the Act at a rate which is not higher than that payable on judgment debts at the date of the writ.]

Commencement 1 October 1966.
Amendments Para (1): words "give notice of intention to defend" and "the prescribed time" substituted by SI 1979/1716, rr 15, 48, Schedule, Pt 1.
Para (2): words from "the claim is for interest" to "date of the writ" substituted by SI 1982/1786, r 6.
Definitions The Act: Supreme Court Act 1981.
Forms Judgment (No 39).

Order 13, r 2 Claim for unliquidated damages

Where a writ is indorsed with a claim against a defendant for unliquidated damages only, then, if that defendant fails to [give notice of intention to defend], the plaintiff may, after [the prescribed time], enter interlocutory judgment against that defendant for damages to be assessed and costs, and proceed with the action against the other defendants, if any.

Commencement 1 October 1966.
Amendments Words "give notice of intention to defend" and "the prescribed time" substituted by SI 1979/1716, rr 15, 48, Schedule, Pt 1.
Forms Judgment (No 40).

[Order 13, r 3 Claim for detention of goods

(1)   Where a writ is indorsed with a claim against a defendant relating to the detention of goods only, then, if that defendant fails to [give notice of intention to defend], the plaintiff may, after [the prescribed time] and subject to Order 42, rule 1A,—
- (a)   at his option enter either—
    - (i)   interlocutory judgment against that defendant for delivery of the goods or their value to be assessed and costs, or
    - (ii)   interlocutory judgment for the value of the goods to be assessed and costs, or
- (b)   apply by summons for judgment against that defendant for delivery of the goods without giving him the alternative of paying their assessed value,

and in any case proceed with action against the other defendants, if any.

(2) A summons under paragraph (1)(b) must be supported by affidavit and notwithstanding Order 65, rule 9, the summons and a copy of the affidavit must be served on the defendant against whom judgment is sought.]

Commencement 1 June 1978.
Amendments This rule was substituted by SI 1978/579, r 2.
Para (1): words "give notice of intention to defend" and "the prescribed time" substituted by SI 1979/1716, rr 15, 48, Schedule, Pt 1.
Forms Judgment (No 41).

Order 13, r 4 Claim for possession of land

(1) Where a writ is indorsed with a claim against a defendant for possession of land only, then [subject to paragraph (2)], if that defendant fails to [give notice of intention to defend] the plaintiff may, after [the prescribed time], and on producing a certificate by his solicitor, or (if he sues in person) an affidavit, stating that he is not claiming any relief in the action of the nature specified in Order 88, rule 1, enter judgment for possession of the land as against that defendant and costs, and proceed with the action against the other defendants, if any.

[(2) Notwithstanding anything in paragraph (1), the plaintiff shall not be entitled, except with the leave of the Court, to enter judgment under that paragraph unless he produces a certificate by his solicitor, or (if he sues in person) an affidavit, stating either that the claim does not relate to a dwelling-house or that the claim relates to a dwelling-house of which the rateable value [on every day specified by [section 4(2) of the Rent Act 1977] in relation to the premises exceeds the sum so specified] [or of which the rent payable in respect of the premises exceeds the sum specified in section 4(4)(b) of the Rent Act 1977].]

(3)   An application for leave to enter judgment under paragraph (2) shall be by summons stating the grounds of the application, and the summons must, unless the Court otherwise orders and notwithstanding anything in Order 65, rule 9, be served on the defendant against whom it is sought to enter judgment.

(4)   If the Court refuses leave to enter judgment, it may make or give any such order or directions as it might have made or given had the application been an application for judgment under Order 14, rule 1.]

[(5)] Where there is more than one defendant, judgment entered under this rule shall not be enforced against any defendant unless and until judgment for possession of the land has been entered against all the defendants.

Commencement 2 January 1967 (paras (2)–(4)); 1 October 1966 (remainder).
Amendments Para (1): words "subject to paragraph (2)" inserted by SI 1966/1514, r 3(1); words "give notice of intention to defend" and "the prescribed time" substituted by SI 1979/1716, rr 15, 48, Schedule, Pt 1.
Para (2): inserted by SI 1966/1514, r 3(2); first words in square brackets substituted by SI 1973/1384, r 3, words therein substituted by SI 1979/1542, r 9(1), Schedule; final words in square brackets inserted by SI 1990/492, r 2(2).
Paras (3), (4): inserted by SI 1966/1514, r 3(2).
Para (5): originally para (2), renumbered as para (5) by SI 1966/1514, r 3(3).
Forms Summmons for judgment for possession (PF9).
Default judgment for possession (No 42).
Judgment in default for possession, damages and costs (PF79).

Order 13, r 5 Mixed claims

Where a writ issued against any defendant is indorsed with two or more of the claims mentioned in the foregoing rules, and no other claim, then, if that defendant fails to [give notice of intention to defend], the plaintiff may, after [the prescribed time], enter against that defendant such judgment in respect of any such claim as he would be entitled to enter under those rules if that were the only claim indorsed on the writ, and proceed with the action against the other defendants, if any.

Commencement 1 October 1966.
Amendments Words "give notice of intention to defend" and "the prescribed time" substituted by SI 1979/1716, rr 15, 48, Schedule, Pt 1.

Order 13, r 6 Other claims

(1) Where a writ is indorsed with a claim of a description not mentioned in rules 1 to 4, then, if any defendant fails to [give notice of intention to defend], the plaintiff may, after [the prescribed time] [and, if that defendant has not acknowledged service, upon filing an affidavit proving due service of the writ on him] and, where the statement of claim was not indorsed on or served with the writ, upon serving a statement of claim on him, proceed with the action as if that defendant [had given notice of intention to defend].

(2) Where a writ issued against a defendant is indorsed as aforesaid but by reason of the defendant's satisfying the claim or complying with the demands thereof or any other like reason it has become unnecessary for the plaintiff to proceed with the action, then, if the defendant fails to [give notice of intention to defend], the plaintiff may, after [the prescribed time], enter judgment with the leave of the Court against that defendant for costs.

(3) An application for leave to enter judgment under paragraph (2) shall be by summons which must, unless the Court otherwise orders, and notwithstanding anything in Order 65, rule 9, be served on the defendant against whom it is sought to enter judgment.

Commencement 1 October 1966.
Amendments Paras (1), (2): words in square brackets substituted by SI 1979/1716, rr 15, 16, 48, Schedule, Pt 1.

[Order 13, r 6A Prescribed time

In the foregoing rules of this Order "the prescribed time" in relation to a writ issued against a defendant means the time limited for the defendant to acknowledge service of the writ or, if within that time the defendant has returned to the appropriate office an acknowledgment of service containing a statement to the effect that he does not intend to contest the proceedings, the date on which the acknowledgment was received at the appropriate office.]

Commencement 3 June 1980.
Amendments This rule was inserted by SI 1979/1716, r 17.

Order 13, r 7 Proof of service of writ

(1) Judgment shall not be entered against a defendant under this Order unless—
    [(a) the defendant has acknowledged service on him of the writ . . . ; or]
    [(b)] an affidavit is filed by or on behalf of the plaintiff proving due service of the writ . . . on the defendant; or
    [(c)] the plaintiff produces the writ indorsed by the defendant's solicitor with a statement that he accepts service of the writ on the defendant's behalf.

(2)   Where, in an action begun by writ, an application is made to the Court for an order affecting a party who has failed to [give notice of intention to defend], the Court hearing the application may require to be satisfied in such manner as it thinks fit that the party [failed to give such notice].

[(3)   Where, after judgment has been entered under this Order against a defendant purporting to have been served by post under Order 10, rule 1(2)(a), the copy of the writ sent to the defendant is returned to the plaintiff through the post undelivered to the addressee, the plaintiff shall, before taking any step or further step in the action or the enforcement of the judgment, either—

(a)   make a request for the judgment to be set aside on the ground that the writ has not been duly served, or

(b)   apply to the Court for directions.

(4)   A request under paragraph (3)(a) shall be made by producing to an officer of the office in which the judgment was entered, and leaving with him for filing, an affidavit stating the relevant facts, and thereupon the judgment shall be set aside and the entry of the judgment and of any proceedings for its enforcement made in the book kept in the office for that purpose shall be marked accordingly.

(5)   An application under paragraph (3)(b) shall be made ex parte by affidavit stating the facts on which the application is founded and any order or direction sought, and on the application the Court may—

(a)   set aside the judgment; or

(b)   direct that, notwithstanding the return of the copy of the writ, it shall be treated as having been duly served, or

(c)   make such other order and give such other direction as the circumstances may require.]

Commencement   24 April 1979 (paras (3)–(5)); 1 October 1966 (remainder).

Amendments   Para (1): sub-para (a) inserted and original sub-paras (a) and (b) renumbered as sub-paras (b) and (c) by SI 1979/1716, r 18; words omitted revoked by SI 1980/2000, r 21.

Para (2): words "give notice of intention to defend" and "failed to give such notice" substituted by SI 1979/1716, r 48, Schedule, Pt 1.

Paras (3)–(5): added by SI 1979/402, r 5.

Forms   Affidavit of service (PF115–126).

Affidavit of substituted service (PF127–129).

[Order 13, r 7A Judgment against a State

(1)   Where the defendant is a State, as defined in section 14 of the State Immunity Act 1978 ("the Act"), the plaintiff shall not be entitled to enter judgment under this Order except with the leave of the Court.

(2)   An application for leave to enter judgment shall be supported by an affidavit—

(a)   stating the grounds of the application,

(b)   verifying the facts relied on as excepting the State from the immunity conferred by section 1 of the Act, and

(c)   verifying that the writ . . . has been served by being transmitted through the Foreign and Commonwealth Office to the Ministry of Foreign Affairs of the State, or in such other manner as may have been agreed to by the State, and that the time for acknowledging service, as extended by section 12(2) of the Act (by two months) where applicable, has expired.

(3)   The application may be made ex parte but the Court hearing the application may direct a summons to be issued and served on that State, for which purpose such

a direction shall include leave to serve the summons and a copy of the affidavit out of the jurisdiction.

(4)   Unless the Court otherwise directs, an affidavit for the purposes of this Rule may contain statements of information or belief with the sources and grounds thereof, and the grant of leave to enter judgment under this Order shall include leave to serve out of the jurisdiction—
  (a)   a copy of the judgment, and
  (b)   a copy of the affidavit, where not already served.

(5)   The procedure for effecting service out of the jurisdiction pursuant to leave granted in accordance with the Rule shall be the same as for the service of . . . the writ under Order 11, rule 7(1), except where section 12(6) of the Act applies and an alternative method of service has been agreed.]

Commencement   3 June 1980.
Amendments   This rule was inserted by SI 1980/629, r 6.
Paras (2), (5): words omitted revoked by SI 1980/2000, r 21.
Cross references   See CCR Order 9, r 6(3).

[Order 13, r 7B Judgments under the Civil Jurisdiction and Judgments Act 1982

(1)   Where a writ has been served out of the jurisdiction under Order 11, rule 1(2)(a) or has been served within the jurisdiction on a defendant domiciled in Scotland or Northern Ireland or in any other Convention territory the plaintiff shall not be entitled to enter judgment under this Order except with the leave of the Court.

(2)   An application for leave to enter judgment may be made ex parte and shall be supported by an affidavit stating that in the deponent's belief—
  (a)   each claim made by the writ is one which by virtue of the Civil Jurisdiction and Judgments Act 1982 the Court has power to hear and determine,
  (b)   no other court has exclusive jurisdiction [under Schedule 1, 3C or 4] to that Act to hear and determine such claim, and
  (c)   where the writ is served out of the jurisdiction under Order 11, rule 1(2)(a), such service satisfied the requirements of [Article 20 of Schedule 1, 3C or 4 of that Act, as the case may require],

and giving in each case the sources and grounds of such belief.

(3)   For the purposes of this rule, domicile is to be determined in accordance with the provisions of sections 41 to 46 of the Civil Jurisdiction and Judgments Act 1982 and "Convention territory" means the territory or territories of any Contracting State, as defined by section 1(3) of that Act, to which [the Brussels Conventions or the Lugano Convention] as defined in section 1(1) of that Act apply.]

Commencement   1 January 1987.
Amendments   This rule was inserted by SI 1983/1181, r 13.
Paras (2), (3): words in square brackets substituted by SI 1992/1907, rr 16–18.
Cross references   This rule is applied to the county court by CCR Order 9, r 6(4).

[Order 13, r 8 Stay of execution on default judgment

Where judgment for a debt or liquidated demand is entered under this Order against a defendant who has returned to the appropriate office an acknowledgment of service containing a statement to the effect that, although he does not intend to contest the proceedings, he intends to apply for a stay of execution of the judgment by writ of fieri facias, execution of the judgment by such a writ shall be stayed for a period of 14 days from the acknowledgment of service and, if within that time the defendant issues and serves on the plaintiff a summons for such a stay supported by an affidavit in accordance with Order 47, rule 1, the stay imposed by this rule shall continue until the summons is heard or otherwise disposed of, unless the Court after giving the parties an opportunity of being heard otherwise directs.]

Commencement 3 June 1980.
Amendments This rule was substituted by SI 1979/1716, r 19.

Order 13, r 9 Setting aside judgment

[Without prejudice to rule 7(3) and (4)] the Court may, on such terms as it thinks just, set aside or vary any judgment entered in pursuance of this Order.

Commencement 1 October 1966.
Amendments Words "Without prejudice to rule 7(3) and (4)" inserted by SI 1979/402, r 6.
Cross references See CCR Order 37, r 4.

ORDER 14
SUMMARY JUDGMENT

Cross references This Order is applied to business list actions in the central London county court instead of CCR Order 19, r 14 by CCR Order 48C, r 10.

Order 14, r 1 Application by plaintiff for summary judgment

(1)   Where in an action to which this rule applies a statement of claim has been served on a defendant and that defendant has [given notice of intention to defend the action], the plaintiff may, on the ground that that defendant has no defence to a claim included in the writ, or to a particular part of such a claim, or has no defence to such a claim or part except as to the amount of any damages claimed, apply to the Court for judgment against that defendant.

[(2)   Subject to paragraph (3), this rule applies to every action begun by writ in the Queen's Bench Division (including the Admiralty Court) or the Chancery Division other than—

    (a)   an action which includes a claim by the plaintiff for libel, slander, malicious prosecution, false imprisonment or seduction,

    (b)   ... or

    (c)   an Admiralty action in rem.]

(3)   This Order shall not apply to an action to which Order 86 applies.

Commencement 1 July 1975 (para (2)); 1 October 1966 (remainder).
Amendments Para (1): words "given notice of intention to defend the action" substituted by SI 1979/1716, r 48, Schedule, Pt 1.
Para (2): substituted by SI 1975/911, r 5(a); sub-para (b) revoked by SI 1992/638, r 5.
Cross references See CCR Order 9, r 14.
Forms Affidavit of service (PF137).

Order 14, r 2 Manner in which application under rule 1 must be made

(1)   An application under rule 1 must be made by summons supported by an affidavit verifying the facts on which the claim, or the part of a claim, to which the application relates is based and stating that in the deponent's belief there is no defence to that claim or part, as the case may be, or no defence except as to the amount of any damages claimed.

(2)   Unless the Court otherwise directs, an affidavit for the purposes of this rule may contain statements of information or belief with the sources and grounds thereof.

(3)   The summons, a copy of the affidavit in support and of any exhibits referred to therein must be served on the defendant not less than [10 clear days] before the return day.

Commencement 1 October 1966.
Amendments Para (3): words "10 clear days" substituted by SI 1969/1894, r 2.
Forms Affidavit (PF10).
Summons (PF11–12).

Order 14, r 3 Judgment for plaintiff

(1)   Unless on the hearing of an application under rule 1 either the Court dismisses the application or the defendant satisfies the Court with respect to the claim, or the

part of a claim, to which the application relates that there is an issue or question in dispute which ought to be tried or that there ought for some other reason to be a trial of that claim or part, the Court may give such judgment for the plaintiff against that defendant on that claim or part as may be just having regard to the nature of the remedy or relief claimed.

(2)   The Court may by order, and subject to such conditions, if any, as may be just, stay execution of any judgment given against a defendant under this rule until after the trial of any counterclaim made or raised by the defendant in the action.

Commencement 1 October 1966.
Cross references This rule is applied to the county court by CCR Order 9, r 14(5).
Forms Judgment (No 44).

Order 14, r 4 Leave to defend

(1)   A defendant may show cause against an application under rule 1 by affidavit or otherwise to the satisfaction of the Court.

(2)   Rule 2(2) applies for the purposes of this rule as it applies for the purposes of that rule.

(3)   The Court may give a defendant against whom such an application is made leave to defend the action with respect to the claim, or the part of a claim, to which the application relates either unconditionally or on such terms as to giving security or time or mode of trial or otherwise as it thinks fit.

(4)   On the hearing of such an application the Court may order a defendant showing cause or, where that defendant is a body corporate, any director, manager, secretary or other similar officer thereof, or any person purporting to act in any such capacity—
    (a)   to produce any document;
    (b)   if it appears to the Court that there are special circumstances which make it desirable that he should do so, to attend and be examined on oath.

Commencement 1 October 1966.
Cross references This rule is applied to the county court by CCR Order 9, r 14(5).
Forms Orders giving leave to defend (PF 13–16).
Orders re solicitor's bill of costs (PF17).
Order, trial by master (PF18).

Order 14, r 5 Application for summary judgment on counterclaim

(1)   Where a defendant to an action in the Queen's Bench Division [(including the Admiralty Court)] or Chancery Division begun by writ has served a counterclaim on the plaintiff, then, subject to paragraph (3), the defendant may, on the ground that the plaintiff has no defence to a claim made in the counterclaim, or to a particular part of such a claim, apply to the Court for judgment against the plaintiff on that claim or part.

(2)   Rules 2, 3 and 4 shall apply in relation to an application under this rule as they apply in relation to an application under rule 1 but with the following modifications, that is to say—
    (a)   references to the plaintiff and defendant shall be construed as references to the defendant and plaintiff respectively;

(b) the words in rule 3(2) "any counterclaim made or raised by the defendant in" shall be omitted; and

(c) the reference in rule 4(3) to the action shall be construed as a reference to the counterclaim to which the application under this rule relates.

(3)   This rule shall not apply to a counterclaim which includes any such claim as is referred to in rule 1(2).

Commencement 1 October 1966.
Amendments Para (1): words "(including the Admiralty Court)" inserted by SI 1975/911, r 5(b).
Cross references This rule is applied to the county court by CCR Order 9, r 14(5).
Forms Judgment for defendant (PF80).

Order 14, r 6 Directions

(1)   Where the Court—
(a) orders that a defendant or a plaintiff have leave (whether conditional or unconditional) to defend an action or counterclaim, as the case may be, with respect to a claim or a part of a claim, or
(b) gives judgment for a plaintiff or a defendant on a claim or part of a claim but also orders that execution of the judgment be stayed pending the trial of a counterclaim or of the action, as the case may be,

the Court shall give directions as to the further conduct of the action, and Order 25, rules 2 to 7, shall, with the omission of so much of rule 7(1) as requires parties to serve a notice specifying the orders and directions which they require and with any other necessary modifications, apply as if the application under rule 1 of this Order or rule 5 thereof, as the case may be, on which the order was made were a summons for directions.

(2)   In particular, and if the parties consent, the Court may direct that the claim in question and any other claim in the action be tried by a master under the provisions of these rules relating to the trial of causes or matters or questions or issues by masters.

[(3)   Without prejudice to paragraph (1), in proceedings to which article 7(1) of the High Court and County Courts Jurisdiction Order 1991 applies, the Court shall, when giving directions under paragraph (1) of this rule, order that—
(a) a statement of the value of the action be lodged and a copy of it served on every other party; and
(b) unless a statement is so lodged within such time as the Court may direct, the action be transferred to a county court.]

Commencement 1 July 1991 (para (3)); 1 October 1966 (remainder).
Amendments Para (3): inserted by SI 1991/1329, r 5.
Cross references See CCR Order 9, r 14(4).
Forms Statement of value (PF204).

Order 14, r 7 Costs

(1)   If the plaintiff makes an application under rule 1 where the case is not within this Order or if it appears to the Court that the plaintiff knew that the defendant relied on a contention which would entitle him to unconditional leave to defend, then, without prejudice to Order 62, and, in particular, [to paragraphs (1) to (3) of

rule 8 of that Order], the Court may dismiss the application with costs and may, if the plaintiff is not an assisted person, require the costs to be paid by him forthwith.

(2)   The Court shall have the same power to dismiss an application under rule 5 as it has under paragraph (1) to dismiss an application under rule 1, and that paragraph shall apply accordingly with the necessary modifications.

Commencement 1 October 1966.
Amendments   Para (1): words "to paragraphs (1) to (3) of rule 8 of that Order" substituted by SI 1986/632, r 4.

Order 14, r 8 Right to proceed with residue of action or counterclaim

(1)   Where on an application under rule 1 the plaintiff obtains judgment on a claim or a part of a claim against any defendant, he may proceed with the action as respects any other claim or as respects the remainder of the claim or against any other defendant.

(2)   Where on an application under rule 5 a defendant obtains judgment on a claim or part of a claim made in a counterclaim against the plaintiff, he may proceed with the counterclaim as respects any other claim or as respects the remainder of the claim or against any other defendant to the counterclaim.

Commencement 1 October 1966.

Order 14, r 9 Judgment for delivery up of chattel

Where the claim to which an application under rule 1 or rule 5 relates is for the delivery up of a specific chattel and the Court gives judgment under this Order for the applicant, it shall have the same power to order the party against whom judgment is given to deliver up the chattel without giving him an option to retain it on paying the assessed value thereof as if the judgment had been given after trial.

Commencement 1 October 1966.

Order 14, r 10 Relief against forfeiture

A tenant shall have the same right to apply for relief after judgment for possession of land on the ground of forfeiture for non-payment of rent has been given under this Order as if the judgment had been given after trial.

Commencement 1 October 1966.

Order 14, r 11 Setting aside judgment

Any judgment given against a party who does not appear at the hearing of an application under rule 1 or rule 5 may be set aside or varied by the Court on such terms as it thinks just.

Commencement 1 October 1966.
Cross references See CCR Order 37, r 2.

[ORDER 14A
DISPOSAL OF CASE ON POINT OF LAW

Cross references This Order is applied to business list actions in the central London county court by CCR Order 48C, r 10.

Order 14A, r 1 Determination of questions of law or construction

(1) The Court may upon the application of a party or of its own motion determine any question of law or construction of any document arising in any cause or matter at any stage of the proceedings where it appears to the Court that—

    (a) such question is suitable for determination without a full trial of the action, and

    (b) such determination will finally determine (subject only to any possible appeal) the entire cause or matter or any claim or issue therein.

(2) Upon such determination the Court may dismiss the cause or matter or make such order or judgment as it thinks just.

(3) The Court shall not determine any question under this Order unless the parties have either—

    (a) has an opportunity of being heard on the question, or

    (b) consented to an order or judgment on such determination.

(4) The jurisdiction of the Court under this Order may be exercised by a master.

(5) Nothing in this Order shall limit the powers of the Court under Order 18, rule 19 or any other provision of these rules.]

Commencement 1 February 1991.
Amendments Order 14A was inserted by SI 1990/2599, r 8.

[Order 14A, r 2 Manner in which application under rule 1 may be made

An application under rule 1 may be made by summons or motion or (notwithstanding Order 32, rule 1) may be made orally in the course of any interlocutory application to the Court.]

Commencement 1 February 1991.
Amendments See the note to Order 14A, r 1.

ORDER 15
CAUSES OF ACTION, COUNTERCLAIMS AND PARTIES

Order 15, r 1 Joinder of causes of action

(1)   Subject to rule 5(1), a plaintiff may in one action claim relief against the same defendant in respect of more than one cause of action—

(a)   if the plaintiff claims, and the defendant is alleged to be liable, in the same capacity in respect of all the causes of action, or

(b)   if the plaintiff claims or the defendant is alleged to be liable in the capacity of executor or administrator of an estate in respect of one or more of the causes of action and in his personal capacity but with reference to the same estate in respect of all the others, or

(c)   with the leave of the Court.

(2)   An application for leave under this rule must be made ex parte by affidavit before the issue of the writ or originating summons, as the case may be, and the affidavit must state the grounds of the application.

Commencement   1 October 1966.
Cross references   See CCR Order 5, r 1.

Order 15, r 2 Counterclaim against plaintiff

(1)   Subject to rule 5(2), a defendant in any action who alleges that he has any claim or is entitled to any relief or remedy against a plaintiff in the action in respect of any matter (whenever and however arising) may, instead of bringing a separate action, make a counterclaim in respect of that matter; and where he does so he must add the counterclaim to his defence.

(2)   Rule 1 shall apply in relation to a counterclaim as if the counterclaim were a separate action and as if the person making the counterclaim were the plaintiff and the person against whom it is made a defendant.

(3)   A counterclaim may be proceeded with notwithstanding that judgment is given for the plaintiff in the action or that the action is stayed, discontinued or dismissed.

(4)   Where a defendant establishes a counterclaim against the claim of the plaintiff and there is a balance in favour of one of the parties, the Court may give judgment for the balance, so, however, that this provision shall not be taken as affecting the Court's discretion with respect to costs.

Commencement   1 October 1966.
Cross references   See CCR Order 9, rr 2, 5.

Order 15, r 3 Counterclaim against additional parties

(1) Where a defendant to an action who makes a counterclaim against the plaintiff alleges that any other person (whether or not a party to the action) is liable to him along with the plaintiff in respect of the subject-matter of the counterclaim, or claims against such other person any relief relating to or connected with the original subject-matter of the action, then, subject to rule 5(2), he may join that other person as a party against whom the counterclaim is made.

(2)   Where a defendant joins a person as a party against whom he makes a counterclaim, he must add that person's name to the title of the action and serve on

him a copy of the counterclaim [and, in the case of a person who is not already a party to the action, [the defendant must issue the counterclaim out of the appropriate office and serve on the person concerned a sealed copy of the counterclaim, together with a form of acknowledgement of service in Form No 14 in Appendix A (with such modifications as the circumstances may require) and a copy of the writ or originating summons by which the action was begun and of all other pleadings served in the action]] and a person on whom a copy of a counterclaim is served under this paragraph shall, if he is not already a party to the action, become a party to it as from the time of service with the same rights in respect of his defence to the counterclaim and otherwise as if he had been duly sued in the ordinary way by the party making the counterclaim.

(3) A defendant who is required by paragraph (2) to serve a copy of the counterclaim made by him on any person who before service is already a party to the action must do so within the period within which, by virtue of Order 18, rule 2, he must serve on the plaintiff the defence to which the counterclaim is added.

(4) The appropriate office for . . . [issuing and acknowledging service of a counterclaim against] a person who is not already a party to the action is the Central Office, except that, where the action is [proceeding in the Chancery Division or a district registry, or is an Admiralty [or commercial] action which is not proceeding in a district registry, the appropriate office is Chancery Chambers, the district registry in question or [the Admiralty and Commercial Registry], as the case may be.]

(5) Where by virtue of paragraph (2) a copy of a counterclaim is required to be served on a person who is not already a party to the action, the following provisions of these rules, namely, [Order 6, rule 7(3) and (5),] Order 10 . . . , Order 11 . . . , Orders 12 and 13 and Order 75, rule 4, shall, subject to the last foregoing paragraph, apply in relation to the counterclaim and the proceedings arising from it as if—
   (a) the counterclaim were a writ and the proceedings arising from it an action; and
   (b) the party making the counterclaim were a plaintiff and the party against whom it is made a defendant in that action.

[(5A) Where by virtue of paragraph (2) a copy of a counterclaim is required to be served on any person other than the plaintiff who before service is already a party to the action, the provisions of Order 14, rule 5 shall apply in relation to the counterclaim and the proceedings arising therefrom, as if the party against whom the counterclaim is made were the plaintiff in the action.]

(6) A copy of a counterclaim required to be served on a person who is not already a party to the action must be indorsed with a notice, in Form No 17 in Appendix A, addressed to that person—
   (a)–(c) . . .

Commencement 1 October 1989 (para (5A)); 1 October 1966 (remainder).
Amendments Para (2): first words in square brackets inserted by SI 1979/1716, r 20(1), words in square brackets therein substituted by SI 1990/1689, r 13(a).
Para (4): word omitted revoked by SI 1980/1908, r 19; words "issuing and acknowledging service of a counterclaim against" substituted by SI 1990/1689, r 13(b); second words in square brackets substituted by SI 1982/1111, r 18, words "or commercial" therein inserted and words "the Admiralty and Commercial Registry" therein substituted by SI 1987/1423, r 6.
Para (5): words "Order 6, rule 7(3) and (5)," inserted by SI 1990/1689, r 13(c); first words omitted revoked by SI 1979/402, r 7; second words omitted revoked by SI 1980/2000, r 21.
Para (5A): inserted by SI 1989/1307, r 9.
Para (6): sub-paras (a)–(c) revoked by SI 1979/1716, r 20(2).
Cross references See CCR Order 9, r 15.

Order 15, r 4 Joinder of parties

(1)   Subject to rule 5(1), two or more persons may be joined together in one action as plaintiffs or as defendants with the leave of the Court or where—

    (a)   if separate actions were brought by or against each of them, as the case may be, some common question of law or fact would arise in all the actions, and

    (b)   all rights to relief claimed in the action (whether they are joint, several or alternative) are in respect of or arise out of the same transaction or series of transactions.

(2)   Where the plaintiff in any action claims any relief to which any other person is entitled jointly with him, all persons so entitled must, subject to the provisions of any Act and unless the Court gives leave to the contrary, be parties to the action and any of them who does not consent to being joined as a plaintiff must, subject to any order made by the Court on an application for leave under this paragraph, be made a defendant.

This paragraph shall not apply to a probate action.

(3)   ...

***

Commencement   1 October 1966.
Amendments   Para (3): revoked by SI 1979/402, r 15.
Cross references   See CCR Order 5, r 2.

Order 15, r 5 Court may order separate trials, etc

(1)   If claims in respect of two or more causes of action are included by a plaintiff in the same action or by a defendant in a counterclaim, or if two or more plaintiffs or defendants are parties to the same action, and it appears to the Court that the joinder of causes of action or of parties, as the case may be, may embarrass or delay the trial or is otherwise inconvenient, the Court may order separate trials or make such other order as may be expedient.

(2)   If it appears on the application of any party against whom a counterclaim is made that the subject-matter of the counterclaim ought for any reason to be disposed of by a separate action, the Court may order the counterclaim to be struck out or may order it to be tried separately or make such other order as may be expedient.

***

Commencement   1 October 1966.
Cross references   See CCR Order 5, r 3, Order 21, r 4(3).

Order 15, r 6 Misjoinder and nonjoinder of parties

(1)   No cause or matter shall be defeated by reason of the misjoinder or nonjoinder of any party; and the Court may in any cause or matter determine the issues or questions in dispute so far as they affect the rights and interests of the persons who are parties to the cause or matter.

(2)   [Subject to the provisions of this rule,] at any stage of the proceedings in any cause or matter the Court may on such terms as it thinks just and either of its own motion or on application—

    (a)   order any person who has been improperly or unnecessarily made a party or who has for any reason ceased to be a proper or necessary party, to cease to be a party;

[(b)   order any of the following persons to be added as a party, namely—
   (i)   any person who ought to have been joined as a party or whose presence before the Court is necessary to ensure that all matters in dispute in the cause or matter may be effectually and completely determined and adjudicated upon, or
   (ii)   any person between whom and any party to the cause or matter there may exist a question or issue arising out of or relating to or connected with any relief or remedy claimed in the cause or matter which in the opinion of the Court it would be just and convenient to determine as between him and that party as well as between the parties to the cause or matter.]

. . .

(3)   An application by any person for an order under paragraph (2) adding him as a [party] must, except with the leave of the Court, be supported by an affidavit showing his interest in the matters in dispute in the cause or matter [or, as the case may be, the question or issue to be determined as between him and any party to the cause or matter.]

[(4)   No person shall be added as a plaintiff without his consent signified in writing or in such other manner as may be authorised.]

[(5)   No person shall be added or substituted as a party after the expiry of any relevant period of limitation unless either—
   (a)   the relevant period was current at the date when proceedings were commenced and it is necessary for the determination of the action that the new party should be added, or substituted, or
   (b)   the relevant period arises under the provisions of section 11 or 12 of the Limitation Act 1980 and the Court directs that those provisions should not apply to the action by or against the new party.

[In this paragraph "any relevant period of limitation" means a time limit under the Limitation Act 1980 or a time limit which applies to the proceedings in question by virtue of the Foreign Limitation Periods Act 1984.]]

[(6)   [Except in a case to which the law of another country relating to limitation applies, and the law of England and Wales does not so apply] the addition or substitution of a new party shall be treated as necessary for the purposes of paragraph (5)(a) [if, and only if, the Court is satisfied] that—
   (a)   the new party is a necessary party to the action in that property is vested in him at law or in equity and the plaintiff's claim in respect of an equitable interest in that property is liable to be defeated unless the new party is joined, or
   (b)   the relevant cause of action is vested in the new party and the plaintiff jointly but not severally, or
   (c)   the new party is the Attorney General and the proceedings should have been brought by relator proceedings in his name, or
   (d)   the new party is a company in which the plaintiff is a shareholder and on whose behalf the plaintiff is suing to enforce a right vested in the company, or
   (e)   the new party is sued jointly with the defendant and is not also liable severally with him and failure to join the new party might render the claim unenforceable.]

Commencement   1 May 1981 (paras (4)–(6)); 1 October 1966 (remainder).
Amendments   Para (2): words "Subject to the provisions of this rule," inserted and words omitted revoked by SI 1981/562, r 2(1); sub-para (b) substituted by SI 1971/1269, r 45(1).

Para (3): word "party" substituted and words from "or, as the case may be" to "cause or matter" added by SI 1971/1269, r 45(2).
Para (4): added by SI 1981/562, r 2(2).
Para (5): added by SI 1981/562, r 2(2); words from "In this paragraph" to "the Foreign Limitation Periods Act 1984" substituted by SI 1985/1277, r 2(a).
Para (6): added by SI 1981/562, r 2(2); words from "Except in a case" to "does not so apply" inserted by SI 1985/1277, r 2(b); words "if, and only if, the Court is satisfied" substituted by SI 1982/1111, r 114.
Cross references See CCR Order 5, r 4, Order 15, r 1.

[Order 15, r 6A Proceedings against estates

(1)   Where any person against whom an action would have lain has died but the cause of action survives, the action may, if no grant of probate or administration has been made, be brought against the estate of the deceased.

(2)   Without prejudice to the generality of paragraph (1), an action brought against "the personal representatives of A.B. deceased" shall be treated, for the purposes of that paragraph, as having been brought against his estate.

[(3)   An action purporting to have been commenced against a person shall be treated, if he was dead at its commencement, as having been commenced against his estate in accordance with paragraph (1), whether or not a grant of probate or administration was made before its commencement.]

(4)   In any such action as is referred to in paragraph (1) or (3)—
    (a)   the plaintiff shall, during the period of validity for service of the writ or originating summons, apply to the Court for an order appointing a person to represent the deceased's estate for the purpose of the proceedings or, if a grant of probate or administration has been made . . . , for an order that the personal representative of the deceased be made a party to the proceedings, and in either case for an order that the proceedings be carried on against the person so appointed or, as the case may be, against the personal representative, as if he had been substituted for the estate;
    (b)   the Court may, at any stage of the proceedings and on such terms as it thinks just and either of its own motion or on application, make any such order as is mentioned in sub-paragraph (a) and allow such amendments (if any) to be made and make such other order as the Court thinks necessary in order to ensure that all matters in dispute in the proceedings may be effectually and completely determined and adjudicated upon.

(5)   Before making an order under paragraph (4) the Court may require notice to be given to any insurer of the deceased who has an interest in the proceedings and to such (if any) of the persons having an interest in the estate as it thinks fit.

[(5A) Where an order is made under paragraph (4) appointing the Official Solicitor to represent the deceased's estate, the appointment shall be limited to his accepting service of the writ or originating summons by which the action was begun unless, either on making such an order or on a subsequent application, the Court, with the consent of the Official Solicitor, directs that the appointment shall extend to taking further steps in the proceedings.]

(6)   Where an order is made under paragraph (4), rules 7(4) and 8(3) and (4) shall apply as if the order had been made under rule 7 on the application of the plaintiff.

(7)   Where no grant of probate or administration has been made, any judgment or order given or made in the proceedings shall bind the estate to the same extent as it

would have been bound if a grant had been made and a personal representative of the deceased had been a party to the proceedings.]

Commencement 1 February 1978 (para (3)); 4 July 1977 (para (5A)); 1 January 1971 (remainder).
Amendments This rule was inserted by SI 1970/1861, r 4.
Para (3): substituted by SI 1977/1955, r 3(1).
Para (4): in sub-para (a) words omitted revoked by SI 1977/1955, r 3(2).
Para (5A): inserted by SI 1977/960, r 2.
Cross references See CCR Order 5, r 8.
Forms Order for judgment against personal representative (PF19).

Order 15, r 7 Change of parties by reason of death, etc

(1)   Where a party to an action dies or becomes bankrupt but the cause of action survives, the action shall not abate by reason of the death or bankruptcy.

(2)   Where at any stage of the proceedings in any cause or matter the interest or liability of any party is assigned or transmitted to or devolves upon some other person, the Court may, if it thinks it necessary in order to ensure that all matters in dispute in the cause or matter may be effectually and completely determined and adjudicated upon, order that other person to be made a party to the cause or matter and the proceedings to be carried on as if he had been substituted for the first mentioned party.

An application for an order under this paragraph may be made ex parte.

(3)   An order may be made under this rule for a person to be made a party to a cause or matter notwithstanding that he is already a party to it on the other side of the record, or on the same side but in a different capacity; but—
  (a) if he is already a party on the other side, the order shall be treated as containing a direction that he shall cease to be a party on that other side, and
  (b) if he is already a party on the same side but in another capacity, the order may contain a direction that he shall cease to be a party in that other capacity.

(4)   The person on whose application an order is made under this rule must procure the order to be noted in the cause book, and after the order has been so noted that person must, unless the Court otherwise directs, serve the order on every other person who is a party to the cause or matter or who becomes or ceases to be a party by virtue of the order and serve with the order on any person who becomes a defendant a copy of the writ or originating summons by which the cause or matter was begun [and of all other pleadings served in the proceedings,] [and a form of acknowledgment of service in Form No 14 or 15 in Appendix A, whichever is appropriate.]

(5)   Any application to the Court by a person served with an order made ex parte under this rule for the discharge or variation of the order must be made within 14 days after the service of the order on that person.

Commencement 1 October 1966.
Amendments Para (4): words "and of all other pleadings served in the proceedings," inserted by SI 1990/1689, r 14; words from "and a form of acknowledgment" to "whichever is appropriate" added by SI 1979/1716, r 21.
Cross references See CCR Order 5, rr 11, 14.

Order 15, r 8 Provisions consequential on making of order under rule 6 or 7

(1)   Where an order is made under rule 6, the writ by which the action in question was begun must be amended accordingly and must be indorsed with—

   (a)   a reference to the order in pursuance of which the amendment is made, and

   (b)   the date on which the amendment is made;

and the amendment must be made within such period as may be specified in the order or, if no period is so specified, within 14 days after the making of the order.

(2)   Where by an order under rule 6 a person is to be made a defendant, the rules as to service of a writ of summons shall apply accordingly to service of the amended writ on him, but before serving the writ on him the person on whose application the order was made must procure the order to be noted in the cause book.

[(2A) Together with the writ of summons served under paragraph (2) shall be served a copy of all other pleadings served in the action.]

(3)   Where by an order under rule 6 or 7 a person is to be made a defendant, the rules as to [acknowledgment of service] shall apply accordingly to entry of appearance by him, subject, in the case of a person to be made a defendant by an order under rule 7, to the modification that the [time limited for acknowledging service] shall begin with the date on which the order is served on him under rule 7(4) or, if the order is not required to be served on him, with the date on which the order is noted in the cause book.

(4)   Where by an order under rule 6 or 7 a person is to be added as a party or is to be made a party in substitution for some other party, that person shall not become a party until—

   (a)   where the order is made under rule 6, the writ has been amended in relation to him under this rule and (if he is a defendant) has been served on him, or

   (b)   where the order is made under rule 7, the order has been served on him under rule 7(4) or, if the order is not required to be served on him, the order has been noted in the cause book;

and where by virtue of the foregoing provision a person becomes a party in substitution for some other party, all things done in the course of the proceedings before the making of the order shall have effect in relation to the new party as they had in relation to the old, except that [acknowledgment of service] by the old party shall not dispense with [acknowledgment of service] by the new.

[(5)   The foregoing provisions of this rule shall apply in relation to an action begun by originating summons as they apply in relation to an action begun by writ.]

Commencement   1 October 1990 (para (2A)); 1 October 1966 (remainder).
Amendments   Para (2A): inserted by SI 1990/1689, r 15.
Paras (3), (4): words in square brackets substituted by SI 1979/1716, r 48, Schedule, Pt 1.
Para (5): added by SI 1966/1055, r 2.

Order 15, r 9 Failure to proceed after death of party

(1)   If after the death of a plaintiff or defendant in any action the cause of action survives, but no order under rule 7 is made substituting as plaintiff any person in whom the cause of action vests or, as the case may be, the personal representatives of

the deceased defendant, the defendant or, as the case may be, those representatives may apply to the Court for an order that unless the action is proceeded with within such time as may be specified in the order the action shall be struck out as against the plaintiff or defendant, as the case may be, who has died; but where it is the plaintiff who has died, the Court shall not make an order under this rule unless satisfied that due notice of the application has been given to the personal representatives (if any) of the deceased plaintiff and to any other interested persons who, in the opinion of the Court, should be notified.

(2)   Where in any action a counterclaim is made by a defendant, this rule shall apply in relation to the counterclaim as if the counterclaim were a separate action and as if the defendant making the counterclaim were the plaintiff and the person against whom it is made a defendant.

Commencement 1 October 1966.
Cross references See CCR Order 5, r 12.

Order 15, r 10 Actions for possession of land

(1)   Without prejudice to rule 6, the Court may at any stage of the proceedings in an action for possession of land order any person not a party to the action who is in possession of the land (whether in actual possession or by a tenant) to be added as a defendant.

(2)   An application by any person for an order under this rule may be made ex parte, supported by an affidavit showing that he is in possession of the land in question and if by a tenant, naming him.

[The affidavit shall specify the applicant's address for service and Order 12, rule 3(2), (3) and (4), shall apply as if the affidavit were an acknowledgment of service.]

(3)   A person added as a defendant by an order under this rule must serve [on the plaintiff a copy of the order giving the added defendant's address for service specified in accordance with paragraph (2).]

Commencement 1 October 1966.
Amendments Para (2): words from "The affidavit" to "acknowledgment of service" added by SI 1979/1716, r 22(1).
Para (3): words from "on the plaintiff" to "in accordance with paragraph (2)" substituted by SI 1979/1716, r 22(2).
Cross references See CCR Order 15, r 3.

[Order 15, r 10A Actions for wrongful interference with goods

(1)   Where the plaintiff in an action for wrongful interference with goods is one of two or more persons having or claiming any interest in the goods, then, unless he has the written authority of every other such person to sue on the latter's behalf, the writ or originating summons by which the action was begun shall be indorsed with a statement giving particulars of the plaintiff's title and identifying every other person who, to his knowledge, has or claims any interest in the goods.

This paragraph shall not apply to an action arising out of an accident on land due to a collision or apprehended collision involving a vehicle.

(2)   A defendant to an action for wrongful interference with goods who desires to show that a third party has a better right than the plaintiff as respects all or any part of the interest claimed by the plaintiff may, at any time after [giving notice of intention to

defend the action] and before any judgment or order is given or made on the plaintiff's claim, apply for directions as to whether any person named in the application (not being a person whose written authority the plaintiff has to sue on his behalf) should be joined with a view to establishing whether he has a better right than the plaintiff, or has a claim as a result of which the defendant might be doubly liable within the meaning of section 7 of the Torts (Interference with Goods) Act 1977.

(3)   An application under paragraph (2) shall be made by summons, which shall be served personally on every person named in it as well as being served on the plaintiff.

(4)   Where a person named in an application under paragraph (2) fails to appear on the hearing of the summons or to comply with any direction given by the Court on the application, the Court may by order deprive him of any right of action against the defendant for the wrong, either unconditionally or subject to such terms and conditions as the Court thinks fit.]

Commencement 1 June 1978.
Amendments This rule was inserted by SI 1978/579, r 7.
Para (2): words "giving notice of intention to defend the action" substituted by SI 1979/1716, r 48, Schedule, Pt 1.
Cross references See CCR Order 15, r 4.

Order 15, r 11 Relator actions

Before the name of any person is used in any action as a relator, that person must give a written authorisation so to use his name to his solicitor and the authorisation must be filed in the Central Office [or Chancery Chambers], or, if the writ or originating summons is to issue out of a district registry, in that registry.

Commencement 1 October 1966.
Amendments Words "or Chancery Chambers" inserted by SI 1982/1111, r 19.

Order 15, r 12 Representative proceedings

(1)   Where numerous persons have the same interest in any proceedings, not being such proceedings as are mentioned in rule 13, the proceedings may be begun, and, unless the Court otherwise orders, continued, by or against any one or more of them as representing all or as representing all except one or more of them.

(2)   At any stage of proceedings under this rule the Court may, on the application of the plaintiff, and on such terms, if any, as it thinks fit, appoint any one or more of the defendants or other persons as representing whom the defendants are sued to represent all, or all except one or more, of those persons in the proceedings; and where, in exercise of the power conferred by this paragraph, the Court appoints a person not named as a defendant, it shall make an order under rule 6 adding that person as a defendant.

(3)   A judgment or order given in proceedings under this rule shall be binding on all the persons as representing whom the plaintiffs sue or, as the case may be, the defendants are sued, but shall not be enforced against any person not a party to the proceedings except with the leave of the Court.

(4)   An application for the grant of leave under paragraph (3) must be made by summons which must be served personally on the person against whom it is sought to enforce the judgment or order.

(5)   Notwithstanding that a judgment or order to which any such application relates is binding on the person against whom the application is made, that person may dispute liability to have the judgment or order enforced against him on the ground that by reason of facts and matters particular to his case he is entitled to be exempted from such liability.

(6)   The Court hearing an application for the grant of leave under paragraph (3) may order the question whether the judgment or order is enforceable against the person against whom the application is made to be tried and determined in any manner in which any issue or question in an action may be tried and determined.

Commencement 1 October 1966.
Cross references See CCR Order 5, r 5.

Order 15, r 13 Representation of interested persons who cannot be ascertained, etc

(1)   In any proceedings concerning—
   (a) ... the estate of a deceased person, or
   (b) property subject to a trust, or
   (c) the construction of a written instrument, including a statute,

the Court, if satisfied that it is expedient so to do, and that one or more of the conditions specified in paragraph (2) are satisfied, may appoint one or more persons to represent any person (including an unborn person) or class who is or may be interested (whether presently or for any future, contingent or unascertained interest) in or affected by the proceedings.

(2)   The conditions for the exercise of the power conferred by paragraph (1) are as follows:—
   (a) that the person, the class or some member of the class, cannot be ascertained or cannot readily be ascertained;
   (b) that the person, class or some member of the class, though ascertained, cannot be found;
   (c) that, though the person or the class and the members thereof can be ascertained and found, it appears to the Court expedient (regard being had to all the circumstances, including the amount at stake and the degree of difficulty of the point to be determined) to exercise the power for the purpose of saving expense.

(3)   Where in any proceedings to which paragraph (1) applies, the Court exercises the power conferred by that paragraph, a judgment or order of the Court given or made when the person or persons appointed in exercise of that power are before the Court shall be binding on the person or class represented by the person or persons so appointed.

(4)   Where, in any such proceedings, a compromise is proposed and some of the persons who are interested in, or who may be affected by, the compromise are not parties to the proceedings (including unborn or unascertained persons) but—
   (a) there is some other person in the same interest before the Court who assents to the compromise or on whose behalf the Court sanctions the compromise, or
   (b) the absent persons are represented by a person appointed under paragraph (1) who so assents,

the Court, if satisfied that the compromise will be for the benefit of the absent persons and that it is expedient to exercise this power, may approve the compromise and order that it shall be binding on the absent persons, and they shall be bound accordingly except where the order has been obtained by fraud or non-disclosure of material facts.

Commencement 1 October 1966.
Amendments Para (1): in sub-para (a) words omitted revoked by SI 1975/911, r 6.
Cross references See CCR Order 5, r 6.

[Order 15, r 13A Notice of action to non-parties

(1)   At any stage in an action to which this rule applies, the Court may, on the application of any party or of its own motion, direct that notice of the action be served on any person who is not a party thereto but who will or may be affected by any judgment given therein.

(2)   An application under this rule may be made ex parte and shall be supported by an affidavit stating the grounds of the application.

(3)   Every notice of an action under this rule shall be in Form No 52 in Appendix A and [shall be issued out of the appropriate office][; and the copy to be served shall be a sealed copy] accompanied by a copy of the originating summons or writ and [of all other pleadings served in the action, and by] a form of acknowledgement of service in Form No 14 or 15 in Appendix A with such modifications as may be appropriate.

(4)   A person may, within 14 days of service on him of a notice under this rule, acknowledge service of the writ or originating summons and shall thereupon become a party to the action, but in default of such acknowledgement and subject to paragraph (5) he shall be bound by any judgment given in the action as if he was a party thereto.

(5)   If at any time after service of such notice on any person the writ or originating summons is amended so as substantially to alter the relief claimed, the Court may direct that the judgment shall not bind such person unless a further notice together with a copy of the amended writ or originating summons is [issued and] served upon him under this rule.

(6)   This rule applies to any action relating to:
    (a)   the estate of a deceased person, or
    (b)   property subject to a trust.

[(7)   Order 6, rule 7(3) and (5) shall apply in relation to a notice of an action under this rule as if the notice were a writ and the person by whom the notice is issued were the plaintiff.]]

Commencement 1 October 1990 (para (7)); 1 October 1986 (remainder).
Amendments This rule was inserted by SI 1986/1187, r 4.
Para (3): words "shall be issued out of the appropriate office" inserted by SI 1990/2599, r 21; words "; and the copy to be served shall be a sealed copy" and "of all other pleadings served in the action, and by" inserted by SI 1990/1689, r 16(a), (b).
Para (5): words "issued and" inserted by SI 1990/1689, r 16(c).
Para (7): added by SI 1990/1689, r 16(d).

Order 15, r 14 Representation of beneficiaries by trustees, etc

(1)   Any proceedings, including proceedings to enforce a security by foreclosure or otherwise, may be brought by or against trustees, executors or administrators in their capacity as such without joining any of the persons having a beneficial interest in the

trust or estate, as the case may be; and any judgment or order given or made in those proceedings shall be binding on those persons unless the Court in the same or other proceedings otherwise orders on the ground that the trustees, executors or administrators, as the case may be, could not or did not in fact represent the interests of those persons in the first-mentioned proceedings.

(2)   Paragraph (1) is without prejudice to the power of the Court to order any person having such an interest as aforesaid to be made a party to the proceedings or to make an order under rule 13.

Commencement 1 October 1966.

Order 15, r 15 Representation of deceased person interested in proceedings

(1)   Where in any proceedings it appears to the Court that a deceased person was interested in the matter in question in the proceedings and that he has no personal representative, the Court may, on the application of any party to the proceedings, proceed in the absence of a person representing the estate of the deceased person or may by order appoint a person to represent that estate for the purposes of the proceedings; and any such order, and any judgment or order subsequently given or made in the proceedings, shall bind the estate of the deceased person to the same extent as it would have been bound had a personal representative of that person been a party to the proceedings.

(2)   Before making an order under this rule, the Court may require notice of the application for the order to be given to such (if any) of the persons having an interest in the estate as it thinks fit.

Commencement 1 October 1966.
Cross references See CCR Order 5, r 7.

Order 15, r 16 Declaratory judgment

No action or other proceeding shall be open to objection on the ground that a merely declaratory judgment or order is sought thereby, and the Court may make binding declarations of right whether or not any consequential relief is or could be claimed.

Commencement 1 October 1966.

Order 15, r 17 Conduct of proceedings

The Court may give the conduct of any action, inquiry or other proceeding to such person as it thinks fit.

Commencement 1 October 1966.

Order 15, r 18 *(added by SI 1971/1955; revoked by SI 1975/128)*

ORDER 16
THIRD PARTY AND SIMILAR PROCEEDINGS

Order 16, r 1 Third party notice

(1)   Where in any action a defendant who has [given notice of intention to defend]—

  (a)   claims against a person not already a party to the action any contribution or indemnity; or

  (b)   claims against such a person any relief or remedy relating to or connected with the original subject-matter of the action and substantially the same as some relief or remedy claimed by the plaintiff; or

  (c)   requires that any question or issue relating to or connected with the original subject-matter of the action should be determined not only as between the plaintiff and the defendant but also as between either or both of them and a person not already a party to the action;

then, subject to paragraph (2), the defendant may issue a notice in Form No 20 or 21 in Appendix A, whichever is appropriate (in this Order referred to as a third party notice), containing a statement of the nature of the claim made against him and, as the case may be, either of the nature and grounds of the claim made by him or of the question or issue required to be determined.

(2)   A defendant to an action may not issue a third party notice without the leave of the Court unless the action was begun by writ and he issues the notice before serving his defence on the plaintiff.

(3)   Where a third party notice is served on the person against whom it is issued, he shall as from the time of service be a party to the action (in this Order referred to as a third party) with the same rights in respect of his defence against any claim made against him in the notice and otherwise as if he had been duly sued in the ordinary way by the defendant by whom the notice is issued.

Commencement 1 October 1966.
Amendments Para (1): words "given notice of intention to defend" substituted by SI 1979/1716, r 48, Schedule, Pt 1.
Cross references See CCR Order 12, r 1.

Order 16, r 2 Application for leave to issue third party notice

(1)   An application for leave to issue a third party notice may be made ex parte but the Court may direct a summons for leave to be issued.

(2)   An application for leave to issue a third party notice must be supported by an affidavit stating—

  (a)   the nature of the claim made by the plaintiff in the action;

  (b)   the stage which proceedings in the action have reached;

  (c)   the nature of the claim made by the applicant or particulars of the question or issue required to be determined, as the case may be, and the facts on which the proposed third party notice is based; and

  (d)   the name and address of the person against whom the third party notice is to be issued.

Commencement 1 October 1966.
Cross references See CCR Order 12, r 1(3).

Order 16, r 3 [Issue, service and acknowledgment of service, of third party notice]

(1)   The order granting leave to issue a third party notice may contain directions as to the period within which the notice is to be issued.

(2)   There must be served with every third party notice a copy of the writ or originating summons by which the action was begun and of the pleadings (if any) [served in the action and a form of acknowledgment of service in Form No 14 in Appendix A] [with such modifications as may be appropriate].

(3)   The appropriate office for [acknowledging service of] a third party notice is the Central Office, except that, where the notice is issued in an action which is [proceeding in the Chancery Division or a district registry, or is an Admiralty [or commercial] action which is not proceeding in a district registry, the appropriate office is Chancery Chambers, the district registry in question or [the Admiralty and Commercial Registry], as the case may be.]

(4)   Subject to the foregoing provisions of this rule, the following provisions of these rules, namely, Order 6, rule 7(3) and (5), Order 10 . . . , Order 11 . . . , Order 12 and Order 75, rule 4, shall apply in relation to a third party notice and to the proceedings begun thereby as if—

    (a)   the third party notice were a writ and the proceedings begun thereby an action; and

    (b)   the defendant issuing the third party notice were a plaintiff and the person against whom it is issued a defendant in that action:

[Provided that in the application of Order 11, r 1(1)(c) leave may be granted to serve a third party notice outside the jurisdiction on any necessary or proper party to the proceedings brought against the defendant].

Commencement   1 October 1966.
Amendments   Rule heading: substituted by SI 1980/629, r 30(1).
Para (2): words from "served in the action" to "Form No 14 in Appendix A" substituted by SI 1979/1716, r 48, Schedule, Pt 1; words "with such modifications as may be appropriate" added by SI 1980/629, r 30(2).
Para (3): words "acknowledging service of" substituted by SI 1979/1716, r 48, Schedule, Pt 1; words "or commercial" inserted and words "the Admiralty and Commercial Registry" substituted by SI 1987/1423, r 7; other words in square brackets substituted by SI 1982/1111, r 18.
Para (4): first words omitted revoked by SI 1979/402, r 7; second words omitted revoked by SI 1980/2000, r 21; proviso added by SI 1983/1181, r 14.
Cross references   See CCR Order 12, r 1(4)–(6).

Order 16, r 4 Third party directions

(1)   If the third party [gives notice of intention to defend], the defendant who issued third party notice must, by summons to be served on all the other parties to the action, apply to the Court for directions.

(2)   If no summons is served on the third party under paragraph (1), the third party may, not earlier than 7 days after [giving notice of intention to defend], by summons to be served on all the other parties to the action, apply to the Court for directions or for an order to set aside the third party notice.

(3)   On an application for directions under this rule the Court may—

    (a)   if the liability of the third party to the defendant who issued the third party notice is established on the hearing, order such judgment as the nature of the case may require to be entered against the third party in favour of the defendant; or

    (b)   order any claim, question or issue stated in the third party notice to be tried in such manner as the Court may direct; or

(c)   dismiss the application and terminate the proceedings on the third party notice;

and may do so either before or after any judgment in the action has been signed by the plaintiff against the defendant.

(4)   On an application for directions under this rule the Court may give the third party leave to defend the action, either alone or jointly with any defendant, upon such terms as may be just, or to appear at the trial and to take such part therein as may be just, and generally may make such orders and give such directions as appear to the Court proper for having the rights and liabilities of the parties most conveniently determined and enforced and as to the extent to which the third party is to be bound by any judgment or decision in the action.

(5)   Any order made or direction given under this rule may be varied or rescinded by the Court at any time.

Commencement   1 October 1966.
Amendments   Paras (1), (2): words in square brackets substituted by SI 1979/1716, r 48, Schedule, Pt 1.
Cross references   See CCR Order 12, r 1(3), (5).
Forms   Summons for third party directions (PF20).
Order for third party directions (PF21).

Order 16, r 5 Default of third party, etc

(1)   If a third party does not [give notice of intention to defend] or, having been ordered to serve a defence, fails to do so—
  (a)   he shall be deemed to admit any claim stated in the third party notice and shall be bound by any judgment (including judgment by consent) or decision in the action in so far as it is relevant to any claim, question or issue stated in that notice; and
  (b)   the defendant by whom the third party notice was issued may, if judgment in default is given against him in the action, at any time after satisfaction of that judgment and, with the leave of the Court, before satisfaction thereof, enter judgment against the third party in respect of any contribution or indemnity claimed in the notice, and, with the leave of the Court, in respect of any other relief or remedy claimed therein.

(2)   If a third party or the defendant by whom a third party notice was issued makes default in serving any pleading which he is ordered to serve, the Court may, on the application by summons of that defendant or the third party, as the case may be, order such judgment to be entered for the applicant as he is entitled to on the pleadings or may make such other order as may appear to the Court necessary to do justice between the parties.

(3)   The Court may at any time set aside or vary a judgment entered under paragraph (1)(b) or paragraph (2) on such terms (if any) as it thinks just.

Commencement   1 October 1966.
Amendments   Para (1): words "give notice of intention to defend" substituted by SI 1979/1716, r 48, Schedule, Pt 1.
Cross references   See CCR Order 12, rr 1(7), 2, 3(3).

Order 16, r 6 Setting aside third party proceedings

Proceedings on a third party notice may, at any stage of the proceedings, be set aside by the Court.

Commencement   1 October 1966.
Cross references   See CCR Order 12, r 4.

Order 16, r 7 Judgment between defendant and third party

(1) Where in any action a defendant has served a third party notice, the Court may at or after the trial of the action or, if the action is decided otherwise than by trial, on an application by summons or motion, order such judgment as the nature of the case may require to be entered for the defendant against the third party or for the third party against the defendant.

[(2) Where judgment is given for the payment of any contribution or indemnity to a person who is under a liability to make a payment in respect of the same debt or damage, execution shall not issue on the judgment without the leave of the Court until that liability has been discharged.

(3) For the purpose of paragraph (2) 'liability' includes liability under a judgment in the same or other proceedings and liability under an agreement to which section 1(4) of the Civil Liability (Contribution) Act 1978 applies.]

Commencement 24 April 1979 (paras (2), (3)); 1 October 1966 (remainder).
Amendments Paras (2), (3): original para (2) revoked and new paras (2), (3) inserted by SI 1979/402, r 16.
Cross references See CCR Order 12, r 3(2)–(4).

Order 16, r 8 Claims and issues between a defendant and some other party

(1) Where in any action a defendant who has [given notice of intention to defend]—
   (a) claims against a person who is already a party to the action any contribution or indemnity; or
   (b) claims against such a person any relief or remedy relating to or connected with the original subject-matter of the action and substantially the same as some relief or remedy claimed by the plaintiff; or
   (c) requires that any question or issue relating to or connected with the original subject-matter of the action should be determined not only as between the plaintiff and himself but also as between either or both of them and some other person who is already a party to the action;

then, subject to paragraph (2), the defendant may, without leave, issue and serve on that person a notice containing a statement of the nature and grounds of his claim or, as the case may be, of the question or issue required to be determined.

(2) Where a defendant makes such a claim as is mentioned in paragraph (1) and that claim could be made by him by counterclaim in the action, paragraph (1) shall not apply in relation to the claim.

(3) [No acknowledgment of service of] such a notice shall be necessary if the person on whom it is served has [acknowledged service of the writ or originating summons in the action] or is a plaintiff therein, and the same procedure shall be adopted for the determination between the defendant by whom, and the person on whom, such a notice is served of the claim, question or issue stated in the notice as would be appropriate under this Order if the person served with the notice were a third party and (where he has [given notice of intention to defend the action] or is a plaintiff) had [given notice of intention to defend the claim, question or issue].

(4) Rule 4(2) shall have effect in relation to proceedings on a notice issued under this rule as if for the words "7 days after [giving notice of intention to defend]" there were substituted the words "14 days after service of the notice on him".

Commencement 1 October 1966.
Amendments Paras (1), (3): words in square brackets substituted by SI 1979/1716, r 48, Schedule, Pt 1.

Para (4): words "giving notice of intention to defend" substituted by SI 1980/629, r 30(3).
Cross references See CCR Order 12, r 5.

Order 16, r 9 Claims by third and subsequent parties

(1)   Where a defendant has served a third party notice and the third party makes such a claim or requirement as is mentioned in rule 1 or rule 8, this Order shall, with the modification mentioned in paragraph (2) and any other necessary modifications, apply as if the third party were a defendant; and similarly where any further person to whom by virtue of this rule this Order applies as if he were a third party makes such a claim or requirement.

(2)   The modification referred to in paragraph (1) is that paragraph (3) shall have effect in relation to the issue of a notice under rule 1 by a third party in substitution for rule 1(2).

(3)   A third party may not issue a notice under rule 1 without the leave of the Court unless the action in question was begun by writ and he issues the notice before the expiration of 14 days after the time [limited for acknowledging service of] the notice issued against him.

Commencement 1 October 1966.
Amendments Para (3): words "limited for acknowledging service of" substituted by SI 1979/1716, r 48, Schedule, Pt 1.
Cross references See CCR Order 12, r 6.

Order 16, r 10 Offer of contribution

[(1)] If, [at any time after he has [acknowledged service], a party to an action] who, . . . stands to be held liable in the action to another party to contribute towards any debt or damages which may be recovered against that other party in the action, makes (without prejudice to his defence) a written offer to that other party to contribute to a specified extent to the debt or damages, then, [subject to paragraph (2) and] notwithstanding that he reserves the right to bring the offer to the attention of the judge at the trial, the offer shall not be brought to the attention of the judge until after all questions of liability and amount of debt or damages have been decided.

[(2)   Where the question of the costs of the issue of liability falls to be decided, that issue having been tried and an issue or question concerning the amount of the debt or damages remaining to be tried separately, any party may bring to the attention of the judge the fact that a written offer under paragraph (1) has or has not been made and the date (but not the amount) of such offer or of the first such offer if more than one.]

Commencement 1 October 1987 (para (2)); 1 October 1966 (remainder).
Amendments Para (1): numbered as such and words "subject to paragraph (2) and" inserted by SI 1987/1423, r 33(1), (2); words from "at any time" to "a party to an action" substituted by SI 1970/944, r 4, words "acknowledged service" therein substituted by SI 1979/1716, r 48, Schedule, Pt 1; words omitted revoked by SI 1980/1908, r 19.
Para (2): inserted by SI 1987/1423, r 33(3).
Cross references See CCR Order 12, r 7.

Order 16, r 11 Counterclaim by defendant

Where in any action a counterclaim is made by a defendant, the foregoing provisions of this Order shall apply in relation to the counterclaim as if the subject-matter of the counterclaim were the original subject-matter of the action, and as if the person making the counterclaim were the plaintiff and the person against whom it is made a defendant.

Commencement 1 October 1966.
Cross references See CCR Order 12, r 8.

ORDER 17
INTERPLEADER

Order 17, r 1 Entitlement to relief by way of interpleader

(1)   Where—

   (a) a person is under a liability in respect of a debt or in respect of any money, goods or chattels and he is, or expects to be, sued for or in respect of that debt or money or those goods or chattels by two or more persons making adverse claims thereto, or

   (b) claim is made to any money, goods or chattels taken or intended to be taken by a sheriff in execution under any process, or to the proceeds or value of any such goods or chattels, by a person other than the person against whom the process is issued,

the person under liability as mentioned in sub-paragraph (a), or (subject to rule 2) the sheriff, may apply to the Court for relief by way of interpleader.

(2)   References in this Order to a sheriff shall be construed as including references to any other officer charged with the execution of process by or under the authority of the High Court.

Commencement   1 October 1966.
Forms   Interpleader summons (PF25, PF26).

Order 17, r 2 Claim to goods, etc, taken in execution

(1)   Any person making a claim to or in respect of any money, goods or chattels taken or intended to be taken in execution under process of the Court, or to the proceeds or value of any such goods or chattels, must give notice of his claim to the sheriff charged with the execution of the process and must include in his notice a statement of his address, and that address shall be his address for service.

(2)   On receipt of a claim made under this rule the sheriff must forthwith give notice thereof to the execution creditor and the execution creditor must, within [7 days] after receiving the notice, give notice to the sheriff informing him whether he admits or disputes the claim.

An execution creditor who gives notice in accordance with this paragraph admitting a claim shall only be liable to the sheriff for any fees and expenses incurred by the sheriff before receipt of that notice.

(3)   Where—

   (a) the sheriff receives a notice from an execution creditor under paragraph (2) disputing a claim, or the execution creditor fails, within the period mentioned in that paragraph, to give the required notice, and

   (b) the claim made under this rule is not withdrawn,

the sheriff may apply to the Court for relief under this Order.

(4)   A sheriff who receives a notice from an execution creditor under paragraph (2) admitting a claim made under this rule shall withdraw from possession of the money, goods or chattels claimed and may apply to the Court for relief under this Order of the following kind, that is to say, an order restraining the bringing of an action against him for or in respect of his having taken possession of that money or those goods or chattels.

Commencement 1 October 1966.
Amendments Para (2): words "7 days" substituted by SI 1983/1181, r 22.
Forms Notice of claim (PF23).
Notice of admission or dispute of title (PF24).

Order 17, r 3 Mode of application

(1)   An application for relief under this Order must be made by originating summons unless made in a pending action, in which case it must be made by summons in the action.

(2)   Where the applicant is a sheriff who has withdrawn from possession of money, goods or chattels taken in execution and who is applying for relief under rule 2(4), the summons must be served on any person who made a claim under that rule to or in respect of that money or those goods or chattels, and that person may attend the hearing of the application.

[(3)   An originating summons under this rule shall be in Form No 10 in Appendix A.]

(4)   Subject to paragraph (5), a summons under this rule must be supported by evidence that the applicant—

(a)   claims no interest in the subject-matter in dispute other than for charges or costs,

(b)   does not collude with any of the claimants to that subject-matter, and

(c)   is willing to pay or transfer that subject-matter into court or to dispose of it as the Court may direct.

(5)   Where the applicant is a sheriff, he shall not provide such evidence as is referred to in paragraph (4) unless directed by the Court to do so.

[(6)   Any person who makes a claim under rule 2 and who is served with a summons under this rule shall within 14 days serve on the execution creditor and the sheriff an affidavit specifying any money and describing any goods and chattels claimed and setting out the grounds upon which such claim is based.

(7)   Where the applicant is a sheriff a summons under this rule must give notice of the requirement in paragraph (6).]

Commencement 1 October 1983 (paras (6), (7)); 3 June 1980 (para (3)); 1 October 1966 (remainder).
Amendments Para (3): substituted by SI 1979/1716, r 48, Schedule, Pt 2.
Paras (6), (7): added by SI 1983/1181, r 23.
Forms Affidavit on interpleader (PF27).

Order 17, r 4 To whom sheriff may apply for relief

An application to the Court for relief under this Order may, if the applicant is a sheriff, be made—

(a)   where the action in question is proceeding in the Royal Courts of Justice, to a master or, if the execution to which the application relates has been or is to be levied in the district of a district registry, either to a master or to the [district judge] of that registry;

(b)   Where the action in question is proceeding in a district registry, to the [district judge] of that registry or, if such execution has been or is to be levied in the district of some other district registry or outside the district of any district registry, either to the said [district judge] or to the [district judge] of that other registry or to a master, as the case may be.

[Where the action in question is proceeding in the Admiralty Court or the Family Division, references in this rule to a master shall be construed as references to the Admiralty registrar or to a [district judge] of that Division.]

Commencement 1 October 1966.
Amendments Words from "Where the action in question" to "a district judge of that Division" substituted by SI 1975/911, r 7.

Order 17, r 5 Powers of Court hearing summons

(1)   Where on the hearing of a summons under this Order all the persons by whom adverse claims to the subject-matter in dispute (hereafter in this Order referred to as "the claimants") appear, the Court may order—

    (a)   that any claimant be made a defendant in any action pending with respect to the subject-matter in dispute in substitution for or in addition to the applicant for relief under this Order, or

    (b)   that an issue between the claimants be stated and tried and may direct which of the claimants is to be plaintiff and which defendant.

(2)   Where—

    (a)   the applicant on a summons under this Order is a sheriff, or

    (b)   all the claimants consent or any of them so requests, or

    (c)   the question at issue between the claimants is a question of law and the facts are not in dispute,

the Court may summarily determine the question at issue between the claimants and make an order accordingly on such terms as may be just.

(3)   Where a claimant, having been duly served with a summons for relief under this Order, does not appear on the hearing of the summons or, having appeared, fails or refuses to comply with an order made in the proceedings, the Court may make an order declaring the claimant, and all persons claiming under him, for ever barred from prosecuting his claim against the applicant for such relief and all persons claiming under him, but such an order shall not affect the rights of the claimants as between themselves.

Commencement 1 October 1966.
Forms Interpleader orders (PF28–38).

Order 17, r 6 Power to order sale of goods taken in execution

Where an application for relief under this Order is made by a sheriff who has taken possession of any goods or chattels in execution under any process, and a claimant alleges that he is entitled, under a bill of sale or otherwise, to the goods or chattels by way of security for debt, the Court may order those goods or chattels or any part thereof to be sold and may direct that the proceeds of sale be applied in such manner and on such terms as may be just and as may be specified in the order.

Commencement 1 October 1966.
Forms Order for sale (PF35, PF36).

Order 17, r 7 Power to stay proceedings

Where a defendant to an action applies for relief under this Order in the action, the Court may by order stay all further proceedings in the action.

Commencement 1 October 1966.

Order 17, r 8 Other powers

Subject to the foregoing rules of this Order, the Court may in or for the purposes of any interpleader proceedings make such order as to costs or any other matter as it thinks just.

Commencement 1 October 1966.

Order 17, r 9 One order in several causes or matters

Where the Court considers it necessary or expedient to make an order in any interpleader proceedings in several causes or matters pending in several Divisions, or before different judges of the same Division, the Court may make such an order; and the order shall be entitled in all those causes or matters and shall be binding on all the parties to them.

Commencement 1 October 1966.

Order 17, r 10 Discovery

Orders 24 and 26 shall, with the necessary modifications, apply in relation to an interpleader issue as they apply in relation to any other cause or matter.

Commencement 1 October 1966.

Order 17, r 11 Trial of interpleader issue

(1)   Order 35 shall, with the necessary modifications, apply to the trial of an interpleader issue as it applies to the trial of an action.

(2)   The Court by whom an interpleader issue is tried may give such judgment or make such order as finally to dispose of all questions arising in the interpleader proceedings.

Commencement 1 October 1966.

Order 17, r 12 *(revoked)*

ORDER 18
PLEADINGS

Cross references This Order is applied to business list actions in the central London county court by CCR Order 48C, r 11(4).

Order 18, r 1 Service of statement of claim

Unless the Court gives leave to the contrary or a statement of claim is indorsed on the writ, the plaintiff must serve a statement of claim on the defendant or, if there are two or more defendants, on each defendant, and must do so either when the writ . . . is served on that defendant or at any time after service of the writ . . . but before the expiration of 14 days after that defendant [gives notice of intention to defend].

Commencement 1 October 1966.
Amendments Words omitted revoked by SI 1980/2000, r 21; words "gives notice of intention to defend" substituted by SI 1979/1716, r 48, Schedule, Pt 1.

Order 18, r 2 Service of defence

(1) Subject to paragraph (2), a defendant who [gives notice of intention to defend], an action must, unless the Court gives leave to the contrary, serve a defence on [every other party to the action who may be affected thereby] before the expiration of 14 days after the time [limited for acknowledging service of the writ] or after the statement of claim is served on him, whichever is the later.

(2) If a summons under Order 14, rule 1, [or under Order 86, rule 1,] is served on a defendant before he serves his defence, paragraph (1) shall not have effect in relation to him unless by the order made on the summons he is given leave to defend the action and, in that case, shall have effect as if it required him to serve his defence within 14 days after the making of the order or within such other period as may be specified therein.

[(3) Where an application is made by a defendant under Order 12, rule 8(1), paragraph (1) of this rule shall not have effect in relation to the defendant unless the application is dismissed or no order is made on the application and, in that case, paragraph (1) shall have effect as if it required him to serve his defence within 14 days after the final determination of the application or within such other period as may be specified by the Court.]

Commencement 1 October 1991 (para (3)); 1 October 1966 (remainder).
Amendments Para (1): words "gives notice of intention to defend" and "limited for acknowledging service of the writ" substituted by SI 1979/1716, r 48, Schedule, Pt 1; words "every other party to the action who may be affected thereby" substituted by SI 1990/2599, r 11(1).
Para (2): words "or under Order 86, rule 1," inserted by SI 1979/35, r 2.
Para (3): inserted by SI 1991/1884, r 29.
Cross references See CCR Order 9, rr 2, 5.

Order 18, r 3 Service of reply and defence to counterclaim

(1) A plaintiff on whom a defendant serves a defence must serve a reply on that defendant if it is needed for compliance with rule 8; and if no reply is served, rule 14(1) will apply.

(2) A plaintiff on whom a defendant serves a counterclaim must, if he intends to defend it, serve on that defendant a defence to counterclaim.

(3)   Where a plaintiff serves both a reply and a defence to counterclaim on any defendant, he must include them in the same document.

(4)   A reply to any defence must be served by the plaintiff before the expiration of 14 days after the service on him of that defence, and a defence to counterclaim must be served by the plaintiff before the expiration of 14 days after the service on him of the counterclaim to which it relates.

Commencement 1 October 1966.
Forms Judgment (No 40).

Order 18, r 4 Pleadings subsequent to reply

No pleading subsequent to a reply or a defence to counterclaim shall be served except with the leave of the Court.

Commencement 1 October 1966.

Order 18, r 5 *(revoked by SI 1990/1689)*

Order 18, r 6 Pleadings: formal requirements

(1)   Every pleading in an action must bear on its face—
    (a)   the year in which the writ in the action was issued and the letter and number of the action,
    (b)   the title of the action,
    (c)   the Division of the High Court to which the action is assigned and the name of he judge (if any) to whom it is assigned . . . ,
    (d)   the description of the pleading, and
    (e)   the date on which it was served.

(2)   Every pleading must, if necessary, be divided into paragraphs numbered consecutively, each allegation being so far as convenient contained in a separate paragraph.

(3)   Dates, sums and other numbers must be expressed in a pleading in figures and not in words.

[(3A) . . .]

(4)   Every pleading of a party must be indorsed—
    (a)   where the party sues or defends in person, with his name and address;
    (b)   in any other case, with the name or firm and business address of the solicitor by whom it was served and also (if the solicitor is the agent of another) the name or firm and business address of his principal.

(5)   Every pleading of a party must be signed by counsel, if settled by him, and, if not, by the party's solicitor or by the party, if he sues or defends in person.

Commencement   1 October 1970 (para (3A)); 1 October 1966 (remainder).
Amendments   Para (1): in sub-para (c) words omitted revoked by SI 1982/1111, r 20.
Para (3A): inserted by SI 1970/1208, r 4; revoked by SI 1976/337, r 4.
Cross references   See CCR Order 50, r 6 (as to para (5)).

Order 18, r 7 Facts, not evidence, to be pleaded

(1)   Subject to the provisions of this rule, and rules [7A] 10, 11 and 12, every pleading must contain, and contain only, a statement in a summary form of the

material facts on which the party pleading relies for his claim or defence, as the case may be, but not the evidence by which those facts are to be proved, and the statement must be as brief as the nature of the case admits.

(2)   Without prejudice to paragraph (1), the effect of any document or the purport of any conversation referred to in the pleading must, if material, be briefly stated, and the precise words of the document or conversation shall not be stated, except in so far as those words are themselves material.

(3)   A party need not plead any fact if it is presumed by law to be true or the burden of disproving it lies on the other party, unless the other party has specifically denied it in his pleading.

(4)   A statement that a thing has been done or that an event has occurred, being a thing or event the doing or occurrence of which, as the case may be, constitutes a condition precedent necessary for the case of a party is to be implied in his pleading.

Commencement 1 October 1966.
Amendments Para (1): figure "7A" inserted by SI 1969/1105, r 3(1).

[Order 18, r 7A Conviction, etc to be adduced in evidence: matters to be pleaded

(1)   If in any action which is to be tried with pleadings any party intends, in reliance on section 11 of the Civil Evidence Act 1968 (convictions as evidence in civil proceedings) to adduce evidence that a person was convicted of an offence by or before a court in the United Kingdom or by a court-martial there or elsewhere, he must include in his pleading a statement of his intention with particulars of—
   (a)   the conviction and the date thereof,
   (b)   the court or court-martial which made the conviction, and
   (c)   the issue in the proceedings to which the conviction is relevant.

(2)   If in any action which is to be tried with pleadings any party intends, in reliance on section 12 of the said Act of 1968 (findings of adultery and paternity as evidence in civil proceedings) to adduce evidence that a person was found guilty of adultery in matrimonial proceedings or [has been found to be the father of a child in relevant proceedings before any court in England and Wales or has been] adjudged to be the father of a child in affiliation proceedings before a court in the United Kingdom, he must include in his pleading a statement of his intention with particulars of—
   (a)   the finding or adjudication and the date thereof,
   (b)   the court which made the finding or adjudication and the proceedings in which it was made, and
   (c)   the issue in the proceedings to which the finding or adjudication is relevant.

(3)   Where a party's pleading includes such a statement as is mentioned in paragraph (1) or (2), then if the opposite party—
   (a)   denies the conviction, finding of adultery or adjudication of paternity to which the statement relates, or
   (b)   alleges that the conviction, finding or adjudication was erroneous, or
   (c)   denies that the conviction, finding or adjudication is relevant to any issue in the proceedings,

he must make the denial or allegation in his pleading.]

Commencement 1 October 1969.
Amendments This rule was inserted by SI 1969/1105, r 3(2).
Para (2): words from "has been found" to "England and Wales or has been" substituted by SI 1989/386, r 12.

Order 18, r 8 Matters which must be specifically pleaded

(1)   A party must in any pleading subsequent to a statement of claim plead specifically any matter, for example, performance, release, [the expiry of any relevant period of limitation], fraud or any fact showing illegality—

- (a) which he alleges makes any claim or defence of the opposite party not maintainable; or
- (b) which, if not specifically pleaded, might take the opposite party by surprise; or
- (c) which raises issues of fact not arising out of the preceding pleading.

(2)   Without prejudice to paragraph (1), a defendant to an action for possession of land must plead specifically every ground of defence on which he relies, and a plea that he is in possession of the land by himself or his tenant is not sufficient.

[(3)   A claim for exemplary damages [or for provisional damages] must be specifically pleaded together with the facts on which the party pleading relies.]

[(4)   A party must plead specifically any claim for interest under section 35A of the Act or otherwise.]

Commencement 1 April 1983 (para (4)); 1 January 1973 (para (3)); 1 October 1966 (remainder).
Amendments Para (1): words "the expiry of any relevant period of limitation" substituted by SI 1985/1277, r 3.
Para (3): added by SI 1972/1898, r 3; words "or for provisional damages" inserted by SI 1985/846, r 3.
Para (4): inserted by SI 1982/1786, r 7.
Definition The Act: Supreme Court Act 1981.
Cross references See CCR Order 6, rr 1A, 1B, Order 9, r 8.

Order 18, r 9 Matter may be pleaded whenever arising

Subject to rules 7(1), 10 and 15(2), a party may in any pleading plead any matter which has arisen at any time, whether before or since the issue of the writ.

Commencement 1 October 1966.

Order 18, r 10 Departure

(1)   A party shall not in any pleading make any allegation of fact, or raise any new ground or claim, inconsistent with a previous pleading of his.

(2)   Paragraph (1) shall not be taken as prejudicing the right of a party to amend, or apply for leave to amend, his previous pleading so as to plead the allegations or claims in the alternative.

Commencement 1 October 1966.

Order 18, r 11 Points of law may be pleaded

A party may by his pleading raise any point of law.

Commencement 1 October 1966.

Order 18, r 12 Particulars of pleading

[(1) Subject to paragraph (2), every pleading must contain the necessary particulars of any claim, defence or other matter pleaded including, without prejudice to the generality of the foregoing,

  (a) particulars of any misrepresentation, fraud, breach of trust, wilful default or undue influence on which the party pleading relies;

  (b) where a party pleading alleges any condition of the mind of any person, whether any disorder or disability of mind or any malice, fraudulent intention or other condition of mind except knowledge, particulars of the facts on which the party relies; and

  (c) where a claim for damages is made against a party pleading, particulars of any facts on which the party relies in mitigation of, or otherwise in relation to, the amount of damages.]

[(1A) Subject to paragraph (1B), a plaintiff in an action for personal injuries shall serve with his statement of claim—

  (a) a medical report, and

  (b) a statement of the special damages claimed.

(1B) Where the documents to which paragraph (1A) applies are not served with the statement of claim, the Court may—

  (a) specify the period of time within which they are to be provided, or

  (b) make such other order as it thinks fit (including an order dispensing with the requirements of paragraph (1A) or staying the proceedings).

(1C) For the purposes of this rule—

"medical report" means a report substantiating all the personal injuries alleged in the statement of claim which the plaintiff proposes to adduce in evidence as part of his case at the trial;

"a statement of the special damages claimed" means a statement giving full particulars of the special damages claimed for expenses and losses already incurred and an estimate of any future expenses and losses (including loss of earnings and of pension rights).]

(2) Where it is necessary to give particulars of debt, expenses or damages and those particulars exceed 3 folios, they must be set out in a separate document referred to in the pleading and the pleading must state whether the document has already been served and, if so, when, or is to be served with the pleading.

(3) The Court may order a party to serve on any other party particulars of any claim, defence or other matter stated in his pleading, or in any affidavit of his ordered to stand as a pleading, or a statement of the nature of the case on which he relies, and the order may be made on such terms as the Court thinks just.

(4) Where a party alleges as a fact that a person had knowledge or notice of some fact, matter or thing, then, without prejudice to the generality of paragraph (3), the Court may, on such terms as it thinks just, order that party to serve on any other party—

  (a) where he alleges knowledge, particulars of the facts on which he relies, and

  (b) where he alleges notice, particulars of the notice.

(5) An order under this rule shall not be made before service of the defence unless, in the opinion of the Court, the order is necessary or desirable to enable the defendant to plead or for some other special reason.

(6)   Where the applicant for an order under this rule did not apply by letter for the particulars he requires, the Court may refuse to make the order unless of opinion that there were sufficient reasons for an application by letter not having been made.

[(7)   Where particulars are given pursuant to a request, or order of the Court, the request or order shall be incorporated with the particulars, each item of the particulars following immediately after the corresponding item of the request or order.]

Commencement   4 June 1990 (paras (1), (1A)–(1C)); 1 October 1980 (para (7)); 1 October 1966 (remainder).
Amendments   Para (1): substituted by SI 1989/2427, r 8.
Paras (1A)–(1C): inserted by SI 1989/2427, r 12.
Para (7): added by SI 1980/1010, r 2.
Cross references   See CCR Order 6, r 1(5)–(7) (as to paras 1A–1C), Order 6, r 7, Order 13, r 2.

Order 18, r 13 Admissions and denials

(1)   . . . any allegation of fact made by a party in his pleading is deemed to be admitted by the opposite party unless it is traversed by that party in his pleading or a joinder of issue under rule 14 operates as a denial of it.

(2)   A traverse may be made either by a denial or by a statement of non-admission and either expressly or by necessary implication.

(3)   . . . every allegation of fact made in a statement of claim or counterclaim which the party on whom it is served does not intend to admit must be specifically traversed by him in his defence or defence to counterclaim, as the case may be; and a general denial of such allegations, or a general statement of non-admission of them, is not a sufficient traverse of them.

(4)   . . .

Commencement   1 October 1966.
Amendments   Paras (1), (3): words omitted revoked by SI 1991/2671, r 8(a).
Para (4): revoked by SI 1991/2671, r 8(b).

Order 18, r 14 Denial by joinder of issue

(1)   If there is no reply to a defence, there is an implied joinder of issue on that defence.

(2)   Subject to paragraph (3)—
   (a)   there is at the close of pleadings an implied joinder of issue on the pleading last served, and
   (b)   a party may in his pleading expressly join issue on the next preceding pleading.

(3)   There can be no joinder of issue, implied or express, on a statement of claim or counterclaim.

(4)   A joinder of issue operates as a denial of every material allegation of fact made in the pleading on which there is an implied or express joinder of issue unless, in the case of an express joinder of issue, any such allegation is excepted from the joinder and is stated to be admitted, in which case the express joinder of issue operates as a denial of every other such allegation.

Commencement   1 October 1966.

Order 18, r 15 Statement of claim

(1)   A statement of claim must state specifically the relief or remedy which the plaintiff claims; but costs need not be specifically claimed.

(2)   A statement of claim shall not contain any allegation or claim in respect of a cause of action unless that cause of action is mentioned in the writ or arises from facts which are the same as, or include or form part of, facts giving rise to a cause of action so mentioned; but, subject to that, a plaintiff may in his statement of claim alter, modify or extend any claim made by him in the indorsement of the writ without amending the indorsement.

(3)   Every statement of claim must bear on its face a statement of the date on which the writ in the action was issued.

Commencement 1 October 1966.
Cross references See CCR Order 6, r 1(1).

Order 18, r 16 Defence of tender

Where in any action a defence of tender before action is pleaded, the defendant must pay into court in accordance with Order 22 the amount alleged to have been tendered, and the tender shall not be available as a defence unless and until payment into court has been made.

Commencement 1 October 1966.
Cross references See CCR Order 9, r 12.

Order 18, r 17 Defence of set-off

Where a claim by a defendant to a sum of money (whether of an ascertained amount or not) is relied on as a defence to the whole or part of a claim made by the plaintiff, it may be included in the defence and set-off against the plaintiff's claim, whether or not it is also added as a counterclaim.

Commencement 1 October 1966.

Order 18, r 18 Counterclaim and defence to counterclaim

Without prejudice to the general application of this Order to a counterclaim and a defence to counterclaim, or to any provision thereof which applies to either of those pleadings specifically,—

    (a)   [rules 12(1A), (1B), and (1C) and 15(1) shall apply] to a counterclaim as if the counterclaim were a statement of claim and the defendant making it a plaintiff;

    (b)   rules 8(2), 16 and 17 shall, with the necessary modifications apply to a defence to counterclaim as they apply to a defence.

Commencement 1 October 1966.
Amendments Words "rules 12(1A), (1B), and (1C) and 15(1) shall apply" substituted by SI 1989/2427, r 13.

Order 18, r 19 Striking out pleadings and indorsements

(1)   The Court may at any stage of the proceedings order to be struck out or amended any pleading or the indorsement of any writ in the action, or anything in

any pleading or in the indorsement, on the ground that—

- (a) it discloses no reasonable cause of action or defence, as the case may be; or
- (b) it is scandalous, frivolous or vexatious; or
- (c) it may prejudice, embarrass or delay the fair trial of the action; or
- (d) it is otherwise an abuse of the process of the court;

and may order the action to be stayed or dismissed or judgment to be entered accordingly, as the case may be.

(2) No evidence shall be admissible on an application under paragraph (1)(a).

(3) This rule shall, so far as applicable, apply to an originating summons and a petition as if the summons or petition, as the case may be, were a pleading.

Commencement 1 October 1966.
Cross references See CCR Order 9, r 10, Order 13, r 5.

Order 18, r 20 Close of pleadings

(1) The pleadings in an action are deemed to be closed—

- (a) at the expiration of 14 days after service of the reply or, if there is no reply but only a defence to counterclaim, after service of the defence to counterclaim, or
- (b) if neither a reply nor a defence to counterclaim is served, at the expiration of 14 days after service of the defence.

(2) The pleadings in an action are deemed to be closed at the time provided by paragraph (1) notwithstanding that any request or order for particulars has been made but has not been complied with at that time.

Commencement 1 October 1966.
Cross references See CCR Order 17, r 11(11)(a).

Order 18, r 21 Trial without pleadings

(1) Where in an action to which this rule applies any defendant has [given notice of intention to defend] in the action, the plaintiff or that defendant may apply to the Court by summons for an order that the action shall be tried without pleadings or further pleadings, as the case may be.

(2) If, on the hearing of an application under this rule, the Court is satisfied that the issues in dispute between the parties can be defined without pleadings or further pleadings, or that for any other reason the action can properly be tried without pleadings or further pleadings, as the case may be, the Court shall order the action to be so tried, and may direct the parties to prepare a statement of the issues in dispute or, if the parties are unable to agree such a statement, may settle the statement itself.

(3) Where the Court makes an order under paragraph (2), it shall, and where it dismisses an application for such an order, it may, give such directions as to the further conduct of the action as may be appropriate, and Order 25, rules 2 to 7, shall, with the omission of so much of rule 7(1) as requires parties to serve a notice specifying the orders and directions which they desire and with any other necessary modifications, apply as if the application under this rule were a summons for directions.

(4) This rule applies to every action begun by writ other than one which includes—

    (a) a claim by the plaintiff for libel, slander, malicious prosecution [or false imprisonment]; or

    (b) a claim by the plaintiff based on an allegation of fraud.

Commencement 1 October 1966.
Amendments Para (1): words "given notice of intention to defend" substituted by SI 1979/1716, r 48, Schedule, Pt 1.
Para (4): in sub-para (a) words "or false imprisonment" substituted by SI 1987/1423, r 63, Schedule.

Order 18, r 22 Saving for defence under Merchant Shipping Acts

Nothing in Order 75, rules 2 and 37 to 40, shall be taken as limiting the right of any shipowner or other person to rely by way of defence on any provision of the [Merchant Shipping Acts 1894 to 1981] which limits the amount of his liability in connection with a ship or other property.

Commencement 1 October 1966.
Amendments Words "Merchant Shipping Acts 1894 to 1981" substituted by SI 1987/1423, r 63, Schedule.

ORDER 19
DEFAULT OF PLEADINGS

Cross references This Order is applied to business list actions in the central London county court by CCR Order 48C, r 11(5).

Order 19, r 1 Default in service of statement of claim

Where the plaintiff is required by these rules to serve a statement of claim on a defendant and he fails to serve it on him, the defendant may, after the expiration of the period fixed by or under these rules for service of the statement of claim, apply to the Court for an order to dismiss the action, and the Court may by order dismiss the action or make such other order on such terms as it thinks just.

Commencement 1 October 1966.
Forms Summons to dismiss (PF39).
Order to dismiss (PF40).

Order 19, r 2 Default of defence: claim for liquidated demand

(1)   Where the plaintiff's claim against a defendant is for a liquidated demand only, then, if that defendant fails to serve a defence on the plaintiff, the plaintiff may, after the expiration of the period fixed by or under these rules for service of the defence, enter final judgment against that defendant for a sum not exceeding that claimed by the writ in respect of the demand and for costs, and proceed with the action against the other defendants, if any.

(2)   Order 13, rule 1(2), shall apply for the purposes of this rule as it applies for the purposes of that rule.

Commencement 1 October 1966.
Cross references See CCR Order 9, rr 6, 7.
Forms Judgment (No 39).

Order 19, r 3 Default of defence: claim for unliquidated damages

Where the plaintiff's claim against a defendant is for unliquidated damages only, then, if that defendant fails to serve a defence on the plaintiff, the plaintiff may, after the expiration of the period fixed by or under these rules for service of the defence, enter interlocutory judgment against that defendant for damages to be assessed and costs, and proceed with the action against the other defendants, if any.

Commencement 1 October 1966.
Cross references See CCR Order 9, r 6(2).

[Order 19, r 4 Default of defence: claim for detention of goods

(1)   Where the plaintiff's claim against a defendant relates to the detention of goods only, then, if that defendant fails to serve a defence on the plaintiff, the plaintiff may, after the expiration of the period fixed by or under these rules for the service of the defence and subject to Order 42, rule 1A,—
- (a)   at his option enter either—
    - (i)   interlocutory judgment against that defendant for delivery of the goods or their value to be assessed and costs, or
    - (ii)   interlocutory judgment for the value of the goods to be assessed and costs, or
- (b)   apply by summons for judgment against that defendant for delivery of the goods without giving him the alternative of paying their assessed value,

and in any case proceed with the action against the other defendants, if any.

(2) A summons under paragraph (1)(b) must be supported by affidavit and, notwithstanding Order 65, rule 9, the summons and a copy of the affidavit must be served on the defendant against whom judgment is sought.]

Commencement 1 June 1978.
Amendments This rule was substituted by SI 1978/579, r 3.
Forms Judgment (No 41).

Order 19, r 5 Default of defence: claim for possession of land

(1) Where the plaintiff's claim against a defendant is for possession of land only, then [subject to paragraph (2)], if that defendant fails to serve a defence on the plaintiff, the plaintiff may, after the expiration of the period fixed by or under these rules for service of the defence, and on producing a certificate by his solicitor, or (if he sues in person) an affidavit, stating that he is not claiming any relief in the action of the nature specified in Order 88, rule 1, enter judgment for possession of the land as against that defendant and for costs, and proceed with the action against the other defendants, if any.

[(2) Notwithstanding anything in paragraph (1), the plaintiff shall not be entitled, except with the leave of the Court, to enter judgment under that paragraph unless he produces a certificate by his solicitor, or (if he sues in person) an affidavit, stating either that the claim does not relate to a dwelling-house or that the claim relates to a dwelling-house of which the rateable value [on every day specified by [section 4(2) of the Rent Act 1977] in relation to the premises exceeds the sum so specified] [or of which the rent payable in respect of the premises exceeds the sum specified in section 4(4)(b) of the Rent Act 1977].

(3) An application for leave to enter judgment under paragraph (2) shall be by summons stating the grounds of the application, and the summons must, unless the Court otherwise orders, be served on the defendant against whom it is sought to enter judgment.

(4) If the Court refuses leave to enter judgment, it may make or give any such order or directions as it might have made or given had the application been an application for judgment under Order 14, rule 1.]

[(5)] Where there is more than one defendant, judgment entered under this rule shall not be enforced against any defendant unless and until judgment for possession of the land has been entered against all the defendants.

Commencement 2 January 1967 (paras (2)–(4)); 1 October 1966 (remainder).
Amendments Para (1): words "subject to paragraph (2)" inserted by SI 1966/1514, r 4(1).
Para (2): inserted by SI 1966/1514, r 4(2) (original para (2) renumbered as para (5) (see below)); words from "on every day" to "sum so specified" substituted by SI 1973/1384, r 3, words "section 4(2) of the Rent Act 1977" therein substituted by SI 1980/1908, r 20; words "or of which the rent payable in respect of the premises exceeds the sum specified in section 4(4)(b) of the Rent Act 1977" inserted by SI 1990/492, r 2(2).
Paras (3), (4): inserted by SI 1966/1514, r 4(2).
Para (5): originally para (2), renumbered as para (5) by SI 1966/1514, r 4(3).
Forms Judgment (No 42).

Order 19, r 6 Default of defence: mixed claims

Where the plaintiff makes against a defendant two or more of the claims mentioned in rules 2 to 5, and no other claim, then, if that defendant fails to serve a defence on the plaintiff, the plaintiff may, after the expiration of the period fixed by or under these rules for service of the defence, enter against that defendant such judgment in respect of any such claim as he would be entitled to enter under those rules if that were the only claim made, and proceed with the action against the other defendants, if any.

Commencement 1 October 1966.

Order 19, r 7 Default of defence: other claims

(1) Where the plaintiff makes against a defendant or defendants a claim of a description not mentioned in rules 2 to 5, then, if the defendant or all the defendants (where there is more than one) fails or fail to serve a defence on the plaintiff, the plaintiff may, after the expiration of the period fixed by or under these rules for service of the defence, apply to the Court for judgment, and on the hearing of the application the Court shall give such judgment as the plaintiff appears entitled to on his statement of claim.

(2) Where the plaintiff makes such a claim as is mentioned in paragraph (1) against more than one defendant, then, if one of the defendants makes default as mentioned in that paragraph, the plaintiff may—
   (a) if his claim against the defendant in default is severable from his claim against the other defendants, apply under that paragraph for judgment against that defendant, and proceed with the action against the other defendants; or
   (b) set down the action on motion for judgment against the defendant in default at the time when the action is set down for trial, or is set down on motion for judgment, against the other defendants.

(3) An application under paragraph (1) must be by summons or motion.

Commencement 1 October 1966.
Cross references See CCR Order 9, rr 4A, 11(1).

Order 19, r 8 Default of defence to counterclaim

A defendant who counterclaims against a plaintiff shall be treated for the purposes of rules 2 to 7 as if he were a plaintiff who had made against a defendant the claim made in the counterclaim and, accordingly, where the plaintiff or any other party against whom the counterclaim is made fails to serve a defence to counterclaim, those rules shall apply as if the counterclaim were a statement of claim, the defence to counterclaim a defence and the parties making the counterclaim and against whom it is made were plaintiffs and defendants respectively, and as if references to the period fixed by or under these rules for service of the defence were references to the period so fixed for service of the defence to counterclaim.

Commencement 1 October 1966.

Order 19, r 9 Setting aside judgment

The Court may, on such terms as it thinks just, set aside or vary any judgment entered in pursuance of this Order.

Commencement 1 October 1966.
Cross references See CCR Order 37, rr 3, 4.

ORDER 20
AMENDMENT

Cross references This Order is applied to business list actions in the central London county court by CCR Order 48C, r 11(5).

Order 20, r 1 Amendment of writ without leave

(1)   Subject to paragraph (3), the plaintiff may, without the leave of the Court, amend the writ once at any time before the pleadings in the action begun by the writ are deemed to be closed.

(2)   Where a writ is amended under this rule after service thereof, then, unless the Court otherwise directs on an application made ex parte, the amended writ must be served on each defendant to the action.

(3)   This rule shall not apply in relation to an amendment which consists of—
    (a)   the addition, omission or substitution of a party to the action or an alteration of the capacity in which a party to the action sues or is sued, or
    (b)   the addition or substitution of a new cause of action, or
    (c)   (without prejudice to rule 3(1)) an amendment of the statement of claim (if any) indorsed on the writ

[unless the amendment is made before service of the writ on any party to the action.]

Commencement 1 October 1966.
Amendments Para (3): words "unless the amendment is made before service of the writ on any party to the action" added by SI 1969/1894, r 3(1).
Forms Praecipe for re-amended writ (PF41).

[Order 20, r 2 Amendment of acknowledgment of service

(1)   Subject to paragraph (2), a party may not amend his acknowledgment of service without the leave of the court.

(2)   A party whose acknowledgment of service contains a statement to the effect that—
    (a)   he does, or
    (b)   he does not

intend to contest the proceedings to which the acknowledgment relates may, without the leave of the court, amend the acknowledgment by substituting for that statement a statement to the opposite effect, provided that in a case falling under sub-paragraph (b) the amendment is made before judgment has been obtained in the proceedings.

(3)   Where an acknowledgment of service is authorised to be amended under this rule, a fresh acknowledgment, amended as so authorised, must be handed in at or sent by post to the [office or district out of which the writ was issued] and Order 12, rule 4, shall apply ....]

Commencement 3 June 1980.
Amendments This rule was substituted by SI 1979/1716, r 23.
Para (3): words "office or district out of which the writ was issued" substituted and word omitted revoked by SI 1982/1111, r 21.
Forms Praecipe for amended acknowledgment of service (PF42).

Order 20, r 3 Amendment of pleadings without leave

(1)   A party may, without the leave of the Court, amend any pleading of his once at

any time before the pleadings are deemed to be closed and, where he does so, he must serve the amended pleading on the opposite party.

(2)   Where an amended statement of claim is served on a defendant—

    (a)   the defendant, if he has already served a defence on the plaintiff, may amend his defence, and

    (b)   the period for service of his defence or amended defence, as the case may be, shall be either the period fixed by or under these rules for service of his defence or a period of 14 days after the amended statement of claim is served on him, whichever expires later.

(3)   Where an amended defence is served on the plaintiff by a defendant—

    (a)   the plaintiff, if he has already served a reply on that defendant, may amend his reply, and

    (b)   the period for service of his reply or amended reply, as the case may be, shall be 14 days after the amended defence is served on him.

(4)   In paragraphs (2) and (3) references to a defence and a reply include references to a counterclaim and a defence to counterclaim respectively.

(5)   Where an amended counterclaim is served by a defendant on a party (other than the plaintiff) against whom the counterclaim is made, paragraph (2) shall apply as if the counterclaim were a statement of claim and as if the party by whom the counterclaim is made were the plaintiff and the party against whom it is made a defendant.

(6)   Where a party has pleaded to a pleading which is subsequently amended and served on him under paragraph (1), then, if that party does not amend his pleading under the foregoing provisions of this rule, he shall be taken to rely on it in answer to the amended pleading, and Order 18, rule 14(2), shall have effect in such a case as if the amended pleading had been served at the time when that pleading, before its amendment under paragraph (1), was served.

Commencement 1 October 1966.
Cross references See CCR Order 15, r 2.

Order 20, r 4 Application for disallowance of amendment made without leave

(1)   Within 14 days after the service on a party [of a writ amended under rule 1(1) or] of a pleading amended under rule 3(1), that party may apply to the Court to disallow the amendment.

(2)   Where the Court hearing an application under this rule is satisfied that if an application for leave to make the amendment in question had been made under rule 5 at the date when the amendment was made under [rule 1(1) or] rule 3(1) leave to make the amendment or part of the amendment would have been refused, it shall order the amendment or that part to be struck out.

(3)   Any order made on an application under this rule may be made on such terms as to costs or otherwise as the Court thinks just.

Commencement 1 October 1966.
Amendments Para (1): words "of a writ amended under rule 1(1) or" added by SI 1969/1894, r 3(2).
Para (2): words "rule 1(1) or" inserted by SI 1969/1894, r 3(3).
Cross references See CCR Order 15, r 2(3).

Order 20, r 5 Amendment of writ or pleading with leave

(1)   Subject to Order 15, rules 6, 7 and 8, and the following provisions of this rule,

the Court may at any stage of the proceedings allow the plaintiff to amend his writ, or any party to amend his pleading, on such terms as to costs or otherwise as may be just and in such manner (if any) as it may direct.

(2)   Where an application to the Court for leave to make the amendment mentioned in paragraph (3), (4) or (5) is made after any relevant period of limitation current at the date of issue of the writ has expired, the Court may nevertheless grant such leave in the circumstances mentioned in that paragraph if it thinks it just to do so.

[In this paragraph "any relevant period of limitation" includes a time limit which applies to the proceedings in question by virtue of the Foreign Limitation Periods Act 1984.]

(3)   An amendment to correct the name of a party may be allowed under paragraph (2) notwithstanding that it is alleged that the effect of the amendment will be to substitute a new party if the Court is satisfied that the mistake sought to be corrected was a genuine mistake and was not misleading or such as to cause any reasonable doubt as to the identity of the party intending to sue or, as the case may be, intended to be sued.

[(4)   An amendment to alter the capacity in which a party sues may be allowed under paragraph (2) if the new capacity is one which that party had at the date of the commencement of the proceedings or has since acquired.]

(5)   An amendment may be allowed under paragraph (2) notwithstanding that the effect of the amendment will be to add or substitute a new cause of action if the new cause of action arises out of the same facts or substantially the same facts as a cause of action in respect of which relief has already been claimed in the action by the party applying for leave to make the amendment.

Commencement 1 May 1981 (para (4)); 1 October 1966 (remainder).
Amendments Para (2): words from "In this paragraph" to "the Foreign Limitation Periods Act 1984" added by SI 1985/1277, r 4.
Para (4): substituted by SI 1981/562, r 3.
Cross references See CCR Order 15, r 1.

Order 20, r 6 *(revoked by SI 1982/1786)*

Order 20, r 7 Amendment of other originating process

Rule 5 shall have effect in relation to an originating summons, a petition and notice of an originating motion as it has effect in relation to a writ.

Commencement 1 October 1966.

Order 20, r 8 Amendment of certain other documents

(1)   For the purpose of determining the real question in controversy between the parties to any proceedings, or of correcting any defect or error in any proceedings, the Court may at any stage of the proceedings and either of its own motion or on the application of any party to the proceedings order any document in the proceedings to be amended on such terms as to costs or otherwise as may be just and in such manner (if any) as it may direct.

(2) This rule shall not have effect in relation to a judgment or order.

Commencement 1 October 1966.
Cross references See CCR Order 15, r 1.

Order 20, r 9 Failure to amend after order

Where the Court makes an order under this Order giving any party leave to amend a writ, pleading or other document, then, if that party does not amend the document in accordance with the order before the expiration of the period specified for that purpose in the order or, if no period is so specified, of a period of 14 days after the order was made, the order shall cease to have effect, without prejudice, however, to the power of the Court to extend the period.

Commencement 1 October 1966.

Order 20, r 10 Mode of amendment of writ, etc

(1) Where the amendments authorised under any rule of this Order to be made in a writ, pleading or other document are so numerous or of such nature or length that to make written alterations of the document so as to give effect to them would make it difficult or inconvenient to read, a fresh document, amended as so authorised, must be prepared and, in the case of a writ or originating summons re-issued, but, except as aforesaid and subject to any direction given under rule 5 or 8, the amendments so authorised may be effected by making in writing the necessary alterations of the document and, in the case of a writ or originating summons, causing it to be re-sealed and filing a copy thereof.

(2) A writ, pleading or other document which has been amended under this Order must be indorsed with a statement that it has been amended, specifying the date on which it was amended, the name of the judge, master or registrar [district judge] by whom the order (if any) authorising the amendment was made and the date thereof, or, if no such order was made, the number of the rule of this Order in pursuance of which the amendment was made.

Commencement 1 October 1966.

Order 20, r 11 Amendment of judgment and orders

Clerical mistakes in judgments or orders, or errors arising therein from any accidental slip or omission, may at any time be corrected by the Court on motion or summons without an appeal.

Commencement 1 October 1966.
Cross references See Order 15, r 5.

[Order 20, r 12 Amendment of pleadings by agreement

(1) Notwithstanding the foregoing provisions of this Order any pleading [in any cause or matter] may, by written agreement between the parties, be amended at any stage of the proceedings.

(2) This rule shall not have effect in relation to an amendment to a counterclaim which consists of the addition, omission or substitution of a party.]

Commencement 1 January 1983.
Amendments This rule was inserted by SI 1982/1786, r 9.
Para (1): words "in any cause or matter" substituted by SI 1987/1423, r 35.

ORDER 21
WITHDRAWAL AND DISCONTINUANCE

[Order 21, r 1 Withdrawal of acknowledgment of service

A party who has acknowledged service in an action may withdraw the acknowledgment at any time with the leave of the Court.]

Commencement 3 June 1980.
Amendments This rule was substituted by SI 1979/1716, r 24.

Order 21, r 2 Discontinuance of action, etc, without leave

(1)   [Subject to paragraph (2A),] the plaintiff in an action begun by writ may, without the leave of the Court, discontinue the action, or withdraw any particular claim made by him therein, as against any or all of the defendants at any time not later than 14 days after service of the defence on him or, if there are two or more defendants, of the defence last served, by serving a notice to that effect on the defendant concerned.

(2)   [Subject to paragraph (2A),] a defendant [to an action begun by writ] may, without the leave of the Court,—
    (a)   withdraw his defence or any part of it at any time,
    (b)   discontinue a counterclaim, or withdraw any particular claim made by him therein, as against any or all of the parties against whom it is made, at any time not later than 14 days after service on him of a defence to counterclaim or, if the counterclaim is made against two or more parties, of the defence to counterclaim last served,

by serving a notice to that effect on the plaintiff or other party concerned.

[(2A) A party in whose favour an interim payment has been ordered, in accordance with Order 29, rule 11, may not discontinue any action or counterclaim, or withdraw any particular claim therein, except with the leave of the Court or the consent of all the other parties.]

(3)   Where there are two or more defendants to an action [begun by writ] not all of whom serve a defence on the plaintiff, and the period fixed by or under these rules for service by any of those defendants of his defence expires after the latest date on which any other defendant serves his defence, paragraph (1) shall have effect as if the reference therein to the service of the defence last served were a reference to the expiration of that period.

This paragraph shall apply in relation to a counterclaim as it applies in relation to an action with the substitution for references to a defence, to the plaintiff and to paragraph (1), of references to a defence to counterclaim, to the defendant and to paragraph (2) respectively.

[(3A) The plaintiff in an action begun by originating summons may, without the leave of the Court, discontinue the action or withdraw any particular question or claim in the originating summons, as against any or all of the defendants at any time not later than 14 days after service on him of the defendant's affidavit evidence filed pursuant to [Order 28, rule 1A(4)] or, if there are two or more defendants, of such evidence last served, by serving a notice to that effect on the defendant concerned.

(3B) When there are two or more defendants to an action begun by originating summons not all of whom serve affidavit evidence on the plaintiff, and the period fixed by or under these rules for service by any of those defendants of his affidavit evidence expires after the latest date on which any other defendant serves his affidavit evidence, paragraph (3A) shall have effect as if the reference therein to the service of the affidavit evidence last served were a reference to the expiration of that period.]

(4)   If all the parties to an action consent, the action may be withdrawn without the leave of the Court at any time before trial by producing—
  (a)   in a case where the action has been set down for trial, to the proper officer, and
  (b)   in any other case, to an officer of the Central Office or, if the action is [a commercial action or is] proceeding in [the Chancery Division or a district registry, to an officer [in the Admiralty and Commercial Registry or to an officer] in Chancery Chambers or the [district judge] of that registry, as the case may be],

a written consent to the action being withdrawn signed by all the parties.

In this paragraph "proper officer" has the meaning assigned to it by Order 34, rule 3(5) . . . .

Commencement   1 January 1983 (paras (3A), (3B)); 1 October 1980 (para (2A)); 1 October 1966 (remainder).
Amendments   Para (1): words "Subject to paragraph (2A)," substituted by SI 1980/1010, r 4(a).
Para (2): words "Subject to paragraph (2A)," substituted by SI 1980/1010, r 4(a); words "to an action begun by writ" inserted by SI 1982/1786, r 10(1).
Para (2A): inserted by SI 1980/1010, r 4(b).
Para (3): words "begun by writ" inserted by SI 1982/1786, r 10(2).
Para (3A): inserted by SI 1982/1786, r 10(3); words "Order 28, rule 1A(4)" substituted by SI 1985/69, r 7(2), Schedule.
Para (3B): inserted by SI 1982/1786, r 10(3).
Para (4): in sub-para (b) words "a commercial action or is" added and words "in the Admiralty and Commercial Registry or to an officer" substituted by SI 1987/1423, r 8, other words in square brackets substituted by SI 1982/1111, r 22; words omitted revoked by SI 1982/1111, r 23.
Cross references   See CCR Order 18, rr 1, 3.

Order 21, r 3 Discontinuance of action, etc, with leave

(1)   Except as provided by rule 2, a party may not discontinue an action (whether begun by writ or otherwise) or counterclaim, or withdraw any particular claim made by him therein, without the leave of the Court, and the Court hearing an application for the grant of such leave may order the action or counterclaim to be discontinued, or any particular claim made therein to be struck out, as against any or all of the parties against whom it is brought or made on such terms as to costs, the bringing of a subsequent action or otherwise as it thinks just.

(2)   An application for the grant of leave under this rule may be made by summons or motion or by notice under Order 25, rule 7.

Commencement   1 October 1966.
Cross references   See CCR Order 18, r 1.

Order 21, r 4 Effect of discontinuance

Subject to any terms imposed by the Court in granting leave under rule 3, the fact that a party has discontinued an action or counterclaim or withdrawn a particular claim made by him therein shall not be a defence to a subsequent action for the same, or substantially the same, cause of action.

Commencement   1 October 1966.

Order 21, r 5 Stay of subsequent action until costs paid

(1)   Where a party has discontinued an action or counterclaim or withdrawn any particular claim made by him therein and he is liable to pay any other party's costs of the action or counterclaim or the costs occasioned to any other party by the claim withdrawn, then if, before payment of those costs, he subsequently brings an action for the same, or substantially the same, cause of action, the Court may order the proceedings in that action to be stayed until those costs are paid.

(2)   An application for an order under this rule may be made by summons or motion or by notice under Order 25, rule 7.

Commencement 1 October 1966.
Cross references See CCR Order 18, r 2(3).

Order 21, r 6 Withdrawal of summons

A party who has taken out a summons in a cause or matter may not withdraw it without the leave of the Court.

Commencement 1 October 1966.

ORDER 22
Payment into and out of Court

Order 22, r 1 Payment into court

(1)   In any action for a debt or damages any defendant may at any time . . . pay into court a sum of money in satisfaction of the cause of action in respect of which the plaintiff claims or, where two or more causes of action are joined in the action, a sum or sums of money in satisfaction of any or all of those causes of action.

(2)   On making any payment into court under this rule, and on increasing any such payment already made, the defendant must give notice thereof in Form No 23 in Appendix A to the plaintiff and every other defendant (if any); and within 3 days after receiving the notice the plaintiff must send the defendant a written acknowledgement of its receipt.

(3)   A defendant may, without leave, give notice of an increase in a payment made under this rule but, subject to that and without prejudice to paragraph (5), a notice of payment may not be withdrawn or amended without the leave of the Court which may be granted on such terms as may be just.

(4)   Where two or more causes of action are joined in the action and money is paid into court under this rule in respect of all, or some only of, those causes of action, the notice of payment—

(a)   must state that the money is paid in respect of all those causes of action or, as the case may be, must specify the cause or causes of action in respect of which the payment is made, and

(b)   where the defendant makes separate payments in respect of each, or any two or more, of those causes of action, must specify the sum paid in respect of that cause or, as the case may be, those causes of action.

(5)   Where a single sum of money is paid into court under this rule in respect of two or more causes of action, then, if it appears to the Court that the plaintiff is embarrassed by the payment, the Court may, subject to paragraph (6), order the defendant to amend the notice of payment so as to specify the sum paid in respect of each cause of action.

(6)   Where a cause of action under [the Fatal Accidents Act 1976] and a cause of action under the Law Reform (Miscellaneous Provisions) Act 1934 are joined in an action, with or without any other cause of action, the causes of action under the said Acts shall, for the purpose of paragraph (5), be treated as one cause of action.

[(7)   Where—

(a)   an action proceeding in a district registry is being tried at [a town] within the district of another district registry or at the Royal Courts of Justice, or

(b)   an action proceeding in the Royal Courts of Justice is being tried at [a town] within the district of a district registry,

any payment into court under this rule made after the trial or hearing has begun may, if the defendant so desires, be made at the district registry within the district of which [the town] is situated or, if the action is being tried at the Royal Courts of Justice, in the same manner as if the action were proceeding there.]

[(8)   For the purposes of this rule, the plaintiff's cause of action in respect of a debt or damages shall be construed as a cause of action in respect, also, of such interest as might be included in the judgment, whether under [section 35A of the Act] or otherwise, if judgment were given at the date of the payment into court.]

Commencement 1 October 1980 (para (8)); 2 January 1967 (para (7)); 1 October 1966 (remainder).
Amendments Para (1): words omitted revoked by SI 1979/1716, r 25.
Para (6): words "the Fatal Accidents Act 1976" substituted by SI 1980/629, r 24.
Para (7): added by SI 1966/1514, r 5; in sub-paras (a), (b) words "a town" and "the town" substituted by SI 1971/1955, r 8.
Para (8): added by SI 1980/1010, r 5; words "section 35A of the Act" substituted by SI 1982/1786, r 8.
Definitions The Act: Supreme Court Act 1981.
Cross references See CCR Order 11, r 1.

Order 22, r 2 Payment in by defendant who has counterclaimed

Where a defendant, who makes by counterclaim a claim against the plaintiff for a debt or damages, pays a sum or sums of money into court under rule 1, the notice of payment must state, if it be the case, that in making the payment the defendant has taken into account and intends to satisfy—

    (a)   the cause of action in respect of which he claims, or

    (b)   where two or more causes of action are joined in the counterclaim, all those causes of action or, if not all, which of them.

Commencement 1 October 1966.
Cross references See CCR Order 11, rr 1, 8.

Order 22, r 3 Acceptance of money paid into court

(1) Where money is paid into court under rule 1, then, subject to paragraph (2), within [21 days] after receipt of the notice of payment or, where more than one payment has been made or the notice has been amended, within [21 days] after receipt of the notice of the last payment or the amended notice but, in any case, before the trial or hearing of the action begins, the plaintiff may—

    (a)   where the money was paid in respect of the cause of action or all the causes of action in respect of which he claims, accept the money in satisfaction of that cause of action or those causes of action, as the case may be, or

    (b)   where the money was paid in respect of some only of the causes of action in respect of which he claims, accept in satisfaction of any such cause or causes of action the sum specified in respect of that cause or those causes of action in the notice of payment,

by giving notice in Form No 24 in Appendix A to every defendant to the action.

(2)   Where after the trial or hearing of an action has begun—

    (a)   money is paid into court under rule 1, or

    (b)   money in court is increased by a further payment into court under that rule,

the plaintiff may accept the money in accordance with paragraph (1) within 2 days after receipt of the notice of payment or notice of the further payment, as the case may be, but, in any case, before the judge begins to deliver judgment or, if the trial is with a jury, before the judge begins his summing up.

(3)   Rule 1(5) shall not apply in relation to money paid into court in an action after the trial or hearing of the action has begun.

(4)   On the plaintiff accepting any money paid into court all further proceedings in the action or in respect of the specified cause or causes of action, as the case may be, to which the acceptance relates, both against the defendant making the payment and against any other defendant sued jointly with or in the alternative to him, shall be stayed.

(5)   Where money is paid into court by a defendant who made a counterclaim and the notice of payment stated, in relation to any sum so paid, that in making the payment the defendant had taken into account and satisfied the cause or causes of action, or the specified cause or causes of action in respect of which he claimed, then, on the plaintiff accepting that sum, all further proceedings on the counterclaim or in respect of the specified cause or causes of action, as the case may be, against the plaintiff shall be stayed.

(6)   A plaintiff who has accepted any sum paid into court shall, subject to rules 4 and 10 and Order 80, rule 12, be entitled to receive payment of that sum in satisfaction of the cause or causes of action to which the acceptance relates.

Commencement 1 October 1966.
Amendments Para (1): words "21 days" in both places substituted by SI 1972/1898, r 4.
Cross references See CCR Order 11, r 3.

Order 22, r 4 Order for payment out of money accepted required in certain cases

(1)   Where a plaintiff accepts any sum paid into court and that sum was paid into court—

   (a)   by some but not all of the defendants sued jointly or in the alternative by him, or
   (b)   with a defence of tender before action, or
   (c)   in an action to which Order 80, rule 12, applies, or
   (d)   in satisfaction either of causes of action arising under [the Fatal Accidents Act 1976] and the Law Reform (Miscellaneous Provisions) Act 1934, or of a cause of action arising under the first mentioned [Act] where more than one person is entitled to the money, the money in court shall not be paid out except under paragraph (2) or in pursuance of an order of the Court, and the order shall deal with the whole costs of the action or of the cause of action to which the payment relates, as the case may be.

(2)   Where an order of the Court is required under paragraph (1) by reason only of paragraph (1)(a), then if, either before or after accepting the money paid into court by some only of the defendants sued jointly or in the alternative by him, the plaintiff discontinues the action against all the other defendants and those defendants consent in writing to the payment out of that sum, it may be paid out without an order of the Court.

(3)   Where after the trial or hearing of an action has begun a plaintiff accepts any money paid into court and all further proceedings in the action or in respect of the specified cause or causes of action, as the case may be, to which the acceptance relates are stayed by virtue of rule 3(4), then, notwithstanding anything in paragraph (2), the money shall not be paid out except in pursuance of an order of the Court, and the order shall deal with the whole costs of the action.

Commencement 1 October 1966.
Amendments Para (1): in sub-para (d) words "the Fatal Accidents Act 1976" substituted by SI 1980/629, r 24, word "Act" substituted by SI 1980/1908, r 20.
Cross references See CCR Order 11, rr 4, 5.

Order 22, r 5 Money remaining in court

[(1)] If any money paid into court in an action is not accepted in accordance with rule 3, the money remaining in court shall not be paid out except in pursuance of an order of the Court which may be made at any time before, at or after the trial or hearing of the action; and where such an order is made before the trial or hearing the money shall not be paid out except in satisfaction of the cause or causes of action in respect of which it was paid in.

[(2)   In a case where a payment into court has been made as mentioned in paragraph 12(2) of Schedule 4 to the Social Security Act 1989 and an application is made for the money remaining in court to be paid out, the court may treat the money in court as being reduced by a sum equivalent to any further relevant benefits (within the meaning of section 22(3) of that Act) paid to the plaintiff since the date of payment into court and direct payment out accordingly.]

Commencement   1 October 1990 (para (2)); 1 October 1966 (remainder).
Amendments   Para (1): numbered as such by SI 1990/1689, r 18(a).
Para (2): inserted by SI 1990/1689, r 18(b).
Cross references   See CCR Order 11, r 5.

Order 22, r 6 Counterclaim

A plaintiff against whom a counterclaim is made and any other defendant to the counterclaim may pay money into court in accordance with rule 1, and that rule and rules 3 (except paragraph (5)), 4 and 5 shall apply accordingly with the necessary modifications.

Commencement   1 October 1966.
Cross references   See CCR Order 11, r 8.

Order 22, r 7 Non-disclosure of payment into court

[(1)] Except in an action to which a defence of tender before action is pleaded, and except in an action all further proceedings in which are stayed by virtue of rule 3(4) after the trial or hearing has begun, [and subject to paragraph (2)] the fact that money has been paid into court under the foregoing provisions of this Order shall not be pleaded and no communication of that fact shall be made to the Court at the trial or hearing of the action or counterclaim or of any question or issue as to the debt or damages until all questions of liability and of the amount of the debt or damages have been decided.

[(2)   Where the question of the costs of the issue of liability falls to be decided, that issue having been tried and an issue or question concerning the amount of the debt or damages remaining to be tried separately, any party may bring to the attention of the Court the fact that a payment into court has or has not been made and the date (but not the amount) of such payment or of the first payment if more than one.]

Commencement   1 October 1987 (para (2)); 1 October 1966 (remainder).
Amendments   Para (1): numbered as such and words "and subject to paragraph (2)" inserted by SI 1987/1423, r 34(1), (2).
Para (2): inserted by SI 1987/1423, r 34(3).
Cross references   See CCR Order 11, r 7.

Order 22, r 8 Money paid into court under order

[(1)   On making any payment into court under an order of the court or a certificate of a master or associate, a party must give notice thereof to every other party to the proceedings.]

[(2)] Subject to [paragraph (3)], money paid into court under an order of the Court or a certificate of a master or associate shall not be paid out except in pursuance of an order of the Court.

[(3)] Unless the Court otherwise orders, a party who has paid money into court in pursuance of an order made under Order 14—

(a) may by notice to the other party appropriate the whole or any part of the money and any additional payment, if necessary, to any particular claim made in the writ or counterclaim, as the case may be, and specified in the notice, or

(b) if he pleads a tender, may by his pleading appropriate the whole or any part of the money as payment into court of the money alleged to have been tendered;

and money appropriated in accordance with this rule shall be deemed to be money paid into court in accordance with rule 1 or money paid into court with a plea of tender, as the case may be, and this Order shall apply accordingly.

Commencement 7 March 1989 (para (1)); 1 October 1966 (remainder).
Amendments Para (1): inserted by SI 1989/177, r 4(2).
Para (2): originally para (1), renumbered as para (2) and words "paragraph (3)" substituted by SI 1989/177, r 4(1).
Para (3): originally para (2), renumbered as para (3) by SI 1989/177, r 4(1).
Cross references See CCR Order 11, r 9.

Order 22, r 9 *(revoked by SI 1979/1725)*

Order 22, r 10 Person to whom payment to be made

(1) Where the party entitled to money in court is a person in respect of whom a certificate is or has been in force entitling him to legal aid under [Part I of the Legal Aid Act 1974], payment shall be made only to that party's solicitor (or, if he is no longer represented by a solicitor, then, if the Court so orders, to the Law Society), without the need for any authority from the party.

(2) Subject to paragraph (1), payment shall be made to the party entitled or . . . to his solicitor . . . .

(3) This rule applies whether the money in court has been paid into court under rule 1 or under an order of the Court or a certificate of a master or associate.

Commencement 1 October 1966.
Amendments Para (1): words "Part I of the Legal Aid Act 1974" substituted by SI 1979/1542, r 9(1), Schedule.
Para (2): words omitted revoked by SI 1969/1894, r 4(1).
Cross references See CCR Order 11, r 4(4).

Order 22, r 11 Payment out: small intestate estates

Where a person entitled to a fund in court, or a share of such fund, dies intestate and the Court is satisfied that no grant or administration of his estate has been made and that the assets of his estate [including the fund or share, do not exceed in value the amount specified in any order for the time being in force under section 6 of the Administration of Estates (Small Payments) Act 1965], it may order that the fund or share shall be paid, transferred or delivered to the person who, being a widower, widow, child, father, mother, brother or sister of the deceased, would have the prior right to a grant of administration of the estate of the deceased.

Commencement 1 October 1966.
Amendments Words from "including the fund or share" to "the Administration of Estates (Small Payments) Act 1965" substituted by SI 1984/1051, r 3.

Order 22, r 12 Payment of hospital expenses

(1)   This rule applies in relation to an action or counterclaim for bodily injury arising out of the use of a motor vehicle on a road or in a place to which the public have a right of access in which the claim for damages includes a sum for hospital expenses.

(2)   Where the party against whom the claim is made, or an authorised insurer within the meaning of [Part VI of the Road Traffic Act 1972] pays the amount for which that party or insurer, as the case may be, is or may be liable under [section 154] of that Act in respect of the treatment afforded by a hospital to the person in respect of whom the claim is made, the party against whom the claim is made must, within 7 days after the payment is made, give notice of the payment to all the other parties to the action.

Commencement1 October 1966.
Amendments Para (2): words "Part VI of the Road Traffic Act 1972" and "section 154" substituted by SI 1979/1542, r 9(1), Schedule.
Cross references See CCR Order 11, r 6.

Order 22, r 13 Investment of money in court

[(1)   Subject to paragraph (2)] cash under the control of or subject to the order of the Court may be invested in any manner specified in [Part I and] paragraphs 1 to 10 and 12 of Part II of Schedule 1 to the Trustee Investments Act 1961, as [supplemented by the provisions of] Part IV of that Schedule.

[(2)   Nothing in paragraph (1) shall restrict the manner of investment of cash transferred to and held by the Public Trustee under a declaration of trust approved by the Court.]

Commencement 10 January 1970 (para (2)); 1 October 1966 (remainder).
Amendments Para (1): numbered as such and words "Subject to paragraph (2)" inserted by SI 1969/1894, r 4(2); words "Part I and" inserted and words "supplemented by the provisions of" substituted by SI 1982/1111, r 113.
Para (2): added by SI 1969/1894, r 4(2).

[Order 22, r 14 Written Offers 'without prejudice save as to costs'

(1)   A party to proceedings may at any time make a written offer to any other party to those proceedings which is expressed to be 'without prejudice save as to costs' and which relates to any issue in the proceedings.

(2)   Where an offer is made under paragraph (1), the fact that such an offer has been made shall not be communicated to the Court until the question of costs falls to be decided . . .]

Commencement 28 April 1986.
Amendments This rule was added by SI 1986/632, r 5.
Para (2): words omitted revoked by SI 1990/1689, r 19.
Cross references See CCR Order 11, r 10.

ORDER 23
SECURITY FOR COSTS

Order 23, r 1 Security for costs of action, etc

(1)   Where, on the application of a defendant to an action or other proceeding in the High Court, it appears to the Court—

    (a)   that the plaintiff is ordinarily resident out of the jurisdiction, or

    (b)   that the plaintiff (not being a plaintiff who is suing in a representative capacity) is a nominal plaintiff who is suing for the benefit of some other person and that there is reason to believe that he will be unable to pay the costs of the defendant if ordered to do so, or

    (c)   subject to paragraph (2), that the plaintiff's address is not stated in the writ or other originating process or is incorrectly stated therein, or

    (d)   that the plaintiff has changed his address during the course of the proceedings with a view to evading the consequences of the litigation,

then if, having regard to all the circumstances of the case, the Court thinks it just to do so, it may order the plaintiff to give such security for the defendant's costs of the action or other proceeding as it thinks just.

(2)   The Court shall not require a plaintiff to give security by reason only of paragraph (1)(c) if he satisfies the Court that the failure to state his address or the mis-statement thereof was made innocently and without intention to deceive.

(3)   The references in the foregoing paragraphs to a plaintiff and a defendant shall be construed as references to the person (howsoever described on the record) who is in the position of plaintiff or defendant, as the case may be, in the proceeding in question, including a proceeding on a counterclaim.

Commencement   1 October 1966.
Cross references   See CCR Order 13, r 8.
Forms   Summons for security (PF43).
Order for security (PF44).

Order 23, r 2 Manner of giving security

Where an order is made requiring any party to give security for costs the security shall be given in such manner, at such time, and on such terms (if any), as the Court may direct.

Commencement   1 October 1966.
Cross references   See CCR Order 50, r 9.

Order 23, r 3 Saving for enactments

This Order is without prejudice to the provisions of any enactment which empowers the Court to require security to be given for the costs of any proceedings.

Commencement   1 October 1966.

ORDER 24
DISCOVERY AND INSPECTION OF DOCUMENTS

Cross references This Order is applied to business list actions in the central London county court by CCR Order 48C, r 12(2).

Order 24, r 1 Mutual discovery of documents

(1)   After the close of pleadings in an action begun by writ there shall, subject to and in accordance with the provisions of this Order, be discovery by the parties to the action of the documents which are or have been in their possession, custody or power relating to matters in question in the action.

(2)   Nothing in this Order shall be taken as preventing the parties to an action agreeing to dispense with or limit the discovery of documents which they would otherwise be required to make to each other.

Commencement 1 October 1966.

Order 24, r 2 Discovery by parties without order

(1)   Subject to the provisions of this rule and of rule 4, the parties to an action between whom pleadings are closed must make discovery by exchanging lists of documents and, accordingly, each party must, within 14 days after the pleadings in the action are deemed to be closed as between him and any other party, make and serve on that other party a list of the documents which are or have been in his possession, custody or power relating to any matter in question between them in the action.

Without prejudice to any directions given by the Court under Order 16, rule 4, this paragraph shall not apply in third party proceedings, including proceedings under that Order involving fourth or subsequent parties.

(2)   Unless the Court otherwise orders, a defendant to an action arising out of an accident on land due to a collision or apprehended collision involving a vehicle shall not make discovery of any documents to the plaintiff under paragraph (1).

(3)   Paragraph (1) shall not be taken as requiring a defendant to an action for the recovery of any penalty recoverable by virtue of any enactment to make discovery of any documents . . . .

(4)   Paragraphs (2) and (3) shall apply in relation to a counterclaim as they apply in relation to an action but with the substitution, for the reference in paragraph (2) to the plaintiff, of a reference to the party making the counterclaim.

(5)   On the application of any party required by this rule to make discovery of documents, the Court may—

    (a)   order that the parties to the action or any of them shall make discovery under paragraph (1) of such documents or classes of documents only, or as to such only of the matters in question, as may be specified in the order, or

    (b)   if satisfied that discovery by all or any of the parties is not necessary, or not necessary at that stage of the action, order that there shall be no discovery of documents by any or all of the parties either at all or at that stage;

and the Court shall make such an order if and so far as it is of opinion that discovery is not necessary either for disposing fairly of the action or for saving costs.

(6)   An application for an order under paragraph (5) must be by summons, and the summons must be taken out before the expiration of the period within which by virtue of this rule discovery of documents in the action is required to be made.

(7) Any party to whom discovery of documents is required to be made under this rule may, at any time before the summons for directions in the action is taken out, serve on the party required to make such discovery a notice requiring him to make an affidavit verifying the list he is required to make under paragraph (1), and the party on whom such a notice is served must, within 14 days after service of the notice, make and file an affidavit in compliance with the notice and serve a copy of the affidavit on the party by whom the notice was served.

Commencement 1 October 1966.
Amendments Para (3): words omitted revoked by SI 1969/1105, r 4.
Cross references See CCR Order 17, r 11(3), (5).
Forms Notice requiring affidavit (PF45).

Order 24, r 3 Order for discovery

(1)   Subject to the provisions of this rule and of rules 4 and 8, the Court may order any party to a cause or matter (whether begun by writ, originating summons or otherwise) to make and serve on any other party a list of the documents which are or have been in his possession, custody or power relating to any matter in question in the cause or matter, and may at the same time or subsequently also order him to make and file an affidavit verifying such a list and to serve a copy thereof on the other party.

(2)   Where a party who is required by rule 2 to make discovery of documents fails to comply with any provision of that rule, the Court, on the application of any party to whom the discovery was required to be made, may make an order against the first-mentioned party under paragraph (1) of this rule or, as the case may be, may order him to make and file an affidavit verifying the list of documents he is required to make under rule 2 and to serve a copy thereof on the applicant.

(3)   An order under this rule may be limited to such documents or classes of document only, or to such only of the matters in question in the cause or matter, as may be specified in the order.

Commencement 1 October 1966.
Cross references See CCR Order 14, r 1.

Order 24, r 4 Order for determination of issue, etc, before discovery

(1)   Where on an application for an order under rule 2 or 3 it appears to the Court that any issue or question in the cause or matter should be determined before any discovery of documents is made by the parties, the Court may order that that issue or question be determined first.

(2)   Where in an action begun by writ an order is made under this rule for the determination of an issue or question, Order 25, rules 2 to 7, shall, with the omission of so much of rule 7(1) as requires parties to serve a notice specifying the orders and directions which they desire and with any other necessary modifications, apply as if the application on which the order was made were a summons for directions.

Commencement 1 October 1966.

Order 24, r 5 Form of list and affidavit

(1)   A list of documents made in compliance with rule 2, or with an order under rule 3, must be in Form No 26 in Appendix A, and must enumerate the documents in a convenient order and as shortly as possible but describing each of them or, in the case of bundles of documents of the same nature, each bundle, sufficiently to enable it to be identified.

(2)   If it is desired to claim that any documents are privileged from production, the claim must be made in the list of documents with a sufficient statement of the grounds of the privilege.

(3)   An affidavit made as aforesaid verifying a list of documents must be in Form No 27 in Appendix A.

Commencement 1 October 1966.

Order 24, r 6 Defendant entitled to copy of co-defendant's list

(1)   A defendant who has pleaded in an action shall be entitled to have a copy of any list of documents served under any of the foregoing rules of this Order on the plaintiff by any other defendant to the action; and a plaintiff against whom a counterclaim is made in an action begun by writ shall be entitled to have a copy of any list of documents served under any of those rules on the party making the counterclaim by any other defendant to the counterclaim.

(2)   A party required by virtue of paragraph (1) to supply a copy of a list of documents must supply it free of charge on a request made by the party entitled to it.

(3)   Where in an action begun by originating summons the Court makes an order under rule 3 requiring a defendant to the action to serve a list of documents on the plaintiff, it may also order him to supply any other defendant to the action with a copy of that list.

(4)   In this rule "list of documents" includes an affidavit verifying a list of documents.

Commencement 1 October 1966.

Order 24, r 7 Order for discovery of particular documents

(1)   Subject to rule 8, the Court may at any time, on the application of any party to a cause or matter, make an order requiring any other party to make an affidavit stating whether any document specified or described in the application or any class of document so specified or described is, or has at any time been, in his possession, custody or power, and if not then in his possession, custody or power when he parted with it and what has become of it.

(2)   An order may be made against a party under this rule notwithstanding that he may already have made or been required to make a list of documents or affidavit under rule 2 or rule 3.

(3)   An application for an order under this rule must be supported by an affidavit stating the belief of the deponent that the party from whom discovery is sought under this rule has, or at some time had, in his possession, custody or power the document,

or class of document, specified or described in the application and that it relates to one or more of the matters in question in the cause or matter.

Commencement 1 October 1966.
Cross references See CCR Order 14, r 2.

[Order 24, r 7A Application under [sections 33(2) or 34(2) of the Act]

(1)   An application for an order under [section 33(2) of the Act] for the disclosure of documents before the commencement of proceedings shall be made by originating summons [(in Form No 10 in Appendix A)] and the person against whom the order is sought shall be made defendant to the summons.

(2)   An application after the commencement of proceedings for an order under [section 34(2)] of the said Act for the disclosure of documents by a person who is not a party to the proceedings shall be made by summons, which must be served on that person personally and on every party to the proceedings other than the applicant.

(3)   A summons under paragraph (1) or (2) shall be supported by an affidavit which must—
- (a)   in the case of a summons under paragraph (1), state the grounds on which it is alleged that the applicant and the person against whom the order is sought are likely to be parties to subsequent proceedings in the High Court in which a claim for personal injuries is likely to be made;
- (b)   in any case, specify or describe the documents in respect of which the order is sought and show, if practicable by reference to any pleading served or intended to be served in the proceedings, that the documents are relevant to an issue arising or likely to arise out of a claim for personal injuries made or likely to be made in the proceedings and that the person against whom the order is sought is likely to have or have had them in his possession, custody or power.

(4)   A copy of the supporting affidavit shall be served with the summons on every person on whom the summons is required to be served.

(5)   An order under the said [section 33(2) or 34(2)] for the disclosure of documents may be made conditional on the applicant's giving security for the costs of the person against whom it is made or on such other terms, if any, as the Court thinks just, and shall require the person against whom the order is made to make an affidavit stating whether any documents specified or described in the order are, or at any time have been, in his possession, custody or power and, if not then in his possession, custody or power, when he parted with them and what has become of them.

(6)   No person shall be compelled by virtue of such an order to produce any documents which he could not be compelled to produce—
- (a)   in the case of a summons under paragraph (1), if the subsequent proceedings had already been begun, or
- (b)   in the case of a summons under paragraph (2), if he had been served with a writ of subpoena duces tecum to produce the documents at the trial.

(7)   In this rule "a claim for personal injuries" means a claim in respect of personal injuries to a person . . . or in respect of a person's death.

(8)   For the purposes of rules 10 and 11 an application for an order under the said [section 33(2) or 34(2)] shall be treated as a cause or matter between the applicant and

the person against whom the order is sought.]

Commencement 31 August 1971.
Amendments This rule was inserted by SI 1971/1269, r 40.
Rule heading: words "sections 33(2) or 34(2) of the Act" substituted by SI 1982/1111, r 115, Schedule.
Para (1): words "section 33(2) of the Act" substituted by SI 1982/1111, r 115, Schedule; words "(in Form No 10 in Appendix A)" inserted by SI 1990/1689, r 22.
Para (2): words "section 34(2)" substituted by SI 1982/1111, r 115, Schedule.
Paras (5), (8): words "section 33(2) or 34(2)" substituted by SI 1982/1111, r 115, Schedule.
Para (7): words omitted revoked by SI 1975/911, r 8.
Definitions The Act: Supreme Court Act 1981.
Cross references This rule is applied to the county court by CCR Order 13, r 7.

Order 24, r 8 Discovery to be ordered only if necessary

On the hearing of an application for an order under [rule 3, 7 or 7A] the Court, if satisfied that discovery is not necessary, or not necessary at that stage of the cause or matter, may dismiss or, as the case may be, adjourn the application and shall in any case refuse to make such an order if and so far as it is of opinion that discovery is not necessary either for disposing fairly of the cause or matter or for saving costs.

Commencement 1 October 1966.
Amendments Words "rule 3, 7 or 7A" substituted by SI 1971/1269, r 41.
Cross references See CCR Order 14, r 8.

Order 24, r 9 Inspection of documents referred to in list

A party who has served a list of documents on any other party, whether in compliance with rule 2 [or 6] or with an order under rule 3, must allow the other party to inspect the documents referred to in the list (other than any which he objects to produce) and to take copies thereof and, accordingly, he must when he serves the list on the other party also serve on him a notice stating a time within 7 days after the service thereof at which the said documents may be inspected at a place specified in the notice.

Commencement 1 October 1966.
Amendments Words "or 6" inserted by SI 1991/531, r 2.
Cross references See CCR Order 14, r 3.

Order 24, r 10 Inspection of documents referred to in pleadings[, affidavits and witness statements]

(1) Any party to a cause or matter shall be entitled at any time to serve a notice on any other party in whose pleadings[, affidavits or witness statements] reference is made to any document requiring him to produce that document for the inspection of the party giving the notice and to permit him to take copies thereof.

(2) The party on whom a notice is served under paragraph (1) must, within 4 days after service of the notice, serve on the party giving the notice a notice stating a time within 7 days after the service thereof at which the documents, or such of them as he does not object to produce, may be inspected at a place specified in the notice, and stating which (if any) of the documents he objects to produce and on what grounds.

Commencement 1 October 1966.
Amendments Rule heading: words ", affidavits and witness statements" substituted by SI 1992/1907, r 7(1).
Para (1): words ", affidavits or witness statements" substituted by SI 1992/1907, r 7(2).

Cross references See CCR Order 14, r 4.
Forms Notice to inspect (PF46).
Notice to produce (PF47).
Notice of objection to inspect (PF48).

Order 24, r 11 Order for production for inspection

(1) If a party who is required by rule 9 to serve such a notice as is therein mentioned or who is served with a notice under rule 10(1)—

    (a) fails to serve a notice under rule 9 or, as the case may be, rule 10(2), or

    (b) objects to produce any document for inspection, or

    (c) offers inspection at a time or place such that, in the opinion of the Court, it is unreasonable to offer inspection then or, as the case may be, there,

then, subject to rule 13(1), the Court may, on the application of the party entitled to inspection, make an order for production of the documents in question for inspection at such time and place, and in such manner, as it thinks fit.

(2) Without prejudice to paragraph (1), but subject to rule 13(1), the Court may, on the application of any party to a cause or matter, order any other party to permit the party applying to inspect any documents in the possession, custody or power of that other party relating to any matter in question in the cause or matter.

(3) An application for an order under paragraph (2) must be supported by an affidavit specifying or describing the documents of which inspection is sought and stating the belief of the deponent that they are in the possession, custody or power of the other party and that they relate to a matter in question in the cause or matter.

Commencement 1 October 1966.
Cross references See CCR Order 14, r 5.
Forms Order for production and inspection (PF49).

[Order 24, r 11A Provision of copies of documents

(1) Any party who is entitled to inspect any documents under any provision of this Order or any order made thereunder may at or before the time when inspection takes place serve on the party who is required to produce such documents for inspection a notice (which shall contain an undertaking to pay the reasonable charges) requiring him to supply a true copy of any such document as is capable of being copied by photographic or similar process.

(2) The party on whom such a notice is served must within 7 days after receipt thereof supply the copy requested together with an account of the reasonable charges.

(3) Where a party fails to supply to another party a copy of any document under paragraph (2), the Court may, on the application of either party, make such order as to the supply of that document as it thinks fit.]

Commencement 1 October 1987.
Amendments This rule was inserted by SI 1987/1423, r 36.
Cross references See CCR Order 14, r 5A.

Order 24, r 12 Order for production to Court

At any stage of the proceedings in any cause or matter the Court may, subject to rule 13(1), order any party to produce to the Court any document in his possession, custody or power relating to any matter in question in the cause or matter and the Court may deal with the document when produced in such manner as it thinks fit.

Commencement 1 October 1966.
Cross references See CCR Order 14, r 7.

Order 24, r 13 Production to be ordered only if necessary, etc

(1)   No order for the production of any documents for inspection or to the Court [or for the supply of a copy of any document] shall be made under any of the foregoing rules unless the Court is of opinion that the order is necessary either for disposing fairly of the cause or matter or for saving costs.

(2)   Where on an application under this Order for production of any document for inspection or to the Court [or for the supply of a copy of any document] privilege from such production [or supply] is claimed or objection is made to such production [or supply] on any other ground, the Court may inspect the document for the purpose of deciding whether the claim or objection is valid.

Commencement 1 October 1966.
Amendments Para (1): words "or for the supply of a copy of any document" inserted by SI 1987/1423, r 37. Para (2): words "or for the supply of a copy of any document" and words "or supply" in both places where they occur inserted by SI 1987/1423, r 37.
Cross references See CCR Order 14, rr 6, 8.

Order 24, r 14 Production of business books

(1)   Where production of any business books for inspection is applied for under any of the foregoing rules, the Court may, instead of ordering production of the original books for inspection, order a copy of any entries therein to be supplied and verified by an affidavit of some person who has examined the copy with the original books.

(2)   Any such affidavit shall state whether or not there are in the original book any and what erasures, interlineations or alterations.

(3)   Notwithstanding that a copy of any entries in any book has been supplied under this rule, the Court may order production of the book from which the copy was made.

Commencement 1 October 1966.

[Order 24, r 14A Use of documents

Any undertaking, whether express or implied, not to use a document for any purposes other than those of the proceedings in which it is disclosed shall cease to apply to such document after it has been read to or by the Court, or referred to, in open court, unless the Court for special reasons has otherwise ordered on the application of a party of the person to whom the document belongs.]

Commencement 1 October 1987.
Amendments This rule was inserted by SI 1987/1423, r 39.
Cross references See CCR Order 14, r 8A.

Order 24, r 15 Document disclosure of which would be injurious to public interest: saving

The foregoing provisions of this Order shall be without prejudice to any rule of law which authorises or requires the withholding of any document on the ground that the disclosure of it would be injurious to the public interest.

Commencement 1 October 1966.
Cross references See CCR Order 14, r 9.

Order 24, r 16 Failure to comply with requirement for discovery, etc

(1)   If any party who is required by any of the foregoing rules, or by any order made thereunder, to make discovery of documents or to produce any documents for the purpose of inspection or any other purpose [or to supply copies thereof] fails to comply with any provision of that rule or with that order, as the case may be, then, without prejudice, in the case of a failure to comply with any such provision, to rules 3(2) and 11(1), the Court may make such order as it thinks just including, in particular, an order that the action be dismissed or, as the case may be, an order that the defence be struck out and judgment be entered accordingly.

(2)   If any party against whom an order for discovery or production of documents is made fails to comply with it, then, without prejudice to paragraph (1), he shall be liable to committal.

(3)   Service on a party's solicitor of an order for discovery or production of documents made against that party shall be sufficient service to found an application for committal of the party disobeying the order, but the party may show in answer to the application that he had no notice or knowledge of the order.

(4)   A solicitor on whom such an order made against his client is served and who fails without reasonable excuse to give notice thereof to his client shall be liable to committal.

Commencement 1 October 1966.
Amendments Para (1): words "or to supply copies thereof" inserted by SI 1987/1423, r 38.
Cross references See CCR Order 14, r 10.

Order 24, r 17 Revocation and variation of orders

Any order made under this Order (including an order made on appeal) may, on sufficient cause being shown, be revoked or varied by a subsequent order or direction of the Court made or given at or before the trial of the cause or matter in connection with which the original order was made.

Commencement 1 October 1966.
Cross references See CCR Order 14, r 12.

ORDER 25
SUMMONS FOR DIRECTIONS

Cross references This Order is applied to business list actions in the central London county court by CCR Order 48C, r 13(1).

Order 25, r 1 Summons for directions

(1)   With a view to providing, in every action to which this rule applies, an occasion for the consideration by the Court of the preparations for the trial of the action, so that—

(a)   all matters which must or can be dealt with on interlocutory applications and have not already been dealt with may so far as possible be dealt with, and

(b)   such directions may be given as to the future course of the action as appear best adapted to secure the just, expeditious and economical disposal thereof,

the plaintiff must, within one month after the pleadings in the action are deemed to be closed, take out a summons (in these rules referred to as a summons for directions) returnable in not less than 14 days.

(2)   This rule applies to all actions begun by writ except—

(a)   actions in which the plaintiff or defendant has applied for judgment under Order 14, or in which the plaintiff has applied for judgment under Order 86, and directions have been given under the relevant Order;

(b)   actions in which the plaintiff or defendant has applied under Order 18, rule 21, for trial without pleadings or further pleadings and directions have been given under that rule;

(c)   actions in which an order has been made under Order 24, rule 4, for the trial of an issue or question before discovery;

(d)   actions in which directions have been given under Order 29, rule 7;

(e)   actions in which an order for the taking of an account has been made under Order 43, rule 1;

(f)   actions in which an application for transfer to the commercial list is pending;

(g)   actions which have been [commenced, or ordered to be tried as, official referees' business]; . . .

(h)   actions for the infringement of a patent;[. . .]

[(i)   . . .]

[(j)   actions for personal injuries for which automatic directions are provided by rule 8;]

[(k)   actions in the Chancery Division in which the parties agree under rule 9 that the only matters to be determined are the mode of trial and time for setting down.]

(3)   Where, in the case of any action in which discovery of documents is required to be made by any party under Order 24, rule 2, the period of 14 days referred to in paragraph (1) of that rule is extended, whether by consent or by order of the Court or both by consent and by order, paragraph (1) of this rule shall have effect in relation to that action as if for the reference therein to one month after the pleadings in the action are deemed to be closed there were substituted a reference to 14 days after the expiration of the period referred to in paragraph (1) of the said rule 2, as so extended.

(4)   If the plaintiff does not take out a summons for directions in accordance with the foregoing provisions of this rule, the defendant or any defendant may do so or apply for an order to dismiss the action.

(5)   On an application by the defendant to dismiss the action under paragraph (4) the Court may either dismiss the action on such terms as may be just or deal with the application as if it were a summons for directions.

(6)   In the case of an action which is proceeding only as respects a counterclaim, references in this rule to the plaintiff and defendant shall be construed respectively as references to the party making the counterclaim and the defendant to the counterclaim.

[(7)   Notwithstanding anything in paragraph (1), any party to an action to which this rule applies may take out a summons for direction at any time after the defendant has given notice of intention to defend, or, if there are two or more defendants, at least one of them has given such notice.]

Commencement   1 January 1983 (para (7)); 1 October 1966 (remainder).
Amendments   Para (1): in sub-para (g) words "commenced, or ordered to be tried as, official referees' business" substituted by SI 1982/1111, r 99, word omitted revoked by SI 1966/1055, r 3; in sub-para (h) word omitted, originally inserted by SI 1966/1055, r 3, revoked by SI 1980/1010, r 6(1) and SI 1982/1786, r 16(1); sub-para (i) added by SI 1966/1055, r 3, revoked by SI 1980/1908, r 13; sub-para (j) added by SI 1980/1010, r 6(1); sub-para (k) inserted by SI 1982/1786, r 16(1).
Para (7): inserted by SI 1982/1786, r 16(2).
Cross references   The county court equivalent of the summons for directions is the pre-trial review as to which see CCR Order 17, rr 1-10.
Forms   Summons for directions (PF50).
Summons to dismiss (PF39).
Order to dismiss (PF40).

Order 25, r 2 Duty to consider all matters

(1)   When the summons for directions first comes to be heard, the Court shall consider whether—
   (a)   it is possible to deal then with all the matters which, by the subsequent rules of this Order, are required to be considered on the hearing of the summons for directions, or
   (b)   it is expedient to adjourn the consideration of all or any of those matters until a later stage.

(2)   If when the summons for directions first comes to be heard the Court considers that it is possible to deal then with all the said matters, it shall deal with them forthwith and shall endeavour to secure that all other matters which must or can be dealt with on interlocutory applications and have not already been dealt with are also then dealt with.

(3)   If, when the summons for directions first comes to be heard, the Court considers that it is expedient to adjourn the consideration of all or any of the matters which, by the subsequent rules of this Order, are required to be considered on the hearing of the summons, the Court shall deal forthwith with such of those matters as it considers can conveniently be dealt with forthwith and adjourn the consideration of the remaining matters and shall endeavour to secure that all other matters which must or can be dealt with on interlocutory applications and have not already been dealt with are dealt with either then or at a resumed hearing of the summons for directions.

(4)   Subject to paragraphs (5) and (6), and except where the parties agree to the making of an order under Order 33 as to the place or mode of trial before all the matters which, by the subsequent rules of this Order, are required to be considered on the hearing of the summons for directions have been dealt with, no such order shall be made until all those matters have been dealt with.

(5)   If, on the summons for directions, an action is ordered to be transferred to the county court or some other court, paragraph (4) shall not apply and nothing in this Order shall be construed as requiring the Court to make any further order on the summons.

(6)　If, on the summons for directions, the action or any question or issue therein is ordered to be tried before an official referee, paragraph (4) shall not apply and the Court may, without giving any further directions, adjourn the summons so that it can be heard by the referee, and the party required by Order 36, rule 6, to apply to the referee for directions may do so by notice without taking out a fresh summons.

(7)　If the hearing of the summons for directions is adjourned without a day being fixed for the resumed hearing thereof, any party may restore it to the list on 2 days' notice to the other parties.

Commencement　1 October 1966.
Forms　Order on summons for directions (PF52).

Order 25, r 3 Particular matters for consideration

[(1)]　On the hearing of the summons for directions the Court shall in particular consider, if necessary of its own motion, whether, . . . , any order should be made [or direction given] in the exercise of the powers conferred by any of the following provisions, that is to say—
　　[(a)　any provision of Part I of the Civil Evidence Act 1968 (hearsay evidence) [or of the Civil Evidence Act 1972 or of Part III or IV] of Order 38];
　　(b)　Order 20, rule 5 [and] Order 38, rules 2 to 7 . . .
　　[(c)　subject to Order 107, rule 2, [section 40 of the County Courts Act 1984]][,
　　(d)　Order 33, rule 4(2).]

[(2)　On the hearing of the summons for directions, the Court shall decide whether the bundle to be provided under Order 34, rule 10 is to include the documents mentioned in paragraph (2)(c) of that rule and direct the parties accordingly.]

Commencement　1 July 1991 (para (2)); 1 October 1966 (remainder).
Amendments　Para (1): numbered as such by SI 1991/1329, r 8; first words omitted revoked and words "or direction given" inserted by SI 1969/1105, r 5(1), (2); sub-para (a) substituted by SI 1969/1105, r 5(3), words "or of the Civil Evidence Act 1972 or of Part III or IV" substituted by SI 1974/295, r 3; in sub-para (b) word "and" substituted and words omitted revoked by SI 1981/1734, r 25(1); sub-para (c) added by SI 1981/1734, r 25(2), words "section 40 of the County Courts Act 1984" substituted by SI 1985/69, r 7(2), Schedule; sub-para (d) added by SI 1989/2427, r 17.
Para (2): inserted by SI 1991/1329, r 8.

Order 25, r 4 Admissions and agreements to be made

At the hearing of the summons for directions, the Court shall endeavour to secure that the parties make all admissions and all agreements as to the conduct of the proceedings which ought reasonably to be made by them and may cause the order on the summons to record any admissions or agreements so made, and (with a view to such special order, if any, as to costs as may be just being made at the trial) any refusal to make any admission or agreement.

Commencement　1 October 1966.

Order 25, r 5 Limitation of right of appeal

Nothing in rule 4 shall be construed as requiring the Court to endeavour to secure that the parties shall agree to exclude or limit any right of appeal, but the order made on the summons for directions may record any such agreement.

Commencement　1 October 1966.

Order 25, r 6 Duty to give all information at hearing

(1)   Subject to paragraph (2), no affidavit shall be used on the hearing of the summons for directions except by the leave or direction of the Court, but, subject to paragraph (4), it shall be the duty of the parties to the action and their advisers to give all such information and produce all such documents on any hearing of the summons as the Court may reasonably require for the purpose of enabling it properly to deal with the summons.

The Court may, if it appears proper so to do in the circumstances, authorise any such information or documents to be given or produced to the Court without being disclosed to the other parties but, in the absence of such authority, any information or document given or produced under this paragraph shall be given or produced to all the parties present or represented on the hearing of the summons as well as to the Court.

(2)   No leave shall be required by virtue of paragraph (1) for the use of an affidavit by any party on the hearing of the summons for directions in connection with any application thereat for any order if, under any of these rules, an application for such an order is required to be supported by an affidavit.

[(2A) In proceedings to which article 7(1) of the High Court and County Courts Jurisdiction Order 1991 applies, a statement of the value of the action shall be lodged by the plaintiff (or, where an action is proceeding only as respects a counterclaim, by the defendant) and a copy shall be served on every other party not later than the day before the hearing of the summons for directions; and, where such a statement is not so lodged and so served, the Court shall at the hearing of the summons for directions order the action to be transferred to a county court.]

(3)   If the Court on any hearing of the summons for directions requires a party to the action or his solicitor or counsel to give any information or produce any document and that information or document is not given or produced, then, subject to paragraph (4), the Court may—

(a)   cause the facts to be recorded in the order with a view to such special order, if any, as to costs as may be just being made at the trial, or

(b)   if it appears to the Court to be just so to do, order the whole or any part of the pleadings of the party concerned to be struck out, or, if the party is plaintiff or the claimant under a counterclaim, order the action or counterclaim to be dismissed on such terms as may be just.

(4)   Notwithstanding anything in the foregoing provisions of this rule, no information or documents which are privileged from disclosure shall be required to be given or produced under this rule by or by the advisers of any party otherwise than with the consent of that party.

Commencement   1 July 1991 (para (2A)); 1 October 1966 (remainder).
Amendments   Para (2A): inserted by SI 1991/1329, r 6.
Forms   Statement of value (PF204).

Order 25, r 7 Duty to make all interlocutory applications on summons for directions

(1)   Any party to whom the summons for directions is addressed must so far as practicable apply at the hearing of the summons for any order or directions which he may desire as to any matter capable of being dealt with on an interlocutory application in the action and must, not less than 7 days before the hearing of the summons, serve on the other parties a notice specifying those orders and directions in

so far as they differ from the orders and directions asked for by the summons.

(2)   If the hearing of the summons for directions is adjourned and any party to the proceedings desires to apply at the resumed hearing for any order or directions not asked for by the summons or in any notice given under paragraph (1), he must, not less than 7 days before the resumed hearing of the summons, serve on the other parties a notice specifying those orders and directions in so far as they differ from the orders and directions asked for by the summons or in any such notice as aforesaid.

(3)   Any application subsequent to the summons for directions and before judgment as to any matter capable of being dealt with on an interlocutory application in the action must be made under the summons by 2 clear days' notice to the other party stating the grounds of the application.

Commencement   1 October 1966.
Forms   Notice under summons (PF51).
Notice for further directions (PF53).

[Order 25, r 8 Automatic directions in personal injury actions

(1)   When the pleadings in any action to which this rule applies are deemed to be closed the following directions shall take effect automatically:—

- (a)   there shall be discovery of documents within 14 days in accordance with Order 24, rule 2, and inspection within seven days thereafter, save that where liability is admitted, or where the action arises out of a road accident, discovery shall be limited to disclosure by the plaintiff of any documents relating to special damages;
- [(b)   subject to paragraph (2), where any party intends to place reliance at the trial on—
  - (i)   expert evidence, he shall, within 14 weeks, disclose the substance of that evidence to the other parties in the form of a written report, which shall be agreed if possible; and
  - (ii)   any other oral evidence, he shall, within 14 weeks, serve on the other parties written statements of all such oral evidence which he intends to adduce;]
- (c)   unless such reports are agreed, the parties shall be at liberty to call as expert witnesses those witnesses the substance of whose evidence has been disclosed in accordance with the preceding sub-paragraph, except that the number of expert witnesses shall be limited in any case to two medical experts and one expert of any other kind;
- (d)   photographs, a sketch plan and the contents of any police accident report book shall be receivable in evidence at the trial, and shall be agreed if possible;
- (e)   subject to Order 77, rule 13, the action shall be tried [at the trial centre for the place in which the action is proceeding or at such other trial centre as the parties may in writing agree];
- (f)   the action shall be tried by Judge alone, as a case of substance or difficulty (Category B), and shall be set down within six months;
- (g)   the Court shall be notified, on setting down, of the estimated length of the trial.

[(1A) Nothing in paragraph (1) shall require a party to produce a further medical report if he proposes to rely at the trial only on the report provided pursuant to Order 18, rule 12(1A) or (1B) but, where a party claiming damages for personal injuries discloses a further report, that report shall be accompanied by a statement of the special damages claimed and, in this paragraph, "statement of the special damages claimed" has the same meaning as in Order 18, rule 12(1C).]

[(2)   Paragraphs (4) to (16) of Order 38, rule 2A shall apply with respect to statements and reports served under sub-paragraph (1)(b) as they apply with respect to statements served under that rule.]

(3)   Nothing in paragraph (1) shall prevent any party to an action to which this rule applies from applying to the Court for such further or different directions or orders as may, in the circumstances, be appropriate [or prevent the making of an order for the transfer of the proceedings to a county court].

(4)   For the purposes of this rule—
   "a road accident" means an accident on land due to a collision or apprehended
      collision involving a vehicle; and
   "documents relating to special damages" include
      (a)   documents relating to any industrial injury, industrial disablement
            or sickness benefit rights, and
      (b)   where the claim is made under the Fatal Accidents Act 1976,
            documents relating to any claim for dependency on the deceased.

(5)   This rule applies to any action for personal injuries except—
   (a)   any Admiralty action; and
   (b)   any action where the pleadings contain an allegation of a negligent act or
         omission in the course of medical treatment.]

Commencement   16 November 1992 (para (2)); 4 June 1990 (para (1A)); 1 October 1980 (remainder).
Amendments   This rule was inserted by SI 1980/1010, r 6(2).
Para (1): sub-para (b) substituted by SI 1992/1907, r 8; in sub-para (e) words from "at the trial centre" to "may in writing agree" substituted by SI 1982/1786, r 16(3).
Para (1A): inserted by SI 1989/2427, r 14.
Para (2): substituted by SI 1992/1907, r 9.
Para (3): words "or prevent the making of an order for the transfer of the proceedings to a county court" inserted by SI 1982/1786, r 16(4).
Cross references   See CCR Order 17, r 11.

[Order 25, r 9 Standard directions by consent in Chancery actions

(1)   Subject to paragraphs (2) and (3), where in any action in the Chancery Division the parties agree, not more than one month after the pleadings are deemed to be closed, that the only directions required are as to the mode of trial and the time for setting down, the provisions of rule 8(1)(e) and (g) shall apply and the action shall be tried by a judge alone and shall be set down within six months.

(2)   In a case where the trial centre for the purpose of rule 8(1)(e) is Birmingham, Bristol or Cardiff the plaintiff or other party having the conduct of the action shall forthwith lodge in Chancery Chambers or, if the case is proceeding in a district registry, that registry, one copy of the pleadings in the action, and the provisions of rule 8(1)(e) shall have effect subject to any direction of the Court given under paragraph (3).

(3)   The Court may give such further directions or orders, whether on application by a party or its own motion, as may, in the circumstances, be appropriate.]

Commencement   1 January 1983.
Amendments   This rule was inserted by SI 1982/1786, r 16(5).

[ORDER 26
Interrogatories

Order 26, r 1 Discovery by interrogatories

(1)   A party to any cause or matter may in accordance with the following provisions of this Order serve on any other party interrogatories relating to any matter in question between the applicant and that other party in the cause or matter which are necessary either—
- (a)   for disposing fairly of the cause or matter, or
- (b)   for saving costs.

(2)   Without prejudice to the provisions of paragraph (1), a party may apply to the Court for an order giving him leave to serve on any other party interrogatories relating to any matter in question between the applicant and that other party in the cause or matter.

(3)   A proposed interrogatory which does not relate to such a matter as is mentioned in paragraph (1) may not be administered notwithstanding that it might be admissible in oral cross-examination of a witness.

(4)   In this Order,
"interrogatories without order" means interrogatories served under paragraph (1);
"ordered interrogatories" means interrogatories served under paragraph (2) or interrogatories which are required to be answered pursuant to an order made on an application under rule 3(2) and, where such an order is made, the interrogatories shall not, unless the Court orders otherwise, be treated as interrogatories without order for the purposes of rule 3(1).

(5)   Unless the context otherwise requires, the provisions of this Order apply to both interrogatories without order and ordered interrogatories.]

Commencement   5 February 1990.
Amendments   Order 26, rr 1–6 were substituted by SI 1989/2427, r 19.
Cross references   This rule is applied to the county court by CCR Order 14, r 11 (subject to the provisions of that rule).
Forms   Notice of application for interrogatories (PF54).
Order for service of interrogatories (PF55).

[Order 26, r 2 Form and nature of interrogatories

(1)   Where interrogatories are served, a note at the end of the interrogatories shall specify—
- (a)   a period of time (not being less than 28 days from the date of service) within which the interrogatories are to be answered;
- (b)   where the party to be interrogated is a body corporate or unincorporate which is empowered by law to sue or be sued whether in its own name or in the name of an officer or other person, the officer or member on whom the interrogatories are to be served; and
- (c)   where the interrogatories are to be served on two or more parties or are required to be answered by an agent or servant of a party, which of the interrogatories each party or, as the case may be, an agent or servant is required to answer, and which agent or servant.

(2)   Subject to rule 5(1), a party on whom interrogatories are served shall, unless the Court orders otherwise on an application under rule 3(2), be required to give within the period specified under rule 2(1)(a) answers, which shall (unless the Court directs otherwise) be on affidavit.]

Commencement5 February 1990.
Amendments See the note to Order 26, r 1.
Cross references This rule is applied to the county court by CCR Order 14, r 11 (subject to the provisions of that rule).
Forms Interrogatories (PF56).
Answer (PF57).

[Order 26, r 3 Interrogatories without order

(1)   Interrogatories without order may be served on a party not more than twice.

(2)   A party on whom interrogatories without order are served may, within 14 days of the service of the interrogatories, apply to the Court for the interrogatories to be varied or withdrawn and, on any such application, the Court may make such order as it thinks fit (including an order that the party who served the interrogatories shall not serve further interrogatories without order).

(3)   Interrogatories without order shall not be served on the Crown.]

Commencement 5 February 1990.
Amendments See the note to Order 26, r 1.
Cross references This rule is applied to the county court by CCR Order 14, r 11 (subject to the provisions of that rule).

[Order 26, r 4 Ordered interrogatories

(1)   Where an application is made for leave to serve interrogatories, a copy of the proposed interrogatories shall be served with the summons or the notice under Order 25, rule 7, by which the application is made.

(2)   In deciding whether to give leave to serve interrogatories, the Court shall take into account any offer made by the party to be interrogated to give particulars, make admissions or produce documents relating to any matter in question and whether or not interrogatories without order have been administered.]

Commencement 5 February 1990.
Amendments See the note to Order 26, r 1.
Cross references This rule is applied to the county court by CCR Order 14, r 11 (subject to the provisions of that rule).

[Order 26, r 5 Objections and insufficient answers

(1)   Without prejudice to rule 3(2), where a person objects to answering any interrogatory on the ground of privilege he may take the objection in his answer.

(2)   Where any person on whom ordered interrogatories have been served answers any of them insufficiently, the Court may make an order requiring him to make a further answer, either by affidavit or on oral examination as the Court may direct.

(3)   Where any person on whom interrogatories without order have been served answers any of them insufficiently, the party serving the interrogatories may ask for

further and better particulars of the answer given and any such request shall not be treated as service of further interrogatories for the purposes of rule 3(1).]

Commencement 5 February 1990.
Amendments See the note to Order 26, r 1.
Cross references This rule is applied to the county court by CCR Order 14, r 11 (subject to the provisions of that rule).

[Order 26, r 6 Failure to comply with order

(1)   If a party fails to answer interrogatories or to comply with an order made under rule 5(2) or a request made under rule 5(3), the Court may make such order as it thinks just including, in particular, an order that the action be dismissed or, as the case may be, an order that the defence be struck out and judgment be entered accordingly.

(2)   Without prejudice to paragraph (1), where a party fails to answer ordered interrogatories or to comply with an order made under rule 5(2), he shall be liable to committal.

(3)   Service on a party's solicitor of an order to answer interrogatories made against the party shall be sufficient service to found an application for committal of the party disobeying the order, but the party may show in answer to the application that he had no notice or knowledge of the order.

(4)   A solicitor on whom an order to answer interrogatories made against his client is served and who fails without reasonable excuse to give notice thereof to his client shall be liable to committal.]

Commencement 5 February 1990.
Amendments See the note to Order 26, r 1.
Cross references This rule is applied to the county court by CCR Order 14, r 11 (subject to the provisions of that rule).

Order 26, r 7 Use of answers to interrogatories at trial

A party may put in evidence at the trial of a cause or matter, or of any issue therein, some only of the answers to interrogatories, or part only of such an answer, without putting in evidence the other answers or, as the case may be, the whole of that answer, but the Court may look at the whole of the answers and if of opinion that any other answer or other part of an answer is so connected with an answer or part thereof used in evidence that the one ought not to be so used without the other, the court may direct that that other answer or part shall be put in evidence.

Commencement 1 October 1966.
Cross references This rule is applied to the county court by CCR Order 14, r 11 (subject to the provisions of that rule)

Order 26, r 8 Revocation and variation of orders

Any order made under this Order (including an order made on appeal) may, on sufficient cause being shown, be revoked or varied by a subsequent order or direction of the Court made or given at or before the trial of the cause or matter in connection with which the original order was made.

Commencement 1 October 1966.
Cross references This rule is applied to the county court by CCR Order 14, r 11 (subject to the provisions of that rule).

ORDER 27
ADMISSIONS

Order 27, r 1 Admission of case of other party

Without prejudice to Order 18, rule 13, a party to a cause or matter may give notice, by his pleading or otherwise in writing, that he admits the truth of the whole or any part of the case of any other party.

Commencement 1 October 1966.
Cross references See CCR Order 9, r 2 and Order 20, r 1.

Order 27, r 2 Notice to admit . . .

(1)   A party to a cause or matter may not later than [21 days] after the cause or matter is set down for trial serve on any other party a notice requiring him to admit, for the purpose of that cause or matter only, [such facts, or such part of his case, as may be] specified in the notice.

(2)   An admission made in compliance with a notice under this rule shall not be used against the party by whom it was made in any cause or matter other than the cause or matter for the purpose of which it was made or in favour of any person other than the person by whom the notice was given, and the Court may at any time allow a party to amend or withdraw an admission so made by him on such terms as may be just.

Commencement 1 October 1966.
Amendments Rule heading: word omitted revoked by SI 1980/1908, r 2(1).
Para (1): words "21 days" substituted by SI 1969/1105, r 6, words "such facts, or such part of his case, as may be" substituted by SI 1980/1908, r 2(2).
Cross references See CCR Order 20, r 2.
Forms Notice to admit facts (PF58).
Admission (PF59).
Affidavit of service (PF138–9).

Order 27, r 3 Judgment on admissions . . .

Where admissions of fact [or of part of a case] are made by a party to a cause or matter either by his pleadings or otherwise, any other party to the cause or matter may apply to the Court for such judgment or order as upon those admissions he may be entitled to, without waiting for the determination of any other question between the parties, and the Court may give such judgment, or make such order, on the application as it thinks just.

An application for an order under this rule may be made by motion or summons.

Commencement 1 October 1966.
Amendments Rule heading: words omitted revoked by SI 1980/1908, r 2(3).
Words "or of part of a case" inserted by SI 1980/1908, r 2(4).

Order 27, r 4 Admission and production of documents specified in list of documents

(1)   Subject to paragraph (2) and without prejudice to the right of a party to object to the admission in evidence of any document, a party on whom a list of documents

is served in pursuance of any provision of Order 24 shall, unless the Court otherwise orders, be deemed to admit—

    (a) that any document described in the list as an original document is such a document and was printed, written, signed or executed as it purports respectively to have been, and

    (b) that any document described therein as a copy is a true copy.

This paragraph does not apply to a document the authenticity of which the party has denied in his pleading.

(2)   If before the expiration of [21 days] after inspection of the documents specified in a list of documents or after the time limited for inspection of those documents expires, whichever is the later, the party on whom the list is served serves on the party whose list it is a notice stating, in relation to any document specified therein, that he does not admit the authenticity of that document and requires it to be proved at the trial, he shall not be deemed to make any admission in relation to that document under paragraph (1).

(3)   A party to a cause or matter by whom a list of documents is served on any other party in pursuance of any provision of Order 24 shall be deemed to have been served by that other party with a notice requiring him to produce at the trial of the cause or matter such of the documents specified in the list as are in his possession, custody or power.

(4)   The foregoing provisions of this rule apply in relation to an affidavit made in compliance with an order under Order 24, rule 7, as they apply in relation to a list of documents served in pursuance of any provision of that Order.

Commencement 1 October 1966.
Amendments Para (2): words "21 days" substituted by SI 1969/1105, r 6.

Order 27, r 5 Notices to admit or produce documents

(1)   Except where rule 4(1) applies, a party to a cause or matter may within [21 days] after the cause or matter is set down for trial serve on any other party a notice requiring him to admit the authenticity of the documents specified in the notice.

(2)   If a party on whom a notice under paragraph (1) is served desires to challenge the authenticity of any document therein specified he must, within [21 days] after service of the notice, serve on the party by whom it was given a notice stating that he does not admit the authenticity of the document and requires it to be proved at the trial.

(3)   A party who fails to give a notice of non-admission in accordance with paragraph (2) in relation to any document shall be deemed to have admitted the authenticity of that document unless the Court otherwise orders.

(4)   Except where rule 4(3) applies, a party to a cause or matter may serve on any other party a notice requiring him to produce the documents specified in the notice at the trial of the cause or matter.

Commencement 1 October 1966.
Amendments Paras (1), (2): words "21 days" substituted by SI 1969/1105, r 6.
Cross references See CCR Order 20, r 3.
Forms Notice to admit documents (PF60).
Notice to produce documents (PF61).
Affidavit of service (PF138–9).

ORDER 28
ORIGINATING SUMMONS PROCEDURE

Order 28, r 1 Application

The provisions of this Order apply to all originating summonses subject, in the case of originating summonses of any particular class, to any special provisions relating to originating summonses of that class made by these rules or by or under any Act; and, subject as aforesaid, Order 32, rule 5, shall apply in relation to originating summonses as it applies in relation to other summonses.

Commencement 1 October 1966.

[Order 28, r 1A Affidavit Evidence

(1)   In any cause or matter begun by originating summons (not being an ex parte summons) the plaintiff must, before the expiration of 14 days after the defendant has acknowledged service, or, if there are two or more defendants, at least one of them has acknowledged service, file with the office of the Court out of which the summons was issued the affidavit evidence on which he intends to rely.

(2)   In the case of an ex parte summons the applicant must file his affidavit evidence not less than 4 clear days before the day fixed for the hearing.

(3)   Copies of the affidavit evidence filed in Court under paragraph (1) must be served by the plaintiff on the defendant, or, if there are two or more defendants, on each defendant, before the expiration of 14 days after service has been acknowledged by that defendant.

(4)   Where a defendant who has acknowledged service wishes to adduce affidavit evidence he must within 28 days after service on him of copies of the plaintiff's affidavit evidence under paragraph (3) file his own affidavit evidence in the office of the Court out of which the summons is issued and serve copies thereof on the plaintiff and on any other defendant who is affected thereby.

(5)   A plaintiff on whom a copy of a defendant's affidavit evidence has been served under paragraph (4) may within 14 days of such service file in Court further affidavit evidence in reply and shall in that event serve copies thereof on that defendant.

(6)   No other affidavit shall be received in evidence without the leave of the Court.

(7)   Where an affidavit is required to be served by one party on another party it shall be served without prior charge.

(8)   The provisions of this rule apply subject to any direction by the Court to the contrary.

(9)   In this rule references to affidavits and copies of affidavits include references to exhibits to affidavits and copies of such exhibits.]

Commencement 1 January 1983.
Amendments This rule was inserted by SI 1982/1786, r 11.

Order 28, r 2 Fixing time for attendance of parties before Court

(1)   [In the case of an originating summons which is in Form No 8 in Appendix A the plaintiff must, within one month of the expiry of the time within which copies of

affidavit evidence may be served under rule 1A,] obtain an appointment for the attendance of the parties before the Court for the hearing of the summons, and a day and time for their attendance shall be fixed by a notice (in Form No 12 in Appendix A) sealed with the seal of the district registry (if any) in which the cause or matter is proceeding and, where the cause or matter is not proceeding in such a registry, sealed with the seal—

> (a) of the Central Office, where the cause or matter is assigned to the Queen's Bench Division;
>
> (b) [of Chancery Chambers], where the cause or matter is assigned to the Chancery Division.
>
> [(c) of the principal registry of the Family Division, where the cause or matter is assigned to the Family Division.]

(2) A day and time for the attendance of the parties before the Court for the hearing of an originating summons [which is in Form No 10 in Appendix A], or for the hearing of an ex parte originating summons, may be fixed on the application of the plaintiff or applicant, as the case may be [and, in the case of a summons which is required to be served, the time limited for acknowledging service shall, where appropriate, be abridged so as to expire on the next day but one before the day so fixed][, and the time limits for lodging affidavits under [rule 1A(1) and (2)] shall, where appropriate, be abridged so as to expire, respectively, on the fifth day before, and the next day but one before, the day so fixed].

(3) Where a plaintiff fails to apply for an appointment under paragraph (1), any defendant may, with the leave of the Court, obtain an appointment in accordance with that paragraph provided that he has [acknowledged service of the originating summons].

Commencement 1 October 1966.
Amendments Para (1): words from the beginning to "rule 1A," substituted by SI 1982/1786, r 12(1); in sub-para (b) words "of Chancery Chambers" substituted by SI 1982/1111, r 24; sub-para (c) inserted by SI 1971/1269, r 6(1).
Para (2): words "which is in Form No 10 in Appendix A" substituted and words from "and, in the case of a summons" to "before the day so fixed" inserted by SI 1979/1716, r 26(2); words from ", and the time limits for lodging affidavits" to the end inserted by SI 1982/1786, r 12(2), words "rule 1A(1) and (2)" therein substituted by SI 1993/2133, r 5.
Para (3): words "acknowledged service of the originating summons" substituted by SI 1979/1716, r 26(3).

Order 28, r 3 [Notice of hearing]

(1) Not less than [14] days before the day fixed under rule 2 for the attendance of the parties before the Court for the hearing of an originating summons [which is in Form No 8 in Appendix A], the party on whose application the day was fixed must serve a copy of the notice fixing it on every other party . . . .

(2) Not less than 4 clear days before the day fixed under rule 2 for the hearing of an originating summons [which is in Form No 10 in Appendix A], the plaintiff must serve the summons on every defendant [or, if any defendant has already been served with the summons, must serve on that defendant notice of the day fixed for the hearing.]

[(3) Where notice in Form No 12 in Appendix A is served in accordance with paragraph (1), such notice shall specify what orders or directions the party serving the notice intends to seek at the hearing; and any party served with such notice who wishes to seek different orders or directions must, not less than 7 days before the hearing, serve on every other party a notice specifying the other orders and directions he intends to seek.

(4)   If the hearing of an originating summons which is in Form No 8 or Form No 10 in Appendix A is adjourned and any party to the proceedings desires to apply at the resumed hearing for any order or direction not previously asked for he must not less than 7 days before the resumed hearing of the summons serve on every other party a notice specifying those orders and directions.

(5)   Where a party is required by any provision of this rule or rule 5(2) to serve a notice or a copy of a notice on "every other party" he must—

(a)   where he is the plaintiff, serve it on every defendant who has acknowledged service of the originating summons; and

(b)   where he is a defendant, serve it on the plaintiff and on every other defendant affected thereby.]

Commencement 1 October 1990 (paras (3)–(5)); 1 October 1966 (remainder).
Amendments Rule heading: substituted by SI 1982/1786, r 13.
Para (1): figure "14" substituted and words omitted revoked by SI 1990/1689, r 23; words "which is in Form No 8 in Appendix A" substituted by SI 1979/1716, r 27(1).
Para (2): words "which is in Form No 10 in Appendix A" substituted and words from "or, if any defendant" to the end added by SI 1979/1716, r 27(2), (3).
Paras (3)–(5): original paras (3), (4) revoked by SI 1982/1786, r 13; new paras (3)–(5) added by SI 1990/1689, r 24.
Forms Affidavit of service of notice (PF133).

Order 28, r 4 Directions, etc, by Court

(1)   The Court by whom an originating summons is heard may, if the liability of the defendant to the plaintiff in respect of any claim made by the plaintiff is established, make such order in favour of the plaintiff as the nature of the case may require, but where the Court makes an order under this paragraph against a defendant who does not appear at the hearing, the order may be varied or revoked by a subsequent order of the Court on such terms as it thinks just.

(2)   [In any case where the Court does not dispose of any originating summons altogether at a hearing or order] the cause or matter begun by it to be transferred to a county court or some other court or [make] an order under rule 8, the Court shall give such directions as to the further conduct of the proceedings as it thinks best adapted to secure the just, expeditious and economical disposal thereof.

(3)   Without prejudice to the generality of paragraph (2), the Court shall, at as early a stage of the proceedings on the summons as appears to it to be practicable, consider whether there is or may be a dispute as to fact and whether the just, expeditious and economical disposal of the proceedings can accordingly best be secured by hearing the summons on oral evidence or mainly on oral evidence and, if it thinks fit, may order that no further evidence shall be filed and that the summons shall be heard on oral evidence or partly on oral evidence and partly on affidavit evidence, with or without cross-examination of any of the deponents, as it may direct.

(4)   Without prejudice to the generality of paragraph (2), and subject to paragraph (3), the Court may give directions as to the filing of evidence and as to the attendance of deponents for cross-examination and any directions which it could give under Order 25 if the cause or matter had been begun by writ and the summons were a summons for directions under that Order.

[(5)   The Court may at any stage of the proceedings order that any affidavit, or any particulars of any claim, defence or other matter stated in any affidavit, shall stand as pleadings or that points of claim, defence or reply be delivered and stand as pleadings.]

Commencement   5 February 1990 (para (5)); 1 October 1966 (remainder).
Amendments   Para (2): words from the beginning to "hearing or order" and the word "make" substituted by SI 1982/1786, r 14.
Para (5): inserted by SI 1989/2427, r 24.

Order 28, r 5 Adjournment of summons

(1)   The hearing of the summons by the Court may (if necessary) be adjourned from time to time, either generally or to a particular date, as may be appropriate, and the powers of the Court under rule 4 may be exercised at any resumed hearing.

[(2)   If the hearing of the summons is adjourned generally, any party may restore it to the list on 14 days' notice to every other party, and rule 3(4) shall apply in relation to any such adjourned hearing.]

Commencement   1 October 1990 (para (2)); 1 October 1966 (remainder).
Amendments   Para (2): substituted by SI 1990/1689, r 25.

Order 28, r 6 Applications affecting party [who has failed to acknowledge service]

Where in a cause or matter begun by originating summons an application is made to the Court for an order affecting a party who has [failed to acknowledge service of the summons], the Court hearing the application may require to be satisfied in such manner as it thinks fit [that the party has so failed].

Commencement   1 October 1966.
Amendments   Rule heading: words "who has failed to acknowledge service" substituted by SI 1979/1716, r 48, Schedule, Pt 1.
Words "failed to acknowledge service of the summons" and "that the party has so failed" substituted by SI 1979/1716, r 48, Schedule, Pt 1.

Order 28, r 7 Counterclaim by defendant

(1)   A defendant to an action begun by originating summons who has [acknowledged service of the summons] and who alleges that he has any claim or is entitled to any relief or remedy against the plaintiff in respect of any matter (whenever and however arising) may make a counterclaim in the action in respect of that matter instead of bringing a separate action.

(2)   A defendant who wishes to make a counterclaim under this rule must at the first or any resumed hearing of the originating summons by the Court but, in any case, at as early a stage in the proceedings as is practicable, inform the Court of the nature of his claim and, without prejudice to the powers of the Court under paragraph (3), the claim shall be made in such manner as the Court may direct under rule 4 or rule 8.

(3)   If it appears on the application of a plaintiff against whom a counterclaim is made under this rule that the subject-matter of the counterclaim ought for any reason to be disposed of by a separate action, the Court may order the counterclaim to be

struck out or may order it to be tried separately or make such other order as may be expedient.

Commencement 1 October 1966.
Amendments Para (1): words "acknowledged service of the summons" substituted by SI 1979/1716, r 48, Schedule, Pt 1.

Order 28, r 8 Continuation of proceedings as if cause or matter begun by writ

(1)   Where, in the case of a cause or matter begun by originating summons, it appears to the Court at any stage of the proceedings that the proceedings should for any reason be continued as if the cause or matter had been begun by writ, it may order the proceedings to continue as if the cause or matter had been so begun and may, in particular, order that any affidavits shall stand as pleadings, with or without liberty to any of the parties to add thereto or to apply for particulars thereof.

(2)   Where the Court decides to make such an order, Order 25, rules 2 to 7, shall, with the omission of so much of rule 7(1) as requires parties to serve a notice specifying the orders and directions which they require and with any other necessary modifications, apply as if there had been a summons for directions in the proceedings and that order were one of the orders to be made thereon.

(3)   This rule applies notwithstanding that the cause or matter in question could not have been begun by writ.

(4)   Any reference in these rules to an action begun by writ shall, unless the context otherwise requires, be construed as including a reference to a cause or matter proceedings in which are ordered under this rule to continue as if the cause or matter had been so begun.

Commencement 1 October 1966.

Order 28, r 9 Order for hearing or trial

(1)   Except where the Court disposes of a cause or matter begun by originating summons in chambers or orders it to be transferred to a county court or some other court or makes an order in relation to it under rule 8 or some other provision of these rules, the Court shall, on being satisfied that the cause or matter is ready for determination, make [such order as to the hearing of the cause or matter as may be appropriate].

[(2)   An order made under paragraph (1) in relation to a cause or matter begun by originating summons in the Chancery Division shall, unless the Court otherwise directs, fix a period within which the plaintiff is to lodge documents and Order 34, rules 1 to 5 and 8 shall apply as they apply in relation to an action begun by writ, with the necessary modifications, and with the further modification that for references therein to the summons for directions there shall be substituted references to the first or any resumed hearing of the originating summons by the Court.]

(3)   . . . the Court shall by order determine the place and mode of the trial, but any such order may be varied by a subsequent order of the Court made at or before the trial.

(4)   Order 33, rule 4(2), and Order 34, rules 1 to 8, shall apply in relation to a cause or matter in the Queen's Bench Division begun by originating summons and to an order made therein under this rule as they apply in relation to an action in that Division begun by writ and to an order made therein under the said rule 4 and shall have effect accordingly with the necessary modifications and with the further modification that for references therein to the summons for directions there shall be substituted references to the first or any resumed hearing of the originating summons by the Court.

Commencement 1 July 1991 (para (2)); 1 October 1966 (remainder).
Amendments Para (1): words "such order as to the hearing of the cause or matter as may be appropriate" substituted by SI 1982/1111, r 25(1).
Para (2): original para (2) revoked by SI 1982/1111, r 25(2); new para (2) inserted by SI 1991/1329, r 9.
Para (3): words omitted revoked by SI 1971/1955, r 9(2).

Order 28, r 10 Failure to prosecute proceedings with despatch

(1)   If the plaintiff in a cause or matter begun by originating summons makes default in complying with any order or direction of the Court as to the conduct of the proceedings, or if the Court is satisfied that the plaintiff in a cause or matter so begun is not prosecuting the proceedings with due despatch, the Court may order the cause or matter to be dismissed or may make such other order as may be just.

(2)   Paragraph (1) shall, with any necessary modifications, apply in relation to a defendant by whom a counterclaim is made under rule 7 as it applies in relation to a plaintiff.

(3)   Where, by virtue of an order made under rule 8, proceedings in a cause or matter begun by originating summons are to continue as if the cause or matter had been begun by writ, the foregoing provisions of this rule shall not apply in relation to the cause or matter after the making of the order.

Commencement 1 October 1966.

Order 28, r 11 Abatement, etc of action

Order 34, rule 9, shall apply in relation to an action begun by originating summons as it applies in relation to an action begun by writ.

Commencement 1 October 1966.

ORDER 29
INTERLOCUTORY INJUNCTIONS, INTERIM PRESERVATION OF PROPERTY, [INTERIM PAYMENTS] ETC

[I INTERLOCUTORY INJUNCTIONS, INTERIM PRESERVATION OF PROPERTY, ETC]

Amendments Words "Interim Payments" and "I Interlocutory Injunctions, Interim Preservation of Property, etc" inserted by SI 1970/944, r 5(1), (2).

Order 29, r 1 Application for injunction

(1)   An application for the grant of an injunction may be made by any party to a cause or matter before or after the trial of the cause or matter, whether or not a claim for the injunction was included in that party's writ, originating summons, counterclaim or third party notice, as the case may be.

(2)   Where the applicant is the plaintiff and the case is one of urgency such application may be made ex parte on affidavit but, except as aforesaid, such application must be made by motion or summons.

(3)   The plaintiff may not make such an application before the issue of the writ or originating summons by which the cause or matter is to be begun except where the case is one of urgency, and in that case the injunction applied for may be granted on terms providing for the issue of the writ or summons and such other terms, if any, as the Court thinks fit.

Commencement 1 October 1966.
Cross references See CCR Order 13, r 6.
Forms Order for interim injunction (PF62).
(see also CCR N16).

[Order 29, r 1A Cross-examination on assets disclosure affidavit

(1)   Where—
   (a) the Court has made an order restraining any party from removing from the jurisdiction of the High Court, or otherwise dealing with, any assets,
   (b) that party has in compliance with the order, or any order made in connection with it, filed affidavit evidence as to his or any other assets, and
   (c) the Court has ordered that that party shall be cross-examined on his affidavit,

the Court may order that the cross-examination shall be conducted otherwise than before a judge, in which case the cross-examination shall take place before a master or, if a master so orders, before an examiner of the Court.

(2)   The following provisions of Order 68 shall apply to a cross-examination of a kind referred to in paragraph (1)(c) as if it were a trial with witnesses in the Queen's Bench or Chancery Division and as if the person presiding were the judge—
   (a) rule 1(1) (except the words "unless the judge otherwise directs"); and
   (b) rules 2(2) and (3) and 8.

(3)   A cross-examination of a kind referred to in paragraph (1)(c) shall take place in chambers and no transcript or other record of it may be used by any person other than the party being cross-examined for any purpose other than the purpose of the

proceedings in which the order for the cross-examination was made, unless and to the extent that that party consents or the Court gives leave.]

Commencement 1 April 1992.
Amendments This rule was inserted by SI 1992/638, r 6.

Order 29, r 2 Detention, preservation, etc, of subject-matter of cause or matter

(1)   On the application of any party to a cause or matter the Court may make an order for the detention, custody or preservation of any property which is the subject-matter of the cause or matter, or as to which any question may arise therein, or for the inspection of any such property in the possession of a party to the cause or matter.

(2)   For the purpose of enabling any order under paragraph (1) to be carried out the Court may by the order authorise any person to enter upon any land or building in the possession of any party to the cause or matter.

(3)   Where the right of any party to a specific fund is in dispute in a cause or matter, the Court may, on the application of a party to the cause or matter, order the fund to be paid into court or otherwise secured.

(4)   An order under this rule may be made on such terms, if any, as the Court thinks just.

(5)   An application for an order under this rule must be made by summons or by notice under Order 25, rule 7.

(6)   Unless the Court otherwise directs, an application by a defendant for such an order may not be made before he [acknowledges service of the writ or originating summons by which the cause or matter was begun].

Commencement 1 October 1966.
Amendments Para (6): words "acknowledges service of the writ or originating summons by which the cause or matter was begun" substituted by SI 1979/1716, r 48, Schedule, Pt 1.
Cross references This rule is applied to the county court by CCR Order 13, r 7.

[Order 29, r 2A Delivery up of goods under s 4 of Torts (Interference with Goods) Act 1977

(1)   Without prejudice to rule 2, the Court may, on the application of any party to a cause or matter, make an order under section 4 of the Torts (Interference with Goods) Act 1977 for the delivery up of any goods which are the subject-matter of the cause or matter or as to which any question may arise therein.

(2)   Paragraphs (2) and (3) of rule 1 shall have effect in relation to an application for such an order as they have effect in relation to an application for the grant of an injunction.]

Commencement 1 June 1978.
Amendments This rule was inserted by SI 1978/579, r 6.
Cross references This rule is applied to the county court by CCR Order 13, r 7.

Order 29, r 3 Power to order samples to be taken, etc

(1)   Where it considers it necessary or expedient for the purpose of obtaining full information or evidence in any cause or matter, the Court may, on the application of

a party to the cause or matter, and on such terms, if any, as it thinks just, by order authorise or require any sample to be taken of any property which is the subject-matter of the cause or matter or as to which any question may arise therein, any observation to be made on such property or any experiment to be tried on or with such property.

(2) For the purpose of enabling any order under paragraph (1) to be carried out the Court may by the order authorise any person to enter upon any land or building in the possession of any party to the cause or matter.

(3) Rule 2(5) and (6) shall apply in relation to an application for an order under this rule as they apply in relation to an application for an order under that rule.

Commencement 1 October 1966.

Order 29, r 4 Sale of perishable property, etc

(1) The Court may, on the application of any party to a cause or matter, make an order for the sale by such person, in such manner and on such terms (if any) as may be specified in the order of any property (other than land) which is the subject-matter of the cause or matter or as to which any question arises therein and which is of a perishable nature or likely to deteriorate if kept or which for any other good reason it is desirable to sell forthwith.

In this paragraph "land" includes any interest in, or right over, land.

(2) Rule 2(5) and (6) shall apply in relation to an application for an order under this rule as they apply in relation to an application for an order under that rule.

Commencement 1 October 1966.

Order 29, r 5 Order for early trial

Where on the hearing of an application, made before the trial of a cause or matter, for an injunction or the appointment of a receiver or an order under rule 2, 3 or 4 it appears to the Court that the matter in dispute can be better dealt with by an early trial than by considering the whole merits thereof for the purposes of the application, the Court may make an order accordingly and may also make such order as respects the period before trial as the justice of the case requires.

Where the Court makes an order for early trial it shall by the order determine the place and mode of the trial.

Commencement 1 October 1966.

Order 29, r 6 Recovery of personal property subject to lien, etc

Where the plaintiff, or the defendant by way of counterclaim, claims the recovery of specific property (other than land) and the party from whom recovery is sought does not dispute the title of the party making the claim but claims to be entitled to retain the property by virtue of a lien or otherwise as security for any sum of money, the Court, at any time after the claim to be so entitled appears from the pleadings (if any) or by affidavit or otherwise to its satisfaction, may order that the party seeking to recover the property be at liberty to pay into court, to abide the event of the action, the amount of money in respect of which the security is claimed and such further sum (if any) for interest and costs as the Court may direct and that, upon such payment being made, the property claimed be given up to the party claiming it, ...

Commencement 1 October 1966.
Amendments Words omitted revoked by SI 1979/1725, r 3(3).
Cross references This rule is applied to the county court by CCR Order 13, r 7.

Order 29, r 7 Directions

(1) Where an application is made under any of the foregoing provisions of this Order, the Court may give directions as to the further proceedings in the cause or matter.

(2) If, in an action begun by writ, not being any such action as is mentioned in sub-paragraphs (a) to (c) and (e) to (h) of Order 25, rule 1(2), the Court thinks fit to give directions under this rule before the summons for directions, rules 2 to 7 of that Order shall, with the omission of so much of rule 7(1) as requires parties to serve a notice specifying the orders and directions which they desire and with any other necessary modifications, apply as if the application were a summons for directions.

Commencement 1 October 1966.
Cross references See CCR Order 13, r 2.

[Order 29, r 7A Inspection etc of property under [section 33(1) of the Act] or [section 34(3) of the Act]

[(1) An application for an order under [section 33(1) of the Act] in respect of property which may become the subject-matter of subsequent proceedings in the High Court or as to which any question may arise in any such proceedings shall be made by originating summons and the person against whom the order is sought shall be made defendant to the summons.]

[(2)] An application after the commencement of proceedings for an order under [section 34(3) of the Act] in respect of property which is not the property of or in the possession of any party to the proceedings shall be made by summons, which must be served on the person against whom the order is sought personally and on every party to the proceedings other than the applicant.

[(3) A summons under paragraph (1) or (2) shall be supported by affidavit which must specify or describe the property in respect of which the order is sought and show, if practicable by reference to any pleading served or intended to be served in the proceedings or subsequent proceedings, that it is property which is or may become the subject-matter of the proceedings or as to which any question arises or may arise in the proceedings.]

[(4)] A copy of the supporting affidavit shall be served with the summons on every person on whom the summons is required to be served.

[(5)] An order made under the said [section 33(1) or 34(3)] may be made conditional on the applicant's giving security for the costs of the person against whom it is made or on such other terms, if any, as the Court thinks just.

[(6)] No such order shall be made if it appears to the Court—
    (a)   that compliance with the order, if made, would result in the disclosure of information relating to a secret process, discovery or invention not in issue in the proceedings, and

    (b) that the application would have been refused on that ground if—
        (i) in the case of a summons under [paragraph (1)], the subsequent proceedings had already been begun, or
        (ii) in the case of a summons under [paragraph (2)], the person against whom the order is sought were a party to the proceedings.]

Commencement 1 January 1972 (paras (1), (3)); 31 August 1971 (remainder).
Amendments This rule was inserted by SI 1971/1269, r 42.
Rule heading: words "section 33(1) of the Act" and "section 34(3) of the Act" substituted by SI 1982/1111, r 115, Schedule.
Original rule revoked and substituted in part, and remaining text renumbered, by SI 1971/1955, r 38.
Para (1): words "section 33(1) of the Act" substituted by SI 1982/1111, r 115, Schedule.
Para (2): words "section 34(3) of the Act" substituted by SI 1982/1111, r 115, Schedule.
Para (5): words "section 33(1) or 34(3)" substituted by SI 1982/1111, r 115, Schedule.
Para (6): words "paragraph (1)" and "paragraph (2)" substituted by SI 1971/1955, r 38(4).
Definitions The Act: Supreme Court Act 1981.
Cross references This rule is applied to the county court by CCR Order 13, r 7.

Order 29, r 8 Allowance of income of property pendente lite

Where any real or personal property forms the subject-matter of any proceedings, and the Court is satisfied that it will be more than sufficient to answer all the claims thereon for which provision ought to be made in the proceedings, the Court may at any time allow the whole or part of the income of the property to be paid, during such period as it may direct, to any or all of the parties who have an interest therein or may direct that any part of the personal property be transferred or delivered to any or all of such parties.

Commencement 1 October 1966.

[II Interim Payments]

Amendments Heading originally added by SI 1970/944, r 5(1), substituted by SI 1980/1010, r 7.

[Order 29, r 9 Interpretation of Part II

In this Part of this Order—
    "interim payments", in relation to a defendant, means a payment on account of any damages, debt or other sum (excluding costs) which he may be held liable to pay to or for the benefit of the plaintiff; and any reference to the plaintiff or defendant includes a reference to any person who, for the purpose of the proceedings, acts as next friend of the plaintiff or guardian of the defendant.]

Commencement 1 October 1980.
Amendments Order 29, Pt II (rr 9–17) added by SI 1970/944, r 5(3); Order 29, Pt III (rr 18–21) added by SI 1977/1955, r 4(2); new Pt II (rr 9–18) substituted, for existing Pts II and III, by SI 1980/1010, r 7.
Cross references The provisions of this part of Order 29 are applied to the county court by CCR Order 13, r 12 (subject to the amendments in that rule).

[Order 29, r 10 Application for interim payment

(1)   The plaintiff may, at any time after the writ has been served on a defendant and the time limited for him to acknowledge service has expired, apply to the Court for

an order requiring that defendant to make an interim payment.

(2)　An application under this rule shall be made by summons but may be included in a summons for summary judgment under Order 14 or Order 86.

(3)　An application under this rule shall be supported by an affidavit which shall—
- (a)　verify the amount of the damages, debt or other sum to which the application relates and the grounds of the application;
- (b)　exhibit any documentary evidence relied on by the plaintiff in support of the application; and
- (c)　if the plaintiff's claim is made under the Fatal Accidents Act 1976, contain the particulars mentioned in section 2(4) of that Act.

(4)　The summons and a copy of the affidavit in support and any documents exhibited thereto shall be served on the defendant against whom the order is sought not less than 10 clear days before the return day.

(5)　Notwithstanding the making or refusal of an order for an interim payment, a second or subsequent application may be made upon cause shown.]

Commencement 1 October 1980.
Amendments See the note to Order 29, r 9.

[Order 29, r 11 Order for interim payment in respect of damages

(1)　If, on the hearing of an application under rule 10 in an action for damages, the Court is satisfied—
- (a)　that the defendant against whom the order is sought (in this paragraph referred to as "the respondent") has admitted liability for the plaintiff's damages, or
- (b)　that the plaintiff has obtained judgment against the respondent for damages to be assessed; or
- (c)　that, if the action proceeded to trial, the plaintiff would obtain judgment for substantial damages against the respondent or, where there are two or more defendants, against any of them,

the Court may, if it thinks fit and subject to paragraph (2), order the respondent to make an interim payment of such amount as it thinks just, not exceeding a reasonable proportion of the damages which in the opinion of the Court are likely to be recovered by the plaintiff after taking into account any relevant contributory negligence and any set-off, cross-claim or counter claim on which the respondent may be entitled to rely.

(2)　No order shall be made under paragraph (1) in an action for personal injuries if it appears to the Court that the defendant is not a person falling within one of the following categories, namely—
- (a)　a person who is insured in respect of the plaintiff's claim;
- (b)　a public authority; or
- (c)　a person whose means and resources are such as to enable him to make the interim payment.]

Commencement 1 October 1980.
Amendments See the note to Order 29, r 9.

[Order 29, r 12 Order for interim payment in respect of sums other than damages

If, on the hearing of an application under rule 10, the Court is satisfied—

(a) that the plaintiff has obtained an order for an account to be taken as between himself and the defendant and for any amount certified due on taking the account to be paid; or

(b) that the plaintiff's action includes a claim for possession of land and, if the action proceeded to trial, the defendant would be held liable to pay to the plaintiff a sum of money in respect of the defendant's use and occupation of the land during the pendency of the action, even if a final judgment or order were given or made in favour of the defendant; or

(c) that, if the action proceeded to trial the plaintiff would obtain judgment against the defendant for a substantial sum of money apart from any damages or costs,

the Court may, if it thinks fit, and without prejudice to any contentions of the parties as to the nature or character of the sum to be paid by the defendant, order the defendant to make an interim payment of such amount as it thinks just, after taking into account any set-off, cross-claim or counterclaim on which the [defendant] may be entitled to rely.]

Commencement 1 October 1980.
Amendments See the note to Order 29, r 9.
Word "defendant" substituted by SI 1980/1908, r 20.

[Order 29, r 13 Manner of payment

(1)   Subject to Order 80, rule 12, the amount of any interim payment ordered to be made shall be paid to the plaintiff unless the order provides for it to be paid into court, and where the amount is paid into court, the Court may, on the application of the plaintiff, order the whole or any part of it to be paid out to him at such time or times as the Court thinks fit.

(2)   An application under the preceding paragraph for money in court to be paid out may be made ex parte, but the Court hearing the application may direct a summons to be issued.

(3)   An interim payment may be ordered to be made in one sum or by such instalments as the Court thinks fit.

(4)   Where a payment is ordered in respect of the defendant's use and occupation of land the order may provide for periodical payments to be made during the pendency of the action.]

Commencement 1 October 1980.
Amendments See the note to Order 29, r 9.

[Order 29, r 14 Directions on application under rule 10

Where an application is made under rule 10, the Court may give directions as to the further conduct of the action, and, so far as may be applicable, Order 25, rules 2 to 7, shall, with the omission of so much of rule 7(1) as requires the parties to serve a notice specifying the orders and directions which they require and with any other necessary modifications, apply as if the application were a summons for directions, and, in particular, the Court may order an early trial of the action.]

Commencement 1 October 1980.
Amendments See the note to Order 29, r 9.

[Order 29, r 15 Non-disclosure of interim payment

The fact that an order has been made under rule 11 or 12 shall not be pleaded and, unless the defendant consents or the Court so directs, no communication of that fact or of the fact that an interim payment has been made, whether voluntarily or pursuant to an order, shall be made to the court at the trial, or hearing, of any question or issue as to liability or damages until all questions of liability and amount have been determined.]

Commencement 1 October 1980.
Amendments See the note to Order 29, r 9.

[Order 29, r 16 Payment into court in satisfaction

Where, after making an interim payment, whether voluntarily or pursuant to an order, a defendant pays a sum of money into Court under Order 22, rule 1, the notice of payment must state that the defendant has taken into account the interim payment.]

Commencement 1 October 1980.
Amendments See the note to Order 29, r 9.

[Order 29, r 17 Adjustment on final judgment or order or on discontinuance

Where a defendant has been ordered to make an interim payment or has in fact made an interim payment, whether voluntarily or pursuant to an order, the Court may, in giving or making a final judgment or order, or granting the plaintiff leave to discontinue his action or to withdraw the claim in respect of which the interim payment has been made, or at any other stage of the proceedings on the application of any party, make such order with respect to the interim payment as may be just, and in particular—

(a) an order for the repayment by the plaintiff of all or part of the interim payment, or
(b) an order for the payment to be varied or discharged, or
(c) an order for the payment by any other defendant of any part of the interim payment which the defendant who made it is entitled to recover from him by way of contribution or indemnity or in respect of any remedy or relief relating to or connected with the plaintiff's claim.]

Commencement 1 October 1980.
Amendments See the note to Order 29, r 9.

[Order 29, r 18 Counterclaims and other proceedings

The preceding rules in this Part of this Order shall apply, with the necessary modifications, to any counterclaim or proceeding commenced otherwise than by writ, where one party seeks an order for an interim payment to be made by another.]

Commencement 1 October 1980.
Amendments See the note to Order 29, r 9.

ORDER 30
RECEIVERS

Order 30, r 1 Application for receiver and injunction

(1)   An application for the appointment of a receiver may be made by summons or motion.

(2)   An application for an injunction ancillary or incidental to an order appointing a receiver may be joined with the application for such order.

(3)   Where the applicant wishes to apply for the immediate grant of such an injunction, he may do so ex parte on affidavit.

(4)   The Court hearing an application under paragraph (3) may grant an injunction restraining the party beneficially entitled to any interest in the property of which a receiver is sought from assigning, charging or otherwise dealing with that property until after the hearing of a summons for the appointment of the receiver and may require such a summons, returnable on such date as the Court may direct, to be issued.

Commencement   1 October 1966.
Cross references   See CCR Order 32, r 1.
Forms   Interim order for receiver (PF63).

Order 30, r 2 Giving of security by receiver

(1)   [A judgment or order directing the appointment of a receiver may include such directions as the Court thinks fit as to the giving security by the person appointed.]

(2)   Where by virtue of . . . any judgment or order appointing a person named therein to be receiver . . . a person is required to give security in accordance with this rule he must give security approved by the Court duly to account for what he receives as receiver and to deal with it as the Court directs.

(3)   Unless the Court otherwise directs, the security shall be by guarantee . . . .

(4)   The guarantee . . . must be filed in the [office of the Supreme Court which has the conduct of the business of the division or court in which the cause or matter is proceeding, or, if it is proceeding in a district registry, that registry], and it shall be kept as of record until duly vacated.

Commencement   1 October 1982 (para (1)); 1 October 1966 (remainder).
Amendments   Para (1): substituted by SI 1982/1111, r 26(1).
Paras (2), (3): words omitted revoked by SI 1982/1111, r 26(2), (3).
Para (4): words omitted revoked and words from "office of the Supreme Court" to the end substituted by SI 1982/1111, r 26(4).
Cross references   See CCR Order 32, r 2.
Forms   Security of receiver or administrator (ChPF30).

[Order 30, r 3 Remuneration of receiver

(1)   A person appointed receiver shall be allowed such proper remuneration, if any, as may be authorised by the Court.

(2)   The Court may direct that such remuneration shall be—
    (a)   fixed by reference to such scales or rates of professional charges as it thinks fit; or
    (b)   assessed by a taxing officer.

(3) Where remuneration is assessed by a taxing officer pursuant to a direction under paragraph (2)(b), Order 62, rule 13 shall apply as it applies to an assessment by a master; and an appeal shall lie from the assessment to a judge in chambers under Order 58, rule 1 (where the assessment was by a taxing master) or rule 3 (where the assessment was by a district judge).

(4) In this rule, "taxing officer" means a taxing master or a district judge.]

Commencement 1 April 1992.
Amendments This rule was substituted by SI 1992/638, r 7.
Cross references This rule is applied to the county court by CCR Order 32, r 3.

[Order 30, r 4 Service of order and notice

A copy of the judgment or order appointing a receiver shall be served by the party having conduct of the proceedings on the receiver and all other parties to the cause matter in which the receiver has been appointed.]

Commencement 1 October 1982.
Amendments This rule was substituted, together with rr 5, 6, for rr 4, 5 as originally enacted, by SI 1982/1111, r 28.
Cross references This rule is applied to the county court by CCR Order 32, r 3.

[Order 30, r 5 Receiver's Accounts

(1) A receiver shall submit such accounts to such parties at such intervals or on such dates as the Court may direct.

(2) Any party to whom a receiver is required to submit accounts may, on giving reasonable notice to the receiver, inspect, either personally or by an agent, the books and other papers relating to such accounts.

(3) Any party who is dissatisfied with the accounts of the receiver may give notice specifying the item or items to which objection is taken and requiring the receiver within not less than 14 days to lodge his accounts with the Court and a copy of such notice shall be lodged in the office of the Supreme Court having the conduct of the business of the division or court in which the cause or matter is proceeding or, if it is proceeding in a district registry, in that registry.

(4) Following an examination by or on behalf of the Court of an item or items in an account to which objection is taken the result of such examination must be certified by a master, the Admiralty registrar, a [district judge] of the Family Division or a [district judge], as the case may be, and an order may thereupon be made as to the incidence of any costs or expenses incurred.]

Commencement 1 October 1982.
Amendments See the note to Order 30, r 4.
Cross references This rule is applied to the county court by CCR Order 32, r 3.

[Order 30, r 6 Payment into court by receiver

The Court may fix the amounts and frequency of payments into court to be made by a receiver.]

Commencement 1 October 1982.
Amendments See the note to Order 30, r 4.
Cross references This rule is applied to the county court by CCR Order 32, r 3.

Order 30, r [7] Default by receiver

(1)   Where a receiver fails to attend for the [examination] of any account of his, or fails to submit any account, [provide access to any books or papers] or do any other thing which he is required to submit, [provide or do], he and any or all of the parties to the cause or matter in which he was appointed may be required to attend in chambers to show cause for the failure, and the Court may, either in chambers or after adjournment into court, give such directions as it thinks proper including, if necessary, directions for the discharge of the receiver and the appointment of another and the payment of costs.

(2)   Without prejudice to paragraph (1), where a receiver fails to attend for the [examination] of any account of his or fails to submit any account or fails to pay into court on the date fixed by the Court any sum [required to be so paid], the Court may disallow any remuneration claimed by the receiver . . . and may, where he has failed to pay any such sum into court, charge him with interest at the rate [currently payable in respect of judgment debts in the High Court] on that sum while in his possession as receiver.

Commencement 1 October 1966.
Amendments Originally r 6, renumbered as r 7 by SI 1982/1111, r 29.
Words in square brackets substituted and words omitted revoked by SI 1982/1111, r 29.
Cross references This rule is applied to the county court by CCR Order 32, r 3.

[Order 30, r 8 Directions to receivers

A receiver may at any time request the Court to give him directions and such request shall state in writing the matters with regard to which directions are required.]

Commencement 1 October 1982.
Amendments This rule was inserted by SI 1982/1111, r 30.
Cross references This rule is applied to the county court by CCR Order 32, r 3.

ORDER 31

SALES, ETC OF LAND BY ORDER OF COURT: CONVEYANCING COUNSEL OF THE COURT

I SALES, ETC OF LAND BY ORDER OF COURT

Order 31, r 1 Power to order sale of land

Where in any cause or matter in the Chancery Division relating to any land it appears necessary or expedient for the purposes of the cause or matter that the land or any part thereof should be sold, the Court may order that land or part to be sold, and any party bound by the order and in possession of that land or part, or in receipt of the rents and profits thereof, may be compelled to deliver up such possession or receipt to the purchaser or to such other person as the Court may direct.

In this Order "land" includes any interest in, or right over, land.

Commencement 1 October 1966.
Cross references This rule is applied to the county court by virtue of CCR Order 22, r 12.

Order 31, r 2 Manner of carrying out sale

(1)   Where an order is made, whether in court or in chambers, directing any land to be sold, the Court may permit the party or person having the conduct of the sale to sell the land in such manner as he thinks fit, or may direct that the land be sold in such manner as the Court may either by the order or [subsequently] direct for the best price that can be obtained, and all proper parties shall join in the sale and conveyance as the Court shall direct.

[(2)] [The Court] may give such directions as it thinks fit for the purpose of effecting the sale, including, without prejudice to the generality of the foregoing words, directions—

(a)   appointing the party or person who is to have the conduct of the sale;
(b)   fixing the manner of sale, whether by contract conditional on the approval of the Court, private treaty, public auction, tender or some other manner;
(c)   fixing a reserve or minimum price;
(d)   requiring payment of the purchase money into court or to trustees or other persons;
(e)   for settling the particulars and conditions of sale;
(f)   for obtaining evidence of the value of the property;
(g)   fixing the security (if any) to be given by the auctioneer, if the sale is to be by public auction, and the remuneration to be allowed him;
(h)   requiring an abstract of the title to be referred to conveyancing counsel of the Court or some other conveyancing counsel for his opinion thereon and to settle the particulars and conditions of sale.

Commencement 1 October 1966.
Amendments Para (1): word "subsequently" substituted by SI 1982/1111, r 31(1).
Para (2): original paras (2), (3) revoked, original para (4) renumbered as para (2) and words "The Court" substituted, by SI 1982/1111, r 31(2), (3).
Cross references This rule is applied to the county court by virtue of CCR Order 22, r 12.

Order 31, r 3 Certifying result of sale

(1)   If either the Court has directed payment of the purchase money into court or the Court so directs, the result of a sale by order of the Court must be certified—

(a)   in the case of a sale by public auction, by the auctioneer who conducted the sale, and

(b)   in any other case, by the solicitor of the party or person having the conduct of the sale;

and the Court may require the certificate to be verified by the affidavit of the auctioneer or solicitor, as the case may be.

(2)   The solicitor of the party or person having the conduct of the sale must . . . file the certificate and any affidavit in [Chancery Chambers].

Commencement 1 October 1966.
Amendments Para (2): words omitted revoked and words "Chancery Chambers" substituted by SI 1982/1111, r 32.
Cross references This rule is applied to the county court by virtue of CCR Order 22, r 12.

Order 31, r 4 Mortgage, exchange or partition under order of the Court

Rules 2 and 3 shall, so far as applicable and with the necessary modifications, apply in relation to the mortgage, exchange or partition of any land under an order of the Court as they apply in relation to the sale of any land under such an order.

Commencement 1 October 1966.
Cross references This rule is applied to the county court by virtue of CCR Order 22, r 12.

II Conveyancing Counsel of the Court

Order 31, r 5 Reference of matters to conveyancing counsel of Court

The Court may refer to the conveyancing counsel of the Court—

(a)   any matter relating to the investigation of the title to any property with a view to an investment of money in the purchase or on mortgage thereof, or with a view to the sale thereof,

(b)   any matter relating to the settlement of a draft of a conveyance, mortgage, settlement or other instrument, and

(c)   any other matter it thinks fit,

and may act upon his opinion in the matter referred.

Commencement 1 October 1966.
Cross references See CCR Order 22, r 7(6).

Order 31, r 6 Objection to conveyancing counsel's opinion

Any party may object to the opinion given by any conveyancing counsel on a reference under rule 5, and if he does so the point in dispute shall be determined by the judge either in chambers or in court as he thinks fit.

Commencement 1 October 1966.

Order 31, r 7 Distribution of references among conveyancing counsel

(1)   The matters referred to conveyancing counsel of the Court shall, subject to paragraph (2), be distributed among them in rotation by [the proper officer in Chancery Chambers].

(2)   The Court may direct or transfer a reference to a particular conveyancing counsel of the Court.

Commencement 1 October 1966.
Amendments Para (1): words "the proper officer in Chancery Chambers" substituted by SI 1982/ 1111, r 33.

[Order 31, r 8 Obtaining Counsel's opinion on reference

The order referring any matter to conveyancing counsel of the Court shall be recorded in the books of the Court and a copy of such order shall be sent by the Court to counsel and shall constitute sufficient authority for him to proceed with the reference.]

Commencement 1 October 1982.
Amendments This rule was substituted by SI 1982/1111, r 34.

ORDER 32
APPLICATIONS AND PROCEEDINGS IN CHAMBERS

I GENERAL

Order 32, r 1 Mode of making application

Except as provided by Order 25, rule 7, every application in chambers not made ex parte must be made by summons.

Commencement 1 October 1966.
Cross references See CCR Order 13, r 1.
Forms Summons (PF64).
Summons (Chancery) (ChPF1).
Order (PF65).
Order dismissing summons (PF66).

Order 32, r 2 Issue of summons

(1) Issue of a summons by which an application in chambers is to be made takes place on its being sealed by an officer of the appropriate office.

(2) A summons may not be amended after issue without the leave of the Court.

(3) In this rule "the appropriate office" means—
    (a) in relation to a summons in a cause or matter proceeding in a district registry, that registry;
    (b) in relation to a cause or matter in the Chancery Division which is not proceeding in a district registry, [Chancery Chambers];
    [(c) in relation to a summons in a cause or matter proceeding in the [principal registry of the Family Division], that registry;]
    (d) in relation to a summons in an Admiralty cause or matter [or a commercial action] which is not proceeding in a district registry, [the Admiralty and Commercial Registry];
    [(dd) in relation to a summons in taxation proceedings in the Supreme Court Taxing Office, that office;]
    (e) in relation to a summons in any other cause or matter, the Central Office.

[For the purposes of this paragraph, a cause or matter in which any jurisdiction is to be exercised by virtue of Order 34, rule 5(4), by a master or by the [district judge] of a district registry shall be treated, in relation to that jurisdiction, as proceeding in the Central Office[, Chancery Chambers or that district registry, as the case may be].]

Commencement 1 October 1966.
Amendments Para (3): in sub-para (b) words "Chancery Chambers" substituted by SI 1982/1111, r 35; sub-para (c) substituted by SI 1968/1244, r 5, words "principal registry of the Family Division" substituted by SI 1971/1269, r 38, Schedule; in sub-para (d) words "or a commercial action" inserted and words "the Admiralty and Commercial Registry" substituted by SI 1987/1423, r 9; sub-para (dd) inserted by SI 1990/1689, r 27; final paragraph added by SI 1971/1955, r 10(1), words ", Chancery Chambers or that district registry, as the case may be" therein substituted by SI 1982/1111, r 35.
Cross references See CCR Order 13, r 1(2).

Order 32, r 3 Service of summons

A summons asking only for the extension or abridgement of any period of time may be served on the day before the day specified in the summons for the hearing thereof but, except as aforesaid and unless the Court otherwise orders or any of these rules otherwise provides, a summons must be served on every other party not less than 2 clear days before the day so specified.

Commencement 1 October 1966.
Cross references See CCR Order 13, r 1(2).

Order 32, r 4 Adjournment of hearing

(1)   The hearing of a summons may be adjourned from time to time, either generally or to a particular date, as may be appropriate.

(2)   If the hearing is adjourned generally, the party by whom the summons was taken out may restore it to the list on 2 clear days' notice to all the other parties on whom the summons was served.

Commencement 1 October 1966.
Cross references See CCR Order 13, r 3.

Order 32, r 5 Proceeding in absence of party failing to attend

(1)   Where any party to a summons fails to attend on the first or any resumed hearing thereof, the Court may proceed in his absence if, having regard to the nature of the application, it thinks it expedient so to do.

(2)   Before proceeding in the absence of any party the Court may require to be satisfied that the summons or, as the case may be, notice of the time appointed for the resumed hearing was duly served on that party.

(3)   Where the Court hearing a summons proceeded in the absence of a party, then, provided that any order made on the hearing has not been perfected, the Court, if satisfied that it is just to do so, may re-hear the summons.

(4)   Where an application made by summons has been dismissed without a hearing by reason of the failure of the party who took out the summons to attend the hearing, the Court, if satisfied that it is just to do so, may allow the summons to be restored to the list.

Commencement 1 October 1966.
Cross references See CCR Order 13, r 1(5).

Order 32, r 6 Order made ex parte may be set aside

The Court may set aside an order made ex parte.

Commencement 1 October 1966.

Order 32, r 7 Subpoena for attendance of witness

(1)   A writ of subpoena ad testificandum or a writ of subpoena duces tecum to compel the attendance of a witness for the purpose of proceedings in chambers may be issued out of the Central Office, the [principal registry of the Family Division], the [Admiralty and Commercial Registry] or a district registry, as the case may be, if the party who desires the attendance of the witness produces a note from a judge or from a master or [district judge], as the case may be, authorising the issue of the writ.

(2)   In the Chancery Division and the Queen's Bench Division any master or [district judge], and in the [Family Division] any [district judge], may give such a note or may direct that the application for it be made to the judge before whom the proceedings are to be heard.

Commencement 1 October 1966.
Amendments Para (1): words "principal registry of the Family Division" substituted by SI 1971/1269, r 38, Schedule; words "Admiralty and Commercial Registry" substituted by SI 1987/1423, r 2.
Para (2): words "Family Division" substituted by SI 1971/1269, r 38, Schedule.

[Order 32, r 8 Officers may administer oaths

The following persons shall have authority to administer oaths and take affidavits for the purpose of proceedings in the Supreme Court, namely—
- (a)   the holder of any office which is listed in column 1 of Part II or III of Schedule 2 to the Act and any person appointed to act as a deputy for a person holding any such office or as a temporary additional officer in any such office, and
- (b)   any [district judge], [deputy district judge] or [assistant district judge], and
- (c)   any officer in the court service established by section 27 of the Courts Act 1971 who is for the time being authorised in that behalf by the Lord Chancellor.]

Commencement 1 October 1983.
Amendments This rule was substituted by SI 1983/1181, r 24.

Order 32, r 9 Application for leave to institute certain proceedings

(1)   The jurisdiction of the High Court—
- (a)   to grant leave for the purpose of section 1 of the Leasehold Property (Repairs) Act 1938, or
- (b)   to grant leave under [section 139 of the Mental Health Act 1983] to bring proceedings against a person, [or
- (c)   to grant leave under section 32A of the Limitation Act 1980 to bring an action for libel or slander,]

may be exercised in chambers but, in the case of the jurisdiction referred to in sub-paragraph (b), only by a judge.

(2)   Notwithstanding anything in Order 7, rule 5, an originating summons by which an application for leave under the said section 1 is made may be issued out of a district registry only if the premises to which the application relates are situated in the district of that registry and, in that case, may be so issued notwithstanding that the proceedings are assigned to the Chancery Division.

[(3)   An originating summons by which an application for leave under the said section 1 or the said [section 139] [or the said section 32A] is made shall be in Form No 10 in Appendix A.]

(4)   The application must be supported by an affidavit setting out the grounds on which such leave is sought and any facts necessary to substantiate those grounds.

Commencement 3 June 1980 (para (3)); 1 October 1966 (remainder).
Amendments Para (1): in sub-para (b) words "section 139 of the Mental Health Act 1983" substituted by SI 1983/1181, r 36, Schedule; sub-para (c) and the word "or" immediately preceding it inserted by SI 1986/632, r 17(1).

Para (3): substituted by SI 1979/1716, r 48, Schedule, Pt 2; words "section 139" substituted by SI 1983/1181, r 36, Schedule; words "or the said section 32A" inserted by SI 1986/632, r 17(2).

[Order 32, r 9A Application for a direction under the Limitation Act 1980

The jurisdiction to direct, under section 33 of the Limitation Act 1980, that section 11 or 12 of that Act should not apply to an action or to any specified cause of action to which the action relates shall be exercisable by the Court.]

Commencement 1 May 1981.
Amendments This rule was inserted by SI 1981/562, r 4.

Order 32, r 10 Application to make order of House of Lords order of High Court

An application to make an order of the House of Lords an order of the High Court may be made ex parte by affidavit to a master [or to the Admiralty Registrar] or to a [district judge] of the [Family Division] or, if the cause or matter in which the order was made proceeded in the High Court in a district registry, to the [district judge] of that registry.

Commencement 1 October 1966.
Amendments Words "or to the Admiralty Registrar" inserted and "Family Division" substituted by SI 1971/1269, rr 7(2), 38, Schedule.
Forms Affidavit in support (PF67).
Order (PF68).

II QUEEN'S BENCH DIVISION AND [FAMILY DIVISION]

Order 32, r 11 Jurisdiction of masters and [district judges]

(1)   The masters of the Queen's Bench Division and the [district judges] of the [Family Division] shall have power to transact all such business and exercise all such authority and jurisdiction as under the Act or these rules may be transacted and exercised by a judge in chambers except in respect of the following matters and proceedings, that is to say—

(a) matters relating to criminal proceedings, other than applications to which [Order 55, rule 6A, Order 56, rule 13 or] Order 79, rule 10(2), relates;
(b) matters relating to the liberty of the subject;
(c) proceedings to which Order 57 applies and with respect to which a judge in chambers has jurisdiction[, other than applications to which Order 55, rule 6A or Order 56, rule 13 applies;]
(d) subject to paragraph (2), [Order 50, rule 9, and Order 51, rule 2], proceedings for the grant of an injunction or other order under [section 37] of the Act;
(e) appeals from [district judges];
(f) applications for review of a taxing officer's decision;
(g) applications under [section 42] of the Act for leave to institute or continue legal proceedings;
(h) any other matter or proceeding which by any of these rules is required to be heard only by a judge.

(2)   Any such master or [district judge] shall have power to grant an injunction in the terms agreed by the parties to the proceedings in which the injunction is sought.

Commencement 1 October 1966.
Amendments Cross-heading: words "Family Division" substituted by virtue of SI 1971/1269, r 38, Schedule.

Para (1): words "Family Division" substituted by SI 1971/1269, r 38, Schedule; in sub-para (a) words "Order 55, rule 6A, Order 56, rule 13 or" inserted by SI 1987/1423, r 44; in sub-para (c) words ", other than applications to which Order 55, rule 6A or Order 56, rule 13 applies" added by SI 1987/1423, r 45; in sub-paras (d) words "Order 50, rule 9, and Order 51, rule 2" and "section 37" substituted by SI 1982/1111, r 115, Schedule; in sub-para (g) words "section 42" substituted by SI 1982/1111, r 115, Schedule.
Definitions The Act: Supreme Court Act 1981.

Order 32, r 12 Reference of matter to judge

Any master of the Queen's Bench Division or [district judge] of the [Family Division] may refer to a judge any matter which he thinks should properly be decided by a judge, and the judge may either dispose of the matter or refer it back to the master or [district judge], as the case may be, with such directions as he thinks fit.

Commencement 1 October 1966.
Amendments Words "Family Division" substituted by SI 1971/1269, r 38, Schedule.
Cross references See CCR Order 13, r 1(7).

Order 32, r 13 Power to direct hearing in court

(1)   The judge in chambers may direct that any summons, application or appeal shall be heard in court or shall be adjourned into court to be so heard if he considers that by reason of its importance or for any other reason it should be so heard.

(2)   Any matter heard in court by virtue of a direction under paragraph (1) may be adjourned from court into chambers.

Commencement 1 October 1966.
Cross references See CCR Order 13, r 1(4).

III CHANCERY DIVISION

[Order 32, r 14 Jurisdiction of masters

(1)   The masters of the Chancery Division shall have power to transact all such business and exercise all such authority and jurisdiction as may be transacted and exercised by a judge in chambers except in respect of the following matters and proceedings, that is to say,—
  (a) matters relating to criminal proceedings,
  (b) matters relating to the liberty of the subject,
  (c) proceedings to which Order 57 applies and with respect to which a judge in chambers has jurisdiction,
  (d) subject to paragraph (2) below, Order 50, rule 9 and Order 51, rule 2, proceedings for the grant of an injunction,
  (e) appeals from [district judges],
  (f) applications for review from a taxing officer's decision,
  (g) applications under section 42 of the Act for leave to institute or continue legal proceedings,
  (h) where an originating summons raises for the determination of the Court a question as to the construction of a document or a question of law, the determination of that question, and
  (i) any other matter or proceeding which by any of these rules or by direction of the Vice-Chancellor is required to be heard only by a judge.

(2)   Any master of the Chancery Division shall have power to grant an injunction in the terms agreed by the parties to the proceedings in which the injunction is sought.

(3)   Rule 12 of this Order shall apply to a master of the Chancery Division as it applies to a master of the Queen's Bench Division.]

Commencement   1 October 1989.
Amendments   This rule was substituted by SI 1989/1307, r 10.
Cross references   See CCR Order 13, r 1(6).

Order 32, r 15 Masters may summon parties, etc

(1)   For the purpose of any proceedings before him, a master of the Chancery Division may—
    (a)   issue a summons requiring any party to the proceedings to attend before him,
    (b)   at the request of any such party, issue a summons requiring any person to attend before him as a witness, . . .
    (c)   require the production of documents [and]
    [(d)   examine any party or witness either orally or on interrogatories.]

(2)   A summons under paragraph (1)(b) must be served personally on the person against whom it is issued.

(3)   If a person refuses or fails to obey a summons duly served on him under this rule the master may make an order requiring that person to attend before him.

(4)   . . .

Commencement   1 October 1966.
Amendments   Para (1): in sub-para (b) word omitted revoked, in sub-para (c) word "and" added, and sub-para (d) added, by SI 1975/911, r 11.
Para (4): revoked by SI 1975/911, r 11.
Forms   Summons by master (ChPF2).

Order 32, r 16 Obtaining assistance of experts

If the Court thinks it expedient in order to enable it better to determine any matter arising in proceedings in chambers, it may obtain the assistance of any person specially qualified to advise on that matter and may act upon his opinion.

Commencement   1 October 1966.

Order 32, r 17 Notice of filing, etc of affidavit

Any party—
    (a)   filing an affidavit intended to be used by him in any proceedings in chambers in the Chancery Division, or
    (b)   intending to use in any such proceedings any affidavit filed by him in previous proceedings,

must give notice to every other party of the filing or, as the case may be, of his intention to do so.

Commencement   1 October 1966.

Order 32, r 18 Adjournment into or from court

The hearing of any summons or other application in chambers may be adjourned from chambers into court and subsequently from court into chambers.

Commencement 1 October 1966.
Cross references See CCR Order 13, r 1(4).

Order 32, r 19 Disposal of matters in chambers

The judge may by any judgment or order made in court in any proceedings direct that such matters (if any) in the proceedings as he may specify shall be disposed of in chambers.

Commencement 1 October 1966.

Order 32, r 20 *(revoked by SI 1982/1111)*

Order 32, r 21 Papers for use of Court, etc

The original of any document which is to be used in evidence in proceedings in chambers must, if it is available, be brought in, and copies of any such document or of any part thereof shall not be made unless the Court directs that copies of that document or part be supplied for the use of the Court or be given to the other parties to the proceedings.

Commencement 1 October 1966.

Order 32, r 22 Notes of proceedings in chambers

A note shall be kept of all proceedings [before masters in Chancery Chambers] with the dates thereof so that all such proceedings in any cause or matter are noted in chronological order with a short statement of the matters decided at each hearing.

Commencement 1 October 1966.
Amendments Words "before masters in Chancery Chambers" substituted by SI 1982/1111, r 39.

IV District Registries

Order 32, r 23 Jurisdiction of [district judges]

Where a cause or matter is proceeding in any Division in a district registry, the [district judge] of that registry may exercise all such authority and jurisdiction in respect thereof as may be exercised by a master of that Division (or, in the case of the [Family Division] a [district judge]) subject—
    (a) to the same limitations as are imposed by or by virtue of these rules on the authority and jurisdiction of a master or [district judge] of that Division; and
    (b) in the case of a cause or matter in the Chancery Division, to any directions to the contrary given by the judges of that Division . . .

and references in these rules to a master or to a [district judge] of the [Family Division] shall (subject to any such directions) be construed accordingly.

Commencement 1 October 1966.
Amendments Words "Family Division" in both places substituted by SI 1971/1269, r 38, Schedule; in sub-para (b) words omitted revoked by SI 1982/1111, r 40.

Order 32, r 24 Proceedings to be taken in district registry

(1)   Where a cause or matter is proceeding in a district registry, then, except where by these rules it is otherwise provided or the Court otherwise orders, all proceedings in that cause or matter shall be taken in that registry.

In this paragraph "Court" does not include a master or a [district judge] of the [Family Division].

(2)   Unless the context otherwise requires, any provision of these rules referring to a thing done, or requiring a thing to be done, in chambers shall, in relation to a cause or matter proceeding in a district registry, be construed as referring to a thing done, or as requiring the thing to be done, in that registry.

Commencement 1 October 1966.
Amendments Para (1): words "Family Division" substituted by SI 1971/1269, r 38, Schedule.

Order 32, r 25 *(revoked by SI 1971/1955)*

Order 32, r 26 *(revoked by SI 1982/1111)*

TRIAL

ORDER 33
PLACE AND MODE OF TRIAL

Order 33, r 1 Place of trial

Subject to the provisions of these rules, the place of trial of a cause or matter, or of any question or issue arising therein, shall be determined by the Court and shall be either the Royal Courts of Justice [or one of the other places at which sittings of the High Court are authorised to be held for the trial of those proceedings or proceedings of the class to which they belong].

Commencement 1 October 1966.
Amendments Words from "or one of the other places" to the end substituted by SI 1971/1955, r 11(1).

Order 33, r 2 Mode of trial

Subject to the provisions of these rules, a cause or matter, or any question or issue arising therein, may be tried before—
    (a) a judge alone, or
    (b) a judge with a jury, or
    (c) a judge with the assistance of assessors, or
    (d) an official referee with or without the assistance of assessors, or
    (e) a master, or
    (f) a special referee.

Commencement 1 October 1966.

Order 33, r 3 Time, etc of trial of questions or issues

The Court may order any question or issue arising in a cause or matter, whether of fact or law or partly of fact and partly of law, and whether raised by the pleadings or otherwise, to be tried before, at or after the trial of the cause or matter, and may give directions as to the manner in which the question or issue shall be stated.

Commencement 1 October 1966.
Cross references See CCR Order 13, r 2(2)(c).

Order 33, r 4 Determining the place and mode of trial

(1)   In every action begun by writ, an order made on the summons for directions shall determine the place and mode of the trial; and any such order may be varied by a subsequent order of the Court made at or before the trial.

(2)   In any such action different questions or issues may be ordered to be tried at different places or by different modes of trial and one or more questions or issues may be ordered to be tried before the others.

[(2A) In an action for personal injuries, the Court may at any stage of the proceedings and of its own motion make an order for the issue of liability to be tried before any issue or question concerning the amount of damages to be awarded and—

(a) notwithstanding the provisions of Order 42, rule 5(5), an order so made in the absence of the parties shall be drawn up by an officer of the Court who shall serve a copy of the order on every party; and

(b) where a party applies within 14 days after service of the order upon him, the Court may confirm or vary the order or set it aside.]

[(3)] The references in this Order to the summons for directions include references to any summons or application to which, under any of these rules, Order 25, rules 2 to 7, are to apply, with or without modifications.

[(4)] ...

Commencement 5 February 1990 (para (2A)); 1 October 1966 (remainder).
Amendments Para (2A): inserted by SI 1989/2427, r 18.
Para (3): original para (3) revoked, and original para (4) renumbered as para (3) by SI 1971/1955, r 11(2).
Para (4): originally para (5), renumbered as para (4) by SI 1971/1955, r 11(2); revoked by SI 1984/1051, r 51.
Cross references See CCR Order 13, r 2(2)(c).

[Order 33, r 4A Split trial: offer on liability

(1) This rule applies where an order is made under rule 4(2) for the issue of liability to be tried before any issue or question concerning the amount of damages to be awarded if liability is established.

(2) After the making of an order to which paragraph (1) applies, any party against whom a finding of liability is sought may (without prejudice to his defence) make a written offer to the other party to accept liability up to a specified proportion.

(3) Any offer made under the preceding paragraph may be brought to the attention of the Judge after the issue of liability has been decided, but not before.]

Commencement 1 October 1980.
Amendments This rule was inserted by SI 1980/1010, r 8.

Order 33, r 5 Trial with jury

(1) The provisions of rule 4(1) and (2) are, as respects any action to be tried in the Queen's Bench Division and as respects any question of fact arising in such an action, subject to the provisions of [section 69 of the Act], but an application for trial with a jury under that section (the time for making which is, under that section, to be limited by rules of court) must be made before the place and mode of the trial is fixed under rule 4.

(2) The powers conferred by the said [section 69] on a judge may be exercised by a master.

Commencement 1 October 1966.
Amendments Para (1): words "section 69 of the Act" substituted by SI 1982/1111, r 115, Schedule.
Para (2): words "section 69" substituted by SI 1982/1111, r 115, Schedule.
Definitions The Act: Supreme Court Act 1981.
Cross references See CCR Order 13, r 10.

Order 33, r 6 Trial with assistance of assessors

A trial of a cause or matter with the assistance of assessors under [section 70] of the Act shall take place in such manner and on such terms as the Court may direct.

Commencement 1 October 1966.
Amendments Words "section 70" substituted by SI 1982/1111, r 115, Schedule.
Definitions The Act: Supreme Court Act 1981.
Cross references See CCR Order 13, r 11.

Order 33, r 7 Dismissal of action, etc after decision of preliminary issue

If it appears to the Court that the decision of any question or issue arising in a cause or matter and tried separately from the cause or matter substantially disposes of the cause or matter or renders the trial of the cause or matter unnecessary, it may dismiss the cause or matter or make such other order or give such judgment therein as may be just.

Commencement 1 October 1966.
Forms Judgment (No 48).

ORDER 34

SETTING DOWN FOR TRIAL ACTION BEGUN BY WRIT

Order 34, r 1 Application and interpretation

This Order applies to actions begun by writ and, accordingly, references in this Order to an action shall be construed as references to an action so begun.

. . .

Commencement 1 October 1966.
Amendments Words omitted revoked by SI 1971/1955, r 12(1).

Order 34, r 2 Time for setting down action

(1) Every order made in an action which provides for trial before a judge shall, whether the trial is to be with or without a jury and wherever the trial is to take place, fix a period within which the plaintiff is to set down the action for trial.

(2) Where the plaintiff does not, within the period fixed under paragraph (1), set the action down for trial, the defendant may set the action down for trial or may apply to the Court to dismiss the action for want of prosecution and, on the hearing of any such application, the Court may order the action to be dismissed accordingly or may make such order as it thinks just.

(3) Every order made in an action in the Queen's Bench Division which provides for trial before a judge (otherwise than in the commercial list or the special paper or any corresponding list which may be specified for the purposes of this paragraph by directions under rule 4) shall contain an estimate of the length of the trial and, if the action is to be tried at the Royal Courts of Justice, shall, subject to any such directions, specify the list in which the action is to be put.

Commencement 1 October 1966.

Order 34, r 3 Lodging documents when setting down

[(1) In order to set down for trial an action which is to be tried before a judge, the party setting it down must, subject to any order of the Court to the contrary, deliver to the proper officer, by post or otherwise, a request that the action be set down for trial at the place determined in accordance with automatic directions or by order of the Court and lodge two bundles consisting of one copy of each of the following documents—

    (a) the writ,
    (b) the pleadings (including any affidavits ordered to stand as pleadings),
    (c) any request or order for particulars and the particulars given, and any interrogatories and answers thereto,
    (d) all orders made in the action except only any order relating only to time,
    (e) in proceedings to which article 7(1) of the High Court and County Courts Jurisdiction Order 1991 applies, a statement of the value of the action,
    (f) a note agreed by the parties or, failing agreement, a note by each party giving (in the following order)—
        (i) an estimate of the length of the trial,
        (ii) the list in which the action is to be included,

(g)   the requisite legal aid documents, if any.

(1A)   Nothing in paragraph (1) shall alter the practice under Order 19, rule 7 and Order 82, rule 5.

(1B)   Where a statement under paragraph (1)(e) is not lodged and a copy of it served on every other party, the Court may give notice to the parties to show cause why the action should not be transferred to a county court for trial.]

(2)   Each of the said bundles must be bound up in the proper chronological order[, save that voluntary particulars of any pleading and particulars to which Order 18, rule 12(7) applies shall be placed immediately after the pleading to which they relate;] and the bundle which is to serve as the record must be stamped with the stamp denoting payment of the fee payable on setting down the action and have indorsed thereon the names, addresses and telephone numbers of the solicitors for the parties or, in the case of a party who has no solicitor, of the party himself.

[(3)   In this rule "the requisite legal aid documents" means any documents which are required by regulations made under Part IV of the Legal Aid Act 1988 to be included in the papers for the use of the court.]

(4)   Where a new trial becomes necessary in the case of any action, the procedure for setting down the action for the new trial shall be that specified in the foregoing provisions except that—
  (a)   the bundle which is to serve as the record must be bespoken from the person in whose custody it is and sent to the proper officer, and
  (b)   there must be delivered, along with the request that the action may be set down, a backsheet with the title of the action thereon, and the names, addresses and telephone numbers of the solicitors for the parties or, in the case of a party who has no solicitor, of the party himself, stamped with the stamp denoting payment of the fee payable on setting down the action for the new trial.

(5)   In this rule "the proper officer" means—
  (a)   in relation to an action in the Queen's Bench Division which is to be tried at the Royal Courts of Justice, the head clerk of the Crown Office [or the chief clerk of the Admiralty and Commercial Registry];
  [(b)   in relation to an action (in whatever Division) which is to be tried outside the Royal Courts of Justice, [an officer of the district registry] for the district comprising the place of trial;]
  [(c)]   in relation to an action in the Chancery Division which is to be tried at the Royal Courts of Justice, the cause clerk [in Chancery Chambers].

Commencement 1 July 1991 (paras (1)–(1B), (3)); 1 October 1966 (remainder).
Amendments Paras (1), (1A), (1B): substituted for para (1) as originally enacted, by SI 1991/1329, r 10.
Para (2): words from ", save that" to "relate;" inserted by SI 1980/1010, r 3.
Para (3): substituted by SI 1991/1329, r 11.
Para (5): original sub-paras (a)–(f) partially revoked and renumbered as sub-paras (a)–(d) by SI 1970/1861, r 5(1), SI 1971/1269, r 8(1); in sub-para (a) words "or the chief clerk of the Admiralty and Commercial Registry" inserted by SI 1987/1423, r 10; sub-para (b) substituted for sub-paras (b) and (c) by SI 1971/1955, r 12(2), words "an officer of the district registry" substituted by SI 1991/1329, r 12; sub-para (d) renumbered as sub-para (c) by SI 1971/1955, r 12(2), and words "in Chancery Chambers" substituted by SI 1982/1111, r 42.
Forms Statement to be lodged with pleadings outside London (PF69).
Statement of value (PF204).

Order 34, r 4 Directions relating to lists

Nothing in this Order shall prejudice any powers of—
  (a) the Lord Chief Justice, as respects actions in the Queen's Bench Division,
       [or]
  (b) [the Vice-Chancellor], as respects actions in [the Chancery Division] . . .
  (c) . . .

to give directions—
  (i)   specifying the lists in which actions, or actions of any class or description,
        are to be set down for trial and providing for the keeping and publication
        of the lists;
  (ii) providing for the determination of a date for the trial of any action which
        has been set down or a date before which the trial thereof is not to take
        place; and
  (iii) as to the making of applications (whether to a Court or a judge or an
        officer of a Court) to fix, vacate or alter any such date, and, in particular,
        requiring any such application to be supported by an estimate of the length
        of the trial and any other relevant information.

Commencement 1 October 1966.

Amendments Word "or" inserted, words "the Vice Chancellor" substituted, and words omitted revoked, by SI 1971/1269, r 8(2); words "the Chancery Division" substituted by SI 1971/1955, r 12(3).

[Order 34, r 5 Further provisions as to lists

(1)   The [district judge] for the district comprising each place at which sittings of the High Court are held outside the Royal Courts of Justice shall keep a list of the actions for the time being set down for trial before a judge at that place.

(2)   Where, after an action has been set down for trial—
  (a) an order is made under Order 33, rule 4(1), varying the order determining
       the place of trial; or
  (b) the place of trial is changed under paragraph (5) of this rule,

the action shall be treated, unless the Court otherwise directs, as having been set down at the new place of trial on the date on which it was first set down for trial elsewhere.

(3)   At any time after an action has been set down for trial and before it is tried, the Court may require the parties to furnish the Court or an officer thereof, by personal attendance or otherwise, with such information as may be necessary to show whether the action is ready for trial, and if any party fails to comply with any such requirement, the Court may—
  (a) of its own motion, on 7 days' notice to the parties, direct that the action be
       removed from the list, or
  (b) on the application of any party, dismiss the action for want of prosecution
       or strike out the defence or counterclaim or make such other order as the
       Court thinks fit.

Where a direction is given under sub-paragraph (a), the Court may subsequently direct the action to be restored to the list on such terms, if any, as it thinks fit.

(4)   Where an action proceeding in a district registry has been set down for trial at the Royal Courts of Justice or at a place comprised in the district of another district registry, or an action proceeding in the Central Office [or Chancery Chambers] has

been set down for trial outside the Royal Courts of Justice, a master or the [district judge] at the place where the action has been set down for trial may, if it appears to him to be desirable having regard to the proximity of the date of trial or otherwise, exercise any jurisdiction which is exercisable in the action by a master or the [district judge] at the place where the action is proceeding.

(5) Without prejudice to Order 33, rule 4(1), a judge, or a master or the [district judge] at the place where an action has been set down for trial, may, if it appears to him that the action cannot conveniently be tried at the place of trial which has been ordered, change the place of trial to some other place mentioned in Order 33, rule 1.

(6) The power conferred by paragraph (5) may be exercised by the Court of its own motion or on the application of a party, but before acting of its own motion the Court shall give to every party concerned an opportunity of being heard on the question whether the power should be exercised and for that purpose the Court may cause him to be given notice of a date, time and place at which the question will be considered.]

Commencement 1 January 1972.
Amendments This rule was substituted by SI 1971/1955, r 12(4).
Para (4): words "or Chancery Chambers" inserted by SI 1982/1111, r 43.

Order 34, r 6 *(revoked by SI 1970/1861)*

Order 34, r 7 *(revoked by SI 1971/1955)*

Order 34, r 8 Notification of setting down

(1) A party to an action who sets it down for trial must, within 24 hours after doing so, notify the other parties to the action that he has done so . . . .

(2) It shall be the duty of all parties to an action entered in any list to furnish without delay to the officer who keeps the list all available information as to the action being or being likely to be settled, or affecting the estimated length of the trial, and, if the action is settled or withdrawn, to notify that officer of the fact without delay and take such steps as may be necessary to withdraw the record.

[(3) In performance of the duty imposed by paragraph (2), a plaintiff who gives notice of acceptance of a payment into court in accordance with Order 22, rule 3(1), shall at the same time lodge a copy of the notice with the officer mentioned in that paragraph.]

Commencement 1 January 1973 (para (3)); 1 October 1966 (remainder).
Amendments Para (1): words omitted revoked by SI 1971/1955, r 12(6).
Para (3): added by SI 1972/1898, r 5.

Order 34, r 9 Abatement, etc, of action

(1) Where after an action has been set down for trial the action becomes abated, or the interest or liability of any party to the action is assigned or transmitted to or devolves on some other person, the solicitor for the plaintiff or other party having the conduct of the action must, as soon as practicable after becoming aware of it, certify the abatement or change of interest or liability and send the certificate to the proper officer, and that officer shall cause the appropriate entry to be made in the list of actions set down for trial.

(2)   Where in any such list an action stands for one year marked as abated or ordered to stand over generally, the action shall on the expiration of that year be struck out of the list unless, in the case of an action ordered to stand over generally, the order otherwise provides.

[(3)   In this rule "proper officer" has the same meaning as in rule 3.]

Commencement   2 November 1987 (para (3)); 1 October 1966 (remainder).
Amendments   Para (3): substituted by SI 1987/1423, r 11.

[Order 34, r 10 The Court bundle

(1)   At least 14 days before the date fixed for the trial or, in the case of an action entered in any running list, within 3 weeks of the defendant's receiving notice of such entry, the defendant shall identify to the plaintiff those documents central to his case which he wishes included in the bundle to be provided under paragraph (2).

(2)   At least 2 clear days before the date fixed for the trial the plaintiff shall lodge two bundles consisting of one copy of each of the following documents—
  (a)   witness statements which have been exchanged, and experts' reports which have been disclosed, together with an indication of whether the contents of such documents are agreed,
  (b)   those documents which the defendant wishes to have included in the bundle and those central to the plaintiff's case, and
  (c)   where a direction has been given under Order 25, rule 3(2), a note agreed by the parties or, failing agreement, a note by each party giving (in the following order)—
     (i)   a summary of the issues involved,
     (ii)   a summary of any propositions of law to be advanced together with a list of the authorities to be cited, and
     (iii) a chronology of relevant events.

(3)   Nothing in this rule shall—
  (a)   prevent the Court from giving, whether before or after the documents have been lodged, such further or different directions as to the documents to be lodged as may, in the circumstances, be appropriate; or
  (b)   prevent the making of an order for the transfer of the action to a county court.

(4)   Where an action is to be tried with the assistance of assessors, additional copies of the bundles to be lodged under paragraph (2) shall be provided for the use of the assessors.

(5)   For the purposes of this rule, "plaintiff" includes a defendant where an action is proceeding on a counterclaim and "defendant" includes any other party who is entitled under any order of the Court or otherwise to be heard at the trial.]

Commencement   1 July 1991.
Amendments   This rule was inserted by SI 1991/1329, r 13.
Cross references   See CCR Order 17, r 12.

ORDER 35
PROCEEDINGS AT TRIAL

Order 35, r 1 Failure to appear by both parties or one of them

(1)   If, when the trial of an action is called on, neither party appears, the action may be struck out of the list, without prejudice, however, to the restoration thereof, on the direction of a judge.

(2)   If, when the trial of an action is called on, one party does not appear, the judge may proceed with the trial of the action or any counterclaim in the absence of that party.

Commencement 1 October 1966.
Cross references See CCR Order 21, rr 1, 3.

Order 35, r 2 Judgment, etc given in absence of party may be set aside

(1)   Any judgment, order or verdict obtained where one party does not appear at the trial may be set aside by the Court, on the application of that party, on such terms as it thinks just.

(2)   An application under this rule must be made within 7 days after the trial.

Commencement 1 October 1966.
Cross references See CCR Order 37, r 2.

Order 35, r 3 Adjournment of trial

The judge may, if he thinks it expedient in the interest of justice, adjourn a trial for such time, and to such place, and upon such terms, if any, as he thinks fit.

Commencement 1 October 1966.
Cross references See CCR Order 13, r 3.

Order 35, rr 4–6 *(revoked by SI 1971/1955)*

Order 35, r 7 Order of speeches

[(1)   The judge before whom an action is tried (whether with or without a jury) may give directions—
    (a)   as to the party to begin,
    (b)   as to the order of speeches at the trial, and
    (c)   in an action tried without a jury, dispensing with opening speeches;

and, subject to any such directions, the party to begin and the order of speeches shall be that provided by this rule.]

(2)   Subject to paragraph (6), the plaintiff shall begin by opening his case.

(3)   If the defendant elects not to adduce evidence, then, whether or not the defendant has in the course of cross-examination of a witness for the plaintiff or otherwise put in a document, the plaintiff may, after the evidence on his behalf has been given, make a second speech closing his case and the defendant shall then state his case.

(4)   If the defendant elects to adduce evidence, he may, after any evidence on behalf of the plaintiff has been given, open his case and, after the evidence on his behalf has been given, make a second speech closing his case, and at the close of the defendant's case the plaintiff may make a speech in reply.

(5)   Where there are two or more defendants who appear separately or are separately represented, then—

(a) if none of them elects to adduce evidence, each of them shall state his case in the order in which his name appears on the record;

(b) if each of them elects to adduce evidence, each of them may open his case and the evidence on behalf of each of them shall be given in the order aforesaid and the speech of each of them closing his case shall be made in that order after the evidence on behalf of all the defendants has been given;

(c) if some of them elect to adduce evidence and some do not, those who do not shall state their cases in the order aforesaid after the speech of the plaintiff in reply to the other defendants.

(6)   Where the burden of proof of all the issues in the action lies on the defendant or, where there are two or more defendants and they appear separately or are separately represented, on one of the defendants, the defendant or that defendant, as the case may be, shall be entitled to begin, and in that case paragraphs (2), (3) and (4) shall have effect in relation to, and as between, him and the plaintiff as if for references to the plaintiff and the defendant there were substituted references to the defendant and the plaintiff respectively.

(7)   Where, as between the plaintiff and any defendant, the party who would, but for this paragraph, be entitled to make the final speech raises any fresh point of law in that speech or cites in that speech any authority not previously cited, the opposite party may make a further speech in reply, but only in relation to that point of law or that authority, as the case may be.

Commencement 1 July 1991 (para (1)); 1 October 1966 (remainder).
Amendments Para (1): substituted by SI 1991/1329, r 14.
Cross references See CCR Order 21, r 5A.

Order 35, r 8 Inspection by judge or jury

(1)   The judge by whom any cause or matter is tried may inspect any place or thing with respect to which any question arises in the cause or matter.

(2)   Where a cause or matter is tried with a jury and the judge inspects any place or thing under paragraph (1), he may authorise the jury to inspect it also.

Commencement 1 October 1966.
Cross references See CCR Order 21, r 6.

Order 35, r 9 Death of party before giving of judgment

Where a party to any action dies after the verdict or finding of the issues of fact and before judgment is given, judgment may be given notwithstanding the death, but the foregoing provision shall not be taken as affecting the power of the judge to make an order under Order 15, rule 7(2), before giving judgment.

Commencement 1 October 1966.

Order 35, r 10 Certificate of associate

At the conclusion of the trial of any action in the Queen's Bench Division, . . . , the associate in attendance at the trial shall make a certificate in which he shall certify—

(a) the time actually occupied by the trial,

(b) any order made by the judge under Order 38, rule 5 or 6,

(c) every finding of fact by the jury, where the trial was with a jury,

(d) the judgment given by the judge, and

(e) any order made by the judge as to costs.

Commencement 1 October 1966.
Amendments Words omitted revoked by SI 1971/1269, r 9(1) and SI 1982/1111, r 44.
Forms Certificate (PF70–71).

[Order 35, r 10A Reductions in costs under section 51(8) of the Act

At the conclusion of the trial of an action, the associate in attendance at the trial shall record in his certificate under rule 10 any opinion expressed by the judge under section 51(8) of the Act (reduction in costs where proceedings should have been commenced in a county court).]

Commencement 1 October 1991.
Amendments This rule was inserted by SI 1991/1884, r 9.
Definitions The Act: Supreme Court Act 1981.

Order 35, r 11 List of exhibits

(1) The associate shall take charge of every document or object put in as an exhibit during the trial of any action and shall mark or label every exhibit with a letter or letters indicating the party by whom the exhibit is put in or the witness by whom it is proved, and with a number, so that all the exhibits put in by a party, or proved by a witness, are numbered in one consecutive series.

In this paragraph a witness by whom an exhibit is proved includes a witness in the course of whose evidence the exhibit is put in.

(2) The associate shall cause a list to be made of all the exhibits in the action, and any party may, on payment of the prescribed fee, have an office copy of that list.

(3) The list of exhibits when completed shall be attached to the pleadings and shall form part of the record of the action.

(4) For the purpose of this rule a bundle of documents may be treated and counted as one exhibit.

Commencement 1 October 1966.
Forms List of exhibits (PF72).

Order 35, r 12 Custody of exhibit after trial

It shall be the duty of every party to an action [. . .] who has put in any exhibit to apply to the associate immediately after the trial for the return of the exhibit, and, so far as is practicable regard being had to the nature of the exhibit, to keep it duly marked and labelled as before, so that in the event of an appeal to the Court of Appeal or the House of Lords, he may be able to produce the exhibit so marked and labelled at the hearing of the appeal in case he is required by the Court of Appeal or the House of Lords to do so.

Commencement 1 October 1966.
Amendments Words omitted originally inserted by SI 1971/1269, r 9(2), subsequently revoked by SI 1982/1111, r 45.

Order 35, r 13 Impounded documents

(1) Documents impounded by order of the Court shall not be delivered out of the custody of the Court except in compliance with an order made by a judge on an application made by motion:

Provided that where a Law Officer or the Director of Public Prosecutions makes a written request in that behalf, documents so impounded shall be delivered into his custody.

(2) Documents impounded by order of the Court, while in the custody of the Court, shall not be inspected except by a person authorised to do so by an order signed by a judge.

Commencement 1 October 1966.

ORDER 36

TRIALS BEFORE, AND INQUIRIES BY, REFEREES AND MASTERS

[Order 36, r 1 Application and interpretation

(1)   This Order applies to official referees' business in the Chancery Division or Queen's Bench Division, and the other provisions of these rules apply to such business subject to the provisions of this Order.

(2)   In this Order official referees' business includes, without prejudice to any right to a trial with a jury, any cause or matter commenced in the Chancery Division or Queen's Bench Division, being a cause or matter—

(a)   which involves a prolonged examination of documents or accounts, or a technical scientific or local investigation such as could more conveniently be conducted by an official referee; or

(b)   for which trial by an official referee is desirable in the interests of one or more of the parties on grounds of expedition, economy or convenience or otherwise.]

Commencement   1 October 1982.
Amendments   This rule was substituted by SI 1982/1111, r 100(1).
Forms   Order referring official referee (PF73).

[Order 36, r 2 Commencement of official referees' business

(1)   Before the issue of a writ or originating summons by which official referees' business is to be begun, it may be marked in the top left hand corner with the words "official referees' business" and, on the issue of the writ or summons so marked, the cause or matter begun thereby shall be treated as official referees' business.

(2)   If the plaintiff intends to issue a writ or originating summons for service out of the jurisdiction and to mark it in accordance with paragraph (1), an application for leave to issue the writ or summons and to serve it out of the jurisdiction may be made to an official referee.

(3)   The affidavit in support of an application under paragraph (2) must, in addition to the matters required to be stated by Order 11, rule 4(1), state that the plaintiff intends to mark the writ or summons in accordance with paragraph (1) of this rule.

(4)   If the official referee hearing an application under paragraph (2) is of opinion that the cause or matter should not be dealt with as official referees' business, he may adjourn the application to be heard by a master.]

Commencement   1 October 1982.
Amendments   Original r 2 renumbered as r 8 and new r 2 inserted by SI 1982/1111, r 100(1).

[Order 36, r 3 Transfer of official referees' business

(1)   At any stage before the trial of a cause or matter in the Chancery Division or Queen's Bench Division, any party may apply by summons to the Court to transfer the proceedings to be dealt with as official referees' business.

(2)   If the Court considers that any cause or matter in the Chancery Division or Queen's Bench Division may more appropriately be dealt with as official referees' business, the Court may of its own motion, but subject to any right to a trial with a

jury, order that the cause or matter, or any question or issue of fact arising therein, shall be tried by an official referee.

(3)   An official referee may of his own motion or on the application of any party, order a cause or matter which is proceeding as official referees' business to be transferred to the Chancery Division or Queen's Bench Division if he considers that it may more appropriately be tried by a master or judge.

(4)   No order for the transfer of proceedings shall be made by the Court or an official referee under this rule unless the parties have either—
    (a) had an opportunity of being heard on the issue, or
    (b) consented to such an order.]

Commencement 1 October 1982.
Amendments Original r 3 renumbered as r 9 and new r 3 inserted by SI 1982/1111, r 100(1).

Order 36, r 4 Powers, etc of official referees

(1)   Subject to any directions contained in the order referring any business to an official referee—
    (a) the official referee shall for the purpose of disposing of any cause or matter (including any interlocutory application therein) or any other business referred to him have the same jurisdiction, powers and duties (including the power of committal and discretion as to costs) as a judge, exercisable or, as the case may be, to be performed as nearly as circumstances admit in the like cases, in the like manner and subject to the like limitations; and
    (b) every trial and all other proceedings before an official referee shall, as nearly as circumstances admit, be conducted in the like manner as the like proceedings before a judge.

(2)   Without prejudice to the generality of paragraph (1), but subject to any such directions as are mentioned therein, an official referee before whom any cause or matter is tried shall have the like powers as the Court with respect to claims relating to or connected with the original subject-matter of the cause or matter by any party thereto against any other person, and Order 15, rule 5(2) and Order 16 shall with any necessary modifications apply in relation to any such claim accordingly.

(3)   An official referee may hold any trial or any other proceeding before him at any place which appears to him to be convenient and may adjourn the proceedings from place to place as he thinks fit.

Commencement 1 October 1966.

Order 36, r 5 Allocation of business to official referees

(1)   [No writ or originating summons by which official referees' business is to be begun and no] order referring any business to an official referee under these rules shall specify any particular referee.

(2)   . . .

[(3)   Official referees' business in the Royal Courts of Justice shall be allocated by the rota clerk to the official referees in rotation.]

(4)   . . .

Commencement 1 October 1982 (para (3)); 1 October 1966 (remainder).
Amendments Para (1): words from the beginning to "and no" substituted by SI 1982/1111, r 100(2)(a).
Para (2): revoked by SI 1991/531, r 3.
Para (3): substituted by SI 1982/1111, r 100(2)(b).
Para (4): revoked by SI 1982/1111, r 100(2)(c).

Order 36, r 6 Entry of business and application for directions

[(1) An application for directions (including an application for a fixed date for hearing) shall be made by the plaintiff to the official referee to whom the business has been allocated within 14 days of—

    (a)   the giving by a defendant of notice of intention to defend, or

    (b)   the date of the order transferring the cause or matter,

whichever is the later.]

[(2)] If that party does not make an application for directions to the official referee in accordance with paragraph (2), any other interested party may do so or may apply to the official referee—

    (a)   in the case of any cause or matter referred for trial, for an order to strike out the pleadings of the party in default or, where the party in default is the plaintiff or has made a counterclaim, an order to dismiss the action or counterclaim;

    (b)   in the case of any question or issue referred for trial or inquiry and report, to have the matter referred back to the Court.

[(3)] Upon application by any party for an order under paragraph (3)(a), the official referee may make the order asked for on such terms as may be just or deal with the application as if it were an application for directions.

[(4)] Order 25, rules 2 to 7, shall, with the omission of so much of rule 7(1) as requires parties to serve a notice specifying the orders and directions which they desire and with any other necessary modifications, apply as if any application under this rule were a summons for directions under that Order.

Commencement 1 October 1982 (para (1)); 1 October 1966 (remainder).
Amendments Para (1): substituted, for paras (1), (2) as originally enacted, by SI 1982/1111, r 100(3).
Paras (2)-(4): originally paras (3)-(5), renumbered as paras (2)-(4) by SI 1982/1111, r 100(3).

Order 36, r 7 Transfer of business from one official referee to another

(1)   If, in the opinion of the Lord Chancellor or the Lord Chief Justice, it is expedient so to do having regard to the state of the business pending before the official referees, he may order the transfer of any business from any official referee to any other official referee.

(2)   Any official referee may order the transfer of any business from himself to any other official referee who consents to the transfer.

(3)   In the absence, or with the consent, of the official referee to whom any business was allocated or has been transferred, any interlocutory application may be made to any other official referee and that other referee may deal with the application and make any order thereon which could have been made by the first-mentioned referee.

Commencement 1 October 1966.

Order 36, r [8] Reference to official referee of question of fact for inquiry, etc

In any cause or matter in the Chancery Division or Queen's Bench Division other than a criminal proceeding by the Crown the Court may, subject to any right to a trial with a jury, refer to an official referee for inquiry and report any question or issue of fact arising therein; and, unless the Court otherwise orders, the further consideration of the cause or matter shall stand adjourned until the receipt of the official referee's report.

Commencement 1 October 1966.
Amendments Originally r 2, renumbered as r 8 and original r 8 renumbered as r 10 by SI 1982/1111, r 100(4).

Order 36, r [9] Report on reference under r [8]

(1)   The report made by an official referee in pursuance of a reference under [rule 8] shall be made to the Court and notice thereof served on the parties to the reference.

(2)   The official referee may in his report submit any question arising therein for the decision of the Court or make a special statement of facts from which the Court may draw such inferences as it thinks fit.

(3)   On the receipt of the official referee's report, the Court may—
    (a)   adopt the report in whole or in part;
    (b)   vary the report;
    (c)   require an explanation from him;
    (d)   remit the whole or any part of the question or issue originally referred to him for further consideration by him or any other official referee; or
    (e)   decide the question or issue originally referred to him on the evidence taken before him, either with or without additional evidence.

(4)   When the report of the official referee has been made, an application to vary the report or remit the whole or any part of the question or issue originally referred may be made on the hearing by the Court of the further consideration of the cause or matter, after giving not less than 4 days' notice thereof, and any other application with respect to the report may be made on that hearing without notice.

(5)   Where on a reference under [rule 8] the Court orders that the further consideration of the cause or matter in question shall not stand adjourned until the receipt of the official referee's report, the order may contain directions with respect to the proceedings on the receipt of the report, and the foregoing provisions of this rule shall have effect subject to any such directions.

Commencement 1 October 1966.
Amendments Originally r 3, renumbered as r 9 and original r 9 renumbered as r 11 by SI 1982/1111, r 100(4).
Rule heading: number "8" substituted by SI 1982/1111, r 100(4)(a).
Paras (1), (5): words "rule 8" substituted by SI 1982/1111, r 100(4)(a).

Order 36, r [10] Trial before, and inquiry by, special referee

(1)   An order under [rule 3] may, with the consent of the parties to the cause or matter, order that the cause or matter, or any question or issue of fact arising therein, be tried before a special referee instead of an official referee and that rule shall have effect accordingly with the omission of the reference to assessors.

(2)   A reference under [rule 8] may be made to a special referee instead of an official referee, and that rule and [rule 9] shall have effect accordingly.

(3)   Rule 4 shall apply in relation to a special referee, and the conduct of proceedings before a special referee, as it applies in relation to an official referee and the conduct of proceedings before an official referee, except that a special referee shall not have power to make orders of committal or the powers conferred on an official referee by rule 4(2).

Commencement 1 October 1966.
Amendments Originally r 8, renumbered as r 10 by SI 1982/1111, r 100(4).
Para (1): words "rule 3" substituted by SI 1982/1111, r 100(4)(b).
Para (2): words "rule 8" and "rule 9" substituted by SI 1982/1111, r 100(4)(b).

Order 36, r [11] Trial before, and inquiry by, master

(1)   An order under rule [3] may, with the consent of the parties to the cause or matter, order that the cause or matter, or any question or issue of fact arising therein, be tried before a master [or the Admiralty Registrar] instead of an official referee and that rule shall have effect accordingly with the omission of the reference to assessors.

(2)   Without prejudice to Orders 43 and 44, and subject to the provisions of those Orders, a reference under rule [8] may be made by the judge to a master instead of an official referee and that rule and rule [9] shall have effect accordingly.

(3)   Rule 4 shall apply in relation to a master, and the conduct of any proceedings before a master at a trial before, or reference to, him under this Order as it applies in relation to an official referee and the conduct of proceedings before an official referee, except that a master shall not have power to make orders of committal or the power conferred on an official referee by rule 4(3).

[(4)   Rule 4 shall apply in relation to the Admiralty Registrar and the conduct of any proceedings before the Admiralty Registrar at a trial before him under this Order as it applies in relation to an Official Referee and the conduct of proceedings before an Official Referee, except that the Admiralty Registrar shall not have power to make orders of committal.]

Commencement 7 March 1989 (para (4)); 1 October 1966 (remainder).
Amendments Originally r 9, renumbered as r 11 by SI 1982/1111, r 100(4).
Para (1): figure "3" substituted by SI 1982/1111, r 100(4)(c); words "or the Admiralty Registrar" inserted by SI 1989/177, r 5.
Para (2): figures "8" and "9" substituted by SI 1982/1111, r 100(4)(c).
Para (4): added by SI 1989/177, r 6.
Cross references See CCR Order 21, r 5 and Order 19, rr 11-14.
Forms Order for trial by master (PF74).

Order 36, r [12] Restriction of power to order trial before referee, etc

Notwithstanding anything in this Order, no cause or matter to which Her Majesty or the Duke of Cornwall is a party or any question or issue therein shall be . . . tried before an official referee except with the consent of Her Majesty or the Duke of Cornwall, as the case may be, and no question or issue in such cause or matter shall be referred for inquiry and report to a referee or master except with such consent.

Commencement 1 October 1966.
Amendments Originally r 10, renumbered as r 12 by SI 1982/1111, r 100(4).
Words omitted revoked by SI 1982/1111, r 100(4)(d).

ORDER 37

[DAMAGES: ASSESSMENT AFTER JUDGMENT AND ORDERS FOR PROVISIONAL DAMAGES]

[I ASSESSMENT OF DAMAGES AFTER JUDGMENT]

Amendments Words "Damages: Assessment after Judgment and Orders for Provisional Damages" substituted and words "I Assessment of Damages after Judgment" inserted by SI 1985/846, r 4(1), (2).

Order 37, r 1 Assessment of damages by Chancery or Queen's Bench master

(1)   Where judgment is given in the Chancery Division or the Queen's Bench Division for damages to be assessed and no provision is made by the judgment as to how they are to be assessed, the damages shall, subject to the provisions of this Order, be assessed by a master [or, in an Admiralty cause or matter, by the Admiralty Registrar], and the party entitled to the benefit of the judgment may, after obtaining the necessary appointment from the master and, at least 7 days before the date of the appointment, serving notice of the appointment on the party against whom the judgment is given, proceed accordingly.

(2)   Notwithstanding anything in Order 65, rule 9, a notice under this rule must be served on the party against whom the judgment is given.

(3)   Without prejudice to the powers of a master of the Chancery Division under Order 32, rule 15, the attendance of witnesses and the production of documents before the master in proceedings under this Order may be compelled by writ of subpoena, and the provisions of Order 35 shall, with the necessary adaptations, apply in relation to those proceedings as they apply in relation to proceedings at a trial.

[(4)   In relation to an Admiralty cause or matter, for the references in this rule and rule 2 to a master there shall be substituted references to the Admiralty Registrar.]

Commencement   1 September 1978 (para (4)); 1 October 1966 (remainder).
Amendments   Para (1): words "or, in an Admiralty cause or matter, by the Admiralty Registrar" inserted by SI 1971/1269, r 10(1).
Para (4): added by SI 1978/1066, r 3(1).
Cross references   See CCR Order 22, r 6.
Forms   Judgment for amount to be ascertained (PF81).
Final judgment after assessment (No 43).

Order 37, r 2 Certificate of amount of damages

Where in pursuance of this Order or otherwise damages are assessed by a master, he shall certify the amount of the [damages and the certificate shall be filed in the office of the Supreme Court which has the conduct of the business of the division or court in which the cause or matter is proceeding, or, if it is proceeding in a district registry, that registry.]

Commencement   1 October 1966.
Amendments   Words from "damages and" to the end substituted by SI 1982/1111, r 46.

Order 37, r 3 Default judgment against some but not all defendants

Where any such judgment as is mentioned in rule 1 is given [on failure to give notice of intention to defend] or in default of defence, and the action proceeds against other defendants, the damages under the judgment shall be assessed at the trial unless the Court otherwise orders.

Commencement 1 October 1966.
Amendments Words "on failure to give notice of intention to defend" substituted by SI 1979/1716, r 48, Schedule, Pt 1.

[Order 37, r 4 Power to order assessment by referee, etc

(1)   Where judgment is given in the Chancery Division or the Queen's Bench Division for damages to be assessed, the Court may—

    (a) order that the assessment of the damages be referred to an official referee or to a special referee, or

    (b) except in a case to which sub-paragraph (c) applies, order that the damages be assessed by a master, or

    (c) in the case of an Admiralty cause or matter, or in the case of an action in the commercial list where the claim is of such a nature that in the opinion of the court it would be appropriate for the damages to be assessed by the Admiralty Registrar, order that the damages be assessed by him, or

    (d) order that the action shall proceed to trial before a judge (with or without a jury) as respects the damages.

(2)   Where damages are ordered to be assessed by the Admiralty Registrar pursuant to paragraph (1)(c), rule 1 shall apply as it applies to an Admiralty cause or matter.

(3)   Where the Court orders that the action shall proceed to trial, Order 25, rules 2 to 7, shall, with the omission of so much of rule 7(1) as requires the parties to serve a notice specifying the orders and directions which they desire and with any other necessary modifications, apply as if the application to the Court in pursuance of which the Court makes the order, were a summons for directions under Order 25.]

Commencement 1 September 1978.
Amendments This rule was substituted by SI 1978/1066, r 3(2).

Order 37, r 5 Assessment of value

The foregoing provisions of this Order shall apply in relation to a judgment for the value of goods to be assessed, with or without damages to be assessed, as they apply to a judgment for damages to be assessed, and references in those provisions to the assessment of damages shall be construed accordingly.

Commencement 1 October 1966.

Order 37, r 6 Assessment of damages to time of assessment

Where damages are to be assessed (whether under this Order or otherwise) in respect of any continuing cause of action, they shall be assessed down to the time of the assessment.

Commencement 1 October 1966.

[II ORDERS FOR PROVISIONAL DAMAGES FOR PERSONAL INJURIES

Order 37, r 7 Application and Interpretation

(1)   This Part of this Order applies to actions to which section 32A of the Act (in this Part of this Order referred to as "section 32A") applies.

(2)   In this Part of this Order "award of provisional damages" means an award of damages for personal injuries under which—

    (a) damages are assessed on the assumption that the injured person will not develop the disease or suffer the deterioration referred to in section 32A; and

    (b) the injured person is entitled to apply for further damages at a future date if he develops the disease or suffers the deterioration.]

Commencement 1 July 1985.
Amendments Order 37, Pt II (rr 7–10) was added by SI 1985/846, r 4(3).
Definitions The Act: Supreme Court Act 1981.
Cross references Para (2) of this rule is applied to the county court by CCR Order 22, r 6A.

[Order 37, r 8 Order for provisional damages

(1)   The Court may on such terms as it thinks just and subject to the provisions of this rule make an award of provisional damages if—

    (a) the plaintiff has pleaded a claim for provisional damages, and

    (b) the Court is satisfied that the action is one to which section 32A applies.

(2)   An order for an award of provisional damages shall specify the disease or type of deterioration in respect of which an application may be made at a future date, and shall also, unless the Court otherwise determines, specify the period within which such application may be made.

(3)   The Court may, on the application of the plaintiff made within the period, if any, specified in paragraph (2), by order extend that period if it thinks it just to do so, and the plaintiff may make more than one such application.

(4)   An order for an award of provisional damages may be made in respect of more than one disease or type of deterioration and may in respect of each disease or deterioration specify a different period within which an application may be made at a future date.

(5)   Orders 13 and 19 shall not apply in relation to an action in which the plaintiff claims provisional damages.]

Commencement 1 July 1985.
Amendments See the note to Order 37, r 7.
Definitions Section 32A: Supreme Court Act 1981, s 32A.
Cross references This rule is applied to the county court by CCR Order 22, r 6A.

[Order 37, r 9 Offer to submit to an award

(1)   Where an application is made for an award of provisional damages, any defendant may at any time (whether or not he makes a payment into court) make a written offer to the plaintiff—

    (a) to tender a sum of money (which may include an amount, to be specified, in respect of interest) in satisfaction of the plaintiff's claim for damages assessed on the assumption that the injured person will not develop the disease or suffer the deterioration referred to in section 32A [and identifying the disease or deterioration in question]; and

(b) to agree to the making of an award of provisional damages.

(2) Any offer made under paragraph (1) shall not be brought to the attention of the Court until after the Court has determined the claim for an award of provisional damages.

(3) Where an offer is made under paragraph (1), the plaintiff may, within 21 days after receipt of the offer, give written notice to the defendant of his acceptance of the offer and shall on such acceptance make an application to the Court for an order in accordance with the provisions of rule 8(2).]

Commencement 1 July 1985.
Amendments See the note to Order 37, r 7.
Para (1): words "and identifying the disease or deterioration in question" inserted by SI 1989/2427, r 21.
Definitions Section 32A: Supreme Court Act 1981, s 32A.
Cross references This rule is applied to the county court by CCR Order 22, r 6A.

[Order 37, r 10 Application for award of further damages

(1) This rule applies where the plaintiff, pursuant to an award of provisional damages, claims further damages.

(2) No application for further damages may be made after the expiration of the period, if any, specified under rule 8(2), or of such period as extended under rule 8(3).

(3) The plaintiff shall give not less than three months' written notice to the defendant of his intention to apply for further damages and, if the defendant is to the plaintiff's knowledge insured in respect of the plaintiff's claim, to the insurers.

(4) The plaintiff must take out a summons for directions as to the future conduct of the action within 21 days after the expiry of the period of notice referred to in paragraph (3).

(5) On the hearing of the summons for directions the Court shall give such directions as may be appropriate for the future conduct of the action, including, but not limited to, the disclosure of medical reports and the place, mode and date of the hearing of the application for further damages.

(6) Only one application for further damages may be made in respect of each disease or type of deterioration specified in the order for the award of provisional damages.

(7) The provisions of Order 29 with regard to the making of interim payments shall, with the necessary modifications, apply where an application is made under this rule.

(8) The Court may include in an award of further damages simple interest at such rate as it thinks fit on all or any part thereof for all or any part of the period between the date of notification of the plaintiff's intention to apply for further damages and the date of the award.]

Commencement 1 July 1985.
Amendments See the note to Order 37, r 7.
Cross references This rule is applied to the county court by CCR Order 22, r 6A.

ORDER 38
[EVIDENCE]

[I GENERAL RULES]

Amendments Word "Evidence" substituted and words "I General Rules" inserted by SI 1969/1105, r 7(1), (2).

Order 38, r 1 General rule: witnesses to be examined orally

Subject to the provisions of these rules and of the [Civil Evidence Act 1968] [and the Civil Evidence Act 1972] and any other enactment relating to evidence, any fact required to be proved at the trial of any action begun by writ by the evidence of witnesses shall be proved by the examination of the witnesses orally and in open court.

Commencement 1 October 1966.
Amendments Words "Civil Evidence Act 1968" substituted by SI 1969/1105, r 7(3); words "and the Civil Evidence Act 1972" inserted by SI 1979/1542, r 9(2).
Cross references See CCR Order 20, r 4.

Order 38, r 2 Evidence by affidavit

(1)   The Court may, at or before the trial of an action begun by writ, order that the affidavit of any witness may be read at the trial if in the circumstances of the case it thinks it reasonable so to order.

(2)   An order under paragraph (1) may be made on such terms as to the filing and giving of copies of the affidavits and as to the production of the deponents for cross-examination as the Court thinks fit but, subject to any such terms and to any subsequent order of the Court, the deponents shall not be subject to cross-examination and need not attend the trial for the purpose.

(3)   In any cause or matter begun by originating summons, originating motion or petition, and on any application made by summons or motion, evidence may be given by affidavit unless in the case of any such cause, matter or application any provision of these rules otherwise provides or the Court otherwise directs, but the Court may, on the application of any party, order the attendance for cross-examination of the person making any such affidavit, and where, after such an order has been made, the person in question does not attend, his affidavit shall not be used as evidence without the leave of the Court.

Commencement 1 October 1966.
Cross references See CCR Order 20, r 6 (see also rr 5, 7, 10).
Forms Order for cross-examination of deponent on affidavit (ChPF33).

[Order 38, r 2A Exchange of witness statements

(1)   The powers of the Court under this rule shall be exercised for the purpose of disposing fairly and expeditiously of the cause or matter before it, and saving costs, having regard to all the circumstances of the case, including (but not limited to)—
    (a)   the extent to which the facts are in dispute or have been admitted;
    (b)   the extent to which the issues of fact are defined by the pleadings;
    (c)   the extent to which information has been or is likely to be provided by further and better particulars, answers to interrogatories or otherwise.

(2)   At the summons for directions in an action commenced by writ the Court shall direct every party to serve on the other parties, within 14 weeks (or such other period as the Court may specify) of the hearing of the summons and on such terms as the Court may specify, written statements of the oral evidence which the party intends to adduce on any issues of fact to be decided at the trial.

The Court may give a direction to any party under this paragraph at any other stage of such an action and at any stage of any other cause or matter.

Order 3, rule 5(3) shall not apply to any period specified by the Court under this paragraph.

(3)   Directions under paragraph (2) or (17) may make different provision with regard to different issues of fact or different witnesses.

(4)   Statements served under this rule shall–
   (a)   be dated and, except for good reason (which should be specified by letter accompanying the statement), be signed by the intended witness and shall include a statement by him that the contents are true to the best of his knowledge and belief;
   (b)   sufficiently identify any documents referred to therein; and
   (c)   where they are to be served by more than one party, be exchanged simultaneously.

(5)   Where a party is unable to obtain a written statement from an intended witness in accordance with paragraph (4)(a), the Court may direct the party wishing to adduce that witness's evidence to provide the other party with the name of the witness and (unless the Court otherwise orders) a statement of the nature of the evidence intended to be adduced.

(6)   Subject to paragraph (9), where the party serving a statement under this rule does not call the witness to whose evidence it relates, no other party may put the statement in evidence at the trial.

(7)   Subject to paragraph (9), where the party serving the statement does call such a witness at the trial–
   (a)   except where the trial is with a jury, the Court may, on such terms as it thinks fit, direct that the statement served, or part of it, shall stand as the evidence in chief of the witness or part of such evidence;
   (b)   the party may not without the consent of the other parties or the leave of the Court adduce evidence from that witness the substance of which is not included in the statement served, except–
      (i)   where the Court's directions under paragraph (2) or (17) specify that statements should be exchanged in relation to only some issues of fact, in relation to any other issues:
      (ii)   in relation to new matters which have arisen since the statement was served on the other party;
   (c)   whether or not the statement or any part of it is referred to during the evidence in chief of the witness, any party may put the statement or any part of it in cross-examination of that witness.

(8)   Nothing in this rule shall make admissible evidence which is otherwise inadmissible.

(9)   Where any statement served is one to which the Civil Evidence Acts 1968 and 1972 apply, paragraphs (6) and (7) shall take effect subject to the provisions of those Acts and Parts III and IV of this Order.

The service of a witness statement under this rule shall not, unless expressly so stated by the party serving the same, be treated as a notice under the said Acts of 1968 and 1972; and where a statement or any part thereof would be admissible in evidence by virtue only of the said Act of 1968 or 1972 the appropriate notice under Part III or Part IV of this Order shall be served with the statement notwithstanding any provision of those Parts as to the time for serving such a notice. Where such a notice is served a counter-notice shall be deemed to have been served under Order 38, rule 26(1).

(10) Where a party fails to comply with a direction for the exchange of witness statements he shall not be entitled to adduce evidence to which the direction related without the leave of the Court.

(11) Where a party serves a witness statement under this rule, no other person may make use of that statement for any purpose other than the purpose of the proceedings in which it was served–
   (a) unless and to the extent that the party serving it gives his consent in writing or the Court gives leave; or
   (b) unless and to the extent that it has been put in evidence (whether pursuant to a direction under paragraph (7)(a) or otherwise).

(12) Subject to paragraph (13), the judge shall, if any person so requests during the course of the trial, direct the associate to certify as open to inspection any witness statement which was ordered to stand as evidence in chief under paragraph (7)(a).

A request under this paragraph may be made orally or in writing.

(13) The judge may refuse to give a direction under paragraph (12) in relation to a witness statement, or may exclude from such a direction any words or passages in a statement, if he considers that inspection should not be available–
   (a) in the interests of justice or national security,
   (b) because of the nature of any expert medical evidence in the statement, or
   (c) for any other sufficient reason.

(14) Where the associate is directed under paragraph (12) to certify a witness statement as open to inspection he shall–
   (a) prepare a certificate which shall be attached to a copy ("the certified copy") of that witness statement; and
   (b) make the certified copy available for inspection.

(15) Subject to any conditions which the Court may by special or general direction impose, any person may inspect and (subject to payment of the prescribed fee) take a copy of the certified copy of a witness statement from the time when the certificate is given until the end of 7 days after the conclusion of the trial.

(16) In this rule–
   (a) any reference in paragraphs (12) to (15) to a witness statement shall, in relation to a witness statement of which only part has been ordered to stand as evidence in chief under paragraph (7)(a), be construed as a reference to that part;
   (b) any reference to inspecting or copying the certified copy of a witness statement shall be construed as including a reference to inspecting or copying a copy of that certified copy.

(17) The Court shall have power to vary or override any of the provisions of this rule (except paragraphs (1), (8) and (12) to (16)) and to give such alternative directions as it thinks fit.]

Commencement 16 November 1992.
Amendments This rule was inserted by SI 1986/1187, r 6; it was subsequently substituted by SI 1992/1907, r 10.
Cross references See CCR Order 20, r 12A.

Order 38, r 3 Evidence of particular facts

(1)   Without prejudice to rule 2, the Court may, at or before the trial of any action, order that evidence of any particular fact shall be given at the trial in such manner as may be specified by the order.

(2)   The power conferred by paragraph (1) extends in particular to ordering that evidence of any particular fact may be given at the trial—

    (a)   by statement on oath of information or belief, or

    (b)   by the production of documents or entries in books, or

    (c)   by copies of documents or entries in books, or

    (d)   in the case of a fact which is or was a matter of common knowledge either generally or in a particular district, by the production of a specified newspaper which contains a statement of that fact.

Commencement 1 October 1966.
Cross references See CCR Order 20 r, 8.

Order 38, r 4 Limitation of expert evidence

The Court may, at or before the trial of any action, order that the number of medical or other expert witnesses who may be called at the trial shall be limited as specified by the order.

Commencement 1 October 1966.

Order 38, r 5 Limitation of plans, etc in evidence

Unless, at or before the trial, the Court for special reasons otherwise orders, no plan, photograph or model shall be receivable in evidence at the trial of an action unless at least 10 days before the commencement of the trial the parties, other than the party producing it, have been given an opportunity to inspect it and to agree to the admission thereof without further proof.

Commencement 1 October 1966.

[Order 38, r 6 Revocation or variation of orders under rules 2 to 5

Any order under rules 2 to 5 (including an order made on appeal) may, on sufficient cause being shown, be revoked or varied by a subsequent order of the Court made at or before the trial.]

Commencement 1 June 1974.
Amendments This rule was substituted by SI 1974/295, r 5(1).
Cross references See CCR Order 20, r 9(2), (3).

[Order 38, r 7 Evidence of finding on foreign law

(1)   A party to any cause or matter who intends to adduce in evidence a finding or decision on a question of foreign law by virtue of section 4(2) of the Civil Evidence

Act 1972 shall—

    (a) in the case of an action to which Order 25, rule 1, applies, within 14 days after the pleadings in the action are deemed to be closed, and

    (b) in the case of any other cause or matter, within 21 days after the date on which an appointment for the first hearing of the cause or matter is obtained,

or, in either case, within such other period as the Court may specify, serve notice of his intention on every other party to the proceedings.

(2)   The notice shall specify the question on which the finding or decision was given or made and specify the document in which it is reported or recorded in citable form.

(3)   In any cause or matter in which evidence may be given by affidavit, an affidavit specifying the matters contained in paragraph (2) shall constitute notice under paragraph (1) if served within the period mentioned in that paragraph.]

Commencement 1 June 1974.
Amendments This rule was substituted by SI 1974/295, r 5(1).
Cross references See CCR Order 20, r 25.

Order 38, r 8 Application to trials of issues, references, etc

The foregoing rules of this Order [(other than rule 2A)] shall apply to trials of issues or questions of fact or law, references, inquiries and assessments of damages as they apply to the trial of actions.

Commencement 1 October 1966.
Amendments Words "(other than rule 2A)" inserted by SI 1986/1187, r 7.

Order 38, r 9 Depositions: when receivable in evidence at trial

(1)   No deposition taken in any cause or matter shall be received in evidence at the trial of the cause or matter unless—

    (a) the deposition was taken in pursuance of an order under Order 39, rule 1, and

    (b) either the party against whom the evidence is offered consents or it is proved to the satisfaction of the Court that the deponent is dead, or beyond the jurisdiction of the Court or unable from sickness or other infirmity to attend the trial.

(2)   A party intending to use any deposition in evidence at the trial of a cause or matter must, a reasonable time before the trial, give notice of his intention to do so to the other party.

(3)   A deposition purporting to be signed by the person before whom it was taken shall be receivable in evidence without proof of the signature being the signature of that person.

Commencement 1 October 1966.
Cross references See CCR Order 20 r 13.

Order 38, r 10 Court documents admissible or receivable in evidence

(1)   Office copies of writs, records, pleadings and documents filed in the High

Court shall be admissible in evidence in any cause or matter and between all parties to the same extent as the original would be admissible.

(2)   Without prejudice to the provisions of any enactment, every document purporting to be sealed with the seal of any office or department of the Supreme Court shall be received in evidence without further proof, and any document purporting to be so sealed and to be a copy of a document filed in, or issued out of, that office or department shall be deemed to be an office copy of that document without further proof unless the contrary is shown.

Commencement 1 October 1966.

Order 38, r 11 Evidence of consent of new trustee to act

A document purporting to contain the written consent of a person to act as trustee and to bear his signature verified by some other person shall be evidence of such consent.

Commencement 1 October 1966.
Forms Consent to act as trustee (ChPF31).

Order 38, r 12 Evidence at trial may be used in subsequent proceedings

Any evidence taken at the trial of any cause or matter may be used in any subsequent proceedings in that cause or matter.

Commencement 1 October 1966.

Order 38, r 13 Order to produce document at proceeding other than trial

(1)   At any stage in a cause or matter the Court may order any person to attend any proceeding in the cause or matter and produce any document, to be specified or described in the order, the production of which appears to the Court to be necessary for the purpose of that proceeding.

(2)   No person shall be compelled by an order under paragraph (1) to produce any document at a proceeding in a cause or matter which he could not be compelled to produce at the trial of that cause or matter.

Commencement 1 October 1966.

[II Writs of Subpoena]

Amendments Words "II Writs of Subpoena" inserted by SI 1969/1105, r 7(1), (4).

Order 38, r 14 Form and issue of writ of subpoena

(1)   A writ of subpoena must be in Form No 28, 29 or 30 in Appendix A, whichever is appropriate.

(2)   Issue of a writ of subpoena takes place upon its being sealed by an officer of the office out of which it is issued.

(3)   Where a writ of subpoena is to be issued in a cause or matter which is not proceeding in a district registry, the appropriate office for the issue of the writ is the

Central Office or, if the cause or matter has been set down for trial [outside the Royal Courts of Justice], either the Central Office or the registry for the district comprising the city or town at which the cause or matter has been set down for trial.

(4)   Where a writ of subpoena is to be issued in a cause or matter which is proceeding in a district registry, the appropriate office for the issue of the writ is—

- (a) that registry, or
- (b) if the cause or matter has been set down for trial at a city or town not comprised in the district of that registry, either that registry or the registry for the district comprising that city or town, or
- (c) if the cause or matter has been set down for trial at the Royal Courts of Justice, either the Central Office or the registry in which the cause or matter is proceeding.

(5)   Before a writ of subpoena is issued a praecipe for the issue of the writ must be filed in the office out of which the writ is to issue; and the praecipe must contain the name and address of the party issuing the writ, if he is acting in person, or the name or firm and business address of that party's solicitor and also (if the solicitor is the agent of another) the name or firm and business address of his principal.

Commencement 1 October 1966.
Amendments Para (3) : words "outside the Royal Courts of Justice" substituted by SI 1971/1955, r 14.
Cross references See CCR Order 20, r 12.
Forms Praecipe (PF75).

Order 38, r 15 More than one name may be included in one writ of subpoena

The names of two or more persons may be included in one writ of subpoena ad testificandum.

Commencement 1 October 1966.

Order 38, r 16 Amendment of writ of subpoena

Where there is a mistake in any person's name or address in a writ of subpoena, then, if the writ has not been served, the party by whom the writ was issued may have the writ re-sealed in correct form by filing a second praecipe under rule 14(5) indorsed with the words "Amended and re-sealed".

Commencement 1 October 1966.

Order 38, r 17 Service of writ of subpoena

A writ of subpoena must be served personally and, subject to rule 19, the service shall not be valid unless effected within 12 weeks after the date of issue of the writ [and not less than four days, or such other period as the Court may fix, before the day on which attendance before the Court is required].

Commencement 1 October 1966.
Amendments Words from "and not less than four days" to the end inserted by SI 1980/1010, r 9.
Cross references See CCR Order 20, r 12(5)-(7).

Order 38, r 18 Duration of writ of subpoena

Subject to rule 19, a writ of subpoena continues to have effect until the conclusion of the trial at which the attendance of the witness is required.

Commencement 1 October 1966.

Order 38, r 19 Writ of subpoena in aid of inferior court or tribunal

(1)   The office of the Supreme Court out of which a writ of a subpoena ad testificandum or a writ of subpoena duces tecum in aid of an inferior court or tribunal may be issued is the Crown Office, and no order of the Court for the issue of such a writ is necessary.

(2)   A writ of subpoena in aid of an inferior court or tribunal continues to have effect until the disposal of the proceedings before that court or tribunal at which the attendance of the witness is required.

(3)   A writ of subpoena issued in aid of an inferior court or tribunal must be served personally.

(4)   Unless a writ of subpoena issued in aid of an inferior court or tribunal is duly served on the person to whom it is directed not less than 4 days, or such other period as the Court may fix, before the day on which the attendance of that person before the court or tribunal is required by the writ, that person shall not be liable to any penalty or process for failing to obey the writ.

(5)   An application to set aside a writ of subpoena issued in aid of an inferior court or tribunal may be heard by a master of the Queen's Bench Division.

Commencement 1 October 1966.

[III Hearsay Evidence

Order 38, r 20 Interpretation and application

(1)   In this Part of this Order "the Act" means the Civil Evidence Act 1968 and any expressions used in this Part of this Order and in Part I of the Act have the same meanings in this Part of this Order as they have in the said Part I.

(2)   This Part of this Order shall apply in relation to the trial or hearing of an issue or question arising in a cause or matter, and to a reference, inquiry and assessment of damages, as it applies in relation to the trial or hearing of a cause or matter.]

Commencement 1 October 1969.
Amendments Order 38, Pt III (rr 20–33) was added by SI 1969/1105, r 7(5).
Cross references See CCR Order 20, r 14.

[Order 38, r 21 Notice of intention to give certain statements in evidence

(1)   Subject to the provisions of this rule, a party to a cause or matter who desires to give in evidence at the trial or hearing of the cause or matter any statement which is admissible in evidence by virtue of section 2, 4 or 5 of the Act must—
    (a)   in the case of a cause or matter which is required to be set down for trial or hearing or adjourned into court, within 21 days after it is set down or so adjourned, or within such other period as the Court may specify, and
    (b)   in the case of any other cause or matter, within 21 days after the date on which an appointment for the first hearing of the cause or matter is obtained, or within such other period as the Court may specify,

serve on every other party to the cause or matter notice of his desire to do so, and the notice must comply with the provisions of rule 22, 23 or 24, as the circumstances of the case require.

(2)   Paragraph (1) shall not apply in relation to any statement which is admissible as evidence of any fact stated therein by virtue not only of the said section 2, 4 or 5 but by virtue also of any other statutory provision within the meaning of section 1 of the Act.

(3)   Paragraph (1) shall not apply in relation to any statement which any party to a probate action desires to give in evidence at the trial of that action and which is alleged to have been made by the deceased person whose estate is the subject of the action.

(4)   Where by virtue of any provision of these rules or of any order or direction of the Court the evidence in any proceedings is to be given by affidavit then, without prejudice to paragraph (2), paragraph (1) shall not apply in relation to any statement which any party to the proceedings desires to have included in any affidavit to be used on his behalf in the proceedings, but nothing in this paragraph shall affect the operation of Order 41, rule 5, or the powers of the Court under Order 38, rule 3.

(5)   Order 65, rule 9, shall not apply to a notice under this rule but the Court may direct that the notice need not be served on any party who at the time when service is to be effected is in default as to [acknowledgment of service] or who has no address for service.]

Commencement   1 October 1969.
Amendments   See the note to Order 38, r 20.
Para (5): words "acknowledgement of service" substituted by SI 1979/1716, r 48, Schedule, Pt 1.
Definitions   The Act: Civil Evidence Act 1968.
Cross references   See CCR Order 20, r 15.

[Order 38, r 22 Statement admissible by virtue of section 2 of the Act: contents of notice

(1)   If the statement is admissible by virtue of section 2 of the Act and was made otherwise than in a document, the notice must contain particulars of—
    (a)   the time, place and circumstances at or in which the statement was made;
    (b)   the person by whom, and the person to whom, the statement was made; and
    (c)   the substance of the statement or, if material, the words used.

(2)   If the statement is admissible by virtue of the said section 2 and was made in a document, a copy or transcript of the document, or of the relevant part thereof, must be annexed to the notice and the notice must contain such (if any) of the particulars mentioned in paragraph (1)(a) and (b) as are not apparent on the face of the document or part.

(3)   If the party giving the notice alleges that any person, particulars of whom are contained in the notice, cannot or should not be called as a witness at the trial or hearing for any of the reasons specified in rule 25, the notice must contain a statement to that effect specifying the reason relied on.]

Commencement   1 October 1969.
Amendments   See the note to Order 38, r 20.
Definitions   The Act: Civil Evidence Act 1968.
Cross references   This rule applies to the county court by virtue of CCR Order 20, r 16.

[Order 38, r 23 Statement admissible by virtue of section 4 of the Act: contents of notice

(1) If the statement is admissible by virtue of section 4 of the Act, the notice must have annexed to it a copy or transcript of the document containing the statement, or of the relevant part thereof, and must contain—

    (a) particulars of—

        (i) the person by whom the record containing the statement was compiled;

        (ii) the person who originally supplied the information from which the record was compiled; and

        (iii) any other person through whom that information was supplied to the compiler of that record;

        and, in the case of any such person as is referred to in (i) or (iii) above, a description of the duty under which that person was acting when compiling that record or supplying information from which that record was compiled, as the case may be;

    (b) if not apparent on the face of the document annexed to the notice, a description of the nature of the record which, or part of which, contains the statement; and

    (c) particulars of the time, place and circumstances at or in which that record or part was compiled.

(2) If the party giving the notice alleges that any person, particulars of whom are contained in the notice, cannot or should not be called as a witness at the trial or hearing for any of the reasons specified in rule 25, the notice must contain a statement to that effect specifying the reason relied on.]

Commencement 1 October 1969.
Amendments See the note to Order 38, r 20.
Definitions The Act: Civil Evidence Act 1968.
Cross references This rule applies to the county court by virtue of CCR Order 20, r 16.

[Order 38, r 24 Statement admissible by virtue of section 5 of the Act: contents of notice

(1) If the statement is contained in a document produced by a computer and is admissible by virtue of section 5 of the Act, the notice must have annexed to it a copy or transcript of the document containing the statement, or of the relevant part thereof, and must contain particulars of—

    (a) a person who occupied a responsible position in relation to the management of the relevant activities for the purposes of which the computer was used regularly during the material period to store or process information;

    (b) a person who at the material time occupied such a position in relation to the supply of information to the computer, being information which is reproduced in the statement or information from which the information contained in the statement is derived;

    (c) a person who occupied such a position in relation to the operation of the computer during the material period;

and where there are two or more persons who fall within any of the foregoing subparagraphs and some only of those persons are at the date of service of the notice capable of being called as witnesses at the trial or hearing, the person particulars of whom are to be contained in the notice must be such one of those persons as is at that date so capable.

(2)   The notice must also state whether the computer was operating properly throughout the material period and, if not, whether any respect in which it was not operating properly or was out of operation during any part of that period was such as to affect the production of the document in which the statement is contained or the accuracy of its contents.

(3)   If the party giving the notice alleges that any person, particulars of whom are contained in the notice, cannot or should not be called as a witness at the trial or hearing for any of the reasons specified in rule 25, the notice must contain a statement to that effect specifying the reason relied on.]

Commencement 1 October 1969.
Amendments See the note to Order 38, r 20.
Definitions The Act: Civil Evidence Act 1968.
Cross references This rule applies to the county court by virtue of CCR Order 20, r 16.

[Order 38, r 25 Reasons for not calling a person as a witness

The reasons referred to in rules 22(3), 23(2) and 24(3) are that the person in question is dead, or beyond the seas, or unfit by reason of his bodily or mental condition to attend as a witness or that despite the exercise of reasonable diligence it has not been possible to identify or find him or that he cannot reasonably be expected to have any recollection of matters relevant to the accuracy or otherwise of the statement to which the notice relates.]

Commencement 1 October 1969.
Amendments See the note to Order 38, r 20.
Cross references This rule applies to the county court by virtue of CCR Order 20, r 16.

[Order 38, r 26 Counter-notice requiring person to be called as a witness

(1)   Subject to paragraphs (2) and (3), any party to a cause or matter on whom a notice under rule 21 is served may within 21 days after service of the notice on him serve on the party who gave the notice a counter-notice requiring that party to call as a witness at the trial or hearing of the cause or matter any person (naming him) particulars of whom are contained in the notice.

(2)   Where any notice under rule 21 contains a statement that any person particulars of whom are contained in the notice cannot or should not be called as a witness for the reason specified therein, a party shall not be entitled to serve a counter-notice under this rule requiring that person to be called as a witness at the trial or hearing of the cause or matter unless he contends that that person can or, as the case may be, should be called, and in that case he must include in his counter-notice a statement to that effect.

(3)   Where a statement to which a notice under rule 21 relates is one to which rule 28 applies, no party on whom the notice is served shall be entitled to serve a counter-notice under this rule in relation to that statement, but the foregoing provision is without prejudice to the right of any party to apply to the Court under rule 28 for directions with respect to the admissibility of that statement.

(4)   If any party to a cause or matter by whom a notice under rule 21 is served fails to comply with a counter-notice duly served on him under this rule, then, unless any of the reasons specified in rule 25 applies in relation to the person named in the

counter-notice, and without prejudice to the powers of the Court under rule 29, the statement to which the notice under rule 21 relates shall not be admissible at the trial or hearing of the cause or matter as evidence of any fact stated therein by virtue of section 2, 4 or 5 of the Act, as the case may be.]

Commencement 1 October 1969.
Amendments See the note to Order 38, r 20.
Definitions The Act: Civil Evidence Act 1968.
Cross references See CCR Order 20, r 17.

[Order 38, r 27 Determination of question whether person can or should be called as a witness

(1) Where in any cause or matter a question arises whether any of the reasons specified in rule 25 applies in relation to a person particulars of whom are contained in a notice under rule 21, the Court may, on the application of any party to the cause or matter, determine that question before the trial or hearing of the cause or matter or give directions for it to be determined before the trial or hearing and for the manner in which it is to be so determined.

(2) Unless the Court otherwise directs, the summons by which an application under paragraph (1) is made must be served by the party making the application on every other party to the cause or matter.

(3) Where any such question as is referred to in paragraph (1) has been determined under or by virtue of that paragraph, no application to have it determined afresh at the trial or hearing of the cause or matter may be made unless the evidence which it is sought to adduce in support of the application could not with reasonable diligence have been adduced at the hearing which resulted in the determination.]

Commencement 1 October 1969.
Amendments See the note to Order 38, r 20.
Cross references See CCR Order 20, r 18.

[Order 38, r 28 Directions with respect to statement made in previous proceedings

Where a party to a cause or matter has given notice in accordance with rule 21 that he desires to give in evidence at the trial or hearing of the cause or matter—
- (a) a statement falling within section 2(1) of the Act which was made by a person, whether orally or in a document, in the course of giving evidence in some other legal proceedings (whether civil or criminal), or
- (b) a statement falling within section 4(1) of the Act which is contained in a record of direct oral evidence given in some other legal proceedings (whether civil or criminal),

any party to the cause or matter may apply to the Court for directions under this rule, and the Court hearing such an application may give directions as to whether, and if so on what conditions, the party desiring to give the statement in evidence will be permitted to do so and (where applicable) as to the manner in which that statement and any other evidence given in those other proceedings is to be proved.]

Commencement 1 October 1969.
Amendments See the note to Order 38, r 20.
Definitions The Act: Civil Evidence Act 1968.
Cross references See CCR Order 20, r 19.

[Order 38, r 29 Power of Court to allow statement to be given in evidence

(1)   Without prejudice to section 2(2)(a) and 4(2)(a) of the Act and rule 28, the Court may, if it thinks it just to do so, allow a statement falling within section 2(1), 4(1) or 5(1) of the Act to be given in evidence at the trial or hearing of a cause or matter notwithstanding—

    (a)   that the statement is one in relation to which rule 21(1) applies and that the party desiring to give the statement in evidence has failed to comply with that rule, or

    (b)   that that party has failed to comply with any requirement of a counter-notice relating to that statement which was served on him in accordance with rule 26.

(2)   Without prejudice to the generality of paragraph (1), the Court may exercise its power under that paragraph to allow a statement to be given in evidence at the trial or hearing of a cause or matter if a refusal to exercise that power might oblige the party desiring to give the statement in evidence to call as a witness at the trial or hearing an opposite party or a person who is or was at the material time the servant or agent of an opposite party.]

Commencement   1 October 1969.
Amendments   See the note to Order 38, r 20.
Definitions   The Act: Civil Evidence Act 1968.
Cross references   See CCR Order 20, r 20.

[Order 38, r 30 Restriction on adducing evidence as to credibility of maker, etc of certain statements

Where—

    (a)   a notice given under rule 21 in a cause or matter relates to a statement which is admissible by virtue of section 2 or 4 of the Act, and

    (b)   the person who made the statement, or, as the case may be, the person who originally supplied the information from which the record containing the statement was compiled, is not called as a witness at the trial or hearing of the cause or matter, and

    (c)   none of the reasons mentioned in rule 25 applies so as to prevent the party who gave the notice from calling that person as a witness,

no other party to the cause or matter shall be entitled, except with the leave of the Court, to adduce in relation to that person any evidence which could otherwise be adduced by him by virtue of section 7 of the Act unless he gave a counter-notice under rule 26 in respect of that person or applied under rule 28 for a direction that that person be called as a witness at the trial or hearing of the cause or matter.]

Commencement   1 October 1969.
Amendments   See the note to Order 38, r 20.
Definitions   The Act: Civil Evidence Act 1968.
Cross references   See CCR Order 20, r 21.

[Order 38, r 31 Notice required of intention to give evidence of certain inconsistent statements

(1)   Where a person, particulars of whom were contained in a notice given under rule 21 in a cause or matter, is not to be called as a witness at the trial or hearing of the cause or matter, any party to the cause or matter who is entitled and intends to adduce in relation to that person any evidence which is admissible for the purpose mentioned in

section 7(1)(b) of the Act must, not more than 21 days after service of that notice of him, serve on the party who gave that notice, notice of his intention to do so.

(2)   Rule 22(1) and (2) shall apply to a notice under this rule as if the notice were a notice under rule 21 and the statement to which the notice relates were a statement admissible by virtue of section 2 of the Act.

(3)   The Court may, if it thinks it just to do so, allow a party to give in evidence at the trial or hearing of a cause or matter any evidence which is admissible for the purpose mentioned in the said section 7(1)(b) notwithstanding that that party has failed to comply with the provisions of paragraph (1).]

Commencement 1 October 1969.
Amendments See the note to Order 38, r 20.
Definitions The Act: Civil Evidence Act 1968.
Cross references See CCR Order 20, r 22.

[Order 38, r 32 Costs

If—

(a)   a party to a cause or matter serves a counter-notice under rule 26 in respect of any person who is called as a witness at the trial of the cause or matter in compliance with a requirement of the counter-notice, and

(b)   it appears to the Court that it was unreasonable to require that person to be called as a witness,

then, without prejudice to Order 62 and, in particular, [to rule 10(1)] thereof, the Court may direct that any costs to that party in respect of the preparation and service of the counter-notice shall not be allowed to him and that any costs occasioned by the counter-notice to any other party shall be paid by him to that other party.]

Commencement 1 October 1969.
Amendments See the note to Order 38, r 20.
Words "to rule 10(1)" substituted by SI 1986/632, r 6.
Cross references See CCR Order 20, r 23.

[Order 38, r 33 Certain powers exercisable in chambers

The jurisdiction of the Court under sections 2(2)(a), 2(3), 4(2)(a) and 6(1) of the Act may be exercised in chambers.]

Commencement 1 October 1969.
Amendments See the note to Order 38, r 20.
Definitions The Act: Civil Evidence Act 1968.

[Order 38, r 34 Statements of opinion

Where a party to a cause or matter desires to give in evidence by virtue of Part I of the Act, as extended by section 1(1) of the Civil Evidence Act 1972, a statement of opinion other than a statement to which Part IV of this Order applies, the provisions of rules 20 to 23 and 25 to 33 shall apply with such modifications as the Court may direct or the circumstances of the case may require.]

Commencement 1 June 1974.
Amendments This rule was added by SI 1974/295, r 5(2).
Definitions The Act: Civil Evidence Act 1968.
Cross references See CCR Order 20, r 26.

[IV Expert Evidence

Order 38, r 35 Interpretation

In this Part of this Order a reference to a summons for directions includes a reference to any summons or application to which, under any of these Rules, Order 25, rules 2 to 7, apply and expressions used in this Part of this Order which are used in the Civil Evidence Act 1972 have the same meanings in this Part of this Order as in that Act.]

Commencement1 June 1974.
Amendments Order 38, Pt IV (rr 35–44) was added by SI 1974/295, r 5(2).

[Order 38, r 36 Restrictions on adducing expert evidence

(1)   Except with the leave of the Court or where all parties agree, no expert evidence may be adduced at the trial or hearing of any cause or matter unless the party seeking to adduce the evidence
   [(a)]   has applied to the Court to determine whether a direction should be given under rule 37 . . . or 41 (whichever is appropriate) and has complied with any direction given on the application[, or
   (b)   has complied with automatic directions taking effect under Order 25, rule 8(1)(b).]

(2)   Nothing in paragraph (1) shall apply to evidence which is permitted to be given by affidavit or shall affect the enforcement under any other provision of these Rules (except Order 45, rule 5) of a direction given under this Part of this Order.]

Commencement 1 June 1974.
Amendments See the note to Order 38, r 35.
Para (1): sub-para (a) numbered as such, word "or" and sub-para (b) added, by SI 1980/1010, r 10(1); words omitted revoked by SI 1987/1423, r 40.
Cross references See CCR Order 20, r 27.

[Order 38, r 37 Direction that expert report be disclosed

(1)   Subject to paragraph (2), where in any cause or matter an application is made under rule 36(1) in respect of oral expert evidence, then, unless the Court considers that there are special reasons for not doing so, it shall direct that the substance of the evidence be disclosed in the form of a written report or reports to such other parties and within such period as the Court may specify.

(2)   Nothing in paragraph (1) shall require a party to disclose a further medical report if he proposes to rely at the trial only on the report provided pursuant to Order 18, rule 12(1A) or (1B) but, where a party claiming damages for personal injuries discloses a further report, that report shall be accompanied by a statement of the special damages claimed and, in this paragraph, "statement of the special damages claimed" has the same meaning as in Order 18, rule 12(1C).]

Commencement 4 June 1990.
Amendments See the note to Order 38, r 35.
This rule was subseqently substituted by SI 1989/2427, r 15.
Cross references This rule is applied to the county court by virtue of CCR Order 20, r 28.

[Order 38, r 38 Meeting of experts

In any cause or matter the Court may, if it thinks fit, direct that there be a meeting "without prejudice" of such experts within such periods before or after the disclosure of their reports as the Court may specify, for the purpose of identifying those parts of their evidence which are in issue. Where such a meeting takes place the experts may prepare a joint statement indicating those parts of their evidence on which they are, and those on which they are not, in agreement.]

Commencement 1 October 1987.
Amendments See the note to Order 38, r 35.
This rule was subsequently substituted by SI 1987/1423, r 41.
Cross references This rule is applied to the county court by virtue of CCR Order 20, r 28.

[Order 38, r 39 Disclosure of part of expert evidence

Where the Court considers that any circumstances rendering it undesirable to give a direction under rule 37 . . . relate to part only of the evidence sought to be adduced, the Court may, if it thinks fit, direct disclosure of the remainder.]

Commencement 1 June 1974.
Amendments See the note to Order 38, r 35.
Words omitted revoked by SI 1987/1423, r 42.
Cross references This rule is applied to the county court by virtue of CCR Order 20, r 28.

Order 38, r 40 *(revoked by SI 1980/1010)*

[Order 38, r 41 Expert evidence contained in statement

Where an application is made under rule 36 in respect of expert evidence contained in a statement and the applicant alleges that the maker of the statement cannot or should not be called as a witness, the Court may direct that the provisions of rules 20 to 23 and 25 to 33 shall apply with such modifications as the Court thinks fit.]

Commencement1 June 1974.
Amendments See the note to Order 38, r 35.
Cross references This rule is applied to the county court by virtue of CCR Order 20, r 28.

[Order 38, r 42 Putting in evidence expert report disclosed by another party

A party to any cause or matter may put in evidence any expert report disclosed to him by any other party in accordance with this Part of this Order.]

Commencement 1 June 1974.
Amendments See the note to Order 38, r 35.
Cross references This rule is applied to the county court by virtue of CCR Order 20, r 28.

[Order 38, r 43 Time for putting expert report in evidence

Where a party to any cause or matter calls as a witness the maker of a report which has been disclosed . . . in accordance with a direction given under rule 37 . . . , the report may be put in evidence at the commencement of its maker's examination in chief or at such other time as the Court may direct.]

Commencement 1 June 1974.
Amendments See the note to Order 38, r 35.
First words omitted revoked by SI 1982/1111, r 115, Schedule; second words omitted revoked by SI 1987/1423, r 43.
Cross references This rule is applied to the county court by virtue of CCR Order 20, r 28.

[Order 38, r 44 Revocation and variation of directions

Any direction given under this Part of this Order may on sufficient cause being shown be revoked or varied by a subsequent direction given at or before the trial of the cause or matter.]

Commencement 1 June 1974.
Amendments See the note to Order 38, r 35.

ORDER 39

Evidence by Deposition: Examiners of the Court

Order 39, r 1 Power to order depositions to be taken

(1)　The Court may, in any cause or matter where it appears necessary for the purposes of justice, make an order (in Form No 32 in Appendix A) for the examination on oath before a judge, an officer or examiner of the Court or some other person, at any place, of any person.

(2)　An order under paragraph (1) may be made on such terms (including, in particular, terms as to the giving of discovery before the examination takes place) as the Court thinks fit[, and may contain an order for the production of any document which appears to the Court to be necessary for the purposes of the examination.]

Commencement　1 October 1966.
Amendments　Para (2): words from ", and may contain an order" to the end added by SI 1984/1051, r 4.
Cross references　See CCR Order 20, r 13 (which is limited to examinations in England and Wales) which incorporates Order 39, rr 7–11, 13.

Order 39, r 2 Where person to be examined is out of the jurisdiction

(1)　Where the person in relation to whom an order under rule 1 is required is out of the jurisdiction, an application may be made—
   - (a)　for an order (in Form No 34 in Appendix A) under that rule for the issue of a letter of request to the judicial authorities of the country in which that person is to take, or cause to be taken, the evidence of that person, or
   - (b)　if the government of that country allows a person in that country to be examined before a person appointed by the Court, for an order (in Form No 37 in Appendix A) under that rule appointing a special examiner to take the evidence of that person in that country.

(2)　An application may be made for the appointment as special examiner of a British consul in the country in which the evidence is to be taken or his deputy—
   - (a)　if there subsists with respect to that country a Civil Procedure Convention providing for the taking of the evidence of any person in that country for the assistance of proceedings in the High Court, or
   - (b)　with the consent of the Secretary of State.

Commencement　1 October 1966.

Order 39, r 3 Order for issue of letter of request

(1)　Where an order is made under rule 1 for the issue of a letter of request to the judicial authorities of a country to take, or cause to be taken, the evidence of any person in that country the following provisions of this rule shall apply.

(2)　The party obtaining the order must prepare the letter of request and lodge it in the Central Office, and the letter must be in Form No 35 in Appendix A, with such variations as the order may require.

(3)　If the evidence of the person to be examined is to be obtained by means of written questions, there must be lodged with the letter of request a copy of the interrogatories and cross-interrogatories to be put to him on examination.

(4) . . . , each document lodged under paragraph (2) or (3) must be accompanied by a translation of the document in the official language of [the country in which the examination is to be taken] or, if there is more than one official language of that country, in any one of those languages which is appropriate to the place in that country where the examination is to be taken [unless—

(a) the senior master has given a general direction in relation to that country that no translation need be provided, or

(b) the official language or one of the official languages of that country is English.]

(5) Every translation lodged under paragraph (4) must be certified by the person making it to be a correct translation; and the certificate must contain a statement of that person's full name, of his address and of his qualifications for making the translation.

(6) The party obtaining the order must, when he lodges in the Central Office the documents mentioned in paragraphs (2) to (5), also file in that office an undertaking signed by him or his solicitor to be responsible personally for all expenses incurred by the Secretary of State in respect of the letter of request and, on receiving due notification of the amount of those expenses, to pay that amount to the Finance Officer of the office of the Secretary of State and to produce a receipt for the payment to the proper officer of the High Court.

Commencement 1 October 1966.
Amendments Para (4): words omitted revoked, words "the country in which the examination is to be taken" substituted, word "unless" and subsequent sub-paras (a), (b) added, by SI 1976/337, r 6.
Forms Solicitor's undertaking (PF78).

[Order 39, r 3A Examination otherwise than on oath

Notwithstanding the provisions of rule 1, where the person to be examined is out of the jurisdiction that person may be examined on oath or affirmation or otherwise in accordance with the procedure of the country in which the examination is to take place.]

Commencement 1 October 1984.
Amendments This rule was inserted by SI 1984/1051, r 5.

Order 39, r 4 Enforcing attendance of witness at examination

Where an order has been made under rule 1—

(a) for the examination of any person before an officer or examiner of the Court or some other person (in this rule and rules 5 to 14 referred to as "the examiner"), or

(b) for the cross-examination before the examiner of any person who has made an affidavit which is to be used in any cause or matter,

the attendance of that person before the examiner and the production by him of any document at the examination may be enforced by writ of subpoena in like manner as the attendance of a witness and the production by a witness of a document at a trial may be enforced.

Commencement 1 October 1966.

Order 39, r 5 Refusal of witness to attend, be sworn, etc

(1) If any person, having been duly summoned by writ of subpoena to attend before the examiner, refuses or fails to attend or refuses to be sworn for the purpose of the examination or to answer any lawful question or produce any document

therein, a certificate of his refusal or failure, signed by the examiner, must be filed in the district registry (if any) in which the cause or matter is proceeding and otherwise in the Central Office, and upon the filing of the certificate the party by whom the attendance of that person was required may apply to the Court for an order requiring that person to attend, or to be sworn, or to answer any question or produce any document, as the case may be.

(2)   An application for an order under this rule may be made ex parte.

(3)   If the Court makes an order under this rule it may order the person against whom the order is made to pay any costs occasioned by his refusal or failure.

(4)   A person who wilfully disobeys any order made against him under paragraph (1) is guilty of contempt of court.

Commencement   1 October 1966.

Order 39, r 6 Appointment of time and place for examination

(1)   The examiner must give the party on whose application the order for examination was made by a notice appointing the place and time at which, subject to any application by the parties, the examination shall be taken, and such time shall, having regard to the convenience of the persons to be examined and all the circumstances of the case, be as soon as practicable after the making of the order.

(2)   The party to whom a notice under paragraph (1) is given must, on receiving it, forthwith give notice of the appointment to all the other parties.

Commencement   1 October 1966.
Cross references   See CCR Order 20, r 13(3).

Order 39, r 7 Examiner to have certain documents

The party on whose application the order for examination before the examiner was made must furnish the examiner with copies of such of the documents in the cause or matter as are necessary to inform the examiner of the questions at issue in the cause or matter.

Commencement   1 October 1966.
Cross references   This rule is applied to the county court by virtue of CCR Order 20, r 13.

Order 39, r 8 Conduct of examination

(1)   Subject to any directions contained in the order for examination—
   (a)   any person ordered to be examined before the examiner may be cross-examined and re-examined, and
   (b)   the examination, cross-examination and re-examination of persons before the examiner shall be conducted in like manner as at the trial of a cause or matter.

(2)   The examiner may put any question to any person examined before him as to the meaning of any answer made by that person or as to any matter arising in the course of the examination.

(3)   The examiner may, if necessary, adjourn the examination from time to time.

Commencement   1 October 1966.
Cross references   This rule is applied to the county court by virtue of CCR Order 20, r 13.

Order 39, r 9 Examination of additional witnesses

The examiner may, with the written consent of all the parties to the cause or matter, take the examination of any person in addition to those named or provided for in the order for examination, and must annex such consent to the original deposition of that person.

Commencement 1 October 1966.
Cross references This rule is applied to the county court by virtue of CCR Order 20, r 13.

Order 39, r 10 Objection to questions

(1)   If any person being examined before the examiner objects to answer any question put to him, or if objection is taken to any such question, that question, the ground for the objection and the answer to any such question to which objection is taken must be set out in the deposition of that person or in a statement annexed thereto.

(2)   The validity of the ground for objecting to answer any such question or for objecting to any such question shall be decided by the Court and not by the examiner, but the examiner must state to the parties his opinion thereon, and the statement of his opinion must be set out in the deposition or in a statement annexed thereto.

(3)   If the Court decides against the person taking the objection it may order him to pay the costs occasioned by his objection.

Commencement 1 October 1966.
Cross references This rule is applied to the county court by virtue of CCR Order 20, r 13.

Order 39, r 11 Taking of depositions

(1)   The deposition of any person examined before the examiner must be taken down by the examiner or a shorthand writer or some other person in the presence of the examiner but, subject to paragraph (2) and rule 10(1), the deposition need not set out every question and answer so long as it contains as nearly as may be the statement of the person examined.

(2)   The examiner may direct the exact words of any particular question and the answer thereto to be set out in the deposition if that question and answer appear to him to have special importance.

(3)   The deposition of any person shall be read to him, and he shall be asked to sign it, in the presence of such of the parties as may attend, but the parties may agree in writing to dispense with the foregoing provision.

If a person refuses to sign a deposition when asked under this paragraph to do so, the examiner must sign the deposition.

(4)   The original deposition of any person, authenticated by the signature of the examiner before whom it was taken, must be sent by the examiner to the district registry (if any) in which the cause or matter is proceeding and otherwise to the Central Office and shall be filed therein.

[(5)   Where a deposition is filed in the Central Office and the cause or matter is proceeding in the Chancery Division in the Royal Courts of Justice, a copy of the deposition shall be made in the Central Office and transmitted to Chancery Chambers.]

Commencement 1 October 1982 (para (5)); 1 October 1966 (remainder).
Amendments Para (5): inserted by SI 1982/1111, r 47.
Cross references This rule is applied to the county court by virtue of CCR Order 20, r 13.

Order 39, r 12 Time taken by examination to be indorsed on depositions

Before sending any deposition to a district registry or the Central Office under rule 11(4), the examiner must indorse on the deposition a statement signed by him of the time occupied in taking the examination and the fees received in respect thereof.

Commencement 1 October 1966.

Order 39, r 13 Special report by examiner

The examiner may make a special report to the Court with regard to any examination taken before him and with regard to the absence or conduct of any person thereat, and the Court may direct such proceedings to be taken, or make such order, on the report as it thinks fit.

Commencement 1 October 1966.
Cross references This rule is applied to the county court by virtue of CCR Order 20, r 13.

Order 39, r 14 Order for payment of examiner's fees

(1) If the fees and expenses due to an examiner are not paid he may report that fact to the Court, and the Court may direct the official solicitor to apply for an order against the party on whose application the order for examination was made to pay the examiner the fees and expenses due to him in respect of the examination.

(2) An order under this rule shall not prejudice any determination on the taxation of costs or otherwise as to the party by whom the costs of the examination are ultimately to be borne.

Commencement 1 October 1966.
Cross references This rule is applied to the county court by virtue of CCR Order 20, r 13.

Order 39, r 15 Perpetuation of testimony

(1) Witnesses shall not be examined to perpetuate testimony unless an action has been begun for the purpose.

(2) Any person who would under the circumstances alleged by him to exist become entitled, upon the happening of any future event, to any honour, title, dignity or office, or to any estate or interest in any real or personal property, the right or claim to which cannot be brought to trial by him before the happening of such event, may begin an action to perpetuate any testimony which may be material for establishing such right or claim.

(3) No action to perpetuate the testimony of witnesses shall be set down for trial.

Commencement 1 October 1966.

Order 39, r 16 Examiners of the Court

A sufficient number of barristers, of not less than three years' standing, shall be appointed by the Lord Chancellor to act as examiners of the Court for a period not exceeding five years at a time, but the Lord Chancellor may at any time revoke any such appointment.

Commencement 1 October 1966.

Order 39, r 17 Assignment of examinations to examiners of the Court

(1)　The examinations to be taken before examiners of the Court shall be assigned to them in rotation by [the proper officer in the Central Office].

(2)　If an examiner is unable or declines to take an examination assigned to him, the examination shall be assigned to some other examiner under paragraph (1).

Commencement　1 October 1966.
Amendments　Para (1): words "the proper officer in the Central Office" substituted by SI 1982/1111, r 48.

Order 39, r 18 Obtaining assignment of examiner of the Court

(1)　The party prosecuting an order for examination before an examiner of the Court must take the order or a copy thereof to [the proper officer] mentioned in rule 17 for him to note on it the name of the examiner to whom the examination is to be assigned and must leave a copy of the order with that examiner's clerk.

(2)　A copy of the order for examination is sufficient authority for the examiner whose name is indorsed on it to proceed with the examination.

Commencement　1 October 1966.
Amendments　Para (1): words "the proper officer" substituted by SI 1986/2289, r 2.

[Order 39, r 19 Fees and expenses of examiners of the Court

(1)　The examiners of the Court shall be entitled to charge the fees mentioned in the following Table:—

TABLE OF EXAMINERS' FEES

	£
1. For each day for which an appointment to take an examination is given	[32.00]
2. For each hour or part thereof (after the first hour) occupied in an examination within [5 kilometres] from the principal entrance of the Royal Courts of Justice	[16.00]
3. For each day of 3 hours or part thereof occupied in an examination beyond [5 kilometres] from the principal entrance of the Royal Courts of Justice	[37.00]

(2)　The party prosecuting the order must also pay all reasonable travelling and other expenses, including charges for the room (other than the examiner's chambers) where the examination is taken.

(3)　An examiner shall not be obliged to send any deposition to the Central Office under rule 11(4) until all fees and expenses due to him in respect of the examination have been paid.]

Commencement　1 October 1985.
Amendments　This rule was substituted by SI 1985/1277, r 5.
Para (1): in the Table sums "32.00", "16.00" and "37.00" substituted by SI 1986/2289, r 3; words "5 kilometres" in both places substituted by SI 1991/2671, r 2.

ORDER 40

COURT EXPERT

Order 40, r 1 Appointment of expert to report on certain questions

(1) In any cause or matter which is to be tried without a jury and in which any question for an expert witness arises the Court may at any time, on the application of any party, appoint an independent expert or, if more than one such question arises, two or more such experts, to inquire and report upon any question of fact or opinion not involving questions of law or of construction.

An expert appointed under this paragraph is referred to in this Order as a "court expert".

(2) Any court expert in a cause or matter shall, if possible, be a person agreed between the parties and, failing agreement, shall be nominated by the Court.

(3) The question to be submitted to the court expert and the instructions (if any) given to him shall, failing agreement between the parties, be settled by the Court.

(4) In this rule "expert", in relation to any question arising in a cause or matter, means any person who has such knowledge or experience of or in connection with that question that his opinion on it would be admissible in evidence.

Commencement 1 October 1966.

Order 40, r 2 Report of court expert

(1) The court expert must send his report to the Court, together with such number of copies thereof as the Court may direct, and the proper officer must send copies of the report to the parties or their solicitors.

(2) The Court may direct the court expert to make a further or supplemental report.

(3) Any part of a court expert's report which is not accepted by all the parties to the cause or matter in which it is made shall be treated as information furnished to the Court and be given such weight as the Court thinks fit.

Commencement 1 October 1966.

Order 40, r 3 Experiments and tests

If the court expert is of opinion that an experiment or test of any kind (other than one of a trifling character) is necessary to enable him to make a satisfactory report he shall inform the parties or their solicitors and shall, if possible, make an arrangement with them as to the expenses involved, the persons to attend and other relevant matters; and if the parties are unable to agree on any of those matters it shall be settled by the Court.

Commencement 1 October 1966.

Order 40, r 4 Cross-examination of court expert

Any party may, within 14 days after receiving a copy of the court expert's report, apply to the Court for leave to cross-examine the expert on his report, and on that application the Court shall make an order for the cross-examination of the expert by all the parties either—

(a) at the trial, or

(b) before an examiner at such time and place as may be specified in the order.

Commencement 1 October 1966.

Order 40, r 5 Remuneration of court expert

(1) The remuneration of the court expert shall be fixed by the Court and shall include a fee for his report and a proper sum for each day during which he is required to be present either in court or before an examiner.

(2) Without prejudice to any order providing for payment of the court expert's remuneration as part of the costs of the cause or matter, the parties shall be jointly and severally liable to pay the amount fixed by the Court for his remuneration, but where the appointment of a court expert is opposed the Court may, as a condition of making the appointment, require the party applying for the appointment to give such security for the remuneration of the expert as the Court thinks fit.

Commencement 1 October 1966.

Order 40, r 6 Calling of expert witnesses

Where a court expert is appointed in a cause or matter, any party may, on giving to the other parties a reasonable time before the trial notice of his intention to do so, call one expert witness to give evidence on the question reported on by the court expert but no party may call more than one such witness without the leave of the Court, and the Court shall not grant leave unless it considers the circumstances of the case to be exceptional.

Commencement 1 October 1966.

ORDER 41
AFFIDAVITS

Order 41, r 1 Form of affidavit

(1)   Subject to paragraphs (2) and (3), every affidavit sworn in a cause or matter must be entitled in that cause or matter.

(2)   Where a cause or matter is entitled in more than one matter, it shall be sufficient to state the first matter followed by the words "and other matters", and where a cause or matter is entitled in a matter or matters and between parties, that part of the title which consists of the matter or matters may be omitted.

(3)   Where there are more plaintiffs than one, it shall be sufficient to state the full name of the first followed by the words "and others", and similarly with respect to defendants.

(4)   Every affidavit must be expressed in the first person and[, unless the Court otherwise directs,] must state the place of residence of the deponent and his occupation or, if he has none, his description, and if he is, or is employed by, a party to the cause or matter in which the affidavit is sworn, the affidavit must state that fact.

[In the case of a deponent who is giving evidence in a professional, business or other occupational capacity the affidavit may, instead of stating the deponent's place of residence, state the address at which he works, the position he holds and the name of his firm or employer, if any.]

[(5)   Every affidavit must be bound in book form, and, whether or not both sides of the paper are used, the printed, written or typed sides of the paper must be numbered consecutively.]

(6)   Every affidavit must be divided into paragraphs numbered consecutively, each paragraph being as far as possible confined to a distinct portion of the subject.

(7)   Dates, sums and other numbers must be expressed in an affidavit in figures and not in words.

(8)   Every affidavit must be signed by the deponent and the jurat must be completed and signed by the person before whom it is sworn.

Commencement   1 October 1984 (para (5)); 1 October 1966 (remainder).
Amendments   Para (4): words ", unless the Court otherwise directs" and paragraph beginning "In the case of a deponent" inserted by SI 1979/522, r 3.
Para (5): substituted by SI 1984/1051, r 7.
Cross references   See CCR Order 20, r 10.
This rule is applied to the county court by CCR Order 20, r 10 subject to the alterations in such rule.

Order 41, r 2 Affidavit by two or more deponents

Where an affidavit is made by two or more deponents, the names of the persons making the affidavit must be inserted in the jurat except that, if the affidavit is sworn by both or all the deponents at one time before the same person, it shall be sufficient to state that it was sworn by both (or all) of the "above named" deponents.

Commencement   1 October 1966.
Cross references   This rule is applied to the county court by CCR Order 20, r 10 subject to the alterations in such rule.

Order 41, r 3 Affidavit by illiterate or blind person

Where it appears to the person administering the oath that the deponent is illiterate or blind, he must certify in the jurat that—
- (a) the affidavit was read in his presence to the deponent,
- (b) the deponent seemed perfectly to understand it, and
- (c) the deponent made his signature or mark in his presence;

and the affidavit shall not be used in evidence without such a certificate unless the Court is otherwise satisfied that it was read to and appeared to be perfectly understood by the deponent.

Commencement 1 October 1966.
Cross references This rule is applied to the county court by CCR Order 20, r 10 subject to the alterations in such rule.

Order 41, r 4 Use of defective affidavit

An affidavit may, with the leave of the Court, be filed or used in evidence notwithstanding any irregularity in the form thereof.

Commencement 1 October 1966.
Cross references This rule is applied to the county court by CCR Order 20, r 10 subject to the alterations in such rule.

Order 41, r 5 Contents of affidavit

[(1) Subject to—
- (a) Order 14, rule 2(2) and 4(2);
- (b) Order 86, rule 2(1);
- (c) Order 113, rule 3;
- (d) paragraph (2) of this rule, and
- (e) any Order made under Order 38, rule 3,

an affidavit may contain only such facts as the deponent is able of his own knowledge to prove.]

(2) An affidavit sworn for the purpose of being used in interlocutory proceedings may contain statements of information or belief with the sources and grounds thereof.

Commencement 1 February 1991 (para (1)); 1 October 1966 (remainder).
Amendments Para (1): substituted by SI 1990/2599, r 18.
Cross references This rule is applied to the county court by CCR Order 20, r 10 subject to the alterations in such rule.

Order 41, r 6 Scandalous, etc, matter in affidavit

The Court may order to be struck out of any affidavit any matter which is scandalous, irrelevant or otherwise oppressive.

Commencement 1 October 1966.
Cross references This rule is applied to the county court by CCR Order 20, r 10 subject to the alterations in such rule.

Order 41, r 7 Alterations in affidavits

(1)   An affidavit which has in the jurat or body thereof any interlineation, erasure or other alteration shall not be filed or used in any proceeding without the leave of the Court unless the person before whom the affidavit was sworn has [initialled the alteration and, in the case of an erasure, has re-written in the margin of the affidavit any words or figures written on the erasure and has signed or initialled them.]

(2)   Where an affidavit is sworn at the Central Office or any other office of the Supreme Court, the official stamp of that office may be substituted for the signature or initials required by this rule.

Commencement 1 October 1966.
Amendments Para (1): words from "initialled the alteration" to "or initialled them" substituted by SI 1966/559, r 2.
Cross references This rule is applied to the county court by CCR Order 20, r 10 subject to the alterations in such rule.

Order 41, r 8 Affidavit not to be sworn before solicitor of party, etc

Without prejudice to section 1(3) of the Commissioners for Oaths Act 1889, no affidavit shall be sufficient if sworn before the solicitor of the party on whose behalf the affidavit is to be used or before any agent, partner or clerk of that solicitor.

Commencement 1 October 1966.
Cross references This rule is applied to the county court by CCR Order 20, r 10 subject to the alterations in such rule.

Order 41, r 9 Filing of affidavits

(1)   Every affidavit used in a cause or matter proceeding in a district registry must be filed in that registry.

(2)   Every affidavit used in an Admiralty cause or matter [or in a commercial action] must, subject to paragraph (1), be filed in [the Admiralty and Commercial Registry].

[(3)   Every affidavit used in a cause or matter proceeding in the [principal registry of the Family Division] must be filed in that registry.]

[(3A) Every affidavit used in a cause or matter proceeding in the Chancery Division must, subject to paragraph (1), be filed in Chancery Chambers.]

[(3B) Every affidavit used in proceedings for taxation in the Supreme Court Taxing Office must be filed in that office.]

(4)   Except as otherwise provided by these rules, every affidavit must be filed in the Central Office.

(5)   Every affidavit must be indorsed with a note showing on whose behalf it is filed and the dates of swearing and filing, and an affidavit which is not so indorsed may not be filed or used without the leave of the Court.

Commencement 1 October 1990 (para (3B)); 1 October 1982 (para (3A)); 1 September 1968 (para (3)); 1 October 1966 (remainder).
Amendments Para (2): words "or in a commercial action" inserted and words "the Admiralty and Commercial Registry" substituted by SI 1987/1423, r 12.

Para (3): substituted by SI 1968/1244, r 6; words "principal registry of the Family Division" substituted by SI 1971/1269, r 38(b), Schedule.
Para (3A): inserted by SI 1982/1111, r 49.
Para (3B): inserted by SI 1990/1689, r 28.
Cross references See CCR Order 20, r 10(3).

Order 41, r 10 Use of original affidavit or office copy

(1)   Subject to paragraph (2), an original affidavit may be used in proceedings in the Chancery Division with the leave of the Court, and in any other proceedings without such leave, notwithstanding that it has not been filed in accordance with rule 9.

(2)   . . .

(3)   Where an original affidavit is used then, unless the party whose affidavit it is undertakes to file it, he must immediately after it is used leave it with the proper officer in court or in chambers, as the case may be, and that officer shall send it to be filed.

(4)   Where an affidavit has been filed, an office copy thereof may be used in any proceedings.

Commencement   1 October 1966.
Amendments   Para (2): revoked by SI 1992/638, r 16.

Order 41, r 11 Document to be used in conjunction with affidavit to be exhibited to it

(1)   Any document to be used in conjunction with an affidavit must be exhibited, and not annexed, to the affidavit.

(2)   Any exhibit to an affidavit must be identified by a certificate of the person before whom the affidavit is sworn.

The certificate must be entitled in the same manner as the affidavit and rule 1(1), (2) and (3) shall apply accordingly.

Commencement   1 October 1966.
Cross references   This rule is applied to the county court by CCR Order 20, r 10.

Order 41, r 12 Affidavit taken in Commonwealth country admissible without proof of seal, etc

A document purporting to have affixed or impressed thereon or subscribed thereto the seal or signature of a court, judge, notary public or person having authority to administer oaths in a part of the Commonwealth outside England and Wales in testimony of an affidavit being taken before it or him in that part shall be admitted in evidence without proof of the seal or signature being the seal or signature of that court, judge, notary public or person.

Commencement   1 October 1966.

JUDGMENTS, ORDERS, ACCOUNTS AND INQUIRIES

ORDER 42
JUDGMENTS AND ORDERS

Order 42, r 1 Form of judgment, etc

(1)   If, in the case of any judgment, a form thereof is prescribed by Appendix A the judgment must be in that form.

(2)   The party entering any judgment shall be entitled to have recited therein a statement of the manner in which, and the place at which, the writ or other originating process by which the cause or matter in question was begun was served.

(3)   [Any order other than a consent order to which rule 5A applies] must be marked with the name of the judge, referee or master by whom it was made and must be sealed.

[(4)   . . .]

Commencement   15 February 1971 (para (4)); 1 October 1966 (remainder).
Amendments   Para (3): words "Any order other than a consent order to which rule 5A applies" substituted by SI 1980/1010, r 11(1).
Para (4): added by SI 1970/1208, r 5; revoked by SI 1976 No 337, r 8.
Forms   Judgments (Nos 39–51; PF80–84).

[Order 42, r 1A Judgment in favour of reversioner for detention of goods

(1)   Where a claim relating to the detention of goods is made by a partial owner whose right of action is not founded on a possessory title, any judgment or order given or made in respect of the claim shall, notwithstanding anything in section 3(3) of the Torts (Interference with Goods) Act 1977, be for the payment of damages only.

In this paragraph "partial owner" means one of two or more persons having interests in the goods, unless he has the written authority of every other such person to sue on the latter's behalf.

(2)   This rule is without prejudice to the remedies and jurisdiction mentioned in section 3(8) of the said Act of 1977.]

Commencement   1 June 1978.
Amendments   This rule was inserted by SI 1978/579, r 5.
Cross references   See CCR Order 22, r 4.

Order 42, r 2 Judgment, etc requiring act to be done: time for doing it

(1)   Subject to paragraph (2), a judgment or order which requires a person to do an act must specify the time after service of the judgment or order, or some other time, within which the act is to be done.

(2)   Where the act which any person is required by any judgment or order to do is to pay money to some other person, give possession of any land or deliver any goods, a time within which the act is to be done need not be specified in the judgment or order by virtue of paragraph (1), but the foregoing provision shall not affect the power of the Court to specify such a time and to adjudge or order accordingly.

Commencement 1 October 1966.
Cross references See CCR Order 22, r 3.

Order 42, r 3 Date from which judgment or order takes effect

(1)   [Subject to the provisions of Rule 3A] a judgment or order of the Court or of an official or special referee takes effect from the day of its date.

(2)   Such a judgment or order shall be dated as of the day on which it is pronounced, given or made, unless the Court or referee, as the case may be, orders it to be dated as of some other earlier or later day, in which case it shall be dated as of that other day.

Commencement 1 October 1966.
Amendments Para (1): words "Subject to the provisions of Rule 3A" inserted by SI 1980/629, r 7(1).

[Order 42, r 3A Judgment against a State

(1)   Where judgment on failure to acknowledge service has been entered against a State, as defined in section 14 of the State Immunity Act 1978, the judgment shall not take effect until two months after service on the State of—
   (a)   a copy of the judgment, and
   (b)   a copy of the affidavit in support of the application for leave to enter judgment, unless one has already been served pursuant to a direction under Order 13, rule 7A(3).]

Commencement 3 June 1980.
Amendments This rule was inserted by SI 1980/629, r 7(2).

Order 42, r 4 Orders required to be drawn up

(1)   Subject to paragraph (2), every order of the Court shall be drawn up unless the Court otherwise directs.

(2)   An order—
   (a)   which—
      (i)   extends the period within which a person is required or authorised by these rules, or by any judgment, order or direction, to do any act, or
      (ii)   grants leave for the doing of any of the acts mentioned in paragraph (3), and
   (b)   which neither imposes any special terms nor includes any special directions other than a direction as to costs,

need not be drawn up unless the Court otherwise directs.

(3)   The acts referred to in paragraph (2)(a)(ii) are—
   (a)   the issue of any writ, other than a writ of summons for service out of the jurisdiction;
   (b)   the amendment of a writ of summons or other originating process or a pleading;
   (c)   the filing of any document;
   (d)   any act to be done by an officer of the Court other than a solicitor.

Commencement 1 October 1966

Order 42, r 5 Drawing up and entry of Queen's Bench judgments and orders

(1)   Where a judgment given in a cause or matter in the Queen's Bench Division [(including an Admiralty cause or matter)] is presented for entry in accordance with this rule at the appropriate office, it shall be entered by an officer of that office in the book kept for the purpose.

(2)   The party seeking to have such a judgment entered must draw up the judgment and present it to the proper officer of the appropriate office for entry.

(3)   A party presenting a judgment for entry must—
  (a)   if he is the plaintiff, produce the original of the writ or other originating process by which the cause or matter in question was begun;
  (b)   produce any certificate, order or other document needed to satisfy the proper officer that he is entitled to have the judgment entered and lodge the pleadings (if any) with that officer.

(4)   On entering any such judgment the proper officer shall file the judgment and return a duplicate thereof to the party who presented it for entry.

(5)   Every order made in the Queen's Bench Division and required to be drawn up must be drawn up by the party having the custody of the summons, notice or other document on which the order is indorsed and if that party fails to draw up the order within 7 days after it is made any other party affected by the order may draw it up.

(6)   The order referred to in paragraph (5) must, when drawn up, be produced at the appropriate office, together with a copy thereof, and when passed by the proper officer the order, sealed with the seal of that office, shall be returned to the party producing it and the copy shall be lodged in that office.

(7)   The appropriate office for the purpose of this rule is the Central Office [or the Admiralty and Commercial Registry, as the case may be], except where the cause or matter is proceeding in a district registry in which case it is that registry unless the Court otherwise orders:

  Provided that in the case of an order made on a summons or other application transferred under Order 4, rule 6(4), to a district registry or to the Royal Courts of Justice, the appropriate office shall be that registry or the Central Office, as the case may be, unless the Court otherwise orders.

(8)   Where by virtue of paragraph (7) a judgment or order in a cause or matter proceeding in a district registry is entered in the Central Office, or an order in a cause or matter proceeding in the Royal Courts of Justice is entered in a district registry, the proper officer shall send an office copy of the judgment or order to the registry in which the cause or matter is proceeding or to the Central Office, as the case may be.

Commencement   1 October 1966.
Amendments   Para (1): words "(including an Admiralty cause or matter)" inserted by SI 1987/1423, r 13.
Para (7): words "or the Admiralty and Commercial Registry, as the case may be" inserted by SI 1987/1423, r 14.
Cross references   See CCR Order 22, r 1.

[Order 42, r 5A Consent judgments and orders in the Queen's Bench Division

(1)   Subject to paragraphs (2), (3), (4) and (5), where all the parties to a cause or matter in the Queen's Bench Division are agreed upon the terms in which a

judgment should be given, or an order should be made, a judgment or order in such terms may be given effect as a judgment or order of the Court by the procedure provided in rule 5.

(2) This rule applies to any judgment or order which consists of one or more of the following—

  (a) any judgment or order for—

   (i) the payment of a liquidated sum, or damages to be assessed, or the value of goods to be assessed;

   (ii) the delivery up of goods, with or without the option of paying the value of the goods to be assessed, or the agreed value;

   (iii) the possession of land where the claim does not relate to a dwelling-house;

  (b) any order for—

   (i) the dismissal, discontinuance or withdrawal of any proceedings, wholly or in part;

   (ii) the stay of proceedings, either unconditionally or upon conditions as to the payment of money;

   (iii) the stay of proceedings upon terms which are scheduled to the order but which are not otherwise part of it (a "Tomlin order");

   (iv) the stay of enforcement of a judgment, either unconditionally or upon condition that the money due under the judgment is paid by instalments specified in the order;

   (v) the setting aside of a judgment in default;

   (vi) the transfer of any proceedings to a county court, under [section 40 of the County Courts Act 1984];

   (vii) the payment out of money in court;

   (viii) the discharge from liability of any party;

   (ix) the payment, taxation or waiver of costs, or such other provision for costs as may be agreed;

  (c) any order, to be included in a judgment or order to which the preceding sub-paragraphs apply, for—

   (i) the extension of the period required for the service or filing of any pleading or other document;

   (ii) the withdrawal of the record;

   (iii) liberty to apply, or to restore.

(3) Before any judgment, or order, to which this rule applies may be entered, or sealed, it must be drawn up in the terms agreed and expressed as being "By Consent" and it must be indorsed by solicitors acting for each of the parties.

(4) This rule shall not apply to any judgment or order in proceedings which are pending in the Admiralty Court or in the Commercial Court or before an official referee.

(5) This rule shall not apply to any judgment or order in proceedings in which any of the parties is a litigant in person or a person under a disability.]

Commencement 1 October 1980.

Amendments This rule was inserted by SI 1980/1010, r 11(2).

Para (2): in sub-para (b)(vi) words "section 40 of the County Courts Act 1984" substituted by SI 1985/69, r 7(2), Schedule.

Cross references See CCR Order 22, r 7A.

[Order 42, r 6 Drawing up and filing of Chancery judgments and orders

(1)   Every judgment given in a cause or matter in the Chancery Division and, subject to paragraph (3), every order made in such a cause or matter and required to be drawn up shall be drawn up in the appropriate office of the Court and filed in that office.

(2)   The appropriate office for the purpose of this rule is Chancery Chambers, except where the cause or matter is proceeding in a district registry in which case it is that registry unless the Court otherwise directs.

(3)   Whenever a Chancery Master or [district judge] makes an interlocutory order he shall, having first given the parties an opportunity to be heard in the matter, direct whether or not such order is to be drawn up, and, if so, whether it is to be drawn up in court or by such of the parties as he may direct:

Provided that, where an order is directed to be drawn up by a party and is not presented for entry by that party at the appropriate office within seven days after the order was made, any party may apply to a master for the order to be drawn up in court and the master may make such order as he thinks fit as to the costs of such application and of the hearing which gave rise to the order.]

Commencement   1 October 1982.
Amendments   This rule was substituted, for rr 6–8 as originally enacted, by SI 1982/1111, r 50.

Order 42, r [7] Duplicates of Chancery judgments and orders

(1)   [On the filing of a judgment] under rule 6 a duplicate thereof shall be supplied without fee out of [Chancery Chambers] to the party having the carriage of the judgment.

In this rule "judgment" includes order.

[(2)]   Where by any of these rules or any order of the Court the original judgment is required to be produced or served it shall be sufficient to produce or serve the duplicate.

[(3)]   A judgment shall not be amended except on production of the duplicate thereof last issued, and if the judgment is amended the duplicate so issued shall be similarly amended, and the amendment sealed, under the direction of the [proper officer].

[(4)]   The foregoing provisions of this rule shall have effect in relation to a judgment filed under rule 6 in a district registry as if for the reference to [Chancery Chambers] there were substituted a reference to that registry . . . .

Commencement   1 October 1966.
Amendments   Originally r 9, renumbered as r 7 by SI 1982/1111, r 51.
Original paras (2), (3), (5) revoked, and original paras (4), (6) and (7) renumbered as paras (2)–(4); words in square brackets substituted, and words omitted revoked, by SI 1982/1111, r 51.

ORDER 43
ACCOUNTS AND INQUIRIES

Order 43, r 1 Summary order for account

(1)   Where a writ is indorsed with a claim for an account or a claim which necessarily involves taking an account, the plaintiff may, at any time [after the defendant has acknowledged service of the writ or after the time limited for acknowledging service], apply for an order under this rule.

[(1A) A defendant to an action begun by writ who has served a counterclaim, which includes a claim for an account or a claim which necessarily involves taking an account, on—
- (a)   the plaintiff, or
- (b)   any other party, or
- (c)   any person who becomes a party by virtue of such service may apply for an order under this rule.]

(2)   An application under this rule must be made by summons and, if the Court so directs, must be supported by affidavit or other evidence.

(3)   On the hearing of the application, the Court may, unless satisfied . . . that there is some preliminary question to be tried, order that an account be taken and may also order that any amount certified on taking the account to be due to either party be paid to him within a time specified in the order.

Commencement   1 January 1983 (para (1A)); 1 October 1966 (remainder).
Amendments   Para (1): words from "after the defendant" to "acknowledging service" substituted by SI 1979/1716, r 48, Schedule, Pt 1.
Para (1A): inserted by SI 1982/1786, r 17(1).
Para (3): words omitted revoked by SI 1982/1786, r 17(2).

Order 43, r 2 Court may direct taking of accounts, etc

(1)   The Court may, on an application made by summons at any stage of the proceedings in a cause or matter, direct any necessary accounts or inquiries to be taken or made.

(2)   Every direction for the taking of an account or the making of an inquiry shall be numbered in the judgment or order so that, as far as may be, each distinct account and inquiry may be designated by a number.

Commencement   1 October 1966.
Cross references   This rule is applied to the county court by CCR Order 13, r 7(1)(h).

Order 43, r 3 Direction as to manner of taking account [or making inquiry]

(1)   Where the Court orders an account to be taken [or inquiry to be made] it may by the same or a subsequent order give directions with regard to the manner in which the account is to be taken or vouched [or the inquiry is to be made].

(2)   Without prejudice to the generality of paragraph (1), the Court may direct that in [taking an account] the relevant books of account shall be evidence of the matters contained therein with liberty to the parties interested to take such objections thereto as they think fit.

Commencement 1 October 1966.
Amendments Rule heading: words "or making inquiry" inserted by SI 1982/1111, r 52.
Para (1): words "or inquiry to be made" and "or the inquiry is to be made" inserted by SI 1982/1111, r 52.
Para (2): words "taking an account" substituted by SI 1982/1111, r 52.
Cross references This rule is applied to the county court by CCR Order 13, r 7(1)(h).

Order 43, r 4 Account to be made, verified etc

(1)   Where an account has been ordered to be taken, the accounting party must make out his account and, unless the Court otherwise directs, verify it by an affidavit to which the account must be exhibited.

(2)   The items on each side of the account must be numbered consecutively.

(3)   Unless the order for the taking of the account otherwise directs, the accounting party must lodge the account with the Court and must at the same time notify the other parties that he has done so and of the filing of any affidavit verifying the account and of any supporting affidavit.

Commencement 1 October 1966.
Cross references This rule is applied to the county court by CCR Order 13, r 7(1)(h).

Order 43, r 5 Notice to be given of alleged omissions, etc in account

Any party who seeks to charge an accounting party with an amount beyond that which he has by his account admitted to have received or who alleges that any item in his account is erroneous in respect of amount or in any other respect must give him notice thereof stating, so far as he is able, the amount sought to be charged with brief particulars thereof or, as the case may be, the grounds for alleging that the item is erroneous.

Commencement 1 October 1966.
Cross references This rule is applied to the county court by CCR Order 13, r 7(1)(h).

Order 43, r 6 Allowances

In taking any account directed by any judgment or order all just allowances shall be made without any directions to that effect.

Commencement 1 October 1966.
Cross references This rule is applied to the county court by CCR Order 13, r 7(1)(h).

Order 43, r 7 Delay in prosecution of accounts, etc

(1)   If it appears to the Court that there is undue delay in the prosecution of any accounts or inquiries, or in any other proceedings under any judgment or order, the Court may require the party having the conduct of the proceedings or any other party to explain the delay and may then make such order for staying the proceedings or for expediting them or for the conduct thereof and for costs as the circumstances require.

(2)   The Court may direct any party or the official solicitor to take over the conduct of the proceedings in question and to carry out any directions made by an order under this rule and may make such order as it thinks fit as to the payment of the official solicitor's costs.

Commencement   1 October 1966.
Cross references   This rule is applied to the county court by CCR Order 13, r 7(1)(h).

Order 43, r 8 Distribution of fund before all persons entitled are ascertained

Where some of the persons entitled to share in a fund are ascertained, and difficulty
or delay has occurred or is likely to occur in ascertaining the other persons so
entitled, the Court may order or allow immediate payment of their shares to the
persons ascertained without reserving any part of those shares to meet the subsequent
costs of ascertaining those other persons.

Commencement   1 October 1966.
Cross references   This rule is applied to the county court by CCR Order 13, r 7(1)(h).

[Order 43 r 9 Guardian's accounts

The accounts of a person appointed guardian of a minor's estate must be verified and
passed in [such] manner as the Court may direct.]

Commencement   1 October 1971.
Amendments   This rule was added by SI 1971/1269, r 11.
Word "such" substituted by SI 1982/1111, r 52A.

[ORDER 44

Proceedings under Judgments and Orders: Chancery Division

Order 44 r 1 Application to Orders

In this Order references to a judgment include references to an order.]

Commencement 1 October 1982.
Amendments Order 44 was substituted by SI 1982/1111, r 53.
Cross references This rule is applied to the county court by CCR Order 23, r 2 (subject to the exceptions in that rule).

[Order 44, r 2 Service of notice of judgment on person not a party

(1) Where in an action for—
  (a) the administration of the estate of a deceased person, or
  (b) the execution of a trust, or
  (c) the sale of any property,

the Court gives a judgment or makes a direction which affects persons not parties to the action, the Court may when giving the judgment or at any stage of the proceedings under the judgment direct notice of the judgment to be served on any such person and any person so served shall, subject to paragraph (4), be bound by the judgment as if he had originally been a party to the action.

(2) If it appears that it is not practicable to serve notice of a judgment on a person directed to be served the Court may dispense with service and may also order that such person be bound by the judgment.

[(2A) Order 6, rule 7(3) and (5) shall apply in relation to a notice of judgment under this rule as if the notice were a writ and the person by whom the notice is issued were the plaintiff.]

(3) Every notice of a judgment for service under this rule must be indorsed with a memorandum in [Form No 52A] in Appendix A and accompanied by a form of acknowledgment of service in Form No 15 in Appendix A with such modifications as may be appropriate[; and the copy of the notice to be served shall be a sealed copy].

(4) A person served with notice of a judgment may, within one month after service of the notice on him, and [after acknowledging service] apply to the court to discharge, vary or add to the judgment.

(5) A person served with notice of a judgment may, after acknowledging service of the notice, attend the proceedings under the judgment.

(6) Order 12, rules 1 to 4, shall apply in relation to the acknowledgment of service of a notice of judgment as if the judgment were a writ, the person by whom the notice is served were the plaintiff and the person on whom it is served were a defendant.]

Commencement 1 October 1990 (para (2A)); 1 October 1982 (remainder).
Amendments See the note to Order 44, r 1.
Para (2A): inserted by SI 1990/1689, r 17(a).
Para (3): words "Form No 52A" substituted by SI 1987/1423, r 63, Schedule; words "; and the copy of the notice to be served shall be a sealed copy" added by SI 1990/1689, r 17(b).
Para (4): words "after acknowledging service" substituted by SI 1990/1689, r 17(c).
Cross references See CCR Order 23, r 1.
Forms Affidavit of service of notice (PF140).

[Order 44, r 3 Directions by the Court

(1)   Where a judgment given in a cause or matter in the Chancery Division contains directions which make it necessary to proceed in chambers under the judgment the Court may, when giving the judgment or at any time during proceedings under the judgment, give further directions for the conduct of those proceedings, including, in particular, directions with respect to—

    (a)   the manner in which any account or inquiry is to be prosecuted,

    (b)   the evidence to be adduced in support thereof,

    (c)   the preparation and service on the parties to be bound thereby of the draft of any deed or other instrument which is directed by the judgment to be settled by the Court and the service of any objections to the draft,

    (d)   without prejudice to Order 15, rule 17, the parties required to attend all or any part of the proceedings,

    (e)   the representation by the same solicitor of parties who constitute a class and by different solicitors of parties who ought to be separately represented, and

    (f)   the time within which each proceeding is to be taken, and may fix a day or days for the further attendance of the parties.

(2)   The Court may revoke or vary any directions given under this rule.]

Commencement   1 October 1982.
Amendments   See the note to Order 44, r 1.
Cross references   This rule is applied to the county court by CCR Order 23, r 2 (subject to the exceptions in that rule).

[Order 44, r 4 Application of rr 5 to 8

Rules 5 to 8 apply—

    (a)   where in proceedings for the administration under the direction of the Court of the estate of a deceased person the judgment directs any account of debts or other liabilities of the deceased's estate to be taken or any inquiry for next of kin or other ascertained claimants to be made, and

    (b)   where in proceedings for the execution under the direction of the Court of a trust the judgment directs any such inquiry to be made,

and those rules shall, with the necessary modifications, apply where in any other proceedings the judgment directs an account of debts or other liabilities to be taken or any inquiry to be made.]

Commencement   1 October 1982.
Amendments   See the note to Order 44, r 1.
Cross references   This rule is applied to the county court by CCR Order 23, r 2 (subject to the exceptions in that rule).

[Order 44, r 5 Advertisements for creditors and other claimants

The Court may, when giving a judgment or at any stage of proceedings under a judgment, give directions for the issue of advertisements for creditors or other claimants and may fix the time within which creditors and claimants may respond.]

Commencement   1 October 1982.
Amendments   See the note to Order 44, r 1.
Cross references   This rule is applied to the county court by CCR Order 23, r 2 (subject to the exceptions in that rule).
Forms   Advertisement for creditors (ChPF12).
Advertisement for other claimants (ChPF13).

[Order 44, r 6 Examination of claims

(1)   Where an account of debts or other liabilities of the estate of a deceased person has been directed, such party as the Court may direct must—
  (a)   examine the claims of persons claiming to be creditors of the estate,
  (b)   determine, so far as he is able, to which of such claims the estate is liable, and
  (c)   at least 7 clear days before the time appointed for adjudicating on claims, make an affidavit stating his findings and his reasons for them and listing all the other debts of the deceased which are or may still be due.

(2)   Where an inquiry for next of kin or other unascertained claimants has been directed, such party as the Court may direct must—
  (a)   examine the claims,
  (b)   determine, so far as he is able, which of them are valid, and
  (c)   at least 7 clear days before the time appointed for adjudicating on claims, make an affidavit stating his findings and his reasons for them.

(3)   If the personal representatives or trustees concerned are not the parties directed by the Court to examine claims, they must join with the party directed to examine them in making the affidavit required by this rule.]

Commencement   1 October 1982.
Amendments   See the note to Order 44, r 1.
Forms   Affidavit verifying list of creditor's claims (ChPF14).
List of claims (ChPF15).
List of claims otherwise than through advertisement (ChPF16).
List of sums in respect of which no claim made (ChPF17).
Affidavit verifying list of claims other than creditors (ChPF23, ChPF25).

[Order 44, r 7 Adjudication on claims

For the purpose of adjudicating on claims the Court may—
  (a)   direct any claim to be investigated in such manner as it thinks fit,
  (b)   require any claimant to attend and prove his claim or to furnish further particulars or evidence of it, or
  (c)   allow any claim after or without proof thereof.]

Commencement   1 October 1982.
Amendments   See the note to Order 44, r 1.
Cross references   This rule is applied to the county court by CCR Order 23, r 2 (subject to the exceptions in that rule).
Forms   Notice to creditor to claim (ChPF18).
Notice to claimant other than creditor to claim (ChPF26).
Notice to creditor to produce documents (ChPF19).

[Order 44, r 8 Notice of adjudication

The Court shall give directions that there be served on every creditor whose claim or any part thereof has been allowed or disallowed, and who did not attend when the claim was disposed of, a notice informing him of that fact.]

Commencement   1 October 1982.
Amendments   See the note to Order 44, r 1.
Forms   Notice to creditor of allowance of claim (ChPF20).
Notice of disallowance (ChPF21).

[Order 44, r 9 Interest on debts

(1)   Where an account of debts of a deceased person is directed by any judgment, then, unless the deceased's estate is insolvent or the Court otherwise orders, interest shall be allowed—

    (a)   on any such debt as carries interest, at the rate it carries, and

    (b)   on any other debt, from the date of the judgment at the rate payable on judgment debts at that date.

(2)   A creditor who has established his debt in proceedings under the judgment and whose debt does not carry interest shall be entitled to interest on his debt in accordance with paragraph (1)(b) out of any assets which may remain after satisfying the costs of the cause or matter, the debts which have been established and the interest on such of those debts as by law carry interest.

(3)   For the purposes of this rule "debt" includes funeral, testamentary or administration expenses and, in relation to expenses incurred after the judgment, for the reference in paragraph (1)(b) to the date of the judgment there shall be substituted a reference to the date when the expenses became payable.]

Commencement   1 October 1982.
Amendments   See the note to Order 44, r 1.
Cross references   This rule is applied to the county court by CCR Order 23, r 2 (subject to the exceptions in that rule).

[Order 44, r 10 Interest on Legacies

Where an account of legacies is directed by any judgment, then, subject to any directions contained in the will or codicil in question and to any order made by the Court, interest shall be allowed on each legacy at the rate of [£6] per cent per annum beginning at the expiration of one year after the testator's death.]

Commencement   1 October 1982.
Amendments   See the note to Order 44, r 1.
Figure "£6" substituted by SI 1983/1181, r 25.
Cross references   This rule is applied to the county court by CCR Order 23, r 2 (subject to the exceptions in that rule).

[Order 44, r 11 Master's order

[(1)   Subject to Order 37, rule 2, the result of proceedings before a master under a judgment shall be stated in the form of an order.]

(2)   Subject to any direction of the master under paragraph (3) or otherwise an order under this rule shall have effect as a final order disposing of the cause or matter in which it is made.

(3)   An order under this rule shall contain such directions as the master thinks fit as to the further consideration, either in court or in chambers, of the cause or matter in which it is made.

(4)   Every order made under this rule shall have immediate binding effect on the parties to the cause or matter in which it is made and copies of the order shall be served on such of the parties as the master may direct.]

Commencement   4 April 1988 (para (1)); 1 October 1982 (remainder).
Amendments   See the note to Order 44, r 1.

Para (1): substituted by SI 1988/298, r 3.
Cross references This rule is applied to the county court by CCR Order 23, r 2 (subject to the exceptions in that rule).
Forms Master's order on accounts and inquiries (ChPF29).

[Order 44, r 12 Appeal against master's order

Subject to Order 58, rule 2, rule 1 of that Order shall apply to an order made pursuant to rule 11 above, save that—

(a) except where paragraph (e) below applies, the notice referred to in Order 58, rule 1(2) shall state the grounds of the appeal, and must be issued within 14 days after the order is made;

(b) the hearing shall be in open court unless the Court directs otherwise;

(c) no fresh evidence (other than evidence as to matters which have occurred after the date of the master's order) shall be admitted except on special grounds;

(d) the judge hearing the appeal shall have the same power to draw inferences of fact as has the Court of Appeal under Order 59, rule 10(3);

(e) if the order is to be acted on by the Accountant-General or is an order passing a receiver's account, notice of appeal must be issued not later than two clear days after the making of the order and, where the order is to be acted on by the Accountant-General, a copy of it must be served on the Accountant-General as soon as practicable after it is made.]

Commencement 1 April 1992.
Amendments See the note to Order 44, r 1.
This rule was further substituted by SI 1992/638, r 8.
Cross references See CCR 23, r 3.

ENFORCEMENT OF JUDGMENTS AND ORDERS

ORDER 45
ENFORCEMENT OF JUDGMENTS AND ORDERS: GENERAL

Order 45, r 1 Enforcement of judgment, etc, for payment of money

(1)   Subject to the provisions of these rules, a judgment or order for the payment of money, not being a judgment or order for the payment of money into court, may be enforced by one or more of the following means, that is to say—

    (a)   writ of fieri facias;
    (b)   garnishee proceedings;
    (c)   a charging order;
    (d)   the appointment of a receiver;
    (e)   in a case in which rule 5 applies, an order of committal;
    (f)   in such a case, writ of sequestration.

(2)   Subject to the provisions of these rules, a judgment or order for the payment of money into court may be enforced by one or more of the following means, that is to say—

    (a)   the appointment of a receiver;
    (b)   in a case in which rule 5 applies, an order of committal;
    (c)   in such a case, writ of sequestration.

(3)   Paragraphs (1) and (2) are without prejudice to any other remedy available to enforce such a judgment or order as is therein mentioned or to the power of a court under the Debtors Acts 1869 and 1878 to commit to prison a person who makes default in paying money adjudged or ordered to be paid by him, or to the right of a person prosecuting a judgment or order for the payment of money to a person to apply under [section 105(1) of the County Courts Act 1984] to have the judgment or order enforced in a county court, or to the enactments relating to bankruptcy or the winding up of companies.

(4)   In this Order references to any writ shall be construed as including references to any further writ in aid of the first mentioned writ.

[(5)   . . .]

Commencement   15 February 1971 (para (5)); 1 October 1966 (remainder).
Amendments   Para (3): words "section 105(1) of the County Courts Act 1984" substituted by SI 1985/69, r 7(2), Schedule.
Para (5): added by SI 1970/1208, r 6; revoked by SI 1976/337, r 8.

Order 45, r 2   *(revoked by SI 1979/1725)*

Order 45, r 3 Enforcement of judgment for possession of land

(1)   Subject to the provisions of these rules, a judgment or order for the giving of possession of land may be enforced by one or more of the following means, that is to say—

    (a)   writ of possession;
    (b)   in a case in which rule 5 applies, an order of committal;
    (c)   in such a case, writ of sequestration.

(2)   A writ of possession to enforce a judgment or order for the giving of possession of any land shall not be issued without the leave of the Court except where the judgment or order was given or made in a mortgage action to which Order 88 applies.

(3)   Such leave shall not be granted unless it is shown—

(a)   that every person in actual possession of the whole or any part of the land has received such notice of the proceedings as appears to the Court sufficient to enable him to apply to the Court for any relief to which he may be entitled, and

(b)   if the operation of the judgment or order is suspended by subsection (2) of section 16 of the Landlord and Tenant Act 1954, that the applicant has not received notice in writing from the tenant that he desires that the provisions of paragraphs (a) and (b) of that subsection shall have effect.

(4)   A writ of possession may include provision for enforcing the payment of any money adjudged or ordered to be paid by the judgment or order which is to be enforced by the writ.

Commencement   1 October 1966.
Cross references   See CCR Order 26, r 17.
Forms   Praecipe for writ of possession (PF88).
Praecipe for writ of possession combined with Fi Fa (PF89).
Affidavit to support application for leave to enforce (PF91).

Order 45, r 4 Enforcement of judgment for delivery of goods

(1)   Subject to the provisions of these rules, a judgment or order for the delivery of any goods which does not give a person against whom the judgment is given or order made the alternative of paying the assessed value of the goods may be enforced by one or more of the following means, that is to say—

(a)   writ of delivery to recover the goods without alternative provision for recovery of the assessed value thereof (hereafter in this rule referred to as a "writ of specific delivery");

(b)   in a case in which rule 5 applies, an order of committal;

(c)   in such a case, writ of sequestration.

(2)   Subject to the provisions of these rules, a judgment or order for the delivery of any goods or payment of their assessed value may be enforced by one or more of the following means, that is to say—

(a)   writ of delivery to recover the goods or their assessed value;

(b)   [by order] of the Court, writ of specific delivery;

(c)   in a case in which rule 5 applies, writ of sequestration.

[An application for an order under sub-paragraph (b) shall be made by summons, which must, notwithstanding Order 65, rule 9, be served on the defendant against whom the judgment or order sought to be enforced was given or made.]

(3)   A writ of specific delivery, and a writ of delivery to recover any goods or their assessed value, may include provision for enforcing the payment of any money adjudged or ordered to be paid by the judgment or order which is to be enforced by the writ.

(4)   A judgment or order for the payment of the assessed value of any goods may be enforced by the same means as any other judgment or order for the payment of money.

Commencement 1 October 1966.
Amendments Para (2): in sub-para (b) words "by order" substituted, words from "An application" to the end inserted by SI 1978/579, r 4.
Cross references See CCR Order 26, r 16.
Forms Praecipe for writ of delivery (PF90).
Praecipe for writ of sequestration (PF87).

Order 45, r 5 Enforcement of judgment to do or abstain from doing any act

(1) Where—
- (a) a person required by a judgment or order to do an act within a time specified in the judgment or order refuses or neglects to do it within that time or, as the case may be, within that time as extended or abridged under Order 3, rule 5, or
- (b) a person disobeys a judgment or order requiring him to abstain from doing an act,

then, subject to the provisions of these rules, the judgment or order may be enforced by one or more of the following means, that is to say—
- (i) with the leave of the Court, a writ of sequestration against the property of that person;
- (ii) where that person is a body corporate, with the leave of the Court, a writ of sequestration against the property of any director or other officer of the body;
- (iii) subject to the provisions of the Debtors Acts 1869 and 1878, an order of committal against that person or, where that person is a body corporate, against any such officer.

(2) Where a judgment or order requires a person to do an act within a time therein specified and an order is subsequently made under rule 6 requiring the act to be done within some other time, references in paragraph (1) of this rule to a judgment or order shall be construed as references to the order made under rule 6.

(3) Where under any judgment or order requiring the delivery of any goods the person liable to execution has the alternative of paying the assessed value of the goods, the judgment or order shall not be enforceable by order of committal under paragraph (1), but the Court may, on the application of the person entitled to enforce the judgment or order, make an order requiring the first mentioned person to deliver the goods to the applicant within a time specified in the order, and that order may be so enforced.

Commencement 1 October 1966.

Order 45, r 6 Judgment, etc requiring act to be done: order fixing time for doing it

(1) Notwithstanding that a judgment or order requiring a person to do an act specifies a time within which the act is to be done, the Court shall, without prejudice to Order 3, rule 5, have power to make an order requiring the act to be done within another time, being such time after service of that order, or such other time, as may be specified therein.

(2) Where, notwithstanding Order 42, rule 2(1), or by reason of Order 42, rule 2(2), a judgment or order requiring a person to do an act does not specify a time within

which the act is to be done, the Court shall have power subsequently to make an order requiring the act to be done within such time after service of that order, or such other time, as may be specified therein.

(3)   An application for an order under this rule must be made by summons and the summons must, notwithstanding anything in Order 65, rule 9, be served on the person required to do the act in question.

Commencement   1 October 1966.

Order 45, r 7 Service of copy of judgment, etc, prerequisite to enforcement under r 5

(1)   In this rule references to an order shall be construed as including references to a judgment.

(2)   Subject to Order 24, rule 16(3), Order 26, rule 6(3), and [paragraphs (6) and (7)] of this rule, an order shall not be enforced under rule 5 unless—
  (a) a copy of the order has been served personally on the person required to do or abstain from doing the act in question, and
  (b) in the case of an order requiring a person to do an act, the copy has been so served before the expiration of the time within which he was required to do the act.

(3)   Subject as aforesaid, an order requiring a body corporate to do or abstain from doing an act shall not be enforced as mentioned in rule 5(1)(ii) or (iii) unless—
  (a) a copy of the order has also been served personally on the officer against whose property leave is sought to issue a writ of sequestration or against whom an order of committal is sought, and
  (b) in the case of an order requiring the body corporate to do an act, the copy has been so served before the expiration of the time within which the body was required to do the act.

[(4)   There must be prominently displayed on the front of the copy of an order served under this rule a warning to the person on whom the copy is served that disobedience to the order would be a contempt of court punishable by imprisonment, or (in the case of an order requiring a body corporate to do or abstain from doing an act) punishable by sequestration of the assets of the body corporate and by imprisonment of any individual responsible.]

(5)   With the copy of an order required to be served under this rule, being an order requiring a person to do an act, there must also be served a copy of any order made under Order 3, rule 5, extending or abridging the time for doing the act and, where the first-mentioned order was made under rule 5(3) or 6 of this Order, a copy of the previous order requiring the act to be done.

[(6)   An order requiring a person to abstain from doing an act may be enforced under rule 5 notwithstanding that service of a copy of the order has not been effected in accordance with this rule if the Court is satisfied that, pending such service, the person against whom or against whose property it is sought to enforce the order has had notice thereof either—
  (a) by being present when the order was made, or
  (b) by being notified of the terms of the order, whether by telephone, telegram or otherwise.]

[(7)] Without prejudice to its powers under Order 65, rule 4, the Court may dispense with service of a copy of an order under this rule if it thinks it just to do so.

Commencement   1 June 1992 (para (4)); 1 July 1967 (para (6)); 1 October 1966 (remainder).
Amendments   Para (2): words "paragraphs (6) and (7)" substituted by SI 1967/829, r 4(1).
Para (4): substituted by SI 1992/638, r 10.
Para (6): inserted by SI 1967/829, r 4(2).
Para (7): originally para (6), renumbered as para (7) by SI 1967/829, r 4(3).
Forms   Affidavit of personal service of judgment or order (PF141).

Order 45, r 8 Court may order act to be done at expense of disobedient party

If an order of mandamus, a mandatory order, an injunction or a judgment or order for the specific performance of a contract is not complied with, then, without prejudice to its powers under [section 39] of the Act and its powers to punish the disobedient party for contempt, the Court may direct that the act required to be done may, so far as practicable, be done by the party by whom the order or judgment was obtained or some other person appointed by the Court, at the cost of the disobedient party, and upon the act being done the expenses incurred may be ascertained in such manner as the Court may direct and execution may issue against the disobedient party for the amount so ascertained and for costs.

Commencement1 October 1966.
Amendments   Words "section 39" substituted by SI 1982/1111, r 115, Schedule.
Definitions   The Act: Supreme Court Act 1981.

Order 45, r 9 Execution by or against person not being a party

(1)   Any person, not being a party to a cause or matter, who obtains any order or in whose favour any order is made, shall be entitled to enforce obedience to the order by the same process as if he were a party.

(2)   Any person, not being a party to a cause or matter, against whom obedience to any judgment or order may be enforced, shall be liable to the same process for enforcing obedience to the judgment or order as if he were a party.

Commencement   1 October 1966.

Order 45, r 10 Conditional judgment: waiver

A party entitled under any judgment or order to any relief subject to the fulfilment of any condition who fails to fulfil that condition is deemed to have abandoned the benefit of the judgment or order, and, unless the Court otherwise directs, any other person interested may take any proceedings which either are warranted by the judgment or order or might have been taken if the judgment or order had not been given or made.

Commencement   1 October 1966.

Order 45, r 11 Matters occurring after judgment: stay of execution, etc

Without prejudice to Order 47, rule 1, a party against whom a judgment has been given or an order made may apply to the Court for a stay of execution of the judgment or order or other relief on the ground of matters which have occurred since the date of the judgment or order, and the Court may by order grant such relief, and on such terms, as it thinks just.

Commencement 1 October 1966.
Cross references See CCR Order 25, r 8.

Order 45, r 12 Forms of writs

(1)   A writ of fieri facias must be in such of the Forms Nos 53 to 63 in Appendix A as is appropriate in the particular case.

(2)   A writ of delivery must be in Form No 64 or 65 in Appendix A, whichever is appropriate.

(3)   A writ of possession must be in Form No 66 [or 66A in Appendix A, whichever is appropriate].

(4)   A writ of sequestration must be in Form No 67 in Appendix A.

Commencement 1 October 1966.
Amendments Para (3): words "or 66A in Appendix A, whichever is appropriate" substituted by SI 1970/944, r 6.
Forms Praceipe for writs de bonis ecclesiasticis (PF95, PF96).
Writ de bonis ecclesiasticis (PF94).

Order 45, r 13 Enforcement of judgments and orders for recovery of money, etc

(1)   Rule 1(1) of this Order, with the omission of sub-paragraphs (e) and (f) thereof, and Orders 46 to 51 shall apply in relation to a judgment or order for the recovery of money as they apply in relation to a judgment or order for the payment of money.

(2)   Rule 3 of this Order, with the omission of paragraph (1)(b) and (c) thereof, and Order 47, rule 3(2), shall apply in relation to a judgment or order for the recovery of possession of land as they apply in relation to a judgment or order for the giving or delivery of possession of land.

(3)   Rule 4 of this Order, with the omission of paragraphs 1(b) and (c) and (2)(c) thereof, and Order 47, rule 3(2), shall apply in relation to a judgment or order that a person do have a return of any goods and to a judgment or order that a person do have a return of any goods or do recover the assessed value thereof as they apply in relation to a judgment or order for the delivery of any goods and a judgment or order for the delivery of any goods or payment of the assessed value thereof respectively.

Commencement 1 October 1966.

[Order 45, r 14 Enforcement of decisions of Value Added Tax Tribunals

(1)   An application under section 29 of the Finance Act 1985 for registration of a decision of a Value Added Tax Tribunal on an appeal under section 40 of the Value Added Tax Act 1983 shall be made by a request in writing to the head clerk of the Crown Office—

    (a)   exhibiting the decision or a duly authenticated copy thereof,

    (b)   stating, so far as is known to the deponent, the name and occupation and the usual or last known address or place of business of the person against whom it is sought to enforce the decision, and

(c) stating, to the best of the deponent's information and belief, the amount which as a result of the decision is, or is recoverable as, tax from such person at the date of the application and the amount then remaining unpaid of any costs awarded to the Commissioners of Customs and Excise by the decision.

(2) Notice of the registration of a decision must be served on the person against whom it is sought to enforce the decision by delivering it to him personally or by sending it to him at his usual or last known address or place of business or in such manner as the Court may direct.

(3) There shall be kept in the Central Office under the direction of the Senior Master a register of the decisions registered under section 29 of the Finance Act 1985, and there shall be included in the register particulars of any execution issued on a decision so registered.]

Commencement 1 October 1987.
Amendments This rule was added by SI 1987/1423, r 49.

[Order 45, r 15 Signing judgment for costs [under deemed order]

A party entitled to tax his costs by virtue of paragraphs (3), (4), (5) or (6) of Order 62, rule 5 may, if the taxed costs are not paid within 4 days after taxation, sign judgment for them.]

Commencement 1 October 1987.
Amendments This rule was added by SI 1987/1423, r 50.
Rule heading: words "under deemed order" substituted by SI 1991/1884, r 10.
Forms Judgment (No 51).

ORDER 46
WRITS OF EXECUTION: GENERAL

Order 46, r 1 Definition

In this Order, unless the context otherwise requires, "writ of execution" includes a writ of fieri facias, a writ of possession, a writ of delivery, a writ of sequestration and any further writ in aid of any of the aforementioned writs.

Commencement 1 October 1966.
Forms Writ of restitution (No 68).
Writ of assistance (No 69).
Writ of venditioni exponas (PF92).
Praecipe for writ of venditioni exponas (PF93).

Order 46, r 2 When leave to issue any writ of execution is necessary

(1)   A writ of execution to enforce a judgment or order may not issue without the leave of the Court in the following cases, that is to say:—

(a) where six years or more have elapsed since the date of the judgment or order;

(b) where any change has taken place, whether by death or otherwise, in the parties entitled or liable to execution under the judgment or order;

(c) where the judgment or order is against the assets of a deceased person coming to the hands of his executors or administrators after the date of the judgment or order, and it is sought to issue execution against such assets;

(d) where under the judgment or order any person is entitled to relief subject to the fulfilment of any condition which it is alleged has been fulfilled;

(e) where any goods sought to be seized under a writ of execution are in the hands of a receiver appointed by the Court or a sequestrator.

(2)   Paragraph (1) is without prejudice to section 2 of the Reserve and Auxiliary Forces (Protection of Civil Interests) Act 1951 or any other enactment or rule by virtue of which a person is required to obtain the leave of the Court for the issue of a writ of execution or to proceed to execution on or otherwise to the enforcement of a judgment or order.

(3)   Where the Court grants leave, whether under this rule or otherwise, for the issue of a writ of execution and the writ is not issued within one year after the date of the order granting such leave, the order shall cease to have effect, without prejudice, however, to the making of a fresh order.

Commencement 1 October 1966.
Cross references See CCR Order 26, r 5.
Forms Certificate of application for leave to issue execution on suspended order for possession (ChPF6).

Order 46, r 3 Leave required for issue of writ in aid of other writ

A writ of execution in aid of any other writ of execution shall not issue without the leave of the Court.

Commencement 1 October 1966.

Order 46, r 4 Application for leave to issue writ

(1) An application for leave to issue a writ of execution may be made ex parte unless the Court directs it to be made by summons.

(2) Such an application must be supported by an affidavit—

    (a) identifying the judgment or order to which the application relates and, if the judgment or order is for the payment of money, stating the amount originally due thereunder and the amount due thereunder at the date of the application;

    (b) stating, where the case falls within rule 2(1)(a), the reasons for the delay in enforcing the judgment or order;

    (c) stating, where the case falls within rule 2(1)(b), the change which has taken place in the parties entitled or liable to execution since the date of the judgment or order;

    (d) stating, where the case falls within rule 2(1)(c) or (d), that a demand to satisfy the judgment or order was made on the person liable to satisfy it and that he had refused or failed to do so;

    (e) giving such other information as is necessary to satisfy the Court that the applicant is entitled to proceed to execution on the judgment or order in question and that the person against whom it is sought to issue execution is liable to execution on it.

(3) The Court hearing such application may grant leave in accordance with the application or may order that any issue or question, a decision on which is necessary to determine the rights of the parties, be tried in any manner in which any question of fact or law arising in an action may be tried and, in either case, may impose such terms as to costs or otherwise as it thinks just.

Commencement 1 October 1966.
Cross references See CCR Order 26, r 5(2).
Forms Certificate of application for leave to issue execution on suspended order for possession (ChPF6).

Order 46, r 5 Application for leave to issue writ of sequestration

(1) Notwithstanding anything in rules 2 and 4, an application for leave to issue a writ of sequestration must be made to a judge by motion.

(2) Subject to paragraph (3), the notice of motion, stating the grounds of the application and accompanied by a copy of the affidavit in support of the application, must be served personally on the person against whose property it is sought to issue the writ.

(3) Without prejudice to its powers under Order 65, rule 4, the Court may dispense with service of the notice of motion under this rule if it thinks it just to do so.

(4) The judge hearing an application for leave to issue a writ of sequestration may sit in private in any case in which, if the application were for an order of committal, he would be entitled to do so by virtue of Order 52, rule 6, but, except in such a case, the application shall be heard in open court.

Commencement 1 October 1966.

Order 46, r 6 Issue of writ of execution

(1) Issue of a writ of execution takes place on its being sealed by an officer of the appropriate office.

(2)　Before such a writ is issued a praecipe for its issue must be filed.

(3)　The praecipe must be signed by or on behalf of the solicitor of the person entitled to execution or, if that person is acting in person, by him.

(4)　No such writ shall be sealed unless at the time of the tender thereof for sealing—
- (a)　the person tendering it produces—
  - (i)　the judgment or order on which the writ is to issue, or an office copy thereof,
  - (ii)　where the writ may not issue without the leave of the Court, the order granting such leave or evidence of the granting of it,
  - [(iii)　Where judgment on failure to acknowledge service has been entered against a State, as defined in section 14 of the State Immunity Act 1978, evidence that the State has been served in accordance with Order 42, rule 3A and that the judgment has taken effect] and
- (b)　the officer authorised to seal it is satisfied that the period, if any, specified in the judgment or order for the payment of any money or the doing of any other act thereunder has expired.

(5)　Every writ of execution shall bear the date of the day on which it is issued.

(6)　In this rule "the appropriate office" means—
- (a)　where the cause or matter in which execution is to issue is proceeding in a district registry, that registry;
- [(b)　where that cause or matter is proceeding in the principal registry of the Family Division, that registry;]
- (c)　where that cause or matter is an Admiralty cause or matter [or a commercial action] which is not proceeding in a district registry, [the Admiralty and Commercial Registry];
- [(ca)　where the cause or matter is proceeding in the Chancery Division, Chancery Chambers;]
- (d)　in any other case, the Central Office.

Commencement　1 October 1966.
Amendments　Para (4): original sub-para (iii) revoked by SI 1979/1725, r 3(5), new sub-para (iii) inserted by SI 1980/629, r 8.
Para (6): sub-para (b) substituted by SI 1971/1269, r 12; in sub-para (c) words "or a commercial action" inserted and words "the Admiralty and Commercial Registry" substituted by SI 1987/1423, r 15; sub-para (ca) inserted by SI 1991/1329, r 16.
Cross references　See CCR Order 26, r 1.
Forms　Praecipe (PF86).

Order 46, r 7 *(revoked by SI 1979/1725)*

Order 46, r 8 Duration and renewal of writ of execution

(1)　For the purpose of execution, a writ of execution is valid in the first instance for 12 months beginning with the date of its issue.

(2)　Where a writ has not been wholly executed the Court may by order extend the validity of the writ from time to time for a period of 12 months at any one time beginning with the day on which the order is made, if an application for extension is made to the Court before the day next following that on which the writ would otherwise expire [or such later day (if any) as the Court may allow].

(3)   Before a writ the validity of which has been extended under [paragraph (2)] is executed either the writ must be sealed with the seal of the office out of which it was issued showing the date on which the order extending its validity was made or the applicant for the order must serve a notice (in Form No 71 in Appendix A), sealed as aforesaid, on the sheriff to whom the writ is directed informing him of the making of the order and the date thereof.

(4)   The priority of a writ, the validity of which has been extended under this rule, shall be determined by reference to the date on which it was originally delivered to the sheriff.

(5)   The production of a writ of execution, or of such a notice as is mentioned in paragraph (3), purporting in either case to be sealed as mentioned in that paragraph, shall be evidence that the validity of that writ or, as the case may be, of the writ referred to in that notice, has been extended under [paragraph (2)].

[(6)   If, during the validity of a writ of execution, an interpleader summons is issued in relation to an execution under that writ, the validity of the writ shall be extended until the expiry of 12 months from the conclusion of the interpleader proceedings.]

Commencement   1 October 1989 (para (6)); 1 October 1966 (remainder).
Amendments   Para (2): words "or such later day (if any) as the Court may allow" added by SI 1980/629, r 9.
Paras (3), (5): words "paragraph (2)" substituted by SI 1989/1307, r 11(a).
Para (6): added by SI 1989/1307, r 11(b).
Cross references   See CCR Order 26, r 6.

Order 46, r 9 Return to writ of execution

(1)   Any party at whose instance [or against whom] a writ of execution was issued may serve a notice on the sheriff to whom the writ was directed requiring him, within such time as may be specified in the notice, to indorse on the writ a statement of the manner in which he has executed it and to send to that party a copy of the statement.

(2)   If a sheriff on whom such a notice is served fails to comply with it the party by whom it was served may apply to the Court for an order directing the sheriff to comply with the notice.

Commencement   1 October 1966.
Amendments   Para (1): words "or against whom" inserted by SI 1988/1340, r 4.

ORDER 47
WRITS OF FIERI FACIAS

Order 47, r 1 Power to stay execution by writ of fieri facias

(1) Where a judgment is given or an order made for the payment by any person of money, and the Court is satisfied, on an application made at the time of the judgment or order, or at any time thereafter, by the judgment debtor or other party liable to execution—

    (a) that there are special circumstances which render it inexpedient to enforce the judgment or order, or

    (b) that the applicant is unable from any cause to pay the money,

then, notwithstanding anything in rule 2 or 3, the Court may by order stay the execution of the judgment or order by writ of fieri facias either absolutely or for such period and subject to such conditions as the Court thinks fit.

(2) An application under this rule, if not made at the time the judgment is given or order made, must be made by summons and may be so made notwithstanding that the party liable to execution did not [acknowledge service of the writ or originating summons in the action or did not state in his acknowledgment of service that he intended to apply for a stay of execution under this rule pursuant to Order 13, rule 8].

(3) An application made by summons must be supported by an affidavit made by or on behalf of the applicant stating the grounds of the application and the evidence necessary to substantiate them and, in particular, where such application is made on the grounds of the applicant's inability to pay, disclosing his income, the nature and value of any property of his and the amount of any other liabilities of his.

(4) The summons and a copy of the supporting affidavit must, not less than 4 clear days before the return day, be served on the party entitled to enforce the judgment or order.

(5) An order staying execution under this rule may be varied or revoked by a subsequent order.

Commencement 1 October 1966.
Amendments Para (2): words from "acknowledge service" to "Order 13, rule 8" substituted by SI 1979/1716, r 30.
Cross references See CCR Order 25, r 8.

Order 47, r 2 Two or more writs of fieri facias

(1) A party entitled to enforce a judgment or order by writ of fieri facias may issue two or more such writs, directed to the sheriffs of different counties, at either the same time or different times, to enforce that judgment or order, but no more shall be levied under all those writs together than is authorised to be levied under one of them.

(2) Where a party issues two or more writs of fieri facias directed to the sheriffs of different counties to enforce the same judgment or order he must inform each sheriff of the issue of the other writ or writs.

Commencement 1 October 1966.
Cross references See CCR Order 26, r 4.

Order 47, r 3 Separate writs to enforce payment of costs, etc

(1)   Where only the payment of money, together with costs to be taxed, is adjudged or ordered, then, if when the money becomes payable under the judgment or order the costs have not been taxed, the party entitled to enforce that judgment or order may issue a writ of fieri facias to enforce payment of the sum (other than for costs) adjudged or ordered and, not less than 8 days after the issue of that writ, he may issue a second writ to enforce payment of the taxed costs.

(2)   A party entitled to enforce a judgment or order for the delivery of possession of any property (other than money) may, if he so elects, issue a separate writ of fieri facias to enforce payment of any damages or costs awarded to him by that judgment or order.

Commencement   1 October 1966.

Order 47, r 4 No expenses of execution in certain cases

Where a judgment or order is for less than [£600] and does not entitle the plaintiff to costs against the person against whom a writ of fieri facias to enforce the judgment or order is issued, the writ may not authorise the sheriff to whom it is directed to levy any fees, poundage or other costs of execution.

Commencement   1 October 1966.
Amendments   Figure "£600" substituted by SI 1981/1734, r 28.

Order 47, r 5 Writ of fieri facias de bonis ecclesiasticis, etc

(1)   Where it appears upon the return of any writ of fieri facias that the person against whom the writ was issued has no goods or chattels in the county of the sheriff to whom the writ was directed but that he is the incumbent of a benefice named in the return, then, after the writ and return have been filed, the party by whom the writ of fieri facias was issued may issue a writ of fieri facias de bonis ecclesiasticis or a writ of sequestrari de bonis ecclesiasticis directed to the bishop of the diocese within which that benefice is.

(2)   Any such writ must be delivered to the bishop to be executed by him.

(3)   Only such fees for the execution of any such writ shall be taken by or allowed to the bishop or any diocesan officer as are for the time being authorised by or under any enactment, including any measure of the [General Synod].

Commencement   1 October 1966.
Amendments   Para (3): words "General Synod" substituted by SI 1982/1111, r 115, Schedule.

Order 47, r 6 Order for sale otherwise than by auction

(1)   An order of the Court under section 145 of the Bankruptcy Act 1883 that a sale under an execution may be made otherwise than by public auction may be made on the application of the person at whose instance the writ of execution under which the sale is to be made was issued or the person against whom that writ was issued (in this rule referred to as "the judgment debtor") or the sheriff to whom it was issued.

(2)   Such an application must be made by summons and the summons must contain a short statement of the grounds of the application.

(3) Where the applicant for an order under this rule is not the sheriff, the sheriff must, on the demand of the applicant, send to the applicant a list containing the name and address of every person at whose instance any other writ of execution against the goods of the judgment debtor was issued and delivered to the sheriff (in this rule referred to as "the sheriff's list"); and where the sheriff is the applicant, he must prepare such a list.

(4) Not less than 4 clear days before the return day the applicant must serve the summons on each of the other persons by whom the application might have been made and on every person named in the sheriff's list.

(5) Service of the summons on a person named in the sheriff's list is notice to him for the purpose of section 12 of the Bankruptcy Act 1890 (which provides that the Court shall not consider an application for leave to sell privately goods taken in execution until notice directed by rules of court has been given to any other execution creditor).

(6) The applicant must produce the sheriff's list to the Court on the hearing of the application.

(7) Every person on whom the summons was served may attend and be heard on the hearing of the application.

Commencement 1 October 1966.
Cross references See CCR Order 26, r 15.
Forms Order for sale by private contract (PF97).

ORDER 48
EXAMINATION OF JUDGMENT DEBTOR, ETC

Order 48, r 1 Order for examination of judgment debtor

(1)   Where a person has obtained a judgment or order for the payment by some other person (hereinafter referred to as "the judgment debtor") of money, the Court may, on an application made ex parte by the person entitled to enforce the judgment or order, order the judgment debtor or, if the judgment debtor is a body corporate, an officer thereof, to attend before such master, registrar or nominated officer as the Court may appoint and be orally examined on the questions—

     (a) whether any and, if so, what debts are owing to the judgment debtor, and

     (b) whether the judgment debtor has any and, if so, what other property or means of satisfying the judgment or order;

and the Court may also order the judgment debtor or officer to produce any books or documents in the possession of the judgment debtor relevant to the questions aforesaid at the time and place appointed for the examination.

[In this paragraph "registrar" includes the [district judge] of a district registry or county court, and where the Court appoints such a [district judge] without specifying him personally, the examination may, if he thinks fit, be conducted on his behalf by a nominated officer of that registry or county court.]

(2)   An order under this rule must be served personally on the judgment debtor and on any officer of a body corporate ordered to attend for examination.

(3)   Any difficulty arising in the course of an examination under this rule before a nominated officer, including any dispute with respect to the obligation of the person being examined to answer any question put to him, may be referred to the senior master or practice master [(or, in the case of an examination at the principal registry of the Family Division, a district registry or a county court, a [district judge] of that registry, district registry or county court respectively)] and he may determine it or give such directions for determining it as he thinks fit.

[(4)   In this rule "nominated officer" in relation to an examination which is to take place at the Central Office, the principal registry of the Family Division, a district registry or a county court means such of the officers of that Office, registry, district registry or county court of a grade not lower than that of higher executive officer as may be nominated for the purposes of this rule by the senior master, the senior [district judge] of the Family Division or the [district judge] of that district registry or county court respectively.]

Commencement   1 October 1973 (para (4)); 1 October 1966 (remainder).
Amendments   Para (1): words from "In this paragraph" to the end added by SI 1973/1384, r 4(1).
Para (3): words from "(or in the case" to "county court respectively)" inserted by SI 1973/1384, r 4(2).
Para (4): substituted by SI 1973/1384, r 4(3).
Cross references   See CCR Order 25, r 3.
Forms   Affidavit in support (PF98).
Order (PF99).

Order 48, r 2 Examination of party liable to satisfy other judgment

Where any difficulty arises in or in connection with the enforcement of any judgment or order, other than such a judgment or order as is mentioned in rule 1, the Court may make an order under that rule for the attendance of the party liable to satisfy the judgment or order and for his examination on such questions as may be specified in the order, and that rule shall apply accordingly with the necessary modifications.

Commencement 1 October 1966.
Cross references See CCR Order 25, r 4.

Order 48, r 3 Examiner to make record of debtor's statement

The officer conducting the examination shall take down, or cause to be taken down, in writing the statement made by the judgment debtor or other person at the examination, read it to him and ask him to sign it; and if he refuses the officer shall sign the statement.

Commencement 1 October 1966.
Cross references See CCR Order 25, r 3.

ORDER 49
Garnishee Proceedings

Order 49, r 1 Attachment of debt due to judgment debtor

(1)   Where a person (in this Order referred to as "the judgment creditor") has obtained a judgment or order for the payment by some other person (in this Order referred to as "the judgment debtor") [of a sum of money amounting in value to at least £50, not being a judgment or order] for the payment of money into court, and any other person within the jurisdiction (in this Order referred to as "the garnishee") is indebted to the judgment debtor, the Court may, subject to the provisions of this Order and of any enactment, order the garnishee to pay the judgment creditor the amount of any debt due or accruing due to the judgment debtor from the garnishee, or so much thereof as is sufficient to satisfy that judgment or order and the costs of the garnishee proceedings.

(2)   An order under this rule shall in the first instance be an order to show cause, specifying the time and place for further consideration of the matter, and in the meantime attaching such debt as is mentioned in paragraph (1), or so much thereof as may be specified in the order, to answer the judgment or order mentioned in that paragraph and the costs of the garnishee proceedings.

(3)   Among the conditions mentioned in [section 40 of the Supreme Court Act 1981] (which enables any sum standing to the credit of a person in [certain types of account] to be attached notwithstanding that certain conditions applicable to the account [in question] have not been satisfied) there shall be included any condition that a receipt for money deposited in the account must be produced before any money is withdrawn.

[(4)   An order under this rule shall not require a payment which would reduce below £1 the amount standing in the name of the judgment debtor in an account with a building society or a credit union.]

Commencement   1 January 1982 (para (4)); 1 October 1966 (remainder).
Amendments   Para (1): words from "of a sum of money" to "judgment or order" substituted by SI 1981/ 1734, r 31(1).
Para (3): words "section 40 of the Supreme Court Act 1981" and "certain types of account" substituted and words "in question" inserted by SI 1981/1734, r 31(2).
Para (4): inserted by SI 1981/1734, r 31(3).
Cross references   See CCR Order 30, r 1.
Forms   Garnishee order to show cause (No 72).

Order 49, r 2 Application for order

An application for an order under rule 1 must be made ex parte supported by an affidavit—

[(a)]   stating the name and last known address of the judgment debtor,]

[(b)]   identifying the judgment or order to be enforced and stating the amount [of such judgment or order and the amount] remaining unpaid under it at the time of the application,

[(c)]   stating that to the best of the information or belief of the deponent the garnishee (naming him) is within the jurisdiction and is indebted to the judgment debtor and stating the sources of the deponent's information or the grounds for his belief[, and]

[(d)]   stating, where the garnishee is [a deposit-taking institution] having more than one place of business, the name and address of the branch at which the judgment debtor's account is believed to be held [and the number of that account] or, if it be the case, that [all or part of] this information is not known to the deponent.]

Commencement 1 October 1966.
Amendments Original sub-para (a) renumbered as sub-para (b) and new sub-para (a) added by SI 1981/1734, r 32(1), (2); in sub-para (b) words "of such judgement or order and the amount" inserted by SI 1981/1734, r 32(3); original sub-para (b) renumbered as sub-para (c) by SI 1981/1734, r 32(2), word ", and" inserted by SI 1976/337, r 9; sub-para (d) originally added as sub-para (c) by SI 1976/337, r 9, renumbered as sub-para (d) and words "a deposit-taking institution" substituted and words "and the number of that account" and "all or part of" inserted by SI 1981/1734, r 32(4).
Cross references See CCR Order 30, r 2.
Forms Affidavit in support of garnishee order (PF100).

Order 49, r 3 Service and effect of order to show cause

(1) [Unless the Court otherwise directs, an order] under rule 1 to show cause must ... be served—

   (a) on the garnishee personally, [at least 15 days before the time appointed thereby for the further consideration of the matter,] and

   (b) [on the judgment debtor, at least 7 days after the order has been served on the garnishee and at least 7 days before the time appointed by the order for the further consideration of the matter.]

(2) Such an order shall bind in the hands of the garnishee as from the service of the order on him any debt specified in the order or so much thereof as may be so specified.

Commencement 1 October 1966.
Amendments Para (1): words "Unless the Court otherwise directs, an order" substituted, words omitted revoked, in sub-para (a) words from "at least 15 days" to "of the matter" inserted, and sub-para (b) substituted, by SI 1981/1734, r 33.
Cross references See CCR Order 30, r 3.

Order 49, r 4 No appearance or dispute of liability by garnishee

(1) Where on the further consideration of the matter the garnishee does not attend or does not dispute the debt due or claimed to be due from him to the judgment debtor, the Court may ... make an order absolute under rule 1 against the garnishee.

(2) An order absolute under rule 1 against the garnishee may be enforced in the same manner as any other order for the payment of money.

Commencement 1 October 1966.
Amendments Para (1): words omitted revoked by SI 1981/1734, r 34.
Cross references See CCR Order 30, r 7.
Forms Garnishee order absolute (Nos 73, 74).

Order 49, r 5 Dispute of liability by garnishee

Where on the further consideration of the matter the garnishee disputes liability to pay the debt due or claimed to be due from him to the judgment debtor, the Court may summarily determine the question at issue or order that any question necessary for determining the liability of the garnishee be tried in any manner in which any question or issue in an action may be tried, without, if it orders trial before a master, the need for any consent by the parties.

Commencement 1 October 1966.
Cross references See CCR Order 30 rr 8, 9.
Forms Order for trial of issue (PF102).

Order 49, r 6 Claims of third persons

(1) If in garnishee proceedings it is brought to the notice of the Court that some other person than the judgment debtor is or claims to be entitled to the debt sought to be attached or has or claims to have a charge or lien upon it, the Court may order that person to attend before the Court and state the nature of his claim with particulars thereof.

(2) After hearing any person who attends before the Court in compliance with an order under paragraph (1), the Court may summarily determine the questions at issue between the claimants or make such other order as it thinks just, including an order that any question or issue necessary for determining the validity of the claim of such other person as is mentioned in paragraph (1) be tried in such manner as is mentioned in rule 5.

Commencement 1 October 1966.

Order 49, r 7 *(revoked by SI 1979/1725)*

Order 49, r 8 Discharge of garnishee

Any payment made by a garnishee in compliance with an order absolute under this Order, and any execution levied against him in pursuance of such an order, shall be a valid discharge of his liability to the judgment debtor to the extent of the amount paid or levied notwithstanding that the garnishee proceedings are subsequently set aside or the judgment or order from which they arose reversed.

Commencement 1 October 1966.
Cross references See CCR Order 30, r 11.

Order 49, r 9 Money in court

(1) Where money is standing to the credit of the judgment debtor in court, the judgment creditor shall not be entitled to take garnishee proceedings in respect of that money but may apply to the Court by summons for an order that the money or so much thereof as is sufficient to satisfy the judgment or order sought to be enforced and the costs of the application be paid to the judgment creditor.

(2) On issuing a summons under this rule the applicant must produce the summons at the office of the Accountant General and leave a copy at that office, and the money to which the application relates shall not be paid out of court until after the determination of the application.

If the application is dismissed, the applicant must give notice of that fact to the Accountant General.

(3) Unless the Court otherwise directs, the summons must be served on the judgment debtor at least 7 days before the day named therein for the hearing of it.

(4) Subject to Order 75, rule 24, the Court hearing an application under this rule

may make such order with respect to the money in court as it thinks just.

Commencement　1 October 1966.
Cross references　See CCR Order 30, r 12.

Order 49, r 10 Costs

The costs of any application for an order under rule 1 or 9, and of any proceedings arising therefrom or incidental thereto, shall, unless the Court otherwise directs, be retained by the judgment creditor out of the money recovered by him under the order and in priority to the judgment debt.

Commencement　1 October 1966.
Cross references　See CCR Order 30, r 13.

ORDER 50
CHARGING ORDERS, STOP ORDERS, ETC

[Order 50, r 1 Order imposing a charge on a beneficial interest

(1)   The power to make a charging order under section 1 of the Charging Orders Act 1979 (referred to in this Order as "the Act") shall be exercisable by the Court.

(2)   An application by a judgment creditor for a charging order in respect of a judgment debtor's beneficial interest may be made ex parte, and any order made on such an application shall in the first instance be an order, made in Form No 75 in Appendix A, to show cause, specifying the time and place for further consideration of the matter and imposing the charge in any event until that time.

(3)   The application shall be supported by an affidavit—
(a)   identifying the judgment or order to be enforced and stating the amount unpaid at the date of the application;
(b)   stating the name of the judgment debtor and of any creditor of his whom the applicant can identify;
(c)   giving full particulars of the subject matter of the intended charge, including, in the case of securities other than securities in court, the full title of the securities, their amount and the name in which they stand and, in the case of funds in court, the number of the account; and
(d)   verifying that the interest to be charged is owned beneficially by the judgment debtor.

(4)   Unless the Court otherwise directs, an affidavit for the purposes of this rule may contain statements of information or belief with the sources and grounds thereof.

(5)   An application may be made for a single charging order in respect of more than one judgment or order against the debtor.]

Commencement   3 June 1980.
Amendments   Original rr 1–8 were substituted by new rr 1–7 by SI 1980/629, r 10.
Cross references   See CCR Order 31, r 1.

[Order 50, r 2 Service of notice of order to show cause

(1)   On the making of an order to show cause, notice of the order shall, unless the Court otherwise directs, be served as follows:—
(a)   a copy of the order, together with a copy of the affidavit in support, shall be served on the judgment debtor;
(b)   where the order relates to securities other than securities in court, copies of the order shall also be served
(i)   in the case of government stock for which the Bank of England keeps the register, on the Bank of England;
(ii)   in the case of government stock to which (i) does not apply, on the keeper of the register;
(iii)   in the case of stock of any body incorporated within England and Wales, on that body, or, where the register is kept by the Bank of England, on the Bank of England;
(iv)   in the case of stock of any body incorporated outside England and Wales or of any state or territory outside the United Kingdom, being stock registered in a register kept in England and Wales, on the keeper of the register;

(v) in the case of units of any unit trust in respect of which a register of the unit holders is kept in England and Wales, on the keeper of the register;

(c) where the order relates to a fund in court, a copy of the order shall be served on the Accountant General at the Court Funds Office; and

(d) where the order relates to an interest under a trust, copies of the order shall be served on such of the trustees as the Court may direct.

(2)   Without prejudice to the provisions of paragraph (1), the Court may, on making the order to show cause, direct the service of copies of the order, and of the affidavit in support, on any other creditor of the judgment debtor or on any other interested person as may be appropriate in the circumstances.

(3)   Documents to be served under this Rule must be served at least seven days before the time appointed for the further consideration of the matter.]

Commencement 3 June 1980.
Amendments See the note to Order 50, r 1.
Cross references See CCR Order 31, r 1(5)-(9).

[Order 50, r 3 Order made on further considerations

(1)   On the further consideration of the matter the Court shall either make the order absolute, with or without modifications, or discharge it.

(2)   Where the order is made absolute, it shall be made in Form No 76 in Appendix A, and where it is discharged, the provisions of rule 7, regarding the service of copies of the order of discharge, shall apply.]

Commencement 3 June 1980.
Amendments See the note to Order 50, r 1.
Cross references See CCR Order 31, r 2.

[Order 50, r 4 Order imposing a charge on an interest held by a trustee

(1)   Save as provided by this rule, the provisions of rules 1, 2 and 3 shall apply to an order charging an interest held by a trustee as they apply to an order charging the judgment debtor's beneficial interest.

(2)   Instead of verifying the judgment debtor's beneficial ownership of the interest to be charged, the affidavit required by rule 1(3) shall state the ground on which the application is based and shall verify the material facts.

(3)   On making the order to show cause, the Court shall give directions for copies of the order, and of the affidavit in support, to be served on such of the trustees and beneficiaries, if any, as may be appropriate.

(4)   Rules 5, 6 and 7 shall apply to an order charging an interest held by a trustee as they apply to an order charging the judgment debtor's beneficial interest, except that, where the order is made under subsection (ii) or (iii) of section 2(1)(b) of the Act, references in those rules to "the judgment debtor" shall be references to the trustee.

(5)   Forms No 75 and 76 in Appendix A shall be modified so as to indicate that the interest to be charged is held by the debtor as trustee or, as the case may be, that it is held by a trustee (to be named in the order) on trust for the debtor beneficially.]

Commencement 3 June 1980.
Amendments See the note to Order 50, r 1.

Definitions   The Act: Charging Orders Act 1979.
Cross references   This rule is applied to the county court by CCR Order 31, r 3.

[Order 50, r 5 Effect of order in relation to securities out of court

(1)   No disposition by the judgment debtor of his interest in any securities to which an order to show cause relates made after the making of that order shall, so long as that order remains in force, be valid as against the judgment creditor.

(2)   Until such order is discharged or made absolute, the Bank of England (or other person or body served in accordance with rule 2(1)(b)) shall not permit any transfer of any of the securities specified in the order, or pay any dividend, interest or redemption payment in relation thereto, except with the authority of the Court, and, if it does so, shall be liable to pay the judgment creditor the value of the securities transferred or, as the case may be, the amount of the payment made or, if that value or amount is more than sufficient to satisfy the judgment or order to which such order relates, so much thereof as is sufficient to satisfy it.

(3)   If the Court makes the order absolute, a copy of the order, including a stop notice as provided in Form No 76 in Appendix A, shall be served on the Bank of England, or on such other person or body specified in rule 2(1)(b) as may be appropriate and, save as provided in rule 7(5), rules 11 to 14 shall apply to such a notice as they apply to a stop notice made and served under rule 11.

(4)   This rule does not apply to orders in respect of securities in court.]

Commencement   3 June 1980.
Amendments   See the note to Order 50, r 1.
Cross references   This rule is applied to the county court by CCR Order 31, r 3.

[Order 50, r 6 Effect of order in relation to funds in court

(1)   Where an order to show cause has been made in relation to funds in court (including securities in court) and a copy thereof has been served on the Accountant General in accordance with rule 2, no disposition by the judgment debtor of any interest to which the order relates, made after the making of that order, shall, so long as the order remains in force, be valid as against the judgment creditor.

(2)   If the Court makes the order absolute, a copy of the order shall be served on the Accountant General at the Court Funds Office.]

Commencement   3 June 1980.
Amendments   See the note to Order 50, r 1.
Cross references   This rule is applied to the county court by CCR Order 31, r 3.

[Order 50, r 7 Discharge, etc, of charging order

(1)   Subject to paragraph (2), on the application of the judgment debtor or any other person interested in the subject matter of the charge, the Court may, at any time, whether before or after the order is made absolute, discharge or vary the order on such terms (if any) as to costs or otherwise as it thinks just.

(2)   Where an application is made for the discharge of a charging order in respect of the judgment debtor's land on the ground that the judgment debt has been satisfied, the applicant shall state in his application, and the Court shall specify in its order, the

title number of the land in the case of registered land, and the entry number of any relevant land charge in the case of unregistered land.

(3)   Notice of an application for the discharge or variation of the order shall be served on such interested parties as the Court may direct.

(4)   Where an order is made for the discharge or variation of a charging order in respect of funds in court, a copy thereof shall be served on the Accountant General at the Court Funds Office.

(5)   Where an order is made for the discharge or variation of a charging order in respect of securities other than securities in court, a copy thereof shall be served on the Bank of England or on such other person or body specified in rule 2(1)(b) as may be appropriate, and the service thereof shall discharge, or, as the case may be, vary, any stop notice in respect of such securities which may be in force pursuant to the original order.]

Commencement   3 June 1980.
Amendments   See the note to Order 50, r 1.
Cross references   This rule is applied to the county court by CCR Order 31, r 3.

Order 50, r 8   (*see the note to Order 50, r 1*)

[Order 50, r 9 Jurisdiction of Master, etc to grant injunction . . .

[A master] [and the Admiralty Registrar] and a [district judge] of the [Family Division] shall have power . . . to grant an injunction if, and only so far as, it is ancillary or incidental to an order [under rule 1, 3 or 4], and an application for . . . an injunction under this rule may be joined with the application for the order [under rule 1, 3 or 4] to which it relates.]

Commencement   1 January 1968.
Amendments   This rule was substituted by SI 1967/1809, r 4(2).
Rule heading: words omitted revoked by SI 1980/629, r 11.
Words "A master" substituted by SI 1982/1111, r 54; words "and the Admiralty Registrar" inserted and words "Family Division" substituted by SI 1971/1269, rr 13, 38(a), Schedule; words omitted revoked and words "under rule 1, 3 or 4" in both places substituted by SI 1980/629, r 11.

[Order 50 r 9A Enforcement of Charging Order by Sale

(1)   Proceedings for the enforcement of a charging order by sale of the property charged must be begun by originating summons issued out of Chancery Chambers or out of one of the Chancery district registries.

(2)   The provisions of Order 88 shall apply to all such proceedings.]

Commencement   1 October 1984.
Amendments   This rule was inserted by SI 1984/1051, r 8.
Cross references   See CCR Order 31, r 4.
Forms   Order as to inquiry as to title (ChPF34).

Order 50, r 10 Funds in court: stop order

(1)   The Court, on the application of any person—
    (a)   who has a mortgage or charge on the interest of any person in funds in court, or

(b) to whom that interest has been assigned, or

(c) who is a judgment creditor of the person entitled to that interest,

may make an order prohibiting the transfer, sale, delivery out, payment or other dealing with such funds, or any part thereof, or the income thereon, without notice to the applicant.

(2) An application for an order under this rule must be made by summons in the cause or matter relating to the funds in court, or, if there is no such cause or matter, by originating summons.

(3) The summons must be served on every person whose interest may be affected by the order applied for and on the Accountant General but shall not be served on any other person.

(4) Without prejudice to the Court's powers and discretion as to costs, the Court may order the applicant for an order under this rule to pay the costs of any party to the cause or matter relating to the funds in question, or of any person interested in those funds, occasioned by the application.

Commencement 1 October 1966.
Forms Stop Order (No 79).

Order 50, r 11 Securities not in court: stop notice

(1) Any person claiming to be beneficially entitled to an interest in any securities [of the kinds set out in section 2(2)(b) of the Act], other than securities in court, who wishes to be notified of any proposed transfer or payment of those securities may avail himself of the provisions of this rule.

(2) A person claiming to be so entitled must file in [Chancery Chambers or] in a district registry—
    (a) an affidavit identifying the securities in question and describing his interest therein by reference to the document under which it arises, and
    (b) a notice in Form No 80 in Appendix A, [(a stop notice),] signed by the deponent to the affidavit, and annexed to it, addressed to the Bank of England or, as the case may be, [the body, state, territory or unit trust concerned],

and must serve an office copy of the affidavit, and a copy of the notice sealed with the seal of [Chancery Chambers or the] district registry, on the Bank [or other person or body, as provided in rule 2(1)(b)].

(3) There must be indorsed on the affidavit filed under this rule a note stating the address to which any such notice as is referred to in [rule 12] is to be sent and, subject to paragraph (4), that address shall for the purpose of that rule be the address for service of the person on whose behalf the affidavit is filed.

(4) A person on whose behalf an affidavit under this rule is filed may change his address for service for the purpose of rule 12 by serving on the Bank of England, [or other person or body], a notice to that effect, and as from the date of service of such a notice the address stated therein shall for the purpose of that rule be the address for service of that person.

Commencement 1 October 1966.
Amendments Para (1): words "of the kinds set out in section 2 (2)(b) of the Act" substituted by SI 1980/629, r 12(1).

Para (2): words "Chancery Chambers or" and "Chancery Chambers or the" substituted by SI 1982/1111, r 55; words "(a stop notice)," inserted and words "the body, state, territory or unit trust concerned" and "or other person or body, as provided in rule 2(1)(b)" substituted by SI 1980/629, r 12(2).
Para (3): words "rule 12" substituted by SI 1980/629, r 12(3).
Para (4): words "or other person or body" substituted by SI 1980/629, r 12(4).
Definitions The Act: Charging Orders Act 1979.

[Order 50, r 12 Effect of stop notice

Where a stop notice has been served in accordance with rule 11, then, so long as the stop notice is in force, the Bank of England or other person or body on which it is served shall not register a transfer of the securities or take any other step restrained by the stop notice until 14 days after sending notice thereof, by ordinary first class post, to the person on whose behalf the stop notice was filed, but shall not by reason only of the notice refuse to register a transfer, or to take any other step, after the expiry of that period.]

Commencement 3 June 1980.
Amendments This rule was substituted by SI 1980/629, r 13.

[Order 50, r 13 Amendments of stop notice

If any securities are incorrectly described in a stop notice which has been filed and of which a sealed copy has been served in accordance with rule 11, an amended stop notice may be filed and served in accordance with the same procedure and shall take effect as a stop notice on the day on which the sealed copy of the amended notice is served.]

Commencement 3 June 1980.
Amendments This rule was substituted by SI 1980/629, r 13.

Order 50, r 14 Withdrawal, etc of stop notice

(1)   The person on whose behalf [a stop notice] was filed may withdraw it by serving a request for its withdrawal on the Bank of England [or other person or body] on whom the notice was served.

(2)   Such request must be signed by the person on whose behalf the notice was filed and his signature must be witnessed by a practising solicitor.

(3)   The Court, on the application of any person claiming to be beneficially entitled to an interest in the securities to which [a stop notice] relates, may by order discharge the notice.

(4)   An application for an order under paragraph (3) must be made in the Chancery Division by originating summons, and the summons must be served on the person on whose behalf [a stop notice] was filed.

[The summons shall be in Form No 10 in Appendix A.]

Commencement 1 October 1966.
Amendments Para (1): words "a stop notice" and "or other person or body" substituted by SI 1980/629, r 14.
Para (3): words "a stop notice" substituted by SI 1980/629, r 14.
Para (4): words "a stop notice" substituted by SI 1980/629, r 14; words "The summons shall be in Form No 10 in Appendix A" substituted by SI 1979/1716, r 48, Schedule, Pt 2.

Order 50, r 15 Order prohibiting transfer, etc of securities

[(1) The Court, on the application of any person claiming to be beneficially entitled to an interest in any securities of the kinds set out in section 2(2)(b) of the Act may by order prohibit the Bank of England or other person or body concerned from registering any transfer of the securities or taking any other step to which section 5(5) of the Act applies.

The order shall specify the securities to which the prohibition relates, the name in which they stand and the steps which may not be taken, and shall state whether the prohibition applies to the securities only or to the dividends or interest as well.]

(2) An application for an order under this rule must be made by motion or summons in the Chancery Division.

[An originating summons under this rule shall be in Form No 10 in Appendix A.]

(3) The Court, on the application of any person claiming to be entitled to an interest in any [securities] to which an order under this rule relates, may vary or discharge the order on such terms (if any) as to costs [or otherwise] as it thinks fit.

Commencement   3 June 1980 (para (1)); 1 October 1966 (remainder).
Amendments   Para (1): substituted by SI 1980/629, r 15(1).
Para (2): words from "An originating summons" to "Appendix A" substituted by SI 1979/1716, r 48, Schedule, Pt 2.
Para (3): word "securities" substituted and words "or otherwise" inserted by SI 1980/629, r 15(2).
Definitions   The Act: Charging Orders Act 1979.
Forms   Order restraining transfer (No 81).

ORDER 51
RECEIVERS: EQUITABLE EXECUTION

Order 51, r 1 Appointment of receiver by way of equitable execution

. . . Where an application is made for the appointment of a receiver by way of equitable execution, the Court in determining whether it is just or convenient that the appointment should be made shall have regard to the amount claimed by the judgment creditor, to the amount likely to be obtained by the receiver and to the probable costs of his appointment and may direct an inquiry on any of these matters or any other matter before making the appointment.

. . .

Commencement   1 October 1966.
Amendments   Words omitted revoked by SI 1980/629, r 25.
Cross references   See CCR Order 32, r 1.

Order 51, r 2 Masters and [district judges] may appoint receiver, etc

[A master] [and the Admiralty Registrar] and a [district judge] of the [Family Division] shall have power to make an order for the appointment of a receiver by way of equitable execution and to grant an injunction if, and only so far as, the injunction is ancillary or incidental to such an order.

Commencement   1 October 1966.
Amendments   Words "A master" substituted by SI 1982/1111, r 54; words "and the Admiralty Registrar" inserted and words "Family Division" substituted by SI 1971/1269, rr 14, 38(a), Schedule.
Cross references   See CCR Order 32, r 1(4).

Order 51, r 3 Application of rules as to appointment of receiver, etc

An application for the appointment of a receiver by way of equitable execution may be made in accordance with Order 30, rule 1, and rules 2 to 6 of that Order shall apply in relation to a receiver appointed by way of equitable execution as they apply in relation to a receiver appointed for any other purpose.

Commencement   1 October 1966.
Cross references   See CCR Order 32, r 3.
Forms   Summons for appointment of receiver (No 82).
Order directing summons (No 83).
Order appointing receiver (No 84).

ORDER 52
COMMITTAL

Order 52, r 1 Committal for contempt of court

(1)   The power of the High Court or Court of Appeal to punish for contempt of court may be exercised by an order of committal.

(2)   Where contempt of court—
    (a)   is committed in connection with—
        (i)   any proceedings before a Divisional Court of the Queen's Bench Division, or
        (ii)   criminal proceedings, except where the contempt is committed in the face of the court or consists of disobedience to an order of the court or a breach of an undertaking to the court, or
        (iii) proceedings in an inferior court, or
    (b)   is committed otherwise than in connection with any proceedings,

then, subject to paragraph (4), an order of committal may be made only by a Divisional Court of the Queen's Bench Division.

This paragraph shall not apply in relation to contempt of the Court of Appeal.

(3)   Where contempt of court is committed in connection with any proceedings in the High Court, then, subject to paragraph (2), an order of committal may be made by a single judge of the Queen's Bench Division except where the proceedings were assigned or subsequently transferred to some other Division, in which case the order may be made only by a single judge of that other Division.

The reference in this paragraph to a single judge of the Queen's Bench Division shall, in relation to proceedings in any court the judge or judges of which are, when exercising the jurisdiction of that court, deemed by virtue of any enactment to constitute a court of the High Court, be construed as a reference to a judge of that court.

(4)   Where by virtue of any enactment the High Court has power to punish or take steps for the punishment of any person charged with having done any thing in relation to a court, tribunal or person which would, if it had been done in relation to the High Court, have been a contempt of that Court, an order of committal may be made by a single judge of the Queen's Bench Division.

Commencement   1 October 1966.
Cross references   See CCR Order 29, r 1.

Order 52, r 2 Application to Divisional Court

(1)   No application to a Divisional Court for an order of committal against any person may be made unless leave to make such an application has been granted in accordance with this rule.

(2)   An application for such leave must be made ex parte to a Divisional Court, except in vacation when it may be made to a judge in chambers, and must be supported by a statement setting out the name and description of the applicant, the name, description and address of the person sought to be committed and the grounds on which his committal is sought, and by an affidavit, to be filed before the application is made, verifying the facts relied on.

(3)   The applicant must give notice of the application for leave not later than the preceding day to the Crown Office and must at the same time lodge in that Office copies of the statement and affidavit.

(4)   Where an application for leave under this rule is refused by a judge in chambers, the applicant may make a fresh application for such leave to a Divisional Court.

(5)   An application made to a Divisional Court by virtue of paragraph (4) must be made within 8 days after the judge's refusal to give leave or, if a Divisional Court does not sit within that period, on the first day on which it sits thereafter.

Commencement   1 October 1966.
Forms   Order for committal (No 85).
Warrants for committal (PF103–5).

Order 52, r 3 Application for order after leave to apply granted

(1)   When leave has been granted under rule 2 to apply for an order of committal, the application for the order must be made by motion to a Divisional Court and, unless the Court or judge granting leave has otherwise directed, there must be at least 8 clear days between the service of the notice of motion and the day named therein for the hearing.

(2)   Unless within 14 days after such leave was granted the motion is entered for hearing the leave shall lapse.

(3)   Subject to paragraph (4), the notice of motion, accompanied by a copy of the statement and affidavit in support of the application for leave under rule 2, must be served personally on the person sought to be committed.

(4)   Without prejudice to the powers of the Court or judge under Order 65, rule 4, the Court or judge may dispense with service of the notice of motion under this rule if it or he thinks it just to do so.

Commencement   1 October 1966.

Order 52, r 4 Application to Court other than Divisional Court

(1)   Where an application for an order of committal may be made to a Court other than a Divisional Court, the application must be made by motion and be supported by an affidavit.

(2)   Subject to paragraph (3), the notice of motion, stating the grounds of the application and accompanied by a copy of the affidavit in support of the application, must be served personally on the person sought to be committed.

(3)   Without prejudice to its powers under Order 65, rule 4, the Court may dispense with service of the notice of motion under this rule if it thinks it just to do so.

[(4)   This rule does not apply to proceedings brought before a single judge by virtue of Order 64, rule 4.]

Commencement   1 July 1991 (para (4)); 1 October 1966 (remainder).
Amendments   Para (4): added by SI 1991/1329, r 17(1).

Order 52, r 5 Saving for power to commit without application for purpose

Nothing in the foregoing provisions of this Order shall be taken as affecting the power of the High Court or Court of Appeal to make an order of committal of its own motion against a person guilty of contempt of court.

Commencement 1 October 1966.

Order 52, r 6 Provisions as to hearing

(1) Subject to paragraph (2), the Court hearing an application for an order of committal may sit in private in the following cases, that is to say—

(a) Where the application arises out of proceedings relating to the wardship or adoption of an infant or wholly or mainly to the guardianship, custody, maintenance or upbringing of an infant, or rights of access to an infant;

(b) where the application arises out of proceedings relating to a person suffering or appearing to be suffering from mental disorder within the meaning of the [Mental Health Act 1983];

(c) where the application arises out of proceedings in which a secret process, discovery or invention was in issue;

(d) where it appears to the Court that in the interests of the administration of justice or for reasons of national security the application should be heard in private;

but, except as aforesaid, the application shall be heard in open court.

(2) If the Court hearing an application in private by virtue of paragraph (1) decides to make an order of committal against the person sought to be committed, it shall in open court state—

(a) the name of that person,

(b) in general terms the nature of the contempt of court in respect of which the order of committal is being made, and

(c) [the length of the period for which he is being committed].

(3) Except with the leave of the Court hearing an application for an order of committal, no grounds shall be relied upon at the hearing except the grounds set out in the statement under rule 2 or, as the case may be, in the notice of motion under rule 4.

The foregoing provision is without prejudice to the powers of the Court under Order 20, rule 8.

(4) If on the hearing of the application the person sought to be committed expresses a wish to give oral evidence on his own behalf, he shall be entitled to do so.

Commencement 1 October 1966.
Amendments Para (1): in sub-para (b) words "Mental Health Act 1983" substituted by SI 1983/1181, r 36, Schedule.
Para (2): sub-para (c) substituted by SI 1986/632, r 18.

Order 52, r 7 Power to suspend execution of committal order

(1) The Court by whom an order of committal is made may by order direct that the execution of the order of committal shall be suspended for such period or on such terms or conditions as it may specify.

(2)   Where execution of an order of committal is suspended by an order under paragraph (1), the applicant for the order of committal must, unless the Court otherwise directs, serve on the person against whom it was made a notice informing him of the making and terms of the order under that paragraph.

Commencement   1 October 1966.

Order 52, r 8 Discharge of person committed

(1)   The Court may, on the application of any person committed to prison for any contempt of court, discharge him.

(2)   Where a person has been committed for failing to comply with a judgment or order requiring him to deliver any thing to some other person or to deposit it in court or elsewhere, and a writ of sequestration has also been issued to enforce that judgment or order, then, if the thing is in the custody or power of the person committed, the commissioners appointed by the writ of sequestration may take possession of it as if it were the property of that person and, without prejudice to the generality of paragraph (1), the Court may discharge the person committed and may give such directions for dealing with the thing taken by the commissioners as it thinks fit.

Commencement   1 October 1966.
Cross references   See CCR Order 29, r 3.

Order 52, r 9 Saving for other powers

Nothing in the foregoing provisions of this Order shall be taken as affecting the power of the Court to make an order requiring a person guilty of contempt of court, or a person punishable by virtue of any enactment in like manner as if he had been guilty of contempt of the High Court, to pay a fine or to give security for his good behaviour, and those provisions, so far as applicable, and with the necessary modifications, shall apply in relation to an application for such an order as they apply in relation to an application for an order of committal.

Commencement   1 October 1966.

DIVISIONAL COURTS, COURT OF APPEAL, ETC

[ORDER 53
APPLICATIONS FOR JUDICIAL REVIEW

Order 53, r 1 Cases appropriate for application for judicial review

(1)   An application for—
   (a)   an order of mandamus, prohibition or certiorari, or
   (b)   an injunction under [section 30 of the Act] restraining a person from acting in any office in which he is not entitled to act,

shall be made by way of an application for judicial review in accordance with the provisions of this Order.

(2)   An application for a declaration or an injunction (not being an injunction mentioned in paragraph (1)(b)) may be made by way of an application for judicial review, and on such an application the Court may grant the declaration or injunction claimed if it considers that, having regard to—
   (a)   the nature of the matters in respect of which relief may be granted by way of an order of mandamus, prohibition or certiorari,
   (b)   the nature of the persons and bodies against whom relief may be granted by way of such an order, and
   (c)   all the circumstances of the case,

it would be just and convenient for the declaration or injunction to be granted on an application for judicial review.]

Commencement   11 January 1978.
Amendments   Order 53 was substituted by SI 1977/1955, r 5.
Para (1): in sub-para (b) words "section 30 of the Act" substituted by SI 1982/1111, r 115, Schedule.
Definitions   The Act: Supreme Court Act 1981.

[Order 53, r 2 Joinder of claims for relief

On an application for judicial review any relief mentioned in rule 1(1) or (2) may be claimed as an alternative or in addition to any other relief so mentioned if it arises out of or relates to or is connected with the same matter.]

Commencement   11 January 1978.
Amendments   See the first note to Order 53, r 1.

[Order 53, r 3 Grant of leave to apply for judicial review

(1)   No application for judicial review shall be made unless the leave of the Court has been obtained in accordance with this rule.

[(2)   An application for leave must be made ex parte to a judge by filing in the Crown Office—
   (a)   a notice in Form No 86A containing a statement of
      (i)   the name and description of the applicant,
      (ii)   the relief sought and the grounds upon which it is sought,
      (iii)   the name and address of the applicant's solicitors (if any), and
      (iv)   the applicant's address for service; and
   (b)   an affidavit verifying the facts relied on.

(3)   The judge may determine the application without a hearing, unless a hearing is requested in the notice of application, and need not sit in open court; in any case, the Crown Office shall serve a copy of the judge's order on the applicant.

(4)   Where the application for leave is refused by the judge, or is granted on terms, the applicant may renew it by applying—

    (a)   in any criminal cause or matter, to a Divisional Court of the Queen's Bench Division;

    (b)   in any other case, to a single judge sitting in open court or, if the Court so directs, to a Divisional Court of the Queen's Bench Division;

Provided that no application for leave may be renewed in any non-criminal cause or matter in which the judge has refused leave under paragraph (3) after a hearing.

(5)   In order to renew his application for leave the applicant must, within 10 days of being served with notice of the judge's refusal, lodge in the Crown Office notice of his intention in Form No 86B.]

[(6)]   Without prejudice to its powers under Order 20, rule 8, the Court hearing an application for leave may allow the applicant's statement to be amended, whether by specifying different or additional grounds or relief or otherwise, on such terms, if any, as it thinks fit.

[(7)]   The Court shall not grant leave unless it considers that the applicant has a sufficient interest in the matter to which the application relates.

[(8)]   Where leave is sought to apply for an order of certiorari to remove for the purpose of its being quashed any judgment, order, conviction or other proceeding which is subject to appeal and a time is limited for the bringing of the appeal, the Court may adjourn the application for leave until the appeal is determined or the time for appealing has expired.

[(9)]   If the Courts grants leave, it may impose such terms as to costs and as to giving security as it thinks fit.

(10)   Where leave to apply for judicial review is granted, then—

    (a)   if the relief sought is an order of prohibition or certiorari and the Court so directs, the grant shall operate as a stay of the proceedings to which the application relates until the determination of the application or until the Court otherwise orders;

    (b)   if any other relief is sought, the Court may at any time grant in the proceedings such interim relief as could be granted in an action begun by writ.]

Commencement   12 January 1981 (paras (2)–(5)); 11 January 1978 (remainder).
Amendments   See the first note to Order 53, r 1.
Paras (2)–(5): substituted, for existing paras (2), (3), by SI 1980/2000, r 2(1).
Paras (6)–(9): original paras (8), (9) revoked and original paras (4)–(7) renumbered as paras (6)–(9) by SI 1980/2000, r 2(2).

[Order 53, r 4 Delay in applying for relief

(1)   [An application for leave to apply for judicial review] shall be made promptly and in any event within three months from the date when grounds for the application first arose unless the Court considers that there is good reason for extending the period within which the application shall be made.

(2)   Where the relief sought is an order of certiorari in respect of any judgment,

order, conviction or other proceeding, the date when grounds for the application first arose shall be taken to be the date of that judgment, order, conviction or proceeding.

(3)   Paragraph (1) is without prejudice to any statutory provision which has the effect of limiting the time within which an application for judicial review may be made.]

Commencement   12 January 1981.
Amendments   See the first note to Order 53, r 1.
This rule was further substituted by SI 1980/2000, r 3.
Para (1): words "An application for leave to apply for judicial review" substituted by SI 1987/1423, r 63, Schedule.

[Order 53, r 5 Mode of applying for judicial review

[(1)   In any criminal cause or matter where leave has been granted to make an application for judicial review, the application shall be made by originating motion to a Divisional Court of the Queen's Bench Division.

(2)   In any other such cause or matter, the application shall be made by originating motion to a judge sitting in open court, unless the Court directs that it shall be made—
   (a)   by originating summons to a judge in chambers; or
   (b)   by originating motion to a Divisional Court of the Queen's Bench Division.

Any direction under sub-paragraph (a) shall be without prejudice to the judge's powers under Order 32, rule 13.]

(3)   The notice of motion or summons must be served on all persons directly affected and where it relates to any proceedings in or before a court and the object of the application is either to compel the court or an officer of the court to do any act in relation to the proceedings or to quash them or any order made therein, the notice or summons must also be served on the clerk or registrar of the court and, where any objection to the conduct of the judge is to be made, on the judge.

(4)   Unless the Court granting leave has otherwise directed, there must be at least 10 days between the service of the notice of motion or summons and . . . the hearing.

(5)   A motion must be entered for hearing within 14 days after the grant of leave.

(6)   An affidavit giving the names and addresses of, and the places and dates of service on, all persons who have been served with the notice of motion or summons must be filed before the motion or summons is entered for hearing and, if any person who ought to be served under this rule has not been served, the affidavit must state that fact and the reason for it; and the affidavit shall be before the Court on the hearing of the motion or summons.

(7)   If on the hearing of the motion or summons the Court is of opinion that any person who ought, whether under this rule or otherwise, to have been served has not been served, the Court may adjourn the hearing on such terms (if any) as it may direct in order that the notice or summons may be served on that person.]

Commencement   12 January 1981 (paras (1), (2)); 11 January 1978 (remainder).
Amendments   See the first note to Order 53, r 1.
Paras (1), (2): substituted by SI 1980/2000, r 4(1).
Para (4): words omitted revoked by SI 1980/2000, r 4(2).
Forms   Notice of motion (No 86).
Notice of application (No 86A).
Notice of renewal of application (No 86B).

[Order 53, r 6 Statements and affidavits

(1)   Copies of the statement in support of an application for leave under rule 3 must be served with the notice of motion or summons and, subject to paragraph (2), no grounds shall be relied upon or any relief sought at the hearing except the grounds and relief set out in the statement.

[(2)   The Court may on the hearing of the motion or summons allow the applicant to amend his statement, whether by specifying different or additional grounds or relief or otherwise, on such terms, if any, as it thinks fit and may allow further affidavits to be used by him.]

(3)   Where the applicant intends to ask to be allowed to amend his statement or to use further affidavits, he shall give notice of his intention and of any proposed amendment to every other party.

[(4)   Any respondent who intends to use an affidavit at the hearing shall file it in the Crown Office, and give notice thereof to the applicant, as soon as practicable and in any event, unless the Court otherwise directs, within [56 days] after the service upon him of the documents required to be served by paragraph (1).]

[(5)] Each party to the application must supply to every other party on demand and on payment of the proper charges copies of every affidavit which he proposes to use at the hearing, including, in the case of the applicant, the affidavit in support of the application for leave under rule 3.]

Commencement   1 October 1992 (para (2)); 12 January 1981 (para (4)); 11 January 1978 (remainder).
Amendments   See the first note to Order 53, r 1.
Para (2): substituted by SI 1992/1907, r 11.
Para (4): inserted by SI 1980/2000, r 5(1); words "56 days" substituted by SI 1989/177, r 7.
Para (5): originally para (4), renumbered as para (5) by SI 1980/2000, r 5(2).

[Order 53, r 7 Claim for damages

(1)   On an application for judicial review the Court may, subject to paragraph (2), award damages to the applicant if—
    (a)   he has included in the statement in support of his application for leave under rule 3 a claim for damages arising from any matter to which the application relates, and
    (b)   the Court is satisfied that, if the claim had been made in an action begun by the applicant at the time of making his application, he could have been awarded damages.

(2)   Order 18, rule 12, shall apply to a statement relating to a claim for damages as it applies to a pleading.]

Commencement   11 January 1978.
Amendments   See the first note to Order 53, r 1.

[Order 53, r 8 Application for discovery, interrogatories, cross-examination, etc

(1)   Unless the Court otherwise directs, any interlocutory application in proceedings on an application for judicial review may be made to any judge or a master of the Queen's Bench Division, notwithstanding that the application for judicial review has been made by motion and is to be heard by a Divisional Court.

In this paragraph "interlocutory application" includes an application for an order under Order 24 or 26 or Order 38, rule 2(3), or for an order dismissing the proceedings by consent of the parties.

(2) In relation to an order made by a master pursuant to paragraph (1), Order 58, rule 1, shall, where the application for judicial review is to be heard by a Divisional Court, have effect as if a reference to that Court were substituted for the reference to a judge in chambers.

(3) This rule is without prejudice to any statutory provision or rule of law restricting the making of an order against the Crown.]

Commencement 11 January 1978.
Amendments See the first note to Order 53, r 1.

[Order 53, r 9 Hearing of application for judicial review

(1) On the hearing of any motion or summons under rule 5, any person who desires to be heard in opposition to the motion or summons, and appears to the Court to be a proper person to be heard, shall be heard, notwithstanding that he has not been served with notice of the motion or the summons.

(2) Where the relief sought is or includes an order of certiorari to remove any proceedings for the purpose of quashing them, the applicant may not question the validity of any order, warrant, commitment, conviction, inquisition or record unless before the hearing of the motion or summons he has lodged in the Crown Office a copy thereof verified by affidavit or accounts for his failure to do so to the satisfaction of the Court hearing the motion or summons.

(3) Where an order of certiorari is made in any such case as is referred to in paragraph (2), the order shall, subject to paragraph (4), direct that the proceedings shall be quashed forthwith on their removal into the Queen's Bench Division.

(4) Where the relief sought is an order of certiorari and the Court is satisfied that there are grounds for quashing the decision to which the application relates, the Court may, in addition to quashing it, remit the matter to the court, tribunal or authority concerned with a direction to reconsider it and reach a decision in accordance with the findings of the Court.

(5) Where the relief sought is a declaration, an injunction or damages and the Court considers that it should not be granted on an application for judicial review but might have been granted if it had been sought in an action begun by writ by the applicant at the time of making his application, the Court may, instead of refusing the application, order the proceedings to continue as if they had been begun by writ; and Order 28, rule 8, shall apply as if, in the case of an application made by motion, it had been made by summons.]

Commencement 11 January 1978.
Amendments See the first note to Order 53, r 1.

[Order 53, r 10 Saving for person acting in obedience to mandamus

No action or proceeding shall be begun or prosecuted against any person in respect of anything done in obedience to an order of mandamus.]

Commencement 11 January 1978.
Amendments See the first note to Order 53, r 1.

[Order 53, r 11 Proceedings for disqualification of member of local authority

(1)   Proceedings under section 92 of the Local Government Act 1972 must be begun by originating motion to a Divisional Court of the Queen's Bench Division, ... and, unless otherwise directed, there must be at least 10 days between the service of the notice of motion ... and ... the hearing.

(2)   Without prejudice to ... Order 8, rule 3, the notice of motion ... must set out the name and description of the applicant, the relief sought and the grounds on which it is sought, and must be supported by affidavit verifying the facts relied on.

(3)   Copies of every supporting affidavit must be lodged in the Crown Office before the motion is entered for hearing ... and must be supplied to any other party on demand and on payment of the proper charges.

(4)   The provisions of rules 5, 6 and 9(1) as to the persons on whom the notice ... is to be served and as to the proceedings at the hearing shall apply, with the necessary modifications, to proceedings under the said section 92 as they apply to an application for judicial review.]

Commencement   11 January 1978.
Amendments   See the first note to Order 53, r 1.
Paras (1), (3), (4): words omitted revoked by SI 1980/2000, r 6.
Para (2): first words omitted revoked by SI 1982/1111, r 115, Schedule; second words omitted revoked by SI 1980/2000, r 6(2).

[Order 53, r 12 Consolidation of applications

Where there is more than one application pending under [section 30 of the Act], or section 92 of the Local Government Act 1972, against several persons in respect of the same office, and on the same grounds, the Court may order the applications to be consolidated.]

Commencement   11 January 1978.
Amendments   See the first note to Order 53, r 1.
Words "section 30 of the Act" substituted by SI 1982/1111, r 115, Schedule.
Definitions   The Act: Supreme Court Act 1981.

[Order 53, r 13 Appeal from judge's order

No appeal shall lie from an order made under paragraph (3) of rule 3 on an application for leave which may be renewed under paragraph (4) of that rule.]

Commencement   12 January 1981.
Amendments   See the first note to Order 53, r 1.
This rule was further substituted by SI 1980/2000, r 7.

[Order 53, r 14 Meaning of "Court"

In relation to the hearing by a judge of an application for leave under rule 3 or of an application for judicial review, any reference in this Order to "the Court" shall, unless the context otherwise requires, be construed as a reference to the judge.]

Commencement   11 January 1978.
Amendments   See the first note to Order 53, r 1.

ORDER 54

APPLICATIONS FOR WRIT OF HABEAS CORPUS

Order 54, r 1 Application for writ of habeas corpus ad subjiciendum

[(1)   Subject to rule 11, an application for a writ of habeas corpus ad subjiciendum shall be made to a judge in court, except that—

- (a)   it shall be made to a Divisional Court of the Queen's Bench Division if the Court so directs;
- (b)   it may be made to a judge otherwise than in court at any time when no judge is sitting in court; and
- (c)   any application on behalf of a minor must be made in the first instance to a judge otherwise than in court.]

(2)   An application for such writ may be made ex parte and, subject to paragraph (3), must be supported by an affidavit by the person restrained showing that it is made at his instance and setting out the nature of the restraint.

(3)   Where the person restrained is unable for any reason to make the affidavit required by paragraph (2), the affidavit may be made by some other person on his behalf and that affidavit must state that the person restrained is unable to make the affidavit himself and for what reason.

Commencement   12 January 1981 (para (1)); 1 October 1966 (remainder).
Amendments   Para (1): substituted by SI 1980/2000, r 8.
Forms   Summons for writ (PF106).

Order 54, r 2 Power of Court to whom ex parte application made

(1)   The Court or judge to whom an application under rule 1 is made ex parte may make an order forthwith for the writ to issue, or may—

- (a)   where the application is made to a judge otherwise than in court, direct that an originating summons for the writ be issued, or that an application therefor be made by originating motion to a Divisional Court or to a judge in court;
- (b)   where the application is made to a judge in court, adjourn the application so that notice thereof may be given, or direct that an application be made by originating motion to a Divisional Court;
- (c)   where the application is made to a Divisional Court, adjourn the application so that notice thereof may be given.

(2)   The summons or notice of the motion must be served on the person against whom the issue of the writ is sought and on such other persons as the Court or judge may direct, and, unless the Court or judge otherwise directs, there must be at least 8 clear days between the service of the summons or notice and the date named therein for the hearing of the application.

Commencement   1 October 1966.
Forms   Notice of motion (No 87).
Notice of adjourned hearing (No 88).
Order for writ (PF107).

Order 54, r 3 Copies of affidavits to be supplied

Every party to an application under rule 1 must supply to every other party on demand and on payment of the proper charges copies of the affidavits which he proposes to use at the hearing of the application.

Commencement 1 October 1966.

Order 54, r 4 Power to order release of person restrained

(1)   Without prejudice to rule 2(1), the Court or judge hearing an application for a writ of habeas corpus ad subjiciendum may in its or his discretion order that the person restrained be released, and such order shall be a sufficient warrant to any governor of a prison, constable or other person for the release of the person under restraint.

(2)   Where such an application in a criminal cause or matter is heard by a judge and the judge does not order the release of the person restrained, he shall direct that the application be made by originating motion to a Divisional Court of the Queen's Bench Division.

Commencement 1 October 1966.

Order 54, r 5 Directions as to return to writ

Where a writ of habeas corpus ad subjiciendum is ordered to issue, the Court or judge by whom the order is made shall give directions as to the Court or judge before whom, and the date on which, the writ is returnable.

Commencement 1 October 1966.

Order 54, r 6 Service of writ and notice

(1)   Subject to paragraphs (2) and (3), a writ of habeas corpus ad subjiciendum must be served personally on the person to whom it is directed.

(2)   If it is not possible to serve such writ personally, or if it is directed to a governor of a prison or other public official, it must be served by leaving it with a servant or agent of the person to whom the writ is directed at the place where the person restrained is confined or restrained.

(3)   If the writ is directed to more than one person, the writ must be served in manner provided by this rule on the person first named in the writ, and copies must be served on each of the other persons in the same manner as the writ.

(4)   There must be served with the writ a notice (in Form No 90 in Appendix A) stating the Court or judge before whom and the date on which the person restrained is to be brought and that in default of obedience proceedings for committal of the party disobeying will be taken.

Commencement 1 October 1966.

Order 54, r 7 Return to the writ

(1)   The return to a writ of habeas corpus ad subjiciendum must be indorsed on or annexed to the writ and must state all the causes of the detainer of the person restrained.

(2)   The return may be amended, or another return substituted therefor, by leave of the Court or judge before whom the writ is returnable.

Commencement   1 October 1966.

Order 54, r 8 Procedure at hearing of writ

When a return to a writ of habeas corpus ad subjiciendum is made, the return shall first be read, and motion then made for discharging or remanding the person restrained or amending or quashing the return, and where that person is brought up in accordance with the writ, his counsel shall be heard first, then the counsel for the Crown, and then one counsel for the person restrained in reply.

Commencement   1 October 1966.

Order 54, r 9 Bringing up prisoner to give evidence, etc

(1)   An application for a writ of habeas corpus ad testificandum or of habeas corpus ad respondendum must be made on affidavit to a judge in chambers.

(2)   An application for an order to bring up a prisoner, otherwise than by writ of habeas corpus, to give evidence in any cause or matter, civil or criminal, before any court, tribunal or justice must be made on affidavit to a judge in chambers.

Commencement   1 October 1966.
Forms   Praecipe for writ (PF108).
Order pursuant to Criminal Procedure Act 1853 (PF109).

Order 54, r 10 Form of writ

A writ of habeas corpus must be in Form No 89, 91 or 92 in Appendix A, whichever is appropriate.

Commencement   1 October 1966.

[Order 54, r 11 Applications relative to the custody etc, of minors

An application by a parent or guardian of a minor for a writ of habeas corpus ad subjiciendum relative to the custody, care or control of the minor must be made in the Family Division, and this Order shall accordingly apply to such applications with the appropriate modifications.]

Commencement   1 October 1971.
Amendments   This rule was added by SI 1971/1269, r 15(2).

ORDER 55
APPEALS TO HIGH COURT FROM COURT, TRIBUNAL OR PERSON: GENERAL

Order 55, r 1 Application

(1)   Subject to paragraphs (2), (3) and (4), this Order shall apply to every appeal which by or under any enactment lies to the High Court from any court, tribunal or person.

[(2)   This order shall not apply to an appeal by case stated or to any appeal to which Order 73 applies.]

(3)   The following rules of this Order shall not apply to an appeal from a county court to a [single judge under section 375 of the Insolvency Act 1986] but, subject to the [Insolvency Rules 1986] as amended, Order 59 shall, with the necessary modifications, apply to such an appeal as it applies to an appeal from a county court to the Court of Appeal.

(4)   The following rules of this Order shall, in relation to an appeal to which this Order applies, have effect subject to any provision made in relation to that appeal by any other provision of these rules or by or under any enactment.

(5)   In this Order references to a tribunal shall be construed as references to any tribunal constituted by or under any enactment other than any of the ordinary courts of law.

Commencement   1 October 1989 (para (2)); 1 October 1966 (remainder).
Amendments   Para (2): substituted by SI 1989/1307, r 12.
Para (3): words "single judge under section 375 of the Insolvency Act 1986" and "Insolvency Rules 1986" substituted by SI 1986/2001, art 2, Schedule.

[Order 55, r 2 Court to hear appeal

Except where it is otherwise provided by these rules or by or under any enactment, an appeal to which this Order applies shall be assigned to the Queen's Bench Division and shall be heard and determined—
    (a)   where the decision of the High Court on the appeal is final, by a Divisional Court, and
    (b)   in any other case, by a single judge.]

Commencement   11 January 1978.
Amendments   This rule was substituted by SI 1977/1955, r 6.

Order 55, r 3 Bringing of appeal

(1)   An appeal to which this Order applies shall be by way of rehearing and must be brought by originating motion.

(2)   Every notice of the motion by which such an appeal is brought must state the grounds of the appeal and, if the appeal is against a judgment, order or other decision of a court, must state whether the appeal is against the whole or a part of that decision and, if against a part only, must specify the part.

(3)   The bringing of such an appeal shall not operate as a stay of proceedings on the judgment, determination or other decision against which the appeal is brought unless the Court by which the appeal is to be heard or the court, tribunal or person by which or by whom the decision was given so orders.

Commencement   1 October 1966.

Order 55, r 4 Service of notice of motion and entry of appeal

(1)   The persons to be served with notice of the motion by which an appeal to which this Order applies is brought are the following:—

    (a) if the appeal is against a judgment, order or other decision of a court, the registrar or clerk of the court and any party to the proceedings in which the decision was given who is directly affected by the appeal;

    (b) if the appeal is against an order, determination, award or other decision of a tribunal, Minister of the Crown, government department or other person, the chairman of the tribunal, Minister, government department or other person, as the case may be, and every party to the proceedings (other than the appellant) in which the decision appealed against was given.

(2)   The notice must be served, and the appeal entered, within 28 days after the date of the judgment, order, determination or other decision against which the appeal is brought.

(3)   In the case of an appeal against a judgment, order or decision of a court, the period specified in paragraph (2) shall be calculated from the date of the judgment or order or the date on which the decision was given.

(4)   In the case of an appeal against an order, determination, award or other decision of a tribunal, Minister, government department or other person, the period specified in paragraph (2) shall be calculated from the date on which notice of the decision[, or, in a case where a statement of the reasons for a decision was given later than such notice, on which such a statement] was given to the appellant by the person who made the decision or by a person authorised in that behalf to do so.

Commencement   1 October 1966.
Amendments   Para (4): words from ", or, in a case" to "such a statement" inserted by SI 1982/1111, r 109.

Order 55, r 5 Date of hearing of appeal

Unless the Court having jurisdiction to determine the appeal otherwise directs, an appeal to which this Order applies shall not be heard sooner than 21 days after service of notice of the motion by which the appeal is brought.

Commencement   1 October 1966.

Order 55, r 6 Amendments of grounds of appeal, etc

(1)   The notice of the motion by which an appeal to which this Order applies is brought may be amended by the appellant, without leave, by supplementary notice served not less than 7 days before the day appointed for the hearing of the appeal, on each of the persons on whom the notice to be amended was served.

(2)   Within 2 days after service of a supplementary notice under paragraph (1) the appellant must lodge two copies of the notice in the office in which the appeal is entered.

(3)   Except with the leave of the Court hearing any such appeal, no grounds other than those stated in the notice of the motion by which the appeal is brought or any supplementary notice under paragraph (1) may be relied upon by the appellant at the hearing; but that Court may amend the grounds so stated or make any other order, on such terms as it thinks just, to ensure the determination on the merits of the real question in controversy between the parties.

(4)   The foregoing provisions of this rule are without prejudice to the powers of the Court under Order 20.

Commencement 1 October 1966.

[Order 55, r 6A Interlocutory applications

(1)   Unless the Court otherwise directs, any interlocutory application in proceedings to which this Order applies may be made to any Judge or a Master of the Queen's Bench Division or, as the case may be, any Judge or a [district judge] of the Family Division, notwithstanding that the appeal has been brought by motion and is to be heard by a Divisional Court.

In this paragraph "interlocutory application" includes an application for the extension of time for the service of the notice of motion or the entry of the appeal or for the amendment of the notice of motion.

(2)   In relation to an order made by a Master or [district judge] pursuant to paragraph (1), Order 58, rule 1 shall, where the appeal is to be heard by a Divisional Court, have effect as if a reference to that Court were substituted for the reference to a Judge in chambers.

(3)   This rule is without prejudice to any statutory provision or rule of law restricting the making of an order against the Crown.]

Commencement 1 October 1987.
Amendments This rule was inserted by SI 1987/1423, r 46.

Order 55, r 7 Powers of court hearing appeal

(1)   In addition to the power conferred by rule 6(3), the Court hearing an appeal to which this Order applies shall have the powers conferred by the following provisions of this rule.

(2)   The Court shall have power to receive further evidence on questions of fact, and the evidence may be given in such manner as the Court may direct either by oral examination in court, by affidavit, by deposition taken before an examiner or in some other manner.

(3)   The Court shall have power to draw any inferences of fact which might have been drawn in the proceedings out of which the appeal arose.

(4)   It shall be the duty of the appellant to apply to the judge or other person presiding at the proceedings in which the decision appealed against was given for a signed copy of any note made by him of the proceedings and to furnish that copy for the use of the Court; and in default of production of such a note, or, if such note is incomplete, in addition to such note, the Court may hear and determine the appeal on any other evidence or statement of what occurred in those proceedings as appears to the Court to be sufficient.

Except where the Court otherwise directs, an affidavit or note by a person present at the proceedings shall not be used in evidence under this paragraph unless it was previously submitted to the person presiding at the proceedings for his comments.

(5)   The Court may give any judgment or decision or make any order which ought to have been given or made by the court, tribunal or person and make such further or

other order as the case may require or may remit the matter with the opinion of the Court for rehearing and determination by it or him.

(6)   The Court may, in special circumstances, order that such security shall be given for the costs of the appeal as may be just.

(7)   [The Court shall not be bound to allow the appeal] on the ground merely of misdirection, or of the improper admission or rejection of evidence, unless in the opinion of the Court substantial wrong or miscarriage has been thereby occasioned.

Commencement 1 October 1966.
Amendments Para (7): words "The Court shall not be bound to allow the appeal" substituted by SI 1968/ 1244, r 7(2).

Order 55, r 8 Right of Minister, etc, to appear and be heard

Where an appeal to which this Order applies is against an order, determination or other decision of a Minister of the Crown or government department, the Minister or department, as the case may be, shall be entitled to appear and be heard in the proceedings on the appeal.

Commencement 1 October 1966.

ORDER 56

APPEALS, ETC TO HIGH COURT BY CASE STATED: GENERAL

Order 56, r 1 Appeals from the Crown Court by case stated

(1) [Except where they relate to affiliation proceedings] [or to care proceedings under the Children and Young Persons Act 1969] all appeals from [the Crown Court] by case stated shall be heard and determined

    [(a) in any criminal cause or matter, by a Divisional Court of the Queen's Bench Division;

    (b) in any other cause or matter, by a single judge sitting in court, or if the Court so directs, by a Divisional Court of the Queen's Bench Division.]

(2) ...

(3) An appeal from [the Crown Court] by case stated shall not be entered for hearing unless and until the case and a copy of the judgment, order or decision in respect of which the case has been stated and, if that judgment, order or decision was given or made on an appeal to [the Crown Court], a copy of the judgment, order or decision appealed from, have been lodged in the Crown Office.

(4) No such appeal shall be entered after the expiration of [10 days from the receipt by the appellant of the case] unless the delay is accounted for to the satisfaction of the Divisional Court.

Notice of intention to apply for an extension of time for entry of the appeal must be served on the respondent at least 2 clear days before the day named in the notice for the hearing of the application.

(5) Where any such appeal has not been entered by reason of a default in complying with the provisions of this rule, [the Crown Court] may proceed as if no case had been stated.

Commencement 1 October 1966.
Amendments Para (1): words "Except where they relate to affiliation proceedings" inserted by SI 1971/1269, r 16(1); words from "or to care proceedings" to "Act 1969" inserted by SI 1980/1908, r 3; words "the Crown Court" substituted by SI 1971/1955, r 16(1); sub-paras (a), (b) substituted for original wording by SI 1980/2000, r 9(1).
Para (2): revoked by SI 1971/1955, r 16(2).
Paras (3), (5): words "the Crown Court" wherever they occur substituted by SI 1971/1955, r 16(1).
Para (4): words "10 days from the receipt by the appellant of the case" substituted by SI 1982/1786, r 18.

Order 56, r 2 *(revoked by SI 1978/359)*

Order 56, r 3 *(revoked by SI 1971/1955)*

Order 56, r 4 Notice of entry of appeal

Within 4 days after an appeal from [the Crown Court] by case stated is entered for hearing, the appellant must serve notice of the entry of the appeal on the respondent.

Commencement 1 October 1966.
Amendments Words "the Crown Court" substituted by SI 1971/1955, r 16(1).

[Order 56, r 4A Appeals relating to affiliation proceedings [and care proceedings]

Appeals from [the Crown Court] by case stated which relate to affiliation proceedings [or to care proceedings under the Children and Young Persons Act 1969] shall be heard and determined by [a single judge or, if the court so directs,] a Divisional Court of the Family Division, and the foregoing provisions of this Order shall accordingly apply to such appeals with the substitution of references to the principal registry of the Family Division for references to the Crown Office and such other modifications as may be appropriate.]

Commencement 1 October 1971.
Amendments This rule was inserted by SI 1971/1269, r 16(2).
Rule heading: words "and care proceedings" added by SI 1980/1908, r 4(1).
Words "the Crown Court" substituted by SI 1971/1955, r 16(1); words from "or to care" to "Act 1969" inserted by SI 1980/1908, r 4(2); words "a single judge or, if the court so directs" inserted by SI 1980/2000, r 9(2).

[Order 56, r 5 Appeal from magistrates' court by case stated

(1)   Except as provided by paragraph (2), all appeals from a magistrates' court by case stated shall be heard and determined

> [(a) in any criminal cause or matter, by a Divisional Court of the Queen's Bench Division;
>
> (b) in any other cause or matter, by a single judge sitting in court, or if the Court so directs, by a Divisional Court of the Queen's Bench Division.]

(2)   An appeal by way of case stated against an order or determination of a magistrates' court shall be heard and determined by [a single judge or, if the Court so directs,] a Divisional Court of the Family Division if the order or determination appealed against was made or given in affiliation proceedings [or in care proceedings under the Children and Young Persons Act 1969] or on an application under [section 35 of the Matrimonial Causes Act 1973] or if it relates to the enforcement of—

> (a) an order for the payment of money made by virtue of the Matrimonial Proceedings (Magistrates' Courts) Act 1960[, the Guardianship of Minors Act 1971] [or the Domestic Proceedings and Magistrates' Courts Act 1978], or
>
> (b) an order for the payment of money to a wife or her maintenance or for her maintenance and that of any child or children of hers, registered in a court in England or Wales under Part II of the Maintenance Orders Act 1950 . . . the Maintenance Orders (Facilities for Enforcement) Act 1920 [or the Maintenance Orders (Reciprocal Enforcement) Act 1972 or confirmed by such a court under either of the two last-mentioned Acts], [or registered in such a court under the Civil Jurisdiction and Judgments Act 1982,] or
>
> [(c) an order for periodical or other payments made, or having effect as if made, under Part II of the Matrimonial Causes Act 1973 and registered in a magistrates' court under the Maintenance Orders Act 1958].]

Commencement 1 October 1971.
Amendments This rule was substituted by SI 1971/1269, r 16(3).
Para (1): sub-paras (a), (b) substituted for original wording by SI 1980/2000, r 9(1).
Para (2): words "a single judge or, if the Court so directs," inserted by SI 1980/2000, r 9(2); words from "or to care" to "Act 1969" inserted by SI 1980/1908, r 5; words "section 35 of the Matrimonial Causes Act 1973" substituted by SI 1976/337, r 10(1); in sub-para (a) words ", the Guardianship of Minors Act 1971" inserted by SI 1983/1181, r 26, words "or the Domestic Proceedings and Magistrates' Courts Act 1978"

inserted by SI 1980/1010, r 12; in sub-para (b) words omitted revoked and words from "or the Maintenance" to "last-mentioned Acts" substituted by SI 1976/337, r 10(2), words from "or registered" to "Act 1982," inserted by SI 1988/1340, r 5; sub-para (c) substituted by SI 1976/337, r 10(3).

Order 56, r 6 Case stated by magistrates' court: lodging case, etc

(1)   Where a case has been stated by a magistrates' court the appellant must—
   (a)   within 10 days after receiving the case, lodge it in the Crown Office or, if the appeal falls to be heard by a Divisional Court of the [Family Division], the [principal registry of the Family Division], and
   (b)   within 4 days after lodging the case as aforesaid serve on the respondent a notice of the entry of appeal together with a copy of the case.

(2)   Unless the Court having jurisdiction to determine the appeal otherwise directs, the appeal shall not be heard sooner than 8 clear days after service of notice of the entry of the appeal.

Commencement   1 October 1966.
Amendments   Para (1): in sub-para (a) words "Family Division" and "principal registry of the Family Division" substituted by SI 1971/1269, r 38(a), (b), Schedule.

Order 56, r 7 Case stated by Ministers, tribunal, etc

(1)   The jurisdiction of the High Court under any enactment to hear and determine a case stated by a Minister of the Crown, government department, tribunal or other person, or a question of law referred to that Court by such a Minister or department or a tribunal or other person by way of case stated, [shall be exercised by a single judge of the Queen's Bench Division, except where it is otherwise provided by these rules or by or under any enactment].

(2)   The jurisdiction of the High Court under any enactment to hear and determine an application for an order directing such a Minister or department or a tribunal or other person to state a case for determination by the High Court, or to refer a question of law to that Court by way of case stated, shall be exercised by the Court or judge having jurisdiction to hear and determine that case or question except where by some other provision of these rules or by or under any enactment it is otherwise provided.

(3)   [This rule and rules 8 to 12] of this Order shall apply to proceedings for the determination of such a case, question or application and, in relation to any such proceedings, shall have effect subject to any provision made in relation to those proceedings by any other provision of these rules or by or under any enactment.

(4)   In this Order references to a tribunal shall be construed as references to any tribunal constituted by or under any enactment other than any of the ordinary courts of law.

(5)   In the following rules references to a Minister shall be construed as including references to a government department, and in those rules and this rule "case" includes a special case.

Commencement   1 October 1966.
Amendments   Para (1): words from "shall be exercised" to "any enactment" substituted by SI 1977/1955, r 7.
Para (3): words "This rule and rules 8 to 12" substituted by SI 1987/1423, r 47.

Order 56, r 8 Application for order to state a case

(1)   An application to the Court for an order directing a Minister, tribunal or other person to state a case for determination by the Court or to refer a question of law to the Court by way of case stated must be made by originating motion; and the persons to be served with notice thereof are the Minister, secretary of the tribunal or other person, as the case may be, and every party (other than the applicant) to the proceedings to which the application relates.

(2)   The notice of such motion must state the grounds of the application, the question of law on which it is sought to have the case stated and any reasons given by the Minister, tribunal or other person for his or its refusal to state a case.

(3)   The motion must be entered for hearing, and the notice thereof served, within 14 days after receipt by the applicant of notice of the refusal of his request to state a case.

Commencement   1 October 1966.

Order 56, r 9 Signing and service of case

(1)   A case stated by a tribunal must be signed by the chairman or president of the tribunal, and a case stated by any other person must be signed by him or by a person authorised in that behalf to do so.

(2)   The case must be served on the party at whose request, or as a result of whose application to the Court, the case was stated; and if a Minister, tribunal, arbitrator or other person is entitled by virtue of any enactment to state a case, or to refer a question of law by way of case stated, for determination by the High Court without request being made by any party to the proceedings before that person, the case must be served on such party to those proceedings as the Minister, tribunal, arbitrator or other person, as the case may be, thinks appropriate.

(3)   When a case is served on any party under paragraph (2), notice must be given to every other party to the proceedings in question that the case has been served on the party named, and on the date specified, in the notice.

Commencement   1 October 1966.

Order 56, r 10 Proceedings for determination of case

(1)   Proceedings for the determination by the High Court of a case stated, or a question of law referred by way of case stated, by a Minister, tribunal, arbitrator or other person must be begun by originating motion by the person on whom the case was served in accordance with rule 9(2) [or, where the case is stated without a request being made, by the Minister, secretary of the tribunal, arbitrator or other person by whom the case is stated].

[(2)   The applicant shall serve notice of a motion under paragraph (1), together with a copy of the case, on—
    (a)   the Minister, secretary of the tribunal, arbitrator or other person by whom the case was stated, unless that Minister, tribunal, arbitrator or other person is the applicant,
    (b)   every party (other than the applicant) to the proceedings in which the question of law to which the case relates arose, and
    (c)   any other person (other than the applicant) served with the case under rule 9(2).]

(3)   The notice of such motion must set out the applicant's contentions on the question of law to which the case stated relates.

(4)   The motion must be entered for hearing, and the notice thereof served, within 14 days after the case stated was served on the applicant.

(5)   If the applicant fails to enter the motion within the period specified in paragraph (4), then, after obtaining a copy of the case from the Minister, tribunal, arbitrator or other person by whom the case was stated, any other party to the proceedings in which the question of law to which the case relates arose may, within 14 days after the expiration of the period so specified, begin proceedings for the determination of the case, and paragraphs (1) to (4) shall have effect accordingly with the necessary modifications.

The references in this paragraph to the period specified in paragraph (4) shall be construed as including references to that period as extended by any order of the Court.

(6)   The documents required to be lodged in accordance with Order 57, rule 2, before entry of the motion include a copy of the case stated.

(7)   Unless the Court having jurisdiction to determine the case otherwise directs, the motion shall not be heard sooner than 7 days after service of notice of the motion.

Commencement   1 February 1991 (para (2)); 1 October 1966 (remainder).
Amendments   Para (1): words from "or, where the case" to "case is stated" added by SI 1990/2599, r 12(1). Para (2): substituted by 1990/2599, r 12(2).

Order 56, r 11 Amendment of case

The Court hearing a case stated by a Minister, tribunal, arbitrator or other person may amend the case or order it to be returned to that person for amendment, and may draw inferences of fact from the facts stated in the case.

Commencement   1 October 1966.

Order 56, r 12 Right of Minister to appear and be heard

[In proceedings for the determination of a case stated, or of a question of law referred by way of case stated, the Minister, chairman or president of the tribunal, arbitrator or other person by whom the case was stated shall be entitled to appear and be heard.]

Commencement   1 February 1991.
Amendments   This rule was substituted by SI 1990/2599, r 12(3).

[Order 56, r 12A Extradition

(1)   Rules 5 and 6 of this Order shall apply to appeals by case stated under—
    (a)   section 7 of the Criminal Justice Act 1988, and
    (b)   section 7A of the Fugitive Offenders Act 1967,

as they apply to appeals by case stated from a magistrates' court and references in those rules to appellant and respondent shall be construed as references to the requesting state and the person whose surrender is sought respectively.

(2)   An application for an order under either of the sections mentioned in paragraph (1) or under section 2A of the Backing of Warrants (Republic of Ireland) Act 1965 requiring a court to state a case shall be made in accordance with rule 8 of this Order, the references in that rule to a tribunal and the secretary of a tribunal being construed for this purpose as references to the court and the clerk of the court respectively.]

Commencement   1 October 1989.
Amendments   This rule was inserted by SI 1989/1307, r 13.

[Order 56, r 13 Interlocutory applications

(1)   Unless the Court otherwise directs, any interlocutory application in proceedings to which this Order applies may be made to any Judge or a Master of the Queen's Bench Division or, as the case may be, any Judge or a [district judge] of the Family Division, notwithstanding that the appeal has been brought by case stated and is to be heard by a Divisional Court.

In this paragraph "interlocutory application" includes an application for an order extending the time for entry of the appeal or for service of notice of entry of the appeal.

(2)   In relation to an order made by a Master or [district judge] pursuant to paragraph (1), Order 58, rule 1 shall, where the application is to be heard by a Divisional Court, have effect as if a reference to that Court were substituted for the reference to a Judge in chambers.

(3)   This rule is without prejudice to any statutory provision or rule of law restricting the making of an order against the Crown.]

Commencement   1 October 1987.
Amendments   This rule was inserted by SI 1987/1423, r 48.

ORDER 57
DIVISIONAL COURT PROCEEDINGS, ETC: SUPPLEMENTARY PROVISIONS

Order 57, r 1 Application

(1)   Subject to paragraph (2), this Order shall apply to—
  (a)   any proceedings before a Divisional Court,
  (b)   any proceedings before a single judge under Order 52, rule 2, Order 53, Order 54[, Order 64, rule 4] or Order 79,
  (c)   any proceedings before a single judge, being proceedings which consist of or relate to an appeal to the High Court from any court, tribunal or person including an appeal by case stated and the reference of a question of law by way of case stated.

(2)   The following rules of this Order shall not apply to an appeal from a county court to a [single judge under section 375 of the Insolvency Act 1986].

Commencement   1 October 1966.
Amendments   Para (1): in sub-para (b) words ", Order 64, rule 4" inserted by SI 1991/1329, r 17(2).
Para (2): words "single judge under section 375 of the Insolvency Act 1986" substituted by SI 1986/2001, art 2, Schedule.

Order 57, r 2 Entry of motions

(1)   Every motion in proceedings to which this Order applies must be entered for hearing in the appropriate office; and entry shall be made when a copy of the notice of motion, and any other documents required to be lodged before entry, have been lodged in that office.

(2)   The party entering the motion for hearing must lodge in the appropriate office copies of the proceedings for the use of the judges.

(3)   [Expect where it relates to proceedings in the Admiralty Court] every motion entered for hearing by a Divisional Court of the Queen's Bench Division shall be entered in the Divisional Court list.

(4)   In the rule "the appropriate office" means—
  (a)   in relation to proceedings in the Queen's Bench Division [(including the Admiralty Court)], the Crown Office [or the [Admiralty and Commercial Registry], as the circumstances of the case require];
  (b)   in relation to proceedings in the Chancery Division, [Chancery Chambers];
  (c)   in relation to proceedings in the [Family Division], the [principal registry of the Family Division] ....

Commencement   1 October 1966.
Amendments   Para (3): words "Except where it relates to proceedings in the Admiralty Court" inserted by SI 1971/1269, r 17(1).
Para (4): in sub-para (a) words "(including the Admiralty Court)" inserted and words from "or the" to "case require" inserted by SI 1971/1269, r 17, words "Admiralty and Commercial Registry" substituted by 1987/1423, r 2; in sub-para (b) words "Chancery Chambers" substituted by SI 1982/1111, r 56; in sub-para (c) words "Family Division" and "principal registry of the Family Division" substituted and words omitted revoked by SI 1971/1269, rr 17(2), 38(a), Schedule.

Order 57, r 3 Issue, etc, of originating summons

An originating summons by which any proceedings to which this Order applies are begun must be issued—
  (a)   in the case of proceedings in the [Family Division], out of the [principal

     registry of the Family Division] ..., and

  (b) in the case of any other proceedings, out of the Crown Office[, Chancery Chambers] [or the [Admiralty and Commercial Registry], as the circumstances of the case require];

and [such summons shall be in Form No 10 in Appendix A].

Commencement 1 October 1966.

Amendments In sub-para (a) words "Family Division" and "principal registry of the Family Division" substituted and words omitted revoked by SI 1971/1269, rr 17(2), 38(a), Schedule; in sub-para (b) words ", Chancery Chambers" inserted by SI 1982/1111, r 57, words from "or the" to "case require" inserted by SI 1971/1269, r 17(2), words "Admiralty and Commercial Registry" therein substituted by SI 1987/1423, r 2; words "such summons shall be in Form No 10 in Appendix A" substituted by SI 1979/1716, r 48, Schedule, Pt 2.

Order 57, r 4 Filing of affidavits and drawing up of orders

(1)   Except as provided by Order 41, rule 9(2) and (3), every affidavit used in proceedings to which this Order applies must be filed in the Crown Office[, Chancery Chambers] [or the [Admiralty and Commercial Registry], as the circumstances of the case require].

(2)   Every order made in proceedings to which this Order applies in the Queen's Bench Division shall be drawn up in the Crown Office [or the [Admiralty and Commercial Registry], as the circumstances of the case require], and a copy of any order made by a judge in chambers in any such proceedings must be filed in that office.

Commencement 1 October 1966.

Amendments Para (1): words ", Chancery Chambers" inserted by SI 1982/1111, r 57; words from "or the" to "case require" inserted by SI 1971/1269, r 17(2), words "Admiralty and Commercial Registry" therein substituted by SI 1987/1423, r 2.

Para (2): words from "or the" to "case require" inserted by SI 1971/1269, r 17(2), words "Admiralty and Commercial Registry" therein substituted by SI 1987/1423, r 2.

Order 57, r 5 Issue of writs

(1)   Every writ issued in proceedings to which this Order applies shall be issued out of the Crown Office[, Chancery Chambers] and must be prepared by the party seeking to issue it.

(2)   Every such writ must be filed in the Crown Office[, Chancery Chambers] [or the principal registry of the Family Division, as the circumstances of the case require] together with the return thereto and a copy of any order made thereon.

Commencement 1 October 1966.

Amendments Para (1): words ", Chancery Chambers" inserted by SI 1982/1111, r 57.

Para (2): words ", Chancery Chambers" inserted by SI 1982/1111, r 57; words from "or the principal" to "case require" inserted by SI 1971/1269, r 17(4).

Order 57, r 6 Custody of records

The master of the Crown Office [or the [Admiralty and Commercial Registry], as the circumstances of the case require] shall have the custody of the records of or relating to proceedings in the Queen's Bench Division to which this Order applies.

Commencement 1 October 1966.

Amendments Words from "or the" to "case require" inserted by SI 1971/1269, r 17(2), words "Admiralty and Commercial Registry" therein substituted by SI 1987/1423, r 2.

ORDER 58

APPEALS FROM MASTERS, REGISTRARS [DISTRICT JUDGES], REFEREES AND JUDGES

Order 58, r 1 Appeals from certain decisions of masters, etc to judge in chambers

(1)   Except as provided by rule 2, an appeal shall lie to a judge in chambers from any judgment, order or decision of a master, . . . [the Admiralty Registrar or a] [district judge] of the [Family Division].

(2)   The appeal shall be brought by serving on every other party to the proceedings in which the judgment, order or decision was given or made a notice to attend before the judge on a day specified in the notice [or on such other day as may be directed].

(3)   Unless the Court otherwise orders, the notice must be issued within 5 days after the judgment, order or decision appealed against was given or made [and must be served within 5 days after issue and an appeal to which this rule applies shall not be heard sooner than two clear days after such service.]

(4)   Except so far as the Court may otherwise direct, an appeal under this rule shall not operate as a stay of the proceedings in which the appeal is brought.

Commencement 1 October 1966.
Amendments Para (1): words omitted revoked by SI 1982/1111, r 58(1); words "the Admiralty Registrar or a" inserted and words "Family Division" substituted by SI 1971/1269, rr 18(1), 38(a), Schedule.
Para (2): words "or on such other day as may be directed" inserted by SI 1982/1111, r 58(2).
Para (3): words from "and must be served" to "after such service" substituted by SI 1987/1423, r 56.
Cross references See CCR Order 37, r 6.
Forms Notice of Appeal (PF110).
Application for copy notes (PF111).

Order 58, r 2 Appeals from certain decisions of masters, etc to Court of Appeal

An appeal shall lie to the Court of Appeal from any judgment, order or decision of a master . . . given or made—

(a)   on the hearing or determination of any cause, matter, question or issue tried before or referred to him, [under Order 36, [rule 11]] . . . ; or

[(b)   on an assessment of damages or of the value of goods under Order 37 or otherwise, or an assessment of interest;

and where a judgment, order or decision of a kind referred to in paragraph (b) includes or involves a determination of any other matter, an appeal shall lie to the Court of Appeal in relation to such other matter.]

(c), (d) . . .

[. . .]

Commencement 1 October 1966.
Amendments Originally paras (1)–(3); paras (2), (3) and numbering of para (1) revoked by SI 1978/359, r 3(1)(b).
First words omitted revoked by SI 1982/1111, r 59(1) and SI 1978/359, r 3(1)(a); in sub-para (a) words in square brackets added by SI 1978/359, r 3(1)(a), words "rule 11" therein substituted by SI 1982/1111, r 101(1), words omitted revoked by SI 1971/1269, r 18(2); sub-para (b) and subsequent wording substituted by SI 1992/638, r 9; sub-paras (c), (d) revoked by SI 1978/359, r 3(1)(a); final words omitted originally inserted by SI 1971/1269, r 18(2), subsequently omitted by SI 1982/1111, r 59(3).

Order 58, r [3] Appeals from [district judges]

(1) An appeal shall lie from any judgment, order or decision of a [district judge] in any cause or matter in any Division in the same circumstances and, except as provided by paragraph (2), subject to the same conditions as if the judgment, order or decision were given or made by a master or registrar [district judge] in that cause or matter in that Division, and the provisions of these rules with respect to appeals shall apply accordingly.

(2) In relation to an appeal from a judgment, order or decision of a [district judge], rule 1 shall have effect subject to the modification that [for the first reference therein to 5 days and the reference therein to two clear days] there shall be substituted references to 7 days and 3 clear days respectively.

Commencement 1 October 1966.
Amendments Originally r 4, renumbered as r 3 and original r 3 revoked by SI 1982/1111, r 60.
Para (2): words "for the first reference therein to 5 days and the reference therein to two clear days" substituted by SI 1987/1423, r 57.
Cross references See CCR Order 37, r 6.

[Order 58, r [4] Appeals from official referees

Subject to section 18 of the Act (which shall apply in relation to a decision of an official referee as if he were a judge of the High Court) an appeal shall lie to the Court of Appeal from a decision of an official referee—

    (a) on a question of law or, where section 18(1)(f) does not apply, as to costs only; and

    (b) with the leave of the official referee or the Court of Appeal, on any question of fact or, where section 18(1)(f) applies, as to costs only.]

Commencement 1 October 1988.
Amendments Originally r 5, renumbered as r 4 by SI 1982/1111, r 60.
This rule was substituted by SI 1988/1340, r 6.
Definitions The Act: Supreme Court Act 1981.

Order 58, r [5] Appeals from special referees

An appeal shall lie to the Court of Appeal from any judgment, order or decision of a special referee given or made on the hearing or determination of any cause, matter, question or issue ordered to be tried before him under Order 36, [rule 10].

Commencement 1 October 1966.
Amendments Originally r 6, renumbered as r 5 by SI 1982/1111, r 60.
Words "rule 10" substituted by SI 1982/1111, r 101(3).

Order 58, r [6] Appeal from judge in chambers

[(1) Subject to section 18 of the Act and section 15(2) of the Administration of Justice Act 1960 (which restrict appeals) and to Order 53, rule 13, and without prejudice to section 13 of the said Act of 1960 (which provides for an appeal in cases of contempt of court), an appeal shall lie to the Court of Appeal from any judgment, order or decision of a judge in chambers.]

(2) . . .

Commencement   4 April 1988 (para (1)); 1 October 1966 (remainder).
Amendments   Originally r 7, renumbered as r 6 by SI 1982/1111, r 60.
Para (1): substituted by SI 1988/298, r 4.
Para (2): revoked by SI 1988/298, r 5.
Definitions   The Act: Supreme Court Act 1981.

Order 58, r [7] Appeal from judgment, etc of judge in interpleader proceedings

(1)   Any judgment, order or decision of a judge given or made in summarily determining under Order 17, rule 5(2)(b) or (c), any question at issue between claimants in interpleader proceedings shall be final and conclusive against the claimants and all persons claiming under them unless leave to appeal to the Court of Appeal is given by the judge or the Court of Appeal.

(2)   Where an interpleader issue is tried by a judge (with or without a jury), an appeal shall lie to the Court of Appeal, without the leave of the judge or that Court, from any judgment, order or decision given or made by the judge on the trial.

(3)   The time within which notice of appeal under this rule must be served shall be the same as in the case of an appeal from an interlocutory order.

Commencement   1 October 1966.
Amendments   Originally r 8, renumbered as r 7 by SI 1982/1111, r 60.

ORDER 59
APPEALS TO THE COURT OF APPEAL

Order 59, r 1 Application of Order to appeals

This Order applies, subject to the provisions of these rules with respect to particular appeals, to every appeal to the Court of Appeal (including, so far as it is applicable thereto, any appeal to that Court from an official referee, master or other officer of the Supreme Court or from any tribunal from which an appeal lies to that Court under or by virtue of any enactment) not being an appeal for which other provision is made by these rules[, and references to "the court below" apply to any court, tribunal or person from which such an appeal lies].

Commencement 1 October 1966.
Amendments Words from ", and references" to "appeal lies" inserted by SI 1981/1734, r 4.

[Order 59, r 1A Final and interlocutory orders

(1) For all purposes connected with appeals to the Court of Appeal, a judgment or order shall be treated as final or interlocutory in accordance with the following provisions of this rule.

(2) In this rule, unless the context otherwise requires—
    (a) "order" includes a judgment, decree, decision or direction;
    (b) references to an order giving specified directions or granting a specified form of remedy or relief shall include an order—
        (i) refusing to give such directions or grant such remedy or relief;
        (ii) giving such directions or granting such remedy or relief on terms;
        (iii) varying, suspending or revoking such an order, and
        (iv) determining an appeal from such an order.

(3) A judgment or order shall be treated as final if the entire cause or matter would (subject only to any possible appeal) have been finally determined whichever way the court below had decided the issues before it.

(4) For the purposes of paragraph (3), where the final hearing or the trial of a cause or matter is divided into parts, a judgment or order made at the end of any part shall be treated as if made at the end of the complete hearing or trial.

(5) Notwithstanding anything in paragraph (3), the following orders shall be treated as final—
    (a) an order for discovery of documents made in an action for discovery only;
    (b) an order granting any relief made at the hearing of an application for judicial review;
    (c) an order made on an originating summons under Order 85, rule 2(2)(b) or (c);
    (d) an order for the winding up of a company;
    (e) a decree absolute of divorce or nullity of marriage;
    (f) an order absolute for foreclosure;
    (g) an order as to costs made as part of a final judgment or order;
    (h) an order of committal.

(6) Notwithstanding anything in paragraph (3), but without prejudice to paragraph (5), the following judgments and orders shall be treated as interlocutory—
    (a) an order extending or abridging the period for the doing of any act;
    (b) an order for or relating to the transfer or consolidation of proceedings;

(c) an order for or relating to the validity, service (including service out of the jurisdiction) or renewal of a writ or other originating process;

(d) an order granting leave under section 139 of the Mental Health Act 1983 to bring proceedings against a person;

(e) an order for or relating to the amendment of an acknowledgment of service;

(f) any judgment in default or any "unless" order;

(g) an order for or relating to the joinder of causes of action;

(h) an order for or relating to the addition, substitution or striking out of parties;

(i) subject to Order 58, rule 7, an order granting relief by way of interpleader;

(j) an order for or relating to the service or amendment of any pleading;

(k) an order striking out an action or other proceedings or any pleading under Order 18, rule 19 or under the inherent jurisdiction of the court;

(l) an order dismissing or striking out an action or other proceedings for want of prosecution;

(m) an order staying proceedings or execution;

(n) an order for or relating to a payment into or out of court;

(o) an order for or relating to security for the costs of an action or other proceedings;

(p) subject to paragraph (5)(a), an order for or relating to the discovery or inspection of documents, including an order under Order 24, rule 7A(1) for the disclosure of documents before the commencement of proceedings;

(q) an order for or relating to the service of or answer to interrogatories;

(r) a judgment or order on admissions under Order 27, rule 3;

(s) an order granting an interlocutory injunction or for the appointment of a receiver;

(t) an order for or relating to an interim payment under Order 29;

(u) an order made under or relating to a summons for directions;

(v) an order directing a trial with a jury;

(w) an order for or relating to the fixing or adjournment of trial dates;

(x) an order directing a new trial or a re-hearing;

(y) an order relating to access to, or the custody, care, education or welfare of, a minor whether in matrimonial, wardship, guardianship, custodianship or any other proceedings, or a certificate under section 41 of the Matrimonial Causes Act 1973;

(z) an order for or relating to ancillary relief in matrimonial proceedings, including a property adjustment order, an order for the payment of a lump sum and any other order making or relating to financial provision whether of a capital or income nature;

(aa) . . . a judgment or order under Order 14[, Order 14A] or Order 86 or under Order 9, rule 14 of the County Court Rules 1981;

(bb) an order setting aside or refusing to set aside another judgment or order (whether such other judgment or order is final or interlocutory);

(cc) an order made for or relating to the enforcement of an earlier order (whether such earlier order is final or interlocutory) or giving further directions as to such an order and (without prejudice to the generality of the foregoing)—

(i) a garnishee order nisi or a garnishee order absolute;

(ii) a charging order nisi or a charging order absolute;

(iii) an order for the sale of any property by way of enforcement of an earlier order (whether such earlier order is final or interlocutory) or an order giving directions regarding any such sale or an order designed to regulate or facilitate any such sale;

(dd) an order for or relating to the taxation of costs or the delivery, withdrawal or amendment of bills of costs;

(ee) without prejudice to paragraph (5)(d), an order made in the course of or by way of regulation of a liquidation and any other order ancillary to or consequential on a winding up order;

(ff) an order directing or otherwise determining an issue as to limitation of actions other than as part of a final judgment or order within the meaning of paragraph (3);

(gg) an order made on an originating summons under Order 85, rule 2, other than such an order as is mentioned in paragraph (5)(c).

(7) Notwithstanding anything in paragraph (3)—

(a) orders made on an appeal to the High Court under section 1(2) of the Arbitration Act 1979 shall be treated as final orders;

(b) all other orders made in connection with or arising out of an arbitration or arbitral award shall be treated as interlocutory orders; without prejudice to the generality of the foregoing, such orders shall include—

(i) orders made in connection with the appointment or removal of an arbitrator or umpire;

(ii) orders made on or in connection with applications for an extension of time for commencing arbitration proceedings;

(iii) orders setting aside an arbitral award or remitting the matter to an arbitrator or umpire (other than orders setting aside the award or remitting the matter made on an appeal in pursuance of the said section 1(2)); and

(iv) orders made on or in connection with applications for leave to enforce an award.]

Commencement 1 October 1988.

Amendments This rule was inserted by SI 1988/1340, r 7.

Para (6): in sub-para (aa) words omitted revoked, in relation to proceedings in which an appeal is set down or an application is lodged, on or after 1 October 1993, by SI 1993/2133, rr 6(1), 7, words ", Order 14A" added by SI 1990/2599, r 9.

[Order 59, r 1B Classes of case where leave to appeal is required

(1) The classes of case prescribed for the purposes of section 18(1A) of the Act (appeals subject to leave) are the following—

(a) a determination by a divisional court of any appeal to the High Court;

(b) orders of the High Court or any other court or tribunal made with the consent of the parties or relating only to costs which are by law left to the discretion of the court or tribunal;

(c) an order granting or refusing any relief made at the hearing of an application for judicial review, except in proceedings arising from a decision made by virtue of the Immigration Act 1971, the British Nationality Act 1981, the Immigration Act 1988, the Asylum and Immigration Appeals Act 1993 or any other enactment relating to nationality or immigration which for the time being is in force in any part of the United Kingdom;

(d) orders which include the giving or refusing of possession of land;

(e) orders including the grant or refusal of an application for the grant of a new tenancy under Part II of the Landlord and Tenant Act 1954;

(f) interlocutory orders of the High Court or any other court or tribunal, except in the following cases, namely—

        (i)   where the liberty of the subject is concerned;

       (ii)   where the residence, education or welfare of a minor is concerned;

     (iii)   where an applicant for contact with a minor is refused all contact with the minor;

     (iv)   in the case of a decree nisi in a matrimonial cause.

(2)   For the purposes of sub-paragraph (1)(f), "education" includes training and religious instruction.

(3)   Leave to appeal to the Court of Appeal may be given by the court or tribunal from whose decision the appeal is sought or by the Court of Appeal.]

Commencement 1 October 1993.
Amendments This rule was inserted, in relation to proceedings in which an appeal is set down or an application is lodged, on or after 1 October 1993, by SI 1993/2133, rr 6(2), 7.
Definitions The Act: Supreme Court Act 1981.

Order 59, r 2 Application of Order to applications for new trial

This Order (except so much of rule 3(1) as provides that an appeal shall be by way of rehearing and except rule 11(1)) applies to an application to the Court of Appeal for a new trial or to set aside a verdict, finding or judgment after trial with or without a jury, as it applies to an appeal to that Court, and references in this Order to an appeal and to an appellant shall be construed accordingly.

Commencement 1 October 1966.

[Order 59, r 2A Interpretation

In this Order "a single judge" means a single judge of the Court of Appeal and "the registrar" means the registrar of civil appeals.]

Commencement 20 April 1982.
Amendments This rule was inserted by SI 1981/1734, r 5.

GENERAL PROVISIONS AS TO APPEALS

Order 59, r 3 Notice of appeal

(1)   An appeal to the Court of Appeal shall be by way of rehearing and must be brought by motion, and the notice of the motion is referred to in this Order as "notice of appeal".

(2)   Notice of appeal may be given either in respect of the whole or in respect of any specified part of the judgment or order of the court below; and every such notice must specify the grounds of the appeal and the precise form of the order which the appellant proposes to ask the Court of Appeal to make.

(3)   Except with the leave of the Court of Appeal[, a single judge or the registrar], the appellant shall not be entitled on the hearing of an appeal to rely on any grounds of appeal, or to apply for any relief, not specified in the notice of appeal.

[(4)   Every notice of appeal must specify the list of appeals to which the appellant proposes that the appeal should be assigned.]

(5)   A notice of appeal must be served on all parties to the proceedings in the court below who are directly affected by the appeal; and, subject to rule 8, it shall not be necessary to serve the notice on parties not so affected.

[(6)   No notice of appeal shall be given by a respondent in a case to which rule 6(1) relates.]

Commencement   1 October 1991 (para (4)); 5 February 1979 (para (6)); 1 October 1966 (remainder).
Amendments   Para (3): words ", a single judge or the registrar" inserted by SI 1981/1734, r 6.
Para (4): substituted by SI 1991/1884, r 15.
Para (6): added by SI 1979/35, r 3(1).

[Order 59, r 3A Value of appeal where appeal is from decision of county court

(1)   This rule applies where the determination sought to be appealed from is a determination of a county court in proceedings to which article 2(3) or (4) of the Appeals Order applies and the value of the appeal is not limited by article 2(6) of that Order.

(2)   Every notice of appeal in a case to which this rule applies shall be accompanied by a statement showing, as the case may be, whether the value of the appeal—
   (a)   exceeds the sum for the time being specified in article 2(1) of the Appeals Order in relation to proceedings of that kind; or
   (b)   is not quantifiable.

(3)   In this rule—
   "the Appeals Order" means the County Court Appeals Order 1991;
   "value of the appeal" has the same meaning as in article 2 of the Appeals Order.]

Commencement   1 October 1991.
Amendments   This rule was inserted by SI 1991/1884, r 14.

Order 59, r 4 Time for appealing

[(1)   Except as otherwise provided by this Order, every notice of appeal must be served under rule 3(5) [not later than 4 weeks after] the date on which the judgment or order of the court was [sealed] or otherwise perfected.]

[[(2)] In the case of an appeal from a decision in respect of which a certificate has been granted under section 12 of the Administration of Justice Act 1969 the period referred to in paragraph (1) shall be calculated from the end of the time during which, in accordance with section 13(5) of that Act, no appeal lies to the Court of Appeal.]

[(3)   Where leave to appeal is granted by the Court of Appeal upon an application made within the time limited for serving notice of appeal under paragraph (1), a notice of appeal may, instead of being served within that time, be served within 7 days after the date when leave is granted.]

Commencement   1 October 1984 (para (3)); 20 April 1982 (para (1)); 20 July 1970 (remainder).
Amendments   Para (1): substituted for paras (1) and (2) as originally enacted by SI 1981/1734, r 7(1); words "not later than 4 weeks after" and word "sealed" substituted by SI 1986/1187, r 9(i).
Para (2): added as para (3) by SI 1970/944, r 7(1), renumbered as para (2) by SI 1981/1734, r 7(2).
Para (3): new para (3) added by SI 1984/1051, r 11.

Order 59, r 5 Setting down appeal

(1)   [Within 7 days after the later of (i) the date on which service of the notice of appeal was effected, or (ii) the date on which the judgment or order of the court

below was sealed or otherwise perfected, the appellant must [set down his appeal by lodging] with the registrar]—

    (a)   a copy of the said judgment or order, and

    (b)   two copies of the notice of appeal, one of which shall be . . . indorsed with the amount of the fee paid, and the other indorsed with a certificate of the date of service of the notice. . . .

    (c)   . . .

[(2)   Upon the said documents being so lodged the registrar shall cause the appeal to be entered in the records of the Court and assigned to the appropriate list of appeals.]

(3)   The [appropriate] list of appeals for the purpose of paragraph (2) shall be decided by the [registrar], without prejudice, however, to any decision of the Court of Appeal on the question whether the judgment or order appealed against is interlocutory or final.

[(4)   Within 4 days of receipt of notification from the office of the registrar that the appeal has been entered in the records of the Court, the appellant must give notice to that effect to all parties on whom the notice of appeal was served, specifying the Court of Appeal reference allocated to that appeal.]

(5)   . . .

Commencement   1 October 1991 (paras (2), (4)); 1 October 1966 (remainder).

Amendments   Para (1): words from "Within 7 days" to "the registrar" substituted by SI 1986/1187, r 9(ii)(a), words "set down his appeal by lodging" therein substituted by SI 1991/1884, r 16; in sub-para (b) first words omitted revoked by SI 1972/1194, r 3(1), second words omitted and para (c) revoked by SI 1986/1187, r 9(ii)(b).

Para (2): substituted by SI 1991/1884, r 17.

Para (3): word "appropriate" substituted by SI 1991/1884, r 18; word "registrar" substituted by SI 1981/1734, r 8(1).

Para (4): substituted by SI 1991/1884, r 19.

Para (5): revoked by SI 1981/1734, r 8(4).

[Order 59, r 6 Respondent's notice

(1)   A respondent who, having been served with a notice of appeal, desires—

    (a)   to contend on the appeal that the decision of the court below should be varied, either in any event or in the event of the appeal being allowed in whole or in part, or

    (b)   to contend that the decision of the court below should be affirmed on grounds other than those relied upon by that court, or

    (c)   to contend by way of cross-appeal that the decision of the court below was wrong in whole or in part,

must give notice to that effect, specifying the grounds of his contention and, in a case to which paragraph (a) or (c) relates, the precise form of the order which he proposes to ask the Court to make.

(2)   Except with the leave of the Court of Appeal [or a single judge or the registrar], a respondent shall not be entitled on the hearing of the appeal to apply for any relief not specified in a notice under paragraph (1) or to rely, in support of any contention, upon any ground which has not been specified in such a notice or relied upon by the court below.

(3)   Any notice given by a respondent under this rule (in this Order referred to as a "respondent's notice") must be served on the appellant, and on all parties to the

proceedings in the court below who are directly affected by the contentions of the respondent, [and must be served within 21 days after the service of the notice of appeal on the respondent].

(4)   A party by whom a respondent's notice is given must, [within 4 days after the later of (i) the date on which service of the respondent's notice was effected or (ii) the date on which he was notified under rule 5(4) that the appeal had been set down, lodge with the registrar two copies of the respondent's notice, one of which shall be indorsed with the amount of the fee paid, and the other indorsed with a certificate of the date of service of such respondent's notice.]]

Commencement   5 February 1979.
Amendments   This rule was substituted by SI 1979/35, r 3(3).
Para (2): words "or a single judge or the registrar" inserted by SI 1981/1734, r 9(1).
Para (3): words from "and must be served" to "the respondent" substituted by SI 1981/1734, r 9(2).
Para (4): words from "within 4 days" to "respondent's notice" substituted by SI 1986/1187, r 9(iv).

Order 59, r 7 Amendments of notice of appeal and respondent's notice

(1)   A notice of appeal or respondent's notice may be amended—
  (a) by or with the leave of the Court of Appeal[, a single judge or the registrar], at any time;
  (b) without such leave, by supplementary notice served, before . . . the date on which the appeal first appears in the [List of Forthcoming Appeals referred to in rule 9(1)], on each of the parties on whom the notice to be amended was served.

(2)   A party by whom a supplementary notice is served under this rule must, within 2 days after service of the notice, furnish two copies of the notice to the [registrar].

Commencement   1 October 1966.
Amendments   Para (1): in sub-para (a) words ", a single judge or the registrar" inserted, in sub-para (b) words omitted revoked and words "List of Forthcoming Appeals referred to in rule 9(1)" substituted, by SI 1981/1734, r 10(1), (2).
Para (2): word "registrar" substituted by SI 1981/1734, r 10(3).

Order 59, r 8 Directions of the Court as to service

(1)   The Court of Appeal [or a single judge or the registrar] may in any case direct that [a notice of appeal or respondent's notice] be served on any party to the proceedings in the court below on whom it has not been served, or on any person not party to those proceedings.

[(2)   Where a direction is given under paragraph (1) the hearing of the appeal may be postponed or adjourned for such period and on such terms as may be just and such judgment may be given and such order made on the appeal as might have been given or made if the persons served in pursuance of the direction had originally been parties.]

Commencement   20 April 1982 (para (2)); 1 October 1966 (remainder).
Amendments   Para (1): words "or a single judge or the registrar" inserted by SI 1981/1734, r 11(1); words "a notice of appeal or respondent's notice" substituted by SI 1979/35, r 3(4)(a).
Para (2): original para (2) revoked and original para (3) renumbered as para (2) by SI 1979/35, r 3(4)(b); subsequently substituted by SI 1981/1734, r 11(2).

Order 59, r 9 Documents to be lodged by appellant

(1)   [[Not more than 14 days] after the appeal first appears in a list to be called "the List of Forthcoming Appeals"] the appellant must cause to be lodged with the [registrar] the number of copies for which paragraph (2) provides of each of the following documents, namely—

(a)   the notice of appeal;

(b)   the respondent's notice;

(c)   any supplementary notice served under rule 7;

(d)   the judgment or order of the court below;

(e)   [the originating process by which the proceedings in the court below were begun, any interlocutory or other related process which is the subject of the appeal,] the pleadings (including particulars), if any, and, in the case of an appeal in an Admiralty cause or matter, the preliminary acts, if any;

(f)   [the transcript of the official shorthand note or record, if any, of the judge's reasons for giving the judgment or making the order of the court below or, in the absence of such a note or record, the judge's note of his reasons or, if the judge's note is not available, counsel's note of the judge's reasons approved wherever possible by the judge;]

(g)   [such parts of the transcript of the official shorthand note or record, if any, of the evidence given in the court below as are relevant to any question at issue on the appeal or, in the absence of such a note or record, such parts of the judge's note of the evidence as are relevant to any such question;]

(h)   any list of exhibits made under Order 35, rule 11, or the schedule of evidence, as the case may be;

(i)   such affidavits, exhibits, or parts of exhibits, as were in evidence in the court below and as are relevant to any question at issue on the appeal.

(2)   [Unless otherwise directed, the number] of copies to be lodged in accordance with paragraph (1) is three copies [except—

(a)   where the appeal is to be heard by two judges in which case it is two copies; or

(b)   in the case of an appeal in an Admiralty cause or matter, in which case it is four copies or, if the Court of Appeal is to hear the appeal with assessors, six].

[(2A) When the transcripts, if any, referred to in items (f) and (g) of paragraph (1) have been bespoken by the appellant and paid for, the number of such transcripts required in accordance with paragraph (2) shall be sent by the official shorthand writer or transcriber direct to the registrar.]

[(3)   [At any time after an appeal has been set down in accordance with rule 5 the registrar may] give such directions in relation to the documents to be produced at the appeal, and the manner in which they are to be presented, and as to other matters incidental to the conduct of the appeal, as appear best adapted to secure the just, expeditious and economical disposal of the appeal.

(4)   The directions referred to in paragraph (3) may be given without a hearing provided always that the registrar may at any time issue a summons requiring the parties to an appeal to attend before him and any party to an appeal may apply at any time for an appointment before the registrar.]

Commencement 1 October 1983 (para (2A)); 20 April 1982 (paras (3), (4)); 1 October 1966 (remainder).
Amendments Para (1): words from the beginning to "the List of Forthcoming Appeals" and word "registrar" substituted by SI 1981/1734, r 12(1), words "Not more than 14 days" substituted by SI 1983/1181, r 28(i); in sub-para (e) words from "the originating process" to "the appeal" inserted by SI 1983/1181, r 28(ii); sub-paras (f), (g) substituted by SI 1983/1181, r 28(iii), (iv).

Para (2): words "Unless otherwise directed, the number" and word "except" and sub-paras (a), (b) substituted by SI 1981/1734, r 12(2).
Para (2A): inserted by SI 1983/1181, r 28(v).
Para (3): substituted, together with para (4), for para (3) as originally enacted, by SI 1981/1734, r 12(3); words "At any time after an appeal has been set down in accordance with rule 5 the registrar may" substituted by SI 1983/1181, r 28(vi).
Para (4): substituted, together with para (3), for para (3) as originally enacted, by SI 1981/1734, r 12(3).

Order 59, r 10 General powers of the Court

(1)   In relation to an appeal the Court of Appeal shall have all the powers and duties as to amendment and otherwise of the High Court including, without prejudice to the generality of the foregoing words, the powers of the Court under Order 36 to refer any question or issue of fact for trial before, or inquiry and report by, an official referee.

In relation to a reference made to an official referee, any thing required or authorised under Order 36, [rule 9], to be done by, to or before the Court shall be done by, to or before the Court of Appeal.

(2)   The Court of Appeal shall have power to receive further evidence on questions of fact, either by oral examination in court, by affidavit, or by deposition taken before an examiner, but, in the case of an appeal from a judgment after trial or hearing of any cause or matter on the merits, no such further evidence (other than evidence as to matters which have occurred after the date of the trial or hearing) shall be admitted except on special grounds.

(3)   The Court of Appeal shall have power to draw inferences of fact and to give any judgment and make any order which ought to have been given or made, and to make such further or other order as the case may require.

(4)   The powers of the Court of Appeal under the foregoing provisions of this rule may be exercised notwithstanding that no notice of appeal or respondent's notice has been given in respect of any particular part of the decision of the court below or by any particular party to the proceedings in that court, or that any ground for allowing the appeal or for affirming of varying the decision of that court is not specified in such a notice; and the Court of Appeal may make any order, on such terms as the Court thinks just, to ensure the determination on the merits of the real question in controversy between the parties.

(5)   The Court of Appeal may, in special circumstances, order that such security shall be given for the costs of an appeal as may be just.

(6)   The powers of the Court of Appeal in respect of an appeal shall not be restricted by reason of any interlocutory order from which there has been no appeal.

(7)   Documents impounded by order of the Court of Appeal shall not be delivered out of the custody of that Court except in compliance with an order of that Court:

Provided that where a Law Officer or the Director of Public Prosecutions makes a written request in that behalf, documents so impounded shall be delivered into his custody.

(8)   Documents impounded by order of the Court of Appeal, while in the custody of that Court, shall not be inspected except by a person authorised to do so by an order of that Court.

[(9)   In any proceedings incidental to any cause or matter pending before the Court of Appeal, the powers conferred by this rule on the Court may be exercised by a single judge or the registrar.

Provided that the said powers of the Court of Appeal shall be exercisable only by that Court or a single judge in relation to
  (a) the grant, variation, discharge or enforcement of an injunction, or an undertaking given in lieu of an injunction; and
  (b) the grant or lifting of a stay of execution or proceedings.]

Commencement 20 April 1982 (para (9)); 1 October 1966 (remainder).
Amendments Para (1): words "rule 9" substituted by SI 1982/1111, r 102.
Para (9): added by SI 1981/1734, r 13.
Forms Order to admit to bail (No 99).
Notice of bail (No 100).

Order 59, r 11 Powers of the Court as to new trials

(1) On the hearing of any appeal the Court of Appeal may, if it thinks fit, make any such order as could be made in pursuance of an application for a new trial or to set aside a verdict, finding or judgment of the court below.

(2) [The Court of Appeal shall not be bound to order a new trial] on the ground of misdirection, or of the improper admission or rejection of evidence, or because the verdict of the jury was not taken upon a question which the judge at the trial was not asked to leave to them, unless in the opinion of the Court of Appeal some substantial wrong or miscarriage has been thereby occasioned.

(3) A new trial may be ordered on any question without interfering with the finding or decision on any other question; and if it appears to the Court of Appeal that any such wrong or miscarriage as is mentioned in paragraph (2) affects part only of the matter in controversy, or one or some only of the parties, the Court may order a new trial as to that part only, or as to that party or those parties only, and give final judgment as to the remainder.

[(4) In any case where the Court of Appeal has power to order a new trial on the ground that damages awarded by a jury are excessive or inadequate, the Court may, instead of ordering a new trial, substitute for the sum awarded by the jury such sum as appears to the Court to be proper; but except as aforesaid the Court of Appeal shall not have power to reduce or increase the damages awarded by a jury.]

(5) A new trial shall not be ordered by reason of the ruling of any judge that a document is sufficiently stamped or does not require to be stamped.

Commencement 1 February 1991 (para (4)); 1 October 1966 (remainder).
Amendments Para (2): words "The Court of Appeal shall not be bound to order a new trial" substituted by SI 1968/1244, r 8(1).
Para (4): substituted by SI 1990/2599, r 13(1).

Order 59, r 12 Evidence on appeal

Where any question of fact is involved in an appeal, the evidence taken in the court below bearing on the question shall, subject to any direction of the Court of Appeal [or a single judge or the registrar], be brought before that Court as follows:—
  (a) in the case of evidence taken by affidavit, by the production of [a true copy of such affidavit];
  (b) in the case of evidence given orally, by a copy of so much of the transcript

of the official shorthand note as is relevant or by a copy of the judge's note, where he has intimated that in the event of an appeal his note will be sufficient, or by such other means as the Court of Appeal [or a single judge or the registrar] may direct.

Commencement 1 October 1966.
Amendments Words "or a single judge or the registrar" in both places inserted, words "a true copy of such affidavit" substituted, by SI 1981/1734, r 14.

[Order 59, r 12A Non-disclosure of payment into court

(1)   Where—

(a)   any question on an appeal in an action for a debt, damages or salvage relates to liability for the debt, damages or salvage or to the amount thereof, and

(b)   money was paid into court under Order 22, rule 1, in the proceedings in the court below before judgment,

neither the fact of the payment nor the amount thereof shall be stated in the notice of appeal or the respondent's notice or in any supplementary notice or be communicated to the Court of Appeal until all such questions have been decided.

This rule shall not apply in the case of an appeal as to costs only or an appeal in an action to which a defence of tender before action was pleaded.

(2)   For the purpose of complying with this rule the appellant must cause to be omitted from the copies of the documents lodged by him under rules 9(d) and (f) every part thereof which states . . . that money was paid into court in the proceedings in that court before judgment.]

Commencement 1 April 1976.
Amendments This rule was inserted by SI 1976/337, r 11.
Para (2): words omitted revoked by SI 1981/1734, r 15.

Order 59, r 13 Stay of execution, etc

(1)   Except so far as the court below or the Court of Appeal [or a single judge] may otherwise direct—

(a)   an appeal shall not operate as a stay of execution or of proceedings under the decision of the court below;

(b)   no intermediate act or proceeding shall be invalidated by an appeal.

(2)   On an appeal from the High Court, interest for such time as execution has been delayed by the appeal shall be allowed unless the Court otherwise orders.

Commencement 1 October 1966.
Amendments Para (1): words "or a single judge" inserted by SI 1981/1734, r 16.

Order 59, r 14 Applications to Court of Appeal

[(1) Unless otherwise directed, every application to the Court of Appeal, a single judge or the registrar which is not made ex parte must be made by summons and such summons must be served on the party or parties affected at least 2 clear days before the day on which it is heard or, in the case of an application which is made after the expiration of the time for appealing, at least 7 days before the day on which the summons is heard.]

[(1A) In support of any application (whether made ex parte or inter partes) the applicant shall lodge with the registrar such documents as the Court of Appeal, a single judge or the registrar may direct, and rule 9(3) and (4) shall apply, with any necessary modifications, to applications as they apply to appeals.]

[(2)   An application to the Court of Appeal for leave to appeal shall—
  (a)   include, where necessary, any application to extend the time for appealing, and
  (b)   be made ex parte in writing setting out the reasons why leave should be granted and, if the time for appealing has expired, the reasons why the application was not made within that time;

and the Court may grant or refuse the application or direct that the application be renewed in open court either ex parte or inter partes.

(2A) If an application under paragraph (2) is refused otherwise than after a hearing in open court, the applicant shall be entitled, within 7 days after he has been given notice of the refusal, to renew his application; and such renewed application shall be heard ex parte in open court [before two Lords Justices].

(2B) If an application under paragraph (2) is granted otherwise than after a hearing inter partes, notice of the order shall be served on the party or parties affected by the appeal and any such party shall be entitled, within 7 days after service of the notice, to apply to have the grant of leave reconsidered inter partes in open court [before two Lords Justices].]

(3)   Where an ex parte application has been refused by the court below, an application for a similar purpose may be made to the Court of Appeal ex parte within 7 days after the date of the refusal.

(4)   Wherever under these rules an application may be made either to the court below or to the Court of Appeal, it shall not be made in the first instance to the Court of Appeal, except where there are special circumstances which make it impossible or impracticable to apply to the court below.

[(5)   Where an application is made to the Court of Appeal with regard to arbitration proceedings before a judge-arbitrator or judge-umpire which would, in the case of an ordinary arbitrator or umpire, be made to the High Court, the provisions of Order 73, rule 5, shall apply as if, for the words "the Court", wherever they appear in that rule, there were substituted the words "the Court of Appeal" and as if, for the words "arbitrator" and "umpire", there were substituted the words "judge-arbitrator" and "judge-umpire" respectively.

(6)   Where an application is made to the Court of Appeal under section 1(5) of the Arbitration Act 1979 (including any application for leave), notice thereof must be served on the judge-arbitrator or judge-umpire and on any other party to the reference.]

[(7)   An application, not being an application for leave to appeal, which may be heard by a single judge shall unless otherwise directed be heard in chambers.]

[(8)   An application which may under the provisions of this Order be heard by the registrar shall be heard in chambers.

(9)   The registrar may refer to a single judge any matter which he thinks should properly be decided by a single judge, and, following such reference, the judge may either dispose of the matter or refer it back to the registrar with such direction as the single judge thinks fit.

(10) A single judge may refer to the Court of Appeal any matter which he thinks should properly be decided by that Court, and, following such reference, that Court may either dispose of the matter or refer it back to a single judge or the registrar, with such directions as that Court thinks fit.

(11) An appeal shall lie to a single judge from any determination made by the registrar and shall be brought by way of fresh application made within 10 days of the determination appealed against.]

[(12) An appeal shall lie to the Court of Appeal from any determination by a single judge, not being the determination of an application for leave to appeal, and shall be brought by way of fresh application made within 10 days of the determination appealed against.

Provided that an appeal shall not lie to the Court of Appeal without the leave of that Court in respect of a determination of the registrar which has been reviewed by a single judge.]

Commencement 1 October 1989 (paras (2), (2A), (2B)); 1 October 1986 (para (1A)); 1 October 1983 (paras (1), (7), (12)); 20 April 1982 (paras (8)–(11)); 1 August 1979 (paras (5), (6)); 1 October 1966 (remainder).
Amendments Para (1): substituted by SI 1983/1181, r 29(i).
Para (1A): inserted by SI 1986/1187, r 9(v).
Para (2): substituted, together with paras (2A), (2B), for para (2) as originally enacted, by SI 1989/1307, r 15.
Paras (2A), (2B): substituted, together with para (2), for para (2) as originally enacted, by SI 1989/1307, r 15; words "before two Lords Justices" in both paras inserted, in relation to proceedings in which an appeal is set down or an application is lodged, on or after 1 October 1993, by SI 1993/2133, rr 6(3), 7.
Paras (5), (6): added by SI 1979/522, r 4.
Paras (7), (12): added by SI 1981/1734, r 17; substituted by SI 1983/1181, r 29(iii), (iv).
Paras (8)–(11): added by SI 1981/1734, r 17.

Order 59, r 15 Extension of time

Without prejudice to the power of the Court of Appeal[, a single judge or the registrar] under Order 3, rule 5, to extend [or abridge] the time prescribed by any provision of this Order, the period for serving notice of appeal under rule 4 or for making application ex parte under rule 14(3) may be extended [or abridged] by the court below on application made before the expiration of that period.

Commencement 1 October 1966.
Amendments Words ", a single judge or the registrar", "or abridge" and "or abridged" inserted by SI 1981/1734, r 18.

SPECIAL PROVISIONS AS TO PARTICULAR APPEALS

Order 59, r 16 Appeal against decree nisi

(1)   The following provisions of this rule shall apply to any appeal to the Court of Appeal in a matrimonial cause against a decree nisi of divorce or nullity of marriage.

(2)   The period of [4] weeks specified in rule 4 shall be calculated from the date on which the decree was pronounced and rule 15 shall not apply in relation to that period.

[(2A) The notice of appeal shall be served on the appropriate registrar as well as on the party or parties required to be served under rule 3.]

(3)   The appellant must, within [the period mentioned in paragraph (2)] and after service of the notice of appeal, [produce to the [registrar of civil appeals] a sealed copy of the decree appealed against and leave with him a copy of that decree and two copies of the notice of appeal (one of which shall be) indorsed with the amount of the fee

paid, and the other indorsed with a certificate of the date of service of the notice); and the appeal shall not be competent unless this paragraph has been complied with.

(4)   ... for the purposes of rule 5 the leaving of the said copies shall be sufficient for the setting down of the appeal and rule 5(1) shall not apply.

(5)   A party who intends to apply ex parte to the Court of Appeal to extend the period referred to in paragraphs (2) and (3) must give notice of his intention to [the appropriate registrar] before the application is made; and where any order is made by the Court of Appeal extending the said period, it shall be the duty of the [registrar of civil appeals] forthwith to give notice of the making of the order and of the terms thereof to the appropriate registrar.

[(6)   In this rule "the appropriate registrar" means—
   (a)   in relation to a cause pending in a county court, the [district judge] of that court,
   (b)   in relation to a cause proceeding in the principal registry of the Family Division, the [senior district judge] of that Division, and
   (c)   in relation to a cause proceeding in a district registry, the [district judge] of that registry.]

Commencement   1 October 1972 (paras (2A), (6)); 1 October 1966 (remainder).
Amendments   Para (2): figure "4" substituted by SI 1981/1734, r 19(1).
Para (2A): inserted by SI 1968/1244, r 8(2); substituted by SI 1972/1194, r 3(3).
Para (3): words "the period mentioned in paragraph (2)" substituted by SI 1968/1244, r 8(3); words from "produce to the" to "(one of which shall be" substituted by SI 1972/1194, r 3(4); words "registrar of civil appeals" therein substituted by SI 1981/1734, r 19(2).
Para (4): words omitted revoked by SI 1972/1194, r 3(5).
Para (5): words "the appropriate registrar" substituted by SI 1972/1194, r 3(6); words "registrar of civil appeals" substituted by SI 1981/1734, r 19(3).
Para (6): substituted by SI 1972/1194, r 3(7); in sub-para (b) words "senior registrar" substituted by SI 1981/1734, r 19(4).

Order 59, r 17 Appeal against order for revocation of patent

(1)   The following provisions of this rule shall apply to any appeal to the Court of Appeal from an order for the revocation of a patent ....

(2)   The notice of appeal must be served on the Comptroller-General of Patents, Designs and Trade Marks (in this rule referred to as "the Comptroller") as well as on the party or parties required to be served under rule 3.

(3)   If, at any time before the appeal comes on for hearing, the respondent decides not to appear on the appeal or not to oppose it, he must forthwith serve notice of his decision on the Comptroller and the appellant, and any such notice served on the Comptroller must be accompanied by a copy of the petition or of the pleadings in the action and the affidavits filed therein.

(4)   The Comptroller must, within 14 days after receiving notice of the respondent's decision, serve on the appellant a notice stating whether or not he intends to appear on the appeal.

(5)   The Comptroller may appear and be heard in opposition to the appeal—
   (a)   in any case where he has given notice under paragraph (4) of his intention to appear, and
   (b)   in any other case (including, in particular, a case where the respondent withdraws his opposition to the appeal during the hearing) if the Court of Appeal so directs or allows.

(6) The Court of Appeal may make such orders for the postponement or adjournment of the hearing of the appeal as may appear to the Court necessary for the purpose of giving effect to the foregoing provisions of this rule.

Commencement 1 October 1966.
Amendments Para (1): words omitted revoked by SI 1978/579, r 9(1)(a).

[Order 59, r 18 Appeal from Patents Court on appeal from Comptroller

In the case of an appeal to the Court of Appeal from a decision of the Patents Court on an appeal from a decision of the Comptroller-General of Patents, Designs and Trade Marks the notice of appeal must be served on the Comptroller-General as well as on the party or parties required to be served under rule 3.]

Commencement 1 June 1978.
Amendments This rule was substituted by SI 1978/579, r 9(1)(b).

Order 59, r 19 Appeal from county court

(1) The following provisions of this rule shall apply to any appeal to the Court of Appeal from a county court [other than an appeal against a decree nisi of divorce or nullity of marriage].

(2) [The appellant must, within the time specified in rule 4, serve the notice of appeal on] the [district judge] of the county court as well as on the party or parties required to be served under rule 3.

(3) [In relation to the appeal rule 4(1) and rule 5(1) shall have effect as if for the words "the date on which the judgment or order of the court below was sealed or otherwise perfected" there were substituted the words "the date of the judgment or order of the court below".]

(4) It shall be the duty of the appellant to apply to the judge of the county court for a signed copy of any note made by him of the proceedings and of his decision, and to furnish that copy for the use of the Court of Appeal; and in default of production of such a note, or, if such note is incomplete, in addition to such note, the Court of Appeal may hear and determine the appeal on any other evidence or statement of what occurred before the judge of the county court which appears to the Court of Appeal to be sufficient.

Except where the Court of Appeal [or a single judge or the registrar of civil appeals] otherwise directs, an affidavit or note by a person present in the county court shall not be used in evidence under this paragraph unless it was previously submitted to the judge for his comments.

[(4A) Rule 12A shall apply in any case where money was paid into court by the defendant before judgment in county court proceedings in satisfaction of the plaintiff's cause of action or of one or more causes joined in one action or on account of a sum admitted by the defendant to be due to the plaintiff.]

(5) Rule 13(1)(a) shall not apply, but the appeal shall not operate as a stay of [execution or of] proceedings in the county court unless the judge of that court [or the Court of Appeal] so orders or unless, within 10 days after the date of the judgment or order appealed against, the appellant deposits a sum fixed by the judge not exceeding the amount of the money or the value of the property affected by the judgment or order, or gives such security for the said sum as the judge may direct.

[(5A) Where the Court of Appeal determines that a statement provided pursuant to rule 3A is grossly inaccurate, the Court may, without prejudice to its powers under section 51(6) of the Act, strike out the appeal.]

(6)   In the case of an appeal to the Court of Appeal from the decision of a county court on the hearing of an appeal from a registration officer under [section 56 of the Representation of the People Act 1983], notice of the decision of the Court of Appeal shall be given by the [registrar of civil appeals] to the registration officer, specifying every alteration to be made in pursuance of the decision in the register or list concerned, and a copy of every such notice shall be sent to the [district judge] of the county court.

[(7)   In relation to any proceedings in the principal registry of the Family Division which by virtue of [any statutory provision] are treated as pending in a county court, paragraphs (1) to (5) shall have effect with the necessary modifications as if the principal registry were a county court.]

Commencement 1 October 1991 (para (5A)); 1 October 1986 (para (3)); 20 April 1982 (para (4A)); 1 October 1972 (para (7)); 1 October 1966 (remainder).
Amendments Para (1): words "other than an appeal against a decree nisi of divorce or nullity of marriage" added by SI 1968/1244, r 8(4).
Para (2): words "The appellant must, within the time specified in rule 4, serve the notice of appeal on" substituted by SI 1986/1187, r 9(vi).
Para (3): substituted by SI 1986/1187, r 9(vii).
Para (4): words "or a single judge or the registrar of civil appeals" inserted by SI 1981/1734, r 20(1).
Para (4A): inserted by SI 1981/1734, r 20(2).
Para (5): words "execution or of" and "or the Court of Appeal" inserted by SI 1976/337, r 11(2).
Para (5A): inserted by SI 1991/1884, r 20.
Para (6): words "section 56 of the Representation of the People Act 1983" substituted by SI 1987/1423, r 63, Schedule; words "registrar of civil appeals" substituted by SI 1981/1734, r 20(3).
Para (7): added by SI 1972/1194, r 3(8); words "any statutory provision" substituted by SI 1991/1884, r 4.
Definitions The Act: Supreme Court Act 1981.

Order 59, r 20 Appeals in cases of contempt of court

(1)   In the case of an appeal to the Court of Appeal under section 13 of the Administration of Justice Act 1960, the notice of appeal must be served on the proper officer of the court from whose order or decision the appeal is brought as well as on the party or parties required to be served under rule 3.

This paragraph shall not apply in relation to an appeal to which rule 19 applies.

(2)   Where, in the case of an appeal under the said section 13 to the Court of Appeal or to the House of Lords from the Court of Appeal, the appellant is in custody, the Court of Appeal may order his release on his giving security (whether by recognizance, with or without sureties, or otherwise and for such reasonable sum as that Court may fix) for his appearance within 10 days after the judgment of the Court of Appeal or, as the case may be, of the House of Lords on the appeal shall have been given, before the court from whose order or decision the appeal is brought unless the order or decision is reversed by that judgment.

(3)   An application for the release of a person under paragraph (2) pending an appeal to the Court of Appeal or House of Lords under the said section 13 must be made by motion, and the notice of the motion must, at least 24 hours before the day named therein for the hearing, be served on the proper officer of the court from whose order or decision the appeal is brought and on all parties to the proceedings in that court who are directly affected by the appeal.

(4)   [Order 79, rule 9(6), (6A), (6B) and (8)], shall apply in relation to the grant of bail under this rule by the Court of Appeal [in a case of criminal contempt of court] as they apply in relation to the grant of bail in criminal proceedings by the High Court, but with the substitution for references to a judge in chambers of references to the Court of Appeal and for references to the defendant of references to the appellant.

[(5)   When granting bail under this Rule in a case of civil contempt of court, the Court of Appeal may order that the recognizance or other security to be given by the appellant or the recognizance of any surety shall be given before any person authorised by virtue of [section 119(1) of the Magistrates' Courts Act 1980] to take a recognizance where a magistrates' court having power to take it has, instead of taking it, fixed the amount in which the principal and his sureties, if any, are to be bound.

An order by the Court of Appeal granting bail as aforesaid must be in Form 98 in Appendix A with the necessary adaptations.]

[(6)   Where in pursuance of an order of the Court of Appeal under paragraph (5) of this Rule a recognizance is entered into or other security given before any person, it shall be the duty of that person to cause the recognizance of the appellant or any surety or, as the case may be, a statement of the other security given, to be transmitted forthwith to the clerk of the court which committed the appellant; and a copy of such recognizance or statement shall at the same time be sent to the governor or keeper of the prison or other place of detention in which the appellant is detained, unless the recognizance or security was given before such governor or keeper.

(7)   . . .]

[(8)   [The] powers conferred on the Court of Appeal by paragraphs (2), (4), (5) and (6) of this rule may be exercised by a single judge.]

Commencement   20 April 1982 (para (8)); 17 April 1978 (paras (5)–(7)); 1 October 1966 (remainder).
Amendments   Para (4): words "Order 79, rule 9(6), (6A), (6B) and (8)" substituted and words "in a case of criminal contempt of court" inserted by SI 1978/251, r 2(1).
Para (5): inserted by SI 1978/251, r 2(2); words "section 119(1) of the Magistrates' Courts Act 1980" substituted by SI 1981/1734, r 21(1).
Para (6): inserted by SI 1978/251, r 2(2).
Para (7): inserted by SI 1978/251, r 2(2); revoked by SI 1989/1307, r 16.
Para (8): added by SI 1981/1734, r 21(2); word "The" substituted by SI 1989/1307, r 17.

[Order 59, r 21 Appeals from Social Security Commissioners

(1)   This rule shall apply to any appeal to the Court of Appeal under section 14 of the Social Security Act 1980 (appeal from the decision of a Commissioner on a question of law, with the leave of the Commissioner or of the Court of Appeal).

(2)   The notice of appeal must be served within 6 weeks from the date on which notice of the Commissioner's grant or refusal of leave was given in writing to the appellant and must be served on the Secretary of State and any person appointed by him to proceed with a claim as well as on the party or parties required to be served under rule 3.

[(3)   The provisions of rule 4(3) apply to this rule, with the substitution for the reference in rule 4(3) to paragraph (1) of a reference to paragraph (2).]]

Commencement   1 October 1984 (para (3)); 2 January 1981 (remainder).
Amendments   This rule was inserted by SI 1980/1908, r 6(2).
Para (3): added by SI 1984/1051, r 12.

[Order 59, r 22 Appeals from value added tax tribunals

(1)   An application to the Court of Appeal for leave to appeal from a value added tax tribunal direct to that Court under section 26 of the Finance Act 1985 shall be made within 28 days from the date on which the tribunal certifies that its decision involves a point of law relating wholly or mainly to the construction of an enactment or of a statutory instrument, or of any of the Community Treaties or any Community Instrument, which has been fully argued before it and fully considered by it.

(2)   Such an application shall be made by the parties jointly by lodging a copy of the decision, endorsed with the certificate of the tribunal and a statement of the grounds of the application, with the Registrar of Civil Appeals, and shall be determined by a single judge of the Court of Appeal, who may do so without a hearing.

(3)   In the case of all applications, the Registrar of Civil Appeals shall notify the parties of the determination of the single judge, and
    (a)   where leave to appeal to the Court of Appeal is granted, the appellant shall within 14 days after such notification serve the notice of appeal on the chairman of the tribunal as well as on the party or parties required to be served by rule 3,
    (b)   where leave to appeal to the Court of Appeal is refused, the period specified in Order 55, rule 4(2) for appealing to the High Court shall be calculated from the date of notification of the refusal.]

Commencement   12 January 1987.
Amendments   This rule was added by SI 1986/2289, r 4.

[Order 59, r 23 Dismissal of patient's appeal by consent

Notwithstanding anything in Order 80, rule 10(1) or in Order 10, rule 10(1) of the County Court Rules 1981, where the receiver or other person authorised under Part VII of the Mental Health Act 1983 to conduct legal proceedings in the name of the patient or on his behalf has also been authorised by the Court of Protection under its seal to consent to the dismissal of an appeal to the Court of Appeal by that patient, the appeal may be dismissed by consent without a hearing.]

Commencement   4 April 1988.
Amendments   This rule was added by SI 1988/298, r 6 (this rule was added as rule 22; as there is already a rule 22, this rule has been numbered as rule 23).

[Order 59, r 24 Appeals from Immigration Appeals Tribunals

(1)   This rule shall apply to any appeal to the Court of Appeal under section 9 of the Asylum and Immigration Appeals Act 1993 (appeal on a question of law from a final determination of an Immigration Appeals Tribunal, with the leave of the Immigration Appeals Tribunal or the Court of Appeal).

(2)   Rule 4(1) shall have effect as if for the words "the date on which the judgment or order of the court below was sealed or otherwise perfected" there were substituted the words "the date of the tribunal's written decision to grant or refuse leave to appeal".

(3)   The notice of appeal must be served on the other party or parties to the proceedings before the tribunal, and on the chairman.

(4)   Rule 9 shall have effect as if—

    (a)   for paragraph (1)(e) there were substituted a reference to the following documents—

        (i)   any note recording the original decision or action of the immigration officer or of the Secretary of State, notes of interviews, any documents referred to in the original decision and any explanatory statement;

        (ii)   the notice of appeal to the Adjudicator or Special Adjudicator;

        (iii)   the written decision of the Adjudicator or Special Adjudicator; and

        (iv)   the notice of appeal to the tribunal;

    (b)   for paragraph (1)(f) there were substituted a reference to the written notice or decision and reasons for that decision given to the parties by the tribunal;

    (c)   for paragraph (1)(g) there were substituted a reference to any summary or record taken by the tribunal of the proceedings before it.

(5)   Rule 13 shall not apply.]

Commencement   1 December 1993.
Amendments   This rule was inserted by SI 1993/2760, r 4.

ORDER 60

APPEALS TO COURT OF APPEAL FROM THE RESTRICTIVE PRACTICES COURT

Order 60, r 1 Appeal to be brought by motion

An appeal to the Court of Appeal from the Restrictive Practices Court under the [Restrictive Practices Court Act 1976] must be brought by motion, and the notice of the motion must state [any question of law and, in the case of proceedings under Part III of the Fair Trading Act 1973, any question of fact on which the appeal is brought together in each case with the appellant's contentions thereon].

Commencement 1 October 1966.
Amendments Words "Restrictive Practices Court Act 1976" substituted by SI 1979/1542, r 9(1), Schedule; words from "any question" to "contentions thereon" substituted by SI 1981/1734, r 22(1).

Order 60, r 2 Service of notice of motion

(1)   [Within 28 days] after the appellant receives a copy of the judgment constituting the case stated by the Restrictive Practices Court he must serve the notice of motion and a copy of the judgment on every other party to the proceedings before that Court and must serve the notice of motion on the proper officer of that Court.

(2)   Where the appellant applies to the said Court for the Court's judgment to be amplified or amended—
    (a)   he shall be deemed for the purpose of paragraph (1) to have received a copy of the judgment on the date on which he receives a copy of the order made on his application, and
    (b)   the judgment constituting the case stated shall be the judgment with such amplifications or amendments, if any, as may be specified in that order.

Commencement 1 October 1966.
Amendments Para (1): words "Within 28 days" substituted by SI 1981/1734, r 22(2).

Order 60, r 3 Entry, etc of appeal

(1)   Within 2 days after service of the notice of motion, the appellant must lodge the judgment constituting the case and two copies of the notice with the [registrar of civil appeals] who shall enter the appeal in the appropriate list; and the appeal shall not be heard until after the expiration of 21 days from the date of entry.

(2)   The [registrar of civil appeals] shall notify the proper officer of the Restrictive Practices Court of the decision of the Court of Appeal on the appeal and of any directions given by the Court of Appeal thereon.

Commencement 1 October 1966.
Amendments Paras (1), (2): words "registrar of civil appeals" substituted by SI 1981/1734, r 22(3).

Order 60, r 4 Powers of Court of Appeal

The Court of Appeal shall have power to draw inferences of fact from the facts set forth in the judgment of the Restrictive Practices Court constituting the case.

Commencement 1 October 1966.

ORDER 61

Appeals from Tribunals to Court of Appeal by Case Stated

Order 61, r 1 Statement of case by Lands Tribunal

(1)   The time within which a person aggrieved by a decision of the Lands Tribunal as being erroneous in point of law may under section 3(4) of the Lands Tribunal Act 1949 or any other enactment require the Tribunal to state a case for the decision of the Court of Appeal shall be [4] weeks from the date of the decision, and the application for the statement of the case must be made to the registrar of the Tribunal in writing.

(2)   A case stated by the Tribunal must state the facts on which the decision was based and the decision of the Tribunal and must be signed by the member or members of the Tribunal by whom it was given.

(3)   The case must be stated as soon as may be after the application therefor is made and must be sent by post to the applicant.

(4)   Where the decision of the Lands Tribunal in respect of which a case is stated states all the relevant facts found by the Tribunal and indicates the questions of law to be decided by the Court of Appeal, a copy of the decision signed by the person who presided at the hearing shall be annexed to the case, and the facts so found and the questions of law to be decided shall be sufficiently stated in the case by referring to the statement thereof in the decision.

Commencement   1 October 1966.
Amendments   Para (1): figure "4" substituted by SI 1981/1734, r 23(1).

Order 61, r 2 Statement of case by other tribunals

(1)   Where any tribunal other than the Lands Tribunal is empowered or may be required to state a case on a question of law for determination by the Court of Appeal, any party to the proceedings who is aggrieved by the tribunal's refusal to state a case may apply to the Court of Appeal [or a single judge of that Court] for an order requiring the tribunal to state a case.

(2)   An application under this rule must be made by motion and the notice of the motion, stating in general terms the grounds of the application, together with the question of law on which it is desired that a case shall be stated and any reasons given by the tribunal for its refusal, must within [28] days after the refusal, be served on the clerk or registrar of the tribunal and on every other party to the proceedings before the tribunal.

(3)   Within 2 days after service of the notice of motion, the applicant must lodge two copies of the notice with the [registrar of civil appeals] who shall enter the motion in the appropriate list.

(4)   Where a tribunal is ordered under this rule to state a case, the tribunal must, within such period as may be specified in the order, state a case, stating the facts on which the decision of the tribunal was based and the decision, sign it and cause it to be sent by post to the applicant.

(5)   Rule 1(4) shall apply in relation to a case stated by a tribunal other than the Lands Tribunal as it applies in relation to a case stated by that Tribunal.

[(6)   In this rule, references to a tribunal other than the Lands Tribunal include references to a judge of the Commercial Court acting as an arbitrator or umpire under section 4 of the Administration of Justice Act 1970.]

Commencement   1 October 1971 (para (6)); 1 October 1966 (remainder).
Amendments   Para (1): words "or a single judge of that Court" inserted by SI 1981/1734, r 23(2).
Para (2): figure "28" substituted by SI 1981/1734, r 23(3).
Para (3): words "registrar of civil appeals" substituted by SI 1981/1734, r 23(4).
Para (6): added by SI 1971/1269, r 20.

Order 61, r 3 Proceedings on case stated

(1)   The party at whose instance a case has been stated by any tribunal to which this Order applies must, within 21 days after receiving the case—

   (a)   serve on every other party to the proceedings before the tribunal a copy of the case, together with a notice setting out his contentions on the question of law, and

   (b)   serve a copy of the notice on the clerk or registrar of the tribunal.

(2)   Within 2 days after service of the notice, the said party must lodge the case and two copies of the notice with the [registrar of civil appeals] who shall enter the case in the appropriate list; and the case shall not be heard until after the expiration of 21 days from the date of entry.

(3)   Where any enactment under which the case is stated provides that a Minister or government department shall have a right to be heard in the proceedings on the case, a copy of the case and of the notice served under paragraph (1) must be served on that Minister or department.

(4)   On the hearing of the case, the Court of Appeal may amend the case or order it to be sent back to the tribunal for amendment.

(5)   Order 59, rule 10, shall, so far as applicable, apply in relation to a case stated by a tribunal to which this Order applies.

(6)   The [registrar of civil appeals] shall notify the clerk or registrar of the tribunal of the decision of the Court of Appeal on the case and of any directions given by that Court thereon.

Commencement   1 October 1966.
Amendments   Paras (2), (6): words "registrar of civil appeals" substituted by SI 1981/1734, r 23(4).

[Order 61, r 4 Appeals from Special Commissioners direct to Court of Appeal

(1)   An application to the Court of Appeal for leave for a case stated by the Special Commissioners under section 56 of the Taxes Management Act 1970 to be referred direct to the Court of Appeal shall be made within 30 days after the date on which the party at whose instance the case has been stated receives the case.

(2)   Such an application shall be made by the parties jointly by lodging the case and a statement of the grounds of the application with the Registrar of Civil Appeals.

(3)   Such an application shall be determined by a single Judge of the Court of Appeal, who may do so without a hearing.

(4)   Where leave is refused under this rule the Registrar of Civil Appeals shall forthwith send back the case to the party who required it.

(5)   Where leave is granted under this rule the Registrar of Civil Appeals shall enter the case in the appropriate list and shall forthwith notify the parties of the date of entry; and the case shall not be heard until after the expiration of 21 days from that date.

(6)   Not less than 10 days before the hearing of the case either party must give notice to the other of any point which he intends to take at the hearing and which might take the other by surprise and shall furnish three copies of the notice to the Registrar of Civil Appeals.

(7)   The Registrar of Civil Appeals shall notify the Clerk to the Special Commissioners of the decision of the Court of Appeal on the case and of any directions given by that court thereon.

(8)   Rule 3 shall not apply in relation to a case stated under section 56 of the Taxes Management Act 1970.]

Commencement 1 October 1987.
Amendments This rule was inserted by SI 1987/1423, r 58.

[COSTS

ORDER 62
Costs

Part I Preliminary

Order 62, r 1 Interpretation

(1)   Except where it is otherwise expressly provided, or the context otherwise requires, the following provisions of this rule shall apply for the interpretation of this Order.

(2)   "Certificate" includes allocatur;

"contentious business" and "non-contentious business" have the same meanings respectively as in the Solicitors Act 1974;

"party", in relation to a cause or matter, includes a party who is treated as being a party to that cause or matter by virtue of Order 4, rule 9(2);

"patient" means a person who, by reason of mental disorder within the meaning of Part VII of the Mental Health Act 1983, is incapable of managing and administering his property and affairs;

"proceedings in the Family Division" includes proceedings in the Court of Appeal on an application or appeal made in connection with proceedings in that Division or on an appeal from a judgment, direction, decision or order of a county court given or made in probate proceedings (as defined in section 147 of the County Courts Act 1984) or in family proceedings (as defined in section 32 of the Matrimonial and Family Proceedings Act 1984);

"registrar" means the Admiralty Registrar, a [district judge] of the Family Division or a [district judge] of the High Court;

"the standard basis" and "the indemnity basis" have the meanings assigned to them by rule 12(1) and (2) respectively;

"taxed costs" means costs taxed in accordance with this Order;

"taxing master" means a taxing master of the Supreme Court;

"taxing officer" means a taxing master, a registrar [district judge] and any other person who by virtue of rule 19 has power to tax costs.

(3)   References to a fund, being a fund out of which costs are to be paid or which is held by a trustee or personal representative, include references to any estate or property, whether real or personal, held for the benefit of any person or class of persons; and references to a fund held by a trustee or personal representative include references to any fund to which he is entitled (whether alone or together with any other person) in that capacity, whether the fund is for the time being in his possession or not.

(4)   References to costs shall be construed as including references to fees, charges, disbursements, expenses and remuneration and, in relation to proceedings (including taxation proceedings), also include references to costs . . . of or incidental to those proceedings.]

Commencement   28 April 1986.

Amendments   Order 62 was substituted by SI 1986/632, r 7, Schedule.

Para (4): words omitted revoked by SI 1987/1423, r 51.

[Order 62, r 2 Application

(1)   In addition to the civil proceedings to which this Order applies by virtue of Order 1, rule 2(1) and (2), this Order applies to all criminal proceedings in the High Court and in the civil division of the Court of Appeal.

(2)   This Order shall have effect, with such modifications as may be necessary, where by virtue of any Act the costs of any proceedings before an arbitrator or umpire or before a tribunal or other body constituted by or under any Act, not being proceedings in the Supreme Court, are taxable in the High Court.

(3)   This Order shall have effect subject to sections 19, 20 and 29 of the County Courts Act 1984 (which limit the costs recoverable in relation to certain proceedings which could have been commenced in a county court) and to any other Act.

(4)   The powers and discretion of the Court under section 51 of the Act (which provides that the costs of and incidental to proceedings of the Supreme Court shall be in the discretion of the Court and that the Court shall have full power to determine by whom and to what extent the costs are to be paid) and under the enactments relating to the costs of criminal proceedings to which this Order applies shall be exercised subject to and in accordance with this Order.]

Commencement   28 April 1986.
Amendments   See the first note to Order 62, r 1.
Definitions   The Act: Supreme Court Act 1981.

[PART II ENTITLEMENT TO COSTS

Order 62, r 3 General principles

(1)   This rule shall have effect subject only to the following provisions of this Order.

(2)   No party to any proceedings shall be entitled to recover any of the costs of those proceedings from any other party to those proceedings except under an order of the Court.

(3)   If the Court in the exercise of its discretion sees fit to make any order as to the costs of any proceedings, the Court shall order the costs to follow the event, except when it appears to the Court that in the circumstances of the case some other order should be made as to the whole or any part of the costs.

(4)   The amount of his costs which any party shall be entitled to recover is the amount allowed after taxation on the standard basis where—
     (a)   an order is made that the costs of one party to proceedings be paid by another party to those proceedings, or
     (b)   an order is made for the payment of costs out of any fund (including the legal aid fund), or
     (c)   no order for costs is required,

unless it appears to the Court to be appropriate to order costs to be taxed on the indemnity basis.

(5)   Paragraph (3) does not apply to proceedings in the Family Division.

(6)   Subject to rule 8, a term mentioned in the first column of the table below, when used in an order for costs, shall have the effect indicated in the second column of that table.

Term	Effect
"Costs"	(a) Where this order is made in interlocutory proceedings, the party in whose favour it is made shall be entitled to his costs in respect of those proceedings whatever the outcome of the cause or matter in which the proceedings arise; and
	(b) where this order is made at the conclusion of a cause or matter, the party in whose favour it is made shall be entitled to have his costs taxed forthwith;
"Costs reserved"	(Except in proceedings in the Family Division) the party in whose favour an order for costs is made at the conclusion of the cause or matter in which the proceedings arise shall be entitled to his costs of the proceedings in respect of which this order is made unless the Court orders otherwise;
"Costs in any event"	This order has the same effect as an order for "costs" made in interlocutory proceedings;
"Costs here and below"	The party in whose favour this order is made shall be entitled not only to his costs in respect of the proceedings in which it is made but also to his costs of the same proceedings in any lower court, save that where such an order is made by the Court of Appeal on an appeal from a Divisional Court the party shall not be entitled by virtue of that order to any costs which he has incurred in any court below the Divisional Court;
"Costs in the cause" or "costs in application"	The party in whose favour an order for costs is made at the conclusion of the cause or matter in which the proceedings arise shall be entitled to his costs of the proceedings in respect of which such an order is made;
"Plaintiff's costs in the cause" or "Defendant's costs in the cause"	The plaintiff or defendant, as the case may be, shall be entitled to his costs of the proceedings in respect of which such an order is made if judgment is given in his favour in the cause or matter in which the proceedings arise, but he shall not be liable to pay the costs of any other party in respect of those proceedings if judgment is given in favour of any other party or parties in the cause or matter in question;
"Costs thrown away"	Where proceedings or any part of them have been ineffective or have been subsequently set aside, the party in whose favour this order is made shall be entitled to his costs of those proceedings or that part of the proceedings in respect of which it is made.]

Commencement 28 April 1986.
Amendments See the first note to Order 62, r 1.
Cross references See CCR Order 38, r 1(1), (2).
This rule is applied to the county court by CCR Order 38, r 1(3).

[Order 62, r 4 Cases where no order for costs is to be made

(1)   No order shall be made directing one party to pay to the other any costs of or incidental to an appeal or application for leave to appeal under section 6(2) of the Pensions Appeal Tribunals Act 1943.

(2)   No order shall be made for costs to be paid by or to any person (other than the registration officer) who is respondent to an appeal to the Court of Appeal from the decision of a county court on the hearing of an appeal from the registration officer under section 56 of the Representation of the People Act 1983, unless that person appears in support of the decision of the county court.

(3)   In a probate action where a defendant has given notice with his defence to the party setting up the will that he merely insists upon the will being proved in solemn form of law and only intends to cross-examine the witnesses produced in support of the will, no order for costs shall be made against him unless it appears to the Court that there was no reasonable ground for opposing the will.]

Commencement   28 April 1986.
Amendments   See the first note to Order 62, r 1.
Cross references   This rule is applied to the county court by CCR Order 38, r 1(3).

[Order 62, r 5 [Cases where order for costs deemed to have been made]

[(1)   In each of the circumstances mentioned in this rule an order for costs shall be deemed to have been made to the effect respectively described and, for the purposes of section 17 of the Judgments Act 1838, the order shall be deemed to have been entered up on the date on which the event which gave rise to the entitlement to costs occurred.]

(2)   Where a summons is taken out to set aside any proceedings on the ground of irregularity and the summons is dismissed, the party who issued the summons shall pay the costs of every other party.

(3)   Where a party by notice in writing and without leave discontinues an action or counterclaim or withdraws any particular claim made by him as against any other party, that other party shall be entitled to his costs of the action or counterclaim or his costs occasioned by the claim withdrawn, as the case may be, incurred to the time of receipt of the notice of discontinuance or withdrawal.

(4)   Where a plaintiff by notice in writing in accordance with [Order 22, rule 3(1)] accepts money paid into court in satisfaction of the cause of action or of all the causes of action in respect of which he claims, or accepts money paid in satisfaction of one or more specified causes of action and gives notice that he abandons the others, he shall be entitled to his costs of the action incurred up to the time of giving notice of acceptance.

(5)   Where in an action for libel or slander against several defendants sued jointly a plaintiff, by notice in writing in accordance with [Order 22, rule 3(1)], accepts money paid into court by one of the defendants he shall be entitled to his costs of the action against that defendant incurred up to the time of giving notice of acceptance.

(6)   A defendant who has counterclaimed shall be entitled to the costs of the counterclaim if—
    (a)   he pays money into court and his notice of payment in states that he has taken into account and satisfied the cause or causes of action in respect of which he counterclaims, and
    (b)   the plaintiff accepts the money paid in;

but the costs of such counterclaim shall be limited to those incurred up to the time when the defendant receives notice of acceptance by the plaintiff of the money paid into court.]

Commencement 1 October 1991 (para (1)); 28 April 1986 (remainder).
Amendments See the first note to Order 62, r 1.
Rule heading: substituted by SI 1991/1884, r 11.
Para (1): substituted by SI 1991/1884, r 12.
Paras (4), (5): words "Order 22, rule 3(1)" substituted by SI 1987/1423, r 52.
Cross references This rule is applied to the county court by CCR Order 38, r 1(3). See also, in relation to para (3), CCR Order 18, r 2(1) and in relation to para (4), CCR Order 11, r 3(5).

[Order 62, r 6 Cases where costs do not follow the event

(1)   The provisions of this rule shall apply in the circumstances mentioned in this rule unless the Court orders otherwise.

(2)   Where a person is or has been a party to any proceedings in the capacity of trustee, personal representative or mortgagee, he shall be entitled to the costs of those proceedings, insofar as they are not recovered from or paid by any other person, out of the fund held by him in that capacity or out of the mortgaged property, as the case may be, and the Court may order otherwise only on the ground that he has acted unreasonably or, in the case of a trustee or personal representative, has in substance acted for his own benefit rather than for the benefit of the fund.

(3)   Where any person claiming to be a creditor—
    (a) seeks to establish any claim to a debt under any judgment or order in accordance with Order 44, or
    (b) comes to prove his title, debt or claim in relation to a company in pursuance of any such notice as is mentioned in Order 102, rule 13,

he shall, if his claim succeeds, be entitled to his costs incurred in establishing it; and, if his claim or any part of it fails, he may be ordered to pay the costs of any person incurred in opposing it.

(4)   Where a claimant (other than a person claiming to be a creditor) has established a claim to be entitled under a judgment or order in accordance with Order 44 and has been served with notice of the judgment or order pursuant to rule 2 of that Order, he shall, if he acknowledges service of the notice, be entitled as part of his costs of action (if allowed) to costs incurred in establishing his claim; and where such a claimant fails to establish his claim or any part of it he may be ordered to pay the costs of any person incurred in opposing it.

(5)   The costs of any amendment made without leave in the writ or any pleadings shall be borne by the party making the amendment.

(6)   The costs of any application to extend the time fixed by these rules or by any direction or order thereunder shall be borne by the party making the application.

[(7)   If a party on whom a notice to admit facts is served under Order 27, rule 2, refuses or neglects to admit the facts within 14 days after the service on him of the notice or such longer time as may be allowed by the Court, the costs of proving the facts and the costs occasioned by and thrown away as a result of his failure to admit the fact shall be borne by him.

(8)   If a party—
    (a) on whom a list of documents is served in pursuance of Order 24, or
    (b) on whom a notice to admit documents is served under Order 27, rule 5.

gives notice of non-admission of any of the documents in accordance with Order 27, rule 4(2) or 5(2), as the case may be, the costs of proving that document and the costs occasioned by and thrown away as a result of his non-admission shall be borne by him.]

(9) Where an application is made in accordance with Order 24, rule 7A or Order 29, rule 7A for an order under section 33 or 34 of the Act the person against whom the order is sought shall be entitled to his costs of the application, and of complying with any order made thereon.]

Commencement 5 February 1990 (paras (7), (8)); 28 April 1986 (remainder).
Amendments See the first note to Order 62, r 1.
Paras (7), (8): substituted by SI 1989/2427, r 22.
Definitions The Act: Supreme Court Act 1981.
Cross references This rule is applied to the county court by CCR Order 38, r 1(3). See also, in relation to paras (8), (9), CCR Order 20, r 3(2A) and Order 20, r 2(2) respectively.

[Order 62, r 7 Special circumstances in which costs shall not or may not be taxed

(1) The provisions of this rule shall apply in the circumstances mentioned in this rule.

(2) Costs which by or under any direction of the Court are to be paid to a receiver appointed by the High Court under section 37 of the Act, in respect of his remuneration, disbursements or expenses, shall be allowed in accordance with Order 30, rule 3 and shall not be taxed.

(3) Where a writ in an action is indorsed in accordance with Order 6, rule 2(1)(b), and judgment is entered on failure to give notice of intention to defend or in default of defence for the amount claimed for costs (whether alone or together with any other amount claimed), the plaintiff is not entitled to tax his costs; but if the amount claimed for costs as aforesaid is paid in accordance with the indorsement (or is accepted by the plaintiff as if so paid) the defendant shall be entitled to have those costs taxed.

(4) In awarding costs to any person the Court may order that, instead of his taxed costs, that person shall be entitled—

    (a) to a proportion (specified in the order) of those costs from or up to a stage of the proceedings so specified; or

    (b) to a gross sum so specified in lieu of those costs,

but where the person entitled to such a gross sum is a litigant in person, rule 18 shall apply with the necessary modifications to the assessment of the gross sum as it applies to the taxation of the costs of a litigant in person.

(5) Where a claimant is entitled to costs under rule 6(3) the amount of the costs shall be assessed by the Court unless it thinks fit to order taxation and the amount so assessed or taxed shall be added to the debt due to the claimant.]

[(6) Subject to paragraph (7), where a party is entitled to costs under rule 6(7) or (8) the amount of those costs may be assessed by the Court and be ordered to be paid forthwith.

(7) No order may be made under paragraph (6) in a case where the person against whom the order is made is an assisted person within the meaning of the statutory provisions relating to legal aid.]

Commencement 5 February 1990 (paras (6), (7)); 28 April 1986 (remainder).
Amendments See the first note to Order 62, r 1.
Paras (6), (7): added by SI 1989/2427, r 23.

Definitions The Act: Supreme Court Act 1981.
Cross references This rule is applied to the county court by CCR Order 38, r 1(3). See also, in relation to para (6), CCR Order 20, rr 2(2), 3(2), (2A), Order 38 r 17B and quaere whether para (4) applies to costs on county court scale 1 (for which provision is made for assessment in the county court rules).

[Order 62, r 7A Reimbursement of additional costs under section 53, Administration of Justice Act 1985

(1) In default of agreement between the Lord Chancellor and a person as to the amount of additional costs to be reimbursed under section 53 of the Administration of Justice Act 1985, either of them may make a written request to the appropriate office referred to in rule 29 that such costs be taxed.

(2) Only a taxing master or a registrar [district judge] shall tax such costs.

(3) Notwithstanding rule 3(4), such costs shall be taxed on the indemnity basis.]

Commencement 1 October 1988.
Amendments See the first note to Order 62, r 1.
This rule was inserted by SI 1988/1340, r 9.
Cross references This rule is applied to the county court by CCR Order 38, r 1(3). See also CCR Order 38, r 17A.

[Order 62, r 8 Stage of proceedings at which costs to be taxed

(1) Subject to paragraph (2), the costs of any proceedings shall not be taxed until the conclusion of the cause or matter in which the proceedings arise.

(2) If it appears to the Court when making an order for costs that all or any part of the costs ought to be taxed at an earlier stage it may, except in a case to which paragraph (3) applies, order accordingly.

(3) No order may be made under paragraph (2) in a case where the person against whom the order for costs is made is an assisted person within the meaning of the statutory provisions relating to legal aid.

(4) In the case of an appeal the costs of the proceedings giving rise to the appeal, as well as the costs of the appeal, may be dealt with by the Court hearing the appeal.

(5) In the case of any proceedings transferred or removed to the High Court from any other court, the High Court may (subject to any order of the court ordering the transfer or removal) deal with the costs of the whole proceedings (including the costs before the transfer or removal).

(6) Notwithstanding anything in Part III of this Order, but subject to paragraph (7) below, where the Court makes an order as to the costs of any proceedings before another court under paragraphs (4) or (5), the order—
  (a) shall specify the amount of the costs to be allowed; or
  (b) shall direct that the costs be assessed by the court before which the proceedings took place or be taxed by an officer of that court; or
  (c) may, in the case of an appeal from a county court, direct that the costs be taxed by a taxing officer.

(7) Paragraph (6) shall not apply in relation to the costs of proceedings transferred or removed from a county court.

(8) In relation to an action in which provisional damages are awarded under Part II of Order 37, the reference in paragraph (1) to the conclusion of the cause or matter

329

shall be construed as a reference to the conclusion of the proceedings in which the provisional damages are awarded, notwithstanding the possibility that the plaintiff may claim further damages at a future date.

(9)   Where it appears to a taxing officer on application that there is no likelihood of any further order being made in a cause or matter, he may tax forthwith the costs of any interlocutory proceedings which have taken place.]

Commencement   28 April 1986.
Amendments   See the first note to Order 62, r 1.
Cross references   This rule is applied to the county court by CCR Order 38, r 1(3).

[Order 62, r 9 Matters to be taken into account in exercising discretion

[(1)]   The Court in exercising its discretion as to costs shall take into account—
    (a)   any offer of contribution brought to its attention in accordance with Order 16, rule 10;
    (b)   any payment of money into court and the amount of such payment;
    (c)   any written offer made under Order 33, rule 4A(2); and
    (d)   any written offer made under Order 22, rule 14, provided that[, except in a case to which paragraph (2) applies,] the Court shall not take such an offer into account if, at the time it is made, the party making it could have protected his position as to costs by means of a payment into court under Order 22.

[(2)   This paragraph applies to a case where the party making the offer has applied for, but has not yet received, a certificate of total benefit given in accordance with Schedule 4 to the Social Security Act 1989; but this paragraph shall not apply with respect to any time after 7 days after that party has received the certificate.]]

Commencement   1 October 1990 (para (2)); 28 April 1986 (remainder).
Amendments   See the first note to Order 62, r 1.
Para (1): numbered as such, and in sub-paragraph (d) words ", except in a case to which paragraph (2) applies," inserted, by SI 1990/1689, r 20(a), (b).
Para (2): inserted by SI 1990/1689, r 20(c).
Cross references   This rule is applied to the county court by CCR Order 38, r 1(3). See also CCR Order 12, r 7(2), Order 11, rr 5(4), 10(2).

[Order 62, r 10 Misconduct or neglect in the conduct of any proceedings

(1)   Where it appears to the Court in any proceedings that any thing has been done, or that any omission has been made, unreasonably or improperly by or on behalf of any party, the Court may order that the costs of that party in respect of the act or omission, as the case may be, shall not be allowed and that any costs occasioned by it to any other party shall be paid by him to that other party.

(2)   Instead of making an order under paragraph (1) the Court may refer the matter to a taxing officer, in which case the taxing officer shall deal with the matter under rule 28(1).

(3)   In this rule "taxing officer" means a taxing master or a registrar.]

Commencement   28 April 1986.
Amendments   See the first note to Order 62, r 1.
Cross references   This rule is applied to the county court by CCR Order 38, r 1(3).

[Order 62, r 11 Personal liability of legal representative for costs

(1) (a) Where the Court decides to make an order under section 51(6) of the Supreme Court Act 1981 disallowing wasted costs or ordering a legal representative to meet such costs or part of them, it shall, subject to paragraph (4), specify in the order the costs which are to be so disallowed or met, and may make such other order as it thinks fit;

  (b) before proceeding under sub-paragraph (a), the Court may direct a taxing officer to inquire into the matter and report to the Court.

(2) When conducting an inquiry pursuant to a direction under paragraph (1)(b), the taxing officer shall have all the powers and duties of the Court under paragraphs (6) and (8) of this rule; and references in those paragraphs and paragraphs (4) and (5) to the Court include references to the taxing officer.

(3) Instead of proceeding under paragraph (1) of this rule the Court may refer the matter to a taxing officer, in which case the taxing officer shall deal with the matter under paragraphs (2) and (3) of rule 28.

(4) No order may be made under section 51(6) unless the Court has given the legal representative concerned a reasonable opportunity to appear and show cause why an order should not be made.

(5) Without prejudice to Order 32, rule 5(3), the Court shall not be obliged to give the legal representative a reasonable opportunity to show cause where proceedings fail, cannot conveniently proceed or are adjourned without useful progress being made because the legal representative—

  (a) fails to attend in person or by a proper representative;

  (b) fails to deliver any document for the use of the Court, which ought to have been delivered or to be prepared with any proper evidence or account, or

  (c) otherwise fails to proceed.

(6) The Court may direct the Official Solicitor to attend and take such part in any proceedings or inquiry under this rule as the Court may direct and the Court shall make such order as to the payment of the Official Solicitor's costs as it thinks fit.

(7) If in any proceedings a party who is represented by a legal representative fails to pay the fees or any part of the fees prescribed by the orders as to court fees the Court may order the legal representative personally to pay that amount in the manner so prescribed.

[The power of the Court under this paragraph may be exercised by a taxing officer and rule 28(5) shall apply to an order made by a taxing officer under this paragraph as it applies to a decision made by a taxing officer.]

(8) The Court may direct that notice of any proceedings or order against a legal representative under this rule be given to his client in such manner as may be specified in the direction.

(9) In this rule 'taxing officer' means a taxing master or a district judge.]

Commencement 1 October 1991.
Amendments See the first note to Order 62, r 1.
This rule further substituted by SI 1991/1884, r 13(1).
Para (7): words from "The power" to "a taxing officer" inserted by SI 1992/638, r 11.
Cross references This rule is applied to the county court by CCR Order 38, r 1(3).

[PART III TAXATION AND ASSESSMENT OF COSTS

Order 62, r 12 Basis of Taxation

(1)   On a taxation of costs on the standard basis there shall be allowed a reasonable amount in respect of all costs reasonably incurred and any doubts which the taxing officer may have as to whether the costs were reasonably incurred or were reasonable in amount shall be resolved in favour of the paying party; and in these rules the term "the standard basis" in relation to the taxation of costs shall be construed accordingly.

(2)   On a taxation on the indemnity basis all costs shall be allowed except insofar as they are of an unreasonable amount or have been unreasonably incurred and any doubts which the taxing officer may have as to whether the costs were reasonably incurred or were reasonable in amount shall be resolved in favour of the receiving party; and in these rules the term "the indemnity basis" in relation to the taxation of costs shall be construed accordingly.

(3)   Where the Court makes an order for costs without indicating the basis of taxation or an order that costs be taxed on any basis other than the standard basis or the indemnity basis, the costs shall be taxed on the standard basis.]

Commencement 28 April 1986.
Amendments See the first note to Order 62, r 1.
Cross references This rule is applied to the county court by CCR Order 38, r 19A.

[Order 62, r 13 Assessment or settlement of costs by master or registrar

Where the Court orders that costs are to be assessed or settled by a master or registrar, rules 3(4), 12, 14, 17 and 18 shall apply in relation to such assessment or settlement by a master or [district judge] as they apply in relation to a taxation of costs by a taxing officer.]

Commencement 28 April 1986.
Amendments See the first note to Order 62, r 1.

[Order 62, r 14 Costs payable to a trustee or personal representative out of any fund

(1)   This rule applies to every taxation of a trustee's or personal representative's costs where—
    (a) he is or has been a party to any proceedings in that capacity, and
    (b) he is entitled to be paid his costs out of any fund which he holds in that capacity.

(2)   On a taxation to which this rule applies, costs shall be taxed on the indemnity basis but shall be presumed to have been unreasonably incurred if they were incurred contrary to the duty of the trustee or personal representative as such.]

Commencement 28 April 1986.
Amendments See the first note to Order 62, r 1.
Cross references This rule is applied to the county court by CCR Order 38, r 19A.

[Order 62, r 15 Costs payable to a solicitor by his own client

(1)   This rule applies to every taxation of a solicitor's bill to his own client except a bill which is to be paid out of the legal aid fund under the Legal Aid Act 1974.

(2) On a taxation to which this rule applies costs shall be taxed on the indemnity basis but shall be presumed—

(a) to have been reasonably incurred if they were incurred with the express or implied approval of the client, and

(b) to have been reasonable in amount if their amount was expressly or impliedly approved by the client, and

(c) to have been unreasonably incurred if in the circumstances of the case they are of an unusual nature unless the solicitor satisfies the taxing officer that prior to their being incurred he informed his client that they might not be allowed on a taxation of costs inter partes.

(3) Taxations under this rule may be carried out by a taxing master or a registrar.]

Commencement 28 April 1986.
Amendments See the first note to Order 62, r 1.
Cross references This rule is applied to the county court by CCR Order 38, r 19A.

[Order 62, r 16 Costs payable to solicitor where money claimed by or on behalf of a minor or a patient

(1) This rule applies to any proceedings (including proceedings in the Court of Appeal) in which—

(a) money is claimed or recovered by or on behalf of, or adjudged, or ordered, or agreed to be paid to, or for the benefit of, a minor or a patient; or

(b) money paid into court is accepted by or on behalf of a minor or patient.

(2) The costs of proceedings to which this rule applies which are payable by any plaintiff to his solicitor shall, unless the Court otherwise orders, be taxed under paragraphs (1) and (2) of rule 15 and paragraph (3) of that rule shall not apply.

(3) On a taxation under paragraph (2), the taxing officer shall also tax any costs payable to that plaintiff in those proceedings and shall certify—

(a) the amount allowed on the taxation of the solicitor's bill to his own client, and

(b) the amount allowed on the taxation of any costs payable to that plaintiff in those proceedings, and

(c) the amount (if any) by which the amount mentioned in sub-paragraph (a) exceeds the amount mentioned in sub-paragraph (b), and

(d) where necessary, the proportion of the amount of such excess payable by, or out of money belonging to, respectively any claimant who is a minor or patient and any other party.

(4) Paragraphs (2) and (3) shall apply in relation to any proceedings in the Court of Appeal as if for references to the plaintiff there were substituted references to the party, whether appellant or respondent, who was the plaintiff in the proceedings which gave rise to the appeal proceedings.

(5) Nothing in the foregoing provisions of this rule shall prejudice a solicitor's lien for costs.

(6) The foregoing provisions of this rule shall apply in relation to—

(a) a counterclaim by or on behalf of a person who is a minor or a patient, and

(b) a claim made by or on behalf of a person who is a minor or a patient in an action by any other person for relief under section 504 of the Merchant Shipping Act 1894,

as if for the references to a plaintiff there were substituted references to a defendant.]

Commencement   28 April 1986.
Amendments   See the first note to Order 62, r 1.
Cross references   This rule is applied to the county court by CCR Order 38, r 19A.

[Order 62, r 17 Provisions for ascertaining costs on a taxation

(1)   Subject to the following provisions of this rule, the provisions contained in Appendix 2 to this Order for ascertaining the amount of costs to be allowed on a taxation of costs shall apply to the taxation of all costs with respect to contentious business.

(2)   Where the amount of a solicitor's remuneration in respect of non-contentious business is regulated (in the absence of agreement to the contrary) by any general orders for the time being in force under the Solicitors Act 1974, the amount of the costs to be allowed on taxation in respect of the like contentious business shall be the same notwithstanding anything contained in Appendix 2 to this Order.

(3)   Notwithstanding paragraph (1), costs shall be allowed in the cases to which Appendix 3 to this Order applies in accordance with the provisions of that Appendix unless the Court otherwise orders.

(4)   The foregoing provisions of this rule shall be without prejudice to the powers of the Court under section 19(3) of the County Courts Act 1984.]

Commencement   28 April 1986.
Amendments   See the first note to Order 62, r 1.
Cross references   See CCR Order 38, r 20.

[Order 62, r 18 Litigants in person

[(1)   Subject to the provisions of this rule, on any taxation of the costs of a litigant in person there may be allowed such costs as would have been allowed if the work and disbursements to which the costs relate had been done or made by a solicitor on the litigant's behalf together with any payments reasonably made by him for legal advice relating to the conduct of or the issues raised by the proceedings.]

(2)   The amount allowed in respect of any item shall be such sum as the taxing officer thinks fit but not exceeding, except in the case of a disbursement, two-thirds of the sum which in the opinion of the taxing officer would have been allowed in respect of that item if the litigant had been represented by a solicitor.

(3)   Where it appears to the taxing officer that the litigant has not suffered any pecuniary loss in doing any item of work to which the costs relate, he shall be allowed in respect of the time reasonably spent by him on that item not more than [[£8.25] an hour].

(4)   A litigant who is allowed costs in respect of attending court to conduct his case shall not be entitled to a witness allowance in addition.

(5)   Nothing in Order 6, rule 2(1)(b), or in rule 17(3) of, or Appendix 3 to, this Order shall apply to the costs of a litigant in person.

(6)   For the purposes of this rule a litigant in person does not include a litigant who is a practising solicitor.]

Commencement   1 April 1989 (para (1)); 28 April 1986 (remainder).
Amendments   See the first note to Order 62, r 1.
Para (1): substituted by SI 1989/386, r 9.
Para (3): words in square brackets substituted by SI 1987/1423, r 53, sum "£8.25" therein substituted by SI 1992/638, r 12.
Cross references   See CCR Order 38, r 17.

[PART IV POWERS OF TAXING OFFICERS

Order 62, r 19 Who may tax costs

(1)   Subject to paragraphs (2) and (3), a taxing master and a registrar [district judge] (other than a [district judge of a district registry]) shall have power to tax—
   (a)   the costs of or arising out of any proceedings to which this Order applies,
   (b)   the costs ordered by an award made on a reference to arbitration under any Act or payable pursuant to an arbitration agreement, and
   (c)   any other costs the taxation of which is ordered by the Court.

(2)   Where by or under any Act any costs are to be taxed by a master of the Supreme Court, only a taxing master shall tax those costs.

(3)   The [district judge] of a district registry shall have power to tax—
   (a)   the costs of any proceedings in that registry,
   (b)   the costs ordered by an award made on a reference to arbitration under any Act or payable pursuant to an arbitration agreement,
   (c)   the costs of any application or appeal to a Divisional Court or a single judge of the Family Division if that Court or judge so orders,
   (d)   the costs of any application or appeal to the Court of Appeal in connection with any proceedings which were conducted in that registry, and
   (e)   where an order has been made under any provision of Part III of the Solicitors Act 1974 for the taxation of a bill of costs, the costs to which the order relates if the costs are for contentious business done in a cause or matter which proceeded in that registry or for non-contentious business.

(4)   Except where it is otherwise provided in these rules—
   (a)   a principal or a senior executive officer of the Principal Registry of the Family Division authorised in that behalf by the President of the Family Division shall have power to tax the costs of proceedings in the Family Division; and
   (b)   a principal or a senior executive officer of (i) the Supreme Court Taxing Office, or a principal or a senior executive officer of (ii) a district registry who has previously served in either of such capacities for at least two years in the Supreme Court Taxing Office or in any of the following district registries, namely, Birmingham, Bristol, Cardiff, Leeds, Liverpool or Manchester, authorised in that behalf by the Lord Chancellor shall have power to tax any costs the taxation of which is within the powers of a taxing master or a [district judge] of that registry, as the case may be, and to issue a certificate for any costs taxed by him.

(5)   Where a party to proceedings objects to a bill of costs or any part of it being taxed by a principal or a senior executive officer under paragraph (4), he shall, before the taxation begins, deliver to the taxing master written reasons for his objections and if sufficient reason is shown the taxing master shall direct that the bill or any part of it be taxed by a taxing master.

(6)   On a taxation under paragraph (4), a principal or a senior executive officer shall comply with any directions given to him by a taxing master.

(7)   In paragraphs (5) and (6) references to a taxing master shall, in relation to a taxation in the Principal Registry of the Family Division or a district registry, be construed as references to a [district judge] of the Family Division or the [district judge of a district registry] respectively.]

Commencement   28 April 1986.
Amendments   See the first note to Order 62, r 1.
Cross references   See CCR Order 38, r 2(2).

[Order 62, r 20 Supplementary powers of taxing officers

A taxing officer may, in the discharge of his functions with respect to the taxation of costs,—

(a) take an account of any dealings in money made in connection with the payment of the costs being taxed, if the Court so orders;

(b) require any party represented jointly with any other party in any proceedings before him to be separately represented;

(c) examine any witness in those proceedings; and

(d) order the production of any document which may be relevant in connection with those proceedings.]

Commencement 28 April 1986.
Amendments See the first note to Order 62, r 1.

[Order 62, r 21 Extension of Time

(1) A taxing officer may—

(a) extend the period within which a party is required by or under this Order or by the Court to begin proceedings for taxation or to do any thing in or in connection with those proceedings on such terms (if any) as he thinks just; or

(b) where no period is specified by or under this Order or by the Court for the doing of any thing in or in connection with such proceedings, specify the period within which the thing is to be done.

(2) A taxing officer may extend any such period as is referred to in paragraph (1) of this rule although the application for extension is not made until after the expiration of that period.]

Commencement 28 April 1986.
Amendments See the first note to Order 62, r 1.
Cross references See CCR Order 13, r 4.

[Order 62, r 22 Certificates

(1) A taxing officer—

(a) shall, at the conclusion of taxation proceedings before him, issue a certificate for the costs allowed by him;

(b) may from time to time in the course of the taxation issue an interim certificate for any part of the costs which have been taxed or for any part the amount of which is not in dispute;

(c) may amend or cancel an interim certificate issued by him;

(d) may correct any clerical mistake in any certificate issued by him or any error arising therein from any accidental slip or omission, and

(e) may set aside a certificate issued by him in order to enable him to extend the period provided by rule 33(2).

(2) If, in the course of the taxation of a solicitor's bill to his own client, it appears to the taxing officer that in any event the solicitor will be liable in connection with that bill to pay money to the client, he may from time to time issue an interim certificate specifying an amount which in his opinion is payable by the solicitor to his client.

(3) On the filing of a certificate issued under paragraph (2) the Court may order the amount specified in it to be paid forthwith to the client or into court.]

Commencement 28 April 1986.
Amendments See the first note to Order 62, r 1.

[Order 62, r 23 Power of taxing officer where party liable to be paid and to pay costs

Where a party entitled to be paid costs is also liable to pay costs, the taxing officer may—

(a) tax the costs which that party is liable to pay and set off the amount allowed against the amount he is entitled to be paid and direct payment of any balance; or

(b) delay the issue of a certificate for the costs the party is entitled to be paid until he has paid or tendered the amount he is liable to pay.]

Commencement   28 April 1986.
Amendments   See the first note to Order 62, r 1.

[Order 62, r 24 Taxation of bill of costs comprised in an account

(1)   Where the Court orders an account to be taken and the account consists in part of a bill of costs, the Court may direct a taxing officer to tax those costs and the taxing officer shall after taxation of the bill of costs return it, together with his report on it, to the Court.

(2)   A taxing officer taxing a bill of costs in accordance with a direction under paragraph (1) shall have the same powers, and the same fee shall be payable in connection with the taxation, as if an order for taxation of the costs had been made by the Court.]

Commencement   28 April 1986.
Amendments   See the first note to Order 62, r 1.
Cross references   This rule is applied to the county court by CCR Order 38, r 19A.

[Order 62, r 25 Taxing officer to fix certain fees payable to conveyancing counsel

(1)   Where the Court refers any matter to the conveyancing counsel of the Court or obtains the assistance of any other person under Order 32, rule 16, the fees payable to counsel or that other person in respect of the work done by him in connection with the reference or, as the case may be, in assisting the Court shall be fixed by a taxing officer.

(2)   An appeal from a decision of a taxing officer under paragraph (1) shall lie to the Court and the decision of the Court thereon shall be final.]

Commencement   28 April 1986.
Amendments   See the first note to Order 62, r 1.

[Order 62, r 26 Powers of taxing officers on taxation of costs out of a fund

(1)   Where any costs are to be paid out of a fund the taxing officer may give directions as to the parties who are entitled to attend on the taxation of those costs and may disallow the costs of attendance of any party not entitled to attend by virtue of the directions and whose attendance he considers unnecessary.

(2)   Where the Court has directed that a bill of costs be taxed for the purpose of being paid out of a fund, the taxing officer may direct the party whose bill it is to send to any person having an interest in the fund a copy of the bill, or of any part thereof, free of charge together with a letter containing the following information, that is to say—

(a) that the bill of costs, a copy of which or of part of which is sent with the letter, has been referred to a taxing officer for taxation;

(b)   the name of the taxing officer and the address of the office at which the taxation is proceeding;

(c)   the time appointed by the taxing officer at which the taxation will be continued, and

(d)   such other information, if any, as the taxing officer may direct.]

Commencement   28 April 1986.
Amendments   See the first note to Order 62, r 1.
Cross references   This rule is applied to the county court by CCR Order 38, r 19A.

[Order 62, r 27 Powers of taxing officers in relation to costs of taxation proceedings

(1)   Subject to the provisions of any Act and this Order, the party whose bill is being taxed shall be entitled to his costs of the taxation proceedings.

(2)   Where it appears to the taxing officer that in the circumstances of the case some other order should be made as to the whole or any part of the costs, the taxing officer shall have, in relation to the costs of taxation proceedings, the same powers as the Court has in relation to the costs of proceedings.

(3)   Subject to paragraph (5), the party liable to pay the costs of the proceedings which gave rise to the taxation proceedings may make a written offer to pay a specific sum in satisfaction of those costs which is expressed to be "without prejudice save as to the costs of taxation" at any time before the expiration of 14 days after the delivery to him of a copy of the bill of costs under rule 30(3) and, where such an offer is made, the fact that it has been made shall not be communicated to the taxing officer until the question of the costs of the taxation proceedings falls to be decided.

(4)   The taxing officer may take into account any offer made under paragraph (3) which has been brought to his attention.

(5)   No offer to pay a specific sum in satisfaction of costs may be made in a case where the person entitled to recover his costs is an assisted person within the meaning of the statutory provisions relating to legal aid.

(6)   In this rule any reference to the costs of taxation proceedings shall be construed as including a reference to any fee which is prescribed by the Orders as to Court fees for the taxation of a bill of costs.]

Commencement   28 April 1986.
Amendments   See the first note to Order 62, r 1.
Cross references   This rule is applied to the county court by CCR Order 38, r 19A.

[Order 62, r 28 Powers of taxing officers in relation to misconduct, neglect, etc

(1)   Where, whether or not on a reference by the Court under rule 10(2), it appears to the taxing officer that any thing has been done, or that any omission has been made, unreasonably or improperly by or on behalf of any party in the taxation proceedings or in the proceedings which gave rise to the taxation proceedings, he may exercise the powers conferred on the Court by rule 10(1).

(2)   Where, whether or not on a reference by the Court under rule 11(3), it appears to the taxing officer that costs have been wasted in the taxation proceedings or in the proceedings which gave rise to the taxation proceedings, he may, subject to paragraph (3) of this rule, exercise the powers conferred on the Court by section 51(6) of the Act.

(3)   In relation to the exercise by a taxing officer of the powers of the Court under the said section 51(6), paragraphs (4) to (6) and (8) of rule 11 shall apply as if for references to the Court there were substituted references to the taxing officer.

(4)   Where a party entitled to costs—
    (a)   fails without good reason to commence or conduct proceedings for the taxation of those costs in accordance with this Order or any direction, or
    (b)   delays lodging a bill of costs for taxation,

the taxing officer may—
    (i)   disallow all or part of the costs of taxation that he would otherwise have awarded that party; and
    (ii)   after taking into account all the circumstances (including any prejudice suffered by any other party as a result of such failure or delay, as the case may be, and any additional interest payable under section 17 of the Judgments Act 1838 because of the failure or delay), allow the party so entitled less than the amount he would otherwise have allowed on taxation of the bill or wholly disallow the costs.

(5)   An appeal shall lie to a judge in chambers from the exercise by a taxing officer of the powers conferred by this rule; and Order 58, rule 1 (as modified, in the case of an appeal from a district judge, by Order 58, rule 3(2)) shall apply to such an appeal as it applies to an appeal from a master.

(6)   In exercising his powers under this rule the taxing officer shall have all the powers available to the Court in the exercise of its discretion under rules 10 and 11.

(7)   In this rule 'taxing officer' means a taxing master or a district judge.]

Commencement   1 October 1991.
Amendments   See the first note to Order 62, r 1.
This rule was further substituted by SI 1991/1884, r 13(2).
Definitions   The Act: Supreme Court Act 1981.
Cross references   This rule is applied to the county court by CCR Order 38, r 19A.

[PART V PROCEDURE ON TAXATION]

Order 62, r 29 Commencement of proceedings

(1)   Subject to paragraph (2), where a party is entitled to recover taxed costs or to require any costs to be taxed by a taxing officer by virtue of—
    (a)   a judgment, direction or order given or made in proceedings in the High Court or in the Civil Division of the Court of Appeal; or
    (b)   rule 5(3), (4) or (5); or
    (c)   an award made on an arbitration under any Act or pursuant to an arbitration agreement; or
    (d)   an order, award or other determination of a tribunal or other body constituted by or under any Act,

he must begin proceedings for the taxation of those costs either within 3 months after the judgment, direction, order, award or other determination was entered, signed or otherwise perfected or, in cases to which sub-paragraph (b) applies, within 3 months after service of the notice given to him under Order 21, rule 2 or Order 22, rule 3.

(2)   Paragraph (1) shall have effect, in relation to the taxation of costs pursuant to an order under the Solicitors Act 1974, as if for the period of 3 months first mentioned in that paragraph there were substituted a reference to 14 days.

(3)   Where a party entitled to costs fails to begin proceedings for taxation within the time limit specified in paragraph (1), any other party to the proceedings which gave rise to the taxation proceedings may with the leave of the taxing officer begin taxation proceedings.

(4)   Where leave has been granted under paragraph (3), the party to whom it has been granted shall proceed as if he were the person entitled to begin taxation proceedings.

(5)   Proceedings for the taxation of costs shall be begun by producing the requisite document at the appropriate office.

(6)   For the purposes of this rule—
    (a)   the requisite document shall be ascertained by reference to Appendix 1 to this Order, and
    (b)   the appropriate office is:—
       (i)   in a case where the costs in question are to be taxed by the Admiralty Registrar, by any [district judge] or principal or senior executive officer of the Principal Registry of the Family Division or by a [district judge], or principal or senior executive officer of a district registry, the [Admiralty and Commercial Registry], the Principal Registry of the Family Division or that district registry respectively; and
      (ii)   in any other case, the Supreme Court Taxing Office.

(7)   A party who begins proceedings for taxation must, at the same time, lodge in the appropriate office—
    (a)   a copy of the requisite document produced under paragraph (5), and
    (b)   a statement containing the following particulars:—
       (i)   the name of every party, and the capacity in which he is a party to the proceedings, his position on the record of the proceedings which gave rise to the taxation proceedings and, if any costs to which taxation proceedings relate are to be paid out of a fund, the nature of his interest in the fund; and
      (ii)   the address of any party to the proceedings who acknowledged service in person or who at the conclusion of the proceedings which gave rise to the taxation proceedings was acting in person and the name or firm and business address, telephone number and office reference of the solicitor of any party who did not so acknowledge service or was not so acting in person and also (if the solicitor is the agent of another) the name or firm and business address of his principal; and
    (c)   unless the taxing officer otherwise orders, a bill of costs
       (i)   in which the professional charges and the disbursements are set out in separate columns and each column is cast, and
      (ii)   which is endorsed with the name, or firm and business address of the solicitor whose bill it is, and
      (iii)   which is signed by that solicitor or, if the costs are due to a firm, by a partner of that firm; and
    (d)   unless the taxing officer otherwise orders, the papers and vouchers specified below in the order mentioned—
       (i)   a bundle comprising all civil legal aid certificates and amendments thereto, notices of discharge or revocation thereof and specific legal aid authorities;
      (ii)   unless the relevant information is included in the judgment or order or the parties have agreed the times of the hearings, a certificate of times or a copy of the associate's certificate;

    (iii)   a bundle comprising fee notes of counsel and accounts for other disbursements;

    (iv)   one complete set of pleadings arranged in chronological order, with any interlocutory summonses and lists of documents annexed to it;

    (v)   cases to counsel to advise with his advice and opinions, and instructions to counsel to settle documents and briefs to counsel with enclosures, arranged in chronological order;

    (vi)   reports and opinions of medical and other experts arranged in chronological order;

    (vii)   the solicitor's correspondence and attendance notes; and

    (viii)   any other relevant papers duly bundled and labelled.

(8)   In this rule and in this Part of this Order—

"proper officer" means an officer of the appropriate office within the meaning of paragraph 6(b), and

"party entitled to be heard on the taxation" means—

    (a)   a person who has acknowledged service or taken any part in the proceedings which gave rise to the taxation proceedings and who is directly liable under an order for costs made against him, or

    (b)   a person who has begun proceedings for taxation in accordance with this rule, or

    (c)   a person who has given the party taxing and the proper officer written notice that he has a financial interest in the outcome of the taxation, or

    (d)   a person in respect of whom a direction has been given under rule 26.

(9)   Paragraph (7)(a), (b) and (d)(i), (ii) and (iv) do not apply to proceedings in the Family Division.]

Commencement   28 April 1986.
Amendments   See the first note to Order 62, r 1.
Para (6): in sub-para (b) words "Admiralty and Commercial Registry" substituted by SI 1987/1423, r 2.

[Order 62, r 30 Subsequent procedure

(1)   Subject to rules 31 and 32, where a party has begun proceedings for taxation in accordance with rule 29, the proper officer shall give to that party and to any other party entitled to be heard on the taxation not less than 14 days' notice of the day, time and place appointed for the taxation.

(2)   Subject to rule 32, where a party has begun proceedings for taxation in accordance with rule 29, the proper officer shall as soon as practicable give notice to any other party whose costs are to be taxed in the proceedings of the period within which his bill of costs (together with all necessary papers and vouchers) are to be sent to the taxing officer by whom the bill is to be taxed.

(3)   A party whose costs are to be taxed (except a solicitor whose costs are to be taxed by virtue of an order made under section 70 of the Solicitors Act 1974) must within 7 days after beginning the proceedings for taxation or, as the case may be, receiving notice under paragraph (2),—

    (a)   send a copy of his bill of costs to every other party entitled to be heard on the taxation, and

    (b)   notify the proper officer that he has done so.

(4)   Where, in beginning or purporting to begin any taxation proceedings or at any stage in the course of or in connection with those proceedings, there has been a

failure to comply with the requirements of this Order, whether in respect of time or in any other respect, the failure shall be treated as an irregularity and shall not nullify the taxation proceedings or any step taken in those proceedings.

(5)   The taxing officer may, on the ground that there has been such a failure as is mentioned in paragraph (4), and on such terms as he thinks just, set aside either wholly or in part the taxation proceedings or exercise his powers under this Order to make such order (if any) dealing with the taxation proceedings generally as he thinks fit.

(6)   Order 3, rule 6 shall not apply to taxation proceedings.]

Commencement   28 April 1986.
Amendments   See the first note to Order 62, r 1.
Cross references   See CCR Order 38, r 20.

[Order 62, r 31 Provisional taxation

(1)   Where in taxation proceedings duly begun in accordance with rule 29, only the party who commenced the proceedings is entitled to be heard on the taxation, the proper officer shall, unless the taxing officer otherwise directs, send to that party a notice specifying the amount which the taxing officer proposes to allow in respect of the bill of costs and requiring him to inform the proper officer, within 14 days after receipt of the notice, if he wishes to be heard on the taxation.

(2)   If the party referred to in paragraph (1) informs the proper officer within the time limited that he wishes to be heard on the taxation, the proper officer shall fix a day and time for the taxation and give not less than 14 days' notice thereof to that party.

(3)   Except on the taxation of a solicitor's bill to his own client or where paragraph (1) applies, where in taxation proceedings begun in accordance with rule 29—
    (a)   the party lodging the bill so requests and the taxing officer considers it to be appropriate, or
    (b)   the taxing officer so decides,

the taxing officer may, instead of proceeding under rule 30(1), proceed under paragraphs (4) to (7) of this rule.

(4)   Where the taxing officer decides to proceed under this and the following paragraphs of this rule, the proper officer shall send to each party entitled to be heard on the taxation (except the party whose bill it is), a notice requiring him to inform the proper officer within 14 days after receipt of the notice if he wishes to be heard on the taxation.

(5)   If any party to whom notice has been given under paragraph (4) informs the proper officer within the time limited that he wishes to be heard on the taxation, the proper officer shall fix an appointment for the taxation and give not less than 14 days' notice of the appointment to every party entitled to be heard.

(6)   If no party to whom notice has been given under paragraph (4) informs the proper officer within the time limited that he wishes to be heard on the taxation, the proper officer shall, unless the taxing officer otherwise directs, send to the party lodging the bill a notice specifying the amount which the taxing officer proposes to allow in respect of the bill and requiring that party to inform the proper officer within 14 days after receipt of the notice if he wishes to be heard on the taxation.

(7) If the party lodging the bill informs the proper officer within the time limited under paragraph (6) that he wishes to be heard on the taxation, the proper officer shall fix an appointment for the taxation and give not less than 14 days' notice of the appointment to that party.]

Commencement 28 April 1986.
Amendments See the first note to Order 62, r 1.
Cross references See CCR Order 38, r 20(2)-(3B).

[Order 62, r 32 Short and urgent taxations

(1) Where a party entitled to require the taxation of any costs of or arising out of proceedings to which this Order applies begins proceedings for the taxation of those costs in accordance with rule 29 then if, when he begins such proceedings, he satisfies the proper officer—

(a) that, in view of the amount of any bill of costs to be taxed, the time required for taxation is likely to be short, and

(b) that the speedy completion of the taxation is necessary in the interests of any person concerned in the taxation,

the proper officer shall enter the proceedings for taxation in a list kept for the purposes of this rule and shall forthwith give notice of the day and time appointed for the taxation to the party whose costs are to be taxed.

(2) A party whose costs are to be taxed in proceedings entered in the list referred to in paragraph (1) must not less than 4 days before the day appointed for the taxation send a copy of his bill of costs to every other party entitled to be heard on the taxation with a notice of the day and time appointed for the taxation.]

Commencement 28 April 1986.
Amendments See the first note to Order 62, r 1.

[Part VI Review of Taxation

Order 62, r 33 Application to taxing officer for review

(1) Any party to any taxation proceedings who is dissatisfied with any decision of a taxing officer (other than a decision on a provisional taxation [or a decision under rule 28]) may apply to the taxing officer to review his decision.

(2) An application under this rule for review of a taxing officer's decision must be made within 21 days after that decision or within such other period as may be fixed by the taxing officer.

(3) Every applicant for review under this rule must at the time of making his application deliver to the taxing officer his objections in writing specifying what is objected to and stating concisely the nature and grounds of the objection in each case, and must deliver a copy of the objections to any other party who was entitled to receive notice of the appointment for the taxation pursuant to rules 30 and 31.

(4) Any party to whom a copy of the objections is delivered under this rule may, within 21 days after delivery of the copy to him or such other period as may be fixed by the taxing officer, deliver to the taxing officer answers in writing to the objections stating concisely the grounds on which he will oppose the objections, and must at the same time deliver a copy of the answers to the party applying for review and to any

other party who was entitled to receive notice of the appointment for the taxation pursuant to rules 30 and 31.]

Commencement 28 April 1986.
Amendments See the first note to Order 62, r 1.
Para (1): words "or a decision under rule 28" inserted by SI 1990/1689, r 30.
Cross references See CCR Order 38, r 24.

[Order 62, r 34 Review by taxing officer

(1)   A review under rule 33 shall be carried out by the taxing officer who conducted the taxation, except that, where the taxation was conducted by a principal or a senior executive officer, the review shall be conducted by a taxing master or a registrar, as the case may be.

(2)   On a review under rule 33, a taxing officer may receive further evidence and may exercise all the powers which he might exercise on an original taxation, including the power to award costs of the proceedings before him; and any costs awarded by him to any party may be taxed by him and may be added to or deducted from any other sum payable to or by that party in respect of costs.

(3)   On a hearing of a review under rule 33 a party to whom a copy of objections was delivered under paragraph (3) of that rule shall be entitled to be heard in respect of all or any of the objections notwithstanding that he did not deliver written answers to the objections under paragraph (4) of that rule.

(4)   A taxing officer who issues his certificate [pursuant to rule 22(1)(a) or (b)] after he has conducted a review under this rule, if requested to do so by any party to the proceedings before him, shall state in the certificate or otherwise in writing by reference to the objections the reasons for his decision on the review, and any special facts or circumstances relevant to it.

(5)   A request under paragraph (4) must be made within 14 days after the review or such other period as may be fixed by the taxing officer.]

Commencement 28 April 1986.
Amendments See the first note to Order 62, r 1.
Para (4): words "pursuant to rule 22(1)(a) or (b)" substituted by SI 1987/1423, r 54.
Cross references See CCR Order 38, r 24.

[Order 62, r 35 Review by a judge

(1)   Any party who is dissatisfied with the decision of a taxing officer on a review under rule 33 may apply to a judge for an order to review that decision either in whole or in part, provided that one of the parties to the taxation proceedings has requested that officer to state the reasons for his decision in accordance with rule 34(4).

(2)   An application under this rule may be made at any time within 14 days after the taxing officer has issued a certificate in accordance with rule 34(4).

(3)   An application under this rule shall be made by summons and shall, unless the judge thinks fit to adjourn it into Court, be heard in chambers.

(4)   Unless the judge otherwise directs, no further evidence shall be received on the hearing of an application under this rule, and no ground of objection shall be raised which was not raised on the review by the taxing officer but, save as aforesaid,

on the hearing of any such application the judge may exercise all such powers and discretion as are vested in the taxing officer in relation to the subject matter of the application.

(5)   If the judge thinks fit to exercise in relation to an application under this rule the power of the Court to appoint assessors under section 70 of the Act, the judge shall appoint not less than two assessors, of whom one shall be a taxing officer and one a practising solicitor.

(6)   On an application under this rule the judge may make such order as the circumstances may require and in particular may order the taxing officer's certificate to be amended or, except where the dispute as to the item under review is as to amount only, order the item to be remitted to the same or another taxing officer for taxation.

(7)   In this rule "taxing officer" means a taxing master or a registrar.]

Commencement   28 April 1986.
Amendments   See the first note to Order 62, r 1.
Cross references   See CCR Order 38, r 24.

[APPENDIX 1
REQUISITE DOCUMENT FOR PURPOSES OF RULE 29

1.—(1) Where a party is entitled to require any costs to be taxed by virtue of a judgment or order given or made in any proceedings in the High Court (except proceedings in the Family Division) or in the civil division of the Court of Appeal, the requisite document for the purposes of rule 29 is the judgment or order as the case may be.

(2) Where the entitlement exists by virtue of a judgment or order given or made in proceedings in the Family Division, the requisite document is the bill of costs to be taxed.

(3) Where the entitlement arises by virtue of a direction of the Court given under these rules, the requisite document is that direction.

2. Where a party is entitled by virtue of rule 5(3), (4) or (5) to require any costs to be taxed, the requisite document for the purposes of rule 29 is:—
    (a)   where he is entitled by virtue of rule 5(3), the notice given to him under Order 21, rule 2;
    (b)   where he is so entitled by virtue of rule 5(4) or (5), a certified copy of the notice given by him under Order 22, rule 3.

3. Where a party is entitled to require taxation by a taxing officer of the costs directed to be paid by an award made on the arbitration under any Act or pursuant to an arbitration agreement and no order of the Court for the enforcement of the award has been made, the requisite document for the purposes of rule 29 is the award.

4. Where apart from any order of the Court a party is entitled to require taxation by a taxing officer of the fees and charges payable to a sheriff or an officer of his under the Sheriffs Act 1887, the requisite document for the purposes of rule 29 is the sheriff's bill of fees and charges.

5. Where a party is entitled to require taxation by a taxing officer of any costs directed to be taxed or paid by an order, award or other determination of a tribunal or other body constituted by or under any Act, the requisite document for the purposes of rule 29 is the order, award or other determination, as the case may be.

6. Where a party is entitled by virtue of rule 6(9) to require any costs to be taxed, the requisite document for the purposes of rule 29 is the order made under section 33 or 34 of the Act, as the case may be.

[7. Where a person is entitled by virtue of section 53(4) of the Administration of Justice Act 1985 to require any costs to be taxed, the requisite document for the purposes of rule 29 is the written request made under rule 7A.]]

Commencement 1 October 1988 (para 7); 28 April 1986 (remainder).
Amendments See the first note to Order 62, r 1.
Para 7: inserted by SI 1988/1340, r 10.
Definitions The Act: Supreme Court Act 1981.

[APPENDIX 2

PART I

Amount of Costs

1.—(1) The amount of costs to be allowed shall (subject to rule 18 and to any order of the Court fixing the costs to be allowed) be in the discretion of the taxing officer.

(2) In exercising his discretion the taxing officer shall have regard to all the relevant circumstances, and in particular to—
    (a) the complexity of the item or of the cause or matter in which it arises and the difficulty or novelty of the questions involved;
    (b) the skill, specialised knowledge and responsibility required of, and the time and labour expended by, the solicitor or counsel;
    (c) the number and importance of the documents (however brief) prepared or perused;
    (d) the place and circumstances in which the business involved is transacted;
    (e) the importance of the cause or matter to the client;
    (f) where money or property is involved, its amount or value;
    (g) any other fees and allowances payable to the solicitor or counsel in respect of other items in the same cause or matter, but only where work done in relation to those items has reduced the work which would otherwise have been necessary in relation to the item in question.

(3) The bill of costs shall consist of such of the items specified in Part II as may be appropriate, set out, except for item 4, in chronological order; each such item (other than an item relating only to time spent in travelling or waiting) may include an allowance for general care and conduct having regard to such of the circumstances referred to in paragraph (2) above as may be relevant to that item.

Fees to Counsel

2.—(1) Except in the case of taxations under the Legal Aid Act 1974 and taxation of fees payable by the Crown, no fee to counsel shall be allowed unless—
    (a) before taxation its amount has been agreed by the solicitor instructing counsel; and
    (b) before the taxing officer issues his certificate a receipt for the fees signed by counsel is produced.

(2) Except in taxations under rules 14 and 15—
    (a) no costs shall be allowed in respect of counsel attending before a master or registrar [district judge] in chambers or of more counsel than one attending before a judge in chambers unless the master, registrar [district judge] or judge, as the case may be, has certified the attendance as being proper in the circumstances of the case;
    (b) a refresher fee, the amount of which shall be in the discretion of the taxing officer, shall be allowed to counsel either
      (i) for each period of 5 hours (or part thereof) after the first, during which a trial or hearing is proceeding, or
      (ii) at the discretion of the taxing officer, in respect of any day after the first day, on which the attendance of counsel at the place of trial was necessary.

Items to be authorised, certified etc

3.—(1) In an action arising out of an accident on land due to a collision or apprehended collision, the costs of preparing a plan (other than a sketch plan) of the place where the accident happened shall not be allowed unless—

    (a)   before the trial the Court authorised the preparation of the plan, or

    (b)   notwithstanding the absence of an authorisation under sub-paragraph (a), the taxing officer is satisfied that it was reasonable to prepare the plan for use at the trial.

(2) The costs of calling an expert witness with regard to any question as to which a court expert is appointed under Order 40, or a scientific adviser is appointed under Order 104, rule 11, shall not be allowed on a taxation of costs on the standard basis, unless the Court at the trial has certified that the calling of the witness was reasonable.

(3) Where—

    (a)   an action or counterclaim for the infringement of a patent, or

    (b)   a petition for revocation of a patent under section 32 of the Patents Act 1949, or

    (c)   an application for revocation of a patent under section 72 of the Patents Act 1977, or

    (d)   a counterclaim for the revocation of a patent under section 61 of the Patents Act 1949, or

    (e)   a counterclaim in proceedings for the infringement of a patent under section 61 of the Patents Act 1977,

proceeds to trial, no costs shall be allowed to the parties serving any particulars of breaches or particulars of objection in respect of any issues raised in those particulars and relating to that patent except insofar as those issues or particulars have been certified by the Court to have been proven or to have been reasonable.]

Commencement   28 April 1986.
Amendments   See the first note to Order 62, r 1.

[Part II

1 Interlocutory Attendances

    (a)   (i)   Attending the hearing of any summons or other application at Court or appointment in chambers or elsewhere.

          (ii) Care and conduct.

    (b)   Travelling and waiting.

2 Conferences with Counsel

    (a)   (i)   Attending counsel in conference.

          (ii) Care and Conduct.

    (b)   Travelling and waiting.

3 Attendance at Trial or Hearing

    (a)   (i)   Attending the trial or hearing of a cause or matter, or an appeal or to hear a deferred judgment.

          (ii) Care and conduct.

    (b)   Travelling and waiting.

4 Preparation

Part A: The doing of any work which was reasonably done arising out of or incidental to the proceedings, including:—

          (i)   The Client: taking instructions to sue, defend, counterclaim, appeal or oppose etc, attending upon and corresponding with client; taking and preparing proofs of evidence;

    (ii) Witnesses: interviewing and corresponding with witnesses and potential witnesses, taking and preparing proofs of evidence and, where appropriate, arranging attendance at Court, including issue of subpoena;

    (iii) Expert Evidence: obtaining and considering reports or advice from experts and plans, photographs and models: where appropriate arranging their attendance at Court, including issue of subpoena;

    (iv) Inspections: inspecting any property or place material to the proceedings;

    (v) Searches and Enquiries: making searches at offices of public records and elsewhere for relevant documents: searches in the Companies' Registry and similar matters;

    (vi) Special Damages: obtaining details of special damages and making or obtaining any relevant calculations;

    (vii) Other Parties: attending upon and corresponding with other parties or their solicitors;

    (viii) Discovery: perusing, considering or collating documents for affidavit or list of documents: attending to inspect or produce for inspection any documents required to be produced or inspected by order of the Court or by virtue of Order 24;

    (ix) Documents: preparation and consideration of pleadings and affidavits, cases and instructions to and advice from counsel, any law involved and any other relevant documents including collating and service;

    (x) Negotiations: work done in connection with negotiations with a view to settlement;

    (xi) Agency: correspondence with and attendances upon London or other agents and work done by them;

    (xii) Interest: where relevant, the calculation of interest;

    (xiii) Notices: preparation and service of miscellaneous notices, including notices to witnesses to attend court.

Part B: The general care and conduct of the proceedings.

Part C: Travelling and waiting time in connection with the above matters.

NOTE: the sums sought under each sub-paragraph (i) to (xiii) of Part A should be shown separately against each item followed by the total of all items under Part A; the sums charged under Parts B and C should each be shown separately, and the total of the items under Parts A, B and C should then follow.

5 Taxation

    (a) Taxation of Costs

        (i) preparing the bill (where allowable) and preparing for and attending the taxation;

        (ii) Care and conduct;

        (iii) Travelling and waiting.

    (b) Review

        (i) preparing and delivering objections to decision of taxing officer on taxation or answers to objections, and considering opponent's answers or objections, as the case may be; attending hearing of review.

        (ii) Care and Conduct.

        (iii) Travelling and waiting.]

Commencement 28 April 1986.

Amendments See the first note to Order 62, r 1.

[APPENDIX 3
FIXED COSTS

PART I

Costs on recovery of a liquidated sum without trial

1. The scale of costs following paragraph 2 of this Part of this Appendix shall apply in relation to the following cases if the writ therein was issued on or after January 1st 1982 and was indorsed in accordance with Order 6, rule 2(1)(b), with a claim for a debt or liquidated demand only of £600 or upwards, that is to say—

    (a)   cases in which the defendant pays the amount claimed or a sum of £600 or upwards within the time and in the manner required by the indorsement of the writ;

    (b)   cases in which the plaintiff obtains judgment on failure to give notice of intention to defend under Order 13, rule 1, or under that rule by virtue of Order 83, rule 4, or judgment in default of defence under Order 19, rule 2, or under that rule by virtue of Order 83, rule 4, being in any case judgment for a sum of £600 or upwards;

    (c)   cases in which the plaintiff obtains judgment under Order 14, for a sum of £600 or upwards, either conditionally or unless that sum is paid into court or to the plaintiff's solicitors.

2. There shall be added to the basic costs set out in the said scale—

    (i)   if the amount recovered is less than £3,000 the fee payable on entering a plaint in a county court for that amount, and

    (ii) in any other case, [the appropriate court fees].

Scale of Costs

[A Basic Costs

		Amount to be allowed in cases under following sub-paragraphs of paragraph 1 of this Appendix		
		(a)	(b)	(c)
		£p	£p	£p
If the amount recovered is—				
not less than £600 but less than £2,000—				
(i)	where the writ was served by post	55.00	72.50	127.75
(ii)	where the writ was served on the defendant personally	62.00	78.25	133.50
not less than £2,000 but less than £3,000—				
(i)	where the writ was served by post	62.00	80.25	133.50
(ii)	where the writ was served on the defendant personally	68.00	85.00	140.00
not less than £3,000		80.25	116.00	165.25]

B Additional costs

	Amount to be allowed where the amount recovered is —	
	(i) £ p	(ii) £ p
	not less than £600 but less than £3,000	not less than £3,000
(1) Where there is more than one defendant, in respect of each additional defendant served	[8.50]	[11.00]
(2) Where substituted service is ordered and effected, in respect of each defendant served	[20.00]	[43.00]
(3) Where service out of the jurisdiction is ordered and effected, in the case of service—		
(a) in Scotland, Northern Ireland, the Isle of Man or the Channel Islands	[31.00]	[55.00]
(b) in any other place out of the jurisdiction	[36.50]	[62.00]
(4) In the case of judgment in default of defence or judgment under Order 14, where notice of intention to defend is given after the time limited therefor and the plaintiff makes an affidavit of service for the purpose of a judgment on failure to give notice of intention to defend (the allowance to include the search fee)	[14.50]	[16.50]
(5) In the case of judgment under Order 14 where an affidavit of service of the summons is required	[14.50]	[16.50]
(6) In the case of judgment under Order 14 for each adjournment of the summons	[11.00]	[20.00]]

Commencement 28 April 1986.
Amendments See the first note to Order 62, r 1.
Para 2: in sub-para (ii) words "the appropriate court fees" substituted by SI 1987/1423, r 55(1).
Table A: substituted by SI 1992/638, r 13(1).
Table B: sums in square brackets substituted by SI 1992/638, r 13(2).

[PART II

Costs on judgment without trial for possession of land

1.—(1) Where the writ is indorsed with a claim for the possession of land the plaintiff obtains judgment—
    (a)   under Order 13, rule 4 or 5, on failure to give notice of intention to defend, or
    (b)   under Order 19, rule 5 or 6, in default of defence, or
    (c)   under Order 14,

for possession of the land and costs, then, subject to sub-paragraph (2), there shall be allowed the costs prescribed by paragraph 2 of this Part of this Appendix.

(2) Where the plaintiff is also entitled under the judgment to damages to be assessed, or where the plaintiff claims any relief of the nature specified in Order 88, rule 1, this part of this Appendix shall not apply.

2. The costs to be allowed under this Part of this Appendix shall be the costs which would be allowed under Part 1 (together with the fee paid on the writ) if judgment had been obtained in the same circumstances, that is to say, on failure to give notice of intention to defend or in default of defence or under Order 14 but the writ has been indorsed with a claim for a debt or liquidated demand only of £600 or upwards and judgment for not less than £3,000 has been obtained.]

Commencement 28 April 1986.
Amendments See the first note to Order 62, r 1.

[PART III]

Miscellaneous

1. Where a plaintiff or defendant is entitled to costs by virtue of rule 5(3), (4) or (5) there shall be allowed—

Costs of the judgment ... ... [£7.75]

2. Where a certificate in respect of money provisions contained in a judgment is registered in the High Court in the Register of United Kingdom judgments under Schedule 6 to the Civil Jurisdiction and Judgments Act 1982, there shall be allowed—

Costs of registration . ...[£31.50]

3. Where, upon the application of any person who has obtained a judgment or order against a debtor for the recovery or payment of money, a garnishee order is made under Order 49, rule 1, against a garnishee attaching debts due or accruing due from him to the debtor, the following costs shall be allowed—
- (a) to the garnishee, to be deducted by him from any debt due by him as aforesaid before payment to the applicant .. ..[£18.75]
- (b) to the applicant, to be retained, unless the Court otherwise orders, out of the money recovered by him under the garnishee order and in priority to the amount of the debt owing to him under the judgment or order—
  - [(i) Basic Costs
    If the amount recovered by the applicant from the garnishee is—
    less than £150.00 .... one half of the amount recovered
    not less than £150.00 .... £79.50]
  - (ii) Additional costs
    Where the garnishee fails to attend the hearing of the application and an affidavit of service is required.................... [£14.50]

4. Where a charging order is granted and made absolute there shall be allowed—
Basic costs ... ...[£89.00]
Additional costs where an affidavit of service is required... ... ...[£14.50]

5. Where leave is given under Order 45, rule 3, to enforce a judgment or order for the giving of possession of land by writ of possession, if the costs are allowed on the judgment or order there shall be allowed the following costs, which shall be added to the judgment or order—
Basic costs ... ... [£34.25]
Where notice of the proceedings has been given to more than one person, (in respect of each additional person ... ... [£2.25]

6. Where a writ of execution within the meaning of Order 46, rule 1, is issued against any party, there shall be allowed—
Costs of issuing execution ... ... [£41.75]]

Commencement 28 April 1986.
Amendments See the first note to Order 62, r 1.
Paras 1-6: words and sums in square brackets substituted by SI 1992/638, r 13(3)-(8).

GENERAL AND ADMINISTRATIVE PROVISIONS

ORDER 63
[OFFICES]

Amendments Word "Offices" substituted by SI 1982/1111, r 62.

Order 63, r 1 Distribution of business [in the Central Office]

The Central Office shall be divided into such departments, and the business performed in the Central Office shall be distributed among the departments in such manner, as the Lord Chancellor may direct.

Commencement 1 October 1966.
Amendments Rule heading: words "in the Central Office" inserted by SI 1982/1111, r 63.

Order 63, r 2 Practice master

One of the masters of the Queen's Bench Division shall be present at the Central Office on every day on which the office is open for the purpose of superintending the business performed there and giving any directions which may be required on questions of practice and procedure.

Commencement 1 October 1966.

Order 63, r 3 Date of filing to be marked, etc

(1)   Any document filed in the Central Office in any proceedings must be sealed with a seal showing the date on which the document was filed.

(2)   Particulars of the time of delivery at the Central Office of any document for filing, the date of the document and the title of the cause or matter of which the document forms part of the record shall be entered in books kept in the Central Office for the purpose.

Commencement 1 October 1966.

Order 63, r 4 Right to inspect, etc certain documents filed in Central Office

(1)   Any person shall, on payment of the prescribed fee, be entitled during office hours to search for, inspect and take a copy of any of the following documents filed in the Central Office, namely—

  (a)   the copy of any writ of summons or other originating process,
  (b)   any judgment or order given or made in court or the copy of any such judgment or order, and
  (c)   with the leave of the Court, which may be granted on an application made ex parte, any other document.

[(2)]   Nothing in the foregoing provisions shall be taken as preventing any party to a cause or matter searching for, inspecting and taking or bespeaking a copy of any affidavit or other document filed in the Central Office in that cause or matter or filed therein before the commencement of that cause or matter but made with a view to its commencement.

Commencement 1 October 1966.
Amendments Para (2): originally para (3), renumbered as para (2) and original para (2) revoked by SI 1982/1111, r 64.

Cross references   See CCR Order 50, r 10.
Forms   Search (PF112).

[Order 63, r 4A Date of filing and inspection of documents filed in other offices

Rules 3 and 4 shall apply in relation to documents filed in Chancery Chambers or ... in a district registry as they apply in relation to documents filed in the Central Office.]

Commencement   1 October 1982.
Amendments   This rule was added by SI 1982/1111, r 65.
Words omitted revoked by SI 1991/1884, r 5.

Order 63, r 5 Deposit of documents

Where the Court orders any documents to be lodged in court, [they must, unless otherwise directed,] be deposited in the Central Office.

Commencement   1 October 1966.
Amendments   Words "they must, unless otherwise directed," substituted by SI 1982/1111, r 66.

Order 63, rr 6–8   *(revoked by SI 1971/1269)*

Order 63, r 9 Restriction on removal of documents

No document filed in or in the custody of any office of the Supreme Court shall be taken out of that office without the leave of the Court unless the document is to be sent to another such office or to a county court.

Commencement   1 October 1966.

Order 63, r 10 Enrolment of instruments

Any deed which by virtue of any Act is required or authorised to be enrolled in the Supreme Court may be enrolled in the Central Office.

In this rule "deed" includes assurances and other instruments.

Commencement   1 October 1966.

Order 63, r 11 Practice in district registries

The practice of the Central Office shall be followed in the district registries.

Commencement   1 October 1966.

Order 63, r 12 Filing of documents in district registries

... Where a cause or matter is proceeding in a district registry all documents in that cause or matter which are required to be filed must ... be filed in that registry.

...

Commencement   1 October 1966.
Amendments   Words omitted revoked by SI 1982/1111, r 67.

Order 63, rr 13, 14   *(revoked by SI 1982/1111)*

ORDER 64
SITTINGS, VACATIONS AND OFFICE HOURS

Order 64, r 1 Sittings . . . of Supreme Court

(1)   The sittings of the Court of Appeal and of the High Court shall be four in every year, that is to say—

    (a)   the Michaelmas sittings which shall begin on [1st October] and end on 21st December;

    (b)   the Hilary sittings which shall begin on 11th January and end on the Wednesday before Easter Sunday;

    (c)   the Easter sittings which shall begin on the second Tuesday after Easter Sunday and end on the Friday before [the spring holiday]; and

    (d)   the Trinity sittings which shall begin on the second Tuesday after [the spring holiday] and end on 31st July.

[(2)   In this rule "spring holiday" means the bank holiday falling on the last Monday in May or any day appointed instead of that day under section 1(2) of the Banking and Financial Dealings Act 1971.]

Commencement   1 October 1972 (para (2)); 1 October 1966 (remainder).
Amendments   Rule heading: words omitted revoked by SI 1972/1194, r 5(1).
Para (1): in sub-para (a) words "1st October" and in sub-paras (c), (d) words "the spring holiday" substituted by SI 1972/1194, r 5(2).
Para (2): substituted, for paras (2), (3) as originally enacted, by SI 1972/1194, r 5(3).

[Order 64, r 2 Court of Appeal

(1)   The Court of Appeal shall sit in vacation on such days as the Master of the Rolls may, with the concurrence of the Lord Chancellor, from time to time direct to hear such appeals or applications as require to be immediately or promptly heard and to hear such appeals and applications if the Master of the Rolls determines that sittings are necessary for that purpose.

(2)   Any party to an appeal may at any time apply to the Court of Appeal for an order that the appeal be heard in vacation and, if that Court is satisfied that the appeal requires to be immediately or promptly heard, it may make an order accordingly and fix a date for the hearing.

(3)   The Court of Appeal may hear such other appeals in vacation as that Court may direct.

(4)   The provisions of Order 59, rule 10(9) shall apply to the powers conferred on the Court of Appeal by this rule.]

Commencement   1 September 1982.
Amendments   This rule was substituted by SI 1982/1111, r 2.

[Order 64, r 3 High Court

(1)   One or more judges of each Division of the High Court shall sit in vacation on such days as the senior judge of that Division may, with the concurrence of the Lord Chancellor, from time to time direct to hear such causes, matters or applications as require to be immediately or promptly heard and to hear other causes, matters, or applications if the senior judge of that Division determines that sittings are necessary for that purpose.

(2)   Any party to a cause or matter may at any time apply to the Court for an order that such cause or matter be heard in vacation and, if the Court is satisfied that the cause or matter requires to be immediately or promptly heard, it may make an order accordingly and fix a date for the hearing.

(3)   Any judge of the High Court may hear such other causes or matters in vacation as the Court may direct.]

Commencement 1 September 1982.
Amendments This rule was substituted, for rr 3, 4 as originally enacted, by SI 1982/1111, r 3.

[Order 64, r 4 Divisional Court business during vacation

Proceedings which require to be immediately or promptly heard and which by virtue of the following provisions must be brought in a Divisional Court may, in vacation, be brought before a single judge:
> (a)   Order 52, rules 1(2) and 3(1);
> (b)   Order 53, rules 3(4)(a) and 5(1);
> (c)   Order 55, rule 2(a);
> (d)   Order 56, rule 1(1)(a).]

Commencement 1 July 1991.
Amendments Original r 4 substituted, together with r 3, by new r 3, by SI 1982/1111, r 3; new r 4 subsequently added by SI 1991/1329, r 17(3).

[Order 64, r 5 Exclusion of trial outside Royal Courts of Justice

The foregoing rules of this Order shall not apply in relation to the trial or hearing of causes, matters of applications outside the Royal Courts of Justice.]

Commencement 1 January 1972.
Amendments This rule was substituted by SI 1971/1955, r 19.

Order 64, r 6 Sittings of official referees: applications in Long Vacation

(1)   The sittings of the official referees . . . shall be those specified in rule 1, but nothing in this rule shall prevent an official referee from sitting in vacation if he thinks it expedient so to do.

(2)   Any interlocutory orders or directions required in connection with a cause or matter pending before an official referee may in the Long Vacation be made or given by a master of the Queen's Bench Division.

Commencement 1 October 1966.
Amendments Para (1): words omitted revoked by SI 1972/1194, r 5(4).

Order 64, r 7 Supreme Court Offices: days on which open and office hours

[(1)   The offices of the Supreme Court shall be open on every day of the year except—
> (a)   Saturdays and Sundays,
> (b)   Good Friday and the day after Easter Monday,
> [(c)   Christmas Eve or—
>> (i)   if that day is a Saturday, then 23rd December,
>> (ii)   if that day is a Sunday, then 22nd December,]

  (d)   Christmas Day and, if that day is a Friday or Saturday, then 28th December,

  (e)   bank holidays in England and Wales under the Banking and Financial Dealings Act 1971, and

  (f)   such other days as the Lord Chancellor, with the concurrence of the Lord Chief Justice, the Master of the Rolls and the President of the Family Division, may direct.]

(2)   The hours during which any office of the Supreme Court shall be open to the public shall be such as the Lord Chancellor, with the concurrence of any other President of a Division concerned with the business performed in that office, may from time to time direct.

Commencement   1 October 1972 (para (1)); 1 October 1966 (remainder).
Amendments   Para (1): substituted by SI 1972/1194, r 5(5); sub-para (c) substituted by SI 1991/2671, r 4.
Cross references   See CCR Order 2, rr 2, 3.

Order 64, r 8 District registries: office hours

Every district registry shall be open on such days and during such hours as the Lord Chancellor may from time to time direct and, in the absence of such a direction, shall be open on the days and during the hours when the offices of the county court of the place in which the district registry is situated are required to be open.

Commencement   1 October 1966.

ORDER 65
SERVICE OF DOCUMENTS

Order 65, r 1 When personal service required

(1) Any document which by virtue of these rules is required to be served on any person need not be served personally unless the document is one which by an express provision of these rules or by order of the Court is required to be so served.

(2) Paragraph (1) shall not affect the power of the Court under any provision of these rules to dispense with the requirement for personal service.

Commencement 1 October 1966.
Cross references See CCR Order 7, rr 1, 2.

Order 65, r 2 Personal service: how effected

Personal service of a document is effected by leaving a copy of the document with the person to be served . . . .

Commencement 1 October 1966.
Amendments Words omitted revoked by SI 1979/402, r 9(1).
Cross references See CCR Order 7, rr 1(1)(a), 2.

Order 65, r 3 . . . Service on body corporate

[(1)] Personal service of a document on a body corporate may, in cases for which provision is not otherwise made by any enactment, be effected by serving it in accordance with rule 2 on the mayor, chairman or president of the body, or the town clerk, clerk, secretary, treasurer or other similar officer thereof.

[(2) Where a writ is served on a body corporate in accordance with Order 10, rule 1(2), that rule shall have effect as if for the reference to the usual or last known address of the defendant there were substituted a reference to the registered or principal office of the body corporate and as if for the reference to the knowledge of the defendant there were substituted a reference to the knowledge of a person mentioned in paragraph (1).]

Commencement 24 April 1979 (para (2)); 1 October 1966 (remainder).
Amendments Rule heading: word omitted revoked by SI 1979/402, r 9(2)(a).
Para (1): numbered as such by SI 1979/402, r 9(2)(b).
Para (2): added by SI 1979/402, r 9(2)(b).
Cross references See CCR Order 7, r 14, in relation only to service of summons.

Order 65, r 4 Substituted service

(1) If, in the case of any document which by virtue of any provision of these rules is required to be served personally [or is a document to which Order 10, rule 1, applies], it appears to the Court that it is impracticable for any reason to serve that document [in the manner prescribed], the Court may make an order for substituted service of that document.

(2) An application for an order for substituted service may be made by an affidavit stating the facts on which the application is founded.

(3) Substituted service of a document, in relation to which an order is made under this rule, is effected by taking such steps as the Court may direct to bring the

document to the notice of the person to be served.

Commencement   1 October 1966.
Amendments   Para (1): words "or is a document to which Order 10, rule 1, applies" and "in the manner prescribed" substituted by SI 1979/402, r 9(3).
Cross references   See CCR Order 7, r 8.
Forms   Affidavit for substituted service (PF113).
Order for substituted service (PF114).
Affidavit of substituted service (PF128, PF129).
Form of advertisement (PF130).

Order 65, r 5 Ordinary service: how effected

(1)   Service of any document, not being a document which by virtue of any provision of these rules is required to be served personally [or a document to which Order 10, rule 1, applies], may be effected—

    (a) by leaving the document at the proper address of the person to be served, or

    (b) by post, or

  [[(c) through a document exchange in accordance with paragraph (2A), or

  (ca) by FAX in accordance with paragraph (2B), or]

    (d) in such other manner as the Court may direct.

    ...]

(2)   For the purposes of this rule, and of [section 7 of the Interpretation Act 1978], in its application to this rule, the proper address of any person on whom a document is to be served in accordance with this rule shall be the address for service of that person, but if at the time when service is effected that person has no address for service his proper address for the purposes aforesaid shall be—

    (a) in any case, the business address of the solicitor (if any) who is acting for him in the proceedings in connection with which service of the document in question is to be effected, or

    (b) in the case of an individual, his usual or last known address, or

    (c) in the case of individuals who are suing or being sued in the name of a firm, the principal or last known place of business of the firm within the jurisdiction, or

    (d) in the case of a body corporate, the registered or principal office of the body.

[(2A) Where—

    (a) the proper address for service includes a numbered box at a document exchange, or

    (b) there is inscribed on the writing paper of the party on whom the document is served (where such party acts in person) or on the writing paper of his solicitor (where such party acts by a solicitor) a document exchange box number, and such a party or his solicitor (as the case may be) has not indicated in writing to the party serving the document that he is unwilling to accept service through a document exchange,

service of the document may be effected by leaving the document addressed to that numbered box at that document exchange or at a document exchange which transmits documents every business day to that document exchange; and any document which is left at a document exchange in accordance with this paragraph shall, unless the contrary is proved, be deemed to have been served on the second business day following the day on which it is left.

(2B) Service by FAX may be effected where—

    (a) the party serving the document acts by a solicitor,

    (b) the party on whom the document is served acts by a solicitor and service is effected by transmission to the business address of such solicitor,

    (c) the solicitor acting for the party on whom the document is served has indicated in writing to the solicitor serving the document that he is willing to accept service by FAX at a specified FAX number and the document is transmitted to that number; and for this purpose the inscription of a FAX number on the writing paper of a solicitor shall be deemed to indicate that such a solicitor is willing to accept service by FAX at that number in accordance with this paragraph unless he states otherwise in writing, and

    [(d) as soon as practicable after service by FAX the solicitor acting for the party serving the document dispatches a copy of it to the solicitor acting for the other party by any of the other methods prescribed for service by paragraph (1), and if he fails to do so the document shall be deemed never to have been served by FAX.]

Where the FAX is transmitted on a business day before 4 p.m., it shall, unless the contrary is shown, be deemed to be served on that day, and, in any other case, on the business day next following.]

(3) Nothing in this rule shall be taken as prohibiting the personal service of any document or as affecting any enactment which provides for the manner in which documents may be served on bodies corporate.

    [. . .]

[(4) In this rule—

    (a) "document exchange" means any document exchange for the time being approved by the Lord Chancellor;

    (b) "business day" means any day other than a Saturday, a Sunday, Christmas Day, Good Friday or a bank holiday as defined in Order 3, rule 2(5).]

Commencement 1 February 1991 (paras (2A), (2B), (4)); 1 October 1966 (remainder).

Amendments Para (1): words "or a document to which Order 10, rule 1, applies" inserted by SI 1979/402, r 9(4); sub-paras (c), (d) and the final paragraph substituted, for sub-para (c) as originally enacted, by SI 1986/632, r 14, sub-para (c) further substituted by sub-paras (c), (ca), and the final paragraph revoked, by SI 1990/2599, r 14(2), (3).

Para (2): words "section 7 of the Interpretation Act 1978" substituted by SI 1982/1111, r 115, Schedule.

Para (2A): added by SI 1986/632, r 15; new paras (2A), (2B) substituted for existing para (2A) by SI 1990/2599, r 14(4).

Para (2B): substituted, together with para (2A), for existing para (2A), by SI 1990/2599, r 14(4); sub-para (d) substituted by SI 1991/1884, r 30.

Para (3): words omitted originally added by SI 1986/632, r 16, subsequently revoked by SI 1990/2599, r 14(5).

Para (4): added by SI 1990/2599, r 14(6).

Cross references See CCR Order 7, r 1.

Forms Affidavit of service by post (PF134).

Affidavit of service via document exchange (PF135).

Affidavit of service by other means (PF136).

Affidavit of service of Order 14 summons (PF137).

Order 65, r 6 Service on Minister, etc in proceedings which are not by or against the Crown

Where for the purpose of or in connection with any proceedings in the Supreme Court, not being civil proceedings by or against the Crown within the meaning of Part II of the Crown Proceedings Act 1947, any document is required by any Act or these rules to be served on the Minister of a government department which is an authorised department for the purposes of that Act, or on such a department or on the Attorney General, section 18 of the said Act of 1947 and Order 77, rule 4, shall apply in relation to the service of the document as they apply in relation to the service of documents required to be served on the Crown for the purpose of or in connection with any civil proceedings by or against the Crown.

Commencement 1 October 1966.
Cross references See CCR Order 42, r 7.

Order 65, r 7 Effect of service after certain hours

Any document (other than a writ of summons or other originating process) service of which is effected under rule 2 or under rule 5(1)(a) [between twelve noon on a Saturday and midnight on the following day] or after four in the afternoon on any other weekday shall, for the purpose of computing any period of time after service of that document, be deemed to have been served on the Monday following that Saturday or on the day following that other weekday, as the case may be.

Commencement 1 October 1966.
Amendments Words "between twelve noon on a Saturday and midnight on the following day" substituted by SI 1969/1894, r 6(1).

Order 65, r 8 Affidavit of service

[Except as provided in Order 10, rule 1(3)(b) and Order 81, rule 3(2)(b)] an affidavit of service of any document must state by whom the document was served, the day of the week and date on which it was served, where it was served and how.

Commencement 1 October 1966.
Amendments Words from "Except" to "rule 3(2)(b)" inserted by SI 1979/402, r 9(5).
Cross references See CCR Order 7, r 6.

Order 65, r 9 No service required in certain cases

Where by virtue of these rules any document is required to be served on any person but is not required to be served personally [or in accordance with Order 10, rule 1(2)], and at the time when service is to be effected that person is in default [as to acknowledgment of service] or has no address for service, the document need not be served on that person unless the Court otherwise directs or any of these rules otherwise provides.

Commencement 1 October 1966.
Amendments Words "or in accordance with Order 10, rule 1(2)" inserted by SI 1979/402, r 9(6); words "as to acknowledgement of service" substituted by SI 1979/1716, r 48, Schedule, Pt 1.

[Order 65, r 10 Service of process on Sunday

(1) No process shall be served or executed within the jurisdiction on a Sunday except, in case of urgency, with the leave of the Court.

(2) For the purposes of this rule "process" includes a writ, judgment, notice, order, petition, originating or other summons or warrant.]

Commencement 10 January 1970.
Amendments This rule was added by SI 1969/1894, r 6(2).
Cross references See CCR Order 7, r 3.

ORDER 66
PAPER, PRINTING, NOTICES AND COPIES

Order 66, r 1 Quality and size of paper

[(1)] Unless the nature of the document renders it impracticable, every document prepared by a party for use in the Supreme Court must be [on A4 ISO paper of durable quality] having a margin, not less than [3∫ centimetres] wide, to be left blank on the left side of the face of the paper and on the right side of the reverse:

. . .

[(2) In these rules the expressions "A3", "A4" and "A5" followed by the letters "ISO" mean respectively the size of paper so referred to in the specifications of the International Standards Organisation.]

Commencement   1 October 1970 (para (2)); 1 October 1966 (remainder).
Amendments   Para (1): numbered as such by SI 1970/1208, r 8(1); words "on A4 ISO paper of durable quality" substituted and words omitted revoked by SI 1980/629, r 17; words "3∫ centimetres" substituted by SI 1991/2671, r 3.
Para (2): added by SI 1970/1208, r 8(3).

Order 66, r 2 Regulations as to printing, etc

(1)   Except where these rules otherwise provide, every document prepared by a party for use in the Supreme Court must be produced by one of the following means, that is to say, printing, writing (which must be clear and legible) and typewriting otherwise than by means of a carbon, and may be produced partly by one of those means and partly by another or others of them.

(2)   For the purposes of these rules a document shall be deemed to be printed if it is produced by type lithography or stencil duplicating.

(3)   Any type used in producing a document for use as aforesaid must be such as to give a clear and legible impression and must be not smaller than 11 point type for printing or elite type for type lithography, stencil duplicating or typewriting.

(4)   Any document produced by a photographic or similar process giving a positive and permanent representation free from blemishes shall, to the extent that it contains a facsimile of any printed, written or typewritten matter, be treated for the purposes of these rules as if it were printed, written or typewritten, as the case may be.

(5)   Any notice required by these rules may not be given orally except with the leave of the Court.

Commencement   1 October 1966.

[Order 66, r 3 Copies of documents for other parties

(1)   Where a document has been prepared by a party for use in the Supreme Court, the party by whom it has been prepared must supply any party entitled to a copy of it with a copy of it and, where the document in question is an affidavit, of any document exhibited to it.

(2)   Subject to paragraph (3), the document must be ready for delivery within 48 hours after a written request for it, together with an undertaking to pay the proper charges, is received and must be supplied immediately on payment of those charges.

(3)   Where a party is joined to existing proceedings, the party joined shall be entitled to require the party joining him to supply, without charge, copies of all pleadings, affidavits and exhibits served in the proceedings by or upon the joining party which relate to any issues between the joining party and the party joined, and copies of all orders made in those proceedings.

The documents must be supplied within 48 hours after a written request for them is received.

(4)   Where a document to which paragraph (1) or (3) applies exists in electronic form, a copy must be supplied (at the option of the party entitled to a copy of it) either in electronic form or hard copy, or both, and if supplied in electronic form must be supplied with sufficient technical information to enable the party entitled to such copy to read the document.]

Commencement 1 October 1993.
Amendments This rule was substituted by SI 1993/2133, r 8(1).

Order 66, r 4 Requirements as to copies

(1), (2) . . .

(3)   The party by whom a copy is supplied under rule 3, or, if he sues or appears by a solicitor, his solicitor, shall be answerable for the copy being a true copy of the original or of an office copy, as the case may be.

Commencement 1 October 1966.
Amendments Para (1): revoked by SI 1970/1208, r 9.
Para (2): revoked by SI 1993/2133, r 8(2).

ORDER 67
CHANGE OF SOLICITOR

Order 67, r 1 Notice of change of solicitor

(1)   A party to any cause or matter who sues or defends by a solicitor may change his solicitor without an order for that purpose but, unless and until notice of the change is filed and copies of the notice are lodged and served in accordance with this rule, the former solicitor shall, subject to rules 5 and 6, be considered the solicitor of the party until the final conclusion of the cause or matter, whether in the High Court or the Court of Appeal.

(2)   Notice of a change of solicitor must be filed, and a copy thereof lodged, in the case where the cause or matter is proceeding in a district registry, in that registry and, in the case of any other cause or matter, in the appropriate office indicated in the following table:—

TABLE

Nature of Cause or Matter	Appropriate Office
(a) An action of any other cause or matter begun in the Action Department of the Central Office.	Central Office (Action Department).
(b) [An action or any cause or matter begun in Chancery Chambers.]	[Chancery Chambers.]
(c) An appeal from an inferior court (other than a county court) or other proceeding begun (as regards the High Court) in the Crown Office.	Crown Office.
(d) An appeal from a county court [which does not fall within paragraph (e)] ...	[Office of the Registrar of Civil Appeals.]
(e) A proceeding begun [or appeal set down] in the [Principal Registry of the Family Division].	[Principal Registry of the Family Division.]
(f) A proceeding begun in the [Admiralty and Commercial Registry].	[Admiralty and Commercial Registry.]

(3)   The party giving the notice must serve on every other party to the cause or matter (not being a party in default [as to acknowledgment of service]) and on the former solicitor a copy of the notice indorsed with a memorandum stating that the notice has been duly filed in the appropriate office (naming it).

(4)   The party giving the notice may perform the duties prescribed by this rule in person or by his new solicitor.

Commencement   1 October 1966.

Amendments   Para (2): in sub-para (b) words from "An action" to "Chancery Chambers" and "Chancery Chambers" substituted by SI 1982/1111, r 69(i); in sub-para (d) words "which does not fall within paragraph (e)" insèrted by SI 1968/1244, r 10(1), words omitted revoked and words "Office of the Registrar of Civil Appeals" substituted by SI 1982/1111, r 69(ii); in sub-para (e) words "or appeal set down" inserted by SI 1968/1244, r 10(1), words "Principal Registry of the Family Division" in both places substituted by SI 1971/1269, r 38, Schedule; in sub-para (f) words "Admiralty and Commercial Registry" substituted by SI 1987/1423, r 2.

Para (3): words "as to acknowledgment of service" substituted by SI 1979/1716, r 48, Schedule, Pt 1.

Cross references   See CCR Order 50, r 5(1), (1A).

Forms   Notice of change (PF143, PF144).

Order 67, r 2 Notice of change of agent solicitor

(1)   Where a solicitor for whom some other solicitor is acting as agent in a cause or matter changes the solicitor so acting, notice of the change must be given, and rule 1(2) shall apply in relation to a notice of change of agent as it applies in relation to a notice of change of solicitor.

(2)   The solicitor giving the notice must serve on every party to the cause or matter (not being the party for whom he is acting or a party in default [as to acknowledgment of service]) and on the solicitor formerly acting as agent a copy of the notice indorsed with a memorandum stating that the notice has been duly filed in the appropriate office (naming it).

Commencement   1 October 1966.

Amendments   Para (2): words "as to acknowledgment of service" substituted by SI 1979/1716, r 48, Schedule, Pt 1.

Order 67, r 3 Notice of appointment of solicitor

Where a party, after having sued or defended in person, appoints a solicitor to act in the cause or matter on his behalf, the change may be made without an order for that purpose and rule 1(2), (3) and (4) shall, with the necessary modifications, apply in relation to a notice of appointment of a solicitor as they apply in relation to a notice of change of solicitor.

Commencement   1 October 1966.

Cross references   See CCR Order 50, r 5(2).

Forms   Notice of change (PF144).

Order 67, r 4 Notice of intention to act in person

Where a party, after having sued or defended by a solicitor, intends and is entitled to act in person, the change may be made without an order for that purpose and rule 1 shall, with the necessary modifications, apply in relation to a notice of intention to act in person as it applies in relation to a notice of change of solicitor except that the notice of intention to act in person must contain an address [within the jurisdiction] for service of the party giving it.

Commencement   1 October 1966.

Amendments   Words "within the jurisdiction" inserted by SI 1993/2133, r 9(1).

Cross references   See CCR Order 50, r 5(3).

Forms   Notice of intention (PF146).

Order 67, r 5 Removal of solicitor from record at instance of another party

(1)   Where—

    (a)   a solicitor who has acted for a party in a cause or matter has died or become bankrupt or cannot be found or has failed to take out a practising certificate or has been struck off the roll of solicitors or has been suspended from practising or has for any other reason ceased to practise, and

(b) the party has not given notice of change of solicitor or notice of intention to act in person in accordance with the foregoing provisions of this Order,

any other party to the cause or matter may apply to the Court, or if an appeal to the Court of Appeal is pending in the cause or matter, to the Court of Appeal, for an order declaring that the solicitor has ceased to be the solicitor acting for the first-mentioned party in the cause or matter, and the Court or Court of Appeal, as the case may be, may make an order accordingly.

(2) An application for an order under this rule must be made by summons or, in the case of an application to the Court of Appeal, by motion, and the summons or notice of the motion must, unless the Court or Court of Appeal, as the case may be, otherwise directs, be served on the party to whose solicitor the application relates.

The application must be supported by an affidavit stating the grounds of the application.

(3) Where an order is made under this rule the party on whose application it was made must—

(a) serve on every other party to the cause or matter (not being a party in default [as to acknowledgment of service]) a copy of the order, and

(b) procure the order to be entered in the district registry or other appropriate office mentioned in rule 1(2), and

(c) leave at that office a copy of the order and a certificate signed by him or his solicitor that the order has been duly served as aforesaid.

(4) An order made under this rule shall not affect the rights of the solicitor and the party for whom he acted as between themselves.

Commencement 1 October 1966.
Amendments Para (3): in sub-para (a) words "as to acknowledgment of service" substituted by SI 1979/1716, r 48, Schedule, Pt 1.
Forms Summons to remove from record (PF147).
Order to remove from record (PF146).

Order 67, r 6 Withdrawal of solicitor who has ceased to act for party

(1) Where a solicitor who has acted for a party in a cause or matter has ceased so to act and the party has not given notice of change in accordance with rule 1, or notice of intention to act in person in accordance with rule 4, the solicitor may apply to the Court for an order declaring that the solicitor has ceased to be the solicitor acting for the party in the cause or matter, and the Court or Court of Appeal, as the case may be, may make an order accordingly, but, unless and until the solicitor—

(a) serves on every party to the cause or matter (not being a party in default [as to acknowledgment of service]) a copy of the order, and

(b) procures the order to be entered in the district registry or other appropriate office mentioned in rule 1(2), and

(c) leaves at that office a copy of the order and a certificate signed by him that the order has been duly served as aforesaid,

he shall, subject to the foregoing provisions of this Order, be considered the solicitor of the party till the final conclusion of the cause or matter, whether in the High Court or Court of Appeal.

(2)   An application for an order under this rule must be made by summons or, in the case of an application to the Court of Appeal, by motion, and the summons or notice of the motion must, unless the Court or the Court of Appeal, as the case may be, otherwise directs, be served on the party for whom the solicitor acted.

The application must be supported by an affidavit stating the grounds of the application.

(3)   An order made under this rule shall not affect the rights of the solicitor and the party for whom he acted as between themselves.

(4)   Notwithstanding anything in paragraph (1), where the certificate of an assisted person within the meaning of the [Legal Aid (General) Regulations 1980] is revoked or discharged, the solicitor who acted for the assisted person shall cease to be the solicitor acting in the cause or matter as soon as his retainer is determined under [regulation 84(1)] of the said Regulations; and if the assisted person whose certificate has been revoked or discharged desires to proceed with the cause or matter without legal aid and appoints that solicitor or another solicitor to act on his behalf, the provisions of rule 3 shall apply as if that party had previously sued or defended in person.

Commencement   1 October 1966.
Amendments   Para (1): in sub-para (a) words "as to acknowledgment of service" substituted by SI 1979/1716, r 48, Schedule, Pt 1.
Para (4): words "Legal Aid (General) Regulations 1980" and "regulation 84(1)" substituted by SI 1982/1111, r 115, Schedule.
Cross references   See CCR Order 50, r 5(4), (5).
Forms   Summons for withdrawal of solicitor (PF149).
Order for withdrawal of solicitor (PF150).

[Order 67, r 7 Address for service of party whose solicitor is removed, etc

(1)   Where—
   (a)   an order is made under rule 5, or
   (b)   an order is made under rule 6, and the applicant for that order has complied with rule 6(1), or
   (c)   the certificate of an assisted person within the meaning of the Civil Legal Aid (General) Regulations 1989 is revoked or discharged,

then, unless and until the party to whose solicitor or to whom, as the case may be, the order or certificate relates either appoints another solicitor and complies with rule 3, or being entitled to act in person, gives notice of his intention so to do and complies with rule 4, his last known address within the jurisdiction or, where the party is a body corporate, its registered or principal office shall for the purpose of the service on him of any document not required to be served personally, be deemed to be his address for service.

(2)   Where such party has no last known address or registered or principal office (as the case may be) within the jurisdiction, and the party wishing to serve documents on him does not know, or may not reasonably be expected to know, of any other address for service within the jurisdiction, he shall be deemed to have no address for service for the purposes of Order 65, rule 9.]

Commencement   1 October 1993.
Amendments   This rule was substituted by SI 1993/2133, r 9(2).

Order 67, r 8 Copy of notice or order to be sent to proper officer, etc

(1)   Where the cause or matter in connection with which a notice is given under rule 1, 2, 3 or 4, or in which an order is made under rule 5 or 6—

(a)   is an action proceeding in the Queen's Bench Division which has been entered for trial before a judge, or

[(b)]   is a cause or matter which, or a question or issue of fact arising in which, has been ordered to be tried before a master of the Queen's Bench Division or an official referee,

an officer of the district registry or other office in which a copy of the notice or order is lodged in accordance with the foregoing provisions of this Order shall cause the copy to be sent to the proper officer . . . or to the master or official referee, as the circumstances of the case require.

In this paragraph "proper officer" has the meaning assigned to it by Order 34, rule 3(5) . . . .

(2)   When a party or solicitor presents such a notice or order as is mentioned in paragraph (1) for filing or entry, he must—

(a)   if the cause or matter in connection with which the notice was given or in which the order was made is such an action as is referred to in paragraph (1)(a), state the place of trial, and

(b)   if that cause or matter is such a cause or matter as is referred to in paragraph (1)(c), state that fact.

Commencement   1 October 1966.

Amendments   Para (1): original sub-para (b) revoked and original sub-para (c) relettered as sub-para (b), and first words omitted revoked, by SI 1982/1111, r 70; second words omitted revoked by SI 1971/1955, r 20.

Cross references   See CCR Order 50, r 5(1), (1A).

Order 67, r 9   *(revoked by SI 1968/1244)*

ORDER 68
OFFICIAL SHORTHAND NOTE

Order 68, r 1 Official shorthand note of all evidence, etc

(1) In every action or other proceeding in the Queen's Bench Division or Chancery Division which is tried or heard with witnesses ... [and in every cause or matter taken in the Admiralty Court], an official shorthand note shall, unless the judge otherwise directs, be taken of any evidence given orally in court and of any summing up by the judge and of any judgment delivered by him, and, if any party so requires, the note so taken shall be transcribed and such number of transcripts as any party may demand shall be supplied to him at the charges authorised by any scheme in force providing for the taking of official shorthand notes of proceedings in the High Court.

(2) Nothing in this rule shall be construed as prohibiting the supply of transcripts to persons not parties to the proceedings.

[(3) The powers of the Court of Appeal under this Order may be exercised by a single judge of that Court or by the registrar of civil appeals.]

Commencement 20 April 1982 (para (3)); 1 October 1966 (remainder).
Amendments Para (1): words omitted revoked by SI 1971/1955, r 21; words "and in every cause or matter taken in the Admiralty Court" inserted by SI 1971/1269, r 22.
Para (3): inserted by SI 1981/1734, r 24(1).
Cross references Paras (1), (2) are applied to the county court by CCR Order 50, r 9B, subject to the amendment there set out.

Order 68, r 2 Evidence when not to be transcribed

(1) If the judge intimates that in the event of an appeal his note will be sufficient, the shorthand note of the evidence need not be transcribed for the purposes of an appeal.

(2) If the parties agree or the judge is of opinion that the evidence or some part of the evidence of any witness would, in the event of an appeal, be of no assistance to the Court of Appeal, the shorthand note of such evidence need not be transcribed for the purposes of an appeal.

(3) If any party requires a transcript of any such evidence as aforesaid the charge therefor shall be borne by that party in any event.

Commencement 1 October 1966.
Cross references This rule is applied to the county court by CCR Order 50, r 9B.

Order 68, r 3 Payment for transcripts out of public funds: excepted proceedings

Rules 4 and 5 shall not apply in relation to a transcript of an official shorthand note taken in proceedings in connection with which [legal aid to make or defend an appeal has been given to the appellant or, as the case may be, the respondent under [Part III or IV of the Legal Aid Act 1988.]]

Commencement 1 October 1966.
Amendments Words from "legal aid" to the end substituted by SI 1987/1423, r 59, words "Pt III or IV of the Legal Aid Act 1988" therein substituted by SI 1991/1329, r 18.

Order 68, r 4 Payment for transcripts for Court of Appeal

(1)   An appellant shall not be required to pay for the transcript to which a certificate given under this rule relates but, except as aforesaid, any transcript required for the Court of Appeal shall be paid for by the appellant in the first instance.

(2)   Where the judge by whom any such proceeding as is referred to in rule 1 was tried or heard or the Court of Appeal is satisfied that an appellant in that proceeding is in such poor financial circumstances that the cost of a transcript would be an excessive burden on him, and, in the case of a transcript of evidence, that there is reasonable ground for the appeal, the judge or the Court of Appeal, as the case may be, may certify that the case is one in which it is proper that the said cost should be borne by public funds.

(3)   An application for a certificate under this rule must be made in the first instance to the judge; if the application is refused, the application (if any) to the Court of Appeal must be made within 7 days after the refusal.

(4)   Where an application is made to the Court of Appeal for a certificate under this rule, then, if the Court of Appeal is of opinion that for the purpose of determining the application it is necessary for that Court to see a transcript of the summing up and judgment, with or without a transcript of the evidence, the Court of Appeal may certify that both transcripts or, as the case may be, only a transcript of the summing up and judgment may properly be supplied for the use of that Court at the expense of public funds.

(5)   No transcript supplied for the use of the Court of Appeal under a certificate given under paragraph (4) shall be handed to the appellant except by direction of the Court of Appeal.

(6)   Where the judge or the Court of Appeal certifies under paragraph (2) that there is reasonable ground for the appeal, the appellant may be supplied with as many free copies of the transcript referred to in the certificate as will, together with any free copies already supplied under a certificate given under paragraph (4), make up a total of one for his own use and three for the use of the Court of Appeal.

(7)   References in this rule to an appellant include references to an intending appellant.

Commencement   1 October 1966.

Order 68, r 5 Payment for transcript for poor respondent

(1)   Where the judge by whom any such proceeding as is referred to in rule 1 was tried or heard or the Court of Appeal is satisfied that the respondent to an appeal in that proceeding is in such poor financial circumstances that the cost of obtaining a transcript, or a specified part thereof, for the purpose of resisting the appeal would be an excessive burden on him, the judge or the Court of Appeal, as the case may be, may certify that the case is one in which it is proper that the cost of the transcript or that part thereof, as the case may be, should be borne by public funds, and where such a certificate is given the respondent shall not be required to pay the said cost.

(2)   Rule 4(3) shall apply in relation to an application for a certificate under this rule as it applies in relation to an application for a certificate under that rule.

Commencement   1 October 1966.

[Order 68, r 6 Transcripts for appeals from county courts

In relation to appeals from county courts, references in rules 4 and 5 to rule 1 shall be construed as references to that rule as applied by [Order 50, rule 9B] of the County Court Rules 1981.]

Commencement 1 July 1991.
Amendments Original r 6 revoked by SI 1983/1181, r 30; new r 6 inserted by SI 1991/1329, r 19.
Words "Order 50, rule 9B" substituted by SI 1992/638, r 17.

Order 68, r 7 Trial before official referee

(1)   If in a reference for trial before an official referee the referee certifies that it is desirable for an official shorthand note to be taken, such a note shall be taken of the evidence given orally in court and of any judgment delivered by the referee.

(2)   Where such a note has been taken, the provisions of this Order relating to transcripts shall apply in relation to the reference as they apply in relation to proceedings before a judge.

Commencement 1 October 1966.

Order 68, r 8 Mechanical recording

In this Order any reference to a shorthand note of any proceedings shall be construed as including a reference to a record of the proceedings made by mechanical means . . . .

Commencement 1 October 1966.
Amendments Words omitted revoked by SI 1983/1181, r 30.
Cross references This rule is applied to the county court by CCR Order 50, r 9B.

PROVISIONS AS TO FOREIGN PROCEEDINGS

ORDER 69
SERVICE OF FOREIGN PROCESS

Order 69, r 1 Definitions

In this Order—

["a convention country" means a foreign country in relation to which there subsists a civil procedure convention providing for service in that country of process of the High Court, and includes a country which is a party to the Convention on the Service Abroad of Judicial and Extra-Judicial Documents in Civil or Commercial matters signed at the Hague on 15th November 1965;

"officer of the County Court" means any clerk or bailiff in the service of a County Court;]

"process" includes a citation;

["process server" means the process server appointed under rule 4 or his authorised agent;]

"taxing master" means a taxing master of the Supreme Court.

Commencement 1 October 1966.
Amendments Definitions "a convention country", "officer of the County Court" and "process server" inserted by SI 1980/629, r 19(1).

[Order 69, r 2 Applications

This order applies to the service on a person in England or Wales of any process in connection with civil or commercial proceedings in a foreign court or tribunal where the senior master receives a written request for service—

(a) from Her Majesty's Principal Secretary of State for Foreign and Commonwealth Affairs, with a recommendation by him that service should be effected, or

(b) where the foreign court or tribunal is in a convention country, from a consular or other authority of that country.]

Commencement 3 June 1980.
Amendments This rule was substituted by SI 1980/629, r 19(2).

[Order 69, r 3 Service of process

(1) The request shall be accompanied by a translation thereof in English, two copies of the process and, unless the foreign court or tribunal certifies that the person to be served understands the language of the process, two copies of a translation thereof.

(2) Subject to paragraphs (3) and (5) and to any enactment providing for the manner of service of documents on corporate bodies, the process shall be served by the process server's leaving a copy of the process and a copy of the translation or certificate, as the case may be, with the person to be served.

(3) The provisions of Order 10, rule 1(2)(b) and (3) regarding service by insertion through a letter-box shall apply to the service of foreign process as they apply to the service of writs, except that service may be proved by an affidavit or by a certificate or report in such form as the senior master may direct.

(4) The process server shall send to the senior master a copy of the process and an affidavit, certificate or report proving due service of process or stating the reason why service could not be effected, as the case may be, and shall, if the Court so directs, specify the costs incurred in effecting or attempting to effect service.

(5) Order 65, rule 4 (substituted service) shall apply to the service of foreign process to the service of writs; except that the senior master may make an order for substituted service of foreign process on the basis of the process server's affidavit, certificate or report, without an application being made to him in that behalf.

(6) The senior master shall send a certificate, together with a copy of the process, to the consular or other authority or the Secretary of State, as the case may be, stating—
  (i) when and how service was effected or the reason why service could not be effected, as the case may be;
  (ii) where appropriate, the amount certified by the taxing master to be the costs of effecting or attempting to effect service.

(7) The certificate under paragraph (6) shall be sealed with the seal of the Supreme Court for use out of the jurisdiction.]

Commencement 3 June 1980.
Amendments This rule was substituted by SI 1980/629, r 19(2).
Forms Certificate of service (PF151).

Order 69, r [4] Appointment of process server

The Lord Chancellor may appoint a process server for the purposes of this Order.

Commencement 1 October 1966.
Amendments Originally r 5, renumbered as r 4 and original r 4 revoked by SI 1980/629, r 19(3).

ORDER 70
OBTAINING EVIDENCE FOR FOREIGN COURTS, ETC

[Order 70, r 1 Interpretation and exercise of jurisdiction

(1)　In this Order "the Act of 1975" means the Evidence (Proceedings in Other Jurisdictions) Act 1975 and expressions used in this Order which are used in that Act shall have the same meaning as in that Act.

(2)　The power of the High Court to make an order under section 2 of the Act of 1975 may be exercised by a master of the Queen's Bench Division.]

Commencement　1 April 1976.
Amendments　This rule was substituted by SI 1976/337, r 14(1).

Order 70, r 2 Application for order

(1)　Subject to paragraph (3) and rule 3, an application for an order under the [Act of 1975] must be made ex parte . . . and must be supported by affidavit.

[(2)　There shall be exhibited to the affidavit the request in pursuance of which the application is made, and if the request is not in the English language, a translation thereof in that language.]

[(3)　Where on an application under section 1 of the Act of 1975 as applied by section 92 of the Patents Act 1977 an order is made for the examination of witnesses, the Court may allow an officer of the European Patent Office to attend the examination and examine the witnesses or request the Court or the examiner before whom the examination takes place to put specified questions to them.]

Commencement　1 June 1978 (para (3)); 1 April 1976 (para (2)); 1 October 1966 (remainder).
Amendments　Para (1): words "Act of 1975" substituted and words omitted revoked by SI 1976/337, r 14(2)(a).
Para (2): substituted by SI 1976/337, r 14(2)(b).
Para (3): original para (3) revoked by SI 1976/337, r 14(2)(c); new para (3) added by SI 1978/579, r 10.
Definitions　Act of 1975: Evidence (Proceedings in Other Jurisdictions) Act 1975.
Forms　Affidavit in support of application (PF152).
Order (No 93).

Order 70, r 3 Application by Treasury Solicitor in certain cases

[Where a request]—
- (a)　is received by the Secretary of State and sent by him to the senior master with an intimation that effect should be given to the request without requiring an application for that purpose to be made by the agent in England of any party to the matter [pending or contemplated before the foreign] court or tribunal, or
- (b)　is received by the senior master in pursuance of a Civil Procedure Convention providing for the taking of the evidence of any person in England or Wales for the assistance of a court or tribunal in the foreign country, and no person is named in the document as the person who will make the necessary application on behalf of such party,

the senior master shall send the document to the Treasury Solicitor and the Treasury Solicitor may, with the consent of the Treasury, make an application for an order under the [Act of 1975], and take such other steps as may be necessary, to give effect to the request.

Commencement   1 October 1966.
Amendments   Words "When a request", "pending or contemplated before the foreign" and "Act of 1975" substituted by SI 1976/337, r 14(3).
Definitions   Act of 1975: Evidence (Proceedings in Other Jurisdictions) Act 1975.

Order 70, r 4 Person to take and manner of taking examination

(1)   Any order made in pursuance of this Order for the examination of a witness may order the examination to be taken before any fit and proper person nominated by the person applying for the order or before an examiner of the Court or before such other qualified person as to the Court seems fit.

(2)   Subject to [rule 6 and to] any special directions contained in any order made in pursuance of this Order for the examination of any witness, the examination shall be taken in manner provided by Order 39, rules 5 to 10 and 11(1) to (3), and an order may be made under Order 39, rule 14, for payment of the fees and expenses due to the examiner, and those rules shall apply accordingly with any necessary modifications.

(3)   If the examination is directed to be taken before one of the examiners of the Court, Order 39, rules 17, 18 and 19, shall apply in relation to the examination.

Commencement   1 October 1966.
Amendments   Para (2): words "rule 6 and to" inserted by SI 1976/337, r 14(4).

Order 70, r 5 Dealing with deposition

Unless any order made in pursuance of this Order for the examination of any witness otherwise directs, the examiner before whom the examination was taken must send the deposition of that witness to the senior master, and the senior master shall—

(a)   give a certificate sealed with the seal of the Supreme Court for use out of the jurisdiction identifying the documents annexed thereto, that is to say, [the request], the order of the Court for examination and the deposition taken in pursuance of the order; and

(b)   send the certificate with the documents annexed thereto to the Secretary of State, or, where the [request] was sent to the senior master by some other person in accordance with a Civil Procedure Convention, to that other person, for transmission to [the court or tribunal out of the jurisdiction requesting the examination].

Commencement   1 October 1966.
Amendments   Words "the request" and "request" substituted by SI 1976/337, r 14(5); words from "the court" to "the examination" substituted by SI 1987/1423, r 63, Schedule.
Forms   Certificate (PF153).

[Order 70, r 6 Claim to privilege

(1)   The provisions of this rule shall have effect where a claim by a witness to be exempt from giving any evidence on the ground specified in section 3(1)(b) of the Act of 1975 is not supported or conceded as mentioned in sub-section (2) of that section.

(2)   The examiner may, if he thinks fit, require the witness to give the evidence to which the claim relates and, if the examiner does not do so the Court may do so, on the ex parte application of the person who obtained the order under section 2.

(3) If such evidence is taken—
  (a) it must be contained in a document separate from the remainder of the deposition of the witness;
  (b) the examiner shall send to the senior master with the deposition a statement signed by the examiner setting out the claim and the ground on which it was made;
  (c) on receipt of the statement the senior master shall, notwithstanding anything in rule 5, retain the document containing the part of the witness's evidence to which the claim relates and shall send the statement and a request to determine the claim to the foreign court or tribunal with the documents mentioned in rule 5:
  (d) if the claim is rejected by the foreign court or tribunal, the senior master shall send to that court or tribunal the document containing that part of the witness's evidence to which the claim relates, but if the claim is upheld he shall send the document to the witness, and shall in either case notify the witness and the person who obtained the order under section 2 of the court or tribunal's determination.]

Commencement 1 April 1976.
Amendments This rule was added by SI 1976/337, r 14(6).
Definitions Act of 1975: Evidence (Proceedings in other Jurisdictions) Act 1975.

ORDER 71
[Reciprocal Enforcement of Judgments and Enforcement of
European Community Judgments and Recommendations etc under
the Merchant Shipping (Liner Conferences) Act 1982]

[I Reciprocal Enforcement:
The Administration of Justice Act 1920 and the Foreign Judgments
(Reciprocal Enforcement) Act 1933]

Amendments First words in square brackets substituted by SI 1986/632, r 21; second words in square brackets, originally added by SI 1972/1898, r 8(2), substituted by SI 1983/1181, r 19.

Order 71, r 1 Powers under relevant Acts exercisable by judge or master

The powers conferred on the High Court by Part II of the Administration of Justice Act 1920 ([in this Part of this Order] referred to as the "Act of 1920") or Part I of the Foreign Judgments (Reciprocal Enforcement) Act 1933 ([in this Part of this Order] referred to as the "Act of 1933") may be exercised by a judge in chambers and a master of the Queen's Bench Division.

Commencement 1 October 1966.
Amendments Words "in this Part of this Order" in both places substituted by SI 1972/1898, r 8(3).

Order 71, r 2 Application for registration

(1) An application—
  (a) under section 9 of the Act of 1920, in respect of a judgment obtained in a superior court in any part of Her Majesty's dominions or other territory to which Part II of that Act applies, or
  (b) under section 2 of the Act of 1933, in respect of a judgment to which Part I of that Act applies,

to have the judgment registered in the High Court may be made ex parte, but the Court hearing the application may direct a summons to be issued.

(2) If the Court directs a summons to be issued, the summons shall be an originating summons.

[(3) An originating summons under this rule shall be in Form No 10 in Appendix A.]

Commencement 3 June 1980 (para (3)); 1 October 1966 (remainder).
Amendments Para (3): substituted by SI 1979/1716, r 48, Schedule, Pt 2.
Definitions Act of 1920: Administration of Justice Act 1920.
Act of 1933: Foreign Judgments (Reciprocal Enforcement) Act 1933.

Order 71, r 3 Evidence in support of application

(1) An application for registration must be supported by an affidavit—
  (a) exhibiting the judgment or a verified or certified or otherwise duly authenticated copy thereof and, where the judgment is not in the English language, a translation thereof in that language certified by a notary public or authenticated by affidavit;
  (b) stating the name, trade or business and the usual or last known place of abode or business of the judgment creditor and the judgment debtor respectively, so far as known to the deponent;

(c) stating to the best of the information or belief of the deponent—
  (i) that the judgment creditor is entitled to enforce the judgment;
  (ii) as the case may require, either that at the date of the application the judgment has not been satisfied, or the amount in respect of which it remains unsatisfied;
  (iii) where the application is made under the Act of 1920, that the judgment does not fall within any of the cases in which a judgment may not be ordered to be registered under section 9 of that Act;
  (iv) where the application is made under the Act of 1933, that at the date of the application the judgment can be enforced by execution in the country of the original court and that, if it were registered, the registration would not be, or be liable to be, set aside under section 4 of that Act;
(d) specifying, where the application is made under the Act of 1933, the amount of the interest, if any, which under the law of the country of the original court has become due under the judgment up to the time of registration[;
(e) verifying that the judgment is not a judgment to which section 5 of the Protection of Trading Interests Act 1980 applies].

[(2)] Where a judgment sought to be registered under the Act of 1933 is in respect of different matters, and some, but not all, of the provisions of the judgment are such that if those provisions had been contained in separate judgments, those judgments could properly have been registered, the affidavit must state the provisions in respect of which it is sought to register the judgment.

[(3)] In the case of an application under the Act of 1933, the affidavit must be accompanied by such other evidence with respect to the enforceability of the judgment by execution in the country of the original court, and of the law of that country under which any interest has become due under the judgment, as may be required having regard to the provisions of the Order in Council extending that Act to that country.

Commencement 1 October 1966.
Amendments Para (1): sub-para (e) inserted by SI 1980/629, r 4.
Paras (2), (3): original para (2) revoked, and original paras (3) and (4) renumbered as paras (2), (3), by SI 1977/1955, r 8(1).
Definitions Act of 1920: Administration of Justice Act 1920.
Act of 1933: Foreign Judgments (Reciprocal Enforcement) Act 1933.

Order 71, r 4 Security for costs

Save as otherwise provided by any relevant Order in Council, the Court may order the judgment creditor to give security for the costs of the application for registration and of any proceedings which may be brought to set aside the registration.

Commencement 1 October 1966.

Order 71, r 5 Order for registration

(1) An order giving leave to register a judgment must be drawn up by, or on behalf of, the judgment creditor.

(2) Except where the order is made on summons, no such order need be served on the judgment debtor.

(3)   Every such order shall state the period within which an application may be made to set aside the registration and shall contain a notification that execution on the judgment will not issue until after the expiration of that period.

(4)   The Court may, on an application made at any time while it remains competent for any party to apply to have the registration set aside, extend the period (either as originally fixed or as subsequently extended) within which an application to have the registration set aside may be made.

Commencement   1 October 1966.
Forms   Order (PF154).

Order 71, r 6 Register of judgments

(1)   There shall be kept in the Central Office under the direction of the senior master a register of the judgments ordered to be registered under the Act of 1920 and a register of the judgments ordered to be registered under the Act of 1933.

(2)   There shall be included in each such register particulars of any execution issued on a judgment ordered to be so registered.

Commencement   1 October 1966.
Definitions   Act of 1920: Administration of Justice Act 1920.
Act of 1933: Foreign Judgments (Reciprocal Enforcement) Act 1933.

Order 71, r 7 Notice of registration

(1)   Notice of the registration of a judgment must be served on the judgment debtor [by delivering it to him personally or by sending it to him at his usual or last known place of abode or business or in such other manner as the Court may direct].

(2)   Service of such a notice out of the jurisdiction is permissible without leave, and Order 11, rules 5, 6 and 8, shall apply in relation to such a notice as they apply in relation to . . . a writ.

(3)   The notice of registration must state—
    (a)   full particulars of the judgment registered and the order for registration,
    (b)   the name and address of the judgment creditor or of his solicitor or agent on whom, and at which, any summons issued by the judgment debtor may be served,
    (c)   the right of the judgment debtor to apply to have the registration set aside, and
    (d)   the period within which an application to set aside the registration may be made.

Commencement   1 October 1966.
Amendments   Para (1): words from "by delivering it" to "the Court may direct" substituted by SI 1979/402, r 10(1).
Para (2): words omitted revoked by SI 1980/2000, r 21.

Order 71, r 8   *(revoked by SI 1979/402)*

Order 71, r 9 Application to set aside registration

(1)   An application to set aside the registration of a judgment must be made by summons supported by affidavit.

(2)   The Court hearing such application may order any issue between the judgment creditor and the judgment debtor to be tried in any manner in which an issue in an action may be ordered to be tried.

(3)   Where the Court hearing an application to set aside the registration of a judgment registered under the Act of 1920 is satisfied that the judgment falls within any of the cases in which a judgment may not be ordered to be registered under section 9 of that Act or that it is not just or convenient that the judgment should be enforced in England or Wales or that there is some other sufficient reason for setting aside the registration, it may order the registration of the judgment to be set aside on such terms as it thinks fit.

Commencement 1 October 1966.
Definitions   Act of 1920: Administration of Justice Act 1920.

Order 71, r 10 Issue of execution

(1)   Execution shall not issue on a judgment registered under the Act of 1920 or the Act of 1933 until after the expiration of the period which, in accordance with rule 5(3), is specified in the order for registration as the period within which an application may be made to set aside the registration or, if that period has been extended by the Court, until after the expiration of that period as so extended.

(2)   If an application is made to set aside the registration of a judgment, execution on the judgment shall not issue until after such application is finally determined.

(3)   Any party wishing to issue execution on a judgment registered under the Act of 1920 or the Act of 1933 must produce to the proper officer an affidavit of service of the notice of registration of the judgment and any order made by the Court in relation to the judgment.

Commencement 1 October 1966.
Definitions   Act of 1920: Administration of Justice Act 1920.
Act of 1933: Foreign Judgments (Reciprocal Enforcement) Act 1933.
Forms   Writ of Fi Fa (No 63).

Order 71, r 11 Determination of certain questions

If, in any case under the Act of 1933, any question arises whether a foreign judgment can be enforced by execution in the country of the original court, or what interest is payable under a foreign judgment under the law of the original court, that question shall be determined in accordance with the provisions in that behalf contained in the Order in Council extending Part I of that Act to that country.

Commencement 1 October 1966.
Definitions   Act of 1933: Foreign Judgments (Reciprocal Enforcement) Act 1933.

Order 71, r 12 Rules to have effect subject to Orders in Council

The foregoing rules shall, in relation to any judgment registered or sought to be registered under the Act of 1933, have effect subject to any such provisions contained in the Order in Council extending Part I of that Act to the country of the original court as are declared by the Order to be necessary for giving effect to the agreement made between Her Majesty and that country in relation to matters with respect to which there is power to make those rules.

Commencement   1 October 1966.
Definitions   Act of 1933: Foreign Judgments (Reciprocal Enforcement) Act 1933.

Order 71, r 13 Certified copy of High Court judgment

(1)   An application under section 10 of the Act of 1920 or section 10 of the Act of 1933 for a certified copy of a judgment entered in the High Court must be made ex parte [on affidavit to a master or, in the case of a judgment given in a cause or matter proceeding in the Family Division, to a [district judge] of that Division.]

(2)   An affidavit by which an application under section 10 of the Act of 1920 is made must give particulars of the judgment, show [that the judgment creditor wishes to secure the enforcement of the judgment in a part (stating which) of Her Majesty's dominions outside the United Kingdom] to which Part II of that Act extends and state the name, trade or business and the usual or last known place of abode of the judgment creditor and the judgment debtor respectively, so far as known to the deponent.

(3)   An affidavit by which an application under section 10 of the Act of 1933 is made must—
   (a)   give particulars of the proceedings in which the judgment was obtained;
   (b)   have annexed to it a copy of the writ [originating summons or other process] by which the proceedings were begun, the evidence of service thereof on, . . . , the defendant, copies of the pleadings, if any, and a statement of the grounds on which the judgment was based;
   (c)   state whether the defendant did or did not object to the jurisdiction, and, if so, on what grounds;
   (d)   show that the judgment is not subject to any stay of execution;
   (e)   state that the time for appealing has expired or, as the case may be, the date on which it will expire and in either case whether notice of appeal against the judgment has been entered; and
   (f)   state the rate at which the judgment carries interest.

(4)   The certified copy of the judgment shall be an office copy sealed with the seal of the Supreme Court and indorsed with a certificate signed by a master [or, where appropriate, a [district judge]] certifying that the copy is a true copy of a judgment obtained in the High Court of England and that it is issued in accordance with section 10 of the Act of 1920 or section 10 of the Act of 1933, as the case may be.

(5)   Where the application is made under section 10 of the Act of 1933 there shall also be issued a certificate (signed by a master [or, where appropriate, a [district judge]] and sealed with the seal of the Supreme Court) having annexed to it a copy of the writ [originating summons or other process] by which the proceedings were begun, and stating—
   (a)   the manner in which the writ or such summons [or other process] was served on the defendant or that the defendant [acknowledged service thereof];
   (b)   what objections, if any, were made to the jurisdiction,
   (c)   what pleadings, if any, were served,
   (d)   the grounds on which the judgment was based,
   (e)   that the time for appealing has expired or, as the case may be, the date on which it will expire,
   (f)   whether notice of appeal against the judgment has been entered, and
   (g)   such other particulars as it may be necessary to give to the court in the foreign country in which it is sought to obtain execution of the judgment,

and a certificate (signed and sealed as aforesaid) stating the rate at which the judgment carries interest.

Commencement 1 October 1966.
Amendments Para (1): words from "on affidavit to a master" to "that Division" substituted by SI 1977/1955, r 8(2)(a).
Para (2): words from "that the judgment" to "United Kingdom" substituted by SI 1989/1307, r 18.
Para (3): in sub-para (b) words "originating summons or other process" substituted by SI 1977/1955, r 8(2)(b); words omitted revoked by SI 1979/1716, r 48, Schedule, Pt 1.
Para (4): words "or, where appropriate, a district judge" inserted by SI 1977/1955, r 8(2)(c).
Para (5): words "or, where appropriate, a district judge" and "or other process" inserted, and words "originating summons or other process" substituted, by SI 1977/1955, r 8(2)(c), (d); words "acknowledged service thereof" substituted by SI 1979/1716, r 48, Schedule, Pt 1.
Definitions Act of 1920: Administration of Justice Act 1920.
Act of 1933: Foreign Judgments (Reciprocal Enforcement) Act 1933.
Forms Certificate (PF155).

Order 71, r 14 *(revoked by SI 1983/1181)*

[[II Enforcement of European Community Judgments]

Amendments The heading for Pt II was substituted by SI 1983/1181, r 19.

[Order 71, r 15 Interpretation

In this Part of this Order, "the Order in Council" means the European Communities (Enforcement of Community Judgments) Order 1972, and expressions used in the Order in Council shall, unless the context otherwise requires, have the same meanings as in that Order.]

Commencement 1 January 1973.
Amendments Order 71, Pt II (rr 15–24) was added by SI 1972/1898, r 8(4).
The heading for Pt II was substituted by SI 1983/1181, r 19.

[Order 71, r 16 Functions under Order in Council exercisable by judge or master

The functions assigned to the High Court by the Order in Council may be exercised by a judge in chambers and a master of the Queen's Bench Division.]

Commencement 1 January 1973.
Amendments See the first note to Order 71, r 15.
Definitions Order in Council: European Communities (Enforcement of Community Judgments) Order 1972, SI 1972/1590.

[Order 71, r 17 Application for registration of Community judgment, etc

An application for the registration in the High Court of a Community judgment or Euratom inspection order may be made ex parte.]

Commencement 1 January 1973.
Amendments See the first note to Order 71, r 15.

[Order 71, r 18 Evidence in support of application

(1) An application for registration must be supported by an affidavit exhibiting—

  (a) the Community judgment and the order for its enforcement or, as the case
       may be, the Euratom inspection order or, in either case, a duly authenticated
       copy thereof, and
  (b) where the Community judgment or Euratom inspection order is not in
       the English language, a translation into English certified by a notary public
       or authenticated by affidavit.

(2) Where the application is for registration of a Community judgment under
which a sum of money is payable, the affidavit shall also state—

  (a) the name and occupation and the usual or last known place of abode or
       business of the judgment debtor, so far as known to the deponent; [and]
  (b) to the best of the deponent's information and belief that at the date of the
       application the European Court has not suspended enforcement of the
       judgment and that the judgment is unsatisfied or, as the case may be, the
       amount in respect of which it remains unsatisfied; . . .
  (c) . . .]

Commencement 1 January 1973.
Amendments See the first note to Order 71, r 15.
Para (2): in sub-para (a) word "and" inserted, in sub-para (b) word omitted revoked, and para (c) revoked, by
SI 1977/1955, r 8(3).
Forms Application (PF156).
Order (PF157).

[Order 71, r 19 Register of judgments and orders

(1) There shall be kept in the Central Office under the direction of the Senior
Master a register of the Community judgments and Euratom inspection orders
registered under the Order in Council.

(2) There shall be included in the register particulars of any execution issued on a
judgment so registered.]

Commencement 1 January 1973.
Amendments See the first note to Order 71, r 15.
Definitions Order in Council: European Communities (Enforcement of Community Judgments) Order
1972, SI 1972/1590.

[Order 71, r 20 Notice of registration

(1) Upon registering a Community judgment or Euratom inspection order, the
proper officer of the Court shall forthwith send notice of the registration to every
person against whom the judgment was given or the order was made.

(2) The notice of registration shall have annexed to it a copy of the registered
Community judgment and the order for its enforcement or, as the case may be, a
copy of the Euratom inspection order, and shall state the name and address of the
person on whose application the judgment or order was registered or of his solicitor
or agent on whom process may be served.

(3) Where the notice relates to a Community judgment under which a sum of
money is payable, it shall also state that the judgment debtor may apply within 28 days
of the date of the notice, or thereafter with the leave of the Court, for the variation
or cancellation of the registration on the ground that the judgment had been partly or
wholly satisfied at the date of registration.]

Commencement 1 January 1973.
Amendments See the first note to Order 71, r 15.
Forms Notice (PF158).

[Order 71, r 21 Issue of execution

Execution shall not issue without the leave of the Court on a Community judgment under which a sum of money is payable until the expiration of 28 days after the date of notice of registration of the judgment or, as the case may be, until any application made within that period for the variation or cancellation of the registration has been determined.]

Commencement 1 January 1973.
Amendments See the first note to Order 71, r 15.

[Order 71, r 22 Application to vary or cancel registration

An application for the variation or cancellation of the registration of a Community judgment on the ground that the judgment had been wholly or partly satisfied at the date of registration shall be made by summons supported by affidavit.]

Commencement 1 January 1973.
Amendments See the first note to Order 71, r 15.

[Order 71, r 23 Application for registration of suspension order

An application for the registration in the High Court of an order of the European Court that enforcement of a registered Community judgment be suspended may be made ex parte by lodging a copy of the order in the Central Office.]

Commencement 1 January 1973.
Amendments See the first note to Order 71, r 15.

[Order 71, r 24 Application for enforcement of Euratom inspection order

An application for an order under Article 6 of the Order in Council for the purpose of ensuring that effect is given to a Euratom inspection order may, in case of urgency, be made ex parte on affidavit but, except as aforesaid, shall be made by motion or summons.]]

Commencement 1 January 1973.
Amendments See the first note to Order 71, r 15.
Definitions Order in Council: European Communities (Enforcement of Community Judgments) Order 1972, SI 1972/1590.

[III RECIPROCAL ENFORCEMENT:
THE CIVIL JURISDICTION AND JUDGMENTS ACT 1982

Order 71, r 25 Interpretation

(1)   In this Part of this Order—
        "the Act of 1982" means the Civil Jurisdiction and Judgments Act 1982;
        "Convention territory" means the territory or territories of any Contracting
            State, as defined by section 1(3) of the Act of 1982, to which [the Brussels
            Conventions or the Lugano Convention] as defined in section 1(1) of the
            Act of 1982 apply;

"judgment" is to be construed in accordance with the definition of "judgment" in section 50 of the Act of 1982;

"money provision" means a provision for the payment of one or more sums of money;

"non-money provision" means a provision for any relief or remedy not requiring payment of a sum of money;

"protective measures" means the protective measures referred to in Article 39 of Schedule 1 [or of Schedule 3C] to the Act of 1982.

(2)   For the purposes of this Part of this Order domicile is to be determined in accordance with the provisions of sections 41 to 46 of the Act of 1982.]

Commencement   1 January 1987.
Amendments   Order 71, Pt III (rr 25–29) was added by SI 1983/1181, r 20.
Para (1): in definition "Convention territory" words "the Brussels Conventions or the Lugano Convention" substituted, and in definition "protective measures" words "or of Schedule 3C" inserted, by SI 1992/1907, rr 19, 20.

[Order 71, r 26 Assignment of business and exercise of powers

Any application to the High Court under the Act of 1982 shall be assigned to the Queen's Bench Division and the powers conferred on the Court by that Act shall be exercised in accordance with the provisions of Order 32, rule 11.]

Commencement   1 January 1987.
Amendments   See the first note to Order 71, r 25.
Definitions   Act of 1982: Civil Jurisdiction and Judgments Act 1982.

[Order 71, r 27 Application for registration

An application for registration of a judgment under section 4 of the Act of 1982 shall be made ex parte.]

Commencement   1 January 1987.
Amendments   See the first note to Order 71, r 25.
Definitions   Act of 1982: Civil Jurisdiction and Judgments Act 1982.
Forms   Application (PF159).

[Order 71, r 28 Evidence in support of application

(1)   An application for registration under section 4 of the Act of 1982 must be supported by an affidavit—
   (a) exhibiting—
      (i) the judgment or a verified or certified or otherwise duly authenticated copy thereof together with such other document or documents as may be requisite to show that, according to the law of the State in which it has been given, the judgment is enforceable and has been served;
      (ii) in the case of a judgment given in default, the original or a certified true copy of the document which establishes that the party in default was served with the document instituting the proceedings or with an equivalent document;
      (iii) where it is the case, a document showing that the party making the application is in receipt of legal aid in the State in which the judgment was given;

       (iv) where the judgment or document is not in the English language, a translation thereof into English certified by a notary public or a person qualified for the purpose in one of the Contracting States or authenticated by affidavit;

  (b) stating—

       (i) whether the judgment provides for the payment of a sum or sums of money;

       (ii) whether interest is recoverable on the judgment or part thereof in accordance with the law of the State in which the judgment was given, and if such be the case, the rate of interest, the date from which interest is recoverable, and the date on which interest ceases to accrue;

  (c) giving an address within the jurisdiction of the Court for service of process on the party making the application and stating, so far as is known to the deponent, the name and the usual or last known address or place of business of the person against whom judgment was given;

  (d) stating to the best of the information or belief of the deponent—

       (i) the grounds on which the right to enforce the judgment is vested in the party making the application;

       (ii) as the case may require, either that at the date of the application the judgment has not been satisfied, or the part or amount in respect of which it remains unsatisfied.

(2)   Where the party making the application does not produce the documents referred to in paragraphs (1)(a)(ii) and (iii) of this rule, the Court may—

  (a) fix a time within which the documents are to be produced; or

  (b) accept equivalent documents; or

  (c) dispense with production of the documents.]

Commencement 1 January 1987.
Amendments See the first note to Order 71, r 25.
Definitions Act of 1982: Civil Jurisdiction and Judgments Act 1982.

[Order 71, r 29 Security for costs

Notwithstanding the provisions of Order 23 a party making an application for registration under section 4 of the Act of 1982 shall not be required solely on the ground that he is not domiciled or resident within the jurisdiction, to give security for costs of the application.]

Commencement 1 January 1987.
Amendments See the first note to Order 71, r 25.
Definitions Act of 1982: Civil Jurisdiction and Judgments Act 1982.

[Order 71, r 30 Order for registration

(1)   An order giving leave to register a judgment under section 4 of the Act of 1982 must be drawn up by or on behalf of the party making the application for registration.

(2)   Every such order shall state the period within which an appeal may be made against the order for registration and shall contain a notification that execution on the judgment will not issue until after the expiration of that period.

(3)   The notification referred to in paragraph (2) shall not prevent any application for protective measures pending final determination of any issue relating to enforcement of the judgment.]

Commencement 1 January 1987.
Amendments See the first note to Order 71, r 25.
Definitions Act of 1982: Civil Jurisdiction and Judgments Act 1982.
Forms Order (PF160).

[Order 71, r 31 Register of judgments registered under s 4 of the Act of 1982

There shall be kept in the Central Office under the direction of the senior master a register of the judgments ordered to be registered under section 4 of the Act of 1982.]

Commencement 1 January 1987.
Amendments See the first note to Order 71, r 25.
Definitions Act of 1982: Civil Jurisdiction and Judgments Act 1982.

[Order 71, r 32 Notice of registration

(1)   Notice of the registration of a judgment must be served on the person against whom judgment was given by delivering it to him personally or by sending it to him at his usual or last known address or place of business or in such other manner as the Court may direct.

(2)   Service of such a notice out of the jurisdiction is permissible without leave, and Order 11, rules 5, 6 and 8, shall apply in relation to such a notice as they apply in relation to a writ.

(3)   The notice of registration must state—
    (a) full particulars of the judgment registered and the order for registration,
    (b) the name of the party making the application and his address for service within the jurisdiction,
    (c) the right of the person against whom judgment was given to appeal against the order for registration, and
    (d) the period within which an appeal against the order for registration may be made.]

Commencement 1 January 1987.
Amendments See the first note to Order 71, r 25.
Forms Notice of registration (PF161).

[Order 71, r 33 Appeals

(1)   An appeal under Article 37 or Article 40 of Schedule 1 [or 3C] to the Act of 1982 must be made by summons to a judge.

(2)   A summons in an appeal to which this rule applies must be served—
    (a) in the case of an appeal under the said Article 37 of Schedule 1 [or 3C], within one month of service of notice of registration of the judgment, or two months of service of such notice where that notice was served on a party not domiciled within the jurisdiction;
    (b) in the case of an appeal under the said Article 40 of Schedule 1 [or 3C], within one month of the determination of the application under rule 27.

(3)   If the party against whom judgment was given is not domiciled in a Convention territory and an application is made within two months of service of notice of registration, the Court may extend the period within which an appeal may be made against the order for registration.]

Commencement 1 January 1987.
Amendments See the first note to Order 71, r 25.
Paras (1), (2): words "or 3C" wherever they occur added by SI 1992/1907, r 21.
Definitions Act of 1982: Civil Jurisdiction and Judgments Act 1982.
Forms Summons (PF162).

[Order 71, r 34 Issue of execution

(1)   Execution shall not issue on a judgment registered under section 4 of the Act of 1982 until after the expiration of the period specified in accordance with rule 30(2) or, if that period has been extended by the Court, until after the expiration of the period so extended.

(2)   If an appeal is made under rule 33(1), execution on the judgment shall not issue until after such appeal is determined.

(3)   Any party wishing to issue execution on a judgment registered under section 4 of the Act of 1982 must produce to the proper officer an affidavit of service of the notice of registration of the judgment and of any order made by the Court in relation to the judgment.

(4)   Nothing in this rule shall prevent the Court from granting protective measures pending final determination of any issue relating to enforcement of the judgment.]

Commencement 1 January 1987.
Amendments See the first note to Order 71, r 25.
Definitions Act of 1982: Civil Jurisdiction and Judgments Act 1982.

[Order 71, r 35 Application for recognition

(1)   Registration of the judgment under these rules shall serve for the purposes of the second paragraph of Article 26 of Schedule 1 [or 3C] to the Act of 1982 as a decision that the judgment is recognised.

(2)   Where it is sought to apply for recognition of a judgment, the foregoing rules of this Order shall apply to such application as they apply to an application for registration under section 4 of the Act, with the exception that the applicant shall not be required to produce a document or documents which establish that according to the law of the State in which it has been given the judgment is enforceable and has been served, or the document referred to in rule 28(1)(a)(iii).]

Commencement 1 January 1987.
Amendments See the first note to Order 71, r 25.
Para (1): words "or 3C" inserted by SI 1992/1907, r 21.
Definitions Act of 1982: Civil Jurisdiction and Judgments Act 1982.

[Order 71, r 36 Enforcement of High Court judgments in other Contracting States

(1)   An application under section 12 of the Act of 1982 for a certified copy of a judgment entered in the High Court must be made ex parte on affidavit to the Court.

(2)   An affidavit by which an application under section 12 of the Act of 1982 is made must—

   (a)   give particulars of the proceedings in which the judgment was obtained;

   (b)   have annexed to it a copy of the writ, originating summons or other process by which the proceedings were begun, the evidence of service thereof on the defendant, copies of the pleadings, if any, and a statement of the grounds on which the judgment was based together, where appropriate, with any document under which the applicant is entitled to legal aid or assistance by way of representation for the purposes of the proceedings;

   (c)   state whether the defendant did or did not object to the jurisdiction, and, if so, on what grounds;

   (d)   show that the judgment has been served in accordance with Order 65, rule 5 and is not subject to any stay of execution;

   (e)   state that the time for appealing has expired, or, as the case may be, the date on which it will expire and in either case whether notice of appeal against the judgment has been given; and

   (f)   state—

      (i)   whether the judgment provides for the payment of a sum or sums of money;

      (ii)   whether interest is recoverable on the judgment or part thereof and if such be the case, the rate of interest, the date from which interest is recoverable, and the date on which interest ceases to accrue.

(3)   The certified copy of the judgment shall be an office copy sealed with the seal of the Supreme Court and there shall be issued with the copy of the judgment a certificate in Form 110, signed by one of the persons referred to in Order 1, rule 4(2) and sealed with the seal of the Supreme Court, having annexed to it a copy of the writ, originating summons or other process by which the proceedings were begun.]

Commencement 1 January 1987.
Amendments See the first note to Order 71, r 25.
Definitions Act of 1982: Civil Jurisdiction and Judgments Act 1982.
Forms Application (PF163).

[Order 71, r 37 Enforcement of United Kingdom judgments in other parts of the United Kingdom: money provisions

(1)   An application for registration in the High Court of a certificate in respect of any money provisions contained in a judgment given in another part of the United Kingdom to which section 18 of the Act of 1982 applies may be made by producing at the Central Office, within six months from the date of its issue, a certificate in the appropriate form prescribed under that Act together with a copy thereof certified by the applicant's solicitor to be a true copy.

(2)   A certificate under paragraph (1) must be filed in the Central Office and the certified copy thereof, sealed by an officer of the office in which the certificate is filed, shall be returned to the applicant's solicitor.

(3)   A certificate in respect of any money provisions contained in a judgment of the High Court to which section 18 of the Act of 1982 applies may be obtained by producing the form of certificate prescribed in Form 111 at the office in which the judgment is entered, together with an affidavit made by the party entitled to enforce the judgment—

   (a)   giving particulars of the judgment, stating the sum or aggregate of the sums (including any costs or expenses) payable and unsatisfied under the money provisions contained in the judgment, the rate of interest, if any, payable thereon and the date or time from which any such interest began to accrue;

(b) verifying that the time for appealing against the judgment has expired, or that any appeal brought has been finally disposed of and that enforcement of the judgment is not stayed or suspended; and

(c) stating to the best of the information or belief of the deponent the usual or last known address of the party entitled to enforce the judgment and of the party liable to execution on it.]

Commencement 1 January 1987.
Amendments See the first note to Order 71, r 25.
Definitions Act of 1982: Civil Jurisdiction and Judgments Act 1982.
Forms Application (PF164).

[Order 71, r 38 Enforcement of United Kingdom judgments in other parts of the United Kingdom: non-money provisions

(1)　An application for registration in the High Court of a judgment which contains non-money provisions, being a judgment given in another part of the United Kingdom to which section 18 of the Act of 1982 applies, may be made ex parte, but the Court hearing the application may direct the issue of a summons to which paragraphs (2) and (3) of rule 2 shall apply.

(2)　An application under paragraph (1) must be accompanied by a certified copy of the judgment issued under Schedule 7 to the Act of 1982 and a certificate in [the appropriate form prescribed for the purposes of paragraph 4(1)(b) of that Schedule] issued not more than six months before the date of application.

(3)　Rules 30 and 32 of this Order shall apply to judgments registered under Schedule 7 to the Act of 1982 as they apply to judgments registered under section 4 of that Act.

(4)　Paragraphs (1) and (2) of rule 9 shall apply to applications to set aside registration of a judgment under Schedule 7 to the Act of 1982 as they apply to judgments registered under the Administration of Justice Act 1920 and the Foreign Judgments (Reciprocal Enforcements) Act 1933.

(5)　A certified copy of a judgment of the High Court to which section 18 of the Act of 1982 applies and which contains any non-money provision may be obtained by an ex parte application on affidavit to the Court.

(6)　The requirements in paragraph (3) of rule 37 shall apply with the necessary modifications to an affidavit made in an application under paragraph (5) of this rule.

[(7)　A certified copy of a judgment shall be an office copy sealed with the seal of the Supreme Court to which shall be annexed a certificate in Form 112.]]

Commencement 1 January 1987.
Amendments See the first note to Order 71, r 25.
Para (2): words from "the appropriate form" to "that Schedule" substituted by SI 1984/1051, r 14.
Para (7): substituted by SI 1984/1051, r 15.
Definitions Act of 1982: Civil Jurisdiction and Judgments Act 1982.
Forms Application (PF165).

[Order 71, r 39 Register of United Kingdom judgments

There shall be kept in the Central Office under the direction of the senior master a register of the certificates in respect of judgments and of the judgments ordered to be registered in the Central Office under Schedule 6, or, as the case may be, Schedule 7 to the Act.]

Commencement 1 January 1987.
Amendments See the first note to Order 71, r 25.
Definitions The Act: Supreme Court Act 1981.

[Order 71, r 39A Authentic Instruments and Court Settlements

Rules 27 to 35 inclusive (except rule 28(1)(a)(ii)) shall apply to:
  (1)   an authentic instrument to which either article 50 of Schedule 1 to the Act of 1982 or article 50 of Schedule 3C to that Act applies; and
  (2)   a settlement to which either article 51 of Schedule 1 to the Act of 1982 or article 51 of Schedule 3C to that Act applies,

as they apply to a judgment, subject to any necessary modifications.]

Commencement 1 October 1993.
Amendments This rule was added by SI 1993/2133, r 10.
Definitions Act of 1982: Civil Jurisdiction and Judgments Act 1982.

[IV   Enforcement of Recommendations etc under the Merchant Shipping (Liner Conferences) Act 1982

Order 71, r 40 Exercise of powers

The powers conferred on the High Court under the Merchant Shipping (Liner Conferences) Act 1982 (in this Part of this Order referred to as "the Act of 1982") may be exercised by a Commercial Judge.]

Commencement 28 April 1986.
Amendments Order 71, Pt IV (rr 40–44) was added by SI 1986/632, r 22.

[Order 71, r 41 Application for Registration

An application under section 9 of the Act of 1982 for the registration of a recommendation, determination or award shall be made by originating summons, which shall be in Form No 10 in Appendix A.]

Commencement 28 April 1986.
Amendments See the note to Order 71, r 40.
Definitions Act of 1982: Merchant Shipping (Liner Conferences) Act 1982.

[Order 71, r 42 Evidence in support of application

(1)   An application under section 9 of the Act of 1982 for the registration of a recommendation must be supported by an affidavit—
  (a)   exhibiting a verified or certified or otherwise duly authenticated copy of the recommendation and the reasons therefor and of the record of settlement;
  (b)   where the recommendation and reasons or the record of settlement is not in the English language, a translation thereof into English certified by a notary public or authenticated by affidavit;
  (c)   exhibiting copies of the acceptance of the recommendation by the parties upon whom it is binding, where the acceptance was in writing, or otherwise verifying the acceptance;

(d) giving particulars of the failure to implement the recommendation; and

(e) verifying that none of the grounds which would render the recommendation unenforceable under section 9(2) of the Act of 1982 is applicable.

(2) An application under section 9 of the Act of 1982 for the registration of a determination or award as to costs must be supported by an affidavit—

(a) exhibiting a verified or certified or otherwise duly authenticated copy of the recommendation or other document containing the pronouncement on costs; and

(b) stating that such costs have not been paid.]

Commencement 28 April 1986.
Amendments See the note to Order 71, r 40.
Definitions Act of 1982: Merchant Shipping (Liner Conferences) Act 1982.

[Order 71, r 43 Order for registration

(1) An order giving leave to register a recommendation, determination or award under section 9 of the Act of 1982 must be drawn up by or on behalf of the party making the application for registration.

(2) Such an order shall contain a provision that the reasonable costs of registration be taxed.]

Commencement 28 April 1986.
Amendments See the note to Order 71, r 40.
Definitions Act of 1982: Merchant Shipping (Liner Conferences) Act 1982.

[Order 71, r 44 Register of recommendations etc

(1) There shall be kept [in the Admiralty and Commercial Registry under the direction of the Senior Master] a register of the recommendations, determinations and awards ordered to be registered under section 9 of the Act of 1982.

(2) There shall be included in such register particulars of the enforcement of a recommendation, determination or award so registered.]

Commencement 28 April 1986.
Amendments See the note to Order 71, r 40.
Para (1): words from "in the Admiralty" to "Senior Master" substituted by SI 1987/1423, r 16.
Definitions Act of 1982: Merchant Shipping (Liner Conferences) Act 1982.

SPECIAL PROVISIONS AS TO PARTICULAR PROCEEDINGS

ORDER 72
COMMERCIAL ACTIONS . . .

Amendments Words omitted revoked by SI 1971/1269, r 23(1).

Order 72, r 1 Application and interpretation

(1)   This Order applies to commercial actions in the Queen's Bench Division, and the other provisions of these rules apply to those actions subject to the provisions of this Order.

(2)   In this Order "commercial action" includes any cause arising out of the ordinary transactions of merchants and traders and, without prejudice to the generality of the foregoing words, any cause relating to the construction of a mercantile document, the export or import of merchandise, affreightment, insurance, banking, mercantile agency and mercantile usage.

Commencement 1 October 1966.

Order 72, r 2 The Commercial List

(1)   There shall be a list, which shall be called "the commercial list", in which commercial actions in the Queen's Bench Division may be entered in accordance with the provisions of this Order [for trial in the Commercial Court, and one of the Commercial Judges shall be in charge of that list].

(2)   In this Order references to the judge shall be construed as references to the judge for the time being in charge of the commercial list.

(3)   The judge shall have control of the actions in the commercial list and, subject to the provisions of this Order and to any directions of the judge, the powers of a judge in chambers (including those exercisable by a master or registrar [district judge]) shall, [in relation to any proceedings] [in such an action (including any appeal from any judgment, order or decision of a master or registrar [district judge], given or made prior to transfer of the action to the commercial list), be exercisable by the judge.]

(4)   Paragraph (3) shall not be construed as preventing the powers of the judge being exercised by some other judge.

Commencement 1 October 1966.
Amendments Para (1): words from "for trial" to "that list" substituted by SI 1971/1269, r 23(2).
Para (3): words "in relation to any proceedings" substituted by SI 1971/354, r 4, words from "in such an action" to "the judge" substituted by SI 1982/1786, r 19(1).

Order 72, r 3 Powers, etc of Liverpool and Manchester [district judges]

(1)   All interlocutory applications in an action in the commercial list proceeding in the district registry of Liverpool or the district registry of Manchester, other than an application under rule 6, must be made to the [district judge] of that registry notwithstanding that the action is in the commercial list, and the [district judge] may make such order on any such application as he thinks fit or may adjourn the application to be heard by the judge:

Provided that if any party to any such application requests the [district judge] to adjourn the application to the judge for hearing by him the [district judge] shall adjourn it accordingly.

(2)   It shall be the duty of the [district judge] of each of the said registries to keep the judge's clerk informed of the progress of actions in the commercial list proceeding in that registry and, in particular, to inform him of the making of an order that such an action shall be tried at Liverpool or Manchester, as the case may be, and of the date fixed for the trial.

Commencement 1 October 1966.

Order 72, r 4 Entry of action in commercial list when action begun

(1)   Before a writ or originating summons by which a commercial action in the Queen's Bench Division is to be begun is issued out of [the Admiralty and Commercial Registry], the district registry of Liverpool or the district registry of Manchester, it may be marked in the top left hand corner with the words ["Commercial Court"], and on the issue of a writ or summons so marked the action begun thereby shall be entered in the commercial list.

(2)   If the plaintiff intends to issue the writ or originating summons by which a commercial action in the Queen's Bench Division is to be begun out of [the Admiralty and Commercial Registry] and to mark it in accordance with paragraph (1), and the writ, . . . or the originating summons, as the case may be, is to be served out of the jurisdiction, an application for leave to issue the writ or summons and to serve the writ . . . or the summons out of the jurisdiction may be made to the judge.

(3)   The affidavit in support of an application made to the judge by virtue of paragraph (2) must, in addition to the matters required by Order 11, rule 4(1), to be stated, state that the plaintiff intends to mark the writ or originating summons in accordance with paragraph (1) of this rule.

(4)   If the judge hearing an application made to him by virtue of paragraph (2) is of opinion that the action in question should not be entered in the commercial list, he may adjourn the application to be heard by a master.

Commencement 1 October 1966.
Amendments Para (1): words "the Admiralty and Commercial Registry" substituted by SI 1987/1423, r 17; words ""Commercial Court"" substituted by SI 1971/1269, r 23(3).
Para (2): words "the Admiralty and Commercial Registry" substituted by SI 1987/1423, r 17; words omitted revoked by SI 1980/2000, r 21.

Order 72, r 5 Transfer of action to commercial list after action begun

(1)   At any stage of the proceedings in a commercial action in the Queen's Bench Division . . . any party to the action may apply by summons to the judge or, if the action is proceeding in the district registry of Liverpool or the district registry of Manchester, to the [district judge] of that registry to transfer the action to the commercial list.

(2)   Where an application under paragraph (1) is made to the [district judge] of either of the said registries, the [district judge] may either order the action to be transferred to the commercial list or adjourn the summons to be heard by the judge.

(3)   If, [at any stage of the proceedings] in a commercial action in the Queen's Bench Division, it appears to the Court that the action may be one suitable for trial

in the [Commercial Court] and any party wishes the action to be transferred to [the commercial list], then, subject to paragraph (4), the Court may [adjourn any hearing so that it can proceed before the judge and be treated] by him as a summons to transfer the action to that list.

(4)   The [district judge] of the District registry of Liverpool or the district registry of Manchester may, instead of adjourning a summons under paragraph (3), order the action to be transferred to the commercial list; and if on the hearing of any summons in a commercial action in the Queen's Bench Division by the [district judge] of any district registry any party requests the [district judge] to adjourn the summons under paragraph (3) so that it can be heard by the judge, the [district judge] shall adjourn the summons accordingly, and the adjourned summons shall be treated by the judge as a summons to transfer the action to the commercial list.

(5)   Where the judge orders a commercial action in the Queen's Bench Division proceeding in a district registry to be transferred to the commercial list he may also order the action to be transferred to the Royal Courts of Justice.

Commencement 1 October 1966.
Amendments Para (1): words omitted revoked by SI 1982/1786, r 19(2).
Para (3): words "at any stage of the proceedings" and words from "adjourn any hearing" to "be treated" substituted by SI 1982/1786, r 19(3); words "Commercial Court" and "the commercial list" substituted by SI 1971/1269, r 23(4).

Order 72, r 6 Removal of action from commercial list

(1)   The judge may, of his own motion or on the application of any party, order an action in the commercial list to be removed from that list.

(2)   Where an action is in the commercial list by virtue of rule 4, an application by a defendant or third party for an order under this rule must be made within 7 days after [giving notice of intention to defend] the action.

Commencement 1 October 1966.
Amendments Para (2): words "giving notice of intention to defend" substituted by SI 1979/1716, r 48, Schedule, Pt 1.

Order 72, r 7 Pleadings in commercial list actions

(1)   The pleadings in an action in the commercial list must be in the form of points of claim, or of defence, counterclaim, defence to counterclaim or reply, as the case may be, and must be as brief as possible.

(2)   Without prejudice to Order 18, rule 12(1), no particulars shall be applied for or ordered in an action in the commercial list except such particulars as are necessary to enable the party applying to be informed of the case he has to meet or as are for some other reason necessary to secure the just, expeditious and economical disposal of any question at issue in the action.

(3)   The foregoing provisions are without prejudice to the power of the judge or of the [district judge] of Liverpool or the [district judge] of Manchester to order that an action in the commercial list shall be tried without pleadings or further pleadings, as the case may be.

Commencement 1 October 1966.

Order 72, r 8 Directions in commercial list actions

(1)   Notwithstanding anything in Order 25, rule 1(1), any party to an action in the commercial list may take out a summons for directions in the action before the pleadings in the action are deemed to be closed.

(2)   Where an application is made to transfer an action to the commercial list, Order 25, rules 2 to 7, shall, with the omission of so much of rule 7(1) as requires the parties to serve a notice specifying the orders and directions which they desire and with any other necessary modifications, apply as if the application were a summons for directions.

Commencement 1 October 1966.

Order 72, r 9 *(revoked by SI 1971/1955)*

Order 72, r 10 Production of certain documents in marine insurance actions

(1)   Where in an action in the commercial list relating to a marine insurance policy an application for an order under Order 24, rule 3, is made by the insurer, then, without prejudice to its powers under that rule, the Court, if satisfied that the circumstances of the case are such that it is necessary or expedient to do so, may make an order, either in Form No 94 in Appendix A or in such other form as it thinks fit, for the production of such documents as are therein specified or described.

(2)   An order under this rule may be made on such terms, if any, as to staying proceedings in the action or otherwise, as the Court thinks fit.

(3)   In this rule "the Court" means the judge, the [district judge] of Liverpool or the [district judge] of Manchester, as the case may be.

Commencement 1 October 1966.

[Order 72, r 11 Admiralty and Commercial Registry

(1)   In the application of Order 28, rule 2 to commercial actions begun by originating summons, the reference to the Central Office shall have effect as a reference to the Admiralty and Commercial Registry.

(2)   Order 38, rule 14 shall apply in relation to the issue of a writ of subpoena ad testificandum or subpoena duces tecum in a commercial action as if for references therein to the Central Office there were substituted references to the Admiralty and Commercial Registry.

(3)   Order 39 and Form Nos 31, 32 and 34 in Appendix A shall apply in relation to a commercial action as if for references therein to the Central Office (except the references in rule 3) there were substituted references to the Admiralty and Commercial Registry.

(4)   Order 63, rules 3 and 4 shall apply in relation to documents filed in the Admiralty and Commercial Registry as they apply in relation to documents filed in the Central Office.]

Commencement 2 November 1987.
Amendments This rule was added by SI 1987/1423, r 18.

ORDER 73
ARBITRATION PROCEEDINGS

Order 73, r 1   *(revoked by SI 1983/1181)*

Order 73, r 2 Matters for a judge in court

(1)   Every application to the Court—
   (a)   to remit an award under section 22 of the Arbitration Act 1950, or
   (b)   to remove an arbitrator or umpire under section 23(1) of that Act, or
   (c)   to set aside an award under section 23(2) thereof[, or
   (d)   ...
   (e)   to determine, under [section 2(1) of the Arbitration Act 1979], any question of law arising in the course of a reference,]

must be made by originating motion to a single judge in court.

[(2)   Any appeal to the High Court under section 1(2) of the Arbitration Act 1979 shall be made by originating motion to a single judge in court . . . .]

(3)   An application for a declaration that an award made by an arbitrator or umpire is not binding on a party to the award on the ground that it was made without jurisdiction may be made by originating motion to a single judge in court, but the foregoing provision shall not be taken as affecting the judge's power to refuse to make such a declaration in proceedings begun by motion.

Commencement   1 August 1979 (para (2)); 1 October 1966 (remainder).
Amendments   Para (1): in sub-para (c) word ", or" added, and sub-paras (d), (e) inserted, by SI 1979/522, r 6(1); sub-para (d) subsequently revoked by SI 1983/1181, r 32; in sub-para (e) words "section 2(1) of the Arbitration Act 1979" substituted by SI 1986/632, r 23(1).
Para (2): substituted by SI 1979/522, r 6(2); words omitted revoked by SI 1986/632, r 23(2).

Order 73, r 3 Matters for judge in chambers or master

(1)   Subject to the foregoing provisions of this Order [and the provisions of this rule], the jurisdiction of the High Court or a judge thereof under the Arbitration Act 1950 [and the jurisdiction of the High Court under the Arbitration Act 1975] [and the Arbitration Act 1979] may be exercised by a judge in chambers, a master or the Admiralty registrar.

[[(2)   Any application
   (a)   for leave to appeal under section 1(2) of the Arbitration Act 1979, or
   (b)   under section 1(5) of that Act (including any application for leave), or
   (c)   under section 5 of that Act,
shall be made to a judge in chambers.]

(3)   Any application to which this rule applies shall, where an action is pending, be made by summons in the action, and in any other case by an originating summons [which shall be in Form No 10 in Appendix A].

(4)   Where an application is made under section 1(5) of the Arbitration Act 1979 (including any application for leave), the summons must be served on the arbitrator or umpire and on any other party to the reference.]

Commencement 1 October 1983 (para (2)); 1 August 1979 (paras (3), (4)); 1 October 1966 (remainder).
Amendments Para (1): words "and the provisions of this rule" and "and the Arbitration Act 1979" inserted by SI 1979/522, r 7(1); words "and the jurisdiction of the High Court under the Arbitration Act 1975" inserted by SI 1977/1955, r 9(1).
Para (2): substituted, together with paras (3), (4), for paras (2), (3) as originally enacted, by SI 1979/522, r 7(2), further substituted by SI 1983/1181, r 32.
Para (3): substituted, together with paras (2), (4), for paras (2), (3) as originally enacted, by SI 1979/522, r 7(2); words "which shall be in Form No 10 in Appendix A" substituted by SI 1979/1716, r 48, Schedule, Pt 2.
Para (4): substituted, together with paras (2), (3), for paras (2), (3) as originally enacted, by SI 1979/522, r 7(2).

Order 73, r 4 Applications in district registries

An application under section 12(4) of the Arbitration Act 1950 for an order that a writ of subpoena ad testificandum or of subpoena duces tecum shall issue to compel the attendance before an arbitrator or umpire of a witness may, if the attendance of the witness is required within the district of any district registry, be made at that registry, instead of at [the Admiralty and Commercial Registry], at the option of the applicant.

Commencement 1 October 1966.
Amendments Words "the Admiralty and Commercial Registry" substituted by SI 1987/1423, r 19.

[Order 73, r 5 Time-limits and other special provisions as to appeals and applications under the Arbitration Acts

(1)   An application to the Court—
    (a)   to remit an award under section 22 of the Arbitration Act 1950, or
    (b)   to set aside an award under section 23(2) of that Act or otherwise, or
    (c)   to direct an arbitrator or umpire to state the reasons for an award under section 1(5) of the Arbitration Act 1979,

must be made, and the summons or notice must be served, within 21 days after the award has been made and published to the parties.

(2)   In the case of an appeal to the Court under section 1(2) of the Arbitration Act 1979, [the summons for leave to appeal, where leave is required, and the notice of originating motion must be served, and the appeal entered,] within 21 days after the award has been made and published to the parties:

Provided that, where reasons material to the appeal are given on a date subsequent to the publication of the award, the period of 21 days shall run from the date on which the reasons are given.

(3)   An application, under section 2(1) of the Arbitration Act 1979, to determine any question of law arising in the course of a reference, must be made, and notice thereof served, within 14 days after the arbitrator or umpire has consented to the application being made, or the other parties have so consented.

(4)   For the purpose of paragraph (3) the consent must be given in writing.

(5)   In the case of every appeal or application to which this rule applies, [the notice of originating motion, the originating summons or the summons, as the case may be] must state the grounds of the appeal or application and, where the appeal or application is founded on evidence by affidavit, or is made with the consent of the

arbitrator or umpire or of the other parties, a copy of every affidavit intended to be used, or, as the case may be, of every consent given in writing, must be served with that notice.

[(6)   Without prejudice to paragraph (5), in an appeal under section 1(2) of the Arbitration Act 1979 the statement of the grounds of the appeal shall specify the relevant parts of the award and reasons, and a copy of the award and reasons, or the relevant parts thereof, shall be lodged with the court and served with the notice of originating motion.

(7)   Without prejudice to paragraph (5), in an application for leave to appeal under section 1(2) of the Arbitration Act 1979, any affidavit verifying the facts in support of a contention that the question of law concerns a term of a contract or an event which is not a one-off term or event must be lodged with the court and served with the notice of originating motion.

(8)   Any affidavit in reply to an affidavit under paragraph (7) shall be lodged with the court and served on the applicant not less than two clear days before the hearing of the application.

(9)   A respondent to an application for leave to appeal under section 1(2) of the Arbitration Act 1979 who desires to contend that the award should be upheld on grounds not expressed or not fully expressed in the award and reasons shall not less than two clear days before the hearing of the application lodge with the court and serve on the applicant a notice specifying the grounds of his contention.]]

Commencement   12 January 1987 (paras (6)–(9)); 1 August 1979 (remainder).
Amendments   This rule was substituted by SI 1979/522, r 8.
Para (2): words from "the summons" to "appeal entered," substituted by SI 1986/632, r 23(3).
Para (5): words from "the notice" to "case may be" substituted by SI 1986/632, r 23(4).
Paras (6)–(9): added by SI 1986/2289, r 7.

[Order 73, r 6 Applications and appeals to be heard by Commercial Judges

(1)   Any matter which is required, by rule 2 or 3, to be heard by a judge, shall be heard by a Commercial Judge, unless any such judge otherwise directs.

(2)   Nothing in the foregoing paragraph shall be construed as preventing the powers of a Commercial Judge from being exercised by any judge of the High Court.]

Commencement   1 August 1979.
Amendments   This rule was substituted by SI 1979/522, r 8.

Order 73, r 7 Service out of the jurisdiction of summons, notice, etc

[(1)   Subject to paragraph (1A), service out of the jurisdiction—
   (a)   any originating summons or notice of originating motion under the Arbitration Act 1950 or the Arbitration Act 1979, or
   (b)   any order made on such a summons or motion as aforesaid,

is permissible with the leave of the Court provided that the arbitration to which the summons, motion or order relates is governed by English law or has been, is being, or is to be held within the jurisdiction.]

(1A)   Service out of the jurisdiction of an originating summons for leave to enforce an award is permissible with the leave of the Court whether or not the arbitration is governed by English law.]

(2)   An application for the grant of leave under this rule must be supported by an affidavit stating the grounds on which the application is made and showing in what place or country the person to be served is, or probably may be found; and no such leave shall be granted unless it shall be made sufficiently to appear to the Court that the case is a proper one for service out of the jurisdiction under this rule.

(3)   Order 11, rules 5, 6 and 8, shall apply in relation to any such summons, notice or order as is referred to in paragraph (1) as they apply in relation to . . . a writ.

Commencement   1 October 1987 (para (1)); 1 January 1987 (para (1A)); 1 October 1966 (remainder).
Amendments   Para (1): substituted by SI 1987/1423, r 60.
Para (1A): inserted by SI 1983/1181, r 15.
Para (3): words omitted revoked by SI 1980/2000, r 21.

Order 73, r 8 Registration in High Court of foreign awards

Where an award is made in proceedings on an arbitration in any part of Her Majesty's dominions or other territory to which Part I of the Foreign Judgments (Reciprocal Enforcement) Act 1933 extends, being a part to which Part II of the Administration of Justice Act 1920 extended immediately before the said Part I was extended thereto, then, if the award has, in pursuance of the law in force in the place where it was made, become enforceable in the same manner as a judgment given by a court in that place, Order 71 shall apply in relation to the award as it applies in relation to a judgment given by that court, subject, however, to the following modifications:—

    (a) for references to the country of the original court there shall be substituted references to the place where the award was made; and

    (b) the affidavit required by rule 3 of the said Order must state (in addition to the other matters required by that rule) that to the best of the information or belief of the deponent the award has, in pursuance of the law in force in the place where it was made, become enforceable in the same manner as a judgment given by a court in that place.

Commencement   1 October 1966.

[Order 73, r 9 Registration of awards under Arbitration (International Investment Disputes) Act 1966

(1)   In this rule and in any provision of these rules as applied by this rule—
    "the Act of 1966" means the Arbitration (International Investment Disputes) Act 1966;
    "award" means an award rendered pursuant to the Convention;
    "the Convention" means the Convention referred to in section 1(1) of the Act of 1966;
    "judgment creditor" and "judgment debtor" mean respectively the person seeking recognition or enforcement of an award and the other party to the award.

(2)   Subject to the provisions of this rule, the following provisions of Order 71, namely rules 1, 3(1) (except sub-paragraphs (c)(iv) and (d) thereof) . . . , 7 (except paragraph (3)(c) and (d) thereof) . . . and 10(3), shall apply with the necessary modifications in relation to an award as they apply in relation to a judgment to which Part II of the Foreign Judgments (Reciprocal Enforcement) Act 1933 applies.

(3)   An application to have an award registered in the High Court under section 1 of the Act of 1966 shall be made by originating summons [which shall be in Form No 10 in Appendix A].

(4)   The affidavit required by Order 71, rule 3, in support of an application for registration shall—

    (a)   in lieu of exhibiting the judgment or a copy thereof, exhibit a copy of the award certified pursuant to the Convention, and

    (b)   in addition to stating the matters mentioned in paragraph 3(1)(c)(i) and (ii) of the said rule 3, state whether at the date of the application the enforcement of the award has been stayed (provisionally or otherwise), pursuant to the Convention and whether any, and if so what, application has been made pursuant to the Convention which, if granted, might result in a stay of the enforcement of the award.

(5)   There shall be kept [in the Admiralty and Commercial Registry under the direction of the Senior Master] a register of the awards ordered to be registered under the Act of 1966 and particulars shall be entered in the register of any execution issued on such an award.

(6)   Where it appears to the Court on granting leave to register an award or on an application made by the judgment debtor after an award has been registered—

    (a)   that the enforcement of the award has been stayed (whether provisionally or otherwise) pursuant to the Convention, or

    (b)   that an application has been made pursuant to the Convention which, if granted, might result in a stay of the enforcement of the award,

the Court shall, or, in the case referred to in sub-paragraph (b), may, stay execution of the award for such time as it considers appropriate in the circumstances.

(7)   An application by the judgment debtor under paragraph (6) shall be made by summons and supported by affidavit.]

Commencement   1 September 1968.
Amendments   This rule was added by SI 1968/1244, r 16.
Para (2): first words omitted revoked by SI 1977/1955, r 9(2); second words omitted revoked by SI 1982/1111, r 115, Schedule.
Para (3): words "which shall be in Form No 10 in Appendix A" substituted by SI 1979/1716, r 48, Schedule, Pt 2.
Para (5): words from "in the Admiralty" to "Senior Master" substituted by SI 1987/1423, r 20.

[Order 73, r 9A Registration of awards under Multilateral Investment Guarantee Agency Act 1988

Rule 9 shall apply, with the necessary modifications, in relation to an award rendered pursuant to the Convention referred to in section 1(1) of the Multilateral Guarantee Agency Act 1988 as it applies in relation to an award rendered pursuant to the Convention referred to in section 1(1) of the Arbitration (International Investment Disputes) Act 1966.]

Commencement   1 October 1988.
Amendments   This rule was inserted by SI 1988/1340, r 12.

[Order 73, r 10 [Enforcement of arbitration awards]

(1)   An application for leave under section 26 of the Arbitration Act 1950 [or under

section 3(1)(a) of the Arbitration Act 1975] to enforce an award on an arbitration agreement in the same manner as a judgment or order may be made ex parte but the Court hearing the application may direct a summons to be issued.

(2)   If the Court directs a summons to be issued, the summons shall be an originating summons [which shall be in Form No 10 in Appendix A].

(3)   An application for leave must be supported by affidavit—
  [(a) exhibiting—
    (i)   where the application is under section 26 of the Arbitration Act 1950, the arbitration agreement and the original award or, in either case, a copy thereof;
    (ii) where the application is under section 3(1)(a) of the Arbitration Act 1975, the documents required to be produced by section 4 of that Act,]
  (b) stating the name and the usual or last known place of abode or business of the applicant (hereinafter referred to as "the creditor") and the person against whom it is sought to enforce the award (hereinafter referred to as "the debtor") respectively,
  (c) as the case may require, either that the award has not been complied with or the extent to which it has not been compiled with at the date of the application.

(4)   An order giving leave must be drawn up by or on behalf of the creditor and must be served on the debtor by delivering a copy to him personally or by sending a copy to him at his usual or last known place of abode or business or in such other manner as the Court may direct.

(5)   Service of the order out of the jurisdiction is permissible without leave, and Order 11, rules 5, 6 and 8, shall apply in relation to such an order as they apply in relation to . . . a writ.

(6)   Within 14 days after service of the order or, if the order is to be served out of the jurisdiction, within such other period as the Court may fix, the debtor may apply to set aside the order and the award shall not be enforced until after the expiration of that period or, if the debtor applies within the period to set aside the order, until after the application is finally disposed of.

(7)   The copy of the order served on the debtor shall state the effect of paragraph (6).

(8)   In relation to a body corporate this rule shall have effect as if for any reference to the place of abode or business of the creditor or the debtor there were substituted a reference to the registered or principal address of the body corporate; so, however, that nothing in this rule shall affect any enactment which provides for the manner in which a document may be served on a body corporate.]

Commencement   1 September 1978.
Amendments   This rule was added by SI 1978/1066, r 4.
Rule heading: substituted by SI 1979/35, r 7(1).
Para (1): words "or under section 3(1)(a) of the Arbitration Act 1975" inserted by SI 1979/35, r 7(2).
Para (2): words "which shall be in Form No 10 in Appendix A" substituted by SI 1979/1716, r 48, Schedule, Pt 2.
Para (3): sub-para (a) substituted by SI 1979/35, r 7(3).
Para (5): words omitted revoked by SI 1980/2000, r 21.

[ORDER 74

APPLICATIONS AND APPEALS UNDER THE MERCHANT SHIPPING ACTS 1894 TO 1979

Order 74, r 1 Assignment of proceedings

(1)   Subject to paragraph (2), proceedings by which any application is made to the High Court under the Merchant Shipping Acts 1894 to 1979 shall be assigned to the Queen's Bench Division and taken by the Admiralty Court.

(2)   Proceedings by which an application under section 55 of the Merchant Shipping Act 1894 is made shall be assigned to the Chancery Division.]

Commencement   1 May 1983.
Amendments   Order 74 was substituted by SI 1983/531, r 3.

[Order 74, r 2 Appeals and re-hearings

(1)   An appeal to the High Court under section 28 of the Pilotage Act 1913 against a decision of a county court judge or a magistrate shall be heard and determined by a Divisional Court of the Queen's Bench Division constituted so far as practicable of Admiralty Judges.

(2)   Subject to the provisions of this rule, Orders 55 and 57 shall apply in relation to an appeal to the High Court under the Merchant Shipping Acts 1894 to 1979 and for this purpose a re-hearing and an application under section 52(2) of the Merchant Shipping Act 1970 shall be treated as an appeal.

(3)   In the case of an appeal to which paragraph (2) applies, the documents required to be lodged before entry for the purposes of Order 57, rule 2(1) shall include the report, if any, to the Secretary of State containing the decision from which the appeal is brought.

(4)   Where a re-hearing by the High Court is ordered under section 57 of the Merchant Shipping Act 1970 the Secretary of State shall cause such reasonable notice to be given to the parties whom he considers to be affected by the re-hearing as the circumstances of the case may, in his opinion, permit.]

Commencement   1 May 1983.
Amendments   See the note to Order 74, r 1.

ORDER 75
ADMIRALTY PROCEEDINGS

Order 75, r 1 Application and interpretation

(1) This Order applies to Admiralty causes and matters, and the other provisions of these rules apply to those causes and matters subject to the provisions of this Order.

(2) In this Order—

"action in rem" means an Admiralty action in rem;

"caveat against arrest" means a caveat entered in the caveat book under rule 6;

"caveat against release and payment" means a caveat entered in the caveat book under rule 14;

"caveat book" means the book kept in the registry in which caveats issued under this Order are entered;

"limitation action" means an action by shipowners or other persons under [the Merchant Shipping Act 1979] for the limitation of the amount of their liability in connection with a ship or other property;

"marshal" means the Admiralty marshal;

"registry" (except where the context otherwise requires) means the [Admiralty and Commercial Registry];

"ship" includes any description of vessel used in navigation.

Commencement 1 October 1966.
Amendments Para (2): in definition "limitation action" words "the Merchant Shipping Act 1979" substituted by SI 1986/2289, r 8(1); in definition "registry" words "Admiralty and Commercial Registry" substituted by SI 1987/1423, r 2.
Cross references See CCR Order 40, r 1.

Order 75, r 2 Certain actions to be assigned to Admiralty

(1) Without prejudice to [section 61 and 62(2) of the [Act]], or to any other enactment or rule providing for the assignment of causes and matters to the [Queen's Bench Division]—

(a) every action to enforce a claim for damage, loss of life or personal injury arising out of—

(i) a collision between ships, or

(ii) the carrying out of or omission to carry out a manoeuvre in the case of one or more of two or more ships, or

(iii) non-compliance, on the part of one or more of two or more ships, with the collision regulations, ...

(b) every limitation action, [and

(c) every action to enforce a claim under section 1 of the Merchant Shipping (Oil Pollution) Act 1971 or section 4 of the Merchant Shipping Act 1974.]

shall be assigned to that Division [and taken by the Admiralty Court].

[(2) In this rule "collision regulations" means regulations under section 418 of the Merchant Shipping Act 1894 or section 21 of the Merchant Shipping Act 1979, or any such rules as are mentioned in subsection (1) of section 421 of the Act of 1894 or any rules made under subsection (2) of the said section 421.]

Commencement 1 October 1984 (para (2)); 1 October 1966 (remainder).
Amendments Para (1): words in square brackets beginning with the words "section 61" substituted by SI 1981/1734, r 36, word "Act" therein substituted by SI 1982/1111, r 115, Schedule; words "Queen's Bench

Division" substituted and words "and taken by the Admiralty Court" added by SI 1971/1269, r 25(2); word omitted revoked and sub-para (c) and word "and" immediately preceding it inserted by SI 1979/522, r 10(1).

Para (2): substituted by SI 1984/1051, r 17.

Definitions   The Act: Supreme Court Act 1981.

[Order 75, r 2A Proceedings against, or concerning, the International Oil Pollution Compensation Fund

(1)   All proceedings against the International Oil Pollution Compensation Fund (in this rule referred to as "the Fund") under section 4 of the Merchant Shipping Act 1974 shall be commenced in [the registry].

(2)   For the purposes of section 6(2) of the Merchant Shipping Act 1974, any party to proceedings brought against an owner or guarantor in respect of liability under section 1 of the Merchant Shipping (Oil Pollution) Act 1971 may give notice to the Fund of such proceedings by serving a notice in writing on the Fund together with a copy of the writ and copies of the pleadings (if any) served in the action.

(3)   The Court shall, on the application made ex parte by the Fund, grant leave to the Fund to intervene in any proceedings to which the preceding paragraph applies, whether notice of such proceedings has been served on the Fund or not, and paragraphs (3) and (4) of rule 17 shall apply to such an application.

(4)   Where judgment is given against the Fund in any proceedings under section 4 of the Merchant Shipping Act 1974, the registrar shall cause a stamped copy of the judgment to be sent by post to the Fund.

(5)   The Fund shall notify the registrar of the matters set out in section 4(12)(b) of the Merchant Shipping Act 1974 by a notice in writing, sent by post to, or delivered at, the registry.]

Commencement   7 June 1979.

Amendments   This rule was inserted by SI 1979/522, r 10(2).

Para (1): words "the registry" substituted by SI 1987/1423, r 21.

Order 75, r 3 Issue of writ and [acknowledgment of service]

(1)   An action in rem must be begun by writ; and the writ must be in Form No 1 .. . in Appendix B, ...

[(2)   The writ by which an Admiralty action in personam is begun must be in Form No 1 in Appendix A with the following modifications:—

   (a)   in the heading after the word "Division" there shall be inserted the words "Admiralty Court";
   (b)   where the writ is issued [out of the registry], for the references to the number of the action and to the Central Office there shall be substituted references to the folio number and [to the Admiralty and Commercial Registry] respectively.

(3)   The writ by which a limitation action is begun must be in Form No 2 in Appendix B . . . .]

[(4)]   [Subject to the following paragraphs] Order 6, rule 7, shall apply in relation to a writ by which an Admiralty action is begun, and Order 12 shall apply in relation to such an action, as if for references therein to the Central Office there were substituted references to the registry.

[(5)   An acknowledgment of service in an action in rem or a limitation action shall be in Form No 2B in Appendix B.

(6)   A defendant to an action in rem in which the writ has not been served, or a defendant to a limitation action who has not been served with the writ, may, if he desires to take part in the proceedings, acknowledge the issue of the writ by handing in at, or sending to, the appropriate office an acknowledgment of issue in the same form as an acknowledgment of service but with the substitution for the references therein to service of references to issue of the writ.

(7)   These rules shall apply, with the necessary modifications, in relation to an acknowledgment of issue or service in Form No 2B in Appendix B as they apply in relation to an acknowledgment of service in Form No 14 in Appendix A which contains a statement to the effect that the defendant intends to contest the proceedings to which the acknowledgment relates.]

Commencement   3 June 1980 (paras (2), (3), (5)–(7)); 1 October 1966 (remainder).
Amendments   Rule heading: words "acknowledgment of service" substituted by SI 1982/1111, r 115, Schedule.
Para (1): words omitted revoked by SI 1979/1716, r 32(1).
Para (2): original para (2) renumbered as para (4) and new para (2) inserted by SI 1979/1716, r 32(2), (3); in sub-para (b) words "out of the registry" and "to the Admiralty and Commercial Registry" substituted by SI 1987/1423, r 22.
Para (3): inserted by SI 1979/1716, r 32(2); words omitted revoked by SI 1984/1051, r 18.
Para (4): originally para (2), renumbered as para (4) and words "Subject to the following paragraphs" inserted by SI 1979/1716, r 32(3).
Paras (5)–(7): added by SI 1979/1716, r 32(4).
Cross references   See CCR Order 40, r 3.

Order 75, r 4 Service of writ out of jurisdiction

(1)   Subject to the following provisions of this rule, service out of the jurisdiction of a writ . . . containing any such claim as is mentioned [in rule 2(1)(a) or (b)] is permissible with the leave of the Court if, but only if—

    (a)   the defendant has his habitual residence or a place of business within England and Wales, or

    (b)   the cause of action arose within inland waters of England and Wales or within the limits of a port of England and Wales, or

    (c)   an action arising out of the same incident or series of incidents is proceeding in the High Court or has been heard and determined in the High Court, or

    (d)   the defendant has submitted or agreed to submit to the jurisdiction of the High Court.

    . . .

[(1A) Service out of the jurisdiction of a writ in an action containing any such claim as is mentioned in rule 2(1)(c) is permissible with the leave of the Court.]

(2)   Order 11, . . . rule 4(1), (2) and (4), shall apply in relation to an application for the grant of leave under this rule as they apply in relation to an application for the grant of leave under rule 1 or 2 of that Order.

(3)   [Paragraphs (1) and (1A)] shall not apply to an action in rem.

(4)   The proviso to rule 7(1) of Order 6 and Order 11, rule 1(2), shall not apply to a writ by which any Admiralty action is begun . . . .

Commencement   1 January 1987 (para (1A)); 1 October 1966 (remainder).
Amendments   Para (1): first words omitted revoked by SI 1982/1111, r 115, Schedule; words "in rule 2(1)(a) or (b)" substituted by SI 1983/1181, r 16(1); final words omitted revoked by SI 1981/1734, r 37.
Para (1A): inserted by SI 1983/1181, r 16(2).
Paras (2), (4): words omitted revoked by SI 1980/2000, r 21.
Para (3): words "Paragraphs (1) and (1A)" substituted by SI 1983/1181, r 16(3).
Cross references   See CCR Order 8, r 3.

Order 75, r 5 Warrant of arrest

[(1)   In an action in rem the plaintiff or defendant, as the case may be, may after the issue of the writ in the action and subject to the provisions of this rule issue a warrant in Form No 3 in Appendix B for the arrest of the property against which the action or any counterclaim in the action is brought.]

(2)   Where an action in rem is proceeding in a district registry, a warrant of arrest in the action may be issued out of that registry but, except as aforesaid, a warrant of arrest shall not be issued out of a district registry.

(3)   [Before a warrant to arrest any property is issued the party intending to use it must] procure a search to be made in the caveat book for the purpose of ascertaining whether there is a caveat against arrest in force with respect to that property and, if the warrant is to issue out of a district registry, the [district judge] of that registry shall procure a search to be made in the said book for that purpose.

(4)   A warrant of arrest shall not be issued until the party [intending to issue the same] has filed . . . an affidavit made by him or his agent containing the particulars required [by] [paragraph (9); however, the Court may, if it thinks fit, give leave to issue the warrant] notwithstanding that the affidavit does not contain all those particulars.

(5)   Except with the leave of the Court [or where notice has been given [under paragraph (7)]], a warrant of arrest shall not be issued in an action in rem against a foreign ship belonging to a port of a State having a consulate in London, being an action for possession of the ship or for wages, until notice that the action has been begun has been sent to the consul.

[(6)   A warrant of arrest may not be issued as of right in the case of property whose beneficial ownership has, since the issue of the writ, changed as a result of a sale or disposal by any court exercising Admiralty jurisdiction.]

[[(7)] Where, by any convention or treaty, the United Kingdom has undertaken to minimise the possibility of arrest of ships of another State, [no warrant of arrest shall be issued] against a ship owned by that State until notice in Form No 15 in Appendix B has been served on a consular officer at the consular office of that State in London or the port at which it is intended to cause the ship to be arrested.

. . .]

[(8)   Issue of a warrant of arrest takes place upon its being sealed by an officer of the registry or district registry.]

[[(9)] An affidavit required by paragraph (4) must state—
    (a)   in every case:
        (i)   the nature of the claim or counterclaim and that it has not been satisfied and, if it arises in connection with a ship, the name of that ship; and
        (ii)   the nature of the property to be arrested and, if the property is a ship, the name of the ship and her port of registry; and

(b) in the case of a claim against a ship by virtue of section 21(4) of the Supreme Court Act 1981:

   (i)   the name of the person who would be liable on the claim in an action in personam ("the relevant person"); and

   (ii) that the relevant person was when the cause of action arose the owner or charterer of, or in possession or in control of, the ship in connection with which the claim arose; and

   (iii) that at the time of the issue of the writ the relevant person was either the beneficial owner of all the shares in the ship in respect of which the warrant is required or (where appropriate) the charterer of it under a charter by demise; and

(c) in the case of a claim for possession of a ship or for wages, the nationality of the ship in respect of which the warrant is required and that the notice (if any) required by paragraph (5) has been sent; and

(d) in the case of a claim where notice is required to be served on a consular officer under paragraph (7), that such notice has been served; [and

(e) in the case of a claim in respect of a liability incurred under section 1 of the Merchant Shipping (Oil Pollution) Act 1971, the facts relied on as establishing that the Court is not prevented from entertaining the action by reason of section 13(2) of that Act].

[(10)] The following documents shall, where appropriate, be exhibited to an affidavit required by paragraph (4)—

(a) a copy of any notice sent to a consul under paragraph (5);

(b) . . .

(c) a copy of any notice served on a consular officer under paragraph (7).]

Commencement 12 January 1987 (paras (1), (6), (8)); 1 January 1982 (paras (9), (10)); 1 July 1975 (para (7)); 1 October 1966 (remainder).

Amendments Paras (1), (6): substituted by SI 1986/2289, r 9(1), (4).

Para (3): words from "Before a warrant" to "use it must" substituted by SI 1986/2289, r 9(2).

Para (4): words "intending to use the same" and words from "paragraph (9)" to "issue the warrant" substituted by SI 1986/2289, r 9(3); words omitted revoked and word "by" substituted by SI 1981/1734, r 38(1).

Para (5): words in square brackets beginning with the words "or where notice" inserted by SI 1975/911, r 16(b), words "under paragraph (7)" therein substituted by SI 1981/1734, r 38(2).

Para (7): originally added as para (11) by SI 1975/911, r 16(d); renumbered as para (7) following the omission of original paras (7)–(10), and words omitted revoked by SI 1981/1734, r 38(3), (4); words "no warrant of arrest" substituted by SI 1986/2289, r 9(5).

Para (8): added by SI 1986/2289, r 9(6).

Para (9): originally added as para (8) by SI 1981/1734, r 38(5); renumbered as para (9) by SI 1986/2289, r 9(6); sub-para (e) and word "and" immediately preceding it inserted by SI 1983/1181, r 17.

Para (10): originally added as para (9) by SI 1981/1734, r 38(5); renumbered as para (10) and words omitted revoked by SI 1986/2289, r 9(6), (7).

Cross references See CCR Order 40, r 4.

Order 75, r 6 Caveat against arrest

(1) [Except in a case to which paragraph (1A) applies, a person] who desires to prevent the arrest of any property must file in the registry a praecipe, in Form No 5 in Appendix B, signed by him or his solicitor undertaking—

(a) [to acknowledge issue or service (as may be appropriate) of the writ] in any action that may be begun against the property described in the praecipe, and

(b) within 3 days after receiving notice that such an action has been begun, to give bail in the action in a sum not exceeding an amount specified in the praecipe or to pay the amount so specified into court;

and on the filing of the praecipe a caveat against the issue of a warrant to arrest the property described in the praecipe shall be entered in the caveat book.

[(1A) Where a plaintiff in a limitation action has constituted a limitation fund in accordance with Article 11 of the Convention on Limitation of Liability for Maritime Claims 1976 (as set out in Schedule 4 to the Merchant Shipping Act 1979) and rule 37A of this Order, and desires to prevent the arrest of any property for a claim which may be or has been made against the fund, he must file in the registry a praecipe, in Form No 5A in Appendix B, signed by him or his solicitor—

    (a) stating that a limitation fund in respect of damage arising from the relevant incident has been constituted, and

    (b) undertaking to acknowledge issue or service (as may be appropriate) of the writ in any action that may be begun against the property described in the praecipe;

and on the filing of the praecipe a caveat against the issue of a warrant to arrest the property described in the praecipe shall be entered in the caveat book.]

(2)   The fact that there is a caveat against arrest in force shall not prevent the issue of a warrant to arrest the property to which the caveat relates.

Commencement 1 October 1990 (para (1A)); 1 October 1966 (remainder).
Amendments Para (1): words from "Except in a case" to "a person" substituted by SI 1990/1689, r 3; in sub-para (a) words from "to acknowledge" to "the writ" substituted by SI 1979/1716, r 33.
Para (1A): inserted by SI 1990/1689, r 4.

Order 75, r 7 Remedy where property protected by caveat is arrested

Where any property with respect to which a caveat against arrest is in force is arrested in pursuance of a warrant of arrest, the party at whose instance the caveat was entered may apply to the Court by motion for an order under this rule and, on the hearing of the application, the Court, unless it is satisfied that the party procuring the arrest of the property had a good and sufficient reason for so doing, may by order discharge the warrant and may also order the last-mentioned party to pay to the applicant damages in respect of the loss suffered by the applicant as a result of the arrest.

Commencement 1 October 1966.

Order 75, r 8 Service of writ in action in rem

(1)   Subject to paragraph (2), a writ by which an action in rem is begun must be served on the property against which the action is [brought, save that

    (a) where the property is freight, the writ must be served on the cargo in respect of which the freight is payable or on the ship in which that cargo was carried;

    (b) where the property has been sold by the marshal, the writ may not be served on that property but a sealed copy of it must be filed in the registry or, if the writ was issued out of a district registry, in that registry, and the writ shall be deemed to have been duly served on the day on which the copy was filed.]

(2)   A writ need not be served [or filed as] mentioned in paragraph (1) if the writ is deemed to have been duly served on the defendant by virtue of Order 10, [rule 1(4) or (5)].

(3)   Where by virtue of this rule a writ is required to be served on any property, [the plaintiff may request service of the writ to be effected by the marshal if, but only if, a warrant of arrest has been issued for service against the property or the property is

under arrest, and in that case the plaintiff] [must file in the registry or, where the action is proceeding in a district registry, that registry, a praecipe in Form 6 in Appendix B and lodge—

    (a)   the writ and a copy thereof, and

    (b)   an undertaking to pay on demand all expenses incurred by the marshal or his substitute in respect of the service of the writ,

and thereupon the marshal or his substitute shall serve the writ on the property described in the praecipe.]

[(3A) Where a writ is served on any property by the marshal or his substitute, the person effecting service must indorse on the writ the following particulars, that is to say, where it was served, the property on which it was served, the day of the week and the date on which it was served, the manner in which it was served and the name and the address of the person effecting service, and the indorsement shall be evidence of the facts stated therein.]

(4) Where the plaintiff in an action in rem, or his solicitor, becomes aware that there is in force a caveat against arrest with respect to the property against which the action is brought, he must serve the writ forthwith on the person at whose instance the caveat was entered.

(5) Where a writ by which an action in rem is begun is amended under Order 20, rule 1, after service thereof, Order 20, rule 1(2), shall not apply and, unless the Court otherwise directs on an application made ex parte, [the amended writ must be served on any intervener and any defendant who has acknowledged issue or service of the writ in the action or, if no defendant has acknowledged issue or service of the writ, it must be served or filed in accordance with paragraph (1) of this rule].

Commencement 3 June 1980 (para (3A)); 1 October 1966 (remainder).
Amendments Para (1): words from "bought, save that" to the end substituted by SI 1984/1051, r 19.
Para (2): words "or filed as" substituted by SI 1984/1051, r 20; words "rule 1(4) or (5)" substituted by SI 1979/402, r 11.
Para (3): words from "the plaintiff may" to "the plaintiff" substituted by SI 1975/911, r 16(3); words from "must file in" to the end substituted by SI 1974/1115, r 3(1).
Para (3A): inserted by SI 1979/1716, r 34(1).
Para (5): words from "the amended writ" to the end substituted by SI 1984/1051, r 21.
Cross references See CCR Order 40, r 5.

Order 75, r 9 Committal of solicitor failing to comply with undertaking

Where the solicitor of a party to an action in rem fails to comply with a written undertaking given by him to any other party or his solicitor [to acknowledge issue or service of the writ] in the action, give bail or pay money into court in lieu of bail, he shall be liable to committal.

Commencement 1 October 1966.
Amendments Words "to acknowledge issue or service of the writ" substituted by SI 1979/1716, r 35.

Order 75, r 10 Execution, etc, of warrant of arrest

(1) A warrant of arrest is valid for 12 months beginning with the date of its issue.

(2) A warrant of arrest may be executed only by the marshal or his substitute.

(3) A warrant of arrest shall not be executed until an undertaking [to pay on demand the fees of the marshal and all expenses incurred by him or on his behalf in respect of the arrest of the property and the care and custody of it while under arrest

has been lodged in the marshal's office or, where the action is proceeding in a district registry, in that registry.]

(4)　　A warrant of arrest shall not be executed if the party at whose instance it was issued lodges a written request to that effect with the marshal or, where the action is proceeding in a district registry, the [district judge] of that registry.

(5)　　A warrant of arrest issued against freight may be executed by serving the warrant on the cargo in respect of which the freight is payable or on the ship in which that cargo was carried or on both of them.

(6)　　Subject to paragraph (5), a warrant of arrest must be served on the property against which it is issued.

[(7)]　Within 7 days after the service of a warrant of arrest, the warrant must be filed—
　　　　(a)　where it was issued out of the registry, in the registry by the marshal, and
　　　　(b)　where it was issued out of a district registry, in that registry by the party who procured it to be issued.

Commencement　1 October 1966.
Amendments　Para (3): words from "to pay on demand" to the end substituted by SI 1974/1115, r 3(2). Para (7): original para (7) revoked and original para (8) renumbered as para (7) by SI 1969/1894, r 7(1).
Cross references　See CCR Order 40, r 5.

Order 75, r 11 Service on ships, etc: how effected

(1)　　Subject to paragraph (2), service of a warrant of arrest or writ in an action in rem against a ship, freight or cargo shall be effected by—
　　　　(a)　affixing the warrant or writ for a short time on any mast of the ship or on the outside of any suitable part of the ship's superstructure, and
　　　　(b)　on removing the warrant or writ, leaving a copy of it affixed (in the case of the warrant) in its place or (in the case of the writ) on a sheltered, conspicuous part of the ship.

(2)　　Service of a warrant of arrest or writ in an action in rem against freight or cargo or both shall, if the cargo has been landed or transhipped, be effected—
　　　　(a)　by placing the warrant or writ for a short time on the cargo and, on removing the warrant or writ, leaving a copy of it on the cargo, or
　　　　(b)　if the cargo is in the custody of a person who will not permit access to it, by leaving a copy of the warrant or writ with that person.

[(3)　　Order 65, rule 10, shall not apply in relation to a warrant of arrest or writ in rem.]

[(4)　　Where in an action in rem a writ has been issued pursuant to Order 6, rule 7A and it is desired to serve the writ before it has been sealed by the Court, a copy of it endorsed in accordance with Order 6, rule 7A(3)(a) may be treated as if it were the original writ for the purpose of the foregoing paragraphs of this rule.]

Commencement　1 February 1991 (para (4)); 10 January 1970 (para (3)); 1 October 1966 (remainder).
Amendments　Para (3): added by SI 1969/1894, r 7(2).
Para (4): added by SI 1990/2599, r 5.
Cross references　See CCR Order 40, r 5.

[Order 75, r 12 Directions with respect to property under arrest

(1)　　The marshal may at any time apply to the Court for directions with respect to property under arrest in any action and may, and if the Court so directs shall, give notice of the application to any or all of the persons referred to in paragraph (2).

(2)　The marshal shall send by post a copy of any order made on an application under paragraph (1) to all those persons who, in relation to that property, have—

    (a)　entered a caveat which is still in force; or

    (b)　caused a warrant for the arrest of the property to be executed by the marshal; or

    (c)　acknowledged issue or service of the writ in any action in which the property is under arrest; or

    (d)　intervened in any action in which the property is under arrest.

(3)　A person other than the marshal may make an application under this rule by summons or motion in the action in which the property is under arrest and the summons or notice of motion together with copies of any affidavits in support must be served upon the marshal and all persons referred to in paragraph (2) unless the Court otherwise orders on an application made ex parte.

(4)　A [district judge] by whom any order under paragraph (3) is made shall cause a copy of the order to be sent to the marshal.]

Commencement　1 October 1984.
Amendments　This rule was substituted by SI 1984/1051, r 22.

Order 75, r 13 Release of property under arrest

(1)　Except where property arrested in pursuance of a warrant of arrest is sold under an order of the Court, property which has been so arrested shall only be released under the authority of an instrument of release (in this rule referred to as a "release"), in Form No 7 in Appendix B, issued out of the registry or, where the action in which the warrant was issued is proceeding in a district registry, out of that registry.

(2)　. . .

[(3)　A release shall not be issued with respect to property as to which a caveat against release is in force, unless, either

    (a)　at the time of the issue of the release the property is under arrest in one or more other actions, or

    (b)　the Court so orders.

(4)　A release may be issued at the instance of any party to the action in which the warrant of arrest was issued if the Court so orders, or, subject to paragraph (3), if all the other parties, except any defendant who has not acknowledged issue or service of the writ, consent.]

(5)　Where a release is to issue out of a district registry the [district judge] of that registry shall, before issuing it, procure a search to be made in the caveat book for the purpose of ascertaining whether there is a caveat against release in force as to the property in question.

[(6)　Before a release is issued, the party applying for its issue must, unless paragraph (3)(a) applies, give notice to any person at whose instance a subsisting caveat against release has been entered, or to his solicitor, requiring the caveat to be withdrawn.]

(7)　Before property under arrest is released in compliance with a release issued under this rule, the party at whose instance it was issued must, in accordance with the directions of the marshal or, where the action is proceeding in a district registry, the [district judge] of that registry, [either—

    (a)　pay the fees of the marshal already incurred and lodge in the marshal's office or the district registry, as the case may be, an undertaking to pay on demand the other fees and expenses in connection with the arrest of the property and the care and custody of it while under arrest and of its release, or

(b) lodge in the marshal's office or district registry an undertaking to pay on demand all such fees and expenses, whether incurred or to be incurred.]

(8) The Court, on the application of any party who objects to directions given to him by the marshal under paragraph (7), may vary or revoke the directions.

Commencement   2 January 1981 (paras (3), (4), (6)); 1 October 1966 (remainder).
Amendments   Para (2): revoked by SI 1980/1908, r 11(1).
Paras (3), (4), (6): substituted by SI 1980/1908, r 11(2)–(4).
Para (7): words from "either" to the end substituted by SI 1974/1115, r 3(3).
Cross references   See CCR Order 40, r 12.

Order 75, r 14 [Caveat against release etc]

[(1) Where a person claiming to have a right of action in rem against any property which is under arrest or the proceeds of sale thereof wishes to be served with notice of any application to the Court in respect of that property or those proceeds, he must file in the registry a praecipe in Form No 9 in Appendix B and, on the filling of the praecipe, a caveat shall be entered in the caveat book.]

(2) Where the release of any property under arrest is delayed by the entry of a caveat under this rule, any person having an interest in that property may apply to the Court by motion for an order requiring the person who procured the entry of the caveat to pay to the applicant damages in respect of the loss suffered by the applicant by reason of the delay, and the Court, unless it is satisfied that the person procuring the entry of the caveat had a good and sufficient reason for so doing, may make an order accordingly.

Commencement   1 October 1984 (para (1)); 1 October 1966 (remainder).
Amendments   Rule heading: substituted by SI 1984/1051, r 23.
Para (1): substituted by SI 1984/1051, r 24.

Order 75, r 15 Duration of caveats

(1) Every caveat entered in the caveat book is valid [for 12 months] beginning with the date of its entry but the person at whose instance a caveat was entered may withdraw it by filing a praecipe in Form No 10 in Appendix B.

(2) The period of validity of a caveat may not be extended, but this provision shall not be taken as preventing the entry of successive caveats.

Commencement   1 October 1966.
Amendments   Para (1): words "for 12 months" substituted by SI 1984/1051, r 25.

Order 75, r 16 Bail

[(1) Bail on behalf of a party to an action in rem must be given by bond in Form No 11 in Appendix B; and the sureties to the bond must enter into the bond before a commissioner for oaths (or a solicitor exercising the powers of a commissioner for oaths under section 81 of the Solicitors Act 1974) not being a commissioner (or solicitor) who, or whose partner, is acting as solicitor or agent for the party on whose behalf the bail is to be given.]

(2) Subject to paragraph (3), a surety to a bail bond must make an affidavit stating that he is able to pay the sum for which the bond is given.

(3)   Where a corporation is a surety to a bail bond given on behalf of a party, no affidavit shall be made under paragraph (2) on behalf of the corporation unless the opposite party requires it, but where such an affidavit is required it must be made by a director, manager, secretary or other similar officer of the corporation.

(4)   The party on whose behalf bail is given must serve on the opposite party a notice of bail containing the names and addresses of the persons who have given bail on his behalf and of the commissioner . . . before whom the bail bond was entered into; and after the expiration of 24 hours from the service of the notice (or sooner with the consent of the opposite party) he may file the bond and must at the same time file the affidavits (if any) made under paragraph (2) and an affidavit proving due service of the notice of bail to which a copy of that notice must be exhibited.

Commencement   1 October 1984 (para (1)); 1 October 1966 (remainder).
Amendments   Para (1): substituted by SI 1984/1051, r 26(1).
Para (4): words omitted revoked by SI 1984/1051, r 26(2).
Cross references   See CCR Order 40, r 11.

Order 75, r 17 Interveners

(1)   Where property against which an action in rem is brought is under arrest or money representing the proceeds of sale of that property is in court, a person who has an interest in that property or money but who is not a defendant to the action may, with the leave of the Court, intervene in the action.

(2)   An application for the grant of leave under this rule must be made ex parte by affidavit showing the interest of the applicant in the property against which the action is brought or in the money in court.

[(3)   A person to whom leave is granted under this rule shall thereupon become a party to the action.

(4)   The Court may order that a person to whom it grants leave to intervene in an action shall, within such period or periods as may be specified in the order, serve on any other party to the action such notice of his intervention and such pleading as may be so specified.]

Commencement   3 June 1980 (paras (3), (4)); 1 October 1966 (remainder).
Amendments   Paras (3), (4): substituted by SI 1979/1716, r 37.
Cross references   See CCR Order 40, r 7.

[Order 75, r 18 Preliminary Acts

(1)   In an action to enforce a claim for damage, loss of life or personal injury arising out of a collision between ships, the following provisions of this rule shall apply unless the Court otherwise orders.

(2)   The plaintiff must within two months after service of the writ on any defendant and the defendant must within two months of acknowledging issue or service of the writ file in the appropriate registry a document in two parts (in these rules referred to as a preliminary act) containing a statement of the following:

Part One
   (i)   the names of the ships which came into collision and their ports of registry;
   (ii)   the length, breadth, gross tonnage, horsepower and draught at the material time of the ship and the nature and tonnage of any cargo carried by the ship;

   (iii)   the date and time (including the time zone) of the collision;

   (iv)   the place of the collision;

   (v)   the direction and force of the wind;

   (vi)   the state of the weather;

   (vii)   the state, direction and force of the tidal or other current;

   (viii)   the position, the course steered and speed through the water of the ship when the other ship was first seen or immediately before any measures were taken with reference to her presence, whichever was the earlier;

   (ix)   the lights or shapes (if any) carried by the ship;

   (x)   (a)   the distance and bearing of the other ship if and when her echo was first observed by radar;

        (b)   the distance, bearing and approximate heading of the other ship when first seen;

   (xi)   w other lights or shapes or combinations of lights or shapes (if any) of the other ship were subsequently seen before the collision, and when;

   (xii)   what other lights of shapes or combinations of lights or shapes (if any) of the other ship were subsequently seen before the collision, and when;

   (xiii)   what alterations (if any) were made to the course and speed of the ship after the earlier of the two times referred to in article (viii) up to the time of the collision, and when, and what measures (if any) other than alterations of course or speed, were taken to avoid the collision, and when;

   (xiv)   the heading of the ship, the parts of each ship which first came into contact and the approximate angle between the two ships at the moment of contact;hat light or shape or combination of lights or shapes (if any) of the other ship was first seen;

   (xv)   what sound signals (if any) were given, and when;

   (xvi)   what sound signals (if any) were heard from the other ship, and when.

Part Two

   (i)   a statement that the particulars in Part One are incorporated in Part Two;

   (ii)   any other facts and matters upon which the party filing the preliminary act relies;

   (iii)   all allegations of negligence or other fault which the party filing the preliminary act makes;

   (iv)   the remedy or relief which the party filing the preliminary act claims;

(3)   Part Two of the preliminary act shall be deemed to be the pleading of the person filing the preliminary act (in the case of the plaintiff his statement of claim and in the case of the defendant his defence and, where appropriate, his counterclaim) and the provisions of these rules relating to pleadings shall apply to it save insofar as this rule and rule 20 provide otherwise.

(4)   The Court may order that Part Two of the preliminary act need not be filed by the plaintiff or defendant and give directions for the further conduct of the action.

(5)   Every preliminary act shall before filing be sealed by the proper officer and be filed in a sealed envelope which shall not be opened except as provided in paragraph (7) or by order of the court.

(6)   A plaintiff must serve notice of filing his preliminary act on every defendant who acknowledges issue or service of the writ within 3 days of receiving notice of that acknowledgement or upon filing his preliminary act, whichever is the later. A defendant must, upon filing his preliminary act, serve notice that he has done so on the plaintiff and on every other defendant who has acknowledged issue or service of the writ.

(7)   Any party may inspect and bespeak a copy of the preliminary act of any other party upon filing in the appropriate registry a consent signed by that other party or his solicitor.

(8)   Order 18, rule 20 (close of pleadings) shall not apply; and for the purposes of Order 18, rule 14 (denial by joinder of issue), Order 20, rule 3 (amendment of pleadings without leave) and Order 24, rules 1 and 2 (discovery of documents) the pleadings shall be deemed to be closed—

    (a)   at the expiration of 7 days after service of the reply or, if there is no reply but only a defence to counterclaim, after service of the defence to counterclaim pursuant to leave given under rule 20, or

    (b)   if neither a reply nor a defence to counterclaim is served, at the expiration of 7 days after the last preliminary act in the action was served pursuant to paragraph (9) below.

(9)   Within 14 days after the last preliminary act in the action is filed each party must serve on every other party a copy of his preliminary act.

(10)   At any time after all preliminary acts have been filed any party may apply to the Court for an order that—

    (a)   one or more parties file in the registry particulars of the damages claimed by them and serve a copy thereof on every other party, and

    (b)   that the damages be assessed prior to or at the trial on liability.

The application must be made by summons to the appropriate registrar even if it is made after the issue of a summons for directions.

(11)   When an order is made under paragraph (10) the claim or claims concerned shall be treated as referred to the appropriate registrar for assessment and rules 41 and 42 shall apply unless the registrar otherwise directs.

(12)   In this rule "the appropriate registry" means the Admiralty and Commercial Registry or, if the action is proceeding in a district registry, that registry; and references to "the appropriate registrar" shall be construed accordingly.]

Commencement   1 October 1990.
Amendments   This rule was substituted by SI 1990/1689, r 5.
Cross references   See CCR Order 40, r 9.

Order 75, r 19 Failure to lodge preliminary act: proceedings against party in default

(1)   Where in such an action as is referred to in rule 18(1) the plaintiff fails to lodge a preliminary act within the prescribed period, any defendant who has lodged such an act may apply to the Court by summons for an order to dismiss the action, and the Court may by order dismiss the action or make such other order on such terms as it thinks just.

(2)   Where in such an action, being an action in personam, a defendant fails to lodge a preliminary act within the prescribed period, Order 19, rules 2 and 3, shall apply as if the defendant's failure to lodge the preliminary act within that period were a failure by him to serve a defence on the plaintiff within the period fixed by or under these rules for service thereof, and the plaintiff, if he has lodged a preliminary act may, subject to Order 77, rule 9, accordingly enter judgment against that defendant in accordance with the said rule 2 or the said rule 3, as the circumstances of the case require.

(3)   Where in such an action, being an action in rem, a defendant fails to lodge a preliminary act within the prescribed period, the plaintiff, if he has lodged such an

act, may apply to the Court by motion for judgment against that defendant, and it shall not be necessary for the plaintiff to file or serve a statement of claim or an affidavit before the hearing of the motion.

(4)   On the hearing of a motion under paragraph (3) the Court may make such order as it thinks just, and where the defendant does not appear on the hearing and the Court is of opinion that judgment should be given for the plaintiff provided he proves his case, it shall order the plaintiff's preliminary act to be opened and require the plaintiff to satisfy the Court that his claim is well founded.

The plaintiff's evidence may, unless the Court otherwise orders, be given by affidavit without any order or direction in that behalf.

(5)   Where the plaintiff in accordance with a requirement under paragraph (4) satisfies the Court that his claim is well founded, the Court may give judgment for the claim with or without a reference to the registrar or [district judge] and may at the same time order the property against which the action is brought to be appraised and sold and the proceeds to be paid into court or make such order as it thinks just.

(6)   The Court may, on such terms as it thinks just, set aside any judgment entered in pursuance of this rule.

(7)   In this rule references to the prescribed period shall be construed as references to the period within which by virtue of rule [18(2)] or of any order of the Court the plaintiff or defendant, as the context of the reference requires, is required to lodge a preliminary act.

Commencement   1 October 1966.
Amendments   Para (7): figure "18(2)" substituted by SI 1990/1689, r 6.

Order 75, r 20 Special provisions as to pleadings in collision, etc actions

(1)   Notwithstanding anything in Order 18, rule 3, the plaintiff in any such action as is referred to in rule 2(1)(a) may not serve a reply or a defence to counterclaim on the defendant except with the leave of the Court.

[(2)   Subject to paragraph (3), in any such action Order 18, rule 13(3) shall not apply to any allegation of fact made in—
    (a)   a statement of claim contained in Part Two of a preliminary act, or
    (b)   a counterclaim (whether contained in Part Two of a preliminary act or not),

and notwithstanding Order 18, rule 14(3) but without prejudice to the other provisions of that rule, there is an implied joinder of issue on the statement of claim or counterclaim.

(3)   Paragraph (2) does not apply to a counterclaim if the plaintiff has served a defence to counterclaim pursuant to leave given under paragraph (1).]

Commencement   1 October 1990 (paras (2), (3)); 1 October 1966 (remainder).
Amendments   Paras (2), (3): substituted, for para (2) as originally enacted, by SI 1990/1689, r 7.

Order 75, r 21 Judgment by default

(1)   Where a writ is served under rule 8(4) on a party at whose instance a caveat against arrest was issued, then if—
    (a)   the sum claimed in the action begun by the writ does not exceed the amount specified in the undertaking given by that party or his solicitor to procure the entry of that caveat, and

(b) that party or his solicitor does not within 14 days after service of the writ fulfil the undertaking given by him as aforesaid,

the plaintiff may, after filing an affidavit verifying the facts on which the action is based, apply to the Court for judgment by default.

(2) Judgment given under paragraph (1) may be enforced by the arrest of the property against which the action was brought and by committal of the party at whose instance the caveat with respect to that property was entered.

(3) Where a defendant to an action in rem fails to [acknowledge service of the writ within the time limited for doing so], then, on the expiration of 14 days after service of the writ and upon filing an affidavit proving due service of the writ, an affidavit verifying the facts on which the action is based and, if a statement of claim was not indorsed on the writ, a copy of the statement of claim, the plaintiff may apply to the Court for judgment by default.

Where the writ is deemed to have been duly served on the defendant by virtue of Order 10, [rule 1(4)], or was served . . . [. . . by the marshal or his substitute] under rule 8 of this Order, an affidavit proving due service of the writ need not be filed under this paragraph, but the writ indorsed as mentioned in the said [rule 1(4)] . . . [. . . or indorsed as mentioned in rule 8(3A)] must be lodged with the affidavit verifying the facts on which the action is based.

(4) Where a defendant to an action in rem fails to serve a defence on the plaintiff, then, after the expiration of the period fixed by or under these rules for service of the defence and upon filing an affidavit stating that no defence was served on him by that defendant during that period, an affidavit verifying the facts on which the action is based and, if a statement of claim was not indorsed on the writ, a copy of the statement of claim, the plaintiff may apply to the Court for judgment by default.

(5) Where a defendant to a counterclaim in an action in rem fails to serve a defence to counterclaim on the defendant making the counterclaim, then, subject to paragraph (6), after the expiration of the period fixed by or under these rules for service of the defence to counterclaim and upon filing an affidavit stating that no defence to counterclaim was served on him by the first-mentioned defendant during that period, an affidavit verifying the facts on which the counterclaim is based and a copy of the counterclaim, the defendant making the counterclaim may apply to the Court for judgment by default.

(6) No application may be made under paragraph (5) against the plaintiff in any such action as is referred to in rule 2(1)(a).

(7) An application to the Court under this rule must be made by motion and if, on the hearing of the motion, the Court is satisfied that the applicant's claim is well founded it may give judgment for the claim with or without a reference to the registrar or [district judge] and may at the same time order the property against which the action or, as the case may be, counterclaim is brought to be appraised and sold and the proceeds to be paid into court or may make such other order as it thinks just.

(8) In default actions in rem evidence may, unless the Court otherwise orders, be given by affidavit without any order or direction in that behalf.

(9) The Court may, on such terms as it thinks just, set aside or vary any judgment entered in pursuance of this rule.

(10) Order 13 and Order 19 (except rule 1) shall not apply to actions in rem.

Commencement 1 October 1966.
Amendments Para (3): words from "acknowledge service" to "for doing to", words "rule 1(4)" in both places, and final words in square brackets substituted, third words in square brackets inserted, by SI 1979/1716, r 39; words omitted revoked by SI 1984/1051, r 28.

Order 75, r 22 Order for sale of ship: determination of priority of claims

(1)   Where in an action in rem against a ship the Court has ordered the ship to be sold, any party who has obtained or obtains judgment against the ship or proceeds of sale of the ship may—

    (a)   in a case where the order for sale contains the further order referred to in paragraph (2), after the expiration of the period specified in the order under paragraph (2)(a), or

    (b)   in any other case, after obtaining judgment,

apply to the Court by motion for an order determining the order of priority of the claims against the proceeds of sale of the ship.

(2)   Where in an action in rem against a ship the Court orders the ship to be sold, it may further order—

    (a)   that the order of priority of the claims against the proceeds of sale of the ship shall not be determined until after the expiration of 90 days, or of such other period as the Court may specify, beginning with the day on which the proceeds of sale are paid into court;

    (b)   that any party to the action or to any other action in rem against the ship or the proceeds of sale thereof may apply to the Court in the action to which he is a party to extend the period specified in the order;

    (c)   that within 7 days after the date of payment into court of the proceeds of sale the marshal shall send for publication in Lloyd's List and Shipping Gazette and such other newspaper, if any, as the Court may direct, a notice complying with paragraph (3).

(3)   The notice referred to in paragraph (2)(c) must state—

    (a)   that the ship (naming her) has been sold by order of the High Court in an action in rem, identifying the action;

    (b)   that the gross proceeds of the sale, specifying the amount thereof, have been paid into court;

    (c)   that the order of priority of the claims against the said proceeds will not be determined until after the expiration of the period (specifying it) specified in the order for sale; and

    (d)   that any person with a claim against the ship or the proceeds of sale thereof, on which he intends to proceed to judgment should do so before the expiration of that period.

(4)   The marshal must lodge in the registry or, if the action is proceeding in a district registry, that registry, a copy of each newspaper in which the notice referred to in paragraph (2)(c) appeared.

(5)   The expenses incurred by the marshal in complying with an order of the Court under this rule shall be included in his expenses relating to the sale of the ship.

(6)   An application to the Court to extend the period referred to in paragraph (2)(a) must be made by motion, and a copy of the notice of motion must, at least 3 days before the day fixed for the hearing thereof, be served on each party who has begun an action in rem against the ship or the proceeds of sale thereof.

(7)　In this rule "the Court" means [a judge in person].

Commencement　1 October 1966.
Amendments　Para (7): words "a judge in person" substituted by SI 1971/1269, r 25(3).

Order 75, r 23 Appraisement and sale of property

(1)　A commission for the appraisement and sale of any property under an order of the Court shall not be issued until the party applying for it has filed a praecipe in Form No 12 in Appendix B.

(2)　Such a commission must, unless the Court otherwise orders, be executed by the marshal and must be in Form No 13 in Appendix B.

(3)　A commission for appraisement and sale shall not be executed until an undertaking in writing satisfactory to the marshal to pay the fees and expenses of the marshal on demand has been lodged in the marshal's office.

(4)　The marshal shall pay into court the gross proceeds of the sale of any property sold by him under a commission for sale and shall bring into court the account relating to the sale (with vouchers in support) for taxation.

(5)　On the taxation of the marshal's account relating to a sale any person interested in the proceeds of the sale shall be entitled to be heard, and any decision of a registrar [district judge] made on the taxation to which objection is taken may be reviewed in the same manner and by the same persons as any decision of a registrar [district judge] made in taxation proceedings under Order 62, and rules 33 to 35 of that Order shall apply accordingly with the necessary modifications.

Commencement　1 October 1966.
Cross references　See CCR Order 40, rr 13, 14.

[Order 75, r 23A Undertakings as to expenses, etc

(1)　Every undertaking under rule 8(3), 10(3), 13(7) or 23(3) shall be given in writing to the satisfaction of the marshal or, where the action is proceeding in a district registry, the [district judge].

(2)　Where a party is required by rule 8(3), 10(3), 13(7) or 23(3) to give to the marshal or a [district judge] an undertaking to pay any fees or expenses, the marshal or [district judge] may accept instead of an undertaking the deposit with him of such sum as he considers reasonable to meet those fees and expenses.

(3)　The Court or, where the action is proceeding in a district registry, a judge, may on the application of any party who is dissatisfied with a direction or determination of the marshal or [district judge] under rule 13(7) or this rule, vary or revoke the direction or determination.]

Commencement　27 July 1974.
Amendments　This rule was inserted by SI 1974/1115, r 3(4).

Order 75, r 24 Payment into and out of court

(1)　Order 22 (except rules 3, 4, 5 and 12) shall apply in relation to an Admiralty action [(other than a limitation action)] as it applies to an action for a debt or damages.

(2)   Subject to [paragraphs (3) and (4)], money paid into court shall not be paid out except in pursuance of an order of [a judge in person].

(3)   The registrar or, in the case of an action which is proceeding in a district registry, the [district judge] of that registry may, with the consent of the parties interested in money paid into court, order the money to be paid out to the person entitled thereto in the following cases, that is to say—

(a)   where a claim has been referred to the registrar [district judge] for decision and all the parties to the reference have agreed to accept the registrar [district judge]'s decision and to the payment out of any money in court in accordance with that decision;

(b)   where property has been sold and the proceeds of sale thereof paid into court, and the parties are agreed as to the persons to whom the proceeds shall be paid and the amount to be paid to each of those persons;

(c)   where in any other case there is no dispute between the parties.

[(4)   Where in an Admiralty action money has been paid into court pursuant to an order made under Order 29, rule 12, the registrar or, in the case of an action which is proceeding in a district registry, the [district judge] of that registry, may make an order under [rule 13(1) of that Order] for the money to be paid out to the person entitled thereto.]

Commencement   20 July 1970 (para (4)); 1 October 1966 (remainder).
Amendments   Para (1): words "(other than a limitation action)" inserted by SI 1985/69, r 5.
Para (2): words "paragraphs (3) and (4)" substituted by SI 1970/944, r 8(1); words "a judge in person" substituted by SI 1971/1269, r 25(3).
Para (4): added by SI 1970/944, r 8(2); words "rule 13(1) of that Order" substituted by SI 1982/1111, r 115, Schedule.

Order 75, r 25 Summons for directions

(1)   ... Order 25 shall apply to Admiralty actions (other than limitation actions [...]) as it applies to other actions [except that—

(a)   the summons for directions shall be returnable in not less than [21 days];

(b)   any notice under Order 25, rule 7(1), must be served within [14] days after service of the summons for directions on the party giving the notice; and

(c)   unless a judge in person otherwise directs, the summons for directions shall be heard by a judge in person.]

On [or before] the day on which any party serves on any other party a notice under Order 25, rule 7, he must lodge two copies of the notice in the registry or, if the action is proceeding in a district registry, that registry.

(2)   An order made on the summons for directions shall determine whether the trial is to be without assessors or with one or more assessors, whether Elder Brethren of Trinity House, nautical assessors or other assessors.

(3)   The trial shall be at the Royal Courts of Justice before a judge without a jury unless, on the ground that there are special reasons to the contrary, an order made on the summons for directions otherwise provides.

(4)   ...

(5)   Any such order or direction as is referred to in paragraph (2) [or (3)] (including an order made on appeal) may be varied or revoked by a subsequent order or direction made or given at or before the trial by [a judge in person] or, with the judge's consent, by the registrar or [district judge], as the case may be.

Commencement 1 October 1966.

Amendments Para (1): first words omitted revoked by SI 1969/1105, r 8(1); second words omitted originally inserted by SI 1966/1055, r 4(1), subsequently revoked and words "or before" inserted by SI 1984/1051, r 29; words from "except that" to the end inserted by SI 1969/1105, r 8(1), in sub-para (a) words "21 days" and in sub-para (b) figure "14" substituted by SI 1980/1908, r 12(2).

Para (4): revoked by SI 1980/1908, r 12(3).

Para (5): words "or (3)" substituted by SI 1982/1111, r 115, Schedule; words "a judge in person" substituted by SI 1971/1269, r 25(3).

[Order 75, r 26 Fixing date for trial, etc

(1)   Subject to paragraph (2), the date for trial of an Admiralty action shall be fixed by the judge at the hearing of the summons for directions, unless a judge in person otherwise directs.

(2)   Where an action is ordered to be tried without pleadings or a summons for directions is directed to be heard by a registrar [district judge] the date for trial shall be fixed by the Admiralty registrar whether the action is proceeding in the registry or a district registry.

(3)   Order 34 shall apply to Admiralty actions subject to the following and any other necessary modifications—

    (a)   the bundles referred to in rule 3(1) shall include any preliminary acts and [any particulars filed pursuant to an order under rule 18(10)(a)] of this Order, and where trial with one or more assessors has been ordered an additional bundle shall be lodged for the use of each assessor;

    (b)   "the proper officer" shall mean the chief clerk of [the registry]; and

    (c)   in an action which has been ordered to be tried with an assessor or assessors the solicitor to the party setting it down must file in the registry an undertaking to pay the proper fees and expenses of such assessor or assessors.

(4)   If all the parties to an action consent, the action may be withdrawn without the leave of the Court at any time before trial by producing—

    (a)   in a case where the action has been set down for trial, to the proper officer, and

    (b)   in any other case, to an officer of the registry or, if the action is proceeding in a district registry, to the [district judge] of that registry,

a written consent to the action being withdrawn signed by all the parties.]

Commencement 1 October 1984.

Amendments This rule was substituted by SI 1984/1051, r 30.

Para (3): in sub-para (a) words "any particulars filed pursuant to an order under rule 18(10)(a)" substituted by SI 1990/1689, r 8; in sub-para (b) words "the registry" substituted by SI 1987/1423, r 21.

Order 75, r 27 Stay of proceedings in collision, etc actions until security given

Where an action in rem, being an action to enforce any such claim as is referred to in rule 2(1)(a), is begun and a cross action in rem arising out of the same collision or other occurrence as the first mentioned action is subsequently begun, or a counterclaim arising out of that occurrence is made in the first mentioned action, then—

    (a)   if the ship in respect of or against which the first mentioned action is brought has been arrested or security given to prevent her arrest, but

    (b)   the ship in respect of or against which the cross action is brought or the counterclaim made cannot be arrested and security has not been given to satisfy any judgment given in favour of the party bringing the cross action or making the counterclaim, the Court may stay proceedings in the first mentioned action until security is given to satisfy any judgment given in favour of that party.

Commencement   1 October 1966.

Order 75, r 28 Inspection of ship, etc

Without prejudice to its powers under Order 29, rules 2 and 3, and Order 35, rule 8, the Court may, on the application of any party, make an order for the inspection by the assessors (if the action is tried with assessors), or by any party or witness, of any ship or other property, whether real or personal, the inspection of which may be necessary or desirable for the purpose of obtaining full information or evidence in connection with any issue in the action.

Commencement   1 October 1966.

Order 75, r 29   *(revoked by SI 1971/1269)*

Order 75, r 30 Examination of witnesses and other persons

(1)   The power conferred by Order 39, rule 1, shall extend to the making of an order authorising the examination of a witness or person on oath before a judge sitting in court as if for the trial of the cause or matter, without that cause or matter having been set down for trial or called on for trial.

(2)   The power conferred by the said rule 1 shall also extend to the making of an order, with the consent of the parties, providing for the evidence of a witness being taken as if before an examiner, but without an examiner actually being appointed or being present.

(3)   Where an order is made under paragraph (2), it may make provision for any consequential matters and, subject to any provision so made, the following provisions shall have effect—
  (a)   the party whose witness is to be examined shall provide a shorthand writer to take down the evidence of the witness;
  (b)   any representative, being counsel or solicitor, of either of the parties shall have authority to administer the oath to the witness;
  (c)   the shorthand writer need not himself be sworn but shall certify in writing as correct a transcript of his notes of the evidence and deliver it to the solicitor for the party whose witness was examined, and that solicitor must file it in the registry;
  (d)   unless the parties otherwise agree or the Court otherwise orders, the transcript or a copy thereof shall, before the transcript is filed, be made available to the counsel or other persons who acted as advocates at the examination, and if any of those persons is of opinion that the transcript does not accurately represent the evidence he shall make a certificate specifying the corrections which in his opinion should be made therein, and that certificate must be filed with the transcript.

(4)   In actions in which preliminary acts fall to be filed under rule 18, an order shall not be made under Order 39, rule 1, authorising any examination of a witness before the preliminary acts have been filed, unless for special reasons the Court thinks fit so to direct.

(5)　Order 39 shall apply in relation to an Admiralty cause or matter as if for references therein to the Central Office (except the references in rule 3) there were substituted references to the registry.

[(6)　The [Lord Chief Justice] may appoint such number of barristers or solicitors as he thinks fit to act as examiners of the Court in connection with Admiralty causes and matters, and may revoke any such appointment.

(7)　Order 39, rules 16 to 19, shall not apply in relation to examiners of the Court appointed under [paragraph (6)].]

Commencement　1 October 1966.
Amendments　Para (6): originally para (1) of rule 31, renumbered as para (6) of this rule by SI 1966/1055, r 4(2); words "Lord Chief Justice" substituted by SI 1971/1269, r 25(4).
Para (7): originally para (2) of rule 31, renumbered as para (7) of this rule by SI 1966/1055, r 4(2); words "paragraph (6)" substituted by SI 1966/1055, r 4(2).

[Order 75, r 31 Trial without pleadings

Order 18, rule 21 shall apply to Admiralty actions as it applies to other actions except that the summons must be served on every other party not less than 7 days before the day specified in the summons for the hearing thereof.]

Commencement　2 January 1981.
Amendments　Original r 31(1), (2) became r 30(6), (7) by virtue of SI 1966/1055, r 4(2); new r 31 inserted by SI 1966/1055, r 4(3); substituted by SI 1980/1908, r 12(4).

[Order 75, r 32 Further provisions with respect to evidence

(1)　. . .

(2)　Order 38, rule 14, shall apply in relation to the issue of a writ of subpoena ad testificandum or subpoena duces tecum in an Admiralty cause or matter as if for references therein to the Central Office there were substituted references to the registry.

(3)　Unless the Court otherwise directs, Order 38, rule 21(1), shall not apply in relation to any statement which is admissible in evidence by virtue of section 2, 4 or 5 of the Civil Evidence Act 1968 and which an applicant for judgment in default under rule 19 or 21 desires to give in evidence at the hearing of the motion by which the application for judgment is made.

(4)–(6)　. . .

(7)　Unless the Court otherwise directs, an affidavit for the purposes of rule 19(4), 21 or 38(2) may, except in so far as it relates to the service of a writ, contain statements of information or belief with the sources and grounds thereof.]

Commencement　1 October 1969.
Amendments　This rule was substituted by SI 1969/1105, r 8(3).
Paras (1), (5): revoked by SI 1984/1051, r 31.
Paras (4), (6): revoked by SI 1980/1908, r 12(5).

Order 75, r 33 Proceedings for apportionment of salvage

(1)　Proceedings for the apportionment of salvage the aggregate amount of which has already been ascertained shall be assigned to the [Queen's Bench Division and taken by the Admiralty Court, and shall] be begun by originating motion.

(2) ...

(3) On the hearing of the motion the judge may exercise any of the jurisdiction conferred by section 556 of the Merchant Shipping Act 1894.

Commencement 1 October 1966.
Amendments Para (1): words from "Queen's Bench" to "and shall" substituted by SI 1971/1269, r 25(6). Para (2): revoked by SI 1984/1051, r 31.

[Order 75, r 33A Issue of originating and other motions

(1) Notice of an originating motion in Admiralty must be issued out of the registry.

(2) Notice of any other motion in an Admiralty action must be issued out of the registry or, if the action is proceeding in a district registry, that registry.]

Commencement 1 October 1984.
Amendments This rule was inserted by SI 1984/1051, r 32.

[Order 75, r 34 Notice of motion in actions in rem

(1) The affidavits, if any, in support of a motion in an action in rem must be filed in the appropriate registry before the notice of motion is issued, unless the Court gives leave to the contrary.

(2) A notice of motion, except a motion for judgment in default, must be served on all caveators together with copies of the affidavits, if any, in support of the motion 2 clear days at least before the hearing, unless the Court gives leave to the contrary.]

Commencement 1 October 1984.
Amendments This rule was substituted by SI 1984/1051, r 33.

Order 75, r 35 Agreement between solicitors may be made order of court

(1) Any agreement in writing between the solicitors of the parties to a cause or matter, dated and signed by those solicitors, may, if the registrar thinks it reasonable and such as [a judge] would under the circumstances allow, be filed in the registry, and the agreement shall thereupon become an order of court and have the same effect as if such order had been made by [a judge in person].

(2) Paragraph (1) shall apply in relation to a cause or matter which is proceeding in a district registry as if for the references to the registrar and the registry there were substituted references to the [district judge] and district registry respectively.

Commencement 1 October 1966.
Amendments Para (1): words "a judge" and "a judge in person" substituted by SI 1971/1269, r 25(3).

Order 75, r 36 Originating summons procedure

(1) An originating summons in Admiralty may be issued either out of the registry or out of a district registry.

[(2) In the application of Order 12 and of Order 28, rule 2 to the Admiralty proceedings begun by originating summons, references to the Central Office shall have effect as references to the registry.]

Commencement 1 October 1984 (para (2)); 1 October 1966 (remainder)
Amendments Para (2): substituted, for paras (2)-(4) as originally enacted, by SI 1984/1051, r 34.

Order 75, r 37 Limitation action: parties

(1) In a limitation action the person seeking relief shall be the plaintiff and shall be named in the writ by his name and not described merely as the owner of, or as bearing some other relation to, a particular ship or other property.

(2) The plaintiff must make one of the persons with claims against him in respect of the casualty to which the action relates defendant to the action and may make any or all of the others defendants also.

(3) At least one of the defendants to the action must be named in the writ by his name but the other defendants may be described generally and not named by their names.

(4) The writ must be served on one or more of the defendants who are named by their names therein and need not be served on any other defendant.

(5) In this rule and rules 38, 39 and 40 "name" includes a firm name or the name under which a person carries on his business, and where any person with a claim against the plaintiff in respect of the casualty to which the action relates has described himself for the purposes of his claim merely as the owner of, or as bearing some other relation to, a ship or other property, he may be so described as defendant in the writ and, if so described, shall be deemed for the purposes of the rules aforesaid to have been named in the writ by his name.

Commencement 1 October 1966.

[Order 75, r 37A Limitation action: payment into court

(1) The plaintiff may constitute a limitation fund by paying into court the sterling equivalent of the number of special drawing rights to which he claims to be entitled to limit his liability under [the Merchant Shipping Act 1979 together with interest] thereon from the date of the occurrence giving rise to his liability to the date of payment into court.

(2) Where the plaintiff does not know the sterling equivalent of the said number of special drawing rights on the date of payment into court he may calculate the same on the basis of the latest available published sterling equivalent of a special drawing right as fixed by the International Monetary Fund, and in the event of the sterling equivalent of a special drawing right on the date of payment into court under paragraph (1) being different from that used for calculating the amount of that payment into court the plaintiff may—

    (a) make up any deficiency by making a further payment into court which, if made within 14 days after the payment into court under paragraph (1), shall be treated, except for the purposes of the rules relating to the accrual of interest on money paid into court, as if it had been made on the date of that payment into court, or

    (b) apply to the court for payment out of any excess amount (together with any interest accrued thereon) paid into court under paragraph (1).

(3) An application under paragraph (2)(b) may be made ex parte and must be supported by evidence proving the sterling equivalent of the appropriate number of special drawing rights on the date of payment into court.

(4)   On making any payment into court under this rule, the plaintiff shall give notice thereof in writing to every defendant, specifying the date of payment in [the amount paid in, the amount of interest included therein, the rate of such interest] and the period to which it relates.

The plaintiff shall also give notice in writing to every defendant of any excess amount (and any interest thereon) paid out to him under paragraph (2)(b).

(5)   Order 22, rules 10, 11 and 13 shall apply to a limitation action as they apply to an action for a debt or damages, and rule 24(2) and (3) of this Order shall apply, with the necessary modifications, to the payment out of money paid into court under this rule.]

Commencement   20 February 1985.
Amendments   This rule was inserted by SI 1985/69, r 6.
Para (1): words "the Merchant Shipping Act together with interest" substituted by SI 1986/2289, r 8(2).
Para (4): words from "the amount" to "such interest" substituted by SI 1986/2289, r 8(3).

Order 75, r 38 Limitation action: summons for decree or directions

(1)   Within 7 days after the [acknowledgment of issue or service of the writ by one of the defendants named therein by their names or, if none of them acknowledges issue or service, within 7 days after the time limited for acknowledging service], the plaintiff, without serving a statement of claim, must take out a summons returnable in chambers before the registrar or [district judge], as the case may be, asking for a decree limiting his liability or, in default of such a decree, for directions as to the further proceedings in the action.

(2)   The summons must be supported by an affidavit or affidavits proving—
   (a)   the plaintiff's case in the action, and
   (b)   if none of the defendants named in the writ by their names has [acknowledged service], service of the writ on at least one of the defendants so named.

(3)   The affidavit in support of the summons must state—
   (a)   the names of all the persons who, to the knowledge of the plaintiff, have claims against him in respect of the casualty to which the action relates, not being defendants to the action who are named in the writ by their names, and
   (b)   the address of each of those persons, if known to the plaintiff.

(4)   The summons and every affidavit in support thereof must, at least 7 clear days before the hearing of the summons, be served on any defendant who has [acknowledged issue or service of the writ].

(5)   On the hearing of the summons the registrar [district judge], if it appears to him that it is not disputed that the plaintiff has a right to limit his liability, shall make a decree limiting the plaintiff's liability and fix the amount to which the liability is to be limited.

(6)   On the hearing of the summons the registrar [district judge], if it appears to him that any defendant has not sufficient information to enable him to decide whether or not to dispute that the plaintiff has a right to limit his liability, shall give such directions as appear to him to be appropriate for enabling the defendant to obtain such information and shall adjourn the hearing.

(7)   If on the hearing or resumed hearing of the summons the registrar [district judge] does not make a decree limiting the plaintiff's liability, he shall give such directions as to the further proceedings in the action as appear to him to be appropriate including, in particular, a direction requiring the taking out of a summons

for directions under Order 25 [and, if he gives no such direction, a direction fixing the period within which any notice under Order 38, rule 21, must be served].

(8)   Any defendant who, after the registrar [district judge] has given directions under paragraph (7), ceases to dispute the plaintiff's right to limit his liability must forthwith file a notice to that effect in the registry or district registry, as the case may be, and serve a copy on the plaintiff and on any other defendant who has [acknowledged issue or service of the writ].

(9)   If every defendant who disputes the plaintiff's right to limit his liability serves a notice on the plaintiff under paragraph (8), the plaintiff may take out a summons returnable in chambers before the registrar or [district judge], as the case may be, asking for a decree limiting his liability; and paragraphs (4) and (5) shall apply to a summons under this paragraph as they apply to a summons under paragraph (1).

Commencement   1 October 1966.
Amendments   Para (1): words from "acknowledgment of issue" to "acknowledging service" substituted by SI 1979/1716, r 41(1).
Para (2): in sub-para (b) words "acknowledged service" substituted by SI 1979/1716, r 41(2).
Paras (4), (8): words "acknowledged issue or service of the writ" substituted by SI 1979/1716, r 41(3).
Para (7): words from "and, if he gives" to the end added by SI 1969/1105, r 8(4).

Order 75, r 39 Limitation action: proceedings under decree

(1)   Where the only defendants in a limitation action are those named in the writ by their names and all the persons so named have either been served with the writ or [acknowledged the issue thereof], any decree in the action limiting the plaintiff's liability (whether made by a registrar [district judge] or on the trial of the action)—

(a)   need not be advertised, but
(b)   shall only operate to protect the plaintiff in respect of claims by the persons so named or persons claiming through or under them.

(2)   In any case not falling within paragraph (1), any decree in the action limiting the plaintiff's liability (whether made by a [district judge] or on the trial of the action)—

(a)   shall be advertised by the plaintiff in such manner and within such time as may be provided by the decree;
(b)   shall fix a time within which persons with claims against the plaintiff in respect of the casualty to which the action relates may . . . file their claims, and, in cases to which rule 40 applies, take out a summons, if they think fit, to set the order aside.

(3)   The advertisement to be required under paragraph (2)(a) shall, unless for special reasons the registrar [district judge] or judge thinks fit otherwise to provide, be a single advertisement in each of three newspapers specified in the decree, identifying the action, the casualty and the relation of the plaintiff thereto (whether as owner of a ship involved in the casualty or otherwise as the case may be), stating that the decree has been made and specifying the amounts fixed thereby as the limits of the plaintiff's liability and the time allowed thereby for . . . the filing of claims and the taking out of summonses to set the decree aside.

The plaintiff must within the time fixed under paragraph (2)(b) file in the registry or district registry, as the case may be, a copy of each newspaper in which the advertisement required under paragraph (2)(a) appears.

(4)   The time to be allowed under paragraph (2)(b) shall, unless for special reasons the registrar [district judge] or judge thinks fit otherwise to provide, be not less than 2 months

from the latest date allowed for the appearance of the advertisements; and after the expiration of the time so allowed, [no claim may be filed] or summons taken out to set aside the decree except with the leave of the registrar [district judge] ....

(5)   [Save as aforesaid, on the making of any decree limiting the plaintiff's liability arising out of an occurrence the Court may distribute the limitation fund and may stay any proceedings relating to any claim arising out of that occurrence which are pending against the plaintiff.]

Commencement   12 January 1987 (para (5)); 1 October 1966 (remainder).
Amendments   Para (1): words "acknowledged the issue thereof" substituted by SI 1979/1716, r 42(1).
Paras (2), (3): words omitted revoked by SI 1979/1716, r 42(2), (3).
Para (4): words "no claim may be filed" substituted, and words omitted revoked, by SI 1979/1716, r 42(4).
Para (5): substituted by SI 1986/2289, r 8(4).

Order 75, r 40 Limitation action: proceedings to set aside decree

(1)   Where a decree limiting the plaintiff's liability (whether made by a registrar [district judge] or on the trial of the action) fixes a time in accordance with rule 39(2), any person with a claim against the plaintiff in respect of the casualty to which the action relates, who—

(a)   was not named by his name in the writ as a defendant to the action, or

[(b)   if so named, neither was served with the writ nor has acknowledged the issue thereof]

may, within that time, [after acknowledging issue of the writ], take out a summons returnable in chambers before the registrar or [district judge], as the case may be, asking that the decree be set aside.

(2)   The summons must be supported by an affidavit or affidavits showing that the defendant in question has a bona fide claim against the plaintiff in respect of the casualty in question and that he has sufficient prima facie grounds for the contention that the plaintiff is not entitled to the relief given him by the decree.

(3)   The summons and every affidavit in support thereof must, at least 7 clear days before the hearing of the summons, be served on the plaintiff and any defendant [who has acknowledged issue or service of the writ].

(4)   On the hearing of the summons the registrar [district judge], if he is satisfied that the defendant in question has a bona fide claim against the plaintiff and sufficient prima facie grounds for the contention that the plaintiff is not entitled to the relief given him by the decree, shall set the decree aside and give such directions as to the further proceedings in the action as appear to him to be appropriate including, in particular, a direction requiring the taking out of a summons for directions under Order 25.

Commencement   1 October 1966.
Amendments   Para (1): sub-para (b) and words "after acknowledging service of the writ" substituted by SI 1979/1716, r 43(1).
Para (3): words "who has acknowledged issue or service of the writ" substituted by SI 1979/1716, r 43(2).

Order 75, r 41 References to registrar

(1)   Any party (hereafter in this rule referred to as the "claimant") making a claim which is referred to the registrar for decision must, within 2 months after the order is made, or, in a limitation action, within such other period as the Court may direct, file his claim and, unless the reference is in such an action, serve a copy of the claim on every other party.

(2)   At any time after the claimant's claim has been filed or, where the reference is in a limitation action, after the expiration of the time limited by the Court for the filing of claims but, in any case, not less than 28 days before the day appointed for the hearing of the reference, any party to the cause or matter may apply to the registrar by summons for directions as to the proceedings on the reference, and the registrar shall give such directions, if any, as he thinks fit including, without prejudice to the generality of the foregoing words, a direction requiring any party to serve on any claimant, within such period as the registrar may specify, a defence to that claimant's claim.

(3)   The reference shall be heard on a day appointed by the registrar and, unless the reference is in a limitation action or the parties to the reference consent to the appointment of a particular day, the appointment must be made by order on an application by summons made by any party to the cause or matter.

(4)   An appointment for the hearing of a reference shall not be made until after the claimant has filed his claim or, where the reference is in a limitation action, until after the expiration of the time limited by the Court for the filing of claims.

(5)   Not later than 7 days after an appointment for the hearing of a reference has been made the claimant or, where the reference is in a limitation action, the plaintiff must enter the reference for hearing by lodging in the registry a praecipe requesting the entry of the reference in the list for hearing on the day appointed.

(6)   Not less than 14 days before the day appointed for the hearing of the reference the claimant must file—

(a)   a list, signed by him and every other party, of the items (if any) of his claim which are not disputed, stating the amount (if any) which he and the other parties agree should be allowed in respect of each such item, and

(b)   such affidavits or other documentary evidence as is required to support the items of his claim which are disputed;

and, unless the reference is in a limitation action, he must at the same time serve on every other party a copy of every document filed under this paragraph.

(7)   If the claimant fails to comply with paragraph (1) or (6)(b), the Court may, on the application of any other party to the cause or matter, dismiss the claim.

Commencement 1 October 1966.

Order 75, r 42 Hearing of reference

[(1)   Unless a judge in person otherwise orders, a reference shall be heard in public.

(2)   The registrar may adjourn the hearing of a reference from time to time as he thinks fit.]

(4)   When the hearing of the reference has been concluded, the registrar shall—

(a)   reduce to writing his decision on the questions arising in the reference (including any order as to costs) and cause it to be filed;

(b)   cause to be filed either with his decision or subsequently such statement (if any) of the grounds of the decision as he thinks fit; and

(c)   send to the parties to the reference notice that he has done so.

(5)   Where no statement of the grounds of the registrar's decision is filed with his decision and no intimation has been given by the registrar that he intends to file such a

statement later, any party to the reference may, within 14 days after the filing of the decision, make a written request to the registrar to file such a statement.

Commencement 1 October 1984 (paras (1), (2)); 1 October 1966 (remainder).
Amendments Paras (1), (2): substituted, for paras (1)–(3) as originally enacted, by SI 1984/1051, r 35.

Order 75, r 43 Objection to decision on reference

(1) Any party to a reference to the registrar may, by motion in objection, apply . . . to set aside or vary the decision of the [district judge] on the reference, but notice of the motion, specifying the points of objection to the decision, must be filed within [28 days] after the date on which notice of the filing of the decision was sent to that party under rule 42(4) or, if a notice of the filing of a statement of the grounds of the decision was subsequently sent to him thereunder, within [28 days] after the date on which that notice was sent.

(2) The decision of the registrar shall be deemed to be given on the date on which it is filed, but, unless he or [a judge] otherwise directs, the decision shall not be acted upon until the time has elapsed for filing notice of a motion in objection thereto, ...

(3) A direction shall not be given under paragraph (2) without the parties being given an opportunity of being heard, but may, if the [district judge] announces his intended decision at the conclusion of the hearing of the reference, be incorporated in his decision as reduced to writing under rule 42(4).

Commencement 1 October 1966.
Amendments Para (1): words omitted revoked, words "28 days" in both places substituted, by SI 1984/1051, r 36.
Para (2): words "a judge" substituted, words omitted revoked, by SI 1984/1051, r 37.

Order 75, r 44 References to [district judge]

Rules 41, 42 and 43 shall, with the necessary modifications, apply in relation to a claim referred to a [district judge] as they apply in relation to a claim referred to the registrar.

Commencement 1 October 1966.

Order 75, r 45 *(revoked by SI 1987/1423)*

Order 75, r 46 [Date of filing and inspection of documents in the Registry]

(1) [Order 63, rules 3 and 4], shall apply in relation to documents filed in the registry as they apply in relation to documents filed in the Central Office.

(2) For the purpose of the said rule 4, as applied by paragraph (1), a decree made [by a registrar [district judge] in a limitation action and a decision and any statement of the grounds of that decision filed under rule 42 shall be deemed to have been made or given in court.]

Commencement 1 October 1966.
Amendments Rule heading: substituted by SI 1987/1423, r 24.
Para (1): words "Order 63, rules 3 and 4" substituted by SI 1987/1423, r 24.
Para (2): words from "by a district judge" to the end substituted by SI 1984/1051, r 39.

Order 75, r 47 *(revoked by SI 1984/1051)*

[ORDER 76
CONTENTIOUS PROBATE PROCEEDINGS

Order 76, r 1 Application and interpretation

(1)   This Order applies to probate causes and matters, [including applications for the rectification of a will,] and the other provisions of these Rules apply to those causes and matters subject to the provisions of this Order.

(2)   In these Rules "probate action" means an action for the grant of probate of the will, or letters of administration of the estate, of a deceased person or for the revocation of such a grant or for a decree pronouncing for or against the validity of an alleged will, not being an action which is non-contentious or common form probate business.

(3)   In this Order, "will" includes a codicil.

[(4)   In this Order, "relevant office" means—
    (a)   if the action concerned is proceeding in a Chancery district registry, that registry, and
    (b)   in any other case, Chancery Chambers.]]

Commencement   1 October 1992 (para (4)); 1 October 1971 (remainder).
Amendments   Order 76 was substituted by SI 1971/1269, r 26.
Para (1): words "including applications for the rectification of a will," added by SI 1982/1786, r 20.
Para (4): inserted by SI 1992/1907, r 3.
Cross references   See CCR Order 41, r 1.

[Order 76, r 2 Requirements in connection with issue of writ

(1)   A probate action must be begun by writ, and the writ must be issued out of [Chancery Chambers] [or one of the Chancery district registries].

[(2)   Before a writ beginning a probate action is issued it must be indorsed with a statement of the nature of the interest of the plaintiff and of the defendant in the estate of the deceased to which the action relates.]]

Commencement   1 October 1984 (para (2)); 1 October 1971 (remainder).
Amendments   See the first note to Order 76, r 1.
Para (1): words "Chancery Chambers" substituted by SI 1982/1111, r 71; words "or one of the Chancery district registries" inserted by SI 1992/1907, r 4.
Para (2): substituted by SI 1984/1051, r 43.
Cross references   See CCR Order 41, r 2.

[Order 76, r 3 Parties to action for revocation of grant

Every person who is entitled or claims to be entitled to administer the estate of a deceased person under or by virtue of an unrevoked grant of probate of his will or letters of administration of his estate shall be made a party to any action for revocation of the grant.]

Commencement   1 October 1971.
Amendments   See the first note to Order 76, r 1.
Cross references   This rule is applied to the county court by CCR Order 41, r 4.

[Order 76, r 4 Lodgment of grant in action for revocation

(1)   Where, at the commencement of an action for the revocation of a grant of probate of the will or letters of administration of the estate of a deceased person, the

probate or letters of administration, as the case may be, have not been lodged in court, then—

    (a) if the action is commenced by a person to whom the grant was made, he shall lodge the probate or letters of administration in [relevant office] within 7 days after the issue of the writ;

    (b) if any defendant to the action has the probate or letters of administration in his possession or under his control, he shall lodge it or them in [relevant office] within 14 days after the service of the writ upon him.

In this paragraph "court" includes the principal registry of the Family Division or a district probate registry.

(2)   Any person who fails to comply with paragraph (1) may, on the application of any party to the action, be ordered by the Court to lodge the probate or letters of administration in [relevant office] within a specified time; and any person against whom such an order is made shall not be entitled to take any step in the action without the leave of the Court until he has complied with the order.]

Commencement 1 October 1971.
Amendments See the first note to Order 76, r 1.
Words "relevant office" wherever they occur substituted by SI 1992/1907, r 5(a), (b).
Cross references This rule is applied to the county court by CCR Order 41, r 4.

[Order 76, r 5 Affidavit of testamentary scripts

(1)   Unless the Court otherwise directs, the plaintiff and every defendant who has [acknowledged service of the writ] in a probate action must swear an affidavit—

    (a) describing any testamentary script of the deceased person, whose estate is the subject of the action, of which he has any knowledge or, if such be the case, stating that he knows of no such script, and

    (b) if any such script of which he has knowledge is not in his possession or under his control, giving the name and address of the person in whose possession or under whose control it is or, if such be the case, stating that he does not know the name or address of that person.

(2)   Any affidavit required by this rule must be filed, . . . and any testamentary script referred to therein which is in the possession or under the control of the deponent must be lodged in [relevant office] within 14 days [after the acknowledgment of service by a defendant to the action or, if no defendant acknowledges service] and the Court does not otherwise direct, before an order is made for the trial of the action.

(3)   Where any testamentary script required by this rule to be lodged in [relevant office] or any part thereof is written in pencil, then, unless the Court otherwise directs, a facsimile copy of that script, or of the page or pages thereof containing the part written in pencil, must also be lodged in [relevant office] and the words which appear in pencil in the original must be underlined in red ink in the copy.

(4)   Except with the leave of the Court, a party to a probate action shall not be allowed to inspect an affidavit filed, or any testamentary script lodged, by any other party to the action under this rule, unless and until an affidavit sworn by him containing the information referred to in paragraph (1) has been filed.

(5)   In this rule "testamentary script" means a will or draft thereof, written instructions for a will made by or at the request or under the instructions of the testator and any document purporting to be evidence of the contents, or to be a copy, of a will which is alleged to have been lost or destroyed.]

Commencement 1 October 1971.
Amendments See the first note to Order 76, r 1.
Para (1): words "acknowledged service of the writ" substituted by SI 1979/1716, r 48, Schedule, Pt 1.
Para (2): words omitted revoked by SI 1982/1111, r 73; words "relevant office" substituted by SI 1992/
1907, r 5(c); words from "after the acknowledgment" to "acknowledges service" substituted by SI 1979/
1716, r 48, Schedule, Pt 1.
Para (3): words "relevant office" in both places substituted by SI 1992/1907, r 5(d).
Cross references This rule is applied to the county court by CCR Order 41, r 4.
Forms Affidavit of testamentary scripts (ChPF37).

[Order 76, r 6 [Failure to acknowledge service]

(1)   Order 13 shall not apply in relation to a probate action.

(2)   Where any of several defendants to a probate action fails [to acknowledge service of the writ, the plaintiff may, after the time for acknowledging service has expired and upon filing an affidavit proving due service of the writ . . . on that defendant proceed with the action as if that defendant had acknowledged service].

(3)   Where the defendant, or all the defendants, to a probate action, fails or fail to [acknowledge service of the writ], then, unless on the application of the plaintiff the Court orders the action to be discontinued, the plaintiff may after the time limited [for acknowledging service] by the defendant apply to the Court for an order for trial of the action.

(4)   Before applying for an order under paragraph (3) the plaintiff must file an affidavit proving due service of the writ . . . on the defendant and, if no statement of claim is indorsed on the writ, he must lodge a statement of claim in the judge's chambers.

(5)   Where the Court grants an order under paragraph (3), it may direct the action to be tried an affidavit evidence.]

Commencement 1 October 1971.
Amendments See the first note to Order 76, r 1.
Rule heading: further substituted by SI 1979/1716, r 48, Schedule, Pt 1.
Para (2): words from "to acknowledge service" to the end substituted by SI 1979/1716, r 48, Schedule, Pt 1;
words omitted therein revoked by SI 1980/2000, r 21.
Para (3): words "acknowledge service of the writ" and "for acknowledging service" substituted by SI 1979/
1716, r 48, Schedule, Pt 1.
Para (4): words omitted revoked by SI 1980/2000, r 21.

[Order 76, r 7 Service of statement of claim

The plaintiff in a probate action must, unless the Court gives leave to the contrary or unless a statement of claim is indorsed on the writ, serve a statement of claim on every defendant who [acknowledges service of the writ] the action and must do so before the expiration of 6 weeks after [acknowledgment of service] by that defendant or of 8 days after the filing by that defendant of an affidavit under rule 5, whichever is the later.]

Commencement 1 October 1971.
Amendments See the first note to Order 76, r 1.
Words "acknowledges service of the writ" and "acknowledgment of service" substituted by SI 1979/1716, r
48, Schedule, Pt 1.

[Order 76, r 8 Counterclaim

(1)   Notwithstanding anything in Order 15, rule 2(1), a defendant to a probate action who alleges that he has any claim or is entitled to any relief or remedy in

respect of any matter relating to the grant of probate of the will, or letters of administration of the estate, of the deceased person which is the subject of the action must add to his defence a counterclaim in respect of that matter.

(2)   If the plaintiff fails to serve a statement of claim, any such defendant may, with the leave of the Court, serve a counterclaim and the action shall then proceed as if the counterclaim were the statement of claim.]

Commencement   1 October 1971.
Amendments   See the first note to Order 76, r 1.
Cross references   This rule is applied to the county court by CCR Order 41, r 4.

[Order 76, r 9 Contents of pleadings

(1)   Where the plaintiff in a probate action disputes the interest of a defendant he must allege in his statement of claim that he denies the interest of that defendant.

(2)   In a probate action in which the interest by virtue of which a party claims to be entitled to a grant of letters of administration is disputed, the party disputing that interest must show in his pleading that if the allegations made therein are proved he would be entitled to an interest in the estate.

(3)   Without prejudice to Order 18, rule 7, any party who pleads that at the time when a will, the subject of the action, was alleged to have been executed the testator did not know and approve of its contents must specify the nature of the case on which he intends to rely, and no allegation in support of that plea which would be relevant in support of any of the following other pleas, that is to say:—
    (a)   that the will was not duly executed,
    (b)   that at the time of the execution of the will the testator was not of sound mind, memory and understanding, and
    (c)   that the execution of the will was obtained by undue influence or fraud,

shall be made by that party unless that other plea is also pleaded.]

Commencement   1 October 1971.
Amendments   See the first note to Order 76, r 1.
Cross references   This rule is applied to the county court by CCR Order 41, r 4.

[Order 76, r 10 Default of pleadings

(1)   Order 19 shall not apply in relation to a probate action.

(2)   Where any party to a probate action fails to serve on any other party a pleading which he is required by these Rules to serve on that other party, then, unless the Court orders the action to be discontinued or dismissed, that other party may, after the expiration of the period fixed by or under these Rules for service of the pleading in question, apply to the Court for an order for trial of the action; and if an order is made the Court may direct the action to be tried on affidavit evidence.]

Commencement   1 October 1971.
Amendments   See the first note to Order 76, r 1.

[Order 76, r 11 Discontinuance and dismissal

(1)   Order 21 shall not apply in relation to a probate action.

(2)   At any stage of the proceedings in a probate action the Court may, on the

application of the plaintiff or of any party to the action who has [acknowledged service of the writ] therein, order the action to be discontinued or dismissed on such terms as to costs or otherwise as it thinks just, and may further order that a grant of probate of the will, or letters of administration of the estate, of the deceased person, as the case may be, which is the subject of the action, be made to the person entitled thereto.

(3)   An application for an order under this rule may be made by motion or summons or by notice under Order 25, rule 7.]

Commencement 1 October 1971.
Amendments See the first note to Order 76, r 1.
Para (2): words "acknowledged service of the writ" substituted by SI 1979/1716, r 48, Schedule, Pt 1.

[Order 76, r 12 Compromise of action: trial on affidavit evidence

Where, whether before or after the service of the defence in a probate action, the parties to the action agree to a compromise, the Court may order the trial of the action on affidavit evidence.]

Commencement 1 October 1971.
Amendments See the first note to Order 76, r 1.
Cross references This rule is applied to the county court by CCR Order 41, r 4.
Forms Order involving compromise (ChPF38).

[Order 76, r [13] Application for order to bring in will, etc

(1)   Any application in a probate action for an order under [section 122 of the Act] shall be for an order requiring a person to bring a will or other testamentary paper into [relevant office] or to attend in court for examination.

(2)   An application under paragraph (1) shall be made by summons in the action, which must be served on the person against whom the order is sought.

(3)   Any application in a probate action for the issue of a subpoena under [section 123 of the Act] shall be for the issue of a subpoena requiring a person to bring into [relevant office] a will or other testamentary paper.

(4)   An application under paragraph (3) may be made ex parte and must be supported by an affidavit setting out the grounds of the application.

(5)   An application under paragraph (3) shall be made to a master who may, if the application is granted, authorise the issue of a subpoena accordingly.

(6)   Any person against whom a subpoena is issued under [section 123 of the Act] and who denies that the will or other testamentary paper referred to in the subpoena is in his possession or under his control may file an affidavit to that effect.]

Commencement 1 October 1971.
Amendments See the first note to Order 76, r 1.
Originally r 14, renumbered as r 13 and existing r 13 revoked by SI 1982/1111, r 74.
Para (1): words "section 122 of the Act" substituted by SI 1982/1111, r 115, Schedule; words "relevant office" substituted by SI 1992/1907, r 5(e).
Para (3): words "section 123 of the Act" substituted by SI 1982/1111, r 115, Schedule; words "relevant office" substituted by SI 1992/1907, r 5(e).
Para (6): words "section 123 of the Act" substituted by SI 1982/1111, r 115, Schedule.
Definitions The Act: Supreme Court Act 1981.
Forms Subpoena to bring in script (ChPF35).

[Order 76, r [14] Administration pendente lite

(1)   An application under [section 117] of the Act for an order for the grant of administration may be made by summons issued in the Chancery Division.

(2)   Where an order for a grant of administration is made under the said [section 117], Order 30, rules 2, 4 and 6 and (subject to [sub-section (3)] of the said section) rule 3, shall apply as if the administrator were a receiver appointed by the Court; and every application relating to the conduct of the administration shall be made in the Chancery Division.]

Commencement 1 October 1971.
Amendments See the first note to Order 76, r 1.
Previously r 15, renumbered as r 14 by SI 1982/1111, r 74.
Para (1): words "section 117" substituted by SI 1982/1111, r 115, Schedule.
Para (2): words "section 117" and "sub-section (3)" substituted by SI 1982/1111, r 115, Schedule.
Definitions The Act: Supreme Court Act 1981.
Forms Security of receiver or administrator (ChPF30).
Order appointing administrator pendente lite (ChPF36).

[Order 76, r 15 Probate counterclaim in other proceedings

(1)   In this rule "probate counterclaim" means a counterclaim in any action other than a probate action by which the defendant claims any such relief as is mentioned in rule 1(2).

(2)   Subject to the following paragraphs, this Order shall apply with the necessary modifications to a probate counterclaim as it applies to a probate action.

(3)   A probate counterclaim must contain a statement of the nature of the interest of the defendant and of the plaintiff in the estate of the deceased to which the counterclaim relates.

(4)   . . .

(5)   Unless an application under Order 15, rule 5(2), is made within seven days after the service of a probate counterclaim for the counterclaim to be struck out and the application is granted, the Court shall, if necessary of its own motion, order the transfer of the action to the Chancery Division (if it is not already assigned to that Division) and to [either the Royal Courts of Justice or a Chancery district registry (if it is not already proceeding in one of those places).]]

Commencement 1 April 1976.
Amendments See the first note to Order 76, r 1.
This rule was added as r 16 by SI 1976/337, r 15; subsequently renumbered as r 15 by SI 1982/1111, r 74.
Para (4): revoked by SI 1984/1051, r 44.
Para (5): words from "either the Royal Courts" to the end substituted by SI 1992/1907, r 6.

[Order 76, r 16 Rectification of wills

(1)   Where an application is made for the rectification of a will, and the grant has not been lodged in court, rule 4 shall apply, with the necessary modifications, as if the proceedings were a probate action.

(2)   A copy of every order made for the rectification of a will shall be sent to the principal registry of the Family Division for filing, and a memorandum of the order shall be endorsed on, or permanently annexed to, the grant under which the estate is administered.]

Commencement 1 January 1983.
Amendments This rule was added by SI 1982/1786, r 21.

ORDER 77
PROCEEDINGS BY AND AGAINST THE CROWN

Order 77, r 1 Application and interpretation

(1) These rules apply to civil proceedings to which the Crown is a party subject to the following rules of this Order.

(2) In this Order—

"civil proceedings by the Crown", "civil proceedings against the Crown" and "civil proceedings by or against the Crown" have the same respective meanings as in Part II of the Crown Proceedings Act 1947 and do not include any of the proceedings specified in section 23(3) of that Act;

"civil proceedings to which the Crown is a party" has the same meaning as it has for the purposes of Part IV of the Crown Proceedings Act 1947, by virtue of section 38(4) of that Act;

"order against the Crown" means any order (including an order for costs) made in any civil proceedings by or against the Crown or in any proceedings on the Crown side of the Queen's Bench Division, or in connection with any arbitration to which the Crown is a party, in favour of any person against the Crown or against a government department or against an officer of the Crown as such;

"order" includes a judgment, decree, rule, award or declaration.

Commencement 1 October 1966.
Cross references See CCR Order 42, r 1.

Order 77, r 2 Transfer of proceedings

(1) Subject to paragraph (2), in civil proceedings by or against the Crown no order shall be made under Order 4, rule 6, for the transfer of the proceedings, or of any summons or other application therein, from the Royal Courts of Justice to a district registry, except with the consent of the Crown.

(2) . . . in any civil proceedings against the Crown begun by the issue of a writ out of a district registry [the Crown may acknowledge service of the writ either in the district registry or, at the option of the Crown, in [the appropriate office of the Supreme Court at the Royal Courts of Justice], and where service is [acknowledged in an office of the Supreme Court at the Royal Courts of Justice], the action shall thereafter proceed in the Royal Courts of Justice and], no order shall be made under Order 4, rule 6, for the transfer of any proceedings before the trial from the Royal Courts of Justice to a district registry.

Commencement 1 October 1966.
Amendments Para (2): words omitted revoked and words from "the Crown may" to "Royal Courts of Justice and" substituted by SI 1979/1716, r 44; words in square brackets therein substituted by SI 1982/1111, r 76.

Order 77, r 3 Particulars to be included in indorsement of claim

(1) In the case of a writ which begins civil proceedings against the Crown the indorsement of claim required by Order 6, rule 2, shall include a statement of the circumstances in which the Crown's liability is alleged to have arisen and as to the government department and officers of the Crown concerned.

(2)   If in civil proceedings against the Crown a defendant considers that the writ does not contain a sufficient statement as required by this rule, he may, before the expiration of the [time limited for acknowledging service of the writ], apply to the plaintiff by notice for a further and better statement containing such information as may be specified in the notice.

(3)   Where a defendant gives a notice under this rule, the [time limited for acknowledging service of the writ] shall not expire until 4 days after the defendant has notified the plaintiff in writing that the defendant is satisfied with the statement supplied in compliance with the notice or 4 days after the Court has, on the application of the plaintiff by summons served on the defendant not less than 7 days before the return day, decided that no further information as to the matters referred to in paragraph (1) is reasonably required.

Commencement   1 October 1966.
Amendments   Paras (2), (3): words "time limited for acknowledging service of the writ" substituted by SI 1979/1716, r 48, Schedule, Pt 1.
Cross references   See CCR Order 42, rr 4, 5.

Order 77, r 4 Service on the Crown

(1)   Order 10, Order 11 and any other provision of these rules relating to service out of the jurisdiction shall not apply in relation to the service of any process by which civil proceedings against the Crown are begun.

(2)   Personal service of any document required to be served on the Crown for the purpose of or in connection with any civil proceedings is not requisite; but where the proceedings are by or against the Crown service on the Crown must be effected—
    (a)   by leaving the document at the office of the person who is in accordance with section 18 of the Crown Proceedings Act 1947 to be served, or of any agent whom that person has nominated for the purpose, but in either case with a member of the staff of that person or agent, or
    (b)   by posting it in a prepaid envelope addressed to the person who is to be served as aforesaid or to any such agent as aforesaid.

(3)   In relation to the service of any document required to be served on the Crown for the purpose of or in connection with any civil proceedings by or against the Crown, Order 65, rules 5 and 9, shall not apply, and Order 65, rule 7, shall apply as if the reference therein to rules 2 and 5(1)(a) of that Order were a reference to paragraph (2)(a) of this rule.

Commencement   1 October 1966.
Cross references   See CCR Order 42, r 7.

Order 77, r 5   *(revoked by SI 1979/1716)*

Order 77, r 6 Counterclaim and set-off

(1)   Notwithstanding Order 15, rule 2, and Order 18, rules 17 and 18, a person may not in any proceedings by the Crown make any counterclaim or plead a set-off if the proceedings are for the recovery of, or the counterclaim or set-off arises out of a right or claim to repayment in respect of, any taxes, duties or penalties.

(2)   Notwithstanding Order 15, rule 2, and Order 18, rules 17 and 18, no counterclaim may be made, or set-off pleaded, without the leave of the Court, by the

Crown in proceedings against the Crown, or by any person in proceedings by the Crown—

    (a)   if the Crown is sued or sues in the name of a government department and the subject-matter of the counterclaim or set-off does not relate to that department; or

    (b)   if the Crown is sued or sues in the name of the Attorney-General.

(3)   Any application for leave under this rule must be made by summons.

Commencement   1 October 1966.
Cross references   See CCR Order 42, r 9.

Order 77, r 7 Summary judgment

(1)   [No application shall be made against the Crown—

    (a)   under Order 14, rule 1, or Order 86, rule 1, in any proceedings against the Crown,

    (b)   under Order 14, rule 5, in any proceedings by the Crown, or

    (c)   under Order 14A, rule 1, in any proceedings by or against the Crown.]

(2)   Where an application is made by the Crown under Order 14, rule 1, Order 14, rule 5, or Order 86, rule 1, the affidavit required in support of the application must be made by—

    (a)   the solicitor acting for the Crown, or

    (b)   an officer duly authorised by the solicitor so acting or by the department concerned;

and the affidavit shall be sufficient if it states that in the deponent's belief the applicant is entitled to the relief claimed and there is no defence to the claim or part of a claim to which the application relates or no defence except as to the amount of any damages claimed.

Commencement   1 February 1991 (para (1)); 1 October 1966 (remainder).
Amendments   Para (1): substituted by SI 1990/2599, r 10.
Cross references   See CCR Order 42, r 5(5).

Order 77, r 8 Summary applications to the Court in certain revenue matters

(1)   This rule applies to applications under section 14 of the Crown Proceedings Act 1947.

(2)   An application to which this rule applies may be made by originating motion or originating summons.

(3)   The person from whom any account or information or payment is claimed or by whom any books are required to be produced must be made respondent or, where the application is made by originating summons, defendant to the application.

(4)   An originating summons or notice of originating motion under this rule—

    (a)   must be entitled in the matter or matters out of which the need for the application arises and in the matter of the Crown Proceedings Act 1947; and

    (b)   must refer to the enactment under which the account or information or payment or the production of books is claimed and, where information is claimed, must show (by appropriate questions or otherwise) what information is required.

(5)   Upon any application to which this rule applies an affidavit by a duly authorised officer of the government department concerned setting out the state of facts upon which the application is based and stating that he has reason to think that those facts exist shall be evidence of those facts; and if evidence is filed disputing any of those facts, further evidence may be filed, and the Court may either decide the matter upon the affidavits (after any cross-examination that may have been ordered) or may direct that it be decided by oral evidence in court.

(6)   An order in favour of the Crown on an application to which this rule applies shall, unless the Court otherwise determines, name a time within which each of its terms is to be complied with.

(7)   ...

(8)   Nothing in this rule shall, in relation to any case in which the only relief claimed by the Crown is the payment of money, be construed as requiring the Crown to proceed by way of an application to which this rule applies or as preventing the Crown from availing itself of any other procedure which is open to it under these rules.

Commencement 1 October 1966.
Amendments Para (7): revoked by SI 1982/1111, r 115, Schedule.

[Order 77, r 8A Joinder of Commissioners of Inland Revenue under Order 15, rule 6(2)(b)(ii)

Nothing in Order 15, rule 6(2)(b)(ii), shall be construed as enabling the Commissioners of Inland Revenue to be added as a party to any cause or matter except with their consent signified in writing or in such manner as may be authorised.]

Commencement 31 August 1971.
Amendments This rule was inserted by SI 1971/1269, r 48.

Order 77, r 9 Judgment in default

(1)   Except with the leave of the Court, no judgment in default of [notice of intention to defend] or of pleading shall be entered against the Crown in civil proceedings against the Crown or in third party proceedings against the Crown.

(2)   Except with the leave of the Court, Order 16, rule 5(1)(a), shall not apply in the case of third party proceedings against the Crown.

(3)   An application for leave under this rule may be made by summons or, except in the case of an application relating to Order 16, rule 5, by motion; and the summons or, as the case may be, notice of the motion must be served not less than 7 days before the return day.

Commencement 1 October 1966.
Amendments Para (1): words "notice of intention to defend" substituted by SI 1979/1716, r 48, Schedule, Pt 1.
Cross references See CCR Order 42, r 5.

Order 77, r 10 Third party notices

(1)   Notwithstanding anything in Order 16, a third party notice (including a notice issuable by virtue of Order 16, rule 9) for service on the Crown shall not be issued without the leave of the Court, and the application for the grant of such leave must be made by summons, and the summons must be served on the plaintiff and the Crown.

(2)   Leave to issue such a notice for service on the Crown shall not be granted unless the Court is satisfied that the Crown is in possession of all such information as it reasonably requires as to the circumstances in which is alleged that the liability of the Crown has arisen and as to the departments and officers of the Crown concerned.

Commencement 1 October 1966.
Cross references See CCR Order 42, r 11.

Order 77, r 11 Interpleader: application for order against Crown

No order shall be made against the Crown under Order 17, rule 5(3), except upon an application by summons served not less than 7 days before the return day.

Commencement 1 October 1966.

Order 77, r 12 Discovery and interrogatories

(1)   Order 24, rules 1 and 2, shall not apply in civil proceedings to which the Crown is a party.

(2)   In any civil proceedings to which the Crown is a party any order of the Court made under the powers conferred by section 28(1) of the Crown Proceedings Act 1947 shall be construed as not requiring the disclosure of the existence of any document the existence of which it would, in the opinion of a Minister of the Crown, be injurious to the public interest to disclose.

(3)   Where in any such proceedings an order of the Court directs that a list of documents made in answer to an order for discovery against the Crown shall be verified by affidavit, the affidavit shall be made by such officer of the Crown as the Court may direct.

(4)   Where in any such proceedings an order is made under the said section 28 for interrogatories to be answered by the Crown, the Court shall direct by what officer of the Crown the interrogatories are to be answered.

(5)   ...

Commencement 1 October 1966.
Amendments Para (5): revoked by SI 1989/2427, r 20.
Cross references See CCR Order 42, r 12.

Order 77, r 13 Place of trial

(1)   Civil proceedings by or against the Crown shall not, except with the consent of the Crown, be directed to be tried elsewhere than at the Royal Courts of Justice.

(2)　Nothing in any of these rules shall prejudice the right of the Crown to demand a local venue for the trial of any proceedings in which the Attorney General has waived his right to a trial at bar.

Commencement　1 October 1966.

Order 77, r 14 Evidence

(1)　Civil proceedings against the Crown may be instituted under Order 39, rule 15, in any case in which the Crown is alleged to have an interest or estate in the honour, title, dignity or office or property in question.

(2)　For the avoidance of doubt it is hereby declared that any powers exercisable by the Court in regard to the taking of evidence are exercisable in proceedings by or against the Crown as they are exercisable in proceedings between subjects.

Commencement　1 October 1966.

Order 77, r 15 Execution and satisfaction of orders

(1)　Nothing in Orders 45 to 52 shall apply in respect of any order against the Crown.

(2)　An application under the proviso to subsection (1) of section 25 of the Crown Proceedings Act 1947 for a direction that a separate certificate shall be issued under that subsection with respect to the costs (if any) ordered to be paid to the applicant, may be made to the Court ex parte without summons.

(3)　Any such certificate must be in Form No 95 or 96 in Appendix A, whichever is appropriate.

Commencement　1 October 1966.
Cross references　See CCR Order 42, r 13.

Order 77, r 16 Attachment of debts, etc

(1)　No order—
  (a) for the attachment of debts under Order 49, or
  (b) for the appointment of a sequestrator under Order 45, or
  (c) for the appointment of a receiver under Order 30 or 51,

shall be made or have effect in respect of any money due or accruing due, or alleged to be due or accruing due, from the Crown.

[(1A) No application shall be made under paragraph (2) unless the order of the Court to be enforced is for a sum of money amounting in value to at least £50.]

[(2)　Every application to the Court for an order under section 27(1) of the Crown Proceedings Act 1947 restraining any person from receiving money payable to him by the Crown and directing payment of the money to the applicant or some other person must be made by summons and, unless the Court otherwise directs, served—
  (a) on the Crown at least 15 days before the return day, and
  (b) on the person to be restrained or his solicitor at least 7 days after the summons has been served on the Crown and at least 7 days before the return day.

(2A)   An application under paragraph (2) must be supported by an affidavit—

   (a)   setting out the facts giving rise to the application;

   (b)   stating the name and last known address of the person to be restrained;

   (c)   identifying the order to be enforced and stating the amount of such order and the amount remaining unpaid under it at the time of the application, and

   (d)   identifying the particular debt from the Crown in respect of which the application is made.

(2B)   Where the debt from the Crown in respect of which the application is made is money payable by the Crown to a person on account of a deposit in the National Savings Bank, the affidavit must state the name and address of the branch of the Post Office at which the account is believed to be held and the number of that account or, if it be the case, that all or part of this information is not known to the deponent.]

(3)   Order 49, rules 5 and 6, shall apply in relation to such an application as is mentioned in paragraph (2) for an order restraining a person from receiving money payable to him by the Crown as those rules apply to an application under Order 49, rule 1, for an order for the attachment of a debt owing to any person from a garnishee, except that the Court shall not have power to order execution to issue against the Crown.

Commencement   1 October 1984 (paras (1A), (2), (2A), (2B)); 1 October 1966 (remainder).
Amendments   Para (1A): inserted by SI 1984/1051, r 45(1).
Paras (2)–(2B): substituted, for para (2) as originally enacted, by SI 1984/1051, r 45(2).
Cross references   See CCR Order 42, r 14.

Order 77, r 17 Proceedings relating to postal packets

(1)   An application by any person under [section 30(5) of the Post Office Act 1969] for leave to bring proceedings in the name of the sender or addressee of a postal packet or his personal representatives must be made by originating summons in the Queen's Bench Division.

(2)   The Crown and the person in whose name the applicant seeks to bring proceedings must be made defendants to a summons under this rule.

[(3)   A summons under this rule shall be in Form No 10 in Appendix A.]

Commencement   3 June 1980 (para (3)); 1 October 1966 (remainder).
Amendments   Para (1): words "section 30(5) of the Post Office Act 1969" substituted by SI 1982/1111, r 115, Schedule.
Para (3): substituted by SI 1979/1716, r 48, Schedule, Pt 2.
Cross references   See CCR Order 49, r 15.

Order 77, r 18 Applications under ss 17 and 29 of Crown Proceedings Act

(1)   Every application to the Court under section 17(4) of the Crown Proceedings Act 1947 must be made by summons.

(2)   An application such as is referred to in section 29(2) of the Crown Proceedings Act 1947 may be made to the Court at any time before trial by motion or summons, or may be made at the trial of the proceedings.

Commencement   1 October 1966.

ORDER 78

COUNTY COURT PROCEEDINGS TRANSFERRED OR REMOVED TO HIGH COURT

Order 78, r 1 Application and interpretation

(1)   This Order applies where an order has been made under [section 41 or 42 of the County Courts Act 1984] for the transfer, or under section 20 of the Crown Proceedings Act 1947 for the removal, of proceedings from a county court to the High Court.

(2)   Where . . . only the proceedings on a counterclaim are transferred, this Order shall apply as if the party setting up the counterclaim were the plaintiff and the party resisting it the defendant, and references in this Order to the plaintiff and the defendant shall be construed accordingly.

(3)   References in the following provisions of this Order to the plaintiff and the defendant shall, in relation to proceedings begun in the county court otherwise than by plaint, be construed as references to the applicant and the respondent respectively.

Commencement 1 October 1966.
Amendments Para (1): words "section 41 or 42 of the County Courts Act 1984" substituted by SI 1985/69, r 7(2), Schedule.
Para (2): words omitted revoked by SI 1981/1734, r 26.

Order 78, r 2 Duties of officer

On receipt by the proper officer of the documents referred to in [[Order 16, rule 10] of the County Court Rules 1981], that officer must forthwith—

    (a) file the said documents and make an entry of the filing thereof in the cause book,

    (b) mark the action with the name of the Division to which it should be assigned, and

    (c) give notice to all parties to the proceedings in the county court that the action is proceeding in the High Court at the Royal Courts of Justice or, as the case may be, in the district registry (naming it), if any, specified in the order for transfer as the registry in which the proceedings are to proceed and that the defendant is required to [acknowledge service of the notice].

Commencement 1 October 1966.
Amendments First words in square brackets substituted by SI 1982/1111, r 115, Schedule, words "Order 16, rule 10" therein substituted by SI 1985/69, r 7(2), Schedule; words "acknowledge service of the notice" substituted by SI 1979/1716, r 48, Schedule, Pt 1.

Order 78, r 3 [Acknowledgment of service]

The defendant must, within 7 days after receipt of the notice referred to in rule 2, [acknowledge service thereof] in accordance with Order 12, rules 1 to 4, and Order 12, [rules 1 and 4], shall apply as if the proceedings transferred or removed were an action begun by writ and as if the appropriate office for the purpose of those rules were—

    (a) where the order transferring the proceedings provides that they shall proceed in a district registry, that registry;

    (b) where such order does not so provide, and where the proceedings have been ordered to be removed into the High Court under section 20 of the Crown Proceedings Act 1947, the Central Office[, Chancery Chambers or the [Admiralty and Commercial Registry], as the case may be].

Commencement 1 October 1966.
Amendments Rule heading: substituted by SI 1979/1716, r 48, Schedule, Pt 1.
Words "acknowledge service thereof" and "rules 1 and 4" substituted by SI 1979/1716, r 48, Schedule, Pt 1; words from ", Chancery Chambers" to the end substituted by SI 1982/1111, r 77, words "Admiralty and Commercial Registry" therein substituted by SI 1987/1423, r 2.

Order 78, r 4 Judgment [on failure to give notice of intention to defend]

(1)   If the defendant fails, or all the defendants (if more than one) fail, to [give notice of intention to defend] within the period prescribed by rule 3, the plaintiff, after having caused an address for service to be entered in the cause book, may, with the leave of the Court, enter judgment against the defendant or defendants, as the case may be, with costs.

(2)   An application for leave under this rule must be made by summons which must, notwithstanding anything in Order 65, rule 9, be served on the defendant, and the address for service of the defendant shall be his address for service in the proceedings in the county court.

Commencement 1 October 1966.
Amendments Rule heading: words "on failure to give notice of intention to defend" substituted by SI 1979/1716, r 48, Schedule, Pt 1.
Para (1): words "give notice of intention to defend" substituted by SI 1979/1716, r 48, Schedule, Pt 1.

Order 78, r 5 Summons for directions or summary judgment

(1)   Where a defendant [gives notice of intention to defend] the action the plaintiff must, within 7 days after [such notice is given], cause an address for service to be entered in the cause book and either—
  (a)   take out and serve on the defendant a summons for directions returnable in not less than 21 days, or
  (b)   except where the defendant is the Crown, make an application under Order 14, rule 1, for judgment against the defendant;

and where a summons is served on the defendant under sub-paragraph (a), Order 25, rules 2 to 7, shall, with any necessary modifications, apply as if that summons were a summons for directions under that Order.

(2)   If the plaintiff fails either to take out such a summons, or make such an application, as is referred to in paragraph (1) within the period prescribed thereby the defendant or any defendant may take out such a summons or may apply for an order dismissing the action.

(3)   On the hearing of an application to dismiss the action the Court may either dismiss the action on such terms as may be just or may deal with the application as if it were a summons for directions.

Commencement 1 October 1966.
Amendments Para (1): words "gives notice of intention to defend" and "such notice is given" substituted by SI 1979/1716, r 48, Schedule, Part 1.

ORDER 79
CRIMINAL PROCEEDINGS

Order 79, rr 1–7 *(revoked by SI 1971/1955)*

Order 79, r 8 Estreat of recognizances

(1)　No recognizance acknowledged in or removed into the Queen's Bench Division shall be estreated without the order of a judge.

(2)　Every application to estreat a recognizance in the Queen's Bench Division must be made by summons to a judge in chambers and must be supported by an affidavit showing in what manner the breach has been committed and proving that the summons was duly served.

(3)　A summons under this rule must be served at least 2 clear days before the day named therein for the hearing.

(4)　On the hearing of the application the judge may, and if requested by any party shall, direct any issue of fact in dispute to be tried by a jury.

(5)　If it appears to the judge that a default has been made in performing the conditions of the recognizance, the judge may order the recognizance to be estreated.

Commencement　1 October 1966.

Order 79, r 9 Bail

[(1)　Subject to the provisions of this rule, every application to the High Court in respect of bail in any criminal proceeding—
- (a)　where the defendant is in custody, must be made by summons before a judge in chambers to show cause why the defendant should not be [granted] bail;
- (b)　where the defendant has been [granted] bail, must be made by summons before a judge in chambers to show cause why the variation in the arrangements for bail proposed [by the applicant] should not be made.]

[(2)　Subject to paragraph (5), the summons (in Form No 97 or 97A in Appendix A) must, at least 24 hours before the day named therein for the hearing, be served—
- (a)　where the application was made by the defendant, on the prosecutor and on the Director of Public Prosecutions, if the prosecution is being carried on by him;
- (b)　where the application was made by the prosecutor or a constable under section 3(8) of the Bail Act 1976, on the defendant;

and Order 32, rule 5, shall apply in relation to the summons.]

(3)　Subject to paragraph (5), every application must be supported by affidavit.

(4)　Where a defendant in custody who desires to apply for bail is unable through lack of means to instruct a solicitor, he may give notice in writing to the judge in chambers stating his desire to apply for bail and requesting that the official solicitor shall act for him in the application, and the judge may, if he thinks fit, assign the official solicitor to act for the applicant accordingly.

(5)　Where the official solicitor has been so assigned the judge may, if he thinks fit, dispense with the requirements of paragraphs (1) to (3) and deal with the application in a summary manner.

[(6) Where the judge in chambers by whom an application for bail in criminal proceedings is heard grants the defendant bail, the order must be in Form No 98 in Appendix A and a copy of the order shall be transmitted forthwith—

(a) where the defendant has been committed to the Crown Court for trial or to be sentenced or otherwise dealt with, to the appropriate officer of the Crown Court;

(b) in any other case, to the clerk of the court which committed the defendant.

(6A) The recognizance of any surety required as a condition of bail granted as aforesaid may, where the defendant is in a prison or other place of detention, be entered into before the governor or keeper of the prison or place as well as before the persons specified in section 8(4) of the Bail Act 1976.

(6B) Where under section 3(5) or (6) of the Bail Act 1976 a judge in chambers imposes a requirement to be complied with before a person's release on bail, the judge may give directions as to the manner in which and the person or persons before whom the requirement may be complied with.]

[(7) A person who in pursuance of an order for the grant of bail made by a judge under this rule proposes to enter into a recognizance or give security must, unless the judge otherwise directs, give notice (in Form No 100 in Appendix A) to the prosecutor at least 24 hours before he enters into the recognizance or complies with the requirement as aforesaid.]

[(8) Where in pursuance of such an order as aforesaid a recognizance is entered into or requirement complied with before any person, it shall be the duty of that person to cause the recognizance or, as the case may be, a statement of the requirement complied with to be transmitted forthwith—

(a) where the defendant has been committed to the Crown Court for trial or to be sentenced or otherwise dealt with, to the appropriate officer of the Crown Court;

(b) in any other case, to the clerk of the court which committed the defendant;

and a copy of such recognizance or statement shall at the same time be sent to the governor or keeper of the prison or other place of detention in which the defendant is detained, unless the recognizance was entered into or the requirement complied with before such governor or keeper.]

(9) . . .

[(10) An order by the judge in chambers varying the arrangements under which the defendant has been [granted] bail shall be in Form 98A in Appendix A and a copy of the order shall be transmitted forthwith—

(a) [where the defendant has been committed to the Crown Court for trial or to be sentenced or otherwise dealt with], to the [appropriate officer of the Crown Court];

(b) in any other case, to the clerk of the court which committed the defendant.]

[(11)] Where in pursuance of an order of a judge in chambers or of [the Crown Court] a person is released on bail in any criminal proceeding pending the determination of an appeal to the High Court or House of Lords or an application for an order of certiorari, then, upon the abandonment of the appeal or application, or upon the decision of the High Court or House of Lords being given, any justice (being a justice acting for the same petty sessions area as the magistrates' court by which that person was convicted or sentenced) may issue process for enforcing the decision in respect of which such appeal or application was brought or, as the case may be, the decision of the High Court or House of Lords.

[(12)] If an applicant to the High Court in any criminal proceedings is refused bail by a judge in chambers, the applicant shall not be entitled to make a fresh application for bail to any other judge or to a Divisional Court.

[(13) The record required by section 5 of the Bail Act 1976 to be made by the High Court shall be made by including in the file relating to the case in question a copy of the relevant order of the Court and shall contain the particulars set out in Form No 98 or 98A in Appendix A, whichever is appropriate, except that in the case of a decision to withhold bail the record shall be made by inserting a statement of the decision on the Court's copy of the relevant summons and including it in the file relating to the case in question.]

[(14) In the case of a person whose return is sought under the Fugitive Offenders Act 1967 or whose surrender is sought under Part I of the Criminal Justice Act 1988, this rule shall apply as if references to the defendant were references to that person and references to the prosecutor were references to the state seeking the return or surrender of that person.]

Commencement 1 October 1989 (para (14)); 17 April 1978 (paras (2), (6)–(8), (13)); 1 January 1968 (paras (1), (10)); 1 October 1966 (remainder).
Amendments Para (1): substituted by SI 1967/1809, r 5(1); word "granted" in both places and words "by the applicant" substituted by SI 1978/251, r 3(1).
Paras (2), (7), (8): substituted by SI 1978/251, r 3(2), (4), (5).
Paras (6)–(6B): substituted for para (6) as originally enacted by SI 1978/251, r 3(3).
Para (9): revoked by SI 1978/251, r 3(6).
Para (10): inserted by SI 1967/1809, r 5(4); word "granted" and in sub-para (a) words from "where the defendant" to "dealt with" substituted by SI 1978/251, r 3(7); words "appropriate officer of the Crown Court" substituted by SI 1971/1955, r 23(2).
Para (11): originally para (10), renumbered as para (11) by SI 1967/1809, r 5(5); words "the Crown Court" substituted by SI 1971/1955, r 23(3).
Para (12): originally para (11), renumbered as para (12) by SI 1967/1809, r 5(5).
Para (13): added by SI 1978/251, r 3(8).
Para (14): added by SI 1989/1307, r 14.

Order 79, r 10 Issue of witness summonses, etc

(1)   A witness summons under section 2 of the Criminal Procedure (Attendance of Witnesses) Act 1965 may be issued out of the Crown Office or a district registry.

A witness summons under the said section 2 must be in Form [No 101 or 103] in Appendix A, whichever is appropriate.

(2)   [An originating summons by which an application is made under section 2(2) of the said Act for a direction that a witness summons shall be of no effect shall be in Form No 10 in Appendix A], and the application shall be heard and determined in chambers.

Commencement 1 October 1966.
Amendments Para (1): words "No 101 or 103" substituted by SI 1972/813, r 3.
Para (2): words from "An originating summons" to "Appendix A" substituted by SI 1979/1716, r 48, Schedule, Pt 2.

Order 79, r 11 Application for warrant to arrest witness

(1)   An application to a judge of the High Court under section 4 of the Criminal Procedure (Attendance of Witnesses) Act 1965 for the issue of a warrant to arrest a witness and bring him before the court before which he is required to attend must be made by originating summons, supported by affidavit, and the application may be heard and determined either in court or in chambers.

(2)   [An originating summons by which such an application is made shall be in Form No 10 in Appendix A] and, unless the judge otherwise directs, the summons need not be served on the person sought to be arrested.

Commencement   1 October 1966.
Amendments   Para (2): words from "An originating summons" to "Appendix A" substituted by SI 1979/1716, r 48, Schedule, Pt 2.

ORDER 80
Disability

Order 80, r 1 Interpretation

In this Order—

"the Act" means the [Mental Health Act 1983];

"patient" means a person who, by reason of mental disorder within the meaning of the Act, is incapable of managing and administering his property and affairs;

"person under disability" means a person who is an infant or a patient.

Commencement 1 October 1966.
Amendments Words "Mental Health Act 1983" substituted by SI 1983/1181, r 36, Schedule.

Order 80, r 2 Person under disability must sue, etc by next friend or guardian ad litem

(1)   A person under disability may not bring, or make a claim in, any proceedings except by his next friend and may not [acknowledge service,] defend, make a counter-claim or intervene in any proceedings, or appear in any proceedings under a judgment or order notice of which has been served on him, except by his guardian ad litem.

(2)   Subject to the provision of these rules, anything which in the ordinary conduct of any proceedings is required or authorised by a provision of these rules to be done by a party to the proceedings shall or may, if the party is a person under disability, be done by his next friend or guardian ad litem.

(3)   A next friend or guardian ad litem of a person under disability must act by a solicitor.

Commencement 1 October 1966.
Amendments Para (1): words "acknowledge service," inserted by SI 1979/1716, r 46.
Cross references See CCR Order 10, rr 1, 12.

Order 80, r 3 Appointment of next friend or guardian ad litem

(1)   . . .

(2)   Except as provided by paragraph (4) or (5) or by rule 6, an order appointing a person next friend or guardian ad litem of a person under disability is not necessary.

(3)   Where a person is authorised under [Part VII] of the Act to conduct legal proceedings in the name of a patient or on his behalf, that person shall be entitled to be next friend or guardian ad litem, as the case may be, of the patient in any proceedings to which his authority extends unless, in a case to which paragraph (4) or (6) or rule 6 applies, some other person is appointed by the Court under that paragraph or rule to be next friend or guardian ad litem, as the case may be, of the patient in those proceedings.

(4)   Where a person has been or is next friend or guardian ad litem of a person under disability in any proceedings, no other person shall be entitled to act as such friend or guardian, as the case may be, of the person under disability in those proceedings unless the Court makes an order appointing him such friend or guardian in substitution for the person previously acting in that capacity.

(5)   Where, after any proceedings have been begun, a party to the proceedings becomes a patient, an application must be made to the Court for the appointment of a person to be next friend or guardian ad litem, as the case may be, of that party.

(6)   Except where the next friend or guardian ad litem, as the case may be, of a person under disability has been appointed by the Court—

(a)   the name of any person shall not be used in a cause or matter as next friend of a person under disability,

(b)   [service shall not be acknowledged in a cause or matter] for a person under disability, and

(c)   a person under disability shall not be entitled to appear by his guardian ad litem on the hearing of a petition, summons or motion which, or notice of which, has been served on him,

unless and until the documents listed in paragraph (8) have been filed in the appropriate office.

[(7)   The appropriate office for the purpose of paragraph (6) is the office of the Supreme Court which has the conduct of the business of the division or court in which the cause or matter is proceeding or, if it is proceeding in a district registry, that registry.]

(8)   The documents referred to in paragraph (6) are the following—

(a)   a written consent to be next friend or guardian ad litem, as the case may be, of the person under disability in the cause or matter in question given by the person proposing to be such friend or guardian;

(b)   where the person proposing to be such friend or guardian of the person under disability, being a patient, is authorised under [Part VII] of the Act to conduct the proceedings in the cause or matter in question in the name of the patient or on his behalf, an office copy, sealed with the official seal of the Court of Protection, of the order or other authorisation made or given under the said [Part VII] by virtue of which he is so authorised; and

(c)   except where the person proposing to be such friend or guardian of the person under disability, being a patient, is authorised as mentioned in sub-paragraph (b), a certificate made by the solicitor for the person under disability certifying—

(i)   that he knows or believes, as the case may be, that the person to whom the certificate relates is an infant or a patient, giving (in the case of a patient) the grounds of his knowledge or belief; and

(ii)   where the person under disability is a patient, that there is no person authorised as aforesaid; and

(iii)   except where the person named in the certificate as next friend or guardian ad litem, as the case may be, is the official solicitor, that the person so named has no interest in the cause or matter in question adverse to that of the person under disability.

Commencement   1 October 1982 (para (7)); 1 October 1966 (remainder).
Amendments   Para (1): revoked by SI 1971/1269, r 27.
Para (3): words "Part VII" substituted by SI 1983/1181, r 36, Schedule.
Para (6): in sub-para (b) words "service shall not be acknowledged in a cause or matter" substituted by SI 1979/1716, r 48, Schedule, Pt 1.
Para (7): substituted by SI 1982/1111, r 78.
Para (8): words "Part VII" wherever they occur substituted by SI 1983/1181, r 36, Schedule.
Definitions   The Act: Mental Health Act 1983.
Cross references   See CCR Order 10, rr 1, 2, 5.
Forms   Consent of next friend or guardian ad litem (PF169).
Affidavit in support of application to appoint (ChPF32).

Order 80, rr 4, 5 *(revoked by SI 1971/1269)*

Order 80, r 6 Appointment of guardian where person under disability [does not acknowledge service]

(1)   Where—

    (a)   in an action against a person under disability begun by writ, or by originating summons . . . , [no acknowledgment of service is given] in the action for that person, or

    (b)   the defendant to an action serves a defence and counterclaim on a person under disability who is not already a party to the action, and [no acknowledgment of service is given] for that person,

an application for the appointment by the Court of a guardian ad litem of that person must be made by the plaintiff or defendant, as the case may be, after the time limited (as respects that person) for [acknowledging service] and before proceeding further with the action or counterclaim.

(2)   Where a party to an action has served on a person under disability who is not already a party to the action a third party notice within the meaning of Order 16 and [no acknowledgment of service is given] for that person to the notice, an application for the appointment by the Court of a guardian ad litem of that person must be made by that party after the time limited (as respects that person) for [acknowledging service] and before proceeding further with the third party proceedings.

(3)   Where in any proceedings against a person under disability begun by petition or originating motion . . . that person does not appear by a guardian ad litem at the hearing of the [petition or motion], as the case may be, the Court hearing it may appoint a guardian ad litem of that person in the proceedings or direct that an application be made by the petitioner or applicant, as the case may be, for the appointment of such a guardian.

(4)   At any stage in the proceedings in the Chancery Division under any judgment or order, notice of which has been served on a person under disability, the Court may, if [no acknowledgment of service is given] for that person, appoint a guardian ad litem of that person in the proceedings or direct that an application be made for the appointment of such a guardian.

(5)   An application under paragraph (1) or (2) must be supported by evidence proving—

    (a)   that the person to whom the application relates is a person under disability,

    (b)   that the person proposed as guardian ad litem is willing and a proper person to act as such and has no interest in the proceedings adverse to that of the person under disability,

    (c)   that the writ, originating summons, defence and counterclaim or third party notice, as the case may be, was duly served on the person under disability, and

    (d)   subject to paragraph (6), that notice of the application was, after the expiration of the time limited for [acknowledging service] and at least 7 days before the day named in the notice for hearing of the application, so served on him.

(6)   If the Court so directs, notice of an application under paragraph (1) or (2) need not be served on a person under disability.

(7)   An application for the appointment of a guardian ad litem made in compliance with a direction of the Court given under paragraph (3) or (4) must be supported by evidence proving the matters referred to in paragraph (5)(b).

Commencement 1 October 1966.
Amendments Rule heading: words "does not acknowledge service" substituted by SI 1979/1716, r 48, Schedule, Pt 1.
Para (1): words omitted revoked, words "no acknowledgment of service is given" in both places and words "acknowledging service" substituted by SI 1979/1716, r 48, Schedule, Pt 1.
Para (2): words "no acknowledgment of service is given" and "acknowledging service" substituted by SI 1979/1716, r 48, Schedule, Pt 1.
Para (3): words omitted revoked and words "petition or motion" substituted by SI 1979/1716, r 48, Schedule, Pt 1.
Para (4): words "no acknowledgment of service is given" substituted by SI 1979/1716, r 48, Schedule, Pt 1.
Para (5): in sub-para (d) words "acknowledging service" substituted by SI 1979/1716, r 48, Schedule, Pt 1.
Cross references See CCR Order 10, rr 6, 7 (and see r 8).

Order 80, r 7 Application to discharge or vary certain orders

An application to the Court on behalf of a person under disability served with an order made ex parte under Order 15, rule 7, for the discharge or variation of the order must be made—

(a) if a next friend or guardian ad litem is acting for that person in the cause or matter in which the order is made, within 14 days after the service of the order on that person;

(b) if there is no next friend or guardian ad litem acting for that person in that cause or matter, within 14 days after the appointment of such a friend or guardian to act for him.

Commencement 1 October 1966.

Order 80, r 8 Admission not to be implied from pleading of person under disability

Notwithstanding anything in Order 18, rule 13(1), a person under disability shall not be taken to admit the truth of any allegation of fact made in the pleading of the opposite party by reason only that he has not traversed it in his pleadings.

Commencement 1 October 1966.

Order 80, r 9 Discovery and interrogatories

Orders 24 and 26 shall apply to a person under disability and to his next friend or guardian ad litem.

Commencement 1 October 1966.

Order 80, r 10 Compromise, etc, by person under disability

[(1)] Where in any proceedings money is claimed by or on behalf of a person under disability, no settlement, compromise or payment and no acceptance of money paid into court, whenever entered into or made, shall so far as it relates to that person's claim be valid without the approval of the Court.

[(2) . . .]

Commencement 1 October 1987 (para (2)); 1 October 1966 (remainder).
Amendments Para (1): numbered as such by SI 1987/1423, r 61(1).
Para (2): added by SI 1987/1423, r 61(2); revoked by SI 1988/298, r 7.
Cross references See CCR Order 10, r 10(1).

Order 80, r 11 Approval of settlement

(1)   Where, before proceedings in which a claim for money is made by or on behalf of a person under disability (whether alone or in conjunction with any other person) are begun, an agreement is reached for the settlement of the claim, and it is desired to obtain the Court's approval to the settlement, then, notwithstanding anything in Order 5, rule 2, the claim may be made in proceedings begun by originating summons, and in the summons an application may also be made for—

(a)   the approval of the Court to the settlement and such orders or directions as may be necessary to give effect to it or as may be necessary or expedient under . . . rule 12, or

(b)   alternatively, directions as to the further prosecution of the claim.

(2)   Where in proceedings under this rule a claim is made under the [Fatal Accidents Act 1976], the originating summons must include the particulars mentioned in [section 2(4) of that Act].

(3)   Without prejudice to Order 7, rule 5, and Order 75, rule 36(1), an originating summons under this rule may be issued out of any district registry notwithstanding that the proceedings are assigned to the Chancery Division.

[(4)   An originating summons under this rule shall be in Form No 10 in Appendix A.]

(5)   In this rule "settlement" includes a compromise.

Commencement   3 June 1980 (para (4)); 1 October 1966 (remainder).
Amendments   Para (1): words omitted from para (a) revoked by SI 1986/632, r 8(a).
Para (2): words "Fatal Accidents Act 1976" and "section 2(4) of that Act" substituted by SI 1979/1542, r 9, Schedule.
Para (4): substituted by SI 1979/1716, r 48, Schedule, Pt 2.
Cross references   See CCR Order 10, r 10(2).
Forms   Summons for settlement (PF170, PF171).
Originating summons for settlement (PF172, PF173).
Settlement order (PF174, PF175).

Order 80, r 12 Control of money recovered by person under disability

(1)   Where in any proceedings—

(a)   money is recovered by or on behalf of, or adjudged or ordered or agreed to be paid to, or for the benefit of, a person under disability, or

(b)   money paid into court is accepted by or on behalf of a plaintiff who is a person under disability,

the money shall be dealt with in accordance with directions given by the Court [under] this rule and not otherwise.

(2)   Directions given under this rule may provide that the money shall, as to the whole or any part thereof, be paid into the High Court and invested or otherwise dealt with there.

(3)   Without prejudice to the foregoing provisions of this rule, directions given under this rule may include any general or special directions that the Court thinks fit to give and, in particular, directions as to how the money is to be applied or dealt with and as to any payment to be made, either directly or out of the amount paid into court . . . to the plaintiff, or to the next friend in respect of moneys paid or expenses incurred for or on behalf or for the benefit of the person under disability or for his maintenance or otherwise for his benefit or to the plaintiff's solicitor in respect of costs.

(4)   Where in pursuance of directions given under this rule money is paid into the High Court to be invested or otherwise dealt with there, the money (including any interest thereon) shall not be paid out, nor shall any securities in which the money is invested, or the dividends thereon, be sold, transferred or paid out of court, except in accordance with an order of the Court.

(5)   The foregoing provisions of this rule shall apply in relation to a counterclaim by or on behalf of a person under disability, and a claim made by or on behalf of such a person in an action by any other person for relief under section 504 of the Merchant Shipping Act 1894, as if for references to a plaintiff and a next friend there were substituted references to a defendant and to a guardian ad litem respectively.

Commencement   1 October 1966.
Amendments   Para (1): word "under" substituted by SI 1986/632, r 8(b).
Para (3): words omitted revoked by SI 1986/632, r 8(c).
Cross references   See CCR Order 10, r 11.

[Order 80, r 13 Appointment of guardian of child's estate

(1)   In any of the circumstances described in paragraph (2)(a) to (e) the Court may appoint the Official Solicitor to be a guardian of the estate of a child provided that—
    (a)   the appointment is to subsist only until the child reaches the age of eighteen, and
    (b)   the consent of the persons with parental responsibility for the child (within the meaning of section 3 of the Children Act 1989)—
       (i)   has been signified to the Court, or
      (ii)   in the opinion of the Court, cannot be obtained or may be dispensed with.

(2)   The circumstances referred to in paragraph (1) are:
    (a)   where money is paid into court on behalf of the child in accordance with directions given under rule 12(2) (Control of money recovered by person under disability);
    (b)   where the Criminal Injuries Compensation Board notifies the Court that it has made or intends to make an award to the child either under section 111 of the Criminal Justice Act 1988 or otherwise;
    (c)   where a court or tribunal outside England and Wales notifies the Court that it has ordered or intends to order that money be paid to the child;
    (d)   where the child is absolutely entitled to proceeds of a pension fund;
    (e)   where such an appointment seems desirable to the Court.]

Commencement   1 February 1992.
Amendments   Original r 13 revoked by SI 1986/632, r 8(d); new r 13 inserted by SI 1991/2671, r 6.

Order 80, r 14   *(revoked by SI 1971/1132)*

Order 80, r 15 Proceedings under [Fatal Accidents Act]: apportionment by Court

(1)   Where a single sum of money is paid into court under Order 22, rule 1, in satisfaction of causes of action arising under [the Fatal Accidents Act 1976] and the Law Reform (Miscellaneous Provisions) Act 1934, and that sum is accepted, the money shall be apportioned between the different causes of action by the Court either when giving directions for dealing with it under rule 12 (if that rule applies) or when authorising its payment out of court.

(2)   Where, in an action in which a claim under [the Fatal Accidents Act 1976] is made by or on behalf of more than one person, a sum in respect of damages is adjudged or ordered or agreed to be paid in satisfaction of the claim, or a sum of money paid into court under Order 22, rule 1, is accepted in satisfaction of the cause of action under the said [Act], then, unless the sum has been apportioned between the persons entitled thereto by the jury, it shall be apportioned between those persons by the Court.

The reference in this paragraph to a sum of money paid into court shall be construed as including a reference to part of a sum so paid, being the part apportioned by the Court under paragraph (1) to the cause of action under the said [Act].

Commencement   1 October 1966.
Amendments   Rule heading: words "Fatal Accidents Act" substituted by SI 1982/1111, r 115, Schedule.
Para (1): words "the Fatal Accidents Act 1976" substituted by SI 1980/629, r 24.
Para (2): words "the Fatal Accidents Act 1976" substituted by SI 1980/629, r 24; word "Act" in both places substituted by SI 1980/1908, r 20.

Order 80, r 16 Service of certain documents on person under disability

(1)   Where in any proceedings a document is required to be served personally [or in accordance with Order 10, rule 1(2)] on any person and that person is a person under disability this rule shall apply.

(2)   Subject to the following provisions of this rule and to Order 24, rule 16(3), and Order 26, rule 6(3), the document must be served—
    (a)   in the case of an infant who is not also a patient, on his father or guardian or, if he has no father or guardian, on the person with whom he resides or in whose care he is;
    (b)   in the case of a patient, on the person (if any) who is authorised under [Part VII] of the Act to conduct in the name of the patient or on his behalf the proceedings in connection with which the document is to be served or, if there is no person so authorised, on the person with whom he resides or in whose care he is;
and must be served in the manner required by these rules with respect to the document in question.

(3)   Notwithstanding anything in paragraph (2), the Court may order that a document which has been, or is to be, served on the person under disability or on a person other than a person mentioned in that paragraph shall be deemed to be duly served on the person under disability.

(4)   A judgment or order requiring a person to do, or refrain from doing, any act, a notice of motion or summons for the committal of any person, and a writ of subpoena against any person, must, if that person is a person under disability, be served personally on him unless the Court otherwise orders.

This paragraph shall not apply to an order for interrogatories or for discovery or inspection of documents.

Commencement   1 October 1966.
Amendments   Para (1): words "or in accordance with Order 10, rule 1(2)" inserted by SI 1979/402, r 12.
Para (2): in sub-para (b) words "Part VII" substituted by SI 1983/1181, r 36, Schedule.
Definitions   The Act: Mental Health Act 1983.
Cross references   See CCR Order 10, r 4.

ORDER 81
PARTNERS

Order 81, r 1 Actions by and against firms within jurisdiction

Subject to the provisions of any enactment, any two or more persons claiming to be entitled, or alleged to be liable, as partners in respect of a cause of action and carrying on business within the jurisdiction may sue, or be sued, in the name of the firm (if any) of which they were partners at the time when the cause of action accrued.

Commencement 1 October 1966.
Cross references See CCR Order 5, r 9(1), (3).

Order 81, r 2 Disclosure of partners' names

(1)   Any defendant to an action brought by partners in the name of a firm may serve on the plaintiffs or their solicitor a notice requiring them or him forthwith to furnish the defendant with a written statement of the names and places of residence of all the persons who were partners in the firm at the time when the cause of action accrued; and if the notice is not complied with the Court may order the plaintiffs or their solicitor to furnish the defendant with such a statement and to verify it on oath or otherwise as may be specified in the order, or may order that further proceedings in the action be stayed on such terms as the Court may direct.

(2)   When the names of the partners have been declared in compliance with a notice or order given or made under paragraph (1), the proceedings shall continue in the name of the firm but with the same consequences as would have ensued if the persons whose names have been so declared had been named as plaintiffs in the writ.

(3)   Paragraph (1) shall have effect in relation to an action brought against partners in the name of a firm as it has effect in relation to an action brought by partners in the name of a firm but with the substitution, for references to the defendant and the plaintiffs, of references to the plaintiff and the defendants respectively, and with the omission of the words "or may order" to the end.

Commencement 1 October 1966.
Cross references See CCR Order 5, r 9(2).
Forms Order for written statement (PF177).

Order 81, r 3 Service of writ

(1)   Where by virtue of rule 1 partners are sued in the name of a firm, the writ may, except in the case [mentioned in paragraph (3)], be served—
   (a)   on any one or more of the partners, or
   (b)   at the principal place of business of the partnership within the jurisdiction, on any person having at the time of service the control or management of the partnership business there; [or
   (c)   by sending a copy of the writ by ordinary first-class post (as defined in Order 10, rule 1(2)) to the firm at the principal place of business of the partnership within the jurisdiction];

and [subject to paragraph (2)] where service of the writ is effected in accordance with this paragraph, the writ shall be deemed to have been duly served on the firm, whether or not any member of the firm is out of the jurisdiction.

[(2)   Where a writ is served on a firm in accordance with sub-paragraph (1)(c)—

  (a)   the date of service shall, unless the contrary is shown, be deemed to be the
         seventh day (ignoring Order 3, rule 2(5)) after the date on which the copy
         was sent to the firm; and

  (b)   any affidavit proving due service of the writ must contain a statement to
         the effect that—

     (i)   in the opinion of the deponent (or, if the deponent is the plaintiff's
            solicitor or an employee of that solicitor, in the opinion of the
            plaintiff) the copy of the writ, if sent to the firm at the address in
            question, will have come to the knowledge of one of the persons
            mentioned in paragraph (1)(a) or (b) within 7 days thereafter, and

     (ii)   the copy of the writ has not been returned to the plaintiff through the
            post undelivered to the addressee.]

[(3)] Where a partnership has, to the knowledge of the plaintiff, been dissolved
before an action against the firm is begun, the writ by which the action is begun must
be served on every person within the jurisdiction sought to be made liable in the
action.

[(4)] Every person on whom a writ is served under [paragraph (1)(a) or (b)] must at
the time of service be given a written notice stating whether he is served as a partner
or as a person having the control or management of the partnership business or both
as a partner and as such a person; and any person on whom a writ is so served but to
whom no such notice is given shall be deemed to be served as a partner.

Commencement   24 April 1979 (para (2)); 1 October 1966 (remainder).
Amendments   Para (1): words "mentioned in paragraph (3)" substituted by SI 1982/1111, r 115, Schedule;
sub-para (c) and word "or" immediately preceding it inserted, and words "subject to paragraph (2)" inserted,
by SI 1979/402, r 13(1).
Para (2): inserted by SI 1979/402, r 13(2).
Para (3): originally para (2), renumbered as para (3) by SI 1979/402, r 13(3).
Para (4): originally para (3), renumbered as para (4) and words "paragraph (1)(a) or (b)" substituted by
SI 1979/402, r 13(3).
Cross references   See CCR Order 7, r 13.
Forms   Affidavit of service (PF118, PF121, PF122).
Notice of service on manager (PF176).

Order 81, r 4 [Acknowledgment of service] in an action against firm

(1)   Where persons are sued as partners in the name of their firm, [service may not
be acknowledged] in the name of the firm but only by the partners thereof in their
own names, but the action shall nevertheless continue in the name of the firm.

(2)   Where in an action against a firm the writ by which the action is begun is
served on a person as a partner, that person, if he denies that he was a partner or liable
as such at any material time, may [acknowledge service of the writ and state in his
acknowledgment] that he does so as a person served as a partner in the defendant firm
but who denies that he was a partner at any material time.

[An acknowledgment of service given] in accordance with this paragraph shall,
unless and until it is set aside, be treated as [an acknowledgment by] the defendant firm.

(3)   Where [an acknowledgment of service has been given by] a defendant in
accordance with paragraph (2), then—

  (a)   the plaintiff may either apply to the Court to set it aside on the ground
         that the defendant was a partner or liable as such at a material time or may

leave that question to be determined at a later stage of the proceedings;

(b) the defendant may either apply to the Court to set aside the service of the writ on him on the ground that he was not a partner or liable as such at a material time or may at the proper time serve a defence on the plaintiff denying in respect of the plaintiff's claim either his liability as a partner or the liability of the defendant firm or both.

(4) The Court may at any stage of the proceedings in an action in which a defendant has [acknowledged service] in accordance with paragraph (2), on the application of the plaintiff or of that defendant, order that any question as to the liability of that defendant or as to the liability of the defendant firm be tried in such manner and at such time as the Court directs.

(5) Where in an action against a firm the writ by which the action is begun is served on a person as a person having the control or management of the partnership business, that person may not [acknowledge service of the writ] unless he is a member of the firm sued.

Commencement 1 October 1966.

Amendments Rule heading: words "Acknowledgment of service" substituted by SI 1979/1716, r 48, Schedule, Pt 1.

Para (1): words "service may not be acknowledged" substituted by SI 1979/1716, r 48, Schedule, Pt 1.

Para (2): words from "acknowledge service" to "his acknowledgment", "An acknowledgment of service given" and "an acknowledgment by" substituted by SI 1979/1716, r 48, Schedule, Pt 1.

Para (3): words "an acknowledgment of service has been given by" substituted by SI 1979/1716, r 48, Schedule, Pt 1.

Para (4): words "acknowledged service" substituted by SI 1979/1716, r 48, Schedule, Pt 1.

Para (5): words "acknowledge service of the writ" substituted by SI 1979/1716, r 48, Schedule, Pt 1.

Order 81, r 5 Enforcing judgment or order against firm

(1) Where a judgment is given or order made against a firm, execution to enforce the judgment or order may, subject to rule 6, issue against any property of the firm within the jurisdiction.

(2) Where a judgment is given or order made against a firm, execution to enforce the judgment or order may, subject to rule 6 and to the next following paragraph, issue against any person who—

(a) [acknowledged service of the writ] in the action as a partner, or

(b) having been served as a partner with the writ of summons, [failed to acknowledge service of it] in the action, or

(c) admitted in his pleading that he is a partner, or

(d) was adjudged to be a partner.

(3) Execution to enforce a judgment or order given or made against a firm may not issue against a member of the firm who was out of the jurisdiction when the writ of summons was issued unless he—

(a) [acknowledged service of the writ] in the action as a partner, or

(b) was served within the jurisdiction with the writ as a partner, or

(c) was, with the leave of the Court given under Order 11, served out of the jurisdiction with the writ . . . as a partner;

and, except as provided by paragraph (1) and by the foregoing provisions of this paragraph, a judgment or order given or made against a firm shall not render liable, release or otherwise affect a member of the firm who was out of the jurisdiction when the writ was issued.

(4) Where a party who has obtained a judgment or order against a firm claims that a person is liable to satisfy the judgment or order as being a member of the firm, and the foregoing provisions of this rule do not apply in relation to that person, that party may apply to the Court for leave to issue execution against that person, the application to be made by summons which must be served personally on that person.

(5) Where the person against whom an application under paragraph (4) is made does not dispute his liability, the Court hearing the application may, subject to paragraph (3), give leave to issue execution against that person, and, where that person disputes his liability, the Court may order that the liability of that person be tried and determined in any manner in which any issue or question in an action may be tried and determined.

Commencement 1 October 1966.
Amendments Para (2): in sub-para (a) words "acknowledged service of the writ" and in sub-para (b) words "failed to acknowledge service of it" substituted by SI 1979/1716, r 48, Schedule, Pt 1.
Para (3): in sub-para (a) words "acknowledged service of the writ" substituted by SI 1979/1716, r 48, Schedule, Pt 1; in sub-para (c) words omitted revoked by SI 1980/2000, r 21.
Cross references See CCR Order 25, r 9.

Order 81, r 6 Enforcing judgment or order in actions between partners, etc

(1) Execution to enforce a judgment or order given or made in—
   (a) an action by or against a firm in the name of the firm against or by a member of the firm, or
   (b) an action by a firm in the name of the firm against a firm in the name of the firm where those firms have one or more members in common,

shall not issue except with the leave of the Court.

(2) The Court hearing an application under this rule may give such directions, including directions as to the taking of accounts and the making of inquiries, as may be just.

Commencement 1 October 1966.
Cross references See CCR Order 25, r 10.

Order 81, r 7 Attachment of debts owed by firm

(1) An order may be made under Order 49, rule 1, in relation to debts due or accruing due from a firm carrying on business within the jurisdiction notwithstanding that one or more members of the firm is resident out of the jurisdiction.

(2) An order to show cause under the said rule 1 relating to such debts as aforesaid must be served on a member of the firm within the jurisdiction or on some other person having the control or management of the partnership business.

(3) Where an order made under the said rule 1 requires a firm to appear before the Court, an appearance by a member of the firm constitutes a sufficient compliance with the order.

Commencement 1 October 1966.

Order 81, r 8 Actions begun by originating summons

Rules 2 to 7 shall, with the necessary modifications, apply in relation to an action by or against partners in the name of their firm begun by originating summons as they apply in relation to such an action begun by writ.

Commencement   1 October 1966.

Order 81, r 9 Application to person carrying on business in another name

An individual carrying on business within the jurisdiction in a name or style other than his own name, may [whether or not he is within the jurisdiction,] be sued in that name or style as if it were the name of a firm, and rules 2 to 8 shall, so far as applicable, apply as if he were a partner and the name in which he carries on business were the name of his firm.

Commencement   1 October 1966.
Amendments   Words "whether or not he is within the jurisdiction," inserted by SI 1983/1181, r 18.
Cross references   See CCR Order 5, r 10.

Order 81, r 10 Applications for orders charging partner's interest in partnership property, etc

(1)   Every application to the Court by a judgment creditor of a partner for an order under section 23 of the Partnership Act 1890 (which authorises the High Court or a judge thereof to make certain orders on the application of a judgment creditor of a partner, including an order charging the partner's interest in the partnership property), and every application to the Court by a partner of the judgment debtor made in consequence of the first-mentioned application, must be made by summons.

(2)   A master [or the Admiralty registrar or a [district judge]] may exercise the powers conferred on a judge by the said section 23.

(3)   Every summons issued by a judgment creditor under this rule, and every order made on such a summons, must be served on the judgment debtor and on such of his partners as are within the jurisdiction or, if the partnership is a cost book company, on the judgment debtor and the purser of the company.

(4)   Every summons issued by a partner of a judgment debtor under this rule, and every order made on such a summons, must be served—
   (a)   on the judgment creditor, and
   (b)   on the judgment debtor, and
   (c)   on such of the other partners of the judgment debtor as do not join in the application and are within the jurisdiction or, if the partnership is a cost book company, on the purser of the company.

(5)   A summons or order served in accordance with this rule on the purser of a cost book company or, in the case of a partnership not being such a company, on some only of the partners thereof, shall be deemed to have been served on that company or on all the partners of the partnership, as the case may be.

Commencement   1 October 1966.
Amendments   Para (2): words "or the Admiralty registrar or a district judge" substituted by SI 1971/1269, r 28.

ORDER 82
DEFAMATION ACTIONS

Order 82, r 1 Application

These rules apply to actions for libel or slander subject to the following rules of this Order.

Commencement 1 October 1966.

Order 82, r 2 Indorsement of claim in libel action

Before a writ in an action for libel is issued it must be indorsed with a statement giving sufficient particulars of the publications in respect of which the action is brought to enable them to be identified.

Commencement 1 October 1966.

Order 82, r 3 Obligation to give particulars

(1) Where in an action for libel or slander the plaintiff alleges that the words or matters complained of were used in a defamatory sense other than their ordinary meaning, he must give particulars of the facts and matters on which he relies in support of such sense.

(2) Where in an action for libel or slander the defendant alleges that, in so far as the words complained of consist of statements of fact, they are true in substance and in fact, and in so far as they consist of expressions of opinion, they are fair comment on a matter of public interest, or pleads to the like effect, he must give particulars stating which of the words complained of he alleges are statements of fact and of the facts and matters he relies on in support of the allegation that the words are true.

(3) Where in an action for libel or slander the plaintiff alleges that the defendant maliciously published the words or matters complained of, he need not in his statement of claim give particulars of the facts on which he relies in support of the allegation of malice, but if the defendant pleads that any of those words or matters are fair comment on a matter of public interest or were published on a privileged occasion and the plaintiff intends to allege that the defendant was actuated by express malice, he must serve a reply giving particulars of the facts and matters from which the malice is to be inferred.

(4) This rule shall apply in relation to a counterclaim for libel or slander as if the party making the counterclaim were the plaintiff and the party against whom it is made the defendant.

Commencement 1 October 1966.

Order 82, r 4 Provisions as to payment into court

(1) Where in an action for libel or slander against several defendants sued jointly the plaintiff, in accordance with Order 22, rule 3(1), accepts money paid into court by any of those defendants in satisfaction of his cause of action against that defendant, then, notwithstanding anything in rule 3(4) of that Order, the action shall be stayed as against that defendant only, but—

(a) the sum recoverable under any judgement given in the plaintiff's favour against any other defendant in the action by way of damages shall not exceed the amount (if any) by which the amount of the damages exceeds the amount paid into court by the defendant as against whom the action has been stayed, and

(b) the plaintiff shall not be entitled to his costs of the action against the other defendant after the date of the payment into court unless either the amount of the damages awarded to him is greater than the amount paid into court and accepted by him or the judge is of opinion that there was reasonable ground for him to proceed with the action against the other defendant.

(2) Where in an action for libel a party pleads the defence for which section 2 of the Libel Act 1843 provides, Order 22, rule 7, shall not apply in relation to that pleading.

Commencement 1 October 1966.

Order 82, r 5 Statement in open court

[(1) Where a party wishes to accept money paid into Court in satisfaction of a cause of action for libel or slander, malicious prosecution or false imprisonment, that party may before or after accepting the money apply to a Judge in Chambers by summons for leave to make in open Court a statement in terms approved by the judge.]

(2) Where a party to an action for libel or slander [malicious prosecution or false imprisonment] which is settled before trial desires to make a statement in open court, an application must be made to the Court for an order that the action be set down for trial, and before the date fixed for the trial the statement must be submitted for the approval of the judge before whom it is to be made.

[(3) A Judge in Chambers may approve a statement under paragraph (1) or (2) which refers not only to a cause of action mentioned in those paragraphs but also to any other cause of action joined thereto.]

Commencement 1 February 1992 (para (3)); 5 February 1990 (para (1)); 1 October 1966 (remainder).
Amendments Para (1): substituted by SI 1989/2427, r 25.
Para (2): words "malicious prosecution or false imprisonment" added by SI 1989/2427, r 26.
Para (3): added by SI 1991/2671, r 7.

Order 82, r 6 Interrogatories not allowed in certain cases

In an action for libel or slander where the defendant pleads that the words or matters complained of are fair comment on a matter of public interest or were published on a privileged occasion, no interrogatories as to the defendant's sources of information or grounds of belief shall be allowed.

Commencement 1 October 1966.

Order 82, r 7 *(revoked by SI 1989/2427)*

Order 82, r 8 Fulfilment of offer of amends under s 4 of Defamation Act 1952

(1) An application to the Court under section 4 of the Defamation Act 1952 to determine any question as to the steps to be taken in fulfilment of an offer of amends

made under that section must, unless the application is made in the course of proceedings for libel or slander in respect of the publication to which the offer relates, be made in chambers in the Queen's Bench Division, but only a judge may determine such question.

[(2)   An originating summons by which such an application is made shall be in Form No 10 in Appendix A.]

Commencement   3 June 1980 (para (2)); 1 October 1966 (remainder).
Amendments   Para (2): substituted by SI 1979/1716, r 48, Schedule, Pt 2.

[ORDER 83

Reopening of Agreements under the Consumer Credit Act 1974

Order 83, r 1 Interpretation

In this Order a section referred to by number means the section so numbered in the Consumer Credit Act 1974.]

Commencement　16 May 1977.
Amendments　Order 83 was substituted by SI 1976/1196, r 10.

[Order 83, r 2 Notice to reopen agreement

(1)　Where in any such proceedings in the High Court as are mentioned in section 139(1)(b) the debtor or a surety desires to have a credit agreement reopened, he shall serve a notice to that effect on every other party to the proceedings and file a copy of the notice.

(2)　If at the time of serving a notice under paragraph (1) the debtor or surety [has not acknowledged service of the writ or originating summons] in the proceedings, the notice must specify an address for service as if it were [an acknowledgment of service].]

Commencement　16 May 1977.
Amendments　See the note to Order 83, r 1.
Para (2): words "has not acknowledged service of the writ or originating summons" and "an acknowledgment of service" substituted by SI 1979/1716, r 48, Schedule, Pt 1.
Definitions　Section 139(1)(b): Consumer Credit Act 1974, s 139(1)(b).
Cross references　See CCR Order 49, r 4(14), (15).

[Order 83, r 3 No default judgment without leave

(1)　After a notice under rule 2 has been served in an action begun by writ, judgment [on failure to give notice of intention to defend] or in default of defence shall not be entered except with the leave of the Court.

(2)　An application for the grant of leave under paragraph (1) must be made by summons supported by affidavit, and, notwithstanding anything in Order 65, rule 9, the summons and a copy of the affidavit must be served on every other party to the proceedings.

(3)　If the application is for leave to enter judgment [on failure to give notice of intention to defend], the summons shall not be issued until after the [time limited for acknowledging service of the writ or originating summons in the action].]

Commencement　16 May 1977.
Amendments　See the note to Order 83, r 1.
Para (1): words "on failure to give notice of intention to defend" substituted by SI 1979/1716, r 48, Schedule, Pt 1.
Para (3): words "on failure to give notice of intention to defend" and words from "time limited" to the end substituted by SI 1979/1716, r 48, Schedule, Pt 1.
Forms　Summons to sign judgment (PF178).

[Order 83, r 4 Court's powers on hearing of application

On the hearing of an application under rule 3(2) or of any proceedings in which a notice under rule 2 has been filed, the Court may, whether or not the debtor or surety has [acknowledged service of the writ or originating summons] or appears at the hearing, exercise the powers of the Court under sections 137 to 140 and where, on an application under rule 3(2), the Court refuses leave to enter judgment on a claim or any part of a claim, it may make or give any such order or direction as it might have made or given if the application had been made an application under Order 14, rule 1, for judgment on the claim.]

Commencement   16 May 1977.
Amendments   See the note to Order 83, r 1.
Words "acknowledged service of the writ or originating summons" substituted by SI 1979/1716, r 48, Schedule, Pt 1.
Definitions   Sections 137 to 140: Consumer Credit Act 1974, ss 137–140.

ORDER 84

(revoked by SI 1976/1196)

ORDER 85
ADMINISTRATION AND SIMILAR ACTIONS

Order 85, r 1 Interpretation

In this Order "administration action" means an action for the administration under the direction of the Court of the estate of a deceased person or for the execution under the direction of the Court of a trust.

Commencement   1 October 1966.

Order 85, r 2 Determination of questions, etc, without administration

(1)   An action may be brought for the determination of any question or for any relief which could be determined or granted, as the case may be, in an administration action and a claim need not be made in the action for the administration or execution under the direction of the Court of the estate or trust in connection with which the question arises or the relief is sought.

(2)   Without prejudice to the generality of paragraph (1), an action may be brought for the determination of any of the following questions:—

(a)   any question arising in the administration of the estate of a deceased person or in the execution of a trust;

(b)   any question as to the composition of any class of persons having a claim against the estate of a deceased person or a beneficial interest in the estate of such a person or in any property subject to a trust;

(c)   any question as to the rights or interests of a person claiming to be a creditor of the estate of a deceased person or to be entitled under a will or on the intestacy of a deceased person or to be beneficially entitled under a trust.

(3)   Without prejudice to the generality of paragraph (1), an action may be brought for any of the following reliefs:—

(a)   an order requiring an executor, administrator or trustee to furnish and, if necessary, verify accounts;

(b)   an order requiring the payment into court of money held by a person in his capacity as executor, administrator or trustee;

(c)   an order directing a person to do or abstain from doing a particular act in his capacity as executor, administrator or trustee;

(d)   an order approving any sale, purchase, compromise or other transaction by a person in his capacity as executor, administrator or trustee;

(e)   an order directing any act to be done in the administration of the estate of a deceased person or in the execution of a trust which the Court could order to be done if the estate or trust were being administered or executed, as the case may be, under the direction of the Court.

Commencement   1 October 1966.
Forms   Affidavit verifying accounts (ChPF27).
Administrator's account (ChPF28).

Order 85, r 3 Parties

(1)   All the executors or administrators of the estate or trustees of the trust, as the case may be, to which an administration action or such an action as is referred to in rule 2 relates must be parties to the action, and where the action is brought by executors, administrators or trustees, any of them who does not consent to being joined as a plaintiff must be made a defendant.

(2)   Notwithstanding anything in Order 15, rule 4(2), and without prejudice to the powers of the Court under that Order, all the persons having a beneficial interest in or claim against the estate or having a beneficial interest under the trust, as the case may be, to which such an action as is mentioned in paragraph (1) relates need not be parties to the action; but the plaintiff may make such of those persons, whether all or any one or more of them, parties as, having regard to the nature of the relief or remedy claimed in the action, he thinks fit.

(3)   Where, in proceedings under a judgment or order given or made in an action for the administration under the direction of the Court of the estate of a deceased person, a claim in respect of a debt or other liability is made against the estate by a person not a party to the action, no party other than the executors or administrators of the estate shall be entitled to appear in any proceedings relating to that claim without the leave of the Court, and the Court may direct or allow any other party to appear either in addition to, or in substitution for, the executors or administrators on such terms as to costs or otherwise as it thinks fit.

Commencement 1 October 1966.
Forms Form of inquiry for persons entitled (ChPF7).

Order 85, r 4 Grant of relief in action begun by originating summons

In an administration action or such an action as is referred to in rule 2, the Court may make any certificate or order and grant any relief to which the plaintiff may be entitled by reason of any breach of trust, wilful default or other misconduct of the defendant notwithstanding that the action was begun by originating summons, but the foregoing provision is without prejudice to the power of the Court to make an order under Order 28, rule 8, in relation to the action.

Commencement 1 October 1966.

Order 85, r 5 Judgments and orders in administration actions

(1)   A judgment or order for the administration or execution under the direction of the Court of an estate or trust need not be given or made unless in the opinion of the Court the questions at issue between the parties cannot properly be determined otherwise than under such a judgment or order.

(2)   Where an administration action is brought by a creditor of the estate of a deceased person or by a person claiming to be entitled under a will or on the intestacy of a deceased person or to be beneficially entitled under a trust, and the plaintiff alleges that no or insufficient accounts have been furnished by the executors, administrators or trustees, as the case may be, then, without prejudice to its other powers, the Court may—

    (a) order that proceedings in the action be stayed for a period specified in the order and that the executors, administrators or trustees, as the case may be,

shall within that period furnish the plaintiff with proper accounts;
(b) if necessary to prevent proceedings by other creditors or by other persons claiming to be entitled as aforesaid, give judgment or make an order for the administration of the estate to which the action relates and include therein an order that no proceedings are to be taken under the judgment or order, or under any particular account or inquiry directed, without the leave of the judge in person.

Commencement 1 October 1966.
Forms Judgment in creditor's action (ChPF10–11).

Order 85, r 6 Conduct of sale of trust property

Where in an administration action an order is made for the sale of any property vested in executors, administrators or trustees, those executors, administrators or trustees, as the case may be, shall have the conduct of the sale unless the Court otherwise directs.

Commencement 1 October 1966.

ORDER 86
ACTIONS FOR SPECIFIC PERFORMANCE, ETC: SUMMARY JUDGMENT

Order 86, r 1 Application by plaintiff for summary judgment

(1)   In any action in the Chancery Division begun by writ indorsed with a claim—

- (a)   for specific performance of an agreement (whether in writing or not) for the sale, [purchase, exchange, mortgage or charge] of any property, or for the grant or assignment of a lease of any property, with or without an alternative claim for damages, or
- (b)   for rescission of such an agreement, or
- (c)   for the forfeiture or return of any deposit made under such an agreement,

the plaintiff may, on the ground that the defendant has no defence to the action, apply to the Court for judgment.

(2)   An application may be made against a defendant under this rule whether or not he has [acknowledged service of the writ] in the action.

Commencement   1 October 1966.
Amendments   Para (1): in sub-para (a) words "purchase, exchange, mortgage or charge" substituted by SI 1982/1111, r 79.
Para (2): words "acknowledged service of the writ" substituted by SI 1979/1716, r 48, Schedule, Pt 1.

Order 86, r 2 Manner in which application under rule 1 must be made

[(1)   An application under rule 1 shall be made by summons supported by an affidavit verifying the facts on which the cause of action is based and stating that in the deponent's belief there is no defence to the action.

Unless the Court otherwise directs, an affidavit for the purposes of this paragraph may contain statements of information or belief with the sources and grounds thereof.]

(2)   The summons must set out or have attached thereto minutes of the judgment sought by the plaintiff.

(3)   The summons, a copy of the affidavit in support and of any exhibit referred to therein must be served on the defendant not less than 4 clear days before the return day.

Commencement   1 April 1976 (para (1)); 1 October 1966 (remainder)
Amendments   Para (1): substituted by SI 1976/337, r 16.

Order 86, r [3] Judgment for plaintiff

Unless on the hearing of an application under rule 1 either the Court dismisses the application or the defendant satisfies the Court that there is an issue or question in dispute which ought to be tried or that there ought for some other reason to be a trial of the action, the Court may give judgment for the plaintiff in the action.

Commencement   1 October 1966.
Amendments   Originally r 4, renumbered as r 3 and original r 3 revoked by SI 1982/1111, r 80.

Order 86, r [4] Leave to defend

(1)　A defendant may show cause against an application under rule 1 by affidavit or otherwise to the satisfaction of the Court.

(2)　The Court may give a defendant against whom such an application is made leave to defend the action either unconditionally or on such terms as to giving security or time or mode of trial or otherwise as it thinks fit.

(3)　On the hearing of such an application the Court may order a defendant showing cause or, where that defendant is a body corporate, any director, manager, secretary or other similar officer thereof, or any person purporting to act in any such capacity—

(a)　to produce any document;

(b)　if it appears to the Court that there are special circumstances which make it desirable that he should do so, to attend and be examined on oath.

Commencement　1 October 1966.
Amendments　Originally r 5, renumbered as r 4 by SI 1982/1111, r 80.

Order 86, r [5] Directions

Where the Court orders that a defendant have leave to defend the action, the Court shall give directions as to the further conduct of the action, and Order 25, rules 2 to 7, shall, with the omission of so much of rule 7(1) as requires parties to serve a notice specifying the orders and directions which they require and with any other necessary modifications, apply as if the application under rule 1 were a summons for directions.

Commencement　1 October 1966.
Amendments　Originally r 6, renumbered as r 5 by SI 1982/1111, r 80.

Order 86, r [6] Costs

If the plaintiff makes an application under rule 1 where the case is not within this Order, or if it appears to the Court that the plaintiff knew that the defendant relied on a contention which would entitle him to unconditional leave to defend, then, without prejudice to Order 62, and, in particular, [to paragraphs (1) to (3) of rule 8 of that Order], the Court may dismiss the application with costs and may, if the plaintiff is not an assisted person, require the costs to be paid by him forthwith.

Commencement　1 October 1966.
Amendments　Originally r 7, renumbered as r 6 by SI 1982/1111, r 80.
Words "to paragraphs (1) to (3) of rule 8 of that Order" substituted by SI 1986/632, r 4.

Order 86, r [7] Setting aside judgment

Any judgment given against a defendant who does not appear at the hearing of an application under rule 1 may be set aside or varied by the Court on such terms as it thinks just.

Commencement　1 October 1966.
Amendments　Originally r 8, renumbered as r 7 by SI 1982/1111, r 80.

ORDER 87
DEBENTURE HOLDERS' ACTIONS:
RECEIVER'S REGISTER

Order 87, r 1 Receiver's register

Every receiver appointed by the Court in an action to enforce registered debentures or registered debenture stock shall, if so directed by the Court, keep a register of transfers of, and other transmissions of title to, such debentures or stock (in this Order referred to as "the reciever's register").

Commencement 1 October 1966.

Order 87, r 2 Registration of transfers, etc

(1) Where a receiver is required by rule 1 to keep a receiver's register, then, on the application of any person entitled to any debentures or debenture stock by virtue of any transfer or other transmission of title, and on production of such evidence of identity and title as the receiver may reasonably require, the receiver shall, subject to the following provisions of this rule, register the transfer or other transmission of title in that register.

(2) Before registering a transfer the receiver must, unless the due execution of the transfer is proved by affidavit, send by post to the registered holder of the debentures or debenture stock transferred at his registered address a notice stating—

    (a) that an application for the registration of the transfer has been made, and

    (b) that the transfer will be registered unless within the period specified in the notice the holder informs the receiver that he objects to the registration,

and no transfer shall be registered until the period so specified has elapsed.

The period to be specified in the notice shall in no case be less than 7 days after a reply from the registered holder would in the ordinary course of post reach the receiver if the holder had replied to the notice on the day following the day when in the ordinary course of post the notice would have been delivered at the place to which it was addressed.

(3) On registering a transfer or other transmission of title under this rule the receiver must indorse a memorandum thereof on the debenture or certificate of debenture stock, as the case may be, transferred or transmitted, containing a reference to the action and to the order appointing him receiver.

Commencement 1 October 1966.

Order 87, r 3 Application for rectification of receiver's register

(1) Any person aggrieved by any thing done or omission made by a receiver under rule 2 may apply to the Court for rectification of the receiver's register, the application to be made by summons in the action in which the receiver was appointed.

(2) The summons shall in the first instance be served only on the plaintiff or other party having the conduct of the action but the Court may direct the summons or notice of the application to be served on any other person appearing to be interested.

(3)   The Court hearing an application under this rule may decide any question relating to the title of any person who is party to the application to have his name entered in or omitted from the receiver's register and generally may decide any question necessary or expedient to be decided for the rectification of that register.

Commencement   1 October 1966.

Order 87, r 4 Receiver's register evidence of transfers, etc

Any entry made in the receiver's register, if verified by an affidavit made by the receiver or by such other person as the Court may direct, shall in all proceedings in the action in which the receiver was appointed be evidence of the transfer or transmission of title to which the entry relates and, in particular, shall be accepted as evidence thereof for the purpose of any distribution of assets, notwithstanding that the transfer or transmission has taken place after the making of a certificate in the action certifying the holders of the debentures or debenture stock certificates.

Commencement   1 October 1966.

Order 87, r 5 Proof of title of holder of bearer debenture, etc

(1)   This rule applies in relation to an action to enforce bearer debentures or to enforce debenture stock in respect of which the company has issued debenture stock bearer certificates.

(2)   Notwithstanding that judgment has been given in the action and that a certificate has been made therein certifying the holders of such debentures or certificates as are referred to in paragraph (1), the title of any person claiming to be such a holder shall (in the absence of notice of any defect in the title) be sufficiently proved by the production of the debenture or debenture stock certificate, as the case may be, together with a certificate of identification signed by the person producing the debenture or certificate identifying the debenture or certificate produced and certifying the person (giving his name and address) who is the holder thereof.

(3)   Where such a debenture or certificate as is referred to in paragraph (1) is produced in [Chancery Chambers], the solicitor of the plaintiff in the action must cause to be indorsed thereon a notice stating—

    (a)   that the person whose name and address is specified in the notice (being the person named as the holder of the debenture or certificate in the certificate of identification produced under paragraph (2)) has been recorded in [Chancery Chambers] as the holder of the debenture or debenture stock certificate, as the case may be, and

    (b)   that that person will, on producing the debenture or debenture stock certificate, as the case may be, be entitled to receive payment of any dividend in respect of that debenture or stock unless before payment a new holder proves his title in accordance with paragraph (2), and

    (c)   that if a new holder neglects to prove his title as aforesaid he may incur additional delay, trouble and expense in obtaining payment.

(4)   The solicitor of the plaintiff in the action must preserve any certificates of identification produced under paragraph (2) and must keep a record of the debentures and debenture stock certificates so produced and of the names and addresses of the persons producing them and of the holders thereof, and, if the Court requires it, must verify the record by affidavit.

Commencement   1 October 1966.
Amendments   Para (3): words "Chancery Chambers" in both places substituted by SI 1982/1111, r 81.

Order 87, r 6 Requirements in connection with payments

(1)   Where in an action to enforce any debentures or debenture stock an order is made for payment in respect of the debentures or stock, the Accountant General shall not make a payment in respect of any such debenture or stock unless either there is produced to him the certificate for which paragraph (2) provides or the Court has in the case in question for special reason dispensed with the need for the certificate and directed payment to be made without it.

(2)   For the purpose of obtaining any such payment the debenture or debenture stock certificate must be produced to the solicitor of the plaintiff in the action or to such other person as the Court may direct, and that solicitor or other person must indorse thereon a memorandum of payment and must make and sign a certificate certifying that the statement set out in the certificate has been indorsed on the debenture or debenture stock certificate, as the case may be, and send the certificate to the Accountant General.

Commencement   1 October 1966.

ORDER 88
MORTGAGE ACTIONS

Order 88, r 1 Application and interpretation

(1)   This Order applies to any action (whether begun by writ or originating summons) by a mortgagee or mortgagor or by any person having the right to foreclose or redeem any mortgage, being an action in which there is a claim for any of the following reliefs, namely—

    (a)   payment of moneys secured by the mortgage,

    (b)   sale of the mortgaged property,

    (c)   foreclosure,

    (d)   delivery of possession (whether before or after foreclosure or without foreclosure) to the mortgagee by the mortgagor or by any other person who is or is alleged to be in possession of the property,

    (e)   redemption,

    (f)   reconveyance of the property or its release from the security,

    (g)   delivery of possession by the mortgagee.

(2)   In this Order "mortgage" includes a legal and an equitable mortgage and a legal and an equitable charge, and references to a mortgagor, a mortgagee and mortgaged property shall be construed accordingly.

(3)   An action to which this Order applies is referred to in this Order as a mortgage action.

(4)   These rules apply to mortgage actions subject to the following provisions of this Order.

Commencement   1 October 1966.

Cross references   Rules in the county court dealing with mortgage actions are: CCR Order 6, rr 5, 5A, Order 7, r 15A, Order 9, r 7 and Order 21, r 5(1)(c), (2).

Order 88, r 2 Assignment of certain actions to Chancery Division

Without prejudice to [section 61(1)] of the Act (which provides for the assignment to the Chancery Division of causes or matters for the purposes, among others, of the redemption or foreclosure of mortgages and the sale and distribution of the proceeds of property subject to any lien or charge), any action in which there is a claim for—

    (a)   payment of moneys secured by a mortgage of any real or leasehold property, or

    (b)   delivery of possession (whether before or after foreclosure) to the mortgagee of any such property by the mortgagor or by any other person who is or is alleged to be in possession of the property,

shall be assigned to the Chancery Division.

Commencement   1 October 1966.

Amendments   Words "section 61(1)" substituted by SI 1982/1111, r 115, Schedule.

Definitions   The Act: Supreme Court Act 1981.

Order 88, r 3 Commencement of action . . .

(1)   A writ by which a mortgage action is begun may not be issued out of a district registry [which is not a Chancery district registry], unless the mortgaged property is situated in the district of the registry.

(2) Without prejudice to Order 7, rule 5, in so far as it authorises an originating summons to be issued out of [a Chancery district registry], an originating summons by which a mortgage action is begun may be issued out of any other district registry if, but only if, the property to which the action relates is situated in the district of that other registry.

[(3) The writ or originating summons by which a mortgage action is begun shall be indorsed with or contain a statement showing—
  (a) where the mortgaged property is situated, and
  (b) if the plaintiff claims possession of the mortgaged property and it is situated outside Greater London, whether the property consists of or includes a dwelling house ... ,

[and a certificate that the action is not one to which section 141 of the Consumer Credit Act 1974 applies.]]

[(4) ...]

Commencement 1 April 1976 (para (3)); 1 October 1966 (remainder).
Amendments Rule heading: words omitted revoked by SI 1976/337, r 17(a).
Para (1): words "which is not a Chancery district registry" substituted by SI 1982/1111, r 82.
Para (2): words "a Chancery district registry" substituted by SI 1982/1111, r 82.
Para (3): added by SI 1976/337, r 17(b); words omitted revoked by SI 1991/2671, r 9(a); words from "and a certificate" to the end inserted by SI 1989/177, r 3.
Para (4): inserted by SI 1990/1689, r 32; revoked by SI 1991/2671, r 9(b).
Cross references See CCR Order 6, rr 5, 5A.

Order 88, r [4] Claim for possession: [failure by a defendant to acknowledge service]

(1) Where in a mortgage action in the Chancery Division begun by originating summons, being an action in which the plaintiff is the mortgagee and claims delivery of possession or payment of moneys secured by the mortgage or both, any defendant fails [to acknowledge service of the originating summons], the following provisions of this rule shall apply, and references in those provisions to the defendant shall be construed as references to any such defendant.

This rule shall not be taken as affecting Order 28, rule 3, or rule 5(2), in so far as it requires any document to be served on, or notice given to, a defendant who has [acknowledged service of the originating summons] in the action.

(2) Not less than 4 clear days before the day fixed for the first hearing of the originating summons the plaintiff must serve on the defendant a copy of the notice of appointment for the hearing and a copy of the affidavit in support of the summons.

(3) ...

(4) Where the hearing is adjourned, then, subject to any directions given by the Court, the plaintiff must serve notice of the appointment for the adjourned hearing, together with a copy of any further affidavit intended to be used at that hearing, on the defendant not less than 2 clear days before the day fixed for the hearing.

...

(5) Service under paragraph (2) or (4), and the manner in which it was effected, may be proved by a certificate signed by the plaintiff, if he sues in person, and otherwise by his solicitor.

The certificate may be indorsed on the affidavit in support of the summons or, as the case may be, on any further affidavit intended to be used at an adjourned hearing.

(6)   A copy of any exhibit to an affidavit need not accompany the copy of the affidavit served under paragraph (2) or (4).

(7)   Where the plaintiff gives notice to the defendant under Order 3, rule 6, of his intention to proceed, service of the notice, and the manner in which it was effected, may be proved by a certificate signed as mentioned in paragraph (5).

Commencement   1 October 1966.
Amendments   Originally r 5, renumbered as r 4 and original r 4 revoked by SI 1982/1111, r 83.
Rule heading: words "failure by a defendant to acknowledge service" substituted by SI 1979/1716, r 48, Schedule, Pt 1.
Para (1): words "to acknowledge service of the originating summons" and "acknowledged service of the originating summons" substituted by SI 1979/1716, r 48, Schedule, Pt 1.
Para (3): revoked by SI 1990/2599, r 15(a).
Para (4): words omitted revoked by SI 1990/2599, r 15(b).
Forms   Notice to defendant (ChPF3).
Certificate of solicitor (ChPF4).

Order 88, r [5] Action in Chancery Division for possession or payment: evidence

(1)   The affidavit in support of the originating summons by which an action [(other than an action to which rule 5A applies)] to which this rule applies is begun must comply with the following provisions of this rule.

This rule applies to a mortgage action in the Chancery Division begun by originating summons in which the plaintiff is the mortgagee and claims delivery of possession or payment of moneys secured by the mortgage or both.

(2)   The affidavit must exhibit a true copy of the mortgage and the original mortgage or, in the case of a registered charge, the charge certificate must be produced at the hearing of the summons.

[(2A) Unless the Court otherwise directs, the affidavit may contain statements of information or belief with the sources and grounds thereof.]

(3)   Where the plaintiff claims delivery of possession the affidavit must show the circumstances under which the right to possession arises and, except where the Court in any case or class of case otherwise directs, the state of the account between the mortgagor and mortgagee with particulars of—
    (a)   the amount of the advance,
    (b)   the amount of the [periodic payments required to be made],
    (c)   the amount of any interest or instalments in arrear at the date of issue of the originating summons and at the date of the affidavit, and
    (d)   the amount remaining due under the mortgage.

[(4)   Where the plaintiff claims delivery of possession the affidavit must—
    (a)   give particulars of every person who to the best of the plaintiff's knowledge is in possession of the mortgaged property; and
    (b)   state, in the case of a dwelling house, whether—
        (i)   a land charge of Class F has been registered, or [a notice or caution registered under section 2(7) of the Matrimonial Homes Act 1967 or a notice registered under section 2(8) of the Matrimonial Homes Act 1983] has been entered, and, if so, on whose behalf; and

(ii) he has served notice of the proceedings on the person on whose behalf the land charge is registered or the notice or caution entered.]

(5) If the mortgage creates a tenancy other than a tenancy at will between the mortgagor and mortgagee, the affidavit must show how and when the tenancy was determined and if by service of notice when the notice was duly served.

(6) Where the plaintiff claims payment of moneys secured by the mortgage, the affidavit must prove that the money is due and payable and give the particulars mentioned in paragraph (3).

(7) Where the plaintiff's claim includes a claim for interest to judgment, the affidavit must state the amount of a day's interest.

Commencement 1 October 1993 (para (2A)); 14 February 1983 (para (4)); 1 October 1966 (remainder).
Amendments Originally r 6, renumbered as r 5 by SI 1982/1111, r 83.
Para (1): words "(other than an action to which rule 5A applies)" added by SI 1984/1051, r 9.
Para (2A): inserted by SI 1993/2133, r 11.
Para (3): in sub-para (b) words "periodic payments required to be made" substituted by SI 1977/1955, r 10.
Para (4): substituted by SI 1982/1786, r 22; in sub-para (b) words from "a notice or caution" to "Matrimonial Homes Act 1983" substituted by SI 1985/69, r 7(2), Schedule.
Forms Suspended order for possession (ChPF5).
Re Benjamin order (ChPF9).
Re Benjamin summons (ChPF8).

[Order 88, r 5A Action for the Enforcement of Charging Order by Sale

(1) This rule applies to a mortgage action in the Chancery Division to enforce a charging order by sale of the property charged.

(2) The affidavit in support of the originating summons must—
  (a) identify the charging order sought to be enforced and the subject matter of the charge;
  (b) specify the amount in respect of which the charge was imposed and the balance outstanding at the date of the affidavit;
  (c) verify, so far as known, the debtor's title to the property charged;
  (d) identify any prior incumbrances on the property charged, stating, so far as is known, the names and addresses of the incumbrancers and the amounts owing to them;
  (e) set out the plaintiff's proposals as to the manner of sale of the property charged together with estimates of the gross price which would be obtained on a sale in that manner and of the costs of such a sale; and
  (f) where the property charged consists of land in respect of which the plaintiff claims delivery of possession—
    (i) give particulars of every person who to the best of the plaintiff's knowledge is in possession of the property charged or any part of it; and
    (ii) state, in the case of a dwelling house, whether a land charge of Class F has been registered, or a notice or caution pursuant to section 2(7) of the Matrimonial Homes Act 1967, or a notice pursuant to section 2(8) of the Matrimonial Homes Act 1983 has been entered and, if so, on whose behalf, and whether he has served notice of the proceedings on the person on whose behalf the land charge is registered or the notice or caution entered.]

Commencement 1 October 1984.
Amendments This rule was inserted by SI 1984/1051, r 10.
Cross references See CCR Order 31, r 4.

Order 88, r [6] Action by writ: judgment in default

(1)   Notwithstanding anything in Order 13 or Order 19, in a mortgage action begun by writ judgment [on failure to give notice of intention to defend] or in default of defence shall not be entered except with the leave of the Court.

(2)   An application for the grant of leave under this rule must be made by summons and the summons must, notwithstanding anything in Order 65, rule 9, be served on the defendant.

(3)   Where a summons for leave under this rule is issued in an action in the Chancery Division, [rule 4(2) to (7)] shall apply in relation to the action subject to the modification that for references therein to the originating summons, and for the reference in paragraph (2) to the notice of appointment, there shall be substituted references to the summons.

(4)   Where a summons for leave under this rule is issued in an action to which [rule 5] would apply had the action been begun by originating summons, the affidavit in support of the summons must contain the information required by that rule.

Commencement   1 October 1966.
Amendments   Originally r 7, renumbered as r 6 by SI 1982/1111, r 83.
Para (1): words "on failure to give notice of intention to defend" substituted by SI 1979/1716, r 48, Schedule, Pt 1.
Para (3): words "rule 4(2) to (7)" substituted by SI 1985/69, r 7(2), Schedule.
Para (4): words "rule 5" substituted by SI 1985/69, r 7(2), Schedule.
Cross references   See CCR Order 9, r 7.

Order 88, r [7] Foreclosure in redemption action

Where foreclosure has taken place by reason of the failure of the plaintiff in a mortgage action for redemption to redeem, the defendant in whose favour the foreclosure has taken place may apply by motion or summons for an order for delivery to him of possession of the mortgaged property, and the Court may make such order thereon as it thinks fit.

Commencement   1 October 1966.
Amendments   Originally r 8, renumbered as r 7 by SI 1982/1111, r 83.

SPECIAL PROVISIONS AS TO PARTICULAR PROCEEDINGS

ORDER 89
PROCEEDINGS BETWEEN HUSBAND AND WIFE

Order 89, r 1 *(revoked by SI 1991/1884)*

Order 89, r 2 Provisions as to actions in tort

(1)   This rule applies to any action in tort brought by one of the parties to a marriage against the other during the subsistence of the marriage.

(2)   On the first application by summons or motion in an action to which this rule applies, the Court shall consider, if necessary of its own motion, whether the power to stay the action under section 1(2) of the Law Reform (Husband and Wife) Act 1962 should or should not be exercised.

(3)   Notwithstanding anything in Order 13 or Order 19, judgment [on failure to give notice of intention to defend or in default of defence] shall not be entered in an action to which this rule applies except with the leave of the Court.

(4)   An application for the grant of leave under paragraph (3) must be made by summons and the summons must, notwithstanding anything in Order 65, rule 9, be served on the defendant.

(5)   If the summons is for leave to enter judgment [on failure to give notice of intention to defend], the summons shall not be issued until after the [time limited for acknowledging service of the writ].

Commencement 1 October 1966.
Amendments Para (3): words from "on failure" to "default of defence" substituted by SI 1979/1716, r 48, Schedule, Pt 1.
Para (5): words "on failure to give notice of intention to defend" and "time limited for acknowledging service of the writ" substituted by SI 1979/1716, r 48, Schedule, Pt 1.
Cross references See CCR Order 47, r 3.

Order 89, r 3 *(added by SI 1967/1809; revoked by SI 1973/2016)*

ORDER 90

(original Order 90 was renumbered as Order 91, and a new Order 90 was inserted, by SI 1971/1269, r 30; revoked by SI 1991/1884)

ORDER [91]
REVENUE PROCEEDINGS ...

Amendments Words omitted revoked by SI 1986/2289, r 5.
Originally Order 90, renumbered as Order 91 and original Order 91 revoked by SI 1971/1269, r 30.

[Order 91, r 1 Assignment to Chancery Division, etc

The following proceedings, namely—
(a) any case stated for the opinion of the High Court under section 13 of the Stamp Act 1891, section 56 of the Taxes Management Act 1970[, section 225 of the Inheritance Tax Act 1984 or [Regulation 10 of the Stamp Duty Reserve Tax Regulations 1986];]
(b) any appeal to the High Court under section 53 or [100C(4)] of the Taxes Management Act 1970 or [section 222(3), [249(3)] or 251(2) of the Inheritance Tax Act 1984 or [Regulation 8(3) of the Stamp Duty Reserve Tax Regulations 1986]] or any application for leave to appeal under [the said section 222(3) or the said Regulation 8(3)]; and
(c) proceedings to which the provisions of section 56 of the Taxes Management Act 1970 apply under any enactment or regulation,

shall be assigned to the Chancery Division and heard and determined by a single judge.]

Commencement   11 January 1978.
Amendments   This rule was substituted by SI 1977/1955, r 11(1).
Para (a): first words in square brackets substituted by SI 1986/2289, r 10(1), words "Regulation 10 of the Stamp Duty Reserve Tax Regulations 1986" therein substituted by SI 1987/1423, r 63, Schedule.
Para (b): figure "100C(4)" substituted by SI 1991/1329, r 20(2); words in square brackets beginning with the words "section 222(3)" substituted by SI 1986/2289, r 10(1); figure "249(3)" and words "Regulation 8(3) of the Stamp Duty Reserve Tax Regulations 1986" therein and words "the said section 222(3) or the said Regulation 8(3)" substituted by SI 1987/1423, r 63, Schedule.

[Order 91, r 2 [Appeal under section 222 of the Inheritance Tax Act 1984]

(1)   Order 55 shall not apply in relation to an appeal to the High Court under [section 222(3) of the Inheritance Tax Act 1984 or [Regulation 8(3) of the Stamp Duty Reserve Tax Regulations 1986]].

(2)   Such an appeal must be brought by originating summons which must—
(a) state the date on which the Commissioners of Inland Revenue (in this rule referred to as the "Board") gave notice to the appellant under [section 221 of the said Act or Regulation 6 of the said Regulations] of the determination which is the subject of the appeal;
(b) state the date on which the appellant gave to the Board notice of appeal under [section 222(1) of the said Act or Regulation 8(1) of the said Regulations] and, if the notice was not given within the time limited, whether the Board or the Special Commissioners have given consent to the appeal being brought out of time [and, if they have, the date on which it was given], and

(c) either state that the appellant and the Board have agreed that the appeal may be to the High Court or contain an application for leave to appeal to the High Court.

(3)   At the time of issuing the originating summons the appellant shall lodge in [Chancery Chambers]—

(a) two copies of the notice referred to in paragraph (2)(a);

(b) two copies of the notice of appeal referred to in paragraph (2)(b); and

(c) where the originating summons contains an application for leave to appeal, an affidavit setting out the grounds on which it is alleged that the matters to be decided on the appeal are likely to be substantially confined to questions of law.

(4)   The originating summons must be issued and served on the Board within 30 days of the date [on which the appellant gave to the Board notice of appeal under [section 222(1) of the said Act or Regulation 8(1) of the said Regulations] or, if the Board or the Special Commissioners have given consent to the appeal being brought out of time, within 30 days of the date on which such consent was given.]

(5)   [The originating summons shall be in Form No 10 in Appendix A], but it must specify a date of hearing being not less than 40 days from the issue of the summons.

(6)   Where the originating summons contains an application for leave to appeal to the High Court, a copy of the affidavit lodged pursuant to paragraph (3)(c) shall be served on the Board with the originating summons and the Board may, within 30 days after service, lodge in the judge's chambers an affidavit in answer and a copy of any such affidavit shall be served by the Board on the appellant.

(7)   Except with the leave of the Court, the appellant shall not be entitled on the hearing of an appeal to rely on any grounds of appeal not specified in the notice referred to in paragraph (2)(b).]

Commencement   1 September 1976.

Amendments   See the note to the heading to Order 91, r 1.

This rule was substituted for the existing rr 2–5 by SI 1976/1196, r 12(3).

Rule heading: substituted by SI 1986/2289, r 10(2).

Para (1): words from "section 222(3)" to the end substituted by SI 1986/2289, r 10(3), words "Regulation 8(3) of the Stamp Duty Reserve Tax Regulations 1986" therein substituted by SI 1987/1423, r 63, Schedule.

Para (2): in sub-para (a) words from "section 221" to "said Regulations" substituted by SI 1986/2289, r 10(4); in sub-para (b) words from "section 222(1)" to "said Regulations" substituted by SI 1986/2289, r 10(5), words "and, if they have, the date on which it was given" inserted by SI 1977/1955, r 11(2).

Para (3): words "Chancery Chambers" substituted by SI 1982/1111, r 84.

Para (4): words from "on which the appellant" to the end substituted by SI 1977/1955, r 11(3); words "section 222(1) of the said Act or Regulation 8(1) of the said Regulations" therein substituted by SI 1986/2289, r 10(5).

Para (5): words "The originating summons shall be in Form/10 in Appendix A" substituted by SI 1979/1716, r 48, Schedule, Pt 2.

Order 91, r [3] Setting down case stated under [Taxes Management Act 1970]

(1)   At any time after a case stated under [section 56 of the Taxes Management Act 1970] [or [section 225 of the Inheritance Tax Act 1984 or [Regulation 10 of the Stamp Duty Reserve Tax Regulations 1986]]] has been filed in [Chancery Chambers] either party may set down the case for hearing.

(2)   On setting down the case the party who sets it down must give notice to the other party that he has done so.

Commencement 1 October 1966.
Amendments See the note to the heading to Order 91, r 1.
Originally r 6, renumbered as r 3 by SI 1976/1196, r 12(7).
Rule heading: words "Taxes Management Act 1970" substituted by SI 1972/813, r 5(3).
Para (1): words "section 56 of the Taxes Management Act 1970" substituted by SI 1972/813, r 5(1); words in square brackets beginning with the word "or" inserted by SI 1976/1196, r 12(4), words beginning "section 225 of the Inheritance Tax Act 1984 or" substituted by SI 1986/2289, r 10(6), words "Regulation 10 of the Stamp Duty Reserve Tax Regulations 1986" substituted by SI 1987/1423, r 63, Schedule; words "Chancery Chambers" substituted by SI 1982/1111, r 84.

Order 91, r [4] Case stated: notice to be given of certain matters

Not less than 10 days before the hearing of such a case as is mentioned in [rule 1(a)] either party must give notice to the other of any point which he intends to take at the hearing and which might take the other party by surprise and leave at [Chancery Chambers] two copies of the notice for the use of the Court.

Commencement 1 October 1966.
Amendments See the note to the heading to Order 91, r 1.
Originally r 7, renumbered as r 4 by SI 1976/1196, r 12(7).
Words "rule 1(a)" substituted by SI 1978/579, r 15; words "Chancery Chambers" substituted by SI 1982/1111, r 84.

Order 91, r [5] [Appeals under ss 53 and [100C(4)] of Taxes Management Act 1970]

(1)   The notice of an originating motion by which an appeal under [section 53 or [100C(4)] of the Taxes Management Act 1970] [or [section 249(3) or 251(2) of the Inheritance Tax Act 1984]] is brought must be issued out of [Chancery Chambers].

(2)   Order 55, rule 3(2), shall apply in relation to the notice of such motion as if the [decision, award or determination] appealed against were the decision of a court.

(3)   The persons to be served with the notice are the General or Special Commissioners against whose [decision, award or determination] the appeal is brought and—

   (a)   in the case of an appeal brought under [section [100C(4)] of the Taxes Management Act 1970] [or [section 249(3) of the Inheritance Tax Act 1984]] by any party other than the defendant in the proceedings before the Commissioners, that defendant;

   (b)   in any other case, the Commissioners of Inland Revenue.

(4)   Order 55, rules 4(2) and 5, shall apply in relation to any such appeal as if for the period of 28 days and 21 days therein specified there were substituted a period of 30 days and 35 days respectively.

(5)   Within 30 days after the service on them of notice of the originating motion by which any such appeal is brought, the General or Special Commissioners, as the case may be, must lodge in [Chancery Chambers] two copies of a note of their findings and of the reasons for their [decision, award or determination] and must serve a copy of the note on every other party to the appeal.

(6)   Any document required or authorised to be served on the General or Special Commissioners in proceedings to which this rule relates may be served by delivering or sending it to their clerk.

(7)   Order 57 shall not apply to proceedings to which this rule applies.

Commencement 1 October 1966.
Amendments See the note to the heading to Order 91, r 1.
Originally r 8, renumbered as r 5 by SI 1976/1196, r 12(7).
Rule heading: substituted by SI 1972/813, r 5(4); figure "100C(4)" therein substituted by SI 1991/1329, r 20(2).
Para (1): words from "section 53" to "Act 1970" substituted by SI 1972/813, r 5(2), figure "100C(4)" therein substituted by SI 1991/1329, r 20(2); words in square brackets beginning with the word "or" inserted by SI 1976/1196, r 12(5), words "section 249(3) or 251(2) of the Inheritance Tax Act 1984" substituted by SI 1987/1423, r 63, Schedule; words "Chancery Chambers" substituted by SI 1982/1111, r 84.
Para (2): words "decision, award or determination" substituted by SI 1991/1329, r 20(3).
Para (3): words "decision, award or determination" substituted by SI 1991/1329, r 20(3); words in square brackets beginning with the word "section" and ending with the words "Act 1970" substituted by SI 1972/813, r 5(5), figure "100C(4)" therein substituted by SI 1991/1329, r 20(2); words in square brackets beginning with the word "or" inserted by SI 1976/1196, r 12(6), words "section 249(3) of the Inheritance Tax Act 1984" substituted by SI 1987/1423, r 63, Schedule.
Para (5): words "Chancery Chambers" substituted by SI 1982/1111, r 84; words "decision, award or determination" substituted by SI 1991/1329, r 20(3).

[Order 91, r 6 Appeals from value added tax tribunals

(1)   A party to proceedings before a value added tax tribunal who is dissatisfied in point of law with a decision of the tribunal may appeal under section 13(1) of the Tribunals and Inquiries Act 1971 to the High Court and Order 94, rule 9 shall not apply in relation to such an appeal.

(2)   Such an appeal shall be heard and determined by a single judge of the Queen's Bench Division or, where both parties consent, by a single judge of the Chancery Division.

(3)   Order 55 shall apply to such an appeal, except that the period of 28 days specified in rule 4(2) of that Order shall, where the tribunal has refused to grant a certificate under Article 2(b) of the Value Added Tax Tribunal Appeals Order 1986, be calculated from the date of the release of the decision of the tribunal containing the refusal.

(4)   This rule is without prejudice to the right of the parties to appeal direct to the Court of Appeal in accordance with Order 59, rule 22.]

Commencement 12 January 1987.
Amendments See the note to the heading to Order 91, r 1.
This rule was added by SI 1986/2289, r 6.
Modifications references to "value added tax tribunals" modified by the Finance Act 1994, s 7.

ORDER 92
LODGMENT, INVESTMENT, ETC OF FUNDS IN COURT: CHANCERY DIVISION

Order 92, r 1 Payment into court by life assurance company

(1) A company wishing to make a payment into court under the Life Assurance Companies (Payment into Court) Act 1896 (hereinafter referred to as "the Act of 1896") must file an affidavit, made by its secretary or other authorised officer, setting out—

    (a) a short description of the policy in question and a statement of the persons entitled thereunder with their names and addresses so far as known to the company,

    (b) a short statement of the notices received by the company claiming an interest in or title to the money assured, or withdrawing any such claim, with the dates of receipt thereof and the names and addresses of the persons by whom they were given,

    (c) a statement that, in the opinion of the board of directors of the company, no sufficient discharge can be obtained otherwise than by payment into court under the Act of 1896,

    (d) the submission by the company to pay into court such further sum, if any, as the Court may direct and to pay any costs ordered by the Court to be paid by the company,

    (e) an undertaking by the company forthwith to send to the Accountant General any notice of claim received by the company after the making of the affidavit with a letter referring to the title of the affidavit, and

    (f) an address where the company may be served with any summons or order, or notice of any proceeding, relating to the money paid into court.

(2) The company shall not deduct from the money payable by them under the policy any costs of or incidental to the payment into court.

(3) No payment shall be made into court under the Act of 1896 where any action to which the company is a party is pending in relation to the policy or moneys thereby assured except with the leave of the Court to be obtained by summons in the action.

(4) Unless the Court otherwise directs, a summons by which a claim with respect to money paid into court under the Act of 1896 is made shall not, except where the summons includes an application for payment of a further sum of costs by the company who made the payment, be served on that company, but it must be served on every person who appears by the affidavit on which the payment into court was made to be entitled to, or interested in, the money in court or to have a claim upon it or who has given a notice of claim which has been sent to the Accountant General in accordance with the undertaking referred to in rule 1(1)(e).

Commencement 1 October 1966.

Order 92, r 2 Payment into court under Trustee Act 1925

(1) Subject to paragraph (2), any trustee wishing to make a payment into court under section 63 of the Trustee Act 1925 must make and file an affidavit setting out—

    (a) a short description of the trust and of the instrument creating it or, as the case may be, of the circumstances in which the trust arose,

   (b) the names of the persons interested in or entitled to the money or securities to be paid into court with their addresses so far as known to him,

   (c) his submission to answer all such inquiries relating to the application of such money or securities as the Court may make or direct, and

   (d) an address where he may be served with any summons or order, or notice of any proceedings, relating to the money or securities paid into court.

(2)   Where the money or securities represents a legacy, or residue or any share thereof, to which an infant or a person resident outside the United Kingdom is absolutely entitled, no affidavit need be filed under paragraph (1) and the money or securities may be paid into court in the manner prescribed by the Supreme Court Funds Rules for the time being in force.

Commencement 1 October 1966.

Order 92, r 3 Payment into court under War Damage Act 1943

Where the Commissioners of Inland Revenue wish to make a payment into court under section 33(1) of the War Damage Act 1943 in respect of war damage to a hereditament, they shall cause an affidavit to be made and filed setting out—

   (a) short particulars of the hereditament;

   (b) the name and address of any person who has claimed a payment in respect of war damage to the hereditament or a share of such payment, and

   (c) the grounds on which the Commissioners wish to make the payment into court.

Commencement 1 October 1966.

[Order 92, r 3A Payments into court under section 26, Banking Act 1987

Where the Bank of England, having sold shares in pursuance of an order under section 26 of the Banking Act 1987, pays the proceeds of sale, less the costs of the sale, into court, it shall cause an affidavit to be made and filed setting out the names and, so far as known, the addresses of the persons beneficially entitled to the proceeds of sale and shall lodge a copy of the order.]

Commencement 4 April 1988.
Amendments This rule was inserted by SI 1988/298, r 11.

Order 92, r 4 Notice of lodgment

Any person who has lodged money or securities in court in accordance with rule 1, 2[, 3 or 3A] must forthwith send notice of the lodgment to every person appearing from the affidavit on which the lodgment was made to be entitled to, or to have an interest in, the money or securities lodged.

Commencement 1 October 1966.
Amendments Words ", 3 or 3A" substituted by SI 1988/298, r 12.

Order 92, r 5 Applications with respect to funds in court

(1)   Where an application to the High Court—

   (a) for the payment or transfer to any person of any funds in court standing to the credit of any cause or matter or for the transfer of any such funds to a separate account or for the payment to any person of any dividend of or interest on any securities or money comprised in such funds;

(b) for the investment, or change of investment, of any funds in court;

(c) for payment of the dividends of or interest on any funds in court representing or comprising money or securities lodged in court under any enactment; or

(d) for the payment or transfer out of court of any such funds as are mentioned in sub-paragraph (c);

is made in the Chancery Division the application may be disposed of in chambers.

(2) Subject to paragraph (3), any such application made in the Chancery Division must be made by summons and, unless the application is made in a pending cause or matter or an application for the same purpose has previously been made by petition or originating summons, the summons must be an originating summons.

(3) Where an application under paragraph 1(d) is required to be made by originating summons, then, if the funds to which the application relates do not exceed [[£5000] in value], and subject to paragraph (4), the application may be made ex parte . . . to the chief master, or to such master as he may designate, and the master may dispose of the application or may direct it to be made by originating summons.

[Unless otherwise directed, an ex parte application under this paragraph shall be made by affidavit.]

(4) Where the application to which paragraph (3) applies relates to funds lodged in court in [a Chancery district registry], the application may be made to, and the power conferred by paragraph (3) on a master may be exercised by, the [district judge] of that registry.

(5) This rule does not apply to any application for an order under Order 22.

Commencement 1 October 1966.

Amendments Para (3): first words in square brackets substituted by SI 1969/1894, r 8(1), figure "£5000" therein substituted by SI 1982/1786, r 23; words omitted revoked by SI 1969/1894, r 8(2); paragraph beginning "Unless otherwise directed" added by SI 1969/1894, r 8(3).
Para (4): words "a Chancery district registry" substituted by SI 1982/1111, r 85.

ORDER 93
APPLICATIONS AND APPEALS TO HIGH COURT UNDER VARIOUS ACTS: CHANCERY DIVISION

Order 93, r 1 Notice of petition under s 55 of National Debt Act 1870

Where a petition is presented under section 55 of the National Debt Act 1870, the petitioner must, before the petition is heard, apply to a judge of the Chancery Division in chambers for directions with respect to giving notice of the claim to which the petition relates, and the judge may direct that notice thereof be given by advertisement or in such other manner as he may direct or may dispense with the giving of such notice.

Commencement 1 October 1966.

Order 93, r 2 Application under Public Trustee Act 1906

Without prejudice to sections 10(2) and 13(7) of the Public Trustee Act 1906, the jurisdiction of the High Court under that Act shall be exercised by a judge of the Chancery Division in chambers.

Commencement 1 October 1966.

Order 93, r 3 Reference of question, etc under Electricity (Supply) Act 1919

Proceedings for the determination of any question or difference referred to the High Court under section 22(2) of the Electricity (Supply) Act 1919 by virtue of section 1 of the Railway and Canal Commission (Abolition) Act 1949 shall be assigned to the Chancery Division and be begun by originating summons.

Commencement 1 October 1966.

Order 93, r 4 Proceedings under Trustee Act 1925

All proceedings brought in the High Court under the Trustee Act 1925 shall be assigned to the Chancery Division.

Commencement 1 October 1966.

Order 93, r 5 Application under s 2(3) of Public Order Act 1936

(1)   Proceedings by which an application is made to the High Court under section 2(3) of the Public Order Act 1936 shall be assigned to the Chancery Division.

(2)   The persons to be made defendants to the originating summons by which such an application is made shall be such persons as the Attorney General may determine.

(3)   In the absence of other sufficient representation the Court may appoint the official solicitor to represent any interests which in the opinion of the Court ought to be represented on any inquiry directed by the Court under the said section 2(3).

Commencement 1 October 1966.

Order 93, r 6 Application under Variation of Trusts Act 1958

(1)   Proceedings by which an application is made to the High Court under section 1 of the Variation of Trusts Act 1958 shall be assigned to the Chancery Division.

(2)   In addition to any other persons who are necessary and proper defendants to the originating summons by which an application under the said section 1 is made, the settlor and any other person who provided property for the purposes of the trusts to which the application relates must, if still alive and not the plaintiff, be made a defendant unless the Court for some special reason otherwise directs.

Commencement   1 October 1966.

Order 93, r 7 Application under s 15 of Films Act 1960

(1)   Proceedings by which an application is made to the High Court under section 15 of the Films Act 1960 shall be assigned to the Chancery Division.

(2)   The originating summons by which such an application is made must be issued within one month after the date of the decision of the Board of Trade to which the application relates, and the Board and such other persons (if any) as the Court may direct must be made defendants to the summons.

Commencement   1 October 1966.

Order 93, r 8 Applications under Building Societies Act 1962

Proceedings by which an application is made to the High Court under section 28(4) or 85(5) of the Building Societies Act 1962 shall be assigned to the Chancery Division.

Commencement   1 October 1966.

Order 93, r 9 Right of appeal under Law of Property [Act]

An appeal shall lie to the High Court against a decision of the Minister of Agriculture, Fisheries and Food under paragraph 16 of Schedule 15 to the Law of Property Act 1922 ....

Commencement   1 October 1966.
Amendments   Rule heading: word "Act" substituted by SI 1982/1111, r 115, Schedule.
Words omitted revoked by SI 1982/1111, r 115, Schedule.

Order 93, r 10 Determination of appeal or case stated under various Acts

(1)   An appeal to the High Court against an order of a county court made under the Land Registration Act 1925 shall be heard and determined by a Divisional Court of the Chancery Division.

(2)   Subject to paragraph (1), any appeal to the High Court, and any case stated or question referred for the opinion of that Court, under any of the following enactments, that is to say—
   (a)   [the Friendly Societies Act 1974],
   (b)   ...
   (c)   paragraph 16 of Schedule 15 to the Law of Property Act 1922,
   (d)   the Industrial Assurance Act 1923,
   (e)   ...

    (f)   the Land Registration Act 1925,

    (g)   section 7(6) of the Water Act 1945,

    (h)   . . .

    (i)   section 30 of the Copyright Act 1956,

    (j)   section 38(3) of the Clergy Pensions Measure 1961,

    (k)   the Building Societies Act 1962,

    (l)   . . .

    (m)   the Industrial and Provident Societies Act 1965,

   [(n)   section 86 of the Social Security Act 1973.]

shall be heard and determined by a single judge of the Chancery Division.

(3)   No appeal shall lie from the decision of the Court on an appeal under any of the enactments mentioned in paragraph (2)(c), (e) or (f) except with the leave of the Court or the Court of Appeal.

Commencement 1 October 1966.
Amendments Para (2): sub-para (a) substituted and sub-para (e) revoked by SI 1982/1111, r 115, Schedule; sub-paras (b), (l) revoked by SI 1985/69, r 7(2), Schedule; sub-para (h) revoked by SI 1979/522, r 9; sub-para (n) inserted by SI 1975/911, r 17.

Order 93, r 11 Appeal under s 7 or 17 of Industrial Assurance Act 1923

(1)   An application to the judge for leave to appeal to the High Court under section 7(2) of the Industrial Assurance Act 1923 against a refusal of the Industrial Assurance Commissioner to allow further time for making a deposit under subsection (1)(c) of that section or against a direction of the Commissioner under section 17(3) of that Act must be made within 21 days after the date of the Commissioner's refusal or direction.

(2)   An application for the grant of such leave must be made in chambers ex parte by an affidavit stating the material facts, the effect of the Commissioner's refusal or direction, the grounds on which the application is made and that the deponent is advised and believes that the applicant has good grounds for appealing.

(3)   No order under this rule granting leave to appeal shall be drawn up but [the proper officer] shall indorse on the notice of originating motion by which the appeal is brought a note signed by him stating that leave to appeal was granted by the Court and the date on which it was granted.

    A copy of such note shall appear on any copy of such notice served on a respondent to the appeal.

(4)   Order 55, rule 4(2), shall not apply in relation to an appeal with respect to which leave has been granted under this rule, but the notice of originating motion by which the appeal is brought must be served, and the appeal entered, within 28 days after leave to appeal was granted.

Commencement 1 October 1966.
Amendments Para (3): words "the proper officer" substituted by SI 1982/1111, r 86.

Order 93, r 12 Appeals, etc affecting industrial and provident societies, etc

(1)   At any stage of the proceedings on an appeal under—

    (a)   the Friendly Societies Act 1896,

    (b)   . . .

    (c)   the Industrial Assurance Act 1923,

(d)   the Building Societies Act 1962, or

(e)   the Industrial and Provident Societies Act 1965,

the Court may direct that notice of the originating motion by which the appeal is brought be served on any person or may direct that notice be given by advertisement or otherwise of the bringing of the appeal, the nature thereof and the time when it will or is likely to be heard or may give such other directions as it thinks proper for enabling any person interested in the society, trade union, alleged trade union or industrial assurance company concerned or in the subject-matter of the appeal to appear and be heard on the appeal.

(2)   An application for directions under paragraph (1) may be made by either party to the appeal by summons returnable at [Chancery Chambers].

Commencement 1 October 1966.
Amendments Para (1): sub-para (b) revoked by SI 1985/69, r 7(2), Schedule.
Para (2): words "Chancery Chambers" substituted by SI 1982/1111, r 87.

Order 93, r 13 *(revoked by SI 1975/128)*

Order 93, r 14 Case stated under s 30 of the Copyright Act 1956

(1)   Where the Court makes an order directing the Performing Right Tribunal to refer a question of law to the Court under section 30 of the Copyright Act 1956 by way of case stated it may by the order suspend the operation of any order made by the Tribunal in the proceedings in which the question arose.

(2)   The proper officer shall notify the secretary of the Tribunal of the Court's decision on any application for an order directing the Tribunal to refer a question of law to the Court under the said section 30 and on any case stated by the Tribunal thereunder, and of any directions given by the Court thereon.

Commencement 1 October 1966.

[Order 93, r 15 Application under s 19 or 27 of Leasehold Reform Act 1967

Proceedings by which an application is made to the High Court under section 19 or 27 of the Leasehold Reform Act 1967 shall be assigned to the Chancery Division.]

Commencement 1 September 1968.
Amendments This rule was added by SI 1968/1244, r 18.

[Order 93, r 16 Proceedings under the Commons Registration Act 1965

(1)   Proceedings in the High Court under section 14 or 18 of the Commons Registration Act 1965 shall be assigned to the Chancery Division.

(2)   The time within which a person aggrieved by the decision of a Commons Commissioner may require the Commissioner to state a case for the opinion of the High Court pursuant to the said section 18 shall be six weeks from the date on which notice of the decision was sent to the person aggrieved.

(3)   An appeal by way of case stated under the said section 18 shall be heard and determined by a single judge.]

Commencement 1 January 1971.
Amendments This rule was added by SI 1970/1861, r 6.

[Order 93, r 17 Proceedings under section 21 or 25 of the Law of Property Act 1969

Proceedings in the High Court under section 21 or 25 of the Law of Property Act 1969 shall be assigned to the Chancery Division.]

Commencement 1 January 1971.
Amendments This rule was added by SI 1970/1861, r 6.

[Order 93, r 18 Proceedings under section 16 of the Civil Aviation Act 1968

(1)   Proceedings in the High Court for the amendment of any register of aircraft mortgages kept pursuant to an Order in Council made under section 16 of the Civil Aviation Act 1968 shall be assigned to the Chancery Division.

(2)   Every person, other than the plaintiff, appearing in the register as mortgagee or mortgagor of the aircraft in question shall be made a defendant to the originating summons by which the proceedings are begun.

(3)   A copy of the originating summons shall also be sent to the Civil Aviation Authority and the Authority shall be entitled to be heard in the proceedings.]

Commencement 1 January 1973.
Amendments This rule was added by SI 1972/1898, r 10.

[Order 93, r 19 Proceedings under section 85(7) of the Fair Trading Act 1973 [and the Control of Misleading Advertisements Regulations 1988]

(1)   Proceedings to which this rule applies shall be assigned to the Chancery Division and may be begun by originating motion.

(2)   This rule applies to any application to the High Court for an order under section 85(7) of the Fair Trading Act 1973, or under any provision to which that section applies[, or under the Control of Misleading Advertisements Regulations 1988].]

Commencement 3 June 1980.
Amendments This rule was added by SI 1980/629, r 20.
Rule heading: words "and the Control of Misleading Advertisements Regulations 1988" added by SI 1988/1340, r 13.
Para 2: words from ", or under the Control" to the end inserted by SI 1988/1340, r 13.

[Order 93, r 20 Proceedings under section 50 of the Administration of Justice Act 1985

(1)   Proceedings by which an application is made to the High Court under section 50 of the Administration of Justice Act 1985 for an order appointing a substituted personal representative or terminating the appointment of an existing personal representative shall be assigned to the Chancery Division.

(2)   An application under the said section 50 shall be made by originating summons or, if it is made in a pending action, by summons or motion in that action.

(3)   All the existing personal representatives and, notwithstanding anything in Order 15, rule 4(2) and subject to any direction of the Court, such of the persons having a beneficial interest in the estate as the plaintiff thinks fit, must be made parties to the application.

(4)   Such an application must be supported by:—
    (a)   a sealed or certified copy of the grant of probate or letters of administration, and

    (b) an affidavit containing the grounds of the application and the following particulars so far as the plaintiff can gain information with regard to them:—
- (i) short particulars of the property comprised in the estate, with an appropriate estimate of its income, and capital value;
- (ii) short particulars of the liabilities of the estate;
- (iii) particulars of the persons who are in possession of the documents relating to the estate;
- (iv) the names of the beneficiaries and short particulars of their respective interests; and
- (v) the name, address and occupation of any proposed substituted personal representative;

    (c) where the application is for the appointment of a substituted personal representative:—
- (i) a signed or (in the case of the Public Trustee or a corporation) sealed consent to act, and
- (ii) an affidavit as to the fitness of the proposed substituted personal representative, if an individual, to act.

[(5) On the hearing of an application under the said section 50 the personal representative shall produce to the Court the grant of representation to the deceased's estate and, if an order is made under the said section, the grant (together with a sealed copy of the order) shall be sent to and remain in the custody of the principal registry of the Family Division until a memorandum of the order has been endorsed on or permanently annexed to the grant.]]

Commencement 1 June 1992 (para (5)); 28 April 1986 (remainder).
Amendments This rule was added by SI 1986/632, r 31.
Para (5): inserted by SI 1992/638, r 14.

[Order 93, r 21 Proceedings under section 48 of the Administration of Justice Act 1985

Proceedings by which an application is made to the High Court under section 48 of the Administration of Justice Act 1985 shall be assigned to the Chancery Division and shall be begun by ex parte originating summons.]

Commencement 12 January 1987.
Amendments This rule was added by SI 1986/2289, r 11.

[Order 93, r 22 Proceedings under the Financial Services Act 1986

(1) In this rule "the Act" means the Financial Services Act 1986 and a section referred to by number means the section so numbered in that Act.

(2) Proceedings in the High Court under the Act (other than applications for mandamus) and actions for damages for breach of a statutory duty imposed by the Act shall be assigned to the Chancery Division.

(3) Such proceedings and actions shall be begun by writ, except for—
- (a) applications by petition by the Secretary of State or a designated agency under section 72, and
- (b) applications by Inspectors under section 94 or section 178, which shall be begun by originating notice of motion.

(4) No order shall be made under sections 6, 61, 71, 91, 104, 131, 184 or paragraph 22 of Schedule 11 against any person unless he is a party to the relevant proceedings or action.

(5)   Where there is a question of the construction of any of the rules or regulations referred to in section 61(1)(a) of the Act, the Secretary of State, designated agency, or any person referred to in section 61(1)(a)(iv) may make representation to the Court.]

Commencement   1 October 1987 or, in relation to any section of the Financial Services Act 1986 which is not in force on that date, on the date when that section comes into force, see SI 1987/1423, r 1(1)(c).
Amendments   This rule was added by SI 1987/1423, r 62.

[Order 93, r 23 Proceedings under the Banking Act 1987

(1)   In this rule "the Act" means the Banking Act 1987 and a section referred to by number means the section so numbered in the Act.

(2)   Proceedings in the High Court under the following sections of the Act shall be assigned to the Chancery Division and shall be begun—
   (a)   as to applications under sections 26(3), 71(3) and 77(3) and (5), by originating summons;
   (b)   as to appeals under section 31(1), by originating motion;
   (c)   as to applications under sections 48(1), 49(1) and 93(1) and (2), by writ.

(3)   No order shall be made under section 48(1) against any person unless he is a party to the proceedings.

(4)   Where an application has been made under section 71(3) or (5) or section 77(3) or (5) the Bank of England shall within 28 days after service on it of copies of the plaintiff's affidavit evidence cause an affidavit to be made, filed and served on the plaintiff setting out the reasons for its objection to the plaintiff's name.]

Commencement   4 April 1988.
Amendments   This rule was inserted by SI 1988/298, r 13.

[Order 93, r 24 Applications under section 114, 204 or 231 of the Copyright, Designs and Patents Act 1988

(1)   Where an application is made under section 114, 204 or 231 of the Copyright, Designs and Patents Act 1988, the applicant shall serve notice of the application on all persons so far as reasonably ascertainable having an interest in the copy or other article which is the subject of the application, including any person in whose favour an order could be made in respect of the copy or other article under any of the said sections of the Act of 1988 or under section 58C of the Trade Marks Act 1938.

(2)   An application under the said section 114, 204 or 231 shall be made by originating summons or, if it is made in a pending action, by summons or motion in that action.]

Commencement   1 September 1989.
Amendments   This rule was inserted by SI 1989/1307, r 19.
Cross references   This rule is applied to the county court by CCR Order 49, r 4A.

[Order 93, r 25 Proceedings under the Companies Act 1989

(1)   Proceedings in the High Court under sections 166(8) and 167(5) of the Companies Act 1989 shall be begun by writ and shall be assigned to the Chancery Division.

(2)   No order shall be made under the said sections 166(8) and 167(5) against any person unless he is a party to the relevant proceedings.]

Commencement   1 February 1991.
Amendments   This rule was inserted by SI 1990/2599, r 16.

ORDER 94

APPLICATIONS AND APPEALS TO HIGH COURT UNDER VARIOUS ACTS: QUEEN'S BENCH DIVISION

Order 94, r 1 Jurisdiction of High Court to quash certain orders, schemes, etc

(1)　Where by virtue of any enactment the High Court has jurisdiction, on the application of any person, to quash [or prohibit] any order, scheme, certificate or plan, any amendment or approval of a plan, any decision of a Minister or government department or any action on the part of a Minister or government department, the jurisdiction shall be exercisable by a single judge of the Queen's Bench Division.

(2)　The application must be made by originating motion and, without prejudice to Order 8, rule 3(2), the notice of such motion must state the grounds of the application.

Commencement　1 October 1966.
Amendments　Para (1): words "or prohibit" inserted by SI 1982/1111, r 110.

Order 94, r 2 Entry and service of notice of motion

(1)　Notice of a motion under rule 1 must be entered at the Crown Office, and served, within the time limited by the relevant enactment for making the application made by the motion.

(2)　[Subject to paragraph (4)] notice of the motion must be served on the appropriate Minister or government department, and—
- (a)　if the application relates to a compulsory purchase order made by an authority other than the appropriate Minister or government department, or to a clearance order under the Housing Act 1957, on the authority by whom the order was made;
- (b)　if the application relates to a scheme or order to which Schedule 2 to the Highways Act 1959 applies made by an authority other than the [Secretary of State], on that authority;
- [(c)　If the application relates to a structure plan, local plan of other development plan within the meaning of the Town and Country Planning Act 1971, on the local planning authority who prepared the plan.]
- [(d)]　if the application relates to any decision or order, or any action on the part, of [a Minister of the Crown] to which section 21 of the Land Compensation Act 1961 or [section 245 of the Town and Country Planning Act 1971] applies, on the authority directly concerned with such decision, order or action or, if that authority is the applicant, on every person who would, if he were aggrieved by the decision, order or action, be entitled to apply to the High Court under the said section 21 or the said [section 245], as the case may be;
- [(e)　if the application relates to a scheme to which Schedule 32 to the Local Government, Planning and Land Act 1980 applies, on the body which adopted the scheme.]
- [(f)　if the application relates to a compulsory purchase order authorised by a Minister under section 7 of the Land Commission Act 1967, on the Land Commission.]

(3)　In [paragraph (2)] "the appropriate Minister or government department" means the Minister of the Crown or government department by whom the order, scheme, certificate, plan, amendment, approval or decision in question was [or may be] made, [authorised,] confirmed, approved or given or on whose part the action in question was [or may be] taken.

[(4) Where the application relates to an order made under the Road Traffic Regulation Act 1967, notice of the motion must be served—

    (a) if the order was made by a Minister of the Crown, on that Minister;

    (b) if the order was made by a local authority with the consent, or in pursuance of a direction, of a Minister of the Crown, on that authority and also on that Minister;

    (c) in any other case, on the local authority by whom the order was made.

In this paragraph 'local authority' includes the Greater London Council.]

Commencement 1 October 1969 (para (4)); 1 October 1966 (remainder).

Amendments Para (2): words "Subject to paragraph (4)" inserted by SI 1969/1105, r 12(1); in sub-para (b) words "Secretary of State" substituted by SI 1979/1542, r 9(3)(a)(i); original sub-para (c) revoked and original sub-paras (d)–(f) relettered as sub-paras (c)–(e) by SI 1969/1105, r 12(2), sub-para (c) subsequently substituted by SI 1979/1542, r 9(3)(a)(ii); in sub-para (d) words "a Minister of the Crown" substituted by SI 1967/829, r 7(1), words "section 245 of the Town and Country Planning Act 1971" and "section 245" substituted by SI 1979/1542, r 9(3)(a)(iii); sub-para (e) revoked by SI 1979/1542, r 9(3)(a)(iv), new sub-para (e) inserted by SI 1982/1111, r 111; sub-para (f) added by SI 1967/1809, r 7(1).

Para (3): words "paragraph (2)" substituted by SI 1969/1105, r 12(3); words "or may be" in both places inserted by SI 1982/1111, r 112; word "authorised," inserted by SI 1967/1809, r 7(2).

Para (4): added by SI 1969/1105, r 12(4).

Order 94, r 3 Filing of affidavits, etc

(1)   Without prejudice to the powers of the Court under Order 38, rule 2(3), evidence at the hearing of a motion under rule 1 shall be by affidavit.

(2)   Any affidavit in support of the application made by such motion must be filed by the applicant in the Crown Office within 14 days after service of the notice of motion and the applicant must, at the time of filing, serve a copy of the affidavit and of any exhibit thereto on the respondent.

(3)   Any affidavit in opposition to the application must be filed by the respondent in the Crown Office within 21 days after the service on him under paragraph (2) of the applicant's affidavit and the respondent must, at the time of filing, serve a copy of his affidavit and of any exhibit thereto on the applicant.

(4)   When filing an affidavit under this rule a party must leave a copy thereof and of any exhibit thereto at the Crown Office for the use of the Court.

(5)   Unless the Court otherwise orders, a motion under rule 1 shall not be heard earlier than 14 days after the time for filing an affidavit by the respondent has expired.

Commencement 1 October 1966.

Order 94, r 4 Rectification of register of deeds of arrangement

(1)   Every application to the Court under section 7 of the Deeds of Arrangement Act 1914 for an order—

    (a) that any omission to register a deed of arrangement within the time prescribed by that Act be rectified by extending the time for such registration, or

(b) that any omission or mis-statement of the name, residence or description of any person be rectified by the insertion in the register of his true name, residence or description,

must be made by affidavit ex parte to a master of the Queen's Bench Division.

(2)   The affidavit must set out particulars of the deed of arrangements and of the omission or mis-statement in question and must state the grounds on which the application is made.

Commencement 1 October 1966.

Order 94, r 5 Exercise of jurisdiction under Representation of the People Acts

(1)   Proceedings in the High Court under the Representation of the People Acts shall be assigned to the Queen's Bench Division.

(2)   Subject to paragraphs (3) and (4), the jurisdiction of the High Court under the said Acts in matters relating to parliamentary and local government elections shall be exercised by a Divisional Court.

(3)   Paragraph (2) shall not be construed as taking away from a single judge or a master any jurisdiction under the said Acts which, but for that paragraph, would be exercisable by a single judge or, as the case may be, by a master.

(4)   Where the jurisdiction of the High Court under the said Acts is by a provision of any of those Acts made exercisable in matters relating to parliamentary elections by a single judge, that jurisdiction in matters relating to local government elections shall also be exercisable by a single judge.

[(5)   An originating summons by which any application relating to parliamentary or local government elections is made shall be in Form No 10 in Appendix A.]

Commencement   3 June 1980 (para (5)); 1 October 1966 (remainder).
Amendments   Para (5): substituted by SI 1979/1716, r 48, Schedule, Pt 2.

Order 94, r 6 Appeal to High Court where Court's decision is final

(1)   This rule applies to an appeal to the High Court under any of the following enactments, namely—
(a)   section 9 of the Architects (Registration) Act 1931;
[(b)   sections 82(3) and 83(2) of the Medicines Act 1968;]
[(c)] [section 12(3) of the Legal Aid Act 1974];
[(d)] [section 13 of the Nurses, Midwives and Health Visitors Act 1979]
[(e)] section 10 of the Pharmacy Act 1954;
[(f)], [(g)]. . .
[(h)   [section 38(3) of the Legal Aid Act 1974].]

(2)   Every appeal to which this rule applies must be supported by affidavit and, if the Court so directs, by evidence given orally.

(3)   . . .

(4)   Order 55, rule 4(2), shall apply in relation to an appeal [under the enactments mentioned in paragraph (1)(c) and (h)] as if for the period of 28 days therein specified there were substituted a period of 21 days.

(5)   In the case of an appeal under an enactment specified in column (1) of the following Table, the persons to be made respondents are the persons specified in relation to that enactment in column (2) of that Table and the person to be served with notice of the originating motion by which the appeal is brought is the person so specified in column (3) thereof:—

TABLE

(1)	(2)	(3)
Enactment	*Respondents*	*Person to be served*
Architects (Registration) Act 1931 s 9	The Architects' Registration Council of the United Kingdom	The registrar of the Council
[Medicines Act 1968, s 82(3)] [and s 83(2)]	The Pharmaceutical Society of Great Britain	The registrar of the Society
...	...	...
[Legal Aid Act 1974, s 12(3)]	The appropriate Panel (Complaints) Tribunal set up under para 29 of the Legal Aid Scheme 1950	The clerk of the appropriate tribunal
[Nurses, Midwives and Health Visitors Act 1979, s 13	The United Kingdom Central Council for Nursing, Midwifery and Health Visiting	The Registrar of the Council]
Pharmacy Act 1954 s 10	The Pharmaceutical Society of Great Britain	The registrar of the Society
...	...	...
...	...	...
[[Legal Aid Act 1974, s 38(2)]	The appropriate tribunal set up under rule 2 of the Legal Aid in Criminal Cases (Complaints Tribunal) Rules 1968.	The clerk of the appropriate tribunal.]

Commencement   1 October 1966.

Amendments   Para (1): sub-para (b) substituted by SI 1980/629, r 27(1); original sub-para (c) revoked and sub-paras (d)–(h) re-lettered as sub-paras (c)–(g) by SI 1967/829, r 7(2)(a), text of sub-para (c) subsequently substituted by SI 1979/1542, r 9(3)(b)(i); text of sub-para (d) subsequently substituted, and sub-para (g) subsequently revoked, by SI 1987/1423, r 63, Schedule; sub-para (f) revoked by SI 1979/1542, r 9(3)(b)(ii); sub-para (h) added by SI 1968/1244, r 19(1), text of sub-para (h) subsequently substituted by SI 1979/1542, r 9(3)(b)(iii).

Para (3): revoked by SI 1980/1908, r 19.

Para (4): words "under the enactments mentioned in paragraph (1)(c) and (h)" substituted by SI 1968/1244, r 19(2).

Para (5): in the table, words "Medicines Act 1968, s 82(3)" substituted by SI 1979/1542, r 9(3)(c)(ii), words "and s 83(2)" inserted by SI 1980/629, r 27(2); first entry omitted revoked by SI 1967/829, r 7(2)(c); words "Legal Aid Act 1974, s 12(3)" substituted by SI 1980/629, r 27(2); entry relating to the "Nurses, Midwives and Health Visitors Act 1979, s 13" substituted, and third entry omitted revoked, by SI 1987/1423, r 63, Schedule; second entry omitted revoked by SI 1979/1542, r 9(3)(c)(i); final entry added by SI 1968/1244, r 19(3), words "Legal Aid Act 1974, s 38(2)" therein substituted by SI 1982/1111, r 115, Schedule.

Order 94, r 7 Reference of question of law by Agricultural Land Tribunal

(1)   Any question of law referred to the High Court by an Agricultural Land Tribunal under section 6 of the Agriculture (Miscellaneous Provisions) Act 1954 shall be referred by way of case stated by the Tribunal.

(2)   The notice of the originating motion by which an application is made to the Court for an order under the said section 6 directing such a Tribunal to refer a question of law to the Court, and the notice of the originating motion by which an application is made to the Court to determine a question of law so referred, must, where the proceedings before the Tribunal arose on an application under section 4 of the Agriculture Act 1958, be served on the authority having power to enforce the statutory requirement specified in the application as well as on every other party to those proceedings and on the secretary of the Tribunal.

(3)   Where in accordance with the provisions of this rule notice of an originating motion is served on the authority mentioned in paragraph (2), that authority shall be entitled to appear and be heard in the proceedings on the motion.

Commencement   1 October 1966.

Order 94, r 8 Tribunals and Inquiries Act [1971]: appeal from tribunal

(1)   A person who was a party to proceedings before any such tribunal as is mentioned in [section 13(1)] of the Tribunals and Inquiries Act [1971] and is dissatisfied in point of law with the decision of the tribunal may appeal to the High Court.

(2)   Order 55, rule 4(1)(b), shall apply in relation to such an appeal as if for the reference to the chairman of a tribunal there were substituted—
    (a)   in the case of a tribunal which has no chairman or member who acts as a chairman, a reference to the member or members of the tribunal, and
    (b)   in the case of any such tribunal as is specified in [paragraph 10] of Schedule 1 to the said Act of [1971], a reference to the secretary of the tribunal.

[(3)   Where such an appeal is against the decision of—
    (a)   the tribunal constituted under [section 46 of the National Health Service Act 1977], or
    (b)   a tribunal established under [section 128 of the Employment Protection (Consolidation) Act 1978],

Order 55, rule 4(2), shall apply in relation to the appeal as if for the period of 28 days therein specified there were substituted, in the case of the tribunal mentioned in sub-paragraph (a), a period of 14 days and, in the case of a tribunal mentioned in sub-paragraph (b), a period of 42 days.]

Commencement   1 September 1968 (para (3)); 1 October 1966 (remainder).
Amendments   Rule heading: word "1971" substituted by SI 1979/1542, r 9(3)(d).
Para (1): words "section 13(1)" and "1971" substituted by SI 1979/1542, r 9(3)(d).
Para (2): in sub-para (b) words "paragraph 10" and "1971" substituted by SI 1979/1542, r 9(3)(d).
Para (3): substituted by SI 1968/1244, r 19(4); in sub-para (a) words "section 46 of the National Health Service Act 1977" substituted by SI 1980/1908, r 20; in sub-para (b) words "section 128 of the Employment Protection (Consolidation) Act 1978" substituted by SI 1987/1423, r 63, Schedule.

Order 94, r 9 Tribunals and Inquiries Act [1971]: case stated by tribunal

(1)   Any such tribunal as is mentioned in [section 13(1)] of the Tribunal and Inquiries Act [1971] may, of its own motion or at the request of any party to proceedings before

it, state in the course of proceedings before it in the form of a special case for the decision of the High Court any question of law arising in the proceedings.

(2)   Any party to proceedings before any such tribunal who is aggrieved by the tribunal's refusal to state such a case may apply to the High Court for an order directing the tribunal to do so.

(3)   A case stated by any such tribunal which has no chairman or member who acts as a chairman must be signed by the member or members of the tribunal.

Commencement 1 October 1966.
Amendments Rule heading: word "1971" substituted by SI 1979/1542, r 9(3)(d).
Para (1): words "section 13(1)" and "1971" substituted by SI 1979/1542, r 9(3)(d).

Order 94, r 9A *(inserted by SI 1974/1115; revoked by SI 1977/1955)*

Order 94, r 10 Tribunals and Inquiries Act [1971]: appeal from [Secretary of State]

(1)   A person who is dissatisfied in point of law with a decision of the [Secretary of State] on such an appeal as is mentioned in [section 13(5)] of the Tribunals and Inquiries Act [1971] and had, or if aggrieved would have had, a right to appeal to that [Secretary of State], whether or not he exercised that right, may appeal to the High Court.

(2)   The persons to be served with notice of the originating motion by which such an appeal is brought are the [Secretary of State] and every person who had, or if aggrieved would have had, a right to appeal to the [Secretary of State].

(3)   The Court hearing the appeal may remit the matter to the [Secretary of State] to the extent necessary to enable him to provide the Court with such further information in connection with the matter as the Court may direct.

(4)   If the Court is of opinion that the decision appealed against was erroneous in point of law, it shall not set aside or vary that decision but shall remit the matter to the [Secretary of State] with the opinion of the Court for rehearing and determination by him.

(5)   Order 55, rule 7(5), shall not apply in relation to the appeal.

Commencement 1 October 1966.
Amendments Rule heading: words "1971" and "Secretary of State" substituted by SI 1979/1542, r 9(3)(d), (e).
Para (1): words "Secretary of State" in both places and words "section 13(5)" and "1971" substituted by SI 1979/1542, r 9(3)(d), (e).
Paras (2)–(4): words "Secretary of State" wherever they occur substituted by SI 1979/1542, r 9(3)(d).

[Order 94, r 10A Consumer Credit Act 1974: appeal from Secretary of State

(1)   A person who is dissatisfied in point of law with a decision of the [Secretary of State] on an appeal under section 41 of the Consumer Credit Act 1974 from a determination of the Director General of Fair Trading and had a right to appeal to the Secretary of State, whether or not he exercised that right, may appeal to the High Court.

(2)   The persons to be served with notice of the originating motion by which such an appeal is brought are the Secretary of State and, where the appeal is by a licensee under a group licence against compulsory variation, suspension or revocation of that licence, the original applicant, if any; but the Court may in any case direct that the notice be served on any other person.

(3)   The Court hearing the appeal may remit the matter to the Secretary of State to the extent necessary to enable him to provide the Court with such further information in connection with the matter as the Court may direct.

(4)   If the Court is of the opinion that the decision appealed against was erroneous in point of law, it shall not set aside or vary that decision but shall remit the matter to the Secretary of State with the opinion of the Court for hearing and determination by him.

(5)   Order 55, rule 7(5), shall not apply in relation to the appeal.]

Commencement 1 April 1976.
Amendments This rule was inserted by SI 1976/337, r 18.
Para (1): words "Secretary of State" substituted by SI 1987/1423, r 63, Schedule.

[Order 94, r 11 Case stated by Mental Health Review Tribunal

(1)   In this rule, "the Act" means the Mental Health Act 1983.

(2)   The reference in paragraph (3) to a party to proceedings before a Mental Health Review Tribunal, and the references in Order 56, rules 8(1), 9(2) and 10 to a party to proceedings shall be construed as references to—
   (a) the person who initiated the proceedings; and
   (b) any person to whom, in accordance with rules made under section 78 of the Act, the Tribunal sent notice of the application or reference or a request instead of notice of reference.

(3)   A party to proceedings before a Mental Health Review Tribunal shall not be entitled to apply to the High Court for an order under section 78(8) of the Act directing the Tribunal to state a case for determination by the Court unless—
   (a) within 21 days after the decision of the Tribunal was communicated to him in accordance with rules made under section 78 of the Act he made a written request to the Tribunal to state a case, and
   (b) either the Tribunal failed to comply with the last-mentioned request within 21 days after it was made or the Tribunal refused to comply with it.

(4)   The period for entry of the originating motion by which an application to the Court for such an order as is mentioned in paragraph (3) is made, and for service of notice thereof, shall be—
   (a) where the Tribunal refused the applicant's request to state a case, 14 days after receipt by the applicant of notice of the refusal of his request;
   (b) where the Tribunal failed to comply with that request within the period mentioned in paragraph 3(b), 14 days after the expiration of that period.

(5)   A Mental Health Review Tribunal by whom a case is stated shall be entitled to appear and be heard in the proceedings for the determination of the case.

(6)   If the Court is of opinion that any decision of such a Tribunal on the question of law raised by the case was erroneous, the Court may give any direction which the Tribunal ought to have given under Part V of the Act.]

Commencement 1 October 1983.
Amendments This rule was substituted by SI 1983/1181, r 35.

[Order 94, r 12 Applications for leave under section 289(6) of the Town and Country Planning Act 1990 and section 65(5) of the Planning (Listed Buildings and Conservation Areas) Act 1990

(1)　An application for leave to appeal to the High Court under section 289 of the Town and Country Planning Act 1990 or section 65 of the Planning (Listed Buildings and Conservation Areas) Act 1990 shall be made within 28 days after the date on which notice of the decision was given to the applicant.

(2)　An application shall—
  (a)　include, where necessary, any application to extend the time for applying,
  (b)　be in writing setting out the reasons why leave should be granted, and if the time for applying has expired, the reasons why the application was not made within that time,
  (c)　be made by filing it in the Crown Office together with the decision, a draft originating notice of motion, and an affidavit verifying any facts relied on,
  (d)　before being filed under sub-paragraph (c), be served together with the draft originating notice of motion and a copy of the affidavit to be filed with the application, upon the persons who are referred to in rule 13(5), and
  (e)　be accompanied by an affidavit giving the names and addresses of, and the places and dates of service on, all persons who have been served with the application and, if any person who ought to be served has not been served, the affidavit must state that fact and the reason for it.

(3)　An application shall be heard—
  (a)　by a single judge sitting in open court;
  (b)　unless the Court otherwise orders, not less than 21 days after it was filed at the Crown Office.

Any person served with the application shall be entitled to appear and be heard.

(4)　If on the hearing of an application the Court is of opinion that any person who ought to have been served has not been served, the Court may adjourn the hearing on such terms (if any) as it may direct in order that the application may be served on that person.

(5)　If the Court grants leave—
  (a)　it may impose such terms as to costs and as to giving security as it thinks fit;
  (b)　it may give directions; and
  (c)　the originating notice of motion by which the appeal is to be brought shall be served and entered within 7 days of the grant.

(6)　Any respondent who intends to use an affidavit at the hearing shall file it in the Crown Office and serve a copy thereof on the applicant as soon as is practicable and in any event, unless the Court otherwise allows, at least 2 days before the hearing.

The Court may allow the applicant to use a further affidavit.]

Commencement   1 April 1992.
Amendments   This rule was substituted, together with r 13, for r 12 as originally enacted, by SI 1992/638, r 3.

[Order 94, r 13 Proceedings under sections 289 and 290 of the Town and Country Planning Act 1990 and under section 65 of the Planning (Listed Buildings and Conservation Areas) Act 1990

(1)　In this rule a reference to "section 65" is a reference to section 65 of the Planning (Listed Buildings and Conservation Areas) Act 1990, but, save as aforesaid, a reference to a section by number is a reference to the section so numbered in the Town and Country Planning Act 1990.

(2) An appeal shall lie to the High Court on a point of law against a decision of the Secretary of State under subsection (1) or (2) of section 289 or under subsection (1) of section 65 at the instance of any person or authority entitled to appeal under any of those subsections respectively.

(3) In the case of a decision to which section 290 applies, the person who made the application to which the decision relates, or the local planning authority, if dissatisfied with the decision in point of law, may appeal against the decision to the High Court.

(4) Any appeal under section 289(1) or (2), section 65(1) or section 290, and any case stated under section 289(3) or section 65(2), shall be heard and determined by a single judge unless the Court directs that the matter shall be heard and determined by a Divisional Court.

(5) The persons to be served with notice of the originating motion by which an appeal to the High Court is brought by virtue of section 289(1) or (2), section 65(1) or section 290 are—

(a) the Secretary of State;

(b) the local planning authority who served the notice or gave the decision, as the case may be, or, where the appeal is brought by that authority, the appellant or applicant in the proceedings in which the decision appealed against was given;

(c) in the case of an appeal brought by virtue of section 289(1) or section 65(1), any other person having an interest in the land to which the notice relates, and;

(d) in the case of an appeal brought by virtue of section 289(2), any other person on whom the notice to which those proceedings related was served.

(6) The Court hearing any such appeal may remit the matter to the Secretary of State to the extent necessary to enable him to provide the Court with such further information in connection with the matter as the Court may direct.

(7) Where the Court is of opinion that the decision appealed against was erroneous in point of law, it shall not set aside or vary that decision but shall remit the matter to the Secretary of State with the opinion of the Court for re-hearing and determination by him.

(8) Order 55, rule 7(5) shall not apply in relation to any such appeal.

(9) The Court may give directions as to the exercise, until an appeal brought by virtue of section 289(1) is finally concluded and any re-hearing and determination by the Secretary of State has taken place, of the power to serve, and institute proceedings (including criminal proceedings) concerning—

(a) a stop notice under section 183, and;

(b) a breach of condition notice under section 187A.]

Commencement   27 July 1992 (para (9)(b)); 1 April 1992 (remainder).

Amendments   Original r 13 added by SI 1970/1861, r 7, revoked by SI 1991/1884, r 6(2); new r 13 substituted, together with r 12, for r 12 as originally enacted, by SI 1992/638, r 3.

[Order 94, r 14 Applications under section 13, Coroners Act 1988

(1)   Any application under section 13 of the Coroners Act 1988 shall be heard and determined by a Divisional Court.

(2)   The application must be made by originating motion and, without prejudice to Order 8, rule 3(2), the notice of such motion must state the grounds of the application and, unless the application is made by the Attorney General, shall be accompanied by his fiat.

(3)   Notice of the motion must be entered in the Crown Office and served upon all persons directly affected by the application within six weeks after the grant of the fiat.]

Commencement   1 October 1988.
Amendments   This rule was added by SI 1988/1340, r 14.

[Order 94, r 15 Applications under section 42, Supreme Court Act 1981

(1)   Every application to the High Court by the Attorney General under section 42 of the Supreme Court Act 1981 shall be heard and determined by a Divisional Court.

(2)   The application must be made by originating motion, notice of which, together with an affidavit in support, shall be filed in the Crown Office and served on the person against whom the order is sought.]

Commencement   1 October 1988.
Amendments   This rule was added by SI 1988/1340, r 15.

ORDER 95

The Bills of Sale Acts 1878 and 1882 [and the Industrial and Provident Societies Act 1967]

Amendments   Words "and the Industrial and Provident Societies Act 1967" added by SI 1967/1809, r 8(1).

Order 95, r 1 Rectification of register

(1)   Every application to the Court under section 14 of the Bills of Sale Act 1878 for an order—

    (a)   that any omission to register a bill of sale or an affidavit of renewal thereof within the time prescribed by that Act be rectified by extending the time for such registration, or

    (b)   that any omission or mis-statement of the name, residence or occupation of any person be rectified by the insertion in the register of his true name, residence or occupation,

must be made by affidavit ex parte to a master of the Queen's Bench Division.

(2)   Every application for such an order as is described in paragraph (1) shall be supported by an affidavit setting out particulars of the bill of sale and of the omission or mis-statement in question and stating the grounds on which the application is made.

Commencement   1 October 1966.

Order 95, r 2 Entry of satisfaction

(1)   Every application under section 15 of the Bills of Sale Act 1878 to a master of the Queen's Bench Division for an order that a memorandum of satisfaction be written on a registered copy of a bill of sale must—

    (a)   if a consent to the satisfaction signed by the person entitled to the benefit of the bill of sale can be obtained, be made ex parte;

    (b)   in all other cases, be made by originating summons.

(2)   An ex parte application under paragraph (1)(a) must be supported by—

    (a)   particulars of the consent referred to in that paragraph; and

    (b)   an affidavit by a witness who attested the consent verifying the signature on it.

(3)   An originating summons under paragraph (1)(b) must be served on the person entitled to the benefit of the bill of sale and must be supported by evidence that the debt (if any) for which the bill of sale was made has been satisfied or discharged.

[(4)   An originating summons under paragraph (1)(b) shall be in Form No 10 in Appendix A.]

Commencement   3 June 1980 (para (4)); 1 October 1966 (remainder).
Amendments   Para (4): substituted by SI 1979/1716, r 48, Schedule, Pt 2.
Forms   Affidavit for leave to enter memorandum of satisfaction (PF183).
Summons for order that satisfaction be entered (PF184).
Order for entry of satisfaction (PF185).

Order 95, r 3 Restraining removal on sale of goods seized

[An originating summons by which an application to the Court under the proviso to section 7 of the Bills of Sale Act (1878) Amendment Act 1882 must be made shall be in Form No 10 in Appendix A.]

Commencement   3 June 1980.
Amendments   The text of this rule was substituted by SI 1979/1716, r 48, Schedule, Part 2.

Order 95, r 4 Search of register

Any master of the Queen's Bench Division shall, on a request in writing giving sufficient particulars, and on payment of the prescribed fee, cause a search to be made in the register of bills of sale and issue a certificate of the result of the search.

Commencement   1 October 1966.

[Order 95, r 5 Application under section 1(5) of the Industrial and Provident Societies Act 1967

Every application to the Court under section 1(5) of the Industrial and Provident Societies Act 1967 for an order—

  (a) that the period for making an application for recording a charge be extended, or

  (b) that any omission from or mis-statement in such an application be rectified,

must be made to a Master of the Queen's Bench Division ex parte by affidavit setting out particulars of the charge and of the omission or mis-statement in question and stating the grounds of the application.]

Commencement   1 January 1968.
Amendments   This rule was added by SI 1967/1809, r 8(2).

[Order 95, r 6 Assignment of book debts

(1)   There shall continue to be kept in the Central Office, under the supervision of the registrar, a register of assignments of book debts.

(2)   Every application for registration of an assignment of a book debt under [section 344 of the Insolvency Act 1986] shall be made by producing at the Filing and Record Department of the Central Office—

  (a) a true copy of the assignment, and of every schedule thereto, and

  (b) an affidavit verifying the date and the time, and the due execution of the assignment in the presence of the deponent, and setting out the particulars of the assignment and the parties thereto.

(3)   On an application being made in accordance with the preceding paragraph, the documents there referred to shall be filed, and the particulars of the assignment, and of the parties to it, shall be entered in the register.

(4)   In this rule, "the registrar" has the meaning given in section 13 of the Bills of Sale Act 1878.]

Commencement   2 January 1980.
Amendments   This rule was added by SI 1979/1542, r 7.
Para (2): words "section 344 of the Insolvency Act 1986" substituted by SI 1986/2001, art 2, Schedule.
Forms   Affidavit on registration of assignment (PF186).

ORDER 96
THE [MINES (WORKING FACILITIES AND SUPPORT) ACT 1966], ETC

Amendments   Words "Mines (Working Facilities and Support) Act 1966" substituted by SI 1979/1542, r 9, Schedule.

Order 96, r 1 Assignment to Chancery Division

Any proceedings in which the jurisdiction conferred on the High Court . . . by section 1 of the Railway and Canal Commission (Abolition) Act 1949, other than the jurisdiction under section 22(2) of the Electricity (Supply) Act 1919 or section 7(6) of the Water Act 1945, . . . is invoked shall be assigned to the Chancery Division and be begun by ex parte originating summons.

Commencement   1 October 1966.
Amendments   Words omitted revoked by SI 1979/1542, r 9(4).

Order 96, r 2 Reference by [Secretary of State] of certain applications

Where under any provision of [Mines (Working Facilities and Support) Act 1966] the [Secretary of State] refers any application to the High Court, he shall—
   (a)   lodge the reference, signed by him or by an officer authorised by him for the purpose, in [Chancery Chambers], together with all documents and plans deposited with him by the applicant, and
   (b)   within 3 days after doing so give notice to the applicant of the lodging of the reference.

Commencement   1 October 1966.
Amendments   Rule heading: words "Secretary of State" substituted by SI 1982/1111, r 115, Schedule.
Words "Mines (Working Facilities and Support) Act 1966" substituted by SI 1979/1542, r 9, Schedule; words "Secretary of State" and "Chancery Chambers" substituted by SI 1982/1111, rr 88, 115, Schedule.

Order 96, r 3 Issue of summons

Within 10 days after receipt of the notice mentioned in rule 2(b), the applicant must issue an ex parte originating summons which must state the application of the applicant under [the said Act of 1966] and any other relief sought.

Commencement   1 October 1966.
Amendments   Words "the said Act of 1966" substituted by SI 1979/1542, r 9, Schedule.
Definitions   Act of 1966: Mines (Working Facilities and Support) Act 1966.

Order 96, r 4 Appointment for directions

(1)   Within 7 days after issue of the summons the applicant, having applied at [Chancery Chambers] for the name of the master assigned to hear the summons, must take an appointment before that master for the hearing of the summons and must forthwith serve notice of the appointment on the [Secretary of State].

(2)   Not less than 2 clear days before the day appointed for the first hearing of the summons, the applicant must leave [at Chancery Chambers]—
   (a)   an affidavit of facts in support of the summons, giving particulars of all persons known to the applicant to be interested in or affected by the application, and

(b)   a draft of any proposed advertisement or notice of the application.

(3)   On the appointment the master shall—

(a)   fix a time within which any notice of objection under rule 5 must be given,

(b)   fix a date for the further hearing of the summons, and

(c)   direct what, if any, advertisements and notices of the application and of the date fixed for the further hearing of the summons are to be inserted and given, and what persons, if any, are to be served with a copy of the application and of any other document in the proceedings.

(4)   Any such advertisement or notice must include a statement of the effect of rule 5.

Commencement   1 October 1966.
Amendments   Para (1): words "Chancery Chambers" and "Secretary of State" substituted by SI 1982/1111, rr 88, 115, Schedule.
Para (2): words "at Chancery Chambers" substituted by SI 1982/1111, r 88.

Order 96, r 5 Objections to application

(1)   Any person wishing to oppose the application must, within the time fixed by the master under rule 4(3), serve on the applicant a notice of objection stating—

(a)   his name and address and the name and address of his solicitor, if any,

(b)   the grounds of his objection and any alternative methods of effecting the objects of the application which he alleges may be used, and

(c)   the facts on which he relies.

(2)   Any notice required to be served on a person who has given notice of objection (hereafter in this Order referred to as "the objector") may be served by delivering it or sending it by prepaid post—

(a)   where the name and address of a solicitor is stated in the notice of objection, to the solicitor at that address, and

(b)   in any other case, to the objector at his address stated in the notice of objection.

(3)   An objector shall be entitled . . . to appear in person or by solicitor or counsel at the further hearing of the originating summons and to take such part in the proceedings as the master or judge thinks fit; but if he does not so appear his notice of objection shall be of no effect and he shall not be entitled to take any part in the proceedings unless the master or judge otherwise orders.

Commencement   1 October 1966.
Amendments   Para (3): words omitted revoked by SI 1979/1716, r 48, Schedule, Pt 1.

Order 96, r 6 List of objectors

Not less than 2 clear days before the day fixed for the further hearing of the summons, the applicant must leave [at Chancery Chambers] any notices of objection served on the applicant together with a list arranged in 3 columns stating—

(a)   in column 1, the names and addresses of the objectors,

(b)   in column 2, the names and addresses of their respective solicitors, if any, and

(c)   in column 3, short summaries of their respective grounds of objection.

Commencement   1 October 1966.
Amendments   Words "at Chancery Chambers" substituted by SI 1982/1111, r 88.

Order 96, r 7 Directions on further hearing

At the further hearing of the summons the master shall—
  (a) give directions as to the procedure to be followed before the summons is set down for hearing, including, if he thinks fit, a direction—
      (i) that further particulars be given of any of the grounds or facts relied on in support of or in opposition to the application made by the summons,
      (ii) that the applicant may serve a reply to any notice of objection,
      (iii) that any particular fact be proved by affidavit,
      (iv) that pleadings or points of claim or defence be served, and
  (b) adjourn the summons for hearing before the judge in such manner, that is to say—
      (i) in court or in chambers, and
      (ii) on oral evidence or on affidavit evidence, with or without cross examination of any of the deponents, or partly in one way and partly in the other,

  as he shall think best adapted to secure the just, expeditious and economical disposal of the proceedings.

Commencement 1 October 1966.

Order 96, r 8 Other applications

Rules 2 to 7 shall, so far as applicable and with the necessary adaptations, apply in relation to any other application to the High Court falling within rule 1 as they apply in relation to an application under [the Mines (Working Facilities and Support) Act 1966].

Commencement 1 October 1966.
Amendments Words "the Mines (Working Facilities and Support) Act 1966" substituted by SI 1979/1542, r 9, Schedule.

ORDER 97
[THE LANDLORD AND TENANT ACTS 1927, 1954 AND 1987]

Amendments   Words "The Landlord and Tenant Acts 1927, 1954 and 1987" substituted by SI 1988/298, r 14.

Order 97, r 1 Interpretation

[(1)   In this Order "the Act of 1927" means the Landlord and Tenant Act 1927, "the Act of 1954" means the Landlord and Tenant Act 1954 and "the Act of 1987" means the Landlord and Tenant Act 1987.]

(2)   In relation to any proceedings under Part II of the Act of 1954, any reference in this Order to a landlord shall, if the interest of the landlord in question is subject to a mortgage and the mortgagee is in possession or a receiver appointed by the mortgagee or by the court is in receipt of the rents and profits, be construed as a reference to the mortgagee.

Commencement   18 April 1988 (para (1)); 1 October 1966 (remainder).
Amendments   Para (1): substituted by SI 1988/298, r 15.
Cross references   See CCR Order 43, r 1.

Order 97, r 2 Assignment of proceedings to Chancery Division, etc

All proceedings in the High Court under Part I of the Act of 1927 or Part II of the Act of 1954 [or the Act of 1987] shall be assigned to the Chancery Division and, subject to [rules 9A and 12], be begun by originating summons.

Commencement   1 October 1966.
Amendments   Words "or the Act of 1987" inserted by SI 1988/298, r 16; words "rules 9A and 12" substituted by SI 1970/1861, r 8(1).
Definitions   Act of 1927: Landlord and Tenant Act 1927.
Act of 1954: Landlord and Tenant Act 1954.
Act of 1987: Landlord and Tenant Act 1987.

Order 97, r 3 Issue, etc of originating summons

(1)   Any originating summons by which a claim or application under Part I of the Act of 1927 or Part II of the Act of 1954 [or the Act of 1987] is made may be issued out of the district registry for the district in which the premises to which the claim or application relates are situated instead of [Chancery Chambers].

[(2)   Any such summons shall be in Form No 10 in Appendix A.]

(3)   The day fixed under Order 28, rule 2(2), for the hearing of such a summons shall be a day which will allow an interval of at least 14 days between the date of service of the summons and the day so fixed.

Commencement   3 June 1980 (para (2)); 1 October 1966 (remainder).
Amendments   Para (1): words "or the Act of 1987" inserted by SI 1988/298, r 17; words "Chancery Chambers" substituted by SI 1982/1111, r 89.
Para (2): substituted by SI 1979/1716, r 48, Schedule, Pt 2.
Definitions   Act of 1927: Landlord and Tenant Act 1927.
Act of 1954: Landlord and Tenant Act 1954.
Act of 1987: Landlord and Tenant Act 1987.
Cross references   See CCR Order 43, r 2.

Order 97, r 4 Claim for compensation in respect of improvement

(1)   A claim under section 1 of the Act of 1927 for compensation in respect of any improvement, and a claim by a mesne landlord under section 8 of that Act, must be a written claim, signed by the claimant or his solicitor or agent, containing—

(a) a statement of the name and address of the claimant and of the landlord against whom the claim is made,

(b) a description of the holding in respect of which the claim is made and of the trade or business carried on there,

(c) a concise statement of the nature of the claim,

(d) particulars of the improvement, including the date when it was completed and the cost thereof, and

(e) a statement of the amount claimed.

(2)   Where any document relating to any proposed improvement, or to any claim, is sent to or served on a mesne landlord in pursuance of Part I of the Act of 1927, he must forthwith serve on his immediate superior landlord a copy of the document, together with a notice in writing stating the date on which he received the document, and if the last-mentioned landlord is himself a mesne landlord he must accordingly comply with this paragraph.

Commencement   1 October 1966.
Definitions   Act of 1927: Landlord and Tenant Act 1927.
Cross references   See CCR Order 43, r 3.

Order 97, r 5 Proceedings under Part I of Act of 1927

(1)   Without prejudice to Order 7, rule 3, the originating summons by which any claim or application under Part I of the Act of 1927 is made must state—

(a) the nature of the claim or application or the matter to be determined,

(b) the holding in respect of which the claim or application is made and the trade or business carried on there,

(c) particulars of the improvement or proposed improvement to which the claim or application relates, and

(d) if the claim is for payment of compensation, the amount claimed.

(2)   The plaintiff's immediate landlord shall be made defendant to the summons.

(3)   Without prejudice to the powers of the Court under Order 28, rule 4(4), no affidavit shall be filed in the first instance in support of or in answer to any such summons.

(4)   Any certificate of the Court under section 3 of the Act of 1927 that an improvement is a proper improvement or has been duly executed shall be embodied in an order.

Commencement   1 October 1966.
Definitions   Act of 1927: Landlord and Tenant Act 1927.
Cross references   See CCR Order 43, r 4.

Order 97, r 6 Application for new tenancy under s 24 of Act of 1954

(1)   Without prejudice to Order 7, rule 3, the originating summons by which an application under section 24 of the Act of 1954 for a new tenancy is made must state—

(a) the premises to which the application relates and [where a business is carried on there, the nature of such business],

(b) particulars of the plaintiff's current tenancy of the premises and of every notice or request given or made in respect of that tenancy under section 25 or 26 of that Act, and

(c) the plaintiff's proposals as to the terms of the new tenancy applied for including, in particular, terms as to the duration thereof and as to the rent payable thereunder.

(2) The person who, in relation to the plaintiff's current tenancy, is the landlord as defined by section 44 of the Act of 1954 shall be made defendant to the summons.

[(3) Order 7, rule 6, shall not apply to an originating summons under this rule and Order 6, rule 8(1) and (2) shall apply to such a summons as it applies to a writ but with the substitution for the references to 6 months and to 4 months of references to 2 months.]

Commencement 4 June 1990 (para (3)); 1 October 1966 (remainder).
Amendments Para (1): in sub-para (a) words from "where a business" to "such business" substituted by SI 1982/1111, r 115, Schedule.
Para (3): substituted by SI 1989/2427, r 4.
Definitions Act of 1954: Landlord and Tenant Act 1954.
Cross references See CCR Order 43, r 6.

[Order 97, r 6A Application to authorise agreement

(1) An application under section 38(4) of the Act of 1954 for the authorisation of an agreement shall be made by ex parte originating summons and may be heard and determined in chambers.

(2) Notwithstanding that the application must be made jointly by the landlord or proposed landlord and the tenant or proposed tenant and the originating summons is accordingly issued by one solicitor on behalf of both of them, they may appear and be heard at any hearing of the summons by separate solicitors or counsel or, in the case of an individual applicant, in person; and where at any stage of the proceedings it appears to the Court that one of the applicants is not but ought to be separately represented, the Court may adjourn the proceedings until he is.]

Commencement 29 March 1971.
Amendments This rule was inserted by SI 1971/354, r 5.
Definitions Act of 1954: Landlord and Tenant Act 1954.
Cross references See CCR Order 43, r 15(2).

Order 97, r 7 Evidence on application under s 24 of Act of 1954

(1) [Not less than 14 days before the day fixed for the first hearing of] the originating summons by which an application under section 24 of the Act of 1954 for a new tenancy is made the plaintiff must file an affidavit verifying the statements of fact made in the summons.

(2) Not less than 4 days before the day fixed for the first hearing of the summons the defendant must file an affidavit stating—

(a) whether he opposes the grant of a new tenancy and, if he does, on what grounds;

(b) whether, if a new tenancy is granted, he objects to any of the plaintiff's proposals as to the terms thereof and, if he does, the terms to which he objects and the terms he proposes in so far as they differ from the terms proposed by the plaintiff;

(c) whether he is a tenant under a lease having less than 14 years unexpired at the date of the termination of the plaintiff's current tenancy and, if he is, the name and address of his immediate landlord.

Commencement 1 October 1966.
Amendments Para (1): words from the beginning to "the first hearing of" substituted by SI 1984/1051, r 50.
Definitions Act of 1954: Landlord and Tenant Act 1954.
Cross references See CCR Order 43, r 7 (as to para (1)).

Order 97, r 8 Parties to certain proceedings

(1) Any person affected by any proceedings on an originating summons under rule 5 [6, 14, 15, 16 or 17] may apply in chambers to be made a party to the proceedings and the Court may give such directions on the application as appear necessary.

(2) An application under paragraph (1) must in the first instance be made ex parte but the Court may require notice thereof to be given to the parties to the proceedings before making any order.

(3) The foregoing provisions are without prejudice to the power of the Court, either with or without an application by any party, to order notice of the proceedings to be given to any person or any person to be made a party to the proceedings, but nothing in this rule shall be construed as requiring the Court to make any such order and, if it appears that any person though he is affected by the proceedings is not sufficiently affected for it to be necessary for him to be made a party to the proceedings or given notice thereof, the Court may refuse to make him a party or, as the case may be, to require him to be given notice of the proceedings.

Commencement 1 October 1966.
Amendments Para (1): words "6, 14, 15, 16 or 17" substituted by SI 1988/298, r 18.
Cross references See CCR Order 43, r 14.

Order 97, r 9 Order dismissing application under s 24 which is successfully opposed

Where the Court hearing an application under section 24 of the Act of 1954 is precluded by section 31 of that Act from making an order for the grant of a new tenancy by reason of any of the grounds specified in section 30(1) of that Act, the order dismissing the application shall state all the grounds by reason of which the Court is so precluded.

Commencement 1 October 1966.
Definitions Act of 1954: Landlord and Tenant Act 1954.
Cross references See CCR Order 43, r 8.

[Order 97, r 9A Application to determine interim rent

(1) An application under section 24A of the Act of 1954 to determine an interim rent shall—

(a) if the tenant has begun proceedings for a new tenancy under section 24 of the Act, be made by summons in those proceedings, and

(b)   in any other case, be made by originating summons.

(2)   The application may be heard and determined in chambers.]

Commencement 1 January 1971.
Amendments This rule was inserted by SI 1970/1861, r 8(2).
Definitions Act of 1954, the Act: Landlord and Tenant Act 1954.

Order 97, r 10 Other applications under Part II of Act of 1954

(1)   An application for an order under section 31(2)(b) of the Act of 1954 and, unless made at the hearing of the application under section 24 thereof, an application for a certificate under section 37(4) of that Act must be made ex parte in chambers.

(2)   The mesne landlord to whose consent an application for the determination of any question arising under paragraph 4(3) of Schedule 6 to the Act of 1954 relates shall be made defendant to the originating summons by which the application is made.

Commencement 1 October 1966.
Definitions Act of 1954: Landlord and Tenant Act 1954.
Cross references See CCR Order 43, r 9.

Order 97, r 11 Transfer of proceedings from county court

(1)   Where, under [section 63(4)] of the Act of 1954, proceedings in a county court under Part I of the Act of 1927 or Part II of the Act of 1954 are transferred to the High Court, Order 78, rule 2, shall apply subject to the modification that the words in paragraph (c) thereof from "and that" to the end shall be omitted.

(2)   Any such proceedings so transferred shall proceed in the High Court as if they had been begun by originating summons issued out of [Chancery Chambers], and within 7 days after receipt of the notice referred to in Order 78, rule 2(c), the plaintiff must apply in chambers for the appointment of a day and time for the attendance of the parties before the Court.

(3)   If the plaintiff fails to apply for an appointment within the period prescribed by paragraph (2), the defendant may do so.

Commencement 1 October 1966.
Amendments Para (1): words "section 63(4)" substituted by SI 1992/638, r 18.
Para (2): words "Chancery Chambers" substituted by SI 1982/1111, r 89.
Definitions Act of 1927: Landlord and Tenant Act 1927.
Act of 1954: Landlord and Tenant Act 1954.
Cross references See CCR Order 43, r 12, see also CCR Order 16, Part III.

Order 97, r 12 Application for relief under s 16, etc of Act of 1954

In any such proceedings as are mentioned in section 16(1) of the Act of 1954, paragraph 9(1) of Schedule 5 to that Act or paragraph 10(1) of that Schedule, an application for relief under that section or paragraph, as the case may be, may be made—
    (a)   in the applicant's pleading, or
    (b)   by summons at any time before the trial, or
    (c)   at the trial.

Commencement 1 October 1966.
Definitions Act of 1954: Landlord and Tenant Act 1954.

Order 97, r 13 Evidence of rateable value

Where any dispute as to the rateable value of any holding has been referred under section 37(5) of the Act of 1954 to the Commissioners of Inland Revenue for decision by a valuation officer ... any document purporting to be a statement by the valuation officer of his decision shall be admissible as evidence of the matters contained therein.

Commencement 1 October 1966.
Amendments Words omitted revoked by SI 1992/638, r 19.
Definitions Act of 1954: Landlord and Tenant Act 1954.
Cross references See CCR Order 43, r 11.

[Order 97, r 14 Application under section 19 of the Act of 1987

A copy of the notice served under section 19(2)(a) of the Act of 1987 shall be appended to the originating summons issued under section 19(1) thereof, and an additional copy of the notice shall be filed.]

Commencement 18 April 1988.
Amendments This rule was added by SI 1988/298, r 19.
Definitions Act of 1987: Landlord and Tenant Act 1987.
Cross references See CCR Order 43, r 17.

[Order 97, r 15 Application for order under section 24 of the Act of 1987

(1) An application for an order under section 24 of the Act of 1987 shall state—
   (a) the premises to which the application relates,
   (b) the name and address of the applicant and of the landlord of the premises, or, where the landlord cannot be found or his identity ascertained, the steps taken to find him or ascertain his identity.
   (c) the name and address of every person known to the applicant who is likely to be affected by the application, including, but not limited to, the other tenants of flats contained in the premises, any mortgagee or superior landlord of the landlord, and any tenants' association,
   (d) the name, address and qualifications of the person it is desired to be appointed manager of the premises,
   (e) the functions which it is desired that the manager shall carry out, and
   (f) the grounds of the application,
and a copy of the notice served on the landlord under section 22 of the Act of 1987 shall be appended to the originating summons, unless the requirement to serve such a notice has been dispensed with, and an additional copy of the notice shall be filed.

(2) The defendant to an application for an order under section 24 of the Act of 1987 shall be the landlord of the premises.

(3) A copy of the summons shall be served on—
   (a) each of the persons named by the applicant under paragraph (1)(c), together with a notice stating that he may apply under rule 8 to be made a party to the proceedings, and

(b) the person named under paragraph (1)(d).

(4) Order 30, rules 2 to 8 shall apply to proceedings in which an application is made for an order under section 24 of the Act of 1987 as they apply to proceedings in which an application is made for the appointment of a receiver, and as if for the references in those rules to a receiver there were references to a manager under the Act of 1987.]

Commencement 18 April 1988.
Amendments This rule was added by SI 1988/298, r 19.
Definitions Act of 1987: Landlord and Tenant Act 1987.
Cross references See CCR Order 43, r 18.

[Order 97, r 16 Application for acquisition order under section 29 of the Act of 1987

(1) An application for an acquisition order under section 29 of the Act of 1987 shall—

    (a) identify the premises to which the application relates and give such details of them as are necessary to show that section 25 of the Act of 1987 applies thereto,

    (b) give such details of the applicants as are necessary to show that they constitute the requisite majority of qualifying tenants,

    (c) state the name and address of the applicants and of the landlord of the premises, or, where the landlord cannot be found or his identity ascertained, the steps taken to find him or ascertain his identity,

    (d) state the name and address of the person nominated by the applicants for the purposes of Part III of the Act of 1987,

    (e) state the name and address of every person known to the applicants who is likely to be affected by the application, including, but not limited to, the other tenants of flats contained in the premises (whether or not they could have made an application), any mortgagee or superior landlord of the landlord, and any tenants' association, and

    (f) state the grounds of the application,

and a copy of the notice served on the landlord under section 27 of the Act of 1987 shall be appended to the originating summons, unless the requirement to serve such a notice has been dispensed with, and an additional copy of the notice shall be filed.

(2) The defendants to an application for an acquisition order under section 29 of the Act of 1987 shall be the landlord of the premises and the nominated person, where he is not an applicant.

(3) A copy of the summons shall be served on each of the persons named by the applicant under paragraph (1)(e), together with a notice stating that he may apply under rule 8 to be made a party to the proceedings.

(4) Where the nominated person pays money into court in accordance with an order under section 33(1) of the Act of 1987, he shall file a copy of the certificate of the surveyor selected under section 33(2)(a) thereof.]

Commencement 18 April 1988.
Amendments This rule was added by SI 1988/298, r 19.
Definitions Act of 1987: Landlord and Tenant Act 1987.
Cross references See CCR Order 43, r 19.

[Order 97, r 17 Application for order under section 38 or section 40 of the Act of 1987

(1)   An application for an order under section 38 or section 40 of the Act of 1987 shall state—

  (a)   the name and address of the applicant and of the other current parties to the lease or leases to which the application relates,

  (b)   the date of and parties to the lease or leases, the premises demised thereby, the relevant terms thereof and the variation sought,

  (c)   the name and address of every person who the applicant knows or has reason to believe is likely to be affected by the variation, including, but not limited to, the other tenants of flats contained in the premises of which the demised premises form a part, any mortgagee or superior landlord of the landlord, any mortgagee of the applicant, and any tenants' association, and

  (d)   the grounds of the application.

(2)   The other current parties to the lease or leases shall be made defendants to the application.

(3)   A copy of the application shall be served by the applicant on each of the persons named by the applicant under paragraph (1)(c) and by the defendant on any other person who he knows or has reason to believe is likely to be affected by the variation, together, in each case, with a notice stating that the person may apply under rule 8 to be made a party to the proceedings.

(4)   Any application under section 36 of the Act of 1987 shall be contained in the defendant's affidavit, and paragraphs (1) to (3) shall apply to such an application as if the defendant were an applicant.]

Commencement   18 April 1988.
Amendments   This rule was added by SI 1988/298, r 19.
Definitions   Act of 1987: Landlord and Tenant Act 1987.
Cross references   See CCR Order 43, r 20.

[Order 97, r 18 Service of notices in proceedings under the Act of 1987

Where a notice is to be served in or before proceedings under the Act of 1987, it shall be served in accordance with section 54 and, in the case of service on a landlord, it shall be served at the address furnished under section 48(1).]

Commencement   18 April 1988.
Amendments   This rule was added by SI 1988/298, r 19.
Definitions   Act of 1987: Landlord and Tenant Act 1987.
Cross references   See CCR Order 43, r 21.

[Order 97, r 19 Tenants' associations

In rules 15, 16 and 17 a reference to a tenants' association is a reference to a recognised tenants' association within the meaning of section 29 of the Landlord and Tenant Act 1985 which represents tenants of the flats of which the demised premises form a part.]

Commencement   18 April 1988.
Amendments   This rule was added by SI 1988/298, r 19.
Cross references   See CCR Order 43, r 22.

[ORDER 98
[LOCAL GOVERNMENT FINANCE ACT 1982, PART III]

Order 98, r 1 Interpretation

In this Order "the Act" means the [Local Government Finance Act 1982] and a section referred to by number means the section so numbered in that Act.]

Commencement 27 July 1974.
Amendments Order 98 was substituted by SI 1974/1115, r 5.
In the heading to Order 98, words "Local Government Finance Act 1982" substituted by SI 1985/846, r 13(2).

[Order 98, r 2 [Application by auditor for declaration]

[(1) Any application for a declaration [under section 19(1)] of the Act that an item of account is contrary to law shall be made by originating motion.]

(2) Notice of the motion shall be served on the body to whose accounts the application relates and on any person against whom an order is sought [under section 19(2)].

(3) Not later than seven days after lodging the notice of motion in the Crown Office in accordance with Order 57, rule 2, the applicant shall file in that office an affidavit stating the facts on which he intends to rely at the hearing of the application.

(4) A motion under this rule shall be entered for hearing within six weeks after the notice has been lodged in the Crown Office but, unless the Court otherwise directs, the application shall not be heard sooner than 28 days after service of the notice.]

Commencement 12 January 1981 (para (1)); 27 July 1974 (remainder).
Amendments See the first note to Order 98, r 1.
Rule heading: substituted by SI 1985/846, r 13(3).
Para (1): substituted by SI 1980/2000, r 11; words "under section 19(1)" substituted by SI 1985/846, r 13(4).
Para (2): words "under section 19(2)" substituted by SI 1985/846, r 13(5).
Definitions The Act: Local Government Finance Act 1982.

[Order 98, r 3 Appeal against decision of auditor

(1) Notice of motion by which an appeal is brought under [section 19(4) or section 20(3)] against the decision of [auditor] shall be served on—
   (a) [the auditor] who for the time being has responsibility for the audit of the accounts of the body in relation to whom the appeal relates;
   (b) that body; and
   (c) in the case of an appeal against a decision not to certify under [section 20(1)] that a sum or amount is due from another person, that person.

(2) Order 55, rules 4(2) and 5, shall apply to the appeal with the modification that the period of 28 days mentioned in the said rule 4(2) shall be calculated from the day on which the appellant received the [auditor's] statement of the reasons for his decision pursuant to a requirement under [section 19(4) or section 20(2)].

(3) Not later than seven days after lodging notice of the motion in the Crown Office in accordance with Order 57, rule 2, the appellant must file in that office an affidavit stating—

    (a)   the reasons stated by the [auditor] for his decision;

    (b)   the date on which he received the [auditor's] statement;

    (c)   the facts on which he intends to rely at the hearing of the appeal;

    (d)   in the case of a decision not to apply for a declaration, such facts within the appellant's knowledge as will enable the Court to consider whether to exercise the powers conferred on it by [section 19(2)].]

Commencement   27 July 1974.
Amendments   See the first note to Order 98, r 1.
Para (1): words "section 19(4) or section 20(3)", "auditor", "the auditor" and "section 20(1)" substituted by SI 1985/846, r 13(6).
Para (2): words "auditor's" and "section 19(4) or section 20(2)" substituted by SI 1985/846, r 13(7).
Para (3): words "auditor", "auditor's" and "section 19(2)" substituted by SI 1985/846, r 13(8).

[Order 98, r 4 General provisions

[(1)   Any proceedings in which the jurisdiction conferred on the High Court [by section 19 or section 20] of the Act is invoked shall be assigned to the Queen's Bench Division and be heard by a single judge, unless the Court directs that the matter shall be heard by a Divisional Court; and the Court may, at any stage and without prejudice to its powers under Order 15, direct that any officer or member of the body to whose accounts the application or appeal relates be joined as a respondent.]

(2)   Except in so far as the . . . Court directs that the evidence on any such application or appeal shall be given orally, it shall be given by affidavit.

(3)   The applicant or appellant must forthwith after filing any affidavit under rule 2(3) or 3(3) serve a copy thereof on every respondent and any person intending to oppose the application or appeal must, not less than four days before the hearing, serve on the applicant or appellant a copy of any affidavit filed by him in opposition to the motion.

(4)   Except by leave of the Court, no affidavit may be used at the hearing unless a copy thereof was served in accordance with paragraph (3).]

Commencement   12 January 1981 (para (1)); 27 July 1974 (remainder).
Amendments   See the first note to Order 98, r 1.
Para (1): substituted by SI 1980/2000, r 12(1); words "by section 19 or section 20" substituted by SI 1985/846, r 13(9).
Para (2): words omitted revoked by SI 1980/2000, r 12(2).
Definitions   The Act: Local Government Finance Act 1982.

[ORDER 99
INHERITANCE (PROVISION FOR FAMILY AND DEPENDANTS) ACT 1975

[Order 99, r 1 Interpretation

In this Order "the Act" means the Inheritance (Provision for Family and Dependants) Act 1975 and a section referred to by number means the section so numbered in that Act.]

Commencement 1 April 1976.
Amendments Order 99 was substituted by SI 1976/337, r 19(1).
Cross references See CCR Order 48, r 1.

[Order 99, r 2 Assignment to Chancery or Family Division

Proceedings in the High Court under the Act may be assigned to the Chancery Division or to the Family Division.]

Commencement 1 April 1976.
Amendments See the note to Order 99, r 1.
Definitions The Act: Inheritance (Provision for Family and Dependants) Act 1975.

[Order 99, r 3 Application for financial provision

(1) Any originating summons by which an application under section 1 is made may be issued out of [Chancery Chambers], the principal registry of the Family Division or any district registry.

[(2) The summons shall be in Form No 10 in Appendix A.]

(3) There shall be lodged with the Court an affidavit by the applicant in support of the summons, exhibiting an official copy of the grant of representation to the deceased's estate and of every testamentary document admitted to proof, and a copy of the affidavit shall be served on every defendant with the summons.]

Commencement 3 June 1980 (para (2)); 1 April 1976 (remainder)
Amendments See the note to Order 99, r 1.
Para (1): words "Chancery Chambers" substituted by SI 1982/1111, r 90.
Para (2): substituted by SI 1979/1716, r 48, Schedule, Pt 2.
Definitions Section 1: Inheritance (Provision for Family and Dependants) Act 1975, s 1.
Cross references See CCR Order 48, rr 2, 3.

[Order 99, r 4 Powers of Court as to parties

(1) Without prejudice to its powers under Order 15, the Court may at any stage of proceedings under the Act direct that any person be added as a party to the proceedings or that notice of the proceedings be served on any person.

(2) Order 15, rule 13, shall apply to proceedings under the Act as it applies to the proceedings mentioned in paragraph (1) of that rule.]

Commencement 1 April 1976.
Amendments See the note to Order 99, r 1.
Definitions The Act: Inheritance (Provision for Family and Dependants) Act 1975.
Cross references See CCR Order 48, r 4.

[Order 99, r 5 Affidavit in answer

(1)   A defendant to an application under section 1 who is a personal representative of the deceased shall and any other defendant may, within 21 days after service of the summons on him, inclusive of the day of service, lodge with the Court an affidavit in answer to the application.

(2)   The affidavit lodged by a personal representative pursuant to paragraph (1) shall state to the best of the deponent's ability—

    (a)   full particulars of the value of the deceased's net estate, as defined by section 25(1);

    (b)   the person or classes of persons beneficially interested in the estate, giving the names and (in the case of those who are not already parties) the addresses of all living beneficiaries, and the value of their interests so far as ascertained;

    (c)   if such be the case, that any living beneficiary (naming him) is a minor or a patient within the meaning of Order 80, rule 1; and

    (d)   any facts known to the deponent which might affect the exercise of the Court's powers under the Act.

(3)   Every defendant who lodges an affidavit shall at the same time serve a copy on the plaintiff and on every other defendant who is not represented by the same solicitor.]

Commencement   1 April 1976.
Amendments   See the note to Order 99, r 1.
Definitions   Sections 1, 25(1): Inheritance (Provisions for Family and Dependants) Act 1975, ss 1, 25(1).
The Act: Inheritance (Provision for Family and Dependants) Act 1975.
Cross references   See CCR Order 48, r 5.

[Order 99, r 6 Separate representation

Where an application under section 1 is made jointly by two or more applicants and the originating summons is accordingly issued by one solicitor on behalf of all of them, they may, if they have conflicting interests, appear on any hearing of the summons by separate solicitors or counsel or in person; and where at any stage of the proceedings it appears to the Court that one of the applicants is not but ought to be separately represented, the Court may adjourn the proceedings until he is.]

Commencement   1 April 1976.
Amendments   See the note to Order 99, r 1.
Definitions   Section 1: Inheritance (Provision for Family and Dependants) Act 1975, s 1.

[Order 99, r 7 Endorsement of memorandum on grant

On the hearing of an application under section 1 the personal representative shall produce to the Court the grant of representation to the deceased's estate and, if an order is made under the Act, the grant shall remain in the custody of the Court until a memorandum of the order has been endorsed on or permanently annexed to the grant in accordance with section 19(3).]

Commencement   1 April 1976.
Amendments   See the note to Order 99, r 1.
Definitions   Section 1: Inheritance (Provision for Family and Dependants) Act 1975, s 1.
The Act: Inheritance (Provision for Family and Dependants) Act 1975.
Cross references   See CCR Order 48, r 8.

[Order 99, r 8 Disposal of proceedings in chambers

Any proceedings under the Act may, if the Court so directs, be disposed of in chambers and Order 32, rule 14(1), shall apply in relation to proceedings in the Family Division as if for the words ["The Masters of the Chancery Division shall"] there were substituted the words "A [district judge] of the Family Division shall".]

Commencement   1 April 1976.
Amendments   See the note to Order 99, r 1.
Words ""The Masters of the Chancery Division shall"" substituted by SI 1982/1111, r 91.
Definitions   The Act: Inheritance (Provision for Family and Dependants) Act 1975.
Cross references   See CCR Order 48, r 7.

[Order 99, r 9 Subsequent applications in proceedings under section 1

Where an order has been made on an application under section 1, any subsequent application under the Act, whether made by a party to the proceedings or by any other person, shall be made by summons in those proceedings.]

Commencement   1 April 1976.
Amendments   See the note to Order 99, r 1.
Definitions   Section 1: Inheritance (Provision for Family and Dependants) Act 1975, s 1.
The Act: Inheritance (Provision for Family and Dependants) Act 1975.
Cross references   See CCR Order 48, r 6.

[Order 99, r 10 Drawing up and service of orders

The provisions of the [Family Proceedings Rules] relating to the drawing up and service of orders shall apply to proceedings in the Family Division under this Order as if they were proceedings under those Rules.

[In this rule "Family Proceedings Rules" means rules made under section 40 of the Matrimonial and Family Proceedings Act 1984.]]

Commencement   1 April 1976.
Amendments   See the note to Order 99, r 1.
Words "Family Proceedings Rules" substituted, and paragraph beginning "In this rule" added, by SI 1991/1884, r 7.

Order 99, r 11   *(substituted by SI 1976/337; revoked by SI 1992/638.)*

ORDER 100
[THE TRADE MARKS ACT 1938 AND THE TRADE MARKS (AMENDMENT) ACT 1984]

Amendments Words from "The Trade Marks Act" to "Act 1984" substituted by SI 1986/1187, r 14(1).

Order 100, r 1 Assignment to Chancery Division

Proceedings in the High Court under the Trade Marks Act 1938 shall be assigned to the Chancery Division.

Commencement 1 October 1966.

Order 100, r 2 Appeals and applications under the Trade Marks Act 1938

(1)   Every appeal to the High Court under the Trade Marks Act 1938 shall be heard and determined by a single judge.

(2)   Subject to rule 3, every application to the High Court under the said Act of 1938 must be begun by originating motion.

(3)   Notice of the motion by which any such application is made must be served on the Comptroller-General of Patents, Designs and Trade Marks (in this Order referred to as "the Comptroller").

(4)   Where the Comptroller refers to the High Court an application under the said Act of 1938 made to him, and where the Board of Trade refer to that Court an appeal to the Board under that Act, then, unless within one month after receiving notification of the decision to refer, the applicant or the appellant, as the case may be, makes to that Court the application or appeal referred, he shall be deemed to have abandoned it.

(5)   [The period prescribed by Order 55, rule 4(2), in relation to an appeal to which paragraph (1) applies or the period prescribed by paragraph (4) in relation to an application or appeal to which that paragraph applies] may be extended by the Comptroller on the application of any party interested and may be so extended although the application is not made until after the expiration of that period, but the foregoing provision shall not be taken to affect the power of the Court under Order 3, rule 5, to extend that period.

(6)   Where under subsection (6) of section 17, or subsection (9) of section 18, of the said Act of 1938 an appellant becomes entitled and intends to withdraw his application which is the subject matter of the appeal he must give notice of his intention to the Comptroller and to any other party to the appeal within one month after the Court has given leave under the said subsection (6) or the said subsection (9), as the case may be, for further grounds of objection to be taken.

[(7)   Where an application is made under section 58C of the Trade Marks Act 1938 the applicant shall serve notice of the application on all persons so far as reasonably ascertainable having an interest in the goods or material which are the subject of the application, including any person in whose favour an order could be made in respect of the goods or material under the said section of the Act of 1938 or under section 114, 204 or 231 of the Copyright, Designs and Patents Act 1988.

(8)   An application under the said section 58C shall be made by originating summons or, if it is made in a pending action, by summons or motion in that action.]

Commencement   1 September 1989 (paras (7), (8)); 1 October 1966 (remainder).
Amendments   Para (5): from the beginning to "paragraph applies" substituted by SI 1968/1244, r 20.
Paras (7), (8): inserted by SI 1989/1307, r 20.
Cross references   Paras (7), (8) are applied to the county court by CCR Order 49, r 18B.

Order 100, r 3 Proceedings for infringement of registered trade mark [or registered service mark]: validity of registration disputed

(1)   Where in any proceedings a claim is made for relief for infringement of the right to the use of a registered trade mark [or a registered service mark], the party against whom the claim is made may in his defence put in issue the validity of the registration of that trade mark [or that service mark] or may counterclaim for an order that the register of trade marks be rectified by cancelling or varying the relevant entry or may do both those things.

(2)   A party to any such proceedings who in his pleading (whether a defence or counterclaim) disputes the validity of the registration of a registered trade mark [or of a registered service mark] must serve with the pleading particulars of the objections to the validity of the registration on which he relies in support of the allegation of invalidity.

(3)   A party to any such proceedings who counterclaims for an order that the register of trade marks be rectified must serve on the Comptroller a copy of the counterclaim together with a copy of the particulars mentioned in paragraph (2); and the Comptroller shall be entitled to take such part in the proceedings as he may think fit but need not serve a defence or other pleading unless ordered to do so by the Court.

Commencement   1 October 1966.
Amendments   Rule heading: words "or registered service mark" inserted by SI 1986/1187, r 14(2).
Para (1): words "or a registered service mark" and "or that service mark" inserted by SI 1986/1187, r 14(3).
Para (2): words "or of a registered service mark" inserted by SI 1986/1187, r 14(4).

ORDER 101
THE PENSIONS APPEAL TRIBUNALS ACT 1943

Order 101, r 1 Assignment to Queen's Bench Division

Proceedings in the High Court under the Pensions Appeal Tribunals Act 1943 shall be assigned to the Queen's Bench Division.

Commencement 1 October 1966.

Order 101, r 2 Construction of references to judge

In this Order references to the judge shall be construed as references to the judge nominated by the Lord Chancellor under section 6(2) of the Pensions Appeals Tribunals Act 1943.

Commencement 1 October 1966.

Order 101, r 3 Application for leave to appeal

(1)　An application to the judge for leave to appeal against the decision of a Pensions Appeal Tribunal may not be made unless an application for such leave was made to the Tribunal and was refused and must be made within 28 days after the date of the Tribunal's refusal.

(2)　The application to the judge, which may be made ex parte, must be made by filing in the Crown Office a written statement of—
　(a)　the name and description of the applicant,
　(b)　the point of law as respects which the applicant alleges that the Tribunal's decision was erroneous, and
　(c)　the date of the Tribunal's decision refusing leave to appeal.

(3)　If the application is made with the consent of the other party to the proceedings before the Tribunal, that fact shall be included in the statement.

(4)　On the making of the application the proper officer shall request the chairman of the Tribunal to give the judge a written statement of the reasons for the Tribunal's decision to refuse leave to appeal, and within 7 days after receiving the request the chairman shall give the judge such a statement.

(5)　The judge may determine the application without a hearing or may direct that the application be set down for hearing in chambers.

(6)　Where the application is determined without a hearing, a copy of the judge's order shall be sent from the Crown Office to the applicant and to the other party to the proceedings before the Tribunal; and where the application is to be set down for hearing, notice of the day and time fixed for the hearing shall be sent from that Office to the applicant.

Commencement 1 October 1966.

Order 101, r 4 Appeal

(1)　Without prejudice to Order 55, rule 3(2), the notice of the originating motion by which an appeal against the decision of a Pensions Appeal Tribunal is brought must state the question of law on which the appeal is brought, the date on which leave to appeal was granted and whether such leave was granted by the judge or the Tribunal.

(2) Order 55, rules 3(3) and 4(2), shall not apply in relation to such an appeal, but the notice must be served and the appeal entered within 28 days after leave to appeal was granted.

(3) Within 28 days after service of the notice of motion on him, the chairman of the Tribunal must state a case setting out the facts on which the decision appealed against was based and must file the case in the Crown Office and serve a copy thereof on the appellant and on the respondent.

(4) Order 55, rule 5, shall apply in relation to such an appeal as if for the period of 21 days therein mentioned there were substituted a period of 6 weeks.

(5) At the hearing of the appeal the judge may order the case to be returned to the chairman for amendment.

(6) Order 55, rule 7(2), shall not apply in relation to the appeal.

(7) A copy of the judge's order on the appeal must be sent by the proper officer to the appellant, the respondent and the chairman of the Tribunal.

Commencement   1 October 1966.

[ORDER 102
THE COMPANIES ACT 1985

Order 102, r 1 Definitions

In this Order—

"the Act" means the Companies Act 1985;

"the companies court registrar" means any officer of the High Court who is a registrar within the meaning of any rules for the time being in force relating to the winding up of companies;

"the Court", without prejudice to Order 1, rule 4(2), includes the companies court registrar.]

Commencement   12 January 1987.
Amendments   Order 102 was substituted by SI 1986/2289, r 13, Schedule.

[Order 102, r 2 Applications to be made by originating summons

(1) Except in the case of the applications mentioned in rules 3 and 4, every application under the Act must, in accordance with Order 5, rule 3, be made by originating summons.

(2) An originating summons under this rule shall be in Form No 10 in Appendix A unless the application made by summons is—

    (a) an application under section 427 of the Act for an order to make provision for all or any of the matters mentioned in subsection (3) of that section where an order sanctioning the compromise or arrangement to which the application relates has previously been made, or

    (b) an application under section 713 of the Act for an order directing a company and any officer thereof to make good any such default as is mentioned in that section, or

    (c) an application under [section 242(3)] of the Act for an order directing the directors of a company or any of them to make good any such default as is therein mentioned, or

    (d) an application under section 216 of the Act for an order directing that any shares in a company shall be subject to the restrictions imposed by Part XV of the Act.

(3) An application under section 721 of the Act may be made by ex parte originating summons.

(4) An originating summons under this rule may be issued out of the office of the companies court registrar or any Chancery district registry, and Order 7, rule 5(2), shall not apply in relation to such a summons.]

Commencement   12 January 1987.
Amendments   See the note to Order 102, r 1.
Para (2): in sub-para (c) words "section 242(3)" substituted by SI 1990/2599, r 17(1).
Definitions   The Act: Companies Act 1985.

[Order 102, r 3 Applications to be made by originating motion

(1) The following applications under the Act must be made by originating motion, namely, applications—

(a) under section 88(6) for an order extending the time for delivery to the registrar of companies of any documents required by that section to be delivered,

(b) under section 432 for an order declaring that the affairs of a company ought to be investigated by an inspector appointed by the Secretary of State,

(c) under section 436 for an inquiry into any such case as is therein mentioned,

(d) under section 456(1) for an order directing that any shares in or debentures of a company shall cease to be subject to restrictions imposed by Part XV,

(e) under section 456(4) for an order directing that any shares in or debentures of a company shall, on a sale, cease to be subject to restrictions imposed by Part XV,

(f) under section 651 for an order declaring a dissolution of a company which has not been wound up to have been void,

(g) under section 359(1) for rectification of the register of members of a company, and

(h) under section 217(5) for amendment of the register of interests in shares of a company.

[(i) under section 245B(1) for an order declaring that the annual accounts of a company do not comply with the requirements of the Act and requiring the directors of the company to prepare revised accounts.]

(2) The notice of the motion by which any such application is made may be issued out of the office of the companies court registrar, or any Chancery district registry.]

Commencement 12 January 1987.
Amendments See the note to Order 102, r 1.
Para (1): sub-para (i) inserted by SI 1990/2599, r 17(2).
Definitions The Act: Companies Act 1985.

[Order 102, r 4 Applications to be made by petition

(1) The following applications under the Act must be made by petition, namely, applications—

(a) under section 5 to cancel the alteration of a company's objects,

(b) under section 17 to cancel the alteration of a condition contained in a company's memorandum,

(c) under section 130 to confirm a reduction of the share premium account of a company,

(d) under section 136 to confirm a reduction of the share capital of a company,

(e) under section 127 to cancel any variation or abrogation of the rights attached to any class of shares in a company,

(f) under section 425 to sanction a compromise or arrangement between a company and its creditors or any class of them or between a company and its members or any class of them,

(g) under section 653 for an order restoring the name of a company to the register where the application is made in conjunction with an application for the winding up of the company,

(h) under section 690 to cancel the alteration of the form of a company's constitution,

(i) under section 727 for relief from liability of an officer of a company or a person employed by a company as auditor,

(j) under section 54(1) to cancel a special resolution to which that section applies,

(k) under section 157(2) or section 176(1) to cancel a special resolution to which either of those sections applies, and

(l) under section 170 in relation to the reduction of capital redemption reserve.

(2) A petition by which any such application is made may be presented in the office of the companies court registrar, or any Chancery district registry, and Order 9, rule 3, shall not apply in relation to such a petition.]

Commencement 12 January 1987.
Amendments See the note to Order 102, r 1.
Definitions The Act: Companies Act 1985.
Cross references See CCR Order 49, r 3.

[Order 102, r 5 Assignment and entitlement of proceedings

(1) All proceedings to which this Order relates shall be assigned to the Chancery Division.

(2) Every originating summons, notice of originating motion and petition by which any such proceedings are begun and all affidavits, notices and other documents in those proceedings must be entitled in the matter of the company in question and in the matter of the Companies Act 1985.]

Commencement 12 January 1987.
Amendments See the note to Order 102, r 1.

[Order 102, r 6 Summons for directions

(1) After presentation of a petition by which any such application as is mentioned in rule 4 is made, the petitioner, except where his application is one of those mentioned in paragraph (2), must take out a summons for directions under this rule.

(2) The applications referred to in paragraph (1) are—
   (a) an application under section 425 of the Act to sanction a compromise or arrangement unless there is included in the petition for such sanction an application for an order under section 427 of the Act,
   (b) an application under section 653 of the Act for an order restoring the name of a company to the register,
   (c) an application under section 54(1) of the Act for an order cancelling a special resolution to which that section applies, and
   (d) an application under section 157(2) or 176(1) of the Act for an order cancelling a special resolution to which those sections apply.

(3) On the hearing of the summons the Court may by order give such directions as to the proceedings to be taken before the hearing of the petition as it thinks fit including, in particular, directions for the publication of notices and the making of any inquiry.

(4) Where the application made by the petition is to confirm a reduction of the share capital, the share premium account, or the capital redemption reserve of a company, then, without prejudice to the generality of paragraph (3), the Court may give directions—

    (a) for an inquiry to be made as to the debts of, and claims against, the company or as to any class or classes of such debts or claims;

    (b) as to the proceedings to be taken for settling the list of creditors entitled to object to the reduction and fixing the date by reference to which the list is to be made;

and the power of the Court under section 136(6) of the Act to direct that section 136(3) to (5) thereof shall not apply as regards any class of creditors may be exercised on any hearing of the summons.

(5)   Rules 7 to 12 shall have effect subject to any directions given by the Court under this rule.]

Commencement 12 January 1987.
Amendments See the note to Order 102, r 1.
Definitions The Act: Companies Act 1985.

[Order 102, r 7 Inquiry as to debts: Company to make list of creditors

(1)   Where under rule 6 the Court orders such an inquiry as is mentioned in paragraph (4) thereof, the company in question must, within 7 days after the making of the order, file in the office of the companies court registrar an affidavit made by an officer of the company competent to make it verifying a list containing—

    (a) the name and address of every creditor entitled to any debt or claim to which the inquiry extends,

    (b) the amount due to each creditor in respect of such debt or claim or, in the case of a debt or claim which is subject to any contingency or sounds only in damages or for some other reason does not bear a certain value, a just estimate of the value thereof, and

    (c) the total of those amounts and values.

(2)   The deponent must state in the affidavit his belief that at the date fixed by the Court as the date by reference to which the list is to be made there is no debt or claim which, if that date were the commencement of the winding up of the company, would be admissible in proof against the company, other than the debts or claims set out in the list and any debts or claims to which the inquiry does not extend, and must also state his means of knowledge of the matters deposed to.

(3)   The list must be left at the office mentioned in paragraph (1) not later than one day after the affidavit is filed.]

Commencement 12 January 1987.
Amendments See the note to Order 102, r 1.

[Order 102, r 8 Inspection of list of creditors

(1)   Copies of the list made under rule 7 with the omission, unless the Court otherwise directs, of the amount due to each creditor and the estimated value of any debt or claim to which any creditor is entitled, shall be kept at the registered office of the company and at the office of that company's solicitor and of that solicitor's London agent, if any.

(2)   Any person shall be entitled during ordinary business hours, on payment of a fee of 5p to inspect the said list at any such office and to take extracts therefrom.]

Commencement 12 January 1987.
Amendments See the note to Order 102, r 1.

[Order 102, r 9 Notice to creditors

Within 7 days after filing the affidavit required by rule 7 the company must send by post to each creditor named in the list exhibited to the affidavit, at his last known address, a notice stating—

    (a) the amount of the reduction sought to be confirmed,

    (b) the effect of the order directing an inquiry as to debts and claims,

    (c) the amount or value specified in the list as due or estimated to be due to that creditor, and

    (d) the time fixed by the Court within which, if he claims to be entitled to a larger amount, he must send particulars of his debt or claim and the name and address of his solicitor, if any, to the company's solicitor.]

Commencement 12 January 1987.
Amendments See the note to Order 102, r 1.

[Order 102, r 10 Advertisement of petition and list of creditors

After filing the affidavit required by rule 7 the company must insert, in such newspapers and at such times as the Court directs, a notice stating—

    (a) the date of presentation of the petition and the amount of the reduction thereby sought to be confirmed,

    (b) the inquiry ordered by the Court under rule 6,

    (c) the places where the list of creditors may be inspected in accordance with rule 9, and

    (d) the time within which any creditor not named in the list who claims to be entitled to any debt or claim to which the inquiry extends must send his name and address, the name and address of his solicitor, if any, and particulars of his debt or claim to the company's solicitor.]

Commencement 12 January 1987.
Amendments See the note to Order 102, r 1.

[Order 102, r 11 Affidavit as to claims made by creditors

Within such time as the Court directs the company must file in the office of the companies court registrar an affidavit made by the company's solicitor and an officer of the company competent to make it—

    (a) proving service of the notices mentioned in rule 9 and advertisement of the notice mentioned in rule 10,

    (b) verifying a list containing the names and addresses of the person (if any) who in pursuance of such notices sent in particulars of debts or claims, specifying the amount of each debt or claim,

    (c) distinguishing in such list those debts or claims which are wholly, or as to any and what part thereof, admitted by the company, disputed by the company or alleged by the company to be outside the scope of the inquiry, and

    (d) stating which of the persons named in the list made under rule 7, and which of the persons named in the list made under this rule, have been paid or consent to the reduction sought to be confirmed.]

Commencement 12 January 1987.
Amendments See the note to Order 102, r 1.

[Order 102, r 12 Adjudication of disputed claims

If the company contends that a person is not entitled to be entered in the list of creditors in respect of any debt or claim or in respect of the full amount claimed by him in respect of any debt or claim, then, unless the company is willing to secure payment of that debt or claim by appropriating the full amount of the debt or claim, the company must, if the Court so directs, send to that person by post at his last known address a notice requiring him—

(a) within such time as may be specified in the notice, being not less than 4 clear days after service thereof, to file an affidavit proving his debt or claim or, as the case may be, so much thereof as is not admitted by the company, and

(b) to attend the adjudication of his debt or claim at the place and time specified in the notice, being the time appointed by the Court for the adjudication of debts and claims.]

Commencement   12 January 1987.
Amendments   See the note to Order 102, r 1.

[Order 102, r 13 Certifying lists of creditors entitled to object to reduction

The list of creditors entitled to object to such reduction as is mentioned in rule 6(4), as settled by the Court under section 136(4) of the Act, shall be certified and filed by the companies court registrar and his certificate shall—

(a) specify the debts or claims (if any) disallowed by the court;

(b) distinguish the debts or claims (if any) the full amount of which is admitted by the company, the debts or claims (if any) the full amount of which, though not admitted by the company, the company is willing to appropriate, the debts or claims (if any) the amount of which has been fixed by adjudication of the Court under section 136(4) of the Act and other debts or claims;

(c) specify the total amount of the debts or claims payment of which has been secured by appropriation under the said section 136(4);

(d) show which creditors consent to the reduction and the total amount of their debts or claims;

(e) specify the creditors who sought to prove their debts or claims under rule 12 and state which of such debts or claims were allowed.]

Commencement   12 January 1987.
Amendments   See the note to Order 102, r 1.
Definitions   The Act: Companies Act 1985.

[Order 102, r 14 Evidence of consent of creditor

The consent of a creditor to such reduction as is mentioned in rule 6(4) may be proved in such manner as the Court thinks sufficient.]

Commencement   12 January 1987.
Amendments   See the note to Order 102, r 1.

[Order 102, r 15 Time, etc of hearing of petition for confirmation of reduction

(1)   A petition for the confirmation of any such reduction as is mentioned in rule 6(4) shall not, where the Court has directed an inquiry pursuant to that rule, be heard before

the expiration of at least 8 clear days after the filing of the certificate mentioned in rule 13.

(2)   Before the hearing of such a petition, a notice specifying the day appointed for the hearing must be published at such times and in such newspapers as the Court may direct.]

Commencement   12 January 1987.
Amendments   See the note to Order 102, r 1.

[Order 102, r 16 Affidavits to be filed in district registry

Where an application to which this Order relates is proceeding in any Chancery district registry, all affidavits made in connection with the application must be filed in that registry.]

Commencement   12 January 1987.
Amendments   See the note to Order 102, r 1.

ORDER 103
(*revoked by SI 1984/1051*)

[ORDER [104]
THE PATENTS ACTS 1949 TO 1961 AND 1977; THE REGISTERED DESIGNS ACTS 1949 TO 1971; THE DEFENCE CONTRACTS ACT 1958

Order 104, r 1 Definitions

In this Order—

"the 1949 Act" means the Patents Act 1949;

"the 1977 Act" means the Patents Act 1977;

"the comptroller" means the Comptroller-General of Patents, Designs and Trade Marks;

"the Court", without prejudice to Order 1, rule 4(2), means the Patents Court;

"existing patent" means a patent mentioned in section 127(2)(a) or (c) of the 1977 Act;

"the journal" means the journal published pursuant to rules made under section 123(6) of the 1977 Act;

"1977 Act patent" means a patent under the 1977 Act;

"patent" means an existing patent or a 1977 Act patent.]

Commencement 1 June 1978.
Amendments Original Order 104 renumbered as Order 105 and new Order 104 inserted by SI 1978/579, r 12.
Cross references See CCR Order 48A, r 1.

[Order 104, r 2 Assignment of proceedings

(1)   All proceedings in the High Court under the Patents Acts 1949 to 1961 and 1977, the Registered Designs Acts 1949 to 1961 and the Defence Contracts Act 1958, and all proceedings for the determination of a question or the making of a declaration relating to a patent under the inherent jurisdiction of the High Court, shall be assigned to the Chancery Division and taken by the Court.

(2)   Nothing in Order 4, rule 1, shall apply in relation to any proceedings mentioned in paragraph (1) but every writ, summons, petition, notice, pleading, affidavit or other document relating to such proceedings must be marked in the top left-hand corner with the words "Patents Court".]

Commencement 1 June 1978.
Amendments See the note to Order 104, r 1.

[Order 104, r 3 Application for leave to amend specification under s 30 of the 1949 Act or s 75 of the 1977 Act

(1)   A patentee or the proprietor of a patent intending to apply under section 30 of the 1949 Act or under section 75 of the 1977 Act for leave to amend his specification must give notice of his intention to the comptroller accompanied by a copy of an advertisement—

(a) identifying the proceedings pending before the Court in which it is intended to apply for such leave;

(b) giving particulars of the amendment sought;

(c) stating the applicant's address for service within the United Kingdom, and

(d) stating that any person intending to oppose the amendment who is not a party to the proceedings must within 28 days after the appearance of the advertisement give written notice of his intention to the applicant;

and the comptroller shall insert the advertisement once in the journal.

A person who gives notice in accordance with the advertisement shall be entitled to be heard on the application subject to any direction of the Court as to costs.

(2) As soon as may be after the expiration of 35 days from the appearance of the advertisement the applicant must make his application under the said section 30 or 75, as the case may be, by motion in the proceedings pending before the Court; and notice of the motion, together with a copy of the specification certified by the comptroller and showing in coloured ink the amendment sought, must be served on the comptroller, the parties to the proceedings and any person who has given notice of his intention to oppose the amendment.

(3) On the hearing of the motion the Court shall give such directions for the further conduct of the proceedings on the motion as it thinks necessary or expedient and, in particular, directions—

(a) requiring the applicant and any party or person opposing the amendment sought to exchange statements of the grounds for allowing the amendment and of objections to the amendment;

(b) determining whether the motion shall be heard with the other proceedings relating to the patent in question or separately and, if separately, fixing the date of hearing thereof;

(c) as to the manner in which the evidence shall be given and, if the evidence is to be given by affidavit, fixing the times within which the affidavits must be filed.

(4) Where the Court allows a specification to be amended, the applicant must forthwith lodge with the comptroller an office copy of the order made by the Court and, if so required by the Court or comptroller, leave at the Patent Office a new specification and drawings as amended, prepared in compliance with the 1949 or 1977 Act, whichever is applicable, and the rules made under those Acts respectively.

The comptroller shall cause a copy of the order to be inserted at least once in the journal.]

Commencement 1 June 1978.
Amendments See the note to Order 104, r 1.
Definitions 1949 Act: Patents Act 1949.
1977 Act: Patents Act 1977.
Cross references This rule is applied to the Patents County Court by CCR Order 48A, r 10(1).

[Order 104, r 4 Application for revocation of patent

(1) An application under section 72 of the 1977 Act for the revocation of a patent shall be made by petition.

This paragraph does not apply to an application made in pending proceedings.

(2) The respondent to a petition under section 32 of the 1949 Act or section 72 of the 1977 Act must serve an answer on the petitioner within 21 days after service of the petition on him.]

Commencement 1 June 1978.
Amendments See the note to Order 104, r 1.
Definitions 1977 Act: Patents Act 1977.
1949 Act: Patents Act 1949.

[Order 104, r 5 Action for infringement

(1)   Notwithstanding anything in Order 5, rule 4, proceedings in which a claim is made by the plaintiff in respect of the infringement of a patent shall be begun by writ.

(2)   The plaintiff in such an action must serve with his statement of claim particulars of the infringement relied on, showing which of the claims in the specification of the patent are alleged to be infringed and giving at least one instance of each type of infringement alleged.

(3)   If a defendant in such an action alleges, as a defence to the action, that at the time of the infringement there was in force a contract or licence relating to the patent made by or with the consent of the plaintiff and containing a condition or term void by virtue of section 44 of the 1977 Act, he must serve on the plaintiff particulars of the date of, and parties to, each such contract or licence and particulars of each such condition or term.]

Commencement 1 June 1978.
Amendments See the note to Order 104, r 1.
Definitions 1977 Act: Patents Act 1977.

[Order 104, r 6 Objection to validity of patent

[(1)   A person who presents a petition under section 32 of the 1949 Act or section 72 of the 1977 Act for the revocation of a patent must serve with his petition particulars of the objections to the validity of the patent on which he relies.]

[(1A) A party to an action concerning a patent who either challenges the validity of the patent or applies by counterclaim in the action for revocation of the patent must, notwithstanding Order 18, rule 2, serve his defence or counterclaim (as the case may be), together with particulars of the objections to the validity of the patent on which he relies, within 42 days after service upon him of the statement of claim.]

(2)   Particulars given pursuant to paragraph (1) [or (1A)] must state every ground on which the validity of the patent is [challenged] and must include such particulars as will clearly define every issue which it is intended to raise.

(3)   If the grounds stated in the particulars of objections include want of novelty or want of any inventive step, the particulars must state the manner, time and place of every prior publication or user relied upon and, if prior user is alleged, must—
   (a)   specify the name of every person alleged to have made such user,
   (b)   state whether such user is alleged to have continued until the priority date of the claim in question or of the invention, as may be appropriate, and, if not, the earliest and latest date on which such user is alleged to have taken place,
   (c)   contain a description accompanied by drawings, if necessary, sufficient to identify such user, and
   (d)   if such user relates to machinery or apparatus, state whether the machinery or apparatus is in existence and where it can be inspected.

(4)   If in the case of an existing patent—

(a) one of the grounds stated in the particulars of objections is that the invention, so far as claimed in any claim of the complete specification, is not useful, and

(b) it is intended, in connection with that ground, to rely on the fact that an example of the invention which is the subject of any such claim cannot be made to work, either at all or as described in the specification,

the particulars must state that fact and identify each such claim and must include particulars of each such example, specifying the respects in which it is alleged that it does not work or does not work as described.

[(5) In any action or other proceedings relating to a patent in which the validity of the patent has been put in issue on the ground of obviousness a party who wishes to rely on the commercial success of the patent must state in his answer or in his pleadings the grounds upon which he so relies.]]

Commencement 1 October 1986 (paras (1), (1A), (5)); 1 June 1978 (remainder).
Amendments See the note to Order 104, r 1.
Para (1): substituted by SI 1986/1187, r 15(1).
Paras (1A), (5): inserted by SI 1986/1187, r 15(2), (4).
Para (2): words "or (1A)" added, and word "challenged" substituted, by SI 1986/1187, r 15(3).
Definitions 1949 Act: Patents Act 1949.
1977 Act: Patents Act 1977.
Cross references See CCR Order 48A, r 4.

[Order 104, r 7 Amendment of particulars

Without prejudice to Order 20, rule 5, the Court may at any stage of the proceedings allow a party to amend any particulars served by him under the foregoing provisions of this Order on such terms as to costs or otherwise as may be just.]

Commencement 1 June 1978.
Amendments See the note to Order 104, r 1.

[Order 104, r 8 Further particulars

The Court may at any stage of the proceedings order a party to serve on any other party further or better particulars of infringements or of objections.]

Commencement 1 June 1978.
Amendments See the note to Order 104, r 1.

[Order 104, r 9 Application of rules 10 to 14

Rules 10 to 14 of this Order apply to any action for infringement of a patent (whether or not any other relief is claimed) and to any proceedings by petition for the revocation of a patent.]

Commencement 1 October 1984.
Amendments See the note to Order 104, r 1.
Rule 9 (as added by SI 1978/579, r 12) was renumbered as r 16 and a new r 9 was inserted by SI 1986/1187, r 15(5), (7).

[Order 104, r 10 Admissions

(1) Notwithstanding anything in Order 27, where a party desires any other party to admit any facts, he shall, within 21 days after service of a reply or answer or after the

expiration of the period fixed for the service thereof, serve on that other party a notice requiring him to admit for the purpose of the action or proceedings the facts specified in the notice.

(2)   A party upon whom a notice under paragraph (1) is served shall within 21 days after service thereof serve upon the party making the request a notice stating in respect of each fact specified in the notice whether or not he admits it.]

Commencement   1 October 1986.
Amendments   See the note to Order 104, r 1.
Rule 10 was revoked and a new rule 10 was inserted by SI 1986/1187, r 15(5), (7).

[Order 104, r 11 Discovery of documents

(1)   Order 24, rules 1 and 2 shall apply in an action for infringement of a patent except that the list of documents must be served by each party within 21 days after service of the notice of admissions under rule 10(2), or within 21 days after the close of pleadings.

(2)   Order 24, rules 1 and 2 shall apply in proceedings for the revocation of a patent as they apply to actions begun by writ except that the period prescribed by rule 2(1) shall be that which is prescribed by paragraph (1) of this rule.]

Commencement   1 October 1986.
Amendments   See the note to Order 104, r 1.
Rule 11 (as added by SI 1978/579, r 12) was renumbered as r 15 and a new r 11 was inserted by SI 1986/1187, r 15(5), (7).

[Order 104, r 12 Experiments

(1)   Where a party desires to establish any fact by experimental proof he shall within 21 days after service of the lists of documents under rule 11 serve on the other party a notice stating the facts which he desires to establish and giving full particulars of the experiments proposed to establish them.

(2)   A party upon whom a notice under paragraph (1) is served shall, within 21 days after service thereof, serve upon the other party a notice stating in respect of each fact whether or not he admits it.

(3)   Where any fact which a party desires to establish by experimental proof is not admitted he may at the hearing of the summons for directions apply for directions in respect of such experiments.]

Commencement   1 October 1986.
Amendments   See the note to Order 104, r 1.
Rule 12 (as added by SI 1978/579, r 12) was renumbered as r 17 and a new r 12 was inserted by SI 1986/1187, r 15(5), (7).

[Order 104, r 13 Experts

Where a party intends to adduce oral expert evidence he shall not later than 14 days before the hearing of the summons for directions under rule 14 give notice to every other party and to the Court of the name of each expert he intends to call as a witness.

This rule is without prejudice to the power of the Court to restrict the number of expert witnesses.]

Commencement 1 October 1986.
Amendments See the note to Order 104, r 1.
Rule 13 (as added by SI 1978/579, r 12) was renumbered as r 18 and a new r 13 was inserted by SI 1986/ 1187, r 15(5), (7).

[Order 104, r 14 Summons for directions

(1)   The plaintiff or petitioner must, within 21 days after the expiration of all the periods specified in rules 10 to 12, take out a summons for directions as to the place and mode of trial returnable before a judge of the Patents Court in not less than 21 days, accompanied by minutes of the order proposed, a copy of the specification of any patent in issue, copies of the pleadings and of any documents referred to therein and copies of all documents served under rules 10 and 12 and if the plaintiff or petitioner does not take out such a summons in accordance with this paragraph, the defendant or respondent, as the case may be, may do so.

(2)   The judge hearing a summons under this rule may give such directions:
   (a)   for the service of further pleadings or particulars;
   (b)   for the further discovery of documents;
   (c)   for securing the making of further admissions;
   (d)   for the service of interrogatories and of answers thereto;
   (e)   for the taking by affidavit of evidence relating to matters requiring expert knowledge, and for the filing of such affidavits and the service of copies thereof on the other parties;
   (f)   for the holding of a meeting of such experts as the judge may specify, for the purpose of producing a joint report on the state of the relevant art;
   (g)   for the exchanging of experts' reports, in respect of those matters on which they are not agreed;
   (h)   for the making of experiments, tests, inspections or reports;
   (i)   for the hearing, as a preliminary issue, of any question that may arise (including any questions as to the construction of the specification or other documents)

and otherwise as the judge thinks necessary or expedient for the purpose of defining and limiting the issues to be tried, restricting the number of witnesses to be called at the trial of any particular issue and otherwise securing that the case shall be disposed of, consistently with adequate hearing, in the most expeditious manner. Where the evidence is directed to be given by affidavit, the deponents must attend at the trial for cross-examination unless, with the concurrence of the Court, the parties otherwise agree.

(3)   On the hearing of a summons under this rule the judge shall consider, if necessary of his own motion, whether:
   (a)   the parties' advisers should be required to meet for the purpose of agreeing which documents will be required at the trial and of paginating such documents;
   (b)   an independent scientific adviser should be appointed under rule 15 to assist the court.

(4)   Part IV of Order 38 shall not apply to an action or proceedings to which this rule applies.

(5)   No action or petition to which this rule applies shall be set down for trial unless and until a summons under this rule in the action or proceedings has been taken out

and the directions given on the summons have been carried out or the time fixed by the judge for carrying them out has expired.]

Commencement 1 October 1986.
Amendments See the note to Order 104, r 1.
Rule 14 (as inserted by SI 1978/579, r 12) was renumbered as r 19 and a new r 14 was inserted by SI 1986/1187, r 15(5), (7).
Cross references See CCR Order 48A, r 8.

[Order 104, r [15] Appointment of a scientific adviser

(1) In any proceedings under the 1949 or 1977 Act the Court may at any time, and on or without the application of any party, appoint an independent scientific adviser to assist the Court, either—

 (a) by sitting with the judge at the trial or hearing of the proceedings, or
 (b) by inquiring and reporting on any question of fact or of opinion not involving a question of law or construction,

according as the Court may direct.

(2) The Court may nominate the scientific adviser and, where appropriate, settle any question or instructions to be submitted or given to him.

(3) Where the Court appoints a scientific adviser to inquire and report under paragraph (1)(b), Order 40, rules 2, 3, 4 and 6 shall apply in relation to his report as they apply in relation to a report made by a Court expert.]

Commencement 1 June 1978.
Amendments See the note to Order 104, r 1.
This rule was inserted as r 11 by SI 1978/579, r 12; it was subsequently renumbered as r 15 by SI 1986/1187, r 15(7).
Definitions 1949 Act: Patents Act 1949.
1977 Act: Patents Act 1977.
Cross references See CCR Order 48A, r 7.

[Order 104, r [16] Restrictions on admission of evidence

(1) Except with the leave of the judge hearing any action or other proceeding relating to a patent, no evidence shall be admissible in proof of any alleged infringement, or of any objection to the validity, of the patent, if the infringement or objection was not raised in the particulars of infringements or objections, as the case may be.

(2) In any action or other proceeding relating to a patent, evidence which is not in accordance with a statement contained in particulars of objections to the validity of the patent shall not be admissible in support of such an objection unless the judge hearing the proceeding allows the evidence to be admitted.

(3) If any machinery or apparatus alleged to have been used before the priority date mentioned in rule 6(3)(b) is in existence at the date of service of the particulars of objections, no evidence of its user before that date shall be admissible unless it is proved that the party relying on such user offered, where the machinery or apparatus is in his possession, inspection of it to the other parties to the proceedings or, where it is not, used all reasonable endeavours to obtain inspection of it for those parties.]

Commencement 1 June 1978.
Amendments See the note to Order 104, r 1.

This rule was inserted as r 9 by SI 1978/579, r 12; it was subsequently renumbered as r 16 by SI 1986/1187, r 15(7).
Cross references Para (3) is applied to the county court by CCR Order 48A, r 10(3).

[Order 104, r [17] Determination of question or application where comptroller declines to deal with it

Where the comptroller—

    (a) declines to deal with a question under section 8(7), 12(2), 37(8) or 61(5) of the 1977 Act;

    (b) declines to deal with an application under section 40(5) of that Act, or

    (c) certifies under section 72(7)(b) of that Act that the question whether a patent should be revoked is one which would more properly be determined by the court,

any person entitled to do so may, within 28 days after the comptroller's decision, apply to the Court by originating summons to determine the question or application.]

Commencement 1 June 1978.
Amendments See the note to Order 104, r 1.
This rule was inserted as r 12 by SI 1978/579, r 12; it was subsequently renumbered as r 17 by SI 1986/1187, r 15(7).
Definitions 1977 Act: Patents Act 1977.
Cross references This rule is applied to the county court by CCR Order 48A, r 10(3) with the omission of the words "by originating summons".

[Order 104, r [18] Application by employee for compensation under s 40 of the 1977 Act

(1) An application by an employee for compensation under section 40(1) or (2) of the 1977 Act shall be made by originating summons issued within the period which begins when the relevant patent is granted and which expires one year after it has ceased to have effect:

Provided that, where a patent has ceased to have effect by reason of a failure to pay any renewal fee within the period prescribed for the payment thereof and an application for restoration is made to the comptroller under section 28 of the said Act, the said period shall—

    (a) if restoration is ordered, continue as if the patent had remained continuously in effect, or

    (b) if restoration is refused, be treated as expiring one year after the patent ceased to have effect or six months after the refusal, whichever is the later.

(2) On the day fixed for the hearing of the originating summons under Order 28, rule 2, the Court shall, without prejudice to the generality of Order 28, rule 4, give directions as to the manner in which the evidence (including any accounts of expenditure and receipts relating to the claim) shall be given at the hearing of the summons and, if the evidence is to be given by affidavit, specify the period within which the affidavit must be filed.

(3) The Court shall also give directions as to the provision by the defendant to the plaintiff, or a person deputed by him for the purpose, of reasonable facilities for inspecting and taking extracts from the books of account by which the defendant proposes to verify the accounts mentioned in paragraph (2) or from which those accounts have been derived.]

Commencement 1 June 1978.
Amendments See the note to Order 104, r 1.
This rule was inserted as r 13 by SI 1978/579, r 12; it was subsequently renumbered as r 18 by SI 1986/1187, r 15(7).
Definitions 1977 Act: Patents Act 1977.

[Order 104, r [19] Appeals from the comptroller

(1)   An appeal to the Court from a decision of the comptroller in any case in which a right of appeal is given by the 1949 or 1977 Act must be brought by originating motion and the notice of motion is referred to in this rule as "notice of appeal".

(2)   Notice of appeal shall be lodged with the proper officer—
  (a) in the case of a decision on a matter of procedure, within 14 days after the date of the decision; and
  (b) in any other case, within six weeks after the date of the decision.

(3)   The comptroller may determine whether any decision is on a matter of procedure and any such determination shall itself be a decision on a matter of procedure.

(4)   Notice of appeal may be given in respect of the whole or any specific part of the decision of the comptroller and must specify the grounds of the appeal and the relief which the appellant seeks.

(5)   Except with the leave of the Court the appellant shall not be entitled on the hearing of the appeal to rely on any ground of appeal or to apply for any relief not specified in the notice of appeal.

(6)   The appellant shall, within 5 days of lodging notice of appeal, serve a copy thereof on the comptroller and any other party to the proceedings before the comptroller.

(7)   On receiving notice of appeal the comptroller shall forthwith transmit to the proper officer all the papers relating to the matter which is the subject of the appeal.

(8)   Except by leave of the Court, no appeal shall be entertained unless notice of appeal has been given within the period specified in paragraph (2) or within such further time as the comptroller may allow upon request made to him prior to the expiry of that period.

(9)   A respondent who, not having appealed from the decision of the comptroller, desires to contend on the appeal that the decision should be varied, either in any event or in the event of the appeal being allowed in whole or in part, must give notice to that effect, specifying the grounds of that contention and the relief which he seeks from the Court.

(10) A respondent who desires to contend on the appeal that the decision of the comptroller should be affirmed on grounds other than those set out in the decision must give notice to that effect, specifying the grounds of that contention.

(11) A respondent's notice shall be served on the comptroller and on the appellant and every other party to the proceedings before the comptroller within 14 days after receipt of notice of appeal by the respondent, or within such further time as the Court may direct.

(12) A party by whom a respondent's notice is given must within 5 days after service of the notice on the appellant, furnish 2 copies of the notice to the proper officer.

(13)   The proper officer shall give to the comptroller and to the appellant and every other party to the proceedings before the comptroller not less than seven days' notice of the date appointed for the hearing of the appeal, unless the Court directs shorter notice to be given.

(14)   An appeal shall be by way of rehearing and the evidence used on appeal shall be the same as that used before the comptroller and, except with the leave of the Court, no further evidence shall be given.

(15)   ...

(16)   Any notice given in proceedings under this rule may be signed by or served on any patent agent, or member of the Bar of England and Wales not in actual practice, who is acting for the person giving the notice or, as the case may be, the person on whom the notice is to be served, as if the patent agent or member of the Bar were a solicitor.

(17)   ...

(18)   Nothing in Order 42, rule 7 (except paragraph (1)), Order 55 (except rule 7(2) and (3) and (5) to (7)) or Order 57 shall apply in relation to an appeal under this rule.]

Commencement   1 June 1978.
Amendments   See the note to Order 104, r 1.
This rule was inserted as r 14 by SI 1978/579, r 12; it was subsequently renumbered as r 19 by SI 1986/1187, r 15(7).
Paras (15), (17): revoked by SI 1982/1111, r 93.
Definitions   1949 Act: Patents Act 1949.
1977 Act: Patents Act 1977.

[Order 104, r [20] Communication of information to European Patent Office

(1)   The Court may authorise the communication to the European Patent Office or the competent authority of any country which is a party to the European Patent Convention of any such information in the files of the court as the Court thinks fit.

(2)   Before complying with a request for the disclosure of information under paragraph (1) the Court shall afford to any party appearing to be affected by the request the opportunity of making representations, in writing or otherwise, on the question whether the information should be disclosed.]

Commencement   1 June 1978.
Amendments   See the note to Order 104, r 1.
This rule was inserted as r 15 by SI 1978/579, r 12; it was subsequently renumbered as r 20 by SI 1986/1187, r 15(7).
Cross references   This rule is applied to the county court by CCR Order 48A, r 10(3).

[Order 104, r [21] Proceedings for determination of certain disputes

(1)   The following proceedings must be begun by originating motion, that is to say—
   (a)   proceedings for the determination of any dispute referred to the Court under—
      (i)   section 48 of the 1949 Act or section 58 of the 1977 Act;
      (ii)   paragraph 3 of Schedule 1 to the Registered Designs Act 1949, or
      (iii)   section 4 of the Defence Contracts Act 1958;
   (b)   any application under section 45(3) of the 1977 Act.

(2)   There must be at least 10 clear days between the serving of notice of a motion under this rule and the day named in the notice for hearing the motion.

(3)   On the hearing of a motion under this rule the Court shall give such directions for the further conduct of the proceedings as it thinks necessary or expedient and, in particular, directions for the service of particulars and as to the manner in which the evidence shall be given and as to the date of the hearing.]

Commencement   1 June 1978.
Amendments   See the note to Order 104, r 1.
This rule was inserted as r 16 by SI 1978/579, r 12; it was subsequently renumbered as r 21 by SI 1986/1187, r 15(7).
Definitions   1949 Act: Patents Act 1949.
1977 Act: Patents Act 1977.

[Order 104, r [22] Application for rectification of register of patents or designs

(1)   An application to the Court for an order that the register of patents or the register of designs be rectified must be made by originating motion, except where it is made in a petition for the revocation of a patent or by way of counterclaim in proceedings for infringement or by originating summons in proceedings for an order under section 51 of the Trustee Act 1925.

(2)   Where the application relates to the register of patents, the applicant shall forthwith serve an office copy of the application on the comptroller, who shall be entitled to appear and to be heard on the application.]

Commencement   1 June 1978.
Amendments   See the note to Order 104, r 1.
This rule was inserted as r 17 by SI 1978/579, r 12; it was subsequently renumbered as r 22 by SI 1986/1187, r 15(7).

[Order 104, r [23] Counterclaim for rectification of register of designs

[(1)   Where in any proceedings a claim is made for relief for infringement of the copyright in a registered design, the party against whom the claim is made may in his defence put in issue the validity of the registration of that design or may counterclaim for an order that the register of designs be rectified by cancelling or varying the registration or may do both those things.

(2)   A party to any such proceedings who in his pleading (whether a defence or counterclaim) disputes the validity of the registration of a registered design must serve with the pleading particulars of the objections to the validity of the registration on which he relies in support of the allegation of invalidity.

(3)   A party to any such proceedings who counterclaims for an order that the register of designs be rectified must serve on the comptroller a copy of the counterclaim together with a copy of the particulars mentioned in paragraph (2); and the comptroller shall be entitled to take such part in the proceedings as he thinks fit but need not serve a defence or other pleading unless ordered to do so by the Court.]

Commencement   1 June 1978.
Amendments   See the note to Order 104, r 1.
This rule was inserted as r 18 by SI 1978/579, r 12; it was subsequently renumbered as r 23 by SI 1986/1187, r 15(7).
Cross references   This rule is applied to the county court by CCR Order 48A, r 10(3).

ORDER 105
(original Order 105 revoked by SI 1969/1105; original Order 104 renumbered as Order 105 by SI 1978/579; revoked by SI 1991/1884)

ORDER 106
PROCEEDINGS RELATING TO SOLICITORS: THE SOLICITORS ACT [1974]

Amendments   Figure "1974" substituted by SI 1975/128, r 6(1).

[Order 106, r 1 Interpretation

(1)   In this Order—
"the Act" means the Solicitors Act 1974 and a section referred to by number means the section so numbered in that Act;
"appeal" means an appeal to the High Court against an order made by the Tribunal on an application or complaint under the Act.

(2)   Expressions used in this Order which are used in the Act have the same meanings in this Order as in the Act.]

Commencement   1 May 1975.
Amendments   This rule was substituted by SI 1975/128, r 6(2).

Order 106, r 2 Jurisdiction under Part III of Act . . .

(1)   Subject to rule 4, any application to the High Court under Part III of the Act made in the Chancery Division may be disposed of in chambers.

(2)   In the Queen's Bench Division and the [Family Division], the jurisdiction of the High Court under Part III of the Act may be exercised [by—
    (a)   a judge in chambers,
    (b)   a master, a taxing master or a [district judge] of the Family Division, or
    (c)   a [district judge], if the costs are for contentious business done in a cause or matter which proceeded in the district registry of which he is the [district judge] or for non-contentious business.]

(3)–(6). . .

Commencement   1 October 1966.
Amendments   Rule heading: words omitted revoked by SI 1986/632, r 9(a).
Para (2): words "Family Division" substituted by SI 1971/1269, r 38, Schedule; words from "by" to the end substituted by SI 1986/632, r 9(b).
Paras (3)–(6): revoked by SI 1972/1194, r 7(2).
Definitions   The Act: Solicitors Act 1974.
Cross references   See CCR Order 49, r 18.
Forms   Summons for taxation (PF191, PF193).
Order on taxation (PF192, PF194).
Summons to tax after action commenced (PF195).
Order to tax after action commenced (PF196).

Order 106, r 3 Power to order solicitor to deliver cash account, etc

(1)   Where the relationship of solicitor and client exists or has existed, the Court may,

on the application of the client or his personal representatives, make an order for—

    (a) the delivery by the solicitor of a cash account;

    (b) the payment or delivery up by the solicitor of money or securities;

    (c) the delivery to the plaintiff of a list of the moneys or securities which the solicitor has in his possession or control on behalf of the plaintiff;

    (d) the payment into or lodging in court of any such moneys or securities.

(2)   An application for an order under this rule must be made by originating summons.

(3)   If the defendant alleges that he has a claim for costs, the Court may make such order for the taxation and payment, or securing the payment, thereof and the protection of the defendant's lien, if any, as the Court thinks fit.

Commencement 1 October 1966.
Forms Originating summons for delivery of bill (PF189).
Order for delivery of bill (PF190).

Order 106, r 4 Petition for taxation of costs, etc

In the Chancery Division an application under the Act for an order for taxation of a solicitor's bill of costs or for the delivery of such a bill or for the delivery up of, or otherwise in relation to, any deeds, documents and papers in the possession, custody or power of a solicitor may, if the applicant is entitled as of right to the order, be made by petition.

    The foregoing provision shall not be taken as preventing any such application being made by originating summons.

Commencement 1 October 1966.
Definitions The Act: Solicitors Act 1974.

[Order 106, r 5 Form of originating summons

An originating summons by which any application under the Act, or any application for an order under rule 3, is made shall be in Form No 10 in Appendix A.]

Commencement 3 June 1980.
Amendments This rule was substituted by SI 1979/1716, r 48, Schedule, Pt 2.
Definitions The Act: Solicitors Act 1974.

[Order 106, r 5A Certificate to be submitted with solicitor's application for taxation

A solicitor who applies for an order under the Act for the taxation of his bill of costs shall lodge with his application a certificate that all the relevant requirements of the Act have been satisfied.]

Commencement 28 April 1986.
Amendments This rule was inserted by SI 1986/632, r 9(c).
Definitions The Act: Solicitors Act 1974.

Order 106, r 6 Applications under Schedule 1 to Act

(1)   Proceedings in the High Court under Schedule 1 to the Act shall be assigned to the Chancery Division.

(2)   The originating summons by which an application for an order under the said

Schedule is made must be entitled in the matter of a solicitor [or a deceased solicitor, as the case may be] (without naming him) and in the matter of the Act.

[(3)   Where an order has been made under paragraph 9(4), 9(5) or 10 of the said Schedule an application for an order under paragraph 9(8) or 9(10) may be made by summons in the proceedings in which the first mentioned order was made.]

(4)   ...

Commencement   1 May 1975 (para (3)); 1 October 1966 (remainder).
Amendments   Para (2): words "or a deceased solicitor, as the case may be" inserted by SI 1966/1514, r 8(2).
Para (3): substituted by SI 1975/128, r 6(3)(a).
Para (4): revoked by SI 1975/128, r 6(3)(b).
Definitions   The Act: Solicitors Act 1974.

Order 106, r 7 Defendants to applications under Schedule 1 to Act

The defendant to an originating summons by which an application for an order under Schedule 1 to the Act is made shall be—

[(a) if the application is for an order under paragraph 5 thereof, the solicitor or, as the case may be, every member of the firm, on whose behalf the money in respect of which the order is sought is held;

(b) if the application is for an order under paragraph 6(4) or 9(8) thereof, the Law Society;

(c) if the application is for an order under paragraph 8, 9(4) or 9(5) thereof, the person against whom the order is sought;

(d) if the application is for an order under paragraph 9(10) thereof, the person from whom the Law Society obtained possession of the documents by virtue of paragraph 9 or 10;

(e) if the application is for an order under paragraph 10 thereof for the re-direction of postal packets addressed to a solicitor or his firm, the solicitor or, as the case may be, every member of the firm;

(f) if the application is for an order under paragraph 11 thereof, the solicitor or personal representative in substitution for whom the appointment of a new trustee is sought and, if he is a co-trustee, the other trustee or trustees.]

Commencement   1 October 1966.
Amendments   Paras (a)–(f) substituted by SI 1975/128, r 6(4).
Definitions   The Act: Solicitors Act 1974.

Order 106, r 8 Interim order restricting payment out of banking account

At any time after the issue of an originating summons by which an application for an order under [paragraph 5] of Schedule 1 to the Act is made, the Court may, on the ex parte application of the plaintiff, make an interim order under that paragraph to have effect until the hearing of the summons and include therein a further order requiring the defendant to show cause at the hearing why an order under that paragraph should not be made.

Commencement   1 October 1966.
Amendments   Words "paragraph 5" substituted by SI 1975/128, r 6(5).
Definitions   The Act: Solicitors Act 1974.

Order 106, r 9 Adding parties, etc

Without prejudice to its powers under Order 15, the Court may, at any stage of proceedings under Schedule 1 to the Act, order any person to be added as a party to the proceedings or to be given notice thereof.

Commencement   1 October 1966.
Definitions   The Act: Solicitors Act 1974.

Order 106, r 10 Service of documents

(1)   Any document required to be served on . . . the Law Society in proceedings under this Order shall be served by sending it by prepaid post to the secretary of the Law Society.

(2)   Subject to paragraph (1), an originating summons by which an application under Schedule 1 to the Act is made, an order [under [paragraph 5]] of that Schedule or rule 8 and any other document not required to be served personally which is to be served on a defendant to proceedings under the said Schedule shall, unless the Court otherwise directs, be deemed to be properly served by sending it by prepaid post to the defendant at his last known address.

Commencement   1 October 1966.
Amendments   Para (1): words omitted revoked by SI 1966/1514, r 8(5).
Para (2): first words in square brackets substituted by SI 1966/1514, r 8(6); words "paragraph 5" therein substituted by SI 1975/128, r 6(5).
Definitions   The Act: Solicitors Act 1974.

Order 106, r 11 Constitution of Divisional Court to hear appeals

Every appeal shall be heard by a Divisional Court of the Queen's Bench Division consisting, unless the Lord Chief Justice otherwise directs, of not less than three judges.

Commencement   1 October 1966.

Order 106, r 12 Title, service, etc of notice of motion

(1)   The notice of the originating motion by which an appeal is brought must be entitled in the matter of a solicitor, or, as the case may be, a solicitor's clerk, without naming him, and in the matter of the Act.

(2)   Unless the Court otherwise orders, the persons to be served with such notice are every party to the proceedings before the [Tribunal] and the Law Society.

(3)   Order 55, rule 4(2), shall apply in relation to the appeal as if for the period of 28 days therein specified there were substituted a period of 14 days.

[(4)   Order 55, rule 4(4), shall not apply and the said period of 14 days shall begin with the day on which a statement of the Tribunal's findings was filed pursuant to section 48(1).]

Commencement   1 May 1975 (para (4)); 1 October 1966 (remainder).
Amendments   Para (2): word "Tribunal" substituted by SI 1975/128, r 6(7).
Para (4): substituted by SI 1975/128, r 6(6).
Definitions   The Act: Solicitors Act 1974.

Order 106, r 13 Law Society to produce certain documents

(1)   Within 7 days after being served with notice of the originating motion by which an appeal is brought the Law Society must lodge in the Crown Office three copies of each of the following documents:—
    (a)   the order appealed against, [together with the statement of the Tribunal's findings required by section 48(1)],

(b) any document lodged by a party with the [Tribunal] which is relevant to a matter in issue on the appeal, and

(c) the transcript of the shorthand note, or, as the case may be, the note taken by the chairman of the [Tribunal], of the evidence in the proceedings before [the Tribunal].

(2) At the hearing of the appeal the Court shall direct by whom the costs incurred in complying with paragraph (1) are to be borne and may order them to be paid to the Law Society by one of the parties notwithstanding that the Society does not appear at the hearing.

Commencement 1 October 1966.
Amendments Para (1): in sub-para (a) words from "together with" to "section 48(1)", in sub-para (b) word "Tribunal" and in sub-para (c) words "Tribunal" and "the Tribunal" substituted by SI 1975/128, r 6(7)–(9).
Definitions Section 48(1): Solicitors Act 1974, s 48(1).

Order 106, r 14 Restriction on requiring security for costs

No person other than an appellant who was the applicant in the proceedings before the [Tribunal] . . . shall be ordered to give security for the costs of an appeal.

Commencement 1 October 1966.
Amendments Word "Tribunal" substituted and words omitted revoked by SI 1975/128, r 6(7), (10).

Order 106, r 15 [Tribunal's] opinion may be required

The Court may direct the [Tribunal] to furnish the Court with a written statement of their opinion on the case which is the subject-matter of an appeal or on any question arising therein, and where such a direction is given, the clerk to the [Tribunal] must as soon as may be lodge three copies of such statement in the Crown Office and at the same time send a copy to each of the parties to the appeal.

Commencement 1 October 1966.
Amendments Rule heading: word "Tribunal's" substituted by SI 1975/128, r 6(7).
Word "Tribunal" in both places substituted by SI 1975/128, r 6(7).

Order 106, r 16 Persons entitled to be heard on appeal

A person who has not been served with notice of the originating motion by which an appeal is brought but who desires to be heard in opposition to the appeal shall, if he appears to the Court to be a proper person to be so heard, be entitled to be so heard.

Commencement 1 October 1966.

Order 106, r 17 Discontinuance of appeal

(1) An appellant may at any time discontinue his appeal by serving notice of discontinuance on the clerk to the [Tribunal] and every other party to the appeal and, if the appeal has been entered, by lodging a copy of the notice in the Crown Office.

(2) Where an appeal has been discontinued in accordance with paragraph (1), it shall be treated as having been dismissed with an order for payment by the appellant of the costs of and incidental to the appeal, including any costs incurred by the Law Society in complying with rule 13(1).

Commencement 1 October 1966.
Amendments Para (1): word "Tribunal" substituted by SI 1975/128, r 6(7).

ORDER 107
[THE COUNTY COURTS ACT 1984]

Amendments Words "The County Courts Act 1984" substituted by SI 1985/69, r 7(2), Schedule.

Order 107, r 1 Jurisdiction of master, etc under Act

(1)   Subject to paragraphs (2) and (3), a master, [the Admiralty Registrar or any [district judge] of the Family Division] or [district judge] may exercise the jurisdiction and powers conferred on a judge of the High Court by the [County Courts Act 1984] except the power to make an order of certiorari or prohibition or an order removing into the High Court any proceedings commenced in a county court for the purpose of quashing any judgment or order given or made in those proceedings.

(2)   A [district judge] shall have power by virtue of paragraph (1) to make an order in relation to any proceedings in the High Court if, but only if, the proceedings are proceeding in the registry of which he is [district judge].

(3)   A [district judge] shall have power by virtue of paragraph (1) to transfer any proceedings in a county court to the High Court if, but only if, the district for which the county court is held is comprised in the district of the registry of which he is [district judge].

(4)   Where the Court makes an order transferring any proceedings in a county court to the High Court, it may, on the application of a party to the proceedings, also order that the proceedings shall proceed in the High Court in such district registry as may be specified in the order.

Commencement 1 October 1966.
Amendments Para (1): words from "the Admiralty Registrar" to "Family Division" substituted by SI 1971/1269, r 32; words "County Courts Act 1984" substituted by SI 1985/69, r 7(2), Schedule.

[Order 107, r 2 Transfer of proceedings to or from a county court

(1)   The Court shall not order the transfer of any proceedings to a county court unless the parties have been either (a) had an opportunity of being heard on the issue or (b) consented to such an order.

[(1A) Where an order is made transferring proceedings to a county court, the proper officer shall, on the production of the order and the filing of a copy of it, send by post to the proper officer of the county court to which the proceedings are transferred all pleadings, affidavits and other documents filed in the High Court relating to the proceedings together with a copy of the order for transfer.

(1B) Paragraph (1) shall not apply where default has been made in any obligation imposed under Order 14, rule 6(3)(b) or Order 25, rule 6(2A) to lodge or to serve a statement of the value of the action.]

(2)   Where an application is made under [section 41 of the said Act of 1984] for the transfer of the whole or part of any proceedings from a county court to the High Court, the Court hearing such application may order the proceedings in the county court to be stayed until after the final determination of the application.]

Commencement   1 July 1991 (paras (1A), (1B)); 1 January 1982 (remainder).
Amendments   This rule was substituted by SI 1981/1734, r 27.
Paras (1A), (1B): inserted by SI 1991/1329, r 7.
Para (2): words "section 41 of the said Act of 1984" substituted by SI 1985/69, r 7(2), Schedule.
Definitions   Act of 1984: County Courts Act 1984.
Forms   Order transfer to county court (PF168).
Notice of proposal to transfer or strike out (PF200, PF202).
Notice of objection to transfer or strike out (PF203).

Order 107, r 3 Issue of commission, etc under [s 56]

(1)   [Subject to paragraph (1A), a] master of the Queen's Bench Division may exercise the power conferred on the High Court by [section 56 of the said Act of 1984] to issue a commission, request or order to examine witnesses abroad for the purpose of proceedings in a county court and to order that the proceedings be transferred to the High Court.

[(1A) In relation to family proceedings in a county court, an application relating to the exercise of the powers conferred upon a master of the Queen's Bench Division by paragraph (1) shall be made to a district judge of the principal registry of the Family Division.

(1B) In paragraph (1A) "family proceedings" means family proceedings within the meaning of Part V of the Matrimonial and Family Proceedings Act 1984.]

[(2)   An originating summons by which an application under [the said section 56] is made shall be in Form No 10 in Appendix A.]

Commencement   1 October 1993 (paras (1A), (1B)); 3 June 1980 (para (2)); 1 October 1966 (remainder).
Amendments   Rule heading: words "s 56" substituted by virtue of SI 1985/69, r 7(2), Schedule.
Para (1): words "Subject to paragraph (1A), a" substituted by SI 1993/2133, r 12(1), words "section 56 of the said Act of 1984" substituted by SI 1985/69, r 7(2), Schedule.
Paras (1A), (1B): added by SI 1993/2133, r 12(2).
Para (2): substituted by SI 1979/1716, r 48, Schedule, Pt 2; words "the said section 56 " substituted by SI 1985/69, r 7(2), Schedule.
Definitions   Act of 1984: County Courts Act 1984.

Order 107, r 4 Application under [section 72] for leave to set-off cross judgments

(1)   The jurisdiction of the High Court under [section 72 of the said Act of 1984] to allow set-off of any sums payable under several judgments or orders where one judgment or order was obtained in a county court and the other in the High Court may be exercised by a master or, if the judgment or order obtained in the High Court was obtained in a cause or matter proceeding in a district registry, the [district judge] of that registry, on an application made by summons.

(2)   The applicant must give notice of his intended application to the [district judge] of the county court in which the judgment or order to which the application relates was obtained.

(3)   The [district judge] of the county court shall, on receipt of notice of the application, stay execution on the judgment or order to which the application relates, and retain any money paid into that court in either of the actions or matters affected until after the final determination of the application.

(4)   Where the Court hearing the application orders any sums to be set-off, it shall

by the order direct how any money paid into either court in the actions or matters in question is to be dealt with.

(5)   Where any sums payable under the judgment or order obtained in the county court are ordered to be set-off against any sums payable under the judgment or order obtained in the High Court, the last mentioned judgment or order shall be entered as satisfied to the extent of the amount ordered to be set-off, and that judgment or order shall be enforced only as respects the balance (if any) of the amount payable thereunder.

(6)   The proper officer of the High Court for the purposes of [the said section 72] is the head clerk of [the office of the Supreme Court which has the conduct of the business of the division or court in which the cause or matter is proceeding] or, if the cause or matter in the High Court is proceeding in a district registry, the [district judge] of that registry.

[(7)   In relation to a judgment or order given or made in the Admiralty Court any reference in this rule to a master shall be construed as a reference to the Admiralty registrar . . . .]

Commencement   1 July 1975 (para (7)); 1 October 1966 (remainder).
Amendments   Rule heading: words "section 72" substituted by SI 1987/1423, r 63, Schedule.
Para (1): words "section 72 of the said Act of 1984" substituted by SI 1985/69, r 7(2), Schedule.
Para (6): words "the said section 72" substituted by SI 1985/69, r 7(2), Schedule; words from "the office of the Supreme Court" to "matter is proceeding" substituted by SI 1982/1111, r 94.
Para (7): added by SI 1975/911, r 19; words omitted revoked by SI 1982/1111, r 95.
Definitions   Act of 1984: County Courts Act 1984.

ORDER 108
PROCEEDINGS RELATING TO CHARITIES: THE CHARITIES ACT 1960

Order 108, r 1 Interpretation

(1)　In this Order—

"the Act" means the Charities Act 1960;

"certificate" means a certificate that a case is a proper one for an appeal;

"charity proceedings" means proceedings in the High Court brought under the Court's jurisdiction with respect to charities or brought under the Court's jurisdiction with respect to trusts in relation to the administration of a trust for charitable purposes;

"the Commissioners" means the Charity Commissioners for England and Wales.

(2)　...

Commencement　1 October 1966.
Amendments　Para (2): revoked by SI 1991/531, r 5.

Order 108, r 2 Assignment to Chancery Division

Charity proceedings and proceedings brought in the High Court by virtue of the Act shall be assigned to the Chancery Division . . . .

Commencement　1 October 1966.
Amendments　Words omitted revoked by SI 1982/1786, r 24.
Definitions　The Act: Charities Act 1960.

Order 108, r 3 Application for leave to appeal or to take charity proceedings

(1)　An application shall not be made under section 18(11) of the Act for leave to appeal against an order of the Commissioners unless the applicant has requested the Commissioners to grant a certificate and they have refused to do so.

(2)　An application . . . under section 28(5) of the Act for leave to take charity proceedings must be made within 21 days after the refusal by the Commissioners . . . of an order authorising the taking of proceedings.

(3)　The application must be made by lodging in [Chancery Chambers] a statement showing—

(a)　the name, address and description of the applicant;

(b)　particulars of the order against which it is desired to appeal or of the proceedings which it is desired to take;

(c)　the date of the Commissioners' refusal to grant a certificate or an order authorising the taking of proceedings;

(d)　the grounds on which the applicant alleges that it is a proper case for an appeal or for taking proceedings.

(4)　The application may be made ex parte in the first instance and if it is made with the consent of any other party to the proposed appeal or proposed proceedings that fact shall be mentioned in the statement.

(5)　If the judge on considering the application so directs, the Commissioners shall furnish him with a written statement of their reasons for refusing a certificate or, as the case may be, an order authorising the taking of proceedings, and a copy of any such statement shall be sent from [Chancery Chambers] to the applicant.

(6)   Unless, after considering the applicant's statement and the statement (if any) of the Commissioners, the judge decides to grant the leave applied for without a hearing, the application shall be set down for hearing, and the hearing may be in chambers if the judge so directs.

(7)   Where the application is determined without a hearing, a copy of the judge's order shall be sent from [Chancery Chambers] to the applicant and the Commissioners; and where the application is to be set down for hearing, notice of the day and time fixed for the hearing shall be sent from that Office to the applicant.

Commencement 1 October 1966.
Amendments Para (2): words omitted revoked by SI 1982/1786, r 25.
Paras (3), (5), (7): words "Chancery Chambers" substituted by SI 1982/1111, r 96.
Definitions The Act: Charities Act 1960.

[Order 108, r 4 Application for enforcement of order of Commissioners

Order 52, rule 1(4), shall apply in relation to an application under section 41 of the Act as if for the reference in that rule to a single judge of the Queen's Bench Division there were substituted a reference to a single judge of the Chancery Division.]

Commencement 1 July 1972.
Amendments Original r 4 renumbered as r 5 and new r 4 inserted by SI 1972/813, r 7(2), (3).
Definitions The Act: Charities Act 1960.

Order 108, r [5] Appeal against order, etc of Commissioners

(1)   An appeal against an order or decision of the Commissioners shall be heard and determined by a single judge.

(2)   Such an appeal must be brought by originating summons to which the Attorney General, unless he is the appellant, shall be made a defendant in addition to any other person who is a proper defendant thereto.

(3)   An originating summons under this rule must state the grounds of the appeal and, except with the leave of the judge hearing the appeal, the appellant shall not be entitled to rely on any ground not so stated.

Commencement 1 October 1966.
Amendments Originally r 4, renumbered as r 5 by SI 1972/813, r 7(3).

Order 108, r [6] Service on Commissioners

Any document required or authorised to be served on the Commissioners in proceedings to which this Order relates must be served on the Treasury Solicitor in accordance with Order 77, rule 4(2).

Commencement 1 October 1966.
Amendments Originally r 5, renumbered as r 6 by SI 1972/813, r 7(3).

ORDER 109
The Administration of Justice Act 1960

Order 109, r 1 Applications under Act

(1)   Any of the following applications, that is to say—
   (a) an application under section 2 of the Administration of Justice Act 1960, or under that section as applied by section 13 of that Act, to extend the time within which an application may be made to a Divisional Court for leave to appeal to the House of Lords under section 1 of that Act, or section 13 thereof, from an order or decision of that Court, and
   (b) an application by a defendant under section 9(3) of that Act to a Divisional Court for leave to be present on the hearing of any proceedings preliminary or incidental to an appeal to the House of Lords under section 1 of that Act from a decision of that Court,

must be made to a Divisional Court except in vacation when it may be made to a judge in chambers.

(2)   Any such application to a Divisional Court, if not made in the proceedings before the Divisional Court from whose order or decision the appeal in question is brought, must be made by originating motion in open court.

(3)   Any such application to a judge in chambers must, in the case of such an application as is referred to in paragraph (1)(a), be made by summons and, in the case of such an application as is referred to in paragraph (1)(b), be made ex parte unless, in the latter case, the judge otherwise directs.

(4)   Notwithstanding anything in Order 8, rule 2(1), no notice of a motion by which such an application as is referred to in paragraph (1)(b) is made need be given to any party affected thereby unless the Divisional Court otherwise directs.

(5)   Where any application to which this rule applies is made in vacation to a single judge and the judge refuses the application, the applicant shall be entitled to have the application determined by a Divisional Court.

Commencement   1 October 1966.

Order 109, r 2 Appeals under s 13 of Act

(1)   [An] appeal to a Divisional Court of the High Court under section 13 of the Administration of Justice Act 1960 shall be heard and determined by a Divisional Court of the Queen's Bench Division.

(2)   . . .

(3)   Order 55, rules 4(2) and 5, shall not apply in relation to an appeal to a Divisional Court under the said section 13.

(4)   Unless the Court gives leave to the contrary, there shall be not more than 4 clear days between the date on which the order or decision appealed against was made and the day named in the notice of the originating motion for the hearing of the appeal.

(5)   The notice must be served, and the appeal entered, not less than one clear day before the day named in the notice for the hearing of the appeal.

Commencement 1 October 1966.
Amendments Para (1): word "An" substituted by SI 1991/1884, r 8.
Para (2): revoked by SI 1991/1884, r 6(4).

Order 109, r 3 Release of appellant on bail

(1) Where, in the case of an appeal under section 13 of the Administration of Justice Act 1960 to a Divisional Court or to the House of Lords from a Divisional Court, the appellant is in custody, the High Court may order his release on his giving security (whether by recognizance, with or without sureties, or otherwise and for such reasonable sum as the Court may fix) for his appearance, within 10 days after the judgment of the Divisional Court or, as the case may be, of the House of Lords, on the appeal shall have been given, before the court from whose order or decision the appeal is brought unless the order or decision is reversed by that judgment.

(2) Order 79, rule 9(1) to (6) and (8) shall apply in relation to an application to the High Court for bail pending an appeal under the said section 13 to which this rule applies, and to the admission of a person to bail in pursuance of an order made on the application, as they apply in relation to an application to that Court for bail in criminal proceedings, and to the admission of a person to bail in pursuance of an order made on the application, but with the substitution, for references to the defendant, of references to the appellant, and, for references to the prosecutor, of references to the proper officer of the court from whose order or decision the appeal is brought and to the parties to the proceedings in that court who are directly affected by the appeal.

Commencement 1 October 1966.

[ORDER 110
Environmental Control Proceedings

Order 110, r 1 Injunctions to prevent environmental harm

(1)   An injunction under—
  (a) section 187B or 214A of the Town and Country Planning Act 1990;
  (b) section 44A of the Planning (Listed Buildings and Conservation Areas) Act 1990; or
  (c) section 26AA of the Planning (Hazardous Substances) Act 1990

may be granted against a person whose identity is unknown to the applicant; and in the following provisions of this rule such an injunction against such a person is referred to as "an injunction under paragraph (1)", and the person against whom it is sought is referred to as "the defendant".

(2)   An applicant for an injunction under paragraph (1) shall, in the originating summons commencing the application, describe the defendant by reference to—
  (a) a photograph,
  (b) a thing belonging to or in the possession of the defendant, or
  (c) any other evidence,

with sufficient particularity to enable service to be effected; and the form of originating summons used (which may be in Form No 8, Form No 10 or Form No 11 in Appendix A, as appropriate) shall be modified accordingly.

(3)   An applicant for an injunction under paragraph (1) shall file in support of the originating summons evidence by affidavit—
  (a) verifying that he was unable to ascertain, within the time reasonably available to him, the defendant's identity,
  (b) setting out the action taken to ascertain the defendant's identity, and
  (c) verifying the means by which the defendant has been described in the originating summons and that the description is the best that the applicant is able to provide.

(4)   Paragraph (2) is without prejudice to the power of the Court to make an order for substituted service or dispensing with service.]

Commencement   1 June 1992 (paras (1)(a), (b), (2)–(4)); 2 January 1992 (para (1)(c)).
Amendments   Original Order 110 revoked by SI 1976/337, r 20; new Order 110 (consisting of r 1 only) inserted by SI 1992/638, r 4.

ORDER 111
[THE SOCIAL SECURITY ACTS 1975 TO 1986]

Amendments   Words "The Social Security Acts 1975 to 1986" substituted by SI 1988/298, r 21.

Order 111, r 1 Judge by whom appeals and references to be heard

Any appeal to the High Court against a decision of the [Secretary of State] on a question of law under the [Social Security Act 1975], and any question of law referred to the High Court [by the Secretary of State] under [the Act], shall be heard and determined by a single judge of the Queen's Bench Division.

Commencement   1 October 1966.
Amendments   Words "Secretary of State", "Social Security Act 1975", "by the Secretary of State" and "the Act" substituted by SI 1975/911, r 20(1)(b).

Order 111, r 2 Appeal: preliminary statement of facts by [Secretary of State]

Any person who by virtue of [section 94 or 114(5) of the Social Security Act 1975] is entitled and wishes to appeal against a decision of the [Secretary of State] on a question of law must within the prescribed period or within such further time as the [Secretary of State] may allow serve on the [Secretary of State] a notice requiring him to state a case setting out the facts on which his decision was based and his decision.

If within [28 days] after receipt of notice of the decision a request is made to the [Secretary of State] in accordance with regulations made under the Act . . . to furnish a statement of the grounds of the decision, the prescribed period for the purpose of this rule shall be [28 days] after receipt of that statement, and if no such request is made within [28 days] after receipt of notice of the decision the prescribed period for that purpose shall be [28 days] after receipt of that notice.

Commencement   1 October 1966.
Amendments   Words "section 94 or 114(5) of the Social Security Act 1975" and words "Secretary of State" wherever they occur substituted, and words omitted revoked, by SI 1975/911, r 20(1)(c); words "28 days" wherever they occur substituted by SI 1983/531, r 4(2).

Order 111, r 3 Special provisions as to appeals

Order 55 shall not apply in relation to an appeal under the said [section 94 or 114(5)], but Order 56, rules 9 to 12, shall apply in relation to the case stated by [the Secretary of State] for the purpose of any such appeal as they apply in relation to any other case stated by a Minister except that Order 56, [rule 10(4)] and (7), as so applied, shall have effect as if for the period of 14 days and 7 days therein specified there were substituted a period of [28 days].

Commencement   1 October 1966.
Amendments   Words "section 94 or 114(5)" and "the Secretary of State" substituted by SI 1975/911, r 20(1)(d); words "rule 10(4)" substituted by SI 1967/1809, r 9; words "28 days" substituted by SI 1983/531, r 4(2).
Definitions   Section 94 or 114(5): Social Security Act 1975, ss 94, 114(5).

Order 111, r 4 Reference of question of law

(1)   Where under the said [section 94 or 114(5)][the Secretary of State] refers to the High Court for decision any question of law, he must state that question together with the facts relating thereto in a case.

(2)   Order 56, rules 9(1), 10(1), 11 and 12, shall apply in relation to a case stated under paragraph (1) of this rule as they apply in relation to any other case stated by a Minister.

(3)   Notice of the originating motion by which proceedings for the determination of the question of law stated in the case are begun, together with a copy of the case, must be served by [the Secretary of State] on every person as between whom and [the Secretary of State] the question has arisen.

(4)   Unless the Court having jurisdiction to determine the question of law otherwise directs, the motion shall not be heard sooner than [28 days] after service of notice of the motion.

Commencement   1 October 1966.
Amendments   Para (1): words "section 94 or 114(5)" and "the Secretary of State" substituted by SI 1975/911, r 20(d).
Para (3): words "the Secretary of State" in both places substituted by SI 1975/911, r 20(d)(ii).
Para (4): words "28 days" substituted by SI 1983/531, r 4(2).
Definitions   Section 94 or 114(5): Social Security Act 1975, ss 94, 114(5).

Order 111, r 5 Powers of Court hearing appeal or reference

(1)   Without prejudice to Order 56, rule 11, as applied by rules 3 and 4 of this Order, the Court hearing an appeal or reference under the said [section 94 or 114(5)] may order the case stated by [the Secretary of State] to be returned to [the Secretary of State] for him to hear further evidence.

(2)   The Court hearing such an appeal or reference shall determine all questions arising thereon, and in the case of any such appeal may reverse, affirm or amend the decision appealed against or make such other order as it thinks fit.

Commencement   1 October 1966.
Amendments   Para (1): words "section 94 or 114(5)" and words "the Secretary of State" in both places substituted by SI 1975/911, r 20(1)(d).
Definitions   Section 94 or 114(5): Social Security Act 1975, ss 94, 114(5).

Order 111, r 6   *(added by SI 1983/531; revoked by SI 1988/298)*

[ORDER 112
APPLICATIONS FOR USE OF BLOOD TESTS IN DETERMINING PATERNITY

Cross references See CCR Order 47, r 5 for the matters covered by this Order.

Order 112, r 1 Interpretation

In this Order—
"the Act" means Part III of the Family Law Reform Act 1969;
"blood samples" and "blood tests" have the meanings assigned to them by
section 25 of the Act;
"direction" means a direction for the use of blood tests under section 20(1) of
the Act;
"the proper officer" means the officer of the court who draws up a direction.]

Commencement 1 March 1972.
Amendments Order 112 originally inserted by SI 1968/1244, r 13, subsequently revoked by SI 1971/1269, r 34, new Order 112 inserted by SI 1971/1955, r 42.

[Order 112, r 2 Application for direction

(1) Except with the leave of the Court, an application in any proceedings for a direction shall be made on notice to every party to the proceedings (other than the applicant) and to any other person from whom the direction involves the taking of blood samples.

(2) If the application is made otherwise than at the hearing of the proceedings it shall be made by summons.

(3) Any notice or summons required by this rule to be served on a person who is not a party to the proceedings shall be served on him personally.]

Commencement 1 March 1972.
Amendments See the note to Order 112, r 1.

[Order 112, r 3 Applications involving persons under disability

Where an application is made for a direction in respect of a person (in this rule referred to as a person under disability) who is either—
(a) under 16, or
(b) suffering from a mental disorder within the meaning of the [Mental Health Act 1983] and incapable of understanding the nature and purpose of blood tests,

the notice of application or summons shall state the name and address of the person having the care and control of the person under disability and shall be served on him instead of on the person under disability.]

Commencement 1 March 1972.
Amendments See the note to Order 112, r 1.
Words "Mental Health Act 1983" substituted by SI 1983/1181, r 36, Schedule.

[Order 112, r 4 Joinder of person to be tested

Where an application is made for a direction involving the taking of blood samples from a person who is not a party to the proceedings in which the application is made, the Court may at any time direct that person to be made a party to the proceedings.]

Commencement 1 March 1972.
Amendments See the note to Order 112, r 1.

[Order 112, r 5 Service of direction and adjournment of proceedings

Where the Court gives a direction in any proceedings, the proper officer shall send a copy to every party to the proceedings and to every other person from whom the direction involves the taking of blood samples and, unless otherwise ordered, further consideration of the proceedings shall stand adjourned until the court receives a report pursuant to the direction.]

Commencement 1 March 1972.
Amendments See the note to Order 112, r 1.

[Order 112, r 6 Service of copy of report

On receipt by the court of a report made pursuant to a direction, the proper officer shall send a copy to every party to the proceedings and to every other person from whom the direction involved the taking of blood samples.]

Commencement 1 March 1972.
Amendments See the note to Order 112, r 1.

[ORDER 113
SUMMARY PROCEEDINGS FOR POSSESSION OF LAND

Order 113, r 1 Proceedings to be brought by originating summons

Where a person claims possession of land which he alleges is occupied solely by a person or persons (not being a tenant or tenants holding over after the termination of the tenancy) who entered into or remained in occupation without his licence or consent or that of any predecessor in title of his, the proceedings may be brought by originating summons in accordance with the provisions of this Order.]

Commencement   20 July 1970.
Amendments   Order 113 was inserted by SI 1970/944, r 9.
Cross references   See CCR Order 24, r 1.

[Order 113, r 1A Jurisdiction of masters

Proceedings under this Order may be heard and determined by a master, who may refer them to a judge if he thinks they should properly be decided by the judge.]

Commencement   12 January 1987.
Amendments   See the note to Order 113, r 1.
This rule was subsequently inserted by SI 1986/2289, r 14(1).
Cross references   See CCR Order 24, r 5(2).

[Order 113, r 2 Forms of originating summons

[(1)] [The originating summons shall be in Form No 11A in Appendix A and [no acknowledgement of service of it shall be required].]

[(2) The originating summons shall be endorsed with or contain a statement showing whether possession is claimed in respect of residential premises or in respect of other land.]]

Commencement   5 February 1990 (para (2)); 7 June 1979 (remainder).
Amendments   See the note to Order 113, r 1.
Para (1): text originally substituted by SI 1979/522, r 11, for the existing paras (1)–(3); subsequently numbered as para (1) by SI 1989/2427, r 27; words from "no acknowledgement of service" to the end substituted by SI 1979/1716, r 47.
Para (2): inserted by SI 1989/2427, r 27.

[Order 113, r 3 Affidavit in support

The plaintiff shall file in support of the originating summons an affidavit stating—
    (a)   his interest in the land;
    (b)   the circumstances in which the land has been occupied without licence or consent and in which his claim to possession arises; and
    [(c)   that he does not know the name of any person occupying the land who is not named in the summons;

and, unless the Court otherwise directs, any such affidavit may contain statements of information or belief with the sources and grounds thereof.]]

Commencement   20 July 1970.
Amendments   See the note to Order 113, r 1.
Words from para (c) to the end substituted by SI 1990/2599, r 19.
Cross references   See CCR Order 24, r 2.

[Order 113, r 4 Service of originating summons

(1)   [Where any person in occupation of the land is named in the originating summons, the summons] together with a copy of the affidavit in support shall be served on him—

- [(a)   personally, or]
- (b)   by leaving a copy of the summons and of the affidavit, or sending them to him, at the premises, or
- (c)   in such other manner as the Court may direct.

[(2)   Where any person not named as a defendant is in occupation of the land, the summons shall be served (whether or not it is also required to be served in accordance with paragraph (1)), unless the court otherwise directs, by—

- (a)   affixing a copy of the summons and a copy of the affidavit to the main door or other conspicuous part of the premises and, if practicable, inserting through the letter-box at the premises a copy of the summons and a copy of the affidavit enclosed in a sealed transparent envelope addressed to "the occupiers", or
- (b)   placing stakes in the ground at conspicuous parts of the occupied land, to each of which shall be affixed a sealed transparent envelope addressed to "the occupiers" and containing a copy of the summons and a copy of the affidavit.]

[(2A) Every copy of an originating summons for service under paragraph (1) or (2) shall be sealed with the seal of the Office of the Supreme Court out of which the summons was issued.]

(3)   Order 28, rule 3, shall not apply to proceedings under this Order.]

Commencement   12 January 1987 (para (2)); 3 June 1980 (para 2A)); 20 July 1970 (remainder).
Amendments   See the note to Order 113, r 1.
Para (1): words from the beginning to "the summons" substituted by SI 1977/960, r 6(3); sub-para (a) substituted by SI 1980/629, r 31(1).
Para (2): substituted by SI 1986/2289, r 14(2).
Para (2A): inserted by SI 1980/629, r 31(2).
Cross references   See CCR Order 24, r 3.

[Order 113, r 5 Application by occupier to be made a party

Without prejudice to Order 15, rules 6 and 10, any person not named as a defendant who is in occupation of the land and wishes to be heard on the question whether an order for possession should be made may apply at any stage of the proceedings to be joined as a defendant.]

Commencement   20 July 1970.
Amendments   See the note to Order 113, r 1.
Cross references   See CCR Order 24, r 4.

[Order 113, r 6 Order for possession

(1)   A final order for possession in proceedings under this Order shall, except in case of emergency and by leave of the court, not be made—

- (a)   in the case of residential premises, less than five clear days after the date of service, and
- (b)   in the case of other land, less than two clear days after the date of service.]

(2)   An order for possession in proceedings under this Order shall be in Form No 42A.

[(3)   Nothing in this Order shall prevent the Court from ordering possession to be given on a specified date, in the exercise of any power which could have been exercised if possession had been claimed in an action begun by writ.]

Commencement   12 January 1987 (para (1)); 2 January 1981 (para (3)); 20 July 1970 (remainder).
Amendments   See the note to Order 113, r 1.
Para (1): substituted by SI 1986/2289, r 14(3).
Para (3): added by SI 1980/1908, r 16.
Cross references   See CCR Order 24, r 5(1), (4).

[Order 113, r 7 Writ of possession

[(1)   Order 45, rule 3(2), shall not apply in relation to an order for possession under this Order but no writ of possession to enforce such an order shall be issued after the expiry of three months from the date of the order without the leave of the Court.

An application for leave may be made ex parte unless the Court otherwise directs.]

(2)   The writ of possession shall be in Form No 66A.]

Commencement   4 July 1977 (para (1)); 20 July 1970 (remainder).
Amendments   See the note to Order 113, r 1.
Para (1): substituted by SI 1977/960, r 6(6).
Cross references   See CCR Order 24, r 6.

[Order 113, r 8 Setting aside order

[The Court may, on such terms as it thinks just], set aside or vary any order made in proceedings under this Order.]

Commencement   20 July 1970.
Amendments   See the note to Order 113, r 1.
Words from the beginning to "as it thinks just" substituted by SI 1986/2289, r 14(4).
Cross references   See CCR Order 24, r 7.

[ORDER 114
REFERENCES TO THE EUROPEAN COURT

Order 114, r 1 Interpretation

In this Order—

"the Court" means the court by which an order is made and includes the Court of Appeal;

"the European Court" means the Court of Justice of the European Communities; and

"order" means an order referring a question to the European Court for a preliminary ruling under Article 177 of the Treaty establishing the European Economic Community, Article 150 of the Treaty establishing the European Atomic Energy Community or Article 41 of the Treaty establishing the European Coal and Steel Community[, or for a ruling on the interpretation of [any of the instruments referred to in section 1(1) of the Civil Jurisdiction and Judgments Act 1982 or in section 1 of the Contracts (Applicable Law) Act 1990]].]

Commencement 1 January 1973.
Amendments Order 114 inserted by SI 1972/1898, r 11.
In definition "order" words from ", or for a ruling" to the end inserted by SI 1983/1181, r 21, words from "any of the instruments" to "Contracts (Applicable Law) Act 1990" therein substituted by SI 1990/2599, r 20.
Cross references See CCR Order 19, r 15(1).

[Order 114, r 2 Making of order

(1) An order may be made by the Court of its own motion at any stage in a cause or matter, or on application by a party before or at the trial or hearing thereof.

(2) Where an application is made before the trial or hearing, it shall be made by motion.

(3) In the High Court no order shall be made except by a judge in person.]

Commencement 1 January 1973.
Amendments See the note to Order 114, r 1.
Cross references See CCR Order 19, r 15(2), (6).
Forms Order for references (No 109).

[Order 114, r 3 Schedule to order to set out request for ruling

An order shall set out in a schedule the request for the preliminary ruling of the European Court, and the Court may give directions as to the manner and form in which the schedule is to be prepared.]

Commencement 1 January 1973.
Amendments See the note to Order 114, r 1.
Cross references See CCR Order 19, r 15(3).

[Order 114, r 4 Stay of proceedings pending ruling

The proceedings in which an order is made shall, unless the Court otherwise orders, be stayed until the European Court has given a preliminary ruling on the question referred to it.]

Commencement   1 January 1973.
Amendments   See the note to Order 114, r 1.
Cross references   See CCR Order 19, r 15(4).

[Order 114, r 5 Transmission of order to the European Court

When an order has been made, the Senior Master shall send a copy thereof to the Registrar of the European Court; but in the case of an order made by the High Court, he shall not do so, unless the Court otherwise orders, until the time for appealing against the order has expired or, if an appeal is entered within that time, until the appeal has been determined or otherwise disposed of.]

Commencement   1 January 1973.
Amendments   See the note to Order 114, r 1.
Cross references   See CCR Order 19, r 15(5).

[Order 114, r 6 Appeals from orders made by High Court

An order made by the High Court shall be deemed to be a final decision, and accordingly an appeal against it shall lie to the Court of Appeal without leave; but the period within which a notice of appeal must be served under Order 59, rule 4(1), shall be 14 days.]

Commencement   1 January 1973.
Amendments   See the note to Order 114, r 1.

[ORDER 115
[CONFISCATION AND FORFEITURE IN CONNECTION WITH CRIMINAL PROCEEDINGS]

[I DRUG TRAFFICKING OFFENCES ACT] [AND CRIMINAL JUSTICE (INTERNATIONAL CO-OPERATION) ACT 1990]

Order 115, r 1 Interpretation

(1)　In this Part of this Order, "the Act" means the Drug Trafficking Offences Act 1986 and a section referred to by number means the section so numbered in the Act.

(2)　Expressions used in this Part of this Order which are used in the Act have the same meanings in this Part of this Order as in the Act.]

Commencement　3 April 1989.
Amendments　Order 115 was added by SI 1986/2289, r 17.
In the heading to Order 115, words from "Confiscation" to "Proceedings" substituted by SI 1991/1884, r 21; words "I Drug Trafficking Offences Act" substituted by SI 1989/386, r 4; words "and Criminal Justice (International Co-operation) Act 1990" added by SI 1991/1884, r 22.
This rule was substituted by SI 1989/386, r 4.

[Order 115, r 2 Assignment of proceedings

[Subject to rule 12,] the jurisdiction of the High Court under the Act shall be exercised by a judge of the Chancery Division or of the Queen's Bench Division in chambers.]

Commencement　12 January 1987.
Amendments　See the first note to Order 115, r 1.
Words "Subject to rule 12," inserted by SI 1988/298, r 23.
Definitions　The Act: Drug Trafficking Offences Act 1986.

[Order 115, r 3 Application for restraint order or charging order

(1)　An application for a restraint order under section 8 or for a charging order under section 9 (to either of which may be joined an application for the appointment of a receiver) may be made by the prosecutor ex parte by originating motion.

(2)　An application under paragraph (1) shall be supported by an affidavit, which shall:—

(a)　state the grounds for believing that the defendant has benefited from drug trafficking;

(b)　state, as the case may be, either that proceedings have been instituted against the defendant for a drug trafficking offence (giving particulars of the offence) and that they have not been concluded or [that, whether by the laying of an information or otherwise, a person is to be charged with such an offence];

(c)　to the best of the deponent's ability, give full particulars of the realisable property in respect of which the order is sought and specify the person or persons holding such property;

(d)　where proceedings have not been instituted, verify that the prosecutor is to have the conduct of the proposed proceedings;

(e)　where proceedings have not been instituted, indicate when it is intended that they should be instituted.

(3)   An originating motion under paragraph (1) shall be entitled in the matter of the defendant, naming him, and in the matter of the Act, and all subsequent documents in the matter shall be so entitled.

(4)   Unless the Court otherwise directs, an affidavit under paragraph (2) may contain statements of information or belief with the sources and grounds thereof.]

Commencement 12 January 1987.
Amendments See the first note to Order 115, r 1.
Para (2): in sub-para (b) words from "that, whether by the laying" to the end substituted by SI 1989/386, r 5.
Definitions Sections 8, 9: Drug Trafficking Offences Act 1986, ss 8, 9.
The Act: Drug Trafficking Offences Act 1986.

[Order 115, r 4 Restraint order and charging order

(1)   A restraint order may be made subject to conditions and exceptions, including but not limited to conditions relating to the indemnifying of third parties against expenses incurred in complying with the order, and exceptions relating to living expenses and legal expenses of the defendant, but the [prosecutor] shall not be required to give an undertaking to abide by any order as to damages sustained by the defendant as a result of the restraint order.

(2)   Unless the Court otherwise directs, a restraint order made ex parte shall have effect until a day which shall be fixed for the hearing inter partes of the application and a charging order shall be an order to show cause, imposing the charge until such day.

(3)   Where a restraint order is made the prosecutor shall serve copies of the order and of the affidavit in support on the defendant and on all other named persons restrained by the order and shall notify all other persons or bodies affected by the order of its terms.

(4)   Where a charging order is made the prosecutor shall . . . serve copies of the order and of the affidavit in support on the defendant and, where the property to which the order relates is held by another person, on that person and shall serve a copy of the order on such of the persons or bodies specified in Order 50, rule 2(1)(b) to (d) as shall be appropriate.]

Commencement 12 January 1987.
Amendments See the first note to Order 115, r 1.
Para (1): word "prosecutor" substituted by SI 1989/1307, r 5.
Para (4): words omitted revoked by SI 1990/492, r 5.

[Order 115, r 5 Discharge or variation of order

(1)   Any person or body on whom a restraint order or a charging order is served or who is notified of such an order may apply by summons to discharge or vary the order.

(2)   The summons and any affidavit in support shall be lodged with the court and served on the prosecutor and, where he is not the applicant, on the defendant, not less than two clear days before the date fixed for the hearing of the summons.

(3)   Upon the court being notified that proceedings for the offences have been concluded or that the amount payment of which is secured by a charging order has been paid into court, any restraint order or charging order, as the case may be, shall be discharged.]

Commencement 12 January 1987.
Amendments See the first note to Order 115, r 1.

[Order 115, r 6 Further application by prosecutor

(1)　Where a restraint order or a charging order has been made the prosecutor may apply by summons, or, where the case is one of urgency, ex parte:—
 (a)　to discharge or vary such order, or
 (b)　for a restraint order or a charging order in respect of other realisable property, or
 (c)　for the appointment of a receiver.

(2)　An application under paragraph (1) shall be supported by an affidavit which, where the application is for a restraint order or a charging order, shall to the best of the deponent's ability give full particulars of the realisable property in respect of which the order is sought and specify the person or persons holding such property.

(3)　The summons and affidavit in support shall be lodged with the court and served on the defendant and, where one has been appointed in the matter, on the receiver, not less than two clear days before the date fixed for the hearing of the summons.

(4)　Rule 4(3) and (4) shall apply to the service of restraint orders and charging orders respectively made under this rule on persons other than the defendant.]

Commencement　12 January 1987.
Amendments　See the first note to Order 115, r 1.

[Order 115, r 7 Realisation of property

(1)　An application by the prosecutor under section 11 shall, where there have been proceedings against the defendant in the High Court, be made by summons and shall otherwise be made by originating motion.

(2)　The summons or originating motion, as the case may be, shall be served with the evidence in support not less than 7 days before the date fixed for the hearing of the summons on:—
 (a)　the defendant,
 (b)　any person holding any interest in the realisable property to which the application relates, and
 (c)　the receiver, where one has been appointed in the matter.

(3)　The application shall be supported by an affidavit, which shall, to the best of the deponent's ability, give full particulars of the realisable property to which it relates and specify the person or persons holding such property, and a copy of the confiscation order, of any certificate issued by the Crown Court under section 4(2) and of any charging order made in the matter shall be exhibited to such affidavit.

(4)　The court may, on an application under section 11, exercise the power conferred by section 12(1) to direct the making of payments by the receiver.]

Commencement　12 January 1987.
Amendments　See the first note to Order 115, r 1.
Definitions　Sections 4(2), 11, 12(1): Drug Trafficking Offences Act 1986, ss 4(2), 11, 12(1).

[Order 115, r 8 Receivers

(1)　Subject to the provisions of this rule, the provisions of Order 30, rules 2 to 8 shall apply where a receiver is appointed in pursuance of a charging order or under section 8 or 11.

(2)　Where the receiver proposed to be appointed has been appointed receiver in other proceedings under the Act, it shall not be necessary for an affidavit of fitness to be sworn or for the receiver to give security, unless the Court otherwise orders.

(3)   Where a receiver has fully paid the amount payable under the confiscation order and any sums remain in his hands, he shall apply by summons for directions as to the distribution of such sums.

(4)   A summons under paragraph (3) shall be served with any evidence in support not less than 7 days before the date fixed for the hearing of the summons on:—
    (a)   the defendant, and
    (b)   any other person who held property realised by the receiver.]

Commencement   12 January 1987.
Amendments   See the first note to Order 115, r 1.
Definitions   Section 8 or 11: Drug Trafficking Offences Act 1986, ss 8, 11.
The Act: Drug Trafficking Offences Act 1986.

[Order 115, r 9 Certificate of inadequacy

(1)   The defendant may apply by summons for a certificate under section 14(1).

(2)   A summons under paragraph (1) shall be served with any supporting evidence not less than 7 days before the date fixed for the hearing of the summons on the prosecutor and on the receiver, where one has been appointed in the matter.]

Commencement   12 January 1987.
Amendments   See the first note to Order 115, r 1.
Definitions   Section 14(1): Drug Trafficking Offences Act 1986, s 14(1).

[Order 115, r 10 Compensation

An application for an order under section 19 shall be made by summons, which shall be served, with any supporting evidence, on the person alleged to be in default and on the relevant authority under section 19(4) not less than 7 days before the date fixed for the hearing of the summons.]

Commencement   12 January 1987.
Amendments   See the first note to Order 115, r 1.
Definitions   Section 19: Drug Trafficking Offences Act 1986, s 19.

[Order 115, r 11 Disclosure of information

(1)   An application by the prosecutor under section 30 shall be made by summons, which shall state the nature of the order sought and whether material sought to be disclosed is to be disclosed to a receiver appointed under section 8 or 11 or in pursuance of a charging order or to a person mentioned in section 30(8).

(2)   The summons and affidavit in support shall be served on the authorised Government Department in accordance with Order 77, rule 4 not less than 7 days before the date fixed for the hearing of the summons.

(3)   The affidavit in support of an application under paragraph (1) shall state the grounds for believing that the conditions in section 30(4) and, if appropriate, section 30(7) are fulfilled.]

Commencement   12 January 1987.
Amendments   See the first note to Order 115, r 1.
Definitions   Sections 8, 11, 30: Drug Trafficking Offences Act 1986, ss 8, 11, 30.

[Order 115, r 12 Exercise of powers under sections 24A and [26A]

The powers conferred on the High Court by sections 24A and [26A] may be exercised by a judge in chambers and a master of the Queen's Bench Division.]

Commencement   4 April 1988.
Amendments   See the first note to Order 115, r 1.
This rule was added by SI 1988/298, r 24.
References to "26A" in the rule heading and the text substituted by SI 1989/386, r 6.
Definitions   Sections 24A and 26A: Drug Trafficking Offences Act 1986, ss 24A, 26A.

[Order 115, r 13 Application for registration

An application for registration of an order specified in an Order in Council made under section 24A or of an external confiscation order under section [26A(1)] may be made ex parte.]

Commencement   4 April 1988.
Amendments   See the first note to Order 115, r 1.
This rule was added by SI 1988/298, r 24.
Reference to "26A(1)" substituted by SI 1989/386, r 7.
Definitions   Sections 24A, 26A(1): Drug Trafficking Offences Act 1986, ss 24A, 26A(1).

[Order 115, r 14 Evidence in support of application under section 24A

An application for registration of an order specified in an Order in Council made under section 24A must be supported by an affidavit—
  (i)   exhibiting the order or a certified copy thereof, and
  (ii) stating, to the best of the deponent's knowledge, particulars of what property the person against whom the order was made holds in England and Wales, giving the source of the deponent's knowledge.]

Commencement   4 April 1988.
Amendments   See the first note to Order 115, r 1.
This rule was added by SI 1988/298, r 24.
Definitions   Section 24A: Drug Trafficking Offences Act 1986, s 24A.

[Order 115, r 15 Evidence in support of application under section [26A(1)]

[(1)] [An application for registration of an external confiscation order must be supported by an affidavit—
  (a)   exhibiting the order or a verified or otherwise duly authenticated copy thereof and, where the order is not in the English language, a translation thereof into English certified by a notary public or authenticated by affidavit, and
  (b)   stating—
      (i)   that the order is in force and is not subject to appeal,
      (ii) where the person against whom the order was made did not appear in the proceedings, that he received notice thereof in sufficient time to enable him to defend them,
      (iii) in the case of money, either that at the date of the application the sum payable under the order has not been paid or the amount which remains unpaid, as may be appropriate, or, in the case of other property, the property which has not been recovered, and
      (iv) to the best of the deponent's knowledge, particulars of what property the person against whom the order was made holds in England and Wales, giving the source of the deponent's knowledge.

[(2)   Unless the Court otherwise directs, an affidavit for the purposes of this rule may contain statements of information or belief with the sources and grounds thereof.]]

Commencement   1 October 1991 (para (2)); 4 April 1988 (remainder).
Amendments   See the first note to Order 115, r 1.
This rule was added by SI 1988/298, r 24.
Rule heading: reference to "26A(1)" substituted by SI 1989/386, r 7.
Para (1): numbered as such by SI 1991/1884, r 23.
Para (2): added by SI 1991/1884, r 23.
Definitions   Section 26A(1): Drug Trafficking Offences Act 1986, s 26A(1).

[Order 115, r 16 Register of orders

(1)   There shall be kept in the Central Office under the direction of [the Master of the Crown Office] a register of the orders registered under the Act.

(2)   There shall be included in such register particulars of any variation or setting aside of a registration [and of any execution issued on a registered order.]

Commencement   4 April 1988.
Amendments   See the first note to Order 115, r 1.
This rule was added by SI 1988/298, r 24.
Para (1): words "the Master of the Crown Office" substituted by SI 1991/1884, r 24.
Para (2): words "and of any execution issued on a registered order" substituted by SI 1989/1307, r 6.
Definitions   The Act: Drug Trafficking Offences Act 1986.

[Order 115, r 17 Notice of registration

(1)   Notice of the registration of an order must be served on the person against whom it was obtained by delivering it to him personally or by sending it to him at his usual or last known address or place of business or in such other manner as the Court may direct.

(2)   Service of such a notice out of the jurisdiction is permissible without leave, and Order 11, rules 5, 6 and 8 shall apply in relation to such a notice as they apply in relation to a writ.

(3)   . . .]

Commencement   4 April 1988.
Amendments   See the first note to Order 115, r 1.
This rule was added by SI 1988/298, r 24.
Para (3): revoked by SI 1991/1884, r 25.

[Order 115, r 18 Application to vary or set aside registration

An application by the person against whom an order was made to vary or set aside the registration of an order must be made to a judge by summons supported by affidavit.]

Commencement   4 April 1988.
Amendments   See the first note to Order 115, r 1.
This rule added by SI 1988/298, r 24.

[Order 115, r 19 Enforcement of order

(1)   . . .

(2)   If an application is made under rule 18, an order shall not be enforced until after such application is determined.]

Commencement   4 April 1988.
Amendments   See the first note to Order 115, r 1.
This rule was added by SI 1988/298, r 24.
Para (1): revoked by SI 1991/1884, r 25.

[Order 115, r 20 Variation, satisfaction and discharge of registered order

Upon the court being notified by the applicant for registration that an order which has been registered has been varied, satisfied or discharged, particulars of the variation, satisfaction or discharge, as the case may be, shall be entered in the register.]

Commencement   4 April 1988.
Amendments   See the first note to Order 115, r 1.
This rule was added by SI 1988/298, r 24.

[Order 115, r 21 Rules to have effect subject to Orders in Council

Rules 12 to 20 shall have effect subject to the provisions of the Order in Council made under section 24A or, as the case may be, of the Order in Council made under section 26.]

Commencement   4 April 1988.
Amendments   See the first note to Order 115, r 1.
This rule was added by SI 1988/298, r 24.
Definitions   Sections 24A, 26: Drug Trafficking Offences Act 1986, ss 24A, 26.

[Order 115, r 21A Criminal Justice (International Co-operation) Act 1990: external forfeiture orders

The provisions of this Part of this Order shall, with such modifications as are necessary and subject to the provisions of any Order in Council made under section 9 of the Criminal Justice (International Co-operation) Act 1990, apply to proceedings for the registration and enforcement of external forfeiture orders as they apply to such proceedings in relation to external confiscation orders.

For the purposes of this rule, an external forfeiture order is an order made by a court in a country or territory outside the United Kingdom which is enforceable in the United Kingdom by virtue of any such Order in Council.]

Commencement   1 October 1991.
Amendments   See the first note to Order 115, r 1.
This rule was inserted by SI 1991/1884, r 26.

[II PART VI OF THE CRIMINAL JUSTICE ACT 1988

Order 115, r 22 Interpretation

(1)   In this Part of this Order, "the 1988 Act" means the Criminal Justice Act 1988 and a section referred to by number means the section so numbered in that Act.

(2)   Expressions which are used in this Part of this Order which are used in the 1988 Act have the same meanings in this Part of this Order as in the 1988 Act.]

Commencement   12 October 1988 (insofar as this provision applies to the Criminal Justice Act 1988, ss 96, 97); 3 April 1989 (insofar as it applies to the remaining provisions of the Criminal Justice Act 1988, Pt VI).
Amendments   See the first note to Order 115, r 1.
Order 115, Pt II (rr 22, 23) was inserted by SI 1989/386, r 8.

[Order 115, r 23 Application of Part I of Order 115

Part I of Order 115 (except rule 11) shall apply for the purposes of proceedings under Part VI of the 1988 Act with the necessary modifications and, in particular,–

(a) references to drug trafficking offences and to drug trafficking shall be construed as references to offences to which Part VI of the 1988 Act applies and to committing such an offence;

(b) references to the Drug Trafficking Offences Act 1986 shall be construed as references to the 1988 Act and references to sections 4(2), 8, 9, 11, 12(1), 14(1), 19, 19(4), 26 and 26A of the 1986 Act shall be construed as references to sections 73(6), 77, 78, 80, 81(1), 83(1), 89, 89(5), 96 and 97 of the 1988 Act respectively;

(c) rule 3(2) shall have effect as if the following sub-paragraphs were substituted for sub-paragraphs (a) and (b)—

"(a) state, as the case may be, either that proceedings have been instituted against the defendant for an offence to which Part VI of the 1988 Act applies (giving particulars of the offence) and that they have not been concluded or that, whether by the laying of an information or otherwise, a person is to be charged with such an offence;

(b) state, as the case may be, either that a confiscation order has been made or the grounds for believing that such an order may be made;" and

(d) rule 7(3) shall have effect as if the words "certificate issued by a magistrates' court or the Crown Court" were substituted for the words "certificate issued by the Crown Court".]

Commencement   12 October 1988 (insofar as this provision applies to the Criminal Justice Act 1988, ss 96, 97); 3 April 1989 (insofar as it applies to the remaining provisions of the Criminal Justice Act 1988, Pt VI).
Amendments   See the first note to Order 115, r 1 and the second note to Order 115, r 22.
Definitions   The Act: Criminal Justice Act 1988.

[III   PREVENTION OF TERRORISM (TEMPORARY PROVISIONS) ACT 1989

Order 115 r 24 Interpretation

In this Part of this Order—

(a) "the Act" means the Prevention of Terrorism (Temporary Provisions) Act 1989;

(b) "Schedule 4" means Schedule 4 to the Act; and

(c) expressions used have the same meanings as they have in Part III of, and Schedule 4 to, the Act.]

Commencement   1 September 1989.
Amendments   See the first note to Order 115, r 1
Order 115, Pt III (rr 24–36) added by SI 1989/1307, r 7.

[Order 115, r 25 Assignment of proceedings

(1)   Subject to paragraph (2), the jurisdiction of the High Court under the Act shall be exercised by a judge of the Queen's Bench Division or of the Chancery Division in chambers.

(2)   The jurisdiction conferred on the High Court by paragraph 9 of Schedule 4 may also be exercised by a master of the Queen's Bench Division.]

Commencement 1 September 1989.
Amendments See the first note to Order 115, r 1 and the second note to Order 115, r 24.
Definitions The Act: Prevention of Terrorism (Temporary Provisions) Act 1989.

[Order 115, r 26 Application for restraint order

(1)   An application for a restraint order under paragraphs 3 and 4 of Schedule 4 may be made by the prosecutor ex parte by originating motion.

(2)   An application under paragraph (1) shall be supported by an affidavit, which shall:—

(a)   state, as the case may be, either that proceedings have been instituted against a person for an offence under Part III of the Act and that they have not been concluded or that, whether by the laying of an information or otherwise, a person is to be charged with such an offence; and, in either case, give particulars of the offence;

(b)   state, as the case may be, that a forfeiture order has been made in the proceedings or the grounds for believing that such an order may be made;

(c)   to the best of the deponent's ability, give full particulars of the property in respect of which the order is sought and specify the person or persons holding such property and any other persons having an interest in it;

(d)   where proceedings have not been instituted, verify that the prosecutor is to have the conduct of the proposed proceedings;

(e)   where proceedings have not been instituted, indicate when it is intended that they should be instituted.

(3)   An originating motion under paragraph (1) shall be entitled in the matter of the defendant, naming him, and in the matter of the Act, and all subsequent documents in the matter shall be so entitled.

(4)   Unless the Court otherwise directs, an affidavit under paragraph (2) may contain statements of information or belief with the sources and grounds thereof.]

Commencement 1 September 1989.
Amendments See the first note to Order 115, r 1 and the second note to Order 115, r 24.
Definitions Sch 4: Prevention of Terrorism (Temporary Provisions) Act 1989, Sch 4.
The Act: Prevention of Terrorism (Temporary Provisions) Act 1989.

[Order 115, r 27 Restraint Order

(1)   A restraint order may be made subject to conditions and exceptions, including but not limited to conditions relating to the indemnifying of third parties against expenses incurred in complying with the order, and exceptions relating to living expenses and legal expenses of the defendant, but the prosecutor shall not be required to give an undertaking to abide by any order as to damages sustained by the defendant as a result of the restraint order.

(2)   Unless the Court otherwise directs, a restraint order made ex parte shall have effect until a day which shall be fixed for the hearing inter partes of the application.

(3)   Where a restraint order is made the prosecutor shall serve copies of the order and of the affidavit in support on the defendant and on all other persons affected by the order.]

Commencement 1 September 1989.
Amendments See the first note to Order 115, r 1 and the second note to Order 115, r 24.

[Order 115, r 28 Discharge or variation of order

(1) Subject to paragraph (2), an application to discharge or vary a restraint order shall be made by summons.

(2) Where the case is one of urgency, an application under this rule by the prosecutor may be made ex parte.

(3) The application and any affidavit in support shall be lodged with the court and, where the application is made by summons, shall be served on the following persons (other than the applicant)—

(a) the prosecutor;
(b) the defendant; and
(c) all other persons restrained or otherwise affected by the order;

not less than two clear days before the date fixed for the hearing of the summons.

(4) Where a restraint order has been made and has not been discharged, the prosecutor shall notify the court when proceedings for the offence have been concluded, and the court shall thereupon discharge the restraint order.

(5) Where an order is made discharging or varying a restraint order, the applicant shall serve copies of the order of discharge or variation on all persons restrained by the earlier order and shall notify all other persons affected of the terms of the order of discharge or variation.]

Commencement 1 September 1989.
Amendments See the first note to Order 115, r 1 and the second note to Order 115, r 24.

[Order 115, r 29 Compensation

An application for an order under paragraph 7 of Schedule 4 shall be made by summons, which shall be served, with any supporting evidence, on the person alleged to be in default and on the relevant authority under paragraph 7(5) not less than 7 days before the date fixed for the hearing of the summons.]

Commencement 1 September 1989.
Amendments See the first note to Order 115, r 1 and the second note to Order 115, r 24.
Definitions Sch 4: Prevention of Terrorism (Temporary Provisions) Act 1989, Sch 4.

[Order 115, r 30 Application for registration

An application for registration of a Scottish order, a Northern Ireland order or an Islands order may be made ex parte.]

Commencement 1 September 1989.
Amendments See the first note to Order 115, r 1 and the second note to Order 115, r 24.

[Order 115, r 31 Evidence in support of application

[(1)] An application for registration of any such order as is mentioned in rule 30 must be supported by an affidavit—

    (a)   exhibiting the order or a certified copy thereof, and

    (b)   which shall, to the best of the deponent's ability, give particulars of such property in respect of which the order was made as is in England and Wales, and specify the person or persons holding such property.

[(2)   Unless the Court otherwise directs, an affidavit for the purposes of this rule may contain statements of information or belief with the sources and grounds thereof].]

Commencement 1 October 1991 (para (2)); 1 September 1989 (remainder).
Amendments See the first note to Order 115, r 1 and the second note to Order 115, r 24.
Para (1): numbered as such by SI 1991/1884, r 23.
Para (2): added by SI 1991/1884, r 23.

[Order 115, r 32 Register of orders

(1)   There shall be kept in the Central Office under the direction of [the Master of the Crown Office] a register of the orders registered under the Act.

(2)   There shall be included in such register particulars of any variation or setting aside of a registration, and of any execution issued on a registered order.]

Commencement 1 September 1989.
Amendments See the first note to Order 115, r 1 and the second note to Order 115, r 24.
Para (1): words "the Master of the Crown Office" substituted by SI 1991/1884, r 24.
Definitions The Act: Prevention of Terrorism (Temporary Provisions) Act 1989.

[Order 115, r 33 Notice of registration

(1)   Notice of the registration of an order must be served on the person or persons holding the property referred to in rule 31(b) and any other persons appearing to have an interest in that property.

(2)   Service of such a notice out of the jurisdiction is permissible without leave, and Order 11, rules 5, 6 and 8 shall apply in relation to such a notice as they apply in relation to a writ.

(3)   ...]

Commencement 1 September 1989.
Amendments See the first note to Order 115, r 1 and the second note to Order 115, r 24.
Para (3): revoked by SI 1991/1884, r 25.

[Order 115, r 34 Application to vary or set aside registration

An application to vary or set aside the registration of an order must be made to a judge by summons supported by affidavit.

    This rule does not apply to a variation or cancellation under rule 36.]

Commencement 1 September 1989.
Amendments See the first note to Order 115, r 1 and the second note to Order 115, r 24.

[Order 115, r 35 Enforcement of order

(1)   ...

(2)   If an application is made under rule 34, an order shall not be enforced until after such application is determined.

(3)   This rule does not apply to the taking of steps under paragraph 5 or 6 of Schedule 4, as applied by paragraph 9(6) of that Schedule.]

Commencement 1 September 1989.
Amendments See the first note to Order 115, r 1 and the second note to Order 115, r 24.
Para (1): revoked by SI 1991/1884, r 25.
Definitions Sch 4: Prevention of Terrorism (Temporary Provisions) Act 1989, Sch 4.

[Order 115, r 36 Variation and cancellation of registration

If effect has been given (whether in England and Wales or elsewhere) to a Scottish, Northern Ireland or Islands order, or if the order has been varied or discharged by the court by which it was made, the applicant for registration shall inform the court and—

    (a)   if such effect has been given in respect of all the money or other property to which the order applies, or if the order has been discharged by the court by which it was made, registration of the order shall be cancelled;

    (b)   if such effect has been given in respect of only part of the money or other property, or if the order has been varied by the court by which it was made, registration of the order shall be varied accordingly.]

Commencement 1 September 1989.
Amendments See the first note to Order 115, r 1 and the second note to Order 115, r 24.

APPENDIX A
FORMS

(The following is a list of forms contained in Appendix A. Titles in square brackets, (eg, [Writ of Summons ...]) indicate that a Form has been substituted or inserted.)

Form

No 1   [Writ of Summons (Order 6, r 1)]
        (amended by SI 1979/1716, 1982/1111, 1987/1423, 1990/492)

No 8   [Originating summons–general form (Order 7, r 2)]
        (amended by SI 1979/1716, 1980/2000, 1982/1111, 1990/492)

No 10   [Originating summons–expedited form (Order 7, r 2)]
        (amended by SI 1974/1716, 1980/2000, 1982/1111, 1987/1423, 1990/492)

No 11   Ex parte originating summons (Order 7, r 2)
        (amended by SI 1980/2000, 1987/1423)

No 11A [Originating summons for possession under Order 113 (Order 113, r 2)]
        (amended by SI 1970/944, 1977/960, 1980/2000, 1982/1111)

No 12   [Notice of appointment to hear originating summons (Order 28, r 2)]
        (amended by SI 1990/1689)

No 13   Notice of originating motion (Order 8, r 3)
        (amended by SI 1980/2000, 1982/1111)

No 14   [Acknowledgment of Service of Writ of Summons (Order 12, r 3)]
        (amended by SI 1979/1716, 1980/1908, 1982/1111, 1987/1423, 1989/2427)

No 15   [Acknowledgment of Service of Originating summons (Order 10, r 5)]
        (amended by SI 1979/1716, 1982/1111, 1987/1423)

No 17   [Notice to be indorsed on copy of counterclaim (Order 15, r 3(6))]
        (amended by SI 1979/1716)

No 20   [Third party notice claiming contribution or indemnity or other relief or remedy (Order 16)]
        (amended by SI 1979/1716, 1980/2000)

No 21   [Third party notice where question or issue to be determined (Order 16)]
        (amended by SI 1979/1716)

No 23   Notice of payment into court (Order 22, rr 1, 2)
        (amended by SI 1990/1689)

No 24   Notice of acceptance of money paid into court (Order 22, r 3)

No 26   List of documents (Order 24, r 5)

No 27   Affidavit verifying list of documents (Order 24, r 5)

No 28   Writ of subpoena (Order 38, r 14)
        (amended by SI 1971/1955, 1982/1111)

No 29   Writ of subpoena: proceedings in chambers (Order 38, r 14)

No 30   Writ of subpoena issued under enactment (Order 38, r 14)
        (amended by SI 1980/1908

Form

No 31   Summons for examination within jurisdiction of witness before trial (Order 39, r 1)

No 32   Order for examination within jurisdiction of witness before trial (Order 39, r 1)

No 33   Summons for issue of letter of request to judicial authority out of jurisdiction (Order 39, r 2)

No 34   Order for issue of letter of request to judicial authority out of jurisdiction (Order 39, r 2)

No 35   [Letter of request for examination of witness out of jurisdiction (Order 39, r 3)] (amended by SI 1984/1051)

No 36   Summons for appointment of examiner to take evidence of witness out of jurisdiction (Order 39, r 2)

No 37   Order for appointment of examiner to take evidence of witness out of jurisdiction (Order 39, r 2) (amended by SI 1971/1955, 1982/1111)

No 38   Notice of motion (Order 8, r 3)

No 39   Default judgment in action for liquidated demand (Order 13, r 1; Order 19, r 2; Order 42, r 1) (amended by SI 1979/1716)

No 40   Default judgment in action for unliquidated damages (Order 13, r 2; Order 19, r 3; Order 42, r 1) (amended by SI 1979/1716)

No 41   Default judgment in action relating to detention of goods (Order 13, r 3; Order 19, r 4; Order 42, r 1) (amended by SI 1979/1716)

No 42   Default judgment in action for possession of land (Order 13, r 4; Order 19, r 5; Order 42, r 1) (amended by SI 1979/1716)

No 42A   [Order for possession under Order 113 (Order 113, r 6)] (amended by SI 1970/944, 1980/1908)

No 43   Final judgment after assessment of damages, etc (Order 42, r 1)

No 44   Judgment under Order 14 (Order 14, r 3; Order 42, r 1) (amended by SI 1979/1716, 1992/638)

No 45   Judgment after trial before judge without jury (Order 42, r 1)

No 46   Judgment after trial before judge with jury (Order 42, r 1) (amended by SI 1971/1955)

No 47   Judgment after trial before master or referee (Order 42, r 1)

No 48   Judgment after decision of preliminary issue (Order 33, r 7; Order 42, r 1)

No 49   Judgment for liquidated sum against personal representative (Order 42, r 1)

No 50   Judgment for defendant's costs on discontinuance (Order 62, r 10(1))

Form

No 51   Judgment for costs after acceptance of money paid into court (Order 62, r 10(2), (3))

No 52   [Notice of action (Order 15, r 13A)]
            (amended by SI 1986/1187)

No 52A Notice of judgment or order (Order 44, r 3)
            (amended by SI 1979/1716, 1982/1111, 1986/1187)

No 53   [Writ of fieri facias (Order 45, r 12)]
            (amended by SI 1984/1051)

No 54   [Writ of fieri facias on order for costs (Order 45, r 12)]
            (amended by SI 1984/1051)

No 56   [Writ of fieri facias after levy of part (Order 45, r 12)]
            (amended by SI 1984/1051)

No 57   Writ of fieri facias against personal representative (Order 45, r 12)
            (amended by SI 1972/813)

No 58   Writ of fieri facias de bonis ecclesiasticis (Order 45, r 12)

No 59   Writ of sequestrari facias de bonis ecclesiasticis (Order 45, r 12)

No 62   [Writ of fieri facias to enforce Northern Irish or Scottish judgment (Order 71, r 14)]
            (amended by SI 1993/2133)

No 63   Writ of fieri facias to enforce foreign registered judgment (Order 71)
            (amended by SI 1967/1809, 1983/1181)

No 64   Writ of delivery: delivery of goods, damages and costs (Order 45, r 12)

No 65   Writ of delivery: delivery of goods or value, damages, costs (Order 45, r 12)

No 66   Writ of possession (Order 45, r 12)

No 66A [Writ of possession under Order 113 (Order 113, r 7)]
            (amended by SI 1970/944)

No 67   Writ of sequestration (Order 45, r 12)

No 68   Writ of restitution (Order 46, r 1)

No 69   Writ of assistance (Order 46, r 1)

No 71   Notice of renewal of writ of execution (Order 46, r 8)

No 72   Garnishee order to show cause (Order 49, r 1)
            (amended by SI 1976/337, 1981/1734)

No 73   Garnishee order absolute where garnishee owes more than judgment debt (Order 49, rr 1, 4)
            (amended by SI 1980/1908)

No 74   Garnishee order absolute where garnishee owes less than judgment debt (Order 49 rr 1, 4)
            (amended by SI 1979/1725)

Form

No 75   [Charging order: notice to show cause (Order 50, r 1)]
         (amended by SI 1980/629)

No 76   [Charging order absolute (Order 50, r 3)]
         (amended by SI 1980/629)

No 79   Stop order on capital and income of funds in court (Order 50, r 10)

No 80   Affidavit and notice under Order 50 r 11 (Order 50, r 11)

No 81   Order on originating motion restraining transfer of stock, etc (Order 50, r 15)
         (amended by SI 1982/1111)

No 82   Summons for appointment of receiver (Order 51, r 3)

No 83   Order directing summons for appointment of receiver and granting
         injunction meanwhile (Order 51, r 3)

No 84   Order appointing receiver by way of equitable execution [Supreme Court Act
         1981, s 37; (Order 51)]
         (amended by SI 1982/1111)

No 85   Order of committal (Order 52)
         (amended by SI 1986/632)

No 86   [Notice of motion for judicial review (Order 53, r 5)]
         (amended by SI 1980/2000)

No 86A   [Notice of Application for leave to apply for Judicial Review (Order 53, r 3)]
         (amended by SI 1980/2000)

No 86B   [(Notice of Renewal of application for leave to apply for Judicial Review
         (Order 53, r 3(5))]
         (amended by SI 1980/2000)

No 87   Notice of motion for writ of habeas corpus ad subjiciendum (Order 54, r 2)
         (amended by SI 1980/2000)

No 88   Notice directed by Court of adjourned application for writ of habeas corpus
         (Order 54, r 2)
         (amended by SI 1971/1269)

No 89   Writ of habeas corpus ad subjiciendum (Order 54, r 10)
         (amended by SI 1971/1269)

No 90   Notice to be served with writ of habeas corpus ad subjiciendum (Order 54, r 6)
         (amended by SI 1971/1269)

No 91   Writ of habeas corpus ad testificandum (Order 54, r 10)

No 92   Writ of habeas corpus ad respondendum (Order 54, r 10)

No 93   [Order under the Evidence (Proceedings in Other Jurisdictions) Act 1975
         (Order 70, r 1)]
         (amended by SI 1976/337)

No 94   Order for production of documents in marine insurance action (Order 72, r 10)

No 95   Certificate of order against the Crown (Order 77, r 15)

Form

No 96   Certificate of order for costs against the Crown (Order 77, r 15)

No 97   [Summons to grant bail (Order 79, r 9)]
         (amended by SI 1978/251, 1980/2000)

No 97A   [Summons to vary arrangements for bail in a criminal proceeding (Order 79, r 9)]
         (amended by SI 1967/1809, 1978/251, 1980/2000)

No 98   [Order of judge in chambers to release prisoner on bail (Order 79, r 9)]
         (amended by SI 1978/251)

No 98A   [Order of judge in chambers varying arrangements for bail (Order 79, r 9)]
         (amended by SI 1967/1809, 1978/251)

No 99   Order of Court of Appeal to admit prisoner to bail (Order 59, r 20)

No 100   [Notice of bail (Order 79, r 9)]
         (amended by SI 1978/251)

No 101   Written summons [Crown Court] (Order 79, r 10)
         (amended by SI 1971/1955, 1980/2000)

No 103   Witness summons [Crown Court] (Order 79, r 10)
         (amended by SI 1971/1955, 1980/2000)

No 104   Attachment of earnings order under the [Attachment of Earnings Act 1971]
         ([Order 105], r 15)
         (amended by SI 1971/835, 1971/1269, 1978/579)

No 105   Notice under [section 10(2) of the Attachment of Earnings Act 1971] ([Order
         105], r 17)
         (amended by SI 1971/835, 1978/579)

No 109   [Order for reference to the European Court (Order 114, r 2)]
         (amended by SI 1972/1898, 1983/1181, 1988/298)

No 110   [Certificate under section 12 of the Civil Jurisdiction and Judgments Act 1982]
         (amended by SI 1983/1181, 1991/2671)

No 111   [Certificate of Money Provisions contained in a Judgment for Registration under
         Schedule 6 to the Civil Jurisdiction and Judgments Act 1982 (Order 71, r 37)]
         (amended by SI 1983/1181)

No 112   [Certificate issued under Schedule 7 to the Civil Jurisdiction and Judgments
         Act 1982 in respect of Non-Money Provisions (Order 71, r 38)]
         (amended by SI 1983/1181)

APPENDIX B
ADMIRALTY FORMS

(*The following is a list of forms contained in Appendix B Titles in square brackets, (eg, [Writ of summons ...]) indicate that a Form has been substituted or inserted.*)

Form

No 1   [Writ of summons in action in rem (Order 75, r 3)]
          (amended by SI 1979/1716, 1987/1423, 1990/492)

No 2   [Writ of summons in limitation action (Order 75, r 3(3))]
          (amended by SI 1979/1716, 1987/1423, 1990/492)

No 2B   [Acknowledgment of Service of Writ of Summons in Action in rem or
          Limitation Action] (Order 75, r 3(5))
          (amended by SI 1979/1716, 1987/1423, 1990/1689)

No 2C   [Endorsement on Writ Issued when Admiralty and Commercial Registry is
          Closed (Order 6, r 7A)]
          (amended by SI 1990/2599)

No 3   Warrant of arrest (Order 75, r 5(1))

No 5   Praecipe for caveat against arrest (Order 75, r 6)
          (amended by SI 1979/1716)

No 5A   [Praecipe for caveat against arrest (Order 75, r 6(1A))]
          (amended by SI 1990/1689)

No 6   Praecipe for service of writ in rem by Marshal (Order 75, r 8(3))

No 7   Release (Order 75, r 13(1))

No 8   Praecipe for issue of release (Order 75, r 13(6))
          (amended by SI 1987/1423)

No 9   [Praecipe for caveat against release etc (Order 75, r 14)]
          (amended by SI 1984/1051)

No 10   Praecipe for withdrawal of caveat (Order 75, r 15)

No 11   Bail bond (Order 75, r 16)
          (amended by SI 1984/1051)

No 12   Praecipe for commission for appraisement and sale (Order 75, r 23)

No 13   Commission for Appraisement and Sale (Order 75, r 23)
          (amended by SI 1979/1542)

No 14   Release and Warrant of Possession (Order 75)

No 15   [Notice to Consular Officer of Intention to Apply for Warrant of Arrest
          (Order 75, r 5(11))]
          (amended by SI 1975/911)

SCHEDULE 2
(*contains repeals only and is not reproduced in this work*)

SCHEDULE 3
(*contains revocations only and is not reproduced in this work*)

County Court Rules 1981

COUNTY COURT RULES 1981

(SI 1981/1687)

Amendments References to "district judge", "assistant district judge" and "deputy district judge" substituted by virtue of the Courts and Legal Services Act 1990, s 74, throughout these Rules.
Modification References to solicitors etc modified to include references to bodies recognised under the Administration of Justice Act 1985, s 9, by the Solicitors' Incorporated Practices Order 1991, SI 1991/2684, arts 4, 5, Sch 1, throughout these Rules.
Forms References to forms with the prefix N are to the form so numbered in the County Court (Forms) Rules 1982, SI 1982/586. References to forms with the prefix PF are to High Court Practice Forms and with the prefix ChPF are to Chancery Masters' Practice Forms.

ARRANGEMENT OF ORDERS

Order 21   Hearing of action or matter

Order 22   Judgments and orders

Order 27 Attachment of earnings

Part I General

Part II Consolidated attachment of earnings orders

Order 28 Judgment summonses

Order 39 Administration orders

ORDER 1
CITATION, APPLICATION AND INTERPRETATION

Order 1, r 1 Citation

These rules may be cited as the County Court Rules 1981.

Commencement 1 September 1982.

Order 1, r 2 Application of rules

(1) Subject to paragraph (2), these rules shall apply to all proceedings authorised by or under any existing or future Act to be commenced or taken in a county court.

(2) In relation to proceedings of a particular kind in a county court, these rules shall have effect subject to any rules made by an authority other than the rule committee mentioned in [section 75 of the Act] which apply to proceedings of that kind.

Commencement 1 September 1982.
Amendments Para (2): words "section 75 of the Act" substituted by SI 1984/878, r 12, Schedule.
Cross references See RSC Order 1, r 2.

Order 1, r 3 Definitions

In these rules, unless the context otherwise requires—
  "the Act" means the [County Courts Act 1984];
  "address for service" means the address of a place at or to which any document may be delivered or sent for the party giving the address, being—
   (a) in the case of a party in person, his place of residence or business or, if he has no such place within England or Wales, the address of a place within England or Wales at or to which documents for him may be delivered or sent,
   (b) where the party is represented by a solicitor, the business address of the solicitor;
  "defendant" includes respondent;
  ["document exchange" means any document exchange for the time being approved by the Lord Chancellor;]
  "filed" has the meaning assigned to it by Order 2, rule 4;
  "foreign court" means the court to which process is sent by another court;
  "hire-purchase agreement" has the same meaning as in the [Consumer Credit Act 1974];
  "home court" means the court from which process is originally issued;
  "judgment" means the final decision of the court in an action;
  "mental patient" means a person who, by reason of mental disorder within the meaning of the [Mental Health Act 1983] is incapable of managing and administering his property and affairs;
  "order" means the final decision of the court in a matter and also any decision of the court other than a final decision in any proceedings;
  "originating process" means—
   (a) the summons in a default, fixed date or admiralty action, or
   (b) in relation to a garnishee, an order nisi under Order 30, rule 2, or
   (c) an interpleader summons or notice under Order 33, rule 4, 7 or 8, or
   (d) an originating application, petition or request for the entry of an appeal to a county court;

"person under disability" means a person who is a minor or a mental patient;

"plaintiff" includes applicant, petitioner and appellant;

"pre-trial review" means the preliminary consideration of an action or matter under Order 17;

["proper officer" means the district judge or—

    (a) in relation to any act of a formal or administrative character which is not by statute the responsibility of the district judge, and

    (b) in Order 9, rule 3, Order 22, rules 7A and 10, Order 25, rule 8 and Order 27, rules 7, 7A, 8(1B)[, 19(3C) [20[, Order 39, rule 5 and Order 48B, rule 4]]];]

the chief clerk or any other officer of the court acting on his behalf in accordance with directions given by the Lord Chancellor;]

"records of the court" means such records of and in relation to proceedings in the court as the Lord Chancellor may by regulations prescribe;

"recovery of land" means the recovery or delivery of possession of land;

"residence", in relation to a body corporate, means the registered or principal office of the body;

"senior master" means the senior master of [the Queen's Bench Division];

["trial centre" means a county court designated by the Lord Chancellor as a centre for the hearing of trials;]

["value", in relation to an action or claim, shall be construed in accordance with articles 9 and 10 of the High Court and County Courts Jurisdiction Order 1991.]

Commencement 1 September 1982.

Amendments In definition "the Act" words "County Courts Act 1984" substituted by SI 1984/878, r 12, Schedule; definition "document exchange" inserted by SI 1986/636, r 2; in definition "hire-purchase agreement" words "Consumer Credit Act 1974" substituted by SI 1985/566, r 2; in definition "mental patient" words "Mental Health Act 1983" substituted by SI 1983/1716, r 13, Schedule; definition "proper officer" substituted by SI 1991/1126, r 28, words in first (outer) pair of square brackets substituted by SI 1991/1328, r 3, words in second (middle) pair of square brackets substituted by SI 1993/711, r 2, words in third (inner) pair of square brackets substituted by SI 1993/2150, r 2; in definition "senior master" words "the Queen's Bench Division" substituted by SI 1982/1140, r 2; definition "trial centre" inserted by SI 1991/1328, r 11; definition "value" inserted by SI 1991/1126, r 2.

Cross references See RSC Order 1, r 4.

Order 1, r 4 Construction of references to Orders, rules, etc

Unless the context otherwise requires, and subject to rule 5, any reference in these rules to a specified Order, rule or Appendix is a reference to that Order or rule of, or that Appendix to, these rules, and any reference to a specified rule, paragraph or sub-paragraph is a reference to that rule of the Order, that paragraph of the rule or that sub-paragraph of the paragraph in which the reference appears.

Commencement 1 September 1982.
Cross references See RSC Order 1, r 5.

Order 1, r 5 Construction of references to "RSC"

In these rules the abbreviation "RSC" denotes the Rules of the Supreme Court 1965 and any reference to an Order and rule prefixed by "RSC" is a reference to that Order and rule in those rules.

Commencement 1 September 1982.

Order 1, r 6 Application of RSC to county court proceedings

Where by virtue of these rules or [section 76] of the Act or otherwise any provision of the RSC is applied in relation to proceedings in a county court, that provision shall have effect with the necessary modifications and in particular—

(a) rule 8 of this Order shall apply in relation to any power or jurisdiction conferred by that provision on the Court as it applies in relation to any power or jurisdiction conferred by these rules on the court;

(b) any reference in that provision to a master, [district judge] of the principal registry of the Family Division, the Admiralty [district judge], or a [district judge] . . . or taxing officer shall be construed as a reference to the [district judge] of the county court;

(c) any reference in that provision to an application by summons shall be construed as a reference to an application on notice under Order 13 of these rules;

(d) any reference in that provision to [an office of the Supreme Court having the conduct of the business of a division or court] or a district registry shall be construed as a reference to the county court office.

Commencement 1 September 1982.
Amendments Words "section 76" substituted by SI 1984/878, r 12, Schedule; words omitted revoked by SI 1983/1716, r 13, Schedule; words from "an office" to "division or court" substituted by SI 1984/878, r 2.

Order 1, r 7 Construction of references to other enactments

Unless the context otherwise requires, any reference in these rules to an enactment shall be construed as a reference to that enactment as amended, extended or applied by or under any other enactment.

Commencement 1 September 1982.
Cross references See RSC Order 1, r 5.

Order 1, r 8 Exercise of jurisdiction of court

Where any jurisdiction or power is conferred by any provision of these rules on the court, then—

(a) if the jurisdiction or power is to be exercised at the trial or hearing of an action or matter, it may be exercised by the judge or [district judge] before whom the trial or hearing takes place; and

(b) if the jurisdiction or power is to be exercised at any other stage of the proceedings, it may be exercised either by the judge or by the [district judge].

Commencement September 1982.

Order 1, r 9 Computation of time

(1) Any period of time fixed by these rules or by a judgment, order or direction for doing any act shall be reckoned in accordance with the following provisions of this rule.

[(2) Where the act is required to be done not less than a specified period before a specified date, the period starts immediately after the date on which the act is done and ends immediately before the specified date.]

[(3)] Where the act is required to be done within a specified period after or from a specified date, the period starts immediately after that date.

[(4)] Where, apart from this paragraph, the period in question being a period of 3 days or less would include a day on which the court office is closed, that day shall be excluded.

[(5)] Where the time so fixed for doing an act in the court office expires on a day on which the office is closed, and for that reason the act cannot be done on that day, the act shall be in time if done on the next day on which the office is open.

Commencement 1 September 1982.
Amendments Para (2): substituted, for paras (2), (3) as originally enacted, by SI 1982/1140, r 3(a).
Para (3)–(5): originally paras (4)–(6), renumbered as paras (3)–(5) by SI 1982/1140, r 3(b).
Cross references See RSC Order 3, rr 2–4.

Order 1, r 10 Cost of repairs to be treated as liquidated claim in road accident case

A claim in an action for the cost of repairs executed to a vehicle or to any property in, on or abutting a highway in consequence of damage which it is alleged to have sustained in an accident due to the defendant's negligence shall, unless the court otherwise orders, be treated as a liquidated demand for the purposes of these rules.

Commencement 1 September 1982.

Order 1, r 11 Application of rules to conditional sale agreements

The provisions of these rules relating to hire-purchase agreements shall have effect in relation to conditional sale agreements within the meaning of [section 189(1) of the Consumer Credit Act 1974 with such modifications as the circumstances may require].

Commencement 1 September 1982.
Amendments Words from "section 189(1)" to the end substituted by SI 1985/566, r 3.

[Order 1, r 12 Notices about hearings

References in these rules to giving notice of a day fixed for a hearing shall include notice of the time of the hearing.]

Commencement 1 July 1991.
Amendments This rule was inserted by SI 1991/1126, r 22.

[Order 1, r 13 Automatic transfer

Where under these rules provision is made for automatic transfer to the defendant's or debtor's home court—
  (a) "defendant's home court" means the county court for the district in which is situated the defendant's address as shown on the summons (or, where there are two or more defendants, the first defendant's address);
  (b) "debtor's home court" means the county court for the district in which is situated the debtor's address as shown on the application to which the provision relates;
  (c) automatic transfer will not take place if the defendant's or debtor's address is not situated within England and Wales,

and, where proceedings are transferred automatically, "the proper officer" means the proper officer of the defendant's or debtor's home court.]

Commencement 1 July 1991.
Amendments This rule was inserted by SI 1991/1126, r 39.

ORDER 2
OFFICES

[PART I—GENERAL]

Amendments   Words "Part I—General" inserted by SI 1989/1838, r 54.

Order 2, r 1 Courts to have offices

Every court shall have an office or, if the Lord Chancellor so directs, two or more offices, situated at such place or places as he may direct, for the transaction of the business of the court.

Commencement   1 September 1982.

Order 2, r 2 Days of opening

(1)   Every court office or, if a court has two or more offices, at least one of those offices, shall be open on every day of the year except—
- (a) Saturdays and Sundays,
- (b) the day before Good Friday from noon onwards and Good Friday,
- (c) the Tuesday after the spring holiday,
- [(d) Christmas Eve or—
  - (i) if that day is a Saturday, then 23rd December,
  - (ii) if that day is a Sunday, then 22nd December,]
- (e) Christmas Day and, if that day is a Friday or Saturday, then 28th December,
- (f) bank holidays, and
- (g) such other days as the Lord Chancellor may by general or special order direct.

(2)   In the foregoing paragraph "bank holiday" means a bank holiday in England and Wales under the Banking and Financial Dealings Act 1971 and "spring holiday" means the bank holiday on the last Monday in May or any day appointed instead of that day under section 1(2) of that Act.

Commencement   1 September 1982.
Amendments   Para (1): sub-para (d) substituted by SI 1991/1882, r 4.
Cross references   See RSC Order 64, r 7(1).

Order 2, r 3 Hours of opening

Subject to rule 2(1)(b), the hours during which any court office is open to the public shall be such as the Lord Chancellor may by general or special order direct.

Commencement   1 September 1982.
Cross references   See RSC Order 64, rr 7(2) 8.

Order 2, r 4 Filing of documents

In these rules any reference to filing a document is a reference to filing it in the court office by delivering it to the proper officer for entry by him in the records of the court.

Commencement   1 September 1982.

Order 2, r 5 Conduct of business by post

(1)   Any act that may be done by a party in the office of a county court by attendance at the office may be done by post, provided that the party sends to the court office by prepaid post in an envelope addressed to the proper officer—

(a)   such documents as he would have been required to produce at the court office if he had attended, and

(b)   any court fees which are payable and any money which is to be paid or tendered to a witness in accordance with Order 20, rule 12, or to a judgment debtor in accordance with Order 28, rule 2(4) or 4(2), and

(c)   an envelope addressed to himself,

and they are duly received by the proper officer.

[(1A) References in paragraph (1) to the conduct of business by post and to the sending of documents by prepaid post shall include in any case where the court is a member of a document exchange and the party is represented by a solicitor references to the conduct of business and to the sending of documents through a document exchange.]

(2)   Nothing in this rule shall affect any duty of a party to be present at any proceedings before the judge or the [district judge] in court or in chambers.

Commencement   28 April 1986 (para (1A)); 1 September 1982 (remainder).
Amendments   Para (1A): inserted by SI 1986/636, r 3.
Cross references   See RSC Order 1, r 10.

[PART II SUMMONS PRODUCTION CENTRE]

Order 2, r 6 Interpretation

In this Part of this Order, unless the context otherwise requires,—

"the Centre" means the summons production centre established under rule 7 and "appropriate officer" means the officer in charge of the Centre or another officer of the Centre acting on his behalf;

"Centre number" means the number or reference allotted under rule 8(3); and

"Centre user" means a plaintiff or solicitor who, in accordance with rule 8, has been given permission to commence proceedings through the Centre and from whom such permission has not been withdrawn.]

Commencement   1 December 1989.
Amendments   Order 2, Part II (rr 6–12) was inserted by SI 1989/1838, r 55.

[Order 2, r 7 Establishment of the Centre

(1)   There shall be a summons production centre situated at such place or places as the Lord Chancellor may determine and having such functions relating to the production of summonses and other related matters as he may direct.

(2)   For any purpose connected with the exercise of the Centre's functions—

(a)   the Centre shall be deemed to be part of the office of the court whose name appears on the summons to which the functions relate or in whose name the summons is requested to be issued, and

(b)   any officer of the Centre shall, in exercising its functions, be deemed to act as the proper officer of that court, and these rules shall have effect accordingly.]

Commencement 1 December 1989.
Amendments See the note to Order 2, r 6.

[Order 2, r 8 Issue of summons through the Centre

(1)   A plaintiff or solicitor who desires to commence proceedings through the Centre for the recovery of debt shall give notice of his desire to the appropriate officer.

(2)   Where notice is given under paragraph (1) and the appropriate office so permits, the Centre user may, subject to paragraph (4), commence proceedings through the Centre in accordance with the provisions of this Part of this Order.

(3)   The appropriate office shall allot to a Centre user a distinguishing number or reference and send notice thereof to the Centre user.

(4)   The appropriate officer may at any time withdraw permission given under paragraph (2) and, where he does so, he shall give notice of the withdrawal to the Centre user.]

Commencement 1 December 1989.
Amendments See the note to Order 2, r 6.

[Order 2, r 9 Filing of documents

(1)   Where by or under these rules any document is required to be filed before the issue of a summons and the summons is to be produced by the Centre, that requirement shall be deemed to be satisfied if the information which would be contained in the document is delivered to the Centre in computer-readable form.

(2)   For the purposes of paragraph (1), information which would be contained in a document relating to one case may be combined with information of the same nature relating to another case.

(3)   Information furnished to the Centre shall begin with the Centre number allotted to the Centre user, and he shall be deemed, unless the contrary appears, to have authorised the giving of information beginning with that number.]

Commencement 1 December 1989.
Amendments See the note to Order 2, r 6.

[Order 2, r 10 Security

A Centre user shall not divulge a Centre number allotted to him except to a solicitor authorised to issue proceedings on his behalf.]

Commencement 1 December 1989.
Amendments See the note to Order 2, r 6.

[Order 2, r 11 Court documents

(1)   Where by or under these rules any document is required to be served on any person prior to or immediately after the issue of a summons then, where the summons

is or is to be produced by the Centre, the document may be served by the appropriate officer sending it to him by post and Order 7, rule 10 shall apply, with any necessary modifications, where a document is served in accordance with this paragraph.

(2)   Where by or under these rules or by virtue of any order a document containing information stored in the Centre is required to be produced, that requirement shall be deemed to be satisfied if a copy of the document is produced from the computer records kept by the Centre for storing such information.]

Commencement 1 December 1989.
Amendments See the note to Order 2, r 6.

[Order 2, r 12 Venue

Nothing in this Part of this Order shall affect the provisions of these rules relating to the venue—
    (a)   for bringing particular proceedings, or
    (b)   for hearing or disposing of an action after the issue of a summons.]

Commencement 1 December 1989.
Amendments See the note to Order 2, r 6.

ORDER 3
COMMENCEMENT OF PROCEEDINGS

Order 3, r 1 Proceedings by action

Subject to the provisions of any Act or rule, all proceedings authorised to be brought in a county court; where the object of the proceedings is to obtain relief against any person or to compel any person to do or abstain from doing any act, shall be brought by action and commenced by plaint.

Commencement 1 September 1982.
Cross references See RSC Order 5, r 2.

Order 3, r 2 Classes of action

(1)   An action in which a claim is made for any relief other than the payment of money shall be a fixed date action.

(2)   Except as otherwise provided by these rules, every other action shall be a default action.

(3)   Nothing in this rule applies to an Admiralty action . . . .

Commencement 1 September 1982.
Amendments Para (3): words omitted revoked by SI 1993/2175, r 13.

[Order 3, r 3 Commencement of action

(1)   Subject to [paragraphs (1A) and (1B)], a plaintiff desiring to commence a default or fixed date action shall file a request for the issue of a summons, together with the particulars of claim and copies required by Order 6.

[(1A) If the plaintiff so desires and the proper officer so allows, the summons may be prepared by the plaintiff and in that event the summons with a copy for each defendant shall be filed by the plaintiff with the documents mentioned in paragraph (1) and, where service is to be effected otherwise than by an officer of the court, a copy of the summons shall be filed for the court instead of a request.]

[(1B) Without prejudice to paragraph (1A), the summons in an action for recovery of land, including one in which the mortgagee under a mortgage of land claims possession of the mortgaged land, shall be prepared by the plaintiff and in that event the summons with a copy for each defendant shall be filed by the plaintiff with the documents mentioned in paragraph (1) and, where service is to be effected otherwise than by an officer of the court, a copy of the summons shall be filed for the court instead of a request.]

(2)   On the filing of the documents mentioned in paragraph (1) or paragraph (1A) the proper officer shall—
    [(a)   enter a plaint in the records of the court and in the case of a fixed date action to which Order 17, rule 11 does not apply fix the return day;]
    (b)   if necessary, prepare a summons;
    (bb) issue the summons and make any necessary copies;
    (c)   annex to, or incorporate in, the summons and every copy so made a copy of the particulars of claim and also annex to every copy of the summons for service [a copy of any documents filed under Order 6, rule 1(5) and] a form of admission, defence and counter-claim, and,

(d) deliver to the plaintiff—
(i)   a plaint note and
(ii) if the summons is to be served otherwise than by an officer of the court, the summons and all necessary copies, with any documents required to be annexed thereto, for service in accordance with Order 7.

[(3) In the case of a fixed date action to which Order 17, rule 11 does not apply, the return day shall, unless the court otherwise directs or paragraph (4) applies, be a day fixed for the pre-trial review.]

(4) Paragraph (3) shall not apply to an action for the recovery of land unless a claim is joined for some relief other than the payment of mesne profits or arrears of rent or for moneys secured by a mortgage or charge.

[(5) Where a summons is to be served out of England and Wales, the plaintiff shall certify in his request for the issue of the summons that the conditions of paragraph (6) are satisfied.

(6) No summons shall be served out of England and Wales unless
(a) each claim made in the particulars of claim is either—
(i)   one which by virtue of the Civil Jurisdiction and Judgments Act 1982 the court has power to hear and determine, or
(ii) one which by virtue of any other enactment a county court has power to hear and determine notwithstanding that the person against whom the claim is made is not within England and Wales or that the wrongful act, neglect or default giving rise to the claim did not take place within England and Wales; or
(b) leave to serve the summons out of England and Wales is given under Order 8.

(7) Where a claim made in the particulars of claim is one which the court has power to hear and determine by virtue of the Civil Jurisdiction and Judgments Act 1982, the particulars shall contain a statement that the court has power under that Act to hear and determine the claim, and that no proceedings involving the same cause of action are pending between the parties in Scotland, Northern Ireland or another Convention territory.

(8) For the purposes of this rule, "Convention territory" means the territory or territories of any Contracting State, as defined by section 1(3) of the Civil Jurisdiction and Judgments Act 1982, to which [the Brussels Conventions or the Lugano Convention] as defined in section 1(1) of that Act apply.]]

Commencement 1 November 1993 (para (1B)); 1 July 1991 (para (1A)); 1 October 1990 (para (3)); 1 January 1987 (paras (5)–(8)); 19 May 1985 (remainder).
Amendments This rule was substituted by SI 1985/566, r 11.
Para (1): words in square brackets substituted by SI 1993/2175, r 2.
Para (1A): further substituted by SI 1991/1126, r 9.
Para (1B): inserted by SI 1993/2175, r 3.
Para (2): sub-para (a) substituted by SI 1990/1764, r 2; in sub-para (c) words "a copy of any documents filed under Order 6, rule 1(5) and" inserted by SI 1989/2426, r 2.
Para (3): further substituted by SI 1990/1764, r 3.
Paras (5)–(7): added by SI 1985/1269, r 2.
Para (8): added by SI 1985/1269, r 2; words "the Brussels Conventions or the Lugano Convention" substituted by SI 1992/1965, r 9.
Cross references See RSC Order 6, r 7.
Forms Default summons (NI(D)–2).
Fixed date summons (N3, N4).

Summons for possession (N5).
Possession summons (forfeiture) (N6).
Request for issue of summons (N201–214).
Notice of issue of summons (N205, 206).
Plaint note (N205A).

Order 3, r 4 Originating applications

(1)   Any proceedings authorised to be brought in a county court and not required by any Act or rule to be commenced otherwise shall be brought by originating application.

(2)   An originating application shall be in writing and shall state—

    (a)   the order applied for and sufficient particulars to show the grounds on which the applicant claims to be entitled to the order;

    (b)   the names and addresses of the persons (if any) intended to be served (in this rule called "respondents") or that no person is intended to be served, and

    (c)   the applicant's address for service.

(3)   The applicant shall file—

    (a)   the originating application together with as many copies as there are respondents; and

    (b)   a request for the issue of the originating application.

(4)   On the filing of the documents mentioned in paragraph (1) the proper officer shall—

    (a)   enter the originating application in the records of the court and fix the return day;

    (b)   prepare a notice to each respondent of the return day and annex to each such notice a copy of the application, and

    (c)   deliver a plaint note to the applicant.

(5)   The return day shall be a day fixed for the hearing of the originating application or, if the court so directs, a day fixed for a pre-trial review.

(6)   Rule 3(2)(d)(ii) of this Order and the provisions of Order 7 shall apply, with the necessary modifications, to the service of an originating application as if the notice of the return day were a fixed date summons.

[(7)   Paragraphs (5) to (8) of rule 3 of this Order shall apply, with the necessary modifications, to an originating application which is to be served out of England and Wales.]

Commencement   1 January 1987 (para (7)); 1 September 1982 (remainder)
Amendments   Para (7): added by SI 1985/1269, r 3.
Cross references   See RSC Order 5, r 3, Order 7.
Forms   Originating application (N393).
Notice to respondent of hearing (N8).

Order 3, r 5 Petitions

Where by any Act or rule proceedings in a county court are required to be by petition, rule 4 shall apply to the petition as it applies to an originating application but with the substitution of "petitioner" for "applicant" and "petition" for "originating application" or "application", wherever those expressions occur.

Commencement 1 September 1982.
Cross references See RSC Order 5, r 5, Order 9.
Forms Petition (N208).

Order 3, r 6 Appeals to county court

(1)   Where by or under any Act an appeal lies to a county court from any order, decision or award of any tribunal or person, then, subject to any special provision made by or under that Act, the provisions of this rule shall apply.

(2)   The appellant shall, within 21 days after the date of the order, decision or award, file—
    (a) a request for the entry of the appeal, stating the names and addresses of the persons intended to be served (in this rule called "respondents") and the appellant's address for service, together with as many copies of the request as there are respondents; and
    (b) a copy of the order, decision or award appealed against.

(3)   Where the provision under which the appeal lies requires the appellant to give to the other parties notice in writing of his intention to appeal and of the grounds of his appeal, the appellant shall file a copy of such notice with the request, and in any other case he shall include in his request a statement of the grounds of the appeal.

(4)   On the filing of the documents mentioned in paragraph (2) and (3) the proper officer shall—
    (a) enter the appeal in the records of the court and fix the return day;
    (b) prepare a notice to each respondent of the day on which the appeal will be heard and annex each copy of the request for the entry of the appeal to a copy of the notice; and
    (c) deliver a plaint note to the appellant.

(5)   The return day shall be a day fixed for the hearing of the appeal by the judge (or, if the [district judge] has jurisdiction to hear the appeal, by the [district judge]) or, if the court so directs, a day fixed for a pre-trial review.

(6)   Rule 3(2)(d)(ii) of this Order and the provisions of Order 7 shall apply, with the necessary modifications, to the service of the request for the entry of the appeal as if the notice of the day of hearing were a fixed date summons.

Commencement 1 September 1982.
Forms Appeal (N209).

Order 3, r 7 Title of proceedings

(1)   Every document filed, issued or served in an action or matter shall bear the title of the action or matter and the distinguishing number allotted to it by the court.

(2)   The title of an action or matter shall contain a reference to any Act, other than the [County Courts Act 1984], by which the court is given power to entertain the proceedings.

Commencement 1 September 1982.
Amendments Para (2): words "County Courts Act 1984" substituted by SI 1984/878, r 12, Schedule.
Forms General title of action (N200).

ORDER 4
VENUE FOR BRINGING PROCEEDINGS

Order 4, r 1 Saving for particular provisions, etc

(1)   The provisions of this Order shall have effect subject to any provision made by any Act or rule (including the rules of this Order) in relation to particular proceedings.

(2)   Nothing in this Order shall be taken as affecting any obligation under Order 8 or otherwise to obtain the leave of the court to serve process out of England and Wales.

Commencement 1 September 1982.

Order 4, r 2 General provisions as to actions

(1)   An action may be commenced—
    (a)   in the court for the district in which the defendant or one of the defendants resides or carries on business, . . .
    (b)   in the court for the district in which the cause of action wholly or in part arose [or
    (c)   in the case of a default action, in any county court.]

(2)   Where the plaintiff sues as assignee, the action shall be commenced only in a court in which the assignor might have commenced the action but for the assignment.

(3), (4) . . .

Commencement 1 September 1982.
Amendments Para (1): in sub-para (a) word omitted revoked and sub-para (c) inserted, by SI 1991/1126, r 40. Paras (3), (4): revoked by SI 1991/1126, r 41.

Order 4, r 3 Proceedings relating to land

Proceedings—
    (a)   for the recovery of land, or
    (b)   for the foreclosure or redemption of any mortgage or, subject to Order 31, rule 4, for enforcing any charge or lien on land, or
    (c)   for the recovery of moneys secured by a mortgage or charge on land,

may be commenced only in the court for the district in which the land or any part thereof is situated.

Commencement 1 September 1982.

Order 4, r 4 Proceedings under Settled Land Act 1925 etc

Proceedings—
    (a)   under the Settled Land Act 1925, or
    (b)   under the Trustee Act 1925, or
    (c)   for the administration of the estate of a deceased person,

may, subject to Order 49, rule 20, be commenced in the court which in the opinion of the plaintiff is the most convenient having regard to the places where the parties reside or carry on business or the subject matter of the proceedings is situated.

Commencement 1 September 1982.

Order 4, r 5 Partnership proceedings

Proceedings for the dissolution or winding up of a partnership shall be commenced in the court for the district or one of the districts in which the partnership business was or is carried on.

Commencement 1 September 1982.

Order 4, r 6 Wrongful interference with goods

(1)   Where proceedings are brought in a county court on one of two or more claims for wrongful interference with goods, and are still pending, any proceedings on another of those claims may, if they could be brought in the High Court, be brought in the same county court, notwithstanding that they would otherwise be outside the jurisdiction (financial or territorial) of that court under the Act or these rules.

(2)   Where goods are the subject of two or more claims under section 6 of the Torts (Interference with Goods) Act 1977 this rule shall apply as if any claim under section 6(3) were a claim for wrongful interference.

Commencement 1 September 1982.

Order 4, r 7 Proceedings by or against judge or [district judge]

(1)   If the court in which but for this rule an action would be commenced is a court of which one of the parties is the judge or [district judge], the action shall not be commenced in that court but in the court which in the opinion of the plaintiff is the nearest or most convenient one of which the party concerned is not the judge or [district judge].

(2)   Nothing in this rule shall affect any alternative right to commence the action in another court of which the party in question is not the judge or [district judge].

Commencement 1 September 1982.

Order 4, r 8 Originating applications and petitions

Proceedings by originating application or petition may be commenced—
- (a)   in the court for the district in which—
    - (i)   the respondent or one of the respondents resides or carries on business, or
    - (ii)   the subject-matter of the proceedings is situated, or
- (b)   if no respondent is named in the application or petition, in the court for the district in which the applicant or petitioner or one of the applicants or petitioners resides or carries on business.

Commencement 1 September 1982.

Order 4, r 9 Appeals to county court

An appeal to a county court from an order, decision or award of any tribunal or person shall be brought in the court for the district in which the order, decision or award was made or given.

Commencement 1 September 1982.

ORDER 5
CAUSES OF ACTION AND PARTIES

Order 5, r 1 Joinder of causes of action

Subject to rule 3, a plaintiff may in one action claim relief against the same defendant in respect of more than one cause of action—

- (a) if the plaintiff claims, and the defendant is alleged to be liable, in the same capacity in respect of all the causes of action, or
- (b) if the plaintiff claims or the defendant is alleged to be liable in the capacity of executor or administrator of an estate in respect of one or more of the causes of action and in his personal capacity but with reference to the same estate in respect of all the others, or
- (c) with the leave of the court.

Commencement 1 September 1982.
Cross references See RSC Order 15, r 1.

Order 5, r 2 Joinder of parties

Subject to rule 3, two or more persons may be joined together in one action as plaintiffs or as defendants—

- (a) where all rights to relief claimed in the action (whether they are joint, several or in the alternative) are in respect of or arise out of the same transaction or series of transactions and if separate actions were brought by or against each of those persons, some common question of law or fact would arise, or
- (b) in any other case, with the leave of the court.

Commencement 1 September 1982.
Cross references See RSC Order 15, r 4(1).

Order 5, r 3 Power to order separate trials

If it appears to the court that the joinder of two or more causes of action, or of two or more plaintiffs or defendants, in the same action may embarrass or delay the trial or is otherwise inconvenient, the court may order separate trials or make such other order as may be expedient.

Commencement 1 September 1982.
Cross references See RSC Order 15, r 5.

Order 5, r 4 Misjoinder or nonjoinder of parties

No action or matter shall be defeated by reason of the misjoinder or nonjoinder of any parties and the court may in any action or matter determine the issues or questions in dispute so far as they affect the rights and interests of the persons who are parties to the action or matter.

Commencement 1 September 1982.
Cross references See RSC Order 15, r 6.

Order 5, r 5 Representative proceedings

(1) Where numerous persons have the same interest in any proceedings, not being such proceedings as are mentioned in rule 6, the proceedings may be begun and,

11

unless the court otherwise orders, continued, by or against any one or more of them as representing all or all except one or more of them.

(2)   At any stage of proceedings under this rule the court may—

    (a)   on the application of a plaintiff who is suing in a representative capacity, appoint him to represent all, or all except one or more, of the persons on whose behalf he sues;

    (b)   on the application of the plaintiff or of a defendant who is sued in a representative capacity, appoint any one or more of the defendants or other persons on whose behalf the defendants are sued to represent all, or all except one or more, of those persons.

Where in the exercise of the power conferred by sub-paragraph (b) the court appoints a person not named as a defendant, it shall make an order under Order 15, rule 1, adding that person as a defendant.

(3)   An application under paragraph (2)—

    (a)   if made under sub-paragraph (a), may be ex parte;

    (b)   if made under sub-paragraph (b), shall be made on notice—

        (i)   where the applicant is the plaintiff, to the person sought to be appointed, or

        (ii)   where the applicant is a defendant, to the plaintiff and to any person, other than the applicant, sought to be appointed,

and in each case the notice shall state the facts on which the applicant relies and the names and addresses or, where appropriate a collective description, of the persons to be represented.

(4)   Where an order is made granting an application under paragraph (2)(b), the proper officer shall send notice of the order to the person to whom notice of the application was given and shall notify other persons affected by the order in such manner as the court may direct.

(5)   A judgment or order given or made in proceedings under this rule shall be binding on all persons on whose behalf the plaintiff sues or, as the case may be, the defendant is sued but shall not be enforced against any person not a party to the proceedings except with the leave of the court.

(6)   An application for leave under paragraph (5) shall be made on notice to the person against whom it is sought to enforce the judgment or order and, notwithstanding that the judgment or order is binding on him, he may dispute liability to have it enforced against him on the ground that by reason of facts and matters particular to his case he is entitled to be exempted from such liability.

Commencement   1 September 1982.
Cross references   See RSC Order 15, r 12.
Forms   Order for party to sue in representative capacity (N210).
Notice to such persons (N211).
Notice to other party (N212).

Order 5, r 6 Representation of person or class

(1)   In any proceedings concerning—

    (a)   the estate of a deceased person,

    (b)   property subject to a trust, or

    (c)   the construction of a written instrument, including a statute,

the court may appoint one or more persons to represent any person (including an unborn person) or class who is or may be interested in or affected by the proceedings, if the person, the class or some member of the class cannot readily be ascertained or cannot be found or if it otherwise appears to the court expedient to exercise this power for the purpose of saving expense.

(2) A judgment or order given or made when a person or persons appointed under paragraph (1) is or are before the court shall be binding on the person or class so represented.

(3) Where, in proceedings to which paragraph (1) applies, a compromise is proposed and some of the persons who are interested in or who may be affected by the compromise (including unborn or unascertained persons) are not parties to the proceedings but—

    (a) there is some person in the same interest before the court who assents to the compromise or on whose behalf the court sanctions the compromise, or

    (b) the absent persons are represented by a person appointed under paragraph (1) who so assents,

the court, if satisfied that the compromise will be for the benefit of the absent persons and that it is expedient to exercise this power, may approve the compromise and order that it shall be binding on the absent persons, and they shall be bound accordingly except where the order has been obtained by fraud or non-disclosure of material facts.

Commencement 1 September 1982.
Cross references See RSC Order 15, r 13.

Order 5, r 7 Representation of estate where no personal representative

(1) Where in any proceedings it appears to the court that a deceased person who was interested in the matter in question in the proceedings has no personal representative, the court may, on the application of any party to the proceedings—

    (a) proceed in the absence of a person representing the estate of the deceased person or

    (b) by order appoint a person to represent the estate for the purpose of the proceedings.

(2) Any such order, and any judgment or order subsequently given or made in the proceedings, shall bind the estate of the deceased person to the same extent as if a personal representative of that person had been a party to the proceedings.

(3) Before making an order under this rule, the court may require notice of the application for the order to be given to such of the persons having an interest in the estate as it thinks fit.

Commencement 1 September 1982.
Cross references See RSC Order 15, r 15.

Order 5, r 8 Proceedings against estates

(1) Where any person against whom an action would have laid has died but the cause of action survives, the action may, if no grant of probate or administration has been made, be brought against the estate of the deceased.

(2) Without prejudice to the generality of paragraph (1), an action brought against "the personal representatives of A.B. deceased" shall be treated, for the purposes of that paragraph, as having been brought against his estate.

(3) An action purporting to have been commenced against a person shall be

treated, if he was dead at its commencement, as having been commenced against his estate in accordance with paragraph (1), whether or not a grant of probate or administration was made before its commencement.

(4)   In any such action as is referred to in paragraph (1) or (3)—

    (a)   the plaintiff shall, in the case of a fixed date action, on or before the return day, or, in the case of a default action, within the time allowed for service of the summons, apply to the court for an order appointing a person to represent the deceased's estate for the purpose of the proceedings or, if a grant of probate or administration has been made, for an order that the personal representative of the deceased be made a party to the proceedings, and in either case for an order that the proceedings be carried on against the person so appointed or, as the case may be, against the personal representative, as if he had been substituted for the estate;

    (b)   the court may, at any stage of the proceedings and on such terms as it thinks just and either of its own motion or on application, make any such order as is mentioned in sub-paragraph (a) and allow such amendments (if any) to be made and make such other order as the court thinks necessary in order to ensure that all matters in dispute in the proceedings may be effectually and completely determined and adjudicated upon.

(5)   Before making an order under paragraph (4) the court may require notice to be given to any insurer of the deceased who has an interest in the proceedings and to such (if any) of the persons having an interest in the estate as it thinks fit.

(6)   Where an order is made under paragraph (4), the person against whom the proceedings are to be carried on shall be served with a copy of the order, together with a copy of the summons in the action, in accordance with the rules applicable to the service of such a summons on a defendant.

(7)   Where no grant of probate or administration has been made, any judgment or order given or made in the proceedings shall bind the estate to the same extent as it would have been bound if a grant had been made and a personal representative of the deceased had been a party to the proceedings.

Commencement 1 September 1982.
Cross references See RSC Order 15, r 6A.

Order 5, r 9 Partners may sue and be sued in firm name

(1)   Subject to the provisions of any enactment, any two or more persons claiming to be entitled, or alleged to be liable, as partners in respect of a cause of action and carrying on business within England or Wales may sue or be sued in the name of the firm of which they were partners when the cause of action arose.

(2)   Where partners sue or are sued in the name of the firm, the partners shall, on demand made in writing by any other party, forthwith deliver to the party making the demand and file a statement of the names and places of residence of all the persons who were partners in the firm when the cause of action arose.

(3)   If the partners fail to comply with such a demand, the court, on application by any other party, may order the partners to furnish him with such a statement and to verify it on oath and may direct that in default—

    (a)   if the partners are plaintiffs, the proceedings be stayed on such terms as the court thinks fit, or

    (b)   if the partners are defendants, they be debarred from defending the action.

(4)   When the names and places of residence of the partners have been stated in compliance with a demand or order under this rule, the proceedings shall continue in the name of the firm.

Commencement   1 September 1982.
Cross references   See RSC Order 81, r 1.

Order 5, r 10 Defendant carrying on business in another name

(1)   A person carrying on business in England or Wales in a name other than his own name may[, whether or not he is within the jurisdiction,] be sued—
    (a)   in his own name, followed by the words "trading as A.B.", or
    (b)   in his business name, followed by the words "(a trading name)".

(2)   Where a person is sued in his business name in accordance with paragraph (1)(b), the provisions of these rules relating to actions against firms shall, subject to the provisions of any enactment, apply as if he were a partner and the name in which he carries on business were the name of his firm.

Commencement   1 September 1982.
Amendments   Para (1): words ", whether or not he is within the jurisdiction," inserted by SI 1985/1269, r 4.
Cross references   See RSC Order 81, r 9.

Order 5, r 11 Change of parties by reason of assignment etc

(1)   Where, at any stage of the proceedings in an action or matter, the interest or liability of any party is assigned or transmitted to or devolves upon some other person, the court may, for the purpose of ensuring that all matters in dispute in the action or matter may be effectually and completely disposed of, order that other person to be made a party to the action or matter and the proceedings to be carried on as if he had been substituted for the first-mentioned party.

(2)   An application for an order under paragraph (1) may be made ex parte by filing a notice stating the grounds on which the application is made.

(3)   The notice shall be accompanied by an affidavit verifying the facts stated therein and by as many copies of the notice as there are persons to be served under the next succeeding paragraph.

(4)   If an order is made on the application, the proper officer shall, unless the court otherwise directs, serve notice of the order, together with a copy of the notice given under paragraph (2), on every person, other than the applicant, who is a party to the action or matter or who becomes or ceases to be a party by virtue of the order.

(5)   In the case of a person who becomes a defendant by virtue of the order, the documents mentioned in paragraph (4) shall be accompanied by a copy of the originating process and shall be served on him in accordance with the provisions of these rules relating to service of the process by which the proceedings were commenced.

(6)   Any person served with notice of an order made ex parte under this rule may, within 14 days after service of the order on him, apply for the discharge or the variation of the order, and the notice shall contain a statement to that effect.

(7)   Where, by one and the same event, a person becomes entitled to apply for an order under paragraph (1) in more than one action or matter he may give one notice

of application only, specifying in a schedule the actions or matters in respect of which it is given, and it shall be sufficient for the proper officer, in serving a copy of the notice on any party, to set out only so much of the notice as affects that party.

Commencement 1 September 1982.
Cross references See RSC Order 15, r 7.
Forms Notice of change in plaintiff's title (N213).
Notice of change of party (N214).

Order 5, r 12 Failure to proceed after death of party

(1) If, after the death of a plaintiff or defendant in any action or matter, the cause of action survives but no order is made under rule 11 substituting any person in whom the cause of action vests or, as the case may be, the personal representatives of the deceased defendant, the defendant or, as the case may be, those representatives may apply to the court for an order that unless the action or matter is proceeded with within such time as may be specified in the order the action shall be struck out as against the plaintiff or defendant who has died; but where it is the plaintiff who has died, the court shall not make an order unless satisfied that notice of the application has been given to the personal representatives (if any) of the deceased plaintiff and to any other interested person who the court considers should be notified.

(2) Where a counterclaim is made by a defendant to any action, this rule shall apply in relation to the counterclaim as if the counterclaim were a separate action and as if the defendant making the counterclaim were a plaintiff and the person against whom it is made a defendant.

Commencement 1 September 1982.
Cross references See RSC Order 15, r 9.

Order 5, r 13 Claim to money in court where change in parties after judgment

(1) Where any change has taken place after judgment, by death, assignment or otherwise, in the parties to any action or matter and there is money standing in court to the credit of the action or matter, any person claiming to be entitled to the money may give to the proper officer notice of his claim, accompanied by an affidavit verifying the facts stated in the notice.

(2) The [district judge] may, if satisfied as to the entitlement of the person giving the notice, cause the money to be paid to him or may refer the claim to the judge and may require the claimant to give notice of the claim to any other person.

(3) It shall not be necessary for notice to be given under this rule where the person claiming to be entitled to the money in court has obtained leave under Order 26, rule 5, to issue a warrant of execution.

Commencement 1 September 1982.

Order 5, r 14 Bankruptcy of plaintiff

Rules 11 and 13 shall not apply to any case for which provision is made by [section 49] of the Act.

Commencement 1 September 1982.
Amendments Words "section 49" substituted by SI 1984/878, r 12, Schedule.

ORDER 6
Particulars of Claim

Order 6, r 1 General requirements

(1)   Subject to the provisions of this rule, a plaintiff shall, at the time of commencing an action, file particulars of his claim specifying his cause of action and the relief or remedy which he seeks and stating briefly the material facts on which he relies.

[(1A) In an action for an unliquidated sum the value of the plaintiff's claim shall, for the purposes of Order 21, rule 5(1), be treated as limited to the sum for the time being specified in sub-paragraph (b) of that paragraph, unless—
   (a)   the plaintiff states in his particulars of claim or otherwise that the value of his claim exceeds the said sum; or
   (b)   the court orders otherwise;

and, where a statement is made under sub-paragraph (a), the plaintiff shall forthwith file an amended statement whenever the value of his claim falls to the said sum or less.]

(2)   Where in an action for a debt the particulars of claim can conveniently be incorporated in the form of request for the issue of the summons, they may be incorporated in that form if the proper officer so allows.

(3)   Where a plaintiff desires to abandon, under [section 17(1)] of the Act, the excess of his claim over the sum mentioned in that section, the abandonment of the excess shall be stated at the end of the particulars.

(4)   Except where the particulars are incorporated in the request pursuant to paragraph (2), the plaintiff shall, when filing particulars of his claim, file a copy for each defendant to be served with the summons.

[(5)   Subject to paragraph (6), a plaintiff in an action for personal injuries shall file with his particulars of claim—
   (a)   a medical report, and
   (b)   a statement of the special damages claimed,

together with a copy of those documents for each defendant.

(6)   Where the documents to which paragraph (5) applies are not filed with the particulars of the claim, the Court—
   (a)   may specify the period of time within which they are to be provided, in which case the plaintiff shall within the time so specified file a copy of them and serve further copies on each defendant; or
   (b)   may make such other order as it thinks fit (including an order dispensing with the requirements of paragraph (5) or staying the proceedings).

(7)   For the purposes of this rule,
   "medical report" means a report substantiating all the personal injuries alleged in the particulars of claim which the plaintiff proposes to adduce in evidence as part of his case at the trial;
   "a statement of the special damages claimed" means a statement giving full particulars of the special damages claimed for expenses and losses already incurred and an estimate of any future expenses and losses (including loss of earnings and of pension rights).]

Commencement   1 July 1991 (para (1A)); 4 June 1990 (paras (5)–(7)); 1 September 1982 (remainder).
Amendments   Para (1A): inserted by SI 1991/1126, r 3.

Para (3): words "section 17(1)" substituted by SI 1984/878, r 12, Schedule.
Paras (5)–(7): inserted by SI 1989/2426, r 3.
Cross references See RSC Order 6, r 2, Order 18, r 12(1A)–(1C).

[Order 6, r 1A Claim for interest

Where the plaintiff claims interest under [section 69] of the Act or otherwise his particulars of claim shall contain a statement to that effect.]

Commencement 1 April 1983.
Amendments This rule was inserted by SI 1982/1794, r 2 and SI 1983/275, r 3.
Words "section 69" substituted by SI 1984/878, r 12, Schedule.
Cross references See RSC Order 18, r 8(4).

[Order 6, r 1B Aggravated, exemplary and provisional damages

Where a plaintiff claims aggravated, exemplary or provisional damages, his particulars of claim shall contain a statement to that effect and shall state the facts on which he relies in support of his claim for such damages.]

Commencement 5 February 1990.
Amendments This rule was inserted by SI 1989/2426, r 5.
Cross references See RSC Order 18, r 8(3).

Order 6, r 2 Claim for account

Where the plaintiff desires to have an account taken, his particulars of claim shall contain a statement to that effect and shall specify the amount which the plaintiff claims subject to the taking of the account, and if no such amount is stated the plaintiff shall be deemed to claim the maximum sum which may be recovered in the action.

Commencement 1 September 1982.

[Order 6, r 3 Recovery of land

(1)   In an action for recovery of land the particulars of claim shall—
    (a)   identify the land sought to be recovered;
    (b)   state whether the land consists of or includes a dwelling-house;
    (c)   give details about the agreement or tenancy, if any, under which the land is held, stating when it commenced and the amount of money payable by way of rent or licence fee;
    (d)   in a case to which section 138 of the Act applies (forfeiture for non-payment of rent), state the daily rate at which the rent in arrear is to be calculated, and
    (e)   state the ground on which possession is claimed, whether statutory or otherwise.

(2)   In proceedings for forfeiture where the plaintiff knows of any person entitled to claim relief against forfeiture as underlessee (including a mortgagee) under section 146(4) of the Law of Property Act 1925 or under section 138(9C) of the County Courts Act 1984, the particulars of claim shall give the name and address of that person and the plaintiff shall file a copy of the particulars of claim for service on him.

(3)   Where possession of land which consists of or includes a dwelling-house is claimed because of non-payment of rent, the particulars of claim shall be in the prescribed form and shall also—
  (a)   state the amount due at the commencement of the proceedings;
  (b)   give—
      (i)   (whether by means of a schedule or otherwise) particulars of all the payments which have been missed altogether;
      (ii)   where a history of late or under-payments is relied upon, sufficient details to establish the plaintiff's case;
  (c)   state any previous steps which the plaintiff has taken to recover arrears of rent and, in the case of court proceedings, state
      (i)   the dates when proceedings were commenced and concluded, and
      (ii)   the dates and terms of any orders made;
  (d)   give such relevant information as is known by the plaintiff about the defendant's circumstances and, in particular, whether (and, if so, what) payments on his behalf are made direct to the plaintiff by or under the Social Security Contributions and Benefits Act 1992, and
  (e)   if the plaintiff intends as part of his case to rely on his own financial or other circumstances, give details of all relevant facts or matters.]

Commencement   1 November 1993.
Amendments   This rule was substituted by SI 1993/2175, r 4.

Order 6, r 4 Injunction or declaration relating to land

Where the plaintiff claim ... an injunction or declaration in respect of, or relating to, any land, or the possession, occupation, use or enjoyment of any land, the particulars shall contain the information which would be required under [paragraph 1(a) of the last foregoing rule] if the action were for recovery of the relevant land.

Commencement   1 September 1982.
Amendments   Words omitted revoked by SI 1991/1328, r 14; words "paragraph 1(a) of the last foregoing rule" substituted by SI 1992/1965, r 11.

Order 6, r 5 Mortgage action

[(1)   Where a plaintiff claims as mortgagee payment of moneys secured by a mortgage of real or leasehold property or possession of such property, the particulars of claim shall contain the information required under this rule and, as the case may be, by rule 5A.]

[(1A) ...]

[(2)   Where there is more than one loan secured by the mortgage, the information required under the following paragraphs of this rule and under rule 5A shall be provided in respect of each loan agreement.

(3)   The particulars shall state the date of the mortgage and identify the land sought to be recovered.

(4)   Where possession of the property is claimed, the particulars of claim shall state whether or not the property consists of or includes a dwelling-house within the meaning of section 21 of the Act.

(5)   The particulars shall state whether or not the loan which is secured by the mortgage is a regulated consumer credit agreement and, if so, specify the date on

which any notice required by section 76 or section 87 of the Consumer Credit Act 1974 was given.

(6) The particulars shall show the state of account between the plaintiff and the defendant by including—

    (a) the amount of the advance and of any periodic repayment and any payment of interest required to be made;

    (b) the amount which would have to be paid (after taking into account any adjustment for early settlement) in order to redeem the mortgage at a stated date not more than 14 days after the commencement of proceedings specifying the amount of solicitor's costs and administrative charges which would be payable;

    (c) where the loan which is secured by the mortgage is a regulated consumer credit agreement, the total amount outstanding under the terms of the mortgage;

    (d) the rate of interest payable—

        (i) at the commencement of the mortgage;

        (ii) immediately before any arrears referred to in sub-paragraph (e) accrued, and

        (iii) where it differs from that provided under (ii) above, at the commencement of the proceedings;

    (e) the amount of any interest or instalments in arrear at the commencement of the proceedings.

(7) The particulars of claim shall state any previous steps which the plaintiff has taken to recover the moneys secured by the mortgage or the mortgaged property and, in the case of court proceedings, state—

        (i) the dates when proceedings were commenced and concluded, and

        (ii) the dates and terms of any orders made.]

[(8)] In this rule "mortgage" includes a legal or equitable mortgage and a legal or equitable charge, and references to the mortgaged property and mortgagee shall be construed accordingly.

Commencement 1 November 1993 (paras (1), (2)–(7)); 28 April 1986 (para (1A)); 1 September 1982 (remainder).
Amendments Para (1): substituted by SI 1993/2175, r 5.
Para (1A): substituted, for paras (1A), (1B) as inserted by SI 1982/1794, r 4, by SI 1986/636, r 6; revoked by SI 1993/2175, r 6.
Paras (2)–(7): inserted by SI 1993/2175, r 8.
Para (8): originally para (2), renumbered as para (8) by SI 1993/2175, r 7.
Cross references See RSC Order 88, r 3.

[Order 6, r 5A Mortgage action—dwelling-house

(1) This rule applies where a plaintiff claims as mortgagee possession of land which consists of or includes a dwelling-house and in such a case the particulars of claim shall be in the prescribed form.

(2) Where the plaintiff's claim is brought because of failure to make the periodic payments due, the particulars of claim shall—

    (a) give details (whether by means of a schedule or otherwise) of all the payments which have been missed altogether;

    (b) where a history of late or under-payments is relied upon, provide sufficient details to establish the plaintiff's case;

(c) give details of any other payments required to be made as a term of the mortgage (such as for insurance premiums, legal costs, default interest, penalties, administrative or other charges) together with any other sums claimed stating the nature and amount of each such charge, whether any payment is in arrear and whether or not it is included in the amount of any periodic payment;

(d) give such relevant information as is known by the plaintiff about the defendant's circumstances and, in particular, whether (and, if so, what) payments on his behalf are made direct to the plaintiff by or under the Social Security Contributions and Benefits Act 1992.

(3) In an action to which this rule applies, the plaintiff shall state in his particulars of claim whether there is any person on whom notice of the action is required to be served in accordance with section 8(3) of the Matrimonial Homes Act 1983 and, if so, he shall state the name and address of that person and shall file a copy of the particulars of claim for service on that person.

(4) In this rule "mortgage" has the same meaning as in rule 5(8).]

Commencement 1 November 1993.
Amendments This rule was inserted by SI 1993/2175, r 9.
Forms Notice to chargeholder under the Matrimonial Homes Act 1983 (N438).

[Order 6, r 6 Hire-purchase

(1) Where a plaintiff claims the delivery of goods let under a hire-purchase agreement to a person other than a body corporate, he shall in his particulars state in the order following—

(i) the date of the agreement and the parties to it with the number of the agreement or sufficient particulars to enable the debtor to identify the agreement;

(ii) where the plaintiff was not one of the original parties to the agreement, the means by which the rights and duties of the creditor under the agreement passed to him;

(iii) whether the agreement is a regulated agreement and, if it is not a regulated agreement, the reason why;

(iv) the place where the agreement was signed by the debtor (if known);

(v) the goods claimed;

(vi) the total price of the goods;

(vii) the paid-up sum;

(viii) the unpaid balance of the total price;

(ix) whether a default notice or a notice under section 76(1) or section 98(1) of the Consumer Credit Act 1974 has been served on the debtor, and if it has, the date on which and the manner in which it was so served;

(x) the date when the right to demand delivery of the goods accrued;

(xi) the amount (if any) claimed as an alternative to the delivery of the goods; and

(xii) the amount (if any) claimed in addition to the delivery of the goods or any claim under sub-paragraph (xi), stating the cause of action in respect of which each such claim is made.

(2) Where a plaintiff's claim arises out of a hire-purchase agreement but is not for the delivery of goods, he shall in his particulars state in the order following—

(i) the date of the agreement and the parties to it with the number of the agreement or sufficient particulars to enable the debtor to identify the agreement;

(ii) where the plaintiff was not one of the original parties to the agreement, the means by which the rights and duties of the creditor under the agreement passed to him;

(iii) whether the agreement is a regulated agreement and, if it is not a regulated agreement, the reason why;

(iv) the place where the agreement was signed by the debtor (if known);

(v) the goods let under the agreement;

(vi) the amount of the total price;

(vii) the paid-up sum;

(viii) the amount (if any) claimed as being due and unpaid in respect of any instalment or instalments of the total price; and

(ix) the nature and amount of any other claim and the circumstances in which it arises.

(3) Expressions used in this rule which are defined in the Consumer Credit Act 1974 have the same meanings in this rule as they have in that Act.]

Commencement 19 May 1985.
Amendments This rule was substituted by SI 1985/566, r 5.

Order 6, r 7 Further particulars

(1) The court may, on application or of its own motion, order the plaintiff to give the defendant further particulars of the plaintiff's claim and the order may be made on such terms as the court thinks just.

(2) An order shall not be made under this rule before the filing of a defence unless, in the opinion of the court, the order is necessary or desirable to enable the defendant to plead or for some other special reason.

(3) Where the applicant for an order under this rule did not make a written request for the particulars he desires, the court may refuse to make the order unless of opinion that there were sufficient reasons for not making such a request.

(4) Where further particulars are given pursuant to an order or request—

(a) the order or request shall be incorporated with the particulars, each item of the particulars following immediately after the corresponding item of the order or request, and

(b) the particulars shall be filed and a copy shall forthwith be served on the defendant.

Commencement 1 September 1982.
Cross references See RSC Order 18, r 12.

Order 6, r 8 Signing of particulars and address for service

Particulars of claim shall be signed—

(a) by the plaintiff, if he sues in person;

(b) by the plaintiff's solicitor in his own name or the name of his firm, if the plaintiff sues by solicitor,

and shall state the plaintiff's address for service.

Commencement 1 September 1982.
Cross references See RSC Order 6, r 5(2).

ORDER 7
SERVICE OF DOCUMENTS

PART I GENERALLY

Order 7, r 1 General mode of service

(1) Where by virtue of these rules any document is required to be served on any person and no other mode of service is prescribed by any Act or rule, the document may be served—
- (a) if the person to be served is acting in person, by delivering it to him personally or by delivering it at, or sending it by first-class post to, his address for service or, if he has no address for service—
  - (i) by delivering the document at his residence or by sending it by first-class post to his last known residence, or
  - (ii) in the case of a proprietor of a business, by delivering the document at his place of business or sending it by first-class post to his last known place of business;
- [(b) if the person to be served is acting by a solicitor:—
  - (i) by delivering the document at, or sending it by first-class post to, the solicitor's address for service, or
  - (ii) where the solicitor's address for service includes a numbered box at a document exchange, by leaving the document at that document exchange or at a document exchange which transmits documents daily to that document exchange.]

(2) In this Order "first-class post" means first-class post which has been pre-paid or in respect of which prepayment is not required.

[(3) Any document which is left at a document exchange in accordance with paragraph (1)(b)(ii) shall, unless the contrary is proved, be deemed to have been served on the second day after the day on which it is left.

(4) In determining for the purposes of paragraphs (1)(b)(ii) and (3)—
- (a) whether a document exchange transmits documents daily to another document exchange, and
- (b) the second day after a document is left at a document exchange, any day on which the court office is closed shall be excluded.]

Commencement 28 April 1986 (paras (3), (4)); 1 September 1982 (remainder).
Amendments Para (1): sub-para (b) substituted by SI 1986/636, r 4.
Paras (3), (4): inserted by SI 1986/636, r 5.
Cross references See RSC Order 65, rr 1, 5.

Order 7, r 2 Personal service

Where any document is required by an Act or rule to be served personally—
- (a) service shall be effected by leaving the document with the person to be served;
- (b) the document may be served by—
  - (i) a bailiff of the court or, if the person to be served attends at the office of the court, any other officer of the court; or
  - (ii) a party to the proceedings or some person acting as his agent; or
  - (iii) the solicitor of a party or a solicitor acting as an agent for such solicitor or some person employed by either solicitor to serve the document;

but service shall not be effected by any person under the age of 16 years.

Commencement 1 September 1982.
Cross references See RSC Order 65, r 2.

Order 7, r 3 Days on which no service permitted

Without prejudice to Order 40, rule 5(5), no process shall be served or executed within England or Wales on a Sunday, Good Friday or Christmas Day except, in the case of urgency, with the leave of the court.

Commencement 1 September 1982.
Cross references See RSC Order 65, rr 5(4)(b), 10.

Order 7, r 4 Service beyond boundary of district

(1)   Any process to be served or executed by the bailiff of any court may be served or executed within a distance of not more than [500 metres] beyond the boundary of the district of that court.

(2)   Without prejudice to paragraph (1), any process to be served or executed by bailiff may, if the judge or [district judge] of the court from which it issues so directs be served or executed within the district of any other court by the bailiff of the court from which the process issues.

Commencement 1 September 1982.
Amendments Para (1): words "500 metres" substituted by SI 1991/1882, r 2(1).

Order 7, r 5 Violence or threats

Where a bailiff is prevented by the violence or threats of the person to be served, or any other person acting in concert with him, from serving a document in manner prescribed by this Order, it shall be sufficient service to leave the document as near as practicable to the person to be served.

Commencement 1 September 1982.

Order 7, r 6 Proof of service or non-service

(1)   [Subject to paragraph (1A)] the person effecting service of any document shall—
  (a) if he is an officer of the court, make, sign and file a certificate showing the date, place and mode of service and any conduct money paid or tendered to the person served; and
  (b) if he is not an officer of the court, file an affidavit of service.

[(1A) Where service is effected by the summons production centre established by Order 2, rule 7(1)—
  (a) the appropriate officer (within the meaning of Order 2, rule 6) on the day the document is issued shall be deemed to be the person effecting service; and
  (b) the mode of service need not be shown on the certificate.]

(2)   A bailiff who has failed to effect service of any document to be served by bailiff shall make, sign and file a certificate of non-service showing the reason why service

has not been effected, and the proper officer of the bailiff's court shall send notice of non-service to the person at whose instance the document was issued.

Commencement 7 February 1994 (para (1A)); 1 September 1982 (remainder).
Amendments Para (1): words "Subject to paragraph (1A)" added by SI 1993/3273, r 3(1).
Para (1A): inserted by SI 1993/3273, r 3(2).
Cross references See RSC Order 65, r 8.
Forms Certificate of service (N12, N13).
Affidavit of service (N215).
Notice of non-service (N216).
Affidavit of service by post (RSC PF134).
Affidavit of service through document exchange (RSC PF135).
Affidavit of service by other means (RSC PF136).

Order 7, r 7 Service in foreign district

(1)   Where any document is to be served in the district of a foreign court by a bailiff of that court, the proper officer shall send the document and all necessary copies to the foreign court.

(2)   On the filing of a certificate of service or non-service of a document under rule 6 the proper officer of the foreign court shall forward the certificate to the home court, together with any copies of the document in his possession.

Commencement 1 September 1982.

Order 7, r 8 Substituted service

(1)   If it appears to the court that it is impracticable for any reason to serve a document in any manner prescribed by these rules for the service of that document, the court may, upon an affidavit showing grounds, make an order (in this rule called "an order for substituted service") giving leave for such steps to be taken as the court directs to bring the document to the notice of the person to be served.

(2)   Where a document is to be served by bailiff, the proper officer of the bailiff's court shall, if so requested, take such steps as may be necessary to provide evidence on which an order for substituted service may be made.

Commencement 1 September 1982.
Cross references See RSC Order 65, r 4.
Forms Notice of non-service (N216).
Affidavit for substituted service (RSC PF113).
Order for substituted service (N217).
Affidavits of substituted service (RSC PF127–9).

PART II DEFAULT AND FIXED DATE SUMMONSES

Order 7, r 9 Application of Part II

Except as otherwise provided, this Part of this Order shall apply to both default and fixed date summonses and "summons" shall be construed accordingly.

Commencement 1 September 1982.

Order 7, r 10 Mode of service

[(1)   Subject to the provisions of any Act or rule (including the following paragraphs of this rule), service of a summons shall be effected—
   (a) by the plaintiff delivering the summons to the defendant personally; or
   (b) by an officer of the court sending it by first-class post to the defendant at the address stated in the request for the summons.

(2)   Unless the plaintiff or his solicitor otherwise requests, service shall be effected in accordance with paragraph (1)(b).

(3)   Where a summons is served in accordance with paragraph (1)(b), the date of service shall, unless the contrary is shown, be deemed to be the seventh day after the date on which the summons was sent to the defendant.

(4)   Where a summons has been sent by post in accordance with paragraph (1)(b) to the address stated in the request for the summons and has been returned to the court office undelivered, notice of non-service shall be sent pursuant to rule 6(2) together with a notice informing the plaintiff that he may request bailiff service at that address and, if such service is requested, it shall be effected by a bailiff of the court—
   (a) inserting the summons, enclosed in an envelope addressed to the defendant, through the letterbox at the address stated in the request for the summons, or
   (b) delivering the summons to some person, apparently not less than 16 years old, at the address stated in the request for the summons, or
   (c) delivering the summons to the defendant personally.

(5)   Service of a fixed date summons shall be effected not less than 21 days before the return day; but, without prejudice to the power to abridge that period under Order 13, rule 4, service may be effected at any time before the return day on the plaintiff satisfying the [district judge] by affidavit that the defendant is about to remove from the address stated in the request for the summons.]

Commencement   12 December 1983.
Amendments   This rule was substituted by SI 1983/1716, r 2.
Cross references   See RSC Order 10, rr 1, 5.

[Order 7, r 10A Service by post by solicitors

(1)   In an action for personal injuries, the summons may be served in accordance with the provisions of this rule by the plaintiff's solicitor sending it by first-class post to the defendant at the address stated in the summons.

(2)   Service may be effected under this rule only where the summons has been prepared in accordance with Order 3, rule 3(1A).

(3)   Where a summons is served under this rule—
   (a) rules 10(3) and (4) and 13 and Order 37, rule 3 shall apply, with the necessary modifications, as if the summons had been served by post by an officer of the court;
   (b) rules 6(1)(b) and 10(2) shall not apply, and
   (c) it shall be treated, for the purposes of these rules, as if it had been served by an officer of the court.

(4)   Where a summons has been served under this rule and the plaintiff applies for judgment under Order 9, rule 6(1), his request under paragraph (1A)(a) of that rule

shall be accompanied by an affidavit verifying that service was effected in accordance with this rule and that the summons was not returned undelivered.]

Commencement 1 July 1991.
Amendments This rule was inserted by SI 1991/1126, r 10.

Order 7, r 11 Solicitor accepting service

Where a defendant's solicitor gives a certificate that he accepts service of the summons on behalf of that defendant and stating an address for service, the summons shall be deemed to have been duly served on that defendant on the date on which the certificate was made.

Commencement 1 September 1982.
Cross references See RSC Order 10, r 1(4).

[Order 7, r 12 Presumed service of summons

Where a summons has not been served in accordance with these rules but the defendant delivers a defence, admission or counterclaim, the summons shall be deemed, unless the contrary is shown, to have been duly served on him on the date on which the defence, admission or counterclaim was so delivered.]

Commencement 1 July 1991.
Amendments This rule was substituted by SI 1991/1126, r 11.
Cross references See RSC Order 10, r 1(5).

Order 7, r 13 Partners

[(1) Subject to the following paragraphs of this rule, where partners are sued in the name of their firm, service of a summons shall be good service on all the partners, whether any of them is out of England and Wales or not, if the summons is:—
  (a) delivered by the plaintiff to a partner personally, or
  (b) served by an officer of the court sending it by first-class post to the firm at the address stated in the request for the summons.

(2) Where the partnership has to the knowledge of the plaintiff been dissolved before the commencement of the action, the summons shall be served upon every person within England and Wales sought to be made liable.

(3) Rule 10(2) and (3) shall apply in relation to service by post under paragraph (1)(b) as they apply in relation to service under rule 10.

(4) Rule 10(4) shall apply in relation to service under this rule as it applies in relation to service under rule 10, but with the reference to paragraph (1)(b) being read as a reference to the same paragraph in this rule and with the substitution for paragraphs (b) and (c) of the following paragraphs—

"(b) delivering the summons at the principal place of the partnership business within the district within which the summons is to be served to any person having, or appearing to have, at the time of service, the control or management of the business there or,
  (c) delivering the summons to a partner personally."]

Commencement 12 December 1983.

Amendments The text of this rule was substituted by SI 1983/1716, r 3.
Cross references See RSC Order 81, r 3.
Forms Affidavit of service on partner (RSC PF121).

[Order 7, r 14 Service on body corporate

(1)   Service of a summons on a body corporate may, in cases for which provision is not otherwise made by an enactment, be effected by serving it on the mayor, chairman or president of the body or the chief executive, clerk, secretary, treasurer or other similar officer thereof.

(2)   Service of a summons on a company registered in England and Wales may be effected by serving it at the registered office or at any place of business of the company which has some real connection with the cause or matter in issue.

(3)   Where a summons has been served under paragraph (2) other than at the registered office, and, after judgment has been entered or given or an order has been made, it appears to the court that the summons did not come to the knowledge of an appropriate person within the company in due time, the court may, upon application or of its own motion, set aside the judgment or order and may give such directions as it thinks fit.]

Commencement 18 July 1989.
Amendments This rule was substituted by SI 1989/236, r 3.
Cross references See RSC Order 65, r 3(1).
Forms Affidavit of service (RSC PF119).

Order 7, r 15 Recovery of land

(1)   Where, in the case of a summons for the recovery of land which is to be served by bailiff, the court is of opinion that it is impracticable to serve the summons in accordance with any of the foregoing provisions of this Part of this Order, the summons may be served in a manner authorised by this rule.

(2)   The summons may be served on any person on the premises who is the husband or wife of the defendant or on any person who has or appears to have the authority of the defendant—

    (a) to reside or carry on business in the premises or to manage them on behalf of the defendant or to receive any rents or profits of the premises or to pay any outgoings in respect of the premises; or

    (b) to safeguard or deal with the premises or with the furniture or other goods on the premises,

and service on any such person shall be effected in the manner required by these rules with respect to a fixed date summons.

(3)   Paragraph (2) shall apply to a man and woman who are living with each other in the same household as husband and wife as it applies to the parties to a marriage.

(4)   Where the premises are vacant or are occupied only by virtue of the presence of furniture or other goods, the summons may be served by affixing it to some conspicuous part of the premises.

(5)   Unless the court otherwise orders, service of a summons in accordance with this rule shall be good service on the defendant, but if a claim for the recovery of

money is joined with the claim for recovery of land, the court shall order the summons to be marked "not served" with respect to the money claim unless in special circumstances the court thinks it just to hear and determine both claims.

Commencement 1 September 1982.
Cross references See RSC Order 10, r 4.
Forms Request for service of possession summons on representative (N220).
Order for service where premises vacant (RSC PF5).

[Order 7, r 15A Mortgage possession actions

(1)   After the issue of the summons in a mortgage possession action, the plaintiff shall not less than 14 days before the hearing send to the address of the property sought to be recovered a notice addressed to the occupiers which—

(a)   states that possession proceedings have been commenced in respect of the property;

(b)   shows the name and address of the plaintiff, of the defendant and of the court which issued the summons, and

(c)   gives details of the case number and of the hearing date.

(2)   The plaintiff shall either—

(a)   not less than 14 days before the hearing, file a certificate stating that a notice has been sent in accordance with paragraph (1), or

(b)   exhibit the notice to any affidavit used at the hearing.

(3)   In this rule "mortgage possession action" means an action in which the plaintiff claims as mortgagee possession of land which consists of or includes a dwelling-house and "mortgage" has the same meaning as in Order 6, rule 5(8).]

Commencement 1 November 1993.
Amendments This rule was inserted by SI 1993/2175, r 10.

Order 7, r 16 Late knowledge of service

Where a fixed date summons has been served on a defendant in one of the modes mentioned in this Part of this Order but it appears to have come to his knowledge less than 21 days before the return day, the court may, without prejudice to its powers under rule 10(5) or Order 13, rule 4,—

(a)   allow the action to proceed whether or not the defendant appears on the return day, or

(b)   adjourn the hearing or, as the case may be, the pre-trial review.

Commencement 1 September 1982.

Order 7, r 17 Error in request

(1)   Subject to the following paragraphs of this rule, a summons which has not been served may be amended on the plaintiff filing an amended request for the issue of the summons.

(2)   An amendment may be made under paragraph (1) notwithstanding that it consists of the addition or substitution of a defendant but in that case Order 15, rule 2(3), shall apply to the amendment as it applies to an amendment made under paragraph (1) of that rule.

(3)   If the bailiff by whom a summons is to be served ascertains before notice of

non-service has been sent that the defendant has removed from the address stated on the summons to a new address within the district of the court, it shall be his duty to serve the summons without amendment and to state the new address in his certificate of service.

(4)   Where the defendant's address stated in the request for the issue of the summons was within the district of the court and at the time of the entry of the plaint the defendant was not residing or carrying on business within the district, an amendment of the address shall be allowed only on the plaintiff filing a fresh request for the issue of the summons showing that the court had jurisdiction under Order 4, rule 2, to entertain the action.

Commencement 1 September 1982.

Order 7, r 18 Doubtful service

(1) If it appears from the certificate of service of a default or fixed date summons that the summons has been delivered to a person [under rule 10(4)(b)] but it is doubtful whether the court will be satisfied that the summons has come to the defendant's knowledge in sufficient time, the proper officer of the court for the district in which the summons is to be served shall give to the plaintiff notice of doubtful service.

(2)   Where such a notice has been given and the defendant does not deliver a defence, admission or counterclaim or, in the case of a fixed date summons, does not appear on the return day, the plaintiff may be required to satisfy the court that the summons has come to the defendant's knowledge in sufficient time.

(3)   In this rule "sufficient time" means—
   (a)   in the case of a default summons, sufficient time for the defendant to deliver a defence, admission or counterclaim within 14 days after delivery of the summons [under rule 10(4)(b)], and
   (b)   in the case of a fixed date summons, sufficient time for him to attend on the return day.

Commencement 1 September 1982.
Amendments Paras (1), (3): words "under rule 10(4)(b)" substituted by SI 1983/1716, r 4.

Order 7, r 19 Successive summonses

(1)   Where a fixed date summons has not been served on every defendant, successive summonses may from time to time be issued without entering a new plaint, on the plaintiff filing an amendment request on each occasion when a successive summons is to be issued.

(2)   Where a fixed date summons has not been served by reason of a defendant having, after entry of the plaint, removed out of the district in which the summons was required to be served, successive summonses may from time to time be issued for service in any district to which he has removed.

(3)   A successive summons shall—
   (a)   bear the same date and number as the original summons; and
   (b)   be a continuance of the original summons; and
   (c)   be served in accordance with rule 10.

Commencement 1 September 1982.

Order 7, r 20 Duration and renewal of summons

[(1)   The time within which a summons may be served shall, unless extended under the following provisions of this rule, be limited—

(a)   where leave to serve the summons out of England and Wales is required under Order 8, rule 2, to a period of 6 months;

(b)   in any other case, to a period of 4 months,

beginning with the date of issue of the summons.]

(2)   [Subject to paragraph (3), the court may extend the period for service of a summons from time to time for such period, not exceeding 4 months] at any one time, beginning with the day next following that on which it would otherwise expire, as the court may specify, if an application for extension is made before that day or such later day (if any) as the court may allow.

[(3)   Where the court is satisfied on an application under paragraph (2) that, despite the making of all reasonable efforts, it may not be possible to serve the summons within 4 months, the court may, if it thinks fit, extend the period for service for such period, not exceeding 12 months, as the court may specify.]

Commencement 4 June 1990 (paras (1), (3)); 1 September 1982 (remainder).
Amendments Para (1): substituted by SI 1989/2426, r 7.
Para (2): words from "Subject to paragraph (3)" to "4 months" substituted by SI 1989/2426, r 8.
Para (3): added by SI 1989/2426, r 9.
Cross references See RSC Order 6, r 8.

Order 7, r 21 Notice of service of default summons

Where a default summons has been served by a bailiff or other officer of a county court, the proper officer of that court shall send notice of service to the plaintiff.

Commencement 1 September 1982.

ORDER 8
SERVICE OUT OF ENGLAND AND WALES

Order 8, r 1 Interpretation

In this Order the following words and expressions have the following meanings, unless a contrary intention appears:—

"originating process" includes a third party notice;

"interlocutory process" means a summons, order or notice issued, made or given in proceedings already commenced in or transferred to a county court;

"process" means an originating process or an interlocutory process;

"country" means a foreign country, or any country mentioned in rule 8(5);

"country of service" means the country in which a process is to be served or is served pursuant to leave granted under this Order;

"convention country" means a foreign country with which a convention has been made relating to civil procedure including the service of documents issued from England or Wales in the foreign country and includes a country which is a party to the Hague Convention;

"Hague Convention" means the Convention on the Service Abroad of Judicial and Extra-Judicial Documents in Civil or Commercial matters signed at The Hague on 15th November 1965;

["applicant" means the party applying for or obtaining leave under this Order to serve a process out of England and Wales or, where leave is not required, the party intending to serve such process;

"respondent" means the party on whom the applicant seeks or obtains leave to serve a process or, where leave is not required, the party on whom service is to be effected.]

Commencement   1 September 1982.
Amendments   Definitions "applicant" and "respondent" substituted by SI 1990/1764, r 20.
Cross references   See RSC Order 11, rr 1(4), 5(8).

[Order 8, r 2 Principal cases in which service of originating process out of jurisdiction is permissible

(1)   Except in an action to which paragraph (2) or rule 3 applies, service of an originating process out of England and Wales is permissible with the leave of the court where—

(a)   relief is sought against any person domiciled in England or Wales;

b)   an injunction is sought ordering the defendant to do or refrain from doing anything (whether or not damages are also claimed in respect of a failure to do or the doing of that thing);

(c)   the claim is brought against any person duly served within or out of England and Wales and a person out of England and Wales is a necessary or proper party thereto;

(d)   the claim is founded on any breach or alleged breach of any contract wherever made, which—

(i)   according to its terms ought to be performed in England and Wales, or

(ii)   is by its terms, or by implication, governed by English law, or

(iii)   contains a term to the effect that a court in England or Wales shall have jurisdiction to hear and determine any action in respect of the contract;

(e)   the claim is founded on a tort and the damage was sustained, or resulted from an act committed, within England and Wales;

(f) the whole subject-matter of the proceedings is land (with or without rent or profits) or the perpetuation of testimony relating to land;

(g) the claim is brought to construe, rectify, set aside or enforce an act, deed, will, contract, obligation or liability affecting land;

(h) the claim is made for a debt secured on immovable property or is made to assert, declare or determine proprietary or possessory rights, or rights of security, in or over movable property, or to obtain authority to dispose of movable property;

(i) the claim is brought to execute the trusts of a written instrument, being trusts that ought to be executed according to English law and of which the person to be served with the originating process is a trustee, or for any relief or remedy which might be obtained when such a claim is brought;

(j) the claim is made for the administration of the estate of a person who died domiciled in England or Wales or for any relief or remedy which might be obtained when such a claim is made;

(k) the claim is brought in a probate action within the meaning of Order 41;

(l) the claim is brought to enforce any judgment or arbitral award;

(m) the claim is brought against a defendant not domiciled in Scotland or Northern Ireland in respect of a claim by the Commissioners of Inland Revenue for or in relation to any of the duties or taxes which have been, or are for the time being, placed under their care and management;

(n) the claim is brought in respect of contributions under the Social Security Act 1975;

(o) the claim is made for a sum to which the Directive of the Council of the European Communities dated 15th March 1976 No 76/308/EEC applies, and service is to be effected in a country which is a member state of the European Community.

[(p) the claim is brought for money had and received or for an account or other relief against the defendant as constructive trustee, and the defendant's alleged liability arises out of acts committed, whether by him or otherwise, within the jurisdiction];[

(q) the claim is made under the Immigration (Carriers' Liability) Act 1987.]

(2) Service of an originating process out of England and Wales is permissible without the leave of the court provided that each claim made is either—

(a) a claim which by virtue of the Civil Jurisdiction and Judgments Act 1982 the court has power to hear and determine, made in proceedings to which the following conditions apply—

  (i) no proceedings between the parties concerning the same cause of action are pending in the courts of any other part of the United Kingdom or of any other Convention territory, and

  (ii) either—

    the defendant is domiciled in any part of the United Kingdom or in any other Convention territory, or the proceedings begun by the originating process are proceedings to which Article 16 [of Schedule 1, 3C or 4] to the 1982 Act refers, or

    the defendant is a party to an agreement conferring jurisdiction to which Article 17 of the said [Schedule 1, 3C or 4] applies, or

(b) a claim which by virtue of any other enactment the court has power to hear and determine notwithstanding that the person against whom the claim is made is not within England and Wales or that the wrongful act, neglect or default giving rise to the claim did not take place within England and Wales.

(3)   Where an originating process in [a default action or in a fixed date action to which Order 17, rule 11 applies] is to be served out of England and Wales under paragraph (2), the time fixed for delivering an admission or defence or paying the total amount of the claim and costs into court shall be—

  (a)   21 days where the originating process is to be served out of England and Wales under paragraph (2)(a) in Scotland, Northern Ireland or in the European territory of another Contracting State, or

  (b)   31 days where the originating process is to be served under paragraph (2)(a) in any other territory of a Contracting State, or

  (c)   fixed by the court having regard to the distance of the country of service where the originating process is to be served under paragraph 2(a) in a country not referred to in sub-paragraphs (a) or (b) or under paragraph (2)(b).

[(4)   Where an originating process in a fixed date action to which Order 17, rule 11 does not apply is to be served out of England and Wales under paragraph (2) the court shall fix the return day having regard to the distance of the country of service.]

(5)   For the purposes of this rule domicile is to be determined in accordance with the provisions of sections 41 to 46 of the Civil Jurisdiction and Judgments Act 1982 and "Convention territory" means the territory or territories of any Contracting State, as defined by section 1(3) of that Act, to which [the Brussels Conventions or the Lugano Convention] as defined in section 1(1) of that Act apply.]

Commencement   1 October 1990 (para (4)); 1 January 1987 (remainder).
Amendments   This rule was substituted by SI 1985/1269, r 5.
Para (1): sub-para (p) inserted by SI 1990/1764, r 21; sub-para (q) inserted by SI 1993/3273, r 4(2).
Para (2): words "of Schedule 1, 3C or 4" and "Schedule 1, 3C or 4" substituted by SI 1992/1965, r 12.
Para (3): words from "a default action" to "rule 11 applies" substituted by SI 1990/1764, r 4.
Para (4): further substituted by SI 1990/1764, r 5.
Para (5): words "the Brussels Convention or the Lugano Convention" substituted by SI 1992/1965, r 13.
Definitions   Directive of the Council of the European Communities dated 15 March 1976/76/308/EEC: OJ/L73, 18.3.76, p 18.
Cross references   See RSC Order 11, r 1.

Order 8, r 3 Collision of ships and similar cases

Where an action is brought in a county court to enforce a claim to which [section 30] of the Act applies, the court may allow the summons to be served out of England and Wales if, but only if,—

  (a)   the defendant has his habitual residence or place of business within England and Wales; or

  (b)   the cause of action arose within inland waters of England and Wales or within the limits of a port of England and Wales; or

  (c)   an action arising out of the same incident or series of incidents is proceeding in that court or has been heard and determined in that court; or

  (d)   the defendant has submitted or agreed to submit to the jurisdiction of the court.

. . .

Commencement   1 September 1982.
Amendments   Words "section 30" substituted by SI 1984/878, r 12, Schedule; words omitted revoked by SI 1982/1140, r 2.
Cross references   See RSC Order 75, r 4.

Order 8, r 4 Conditions of allowing service of other process

[Service of an interlocutory process out of England and Wales is permissible with the leave of the court on a person who is already a party to the proceedings and, in the case of a defendant, respondent or third party, has been served with the originating process but leave shall not be required for such service in any proceedings in which the originating process may by these rules or under any Act be served out of England and Wales without leave.]

Commencement 1 January 1987.
Amendments The text of this rule was substituted by SI 1985/1269, r 6.

Order 8 r 5 Scotland and Northern Ireland

(1) [Where leave is asked] from the court under rule 2 to serve a process in Scotland or in Northern Ireland and it appears to the court that there may be a concurrent remedy in Scotland or in Northern Ireland (as the case may be), the court shall have regard to the comparative cost and convenience of proceeding in the district, or in the place of residence of the respondent, and particularly to the powers and jurisdiction of the sheriff courts in Scotland and of the county courts in Northern Ireland, respectively.

(2)   ...

Commencement 1 September 1982.
Amendments Para (1): words "Where leave is asked" substituted by SI 1985/1269, r 7.
Para (2): revoked by SI 1985/1269, r 7.
Cross references See RSC Order 11, r 4.

Order 8, r 6 Application to be supported by evidence

(1)   An application for leave to serve a process on a respondent out of England and Wales shall be supported by affidavit or other evidence—
   (a) stating (in the case of a fixed date summons) that in the belief of the deponent the applicant has a good cause of action; and
   (b) showing (in the case of any process)—
      (i) in what country and place the respondent is or may probably be found; and
      (ii) whether the respondent is a United Kingdom national or not; and
      (iii) the grounds on which the application is [made, and]
      [(iv) where the application is made under rule 2(1)(c), the grounds for the deponent's belief that there is between the applicant and the person on whom an originating process has been served a real issue which the applicant may reasonably ask the court to try.]

(2)   Leave shall not be granted unless it appears to the court that the case is a proper one for service out of England and Wales.

Commencement 1 September 1982.
Amendments Para (1): in sub-para (iii) words "made, and" substituted and sub-para (iv) added, by SI 1985/1269, r 8.
Cross references See RSC Order 11, r 4.
Forms Order for service out of jurisdiction (N223).

Order 8, r 7 Return day etc

[When giving leave to serve a process out of England and Wales the court shall—

(a) in the case of [a default or fixed date summons to which Order 17, rule 11 applies], fix the time for delivering an admission or defence at the court office or paying the total amount of the claim and costs to the plaintiff, and

(b) in any other case, fix the return day,

and in so doing shall have regard to the distance of the country of service.]

Commencement 1 April 1990.
Amendments The text of this rule was substituted by SI 1989/1838, r 3.
In para (a) words "a default or fixed date summons to which Order 17, rule 11 applies" substituted by SI 1990/1764, r 6.
Cross references See RSC Order 11, r 4(4).

Order 8, r 8 Modes of service

(1) Where leave has been given to serve a process out of England and Wales, service may, subject to the provisions of this rule, be effected—

(a) through the court; or
(b) by the applicant or his agent.

(2) Where the country of service is a convention country, service may be effected through the court or, if service by the applicant or his agent is permitted by the convention, by the applicant or his agent.

(3) Where the country of service is neither a convention country nor a country mentioned in paragraph (5), service may be effected through the court.

(4) Where the country of service is not a convention country but is a country mentioned in paragraph (5), service may be effected by the applicant or his agent, if and so far as the law of the country of service permits.

(5) The countries referred to in paragraphs (3) and (4) are:—

(a) Scotland, Northern Ireland, the Isle of Man and the Channel Islands;
(b) any independent Commonwealth country outside the United Kingdom, and any territory administered by the government of such a country;
(c) any associated state;
(d) any colony;
(e) the Republic of Ireland.

(6) Where the respondent is a State, as defined in section 14 of the State Immunity Act 1978, service shall be effected through the court, except where the State has agreed to some other method of service.

Commencement 1 September 1982.
Cross references See RSC Order 11, r 5.

Order 8, r 9 Service by applicant

The process, if served by the applicant or his agent, shall be served on the respondent by delivering it to him personally.

Commencement 1 September 1982.
Cross references See RSC Order 11, r 5.

Order 8, r 10 Service through the court

(1) Where service is to be effected through the court, the applicant shall file a request in that behalf, together with a copy thereof and two copies of the process to be served.

(2)   The request shall indicate whether the applicant wishes service to be effected—
   (a)   through the authority designated under the Hague Convention,
   (b)   through the foreign judicial authority,
   (c)   through a British consular authority,
   (d)   through the foreign government, where it is willing for service to be effected in that way.

(3)   Where the party to be served is a State, as defined in section 14 of the State Immunity Act 1978, the request shall indicate that fact and that the applicant is willing for service to be effected by whatever method the Secretary of State may choose.

(4)   The applicant shall file with the request two copies of a translation of the process in the language of the country of service, certified by or on behalf of the applicant to be a correct translation:

   Provided that this paragraph shall not apply where the official language or one of the official languages of the country of service is English, or service is to be effected on a United Kingdom national directly through the British Consul, unless the country of service is a convention country and the convention requires a translation.

(5)   The proper officer shall seal the two copies of the process and the translations (if any), and shall forward them and the request to the senior master.

(6)   An official certificate or declaration upon oath or otherwise of the judicial authority, central authority or government of the country of service or of the British consular authority in that country, transmitted by the senior master to the proper officer of the county court, shall be received as evidence of the facts certified or declared with regard to the service or attempted service of the process.

(7)   Where the process has been served in accordance with the law of the country of service, or in the manner in which default summonses are required to be served, the service shall be deemed to be good service.

(8)   Where it appears from the certificate or declaration that the process has been duly served upon the respondent, the certificate or declaration shall be an equivalent substitute for any affidavit or certificate of service required by these rules.

(9)   Where, pursuant to an order for substituted service, a document is required to be transmitted through the court to the country of service, the provisions of this rule shall apply with the necessary modifications.

Commencement 1 September 1982.
Cross references See RSC Order 11, rr 6, 10.
Forms Request for service out of jurisdiction (N224).

Order 8, r 11 Proof of service

Where the respondent does not appear on the return day, the applicant shall, before proceeding, file an affidavit or official certificate or declaration, showing that the process has been duly served.

Commencement 1 September 1982.

Order 8, r 12 Setting aside the service

The respondent may apply, on notice, to the court to set aside the service of the process, or to discharge the order giving leave to serve the process out of the jurisdiction.

Commencement 1 September 1982.

ORDER 9
ADMISSION, DEFENCE, COUNTERCLAIM AND ANSWER

Order 9, r 1 Application of Order

Except as otherwise provided, the provisions of this Order relating to actions shall apply to both default and fixed date actions.

Commencement   1 September 1982.

[Order 9, r 2 Admission, defence or counterclaim to be delivered

(1)   This rule applies where a defendant in any action—
    (a)   admits his liability for the whole or part of the plaintiff's claim;
    (b)   desires time for payment of any sum admitted by him;
    (c)   disputes his liability for the whole or part of the plaintiff's claim, or
    (d)   desires to set up a counterclaim.

(2)   In this rule and rules 3 and 6—
    "a request for time for payment" means a request containing a proposal as to the date of payment or, if it is proposed to pay by instalments, the frequency and amount of the instalments;
    "admission" and "a statement of means" means the relevant form appended to the summons completed according to the circumstances of the case;
    "defence" includes a counterclaim and means the relevant form appended to the summons completed according to the circumstances of the case or a defence otherwise than on that form;
    "proper officer" does not include the district judge;

and paragraph (1A) of Order 6, rule 1 shall apply, with the necessary modifications, to a defendant making a counterclaim as it applies to a plaintiff.

(3)   Except where paragraph (5)(a) applies, a defendant in an action for a liquidated sum who—
    (a)   admits his liability for the whole of the plaintiff's claim, and
    (b)   desires time for payment of the sum admitted by him,

shall, within 14 days after the service of the summons on him, deliver to the plaintiff a form of admission together with a statement of his means and a request for time for payment.

(4)   The court may at any time allow a defendant to amend or withdraw an admission made by him under this rule on such terms as may be just.

(5)   A defendant who admits liability—
    (a)   in an action brought by a plaintiff under disability,
    (b)   in an action for an unliquidated sum, or
    (c)   in an action for a liquidated sum, for part of the plaintiff's claim

shall, within 14 days after the service of the summons on him,—
    (i)   deliver at the court office an admission of liability together with, if he so wishes, a request for time for payment and, where such a request is made, a statement of means, and
    (ii)   if he wishes to defend part of the plaintiff's claim or to make a counterclaim, comply with the requirements of paragraph (6).

(6)   A defendant who either—
    (a)   disputes his liability for the whole or part of the plaintiff's claim; or
    (b)   desires to set up a counterclaim,

shall, within 14 days after the service of the summons on him, and in addition to any documents he may provide pursuant to paragraph (5), deliver at the court office a defence—
    (i)   defending the whole or part of the claim, or, as the case may be,
    (ii)   making a counterclaim.

[(7)   On receipt of the admission or defence, the proper officer shall—
    (a)   send a copy to the plaintiff together, in a case to which paragraph (1) of rule 3 relates, with a notice of the requirements of that paragraph; and
    (b)   where the defendant states in his defence that he has paid the amount claimed, request the plaintiff to confirm in writing that he wishes the proceedings to continue.]

[(8)   In an action for a liquidated sum, the proceedings shall be automatically transferred to the defendant's home court if the action was not commenced in that court—
    (a)   except where sub-paragraph (b) applies, on the filing of a defence, or
    (b)   in a case to which paragraph (7)(b) applies, where the plaintiff confirms in writing under that paragraph that he wishes the proceedings to continue.]]]

Commencement   1 July 1991.
Amendments   This rule was substituted by SI 1991/1126, r 29.
Para (7): inserted by SI 1991/1126, r 42.
Para (8): inserted by SI 1991/1126, r 42; substituted by SI 1991/1328, r 18.
Cross references   See RSC Order 18, rr 2, 7, Order 15, r 2.
Forms   Form of admission, defence etc (N9, 9A, 9B, 10).
Notice of reply to admission (N228).
Reply to states paid defence (N236).

[Order 9, r 3 Admission of part or request for time in default action

(1)   Where the defendant admits part of the plaintiff's claim or admits the whole or part of the plaintiff's claim and makes a request for time of payment, the plaintiff may, if he accepts the amount admitted—
    (a)   in an action to which rule 2(3) applies, on filing a request in the appropriate form and certifying the terms of the defendant's admission, have judgment entered for the amount so admitted and costs (less any payments made);
    (b)   where the amount admitted is less than the amount claimed and the plaintiff accepts any proposal as to the time of payment, on filing a request in the appropriate form, stating what (if any) payment has been made, have judgment entered for the amount so admitted and costs (less any payments made); or
    (c)   give notice that he accepts the amount so admitted but not the proposal as to time of payment.

(2)   A plaintiff's notice under paragraph (1)(c) shall be given in the appropriate form and shall—
    (a)   give his reasons for the non-acceptance;
    (b)   state what (if any) payments have been made; and
    (c)   where the defendant sent his admission direct to the plaintiff pursuant to rule 2(3), be accompanied by a copy of the defendant's admission.

(3)   Upon receipt of the plaintiff's notice under paragraph (1)(c), the proper officer shall determine the time of payment and enter judgment accordingly.

(4)   Any party affected by a judgment entered under paragraph (3) may, within 14 days of service of the judgment on him and giving his reasons, apply on notice for the order as to time of payment to be re-considered and, where such an application is made—

   (a) the proceedings shall be automatically transferred to the defendant's home court if the judgment or order was not given or made in that court;

   (b) the proper officer shall fix a day for the hearing of the application before the district judge and give to the plaintiff and the defendant not less than 8 days' notice of the day so fixed.

(5)   On hearing an application under paragraph (4), the district judge may confirm the order or set it aside and make such new order as he thinks fit, and the order so made shall be entered in the records of the court.

(6)   Where the defendant admits part of the plaintiff's claim and the plaintiff notifies the proper officer that he does not accept the amount admitted,

   (a) the proceedings shall be automatically transferred to the defendant's home court if the action was not commenced in that court;

   (b) the proper officer shall fix a day for a pre-trial review or, if he thinks fit, a day for the hearing of the action and give to the plaintiff and defendant not less than 8 days' notice of the day so fixed.

[Nothing in sub-paragraph (b) shall require the proper officer to fix a day for a pre-trial review in proceedings which are referred to arbitration under Order 19.]

(7)   Where the action is for unliquidated damages and the defendant delivers an admission of liability for the claim but disputes or does not admit the amount of the plaintiff's damages, then—

   (a) if the defendant offers to pay in satisfaction of the claim a specific sum which the plaintiff accepts, the provisions of this rule shall apply as if the defendant had admitted part of the plaintiff's claim; and

   (b) in any other case, the plaintiff may apply to the court for such judgment as he may be entitled to upon the admission, and the court may give such judgment, including interlocutory judgment for damages to be assessed and costs, or make such other order on the application as it thinks just.

(8)   Where it appears that the proper officer's notice under rule 2(7) or the judgment under paragraph (3) above did not come to the knowledge of the party to be served in due time, the district judge may of his own motion or on application set aside the judgment and may give such directions as he thinks fit.]

Commencement   1 July 1991.
Amendments   This rule was substituted by SI 1991/1126, r 30.
Para (6): words from "Nothing in sub-paragraph (b)" to the end inserted by SI 1992/1965, r 14.
Forms   Request for judgment (N225).

Order 9, r 4 Admission in fixed date action

(1)   If within the period of 14 days mentioned in rule 2 the defendant in a fixed date action other than an action for the recovery of land delivers at the court office an admission of the whole or part of the plaintiff's claim, the plaintiff may apply to the court for such judgment as he may be entitled to upon the admission, without waiting for the return day or for the determination of any other question between the parties, and the court may give such judgment or make such order on the application as it thinks just.

(2)   An application under paragraph (1) shall, if made before the return day, be made on notice to the defendant.

Commencement   1 September 1982.

[Order 9, r 4A Judgment in default in fixed date action

Where, in a fixed date action to which Order 17, rule 11 applies, the defendant fails to deliver a defence within the period of 14 days mentioned in rule 2, the plaintiff may apply to the court for judgment or directions as to the conduct of the proceedings and the court may, subject to the provisions of these rules, give such judgment or directions on the application as it thinks just.]

Commencement   1 October 1990.
Amendments   This rule was inserted by SI 1990/1764, r 7.
Cross references   See RSC Order 19, r 7.

[Order 9, r 5 Defence or counterclaim in default action

(1)   Subject to paragraph (2), if—
   (a)   within 14 days after service of the summons upon him, the defendant in a default action delivers at the court office either a defence not accompanied by an admission of any part of the plaintiff's claim or a counterclaim; or
   (b)   in a case to which rule 2(7)(b) applies, after the plaintiff has confirmed that he wishes the proceedings to continue,

the proper officer shall—
   (i)   fix a day for a pre-trial review or, if he thinks fit, a day for the hearing of the action, and
   (ii) give to all parties not less than 14 days' notice of the day so fixed for the pre-trial review or, in the case of a day for the hearing of the action, not less than 21 days' notice.

(2)   Nothing in paragraph (1) shall require the proper officer to fix a day in a case to which Order 17, rule 11 applies.]

Commencement   1 July 1991.
Amendments   This rule was substituted by SI 1991/1126, r 43.

Order 9, r 6 Judgment in default or on admission in default action

[(1)   Subject to paragraphs (2), (3) and (4) and rule 7, if the defendant in a default action—
   (a)   does not within 14 days after service of the summons on him pay to the plaintiff the total amount of the claim and costs on the summons,
   (b)   delivers an admission of the whole of the plaintiff's claim unaccompanied by a counterclaim or a request for time for payment, or
   (c)   does not deliver an admission of part of the plaintiff's claim, a defence or counterclaim,

the plaintiff may upon fulfilling the requirements of paragraph (1A) have judgment entered against the defendant for the amount of the claim and costs (less any payments made); and the order shall be for payment forthwith or at such time or times as the plaintiff may specify.

(1A)   The requirements are that the plaintiff shall—

   (a)   file a request for judgment,
   (b)   where the action is for a liquidated sum, certify that the defendant has not
         sent to him any reply to the summons, and
   (c)   state what (if any) payment has been made.

   In this paragraph, "reply to the summons" means—
   (i)   a defence,
   (ii)   a counterclaim,
   (iii) an admission of the whole of the plaintiff's claim accompanied by a
          counterclaim or a request for time for payment,
   (iv)   an admission of part of the plaintiff's claim,

or any other written reply of a similar kind.]

(2)   If the plaintiff's claim is for unliquidated damages, any judgment entered [under
paragraph (1)] shall be an interlocutory judgment for damages to be assessed and costs.

(3)   Where the defendant is a State as defined in section 14 of the State Immunity
Act 1978—
   (a)   the plaintiff may not enter judgment [under paragraph (1)] without the
         leave of the judge and RSC Order 13, rule 7A, shall apply to an
         application for such leave as it applies to an application for leave to enter
         judgment against a State in the High Court;
   (b)   the plaintiff may not enforce a judgment entered pursuant to such leave
         until two months after a copy of it has been served on the State.

[(4)   Where an originating process has been served out of England and Wales under
Order 8, rule 2(2)(a) or has been served within England and Wales on a defendant
domiciled in Scotland or Northern Ireland or in any other Convention territory the
plaintiff may not enter judgment [under paragraph (1)] without the leave of the court
and RSC Order 13, rule 7B shall apply to an application for such leave as it applies to
an application for leave to enter judgment in the High Court.]

Commencement   1 July 1991 (paras (1), (1A)); 1 January 1987 (para (4)); 1 September 1982 (remainder).
Amendments   Paras (1), (1A): substituted, for para (1) as originally enacted, by SI 1991/1126, r 31.
Paras (2), (3): words "under paragraph (1)" substituted by SI 1991/1126, r 32.
Para (4): added by SI 1985/1269, r 9; words "under paragraph (1)" substituted by SI 1991/1126, r 32.
Cross references   See RSC Order 13, rr 1, 2, Order 19, rr 2, 3.
Forms   Interlocutory judgment (N17).
Request for interlocutory judgment (N234).

Order 9, r 7 Default judgment for mortgage money

(1)   No judgment shall be entered [under rule 6(1)] for money secured by a
mortgage except with the leave of the court.

(2)   An application for the grant of leave under this rule shall be made on notice to
the defendant.

(3)   The application may be heard and determined by the [district judge].

(4)   In this rule "mortgage" includes a legal and an equitable mortgage and a legal
and an equitable charge.

Commencement   1 September 1982.
Amendments   Para (1): words "under rule 6(1)" substituted by SI 1991/1126, r 33.
Cross references   See RSC Order 88, r 6.

[Order 9, r 8 Recovery of interest

(1)   The sum for which judgment is entered [under rule 3(3)] or 6(1) may include interest down to the date of the issue of the summons or, where it is claimed at the same rate in respect of the period down to judgment, to the date of the request for entry of judgment, provided that—

    (a)   particulars of the amount claimed down to issue, rate and period are set out in the particulars of claim; and

    (b)   in the case of interest claimed under [section 69] of the Act the rate is not higher than that payable on judgment debts in the High Court at the date of issue of the summons.

(2)   Where, in accordance with paragraph (1), the plaintiff requests the entry of judgment for interest in respect of a period subsequent to issue, he shall enter such interest on the appropriate form of request as an additional item, with particulars of the amount, rate and period.

(3)   Save as provided by paragraph (1), where a judgment is sought [under rule 3(3)] or 6(1) in respect of a claim which includes a claim for interest, and the plaintiff so requests, the judgment shall, as regards the interest, be an interlocutory judgment for interest to be assessed.]

Commencement   1 April 1993.
Amendments   This rule was substituted by SI 1983/275, r 4.
Para (1): words "under rule 3(3)" substituted by SI 1991/1126, r 34; in sub-para (b) words "section 69" substituted by SI 1984/878, r 12, Schedule.
Para (3): words "under rule 3(3)" substituted by SI 1991/1126, r 34.

Order 9, r 9 Failure to deliver admission etc in time

(1)   Notwithstanding that the period of 14 days mentioned in rule 2 has expired, a defendant may deliver an admission, defence or counterclaim at any time before the entry of judgment under rule 6 or, in a fixed date action, before [the entry of judgment under rule 4A or] the return day[, whichever is the earlier], and if time permits the same procedure shall be followed as if the admission, defence or counterclaim had been delivered within the said period of 14 days.

(2)   Notwithstanding that he has failed to deliver a defence, the defendant in a fixed date action may appear on the return day and dispute the plaintiff's claim.

(3)   In any case to which paragraph (1) or (2) applies, the court may order the defendant to pay any costs properly incurred in consequence of his delay or failure.

Commencement   1 September 1982.
Amendments   Para (1): words "the entry of judgment under rule 4A or" and ", whichever is the earlier" added by SI 1990/1764, r 9.

Order 9, r 10 Striking out default action after twelve months

Where 12 months have expired from the date of service of a default summons and—

    (i)   no admission, defence or counterclaim has been delivered and judgment has not been entered against the defendant, or

    (ii)   an admission has been delivered but no judgment has been entered under rule 6(1) or, as the circumstances may require, no notice of acceptance or non-acceptance has been received by the proper officer,

the action shall be struck out and no enlargement of the period of 12 months shall be granted under Order 13, rule 4.

Commencement   1 September 1982.

Order 9, r 11 Particulars of defence

(1)   If the defendant in a fixed date action fails to deliver a defence within the period of 14 days mentioned in rule 2, the court may at any time before the trial order him to do so.

(2)   The court may order the defendant in a default or fixed date action to give the plaintiff further particulars of any defence delivered by the defendant and the order may be made on such terms as the court thinks just.

(3)   An order under paragraph (1) or paragraph (2) may be made by the court on application or of its own motion, but where the applicant for an order under paragraph (2) did not make a written request for the particulars he desires, the court may refuse to make an order unless of opinion that there were sufficient reasons for not making such a request.

(4)   Where further particulars are given pursuant to an order or request—
  (a)   the order or request shall be incorporated with the particulars, each item of the particulars following immediately after the corresponding item of the order or request, and
  (b)   the particulars shall be filed and a copy shall forthwith be served on the plaintiff.

Commencement   1 September 1982.

Order 9, r 12 Defence of tender

Where a defence of tender before action is pleaded, the defendant shall pay into court the amount alleged to have been tendered, and the tender shall not be available as a defence unless and until the payment into court has been made.

Commencement   1 September 1982.
Cross references   See RSC Order 18, r 16.

Order 9, r 13 Delivery of defence not a waiver

(1)   The delivery by a defendant of a defence shall not be treated as a waiver by him of any irregularity in the summons or the service thereof or in any order giving leave to serve the summons out of England and Wales or extending the validity of the summons for the purpose of service.

(2)   No application to set aside any proceedings for such an irregularity shall be granted unless made within a reasonable time, nor if the party applying has taken any step in the proceedings, otherwise than by delivering a defence, after knowledge of the irregularity.

Commencement   1 September 1982.
Cross references   See RSC Order 12, r 7.

Order 9, r 14 Summary judgment where no real defence

[(1)   This rule applies to any action except—
  [(a)   an action which stands referred to arbitration under Order 19, rule 3;]
  (b)   an action in which a claim is made for possession of land or in which the title to any land is in question;

(c) an action which includes a claim by the plaintiff for libel, slander, malicious prosecution or false imprisonment;

(d) ...

(e) an Admiralty action in rem.

(1A) Without prejudice to rule 11 and Order 13, rule 5, where the defendant in an action to which this rule applies has delivered at the court office a document purporting to be a defence, the plaintiff may apply to the court for judgment against the defendant on the ground that, notwithstanding the delivery of that document, the defendant has no defence to the claim or to a particular part of the claim.]

(2) An application under paragraph (1) shall be supported by an affidavit verifying the facts on which the claim or the part of it to which the application relates is based and stating that in the deponent's belief, notwithstanding the document which has been delivered, there is no defence to the claim or that part.

(3) Notice of the application, together with a copy of the affidavit in support and of any exhibits referred to therein, shall be served on the defendant not less than 7 days before the day fixed for the hearing of the application.

(4) Where an application under paragraph (1) is made at a time when a day has been fixed for the pre-trial review of the action, the application shall, unless otherwise directed, be heard on that day, and in any case, if on the hearing of the application the court orders that the defendant do have leave (whether conditional or unconditional) to defend the action with respect to the claim or part of the claim, the court may treat the hearing as a pre-trial review and Order 17 with the necessary modifications shall apply accordingly.

[(5) The provisions of the RSC relating to—

(a) showing cause against an application under Order 14 of those rules,

(b) giving the plaintiff judgment or granting the defendant leave to defend on such an application, and

(c) granting summary judgment on a counterclaim,

shall apply in relation to an application under this rule as they apply in relation to an application under the said Order 14.]

Commencement   5 February 1990 (paras (1), (1A), (5)); 1 September 1982 (remainder).
Amendments   Para (1): substituted, together with para (1A), for para (1) as originally enacted, by SI 1989/2426, r 15; sub-para (a) substituted by SI 1992/1965, r 15; sub-para (d) revoked by SI 1992/793, r 13.
Para (1A): substituted, together with para (1), for para (1) as originally enacted, by SI 1989/2426, r 15.
Para (5): substituted by SI 1989/2426, r 16.
Cross references   See RSC Order 14, (and also Order 14A although this has not been directly applied to the county court).
Forms   Summons in support of application for summary judgment (RSC PF11, PF12).
Affidavit in support of application for summary judgment (RSC PF10).
Orders on summons (RSC PF13–18)

Order 9, r 15 Counterclaim against person other than plaintiff

Where a defendant desires to set up a counterclaim against the plaintiff and some other person who is not a party to the action, he may apply to the court for an order that the other person be added as a defendant to the counterclaim and the court may make an order accordingly and give all such directions as may be necessary to enable the questions at issue between all the parties to be determined at the trial of the action.

Commencement   1 September 1982.
Cross references   See RSC Order 15, r 3.

Order 9, r 16 Admission in action for recovery of land

(1)   A defendant in an action for the recovery of land who admits the plaintiff's right to recover possession of the land may at any time before the return day deliver at the court office an admission to that effect.

(2)   The proper officer shall as soon as practicable after the receipt by him of the admission send notice thereof to the plaintiff accompanied by a copy of the admission, and no costs incurred after the receipt of the notice in respect of the proof of any matter which the admission renders it unnecessary to prove shall be allowed against the defendant who has made the admission.

Commencement 1 September 1982.

Order 9, r 17 Interpretation

In the foregoing provisions of this Order, unless the context otherwise requires, "defence", "admission" and "counterclaim" mean respectively any document which shows that the defendant desires—
-   (a)   to dispute the whole or any part of the plaintiff's claim,
-   (b)   to admit the whole or any part of the plaintiff's claim or ask for time for payment of the amount admitted and costs, or
-   (c)   to set up a counterclaim.

Commencement 1 September 1982.

Order 9, r 18 Answer to originating application

(1)   Where the respondent to an originating application is required by any of these rules to file an answer, the following paragraphs shall apply subject to any special provision made by that rule.

(2)   The answer shall state whether or not the respondent intends to resist the application and, if so, on what grounds.

(3)   The answer shall be filed within 14 days after the date of service of the application on the respondent and shall be accompanied by as many copies as there are other parties to the proceedings.

(4)   On receipt of the answer and copies the proper officer shall send a copy to the applicant and to every other party to the proceedings.

(5)   The notice of the return day given to the respondent under Order 3, rule 4(4)(b), shall contain a notice requiring him to file an answer as aforesaid.

Commencement 1 September 1982.

Order 9, r 19 Signing of admission etc and address for service

Every admission, defence or counterclaim delivered pursuant to rule 2 and every answer to which rule 18 relates shall be signed—
-   (a)   by the defendant if he is acting in person;
-   (b)   by the defendant's solicitor in his own name or in the name of his firm, if the defendant is acting by solicitor,

and shall state the defendant's address for service.

Commencement 1 September 1982.

ORDER 10
PERSONS UNDER DISABILITY

Order 10, r 1 Person under disability to have next friend or guardian ad litem

(1)   Except where a minor brings an action in his own name under [section 47] of the Act, a person under disability may not bring or make a claim in any proceedings except by his next friend.

(2)   A person under disability may not defend or make a counterclaim in any proceedings except by his guardian ad litem.

(3)   Where a person is authorised under [Part VII of the Mental Health Act 1983] (in this Order called "[Part VII]") to conduct legal proceedings in the name of a mental patient or on his behalf, that person shall be entitled to be the next friend or guardian ad litem, as the case may be, of the patient in any proceedings to which his authority extends, unless some other person is appointed by the court to be his next friend or guardian ad litem.

Commencement   1 September 1982.
Amendments   Para (1): words "section 47" substituted by SI 1984/878, r 12, Schedule.
Para (3): words "Part VII of the Mental Health Act 1983" and "Part VII" substituted by SI 1983/1716, r 13, Schedule.
Cross references   See RSC Order 80, rr 2(1), 3(3).

Order 10, r 2 Next friend without appointment

Before proceedings are commenced or a claim in any proceedings is made by a next friend on behalf of a person under disability, the next friend shall deliver at the court office—
  (a)   in a case to which rule 1(3) applies, an office copy, sealed with the official seal of the Court of Protection, of the order or other authorisation made or given under [Part VII] by virtue of which he is authorised to conduct the proceedings on behalf of the patient;
  (b)   in any other case, a written undertaking, attested by a solicitor or by an officer of the court authorised to take affidavits, to be responsible for any costs which the person under disability may be ordered and fail to pay the person against whom the proceedings are brought or the claim is made.

Commencement   1 September 1982.
Amendments   Words "Part VII" substituted by SI 1983/1716, r 13, Schedule.
Definitions   Part VII: Mental Health Act 1983, Part VII.
Cross references   See RSC Order 80, r 3(3), (6), (8)(b).
Forms   Undertaking as to costs by next friend (N235).

Order 10, r 3 Appointment of next friend by court

Where proceedings are commenced or a claim is made by a person under disability without a next friend as required by rule 1, the court may—
  (a)   on application appoint as next friend any person who is authorised as mentioned in paragraph (a), or gives such an undertaking as is mentioned in paragraph (b), of rule 2, or
  (b)   order the proceedings to be struck out.

Commencement   1 September 1982.

Order 10, r 4 Service on person under disability

(1)   Where a defendant is a person under disability, the summons shall be served—
    (a)   in the case of a minor who is not also a mental patient, on one of his parents or his guardian or, if he has no parent or guardian, on the person with whom he resides or in whose care he is;
    (b)   in the case of a mental patient, on the person (if any) who is authorised under [Part VII] to conduct in the name of the mental patient or on his behalf the proceedings in connection with which the summons is to be served or, if there is no person so authorised, on the person with whom he resides or in whose care he is,

and shall be served on the person to be served in the manner required by these rules with respect to the summons in question.

(2)   Notwithstanding anything in paragraph (1), the court may order that any summons which has been, or is to be, served on the person under disability or on a person other than a person mentioned in that paragraph shall be deemed to be duly served on the person under disability.

Commencement   1 September 1982.
Amendments   Para (1): in sub-para (b) words "Part VII" substituted by SI 1983/1716, r 13, Schedule.
Definitions   Part VII: Mental Health Act 1983, Part VII.
Cross references   See RSC Order 80, r 16.

Order 10, r 5 Guardian ad litem without appointment

Where in any action a person proposing to act as guardian ad litem of a defendant under disability delivers at the court office on his behalf an admission of or defence to the plaintiff's claim [or a counterclaim] accompanied by—
    (a)   in a case to which rule 1(3) applies, such an office copy as is mentioned in rule 2(a);
    (b)   in any other case, a certificate made by the proposed guardian ad litem that he is a fit and proper person to act as guardian ad litem of the defendant and has no interest in the matters in question in the proceedings adverse to that of the defendant,

the person delivering the admission or defence shall be the guardian ad litem of the defendant and no order appointing him to act as such shall be necessary.

Commencement   1 September 1982.
Amendments   Words "or a counterclaim" inserted by SI 1982/1140, r 4.
Cross references   See RSC Order 80, r 3(2).

Order 10, r 6 Appointment of guardian ad litem

(1)   Where a defendant under disability has no guardian ad litem acting for him by virtue of rule 5, the plaintiff shall, after the time for delivering an admission or defence has expired and before taking any further step in the proceedings, apply to the court for an order that a person named in the application or some other proper person be appointed guardian ad litem of the defendant.

(2)   The application shall be supported by an affidavit showing that the person proposed by the plaintiff for appointment—
    (a)   is a fit and proper person to act as guardian ad litem of the defendant,

(b) has no interest in the matters in question in the proceedings adverse to that of the defendant, and

(c) consents to act.

(3) Not less than 3 days before the hearing of the application notice of the application, together with a copy of the supporting affidavit, shall be served on the person on whom the summons in the action was required to be served.

(4) On the hearing of the application the court may appoint the person proposed by the plaintiff or, if not satisfied that the person proposed is a proper person to be appointed, may appoint any other person willing to act or in default of any such person may appoint the [district judge].

Commencement 1 September 1982.
Cross references See RSC Order 80, r 6.
Forms Affidavit by plaintiff for appointment of guardian ad litem for defendant (N237).
Notice for application for affidavit by plaintiff for appointment of guardian ad litem for defendant (N238).
Orders appointing guardian ad litem (N239–41).

Order 10, r 7 Appointment of guardian ad litem at hearing

Where a defendant attends the hearing of an action and it appears that he is a minor who has no guardian ad litem, then—

(a) if the defendant names a person as his guardian ad litem who consents to act, that person shall be appointed guardian;

(b) if the defendant does not name a guardian ad litem, the court may appoint as guardian any person present who is willing to act or, in default of any such person, the court may appoint the [district judge] to act.

Commencement 1 September 1982.
Cross references See RSC Order 80, r 6(3).

Order 10, r 8 Application of preceding rules to liquidated sums and matters

(1) Where a minor is sued for a liquidated sum, the court may, on the application of the plaintiff, direct that rule 6 or 7, as the case may be, shall not apply, and if the court directs that rule 6 shall not apply, no appointment of a guardian ad litem under rule 7 shall be necessary.

(2) Rules 5, 6 and 7 and this rule shall have effect in relation to a matter as they have effect in relation to an action, but with the substitution of a reference to an answer for any reference to a defence and with such other modifications as may be appropriate.

Commencement 1 September 1982.

Order 10, r 9 Guardian not liable for costs

A guardian ad litem of a person under disability shall not be personally liable for any costs not occasioned by his personal negligence or misconduct.

Commencement 1 September 1982.

Order 10, r 10 Compromise etc by person under disability

(1) Where in any proceedings money is claimed by or on behalf of a person under

disability, no settlement, compromise or payment and no acceptance of money paid into court, whenever entered into or made, shall so far as it relates to that person's claim be valid without the approval of the court.

(2) Where the sole object of an action in which a claim for money is made by or on behalf of a person under disability is to obtain the approval of the court to a settlement or compromise of the claim, the particulars of claim shall contain a brief statement of the cause of action together with a request for the approval of the settlement or compromise.

(3) Whatever the amount involved, the approval of the court may be given either by the judge or by the [district judge] and either in chambers or in open court.

Commencement   1 September 1982.
Cross references   See RSC Order 80, rr 10, 11.
Forms   Minor's settlement summons (RSC PF170, PF171).
Originating summons for minor's settlement summons (RSC PF172, PF173).
Order on settlement (N292, RSC PF174, PF175).

Order 10, r 11 Control of money recovered by person under disability

(1) Where in any proceedings—
    (a) money is recovered by or on behalf of, or adjudged or ordered or agreed to be paid to, or for the benefit of, a person under disability, or
    (b) money paid into court is accepted by or on behalf of a person under disability,

then, unless the court otherwise directs, the money shall not be paid to the person under disability or to his next friend, guardian ad litem or his solicitor but shall be paid into or remain in court.

(2) The money and any interest thereon shall be invested, applied or otherwise dealt with as the court may from time to time direct.

(3) An application to the court as to the mode of dealing with the money and any interest thereon may be made by or on behalf of any person interested.

(4) Unless the court otherwise directs, the costs payable to his solicitor by any plaintiff in the proceedings shall be taxed as between solicitor and own client and no costs shall be payable to the plaintiff's solicitor except the amount allowed on taxation.

(5) On the taxation of a solicitor's bill to any plaintiff in accordance with paragraph (4), the [district judge] shall also tax any costs payable to that plaintiff in the proceedings and shall certify—
    (a) the amount (if any) by which the amount allowed on the taxation of the solicitor's bill exceeds the amount allowed on the taxation of the costs payable to that plaintiff in the proceedings, and
    (b) where necessary, the proportion of the amount of the excess payable by or out of any money belonging to any party to the proceedings who is a person under disability.

(6) Nothing in this rule shall prejudice a solicitor's lien for costs or apply to a case in which a minor sues as if he were of full age by virtue of [section 47] of the Act.

Commencement   1 September 1982.
Amendments   Para (6): words "section 47" substituted by SI 1984/878, r 12, Schedule.
Cross references   See RSC Order 62, r 16, Order 80, r 12.

Order 10, r 12 Authority of next friend or guardian

Subject to the provisions of these rules, any act which in the ordinary conduct of any proceedings is required or authorised by a provision of these rules to be done by a party to the proceedings shall or may, if the party is a person under disability, be done by his next friend or guardian ad litem.

Commencement   1 September 1982.
Cross references   See RSC Order 80, r 2(2).

ORDER 11
Payment into and out of Court [and between the Parties]

Amendments Words "and between the Parties" added by SI 1989/1838, r 7.

Order 11, r 1 Payment into court before judgment

[(1) In any action for debt or damages any defendant may at any time before judgment pay a sum of money (being a sum less than that which is claimed) into court in satisfaction of the plaintiff's cause of action or, where two or more causes of action are joined in the action, in satisfaction of any or all of those causes of action and, where such a payment is made, the defendant shall state that the money is paid in satisfaction of the said cause or causes of action.]

(3)   Where a payment under paragraph (1) is made by one or more but not all of several defendants, it shall be accompanied by a notice stating the name and address of each defendant making the payment.

(4)   A defendant may, without leave, give notice of an increase in a payment made [under paragraph (1)] but, subject to that and without prejudice to paragraph (6), a notice of payment may not be withdrawn or amended without the leave of the court, which may be granted on such terms as may be just.

[(5)   Where two or more causes of action are joined in the action, a payment under paragraph (1) shall be accompanied by a notice—
- (a)   stating that the payment is made in respect of all those causes of action or specifying the cause or causes of action in respect of which the payment is made; and
- (b)   where the defendant desires to make separate payments in respect of any two or more of the causes of action, specifying the sum paid in respect of each,

and, for the purposes of this paragraph, a payment stated (in whatever terms) to be made in satisfaction of the plaintiff's claim shall, subject to paragraph (6), be treated as being made in satisfaction of all the causes of action.]

(6)   Where a single sum of money is paid into court under this rule in respect of two or more causes of action, then, if it appears to the court that the plaintiff is embarrassed by the payment, the court may, subject to paragraph (7), order the defendant to amend the notice of payment so as to specify the sum paid in respect of each cause of action.

(7)   Where a cause of action under the Fatal Accidents Act 1976 and a cause of action under the Law Reform (Miscellaneous Provisions) Act 1934 are joined in an action, with or without any other cause of action, the causes of action under the said Acts shall, for the purpose of paragraph (6), be treated as one cause of action.

(8)   For the purposes of this rule a plaintiff's cause of action in respect of a debt or damages shall be construed as a cause of action in respect also of such interest as might be included in the judgment, whether under [[section 69] of the Act] or otherwise, if judgment were given at the date of the payment into court.

(9)   Where a payment under paragraph (1) is made by a defendant who makes a counterclaim against the plaintiff for a debt or damages, [the payment shall be accompanied by a notice stating,] if it be the case, that in making the payment the defendant has taken into account and intends to satisfy the cause of action in respect of

which he counterclaims or, if two or more causes of action are joined in the counterclaim, all those causes of action or such of them as may be specified in the notice.

(10)   On receipt of a payment by a defendant under paragraph (1) the proper officer shall, if time permits, send notice thereof to every other party to the action.

Commencement   1 April 1990 (paras (1), (5)); 1 September 1982 (remainder).
Amendments   Para (1): substituted, for paras (1), (2) as originally enacted, by SI 1989/1838, r 8.
Para (4): words "under paragraph (1)" substituted by SI 1989/1838, r 9.
Para (5): substituted by SI 1989/1838, r 10.
Para (8): first words in square brackets substituted by SI 1983/1716, r 13, Schedule, words "section 69" therein substituted by SI 1984/878, r 12, Schedule.
Para (9): words "the payment shall be accompanied by a notice stating," substituted by SI 1989/1838, r 11.
Cross references   See RSC Order 22, r 1.

[Order 11, r 1A Misdirected payments

A party who receives any payment which under rule 1(1) is required to be made to the court shall forthwith notify the proper officer in writing and the money so paid shall be paid into court.]

Commencement   1 April 1990.
Amendments   This rule was inserted by SI 1989/1838, r 12.

Order 11, r 2 Payment of whole sum

(1)   Where the only relief claimed in an action is the payment of money and the whole amount is paid [to the plaintiff], the action shall be stayed except for the purposes of paragraphs (2) and (3) of this rule and rules 4 and 6.

(2)   Where the action is for a debt or liquidated demand and the money was paid by the defendant within 14 days after the service of the summons on him, together with the costs stated on the summons, the defendant shall not be liable for any further costs unless the court otherwise orders.

[(3)   In any case to which paragraph (2) does not apply, the defendant shall not be liable for any costs incurred after receipt by the plaintiff of the payment, but—
   (a)   except as provided in sub-paragraph (b), the plaintiff may lodge for taxation a bill of the costs incurred by him before receipt of the payment and, if the costs allowed on taxation are not paid within 14 days after taxation, may have judgment entered for them and the costs of entering judgment;
   (b)   if an order is required under rule 4(2) for payment of the money out of court, the plaintiff may apply for an order for such costs.]

(4)   Paragraphs (2) and (3) are without prejudice to the provisions of Order 10, rules 10 and 11, [Order 19, rule 4], and Order 38, rule 3(4).

Commencement   1 April 1990 (para (3)); 1 September 1982 (remainder).
Amendments   Para (1): words "to the plaintiff" substituted by SI 1989/1838, r 13.
Para (3): substituted by SI 1989/1838, r 14.
Para (4): words "Order 19, rule 4" substituted by SI 1992/1965, r 16(a).
Forms   Judgment for plaintiff for costs (N22).

Order 11, r 3 Acceptance of lesser sum

(1)   [Where the defendant pays a sum of money into court under rule 1(1)] or there

is also a claim for some relief other than the payment of money, then, subject to paragraph (2), the plaintiff may—

(a) where the money was paid in respect of the cause of action or all of the causes of action in respect of which he claims, accept the money in satisfaction of such cause or causes of action, or

(b) where the money was paid in respect of some only of the causes of action in respect of which he claims, accept in satisfaction of any such cause or causes of action the sum specified in the notice of payment into court,

by giving notice of acceptance to the proper officer and to every other party to the action [within 21 days] after the receipt by the plaintiff of notice of payment into court but in any case not less than 3 days before the hearing of the action begins.

(2) Where after the hearing of an action has begun—

(a) money is paid into court [under rule 1(1)], or

(b) money in court is increased by a further payment into court under that rule,

the plaintiff may accept the money in accordance with paragraph (1) within 14 days after receipt of notice of the payment but in any case before the court begins to deliver judgment.

(3) On receipt by the proper officer of the plaintiff's notice of acceptance, proceedings in respect of the cause or causes of action to which the notice relates shall be stayed except for the purposes of this rule.

(4) Where notice of acceptance is given in a case to which paragraph (1)(a) applies and—

(a) the action is for a debt or liquidated demand, and

(b) the money was paid by the defendant within 14 days after service of the summons on him, together with the costs which would be stated on a summons for that amount,

the defendant shall not be liable for any further costs unless the court otherwise orders.

(5) Where notice of acceptance is given in any case to which paragraph (4) does not apply and the notice relates to the whole claim or, if it relates to one or more of several causes of action, the plaintiff at the same time gives notice that he abandons the other cause or causes of action, then—

(a) except as provided in sub-paragraph (b) the plaintiff may lodge for taxation a bill of the costs incurred by him [up to the time of giving notice of acceptance] and, if the costs allowed on taxation are not paid within 14 days after taxation, may have judgment entered for them and the costs of entering judgment;

(b) if an order is required under rule 4(2) for payment of the money out of court, the plaintiff may apply for an order for such costs.

(6) Where money is paid into court by a defendant who made a counterclaim and the notice of payment stated, in relation to any sum so paid, that in making the payment the defendant had taken into account and satisfied the cause or causes of action, or the specified cause or causes of action in respect of which he claimed, then, on the plaintiff accepting that sum, all further proceedings on the counterclaim or in respect of the specified cause or causes of action, as the case may be, against the plaintiff shall be stayed.

(7) The foregoing paragraphs are without prejudice to the provisions of Order 10, rules 10 and 11, [Order 19, rule 4], and Order 38, rule 3(4).

Commencement 1 September 1982.
Amendments Para (1): words "Where the defendant pays a sum of money into court under rule 1(1)" substituted by SI 1989/1838, r 15; words "within 21 days" substituted by SI 1987/493, r 3.
Para (2): in sub-para (a) words "under rule 1(1)" substituted by SI 1989/1838, r 16.
Para (5): in sub-para (a) words "up to the time of giving notice of acceptance" substituted by SI 1989/236, r 5(1).
Para (7): words "Order 19, rule 4" substituted by SI 1992/1965, r 16(a).
Cross references See RSC Order 22, r 3, Order 62, r 5(4), (6).
Forms Judgment for plaintiff for costs (N22).

Order 11, r 4 Payment out of court

(1)   Where proceedings are stayed [under rule 3(3)], the plaintiff shall, subject to the following paragraphs of this rule, be entitled to have paid out to him the sum paid into court in satisfaction of his claim or, if the stay is in respect of some only of the plaintiff's causes of action, in satisfaction of that cause or those causes of action.

(2)   Subject to the provisions of this rule, money paid into court—
    (a) by one or more but not all of defendants sued jointly or in the alternative;
    (b) with a defence of tender before action;
    (c) in an Admiralty action;
    (d) in proceedings to which Order 10, rule 11, relates, or
    (e) in satisfaction either of causes of action arising under the Fatal Accidents Act 1976 and the Law Reform (Miscellaneous Provisions) Act 1934 or a cause of action arising out of the first-mentioned Act where more than one person is entitled to the money,

shall not be paid out of court except in pursuance of an order of the court.

(3)   Where in a case to which paragraph (2)(a) relates the plaintiff discontinues the action against the other defendants and those defendants consent in writing to the payment out of the money, it may be paid out without an order of the court.

(4)   Where a party entitled to money in court is a person in respect of whom a certificate is or has been in force entitling him to [representation under Part IV of the Legal Aid Act 1988], payment shall be made only to that party's solicitor or, if he is no longer represented by a solicitor, to [the Legal Aid Board].

Commencement 1 September 1982.
Amendments Para (1): words "under rule 3(3)" substituted by SI 1989/1838, r 17.
Para (4): words "representation under Part IV of the Legal Aid Act 1988" and "the Legal Aid Board" substituted by SI 1989/1838, r 52.
Cross references See RSC Order 22, r 4.

Order 11, r 5 Late acceptance

(1)   If in a case to which rule 3(1) relates the plaintiff fails to give notice of acceptance within the time limited by that rule, he may give notice at any subsequent time before the hearing of the action begins and thereupon, subject to the provisions of this rule, rule 3 shall apply as if the notice had been given within the time so limited.

(2)   Paragraph (5)(a) of rule 3 shall not apply but in the circumstances to which that paragraph relates the plaintiff may apply for an order for the costs incurred by him [up to the time of giving notice of acceptance].

(3)   Notwithstanding the provisions of rule 4(1) the money in court shall not be paid out without an order of the court.

[(4)   An application for an order under paragraph (2) or (3) shall be made on notice to the defendant, and on the application—

(a)   in a case where a payment into court has been made as mentioned in paragraph 12(2) of Schedule 4 to the Social Security Act 1989, the court may treat the money in court as being reduced by a sum equivalent to any further relevant benefits (within the meaning of section 22(3) of that Act) paid to the plaintiff since the date of payment into court and direct payment out accordingly; and

(b)   the court may make any order as to costs as it thinks fit including an order that the plaintiff pay any costs reasonably incurred by the defendant since the date of payment into court.]

Commencement   1 October 1990 (para (4)); 1 September 1982 (remainder).
Amendments   Para (2): words "up to the time of giving notice of acceptance" substituted by 1989/236, r 5(2). Para (4): substituted by SI 1990/1764, r 22.
Cross references   See RSC Order 22, r 5(1).

Order 11, r 6 Payment of hospital expenses

Where in an action or counterclaim for bodily injury arising out of the use of a motor vehicle on a road or in a place to which the public have a right of access—

(a)   the claim for damages includes a sum for hospital expenses, and

(b)   the party against whom the claim is made, or an authorised insurer within the meaning of Part VI of the Road Traffic Act 1972, pays the amount for which he is or may be liable under section 154 of that Act in respect of treatment afforded by a hospital to the person in respect of whom the claim is made,

the party against whom the claim is made shall, within 7 days after the payment is made, give notice of the payment to the proper officer and to every other party to the action.

Commencement   1 September 1982.
Cross references   See RSC Order 22, r 12.

Order 11, r 7 Non-disclosure of payment into court

(1)   Subject to paragraph (2), no statement of the fact that money has been paid into court [under rule 1(1)] in satisfaction of the plaintiff's cause or causes of action shall be contained in the pleadings or inserted in the documents for the use of the court at the hearing of the action or of any issue as to debt or damages, and no communication of that fact shall be made to the court at any such hearing, until all questions of liability and of the amount of the debt or damages have been decided, but the court shall, in exercising its discretion as to costs, take into account, to such extent, if any, as may be appropriate in the circumstances, both the fact that money has been paid into court and the amount of the payment.

(2)   Nothing in paragraph (1) shall apply in relation to an action in which—

(a)   a defence of tender before action is pleaded, or

(b)   all further proceedings are stayed by virtue of rule 3(3) after the hearing has begun, or

(c)   the defence for which section 2 of the Libel Act 1843 provides is pleaded.

Commencement   1 September 1982.
Amendments   Para (1): words "under rule 1(1)" substituted by SI 1989/1838, r 16.
Cross references   See RSC Order 22, r 7.

Order 11, r 8 Counterclaim

A plaintiff against whom a counterclaim is made and any other defendant to a counterclaim may pay money into court in accordance with rule 1 and rules 1 to 7 (except rules 2(2) and 3(4) and (6)) shall apply accordingly with the necessary modifications.

Commencement 1 September 1982.
Cross references See RSC Order 22, r 6.

Order 11, r 9 Money paid into court under order

(1) Subject to paragraph (2), money paid into court under an order shall not be paid out except in pursuance of an order of the court.

(2) Unless the court otherwise orders, a party who has paid money into court in pursuance of an order made under Order 9, rule 14, or Order 13, rule 1(8)(c), or Order 37, rule 8(1)—

    (a) may by notice to the proper officer and to every other party appropriate the whole or any part of the money and any additional payment, if necessary, to any particular claim made by the other party and specified in the notice, or

    (b) if he pleads a tender, may by his defence appropriate the whole or part of the money as payment into court of the money alleged to be tendered;

and money appropriated in accordance with this rule shall be deemed to be money paid into court in accordance with rule 1 or money paid into court with a plea of tender, as the case may be, and this Order shall apply accordingly.

Commencement 1 September 1982.
Cross references See RSC Order 22, r 8.

[Order 11, r 10 Written offers "without prejudice save as to costs"

(1) A party to proceedings may at any time make a written offer to any other party to those proceedings which is expressed to be "without prejudice save as to costs" and which relates to any issue in the proceedings.

(2) A party who makes such an offer shall file a copy [in a sealed envelope], but the offer shall not be brought to the attention of the court at the hearing until the question of costs falls to be decided and the court shall, in exercising its discretion as to costs, take into account any offer which has been brought to its attention:

    Provided that[, except in a case to which paragraph (3) applies,] the court shall not take such an offer into account if, at the time it is made, the party making it could have protected his position as to costs by means of a payment into court.

[(3) This paragraph applies to a case where the party making the offer has applied for, but has not yet received, a certificate of total benefit given in accordance with Schedule 4 to the Social Security Act 1989; but this paragraph shall not apply with respect to any time after 7 days after that party has received the certificate.]]

Commencement 1 October 1990 (para (3)); 28 April 1986 (remainder).
Amendments This rule was added by SI 1986/636, r 7.
Para (2): words "in a sealed envelope" added by SI 1989/236, r 5(3); words ", except in a case to which paragraph (3) applies," inserted by SI 1990/1764, r 23.
Para (3): inserted by SI 1990/1764, r 24.
Cross references See RSC Order 22, r 14.

ORDER 12
THIRD PARTY AND SIMILAR PROCEEDINGS

Order 12, r 1 Third party notice

(1)   Where in any action a defendant—

(a)   claims against a person not already a party to the action any contribution or indemnity, or

(b)   claims against such a person any relief or remedy relating to or connected with the original subject-matter of the action and substantially the same as some remedy or relief claimed by the plaintiff, or

(c)   requires any question or issue relating to or connected with the original subject-matter of the action to be determined not only as between the plaintiff and the defendant but also as between either or both of them and a person not already a party to the action,

then, subject to paragraph (2), the defendant may issue a notice (in this Order referred to as a third-party notice) containing a statement of the nature and grounds of the claim made by the defendant or, as the case may be, of the question or issue required to be determined.

[(2)   A third party notice shall not be issued without the leave of the court—

(a)   in a fixed date action,

(b)   in a default action where a day has been fixed [under rule 3(6)(b)] or 5 of Order 9 for the hearing or pre-trial review of the action, or

(c)   in an action to which Order 17, rule 11 applies, after the pleadings are deemed to be closed in accordance with paragraph (11)(a) of that rule.]

(3)   An application for leave to issue a third party notice shall be made on notice to the plaintiff, and on the hearing of the application the court, if it grants leave, shall give directions as to the service of the third party notice and as to the further conduct of the proceedings.

(4)   The defendant shall file a copy of the third party notice when it is issued or, if leave to issue the notice is required, when he gives the proper officer notice of his application for leave.

(5)   Where a third party notice is issued pursuant to paragraph (1) without the leave of the court, the proper officer shall fix a day for the pre-trial review of the action and notice of the day so fixed shall be contained in or indorsed on every copy of the third party notice for service under paragraph (6).

(6)   Subject to any directions given under paragraph (3), the third party notice accompanied by a copy of the summons in the action and of the particulars of claim annexed thereto and any pleading delivered by the defendant shall be served on the third party in accordance with the rules applicable to the service of the summons in a fixed date action and, where the notice is issued pursuant to paragraph (1) without leave, a copy shall also be served on the plaintiff.

(7)   Where a third party notice is issued in a default action, judgment on admission or in default shall not be entered against the defendant under Order 9, rule 3(2) or 6.

Commencement   1 October 1990 (para (2)); 1 September 1982 (remainder).

Amendments   Para (2): substituted by SI 1990/1764, r 10; in sub-para (b) words "under rule 3(6)(b)" substituted by SI 1993/3273, r 7.

Cross references   See RSC Order 16, rr 1–3.

Forms Third party notice (N15).
Directions (RSC PF21).

Order 12, r 2 Admission or defence by third party

Order 9, rules 2, 9 and 11, shall apply, with the necessary modifications, in relation to
a third party notice as if—

(a) the third party notice were a summons and the proceedings begun thereby
an action, and

(b) the defendant issuing the third party notice were a plaintiff and the person
against whom it is issued a defendant in that action.

Commencement 1 September 1982.

Order 12, r 3 Hearing of action

(1) Subject to any directions given under rule 1(3) or otherwise, the court shall
have power at the hearing of the action to determine what part the third party shall
take in the trial and generally how the trial shall be conducted.

(2) As between the defendant by whom the third party notice was issued and the
third party, the court may grant to either party any relief or remedy which might
properly have been granted if the claim against the third party had been made in a
separate action and may give such judgment for either party against the other as may
be just.

(3) If the third party does not appear at the hearing, he shall be deemed to admit
any claim stated in the third party notice and shall be bound by any judgment
(including judgment by consent) or decision in the action in so far as it is relevant to
any claim, question or issue stated in the notice.

(4) Where judgment is given for the payment of any contribution or indemnity to
a person who is under a liability to make a payment in respect of the same debt or
damage, execution shall not issue on the judgment without the leave of the court
until that liability has been discharged.

In this paragraph "liability" includes liability under a judgment in the same or
other proceedings and liability under an agreement to which section 1(4) of the Civil
Liability (Contribution) Act 1978 applies.

Commencement 1 September 1982.

Order 12, r 4 Setting aside third party proceedings

Proceedings on a third party notice may be set aside by the court at any stage of the
proceedings.

Commencement 1 September 1982.
Cross references See RSC Order 16, r 6.

Order 12, r 5 Claim against person already a party

(1) Subject to paragraph (3), a defendant in any action who makes against a person
already a party to the action a claim or requirement to which rule 1(1) would apply if
that person were not a party may, without leave, issue and serve on that person a

notice containing a statement of the nature and grounds of his claim or, as the case may be, of the question or issue required to be determined and the same procedure shall be adopted for the determination of the claim, question or issue as would be appropriate under this Order if the person served with the notice were a third party.

(2)   A defendant who issues a notice under paragraph (1) shall at the same time file a copy.

(3)   Nothing in paragraph (1) shall apply in relation to a claim which could be made by the defendant by counterclaim in the action.

Commencement   1 September 1982.
Cross references   See RSC Order 16, r 8.

Order 12, r 6 Fourth and subsequent parties

Where a defendant has issued a third party notice and the third party makes such a claim or requirement as is mentioned in rule 1(1) or 5(1), this Order shall apply, with any necessary modifications, as if the third party were a defendant; and where the person against whom the claim or requirement is made makes such a claim or requirement against a further person, this Order shall similarly apply and so on successively.

Commencement   1 September 1982.
Cross references   See RSC Order 16, r 9.

Order 12, r 7 Offer of contribution

(1)   A party to an action who stands to be held liable in the action to another party to contribute towards any debt or damages which may be recovered against that other party in the action may make, without prejudice to his defence, a written offer to that other party to contribute to a specified extent to the debt or damages and reserve the right to bring the offer to the attention of the court at the hearing.

(2)   A defendant who makes such an offer shall file a copy, but the offer shall not be brought to the attention of the court at the hearing until after all questions of liability and amount of debt or damages have been decided, and if the offer is then brought to the attention of the court in pursuance of the right reserved by the defendant to do so, the court shall take the offer into account, to such extent, if any, as may be appropriate in the circumstances, in exercising its discretion as to costs.

Commencement   1 September 1982.
Cross references   See RSC Order 16, r 10.
Forms   Notice claiming contribution (RSC PF22).

Order 12, r 8 Application to counterclaim

The foregoing provisions of this Order shall apply in relation to a counterclaim by a defendant as if the subject-matter of the counterclaim were the original subject-matter of the action and as if the person making the counterclaim were the plaintiff and the person against whom it is made a defendant.

Commencement   1 September 1982.
Cross references   See RSC Order 16, r 11.

ORDER 13
APPLICATIONS AND ORDERS IN THE COURSE OF PROCEEDINGS

Order 13, r 1 General provisions

(1) Except as otherwise provided, the following paragraphs of this rule shall have effect in relation to any application authorised by or under any Act or rule to be made in the course of an action or matter before or after judgment.

(2) Unless allowed or authorised to be made ex parte, the application shall be made on notice, which shall be filed and served on the opposite party not less than two days before the hearing of the application.

(3) Where the application is made ex parte, notice of the application shall be filed a reasonable time before the application is heard, unless the court otherwise directs.

(4) Unless allowed or authorised to be made otherwise, every application shall be heard in chambers.

(5) Where any party to the application fails to attend on the hearing the court may proceed in his absence if, having regard to the nature of the application, the court thinks it expedient to do so.

(6) The jurisdiction of the court to hear and determine the application may be exercised by the [district judge] and the applicant shall, unless the judge otherwise directs, make the application to the [district judge] in the first instance.

(7) Where the application is made to the [district judge], he may refer to the judge any matter which he thinks should properly be decided by the judge, and the judge may either dispose of the matter or refer it back to the [district judge] with such directions as he thinks fit.

(8) The court may, as a condition of granting any application, impose such terms and conditions as it thinks fit, including a term or condition requiring any party to—

    (a) give security,

    (b) give an undertaking,

    (c) pay money into court,

    (d) pay all or any part of the costs of the proceedings, or

    (e) give a power of re-entry.

(9) Unless the court otherwise directs, the costs of the application shall not be taxed until the general taxation of the costs of the action or matter and, where an earlier taxation is directed, Order 38 shall apply as if the word "claimed" were substituted for the word "recovered" wherever it appears.

(10) An appeal shall lie to the judge from any order made by the [district judge] on the application and the appeal shall be disposed of in chambers unless the judge otherwise directs.

(11) An appeal under paragraph (10) shall be made on notice, which shall be filed and served on the opposite party within 5 days after the order appealed from or such further time as the judge may allow.

Commencement 1 September 1982.
Cross references See RSC Order 32.
Forms General form of application (N244).

Order 13, r 2 Directions

(1)   In any action or matter the court may at any time, on application or of its own motion, give such directions as it thinks proper with regard to any matter arising in the course of the proceedings.

[(2)   In the exercise of the power conferred by paragraph (1) the court may, in particular,
- (a)   order any party to deliver any pleading or give any particulars which the court thinks necessary for defining the issues in the proceedings; and
- (b)   at the same or any subsequent time direct that the action or matter be dismissed or, as the case may be, the defendant be debarred from defending altogether or that anything in any pleading of which particulars have been ordered be struck out unless the order is obeyed within such time as the court may allow; and
- (c)   order one or more questions or issues to be tried before the others.]

(3)   Where the same judge is the judge for two or more districts and proceedings which are to be heard and determined by him are pending in the court for one of those districts, the judge or [district judge] may, in the exercise of the power conferred by paragraph (1), direct that the hearing in those proceedings shall take place in the court for another of those districts, and notice of any such direction shall be given by the proper officer to all parties who were not present when the direction was given.

(4)   Where an application under paragraph (1) is made at a time when no day has been fixed for a pre-trial review, the court may, if it thinks it appropriate to do so, treat the hearing of the application as a day fixed for that purpose and the provisions of Order 17 shall apply accordingly.

(5)   The provisions of this rule are without prejudice to Order 6, rule 7, Order 9, rule 11, and Order 17, rules 3 and 10.

Commencement   5 February 1990 (para (2)); 1 September 1982 (remainder).
Amendments   Para (2): substituted by SI 1989/2426, r 17.
Cross references   See RSC Order 18, r 12, Order 32.
Forms   Notice of directions appointment (N233).
Notice of application (N244).

Order 13, r 3 Adjournment

(1)   The court may at any time and from time to time, upon application or of its own motion, by order adjourn or advance the date of the hearing of any proceedings.

(2)   Notice of any such adjournment or advancement shall be given by the proper officer to all parties who were not present when the order was made.

(3)   If the hearing of any action or matter is adjourned generally, any party may apply to have a day fixed for the hearing and the proper officer shall fix a day and give notice of it to all parties.

(4)   If no application is made under paragraph (3) within 12 months of the day on which the order was made adjourning the action or matter generally, the proper officer may give notice to all parties under this paragraph and, unless any party applies within 14 days after receipt of the notice to have a day fixed for the hearing or to have the hearing again adjourned and the application is granted, the action or matter shall be struck out.

[(5)　An application under paragraph (4) stating the grounds upon which it is made shall be sent in writing to the proper officer.

(6)　The [district judge] may determine an application under paragraph (4) without the attendance of either party or direct the proper officer to fix a day for the hearing of the application.]

Commencement　28 March 1989 (paras (5), (6)); 1 September 1982 (remainder).
Amendments　Paras (5), (6): added by SI 1989/236, r 6.
Cross references　See RSC Order 32, Order 35, r 3.

Order 13, r 4 Extension or abridgment of time

(1)　Except as otherwise provided, the period within which a person is required or authorised by these rules or by any judgment, order or direction to do any act in any proceedings may be extended or abridged by consent of all the parties or by the court on the application of any party.

(2)　Any such period may be extended by the court although the application for extension is not made until after the expiration of the period.

Commencement　1 September 1982.
Cross references　See RSC Order 3, r 5, Order 32.
Forms　Summons for time (RSC PF1).
Order for time (RSC PF2)

Order 13, r 5 Striking out pleadings

(1)　The court may at any stage of the proceedings in an action order the whole or any part of any pleading to be struck out or amended on the ground that—
>   (a)　it discloses no reasonable cause of action or defence, as the case may be; or
>   (b)　it is scandalous, frivolous or vexatious; or
>   (c)　it may prejudice, embarrass or delay the fair trial of the action; or
>   (d)　it is otherwise an abuse of the process of the court;

and may order the action to be stayed or dismissed or judgment to be entered accordingly, as the case may be.

(2)　Any application for an order under paragraph (1) shall be made on notice to the party affected by it.

(3)　This rule shall apply with the necessary modifications to a matter as it applies to an action.

Commencement　1 September 1982.
Cross references　See RSC Order 18, r 19(1), Order 32.

Order 13, r 6 Application for injunction

(1)　An application for the grant of an injunction may be made by any party to an action or matter before or after the trial or hearing, whether or not a claim for the injunction was included in that party's particulars of claim, originating application, petition, counterclaim or third party notice, as the case may be.

[(2)　Except where the district judge has power under Order 21, rule 5 or otherwise to hear and determine the proceedings in which the application is made, the application shall be made to the judge and rule 1(6) shall not apply.]

[(3) The application shall be made in the appropriate prescribed form and shall—
  (a) state the terms of the injunction applied for; and
  (b) be supported by an affidavit in which the grounds for making the application are set out,

and a copy of the affidavit and a copy of the application shall be served on the party against whom the injunction is sought not less than 2 days before the hearing of the application.

(3A) Where an order is sought ex parte before a copy of the application has been served on the other party, the affidavit shall explain why the application is so made and a copy of any order made ex parte shall be served with the application and affidavit in accordance with paragraph (3).

(4) An application may not be made before the issue of the summons, originating application or petition by which the action or matter is to be commenced except where the case is one of urgency, and in that case—
  (a) the affidavit in support of the application shall show that the action or matter is one which the court to which the application is made has jurisdiction to hear and determine, and
  (b) the injunction applied for shall, if granted, be on terms providing for the issue of the summons, originating application or petition in the court granting the application and on such other terms, if any, as the court thinks fit.

(4A) Paragraph (4)(a) and (b) shall apply, with the necessary modifications, where an application for an injunction is made by a defendant in a case of urgency before issuing a counterclaim or cross-application.]

(5) Unless otherwise directed, every application not made ex parte shall be heard in open court.

(6) Except where the case is one of urgency, a draft of the injunction shall be prepared beforehand by the party making an application to the judge under paragraph (1) and, if the application is granted, the draft shall be submitted to the judge by whom the application was heard and shall be settled by him.

(7) The injunction, when settled, shall be forwarded to the proper officer for filing.

Commencement 1 July 1991 (para (2)); 1 May 1991 (paras (3)–(4A)); 1 September 1982 (remainder).
Amendments Para (2): substituted by SI 1991/1126, r 12.
Paras (3)–(4A): substituted, for paras (3), (4) as originally enacted, by SI 1991/525, r 2.
Cross references See RSC Order 29, rr 1–8, Order 32.
Forms General form of injunction (N16).
Application for injunction (N16A).

Order 13, r 7 Application of RSC relating to other interlocutory matters

(1) Subject to the following paragraphs of this rule, the provisions of the RSC with regard to—
  (a) the payment into court of money in respect of which the defendant claims a lien on or other right to retain specific property (other than land) which the plaintiff seeks to recover;
  (b) the detention, custody, preservation or inspection of any relevant property;
  (c) the payment into court or securing of a specific fund which is in dispute in an action or matter;

(d)   the delivery up of any relevant goods under [section 4] of the Torts (Interference with Goods) Act 1977;

(e)   the taking of any sample of or the making of any observation or experiment on any relevant property;

(f)   the sale of any relevant property (other than land) which is of a perishable nature or likely to deteriorate if kept or which for any other good reason it is desirable to sell forthwith;

(g)   the exercise of the powers conferred by [sections 33 to 35 of the Supreme Court Act 1981];

(h)   the taking or making of any necessary accounts or inquiries,

shall apply in relation to proceedings or, as the case may be, subsequent proceedings in a county court as they apply in relation to proceedings or subsequent proceedings in the High Court.

In this paragraph "relevant property" and "relevant goods" mean property or, as the case may be, goods which is or are the subject matter of an action or matter or as to which any question may arise therein.

(2)   Rule 6(3) and (4) shall apply with the necessary modifications to an application for the relief mentioned in sub-paragraph (d) of paragraph (1) as they apply to an application for an injunction.

[(2A) The provisions of the RSC mentioned in sub-paragraph (g) of paragraph (1) shall apply as if for any reference therein to section 33 or section 34 of the Supreme Court Act 1981 there were substituted a reference to section 52 or section 53 respectively of the County Courts Act 1984.]

(3)   An application for the exercise of the powers conferred by [section 52(1) or 52(2) of the Act] shall be made by originating application and the affidavit in support of the application shall show that the subsequent proceedings are such as the court to which the application is made has jurisdiction to hear and determine.

(4)   An application for any other relief mentioned in paragraph (1) shall be made by notice and, in the case of an application for the exercise of the powers conferred by [section 53 of the Act], the notice shall be served on the person against whom the order is sought.

Commencement   1 August 1984 (para (2A)); 1 September 1982 (remainder).
Amendments   Para (1): in sub-para (d) words "section 4" substituted by SI 1982/1140, r 2, in sub-para (g) words "sections 33 to 35 of the Supreme Court Act 1981" substituted by SI 1982/1794, r 6.
Para (2A): inserted by SI 1984/878, r 9(a).
Para (3): words "section 52(1) or 52(2) of the Act" substituted by SI 1984/878, r 9(b).
Para (4): words "section 53 of the Act" substituted by SI 1984/878, r 9(c).
Cross references   See RSC Order 32, and in relation to para (1) as to sub-para (a) see RSC Order 29, r 6, as to sub-paras (b), (c) see RSC Order 29, r 2, as to sub-para (d) see RSC Order 29, r 2A, as to sub-para (e) see RSC Order 29, r 3, as to sub-para (f) see RSC Order 29, r 4, as to sub-para (g) see RSC Order 24, r 7A, Order 29, r 7A, and as to sub-para (h) see RSC Order 43, r 2.

Order 13, r 8 Security for costs where plaintiff resident out of England and Wales

(1)   Where, on the application of a defendant to an action or other proceeding, it appears to the court that the plaintiff is ordinarily resident out of England and Wales, then if, having regard to all the circumstances of the case, the court thinks it reasonable to do so, it may order the plaintiff to give such security for the defendant's costs of the action or other proceeding as it thinks just.

(2)   The references in paragraph (1) to a plaintiff and a defendant shall be construed

as references to the person (however described on the record) who is in the position of plaintiff or defendant, as the case may be, in the proceedings in question, including proceedings on a counterclaim.

(3)   The foregoing paragraphs are without prejudice to the provisions of any enactment by or under which the court is empowered to require security to be given for the costs of any proceedings.

Commencement 1 September 1982.
Cross references See RSC Order 23, r 1(1)(a), Order 32.
Forms Summons for security (RSC PF43).
Order for summons for security (RSC PF44).

Order 13, r 9 Order for consolidation etc

(1)   Where two or more actions or matters are pending in the same county court and it appears to the court—
    (a) that some common question of law or fact arises in both or all of them, or
    (b) that the rights to relief claimed are in respect of or arise out of the same transaction or series of transactions, or
    (c) that for some other reason it is desirable to make an order under this rule,

the court may order that the actions or matters be consolidated or may order them to be tried at the same time or one immediately after another or may order any of them to be stayed until the determination of any other of them.

(2)   An order under paragraph (1) may be made by the court of its own motion or on the application of any party on notice to all other parties to the actions or matters affected.

Commencement 1 September 1982.
Cross references See RSC Order 4, r 9, Order 32.
Forms Order for consolidation (N257).
Order staying proceedings (N258)

Order 13, r 10 Juries

(1)   An application for an order for trial with a jury may be made by any party on notice stating the grounds of the application.

(2)   Notice shall, if time permits, be given not less than 10 days before the return day, and where notice is given later or where for that or any other reason the application is not heard in time for a jury to be summoned, the judge or [district judge] may, on such terms as he thinks fit, postpone the trial so as to allow time for a jury to be summoned.

(3)   Notice of any order for trial with a jury shall be given by the proper officer to any party who was not present when the order was made.

Commencement 1 September 1982.
Cross references See RSC Order 32, Order 33, r 5.

Order 13, r 11 Assessors

(1)   A party to any proceedings who desires an assessor to be summoned to assist the judge at the hearing shall, not less than 14 days before the day fixed for the hearing, file an application in that behalf.

(2)   The proper officer shall submit to the judge any application made under paragraph (1) and, if the judge grants the application, the proper officer shall give to the parties notice stating the name of the person proposed to be summoned as assessor.

(3)   A party who objects to the person proposed to be summoned as assessor shall, within 4 days after service on him of the notice under paragraph (2), give to the proper officer notice of his objection stating the grounds thereof and on receipt of the notice the proper officer shall fix a day for the hearing of the objection and give notice thereof to the parties including, except in the notice to the party objecting, a statement of the grounds of the objection.

(4)   Where no notice of objection is given within the time limited or where an objection has been heard and an assessor has been selected, the applicant shall deposit in the court office such sum as the [district judge] thinks reasonable in respect of the assessor's fee for the day of hearing and thereupon the proper officer shall summon the assessor.

(5)   If an application for an assessor is refused, the proper officer shall give notice of the refusal to the parties.

(6)   An order summoning an assessor may be varied or revoked by the judge on application or of his own motion.

(7)   An assessor shall be entitled to such fee for attending court as would be allowed on taxation in respect of an expert witness.

(8)   Where the hearing of proceedings in which an assessor has been summoned is adjourned, the party on whose application the assessor was summoned shall forthwith deposit in the court office such sum as the [district judge] thinks reasonable in respect of the assessor's fee for the day of the adjourned hearing.

Commencement   1 September 1982.
Cross references   See RSC Order 32, Order 33, r 6.
Forms   Application for assessor (N259).

[Order 13, r 12 Interim payments

(1)   Subject to the following paragraphs of this rule, the provisions of RSC Order 29 Part II shall apply in relation to proceedings in a county court [except where those proceedings stand referred for arbitration under [Order 19, rule 3]].

(2)   ...

(3)   RSC Order 29, rule 13(1) shall apply with the substitution, for the reference to RSC Order 80, rule 12, of a reference to Order 10, rule 11 of these Rules.

(4)   RSC Order 29, rule 14 shall not apply but where an application is made for an order requiring the defendant to make an interim payment the court may treat the hearing of the application as a pre-trial review and Order 17 with the necessary modifications shall apply accordingly.]

Commencement   1 January 1983.
Amendments   This rule was added by SI 1982/1794, r 10.
Para (1): first words in square brackets substituted by SI 1991/1882, r 6, words "Order 19, rule 3" therein substituted by SI 1992/1965, r 17(a).
Para (2): amends SI 1965/1776, Order 29, r 10(4).
Cross references   See RSC Order 29, Part II, Order 32.

ORDER 14
DISCOVERY AND INTERROGATORIES

Order 14, r 1 Discovery of documents

(1)   Subject to the provisions of this rule and of rule 8, the court may, on the application on notice of any party to an action or matter, make an order (in these rules referred to as an "order for discovery") directing any other party to make a list of the documents which are or have been in his possession, custody or power relating to any matter in question in the proceedings and may at the same time or subsequently also order him to make an affidavit verifying such a list.

(2)   Where the applicant for an order for discovery did not make a written request for the discovery he desires, the court may refuse to make the order unless satisfied that there were sufficient reasons for not making such a request.

(3)   An order under this rule may be limited to such documents or classes of document only, or to such only of the matters in question in the proceedings, as may be specified in the order.

(4)   An order under this rule shall be drawn up by the proper officer and shall be served on the party against whom it is made.

[(5)   A copy of a list of documents made in compliance with an order or request, and any affidavit verifying such a list, shall be served on the applicant.]

Commencement   1 October 1990 (para (5)); 1 September 1982 (remainder).
Amendments   Para (5): substituted by SI 1990/1764, r 11.
Cross references   See RSC Order 24, r 3.
Forms   Order for discovery (N264).
List of documents (N265).
Affidavit verifying list of documents (N265(1)).

Order 14, r 2 Disclosure of particular documents

(1)   Subject to rule 8, the court may, on the application on notice of any party to an action or matter, make an order directing any other party to make an affidavit stating whether any document, or any class of document, specified or described in the application is or has at any time been in his possession, custody or power and, if not still in his possession, custody or power, when he parted with it and what has become of it.

(2)   An order may be made against a party under this rule notwithstanding that he has already made or been required to make a list of documents or affidavit under rule 1.

(3)   An application under this rule shall be supported by an affidavit stating that in the belief of the deponent the party against whom an order is sought has or at some time had in his possession, custody or power the document, or class of document, specified or described in the application and that it relates to one or more of the matters in question in the proceedings.

Commencement   1 September 1982.
Cross references   See RSC Order 24, r 7.

Order 14, r 3 Inspection of documents referred to in list

A party who makes a list of documents in compliance with an order or request under rule 1 shall allow the applicant to inspect the documents referred to in the list (other than any which he objects to produce) and to take copies thereof and accordingly, when he serves the list on the applicant, he shall also serve on him a notice stating a time within 7 days after service at which the documents may be inspected at a place specified in the notice.

Commencement 1 September 1982.
Cross references See RSC Order 24, r 9.

Order 14, r 4 Inspection of documents referred to in pleadings[, affidavits and witness statements]

(1)   Any party to an action or matter shall be entitled at any time to serve on any other party in whose pleadings[, affidavits or witness statements] reference is made to any document a notice requiring him to produce it for the inspection of the party giving the notice and to permit him to take copies thereof.

(2)   The party on whom a notice is served under paragraph (1) shall, within 4 days after service, serve on the party giving the notice a notice stating a time within 7 days after service thereof at which the documents, or such of them as he does not object to produce, may be inspected at a place specified in the notice and stating which (if any) of the documents he objects to produce and on what grounds.

Commencement 1 September 1982.
Amendments Rule heading: words ", affidavits and witness statements" substituted by SI 1992/1965, r 2(1).
Para (1): words ", affidavits and witness statements" substituted by SI 1992/1965, r 2(2).
Cross references See RSC Order 24, r 10.
Forms Notice to produce for inspection (N266).
Notice of objections to produce (RSC PF48).
Notice when documents may be inspected (N267).
Order for production of documents and inspection (RSC PF49).

Order 14, r 5 Order for production for inspection

(1)   If a party who is required to serve such a notice as is mentioned in rule 3 or who is served with a notice under rule 4(1)—
  (a)   fails to serve a notice under rule 3 or, as the case may be, rule 4(2), or
  (b)   objects to produce any documents for inspection, or
  (c)   offers inspection at a time or place which in the opinion of the court is unreasonable,

then, subject to rule 8, the court may, on the application on notice of the party entitled to inspection, make an order for production of the documents for inspection at such time and place, and in such manner, as the court thinks fit.

(2)   Without prejudice to paragraph (1), but subject to rule 8, the court may, on the application on notice of any party to an action or matter, order any other party to permit the applicant to inspect any documents in the possession, custody or power of the other party relating to any matter in question in the proceedings.

  An application for an order under this paragraph shall be supported by an affidavit specifying or describing the documents of which inspection is sought and stating the belief of the deponent that they are in the possession, custody or power of the other party and that they relate to a matter in question in the proceedings.

Commencement 1 September 1982.
Cross references See RSC Order 24, r 11.
Forms Order for production/inspection (RSC PF49).

[Order 14, r 5A Provision of copies of documents

(1)   Any party who is entitled to inspect any documents under any provision of this Order, or of any order made thereunder, may, at or before the time when inspection takes place, serve on the party who is required to produce such documents for inspection a notice (which shall contain an undertaking to pay the proper charges) requiring him to supply a true copy of any such document as is capable of being copied by photographic or similar process.

(2)   The party on whom such a notice is served must within 7 days after receipt thereof supply the copy requested together with an account of the proper charges.

(3)   Where a party fails to supply to another party a copy of any document under paragraph (2), the Court may, on the application of either party, make such order as to the supply of that document as it thinks fit.

(4)   The proper charges referred to in paragraph (1) shall not exceed the sum shown in Appendix A Item 4.]

Commencement 11 May 1988.
Amendments This rule was inserted by SI 1988/278, r 3.
Cross references See RSC Order 24, r 11A.

Order 14, r 6 Inspection by court before order

Where, on an application for an order for the production of any document for inspection, privilege from production is claimed or objection to production is made on any other ground, the court may inspect the document for the purpose of deciding whether the claim or objection is valid.

Commencement 1 September 1982.
Cross references See RSC Order 24, r 13(2).

Order 14, r 7 Order for production to court

At any stage of the proceedings in an action or matter the court may, subject to rule 8, order any party to produce to the court any document in his possession, custody or power relating to any matter in question in the proceedings and the court may deal with the document when produced in such manner as it thinks fit.

Commencement 1 September 1982.
Cross references See RSC Order 24, r 12.

Order 14, r 8 Discovery etc to be ordered only if necessary

(1)   On the hearing of an application under rule 1, [2, 5 or 5A], the court, if satisfied that the discovery, [disclosure, production or supply] sought is not necessary, or not necessary at that stage of the action or matter, may dismiss or adjourn the

application and shall in any case refuse to make an order if and so far as it is of opinion that discovery, [disclosure, production or supply], as the case may be, is not necessary either for disposing fairly of the action or matter or for saving costs.

(2)   No order shall be made under rule 7 unless the court is of opinion that production of the document is necessary as aforesaid.

Commencement   1 September 1982.
Amendments   Para (1): words "2, 5 or 5A" and "disclosure, production or supply" substituted by SI 1988/278, rr 4, 5.
Cross references   See RSC Order 24, rr 8, 13(1).

[Order 14, r 8A Use of documents

Any undertaking, whether express or implied, not to use a document for any purposes other than those of the proceedings in which it is disclosed shall cease to apply to such document after it has been read to or by the Court, or referred to, in open court, unless the Court for special reasons has otherwise ordered on the application of a party or of the person to whom the document belongs.]

Commencement   11 May 1988.
Amendments   This rule was inserted by SI 1988/278, r 7.
Cross references   See RSC Order 24, r 14A.

Order 14, r 9 Saving for public interest

The foregoing provisions of this Order shall be without prejudice to any rule of law which authorises or requires the withholding of any document on the ground that the disclosure of it would be injurious to the public interest.

Commencement   1 September 1982.
Cross references   See RSC Order 24, r 15.

Order 14, r 10 Failure to comply with order for discovery etc

(1)   If any party who is required by an order under any of the foregoing rules to make discovery of or disclose any documents or to produce any documents for inspection or for any other purpose [or to supply a copy of any document] fails to comply with the order, the court may make such order as it thinks just, including in particular an order that the action be dismissed or, as the case may be, an order that the defence be struck out and judgment entered accordingly.

(2)   Without prejudice to paragraph (1), a party who fails to comply with any order for discovery, disclosure or production of documents shall be liable to committal.

(3)   Notwithstanding anything in Order 29, rule 1(2), service on a party's solicitor of an order for discovery, disclosure or production or documents shall be sufficient service to found an application for committal of the party disobeying the order, but the party may show in answer to the application that he had no notice or knowledge of the order.

(4)   A solicitor on whom such an order is served and who fails without reasonable excuse to give notice thereof to his client shall be liable to committal.

Commencement 1 September 1982.
Amendments Para (1): words "or to supply a copy of any document" added by SI 1988/278, r 6.
Cross references See RSC Order 24, r 16.

Order 14, r 11 Interrogatories

(1) Subject to the following paragraphs, the provisions of the RSC with regard to the administration of interrogatories shall apply in relation to an action or matter in the county court as they apply in relation to a cause or matter in the High Court.

[(1A) Subject to paragraph (1B), where interrogatories without order are administered, a note at the end of the interrogatories shall set out the effect of RSC Order 26, rule 3(2) (right of the party served to apply to the court for the interrogatories to be varied or withdrawn).

(1B) Interrogatories without order shall not be administered in proceedings which stand referred for arbitration under [Order 19, rule 3].]

(2) An application for leave to serve interrogatories shall be made on notice to the party by whom the interrogatories are to be answered.

(3) If leave is granted, an order shall be drawn up by the proper officer and, subject to paragraph (4), shall be served on the party against whom it is made.

(4) The provisions of the RSC making service of the order on a party's solicitor sufficient to found an application for committal of the party disobeying the order shall apply notwithstanding anything in Order 29, rule 1(2).

(5) A solicitor on whom such an order is served and who fails without reasonable excuse to give notice thereof to his client shall be liable to committal.

Commencement 5 February 1990 (paras (1A), (1B)); 1 September 1982 (remainder).
Amendments Para (1A): inserted by SI 1989/2426, r 18.
Para (1B): inserted by SI 1989/2426, r 18; words "Order 19, rule 3" substituted by SI 1992/1965, r 17(b).
Cross references See RSC Order 26.
Forms Notice of application for interrogatories (RSC PF54).
Order for interrogatories (N269, RSC PF55).
Interrogatories (RSC PF56).
Answers (RSC PF57).

Order 14, r 12 Revocation and variation of orders

Any order made under a power conferred by this Order (including an order made on appeal from the [district judge] to the judge) may, on sufficient cause being shown, be revoked or varied by a subsequent order or direction of the court made or given at or before the hearing of the action or matter in connection with which the original order was made.

Commencement 1 September 1982.

ORDER 15
AMENDMENT

Order 15, r 1 Amendment by order

(1) Without prejudice to Order 5, rules 8 and 11, and rule 2 of this Order, but subject to the following paragraphs of this rule, the court may, in any action or matter, by order allow or direct—

(a) any originating process, pleading or any other document in the proceedings to be amended, or

(b) any person to be added, struck out or substituted as a party to the proceedings,

if the amendment, whether falling within sub-paragraph (a) or (b), is such that the High Court would have power to allow in a like case.

(2) In any case where a relevant limitation period has expired, the reference in paragraph (1) to the power of the High Court to allow the amendment shall be construed, in particular, as a reference to its power to do so subject to the conditions and restrictions imposed by section 35 of the Limitation Act 1980 and the RSC made thereunder.

(3) An order under paragraph (1) may be made on application at the hearing of the action or matter or before the hearing on notice or by the court of its own motion at any stage of the proceedings.

(4) No person shall be added as a plaintiff without his consent signified in writing or in such other manner as may be authorised.

(5) If a summons or other document issued by the court is to be amended pursuant to an order under paragraph (1), the amendment shall be made by the proper officer, and if any other document is to be amended, the amendment shall be made by the party whose document it is and he shall, if authorised or required to do so, file and serve on every other party to the proceedings a copy of the document as so amended.

(6) Where by an order under paragraph (1) a person is added or substituted as a defendant, the amended originating process shall, unless the court otherwise directs, be served on him in accordance with the rules applicable to the service of the originating process.

In relation to a person added or substituted as a defendant to a counterclaim this paragraph shall have effect as if for the reference to the amended originating process there were substituted a reference to the amended counterclaim.

Commencement 1 September 1982.
Cross references This order is broadly the equivalent of RSC Order 20 and the rule entitles the county court to allow amendment of pleadings or "any other document in the proceedings" in the same circumstances as the High Court could.

Order 15, r 2 Amendment of pleadings without order

[(1) Subject to Order 9, rule 2(3) and the following provisions of this rule, in any action or matter . . . a party may, without an order, amend any pleading of his—

(a) at any time before the return day, by filing the amended pleading and serving a copy on every other party, or

(b) at any stage of the proceedings, by filing the amended pleading endorsed with the consent of every party to the proceedings.

Where a day has been fixed for the pre-trial review of the action or matter, that day shall be treated as the return day for the purpose of this paragraph.]

(2) Where in a default action the plaintiff's claim is amended under paragraph (1) by adding or substituting a claim which could not be made in a default action, the action shall continue as if it had been commenced as a fixed date action.

(3) The court may, of its own motion or on the application of the opposite party, disallow an amendment made under paragraph (1) and shall do so where it is satisfied that, if an application for leave to make the amendment had been made under rule 1, leave would have been refused.

[(4) Where the plaintiff amends any pleading under paragraph (1)(a) he shall not apply for judgment under Order 9, rule 6 until 14 days after service of the amendment on the defendant.]

Commencement 28 March 1989 (para (4)); 11 May 1988 (para (1)); 1 September 1982 (remainder)
Amendments Para (1): substituted by SI 1988/278, r 8; words omitted revoked by SI 1989/236, r 7(1).
Para (4): added by SI 1989/236, r 7(2).
Cross references See the note to Order 15, r 1 above, and in particular RSC Order 20, r 3.

Order 15, r 3 Joinder of defendant in action for recovery of land

(1) Without prejudice to rule 1, the court may at any stage of the proceedings in an action for the recovery of land order any person who is in possession of the land (whether in actual possession or by a tenant) and is not a party to the action to be added as a defendant.

(2) An application by any person for an order adding him as a defendant under this rule may be made ex parte in writing stating the grounds of the application and showing that the applicant is in possession of the land in question and, if by a tenant, naming him.

(3) Where an order is made adding a person as a defendant under this rule, the proper officer shall send notice of the order, together with a copy of the application, to every other party to the proceedings.

Commencement 1 September 1982.
Cross references See the note to Order 15, r 1 above, and RSC Order 15, r 10.

Order 15, r 4 Actions for wrongful interference with goods

(1) Where the plaintiff in an action for wrongful interference with goods is one of two or more persons having or claiming any interest in the goods, then unless he has the written authority of every other such person to sue on the latter's behalf, the particulars of claim shall contain particulars of the plaintiff's title and identify every other person who, to his knowledge, has or claims any interest in the goods.

This paragraph shall not apply to an action arising out of an accident on land due to a collision or apprehended collision involving a vehicle.

(2) A defendant to an action for wrongful interference with goods who desires to show that a third party has a better right than the plaintiff as respects all or any part of the interest claimed by the plaintiff may, at any time after service of the summons on the

defendant and before any judgment or order is given or made on the plaintiff's claim, apply to the court on notice for directions as to whether any person named in the application (not being a person whose written authority the plaintiff has to sue on his behalf) should be joined with a view to establishing whether he has a better right than the plaintiff, or has a claim as a result of which the defendant might be doubly liable within the meaning of section 7 of the Torts (Interference with Goods) Act 1977.

Notice of any application under this paragraph shall, as well as being served on the plaintiff, be served on every person named in the application in accordance with the rules applicable to the service of a fixed date summons.

(3)   Where a person named in an application under paragraph (2) fails to appear on the hearing of the application or to comply with any direction given by the court on the application, the court may by order deprive him of any right of action against the defendant for the wrong, either unconditionally or subject to such terms and conditions as the court thinks fit.

Commencement 1 September 1982.
Cross references See the note to Order 15, r 1 above, and RSC Order 15, r 10A.

Order 15, r 5 Clerical mistakes and errors

Clerical mistakes in judgments or orders or errors arising therein from any accidental slip or omission may at any time be corrected by the court.

Commencement 1 September 1982.
Cross references See the note to Order 15, r 1 above, and in particular RSC Order 20, r 11.

ORDER 16
Transfer of Proceedings

Part I—From One County Court to Another

Order 16, r 1 General power of transfer

If the judge or [district judge] of any court is satisfied that—

    (a)   any action or matter in that court could be more conveniently or fairly heard and determined in some other court, or

    (b)   ...

    (c)   any pre-trial review or interlocutory application in an action or matter in that court could be more conveniently or fairly conducted or heard in some other court, or

    (d)   any proceedings for the enforcement of a judgment or order in an action or matter in that court could be more conveniently or fairly taken in some other court, or

    (e)   any payments required to be made into court under a judgment or order in an action or matter in that court could be more conveniently made into some other court,

then, subject to rule 3 and without prejudice, as respects paragraph (d), to Order 25, rule 2, the judge or [district judge] may order the action or matter to be transferred to that other court.

Commencement 1 September 1982.
Amendments Sub-para (b) revoked by SI 1991/1126, r 35(a).

Order 16, r 2 Proceedings commenced in wrong court

Where proceedings are commenced in the wrong court, the judge or [district judge] may, subject to rule 3,—

    (a)   transfer the proceedings to the court in which they ought to have been commenced, or

    (b)   order the proceedings to continue in the court in which they have been commenced, or

    (c)   order the proceedings to be struck out.

Commencement 1 September 1982.

Order 16, r 3 Saving for statutory provisions

Where an action or matter is required by any Act or statutory instrument other than these rules to be commenced in a particular court, nothing in rule 1 or 2 shall authorise the making of an order for the transfer of the action or matter to, or its continuance in, another court.

Commencement 1 September 1982.

Order 16, r 4 Making and carrying out of order for transfer

(1)   Subject to paragraph (2), an order for the transfer of proceedings under rule 1 or 2 may be made by the judge or, as the case may be, the [district judge] of his own motion or on the application of any party on notice to all other parties.

[(2) (a) A defendant who does not reside or carry on business within the district of the court in which an action has been commenced and who has delivered a defence; or

(b) a plaintiff who does not reside or carry on business within the district of the court to which an action has been automatically transferred under Order 9, rule 2(8),

may apply ex parte in writing to that court for an order under rule 1(a) or (c) transferring the action to another county court; and the judge or district judge of the first-mentioned court may, if he thinks fit, grant the application after considering any representations which he may give the other party to the application an opportunity of making.

In this paragraph "defence" includes a counterclaim.]

(3) Where a transfer is ordered under any of the foregoing provisions the proper officer of the court in which the action or matter is pending shall give notice of the transfer to all parties and shall send to the proper officer of the other court a certified copy of all the relevant entries in the records of the first-mentioned court.

(4) If the transfer is ordered under [rule 1(a) or (c)] or rule 2(a), or the proper officer of the other court so requests, the proper officer sending the certified copy mentioned in paragraph (3) shall also send all the documents in his custody relating to the action or matter.

(5) On receipt of the certified copy and any documents sent under paragraph (4) the proper officer of the court to which the action or matter has been transferred shall, if the transfer was ordered under [rule 1(a) or (c)], fix a day for the pre-trial review or, as may be appropriate, the hearing or disposal of the action or matter and send notice thereof . . . to all the parties.

In this paragraph a day for the hearing of the action or matter means, in the case of an action or matter which is to be referred to the arbitration of the judge or [district judge], the day on which the arbitration will be proceeded with.

[(5A) Nothing in paragraph (5) shall require the proper officer to fix a day in an action to which Order 17, rule 11 applies.]

(6) All subsequent proceedings shall be taken in the court to which the action or matter has been transferred except that, where the transfer was ordered under rule 1(d) or (e), any application or appeal under any of the provisions of Order 37 shall be made to the court in which the judgment or order was given or made.

Commencement 1 July 1991 (para (2)); 1 October 1990 (para (5A)); 1 September 1982 (remainder).
Amendments Para (2): substituted by SI 1991/1126, r 44.
Para (4): words "rule 1(a) or (c)" substituted by SI 1991/1126, r 35(b).
Para (5): words "rule 1(a) or (c)" substituted by SI 1991/1126, r 35(b); words omitted revoked by SI 1982/1140, r 2.
Para (5A): inserted by SI 1990/1764, r 12.

Order 16, r 5 Transfer of money in court

(1) The judge or [district judge] of any county court may, at any time, on application or of his own motion, order any money held by that court under Order 10, rule 11(1) . . . to be transferred to another county court if he is of opinion that it may be more conveniently dealt with in that court.

(2) Where such an order is made, the proper officer of the court holding the money shall transfer it to the other court in accordance with the [Court Funds Rules

1987] and shall send to the proper officer of the other court a certified copy of the relevant entries in the records of the first-mentioned court and, if so requested by that officer, all the documents in his custody relating to the proceedings.

Commencement   1 September 1982.
Amendments   Para (1): words omitted revoked by SI 1989/1838, r 18.
Para (2): words "Court Funds Rules 1987" substituted by SI 1989/1838, r 19.

PART II—FROM THE HIGH COURT TO A COUNTY COURT

Order 16, r 6 General provisions on transfer from High Court

(1)   Where by an order of the High Court—
   (a)   any proceedings are to be transferred to a county court, or
   (b)   an issue is directed to be tried in a county court,

the proper officer of the county court, on receipt of [the relevant documents] [shall either refer them to the [district judge] for directions or] shall enter the proceedings or issue in the records of the court and . . . fix a day for the hearing of the proceedings or issue or, if he thinks fit, a day for a pre-trial review and give 21 days' notice thereof to every party.

   [In this paragraph "the relevant documents" means—
   (a)   the writ (or a copy thereof),
   (b)   the order transferring the proceedings to the county court (or a copy thereof),
   (c)   all pleadings and affidavits filed in the High Court, and
   (d)   any documents required by the order for transfer to be filed in the county court.]

[(1A) Nothing in paragraph (1) shall require the proper officer to fix a day in an action to which Order 17, rule 11 applies unless
   (a)   before it was transferred to a county court the action had been set down for hearing in the High Court; or
   (b)   a request for a day to be fixed is made pursuant to directions under Order 17, rule 11

[and, where proceedings are transferred down from the High Court, the pleadings shall, for the purposes of the said rule 11, be deemed to be closed 14 days after the date of transfer.]]

(2)   The party lodging or causing to be lodged with the proper officer the documents aforesaid shall at the same time file—
   (a)   a statement of the names and addresses of the parties and of their solicitors;
   (b)   if he is the plaintiff and has not indorsed a statement of claim on the writ or served a statement of claim in the High Court, particulars of his claim, together with a copy for each defendant;
   (c)   if he is the defendant and only a counterclaim is transferred and the counterclaim has not been served in the High Court, particulars of the counterclaim, together with a copy for the plaintiff;
   (d)   where money has been paid into the High Court, a copy of the notice of payment into court, and
   (e)   a copy of any other pleading served but not filed in the High Court.
(3)   Where—
   (a)   a statement of claim has been indorsed on the writ or served in the High Court but no defence has been served there, or

(b) particulars of claim have been filed in the county court pursuant to paragraph (2)(b),

the defendant shall, within 14 days after receipt of the notice given under paragraph (1), deliver at the court office a defence and, if he has a counterclaim, particulars of the counterclaim, together with a copy for the plaintiff.

(4) Where only a counterclaim is transferred, paragraph (3) shall apply, with the necessary modifications, to the counterclaim as it applies to a claim.

(5) On receipt of any document filed by the plaintiff pursuant to paragraph (2)(b) or by the defendant pursuant to paragraph (2)(c) or (3), the proper officer shall send a copy to each defendant or, as the case may be, to the plaintiff.

(6) For the purpose of enabling a party to obtain further particulars, Order 6, rule 7, Order 9, rule 11(2) to (4), and Order 13, rule 2(2), shall apply in relation to—

(a) a statement of claim indorsed on the writ or served in the High Court,

(b) particulars of claim or counterclaim filed pursuant to paragraph (2), or

(c) a defence or counterclaim filed pursuant to paragraph (3),

as they apply in relation to particulars of claim, defence or counterclaim delivered in an action commenced in the county court.

Commencement 1 October 1990 (para (1A)); 1 September 1982 (remainder).
Amendments Para (1): words "the relevant documents" substituted, and words from "In this paragraph" to the end added, by SI 1991/1126, rr 18, 19; words from "shall either refer them" to "directions or" added by SI 1989/236, r 8; word omitted revoked by SI 1989/236, r 8.
Para (1A): inserted by SI 1990/1764, r 13; words from "and, where proceedings are transferred" to the end inserted by SI 1991/1882, r 7.

Order 16, r 7 Interpleader proceedings under execution

(1) In relation to interpleader proceedings under an execution which are ordered to be transferred from the High Court . . . , rule 6 shall have effect subject to the provisions of this rule.

(2) Notice of the hearing or pre-trial review of the proceedings shall be given by the proper officer to the sheriff as well as to every other party to the proceedings.

(3) The claimant shall, within 8 days of the receipt by him of the notice referred to in paragraph (2), file in triplicate particulars of any goods alleged to be his property and the grounds of his claim and the proper officer shall send a copy to the execution creditor and to the sheriff, but the judge may hear the proceedings or, as the case may be, the registrar may proceed with the pre-trial review, if he thinks fit, notwithstanding that the particulars have not been filed.

(4) Subject to any directions in the order of the High Court, damages may be claimed against the execution creditor in the same manner as in interpleader proceedings commenced in a county court.

(5) On any day fixed for the [pre-trial review] of the proceedings or for the hearing of any application by the sheriff or other party for directions the court may order the sheriff—

(a) to postpone the sale of the goods seized, or

(b) to remain in possession of such goods until the hearing of the proceedings, or

(c) to hand over possession of such goods to the registrar,

and, where a direction is given under sub-paragraph (c), the [district judge] shall be allowed reasonable charges for keeping possession of the goods, not exceeding those which might be allowed to the sheriff, and, if the [district judge] is directed to sell the goods, such charges for the sale as would be allowed under an execution issued by the county court.

(6)   No order made in the proceedings shall prejudice or affect the rights of the sheriff to any proper charges and the judge may make such order with respect to them as may be just.

(7)   The charges referred to in paragraphs (5) and (6) shall ultimately be borne in such manner as the judge shall direct.

(8)   The order made at the hearing of the proceedings shall direct how any money in the hands of the sheriff is to be disposed of.

Commencement 1 September 1982.
Amendments Para (1): words omitted revoked by SI 1991/1328, r 15.
Para (5): words "pre-trial review" substituted by SI 1982/1140, r 2.

Order 16, r 8 (*revoked by SI 1989/1383*)

PART III—FROM A COUNTY COURT TO THE HIGH COURT

[Order 16, r 9 Application for transfer

[(1)] An application for the transfer of proceedings to the High Court shall be made on notice stating the grounds of the application.

[(2) In a case to which article 7(1) of the High Court and County Courts Jurisdiction Order 1991 applies—
- (a) the grounds of the application shall be stated by reference to the criteria mentioned in article 7(5) of that Order; and
- (b) the application shall be supported by a statement showing whether or not the value of the action exceeds the sum for the time being specified in article 7(3) of the Order.]]

Commencement 1 July 1991 (para (2)); 1 September 1982 (remainder).
Amendments This rule was substituted, for rules 9, 10 as originally enacted, by SI 1982/436, r 2(2).
Para (1): numbered as such by SI 1991/1126, r 20.
Para (2): inserted by SI 1991/1126, r 20.

Order 16, r [10] Procedure on transfer or removal

Where an order is made by the High Court or a county court for the transfer or removal of any proceedings from a county court to the High Court, the proper officer shall—
- (a) send notice of the transfer or removal to all parties to the proceedings, and
- (b) make copies of all entries in the records of the court relating to the proceedings and send them, certified by the [district judge], to the proper officer of the High Court, together with—
  - (i) all documents filed in the proceedings,
  - (ii) the order of transfer if made by the county court, and

(iii) in the case of legitimacy proceedings, a certificate by the [district judge] showing the state of the proceedings and the steps which have been taken therein.

Commencement   1 September 1982.
Amendments   Originally rule 11, renumbered as rule 10 by SI 1982/436, r 2(3).

Order 16, r [11] Certiorari or prohibition

A party obtaining from the High Court, on an ex parte application, an order giving leave to make an application for an order of certiorari to remove proceedings from a county court or an order of prohibition to any such court shall forthwith serve a copy of the order on the opposite party and on the proper officer of the county court.

Commencement   1 September 1982.
Amendments   Originally rule 12, renumbered as rule 11 by SI 1982/436, r 2(3).

Order 16, r 12   *(added by SI 1986/636; revoked by SI 1991/1882)*

ORDER 17
Pre-trial Review

Order 17, r 1 Matters to be considered on pre-trial review

On any day fixed for the pre-trial review of an action or matter the [district judge] shall, subject to the following provisions of this Order, consider the course of the proceedings and give all such directions as appear to be necessary or desirable for securing the just, expeditious and economical disposal of the action or matter.

Commencement 1 September 1982.
Cross references This order is broadly the equivalent of and has the same intention as the provisions of RSC Order 25 relating to a summons for directions in the High Court.

Order 17, r 2 Securing admissions and agreements

On the pre-trial review the registrar shall endeavour to secure that the parties make all such admissions and agreements as ought reasonably to be made by them in relation to the proceedings and may record in the order made on the review any admission or agreement so made or any refusal to make any admission or agreement.

Commencement 1 September 1982.
Cross references See the note to Order 17, r 1 above.

Order 17, r 3 Application for particular direction

Every party shall, so far as practicable, apply on the pre-trial review for any particular direction he may desire and shall file and give to every other party notice of his intention to do so, and if an application which might have been made on the review is made subsequently, the applicant shall pay the costs of and occasioned by the application, unless the court otherwise directs.

Commencement 1 September 1982.
Cross references See the note to Order 17, r 1 above.

Order 17, r 4 Rules as to interlocutory applications to apply

The provisions of these rules relating to interlocutory application shall have effect as if the pre-trial review were the hearing of an interlocutory application and accordingly the [district judge] may, on the review, exercise any of the powers exercisable by him on an interlocutory application and may do so of his own motion if no application is made for the exercise of the power.

Commencement 1 September 1982.
Cross references See the note to Order 17, r 1 above.

Order 17, r 5 Non-appearance by plaintiff

(1) If the plaintiff does not appear on the pre-trial review, the [district judge] may, without prejudice to any other power, proceed with the review in his absence or order the action or matter to be struck out.

(2) Order 21, rules 1(2) and (3) and 2(2), shall apply, with the necessary modifications, in relation to the striking out of an action or matter under paragraph (1) as they apply in relation to the striking out of proceedings under Order 21, rule 1(1).

Commencement 1 September 1982.
Cross references See the note to Order 17, r 1 above.

Order 17, r 6 Admission by defendant of plaintiff's claim

If, on or before the pre-trial review, the defendant admits the plaintiff's claim or such part thereof as the plaintiff accepts in satisfaction of his claim, the [district judge] may give such judgment or make such order as he thinks just.

Commencement 1 September 1982.
Cross references See the note to Order 17, r 1 above.

Order 17, r 7 Non-appearance by defendant who has not delivered admission or defence

(1) If the defendant does not appear on the pre-trial review of an action and has not delivered an admission or defence, the [district judge] may, if he thinks fit, enter judgment for the plaintiff.

(2) If the plaintiff's claim is for unliquidated damages, any judgment entered under paragraph (1) shall be an interlocutory judgment for damages to be assessed, unless at the time of the entry of judgment the plaintiff adduces evidence as to the amount of his damages.

Commencement 1 September 1982.
Cross references See the note to Order 17, r 1 above.
Forms Interlocutory judgment (N17).

Order 17, r 8 Non-appearance by defendant who has delivered defence

If the defendant has delivered a defence but does not appear on the pre-trial review of an action, the registrar may, at the request of the plaintiff and upon proof of facts entitling him to relief, give such judgment or make such order as the [district judge] thinks fit.

Commencement 1 September 1982.
Cross references See the note to Order 17, r 1 above.

Order 17, r 9 Fixing date of hearing

On or as soon as practicable after the completion by the [district judge] of his consideration of the matters referred to in rule 1 the proper officer shall, if the action or matter remains to be heard and determined, fix a day for the hearing and give notice thereof to every party.

Commencement 1 September 1982.
Cross references See the note to Order 17, r 1 above.

Order 17, r 10 Pre-trial review in other proceedings

If in any proceedings in which no pre-trial review has been fixed the [district judge] is nevertheless of opinion that the question of giving directions ought to be considered, then, without prejudice to Order 13, rule 2(4), he may, with a view to obtaining assistance in such consideration, cause notice to be given to the parties requiring them to appear before him on a day named in the notice and thereupon the provisions of this Order shall have effect, with the necessary modifications, as if that day were the day fixed for a pre-trial review.

Commencement   1 September 1982.
Cross references   See the note to Order 17, r 1 above.

[Order 17, r 11 Automatic directions

(1)   This rule applies to any default or fixed date action except—
   - (a)   an action for the administration of the estate of a deceased person;
   - (b)   an Admiralty action;
   - (c)   proceedings which are referred for arbitration under Order 19;
   - (d)   an action arising out of a regulated consumer credit agreement within the meaning of the Consumer Credit Act 1974;
   - (e)   an action for the delivery of goods;
   - (f)   an action for the recovery of income tax;
   - (g)   interpleader proceedings or an action in which an application is made for relief by way of interpleader;
   - (h)   an action of a kind mentioned in section 66(3) of the Act (trial by jury);
   - (i)   an action for the recovery of land;
   - (j)   a partnership action;
   - (k)   an action to which Order 48A applies (patent actions);
   - (l)   a contentious probate action;
   - (m)   ...
   - (n)   an action to which Order 5, rule 5 applies (representative proceedings);
   - (o)   an action to which [Order 9, rule 3(6)] applies (admission of part of plaintiff's claim);
   - (p)   an action on a third party notice or similar proceedings under Order 12;
   - (q)   an action to which Order 47, rule 3 applies (actions in tort between husband and wife);
   - [(r)   an action to which Order 48C applies (the Central London County Court Business List)].

[(1A) This rule applies to actions transferred from the High Court as it applies to actions commenced in a county court but (without prejudice to paragraph (2)) where directions have been given by the High Court, directions taking effect automatically under this rule shall have effect subject to any directions given by the High Court.]

[(2)   In an action to which this rule applies—
   - (a)   except where a pre-trial review is ordered pursuant to a direction given under paragraph (4)(a), the foregoing provisions of this Order shall not apply and directions shall take effect automatically in accordance with the following paragraphs of this rule;
   - (b)   where the court gives directions with regard to any matter arising in the course of proceedings, directions taking effect automatically under this rule shall have effect subject to any directions given by the court.]

(3)   When the pleadings are deemed to be closed, the following directions shall take effect—

    (a) there shall be discovery of documents within 28 days, and inspection within 7 days thereafter, in accordance with paragraph (5);

[(b) except with the leave of the court or where all parties agree—

    (i) no expert evidence may be adduced at the trial unless the substance of that evidence has been disclosed to the other parties in the form of a written report within 10 weeks;

    (ii) subject to paragraph (7), the number of expert witnesses of any kind shall be limited to two; and

    (iii) any party who intends to place reliance at the trial on any other oral evidence shall, within 10 weeks, serve on the other parties written statements of all such oral evidence which he intends to adduce;]

    (c) photographs and sketch plans and, in an action for personal injuries, the contents of any police accident report book shall be receivable in evidence at the trial and shall be agreed if possible;

    (d) unless a day has already been fixed, the plaintiff shall within 6 months request the proper officer to fix a day for the hearing and rule 12 shall apply where such request is made.

[(3A) Paragraphs (4) to (16) of Order 20, rule 12A shall apply with respect to statements and reports served under sub-paragraph (3)(b) as they apply with respect to statements served under that rule.]

[(4) Nothing in paragraph (3) shall—

    (a) prevent the court from giving, of its own motion or on the application of any party, such further or different directions or orders as may in the circumstances be appropriate (including an order that a pre-trial review be held or fixing a date for the hearing or dismissing the proceedings or striking out any claim made therein); or

    (b) prevent the making of an order for the transfer of the proceedings to the High Court or another county court;

and rule 3 shall apply where an application is made under this paragraph as it applies to applications made on a pre-trial review.]

(5) Subject to paragraph (6), the parties must make discovery by serving lists of documents and—

    (a) subject to sub-paragraph (c), each party must make and serve on every other party a list of documents which are or have been in his possession, custody or power relating to any matter in question between them in the action;

    (b) the court may, on application,—

    (i) order that discovery under this paragraph shall be limited to such documents or classes of documents only, or as to such only of the matters in question, as may be specified in the order, or

    (ii) if satisfied that discovery by all or any of the parties is not necessary, order that there shall be no discovery of documents by any or all of the parties;

    and the court shall make such an order if and so far as it is of opinion that discovery is not necessary either for disposing fairly of the action or for saving costs;

    (c) where liability is admitted or in an action for personal injuries arising out of a road accident, discovery shall be limited to disclosure of any documents relating to the amount of damages;

    (d) the provisions of Order 14 of these rules relating to inspection of documents shall apply where discovery is made under this paragraph as it applies where discovery is made under that Order.

(6) Discovery under paragraph (5) shall not apply in proceedings to which the Crown is a party.

(7) In an action for personal injuries—
  (a) the number of expert witnesses shall be limited in any case to two medical experts and one expert of any other kind;
  (b) nothing in paragraph (3) shall require a party to produce a further medical report if he proposes to rely at the trial only on the report provided pursuant to Order 6, rule 1(5) or (6) but, where a further report is disclosed, that report shall be accompanied by an amended statement of the special damages claimed, if appropriate.

(8) Where the plaintiff makes a request pursuant to paragraph (3)(d) for the proper officer to fix a day for the hearing, he shall file a note which shall if possible be agreed by the parties giving—
  (a) an estimate of the length of the trial, and
  (b) the number of witnesses to be called.

(9) If no request is made pursuant to paragraph (3)(d) within 15 months of the day on which pleadings are deemed to be closed (or within 9 months after the expiry of any period fixed by the court for making such a request), the action shall be automatically struck out.

(10) Where the proper officer fixes a day for the hearing, he shall give not less than 21 days' notice thereof to every party.

(11) For the purposes of this rule,—
  (a) pleadings shall be deemed to be closed 14 days after the delivery of a defence in accordance with Order 9, rule 2 or, where a counterclaim is served with the defence, 28 days after the delivery of the defence;
  (b) "a road accident" means an accident on land due to a collision or apprehended collision involving a vehicle;
  (c) "a statement of the special damages claimed" has the same meaning as in Order 6, rule 1(7).

(12) Unless the context otherwise requires, references in these rules to the return day in relation to a fixed date action to which this rule applies shall be construed as references to the date on which directions take effect under this rule.]

Commencement 16 November 1992 (para (3A)); 1 July 1991 (paras (1A), (2), (4)); 1 October 1990 (remainder).
Amendments This rule was inserted by SI 1989/2426, r 13, it was then substituted by SI 1990/1764, r 14. Para (1): sub-para (m) revoked by SI 1993/2175, r 14; in sub-para (o) words "Order 9, rule 3(6)" substituted by SI 1991/1126, r 36; sub-para (r) inserted by SI 1994/1288, r 2.
Para (1A): inserted by SI 1991/1328, r 19.
Paras (2), (4): substituted by SI 1991/1126, rr 23, 24.
Para (3): sub-para (b) substituted by SI 1992/1965, r 3.
Para (3A): inserted by SI 1992/1965, r 4.
Cross references See the note to Order 17, r 1 above and RSC Order 25, r 8.

[Order 17, r 12 Arrangements for trial

(1) This rule applies, subject to any order of the court, where a day has been fixed for the hearing of an action or matter—
  (a) to which rule 11 applies; or
  (b) in which a pre-trial review has been held.

(2)   At least 14 days before the day fixed for the hearing the defendant shall inform the plaintiff of the documents which he wishes to have included in the bundle to be provided under paragraph (3).

(3)   At least 7 days before the day fixed for the hearing the plaintiff shall file one copy of a paginated and indexed bundle comprising the documents on which either of the parties intends to rely or which either party wishes to have before the court at the hearing together with two copies of each of the following documents—

    (a)   any request for particulars and the particulars given, and any answer to interrogatories,

    (b)   witness statements which have been exchanged, and experts' reports which have been disclosed, together with an indication of whether the contents of such documents are agreed,

    (c)   the requisite legal aid documents.

(4)   Nothing in this rule shall—

    (a)   prevent the court from giving, whether before or after the documents have been filed, such further or different directions as to the documents to be filed as may, in the circumstances, be appropriate; or

    (b)   prevent the making of an order for the transfer of the proceedings to the High Court or to another county court.

(5)   For the purposes of this rule—

    (a)   "plaintiff" includes a defendant where an action is proceeding on a counterclaim;

    (b)   "the requisite legal aid documents" means any documents which are required by regulations made under Part IV of the Legal Aid Act 1988 to be included in the papers for the use of the court.]

Commencement   2 January 1991.
Amendments   This rule was inserted by SI 1990/1764, r 25.
Cross references   See the note to Order 17, r 1 above, and Order 34, r 10.

ORDER 18
DISCONTINUANCE OF PROCEEDINGS

Order 18, r 1 Notice of discontinuance

The plaintiff in an action or matter may, at any time before judgment or final order, discontinue the proceedings wholly or in part against all or any of the defendants thereto by giving notice to the proper officer and to every defendant against whom he desires to discontinue, and the notice to the proper officer shall contain a certificate by the plaintiff that he has also given notice to the defendant.

Commencement   1 September 1982.
Cross references   See RSC Order 21, rr 2, 3.
Forms   Notice of discontinuance (N279).

Order 18, r 2 Effect of discontinuance

(1)   Subject to the following paragraphs of this rule and to [Order 19, rule 4], and Order 38, rule 3(4), a defendant served with a notice of discontinuance under rule 1 may, unless the court on the application of the plaintiff otherwise directs, lodge for taxation a bill of the costs incurred by him before the receipt of the notice or, if the proceedings are not wholly discontinued against him, his costs so incurred in relation to the part discontinued and, if the costs allowed on taxation are not paid within 14 days after taxation, he may have judgment entered for the taxed costs and the costs of entering judgment.

(2)   Where the proceedings are not wholly discontinued against a defendant entering judgment for costs pursuant to paragraph (1), execution shall not issue for such costs, without the leave of the court, before the proceedings are determined.

(3)   Discontinuance of any action or matter or a particular claim therein under rule 1 shall not be a defence to subsequent proceedings for the same or substantially the same cause of action; but if any such proceedings are subsequently brought before payment of any costs taxed under paragraph (1), the court may order them to be stayed until those costs have been paid.

Commencement   1 September 1982.
Amendments   Para (1): words "Order 19, rule 4" substituted by SI 1992/1965, r 16(b).
Cross references   See RSC Order 21, rr 4, 5 , Order 62, r 5(3).

Order 18, r 3 Discontinuance of counterclaim

Rules 1 and 2 shall apply, with the necessary modifications, in relation to the discontinuance by a defendant of a counterclaim as they apply in relation to the discontinuance by a plaintiff of an action or matter.

Commencement   1 September 1982.
Cross references   See RSC Order 21, r 2(2) , Order 62, r 5(3).

[ORDER 19

REFERENCE TO ARBITRATION OR FOR INQUIRY AND REPORT OR TO EUROPEAN COURT

PART I—COUNTY COURT ARBITRATION

Interpretation and application

Order 19, r 1

In this Part of this Order, unless the context otherwise requires—

"lay representative" means a person exercising a right of audience by virtue of an order made under section 11 of the Courts and Legal Services Act 1990 (representation in county courts),

"reference" means the reference of proceedings to arbitration under section 64 of the Act,

"order" means an order referring proceedings to arbitration under that section and

"outside arbitrator" means an arbitrator other than the judge or district judge.]

Commencement   26 October 1992.
Amendments   Order 19, rr 1–10 were substituted, for Order 19, rr 1–6 as originally enacted, by SI 1992/1965, r 6.

[Order 19, r 2

In this Part of this Order—

(a) Rules 3 and 4 apply only to small claims automatically referred to arbitration under rule 3, and

(b) Rules 5 to 10 apply to all arbitrations.]

Commencement   26 October 1992.
Amendments   See the note to Order 19, r 1.

[Order 19, r 3 Automatic reference of small claims

(1)   Any proceedings in which the sum claimed or amount involved does not exceed £1000 (leaving out of account the sum claimed or amount involved in any counterclaim) shall stand referred for arbitration by the district judge upon the receipt by the court of a defence to the claim.

(2)   Where any proceedings are referred for arbitration by the district judge under paragraph (1), he may, after considering the defence and whether on the application of any party or of his own motion, order trial in court if he is satisfied—

(a) that a difficult question of law or a question of fact of exceptional complexity is involved; or

(b) that fraud is alleged against a party; or

(c) that the parties are agreed that the dispute should be tried in court; or

(d) that it would be unreasonable for the claim to proceed to arbitration having regard to its subject matter, the size of any counterclaim, the circumstances of the parties or the interests of any other person likely to be affected by the award.

(3)   Where the district judge is minded to order trial in court of his own motion—

    (a)   the proper officer shall notify the parties in writing specifying on which of the grounds mentioned in paragraph (2) the district judge is minded to order trial in court;

    (b)   within 14 days after service of the proper officer's notice on him, a party may give written notice stating his reasons for objecting to the making of the order;

    (c)   if in any notice under sub-paragraph (b) a party so requests, the proper officer shall fix a day for a hearing at which the district judge—

        (i)   shall decide whether to order trial in court, and

        (ii)   may give directions regarding the steps to be taken before or at any subsequent hearing as if he were conducting a preliminary appointment or, as the case may be, a pre-trial review;

and, in the absence of any request under sub-paragraph (c), the district judge may, in the absence of the parties, order trial in court.

(4)   For the purposes of paragraph (1), "a defence to the claim" includes a document admitting liability for the claim but disputing or not admitting the amount claimed.]

Commencement   26 October 1992.
Amendments   See the note to Order 19, r 1.
Forms   Notice of arbitration hearing (N18A–19A).
Notice of intention to remove case from small claims procedure (N451).

[Order 19, r 4 Restriction on allowance of costs in small claims

(1)   In this rule, "costs" means—

    (a)   solicitors' charges,

    (b)   sums allowed to a litigant in person pursuant to Order 38, rule 17,

    (c)   a fee or reward charged by a lay representative for acting on behalf of a party in the proceedings.

(2)   No costs shall be allowed as between party and party in respect of any proceedings referred to arbitration under rule 3, except—

    (a)   the costs which were stated on the summons or which would have been stated on the summons if the claim had been for a liquidated sum;

    (b)   the costs of enforcing the award, and

    (c)   such further costs as the district judge may direct where there has been unreasonable conduct on the part of the opposite party in relation to the proceedings or the claim therein.

(3)   Nothing in paragraph (2) shall be taken as precluding the award of the following allowances—

    (a)   any expenses which have been reasonably incurred by a party or a witness in travelling to and from the hearing or in staying away from home;

    (b)   a sum not exceeding £29.00 in respect of a party's or a witness's loss of earnings when attending a hearing;

    (c)   a sum not exceeding £112.50 in respect of the fees of an expert.

(4)   Where trial in court is ordered, paragraph (2) shall not apply to costs incurred after the date of the order.

(5)   Where costs are directed under paragraph (2)(c), those costs shall not be taxed and the amount to be allowed shall be specified by the arbitrator or the district judge.]

Commencement   26 October 1992.
Amendments   See the note to Order 19, r 1.

[Order 19, r 5 The arbitrator

(1)   Unless the court otherwise orders, the district judge shall be the arbitrator.

(2)   An order shall not be made referring proceedings to the Circuit judge except by or with the leave of the judge.

(3)   An order shall not be made referring proceedings to an outside arbitrator except with the consent of the parties.

(4)   Where proceedings are referred to an outside arbitrator, the order shall be served on the arbitrator as well as on the parties, but it shall not, unless the court directs, be served on anyone until each party has paid into court such sum as the district judge may determine in respect of the arbitrator's remuneration.]

Commencement   26 October 1992.
Amendments   See the note to Order 19, r 1.

[Order 19, r 6 Preparation for the hearing

(1)   Paragraph (2) of this rule shall apply unless the district judge—
    (a)   is minded to order trial in court under rule 3(3) or
    (b)   decides that a preliminary appointment should be held.

(2)   Upon the reference to arbitration the district judge shall consider the documents filed and give an estimate of the time to be allowed for the hearing and the proper officer shall—
    (a)   give the parties not less than 21 days' notice of the day fixed for the hearing; and
    (b)   issue directions under paragraph (3) in the appropriate form regarding the steps to be taken before or at any subsequent hearing.

(3)   Where proceedings stand referred to arbitration, the following directions shall take effect—
    (a)   each party shall not less than 14 days before the date fixed for the hearing send to every other party copies of all documents which are in his possession and on which that party intends to rely at the hearing;
    (b)   each party shall not less than 7 days before the date fixed for the hearing send to the court and to every other party a copy of any expert report on which that party intends to rely at the hearing and a list of the witnesses whom he intends to call at the hearing.

(4)   A preliminary appointment shall only be held—
    (a)   where directions under paragraph (3) are not sufficient and special directions can only be given in the presence of the parties, or
    (b)   to enable the district judge to dispose of the case where the claim is ill-founded or there is no reasonable defence.

In deciding whether to hold a preliminary appointment, the district judge shall have regard to the desirability of minimising the number of court attendances by the parties.

(5)   Where the district judge decides to hold a preliminary appointment, the proper

officer shall fix a date for the appointment and give to the plaintiff and the defendant not less than 8 days' notice of the day so fixed.

(6)   On the preliminary appointment the district judge shall have the same powers as he has under Order 17 on a pre-trial review and he shall—

(a)   give an estimate of the time to be allowed for the hearing (unless the parties consent to his deciding the dispute on the statements and documents submitted to him); and

(b)   whether of his own motion or at the request of a party, give such additional directions regarding the steps to be taken before and at the hearing as may appear to him to be necessary or desirable.

Directions given under sub-paragraph (b) may include (but shall not be limited to) a requirement that a party should clarify his claim or, as the case may be, his defence.

(7)   After the preliminary appointment, the proper officer shall—

(a)   give the parties not less than 21 days' notice of the day fixed for the hearing; and

(b)   issue directions under paragraph (3) in the appropriate form regarding the steps to be taken before or at that hearing together with any additional directions given pursuant to paragraph (6)(b).

(8)   The district judge may from time to time whether on application or of his own motion amend or add to any directions issued if he thinks it necessary to do so in the circumstances of the case.

(9)   The following provisions of these rules shall not apply where proceedings stand referred to arbitration:

(a)   Order 6, rule 7 (further particulars),

(b)   Order 9, rule 11 (particulars of defence),

(c)   Order 14, rules 1(2), 3 to 5, 5A and 11 (discovery and interrogatories), and

(d)   Order 20, rules 2 and 3 (notices to admit facts and documents),

(e)   Order 20, rule 12A (exchange of witness statements).

Order 11, rules 1, 1A, 3 to 5, 7, 8 and 10 (payments into court) and Order 13, rule 1(8)(a) (security for costs) shall not apply where proceedings stand referred to arbitration under rule 3.

(10) If it appears to the court at any time after a reference has been made (whether by order or otherwise) that there are any other matters within the jurisdiction of the court in dispute between the parties, the court may order them also to be referred to arbitration.]

Commencement   26 October 1992.

Amendments   See the note to Order 19, r 1.

Forms   Notice of Preliminary hearing (N18–19).

[Order 19, r 7 Conduct of hearing

(1)   Any proceedings referred to arbitration shall be dealt with in accordance with the following paragraphs of this rule unless the arbitrator otherwise orders.

(2)   The hearing may be held at the court house, at the court office or at any other place convenient to the parties.

(3)   The hearing shall be informal and the strict rules of evidence shall not apply;

unless the arbitrator orders otherwise, the hearing shall be held in private and evidence shall not be taken on oath.

(4)   At the hearing the arbitrator may adopt any method of procedure which he may consider to be fair and which gives to each party an equal opportunity to have his case presented; having considered the circumstances of the parties and whether (or to what extent) they are represented, the arbitrator—

   (a)   may assist a party by putting questions to the witnesses and the other party; and
   (b)   should explain any legal terms or expressions which are used.

(5)   If any party does not appear at the arbitration, the arbitrator may, after taking into account any pleadings or other documents filed, make an award on hearing any other party to the proceedings who may be present.

(6)   With the consent of the parties and at any time before giving his decision, the district judge may consult any expert or call for an expert report on any matter in dispute or invite an expert to attend the hearing as assessor.

(7)   The arbitrator may require the production of any document or thing and may inspect any property or thing concerning which any question may arise.

(8)   The arbitrator shall inform the parties of his award and give his reasons for it to any party who may be present at the hearing.]

Commencement   26 October 1992.
Amendments   See the note to Order 19, r 1.

[Order 19, r 8 Setting awards aside

(1)   Where proceedings are referred to arbitration, the award of the arbitrator shall be final and may only be set aside pursuant to paragraph (2) or on the ground that there has been misconduct by the arbitrator or that the arbitrator made an error of law.

(2)   Where an award has been given in the absence of a party, the arbitrator shall have power, on that party's application, to set the award aside and to order a fresh hearing as if the award were a judgment and the application were made pursuant to Order 37, rule 2.

(3)   An application by a party to set aside an award made by a district judge or an outside arbitrator on the ground mentioned in paragraph (1) shall be made on notice and the notice shall be served within 14 days after the day on which the award was entered as the judgment of the court.

(4)   An application under paragraph (3) shall, giving sufficient particulars, set out the misconduct or error of law relied upon.

(5)   Order 37, rule 1 (rehearing of proceedings tried without a jury) shall not apply to proceedings referred to arbitration.]

Commencement   26 October 1992.
Amendments   See the note to Order 19, r 1.

[Order 19, r 9 Mode of voluntary reference

(1)   Except as provided by rule 3, a reference shall be made only on the application of a party to the proceedings sought to be referred.

(2)   Unless the court otherwise directs, an application by a party to any proceedings for a reference may be made—
- (a)   in the case of a plaintiff, by request incorporated in his particulars of claim;
- (b)   in the case of a defendant, by request incorporated in any defence or counterclaim of his;
- (c)   in any case, on notice under Order 13, rule 1.

(3)   Where an application for a reference is made under paragraph (1) and the proceedings are not referred to arbitration under rule 3, the following provisions shall apply:—
- (a)   Subject to rule 5(2) and sub-paragraphs (b) and (c) below, an order may be made by the district judge.
- (b)   If the court is satisfied that an allegation of fraud against a party is in issue in the proceedings, an order shall not be made except with the consent of that party.
- (c)   Where the district judge is minded to grant an application under paragraph (1), the proper officer shall notify the parties in writing accordingly and within 14 days after service of the proper officer's notice on him, a party may give written notice stating his reasons for objecting to the reference; if in any such notice a party so requests, the proper officer shall fix a day for a hearing at which the district judge shall decide whether to grant the application and, in the absence of any such request, the district judge may consider the application in the absence of the parties.]

Commencement   26 October 1992.
Amendments   See the note to Order 19, r 1.

[Order 19, r 10 Costs

Subject to rule 4, the costs of the action up to and including the entry of judgment shall be in the discretion of the arbitrator to be exercised in the same manner as the discretion of the court under the provisions of the County Court Rules.]

Commencement   26 October 1992.
Amendments   See the note to Order 19, r 1.

PART II—REFERENCE FOR INQUIRY AND REPORT

Order 19, r [11] Mode of making order for reference

An order under [section 65] of the Act for the reference of any proceedings or questions to the [district judge] or a referee for inquiry and report may be made—
- (a)   on an application by any party before the hearing on notice; or
- (b)   on an application by any party at the hearing; or
- (c)   at any stage of the proceedings by the court of its own motion.

Commencement   1 September 1982.
Amendments   Originally rule 7, renumbered as rule 11 by SI 1992/1965, r 7.
Words "section 65" substituted by SI 1984/878, r 12, Schedule.
Cross references   See RSC Order 36, rr 8, 11.

Order 19, r [12] [District judge's] power to make order

An order referring any question arising in any proceedings to a referee for inquiry and report may be made by the [district judge] if the sum claimed or amount involved in the proceedings does not exceed the sum mentioned in Order 21, rule 5(1)(b), or in any other case with the consent of the parties.

Commencement 1 September 1982.
Amendments Originally rule 8, renumbered as rule 12 by SI 1992/1965, r 7.

Order 19, r [13] Conduct of reference

Subject to any order as to the conduct of the reference—
  (a) the [district judge] may hold the inquiry at the court house or at the court office or at any place convenient to the parties;
  (b) a referee, other than the [district judge], may hold the inquiry at any place convenient to the parties;
  (c) the [district judge] or referee may inspect any property or thing concerning which any question may arise;
  (d) the attendance of witnesses may be enforced by summons and the inquiry shall be conducted in the same manner, as nearly as circumstances will permit, as if the inquiry were the hearing of an action;
  (e) subject to rule 10, the [district judge] or referee shall have the powers of a judge with respect to discovery and production of documents and in the conduct of the inquiry;
  (f) the [district judge] or referee may submit any question arising in the inquiry for the decision of the court;
  (g) the report shall be in writing and filed and—
    (i) the proper officer shall give notice to all parties of the filing of the report;
    (ii) subject to the right of the referee or any party to appeal to the judge, the [district judge] shall fix the remuneration of the referee unless it has been agreed;
    (iii) upon payment into court by any party of the amount fixed for the remuneration of the referee, without prejudice as to how it shall ultimately be borne, the parties shall be at liberty to inspect the report;
  (h) when the report has been filed—
    (i) if the further consideration of the proceedings has not been adjourned to a day named, the proper officer shall fix a day and give not less than 10 days' notice thereof to all parties;
    (ii) on the day named or fixed any party may apply to the court to adopt the report or, on giving not less than 5 days' notice of his intention to do so, may apply to the court to vary the report or to remit it or any part of it for further inquiry and report, and any such notice shall contain particulars of the variation or remission sought;
    (iii) the court may at any time on the application of any party or the referee determine by whom and (if by more than one person) in what proportions the remuneration and expenses of the referee shall be borne, whether or not any payment or deposit has been made for or on account of such remuneration and expenses, and may make all orders and give all directions necessary to give effect to the determination.

Commencement 1 September 1982.
Amendments Originally rule 9, renumbered as rule 13 by SI 1992/1965, r 7.

Order 19, r [14] Saving for power of committal

Nothing in this Part of this Order shall authorise the [district judge] or referee to commit any person to prison or to enforce any order by committal.

Commencement 1 September 1982.
Amendments Originally rule 10, renumbered as rule 14 by SI 1992/1965, r 7.

PART III—REFERENCE TO EUROPEAN COURT

Order 19, r [15] Making and transmission of order

(1)   In this rule "the European Court" means the Court of Justice of the European Communities and "order" means an order referring a question to the European Court for a preliminary ruling under Article 177 of the Treaty establishing the European Economic Community, Article 150 of the Treaty establishing the European Atomic Energy Community or Article 41 of the Treaty establishing the European Coal and Steel Community.

(2)   An order may be made by the judge before or at the trial or hearing of any action or matter and either of his own motion or on the application of any party.

(3)   An order shall set out in a schedule the request for the preliminary ruling of the European Court, and the judge may give directions as to the manner and form in which the schedule is to be prepared.

(4)   The proceedings in which an order is made shall, unless the judge otherwise orders, be stayed until the European Court has given a preliminary ruling on the question referred to it.

(5)   When an order has been made, the proper officer shall send a copy thereof to the senior master for transmission to the [district judge] of the European Court; but, unless the judge otherwise orders, the copy shall not be sent to the senior master until the time for appealing to the Court of Appeal against the order has expired or, if an appeal is entered within that time, until the appeal has been determined or otherwise disposed of.

(6)   Nothing in these rules shall authorise the [district judge] to make an order.

Commencement 1 September 1982.
Amendments Originally rule 11, renumbered as rule 15 by SI 1992/1965, r 7.
Cross references See RSC Order 114, rr 1–5.

ORDER 20
EVIDENCE

PART I—ADMISSIONS

Order 20, r 1 Admission of other party's case

A party to an action or matter may give notice, by his pleading or otherwise in writing, that he admits the truth of the whole or any part of the case of any other party, and no costs incurred after receipt of the notice in respect of the proof of any matters which the admission renders it unnecessary to prove shall be allowed.

Commencement 1 September 1982.
Cross references See RSC Order 27, r 1

Order 20, r 2 Notice to admit facts

(1)   A party to an action or matter may, not later than 14 days before the trial or hearing, serve on any other party a notice requiring him to admit, for the purpose of that action or matter only, such facts, or such part of his case, as may be specified in the notice.

[(2) If the party served with a notice to admit facts under paragraph (1) does not deliver a written admission of the facts within 7 days after service of the notice on him, the costs of proving the facts and the costs occasioned by and thrown away as a result of his failure to admit the facts shall, unless the court otherwise directs, be borne by him.]

(3)   An admission made in compliance with a notice under paragraph (1) shall not be used against the party by whom it was made in any action or matter other than the one for the purpose of which it was made or in favour of any person other than the one by whom the notice was given and the court may at any time allow a party to amend or withdraw an admission so made by him on such terms as may be just.

Commencement 5 February 1990 (para (2)); 1 September 1982 (remainder).
Amendments Para (2): substituted by SI 1989/2426, r 19.
Cross references See RSC Order 27, r 2, Order 62, r 6(7).
Forms Notice to admit facts (N281).
Admission of facts (N282).

Order 20, r 3 Notice to admit or produce documents

(1)   Without prejudice to rule 11 and any presumption of law as to the authenticity of a document, a party to an action or matter who desires to adduce any document in evidence may, not later than 14 days before the trial or hearing, serve on any other party a notice requiring him to admit the authenticity of the document.

[(2) If the party served with a notice under paragraph (1) desires to challenge the authenticity of the document, he must, within 7 days after service of the notice, serve on the party by whom it was given a notice that he does not admit the authenticity of the document and requires it to be proved at the trial.

(2A) Where a party serves a notice under paragraph (2) and the document to which it relates is proved at the trial, the costs of proving the document and the costs occasioned by and thrown away as a result of that party's non-admission shall, unless the court otherwise directs, be borne by him.]

(3) A party who fails to give notice of non-admission under paragraph (2) shall be deemed to have admitted the authenticity of the document unless the court otherwise orders.

(4) A party to an action or matter may serve on any other party a notice requiring him to produce the document specified in the notice at the trial or hearing of the action or matter.

Commencement 5 February 1990 (paras (2), (2A)); 1 September 1982 (remainder).
Amendments Paras (2), (2A): substituted, for para (2) as originally enacted, by SI 1989/2426, r 20.
Cross references See RSC Order 27, r 5, Order 62, r 6(8).
Forms Notice to admit documents (N283).
Notice to produce documents (N284).
Admission of document (BCCPP [B] 1822).

PART II—EVIDENCE GENERALLY

Order 20, r 4 Evidence generally to be given orally and in open court

Subject to any provision made by or under any Act or rule and to any rule of law, any fact required to be proved at the hearing of an action or matter by the evidence of witnesses shall be proved by the examination of the witnesses orally and in open court.

Commencement 1 September 1982.
Cross references See RSC Order 38, r 1.

Order 20, r 5 Evidence in chambers

In any proceedings in chambers evidence may be given by affidavit unless by any provision of these rules it is otherwise provided or the court otherwise directs, but the court may, on the application of any party, order the attendance for cross-examination of the person making any such affidavit, and where, after such an order has been made, the person in question does not attend, his affidavit shall not be used in evidence without the leave of the court.

Commencement 1 September 1982.
Cross references See RSC Order 38, r 2(3).

Order 20, r 6 Evidence by affidavit on order

(1) In any case to which rule 5 does not apply the court may, at or before the hearing of an action or matter, order that the affidavit of any witness may be read at the hearing if in the circumstances of the case it thinks it reasonable to do so.

(2) An order under paragraph (1) may be made on such terms as to the filing and giving of copies of the affidavit and as to the production of the deponent for cross-examination as the court thinks fit but, subject to such terms and to any subsequent order of the court, the deponent shall not be subject to cross-examination and need not attend the hearing for the purpose.

Commencement 1 September 1982.

Order 20, r 7 Use of affidavit on notice

(1)   Where a party desires to use at the hearing of an action or matter an affidavit which is not rendered admissible by rule 5 and in respect of which no order has been made under rule 6, he may, not less than 14 days before the hearing, give notice of his desire, accompanied by a copy of the affidavit, to the party against whom it is to be used, and unless that party, [within 7 days] after receipt of the notice, gives notice to the other party that he objects to the use of the affidavit, he shall be taken to have consented to its use and accordingly the affidavit may be used at the hearing.

(2)   Where—
   (a)   the defendant in a fixed date action has not delivered a defence within the time limited by Order 9, rule 2, or
   (b)   the defendant in a default or fixed date action does not appear on a pre-trial review of the action,

evidence by affidavit shall be admissible in support of the plaintiff's claim without notice being given under paragraph (1), unless the court otherwise orders.

Commencement   1 September 1982.
Amendments   Para (1): words "within 7 days" substituted by SI 1982/1794, r 9.

Order 20, r 8 Evidence of particular facts

The court may, at or before the trial or hearing of any action or matter and on or before any application in the course of proceedings or any pre-trial review, order that evidence of any particular fact shall be given at the hearing of the action or matter or, as the case may be, on the application or pre-trial review in such manner as may be specified in the order, and in particular—
   (a)   by the production of documents or entries in books, or
   (b)   by copies of documents or entries in books, or
   (c)   in the case of a fact which is or was a matter of common knowledge either generally or in a particular district, by the production of a specified newspaper which contains a statement of that fact.

Commencement   1 September 1982.
Cross references   See RSC Order 38, r 3.

Order 20, r 9 Savings and revocation or variation of orders

(1)   Nothing in rules 5 to 8 or in any order made thereunder shall affect the weight, if any, to be attached to a statement admissible in evidence under any of those rules or under any such order, or the power of the court, when the statement is tendered in evidence, to refuse to admit it if in the interest of justice the court thinks fit to do so.

(2)   Subject to paragraph (3), any order under rules 5 to 8 (including an order made on appeal from the [district judge] to the judge) may, on sufficient cause being shown, be revoked or varied by a subsequent order of the court made at or before the hearing of the proceedings.

(3)   Nothing in paragraph (2) shall enable the [district judge] to revoke or vary an order made by the judge.

Commencement 1 September 1982.

Order 20, r 10 Form and contents of affidavit

(1) Subject to the following paragraphs of this rule, the provisions of the RSC with respect to—

    (a) the form and contents of an affidavit;

    (b) the making of an affidavit by two or more deponents or by a blind or illiterate deponent;

    (c) the use of any affidavit which contains an interlineation, erasure or other alteration or is otherwise defective;

    (d) the striking out of any matter which is scandalous, irrelevant or otherwise oppressive;

    (e) the insufficiency of an affidavit sworn before any agent, partner or clerk of a party's solicitor; and

    (f) the making and marking of exhibits to an affidavit,

shall apply in relation to an affidavit for use in a county court as they apply in relation to an affidavit for use in the High Court.

(2) Before any affidavit is used in evidence it must be filed, but in an urgent case the court may make an order upon the undertaking of a party to file, within such time as the court may require, any affidavit used by him before it is filed.

[(3) Every affidavit must be marked in the top right hand corner of the first page and in the top right hand corner of the back sheet with—

    (a) the party on whose behalf the affidavit is filed;

    (b) the initials and surname of the deponent;

    (c) the number of the affidavit in relation to the deponent;

    (d) the date on which it is sworn, and

    (e) the date on which it is filed.]

(4) Unless the court otherwise orders, an affidavit may be used notwithstanding that it contains statements of information or belief.

(5) Every affidavit shall state which of the facts deposed to are within the deponent's knowledge and which are based on information or belief and shall give, in the former case, his means of knowledge and, in the latter case, the sources and grounds of the information or belief.

Commencement 1 May 1991 (para (3)); 1 September 1982 (remainder).
Amendments Para (3): substituted by SI 1991/525, r 10.
Cross references See RSC Order 41.
Forms Affidavit (N285).

Order 20, r 11 Documents produced from proper custody

(1) Where a document which would, if duly proved, be admissible in evidence is produced to the court from proper custody, it shall be admitted without further proof if—

    (a) in the opinion of the court it appears genuine; and

    (b) no objection is taken to its admission.

(2) If objection is taken to the admission of any document so produced, the court may adjourn the hearing of the action or matter for proof of the document and, if it

is proved, the party objecting shall pay the costs occasioned by the objection unless the court otherwise orders.

Commencement 1 September 1982.

PART III—SUMMONING AND EXAMINATION OF WITNESSES

Order 20, r 12 Witness summons

(1)   Where a party to an action or matter desires a person to be summoned as a witness to give oral evidence or to produce a document in his possession, custody or power, the proper officer shall, on an application made by a party in accordance with paragraph (2), issue a witness summons, together with a copy.

(2)   The applicant shall file a request for the issue of the summons and, if the summons is to be served by an officer of the court, deposit in the court office the money to be paid or tendered under paragraph (7).

(3)   The summons shall contain the name of one witness only but may, as regards such name, be issued in blank.

[(4)   (a)   The summons shall be issued not less than 7 days before the date upon which attendance before the court is required unless the judge or [district judge] otherwise directs and shall be served on the witness not less than 4 days before the date upon which attendance before the court is required unless the judge or [district judge] otherwise directs.

    (b)   Service under this paragraph shall, subject to paragraph (5), be effected by delivering the summons to the witness personally.]

(5)   Where the applicant or his solicitor gives a certificate for postal service, the summons shall, unless the [district judge] otherwise directs, be served on the witness by an officer of the court sending it to him by first-class post at the address stated in the request for the summons and, unless the contrary is shown, the date of service shall be deemed to be the seventh day after the date on which the summons was sent to the witness.

(6)   Where the summons has been served by post, the witness shall not be fined for failing to appear on the return day unless the judge is satisfied that—

    (a)   the summons came to his knowledge in sufficient time for him to appear on that day, and

    (b)   the money to be paid or tendered under paragraph (7) was sent to him with the summons.

(7)   At the time of service of the summons there shall be paid or tendered to the witness the sum of £6 for a police officer and £8.50 for any other person and, in addition, a sum reasonably sufficient to cover his expenses in travelling to and from the court.

[(8)   No summons shall be issued to require a witness to give evidence at a hearing in chambers for directions without leave of the judge or [district judge], the application for which shall be made ex parte.]

Commencement   28 March 1989 (paras (4), (8)); 1 September 1982 (remainder).
Amendments   Para (4): substituted by SI 1989/236, r 9(1).
Para (8): added by SI 1989/236, r 9(2).
Cross references   See RSC Order 38, Pt II.

Forms   Request for witness summons (N286).
Witness summons (N20).
Service certificate of same (N20(1))

[Order 20, r 12A Exchange of witness statements

(1)   The powers of the court under this rule shall be exercised for the purpose of disposing fairly and expeditiously of the action or matter before it, and saving costs, having regard to all the circumstances of the case, including (but not limited to)—
  (a) the extent to which the facts are in dispute or have been admitted;
  (b) the extent to which the issues of fact are defined by the pleadings;
  (c) the extent to which information has been or is likely to be provided by further and better particulars, answers to interrogatories or otherwise.

(2)   At the pre-trial review the court shall direct every party to serve on the other parties, within 10 weeks (or such other period as the court may specify) thereafter and on such terms as the court may specify, written statements of the oral evidence which the party intends to adduce on any issues of fact to be decided at the trial.

The court may give a direction to any party under this paragraph at any other stage of such an action or matter.

(3)   Directions under paragraph (2) or (17) may make different provision with regard to different issues of fact or different witnesses.

(4)   Statements served under this rule shall—
  (a) be dated and, except for good reason (which should be specified by letter accompanying the statement), be signed by the intended witness and shall include a statement by him that the contents are true to the best of his knowledge and belief;
  (b) sufficiently identify any documents referred to therein; and
  (c) where they are to be served by more than one party, be exchanged simultaneously.

(5)   Where a party is unable to obtain a written statement from an intended witness in accordance with paragraph (4)(a), the court may direct the party wishing to adduce that witness's evidence to provide the other party with the name of the witness and (unless the court otherwise orders) a statement of the nature of the evidence intended to be adduced.

(6)   Subject to paragraph (9), where the party serving a statement under this rule does not call the witness to whose evidence it relates, no other party may put the statement in evidence at the trial.

(7)   Subject to paragraph (9), where the party serving the statement does call such a witness at the trial—
  (a) except where the trial is with a jury, the trial judge may, on such terms as he thinks fit, direct that the statement served, or part of it, shall stand as the evidence in chief of the witness or part of such evidence;
  (b) the party may not without the consent of the other parties or the leave of the trial judge adduce evidence from that witness the substance of which is not included in the statement served, except—
    (i) where the court's directions under paragraph (2) or (17) specify that statements should be exchanged in relation to only some issues of fact, in relation to any other issues;

(ii)   in relation to new matters which have arisen since the statement was
served on the other party;

(c)   whether or not the statement or any part of it is referred to during the
evidence in chief of the witness, any party may put the statement or any
part of it in cross-examination of that witness.

(8)   Nothing in this rule shall make admissible evidence which is otherwise
inadmissible.

(9)   Where any statement served is one to which the Civil Evidence Acts 1968 and
1972 apply, paragraphs (6) and (7) shall take effect subject to the provisions of those
Acts and Parts III and IV of this Order.

The service of a witness statement under this rule shall not, unless expressly so
stated by the party serving the same, be treated as a notice under the said Acts of 1968
and 1972; and where a statement or any part thereof would be admissible in evidence
by virtue only of the said Act of 1968 or 1972 the appropriate notice under Part IV
of this Order shall be served with the statement notwithstanding any provision of that
Part as to the time for serving such a notice. Where such a notice is served a counter-
notice shall be deemed to have been served under Order 20, rule 17(1).

(10)   Where a party fails to comply with a direction for the exchange of witness
statements he shall not be entitled to adduce evidence to which the direction related
without the leave of the court.

(11)   Where a party serves a witness statement under this rule, no other person may
make use of that statement for any purpose other than the purpose of the proceedings
in which it was served—

(a)   unless and to the extent that the party serving it gives his consent in
writing or the court gives leave; or

(b)   unless and to the extent that it has been put in evidence (whether pursuant
to a direction under paragraph (7)(a) or otherwise).

(12)   Subject to paragraph (13), the judge shall, if any person so requests during the
course of the trial, direct that any witness statement which was ordered to stand as
evidence in chief under paragraph (7)(a) shall be certified as open to inspection.

A request under this paragraph may be made orally or in writing.

(13)   The judge may refuse to give a direction under paragraph (12) in relation to a
witness statement, or may exclude from such a direction any words or passages in a
statement, if he considers that inspection should not be available—

(a)   in the interests of justice or national security,

(b)   because of the nature of any expert medical evidence in the statement, or

(c)   for any other sufficient reason.

(14)   Where a direction is given under paragraph (12) that a witness statement shall
be certified as open to inspection—

(a)   a certificate shall be attached by the proper officer to a copy ("the certified
copy") of that witness statement; and

(b)   the certified copy shall be made available for inspection.

(15)   Subject to any directions issued by the Lord Chancellor under Order 50, rule 1
and to any conditions which the court may by special direction impose, any person
may inspect and (subject to payment of the prescribed fee) take a copy of the certified
copy of a witness statement during office hours from the time when the certificate is
given until the end of 7 days after the conclusion of the trial.

(16)   In this rule—

    (a)   any reference in paragraphs (12) to (15) to a witness statement shall, in relation to a witness statement of which only part has been ordered to stand as evidence in chief under paragraph (7)(a), be construed as a reference to that part;

    (b)   any reference to inspecting or copying the certified copy of a witness statement shall be construed as including a reference to inspecting or copying a copy of that certified copy.

(17)   The court shall have power to vary or override any of the provisions of this rule (except paragraphs (1), (8) and (12) to (16)) and to give such alternative directions as it thinks fit.]

Commencement   16 November 1992.
Amendments   This rule was inserted by SI 1989/2426, r 22; it was subsequently substituted by SI 1992/1965, r 5.
Cross references   See RSC Order 38, r 2A.

Order 20, r 13 Evidence by deposition

(1)   The court may, in any action or matter where it appears necessary for the purposes of justice, make an order in the appropriate form for the examination on oath of any person (in this rule called "the witness") at any place in England and Wales.

(2)   The examination may be ordered to take place before any of the following persons (in this rule called "the examiner"), that is to say—

    (a)   any officer of the court making the order, or

    (b)   any officer of the court for the district in which the witness resides or carries on business, or

    (c)   such other person as the court may appoint.

(3)   The order shall specify the day and place fixed for the examination and shall be served on the witness personally a reasonable time before the day so fixed and at the same time there shall be paid or tendered to the witness the sums prescribed by rule 12(7).

    A copy of the order shall also be sent to every party to the action or matter.

(4)   Where the examination is to take place before an officer of a court other than the court making the order, the proper officer of the last-mentioned court shall supply the proper officer of the first-mentioned court with sufficient copies of the order to enable paragraph (3) to be complied with.

(5)   Subject to the following paragraphs of this rule, the provisions of the RSC with respect to—

    (a)   the documents to be furnished to the examiner,

    (b)   the conduct of the examination,

    (c)   the making of objections to questions put to the witness,

    (d)   the taking and signing of the deposition,

    (e)   the making of a special report by the examiner, and

    (f)   the reception of the deposition in evidence at the hearing of the action or matter,

shall apply in relation to the examination of a witness pursuant to an order under paragraph (1) as they apply in relation to the examination of a witness pursuant to an order made in a cause or matter in the High Court.

(6)   Order 29, rule 1, shall have effect in relation to an order under paragraph (1) as if it were an order in the nature of an injunction.

(7)   If the witness refuses to be sworn for the purpose of the examination or to answer any lawful question or produce any document, a certificate of his refusal, signed by the examiner, shall be filed in the office of the court by which the order under paragraph (1) was made, and the party by whom the attendance of the witness was required may apply to the court ex parte for an order requiring the witness to be sworn or to answer any question or produce any document, as the case may be.

(8)   The original deposition of the witness, authenticated by the signature of the examiner, shall be filed in the office of the court by which the order under paragraph (1) was made.

Commencement   1 September 1982.
Cross references   See RSC Order 39 r 1; para (5) incorporates RSC Order 39 rr 7–11, 13.
Forms   Order for examination of witness out of court (N 21).

PART IV—HEARSAY EVIDENCE

Order 20, r 14 Interpretation and application

(1)   In this Part of this Order "the Act of 1968" means the Civil Evidence Act 1968 and any expressions used in this Part of this Order and in Part I of the Act of 1968 have the same meanings in this Part of this Order as they have in the said Part I.

(2)   This Part of this Order shall apply in relation to the trial or hearing of an issue arising in an action or matter and to a reference under [section 65] of the Act as it applies to the trial or hearing of an action or matter.

(3)   Nothing in this Part of this Order shall apply in relation to a reference under [section 64] of the Act.

Commencement   1 September 1982.
Amendments   Para (2): words "section 65" substituted by SI 1984/878, r 12, Schedule.
Para (3): words "section 64" substituted by SI 1984/878, r 12, Schedule.
Cross references   See RSC Order 38, r 20.

Order 20, r 15 Notice of intention to give certain statements in evidence

(1)   Subject to the provisions of this rule, a party to an action or matter who desires to give in evidence at the trial or hearing any statement which is admissible in evidence by virtue of section 2, 4 or 5 of the Act of 1968 shall, not less than 14 days before the day fixed for the trial or hearing, give notice of his desire to do so to the [district judge] and to every other party.

(2)   Unless in any particular case the court otherwise directs, paragraph (1) shall not apply to an action or matter in which no defence or answer has been filed; and where a defence or answer is filed less than 14 days before the day fixed for the trial or hearing, any party required to give notice pursuant to paragraph (1) shall apply to the court for an adjournment of the trial or hearing or for such other directions as may be appropriate.

(3)   Paragraph (1) shall not apply in relation to any statement which is admissible as evidence of any fact stated therein by virtue not only of the said section 2, 4 or 5 but by virtue also of any other statutory provision within the meaning of section 1 of the Act of 1968.

(4)   Paragraph (1) shall not apply in relation to any statement which any party to a probate action desires to give in evidence at the trial of that action and which is alleged to have been made by the deceased person whose estate is the subject of the action.

(5)   Where, by virtue of any provision of these rules or of any order or direction of the court, the evidence in any proceedings is to be given by affidavit then, without prejudice to paragraph (3), paragraph (1) shall not apply in relation to any statement which any party to the proceedings desires to have included in any affidavit to be used on his behalf in the proceedings.

Commencement   1 September 1982.
Definitions   Act of 1968: Civil Evidence Act 1968.
Cross references   See RSC Order 38, r 21.

Order 20, r 16 Application of RSC

RSC Order 38, rules 22 to 25, shall apply to a notice under the last foregoing rule as they apply to a notice under rule 21 of the said Order 38.

Commencement   1 September 1982.

Order 20, r 17 Counter-notice requiring person to be called as a witness

(1)   Subject to paragraphs (2) and (3), any party on whom a notice under rule 15 is served may, within 7 days after service of the notice on him, give to the proper officer and to the party who gave the notice a counter-notice requiring that party to call as a witness at the trial or hearing any person (naming him) particulars of whom are contained in the notice.

(2)   Where any notice under rule 15 contains a statement that any person particulars of whom are contained in the notice cannot or should not be called as a witness for the reason specified therein, a party shall not be entitled to serve a counter-notice under this rule requiring that person to be called as a witness at the trial or hearing unless he contends that that person can or, as the case may be, should be called, and in that case he must include in his counter-notice a statement to that effect.

(3)   Where a statement to which a notice under rule 15 relates is one to which rule 19 applies, no party on whom the notice is served shall be entitled to serve a counter-notice under this rule in relation to that statement, but the foregoing provision is without prejudice to the right of any party to apply to the court under rule 19 for directions with respect to the admissibility of that statement.

(4)   If any party by whom a notice under rule 15 is served fails to comply with a counter-notice duly served on him under this rule, then, unless any of the reasons specified in paragraph (5) applies in relation to the person named in the counter-notice, and without prejudice to the powers of the court under rule 20, the statement to which the notice under rule 15 relates shall not be admissible at the trial or hearing as evidence of any fact stated therein by virtue of section 2, 4 or 5 of the Act of 1968, as the case may be.

(5)   The reasons referred to in paragraph (4) are that the person in question is dead, or beyond the seas, or unfit by reason of his bodily or mental condition to attend as a witness or that despite the exercise of reasonable diligence it has not been possible to identify or find him or that he cannot reasonably be expected to have any recollection of matters relevant to the accuracy or otherwise of the statement to which the notice relates.

Commencement 1 September 1982.
Definitions Act of 1968: Civil Evidence Act 1968.
Cross references See RSC Order 38, r 26.

Order 20, r 18 Determination of question whether person can or should be called as a witness

(1)   Where a question arises whether any of the reasons specified in rule 17(5) applies in relation to a person particulars of whom are contained in a notice under rule 15, the court may, on the application of any party to the action or matter, determine that question before the trial or hearing or give directions for it to be determined before the trial or hearing and for the manner in which it is to be determined.

(2)   Unless the court otherwise directs, notice of any application under paragraph (1) must be served on every other party to the action or matter.

(3)   Where any such question as is referred to in paragraph (1) has been determined under or by virtue of that paragraph, no application to have it determined afresh at the trial or hearing may be made unless the evidence which it is sought to adduce in support of the application could not with reasonable diligence have been adduced at the hearing which resulted in the determination.

Commencement 1 September 1982.
Cross references See RSC Order 38, r 27.

Order 20, r 19 Directions with respect to statement made in previous proceedings

(1)   Where a party has given notice in accordance with rule 15 that he desires to give in evidence at the trial or hearing—
- (a)   a statement falling within section 2(1) of the Act of 1968 which was made by a person, whether orally or in a document, in the course of giving evidence in some other legal proceedings (whether civil or criminal), or
- (b)   a statement falling within section 4(1) of the Act of 1968 which is contained in a record of direct oral evidence given in some other legal proceedings (whether civil or criminal),

any party to the action or matter may apply to the court for directions as to whether, and if so on what conditions, the party desiring to give the statement in evidence will be permitted to do so and (where applicable) as to the manner in which that statement and any other evidence given in those other proceedings is to be proved.

Commencement 1 September 1982.
Amendments This rule contains para (1) only.
Definitions Act of 1968: Civil Evidence Act 1968.
Cross references See RSC Order 38, r 28.

Order 20, r 20 Power of court to allow statement to be given in evidence

(1)   Without prejudice to sections 2(2)(a) and 4(2)(a) of the Act of 1968 and rule 19, the court may, if it thinks it just to do so, allow a statement falling within section 2(1), 4(1) or 5(1) of the Act of 1968 to be given in evidence at the trial or hearing of an action or matter notwithstanding—

(a) that the statement is one in relation to which rule 15(1) applies and that the party desiring to give the statement in evidence has failed to comply with that rule, or

(b) that that party has failed to comply with any requirement of a counter-notice relating to that statement which was served on him in accordance with rule 17.

(2) Without prejudice to the generality of paragraph (1), the court may exercise its power under that paragraph to allow a statement to be given in evidence at the trial or hearing if a refusal to exercise that power might oblige the party desiring to give the statement in evidence to call as a witness at the trial or hearing an opposite party or a person who is or was at the material time the servant or agent of an opposite party.

Commencement 1 September 1982.
Definitions Act of 1968: Civil Evidence Act 1968.
Cross references See RSC Order 38, r 29.

Order 20, r 21 Restriction on adducing evidence as to credibility of maker etc of certain statements

Where—

(a) a notice given under rule 15 in an action or matter relates to a statement which is admissible by virtue of section 2 or 4 of the Act of 1968, and

(b) the person who made the statement, or, as the case may be, the person who originally supplied the information from which the record containing the statement was compiled, is not called as a witness at the trial or hearing of the action or matter, and

(c) none of the reasons mentioned in rule 17(5) applies so as to prevent the party who gave the notice from calling that person as a witness,

no other party to the action or matter shall be entitled, except with the leave of the court, to adduce in relation to that person any evidence which could otherwise be adduced by him by virtue of section 7 of the Act of 1968 unless he gave a counter-notice under rule 17 in respect of that person or applied under rule 19 for a direction that that person be called as a witness at the trial or hearing of the action or matter.

Commencement 1 September 1982.
Definitions Act of 1968: Civil Evidence Act 1968.
Cross references See RSC Order 38, r 30.

Order 20, r 22 Notice required of intention to give evidence of certain inconsistent statements

(1) Where a person, particulars of whom were contained in a notice given under rule 15, is not to be called as a witness at the trial or hearing, any party who is entitled and intends to adduce in relation to that person any evidence which is admissible for the purpose mentioned in section 7(1)(b) of the Act of 1968 must, not more than 7 days after service of that notice on him, give notice of his intention to do so to the proper officer and to the party who gave the notice under rule 15.

(2) RSC Order 38, rule 22(1) and (2), shall apply to a notice under this rule as if the notice were a notice under rule 15 and the statement to which the notice relates were a statement admissible by virtue of section 2 of the Act of 1968.

(3)   The court may, if it thinks it just to do so, allow a party to give in evidence at the trial or hearing of an action or matter any evidence which is admissible for the purposes mentioned in the said section 7(1)(b) notwithstanding that that party has failed to comply with the provisions of paragraph (1).

Commencement   1 September 1982.
Definitions   Act of 1968: Civil Evidence Act 1968.
Cross references   See RSC Order 38, r 31.

Order 20, r 23 Costs

If—

(a)   a party to an action or matter serves a counter-notice under rule 17 in respect of any person who is called as a witness at the trial of the action or matter in compliance with a requirement of the counter-notice, and

(b)   it appears to the court that it was unreasonable to require that person to be called as a witness,

then without prejudice to Order 38, and, in particular, to rule 6 thereof, the court may direct that any costs to that party in respect of the preparation and service of the counter-notice shall not be allowed to him and that any costs occasioned by the counter-notice to any other party shall be paid by him to that other party.

Commencement   1 September 1982.
Cross references   See RSC Order 38, r 32.

Order 20, r 24 Exercise of jurisdiction

Order 1, rule 8, shall have effect in relation to the jurisdiction of the court under sections 2(2)(a), 2(3), 4(2)(a) and 6(1) of the Act of 1968 as it has effect in relation to any jurisdiction conferred by these rules.

Commencement   1 September 1982.
Definitions   Act of 1968: Civil Evidence Act 1968.

Order 20, r 25 Evidence of findings on foreign law

(1)   Subject to the provisions of this rule, a party who intends to adduce in evidence a finding or decision on a question of foreign law by virtue of section 4(2) of the Civil Evidence Act 1972 shall, not less than 14 days before the day fixed for the trial or hearing or within such other period as the court may specify, serve notice of his intention on every other party to the proceedings.

(2)   The notice shall specify the question on which the finding or decision was given or made and specify the document in which it is reported or recorded in citable form.

(3)   In any action or matter in which evidence may be given by affidavit, an affidavit specifying the matters contained in paragraph (2) shall constitute notice under paragraph (1) if served within the period mentioned in that paragraph.

(4)   Unless in any particular case the court otherwise directs, paragraph (1) shall not apply to an action or matter in which no defence or answer has been filed.

Commencement   1 September 1982.
Cross references   See RSC Order 38, r 7.

Order 20, r 26 Statements of opinion

Where a party to an action or matter desires to give in evidence by virtue of Part I of the Act of 1968 as extended by section 1(1) of the Civil Evidence Act 1972, a statement of opinion other than a statement to which Part III of this Order applies, the provisions of rules 14 to 24 of this Order (except so much of rule 16 as applies RSC Order 38, rule 24) shall apply with such modifications as the court may direct or the circumstances of the case may require.

Commencement 1 September 1982.
Definitions Act of 1968: Civil Evidence Act 1968.
RSC: Rules of the Supreme Court (Revision) 1965, SI 1965/1776.
Cross references See RSC Order 38, r 34.

PART V—EXPERT EVIDENCE

Order 20, r 27 Restrictions on adducing expert evidence

(1)   [Except—
   (a)   with the leave of the court,
   (b)   in accordance with the provisions of Order 17, rule 11, or
   (c)   where all parties agree,]

no expert evidence may be adduced at the trial or hearing of an action or matter, unless the party seeking to adduce the evidence has applied to the court to determine whether a direction should be given under rule 37, 38 or 41 (whichever is appropriate) of RSC Order 38, as applied by rule 28 of this Order, and has complied with any direction given on the application.

(2)   Nothing in paragraph (1) shall apply to expert evidence which is permitted to be given by affidavit or which is to be adduced in an action or matter in which no defence or answer has been filed or in proceedings referred to arbitration under [section 64] of the Act.

(3)   Nothing in paragraph (1) shall affect the enforcement under any other provision of these rules (except Order 29, rule 1) of a direction given under this Part of this Order.

Commencement 1 September 1982.
Amendments Para (1): words from "Except" to "all parties agree," substituted by SI 1990/1764, r 15.
Para (2): words "section 64" substituted by SI 1984/878, r 12, Schedule.
Cross references See RSC Order 38, r 36.

Order 20, r 28 Application of RSC

RSC Order 38, rules 37 to 44 shall apply in relation to an application under rule 27 of this Order as they apply in relation to an application under rule 36(1) of the said Order 38.

Commencement 1 September 1982.

ORDER 21
HEARING OF ACTION OR MATTER

Order 21, r 1 Non-appearance by plaintiff

(1)   If the plaintiff does not appear on the day fixed for the hearing of an action or matter, the court may, without prejudice to any other power, strike out the proceedings or, if the defendant appears, proceed with the hearing in the plaintiff's absence.

(2)   Where the court has received from the plaintiff an affidavit which is admissible in evidence by virtue of any Act or rule, he shall be deemed for the purposes of paragraph (1) to have appeared on the day aforesaid and to have tendered the evidence in the affidavit.

(3)   Where any proceedings have been struck out under paragraph (1), the court may restore them to the list on application or of its own motion.

Commencement   1 September 1982.
Cross references   See RSC Order 35, r 1.

Order 21, r 2 Failure by plaintiff to prove claim

(1)   If the plaintiff appears at the hearing of an action or matter but fails to prove his claim to the satisfaction of the court, it may, without prejudice to any other power, either nonsuit him or give judgment for the defendant.

(2)   Where, after a plaintiff has been nonsuited, or proceedings have been struck out, and costs have been awarded to the defendant, a subsequent action or matter for the same or substantially the same cause of action is brought before payment of those costs, the court may stay the subsequent action or matter until they have been paid.

Commencement   1 September 1982.
Forms   Judgment for defendant (N289, 291).
Order for costs against Plaintiff (N290).

Order 21, r 3 Non-appearance or admission by defendant

If on the day fixed for the hearing of an action or matter the defendant—
  (a)   does not appear but the plaintiff proves his claim to the satisfaction of the court, or
  (b)   appears and admits the plaintiff's claim,

the court may give such judgment or make such order as may be just.

Commencement   1 September 1982.
Cross references   See RSC Order 35, r 1.

[Order 21, r 3A Payments received after hearing fixed

Where, after a day has been fixed for the hearing of an action or matter, payment of all or part of the amount claimed is made, the plaintiff shall forthwith inform the proper officer.]

Commencement   1 April 1990.
Amendments   This rule was inserted by SI 1989/1838, r 21.

Order 21, r 4 Counterclaims

(1)   The foregoing provisions of this Order shall have effect, with the necessary modifications, in relation to a counterclaim as they have effect in relation to a claim.

(2)   A counterclaim may be proceeded with notwithstanding that judgment is given for the plaintiff in the action or that the action is stayed, discontinued, struck out or dismissed.

(3)   Where it appears that the subject-matter of a counterclaim ought for any reason to be disposed of by a separate action, the court may of its own motion or on the application of any party order the counterclaim to be struck out or to be tried separately or may make such other order as may be expedient.

(4)   Where a defendant establishes a counterclaim against the claim of the plaintiff and there is a balance in favour of one of the parties, the court may give judgment for the balance, but nothing in this provision shall be taken as affecting the court's discretion as to costs.

Commencement   1 September 1982.
Cross references   As to para (2) see RSC Order 15, r 2(3), as to para (3) see RSC Order 15, r 5, as to para (4) see RSC Order 15, r 2(4).
Forms   Judgment where counterclaim made (N23).

Order 21, r 5 [District judge's] jurisdiction

(1)   The [district judge] shall have power to hear and determine—
   (a)   any action or matter in which the defendant fails to appear at the hearing or admits the claim;
   [(b)   any action or matter the value of which does not exceed £5,000;]
   [(c)   any action for recovery of land regardless of the value of any other claim which is brought in the same action and including one in which the mortgagee under a mortgage of land claims possession of the mortgaged land; and]
   [(d)]   by leave of the judge and with the consent of the parties, any other action or matter.

(2)   In relation to an action brought to enforce a right to recover possession of goods, or to enforce such a right and to claim payment of a debt or other demand or damages, [the value of the action or matter] shall be construed as a reference to the aggregate amount claimed by the plaintiff, including the value of the goods or, in the case of goods let under a hire-purchase agreement, the unpaid balance of the [total price].

[(2A) In paragraph (1)(c) "mortgage" and "mortgagee" have the meanings assigned to them by section 21(7) of the Act.]

[(2B) Without prejudice to Order 50, rule 2, a district judge may, at any stage of an action or matter which he has power to hear and determine under paragraph (1) and subject to any right of appeal to the judge, exercise the same powers under section 38 of the Act as the court; but nothing in this paragraph shall authorise the district judge to commit any person to prison.]

(3)   Nothing in this rule shall prejudice any power conferred by any Act or rule on the [district judge] to hear and determine any other action or matter or authorise the [district judge] to exercise any jurisdiction conferred by any Act or rule on the judge alone.

Commencement 1 July 1991 (para (2B)); 1 August 1984 (para (2A)); 1 September 1982 (remainder).
Amendments Para (1): sub-para (b) substituted by SI 1991/1126, r 7; original sub-para (c) re-lettered as
sub-para (d) and new sub-para (c) inserted, by SI 1984/878, r 10(2), (3), sub-para (c) further substituted by
SI 1993/2175, r 11.
Para (2): words "the value of the action or matter" substituted by SI 1993/2175, r 12; words "total price"
substituted by SI 1985/566, r 6.
Para (2A): inserted by SI 1984/878, r 11.
Para (2B): inserted by SI 1991/1126, r 13.

[Order 21, r 5A Order of speeches

The judge before whom an action is tried may give directions—

(a) as to the party to begin,

(b) as to the order and number of speeches at the trial, and

(c) in an action tried without a jury, dispensing with opening speeches.]

Commencement 2 January 1991.
Amendments This rule was inserted by SI 1990/1764, r 26.
Cross references See RSC Order 35, r 7.

Order 21, r 6 Inspection by judge or jury

(1) The judge by whom any action or matter is heard may inspect any place or
thing with respect to which any question arises in the proceedings.

(2) Where an action or matter is tried with a jury and the judge inspects any place
or thing under paragraph (1), he may authorise the jury to inspect it also.

Commencement 1 September 1982.
Cross references See RSC Order 35, r 8.

ORDER 22
JUDGMENTS AND ORDERS

Order 22, r 1 Drawing up and service of judgments and orders

[(1) Subject to the provisions of these rules with respect to particular judgments and orders, every judgment or final order and every order for directions made under Order 13, rule 2, or Order 17, rule 1, shall, unless the court otherwise directs, be drawn up and served by the proper officer on all parties to the proceedings.]

(2) Service shall be effected in accordance with Order 7, rule 1, and it shall not be necessary for the party in whose favour the judgment or order was made to prove that it reached the party to be served.

[(3) Where judgment is entered in a default action under Order 9, rule 6(1), for payment forthwith, it shall not be necessary to draw up and serve the judgment where a request for the issue of a warrant of execution has been made.]

(4) ...

(5) Where a party to be served with a judgment or order is acting by a solicitor, service may, if the court thinks fit, be effected on the party as if he were acting in person.

Commencement   1 July 1991 (para (3)); 1 April 1990 (para (1)); 1 September 1982 (remainder).
Amendments   Para (1): substituted by SI 1989/1838, r 22.
Para (3): substituted by SI 1991/1126, r 25.
Para (4): revoked by SI 1989/1838, r 24.
Cross references   See RSC Order 42, r 5.
Forms   General form of judgment/order (N24).
Judgment for plaintiff, costs to be taxed (N25)
Judgment for plaintiff — possession (N26–29, 31)
Default judgment plaintiff (N30).
Judgment delivery of goods (N32, 33).
Judgment after assessment of damages (N34).

[Order 22, r 1A Payment of money under judgments

Except where under these rules or the Court Funds Rules 1987 money is authorised or required to be paid into court, all monies payable under a judgment or order shall be paid to the party in whose favour the judgment or order is given or made.]

Commencement   1 April 1990.
Amendments   This rule was inserted by SI 1989/1838, r 25.

Order 22, r 2 Time for payment of money judgments

(1) Where judgment is given or an order is made for the payment of money (including costs) otherwise than by instalments, then, subject to paragraph (2) and to rule 7(5) and Order 9, rule 6, the money shall, if no day for payment is specified in the judgment or order, be payable at the expiration of 14 days from the date of the judgment or order.

(2) Where costs to be taxed are payable and the costs have not been taxed before the day on which they would otherwise be payable, the costs shall, unless the court otherwise directs, be payable at the expiration of 14 days from the date of taxation.

Commencement   1 September 1982.

Order 22, r 3 Time for complying with other judgments

Every judgment or order requiring any person to do an act other than the payment of money shall state the time within which the act is to be done.

Commencement 1 September 1982.
Cross references See RSC Order 42, r 2(1).

Order 22, r 4 Judgment in favour of reversioner for detention of goods

(1) Where a claim relating to the detention of goods is made by a partial owner whose right of action is not founded on a possessory title, any judgment or order given or made in respect of the claim shall, notwithstanding anything in section 3(3) of the Torts (Interference with Goods) Act 1977, be for the payment of damages only.

In this paragraph "partial owner" means one of the two or more persons having interests in the goods, unless he has the written authority of every other such person to sue on the latter's behalf.

(2) This rule is without prejudice to the remedies and jurisdiction mentioned in section 3(8) of the said Act of 1977.

Commencement 1 September 1982.
Cross references See RSC Order 42, r 1A.

Order 22, r 5 Entry of judgment on plaintiff's request where defendant debarred etc

(1) Where a defendant is debarred from defending altogether or the whole of his defence is struck out, the plaintiff may have judgment entered for the amount of his claim and costs on filing a request in that behalf showing, where appropriate, that any condition subject to which the defendant was debarred or the defence was to be struck out has been fulfilled.

(2) If the plaintiff's claim is for unliquidated damages, any judgment entered under paragraph (1) shall be an interlocutory judgment for damages to be assessed and costs.

(3) Where a plaintiff or defendant is entitled under Order 11, rule 2(3)(a) or 3(5)(a), or under Order 18, rule 2(1), to have judgment entered for his taxed costs, he may have judgment entered on filing a request in that behalf showing that the costs have not been paid.

Commencement 1 September 1982.

Order 22, r 6 Assessment of damages under interlocutory judgment

(1) Where an interlocutory judgment has been entered for damages to be assessed and no date has been fixed by the court for the assessment, an application by the plaintiff for such assessment shall be made on 7 days' notice to the defendant.

[(2) The district judge may hear and determine an application under paragraph (1).]

Commencement 1 July 1991 (para (2)); 1 September 1982 (remainder).
Amendments Para (2): substituted by SI 1991/1126, r 14.
Cross references See RSC Order 37, rr 1–6.
Forms Judgment after assessment of damages (N34).

[Order 22, r 6A Provisional damages

(1)   This rule applies to actions to which section 51 of the Act applies.

(2)   Subject to paragraph (3), rules 7(2) and 8 to 10 of RSC Order 37 shall apply to actions to which this rule applies as they apply in relation to proceedings or subsequent proceedings in the High Court with the following modifications—
    (a)   references to section 32A of the Supreme Court Act 1981 shall be construed as references to section 51 of the Act;
    (b)   the reference in the said rule 8 to RSC Orders 13 and 19 shall be construed as a reference to rules 3 and 6 of Order 9 in these rules;
    (c)   references in the said rule 10 to the provisions of RSC Order 29 relating to the making of interim payments shall be construed as references to Part II of RSC Order 29 as applied to proceedings in a county court by Order 13, rule 12 of these rules;
    (d)   references in the said rule 10 to a summons for directions shall be construed as references to an application for directions as to the future conduct of the action.

(3)   Where a defendant delivers an admission of whole or part of the plaintiff's claim, Order 9, rule 4 of these rules shall apply as if the action were a fixed date action; and that rule shall also so apply, with the necessary modifications, where the defendant fails to deliver a defence within the period of 14 days mentioned in that rule.]

Commencement   5 February 1990.
Amendments   This rule was inserted by SI 1989/2426, r 6.

Order 22, r 7 Settlement of judgment and preparation of deed

(1)   Where a judgment or order is of such a nature that it should, in the opinion of the [district judge], be settled in the presence of the parties, the judgment or order shall be prepared by the proper officer and a draft thereof, together with notice of an appointment before the [district judge] to settle the judgment or order, shall be sent by the proper officer to every party to the proceedings not less than 7 days before the day of the appointment.

(2)   The [district judge] shall settle the judgment or order in the presence of such of the parties as attend the appointment.

(3)   When the judgment or order has been settled, it shall be filed and a minute of the judgment or order, showing the date thereof shall be entered in the records of the court.

(4)   Any party dissatisfied with the judgment or order as settled may apply to the judge, on notice to be served within 7 days after the settling of the judgment or order, to vary it, but the notice shall not operate as a stay of proceedings unless the court otherwise orders.

(5)   Any money payable under a judgment or order settled under this rule shall be payable forthwith unless the court otherwise orders.

(6)   Where a judgment or order directs any deed to be prepared and executed, it shall state by whom the deed is to be prepared and by whom, if anyone, it is to be approved, and if the parties to the deed cannot agree upon its form, the judge may, upon the application of any of them on notice, settle the deed himself or refer it to

the [district judge] or to conveyancing counsel to be settled, subject to the final approval of the judge.

Commencement   1 September 1982.
Cross references   See RSC Order 31, r 5–8.

[Order 22, r 7A Consent judgments and orders

(1)   Where all the parties to an action or matter are agreed upon the terms in which a judgment or order to which this rule applies should be given or made, a judgment or order in such terms may be entered as a judgment or order of the court by the procedure provided in this rule.

(2)   This rule applies to any judgment or order which consists of one or more of the following—
  (a)   any judgment or order for—
    (i)   the payment of a liquidated sum or damages to be assessed;
    (ii)   the delivery up of goods with or without the option of paying their value whether suspended or not;
    (iii) the possession of land other than land which includes any residential premises or where the order is suspended;
  (b)   any order for—
    (i)   the stay of proceedings, either unconditionally or upon conditions as to the payment of money or upon terms which are scheduled to the order but which are not otherwise part of it (a "Tomlin order");
    (ii)   the dismissal of any proceedings, whether wholly or in part;
    (iii) the setting aside of a judgment entered in default;
    (iv)   the transfer of proceedings to another county court;
    (v)   the payment out of money in court;
    (vi)   the discharge from liability of any party;
    (vii) the payment or waiver of costs, or such other provision for costs as may be agreed;
  (c)   any order, to be included in a judgment or order to which the preceding sub-paragraphs apply, for—
    (i)   the extension of the period required for doing any act;
    (ii)   liberty to apply, or to restore.

(3)   This rule shall not apply to any judgment or order—
  (a)   in Admiralty proceedings;
  (b)   in proceedings in which one of the parties is a litigant in person;
  (c)   in proceedings in which one of the parties is a person under disability;
  (d)   relating to custody of or access to a child;
  (e)   relating to the maintenance of or financial provision for a spouse or a child.

(4)   Before any judgment or order to which this rule applies may be entered in the records of the court, it must be—
  (a)   drawn up in the terms agreed and expressed as being "By Consent";
  (b)   signed by the solicitors acting for each of the parties;

and the solicitor filing the judgment or order shall supply the necessary copies for service under paragraph (5).

(5)   A copy of a judgment or order entered under paragraph (4) shall be sealed and served by the proper officer on every party to the proceedings.

(6)   The proper officer shall refer to the district judge any judgment or order presented for entry in the records of the court which is contradictory or unclear in its terms, appears to fail to give effect to the intention of the parties or is otherwise unsatisfactory.]

Commencement 1 July 1991.
Amendments This rule was inserted by SI 1991/1126, r 48.
Cross references See RSC Order 42, r 5A.

Order 22, r 8 Certificate of judgment

(1)   Any person who desires to have a certificate of any judgment or order given or made in an action or matter shall make a request in writing to the proper officer stating—
   (a)   if he is a party to the action or matter, whether the certificate is required for the purpose of taking proceedings on the judgment or order in another court [or enforcing the judgment or order in the High Court,] or is for the purpose of evidence only, or
   (b)   if he is not a party to the action or matter, the purpose for which the certificate is required, the capacity in which he asks for it and any other facts showing that the certificate may properly be granted.

(2)   Where the request is made by a person who is not a party to the action or matter, the request shall be referred to the [district judge], who may, if he thinks fit, refer it to the judge.

[(3)   Without prejudice to paragraph (2), for the purposes of section 12(2) of the Act a certificate under this rule may be signed by the chief clerk or any other officer of the court acting on his behalf.]

Commencement 1 April 1990 (para (3)); 1 September 1982 (remainder).
Amendments Para (1): in sub-para (a) words "or enforcing the judgment or order in the High Court," inserted by SI 1984/878, r 14.
Para (3): inserted by SI 1989/2426, r 23.
Forms Certificate of judgment (N293).

[Order 22, r 9 Misdirected payments

A party who receives any payment which is, by or under these rules or the Court Funds Rules 1987, required to be made to the court shall forthwith notify the proper officer in writing and, where the payment is—
   (a)   made by or on behalf or in respect of a person under disability; or
   (b)   ordered to be paid into court to abide the event or as a condition of granting an application; or
   (c)   required to be paid into court by Order 31, rule 4(5),

the money so paid shall be paid into court.]

Commencement 1 April 1990.
Amendments This rule was substituted by SI 1989/1838, r 26.

[Order 22, r 10 Variation of payment

(1)   Where a judgment or order has been given or made for the payment of money, the person entitled to the benefit of the judgment or order or, as the case may be, the

person liable to make the payment (in this rule referred to as "the judgment creditor" and "the debtor" respectively) may apply in accordance with the provisions of this rule for a variation in the date or rate of payment.

(2) The judgment creditor may apply ex parte in writing for an order that the money, if payable in one sum, be paid at a later date than that by which it is due or by instalments or, if the money is already payable by instalments, that it be paid by the same or smaller instalments, and the proper officer may make an order accordingly unless no payment has been made under the judgment or order for 6 years before the date of the application in which case he shall refer the application to the district judge.

(3) The judgment creditor may apply to the district judge on notice for an order that the money, if payable in one sum, be paid at an earlier date than that by which it is due or, if the money is payable by instalments, that it be paid in one sum or by larger instalments, and any such application shall be made in writing stating the proposed terms and the grounds on which it is made.

(4) Where an application is made under paragraph (3)—
    (a) the proceedings shall be automatically transferred to the debtor's home court if the judgment or order was not given or made in that court;
    (b) the proper officer shall fix a day for the hearing of the application before the district judge and give to the judgment creditor and the debtor not less than 8 days' notice of the day so fixed

and at the hearing the district judge may make such order as seems just.

(5) The debtor may apply for an order that the money, if payable in one sum, be paid at a later date than that by which it is due or by instalments or, if the money is already payable by instalments, that it be paid by smaller instalments, and any such application shall be in the appropriate form stating the proposed terms, the grounds on which it is made and including a signed statement of the debtor's means.

(6) Where an application is made under paragraph (5), the proper officer shall—
    (a) send the judgment creditor a copy of the debtor's application (and statement of means); and
    (b) require the judgment creditor to notify the court in writing, within 14 days of service of notification upon him, giving his reasons for any objection he may have to the granting of the application.

(7) If the judgment creditor does not notify the court of any objection within the time stated, the proper officer shall make an order in the terms applied for.

(8) Upon receipt of a notice from the judgment creditor under paragraph (6), the proper officer may determine the date and rate of payment and make an order accordingly.

(9) Any party affected by an order under paragraph (8) may, within 14 days of service of the order on him and giving his reasons, apply on notice for the order to be re-considered and, where such an application is made—
    (a) the proceedings shall be automatically transferred to the debtor's home court if the judgment or order was not given or made in that court;
    (b) the proper officer shall fix a day for the hearing of the application before the district judge and give to the judgment creditor and the debtor not less than 8 days' notice of the day so fixed.

(10) On hearing an application under paragraph (9), the district judge may confirm

the order or set it aside and make such new order as he thinks fit and the order so made shall be entered in the records of the court.

(11) Any order made under any of the foregoing paragraphs may be varied from time to time by a subsequent order made under any of those paragraphs.

(12) In this rule "proper officer" does not include the district judge.]

Commencement 1 July 1991.
Amendments This rule was substituted by SI 1991/1126, r 49.
Forms Application to suspend warrant/vary order (N245).
Plaintiff's reply (N246).
Plaintiff application to vary (N294).
Variation order (N35).

Order 22, r 11 Set-off of cross judgments

(1) An application under [section 72] of the Act for leave to set off any sums, including costs, payable under several judgments or orders each of which was obtained in a county court shall be made in accordance with this rule.

(2) Where the judgments or orders have been obtained in the same county court, the application may be made to that court on the day when the last judgment or order is obtained, if both parties are present, and in any other case shall be made on notice.

(3) Where the judgments or orders have been obtained in different county courts, the application may be made to either of them on notice, and notice shall be given to the proper officer of the other court.

(4) The [district judge] of the court to which the application is made and the [district judge] of any other court to which notice is given under paragraph (3) shall forthwith stay execution on any judgment or order in his court to which the application relates and any money paid into court under the judgment or order shall be retained until the application has been disposed of.

(5) The application may be heard and determined by the court and any order giving leave shall direct how any money paid into court is to be dealt with.

(6) Where the judgments or orders have been obtained in different courts, the proper officer of the court in which an order giving leave is made shall send a copy of the order to the proper officer of the other court, who shall deal with any money paid into that court in accordance with the order.

(7) The proper officer or, as the case may be, each of the proper officers affected shall enter satisfaction in the records of his court for any sums ordered to be set off, and execution or other process for the enforcement of any judgment or order not wholly satisfied shall issue only for the balance remaining payable.

(8) Where an order is made by the High Court giving leave to set off sums payable under several judgments and orders obtained respectively in the High Court and a county court, the proper officer of the county court shall, on receipt of a copy of the order, proceed in accordance with paragraph (7).

Commencement 1 September 1982.
Amendments Para (1): words "section 72" substituted by SI 1984/878, r 12, Schedule.
Cross references See RSC Order 107, r 4 (as to set off between cross judgments in High Court and county court).

Order 22, r 12 Sale etc by order of court

(1)   Subject to paragraph (2), the provisions of the RSC with regard to the sale, mortgage, exchange or partition of land by order of the Court shall apply in relation to an action or matter in the county court as they apply in relation to a cause or matter in the Chancery Division of the High Court.

[(2)   Any reference in the said provisions to conveyancing counsel of the Court shall be omitted.]

Commencement   1 September 1984 (para (2)); 1 September 1982 (remainder).
Amendments   Para (2): substituted by SI 1984/878, r 3.
Cross references   RSC Order 31, rr 1–4.
Forms   Order for sale of land (N295).

Order 22, r 13 Order of appellate court

Where the Court of Appeal or High Court has heard and determined an appeal from a county court, the party entitled to the benefit of the order of the Court of Appeal or High Court shall deposit the order or an office copy thereof in the office of the county court.

Commencement   1 September 1982.

ORDER 23
ACCOUNTS AND INQUIRIES IN EQUITY PROCEEDINGS

Order 23, r 1 Service of notice of judgment

(1) Where in any action or matter for—
- (a) the administration of the estate of a deceased person, or
- (b) the execution of a trust, or
- (c) the sale of any property,

the court gives a judgment or makes an order which affects the rights or interests of persons who are not parties to the action or matter or directs any account to be taken or inquiry made, the court may direct notice of the judgment or order to be served on any person interested in the estate or under the trust or in the property, as the case may be.

(2) The notice shall be prepared by the proper officer and shall have annexed to it a copy of the judgment or order.

(3) The notice shall be served in the same manner as a fixed date summons, but if it appears to the court that it is impracticable to serve the notice on any person directed to be served, the court may dispense with service on him.

(4) Where the court dispenses with service of the notice on any person, it may also direct that he shall be bound by the judgment or order to the same extent as if he had been served with notice of it and he shall be bound accordingly except where the judgment has been obtained by fraud or non-disclosure of material facts.

(5) Any person served with notice under this rule shall be bound by the judgment or order and shall be entitled to attend the proceedings under it, but he may, within one month after service of the notice on him, apply to the judge (or, if the judgment or order was given or made by the [district judge], to the [district judge]) to discharge, vary or add to the judgment or order.

Commencement   1 September 1982.
Cross references   RSC Order 44, r 2.
Forms   Notice of judgment to person interested (N296).
Order for accounts and inquiries (N297).
Affidavit verifying accounts (RSC ChPF27).
Account referred to in same (RSC ChPF28).
Order for administration (N298).
Order for foreclosure nisi (N299).
Order for sale by equitable mortgagee (N300)
Judgment in action for specific performance (N302).
Order for dissolution of partnership (N303).

Order 23, r 2 Application of RSC

(1) Subject to the following paragraphs of this rule and to rule 3, the provisions of the RSC relating to proceedings under a judgment in the Chancery Division (except [RSC Order 44, rule 2] to which rule 1 of this Order corresponds[, and rules 6, 8 and 12 of that Order]) shall apply to proceedings under a judgment or order given or made by a county court in the exercise of its equity jurisdiction.

(2) The proper officer shall fix a day for proceeding under the judgment or order and shall give notice thereof to all parties entitled to attend the proceedings.

(3)   Where the judgment or order directs an account to be taken or inquiry made and does not otherwise provide, the account shall be taken or the inquiry made by the [district judge] and [Order 19, rule 13(a), (d) and (e)] shall apply as if there had been a reference to the [district judge] for inquiry and report.

(4)   The person to whom a claimant is required by any advertisement to send his name and address and particulars of his claim shall be the proper officer.

(5)   Where a claimant is required to make an affidavit or produce documents in support of his claim or to attend court for adjudication on the claim, the person by whom notice to that effect is to be given shall be the proper officer.

(6)   The proper officer shall give to every creditor whose claim or any part thereof has been allowed or disallowed, and who did not attend when the claim was disposed of, a notice informing him of that fact.

Commencement   1 September 1982.
Amendments   Para (1): words "RSC Order 44, rule 2" substituted and words ", and rules 6, 8 and 12 of that Order" inserted, by SI 1984/878, r 4.
Para (3): words "Order 19, rule 13(a), (d) and (e)" substituted by SI 1992/1965, r 18.
Cross references   See RSC Order 44, rr 1, 3–5, 7, 8, 10, 11.
Forms   District judges' order on accounts and inquiries (N307).
Order foreclosure absolute (N309).
Partnership, order on further consideration (N310).
Administration action, order on further consideration (N311).

[Order 23, r 3 Appeals

An appeal shall lie to the judge from any order made by the [district judge] under rule 2 (including an order as to the further consideration of the proceedings).]

Commencement   1 September 1984.
Amendments   This rule was substituted by SI 1984/878, r 5.

ORDER 24
SUMMARY PROCEEDINGS FOR THE RECOVERY OF LAND OR RENT

PART I—LAND

Order 24, r 1 Proceedings to be by originating application

Where a person claims possession of land which he alleges is occupied solely by a person or persons (not being a tenant or tenants holding over after the termination of the tenancy) who entered into or remained in occupation without his licence or consent or that of any predecessor in title of his, the proceedings may be brought by originating application in accordance with the provisions of this Order.

Commencement 1 September 1982.
Cross references See RSC Order 113, r 1.
Forms Originating application for possession (N312).

Order 24, r 2 Affidavit in support

[(1)] The applicant shall file in support of the originating application an affidavit stating—
    (a) his interest in the land;
    (b) the circumstances in which the land has been occupied without licence or consent and in which his claim to possession arises; and
    (c) that he does not know the name of any person occupying the land who is not named in the originating application.

[(2) Where the applicant considers that service in accordance with rule 3(2)(b) may be necessary, he shall provide, together with the originating application, sufficient stakes and sealable transparent envelopes for such service.]

Commencement 28 March 1989 (para (2)); 1 September 1982 (remainder).
Amendments Para (1): numbered as such by SI 1989/236, r 11(1).
Para (2): added by SI 1989/236, r 11(2).
Cross references See RSC Order 113, r 3.

Order 24, r 3 Service of originating application

(1) Where any person in occupation of the land is named in the originating application, the application shall be served on him—
    (a) by delivering to him personally a copy of the originating application, together with the notice of the return day required by Order 3, rule 4(4)(b), and a copy of the affidavit in support, or
    (b) by an officer of the court leaving the documents mentioned in subparagraph (a), or sending them to him, at the premises, or
    (c) in accordance with Order 7, rule 11, as applied to originating applications by Order 3, rule 4(6), or
    (d) in such other manner as the court may direct.

[(2) Where any person not named as a respondent is in occupation of the land, the originating application shall be served (whether or not it is also required to be served in accordance with paragraph (1)), unless the court otherwise directs, by—
    (a) affixing a copy of each of the documents mentioned in paragraph (1)(a) to the main door or other conspicuous part of the premises, and, if practicable,

inserting through the letter-box at the premises a copy of those documents enclosed in a transparent sealed envelope addressed to "the occupiers," or
(b) placing stakes in the ground at conspicuous parts of the occupied land, to each of which shall be affixed a sealed transparent envelope addressed to "the occupiers" and containing a copy of each of the documents mentioned in paragraph (1)(a).]

Commencement 13 April 1987 (para (2)); 1 September 1982 (remainder).
Amendments Para (2): substituted by SI 1987/493, r 4(1).
Cross references See RSC Order 113, r 4.

Order 24, r 4 Application by occupier to be made a party

Without prejudice to Order 15, rule 1, any person not named as a respondent who is in occupation of the land and wishes to be heard on the question whether an order for possession should be made may apply at any stage of the proceedings to be joined as respondent, and the notice of the return day required by Order 3, rule 4(4)(b), shall contain a notice to that effect.

Commencement 1 September 1982.
Cross references See RSC Order 113, r 5.
Forms Notice to respondent of hearing (N8(1)).

Order 24, r 5 Hearing of originating application

(1) Except in case of urgency and by leave of the court, the day fixed for the hearing of the originating application[—
(a) in the case of residential premises, shall not be less than five days after the day of service, and
(b) in the case of other land, shall not be less than two days after the day of service.]

(2) Notwithstanding anything in Order 21, rule 5, no order for possession shall be made on the originating application except by the judge or, with the leave of the judge, by the [district judge].

(3) An order for possession in proceedings under this Order shall be to the effect that the plaintiff do recover possession of the land mentioned in the originating application.

(4) Nothing in this Order shall prevent the court from ordering possession to be given on a specified date, in the exercise of any power which could have been exercised if the proceedings had been brought by action.

Commencement 1 September 1982.
Amendments Para (1): words from "— (a) in the case of" to the end substituted by SI 1987/493, r 4(2).
Cross references See RSC Order 113 r 6(1), (3).
Forms Order for possession (N36).

Order 24, r 6 Warrant of possession

(1) [Subject to paragraphs (2) and (3)], a warrant of possession to enforce an order for possession under this Order may be issued at any time after the making of the order and subject to the provisions of Order 26, rule 17, a warrant of restitution may be issued in aid of the warrant of possession.

(2)   No warrant of possession shall be issued after the expiry of 3 months from the date of the order without the leave of the court, and an application for such leave may be made ex parte unless the court otherwise directs.

[(3)   Nothing in this rule shall authorise the issue of a warrant of possession before the date on which possession is ordered to be given.]

Commencement   12 December 1983 (para (3)); 1 September 1982 (remainder)
Amendments   Para (1): words "Subject to paragraphs (2) and (3)" substituted by SI 1983/1716, r 6(1). Para (3): added by SI 1983/1716, r 6(2).
Cross references   See RSC Order 113, r 7.
Forms   Warrant for possession (N52).
Warrant of restitution (N51).

Order 24, r 7 Setting aside order

The judge may, on such terms as he thinks just, set aside or vary any order made in proceedings under this Order.

Commencement   1 September 1982.
Cross references   See RSC Order 113, r 8.

PART II—RENT

Order 24, rr 8–11   *(revoked by SI 1993/2175)*

ORDER 25
ENFORCEMENT OF JUDGMENTS AND ORDERS: GENERAL

Order 25, r 1 Judgment creditor and debtor

In this Order and Orders 26 to 29 "judgment creditor" means the person who has obtained or is entitled to enforce a judgment or order and "debtor" means the person against whom it was given or made.

Commencement 1 September 1982.

Order 25, r 2 Transfer of proceedings for enforcement

(1)   Where, with a view to enforcing a judgment or order obtained by him in a county court, a judgment creditor desires to apply for—

    (a)   the oral examination of the debtor,

    (b)   a charging order under section 1 of the Charging Orders Act 1979,

    (c)   an attachment of earnings order, or

    (d)   the issue of a judgment summons,

and the application is required by any provision of these rules to be made to another county court, the judgment creditor shall make a request in writing to the [district judge] of the court in which the judgment or order was obtained for the transfer of the action or matter to the other court.

(2)   On receipt of a request under paragraph (1) the [district judge] shall make an order transferring the action or matter to the other court and the proper officer shall—

    (a)   make an entry of the transfer in the records of his court; and

    (b)   send to the proper officer of the court to which the action or matter has been transferred a certificate of the judgment or order, stating the purpose for which it has been issued, and, if requested by that officer, all the documents in his custody relating to the action or matter.

(3)   When the action or matter has been transferred to the other court—

    (a)   the proper officer of that court shall give notice of the transfer to the judgment creditor and the debtor,

    [(b)   any payment which, by or under these rules or the Court Funds Rules 1987, is authorised or required to be made into court shall be made into that court, and]

    (c)   subject to sub-paragraph (d), any subsequent proceedings in the action or matter shall be taken in that court, but

    (d)   any application or appeal under Order 37 shall be made to the court in which the judgment or order was obtained.

(4)   If the judgment creditor desires to make a subsequent application for any of the remedies mentioned in paragraph (1)(a) to (d) and the application is required to be made to another court, he may make a request under paragraph (1) to the court to which the action or matter has been transferred and paragraphs (2) and (3) shall apply with the necessary modifications.

Commencement 1 September 1982.
Para (3): sub-para (b) substituted by SI 1989/1838, r 27.

Order 25, r 3 Oral examination of debtor

(1)   Where a person has obtained a judgment or order in a county court for the

payment of money, the appropriate court may, on an application made ex parte by the judgment creditor, order the debtor or, if the debtor is a body corporate, an officer thereof to attend before the [district judge] or such other officer of the court not below the rank of higher executive officer as the court may appoint and be orally examined as to the debtor's means of satisfying the judgment or order, and may also order the person to be examined to produce at the time and place appointed for the examination any books or documents in his possession relevant to the debtor's means.

[(1A) An application under paragraph (1) shall certify the amount of money remaining due under the judgment or order . . . .]

(2)   The appropriate court for the purposes of paragraph (1) shall be the court for the district in which the person to be examined (or, if there are more such persons than one, any of them) resides or carries on business.

(3)   The order shall be served in the same manner as a default summons.

(4)   If the person to be examined fails to attend at the time and place fixed for the examination, the court may adjourn the examination and make a further order for his attendance [and any such order shall direct that any payments made thereafter shall be paid into court and not direct to the judgment creditor].

[(5)   Nothing in Order 29, rule 1(2) to (7) shall apply to an order made under paragraph (4), but Order 27, rule 8 shall apply, with the necessary modifications, as it applies to orders made under section 23(1) of the Attachment of Earnings Act 1971, except that for the period of 5 days specified in paragraph (1) thereof there shall be substituted a period of 10 days.]

[(5A) Where an examination has been adjourned, the judgment creditor, if requested to do so by the person to be examined not less than 7 days before the day fixed for the adjourned examination, shall pay to him a sum reasonably sufficient to cover his expenses in travelling to and from the court, unless such a sum was paid to him at the time of service of the order for oral examination.

(5B) The judgment creditor shall, not more than 4 days before the day fixed for the adjourned examination, file a certificate stating either that no request has been made under paragraph (5A) or that a sum has been paid in accordance with such a request.

(5C) Where the person to be examined has made a request under paragraph (5A), he shall not be committed to prison under Order 29, rule 1(1) for having failed to attend at the time and place fixed for the adjourned examination unless the judgment creditor has paid to him a sum reasonably sufficient to cover his travelling expenses before the day fixed for the adjourned examination.]

(6)   Order 20, rule 13, shall apply with the necessary modifications, to an examination under this rule as it applies to an examination under that rule.

(7)   Nothing in this rule shall be construed as preventing the court, before deciding whether to make an order under paragraph (1), from giving the person to be examined an opportunity of making a statement in writing or an affidavit as to the debtor's means.

Commencement 1 April 1990 (para (1A)); 11 May 1988 (paras (5)–(5C)); 1 September 1982 (remainder).
Amendments Para (1A): inserted by SI 1989/1838, r 28; words omitted repealed by SI 1989/2426, r 24.
Para (4): words from "and any such order" to the end inserted by SI 1989/2426, r 25.
Para (5): substituted by SI 1988/278, r 9.
Paras (5A)–(5C): inserted by SI 1988/278, r 10.

Cross references See RSC Order 48 rr 1, 3.
Forms Request for oral examination (N316).
Order for oral examination (N37–8).
Order for attendance at adjourned hearing (N39).
Warrant of committal (N40).

Order 25, r 4 Examination of debtor under judgment not for money

Where any difficulty arises in or in connection with the enforcement of any judgment or order for some relief other than the payment of money, the court may make an order under rule 3 for the attendance of the debtor and for his examination on such questions as may be specified in the order, and that rule shall apply accordingly with the necessary modifications.

Commencement 1 September 1982.
Cross references See RSC Order 48, r 2.

[Order 25, r 5 Production of plaint note and other information

[(1) The requests and applications mentioned in paragraph (2) are—
  (a) a request for a warrant of execution, delivery or possession,
  (b) a request for a judgment summons or warrant of committal,
  (c) an application for a garnishee order under Order 30, rule 1, and
  (d) an application for a charging order.]

(2) Where the judgment creditor has filed any request or application referred to in paragraph (1) or is seeking to enforce a judgment or order by making an application under rule 3 or under Order 27 or 32, he shall forthwith notify the proper officer of any payment received from the debtor in respect of the judgment to be enforced after the date of the application and before—
  (a) the final return to the warrant of execution, delivery or possession; or
  (b) in any other case, the date fixed for the hearing of the application.

(3) Without prejudice [to rule 8(9)], where the judgment creditor applies to re-issue enforcement proceedings, he shall file a request in that behalf certifying the amount of money remaining due under the judgment or order and that the whole or part of any instalment due remains unpaid and stating why re-issue is necessary.]

Commencement 16 September 1991 (para (1)); 1 April 1990 (remainder).
Amendments This rule was substituted by SI 1989/1838, r 29.
Para (1): substituted by SI 1991/1882, r 9.
Para (3): words "to rule 8(9)" substituted by SI 1991/1882, r 10.
Forms Request for reissue of process (N446).

[Order 25, r 5A Interest on judgment debts

Where the judgment creditor claims interest pursuant to the County Courts (Interest on Judgment Debts) Order 1991 and takes proceedings to enforce payment under the relevant judgment (within the meaning of article 4(1) of that Order), any request or application for enforcement made in those proceedings shall be accompanied by two copies of a certificate giving details of—
  (a) the amount of interest claimed and the sum on which it is claimed,
  (b) the dates from and to which interest has accrued, and
  (c) the rate of interest which has been applied and, where more than one rate of interest has been applied, the relevant dates and rates.]

Commencement 1 July 1991.
Amendments This rule was inserted by SI 1991/1328, r 2.

Order 25, r 6 Description of parties

Where the name or address of the judgment creditor or the debtor as given in the request for the issue of a warrant of execution or delivery, judgment summons or warrant of committal differs from his name or address in the judgment or order sought to be enforced and the judgment creditor satisfies the proper officer that the name or address as given in the request is applicable to the person concerned, the judgment creditor or debtor, as the case may be, shall be described in the warrant or judgment summons as "C.D. of (name and address as given in the request) suing (or sued) as A.D. of (name and address in the judgment or order)".

Commencement 1 September 1982.

Order 25, r 7 Recording and giving information as to warrants and orders

(1)   Every [district judge] by whom a warrant or order is issued or received for execution shall from time to time state in the records of his court what has been done in the execution of the warrant or order.

(2)   If the warrant or order has not been executed within one month from the date of its issue or receipt by him, the proper officer of the court responsible for its execution shall, at the end of that month and every subsequent month during which the warrant remains outstanding, send notice of the reason for non-execution to the judgment creditor and, if the warrant or order was received from another court, to the proper officer of that court.

(3)   The [district judge] responsible for executing a warrant or order shall give such information respecting it as may reasonably be required by the judgment creditor and, if the warrant or order was received by him from another court, by the [district judge] of that court.

(4)   Where money is received in pursuance of a warrant of execution or committal sent by one court to another court, the proper officer of the foreign court shall, subject to paragraph (5) and to [section 346 of the Insolvency Act 1986] and section 326 of the Companies Act 1948, [send the money to the judgment creditor in the manner prescribed by the County Court Funds Rules and make a return to the proper officer of the home court.]

(5)   Where interpleader proceedings are pending, the proper officer shall not proceed in accordance with paragraph (4) until the interpleader proceedings are determined and the [district judge] shall then make a return showing how the money is to be disposed of and, if any money is payable to the judgment creditor, the proper officer shall proceed in accordance with paragraph (4).

(6)   Where a warrant of committal has been received from another court, the proper officer of the foreign court shall, on the execution of the warrant, send notice thereof to the proper officer of the home court.

Commencement 1 September 1982.
Amendments Para (4): words "section 346 of the Insolvency Act 1986" substituted by SI 1986/2001, art 2, Schedule; words from "send the money" to the end substituted by SI 1982/1794, r 11.

[Order 25, r 8 Suspension of judgment or execution

(1)   The power of the court to suspend or stay a judgment or order or to stay execution of any warrant may be exercised by the district judge or, in the case of the power to stay execution of a warrant of execution and in accordance with the provisions of this rule, by the proper officer.

(2)   An application by the debtor to stay execution of a warrant of execution shall be in the appropriate form stating the proposed terms, the grounds on which it is made and including a signed statement of the debtor's means.

(3)   Where the debtor makes an application under paragraph (2), the proper officer shall—

(a)   send the judgment creditor a copy of the debtor's application (and statement of means); and

(b)   require the creditor to notify the court in writing, within 14 days of service of notification upon him, giving his reasons for any objection he may have to the granting of the application.

(4)   If the judgment creditor does not notify the court of any objection within the time stated, the proper officer may make an order suspending the warrant on terms of payment.

(5)   Upon receipt of a notice by the judgment creditor under paragraph (3)(b), the proper officer may, if the judgment creditor objects only to the terms offered, determine the date and rate of payment and make an order suspending the warrant on terms of payment.

(6)   Any party affected by an order made under paragraph (5) may, within 14 days of service of the order on him and giving his reasons, apply on notice for the order to be re-considered and the proper officer shall fix a day for the hearing of the application before the district judge and give to the judgment creditor and the debtor not less than 8 days' notice of the day so fixed.

(7)   On hearing an application under paragraph (6), the district judge may confirm the order or set it aside and make such new order as he thinks fit and the order so made shall be entered in the records of the court.

(8)   Where the judgment creditor states in his notice under paragraph (3)(b) that he wishes the bailiff to proceed to execute the warrant, the proper officer shall fix a day for a hearing before the district judge of the debtor's application and give to the judgment creditor and to the debtor not less than 2 days' notice of the day so fixed.

(9)   Subject to any directions given by the district judge, where a warrant of execution has been suspended, it may be re-issued on the judgment creditor's filing a request pursuant to rule 5(3) showing that any condition subject to which the warrant was suspended has not been complied with.

(10)   Where an order is made by the district judge suspending a warrant of execution, the debtor may be ordered to pay the costs of the warrant and any fees or expenses incurred before its suspension and the order may authorise the sale of a sufficient portion of any goods seized to cover such costs, fees and expenses and the expenses of sale.

(11)   In this rule "proper officer" does not include the district judge.]

Commencement   1 July 1991.

Amendments   This rule was substituted by SI 1991/1126, r 50.

Cross references   See RSC Order 45, r 11, Order 47, r 1.

Forms Application to suspend warrant/vary order (N245).
Plaintiff's reply (N246A).
Order suspending judgment/warrant (N41–41A).
Request for re-issue of warrant (N445).

Order 25, r 9 Enforcement of judgment or order against firm

(1) Subject to paragraph (2), a judgment or order against a firm may be enforced against—

    (a) any property of the firm,

    (b) any person who admitted in the action or matter that he was a partner or was adjudged to be a partner,

    (c) any person who was served as a partner with the originating process if—

        (i) the proceeding is a default action and judgment was entered under Order 9, rule 6, in default of defence or on admission, or

        (ii) the person so served did not appear on a pre-trial review and judgment was entered or given under Order 17, rule 7 or 8, or

        (iii) the person so served did not appear at the trial or hearing of the action or matter.

(2) A judgment or order may not be enforced under paragraph (1) against a member of the firm who was out of England and Wales when the originating process was issued unless he—

    (a) was served within England and Wales with the originating process as a partner, or

    (b) was, with the leave of the court under Order 8, rule 2, served out of England and Wales with the originating process as a partner,

and, except as provided by paragraph (1)(a) and by the foregoing provisions of this paragraph, a judgment or order obtained against a firm shall not render liable, release or otherwise affect a member of the firm who was out of England and Wales when the originating process was issued.

(3) A judgment creditor who claims to be entitled to enforce a judgment or order against any other person as a partner may apply to the court for leave to do so.

(4) Notice of any application under paragraph (3) shall be served on the alleged partner, not less than three days before the hearing of the application, in the manner prescribed by Order 7, rule 10, for a fixed date summons, and on the hearing of the application, if the alleged partner does not dispute his liability, the court may, subject to paragraph (2), give leave to enforce the judgment or order against him and, if he disputes liability, the court may order that the question of his liability be tried and determined in such a manner as the court thinks fit.

(5) The foregoing provisions of this rule shall not apply where it is desired to enforce in a county court a judgment or order of the High Court, or a judgment, order, decree or award of any court or arbitrator which is or has become enforceable as if it were a judgment or order of the High Court, and in any such case the provisions of the RSC relating to the enforcement of a judgment or order against a firm shall apply.

Commencement 1 September 1982.
Cross references See RSC Order 81, r 5.

Order 25, r 10 Enforcing judgment between a firm and its members

(1)   Execution to enforce a judgment or order given or made in—
    (a)   proceedings by or against a firm in the name of the firm against or by a member of the firm, or
    (b)   proceedings by a firm in the name of the firm against a firm in the name of the firm where those firms have one or more members in common.

shall not issue without the leave of the court.

(2)   On an application for leave the court may give such directions, including directions as to the taking of accounts and the making of inquiries, as may be just.

Commencement   1 September 1982.
Cross references   See RSC Order 81, r 6.

[Order 25, r 11 Enforcement of High Court judgment

(1)   A judgment creditor who desires to enforce a judgment or order of the High Court, or a judgment, order, decree or award of any court or arbitrator which is or has become enforceable as if it were a judgment or order of the High Court, shall file in the appropriate court (with such documents as are required to be filed for the purpose of enforcing a judgment or order of a county court)—
    (a)   an office copy of the judgment or order or, in the case of a judgment, order, decree or award of a court other than the High Court or an arbitrator, such evidence of the judgment, order, decree or award and of its enforceability as a judgment of the High Court as the [district judge] may require;
    (b)   an affidavit verifying the amount due under the judgment, order, decree or award, and
    (c)   where a writ of execution has been issued to enforce it, a copy of the sheriff's return to the writ.

(2)   In this rule the "appropriate court" means the county court in which the relevant enforcement proceedings might, 'by virtue of these rules, be brought if the judgment or order had been obtained in proceedings commenced in a county court.

Provided that if under these rules the court in which the relevant enforcement proceedings might be brought is identified by reference to the court in which the judgment or order has been obtained the appropriate court shall be the court for the district in which the debtor resides or carries on business.

(3)   The provisions of this rule are without prejudice to Order 26, rule 2.]

Commencement   1 September 1984.
Amendments   This rule was substituted by SI 1984/878, r 15.
Forms   Affidavit verifying amount due under judgment not of county court (N321).

Order 25, r 12 Enforcement of award of tribunal

(1)   Where by any Act or statutory instrument other than these rules a sum of money is, if the county court so orders, recoverable as if payable under an order of that court, an application for such an order shall be made ex parte by filing an affidavit verifying the amount remaining due to the applicant and by producing any award, order or agreement under which the sum is payable, or a duplicate thereof, and filing a copy.

(2)   Unless otherwise provided, the application shall be made to the court for the district in which the person by whom the sum is payable resides or carries on business.

(3)   The application may be heard and determined by the [district judge].

Commencement 1 September 1982.
Forms Order for recovery of money ordered by tribunal (N322).

[Order 25, r 13 Transfer to High Court for enforcement

[(1)   Where a judgment or order is to be enforced in the High Court, the judgment creditor shall make a request to the proper officer for a certificate of judgment under Order 22, rule 8(1) and the transfer shall have effect on the grant of that certificate.]

(2)   On the transfer of a judgment or order in accordance with paragraph (1), the proper officer shall give notice to the debtor that the judgment or order has been transferred to the High Court and shall make an entry of that fact in the records of his court.

(3)   In a case where a request for a certificate of judgment is made under Order 22, rule 8(1) for the purpose of enforcing a judgment or order in the High Court and
  (a)   an application under Order 22, rule 10, or
  (b)   an application under either rule 2 or rule 4 of Order 37, or
  (c)   a request for an administration order, or
  (d)   an application for a stay of execution under section 88 of the Act,

is pending, the request for the certificate shall not be dealt with until those proceedings are determined.]

Commencement 1 July 1991 (para (1)); 1 September 1984 (remainder).
Amendments This rule was added by SI 1984/878, r 16.
Para (1): substituted by SI 1991/1126, r 21.

ORDER 26
WARRANTS OF EXECUTION, DELIVERY AND POSSESSION

Order 26, r 1 Application for warrant of execution

[(1) A judgment creditor desiring a warrant of execution to be issued shall file a request in that behalf certifying—
  (a) the amount remaining due under the judgment or order; and
  (b) where the order made is for payment of a sum of money by instalments,
    (i)   that the whole or part of any instalment due remains unpaid; and
    (ii) the amount for which the warrant is to be issued.]

(2) Where the court has made an order for payment of a sum of money by instalments and default has been made in payment of such an instalment, a warrant of execution may be issued for the whole of the said sum of money and costs then remaining unpaid or, subject to paragraph (3), for such part as the judgment creditor may request, not being in the latter case less than [£50] or the amount of one monthly instalment or, as the case may be, four weekly instalments, whichever is the greater.

(3) In any case to which paragraph (2) applies no warrant shall be issued unless at the time when it is issued—
  (a) the whole or part of an instalment which has already become due remains unpaid, and
  (b) any warrant previously issued for part of the said sum of money and costs has expired or has been satisfied or abandoned.

[(4) Where a warrant is issued for the whole or part of the said sum of money and costs, the proper officer shall, unless the [district judge] responsible for execution of the warrant directs otherwise, send a warning notice to the person against whom the warrant is issued and, where such a notice is sent, the warrant shall not be levied until 7 days thereafter.]

(5) Where judgment is given or an order made for payment otherwise than by instalments of a sum of money and costs to be taxed and default is made in payment of the sum of money before the costs have been taxed, a warrant of execution may issue for recovery of the sum of money and a separate warrant may issue subsequently for the recovery of the costs if default is made in payment of them.

Commencement 1 April 1990 (paras (1), (4)); 1 September 1982 (remainder).
Amendments Para (1): substituted by SI 1989/1838, r 31.
Para (4): substituted by SI 1989/1383, r 32.
Para (2): sum "£50" substituted by SI 1983/1716, r 7.
Cross references See RSC Order 46, r 6.
Forms Request for warrant of execution (N323).
Notice of issue of warrant (N326).

Order 26, r 2 Execution of High Court judgment

(1) Where it is desired to enforce by warrant of execution a judgment or order of the High Court, or a judgment, order, decree or award which is or has become enforceable as if it were a judgment of the High Court, the request referred to in rule 1(1) may be filed in any court in the district of which execution is to be levied.

(2) Subject to Order 25, rule 9(5), any restriction imposed by these rules on the issue of execution shall apply as if the judgment, order, decree or award were a

judgment or order of the county court, but leave to issue execution shall not be required if leave has already been given by the High Court.

(3) Notice of the issue of the warrant shall be sent by the proper officer of the county court to the proper officer of the High Court.

Commencement 1 September 1982.

Order 26, r 3 Execution against farmer

If after the issue of a warrant of execution the [district judge] for the district in which the warrant is to be executed has reason to believe that the debtor is a farmer, the execution creditor shall, if so required by the [district judge], furnish him with an official certificate, dated not more than three days beforehand, of the result of a search at the Land Registry as to the existence of any charge registered against the debtor under the Agricultural Credits Act 1928.

Commencement 1 September 1982.

Order 26, r 4 Concurrent warrants

Two or more warrants of execution may be issued concurrently for execution in different districts, but—

    (a) no more shall be levied under all the warrants together than is authorised to be levied under one of them, and

    (b) the costs of more than one such warrant shall not be allowed against the debtor except by order of the court.

Commencement 1 September 1982.
Cross references See RSC Order 47, r 2.

Order 26, r 5 Leave to issue certain warrants

(1) A warrant of execution shall not issue without the leave of the court where—

    (a) six years or more have elapsed since the date of the judgment or order;

    (b) any change has taken place, whether by death or otherwise in the parties entitled to enforce the judgment or order or liable to have it enforced against them;

    (c) the judgment or order is against the assets of a deceased person coming to the hands of his executors or administrators after the date of the judgment or order and it is sought to issue execution against such assets; or

    (d) any goods to be seized under a warrant of execution are in the hands of a receiver appointed by a court.

(2) An application for leave shall be supported by an affidavit establishing the applicant's right to relief and may be made ex parte in the first instance but the court may direct notice of the application to be served on such persons as it thinks fit.

(3) Where, by reason of one and the same event, a person seeks leave under paragraph (1)(b) to enforce more judgments or orders than one, he may make one application only, specifying in a schedule all the judgments or orders in respect of which it is made, and if notice is directed to be given to any person, it need set out only such part of the application as affects him.

(4)   Paragraph (1) is without prejudice to any enactment, rule or direction by virtue of which a person is required to obtain the leave of the court for the issue of a warrant or to proceed to execution or otherwise to the enforcement of a judgment or order.

Commencement 1 September 1982.
Cross references See RSC Order 46, r 2.

Order 26, r 6 Duration and renewal of warrant

(1)   A warrant of execution shall, for the purpose of execution, be valid in the first instance for 12 months beginning with the date of its issue, but if not wholly executed, it may be renewed from time to time, by order of the court, for a period of 12 months at any one time, beginning with the day next following that on which it would otherwise expire, if an application for renewal is made before that day or such later day (if any) as the court may allow.

(2)   A note of any such renewal shall be indorsed on the warrant and it shall be entitled to priority according to the time of its original issue or, where appropriate, its receipt by the [district judge] responsible for its execution.

Commencement 1 September 1982.
Cross references See RSC Order 46, r 8.

Order 26, r 7 Notice on levy

Any bailiff upon levying execution shall deliver to the debtor or leave at the place where execution is levied a notice of the warrant.

Commencement 1 September 1982.

Order 26, r 8 Bankruptcy or winding up of debtor

(1)   Where the [district judge] responsible for the execution of a warrant is required by [any provision of the Insolvency Act 1986 or any other enactment relating to insolvency] to retain the proceeds of sale of goods sold under the warrant or money paid in order to avoid a sale, the proper officer shall, as soon as practicable after the sale or the receipt of the money, send notice to the execution creditor and, if the warrant issued out of another court, to the proper officer of that court.

(2)   Where the [district judge] responsible for the execution of a warrant—
  (a) receives notice that a [bankruptcy order] has been made against the debtor or, if the debtor is a company, that a provisional liquidator has been appointed or that an order has been made or a resolution passed for the winding up of the company, and
  (b) withdraws from possession of goods seized or pays over to the official receiver or trustee in bankruptcy or, if the debtor is a company, to the liquidator the proceeds of sale of goods sold under the warrant or money paid in order to avoid a sale or seized or received in part satisfaction of the warrant,

the proper officer shall send notice to the execution creditor and, if the warrant issued out of another court, to the proper officer of that court.

(3)   Where the proper officer of a court to which a warrant issued out of another court has been sent for execution receives any such notice as is referred to in

paragraph (2)(a) after he has sent to the proper officer of the home court any money seized or received in part satisfaction of the warrant, he shall forward the notice to the proper officer of that court.

Commencement 1 September 1982.
Amendments Para (1): words "any provision of the Insolvency Act 1986 or any other enactment relating to insolvency" substituted by SI 1989/236, r 13.
Para (2): in sub–para (a) words "bankruptcy order" substituted by SI 1986/2001, art 2, Schedule.

Order 26, r 9 *(revoked by SI 1991/1126)*

Order 26, r 10 Withdrawal and suspension of warrant at creditor's request

(1) Where an execution creditor requests the [district judge] responsible for executing a warrant to withdraw from possession, he shall, subject to the following paragraphs of this rule, be treated as having abandoned the execution, and the proper officer shall mark the warrant as withdrawn by request of the execution creditor.

(2) Where the request is made in consequence of a claim having been made under Order 33, rule 1, to goods seized under the warrant, the execution shall be treated as being abandoned in respect only of the goods claimed.

(3) If the [district judge] responsible for executing a warrant is requested by the execution creditor to suspend it in pursuance of an arrangement between him and the debtor, the proper officer shall mark the warrant as suspended by request of the execution creditor and the execution creditor may subsequently apply to the [district judge] holding the warrant for it to be re-issued and, if he does so, the application shall be deemed for the purpose of [section 85(3)] of the Act to be an application to issue the warrant.

(4) Nothing in this rule shall prejudice any right of the execution creditor to apply for the issue of a fresh warrant or shall authorise the re-issue of a warrant which has been withdrawn or has expired or has been superseded by the issue of a fresh warrant.

Commencement 1 September 1982.
Amendments Para (3): words "section 85(3)" substituted by SI 1984/878, r 12, Schedule.

Order 26, r 11 Suspension of part warrant

Where a warrant issued for part of a sum of money and costs payable under a judgment or order is suspended on payment of instalments, the judgment or order shall, unless the court otherwise directs, be treated as suspended on those terms as respects the whole of the sum of money and costs then remaining unpaid.

Commencement 1 September 1982.

Order 26, r 12 Inventory and notice where goods removed

(1) Where goods seized in execution are removed, the proper officer shall forthwith deliver or send to the debtor a sufficient inventory of the goods removed and shall, not less than 4 days before the time fixed for the sale, give him notice of the time and place at which the goods will be sold.

(2)   The inventory and notice shall be given to the debtor by delivering them to him personally or by sending them to him by post at his place of residence or, if his place of residence is not known, by leaving them for him, or sending them to him by post, at the place from which the goods were removed.

Commencement   1 September 1982.

Order 26, r 13 Account of sale

Where goods are sold under an execution, the proper officer shall furnish the debtor with a detailed account in writing of the sale and of the application of the proceeds.

Commencement   1 September 1982.

[Order 26, r 14 [Notification to foreign court of payment made]

Where, after a warrant has been sent to a foreign court for execution but before a final return has been made to the warrant, the home court is notified of a payment made in respect of the sum for which the warrant is issued, the proper officer of the home court shall send notice of the payment to the proper officer of the foreign court.]

Commencement   1 April 1990.
Amendments   The text of this rule was substituted by SI 1989/1838, r 33.
Rule heading: substituted by SI 1989/2426, r 26.

Order 26, r 15 Order for private sale

(1)   Subject to paragraph (6), an order of the court under [section 97] of the Act that a sale under an execution may be made otherwise than by public auction may be made on the application of the execution creditor or the debtor or the [district judge] responsible for the execution of the warrant.

(2)   Where he is not the applicant for an order under this rule, the [district judge] responsible for the execution of the warrant shall, on the demand of the applicant, furnish him with a list containing the name and address of every execution creditor under any other warrant or writ of execution against the goods of the debtor of which the [district judge] has notice, and where the [district judge] is the applicant, he shall prepare such a list.

(3)   Not less than 4 days before the day fixed for the hearing of the application, the applicant shall give notice of the application to each of the other persons by whom the application might have been made and to every person named in the list referred to in paragraph (2).

(4)   The applicant shall produce the list to the court on the hearing of the application.

(5)   Every person to whom notice of the application was given may attend and be heard on the hearing of the application.

(6)   Where the [district judge] responsible for the execution of the warrant is the [district judge] by whom it was issued and he has no notice of any other warrant or writ of execution against the goods of the debtor, an order under this rule may be

made by the court of its own motion with the consent of the execution creditor and the debtor or after giving them an opportunity of being heard.

Commencement 1 September 1982.
Amendments Para (1): words "section 97" substituted by SI 1984/878, r 12, Schedule.
Cross references See RSC Order 47, r 6.
Forms Order for sale by private contract (RSC PF97).

Order 26, r 16 Warrant of delivery

(1)　Except where by any Act or rule it is otherwise provided, a judgment or order for the delivery of any goods shall be enforceable by warrant of delivery in accordance with this rule.

(2)　If the judgment or order does not give the person against whom it was given or made the alternative of paying the value of the goods, it may be enforced by a warrant of specific delivery, that is to say, a warrant to recover the goods without alternative provision for recovery of their value.

(3)　If the judgment or order is for the delivery of the goods or payment of their value, it may be enforced by a warrant of delivery to recover the goods or their value.

(4)　Where a warrant of delivery is issued, the judgment creditor shall be entitled, by the same or a separate warrant, to execution against the debtor's goods for any money payable under the judgment or order which is to be enforced by the warrant of delivery.

[(4A) Where a judgment or order is given or made for the delivery of goods or payment of their value and a warrant is issued to recover the goods or their value, money paid into court under the warrant shall be appropriated first to any sum of money and costs awarded.]

(5)　The foregoing provisions of this Order, so far as applicable, shall have effect, with the necessary modifications, in relation to warrants of delivery as they have effect in relation to warrants of execution.

Commencement 1 April 1990 (para (4A)); 1 September 1982 (remainder).
Amendments Para (4A): inserted by SI 1989/1838, r 34.
Cross references See RSC Order 45, r 4.
Forms Request for warrant of delivery (N324).
Warrant of delivery (N46, 48).

Order 26, r 17 Warrant of possession

(1)　A judgment or order for the recovery of land shall be enforceable by warrant of possession.

[(2)　Without prejudice to paragraph (3A), the person desiring a warrant of possession to be issued shall file a request in that behalf certifying that the land has not been vacated in accordance with the judgment or order for the recovery of the said land.]

(3)　Where a warrant of possession is issued, the judgment creditor shall be entitled, by the same or a separate warrant, to execution against the debtor's goods for any money payable under the judgment or order which is to be enforced by the warrant of possession.

[(3A) In a case to which paragraph (3) applies or where an order for possession has been suspended on terms as to payment of a sum of money by instalments, the judgment creditor shall in his request certify—

    (a)   the amount of money remaining due under the judgment or order, and

    (b)   that the whole or part of any instalment due remains unpaid.]

(4)   A warrant of restitution may be issued, with the leave of the court, in aid of any warrant of possession.

(5)   An application for leave under paragraph (4) may be made ex parte and shall be supported by evidence of wrongful re-entry into possession following the execution of the warrant of possession and of such further facts as would, in the High Court, enable the judgment creditor to have a writ of restitution issued.

(6)   Rules 5 and 6 shall apply, with the necessary modifications, in relation to a warrant of possession and any further warrant in aid of such a warrant as they apply in relation to a warrant of execution.

Commencement   1 June 1992 (para (2)); 1 April 1990 (para (3A)); 1 September 1982 (remainder).
Amendments   Para (2): substituted by SI 1992/793, r 2.
Para (3A): inserted by SI 1989/1838, r 35.
Cross references   See RSC Order 45, r 3.
Forms   Request for warrant of possession (N325)
Warrant for possession (N49).
Warrant of restitution (N50).

Order 26, r 18 Saving for enforcement by committal

Nothing in rule 16 or 17 shall prejudice any power to enforce a judgment or order for the delivery of goods or the recovery of land by an order of committal.

Commencement   1 September 1982.

ORDER 27
ATTACHMENT OF EARNINGS

PART I—GENERAL

[Order 27, r 1 Interpretation

(1)   In this Order—
"the Act of 1971" means the Attachment of Earnings Act 1971 and, unless the
     context otherwise requires, expressions used in this Act have the same
     meanings as in that Act;
"proper officer" does not include the district judge.

(2)   Order 1, rule 8 shall apply in relation to any power conferred by the Act of 1971
as it applies in relation to any power conferred by these rules.]

Commencement 1 July 1991.
Amendments This rule was substituted by SI 1991/1126, r 51.

Order 27, r 2 Index of orders

(1)   The proper officer of every court shall keep a nominal index of the debtors
residing within the district of his court in respect of whom there are in force
attachment of earnings orders which have been made by that court or of which the
proper officer has received notice from another court.

(2)   Where a debtor in respect of whom a court has made an attachment of earnings
order resides within the district of another court, the proper officer of the first-
mentioned court shall send a copy of the order to the proper officer of the other
court for entry in his index.

(3)   The proper officer of a court shall, on the request of any person having a
judgment or order against a person believed to be residing within the district of the
court, cause a search to be made in the index of the court and issue a certificate of the
result of the search.

Commencement 1 September 1982.
Forms Request for search (N336).

Order 27, r 3 Appropriate court

(1)   Subject to paragraphs (2) and (3), an application for an attachment of earnings
order may be made to the court for the district in which the debtor resides.

(2)   If the debtor does not reside within England or Wales, or the creditor does not
know where he resides, the application may be made to the court in which, or for the
district in which, the judgment or order sought to be enforced was obtained.

(3)   Where the creditor applies for attachment of earnings orders in respect of two
or more debtors jointly liable under a judgment or order, the application may be
made to the court for the district in which any of the debtors resides, so however that
if the judgment or order was given or made by any such court, the application shall
be made to that court.

Commencement 1 September 1982.

Order 27, r 4 Mode of applying

[(1) A judgment creditor who desires to apply for an attachment of earnings order shall file his application certifying the amount of money remaining due under the judgment or order and that the whole or part of any instalment due remains unpaid] .
. . and, where it is sought to enforce an order of magistrates' court,—

(a) a certified copy of the order, and

(b) an affidavit verifying the amount due under the order or, if payments under the order are required to be made to the clerk to the magistrates' court, a certificate by that clerk to the same effect.

(2) On the filing of the documents mentioned in paragraph (1) the proper officer shall[, where the order to be enforced is a maintenance order,] fix a day for the hearing of the application.

Commencement 1 September 1982.
Amendments Para (1): words from the beginning to "remains unpaid" substituted by SI 1989/1838, r 36; words omitted revoked by SI 1982/1140, r 2.
Para (2): words ", where the order to be enforced is a maintenance order," inserted by SI 1991/1126, r 52.
Forms Request for attachment of earnings order (N337).

Order 27, r 5 Service and reply

(1) [Notice of the application, together with] a form of reply [in the appropriate form], shall be served on the debtor in the manner prescribed by these rules for the service of a [default summons].

(2) The debtor shall, within 8 days after service on him of the documents mentioned in paragraph (1), file a reply in the form provided, and the instruction to that effect in the notice to the debtor shall constitute a requirement imposed by virtue of section 14(4) of the Act of 1971:

Provided that no proceedings shall be taken for an offence alleged to have been committed under section 23(2)(c) or (f) of the Act of 1971 in relation to the requirement unless the said documents have been served on the debtor personally or the court is satisfied that they came to his knowledge in sufficient time for him to comply with the requirement.

[(2A) Nothing in paragraph (2) shall require a defendant to file a reply if, within the period of time mentioned in that paragraph, he pays to the judgment creditor the money remaining due under the judgment or order and, where such payment is made, the judgment creditor shall so inform the proper officer.]

(3) On receipt of a reply the proper officer shall send a copy to the applicant.

Commencement 1 July 1991 (para (2A)); 1 September 1982 (remainder).
Amendments Para (1): words "Notice of the application, together with" substituted by SI 1982/1140, r 2; words "in the appropriate form" added and words "default summons" substituted, by SI 1991/1126, r 53.
Para (2A): inserted by SI 1991/1126, r 54.
Definitions Act of 1971: Attachment of Earnings Act 1971.
Forms Application for attachment of earnings order (N55).
Application for attachment of earnings order (maintenance)(N55(A)).
Reply to application (N56).

Order 27, r 6 Notice to employer

Without prejudice to the powers conferred by section 14(1) of the Act of 1971, the proper officer may, at any stage of the proceedings, send to any person appearing to have the debtor in his employment a notice requesting him to give to [the court], within such period as may be specified in the notice, a statement of the debtor's earnings and anticipated earnings with such particulars as may be so specified.

Commencement 1 September 1982.
Amendments Words "the court" substituted by SI 1991/1126, r 55.
Definitions Act of 1971: Attachment of Earnings Act 1971.
Forms Request for statement of earnings (N338).

[Order 27, r 7 Attachment of earnings order

(1)   On receipt of the debtor's reply, the proper officer may, if he has sufficient information to do so, make an attachment of earnings order and a copy of the order shall be sent to the parties and to the debtor's employer.

(2)   Where an order is made under paragraph (1), the judgment creditor or the debtor may, within 14 days of service of the order on him and giving his reasons, apply on notice for the order to be re-considered and the proper officer shall fix a day for the hearing of the application and give to the judgment creditor and the debtor not less than 2 days' notice of the day so fixed.

(3)   On hearing an application under paragraph (2), the district judge may confirm the order or set it aside and make such new order as he thinks fit and the order so made shall be entered in the records of the court.

(4)   Where an order is not made under paragraph (1), the proper officer shall refer the application to the district judge who shall, if he considers that he has sufficient information to do so without the attendance of the parties, determine the application.

(5)   Where the district judge does not determine the application under paragraph (4), he shall direct that a day be fixed for the hearing of the application whereupon the proper officer shall fix such a day and give to the judgment creditor and the debtor not less than 8 days' notice of the day so fixed.

(6)   Where an order is made under paragraph (4), the judgment creditor or the debtor may, within 14 days of service of the order on him and giving his reasons, apply on notice for the order to be re-considered; and the proper officer shall fix a day for the hearing of the application and give to the judgment creditor and the debtor not less than 2 days' notice of the day so fixed.

(7)   On hearing an application under paragraph (6), the district judge may confirm the order or set it aside and make such new order as he thinks fit and the order so made shall be entered in the records of the court.

(8)   If the creditor does not apply at the hearing of the application under paragraph (5) but—

    (a)   the court has received an affidavit of evidence from him, or
    (b)   the creditor requests the court in writing to proceed in his absence,

the court may, notwithstanding anything in Order 21, rule 1, proceed to hear the application and to make an order thereon.

(9)   An attachment of earnings order may be made to secure the payment of a judgment debt if the debt is—

    (a)   of not less than £50, or
    (b)   for the amount remaining payable under a judgment for a sum of not less than £50.]

Commencement 1 July 1991.
Amendments This rule was substituted by SI 1991/1126, r 56.

[Order 27, r 7A Failure by debtor

(1)   If the debtor has failed to comply with rule 5(2) or to make payment to the judgment creditor, the proper officer may issue an order under subsection 14(1) of the Act of 1971 which shall—

(a) be indorsed with or incorporate a notice warning the debtor of the consequences of disobedience to the order,

(b) be served on the debtor personally, and

(c) direct that any payments made thereafter shall be paid into the court and not direct to the judgment creditor.

(2)   Without prejudice to rule 16, if the person served with an order made pursuant to paragraph (1) fails to obey it or to file a statement of his means or to make payment, the proper officer shall issue a notice calling on that person to show good reason why he should not be imprisoned and any such notice shall be served on the debtor personally not less than 5 days before the hearing.

(3)   Order 29, rule 1 shall apply, with the necessary modifications and with the substitution of references to the district judge for references to the judge, where a notice is issued under paragraph (2) as it applies where a notice is issued under paragraph (4) of that rule.

(4)   In this rule "statement of means" means a statement given under section 14(1) of the Act of 1971.]

Commencement 1 July 1991.
Amendments This rule was inserted by SI 1991/1126, r 57.
Definitions Act of 1971: Attachment of Earnings Act 1971.
Forms Order for statement of means (N61)
Notice to show cause (N63).
Order for arrest (N112).
Power of arrest (N112A).

Order 27, r 8 [Failure by debtor—maintenance orders]

[(1)   An order made under section 23(1) of the Act of 1971 for the attendance of the debtor at an adjourned hearing of an application for an attachment of earnings order [to secure payments under a maintenance order] shall—

(a) be served on the debtor personally not less than 5 days before the day fixed for the adjourned hearing; and

(b) direct that any payments made thereafter shall be paid into the court and not direct to the judgment creditor.]

[(1A) If the debtor fails to attend at an adjourned hearing of an application for an attachment of earnings order and a committal order is made, the district judge may direct that the order shall not be enforced so long as the debtor attends at the time and place specified in the order and paragraphs (2), (4) and (5) of Order 28, rule 7 shall apply where such a direction is given as they apply where a direction is given under paragraph (1) of that rule.

(1B) Where a committal order is suspended under paragraph (1A) and the debtor fails to attend at the time and place so specified, a certificate to that effect given by the proper officer shall be sufficient authority for the issue of a warrant of committal.]

(2)   An application by a debtor for the revocation of an order committing him to prison and, if he is already in custody, for his discharge under subsection (7) of the said section 23 shall be made to the judge [or district judge] ex parte in writing showing the reasons for the debtor's failure to attend the court or his refusal to be sworn or to give evidence, as the case may be, and containing an undertaking by the debtor to attend the court or to be sworn or to give evidence when next ordered or required to do so.

(3)   The application shall, if the debtor has already been lodged in prison, be attested by the governor of the prison (or any other officer of the prison not below the rank of principal officer) and in any other case be made on affidavit.

(4)   Before dealing with the application the judge [or district judge] may, if he thinks fit, cause notice to be given to the judgment creditor that the application has been made and of a day and hour when he may attend and be heard.

Commencement   1 July 1991 (paras (1A), (1B)); 1 April 1990 (para (1)); 1 September 1982 (remainder).
Amendments   Rule heading: substituted by SI 1991/1126, r 58.
Para (1): substituted by SI 1989/1838, r 38; words "to secure payments under a maintenance order" inserted by SI 1991/1126, r 59.
Paras (1A), (1B): inserted by SI 1991/1126, r 60.
Paras (2), (4): words "or district judge" inserted by SI 1991/1126, r 61.
Definitions   Act of 1971: Attachment of Earnings Act 1971.
Forms   Order for attendance at adjourned hearing (N58).
Warrant of committal under s 23 (N59).
Notice of suspended committal order (N118).

Order 27, r 9 Costs

(1)   Where costs are allowed to the judgment creditor on an application for an attachment of earnings order, there may be allowed—

  (a)   a charge of a solicitor for attending the hearing and, if the court so directs, for serving the application;
  (b)   if the court certifies that the case is fit for counsel, a fee to counsel, and
  (c)   the court fee on the issue of the application.

(2)   For the purposes of paragraph (1)(a) a solicitor who has prepared on behalf of the judgment creditor an affidavit or request under rule 7(5) shall be treated as having attended the hearing.

(3)   The costs may be fixed and allowed without taxation and the scale shall be determined by the amount payable under the relevant adjudication (or so much of that amount as remains unpaid), including any relevant costs.

Commencement   1 September 1982.

Order 27, r 10 Contents and service of order

(1)   An attachment of earnings order shall contain such of the following particulars relating to the debtor as are known to the court, namely—

  (a)   his full name and address,
  (b)   his place of work and
  (c)   the nature of his work and his works number, if any,

and those particulars shall be the prescribed particulars for the purposes of section 6(3) of the Act of 1971.

(2)   An attachment of earnings order and any order varying or discharging such an order shall be served on the debtor and on the person to whom the order is directed, and Order 7, rule 1, shall apply with the modification contained in Order 22, rule 1(5), and with the further modification that where the order is directed to a corporation which has requested the court that any communication relating to the debtor or to the class of persons to whom he belongs shall be directed to the corporation at a particular address, service may, if the [district judge] thinks fit, be effected on the corporation at that address.

(3)   Where an attachment of earnings order is made to enforce a judgment or order of the High Court or a magistrates' court, a copy of the attachment of earnings order and of any order discharging it shall be sent by the proper officer of the county court to the proper officer of the High Court or, as the case may be, the clerk of the magistrates' court.

Commencement   1 September 1982.
Definitions   Act of 1971: Attachment of Earnings Act 1971.
Forms   Attachment of earnings order (N60)
Suspended attachment of earnings order (N64).
Attachment of earnings order (maintenance)(N64A).

Order 27, r 11 Application to determine whether particular payments are earnings

An application to the court under section 16 of the Act of 1971 to determine whether payments to the debtor of a particular class or description are earnings for the purpose of an attachment of earnings order may be made to the [district judge] in writing and the proper officer shall thereupon fix a date and time for the hearing of the application by the court and give notice thereof to the persons mentioned in the said section 16(2)(a), (b) and (c).

Commencement   1 September 1982.
Definitions   Act of 1971: Attachment of Earnings Act 1971.

Order 27, r 12 Notice of cesser

Where an attachment of earnings order ceases to have effect under section 8(4) of the Act of 1971, the proper officer of the court in which the matter is proceeding shall give notice of the cesser to the person to whom the order was directed.

Commencement   1 September 1982.
Definitions   Act of 1971: Attachment of Earnings Act 1971.

Order 27, r 13 Variation and discharge by court of own motion

(1)   Subject to paragraph (9), the powers conferred by section 9(1) of the Act of 1971 may be exercised by the court of its own motion in the circumstances mentioned in the following paragraphs.

(2)   Where it appears to the court that a person served with an attachment of earnings order directed to him has not the debtor in his employment, the court may discharge the order.

(3)   Where an attachment of earnings order which has lapsed under section 9(4) of the Act of 1971 is again directed to a person who appears to the court to have the

debtor in his employment, the court may make such consequential variations in the order as it thinks fit.

(4)   Where, after making an attachment of earnings order, the court makes or is notified of the making of another such order in respect of the same debtor which is not to secure the payment of a judgment debt or payments under an administration order, the court may discharge or vary the first-mentioned order having regard to the priority accorded to the other order by paragraph 8 of Schedule 3 to the Act of 1971.

(5)   Where, after making an attachment of earnings order, the court makes an order under section 4(1)(b) of the Act of 1971 or makes an administration order, the court may discharge the attachment of earnings order or, if it exercises the power conferred by section 5(3) of the said Act, may vary the order in such manner as it thinks fit.

(6)   On making a consolidated attachment of earnings order the court may discharge any earlier attachment of earnings order made to secure the payment of a judgment debt by the same debtor.

(7)   Where it appears to the court that a [bankruptcy order] has been made against a person in respect of whom an attachment of earnings order is in force to secure the payment of a judgment debt, the court may discharge the attachment of earnings order.

(8)   Where an attachment of earnings order has been made to secure the payment of a judgment debt and the court grants leave to issue execution for the recovery of the debt, the court may discharge the order.

(9)   Before varying or discharging an attachment of earnings order of its own motion under any of the foregoing paragraphs of this rule, the court shall, unless it thinks it unnecessary in the circumstances to do so, give the debtor and the person on whose application the order was made an opportunity of being heard on the question whether the order should be varied or discharged, and for that purpose the proper officer may give them notice of a date, time and place at which the question will be considered.

Commencement 1 September 1982.
Amendments Para (7): words "bankruptcy order" substituted by SI 1986/2001, art 2, Schedule.
Definitions Act of 1971: Attachment of Earnings Act 1971.

Order 27, r 14 Transfer of attachment order

(1)   Where the court by which the question of making a consolidated attachment order falls to be considered is not the court by which any attachment of earnings order has been made to secure the payment of a judgment debt by the debtor, the [district judge] of the last-mentioned court shall, at the request of the [district judge] of the first-mentioned court, transfer to that court the matter in which the attachment of earnings order was made.

(2)   Without prejudice to paragraph (1), if in the opinion of the judge or [district judge] of any court by which an attachment of earnings order has been made, the matter could more conveniently proceed in some other court, whether by reason of the debtor having become resident in the district of that court or otherwise, he may order the matter to be transferred to that court.

(3)   The court to which proceedings arising out of an attachment of earnings are transferred under this rule shall have the same jurisdiction in relation to the order as if it has been made by that court.

Commencement 1 September 1982.

Order 27, r 15 Exercise of power to obtain statements of earnings etc

(1)   An order under section 14(1) of the Act of 1971 shall be indorsed with or incorporate a notice warning the person to whom it is directed of the consequences of disobedience to the order and shall be served on him personally.

(2)   Order 34, rule 2, shall apply, with the necessary modifications, in relation to any penalty for failure to comply with an order under the said section 14(1) or, subject to the proviso to rule 5(2), any penalty for failure to comply with a requirement mentioned in that rule, as it applies in relation to a fine under [section 55 of the County Courts Act 1984].

Commencement 1 September 1982.
Amendments Para (2): words "section 55 of the County Courts Act 1984" substituted by SI 1984/878, r 12, Schedule.
Definitions Act of 1971: Attachment of Earnings Act 1971.
Forms Order for statement of means (N61).
Order for statement of earnings (N61A).

Order 27, r 16 Offences

(1)   Where it is alleged that a person has committed any offence mentioned in section 23(2)(a), (b), (d), (e) or (f) of the Act of 1971 in relation to proceedings in, or to an attachment of earnings order made by, a county court, the [district judge] shall, unless it is decided to proceed against the alleged offender summarily, issue a summons calling upon him to show cause why he should not be punished for the alleged offence.

The summons shall be served on the alleged offender personally not less than 14 days before the return day.

(2)   Order 34, rules 3 and 4, shall apply, with the necessary modifications, to proceedings for an offence under section 23(2) of the Act of 1971 as they apply to proceedings for offences under the [County Courts Act 1984].

Commencement 1 September 1982.
Amendments Para (2): words "County Courts Act 1984" substituted by SI 1984/878, r 12, Schedule.
Definitions Act of 1971: Attachment of Earnings Act 1971.
Forms Summons for offence under s 23 (N62).

Order 27, r 17 Maintenance orders

(1)   The foregoing rules of this Order shall apply in relation to maintenance payments as they apply in relation to a judgment debt, subject to the following paragraphs.

(2)   An application for an attachment of earnings order to secure payments under a maintenance order made by a county court shall be made to that county court.

(3)   Any application under section 32 of the Matrimonial Causes Act 1973 for leave to enforce the payment of arrears which became due more than 12 months before the application for an attachment of earnings order shall be made in that application.

[(3A) Rule 5(1) shall apply as if for the reference to a default summons there were substituted a reference to a fixed date summons and rule 5(2A) shall not apply.]

(4)   An application by the debtor for an attachment of earnings order to secure payments under a maintenance order may be made on the making of the maintenance order or an order varying the maintenance order, and rules 4 and 5 shall not apply.

[(5)   Rule 7 shall have effect as if for paragraphs (1) to (8) there were substituted the following paragraph—

> "(1) An application for an attachment of earnings order may be heard and determined by the district judge, who shall hear the application in chambers."].

(6)   Rule 9 shall apply as if for the reference to the amount payable under the relevant adjudication there were substituted a reference to the arrears due under the related maintenance order.

(7)   Where an attachment of earnings order made by the High Court designates the proper officer of a county court as the collecting officer, that officer shall, on receipt of a certified copy of the order from the proper officer of the High Court, send to the person to whom the order is directed a notice as to the mode of payment.

(8)   Where an attachment of earnings order made by a county court to secure payments under a maintenance order ceases to have effect and—
   (a)   the related maintenance order was made by that court, or
   (b)   the related maintenance order was an order of the High Court and—
      (i)   the proper officer of the county court has received notice of the cessation from the proper officer of the High Court, or
      (ii)   a committal order has been made in the county court for the enforcement of the related maintenance order,

the proper officer of the county court shall give notice of the cessation to the person to whom the attachment of earnings order was directed.

(9)   Where an attachment of earnings order has been made by a county court to secure payments under a maintenance order, notice under section 10(2) of the Act of 1971 to the debtor and to the person to whom the [district judge] is required to pay sums received under the order shall be in the form provided for that purpose, and if the debtor wishes to request the court to discharge the attachment of earnings order or to vary it otherwise than by making the appropriate variation, he shall apply to the court, within 14 days after the date of the notice, for the relief desired.

(10)   Rule 13 shall have effect as if for paragraphs (4) to (7) there were substituted the following paragraph:—

> "(4) Where it appears to the court by which an attachment of earnings order has been made that the related maintenance order has ceased to have effect, whether by virtue of the terms of the maintenance order or under section 28 of the Matrimonial Causes Act 1973 or otherwise, the court may discharge or vary the attachment of earnings order."

(11)   . . .

Commencement   1 July 1991 (paras (3A), (5)); 1 September 1982 (remainder).
Amendments   Para (3A): inserted by SI 1991/1126, r 62.
Para (5): substituted by SI 1991/1126, r 63.
Para (11): revoked by SI 1991/1126, r 64.
Definitions   Act of 1971: Attachment of Earnings Act 1971.
Forms   Attachment of earnings order (maintenance) (N65).

Order 27, r 18 Cases in which consolidated order may be made

Subject to the provisions of rules 19 to 21, the court may make a consolidated attachment order where—

(a) two or more attachment of earnings orders are in force to secure the payment of judgment debts by the same debtor, or

(b) on an application for an attachment of earnings order to secure the payment of a judgment debt, or for a consolidated attachment order to secure the payment of two or more judgment debts, it appears to the court that an attachment of earnings order is already in force to secure the payment of a judgment debt by the same debtor.

Commencement 1 September 1982.
Forms Consolidated attachment of earnings order (N66).

Order 27, r 19 Application for consolidated order

(1) An application for a consolidated attachment order may be made—

(a) by the debtor in respect of whom the order is sought, or

(b) by any person who has obtained or is entitled to apply for an attachment of earnings order to secure the payment of a judgment debt by that debtor.

[(2) An application under paragraph (1) may be made in the proceedings in which any attachment of earnings order (other than a priority order) is in force and rules 3, 4 and 5 of this Order shall not apply.

(3) Where the judgment which it is sought to enforce was not given by the court which made the attachment of earnings order, the judgment shall be automatically transferred to the court which made the attachment of earnings order.

(3A) An application under paragraph (1)(b) shall certify the amount of money remaining due under the judgment or order and that the whole or part of any instalment due remains unpaid.

(3B) Where an application for a consolidated attachment of earnings order is made, the proper officer shall—

(a) notify any party who may be affected by the application of its terms; and

(b) require him to notify the court in writing, within 14 days of service of notification upon him, giving his reasons for any objection he may have to the granting of the application.

(3C) If notice of any objection is not given within the time stated, the proper officer shall make a consolidated attachment of earnings order.

(3D) If any party objects to the making of a consolidated attachment of earnings order, the proper officer shall refer the application to the district judge who may grant the application after considering the objection made and the reasons given.

(3E) In the foregoing paragraphs of this rule, a party affected by the application means—

(a) where the application is made by the debtor, the creditor in the proceedings in which the application is made and any other creditor who has obtained an attachment of earnings order which is in force to secure the payment of a judgment debt by the debtor;

(b) where the application is made by the judgment creditor, the debtor and every person who, to the knowledge of the applicant, has obtained an attachment of earnings order which is in force to secure the payment of a judgment debt by the debtor.]

(4)   A person to whom two or more attachment of earnings orders are directed to secure the payment of judgment debts by the same debtor may request the court in writing to make an consolidated attachment order to secure the payment of those debts, and on receipt of such a request [paragraphs (3B) to (3E) shall apply, with the necessary modifications, as if the request were an application by the judgment creditor.]

Commencement   1 July 1991 (paras (2)–(3E)); 1 September 1982 (remainder).
Amendments   Paras (2)–(3E): substituted, for paras (2), (3) as originally enacted, by SI 1991/1126, r 65.
Para (4): words from "paragraphs (3B) to (3E)" to the end substituted by SI 1991/1126, r 66.
Forms   Application for consolidated order (N66A).

Order 27, r 20 Making of consolidated order by court of its own motion

Where an application is made for an attachment of earnings order to secure the payment of a judgment debt by a debtor in respect of whom an attachment of earnings order is already in force to secure the payment of another judgment debt and no application is made for a consolidated attachment order, [the proper officer may make such an order of his own motion] after giving all persons concerned an opportunity [of submitting written objections].

Commencement   1 September 1982.
Amendments   Words "the proper officer may make such an order of his own motion" substituted by SI 1991/1328, r 4; words "of submitting written objections" substituted by SI 1991/1126, r 67.

Order 27, r 21 Extension of consolidated order

(1)   Where a consolidated attachment order is in force to secure the payment of two or more judgment debts, any creditor to whom another judgment debt is owed by the same judgment debtor may apply to the court by which the order was made for it to be extended so as to secure the payment of that debt as well as the first-mentioned debts and, if the application is granted, the court may either vary the order accordingly or may discharge it and make a new consolidated attachment order to secure payment of all the aforesaid judgment debts.

(2)   An application under this rule shall be treated for the purposes of rules 19 and 20 as an application for a consolidated attachment order.

Commencement   1 September 1982.

Order 27, r 22 Payments under consolidated order

Instead of complying with section 13 of the Act of 1971, a proper officer who receives payments made to him in compliance with a consolidated attachment order shall, after deducting such court fees, if any, in respect of proceedings for or arising out of the order as are deductible from those payments, deal with the sums paid as he would if they had been paid by the debtor to satisfy the relevant adjudications in proportion to the amounts payable thereunder, and for that purpose dividends may from time to time be declared and distributed among the creditors entitled thereto.

Commencement   1 September 1982.
Definitions   Act of 1971: Attachment of Earnings Act 1971.

ORDER 28
JUDGMENT SUMMONSES

Order 28, r 1 Application for judgment summons

(1)   An application for the issue of a judgment summons may be made to the court for the district in which the debtor resides or carries on business or, if the summons is to issue against two or more persons jointly liable under the judgment or order sought to be enforced, in the court for the district in which any of the debtors resides or carries on business.

[(2)   The judgment creditor shall make his application by filing a request in that behalf certifying the amount of money remaining due under the judgment or order[, the amount in respect of which the judgment summons is to issue] and that the whole or part of any instalment due remains unpaid.]

Commencement   1 April 1990 (para (2)); 1 September 1982 (remainder).
Amendments   Para (2): substituted by SI 1989/1838, r 39; words ", the amount in respect of which the judgment summons is to issue" inserted by SI 1989/2426, r 27.
Forms   Request for judgment summons (N342).
Judgment summons (N67).

Order 28, r 2 Mode of service

(1)   Subject to paragraph (2), a judgment summons shall be served personally on every debtor against whom it is issued.

(2)   Where the judgment creditor or his solicitor gives a certificate for postal service in respect of a debtor residing or carrying on business within the district of the court, the judgment summons shall, unless the [district judge] otherwise directs, be served on that debtor by an officer of the court sending it to him by first-class post at the address stated in the request for the judgment summons and, unless the contrary is shown, the date of service shall be deemed to be the seventh day after the date on which the judgment summons was sent to the debtor.

(3)   Where a judgment summons has been served on a debtor in accordance with paragraph (2), no order of commitment shall be made against him unless—
    (a)   he appears at the hearing, or
    (b)   the judge is satisfied that the summons came to his knowledge in sufficient time for him to appear at the hearing.

(4)   Where a judgment summons is served personally, there may, if the judgment creditor so desires, be paid to the debtor at the time of service a sum reasonably sufficient to cover his expenses in travelling to and from the court.

Commencement   1 September 1982.
Forms   Certificate of service (N68).

Order 28, r 3 Time for service

(1)   A judgment summons shall be served not less than 14 days before the day fixed for the hearing.

(2)   A notice of non-service shall be sent pursuant to Order 7, rule 6(2), in respect of a judgment summons which has been sent by post under rule 2(2) and has been returned to the court office undelivered.

(3)   Order 7, rules 19 and 20, shall apply, with the necessary modifications, to a judgment summons as they apply to a fixed date summons.

Commencement   1 September 1982.

Order 28, r 4 Enforcement of debtor's attendance

(1)   Order 27, rule 8, shall apply, with the necessary modifications, to an order made under [section 110(1)] of the Act for the attendance of the debtor at an adjourned hearing of a judgment summons as it applies to an order made under section 23(1) of the Attachment of Earnings Act 1971 for the attendance of the debtor at an adjourned hearing of an application for an attachment of earnings order.

(2)   At the time of service of the order there shall be paid or tendered to the debtor a sum reasonably sufficient to cover his expenses in travelling to and from the court, unless such a sum was paid to him at the time of service of the judgment summons.

Commencement   1 September 1982.
Amendments   Para (1): words "section 110(1)" substituted by SI 1984/878, r 12, Schedule.
Forms   Order for debtors attendance at adjourned hearing (N69).
Committal order (N70).
Order revoking commitment (N71).

Order 28, r 5 Evidence by affidavit

Where the judgment creditor does not reside or carry on business within the district of the court from which the judgment summons issued, evidence by affidavit shall be admissible on his behalf without any such notice as is required by Order 20, rule 7, having been given, unless the judge otherwise directs.

Commencement   1 September 1982.

Order 28, r 6   *(revoked by SI 1989/1838)*

Order 28, r 7 Suspension of committal order

(1)   If on the hearing of a judgment summons a committal order is made, the judge may direct execution of the order to be suspended to enable the debtor to pay the amount due.

(2)   A note of any direction given under paragraph (1) shall be entered in the records of the court and notice of the suspended committal order shall be sent to the debtor.

(3)   Where a judgment summons is issued in respect of one or more but not all of the instalments payable under a judgment or order for payment by instalments and a committal order is made and suspended under paragraph (1), the judgment or order shall, unless the judge otherwise orders, be suspended for so long as the execution of the committal order is suspended.

(4)   Where execution of a committal order is suspended under paragraph (1) and the debtor subsequently desires to apply for a further suspension, the debtor shall attend at or write to the court office and apply for the suspension he desires, stating

the reasons for his inability to comply with the terms of the original suspension, and the proper officer shall fix a day for the hearing of the application by the judge and give at least 3 days' notice thereof to the judgment creditor and the debtor.

(5)   The [district judge] may suspend execution of the committal order pending the hearing of an application under paragraph (4).

Commencement   1 September 1982.
Forms   Notice to debtor of suspended order (N72).

Order 28, r 8 New order on judgment summons

(1)   Where on the hearing of a judgment summons, the judge makes a new order for payment of the amount of the judgment debt remaining unpaid, there shall be included in the amount payable under the order for the purpose of any enforcement proceedings, otherwise than by judgment summons, any amount in respect of which a committal order has already been made and the debtor imprisoned.

(2)   No judgment summons under the new order shall include any amount in respect of which the debtor was imprisoned before the new order was made, and any amount subsequently paid shall be appropriated in the first instance to the amount due under the new order.

Commencement   1 September 1982.
Forms   New order (N73).

Order 28, r 9 Notification of order on judgment of High Court

(1)   Notice of the result of the hearing of a judgment summons on a judgment or order of the High Court shall be sent by the proper officer of the county court to the proper officer of the High Court.

(2)   If a committal order or a new order for payment is made on the hearing, the office copy of the judgment or order filed under Order 25, rule 11, shall be deemed to be a judgment or order of the court in which the judgment summons is heard, and if the judgment creditor subsequently desires to issue a judgment summons in another county court, Order 25, rule 2, shall apply with the necessary modifications.

Commencement   1 September 1982.

Order 28, r 10 Costs on judgment summons

(1)   No costs shall be allowed to the judgment creditor on the hearing of a judgment summons unless—
    (a)   a committal order is made, or
    (b)   the sum in respect of which the judgment summons was issued is paid before the hearing.

(2)   Where costs are allowed to the judgment creditor,
    (a)   there may be allowed—
        (i)   a charge of the judgment creditor's solicitor for attending the hearing and, if the judge so directs, for serving the judgment summons;
      [(ii)   a fee to counsel if the court certifies that the case is fit for counsel;]

[(iii)] any travelling expenses paid to the debtor, and

[(iv)] the court fee on the issue of the judgment summons;

(b)   the costs may be fixed and allowed without taxation; and

(c)   the scale shall be determined by the sum in respect of which the judgment summons was issued.

(3)   For the purposes of paragraph (2)(a)(i) a solicitor who has prepared on behalf of the judgment creditor an affidavit under rule 5 shall be treated as having attended the hearing.

Commencement 1 September 1982.
Amendments Para (2): in sub-para (a) para (ii) added and original paras (ii), (iii) re-lettered as paras (iii), (iv), by SI 1982/1794, r 12.

Order 28, r 11 Issue of warrant of committal

(1)   A judgment creditor desiring a warrant to be issued pursuant to a committal order shall file a request in that behalf.

(2)   Where two or more debtors are to be committed in respect of the same judgment or order, a separate warrant of committal shall be issued for each of them.

(3)   Where a warrant of committal is sent to a foreign court for execution, the proper officer of that court shall indorse on it a notice as to the effect of [section 122(3)] of the Act addressed to the governor of the prison of that court.

Commencement 1 September 1982.
Amendments Para (3): words "section 122(3)" substituted by SI 1984/878, r 12, Schedule.
Forms Request for warrant of committal (N344).
Warrant of committal (N74).
Indorsement on committal (N75).

Order 28, r 12 Notification to foreign court of part payment before debtor lodged in prison

[Where, after a warrant of committal has been sent to a foreign court for execution but before the debtor is lodged in prison, the home court is notified that an amount which is less than the sum on payment of which the debtor is to be discharged, has been paid, the proper officer of the home court shall send notice of the payment to the proper officer of the foreign court.]

Commencement 1 April 1990.
Amendments This rule was substituted by SI 1989/1838, r 41.

Order 28, r 13 Payment after debtor lodged in prison

(1)   Where, after the debtor has been lodged in prison under a warrant of committal, payment is made of the sum on payment of which the debtor is to be discharged then—

(a)   if the payment is made to the proper officer of the court responsible for the execution of the warrant, he shall make and sign a certificate of payment and send it by post or otherwise to the gaoler;

(b)   if the payment is made to the proper officer of the court which issued the warrant of committal after the warrant has been sent to a foreign court for execution, the proper officer of the home court shall send notice of the payment to the proper officer of the foreign court, who shall make and sign a certificate of payment and send it by post or otherwise to the gaoler;

(c) if the payment is made to the gaoler, he shall sign a certificate of payment and send the amount to the proper officer of the court which made the committal order.

(2) Where, after the debtor has been lodged in prison under a warrant of committal, payment is made of an amount less than the sum on payment of which the debtor is to be discharged, then, subject to paragraph (3), paragraph (1)(a) and (b) shall apply with the substitution of references to a notice of payment for the references to a certificate of payment and paragraph (1)(c) shall apply with the omission of the requirement to make and sign a certificate of payment.

(3) Where, after the making of a payment to which paragraph (2) relates, the balance of the sum on payment of which the debtor is to be discharged is paid, paragraph (1) shall apply without the modifications mentioned in paragraph (2).

Commencement 1 September 1982.

Order 28, r 14 Discharge of debtor otherwise than on payment

(1) Where the judgment creditor lodges with the [district judge] a request that a debtor lodged in prison under a warrant of committal may be discharged from custody, the [district judge] shall make an order for the discharge of the debtor in respect of the warrant of committal and the proper officer shall send the gaoler a certificate of discharge.

(2) Where a debtor who has been lodged in prison under a warrant of committal desires to apply for his discharge under [section 121] of the Act, the application shall be made to the judge ex parte in writing showing the reasons why the debtor alleges that he is unable to pay the sum in respect of which he has been committed and ought to be discharged and stating any offer which he desires to make as to the terms on which his discharge is to be ordered, and Order 27, rule 8(3) and (4), shall apply, with the necessary modifications, as it applies to an application by a debtor for his discharge from custody under section 23(7) of the Attachment of Earnings Act 1971.

(3) If in a case to which paragraph (2) relates the debtor is ordered to be discharged from custody on terms which include liability to re-arrest if the terms are not complied with, the judge may, on the application of the judgment creditor if the terms are not complied with, order the debtor to be re-arrested and imprisoned for such part of the term of imprisonment as remained unserved at the time of discharge.

(4) Where an order is made under paragraph (3), a duplicate warrant of committal shall be issued, indorsed with a certificate signed by the proper officer as to the order of the judge.

Commencement 1 September 1982.
Amendments Para (2): words "section 121" substituted by SI 1984/878, r 12, Schedule.
Forms Certificate on duplicate warrant (N76).

ORDER 29
COMMITTAL FOR BREACH OF ORDER OR UNDERTAKING

Order 29, r 1 Enforcement of judgment to do or abstain from doing any act

(1)   Where a person required by a judgment or order to do an act refuses or neglects to do it within the time fixed by the judgment or order or any subsequent order, or where a person disobeys a judgment or order requiring him to abstain from doing an act, then, subject to the Debtors Acts 1869 and 1878 and to the provisions of these rules, the judgment or order may be enforced, by order of the judge, by a committal order against that person or, if that person is a body corporate, against any director or other officer of the body.

(2)   Subject to paragraphs (6) and (7), a judgment or order shall not be enforced under paragraph (1) unless—

    (a)   a copy of the judgment or order has been served personally on the person required to do or abstain from doing the act in question and also, where that person is a body corporate, on the director or other officer of the body against whom a committal order is sought, and

    (b)   in the case of a judgment or order requiring a person to do an act, the copy has been so served before the expiration of the time within which he was required to do the act and was accompanied by a copy of any order, made between the date of the judgment or order and the date of service, fixing that time.

(3)   Where a judgment or order enforceable by committal order under paragraph (1) has been given or made, the proper officer shall, if the judgment or order is in the nature of an injunction, at the time when the judgment or order is drawn up, and in any other case on the request of the judgment creditor, issue a copy of the judgment or order, indorsed with or incorporating a notice as to the consequences of disobedience, for service in accordance with paragraph (2).

(4)   If the person served with the judgment or order fails to obey it, the proper officer shall, at the request of the judgment creditor, issue a notice [warning him that an application will be made for him to be committed], and subject to paragraph (7) the notice shall be served on him personally.

[(4A) The request for issue of the notice under paragraph (4) shall—

    (a)   identify the provisions of the injunction or undertaking which it is alleged have been disobeyed or broken;

    (b)   list the ways in which it is alleged that the injunction has been disobeyed or the undertaking has been broken,

    (c)   be supported by an affidavit stating the grounds on which the application is made,

and, unless service is dispensed with under paragraph (7), a copy of the affidavit shall be served with the notice.]

[(5)   If a committal order is made, the order shall be for the issue of a warrant of committal and, unless the judge otherwise orders—

    (a)   a copy of the order shall be served on the person to be committed either before or at the time of the execution of the warrant; or

    (b)   where the warrant has been signed by the judge, the order for issue of the warrant may be served on the person to be committed at any time within 36 hours after the execution of the warrant.]

(6)   A judgment or order requiring a person to abstain from doing an act may be enforced under paragraph (1) notwithstanding that service of a copy of the judgment or order has not been effected in accordance with paragraph (2) if the judge is satisfied that, pending such service, the person against whom it is sought to enforce the judgment or order has had notice thereof either—

(a) by being present when the judgment or order was given or made, or

(b) by being notified of the terms of the judgment or order whether by telephone, telegram or otherwise.

(7)   Without prejudice to its powers under Order 7, rule 8, the court may dispense with service of a copy of a judgment or order under paragraph (2) or a notice . . . under paragraph (4), if the court thinks it just to do so.

[(8)   Where service of a notice to show cause is dispensed with under paragraph (7) and a committal order is made, the judge may of his own motion fix a date and time when the person to be committed is to be brought before him or before the court.]

Commencement   1 May 1991 (paras (4A), (5)); 11 May 1988 (para (8)); 1 September 1982 (remainder).
Amendments   Para (4): words "warning him that an application will be made for him to be committed" substituted by SI 1991/525, r 3.
Para (4A): inserted by SI 1991/525, r 4.
Para (5): substituted by SI 1991/525, r 5.
Para (7): words omitted revoked by SI 1991/525, r 6.
Para (8): added by SI 1988/278, r 11.
Cross references   See RSC Order 52, rr 1, 6.
Forms   Penal notice (N77).
Notice to show cause (N78).
Committal order (N79).
Warrant for committal (N80).

[Order 29, r 1A Undertaking given by party

Rule 1 (except paragraph (6)) shall apply to undertakings as it applies to orders with the necessary modifications and as if—

(a) for paragraph (2) of that rule there were substituted the following—

"(2) A copy of the document recording the undertaking shall be delivered by the proper officer to the party giving the undertaking—

(a) by handing a copy of the document to him before he leaves the court building; or

(b) where his place of residence is known, by posting a copy to him at his place of residence; or

(c) through his solicitor,

and, where delivery cannot be effected in this way, the proper officer shall deliver a copy of the document to the party for whose benefit the undertaking is given and that party shall cause it to be served personally as soon as is practicable.";

(b) in paragraph (7), the words from "a copy of" to "paragraph (2) or" were omitted.]

Commencement   1 May 1991.
Amendments   This rule was inserted by SI 1991/525, r 7.
Forms   General form of undertaking (N117).

Order 29, r 2 Solicitor's undertaking

(1)   An undertaking given by a solicitor in relation to any proceeding in a county court may be enforced, by order of the judge of that court, by committal order against the solicitor.

(2)   Where it appears to the judge that a solicitor has failed to carry out any such undertaking, he may of his own motion direct the proper officer to issue a notice calling on the solicitor to show cause why he should not be committed to prison.

(3)   Where any party to the proceedings desires to have the undertaking enforced by committal order, the proper officer shall, on the application of the party supported by an affidavit setting out the facts on which the application is based, issue such a notice as is referred to in paragraph (2).

(4)   A notice to show cause issued under paragraph (2) or (3) shall be served on the solicitor personally, together with a copy of any affidavit filed under paragraph (3), but rule 1(5) and (7) shall apply in relation to the notice as they apply in relation to a notice to show cause issued under rule 1(4).

Commencement   1 September 1982.
Forms   Notice to solicitor to show cause (N81).
Order committing solicitor (N82).

Order 29, r 3 Discharge of person in custody

(1)   Where a person in custody under a warrant or order, other than a warrant of committal to which Order 27, rule 8, or Order 28, rule 4 or 14, relates, desires to apply to the court for his discharge, he shall make his application in writing attested by the governor of the prison (or any other officer of the prison not below the rank of principal officer) showing that he has purged or is desirous of purging his contempt and shall, not less than one day before the application is made, serve notice of it on the party, if any, at whose instance the warrant or order was issued.

[(2)   If the committal order—
  (a)   does not direct that any application for discharge shall be made to a judge; or
  (b)   was made by the district judge under section 118 of the Act,

any application for discharge may be made to the district judge.]

(3)   Nothing in paragraph (1) shall apply to an application made by the Official Solicitor in his official capacity for the discharge of a person in custody.

Commencement   1 July 1991 (para (2)); 1 September 1982 (remainder).
Amendments   Para (2): substituted by SI 1991/1126, r 15.
Cross references   See RSC Order 52, r 8.
Forms   Order discharge from custody (N83).

ORDER 30
GARNISHEE PROCEEDINGS

Order 30, r 1 Attachment of debt due to judgment debtor

(1)   Where a person (in this Order called "the judgment creditor") has obtained in a county court a judgment or order for the payment [of a sum of money amounting in value to at least £25] by some other person ("the judgment debtor") and any person within England and Wales ("the garnishee") is indebted to the judgment debtor, that court may, subject to the provisions of this Order and of any enactment, order the garnishee to pay the judgment creditor the amount of any debt due or accruing due from the garnishee to the judgment debtor or so much thereof as is sufficient to satisfy the judgment or order against the judgment debtor and the costs of the garnishee proceedings.

(2)   An order under this rule shall in the first instance be an order to show cause, specifying the place and time for the further consideration of the matter (in this Order called "the return day") and in the meantime attaching the debt due or accruing due from the garnishee or so much thereof as is sufficient for the purpose aforesaid.

(3)   Among the conditions mentioned in [section 108(3)] of the Act (which enables any sum standing to the credit of a person in [certain types of account] to be attached notwithstanding that certain conditions applicable to the account [in question] have not been satisfied) there shall be included any condition that a receipt for money deposited in the account must be produced before any money is withdrawn.

(4)   . . .

[(5)   An order under this rule shall not require a payment which would reduce below £1 the amount standing in the name of the judgment debtor in an account with a building society or a credit union.]

Commencement   1 September 1982.
Amendments   Para (1): words "of a sum of money amounting in value to at least £25" substituted by SI 1982/436, r 4(1).
Para (3): words "section 108(3)" substituted by SI 1984/878, r 12, Schedule; words "certain types of account" substituted and words "in question" inserted, by SI 1982/436, r 4(2)
Para (4): revoked by SI 1991/1328, r 16.
Para (5): added by SI 1982/436, r 4(3).
Cross references   See RSC Order 49, r 1.

Order 30, r 2 Application for order

An application for an order under rule 1 may be made ex parte by filing an affidavit—
   [(a)   stating the name and last known address of the judgment debtor;
   (b)   identifying the judgment or order to be enforced and stating the amount of such judgment or order . . . ;]
   [(c)]   stating that, to the best of the information or belief of the deponent, the garnishee (giving his name and address) is indebted to the judgment debtor, . . .
   [(d)]   where the garnishee is a [deposit-taking institution] having more than one place of business, giving the name and address of the branch at which the judgment debtor's account is believed to be held [and the number of that account] or, if it be the case, that [all or part of] this information is unknown to the deponent[, and

765

    (e)   certifying the amount of money remaining due under the judgment or order and that the whole or part of any instalment due remains unpaid.]

Commencement   1 September 1982.
Amendments   Sub-paras (a), (b) inserted, original sub-paras (a), (b) re-lettered as sub-paras (c), (d), in sub-para (d) words "deposit-taking institution" substituted and words "and the number of that account" and "all or part of" inserted, by SI 1982/436, r 4(4); in sub-paras (b), (c) words omitted revoked and sub-para (e) inserted, by SI 1989/1838, r 42.
Cross references   See RSC Order 49, r 2.

Order 30, r 3 Preparation, service and effect of order to show cause

(1)   An order under rule 1 to show cause shall be drawn up by the proper officer with sufficient copies for service under this rule.

[(2)   Unless otherwise directed, a copy of the order shall be served—
    (a)   on the garnishee in the same manner as a fixed date summons at least 15 days before the return day, and
    (b)   on the judgment debtor in accordance with Order 7, rule 1, at least 7 days after a copy has been served on the garnishee and at least 7 days before the return day,]

and as from such service on the garnishee the order shall bind in his hands any debt due or accruing due from the garnishee to the judgment debtor, or so much thereof as is sufficient to satisfy the judgment or order obtained by the judgment creditor against the judgment debtor, and the costs entered on the order to show cause.

Commencement   1 September 1982.
Amendments   Para (2): words from the beginning to "before the return day," substituted by SI 1982/436, r 4(5).
Cross references   See RSC Order 49, rr 2, 3.
Forms   Affidavit supporting application garnishee order (N349).
Garnishee order to show cause (N84).

Order 30, r 4   *(revoked by SI 1989/1838)*

Order 30, r 5 Notice by [deposit-taking institution] denying indebtedness

Where the garnishee being a [deposit-taking institution] alleges that it does not hold any money to the credit of the judgment debtor, the garnishee may, at any time before the return day, give notice to that effect to the proper officer and to the judgment creditor and thereupon, subject to rule 8, the proceedings against the garnishee shall be stayed.

Commencement   1 September 1982.
Amendments   Words "deposit-taking institution" substituted by SI 1982/436, r 4(6).

Order 30, r 6   *(revoked by SI 1989/1838)*

Order 30, r 7 [Order where no notice given etc]

(1)   Where the garnishee—
    (a)   does not . . . give notice under rule 5, and
    (b)   does not on the return day appear or dispute the debt due or claimed to be due from him to the judgment debtor,

then, if the judgment debtor does not appear or show cause to the contrary, the court may, if it thinks fit, make an order absolute under rule 1 against the garnishee.

(2)   An order absolute under rule 1 may be enforced in the same manner as any other order for the payment of money.

Commencement   1 September 1982.
Amendments   Rule heading: substituted by SI 1989/1838, r 44.
Para (1): words omitted revoked by SI 1989/1838, r 45.
Cross references   See RSC Order 49, r 4.
Forms   Garnishee order absolute (N85).

[Order 30, r 8 Directions where dispute as to notice under rule 5

Where the garnishee in a notice given under rule 5 makes an allegation which the judgment creditor disputes, the court shall on the return day give directions for the determination of the question at issue.]

Commencement   1 April 1990.
Amendments   This rule was substituted by SI 1989/1838, r 46.
Cross references   See RSC Order 49, r 5.

Order 30, r 9 Determination of liability in other cases

Where in a case in which . . . no notice has been given under rule 5 the garnishee on the return day disputes liability to pay the debt due or claimed to be due from him to the judgment debtor, the court may summarily determine the question at issue or order that any question necessary for determining the liability of the garnishee be tried in any manner in which any question or issue in an action may be tried.

Commencement   1 September 1982.
Amendments   Words omitted revoked by SI 1989/1838, r 47.
Cross references   See RSC Order 49, r 5.

Order 30, r 10 Transfer of proceedings

A garnishee who does not reside or carry on business within the district of the court in which the garnishee proceedings have been commenced and who desires to dispute liability for the debt due or claimed to be due from him to the judgment debtor may apply ex parte in writing to that court for an order transferring the action in which the judgment or order sought to be enforced was obtained to the court for the district in which the garnishee resides or carries on business, and the court applied to may, if it thinks fit, grant the application after considering any representations which it may give the judgment creditor and the judgment debtor an opportunity of making.

Commencement   1 September 1982.

Order 30, r 11 Discharge of garnishee

Any payment made by a garnishee . . . in compliance with an order absolute in garnishee proceedings, and any execution levied against him in pursuance of such an order, shall be a valid discharge of his liability to the judgment debtor to the extent of the amount paid or levied (otherwise than in respect of any costs ordered to be paid by the garnishee personally), notwithstanding that the garnishee proceedings are subsequently set aside or the judgment or order from which they arise is reversed.

Commencement 1 September 1982.
Amendments Words omitted revoked by SI 1989/1838, r 48.
Cross references See RSC Order 49, r 8.

Order 30, r 12 Money in court

(1) Where money is standing to the credit of the judgment debtor in any county court, the judgment creditor shall not be entitled to take garnishee proceedings in respect of the money but may apply to the court on notice for an order that the money or so much thereof as is sufficient to satisfy the judgment or order sought to be enforced and the costs of the application be paid to the judgment creditor.

(2) On receipt of notice of an application under paragraph (1) the proper officer shall retain the money in court until the application has been determined.

(3) The court hearing [an] application under paragraph (1) may make such order with respect to the money in court as it thinks just.

Commencement 1 September 1982.
Amendments Para (3): word "an" substituted by SI 1982/1140, r 2.
Cross references See RSC Order 49, r 9.

Order 30, r 13 Costs of judgment creditor

Any costs allowed to the judgment creditor on an application for an order under rule 1 or 12 which in the former case are not ordered to be paid by the garnishee personally shall, unless the court otherwise directs, be retained by the judgment creditor out of the money recovered by him under the order in priority to the amount due under the judgment or order obtained by him against the judgment debtor.

Commencement 1 September 1982.
Cross references See RSC Order 49, r 10.

Order 30, r 14 Attachment of debt owed by firm

(1) An order may be made under rule 1 in relation to a debt due or accruing due from a firm carrying on business within England and Wales, notwithstanding that one or more members of the firm may be resident out of England and Wales.

(2) An order to show cause under rule 1 relating to such a debt shall be served on a member of the firm within England and Wales or on some other person having the control or management of the partnership business.

Commencement 1 September 1982.
Cross references See RSC Order 81, r 7.

Order 30, r 15 Powers of [district judge]

The powers conferred on the court by any provision of this Order may be exercised by the judge or [district judge].

Commencement 1 September 1982.

ORDER 31
CHARGING ORDERS

Order 31, r 1 Application for charging order

(1)   An application to a county court for a charging order under section 1 of the Charging Orders Act 1979 may be made—

    (a) if the order is sought in respect of a fund in court, to the court where the money is lodged;

    (b) subject to (a), if the judgment or order sought to be enforced is that of a county court, to the court in which the judgment or order was obtained or, if the action or matter has been transferred to another court under Order 16, rule 1(d) or (e), or Order 25, rule 2, the court to which it has been transferred;

    (c) subject to (a) and (b), to the court for the district in which the debtor resides or carries on business or, if there is no such district, to the court for the district in which the judgment creditor resides or carries on business.

[(1A) An application for a charging order under paragraph 11 of Schedule 4 to the Local Government Finance Act 1992 shall be made to the court for the district in which the relevant dwelling (within the meaning of section 3 of that Act) is situated.]

(2)   The application may be made ex parte by filing an affidavit—

    (a) stating the name and address of the debtor and, if known, of every creditor of his whom the applicant can identify;

  [(aa) certifying the amount of money remaining due under the judgment or order and that the whole or part of any instalment due remains unpaid;]

    (b) identifying the subject matter of the intended charge;

   [(c) either verifying the debtor's beneficial ownership of the asset to be charged or, where the asset is held by one or more trustees (including where the asset is land which is jointly owned) and the applicant relies on paragraph (b) of section 2(1) of the said Act [of 1979], stating on which of the three grounds appearing in that paragraph the application is based and verifying the material facts;]

    (d) stating, in the case of securities other than securities in court, the name and address of the person or body to be served for the purpose of protecting the intended charge;

    (e) stating, where the subject matter is an interest under a trust, or held by a trustee, the names and addresses of such trustees and beneficiaries as are known to the applicant.

Where the judgment or order to be enforced is a judgment or order of the High Court or a judgment, order, decree or award of a court or arbitrator which is or has become enforceable as if it were a judgment or order of the High Court, the applicant shall file with his affidavit the documents mentioned in Order 25, rule 11(a) and (c), and the affidavit shall verify the amount unpaid at the date of the application.

(3)   Subject to paragraph (1), an application may be made for a single charging order in respect of more than one judgment or order against a debtor.

(4)   Upon the filing of the affidavit mentioned in paragraph (2), the application shall be entered in the records of the court, and if, in the opinion of the [district judge], a sufficient case for such an order is made in the affidavit, the [district judge] shall make a charging order nisi fixing a day for the further consideration of the matter by the court.

(5)   A copy of the order shall be sent by the proper officer to the judgment creditor and, where funds in court are to be charged, shall be served by the proper officer on the Accountant-General at the Court Funds Office.

(6)   Copies of the order and of the affidavit shall be served [by the judgment creditor] on the debtor and on such of the debtor's other creditors, and, where a trust is involved, [on any trustee holding the asset to be charged, where the applicant relies on paragraph (b) of section 2(1) of the said Act, and on such other trustees] and beneficiaries as the [district judge] may direct.

(7)   Where an interest in securities not in court is to be charged, copies of the order nisi shall be served [by the judgment creditor] on the person or body required to be served in like circumstances by RSC Order 50, rule 2(1)(b).

(8)   The documents required by the foregoing paragraphs to be served shall be served in accordance with Order 7, rule 1, not less than 7 days before the day fixed for the further consideration of the matter.

[(9)   Upon further consideration of the matter service required under paragraph (6) or (7) shall be proved by affidavit.]

Commencement   17 January 1994 (para (1A)); 28 March 1989 (para (9)); 1 September 1982 (remainder).
Amendments   Para (1A): inserted by SI 1993/3273, r 5(1).
Para (2): sub-para (aa) inserted by SI 1989/1838, r 49; sub-para (c) substituted by SI 1991/1328, r 5, words "of 1979" therein inserted by SI 1993/3273, r 5(2).
Para (6): words "by the judgment creditor" substituted by SI 1989/236, r 14(1); words from "on any trustee" to "other trustees" substituted by SI 1991/1328, r 6.
Para (7): words "by the judgment creditor" substituted by SI 1989/236, r 14(2).
Para (9): added by SI 1989/236, r 14(3).
Cross references   See RSC Order 50, rr 1, 2.
Forms   Charging order nisi (N86).

Order 31, r 2 Order on further consideration of application for charging order

(1)   On the day fixed under rule 1(4) for the further consideration of the matter, the court shall either make the order absolute, with or without modifications, or discharge it.

(2)   If an order absolute is made, a copy shall be served by the proper officer, in accordance with Order 7, rule 1, on each of the following persons, namely—
    (a)   the debtor,
    (b)   the applicant for the order,
    (c)   where funds in court are charged, the Accountant General at the Court Funds Office, and
    (d)   unless otherwise directed, any person or body on whom a copy of the order nisi was served pursuant to rule 1(7).

(3)   Every copy of an order served on a person or body under paragraph (2)(d) shall contain a stop notice.

Commencement   1 September 1982.
Cross references   See RSC Order 50, r 3.
Forms   Charging order absolute (N87).

Order 31, r 3 Effect of charging order, etc

(1)   Where a charging order nisi or a charging order absolute has been made and served in accordance with rule 1 or 2, it shall have the same effect as an order made and served in like circumstances under RSC Order 50.

(2)   The court may vary or discharge a charging order in the like circumstances and in accordance with the same procedure, with the necessary modifications, as a like order made by the High Court.

(3)   The powers of the court under rule 2 or the last preceding paragraph, except the power to vary an order made by the judge, may be exercised by the [district judge].

Commencement   1 September 1982.
Cross references   See RSC Order 50 rr 4–7.

Order 31, r 4 Enforcement of charging order by sale

(1)   Proceedings in a county court for the enforcement of a charging order by sale of the property charged shall be commenced by originating application, which shall be filed in the appropriate court, together with an affidavit and a copy thereof—

   (a)   identifying the charging order sought to be enforced and the subject matter of the charge;

   (b)   specifying the amount in respect of which the charge was imposed and the balance outstanding at the date of the application;

   (c)   verifying, so far as known, the debtor's title to the property charged;

   (d)   identifying any prior incumbrances on the property charged, with, so far as known, the names and addresses of the incumbrancers and the amounts owing to them; and

   (e)   giving an estimate of the price which would be obtained on sale of the property.

(2)   The appropriate court shall be—

   (a)   if the charging order was made by a county court, that court;

   (b)   in any other case, the court for the district in which the debtor resides or carries on business or, if there is no such district, the court for the district in which the judgment creditor resides or carries on business.

(3)   A copy of the affidavit filed under paragraph (1) shall be served on the respondent with the documents mentioned in Order 3, rule 4(4)(b).

(4)   The proceedings may be heard and determined by the [district judge].

[(5)   The net proceeds of sale, after discharging any prior incumbrances and deducting the amount referred to in paragraph (1)(b) and the costs of the sale, shall be paid into court.]

Commencement   1 April 1990 (para (5)); 1 September 1982 (remainder).
Amendments   Para (5): inserted by SI 1989/1838, r 50.
Cross references   See RSC Order 50, r 9A, Order 88, r 5A.

ORDER 32
RECEIVERS

Order 32, r 1 Application for appointment

(1)   An application for the appointment of a receiver may be made before, at or after the trial or hearing of any proceedings.

(2)   An application for an injunction ancillary or incidental to an order appointing a receiver may be joined with the application for such an order.

(3)   Where the applicant wishes to apply for the immediate grant of such an injunction pending the hearing of his application for the appointment of a receiver, he may do so ex parte on affidavit.

(4)   The power to make an order for the appointment of a receiver shall be exercisable by the court and, without prejudice to Order 21, rule 5, the [district judge] shall have power to grant an injunction if, and only so far as, it is ancillary or incidental to an order for the appointment of a receiver by way of execution.

In this paragraph "receiver by way of execution" means a receiver appointed by way of equitable execution in relation either to an equitable interest or to a legal estate or interest in land.

Commencement   1 September 1982.
Cross references   See RSC Order 30, r 1, Order 51, rr 1–3.

Order 32, r 2 Receiver to give security

Unless the court otherwise orders, a person other than an officer of the court who is appointed a receiver shall not act as such until he has given security duly to account for what he receives and to deal with it as the court directs.

Commencement   1 September 1982.
Cross references   See RSC Order 30, r 2.
Forms   Order appointing receiver (N353–6).
Security of receiver (RSC ChPF30).

Order 32, r 3 Application of RSC

(1)   Subject to the following paragraphs of this rule, the provisions of the RSC with regard to—
   [(a)   the remuneration of receivers,
   (b)   service of an order appointing a receiver,
   (c)   receivers' accounts,
   (d)   payments into court by receivers,
   (e)   default by receivers, and
   (f)   directions to receivers,]

shall apply in relation to a receiver appointed by a county court as they apply in relation to a receiver appointed by the High Court.

[(2)   The application of RSC Order 30, rule 4 by paragraph (1)(b) shall have effect with the modification that the reference in that rule to the party having conduct of the proceedings shall be construed as a reference to the proper officer.]

(3)   . . .

(4)   Where the order for the appointment of a receiver was made by the judge, the power on any default by the receiver to direct his discharge and the appointment of another receiver shall be exercised only by the judge.

Commencement   1 September 1984 (para (2)); 1 September 1982 (remainder).
Amendments   Para (1): sub-paras (a)–(f) substituted, for paras (a)–(c) as originally enacted, by SI 1984/878, r 6.
Para (2): substituted by SI 1984/878, r 7.
Para (3): revoked by SI 1984/878, r 8.
Cross references   See RSC Order 30 rr 3–8.
Forms   Notice of time fixed for passing receiver's accounts (N357).

ORDER 33
INTERPLEADER PROCEEDINGS

PART I—UNDER EXECUTION

Order 33, r 1 Notice of claim

(1)   Any person making a claim to or in respect of goods seized in execution or the proceeds or value thereof shall deliver to the bailiff holding the warrant of execution, or file in the office of the court for the district in which the goods were seized, notice of his claim stating—

    (a)   the grounds of the claim or, in the case of a claim for rent, the particulars required by [section 102(2)] of the Act, and

    (b)   the claimant's full name and address . . . .

(2)   On receipt of a claim made under this rule, the proper officer shall—

    (a)   send notice thereof to the execution creditor, and

    (b)   except where the claim is to the proceeds or value of the goods, send to the claimant a notice requiring him to make a deposit or give security in accordance with [section 100] of the Act.

Commencement   1 September 1982.
Amendments   Para (1): in sub-para (a) words "section 102(2)" substituted by SI 1984/878, r 12, Schedule; in sub-para (b) words omitted revoked by SI 1982/1140, r 2.
Para (2): words "section 100" substituted by SI 1984/878, r 12, Schedule.
Cross references   The equivalent rule in the RSC is Order 17 but the procedures are substantially different due to the fact that in the county court the district judge is notionally the High Bailiff.

Order 33, r 2 Reply to claim

(1)   Within 4 days after receiving notice of a claim under rule 1(2) the execution creditor shall give notice to the proper officer informing him whether he admits or disputes the claim or requests the [district judge] to withdraw from possession of the goods or money claimed.

(2)   If, within the period aforesaid, the execution creditor gives notice to the proper officer admitting the claim or requesting the [district judge] to withdraw from possession of the goods or money claimed, the execution creditor shall not be liable to the [district judge] for any fees or expenses incurred after receipt of the notice.

Commencement   1 September 1982.

Order 33, r 3 Order protecting [district judge]

Where the execution creditor gives the proper officer such a notice as is mentioned in rule 2(2), the [district judge] shall withdraw from possession of the goods or money claimed and may apply to the judge, on notice to the claimant, for an order restraining the bringing of an action against the [district judge] for or in respect of his having taken possession of the goods or money and on the hearing of the application the judge may make such order as may be just.

Commencement   1 September 1982.

Order 33, r 4 Issue of interpleader proceedings

(1)   Where the execution creditor gives notice under rule 2(1) disputing a claim

made under rule 1 or fails, within the period mentioned in rule 2(1), to give the notice required by that rule, the [district judge] shall, unless the claim is withdrawn, issue an interpleader summons to the execution creditor and the claimant.

(2) On the issue of an interpleader summons under paragraph (1) the proper officer shall enter the proceedings in the records of the court, fix a day for the hearing by the judge and prepare sufficient copies of the summons for service under this rule.

(3) Subject to paragraph (4), the summons shall be served on the execution creditor and the claimant in the same manner as a fixed date summons.

(4) Without prejudice to Order 13, rule 4, service shall be effected not less than 14 days before the return day.

Commencement 1 September 1982.
Forms Interpleader Summons (N88, 88(1)–89).

Order 33, r 5 Claim for damages

Where in interpleader proceedings under an execution the claimant claims from the execution creditor or the [district judge], or the execution creditor claims from the [district judge], damages arising or capable of arising out of the execution—·

- (a) the party claiming damages shall, within 8 days after service of the summons on him, give notice of his claim to the proper officer and to any other party against whom the claim is made, stating the amount and the grounds of the claim; and
- (b) the party from whom damages are claimed may pay money into court in satisfaction of the claim as if the interpleader proceedings were an action brought by the person making the claim.

Commencement 1 September 1982.

PART II—OTHERWISE THAN UNDER EXECUTION

Order 33, r 6 Application for relief

(1) Where a person (in this Part of this Order called "the applicant") is under a liability in respect of a debt or any money or goods and he is, or expects to be, sued for or in respect of the debt, money or goods by two or more persons making adverse claims thereto ("the claimants"), he may apply to the court, in accordance with these rules, for relief by way of interpleader.

(2) The application shall be made to the court in which the action is pending against the applicant or, if no action is pending against him, to the court in which he might be sued.

(3) The application shall be made by filing an affidavit showing that—
- (a) the applicant claims no interest in the subject-matter in dispute other than for charges or costs,
- (b) the applicant does not collude with any of the claimants,
- (c) the applicant is willing to pay or transfer the subject-matter into court or to dispose of it as the court may direct, and
- (d) . . .

together with as many copies of the affidavit as there are claimants.

Commencement 1 September 1982.
Amendments Para (3): sub-para (d) revoked by SI 1991/1328, r 17.
Cross references See RSC Order 17, rr 1(1)(a), (4), 3(1).
Forms Affidavit supporting interpleader summons (not on execution) (N360).

Order 33, r 7 Relief in pending action

Where the applicant is a defendant in a pending action—
- (a) the affidavit and copies required by rule 6(3) shall be filed within 14 days after service on him of the summons in the action;
- (b) the return day of the application shall be a day fixed for the pre-trial review of the action including the interpleader proceedings and, if a day has already been fixed for the pre-trial review or hearing of the action, the proper officer shall, if necessary, postpone it;
- (c) the claimant, the applicant and the plaintiff in the action shall be given notice of the application, which shall be prepared by the proper officer together with sufficient copies for service;
- (d) the notice to the claimant shall be served on him, together with a copy of the affidavit filed under rule 6(3) and of the summons and particulars of claim in the action, not less than 21 days before the return day in the same manner as a fixed date summons;
- (e) the notices to the applicant and the plaintiff shall be sent to them by the proper officer and the notice to the plaintiff shall be accompanied by a copy of the said affidavit.

Commencement 1 September 1982.
Forms Notice of application for relief in pending action (N361).

Order 33, r 8 Relief otherwise than in pending action

Where the applicant is not a defendant in a pending action—
- (a) the proper officer shall enter the proceedings in the records of the court;
- (b) the proper officer shall fix a day for the pre-trial review or, if the court so directs, a day for the hearing of the proceedings and shall prepare and issue an interpleader summons, together with sufficient copies for service;
- (c) the summons, together with a copy of the affidavit filed under rule 6(3), shall be served on each of the claimants not less than 21 days before the return day in the same manner as a fixed date summons; and
- (d) the proper officer shall deliver or send a plaint note to the applicant.

Commencement 1 September 1982.

Order 33, r 9 Payment into court etc

Before or after the proper officer proceeds under rule 7 or 8 the [district judge] may direct the applicant to bring the subject-matter of the proceedings into court, or to dispose of it in such manner as the [district judge] thinks fit, to abide the order of the court.

Commencement 1 September 1982.

Order 33, r 10 Reply by claimant

(1)   A claimant shall, within 14 days after service on him of the notice under rule 7(c) or the summons under rule 8(c), file—
  (a)   a notice that he makes no claim, or
  (b)   particulars stating the grounds of his claim to the subject matter,

together in either case with sufficient copies for service under paragraph (2).

(2)   The proper officer shall send to each of the other parties a copy of any notice or particulars filed under paragraph (1).

(3)   The court may, if it thinks fit, hear the proceedings although no notice or particulars have been filed.

Commencement 1 September 1982.

Order 33, r 11 Order barring claim etc

(1)   Where a claimant does not appear on any day fixed for a pre-trial review or the hearing of interpleader proceedings, or fails or refuses to comply with an order made in the proceedings, the court may make an order barring his claim.

(2)   If, where the applicant is a defendant in a pending action, the plaintiff does not appear on any day fixed for a pre-trial review or the hearing of the inter-pleader proceedings, the action including the interpleader proceedings may be struck out.

(3)   In any other case where a day is fixed for the hearing of interpleader proceedings, the court shall hear and determine the proceedings and give judgment finally determining the rights and claims of the parties.

(4)   Where the court makes an order barring the claim of a claimant, the order shall declare the claimant, and all persons claiming under him, for ever barred from prosecuting his claim against the applicant and all persons claiming under him, but unless the claimant has filed a notice under rule 10 that he makes no claim, such an order shall not affect the rights of the claimants as between themselves.

Commencement 1 September 1982.
Forms Orders on Interpleader summons (N362–5).

Order 33, r 12 Relief in pending matter

The provisions of this Part of this Order relating to an application for interpleader relief by the defendant to an action shall apply with the necessary modifications to an application for such relief by the respondent to a matter.

Commencement 1 September 1982.

ORDER 34
PENAL AND DISCIPLINARY PROVISIONS

Order 34, r 1 Issue and service of summons for offence under [s 14, 92 or 124] of the Act

Where—

(a) it is alleged that any person has committed an offence under [section 14 or 92] of the Act by assaulting an officer of the court while in the execution of his duty, or by rescuing or attempting to rescue any goods seized in execution, and the alleged offender has not been taken into custody and brought before the judge, or

(b) ...

(c) a complaint is made against an officer of the court under [section 124] of the Act for having lost the opportunity of levying execution,

the proper officer shall issue a summons, which shall be served on the alleged offender personally not less than 8 days before the return day appointed in the summons.

Commencement 1 September 1982.
Amendments Rule heading: words "s 14, 92 or 124" substituted by SI 1984/878, r 12, Schedule.
Words "section 14 or 92" and "section 124" substituted by SI 1984/878, r 12, Schedule; words omitted revoked by SI 1982/1140, r 2.
Forms Summons for assault on officer of court or rescue (N90).
Order of commitment (N91).
Summons for neglect to levy (N366).

[Order 34, r 1A Committal under section 14, 92 or 118 of the Act

Rule 1(5) of Order 29 shall apply, with the necessary modifications, where an order is made under section 14, 92 or 118 of the Act committing a person to prison.]

Commencement 1 July 1991.
Amendments This rule was added by SI 1991/1126, r 16.

Order 34, r 2 Notice to show cause before or after fine under [s 55] of the Act

Before or after imposing a fine on any person under [section 55] of the Act for disobeying a witness summons or refusing to be sworn or give evidence, the judge may direct the proper officer to give to that person notice that if he has any cause to show why a fine should not be or should not have been imposed on him, he may show cause in person or by affidavit or otherwise on a day named in the notice, and the judge after considering the cause shown may make such order as he thinks fit.

Commencement 1 September 1982.
Amendments Rule heading: words "s 55" substituted by SI 1984/878, r 12, Schedule.
Words "section 55" substituted by SI 1984/878, r 12, Schedule.

Order 34, r 3 Non-payment of fine

(1) If a fine is not paid in accordance with the order imposing it, the proper officer shall forthwith report the matter to the judge.

(2) Where by an order imposing a fine, the amount of the fine is directed to be paid

by instalments and default is made in the payment of any instalment, the same proceedings may be taken as if default had been made in payment of the whole of the fine.

(3)   If the judge makes an order for payment of a fine to be enforced by warrant of execution, the order shall be treated as an application made to the [district judge] for the issue of the warrant at the time when the order was received by him.

Commencement   1 September 1982.

Order 34, r 4 Repayment of fine

If, after a fine has been paid, the person on whom it was imposed shows cause sufficient to satisfy the judge that, if it had been shown at an earlier date, he would not have imposed a fine or would have imposed a smaller fine or would not have ordered payment to be enforced, the judge may order the fine or any part thereof to be repaid.

Commencement   1 September 1982.

[Order 34, r 5 Exercise of powers by district judges

In relation to proceedings under section 14 or 55 of the Act, references in rules 1, 2 and 4 to the judge shall include references to the district judge.]

Commencement   1 July 1991.
Amendments   This rule was inserted by SI 1991/1126, r 17.

[ORDER 35
ENFORCEMENT OF COUNTY COURT JUDGMENTS
OUTSIDE ENGLAND AND WALES

PART I—ENFORCEMENT OUTSIDE UNITED KINGDOM

Order 35, r 1 Interpretation of Part I

In this Part of this Order "the Act of 1933" means the Foreign Judgments (Reciprocal Enforcement) Act 1933, "the Act of 1982" means the Civil Jurisdiction and Judgments Act 1982 and expressions which are defined in those Acts have the same meaning in this Part of this Order as they have in those Acts.]

Commencement   1 January 1987.
Amendments   Order 35 was substituted by SI 1985/1269, r 11.

[Order 35, r 2 Application under s 10 of the Act of 1933 for certified copy of county court judgment

(1)   An application under section 10 of the Act of 1933 for a certified copy of a judgment of a county court may be made by filing an affidavit, made by the solicitor of the party entitled to enforce the judgment, or by the party himself, if he is acting in person.

(2)   An affidavit by which an application under section 10 of the Act of 1933 is made must—

(a)   give particulars of proceedings in which the judgment was obtained,

(b)   have annexed to it evidence of service on the defendant of the summons or other process by which the proceedings were begun (where service was effected otherwise than through the court), copies of the pleadings, if any, and a statement of the grounds on which the judgment was based,

(c)   state whether the defendant did or did not object to the jurisdiction, and, if so, on what grounds,

(d)   show that the judgment is not subject to any stay of execution,

(e)   state that the time for appealing or applying for a re-hearing has expired, or, as the case may be, the date on which it will expire and in either case whether notice of appeal against the judgment has been given or an application for a re-hearing has been made, and

(f)   state whether interest is recoverable on the judgment or part thereof and, if so, the rate and period in respect of which it is recoverable.

(3)   The certified copy of the judgment shall be a sealed copy indorsed with a certificate signed by the [district judge] certifying that the copy is a true copy of a judgment obtained in the county court and that it is issued in accordance with section 10 of the Act of 1933.

(4)   There shall also be issued a sealed certificate signed by the [district judge] and having annexed to it a copy of the summons or other process by which the proceedings were begun and stating—

(a)   the manner in which the summons or other process was served on the defendant or that the defendant has delivered to the court an admission, defence or counterclaim,

(b)   what objections, if any, were made to the jurisdiction,

(c)   what pleadings, if any, were filed,

(d) the grounds on which the judgment was based,

(e) that the time for appealing or applying for a re-hearing has expired or, as the case may be, the date on which it will expire,

(f) whether notice of appeal against the judgment has been given or an application for a re-hearing has been made,

(g) whether interest is recoverable on the judgment or part thereof and, if such be the case, the rate of interest, the date from which interest is recoverable, and the date on which interest ceases to accrue, and

(h) such other particulars as it may be necessary to give to the court in the foreign country in which it is sought to obtain execution of the judgment.]

Commencement 1 January 1987.
Amendments See the note to Order 35, r 1.
Definitions Act of 1933: Foreign Judgments (Reciprocal Enforcement) Act 1933.

[Order 35, r 3 Application under s 12 of the Act of 1982 for certified copy of county court judgment

(1) An application under section 12 of the Act of 1982 for a certified copy of a judgment of a county court may be made by filing an affidavit made by the solicitor of the party entitled to enforce the judgment, or by the party himself, if he is acting in person.

(2) An affidavit by which an application under section 12 of the Act of 1982 is made must—

(a) give particulars of the proceedings in which the judgment was obtained,

(b) have annexed to it evidence of service on the defendant of the summons or other process by which the proceedings were begun (where service was effected otherwise than through the court), copies of the pleadings, if any, and a statement of the grounds on which the judgment was based together with, where appropriate, any document under which the applicant is entitled to legal aid or assistance by way of representation for the purposes of the proceedings,

(c) state whether the defendant did or did not object to the jurisdiction, and, if so, on what grounds,

(d) show that the judgment has been served in accordance with Order 22, rule 1 and is not subject to any stay of execution;

(e) state that the time for appealing or applying for a re-hearing has expired, or, as the case may be, the date on which it will expire and in either case whether notice of appeal against the judgment has been given or an application for re-hearing has been made, and

(f) state—

(i) whether the judgment provides for the payment of a sum or sums of money,

(ii) whether interest is recoverable on the judgment or part thereof and, if such be the case, the rate of interest, the date from which interest is recoverable, and the date on which interest ceases to accrue.

(3) The certified copy of the judgment shall be a sealed copy and there shall be issued with the copy of the judgment a sealed certificate signed by the [district judge] and having annexed to it a copy of the summons or other process by which the proceedings were begun.]

Commencement 1 January 1987.
Amendments See the note to Order 35, r 1.
Definitions Act of 1982: Civil Jurisdiction and Judgments Act 1982.

[Part II Enforcement in other Parts of the United Kingdom]

Order 35, r 4 Interpretation of Part II

In this Part of this Order—

"the Act of 1982" means the Civil Jurisdiction and Judgments Act 1982,

"money provision" means a provision in any judgment to which section 18 of the Act of 1982 applies for the payment of one or more sums of money,

"non-money provision" means a provision in any judgment to which section 18 of the Act of 1982 applies for any relief or remedy not requiring payment of a sum of money.]

Commencement 1 January 1987.
Amendments See the note to Order 35, r 1.

[Order 35, r 5 Application for certificate of money provision

(1) A certificate in respect of any money provision contained in a judgment of the county court may be obtained by filing an affidavit made by the solicitor of the party entitled to enforce the judgment, or by the party himself if he is acting in person, together with a form of certificate.

(2) An affidavit by which an application under paragraph (1) is made must—
   (a) give particulars of the judgment, stating the rate of payment, if any, specified under the money provisions contained in the judgment, the sum or aggregate of sums (including any costs or expenses) remaining unsatisfied, the rate of interest, if any, applicable and the date or time from which any such interest began to accrue,
   (b) verify that the time for appealing against the judgment or for applying for a re-hearing has expired, or that any appeal or re-hearing has been finally disposed of and that enforcement of the judgment is not stayed or suspended, and
   (c) state to the best of the information or belief of the deponent the usual or last known address of the party entitled to enforce the judgment and of the party liable to execution on it.

(3) The proper officer shall enter on the certificate—
   (a) the number of the action,
   (b) the amount remaining due under the judgment,
   (c) the rate of interest payable on the judgment debt, and the date or time from which any such interest began to accrue,
   (d) a note of the costs, if any, allowed for obtaining the certificate, and
   (e) the date on which the certificate is issued.]

Commencement 1 January 1987.
Amendments See the note to Order 35, r 1.

[Order 35, r 6 Application for certified copy of judgment containing non-money provision

(1) A certified copy of a judgment of a county court which contains any non-money provision may be obtained by filing an affidavit made by the solicitor of the party entitled to enforce the judgment, or by the party himself, if he is acting in person.

(2)   The requirements in paragraph (2) of rule 5 shall apply with the necessary modifications to an affidavit made in an application under paragraph (1) of this rule.

(3)   The certified copy of a judgment shall be a sealed copy to which shall be annexed a certificate signed by the proper officer and stating that the conditions specified in paragraph 3(a) and (b) of Schedule 7 to the Act of 1982 are satisfied in relation to the judgment.]

Commencement   1 January 1987.
Amendments   See the note to Order 35, r 1.
Definitions   Act of 1982: Civil Jurisdiction and Judgments Act 1982.

ORDER 36
(revoked by SI 1992/1965)

ORDER 37
REHEARING, SETTING ASIDE AND APPEAL FROM [DISTRICT JUDGE]

Order 37, r 1 Rehearing

(1)   In any proceedings tried without a jury the judge shall have power on application to order a rehearing where no error of the court at the hearing is alleged.

(2)   Unless the court otherwise orders, any application under paragraph (1) shall be made to the judge by whom the proceedings were tried.

(3)   A rehearing may be ordered on any question without interfering with the finding or decision on any other question.

(4)   Where the proceedings were tried by the [district judge], the powers conferred on the judge by paragraphs (1) and (3) shall be exercisable by the [district judge] and paragraph (2) shall not apply.

(5)   Any application for a rehearing under this rule shall be made on notice stating the grounds of the application and the notice shall be served on the opposite party not more than 14 days after the day of the trial and not less than 7 days before the day fixed for the hearing of the application.

(6)   On receipt of the notice, the proper officer shall, unless the court otherwise orders, retain any money in court until the application has been heard.

Commencement   1 September 1982.

Order 37, r 2 Setting aside judgment given in party's absence

(1)   Any judgment or order obtained against a party in his absence at the hearing may be set aside by the court on application by that party on notice.

(2)   The application shall be made to the judge if the judgment or order was given or made by the judge and in any other case shall be made to the [district judge].

Commencement   1 September 1982.
Cross references   See RSC Order 35, r 2.

Order 37, r 3 Setting aside on failure of postal service

(1)   Where in an action or matter the originating process has been sent to the defendant or inserted in his letter-box [in accordance with Order 7, rule 10(1)(b) or (4)(a) or 13(1)(b) or (4) and after judgment] has been entered or given or an order has been made it appears to the court that the process did not come to the knowledge of the defendant in due time, the court may of its own motion set aside the judgment or order and may give any such directions as the court thinks fit.

(2)   The proper officer shall give notice to the plaintiff of the setting aside of any judgment or order under this rule.

Commencement 1 September 1982.
Amendments Para (1): words "in accordance with Order 7, rule 10(1)(b) or (4)(a) or 13(1)(b) or (4) and after judgment" substituted by SI 1983/1716, r 5.

Order 37, r 4 Setting aside default judgment

(1) Without prejudice to rule 3, the court may, on application or of its own motion, [set aside, vary or confirm] any judgment entered in a default action pursuant to Order 9, rule 6.

[(2) An application under paragraph (1) shall be made on notice and, where such an application is made in a default action for a liquidated sum, the proceedings shall be automatically transferred to the defendant's home court if the judgment or order was not given or made in that court.]

Commencement 1 July 1991 (para (2)); 1 September 1982 (remainder).
Amendments Para (1): words "set aside, vary or confirm" substituted by SI 1991/1126, r 45.
Para (2): substituted by SI 1991/1126, r 46.
Cross references See RSC Order 13, r 9.

Order 37, r 5 Non-compliance with rules

(1) Where there has been a failure to comply with any requirement of these rules, the failure shall be treated as an irregularity and shall not nullify the proceedings, but the court may set aside the proceedings wholly or in part or exercise its powers under these rules to allow any such amendments and to give any such directions as it thinks fit.

(2) No application to set aside any proceedings for irregularity shall be granted unless made within a reasonable time, nor if the party applying has taken any step in the proceedings after knowledge of the irregularity.

(3) Where any such application is made, the grounds of objection shall be stated in the notice.

(4) The expression "proceedings" in paragraph (1), and where it first occurs in paragraph (2), includes any step taken in the proceedings and any document, judgment or order therein.

Commencement 1 September 1982.
Cross references See RSC Order 2, rr 1, 2.

Order 37, r 6 Appeal from [district judge]

(1) Any party affected by a judgment or final order of the [district judge] may, except where he has consented to the terms thereof, appeal from the judgment or order to the judge, who may, upon such terms as he thinks fit,—
   (a) set aside or vary the judgment or order or any part thereof, or
   (b) give any other judgment or make any other order in substitution for the judgment or order appealed from, or
   (c) remit the action or matter or any question therein to the [district judge] for rehearing or further consideration, or
   (d) order a new trial to take place before himself or another judge of the court on a day to be fixed.

(2) The appeal shall be made on notice, which shall state the grounds of the appeal

and be served within 14 days after the day on which judgment or order appealed from was given or made.

Commencement 1 September 1982.
Amendments Rule heading: words "district judge" substituted by SI 1991/1882, r 11.
Para (1): words "district judge" substituted by SI 1991/1882, r 11.
Cross references See RSC Order 58, rr 1, 3.

Order 37 r 7 *(revoked by SI 1990/1965)*

Order 37, r 8 Imposition of terms and stay of execution

(1) An application to the judge or [district judge] under any of the foregoing rules may be granted on such terms as he thinks reasonable.

(2) Notice of any such application shall not of itself operate as a stay of execution on the judgment or order to which it relates but the court may order a stay of execution pending the hearing of the application or any rehearing or new trial ordered on the application.

(3) If a judgment or order is set aside under any of the foregoing rules, any execution issued on the judgment or order shall cease to have effect unless the court otherwise orders.

Commencement 1 September 1982.

ORDER 38
COSTS

[Order 38, r 1 Entitlement to costs

(1)   This rule shall have effect subject to the provisions of any Act or rule and to the following provisions of this Order.

(2)   The costs of and incidental to all proceedings in a county court shall be in the discretion of the court.

(3)   Save where provision is otherwise made by these rules, the provisions of Part II of RSC Order 62 relating to entitlement to costs (except such of those provisions as refer to the Official Solicitor or court fees) shall apply in relation to the costs of and incidental to any proceedings in a county court as they apply in relation to the costs of any like proceedings to which that Order applies.

(4)   For the purposes of paragraph (3), any reference in a provision of the said Part II to any other provision of the RSC shall be construed as a reference to the corresponding provision (if any) in these rules.

[(5)   For the purpose of applying RSC Order 62, rule 5(1) to costs of and incidental to proceedings in a county court, the following words in the said rule 5(1) shall be omitted: "and, for the purposes of section 17 of the Judgments Act 1838, the order shall be deemed to have been entered up".]]

Commencement   1 April 1992 (para (5)); 28 April 1986 (remainder).
Amendments   This rule was substituted by SI 1986/636, r 8.
Para (5): inserted by SI 1992/793, r 3.
Cross references   See RSC Order 62, r 3(1)–(3).

Order 38, r 2 Taxation of costs

(1)   Subject to this Order, where by or under these rules or any order or direction of the court costs are to be paid to any person, that person shall be entitled to his taxed costs.

(2)   The [district judge] shall be the taxing officer of the court.

Commencement   1 September 1982.
Cross references   RSC Order 62, r 3(4) (para 1) and r 19 (para 2).

Order 38, r 3 Costs to be regulated by scales

(1)   For the regulation of solicitors' charges and disbursements otherwise than for the purposes of rule 18 or 19, there shall be [three scales of costs, namely a lower scale, scale 1 as set out in Appendix A and scale 2].

(2)   The scales shall have effect subject to and in accordance with the provisions of this Order and any directions contained in the scales.

[(2A) Scales 1 and 2 shall not apply to determine the amount of costs to be allowed to the extent that regulations made under the Legal Aid Act 1988 determine the amount of costs payable to legal representatives in relation to proceedings to which this Order applies.]

[(3)   In relation to a sum of money only, the scales shall apply as follows:—

Sum of money	*Scale applicable*
Exceeding £25 but not exceeding £100	lower scale
Exceeding £100 but not exceeding £3,000	scale 1
Exceeding £3,000	scale 2.]

[(3A) The amount of costs to be assessed under the lower scale pursuant to rule 19 shall be determined in accordance with Appendix C and the amount of costs to be allowed on any taxation under scale 1 shall be determined in accordance with Appendix A.

(3B) The amount of costs to be allowed on any taxation of costs under scale 2 shall be in the discretion of the taxing officer and, in exercising his discretion, the taxing officer shall have regard to all the relevant circumstances, and in particular to the circumstances referred to in paragraph 1(2) of Part I of Appendix 2 to RSC Order 62.

(3C) Where costs are to be allowed on scale 2—
  (a)   the bill of costs shall consist of such of the items specified in Part II of Appendix 2 to RSC Order 62 as may be appropriate, set out, except for item 4, in chronological order; and each such item (other than an item relating only to time spent in travelling or waiting) may include an allowance for general care and conduct having regard to such of the circumstances referred to in paragraph 1(2) of Part I of Appendix 2 to RSC Order 62 as may be relevant to that item;
  (b)   rules 5, 9, 12 to 16, 17(3) and 19 of this Order shall not apply on any taxation under that scale;
  (c)   rule 21(4) of this Order shall apply as if the words after "party and party" in paragraph (4)(c) were omitted.

(3D) Where costs are awarded on scale 2 to any person, the court may order that, instead of his taxed costs, that person shall be entitled to a gross sum (specified in the order) in lieu of those costs; but where the court so orders and the person entitled to the gross sum is a litigant in person, rule 17 shall apply as if for paragraph (3) there were substituted the following—

   "(3) The costs of a litigant in person shall be assessed in accordance with rule 3(3D) unless the court otherwise orders.".]

(4)   Where the sum of money does not exceed £25, no solicitors' charges shall be allowed as between party and party, unless a certificate is granted under rule 4(6).

(5)   In addition to the disbursements shown in the scales the appropriate court fees shall be allowable.

(6)   In relation to proceedings referred to arbitration under [Order 19, rule 3], this rule is without prejudice to [rule 4] of that Order.

Commencement   7 March 1994 (para (2A)); 1 July 1991 (paras (3)-(3D)); 1 September 1982 (remainder)
Amendments   Para (1): words from "three scales of costs" to the end substituted by SI 1991/1328, r 7(1).
Para (2A): inserted by SI 1994/306, r 2.
Para (3): substituted by SI 1991/1328, r 7(2).
Paras (3A)-(3D): inserted by SI 1991/1328, r 7(3).
Para (6): words "Order 19, rule 3" substituted by SI 1992/1965, r 17(c); words "rule 4" substituted by virtue of SI 1992/1965, r 16(c).

Order 38, r 4 Determination of scale

(1)   Subject to this Order, the scale of costs in an action for the recovery of a sum of money only shall be determined—
    (a)   as regards the costs of the plaintiff, by the amount recovered;
    (b)   as regards the costs of the defendant, by the amount claimed;

but nothing in this paragraph shall apply to an action under the equity jurisdiction or to an admiralty action or an action in which the title to a hereditament comes in question.

(2)   In relation to third party proceedings, paragraph (1) shall have effect as if the defendant issuing the third party notice were the plaintiff and the third party were the defendant.

(3)   Where in an action to which paragraph (1) applies there is a counterclaim for a sum of money only, that paragraph shall have effect in relation to the costs exclusively referable to the counterclaim as if the references therein to the amount recovered and the amount claimed were references to the amount recovered on the counterclaim and the amount of the counterclaim respectively.

(4)   Where an action to which paragraph (1) applies has been transferred from the High Court to a county court and the amount remaining in dispute at the date on which the [district judge] receives [the relevant documents (within the meaning of Order 16, rule 6(1))] is less than the amount originally claimed, paragraph (1)(b) shall have effect as if the reference therein to the amount claimed were a reference to the amount remaining in dispute at that date.

(5)   Paragraph (1) shall have effect in relation to garnishee proceedings as if the judgment creditor were the plaintiff and the garnishee or, as the case may be, the judgment debtor were the defendant.

(6)   In any proceedings in which the judge certifies that a difficult question of law or a question of fact of exceptional complexity is involved, he may award costs on such scale as he thinks fit.

(7)   In proceedings to which none of the foregoing paragraphs applies, costs shall be on such scale as the judge when awarding the costs, or the [district judge] when taxing or assessing them, may determine.

Commencement   1 September 1982.
Amendments   Para (4): words "the relevant documents (within the meaning of Order 16, rule 6(1))" substituted by SI 1991/1328, r 7(4).

Order 38, r 5 Discretionary allowances

Where in the scales of costs—
    (a)   an upper and a lower sum of money are specified against an item, or
    (b)   the amount to be allowed in respect of an item is directed not to exceed a specified sum, or
    (c)   no amount is specified against an item,

the amount of costs to be allowed in respect of that item shall, subject to rules 9 and 17, be in the discretion of the [district judge] within the limits of the sums, if any, so specified, and [in exercising his discretion the [district judge] shall have regard to all the circumstances to which a taxing officer of the Supreme Court is required to have regard when determining the amount of costs to be allowed in accordance with the provisions contained in paragraph 1(2) of Appendix 2 to RSC Order 62].

Commencement 1 September 1982.
Amendments Words from "in exercising his discretion" to the end substituted by SI 1986/636, r 9.

Order 38, r 6 Allowance or disallowance of items by judge

Where the costs of any action or matter are to be taxed, the judge may direct that any item in the scale be allowed or disallowed on taxation.

Commencement 1 September 1982.

Order 38, r 7 Value added tax

In addition to the amount of costs allowed to a party on taxation or assessment in respect of the supply of goods or services on which value added tax is chargeable there may be allowed as a disbursement a sum equivalent to value added tax at the appropriate rate on that amount in so far as the tax is not deductible as input tax by that party.

Commencement 1 September 1982.

Order 38, r 8 Restrictions on allowance of counsel's fees

(1)   No costs shall be allowed on taxation in respect of counsel attending before the judge or [district judge] on an interlocutory application, or in respect of more counsel than one attending before the judge or [district judge] on any occasion, unless the judge or [district judge], as the case may be, has certified the attendance as proper in the circumstances of the case.

(2)   Unless the judge or [district judge] at the hearing otherwise orders, no fee to counsel with brief shall be allowed in an action for the recovery of a sum of money only where no defence has been delivered and the defendant does not appear at the hearing to resist the claim.

(3)   Where a party appearing by counsel is awarded costs but the costs of employing counsel are not allowed, he may be allowed such costs as he might have been allowed if he had appeared by a solicitor and not by counsel.

Commencement 1 September 1982.
Cross references See RSC Order 62, Appendix 2, Pt 1, para 2(2).

Order 38, r 9 Allowance of increased sums on taxation

(1)   Where in any proceedings in which the costs are to be taxed, the judge is satisfied from the nature of the case or the conduct of the proceedings that the costs which may be allowed on taxation may be inadequate in the circumstances, he may give a certificate under this rule.

(2)   Where a certificate is given under this rule, the register may, if he thinks fit, allow on taxation such larger sum as he thinks reasonable in respect of all or any of the items in the relevant scale except item 5.

(3)   If he decides to exercise his powers under paragraph (2), the [district judge], in determining the sum to be allowed in respect of any item, shall have regard to, but

shall not be limited by, the amount allowable in respect of that item in the next higher scale, if any.

(4) Subject to paragraph (5), an application for a certificate under this rule may be made at the trial or hearing of the action or matter or on notice to be served on the party by whom the costs are payable within 14 days after the making of the order or direction for their payment:

Provided that where an application which could have been made at the trial or hearing is made subsequently, the judge may refuse the application on the ground that it ought to have been made at the hearing.

(5) Where no direction has been given by the judge that this paragraph shall not apply, the [district judge] may, if satisfied as to the matters mentioned in paragraph (1), exercise on taxation the powers conferred by paragraph (2) as if a certificate had been given under this rule.

Commencement 1 September 1982.

Order 38, r 10 Plans in collision actions

In an action arising out of an accident on land due to a collision or apprehended collision, the costs of preparing a plan (other than a sketch plan) of the place where the accident happened shall not be allowed on taxation unless—
(a) before the trial the court authorised the preparation of the plan, or
(b) notwithstanding the absence of an authorisation under paragraph (a), the [district judge] is satisfied that it was reasonable to prepare the plan for use at the trial.

Commencement 1 September 1982.

Order 38, r 11 Expenses of inspection

The expenses of any inspection of a place or thing by the judge or a jury under Order 21, rule 6, shall be paid in the first instance by the party on whose application the inspection is made or ordered or, if made or ordered without an application, by the plaintiff and shall be costs in the proceedings unless the judge otherwise orders.

Commencement 1 September 1982.

Order 38, r 12 Allowance of items not in scale

(1) Subject to paragraph (2) and rule 9, where costs are to be taxed in a matter for which no item appears in the relevant scale, reasonable costs may be allowed on taxation, not exceeding those appearing in the scale for a matter of a similar nature.

(2) Where the amount of a solicitor's remuneration in respect of the sale, purchase, lease or mortgage of land or other conveyancing matter or in respect of any other non-contentious business is regulated (in the absence of agreement to the contrary) by general orders for the time being in force under the Solicitors Act 1974, the amount of the costs to be allowed on taxation in respect of the like contentious business shall be the same notwithstanding anything in the scales contained in Appendix A.

Commencement 1 September 1982.

Order 38, r 13 Attendance allowance for witness of fact

(1)   Subject to paragraph (2), there may be allowed such sum as the judge or [district judge] thinks reasonable in respect of the attendance at court of any person (including a party to the proceedings) as a witness of fact or as a witness producing a document.

(2)   The sum allowed under paragraph (1) shall not exceed [£20.25] for a police officer or [£29.00] for any other person, unless the [district judge] on taxing or assessing the costs is satisfied that such sum may be inadequate in the circumstances.

Commencement   1 September 1982.
Amendments   Para (2): sums "£20.25" and "£29.00" substituted by SI 1992/793, r 4.

Order 38, r 14 Expert witness's fees

(1)   Subject to paragraphs (2) and (3), the fees allowable in respect of an expert witness shall be in accordance with the following table:—

Fee	*Amount allowable*
1. For attending court	not less than [£29.00] nor more than [£57.00] (or [£112.50] [on scale 1])
2. For qualifying to give evidence if the judge thinks fit to allow such a fee and the witness has attended court or the judge thinks that the fee should be allowed notwithstanding that the witness did not attend court.	not more than [£29.00] (or [£57.00] [on scale 1])
3. For a report in writing from an expert who is not allowed a qualifying fee, if the judge thinks the report was reasonably necessary.	not more than [£29.00] (or [£57.00] [on scale 1])

(2)   Where in any proceedings the judge is satisfied that any of the fees specified in paragraph (1) ought not to be limited as therein mentioned, he may give a certificate under this rule.

(3)   Rule 9(2), (4) and (5) shall apply, with the necessary modifications, in relation to a certificate under this rule as they apply in relation to a certificate under rule 9.

Commencement   1 September 1982.
Amendments   Para (1): in the table sums in square brackets substituted by SI 1992/793, r 5; words "on scale 1" substituted by SI 1991/1328, r 7(5).

Order 38, r 15 Further provisions as to witnesses' allowances

(1)   There may be allowed in respect of a witness or party who has attended the trial or hearing of an action or matter, in addition to any sum allowed under rule 13 or 14, any expenses which the witness or party has actually and reasonably incurred in travelling to and from the court or in staying in an hotel.

(2)   Where a witness or party attends the court in respect of two or more actions or matters, the sum which might be allowed to him under rule 13 or 14 or paragraph (1) in respect of one action or matter may be apportioned between the several actions or matters.

(3)   Allowances may be made in respect of a witness whether he was called or not, if his attendance was necessary.

Commencement   1 September 1982.

Order 38, r 16 Interpreters

(1)   Subject to paragraph (2), where on the trial or hearing of an action or matter a person attends the court for the purpose of interpreting evidence, there may be allowed in respect of his attendance such sum as might be allowed if he had attended the court as a witness of fact or, if the judge thinks fit, such sum as might be allowed if he had attended the court as an expert witness.

(2)   Nothing in paragraph (1) shall apply to an interpreter who is employed and remunerated in accordance with rules made under section 3 of the Welsh Courts Act 1942.

Commencement   1 September 1982.

Order 38, r 17 Litigant in person

(1)   Where in any proceedings any costs of a litigant in person are ordered to be paid by any other party or in any other way, then, subject to the following paragraphs of this rule, there may be allowed to the litigant in person such costs as would have been allowed if the work and disbursements to which the costs relate had been done or made by a solicitor on his behalf [together with any payments reasonably made by him for legal advice relating to the conduct of or the issues raised by the proceedings], and the provisions of these rules shall apply with the necessary modifications to the costs of a litigant in person as they apply to solicitors' charges and disbursements.

(2)   Nothing in rule 18 or Appendix B shall apply where the plaintiff is a litigant in person.

(3)   In relation to the costs of a litigant in person, rule 19(1) shall have effect as if for the words "and the solicitor for the party to whom they are payable so desires" there were substituted the words "and the court does not otherwise order".

(4)   Where the costs of a litigant in person are taxed or assessed without taxation—
    (a) he shall not be allowed more than such sum as would be allowed in the High Court in respect of the time reasonably spent by him in doing any work to which the costs relate if in the opinion of the court he has not suffered any pecuniary loss in doing the work, and
    (b) the amount allowed in respect of any work done by the litigant in person shall not in any case exceed two-thirds of the sum which in the opinion of the court would have been allowed in respect of that work if the litigant had been represented by a solicitor.

(5)   Where the costs of a litigant in person are assessed under Appendix C, or where on the taxation of the costs of a litigant in person he is allowed a charge for attending court to conduct his own case, then, notwithstanding anything in rule 13, he shall not be entitled to a witness allowance for himself in addition.

[(6)   For the purposes of this rule a litigant in person does not include a litigant who is a practising solicitor.]

Commencement   12 December 1983 (para (6)); 1 September 1982 (remainder).
Amendments   Para (1): words from "together with any payments" to "raised by the proceedings" added by SI 1989/236, r 15.
Para (6): added by SI 1983/1716, r 9.
Cross references   See RSC Order 62, r 18.

[Order 38, r 17A Reimbursement of additional costs under section 53, Administration of Justice Act 1985

(1)   In default of agreement between the Lord Chancellor and a person as to the amount of additional costs to be reimbursed under section 53 of the Administration of Justice Act 1985, either of them may make a written request to the proper officer that such costs be taxed.

(2)   Notwithstanding RSC Order 62, rule 3(4), such costs shall be taxed on an indemnity basis.]

Commencement   1 October 1988.
Amendments   This rule was inserted by SI 1988/278, r 12.
Cross references   See RSC Order 62, r 7A.

[Order 38, r 17B Assessment of costs for failure to admit facts or documents

(1)   Subject to paragraph (3), where a party is entitled to costs under Order 20, rule 2(2) or 3(2A) the amount of those costs may be assessed by the court without taxation and may be ordered to be paid forthwith.

(2)   Where costs are assessed under paragraph (1), the court may allow such sums as it thinks reasonable.

(3)   No order may be made under paragraph (1) in a case where the person against whom the order is made is an assisted person within the meaning of the statutory provisions relating to legal aid.]

Commencement   5 February 1990.
Amendments   This rule was inserted by SI 1989/2426, r 21.
Cross references   See RSC Order 62, r 7(6).

Order 38, r 18 Fixed costs

(1)   Appendix B shall effect for the purpose of showing the total amount which, in the several cases to which Appendix B applies, shall be allowed to the solicitor for the plaintiff as fixed costs without taxation, unless the court otherwise orders.

(2)   In a case to which Appendix B does not apply no amount shall be entered on the summons for the charges of the solicitor for the plaintiff, but the words "to be taxed" shall be inserted.

Commencement   1 September 1982.
Cross references   See RSC Order 62, App 3.

Order 38, r 19 Assessed or agreed costs

(1)   Where costs are payable on the lower scale, or where costs are payable [on scale 1] and the solicitor for the party to whom they are payable so desires, the costs shall be assessed without taxation, and on the assessment the court may allow such sums as it thinks reasonable within the limits of the sums appearing in Appendix C opposite [the

scale applicable to or the amount recovered in the proceedings], together with such additions, if any, as are authorised by that Appendix.

(2)   In relation to costs which fall to be assessed pursuant to paragraph (1), any reference in these rules to taxation shall be treated as a reference to assessment under that paragraph.

(3)   Where costs payable [on scale 1] in respect of an interlocutory application are not included in the general costs of the action or matter, they may be assessed without taxation unless the court otherwise orders, and on the assessment the court may allow such sums as it thinks reasonable within the limits appearing in [the scale applicable to or the amount recovered in the proceedings] opposite the relevant items.

(4)   Before assessing any costs pursuant to paragraph (1) or (3) the court may require the party to whom the costs are payable to give to the court a note of the sums which he claims to be allowed on the assessment.

(5)   Where the sum to be paid by one party to another party in respect of the costs of an action or matter has been agreed between them, the court may direct payment of that sum in lieu of taxed costs.

Commencement   1 September 1982.
Amendments   Paras (1), (3): words "on scale 1" and "the scale applicable to or the amount recovered in the proceedings" substituted by SI 1991/1328, r 7(6).
Cross references   See RSC Order 62, r 7(4).

[Order 38, r 19A Taxation of costs and powers exercisable on taxation

Save where provision is otherwise made by these rules, the provisions of RSC Order 62, rules 12, 14, 15, 16, 24 and 26 to 28, relating to the bases of taxation and the powers of taxing masters and taxing officers (except such of those provisions as refer to the Official Solicitor or court fees) shall apply in relation to proceedings in a county court as they apply in relation to proceedings in the High Court.]

Commencement   28 April 1986.
Amendments   This rule was inserted by SI 1986/636, r 12.

Order 38, r 20 [Taxation of costs inter partes]

(1)   Where a party (in this rule called "the applicant") is entitled to require any costs to be taxed by virtue of any order or direction of the court or by or under any provision of these rules, he shall, within 3 months after the order or direction or, as the case may be, the event entitling him to tax his costs, lodge in the court office his bill of costs, together with all necessary papers and vouchers, and sufficient copies of the bill for service under paragraph (2).

[(2)   On receipt of the documents mentioned in paragraph (1) the proper officer shall send a copy of the bill to every other party entitled to be heard on the taxation together with a notice requiring him to inform the proper officer, within 14 days after receipt of the notice, if he wishes to be heard on the taxation.

(3)   If a party to whom notice has been given under paragraph (2) informs the proper officer within the time limited that he wishes to be heard on the taxation, the proper officer shall fix a day and time for the taxation and give not less than 7 days' notice to the applicant and that party.

(3A) If no party to whom notice has been given under paragraph (2) informs the proper officer within the time limited that he wishes to be heard on the taxation, the proper officer shall, unless the [district judge] directs that an appointment to tax is necessary, send to the applicant a notice specifying the amount which the [district judge] proposes to allow in respect of the bill and requiring him to inform the proper officer, within 14 days after receipt of the notice, if he wishes to be heard on the taxation.

(3B) If the applicant informs the proper officer within the time limited that he wishes to be heard on the taxation, the proper officer shall fix a day and time for the taxation and give not less than 7 days' notice to the applicant.]

[(4) In this rule, "party entitled to be heard on the taxation" means—

  (a) a person who has taken any part in the proceedings which give rise to the taxation and who is directly liable under an order for costs made against him, or

  (b) a person who has given the applicant and the proper officer written notice that he has a financial interest in the outcome of the taxation, or

  (c) a person who is so entitled by virtue of a direction given by the [district judge].]

Commencement 28 April 1986 (para (4)); 1 September 1984 (paras (2)–(3B)); 1 September 1982 (remainder).

Amendments Rule heading: substituted by SI 1986/636, r 13.

Paras (2), (3), (3A), (3B): substituted, for paras (2), (3) as originally enacted, by SI 1984/878, r 19.

Para (3A): substituted, together with paras (2), (3), (3B), for paras (2), (3) as originally enacted, by SI 1984/878, r 19.

Para (4): substituted, for paras (4), (5) as originally enacted, by SI 1986/636, r 14.

Cross references See RSC Order 62, rr 17, 30, 31.

Forms Notice of bill lodged for taxation (N252).

Notice of amount allowed on provisional taxation (N253).

Notice of date of taxation (N254).

Notification of amount of taxed costs (N255).

Order 38, r 21 Taxation as between solicitor and client

[(1) In this rule references to a taxation of costs as between solicitor and client include references to the taxation of—

  (a) costs payable to a solicitor by his own client;

  (b) costs payable to a solicitor out of the legal aid fund, and

  (c) costs payable to a trustee or personal representative out of any fund.]

(2) Rule 4 shall apply to costs as between solicitor and client as if for the reference in paragraph (1)(a) thereof to the amount recovered there were substituted a reference to the amount claimed.

(3) The judge by whom any order is made for the taxation of costs as between solicitor and client may, after affording to the solicitor an opportunity of making any representations that he desires to make,—

  (a) determine the scale on which the costs are to be taxed under rule 4 as applied by paragraph (2) of this rule, and

  (b) exercise any discretion, whether as to scale or any other matter, give any direction and grant any certificate that the judge could have exercised, given or granted in relation to costs as between party and party.

(4) On taxation of costs as between solicitor and client the [district judge] shall not be bound to follow any determination of the judge or [district judge] in relation to

the costs as between party and party and accordingly, subject to any determination made under paragraph (3), the [district judge] may—

    (a)   exercise any of the powers conferred on the judge by that paragraph;

    (b)   allow items disallowed as between party and party, and

    (c)   allow a higher sum in respect of any item than the sum allowed as between party and party, not exceeding the maximum sum prescribed for that item in the scale on which the costs are being taxed.

[(5)   Subject to paragraphs (5A) and (7), rule 20 shall apply in relation to costs as between solicitor and client as it applies in relation to costs as between party and party with the necessary modifications and in particular—

    (a)   for paragraph (2) of that rule there shall be substituted the following paragraph:

    "(2) On receipt of the documents mentioned in paragraph (1) the proper officer shall send a copy of the bill to every other party entitled to be heard on the taxation and shall give to the applicant and that party not less than 14 days' notice of the day and time appointed for the taxation.";

    (b)   paragraphs (3) to (3B) of rule 20 shall not apply.

(5A) [Paragraphs (1), (2), (3), (3A), (3B) and (4)] of rule 20 shall apply to the taxation of a bill which is to be paid out of the legal aid fund subject to the modification that, if the bill is not also to be taxed as between party and party, then—

    (a)   paragraphs (2) and (3) of that rule shall not apply, and

    (b)   for paragraph (3A) of rule 20, there shall be substituted the following paragraph:

    "(3A) The proper officer shall, unless the [district judge] directs that an appointment to tax is necessary, send to the applicant a notice specifying the amount which the [district judge] proposes to allow in respect of the bill and requiring him to inform the proper officer, within 14 days after receipt of the notice, if he wishes to be heard on the taxation.".]

(6)   In relation to the taxation of costs pursuant to an order under the Solicitors Act 1974, rule 20(1) shall have effect as if for the period of 3 months mentioned in that rule there were substituted a [period of 14 days].

(7)   The costs of a taxation under the Solicitors Act 1974 shall be dealt with by the [district judge] in accordance with the provisions of that Act and shall be added to or deducted from the amount certified to be due.

Commencement   28 April 1986 (para (1)); 1 September 1984 (paras (5), (5A)); 1 September 1982 (remainder).

Amendments   Para (1): substituted by SI 1986/636, r 15.

Para (5): substituted, together with para (5A), for para (5) as originally enacted, by SI 1984/878, r 20.

Para (5A): substituted, together with para (5), for para (5) as originally enacted, by SI 1984/878, r 20; words "Paragraphs (1), (2), (3), (3A), (3B) and (4)" substituted by SI 1986/636, r 16.

Para (6): words "period of 14 days" substituted by SI 1986/636, r 17.

Order 38, r 22 Taxation of costs awarded by tribunal

(1)   Rule 20 shall not apply to an application for the taxation of costs, fees or expenses which by or under any Act or statutory instrument other than these rules fall to be taxed by a county court but any such application shall be made by originating application.

(2)   The applicant shall lodge with his originating application a bill of the costs, fees or expenses to be taxed and annex a copy of the bill to every copy of the originating application for service.

(3)   The application may be made to the [district judge] and the rules relating to originating applications shall apply as if the taxation were the hearing of the application.

(4)   On the taxation the [district judge] may exercise in relation to the costs any power which he could have exercised if the costs had been awarded in proceedings in the county court.

(5)   On the completion of the taxation (or, in the case of a review by the judge, after the review) the proper officer shall send to every party a certificate of the result of the taxation.

(6)   Nothing in this rule shall apply to an application under [section 30 of the Representation of the People Act 1983] for the taxation of a returning officer's account.

Commencement   1 September 1982.
Amendments   Para (6): words "section 30 of the Representation of the People Act 1983" substituted by SI 1983/1716, r 13, Schedule.

Order 38, r 23   *(revoked by SI 1986/636)*

Order 38, r 24 Review of taxation

(1)   Any party to a taxation who is dissatisfied with the [district judge]'s allowance or disallowance of the whole or part of any item or with the amount allowed by the [district judge] in respect of any item may, within 14 days after the taxation, request the [district judge] to reconsider his decision in respect of that item.

(2)   A request under paragraph (1) shall be made in writing specifying the item or items objected to and the nature and grounds of the objection, and the party making the request shall serve a copy on each other party to the taxation.

(3)   On the making of a request under paragraph (1) the [district judge] shall reconsider his decision as to the item or items objected to and shall notify each party of his decision on the reconsideration and of his reasons for it.

(4)   Any party who is dissatisfied with the [district judge]'s decision on the reconsideration may, within 14 days, after being notified of it, apply to the judge to review the taxation as to the item or items to which it relates.

(5)   An application for a review under paragraph (4) shall be made on notice stating the nature and grounds of the applicant's objection to the [district judge]'s decision.

(6)   Unless the judge otherwise directs, no further evidence shall be received on the hearing of an application under paragraph (4), and no ground of objection shall be raised which has not been raised in the applicant's notice, but, save as aforesaid, on the hearing of the application the judge may exercise all such powers and discretion as are vested in the [district judge] in relation to the subject matter of the application.

(7)   If the judge sees fit to exercise in relation to the application his power to appoint assessors under [section 63] of the Act without any application being made by any party to the proceedings, he shall appoint two assessors, of whom one shall be a [district judge], and Order 13, rule 11 (with the omission of so much of paragraphs

(4) and (8) thereof as requires the applicant to deposit a sum in respect of the assessor's fee), shall apply as if the assessor had been summoned on the application of a party.

(8)   On an application under this rule the judge may make such order as the circumstances require and in particular may order the [district judge]'s certificate of the result of the taxation to be amended or, except where the dispute as to the item under review is as to amount only, order the item to be remitted to the [district judge] for re-taxation.

Commencement 1 September 1982.
Amendments Para (7): words "section 63" substituted by SI 1984/878, r 12, Schedule.
Cross references See RSC Order 62, rr 33–5.

Order 38, r 25 *(revoked by SI 1992/1965)*

ORDER 39
ADMINISTRATION ORDERS

Order 39, r 1 Exercise of powers by [district judge]

Any powers conferred on the court by [Part VI] of the Act, section 4 of the Attachment of Earnings Act 1971 or this Order may be exercised by the [district judge or, in the circumstances mentioned in this Order, by the proper officer].

Commencement 1 September 1982.
Amendments Words "Part VI" substituted by SI 1984/878, r 12, Schedule; words from "district judge" to the end substituted by SI 1993/711, r 3.

Order 39, r 2 Request and list of creditors

(1) A debtor who desires to obtain an administration order under [Part VI] of the Act shall file a request in that behalf [in the court for the district in which he resides or carries on business].

(2) Where on his examination under Order 25, rule 3, or otherwise, a debtor furnishes to the court on oath a list of his creditors and the amounts which he owes to them respectively and sufficient particulars of his resources and needs, the court may proceed as if the debtor had filed a request under paragraph (1).

(3) Where a debtor is ordered to furnish a list under section 4(1)(b) of the said Act of 1971, then, unless otherwise directed, the list shall be filed within 14 days after the making of the order.

Commencement 1 September 1982.
Amendments Para (1): words "Part VI" and words from "in the court" to the end substituted by SI 1984/878, rr 12, 17, Schedule.
Definitions Act of 1971: Attachment of Earnings Act 1971.
Forms Request for administration order (N92).
List of creditors under 1971 Act (N93).

Order 39, r 3 Verification on oath

The statements in the request mentioned in rule 2(1) and the list mentioned in rule 2(3) shall be verified by the debtor on oath.

Commencement 1 September 1982.

Order 39, r 4   *(revoked by SI 1984/878)*

[Order 39, r 5 Orders made by the proper officer

(1) The question whether an administration order should be made, and the terms of such an order, may be decided by the proper officer in accordance with the provisions of this rule.

(2) On the filing of a request or list under rule 2, the proper officer may, if he considers that the debtor's means are sufficient to discharge in full and within a reasonable period the total amount of the debts included in the list, determine the amount and frequency of the payments to be made under such an order ("the proposed rate") and—

(a) notify the debtor of the proposed rate requiring him to give written reasons for any objection he may have to the proposed rate within 14 days of service of notification upon him;

(b) send to each creditor mentioned in the list provided by the debtor a copy of the debtor's request or of the list together with the proposed rate;

(c) require any such creditor to give written reasons for any objection he may have to the making of an administration order within 14 days of service of the documents mentioned in sub-paragraph (b) upon him.

Objections under sub-paragraph (c) may be to the making of an order, to the proposed rate or to the inclusion of a particular debt in the order.

(3) Where no objection under paragraph (2)(a) or (c) is received within the time stated, the proper officer may make an administration order providing for payment in full of the total amount of the debts included in the list.

(4) Where the debtor or a creditor notifies the court of any objection within the time stated, the proper officer shall fix a day for a hearing at which the district judge will decide whether an administration order should be made and the proper officer shall give not less than 14 days' notice of the day so fixed to the debtor and to each creditor mentioned in the list provided by the debtor.

(5) Where the proper officer is unable to fix a rate under paragraph (2) (whether because he considers that the debtor's means are insufficient or otherwise), he shall refer the request to the district judge.

(6) Where the district judge considers that he is able to do so without the attendance of the parties, he may fix the proposed rate providing for payment of the debts included in the list in full or to such extent and within such a period as appears practicable in the circumstances of the case.

(7) Where the proposed rate is fixed under paragraph (6), paragraphs (2) to (4) shall apply with the necessary modifications as if the rate had been fixed by the proper officer.

(8) Where the district judge does not fix the proposed rate under paragraph (6), he shall direct the proper officer to fix a day for a hearing at which the district judge will decide whether an administration order should be made and the proper officer shall give not less than 14 days' notice of the day so fixed to the debtor and to each creditor mentioned in the list provided by the debtor.

(9) Where an administration order is made under paragraph (3), the proper officer may exercise the power of the court under section 5 of the Attachment of Earnings Act 1971 to make an attachment of earnings order to secure the payments required by the administration order.

(10) In this rule "proper officer" does not include the district judge.]

Commencement 31 March 1993.
Amendments This rule was substituted by SI 1993/711, r 4.

Order 39, r 6 Notice of objection by creditor

(1) Any creditor to whom notice has been given [under rule 5(8)] and who objects to any debt included in the list furnished by the debtor shall, not less than 7 days before the day of hearing, give notice of his objection, stating the grounds thereof, to the proper officer, to the debtor and to the creditor to whose debt he objects.

(2)   Except with the leave of the court, no creditor may object to a debt unless he has given notice of his objection under paragraph (1).

Commencement 1 September 1982.
Amendments Para (1): words "under rule 5(8)" substituted by SI 1993/711, r 5.

Order 39, r 7 Procedure on day of hearing

On the day of hearing—

(a)   any creditor, whether or not he is mentioned in the list furnished by the debtor, may attend and prove his debt or, subject to rule 6, object to any debt included in that list;

(b)   every debt included in that list shall be taken to be proved unless it is objected to by a creditor or disallowed by the court or required by the court to be supported by evidence;

(c)   any creditor whose debt is required by the court to be supported by evidence shall prove his debt;

(d)   the court may adjourn proof of any debt and, if it does so, may either adjourn consideration of the question whether an administration order should be made or proceed to determine the question, in which case, if an administration order is made, the debt, when proved, shall be added to the debts scheduled to the order;

(e)   any creditor whose debt is admitted or proved, and, with the leave of the court, any creditor the proof of whose debt has been adjourned, shall be entitled to be heard and to adduce evidence on the question whether an administration order should be made and, if so, in what terms.

Commencement 1 September 1982.

Order 39, r 8 Direction for order to be subject to review

(1)   The court may, on making an administration order or at any subsequent time, direct that the order shall be subject to review at such time or at such intervals as the court may specify.

(2)   Where the court has directed that an administration order shall be subject to review, the proper officer shall give to the debtor and to every creditor who appeared when the order was made not less than 7 days' notice of any day appointed for such a review.

[(3)   Nothing in this rule shall require the proper officer to fix a day for a review under rule 13A.]

Commencement 31 March 1993 (para (3)); 1 September 1982 (remainder).
Amendments Para (3): inserted by SI 1993/711, r 6.

Order 39, r 9 Service of order

Where an administration order is made, the proper officer shall send a copy to—

(a)   the debtor,

(b)   every creditor whose name was included in the list furnished by the debtor,

(c)   any other creditor who has proved his debt, and

(d) every other court in which, to the knowledge of the [district judge], judgment has been obtained against the debtor or proceedings are pending in respect of any debt scheduled to the order.

Commencement   1 September 1982.
Forms   Administration order (N94).

Order 39, r 10 Subsequent objection by creditor

(1)   After an administration order has been made, a creditor who has not received notice under rule 5 and who wishes to object to a debt scheduled to the order, or to the manner in which payment is directed to be made by instalments, shall give notice to the proper officer of his objection and of the grounds thereof.

(2)   On receipt of such notice the court shall consider the objection and may—
  (a) allow it,
  (b) dismiss it, or
  (c) adjourn it for hearing on notice being given to such persons and on such terms as to security for costs or otherwise as the court thinks fit.

(3)   Without prejudice to the generality of paragraph (2), the court may dismiss an objection if it is not satisfied that the creditor gave notice of it within a reasonable time of his becoming aware of the administration order.

Commencement   1 September 1982.

Order 39, r 11 Subsequent proof by creditor

(1)   Any creditor whose debt is not scheduled to an administration order, and any person who after the date of the order became a creditor of the debtor, shall, if he wishes to prove his debt, send particulars of his claim to the proper officer, who shall give notice thereof to the debtor and to every creditor whose debt is so scheduled.

(2)   If neither the debtor nor any creditor gives notice to the proper officer, within 7 days after receipt of notice under paragraph (1), that he objects to the claim, then, unless it is required by the court to be supported by evidence, the claim shall be taken to be proved.

(3)   If the debtor or a creditor gives notice of objection within the said period of 7 days or the court requires the claim to be supported by evidence, the proper officer shall fix a day for consideration of the claim and give notice thereof to the debtor, the creditor by whom the claim was made and the creditor, if any, making the objection, and on the hearing the court may either disallow the claim or allow it in whole or in part.

(4)   If a claim is taken to be proved under paragraph (2) or allowed under paragraph (3), the debt shall be added to the schedule to the order and a copy of the order shall then be sent to the creditor by whom the claim was made.

Commencement   1 September 1982.

Order 39, r 12 Leave to present bankruptcy petition

An application by a creditor under [section 112(4) of the Act] for leave to present or join in a bankruptcy petition shall be made on notice to the debtor in accordance with Order 13, rule 1, but the court may, if it thinks fit, order that notice be given to any other creditor whose debt is scheduled to the administration order.

Commencement   1 September 1982.
Amendments   Words "section 112(4) of the Act" substituted by SI 1984/878, r 12, Schedule.

Order 39, r 13 Conduct of order

(1)   The chief clerk or such other officer of the court as the court making an administration order shall from time to time appoint shall have the conduct of the order and shall take all proper steps to enforce the order [(including exercising the power of the court under section 5 of the Attachment of Earnings Act 1971 to make an attachment of earnings order to secure the payments required by the administration order)] or to bring to the attention of the court any matter which may make it desirable to review the order.

(2)   Without prejudice to [section 115] of the Act, any creditor whose debt is scheduled to the order may, with the leave of the court, take proceedings to enforce the order.

(3)   The debtor or, with the leave of the court, any such creditor may apply to the court to review the order.

(4)   When on a matter being brought to its attention under paragraph (1) the court so directs or the debtor or a creditor applies for the review of an administration order, rule 8(2) shall apply as if the order were subject to review under that rule.

[(5)   Nothing in this rule shall require the proper officer to fix a day for a review under rule 13A.]

Commencement   31 March 1993 (para (5)); 1 September 1982 (remainder).
Amendments   Para (1): words from "(including exercising the power of the court" to "administration order)" inserted by SI 1993/711, r 7.
Para (2): words "section 115" substituted by SI 1984/878, r 12, Schedule.
Para (5): inserted by SI 1993/711, r 8.

[Order 39, r 13A Review by proper officer by default of payment

(1)   Where it appears that the debtor is failing to make payments in accordance with the order, the proper officer shall (either of his own motion or on the application of a creditor whose debt is scheduled to the administration order) send a notice to the debtor—

    (a)   informing him of the amounts which are outstanding; and
    (b)   requiring him (within 14 days of service of the notice upon him) to
        (i)   make the payments as required by the order; or
        (ii)   explain his reasons for failing to make the payments; and
        (iii)   make a proposal for payment of the amounts outstanding, or
        (iv)   make a request to vary the order.

(2)   If the debtor does not comply with paragraph (1)(b) within the time stated, the proper officer shall revoke the administration order.

(3)   The proper officer shall refer a notice given by a debtor under paragraph (1)(b)(ii), (iii) or (iv) to the district judge who may—

    (a)   without requiring the attendance of the parties—

(i)　the administration order or vary it so as to provide for payment of the debts included in the order in full or to such extent and within such a period as appears practicable in the circumstances of the case; or

(ii)　suspend the operation of the administration order for such time and on such terms as he thinks fit, or

(b)　require the proper officer to fix a day for the review of the administration order and to give to the debtor and to every creditor whose debt is scheduled to the administration order not less than 8 days' notice of the day so fixed.

(4)　Any party affected by an order made under paragraph (2) or (3)(a) may, within 14 days of service of the order on him and giving his reasons, apply on notice for the district judge to consider the matter afresh and the proper officer shall fix a day for the hearing of the application before the district judge and give to the debtor and to every creditor whose debt is scheduled to the administration order not less than 8 days' notice of the day so fixed.

(5)　On hearing an application under paragraph (4), the district judge may confirm the order or set it aside and make such new order as he thinks fit and the order so made shall be entered in the records of the court.

(6)　In this rule "proper officer" does not include the district judge.]

Commencement　31 March 1993.
Amendments　This rule was inserted by SI 1993/711, r 9.

Order 39, r 14 Review of order

(1)　On the review of an administration order the court may—

(a)　if satisfied that the debtor is unable from any cause to pay any instalment due under the order, suspend the operation of the order for such time and on such terms as it thinks fit;

(b)　if satisfied that there has been a material change in any relevant circumstances since the order was made, vary any provision of the order made by virtue of [section 112(6)] of the Act;

(c)　if satisfied that the debtor has failed without reasonable cause to comply with any provision of the order or that it is otherwise just and expedient to do so, revoke the order, either forthwith or on failure to comply with any condition specified by the court; or

(d)　make an attachment of earnings order to secure the payments required by the administration order or vary or discharge any such attachment of earnings order already made.

(2)　The proper officer shall send a copy of any order varying or revoking an administration order to the debtor, to every creditor whose debt is scheduled to the administration order and, if the administration order is revoked, to any other court to which a copy of the administration order was sent pursuant to rule 9.

Commencement　1 September 1982.
Amendments　Para (1): in sub-para (b) words "section 112(6)" substituted by SI 1984/878, r 12, Schedule.
Forms　Order revoking administration order (N95).
Order suspending/varying same (N95A).

Order 39, r 15　*(revoked by SI 1986/2001)*

Order 39, r 16 Discharge of attachment of earnings order

On the revocation of an administration order any attachment of earnings order made to secure the payments required by the administration order shall be discharged.

Commencement 1 September 1982.

Order 39, r 17 Declaration of dividends

(1) The officer having the conduct of an administration order shall from time to time declare dividends and distribute them among the creditors entitled thereto.

(2) When a dividend is declared, notice shall be sent by the officer to each of the said creditors.

Commencement 1 September 1982.

Order 39, r 18 Creditors to rank equally

All creditors scheduled under [section 113(d)] of the Act before an administration order is superseded under [section 117(2)] of the Act shall rank equally in proportion to the amount of their debts subject to the priority given by the said paragraph (d) to those scheduled as having been creditors before the date of the order, but no payment made to any creditor by way of dividend or otherwise shall be disturbed by reason of any subsequent proof by any creditor under the said paragraph (d).

Commencement 1 September 1982.
Amendments Words "section 113(d)" and "section 117(2)" substituted by SI 1984/878, r 12, Schedule.

Order 39, r 19 Change of debtor's address

(1) A debtor who changes his residence shall forthwith inform the court of his new address.

(2) Where the debtor becomes resident in the district of another court, the court in which the administration order is being conducted may transfer the proceedings to that other court.

Commencement 1 September 1982.

ORDER 40
ADMIRALTY PROCEEDINGS

Order 40, r 1 Application and interpretation

(1) This Order applies to Admiralty proceedings and, subject to the provisions of this Order, the other provisions of these rules apply to those proceedings as they apply to default actions.

(2) In this Order "court" means an Admiralty county court and "district" means the district assigned to such a court for Admiralty purposes.

Commencement 1 September 1982.
Cross references See RSC Order 75, r 1.
Forms Request to issue Admiralty action (N378).

Order 40, r 2 Venue for commencement of action

(1) An action in rem may be commenced in the court for the district in which the property against which the action is brought is situated at the time of the commencement of the proceedings . . . .

(2) An action in personam may be commenced—
    (a) if an action in rem could have been brought in respect of the claim, in the court for the district in which the owner, or one of the owners, of the property against which such an action would have lain or the agent in England or Wales of the owner resides or carries on business . . . ; or
    (b) if sub-paragraph (a) is not applicable, then in the court for the district in which the defendant or one of the defendants resides or carries on business . . . ; or
    (c) by leave of the judge or [district judge], in the court for the district in which the cause of action wholly or in part arose.

Commencement 1 September 1982.
Amendments Para (1): words omitted revoked by SI 1983/1716, r 10.
Para (2): in sub-paras (a), (b) words omitted revoked by SI 1983/1716, r 10.

Order 40, r 3 Particulars of claim in action in rem

When filing particulars of his claim pursuant to Order 6, rule 1, the plaintiff in an action in rem shall file a copy for service with the summons.

Commencement 1 September 1982.
Cross references See RSC Order 75, r 3.

Order 40, r 4 Warrant of arrest

(1) Where, after the commencement of an action in rem, it is desired to arrest the property against which the action or any counterclaim in the action is brought, the plaintiff or defendant, as the case may be, shall file an affidavit, stating—
    (a) where the action is brought by virtue of [section 28(3)] of the Act, the grounds on which it is alleged that there is a maritime lien or other charge on the property for the amount claimed;

(b) where the action is brought by virtue of [section 28(4)] of the Act—
   (i) whether or not the ship proceeded against is the ship in connection with which the claim arose,
   (ii) that in the belief of the deponent the person who would, apart from [section 30] of the Act, be liable on the claim in an action in personam was, at the time when the cause of action arose, the owner or charterer, or in possession or control, of the ship in connection with which the claim arose and [was, at the time of the issue of the summons, either the beneficial owner of all the shares in the ship in respect of which the warrant is required or (where appropriate) the charterer of it under a charter by demise];
(c) ...
(d) in an action for wages, the nationality of the ship.

(2) Where upon the filing of the affidavit the court is satisfied with the evidence, it may, subject to paragraphs (3) and (4), issue a warrant of arrest in duplicate and, where the court is not satisfied, it may require further evidence to be adduced and may order the detention of the property for the purpose of adducing such evidence.

(3) Except with the leave of the court or where notice has been given under paragraph (4), a warrant of arrest shall not be issued in an action for wages against a foreign ship belonging to a port of a State having a consulate within the district of the court until notice that the action has been begun has been sent to the consul.

(4) Where by any convention or treaty the United Kingdom has undertaken to minimise the possibility of arrest of ships of another State, no warrant of arrest in an action in rem against a ship owned by that State shall be issued until notice of intention to ask for the ship to be arrested has been served on a consular officer at the consular office of that State in London or the port at which it is intended to cause the ship to be arrested.

(5) In a case to which paragraph (3) or (4) relates the affidavit mentioned in paragraph (1) shall state that the notice required by paragraph (3) or (4), as the case may be, has been served, and a copy of the notice shall be exhibited to the affidavit.

Commencement 1 September 1982.
Amendments Para (1): in sub-paras (a), (b) words "section 28(3)", "section 28(4)" and "section 30" substituted by SI 1984/878, r 12, Schedule; in sub-para (b) words from "was, at the time of the issue" to the end substituted by SI 1982/436, r 5(2); sub-para (c) revoked by SI 1983/1716, r 11.
Cross references See RSC Order 75, r 5.
Forms Warrant of arrest and detention (N100).
Notice to consular office (N379).

Order 40, r 5 Service of summons or warrant in action in rem

(1) Subject to paragraph (6), the summons and any warrant of arrest issued in an action in rem shall be served on the property against which it is issued, except that, where the property is freight, the summons or warrant shall be served on the cargo in respect of which the freight is payable or on the ship in which the cargo was carried.

(2) Subject to paragraph (3), service shall be effected by—
   (a) affixing the summons or duplicate warrant on any mast of the ship or on the outside of any part of the ship's superstructure, or
   (b) delivering the summons or duplicate of the warrant to the person who is, at the time of service, apparently in charge of the ship or other property.

(3)   Service of a summons or warrant of arrest in an action in rem against freight or cargo shall, if the cargo has been landed or transhipped, be effected—
   (a)   by leaving the summons or duplicate warrant on the cargo, or
   (b)   if the cargo is in the custody of a person who will not permit access to it, by leaving the summons or duplicate warrant with that person.

(4)   Service of the summons in an action in rem may be effected by any of the persons mentioned in Order 7, rule 2(b).

(5)   The summons and any warrant of arrest in an action in rem may be served on a Sunday, Good Friday or Christmas Day, as well as on any other day.

(6)   A summons in an action in rem need not be served on the property mentioned in paragraph (1) if the summons is deemed to have been duly served on the defendant by virtue of Order 7, rule 11.

Commencement   1 September 1982.
Cross references   See RSC Order 75, rr 8, 10(6), 11.
Forms   Summons in rem (N97, 99).

Order 40, r 6 Service of summons in action in personam

(1)   The summons in an action in personam may be served in any manner prescribed by these rules for the service of a default summons.

(2)   Where an action in personam is commenced under rule 2(2)(a) in the court for the district in which an agent resides or carries on business, the summons shall be served on the agent.

Commencement   1 September 1982.
Cross references   See RSC Order 10.
Forms   Summons in personam (N96, 98).

Order 40, r 7 Interveners

(1)   In an action in rem any person not named in the summons who claims to be interested in the property against which the action is brought or in money paid into court in the action may, with the leave of the court, intervene in the action.

(2)   An application for the grant of leave under this rule shall be made ex parte by affidavit showing the interest of the applicant in the property against which the action is brought or in the money in court.

(3)   A person to whom leave is granted under this rule shall thereupon become a party to the action.

(4)   The court may order that a person to whom it grants leave to intervene in an action shall, within such period or periods as may be specified in the order, serve on any other party to the action such notice of his intervention and deliver such pleading as may be so specified.

(5)   If the interest claimed by the intervener is not cognisable by the court, any party may apply to the court for an order transferring the action to the High Court.

Commencement   1 September 1982.
Cross references   See RSC Order 75, r 17.

Order 40, r 8 Delivery of defence etc

Order 9, rules 2, 5 and 9, shall apply with the necessary modifications to an Admiralty action as they apply to a default action, and if the defendant fails to deliver a defence or counterclaim within the time prescribed by the said rule 2, the plaintiff may—

(a) except where the claim is in the nature of salvage or towage, proceed under Order 9, rule 6, as if the action were a default action, or

(b) request the proper officer to set the action down for hearing,

and where such a request is made, the proper officer shall fix a day for the hearing of the action and give notice thereof to both parties.

Commencement   1 September 1982.

Forms   Notice of hearing (N380).

Order 40, r 9 Particulars in collision actions

(1) This rule applies, unless the court otherwise orders, to any action to enforce a claim for damage, loss of life or personal injury arising out of a collision between ships.

(2) If the plaintiff's claim is stated not to exceed £500, the plaintiff in his particulars of claim and the defendant in his defence shall give the particulars mentioned in paragraph (4).

(3) In any other case the plaintiff's particulars of claim shall contain only a concise statement of the nature of his claim and the plaintiff shall, when filing his particulars of claim, and the defendant shall, within 14 days after service of the summons on him, file a document, to be called "a preliminary act", containing the particulars mentioned in paragraph (4).

(4) The particulars referred to in paragraphs (2) and (3) are the particulars which would be required to be stated in a preliminary act if the action were proceeding in the High Court and also—

(a) what act of negligence or what breach of any navigation rule, bye-law or regulation is alleged to have been committed by those in charge of the other ship, and

(b) in the case of a defendant, the name of any ship, other than the plaintiff's ship, which is alleged by the defendant to have caused the collision or damage or with reference to which those in charge of the defendant's ship had to act.

(5) Every preliminary act filed pursuant to paragraph (3) shall be sealed by the proper officer and filed in a closed envelope, and, unless the court otherwise orders, no envelope shall be opened until every other preliminary act required to be filed in the action has been filed or all the parties to the action consent in writing to the opening of the preliminary acts.

(6) On filing a preliminary act pursuant to paragraph (3) a defendant shall give notice to the plaintiff that he has done so.

(7) Subject to paragraphs (8) and (9), any action in which preliminary acts are required shall be tried on the preliminary acts without pleadings unless the court otherwise directs.

(8) Where in an action in which preliminary acts are required the defendant has a set-off or counterclaim, he shall, in addition to filing a preliminary act, file a defence in respect of the set-off or a counterclaim.

(9)   In relation to an action in which preliminary acts are required, rule 8 of this Order and Order 9, rules 5 and 9, shall have effect as if the references in them to a defence included references to a preliminary act.

Commencement   1 September 1982.
Cross references   See RSC Order 75, r 18(1).

Order 40, r 10 Examination of witness before trial

In an Admiralty action the power conferred by Order 20, rule 13, shall extend to the making of an order authorising the examination of a person on oath before the judge sitting in court as if for the trial of the action without the action having been fixed for hearing or called on for hearing.

Commencement   1 September 1982.

Order 40, r 11 Bail

(1)   The provisions of the RSC with respect to the giving of bail shall apply in relation to an action in rem in a county court as they apply in relation to an action in rem in the High Court.

(2)   Where the solicitor of a party to an action in rem fails to comply with a written undertaking given by him to any other party or his solicitor to give bail or pay money into court in lieu of bail, he shall be liable to committal.

Commencement   1 September 1982.
Cross references   See RSC Order 75, r 16.

Order 40, r 12 Release of property under arrest

(1)   Except where property arrested in pursuance of a warrant of arrest is sold under an order of the court, it shall only be released—
    (a)   on the written request of a party at whose instance the property was arrested, or
    (b)   if the court so orders or if all the other parties to the action consent, on the written request of a party interested in the property.

(2)   Before property is released under paragraph (1), the party requesting the release shall pay or give an undertaking to pay all the costs, charges and expenses incurred or to be incurred in connection with the arrest of the property, the care and custody of it while under arrest and its release.

Commencement   1 September 1982.
Cross references   See RSC Order 75, r 13.
Forms   Request for release of property under arrest (N381).
Release of property under arrest (N101).

Order 40, r 13 Sale of property after judgment in action in rem

(1)   Where a judgment or order has been obtained in an action in rem, the court may, on an application made by the judgment creditor in accordance with the provisions of this rule, order—
    (a)   if the property to which the action relates is under arrest, that the property be sold;

(b) if the property has not been arrested, that the property be taken and sold in execution.

(2) Where at the time when the judgment or order is obtained the owners of the property are known, then—

(a) except as provided in sub-paragraph (b), an application under paragraph (1) may be made ex parte but the court may, before making an order, direct that notice be given to the owners;

(b) if the property is a British-owned ship, the judgment creditor shall file a certified copy of the ship's register and, if the name of any person not before the court appears on the register as having an interest in the ship, he shall be given notice of any application under paragraph (1).

(3) Where at the time when the judgment or order is obtained the owners of the property are unknown, then—

(a) if the owners are subsequently ascertained and the judgment creditor files a list of their names and addresses accompanied, if the property is a British-owned ship, by a certified copy of the ship's register, an application may be made under paragraph (1) on notice to every owner and, in the case of a British-owned ship, to every person appearing in the ship's register as having an interest in the ship;

(b) if the owners cannot be ascertained, the court may, on an affidavit showing grounds, allow an application under paragraph (1) to be made on notice given by advertisement or otherwise to all the owners of, and all persons having an interest in, the property to which an application relates.

(4) Any notice required to be given to a person by or under paragraph (2) or (3)(a) shall be served on him in the manner prescribed by these rules for service of a default summons.

(5) Where an order is made under paragraph (1)(b), the proper officer shall, on a request in that behalf being filed by the judgment creditor, issue a warrant of execution.

(6) Where an order is made under paragraph (1) in an action in rem against a ship, any party who has obtained judgment against the ship or proceeds of sale may apply to the judge to determine the order of priority of the claims against the proceeds of sale.

(7) Subject to paragraph (8), the proceeds of sale shall not be paid out of court except in pursuance of an order of the judge.

(8) Where the order of priority of claims against the proceeds has been determined and the parties are agreed as to the persons to whom the proceeds shall be paid and the amount to be paid to each, the [district judge] may make an order for payment out in accordance with the agreement.

Commencement 1 September 1982.
Cross references See RSC Order 75, r 23.
Forms Order for sale after judgment (N102).
Order for notice by advertisement (N103).
Notice by advertisement or otherwise (N382).
Notice of judgment or order in rem (N104).
Request for warrant of execution in rem (N383).
Warrant of execution in rem (N105).

Order 40, r 14 Appraisement

Where a ship is ordered to be sold or is seized under a warrant of execution, the [district judge] shall, before selling it, cause the property to be valued by an appraiser and the property shall not be sold for less than the appraised value except by leave of the court.

Commencement 1 September 1982.
Cross references See RSC Order 75, r 23.
Forms Certificate of appraisement (N385).

Order 40, r 15 Completion of sale

(1)   On the completion of the sale of any property in an action in rem, the [district judge] shall—
    (a) deliver up the property to the purchaser and, if required to do so, execute a bill of sale to him at his expense;
    (b) file an account of the sale and the fees thereon, together with the certificate of appraisement signed by the appraiser.

(2)   Any person interested in the proceeds of sale may inspect the account filed under paragraph (1)(b) and, if dissatisfied with any item in the account, may apply to the judge for a review of the account and thereupon Order 38, rule 24, shall apply with the necessary modifications as if the account had been taxed by the [district judge].

Commencement 1 September 1982.

Order 40, r 16 Costs of order for sale

In an action in rem the costs incurred by the plaintiff in obtaining an order for the sale of property and in the execution of the order shall be allowed and recoverable against the property.

Commencement 1 September 1982.

Order 40, r 17 Transfer of proceedings for sale to High Court

(1)   Where, pursuant to [section 28(11)] of the Act, the owner of property liable to be sold in Admiralty proceedings desires that the sale should be conducted in the High Court instead of in the county court, he may, on giving security in the sum of £100, apply to the judge ex parte in writing for an order for the transfer of the proceedings for sale to the High Court.

(2)   Where an order under paragraph (1) relates to a ship which is in the custody of the court, the ship shall be retained by the [district judge] until the Admiralty marshal takes possession of it by order of the High Court.

Commencement 1 September 1982.
Amendments Para (1): words "section 28(11)" substituted by SI 1984/878, r 12, Schedule.
Forms Order for transfer of sale to High Court (N106).

Order 40, r 18 Retention of money where more than one action

Where more actions than one have been commenced against any property and the property has been sold, the proceeds of sale shall, unless the judge otherwise orders, be retained in court to abide the decision of the court in each action.

Commencement 1 September 1982.

Order 40, r 19 Reference to [district judge]

(1)   Where the defendant to a claim or counterclaim in an Admiralty action admits liability before the trial, the parties may agree that the amount to be recovered shall be assessed by the [district judge] with or without assessors.

(2)   On the hearing by the judge of an Admiralty action the judge may, instead of giving judgment for a particular amount, give judgment settling the rights of the parties and order a reference to the [district judge], with or without assessors, as to the amount to be recovered.

(3)   Where the parties are agreed as mentioned in paragraph (1) or an order has been made under paragraph (2), the [district judge] shall proceed as if the assessment of the amount to be recovered were a question referred to him for inquiry and report, and Order 19, rule 9, shall apply with the modification that, unless any party, within 7 days after service on him of notice of the filing of the report, gives notice of an application to vary the report and of the grounds of the application, the report shall become binding on all the parties and judgment shall be entered accordingly.

(4)   Nothing in this rule shall apply to a claim in the nature of salvage or prejudice the power of the [district judge] to hear and determine an action or matter under Order 21, rule 5.

Commencement   1 September 1982.
Forms   Interlocutory judgment (N107).
Final judgment in personam (N108).
Final judgment in rem (N109).
District judge's report (N386).
Notice of filing same (N387).

ORDER 41
PROBATE ACTIONS

Order 41, r 1 Interpretation

In this Order "probate action" means an action in respect of any contentious matter arising in connection with an application through the principal registry of the Family Division [or a district probate registry] for the grant or revocation of probate or administration.

Commencement   1 September 1982.
Amendments   Words "or a district probate registry" inserted by SI 1986/1189, r 3.
Cross references   See RSC Order 76, r 1.

Order 41, r 2 Commencement of probate action

[On issuing a summons in a probate action the proper officer of the county court shall send to the principal registry a notice requesting all documents in the principal registry or any district probate registry relating to the matter to be sent to him.]

Commencement   1 October 1986.
Amendments   This rule was substituted by SI 1986/1189, r 4.
Cross references   See RSC Order 76, r 2.
Forms   Notice to probate registry to produce documents (N388).

Order 41, r 3 Judgment to be sent to every party

A copy of any judgment given in a probate action brought in or transferred to a county court under [section 32 or 40] of the Act shall be sent by the proper officer to every party to the proceedings.

Commencement   1 September 1982.
Amendments   Words "section 32 or 40" substituted by SI 1984/878, r 12, Schedule.
Forms   Judgment in probate action (N389).

Order 41, r 4 Application of RSC

Except as otherwise provided by these rules, the provisions of the RSC relating to contentious probate proceedings shall, so far as appropriate, apply to probate actions in the county court as they apply to probate actions in the High Court.

Commencement   1 September 1982.
Cross references   See RSC Order 76, rr 3–5, 8, 9, 12.

ORDER 42
PROCEEDINGS BY AND AGAINST THE CROWN

Order 42, r 1 Application and interpretation

(1)   These rules apply to any proceedings, so far as they are civil proceedings to which the Crown is a party, subject to the following rules of this Order.

(2)   Except where the context otherwise requires, references in these rules to an action or claim for the recovery of land or other property shall be construed as including references to proceedings against the Crown for an order declaring that the plaintiff is entitled as against the Crown to the land or property or to the possession thereof.

(3) ...

(4)   In this Order—
   "the Act of 1947" means the Crown Proceedings Act 1947;
   "civil proceedings by the Crown" and "civil proceedings against the Crown" and "civil proceedings by or against the Crown" have the same respective meanings as in Part II of the Act of 1947 and do not include any of the proceedings specified in section 23(3) of that Act;
   "civil proceedings to which the Crown is a party" has the same meaning as it has for the purposes of Part IV of the Act of 1947 by virtue of section 38(4) of that Act.

Commencement   1 September 1982.
Amendments   Para (3): revoked by SI 1993/2175, r 16.
Cross references   See RSC Order 77, r 1.

Order 42, r 2 Venue in proceedings against the Crown

(1)   In relation to an action against the Crown Order 4, rule 2, shall have effect as if paragraph (1)(a) thereof were omitted and in relation to an originating application to which the Crown is a respondent Order 4, rule 8, shall have effect as if paragraph (a)(i) thereof were omitted.

(2)   For the purposes of Order 40, rule 2, the Crown shall be deemed to reside in the district of every court.

(3)   If there is any reasonable doubt as to the court in which any proceedings should be commenced pursuant to Order 4 as modified by this rule, they may be commenced in the court for the district in which the plaintiff or one of the plaintiffs resides or carries on business.

Commencement   1 September 1982.

Order 42, r 3 Venue in proceedings for recovery of tax

In the case of proceedings for the recovery of income tax, the cause of action shall, for the purposes of Order 4, rule 2(1)(b), be deemed to have arisen in part at the office of any collector of taxes by whom demand of the sum claimed has been made from the defendant.

Commencement   1 September 1982.

Order 42, r 4 Particulars of claim in action against the Crown

The particulars of claim required by Order 6, rule 1, to be filed at the commencement of an action shall, in the case of civil proceedings against the Crown, include a statement of the circumstances in which the Crown's liability is said to have arisen and as to the government department and officers of the Crown concerned.

Commencement 1 September 1982.
Cross references See RSC Order 77, r 3(1).

Order 42, r 5 Subsequent procedure in default action

(1)   If in a default action against the Crown the defendant considers that the particulars of claim do not contain a sufficient statement as required by rule 4, he may, before the time for delivering a defence has expired, file two copies of a demand for further information as specified in the demand and thereupon the proper officer shall serve one copy on the plaintiff.

(2)   Where the defendant files a demand under paragraph (1), the time for delivering a defence shall not expire until 4 days after the defendant has given notice to the proper officer and the plaintiff that the defendant is satisfied with the information supplied in compliance with the demand or 4 days after the court has, on the application of the plaintiff of which not less than 7 days' notice has been given to the defendant, decided that no further information as to the matters referred to in rule 4 is reasonably required.

(3)   Except with the leave of the court, no judgment shall be entered under Order 9, rule 6(1)(a), in a default action against the Crown.

(4)   An application for leave under paragraph (3) shall be made on not less than 7 days' notice to the defendant.

(5)   No application against the Crown shall be made under Order 9, rule 14.

Commencement 1 September 1982.
Cross references See RSC Order 77, rr 3(2), (3), 7(1), 9(1).

Order 42, r 6 Subsequent procedure in fixed date action

(1)   In the case of a fixed date action against the Crown, Order 3, rule 3(2), shall not apply but on the filing of the documents required by Order 3, rule 3(1), the proper officer shall—
   (a)   enter a plaint in the records of the court and deliver to the plaintiff a plaint note omitting any reference to a return day;
   (b)   serve on the defendant a copy of the particulars of claim and a notice of the entry of the plaint and of the effect of paragraphs (3) and (5).

(2)   Upon the service of the notice mentioned in paragraph (1)(b) all further proceedings in the action shall be stayed except as provided in this rule.

(3)   If the defendant considers that the particulars of claim do not contain a sufficient statement as required by rule 4, he may, within 21 days after service on him of the notice mentioned in paragraph (1)(b), file in the court office two copies of a demand for further information as specified in the demand and thereupon the proper officer shall serve one copy on the plaintiff.

(4)   If within the said period the defendant does not file two copies of such a

demand, then, subject to paragraph (5), the stay of proceedings provided for by paragraph (2) shall cease to have effect at the end of that period.

(5)   If within the said period the defendant files a statement that no such demand will be made, the stay of proceedings provided for by paragraph (2) shall cease to have effect forthwith.

(6)   If within the said period the defendant files two copies of such a demand, the stay of proceedings provided for by paragraph (2) shall cease to have effect when the defendant gives notice to the proper officer and the plaintiff that the defendant is satisfied with the information supplied in compliance with the demand or when the court decides, on the application of the plaintiff of which not less than 7 days' notice has been given to the defendant, that no further information as to the matters referred to in rule 4 is reasonably required.

(7)   When the stay of proceedings provided for by paragraph (2) ceases to have effect, the proper officer shall[, except in a case to which Order 17, rule 11 applies,] fix a return day and give notice thereof to the plaintiff and shall proceed in accordance with Order 3, rule 3(2)(b), (c) (omitting the words from the beginning to "and also") and (d)(ii).

Commencement 1 September 1982.
Amendments Para (7): words " , except in a case to which Order 17, rule 11 applies," inserted by SI 1990/1764, r 16.

Order 42, r 7 Service on the Crown

(1)   Order 8 and any other provision of these rules relating to service of process out of England and Wales shall apply in relation to civil proceedings by the Crown but shall not apply in relation to civil proceedings against the Crown.

(2)   Personal service of any document which is to be served on the Crown for the purpose of or in connection with civil proceedings by or against the Crown shall not be requisite.

(3)   Any such document may be served on the Crown—
   (a)   by leaving the document at the office of the person to be served in accordance with section 18 of the Act of 1947, or any agent whom he has nominated for the purpose, but in either case with a member of the staff of that person or agent, or
   (b)   by posting it in a prepaid envelope addressed to the person to be served in accordance with the said section 18 or to any such agent as aforesaid.

Commencement 1 September 1982.
Definitions Act of 1947: Crown Proceedings Act 1947.
Cross references See RSC Order 77, r 4.

Order 42, r 8 Summary judgment in Admiralty actions etc

(1)   In an Admiralty action no judgment shall be entered against the Crown under Order 40, rule 8, except with the leave of the court to be obtained on application of which not less than 7 days' notice has been given to the Crown.

(2)   No order shall be made against the Crown by the court of its own motion under Order 13, rule 2(2), or Order 17, rule 4.

Commencement 1 September 1982.

Order 42, r 9 Counterclaim in proceedings by or against the Crown

(1)   In proceedings by the Crown for the recovery of taxes, duties or penalties the defendant shall not be entitled to avail himself of any set-off or counterclaim and accordingly the form of summons to be served on the defendant and the form of admission, defence or counterclaim to be annexed to the summons shall omit any reference to a counterclaim.

(2)   In proceedings of any other nature by the Crown the defendant shall not be entitled to avail himself of any set-off or counterclaim arising out of a right or claim to repayment in respect of any taxes, duties or penalties.

(3)   In any proceedings by the Crown the defendant shall not be entitled, and in any proceedings against the Crown the Crown shall not be entitled, without the leave of the court to be obtained on application of which not less than 7 days' notice has been given to the plaintiff, to make any counterclaim or plead any set-off if—
  (a)   the Crown sues or is sued in the name of a Government department and the subject-matter of the set-off or counterclaim does not relate to that department; or
  (b)   the Crown sues or is sued in the name of the Attorney-General.

Commencement   1 September 1982.
Cross references   See RSC Order 77, r 6.

Order 42, r 10 Adjustment of liability under judgment for taxes

Where the Crown has obtained a judgment for taxes but subsequently the tax liability is reduced, whether by reason of an appeal against an assessment or otherwise, and the Crown has given notice of the reduction to the court and to the debtor, the sum remaining unsatisfied under the judgment shall be reduced accordingly, but the amount of the reduction shall not rank as a payment under the judgment.

Commencement   1 September 1982.

Order 42, r 11 Third party notice against the Crown

(1)   Notwithstanding anything in Order 12, rule 1(1), a third party notice (including a notice issuable by virtue of Order 12, rule 6) for service on the Crown shall not be issued without the leave of the court to be obtained on application of which 7 days' notice has been given to the Crown and to the plaintiff.

(2)   Leave shall not be granted under paragraph (1) unless the court is satisfied that the Crown is in possession of all such information as it reasonably requires as to the circumstances in which it is alleged that the liability of the Crown has arisen and as to the departments and officers of the Crown concerned.

Commencement   1 September 1982.
Cross references   See RSC Order 77, r 10.

Order 42, r 12 Discovery against the Crown

(1)   In any civil proceedings to which the Crown is a party any order of the court made under the powers conferred by section 28(1) of the Act of 1947 shall be construed as not requiring disclosure of the existence of any document the existence

of which would, in the opinion of a Minister of the Crown, be injurious to the public interest.

(2) Where in any such proceedings an order of the court directs that a list of documents made in answer to an order for discovery against the Crown shall be verified by affidavit, the affidavit shall be made by such officer of the Crown as the court may direct.

Commencement 1 September 1982.
Definitions Act of 1947: Crown Proceedings Act 1947.
Cross references See RSC Order 77, r 12.

Order 42, r 13 Execution and satisfaction of orders against Crown

(1) Nothing in Orders 25 to 32 shall apply in respect of any order against the Crown.

(2) A certificate issued under section 25(1) of the Act of 1947 shall be in the form used under Order 22, rule 8, with such variations as the circumstances of the case may require.

Commencement 1 September 1982.
Definitions Act of 1947: Crown Proceedings Act 1947.
Cross references See RSC Order 77, r 15.

Order 42, r 14 Attachment of debts, etc

(1) No order for the attachment of a debt under Order 30 or for the appointment of a receiver under Order 32 shall be made or have effect in respect of any money due or accruing due, or alleged to be due or accruing due, from the Crown.

(2) Where such an order could have been obtained in a county court if the money had been due or accruing due from a subject, an application may be made to that county court in accordance with Order 13, rule 1, for an order under section 27 of the Act of 1947 restraining the person to whom the money is payable by t⌐ ⌐own from receiving the money and directing payment to the applicant or to the receiver.

(3) The application shall be supported by an affidavit setting out the facts giving rise to it and in particular identifying the particular debt from the Crown in respect of which it is made.

(4) Notice of the application together with a copy of the affidavit shall be served on the Crown and, unless the court otherwise directs, on the person to be restrained or his solicitor at least 7 days before the day fixed for the hearing.

(5) [Order 30, rules 7 to 9], shall apply, with the necessary modifications, in relation to an application under the said [section 27] as they apply in relation to an application for an order under Order 30, rule 1, except that the court shall not have power to issue execution against the Crown.

Commencement 1 September 1982.
Amendments Para (5): words "Order 30, rules 7 to 9" substituted by SI 1989/1838, r 51; words "section 27" substituted by SI 1982/1140, r 2.
Definitions Act of 1947: Crown Proceedings Act 1947.
Cross references See RSC Order 77, r 16.
Forms Affidavit supporting payment by Crown of money to judgment creditor (N391).
Notice of application for payment by Crown (N392).

ORDER 43
[THE LANDLORD AND TENANT ACTS 1927, 1954, 1985 AND 1987]

Amendments   Heading substituted by SI 1988/278, r 13.

Order 43, r 1 Interpretation

[(1)   In this Order "the Act of 1927" means the Landlord and Tenant Act 1927, "the Act of 1954" means the Landlord and Tenant Act 1954, "the Act of 1985" means the Landlord and Tenant Act 1985 and "the Act of 1987" means the Landlord and Tenant Act 1987.]

(2)   In relation to any proceedings under the Act of 1954 any reference in this Order to a landlord shall, if the interest of the landlord in question is subject to a mortgage and the mortgagee is in possession or a receiver appointed by the mortgagee or by the court is in receipt of the rents and profits, be construed as a reference to the mortgagee.

Commencement   18 April 1988 (para (1)); 1 September 1982 (remainder).
Amendments   Para (1): substituted by SI 1988/278, r 14.
Cross references   See RSC Order 97, r 1.

Order 43, r 2 Commencement of proceedings and answer

(1)   Except as provided in rule 5(2), proceedings in a county court under the Act of 1927 [or of 1954, or of 1985 or of 1987] shall be commenced by originating application, and the respondent shall file an answer.

(2)   Unless the court otherwise directs, the return day shall be a day fixed for the pre-trial review of the proceedings.

Commencement   1 September 1982.
Amendments   Para (1): words "or of 1954, or of 1985 or of 1987" substituted by SI 1988/278, r 15.
Definitions   Act of 1927: Landlord and Tenant Act 1927.
Act of 1954: Landlord and Tenant Act 1954.
Act of 1985: Landlord and Tenant Act 1985.
Act of 1987: Landlord and Tenant Act 1987.
Cross references   See RSC Order 97, r 3.
Forms   Originating application (N394–6).
Notice to respondent (N8(2)).

Order 43, r 3 Claim for compensation in respect of improvement

(1)   A claim under section 1 of the Act of 1927 for compensation in respect of any improvement, or a claim by a mesne landlord under section 8(1) of that Act, shall be in writing, signed by the claimant, his solicitor or agent, and shall contain—
   (a)   a statement of the name and address of the claimant and of the landlord against whom the claim is made;
   (b)   a description of the holding in respect of which the claim arises and of the trade or business carried on there;
   (c)   a concise statement of the nature of the claim;
   (d)   particulars of the improvement including the date when it was completed and the cost thereof, and
   (e)   a statement of the amount claimed.

(2) Where any document relating to any proposed improvement, or to any claim, is sent to or served on a mesne landlord in pursuance of Part I of the Act of 1927, he shall forthwith serve on his immediate landlord a copy of the document, together with a notice in writing stating the date when the document was received by the mesne landlord, and if the immediate landlord is himself a mesne landlord, he shall, forthwith on receipt of the documents aforesaid, serve on his immediate landlord a similar copy and notice, and so on from landlord to landlord.

(3) Any document required to be served under paragraph (2) shall be served in the manner prescribed by section 23 of the Act of 1927.

Commencement   1 September 1982.
Definitions   Act of 1927: Landlord and Tenant Act 1927.
Cross references   See RSC Order 97, r 4.

Order 43, r 4 Proceedings under Part I of the Act of 1927

(1) Subject to paragraph (2), the originating application by which proceedings under Part I of the Act of 1927 are commenced shall state—
- (a) the nature of the claim or application or matter to be determined,
- (b) the holding in respect of which the claim or application is made, its rateable value and the trade or business carried on there,
- (c) particulars of the improvement or proposed improvement to which the claim or application relates, and
- (d) if the claim is for payment of compensation, the amount claimed.

(2) In any case to which rule 3(1) relates the particulars required by paragraph (1) may, so far as they are contained in a claim made in accordance with that rule, be given by appending a copy of the claim to the originating application.

(3) The applicant's immediate landlord shall be made respondent to the application.

(4) Any certificate of the court under section 3 of the Act of 1927 that an improvement is a proper improvement or has been duly executed shall be embodied in an order.

Commencement   1 September 1982.
Definitions   Act of 1927: Landlord and Tenant Act 1927.
Cross references   See RSC Order 97, r 5.
Forms   Order re certificate of improvement (N398).
Final order (N399).

Order 43, r 5 Proceedings under Part I of the Act of 1954

(1) A respondent to an application under section 7 of the Act of 1954 who resists any of the applicant's proposals as to the terms of a statutory tenancy shall state in his answer the terms which he proposes in their place.

(2) An application under section 13 of the Act of 1954 for the recovery of possession shall be brought by action and the particulars shall state, in addition to the matters set out in Order 6, rule 3,—
- (a) the date and term of the lease under which the tenant holds or has held the property;
- (b) the date of service upon the tenant of the landlord's notice to resume possession and the date of termination specified in the notice;
- (c) where the tenant has notified the landlord that he is not willing to give up possession, the date of the notification; and

(d)   where the plaintiff is not both the freeholder of the property comprised in the tenancy and the immediate landlord of the defendant, details of the interest constituting him the landlord for the purpose of proceedings under Part I of the Act of 1954.

(3)   Where an order has been made under paragraph 1 of the Second Schedule to the Act of 1954 for the reduction of rent of any premises on the ground of failure by the landlord to do initial repairs, and it is subsequently agreed between the landlord and the tenant that the repairs to which the order relates have been carried out, the landlord shall file a copy of the agreement, and a note thereof shall be entered in the records of the court.

(4)   Where the court makes an order for the recovery of possession of property in proceedings to which paragraph 9 of the Fifth Schedule to the Act of 1954 applies, the plaintiff shall, if the occupying tenant is not a party to the proceedings, forthwith notify him of the terms of the order and inform him of his rights to obtain relief under sub-paragraph (2) of that paragraph.

(5)   If a copy of a notice under section 16(2) of the Act of 1954 or paragraph 9(2) or 10(2) of the Fifth Schedule to that Act is lodged in court, a note of the lodgment shall be entered in the records of the court.

Commencement   1 September 1982.
Definitions   Act of 1954: Landlord and Tenant Act 1954.

Order 43, r 6 Application for new tenancy under s 24 of the Act of 1954

(1)   An application under section 24 of the Act of 1954 for a new tenancy shall state—
   (a)   the premises to which the application relates, their rateable value and the business carried on there,
   (b)   particulars of the applicant's current tenancy of the premises and of every notice or request given or made in respect of that tenancy under section 25 or 26 of that Act,
   (c)   the applicant's proposals as to the terms of the new tenancy applied for, including, in particular, terms as to the duration thereof and as to the rent payable thereunder,
   (d)   the name and address of any person other than the respondent who, to the knowledge of the applicant, has an interest in reversion in the premises expectant (whether immediately or in not more than 14 years) on the termination of the applicant's current tenancy; and
   (e)   the name and address of any person having an interest in the premises other than a freehold interest or tenancy who, to the knowledge of the applicant, is likely to be affected by the grant of a new tenancy.

(2)   The person who, in relation to the applicant's current tenancy, is the landlord as defined by section 44 of the Act of 1954 shall be made respondent to the application.

[(3)   The provisions of Order 7, rule 20(1) and (2) shall apply to an originating application under this rule with the substitution of references to two months for the references therein to 6 months and to 4 months.]

Commencement   4 June 1990 (para (3)); 1 September 1982 (remainder).
Amendments   Para (3): substituted by SI 1989/2426, r 10.
Definitions   Act of 1954: Landlord and Tenant Act 1954.
Cross references   See RSC Order 97, r 6.
Forms   Originating application (new tenancy) (N397).

Order 43, r 7 Answer to application for new tenancy under s 24 of Act of 1954

Every answer by a respondent to an application to which rule 6 relates shall state—
- (a) whether or not the respondent opposes the grant of a new tenancy and, if so, on what grounds;
- (b) whether or not, if a new tenancy is granted, the respondent objects to any of the terms proposed by the applicant and, if so, the terms to which he objects and the terms which he proposes in so far as they differ from those proposed by the applicant;
- (c) whether the respondent is a tenant under a lease having less than 14 years unexpired at the date of the termination of the applicant's current tenancy and, if he is, the name and address of any person who, to the knowledge of the respondent, has an interest in reversion in the premises expectant (whether immediately or in not more than 14 years from the said date) on the termination of the respondent's tenancy;
- (d) the name and address of any person having an interest in the premises other than a freehold interest or tenancy who is likely to be affected by the grant of a new tenancy, and
- (e) if the applicant's current tenancy is one to which section 32(2) of the Act of 1954 applies, whether the respondent requires that any new tenancy ordered to be granted shall be a tenancy of the whole of the property comprised in the applicant's current tenancy.

Commencement   1 September 1982.
Definitions   Act of 1954: Landlord and Tenant Act 1954.
Cross references   See RSC Order 97, r 7(2).
Forms   Answer (new tenancy) (N400).

Order 43, r 8 Order dismissing application under section 24 which is successfully opposed

Where the court hearing an application under section 24 of the Act of 1954 is precluded by section 31 of that Act from ordering the grant of a new tenancy by reason of any of the grounds specified in section 30(1) of that Act, the order dismissing the application shall state all the grounds by reason of which the court is so precluded.

Commencement   1 September 1982.
Definitions   Act of 1954: Landlord and Tenant Act 1954.
Cross references   See RSC Order 97, r 9.
Forms   Order (new tenancy) (N401).

Order 43, r 9 Other applications under Part II of Act of 1954

An application for an order under section 31(2)(b) of the Act of 1954 and, unless made at the hearing of the application under section 24, an application for a certificate under section 37(4) of that Act may be made ex parte to the [district judge].

Commencement   1 September 1982.
Definitions   Act of 1954: Landlord and Tenant Act 1954.
Cross references   See RSC Order 97, r 10(1).
Forms   Application for certificate of ground for refusal (N403).
Certificate of ground for refusal (N404).

Order 43, r 10 Service of order in proceedings under Part II of Act of 1954

A copy of any order made on an application to which rule 6 or 9 relates shall be sent by the proper officer to every party to the proceedings.

Commencement 1 September 1982.
Definitions Act of 1954: Landlord and Tenant Act 1954.
Forms Order substituting new date (N402).

Order 43, r 11 Proof of determination of rateable value

Where pursuant to section 37(5) of the Act of 1954 any dispute as to the rateable value of any premises has been referred to the Commissioners of Inland Revenue for decision by a valuation officer, whether for the purpose of section 37(2) or of section 63 of that Act, any document purporting to be a notification by the valuation officer of his decision shall be admissible in any proceedings in a county court as evidence of the matters contained therein.

Commencement 1 September 1982.
Definitions Act of 1954: Landlord and Tenant Act 1954.
Cross references See RSC Order 97, r 13.

Order 43, r 12 Transfer of jurisdiction to High Court

Where under section 63(3) of the Act of 1954 the parties to any proceedings agree in writing that the jurisdiction of the court under Part I of the Act of 1927 or Part II of the Act of 1954 with respect to those proceedings shall be transferred to the High Court, either party may file the agreement and thereupon the provisions of Order 16, rule 11, shall apply, with such modifications as may be necessary, as if an order had been made for the transfer of the proceedings to the High Court.

Commencement 1 September 1982.
Definitions Act of 1954: Landlord and Tenant Act 1954.
Act of 1927: Landlord and Tenant Act 1927.
Cross references See RSC Order 97, r 11.

Order 43, r 13 Provisions as to assessors

(1)   Where, in any proceedings under Part I of the Act of 1927 or Part I or II of the Act of 1954, an assessor is summoned by the judge under [section 63(1) of the County Courts Act 1984], as extended by section 63 of the Act of 1954, then, whether or not the summons was issued pursuant to an application by one of the parties, the provisions of Order 13, rule 11(4) and (8), shall not apply.

(2)   In relation to any such proceedings, Order 13, rule 11(2), shall have effect where the judge decides to exercise his power to appoint an assessor without any application being made in that behalf by a party to the proceedings as it has effect where the judge grants such an application.

(3)   Any report made by the assessor pursuant to paragraph (a) of section 63(6) of the Act of 1954 shall be filed by the assessor, together with a copy for each party to the proceedings, and thereupon the proper officer shall send a copy to each party and shall, if the further consideration of the proceedings has not been adjourned to a day named, fix a day for further consideration and give notice thereof to all parties.

Commencement 1 September 1982.
Amendments Para (1): words "section 63(1) of the County Courts Act 1984" substituted by SI 1984/878, r 12, Schedule.
Definitions Act of 1927: Landlord and Tenant Act 1927.
Act of 1954: Landlord and Tenant Act 1954.

Order 43, r 14 Joinder of and notice to persons affected

(1) Any person affected by any proceedings on an originating application under Part I of the Act of 1927 or Part I or II of the Act of 1954 [or the Act of 1987] may apply to the court to be made a party to the proceedings and the court may give such directions on the application as appear to be necessary.

(2) An application under paragraph (1) may be made ex parte in the first instance but the court may require notice thereof to be given to the parties to the proceedings before making any order.

(3) The foregoing provisions are without prejudice to the power of the court, either with or without an application by any party, to order notice of the proceedings to be given to any person or any person to be made a party to the proceedings but nothing in this rule shall be construed as requiring the court to make any such order and, if it appears that any person though he is affected by the proceedings is not sufficiently affected for it to be necessary for him to be made a party or given notice of the proceedings, the court may refuse to make him a party or, as the case may be, to require him to be given notice of the proceedings.

Commencement 1 September 1982.
Amendments Para (1): words "or the Act of 1987" inserted by SI 1988/278, r 16.
Definitions Act of 1927: Landlord and Tenant Act 1927.
Act of 1954: Landlord and Tenant Act 1954.
Act of 1987: Landlord and Tenant Act 1987.
Cross references See RSC Order 97, r 8.
Forms Notice of proceedings (N405).

Order 43, r 15 [District judge's] jurisdiction

(1) If on the day fixed for the hearing of an application under section 7 or section 24 of the Act of 1954 the [district judge] is satisfied that—
    (a) the parties to the application have agreed, in the case of an application under section 7, on the matters specified in subsection (2) of that section, or, in the case of an application under section 24, on the subject, period and terms of the new tenancy;
    (b) the owner of any reversionary interest in the property consents thereto, and
    (c) there are no other persons with interests in the property who are likely to be affected,

the [district judge] shall have power to make an order giving effect to the agreement.

(2) An application under section 38(4) of the Act of 1954 for the authorisation of an agreement may be heard and determined by the [district judge] and may be dealt with in chambers.

Commencement 1 September 1982.
Definitions Act of 1954: Landlord and Tenant Act 1954.
Cross references See RSC Order 97, r 6A.
Forms Order authorising agreement excluding Act (N404(1)).

[Order 43, r 16 Application under section 12(2) of the Act of 1985

An application under section 12(2) of the Act of 1985 for an order authorising the inclusion in a lease of provisions excluding or modifying the provisions of section 11 of that Act may be heard and determined by the [district judge] and may, if the court thinks fit, be dealt with in chambers.]

Commencement   18 April 1988.
Amendments   This rule was added by SI 1988/278, r 17.
Definitions   Act of 1985: Landlord and Tenant Act 1985.

[Order 43, r 17 Application under section 19 of the Act of 1987

A copy of the notice served under section 19(2)(a) of the Act of 1987 shall be appended to the originating application under section 19(1) thereof, and an additional copy of the notice shall be filed.]

Commencement   18 April 1988.
Amendments   This rule was added by SI 1988/278, r 18.
Definitions   Act of 1987: Landlord and Tenant Act 1987.
Cross references   See RSC Order 97, r 14.

[Order 43, r 18 Application under section 24 of the Act of 1987

(1)   An application for an order under section 24 of the Act of 1987 shall state—
    (a)   the premises to which the application relates,
    (b)   the name and address of the applicant and of the landlord of the premises, or, where the landlord cannot be found or his identity ascertained, the steps taken to find him or ascertain his identity,
    (c)   the name and address of every person known to the applicant who is likely to be affected by the application, including, but not limited to, the other tenants of flats contained in the premises, any mortgagee or superior landlord of the landlord, and any tenants' association,
    (d)   the name, address and qualifications of the person it is desired to be appointed manager of the premises,
    (e)   the functions which it is desired that the manager should carry out, and
    (f)   the grounds of the application,

and a copy of the notice served on the landlord under section 22 of the Act of 1987 shall be appended to the originating application, unless the requirement to serve such a notice has been dispensed with, and an additional copy of the notice shall be filed.

(2)   The respondent to an application for an order under section 24 of the Act of 1987 shall be the landlord of the premises.

(3)   A copy of the application shall be served on—
    (a)   each of the persons named by the applicant under paragraph (1)(c), together with a notice stating that he may apply under rule 14 to be made a party to the proceedings, and
    (b)   the person named under paragraph (1)(d).

(4)   Order 32, rules 2 and 3 shall apply to proceedings in which an application is made for an order under section 24 of the Act of 1987 as they apply to proceedings in which an application is made for the appointment of a receiver, and as if for the references in those rules to a receiver there were references to a manager under the Act of 1987.]

Commencement   18 April 1988.
Amendments   This rule was added by SI 1988/278, r 18.
Definitions   Act of 1987: Landlord and Tenant Act 1987.
Cross references   See RSC Order 97, r 15.

[Order 43, r 19 Application for acquisition order under section 29 of the Act of 1987

(1)   An application for an acquisition order under section 29 of the Act of 1987 shall—

   (a)   identify the premises to which the application relates and give such details of them as are necessary to show that section 25 of the Act of 1987 applies thereto,

   (b)   give such details of the applicants as are necessary to show that they constitute the requisite majority of qualifying tenants,

   (c)   state the name and address of the applicants and of the landlord of the premises, or, where the landlord cannot be found or his identity ascertained, the steps taken to find him or ascertain his identity,

   (d)   state the name and address of the person nominated by the applicants for the purposes of Part III of the Act of 1987,

   (e)   state the name and address of every person known to the applicants who is likely to be affected by the application, but not limited to, the other tenants of flats contained in the premises (whether or not they could have made an application), any mortgagee or superior landlord of the landlord, and any tenants' association, and

   (f)   state the grounds of the application,

and a copy of the notice served on the landlord under section 27 of the Act of 1987 shall be appended to the originating application unless the requirement to serve such a notice has been dispensed with, and an additional copy of the notice shall be filed.

(2)   The respondents to an application for an acquisition order under section 29 of the Act of 1987 shall be the landlord of the premises and the nominated person, where he is not an applicant.

(3)   A copy of the application shall be served on each of the persons named by the applicant under paragraph (1)(e), together with a notice stating that he may apply under rule 14 to be made a party to the proceedings.

(4)   Where the nominated person pays money into court in accordance with an order under section 33(1) of the Act of 1987, he shall file a copy of the certificate of the surveyor selected under section 33(2)(a) thereof.]

Commencement   18 April 1988.
Amendments   This rule was added by SI 1988/278, r 18.
Definitions   Act of 1987: Landlord and Tenant Act 1987.
Cross references   See RSC Order 97, r 16.

[Order 43, r 20 Application for order under section 38 or section 40 of the Act of 1987

(1)   An application for an order under section 38 or section 40 of the Act of 1987 shall state—

(a) the name and address of the applicant and of the other current parties to the lease or leases to which the application relates,

(b) the date of the lease or leases, the premises demised thereby, the relevant terms thereof and the variation sought,

(c) the name and address of every person who the applicant knows or has reason to believe is likely to be affected by the variation, including but not limited to, the other tenants of flats contained in the premises of which the demised premises form a part, any previous parties to the lease, any mortgagee or superior landlord of the landlord, any mortgagee of the applicant, and any tenants' association, and

(d) the grounds of the application.

(2) The other current parties to the lease or leases shall be made respondents to the application.

(3) A copy of the application shall be served by the applicant on each of the persons named by the applicant under paragraph (1)(c) and by the respondent on any other person who he knows or has reason to believe is likely to be affected by the variation, together, in each case, with a notice stating that the person may apply under rule 14 to be made a party to the proceedings.

(4) Any application under section 36 of the Act of 1987 shall be contained in the respondent's answer, and paragraphs (1) to (3) shall apply to such an application as if the respondent were an applicant.]

Commencement 18 April 1988.
Amendments This rule was added by SI 1988/278, r 18.
Definitions Act of 1987: Landlord and Tenant Act 1987.
Cross references See RSC Order 97, r 17.

[Order 43, r 21 Service of documents in proceedings under the Act of 1987

(1) Where an originating application or answer is to be served in proceedings under the Act of 1987 it shall be served by the applicant or, as the case may be, by the respondent.

(2) Where a notice is to be served in or before proceedings under the Act of 1987, it shall be served in accordance with section 54 and, in the case of service on a landlord, it shall be served at the address furnished under section 48(1).]

Commencement 18 April 1988.
Amendments This rule was added by SI 1988/278, r 18.
Definitions Act of 1987: Landlord and Tenant Act 1987.
Cross references See RSC Order 97, r 18.

[Order 43, r 22 Tenants' associations

In rules 18, 19 and 20 a reference to a tenants' association is a reference to a recognised tenants' association within the meaning of section 29 of the Act of 1985 which represents tenants of the flats of which the demised premises form a part.]

Commencement 18 April 1988.
Amendments This rule was added by SI 1988/278, r 18.
Definitions Act of 1985: Landlord and Tenant Act 1985.
Cross references See RSC Order 97, r 19.

ORDER 44
[THE AGRICULTURAL HOLDINGS ACT 1986]

Amendments Heading substituted by SI 1987/493, r 12(1).

Order 44, r 1 Order to arbitrator to state case

(1)   An application under [paragraph 26 of Schedule 11 to the Agricultural Holdings Act 1986] for an order directing an arbitrator to state, in the form of a special case for the opinion of the court, a question of law arising in the course of the arbitration shall include a concise statement of the question of law.

(2)   The arbitrator shall not be made a respondent to the application, but if the judge grants the application, a copy of the order shall be served on the arbitrator.

Commencement 1 September 1982.
Amendments Para (1): words "paragraph 26 of Schedule 11 to the Agricultural Holdings Act 1986" substituted by SI 1987/493, r 12(2).

Order 44, r 2 Special case stated by arbitrator

(1)   Where, pursuant to [the said paragraph 26], an arbitrator states, in the form of a special case for the opinion of the court, any question of law arising in the course of the arbitration, the case shall contain a statement of such facts and reference to such documents as may be necessary to enable the judge to decide the question of law.

(2)   The case shall be signed by the arbitrator and shall be lodged in the court office by the arbitrator or any party to the arbitration, together with a copy for the use of the judge.

(3)   The proper officer shall fix a day for the hearing of the special case and give notice thereof to the parties.

(4)   On the hearing the judge shall be at liberty to draw any inferences of fact from the case and the documents referred to therein.

(5)   The judge may remit the case to the arbitrator for restatement or further statement.

(6)   A copy of the order made by the judge on the hearing shall be served on the parties to the arbitration and on the arbitrator.

Commencement 1 September 1982.
Amendments Para (1): words "the said paragraph 26" substituted by SI 1987/493, r 12(3).
Definitions Paragraph 26: Agricultural Holdings Act 1986, Sch 11, para 26.

Order 44, r 3 Removal of arbitrator or setting aside award

(1)   An application under [paragraph 27 of Schedule 11 to the said Act of 1986] for the removal of an arbitrator on the ground of his misconduct or for an order setting aside an award on the ground that the arbitrator has misconducted himself or that an arbitration or award has been improperly procured or that there is an error of law on the face of the award shall be made within 21 days after the date of the award.

(2)   The arbitrator and all parties to the arbitration, other than the applicant, shall be made respondents.

Commencement   1 September 1982.
Amendments   Para (1): words "paragraph 27 of Schedule 11 to the said Act of 1986" substituted by SI 1987/493, r 12(4).
Definitions   Act of 1986: Agricultural Holdings Act 1986.

Order 44, r 4 Enforcement of order imposing penalty

(1)   When taking any proceedings for the enforcement in a county court of an order under [section 27 of the Agricultural Holdings Act 1986], the party in whose favour the order was made shall file—

   (a)   a certified copy of the order and
   (b)   an affidavit verifying the amount due under the order and stating whether any previous proceedings have been taken for its enforcement and, if so, the nature of the proceedings and their result.

(2)   Where it is desired to enforce the order by warrant of execution, the proceedings may be taken in any court in the district of which execution is to be levied.

Commencement   1 September 1982.
Amendments   Para (1): words "section 27 of the Agricultural Holdings Act 1986" substituted by SI 1987/493, r 12(5).

ORDER 45
[THE REPRESENTATION OF THE PEOPLE ACT 1983]

Amendments   Heading substituted by SI 1983/1716, r 13, Schedule.

Order 45, r 1 Application for taxation of returning officer's account

(1)   An application by [the Secretary of State] under [section 30 of the Representation of the People Act 1983] for the taxation of a returning officer's account shall be made by originating application and the day fixed for the hearing shall be a day for proceeding with the taxation if the application is granted.

(2)   Where on the application the returning officer desires to apply to the court to examine any claim made against him in respect of matters charged in the account, the application shall be made in writing and filed, together with a copy thereof, within 7 days after service on the returning officer of the copy of the application for taxation.

(3)   On the filing of an application under paragraph (2) the proper officer shall fix a day for the hearing and give notice thereof to the returning officer, and a copy of the application and of the notice shall be served on the claimant in the manner prescribed for a fixed date summons.

(4)   The examination and taxation may, if the court thinks fit, take place on the same day, but the examination shall be determined before the taxation is concluded.

(5)   The application for taxation and any application under paragraph (2) may be heard and determined by the [district judge] and a copy of the order made on the application shall be served on [the Secretary of State] and the returning officer and, in the case of an application under paragraph (2), on the claimant.

Commencement   1 September 1982.
Amendments   Para (1): words "the Secretary of State" substituted by SI 1992/1965, r 19; words "section 30 of the Representation of the People Act 1983" substituted by SI 1983/1716, r 13, Schedule.
Para (5): words "the Secretary of State" substituted by SI 1992/1965, r 19.

Order 45, r 2 Appeal from decision of registration officer

(1)   Where notice of appeal from a decision of a registration officer is given pursuant to regulations made under [section 53 of the said Act of 1983], the registration officer shall, within 7 days after receipt of the notice by him, forward the notice by post to the proper officer of the court in which the appeal is required to be brought, together with the statement mentioned in those regulations.

(2)   The appeal shall be brought in the court for the district in which the qualifying premises are situated.

[In this paragraph "qualifying premises" means the premises in respect of which—
   (a)   the person whose right to be registered in the register of electors is in question on the appeal is entered on the electors' list or is registered or claims to be entitled to be registered, or
   (b)   the person whose right to vote by proxy or by post is in question on the appeal is or will be registered in the register of electors, or
   (c)   the elector whose proxy's right to vote by post is in question on the appeal is or will be registered in the register of electors,

as the case may be.]

(3)   The respondents to the appeal shall be the registration officer and the party (if any) in whose favour the decision of the registration officer was given.

(4)   On the hearing of the appeal—
   (a)   the statement forwarded to the proper officer by the registration officer and any document containing information furnished to the court by the registration officer pursuant to the regulations mentioned in paragraph (1) shall be admissible as evidence of the facts stated therein;
   (b)   the judge shall have power to draw all inferences of fact which might have been drawn by the registration officer and to give any decision and make any order which ought to have been given or made by the registration officer.

(5)   A respondent to an appeal other than the registration officer shall not be liable for or entitled to costs, unless he appears before the court in support of the decision of the registration officer.

Commencement   1 September 1982.
Amendments   Para (1): words "section 53 of the said Act of 1983" substituted by SI 1983/1716, r 13, Schedule.
Para (2): words from "In this paragraph" to the end substituted by SI 1989/2426, r 28.
Definitions   Act of 1983: Representation of the People Act 1983.

Order 45, r 3 Selected appeal

(1)   Where two or more appeals to which rule 2 relates involve the same point of law, the judge may direct that one appeal shall be heard in the first instance as a test case and thereupon the proper officer shall send a notice of the direction to the parties to the selected appeal and the parties to the other appeals.

(2)   If within 7 days after service of such notice on him any party to an appeal other than the selected appeal gives notice to the proper officer that he desires the appeal to which he is a party to be heard—
   (a)   the appeal shall be heard after the selected appeal is disposed of;
   (b)   the proper officer shall give the parties to the appeal notice of the day on which it will be heard;
   (c)   the party giving notice under this paragraph shall not be entitled to receive any costs occasioned by the separate hearing of the appeal to which he is a party, unless the judge otherwise orders.

(3)   If no notice is given under paragraph (2) within the time limited—
   (a)   the decision on the selected appeal shall bind the parties to each other appeal without prejudice to their right to appeal to the Court of Appeal;
   (b)   an order similar to the order in the selected appeal shall be made in each other appeal without further hearing;
   (c)   the party to each other appeal who is in the same interest as the unsuccessful party to the selected appeal shall be liable for the costs of the selected appeal in the same manner and to the same extent as the unsuccessful party to that appeal and an order directing him to pay such costs may be made and enforced accordingly.

Commencement   1 September 1982.

ORDER 46

(spent consequential on the repeal of the Matrimonial Causes Act 1973, s 45)

ORDER 47
DOMESTIC AND MATRIMONIAL PROCEEDINGS

Order 47, rr 1, 2 *(revoked by SI 1991/1882)*

Order 47, r 3 Law Reform (Husband and Wife) Act 1962, s 1(1)

(1)   In any action in tort brought by one of the parties to a marriage against the other during the subsistence of the marriage, the jurisdiction of the court under section 1(2) of the Law Reform (Husband and Wife) Act 1962 may be exercised by the [district judge]—
     (a) if the action is to be heard by the judge, at any time before the hearing, or
     (b) if the action is to be heard by the [district judge], at any stage of the proceedings.

(2)   In every such action the court shall, after a defence has been filed or, in a fixed date action, after the time for filing a defence has expired, consider whether the power to stay the action under the said section 1(2) should or should not be exercised and for the purpose of such consideration the proper officer shall, if he has not already done so, fix a day for a pre-trial review.

(3)   Where the action is a default action, judgment shall not be entered under Order 9, rule 6(1)(a), except with the leave of the court.

(4)   An application for the grant of leave under paragraph (3) shall be made on notice to the defendant and on the hearing of the application, which may be dealt with by the [district judge], the court shall consider whether the power to stay the action under the said section 1(2) should or should not be exercised.

Commencement 1 September 1982.
Cross references See RSC Order 89, r 2.

Order 47, r 4 *(revoked by SI 1991/1882)*

Order 47, r 5 Family Law Reform Act 1969

(1)   In this rule—
     "blood samples" and "blood tests" have the meanings assigned to them by section 25 of the Family Law Reform Act 1969, and
     "direction" means a direction for the use of blood tests under section 20(1) of that Act.

(2)   Except with the leave of the court, an application in any proceedings for a direction shall be made on notice to every party to the proceedings (other than the applicant) and to any other person from whom the direction involves the taking of blood samples.

(3)   Where an application is made for a direction involving the taking of blood samples from a person who is not a party to the proceedings in which the application is made, the notice of application shall be served on him personally and the court may at any time direct him to be made a party to the proceedings.

(4)   Where an application is made for a direction in respect of a person (in this paragraph referred to as a person under disability) who is either—

    (a)   under 16, or

    (b)   suffering from mental disorder within the meaning of the [Mental Health Act 1983] and incapable of understanding the nature and purpose of blood tests,

the notice of application shall state the name and address of the person having the care and control of the person under disability and shall be served on him instead of on the person under disability.

(5)   Where the court gives a direction in any proceedings, the proper officer shall send a copy to every party to the proceedings and to every other person from whom the direction involves the taking of blood samples and, unless otherwise ordered, the proceedings shall stand adjourned until the court receives a report pursuant to the direction.

(6)   On receipt by the court of a report made pursuant to a direction, the proper officer shall send a copy to every party to the proceedings and to every other person from whom the direction involved the taking of blood samples.

Commencement   1 September 1982.
Amendments   Para (4): words "Mental Health Act 1983" substituted by SI 1983/1716, r 13, Schedule.
Cross references   See RSC Order 112.

Order 47, rr 6–9   *(revoked by SI 1991/1882)*

Order 47, r 10   *(added by SI 1986/1189; revoked by SI 1991/1882)*

Order 47, r 11   *(added by SI 1988/278; revoked by SI 1991/1882)*

ORDER 48
FAMILY PROVISION

Order 48, r 1 Interpretation

In this Order—

> . . .
>
> "the Act of 1975" means the Inheritance (Provision for Family and Dependants) Act 1975;
>
> "the deceased" means, . . . in the case of an application under section 1 of the Act of 1975, the person to whose estate the application relates.

Commencement   1 September 1982.
Amendments   Words omitted revoked by SI 1991/1882, r 3(d)(i).
Cross references   See RSC Order 99, r 1.

Order 48, r 2 Mode of application

. . . An application to a county court under section 1 of the Act of 1975 for provision to be made out of the estate of a deceased person shall be made by originating application stating—

(a) the name of the deceased, the date of his death and his country of domicile at that date;

(b) the relationship of the applicant to the deceased or other qualification of the applicant for making the application;

(c) the date on which representation with respect to the deceased's estate was first taken out and the names and addresses of the personal representatives;

(d) . . .

(e) whether the disposition of the deceased's estate effected by his will or the law relating to intestacy was such as to make any provision for the applicant and, if it was, the nature of the provision;

(f) to the best of the applicant's knowledge and belief, the persons or classes of persons interested in the deceased's estate and the nature of their interests;

(g) particulars of the applicant's present and foreseeable financial resources and financial needs and any other information which he desires to place before the court on the matters to which the court is required to have regard under section 3 of the Act of 1975;

(h) where appropriate, a request for the court's permission to make the application notwithstanding that the period of six months has expired from the date on which representation in regard to the estate of the deceased was first taken out, and the grounds of the request; and

(i) the nature of the provision applied for.

. . .

Commencement   1 September 1982.
Amendments   This rule originally stood as paras (1), (2), para (2) revoked and former para (1) now stands alone as the text of this rule by virtue of SI 1991/1882, r 3(2)(ii); sub-para (d) revoked by SI 1992/793, r 14.
Definitions   Act of 1975: Inheritance (Provision for Family and Dependants) Act 1975.
Cross references   See RSC Order 99, r 3.
Forms   Originating application (N423).

Order 48, r 3 Filing of application

(1)   An application to which rule 2 . . . relates shall be filed—

    (a)   in the court for the district in which the deceased resided at the date of his death, or

    (b)   if the deceased did not then reside in England or Wales, in the court for the district in which the respondent or one of the respondents resides or carries on business or the estate or part of the estate is situate, or

    (c)   if neither of the foregoing sub-paragraphs is applicable, in the court for the district in which the applicant resides or carries on business.

(2)   The applicant shall file with his originating application . . . an official copy of the grant of representation to the deceased's estate and of every testamentary document admitted to proof, ...

(3)   Unless the court otherwise directs, the return day of the originating application shall be a day fixed for the pre-trial review of the proceedings.

Commencement 1 September 1982.
Amendments Paras (1), (2): words omitted revoked by SI 1991/1882, r 3(d)(iii), (iv).
Cross references See RSC Order 99, r 3.

Order 48, r 4 Parties

(1)   Without prejudice to its powers under Orders 5 and 15, the court may, at any stage of the proceedings, direct that any person be added as a party to the proceedings or that notice of the proceedings be served on any person.

(2)   Order 5, rule 6, shall apply to an application under section 1 of the Act of 1975 . . . as it applies to the proceedings mentioned in that rule.

Commencement 1 September 1982.
Amendments Para (2): words omitted revoked by SI 1991/1882, r 3(d)(v).
Definitions Act of 1975: Inheritance (Provision for Family and Dependants) Act 1975.
Cross references See RSC Order 99, r 4.

Order 48, r 5 Answer

Every respondent shall, within 21 days after service of the originating application on him, file an answer, which, if the respondent is a personal representative, shall state to the best of his ability—

    (a)   full particulars of the value of the deceased's net estate, as defined by section 25(1) of the Act of 1975;

    (b)   the persons or classes of persons beneficially interested in the estate, giving the names and (in the case of those who are not already parties) the addresses of all living beneficiaries, and the value of their interests so far as ascertained;

    (c)   if such be the case, that any living beneficiary (naming him) is a minor or a mental patient; and

    (d)   in the case of an application under section 1 of the Act of 1975, any facts known to the personal representative which might affect the exercise of the court's powers under that Act.

Commencement 1 September 1982.
Definitions Act of 1975: Inheritance (Provision for Family and Dependants) Act 1975.
Cross references See RSC Order 99, r 5.

Order 48, r 6 Subsequent application

Where an order has been made on an application under section 1 of the Act of 1975, any subsequent application, whether made by a party to the proceedings or by any other person, shall be made in those proceedings in accordance with Order 13, rule 1.

Commencement   1 September 1982.
Definitions   Act of 1975: Inheritance (Provision for Family and Dependants) Act 1975.
Cross references   See RSC Order 99, r 9.

Order 48, r 7 Hearing

Any application under section 1 of the Act of 1975 ... may be heard and determined by the [district judge] and may, if the court thinks fit, be dealt with in chambers.

Commencement   1 September 1982.
Amendments   Words omitted revoked by SI 1991/1882, r 3(d)(v).
Definitions   Act of 1975: Inheritance (Provision for Family and Dependants) Act 1975.
Cross references   See RSC Order 99, r 8.

Order 48, r 8 Endorsement of memorandum on grant

On the hearing of an application under section 1 of the Act of 1975, the personal representative shall produce to the court the grant of representation to the deceased's estate and, if an order is made under the Act, the proper officer shall send a sealed copy thereof, together with the grant of representation, to the principal registry of the Family Division for a memorandum of the order to be endorsed on, or permanently annexed to, the grant in accordance with section 19(3) of the Act of 1975.

Commencement   1 September 1982.
Definitions   Act of 1975: Inheritance (Provision for Family and Dependants) Act 1975.
Cross references   See RSC Order 99, r 7.

[Order 48, r 9 Transfer to High Court

An order transferring an application under section 1 of the Act of 1975 to the High Court shall state whether it is desired that the proceedings be assigned to the Chancery Division or to the Family Division of the High Court.]

Commencement   1 April 1992.
Amendments   This rule was substituted by SI 1992/793, r 15.
Definitions   Act of 1975: Inheritance (Provision for Family and Dependants) Act 1975.

[ORDER 48A
PATENTS AND DESIGNS

Order 48A, r 1 Application and Interpretation

[(1)　This Order applies to proceedings in respect of which patents county courts have jurisdiction under section 287(1) of the 1988 Act.

(2)　In this Order:—

"The 1988 Act" means the Copyright, Designs and Patents Act 1988;

"patents county court" means a county court designated as a patents county court under section 287(1) of the 1988 Act;

"patents judge" means a person nominated under section 291(1) of the 1988 Act as the patents judge of a patents county court.]

Commencement　3 September 1990.
Amendments　Order 48A was inserted by SI 1990/1495, r 2.
Cross references　See RSC Order 104, r 1.

[Order 48A, r 2 Patents Judge

(1)　Subject to paragraph (2), proceedings to which this Order applies shall be dealt with by the patents judge.

(2)　When an interlocutory matter needs to be dealt with urgently and the patents judge is not available, the matter may be dealt with by another judge.]

Commencement　3 September 1990.
Amendments　See the note to Order 48A, r 1.

[Order 48A, r 3 Commencement

Every summons, notice, pleading, affidavit or other document relating to proceedings to which this Order applies must be marked in the top left hand corner with the words "patents county court".]

Commencement　3 September 1990.
Amendments　See the note to Order 48A, r 1.
Cross references　See RSC Order 104, r 2.

[Order 48A, r 4 Pleadings

(1)　Every summons issued in accordance with rule 3 above shall be endorsed with or accompanied by a statement of case.

(2)　Where a claim is made by the plaintiff in respect of the infringement of a patent, the statement of case shall give full particulars of the infringement relied on, setting out:—

(a)　which of the claims in the specification of the patent are alleged to be infringed; and

(b)　in respect of each claim alleged to be infringed the grounds relied on in support of the allegations that such claim has been infringed; and all facts, matters and arguments relied on as establishing those grounds, including at least one example of each type of infringement alleged.

(3)　Where, in any proceedings, the validity of a patent is put in issue, the statement of case shall give particulars of the objections to the validity of the patent which are relied on; and in particular shall explain the relevance of every citation to each claim, with identification of the significant parts of each citation, and shall give all facts, matters and arguments which are relied on for establishing the invalidity of the patent.

(4)   Without prejudice to paragraph (3) above, RSC Order 104, rule 6(2) to (4) shall apply to particulars of objections given under paragraph (3) as they apply to particulars given under paragraph (1) of that rule.

(5)   Every statement of case shall be signed:—
    (a) by the plaintiff, if he sues in person; or
    (b) by the plaintiff's solicitor in his own name or the name of his firm;

and shall state the plaintiff's address for service.

(6)   Where a defendant wishes to serve a defence to any claim he shall serve it, together with any counterclaim including a statement of case under paragraph (2) or (3) above, upon the plaintiff within 42 days of service upon him of the summons.

(7)   Where a party wishes to serve a reply or a defence to counterclaim, he shall do so within 28 days of the service of the previous pleading upon him.

(8)   Pleadings will close seven days after the expiry of the time for service of a reply.

(9)   No time limit mentioned in this rule may be extended more than once (and then by no more than 42 days) save by order of the court; and such order shall, in the first place, be applied for in writing, whereupon the judge shall either grant the application, refuse it or order a hearing.

(10)   The parties to proceedings shall notify the court of any agreed extension of any time limit mentioned in this rule.]

Commencement   3 September 1990.
Amendments   See the note to Order 48A, r 1.
Cross references   See RSC Order 104, r 6.

[Order 48A, r 5 Service

(1)   In their application to proceedings to which this Order applies, rules 10 and 13 of Order 7 shall apply as if:—
    (a) before the words "an officer" in paragraph (1)(b) of each rule there were inserted the words "the plaintiff or"; and
    (b) in paragraph (4) of rule 10 (and in that paragraph as applied by rule 13) after the words "sent by post" there were inserted the words "by an officer of the court".

(2)   Where a pleading is served which refers to any document, the party serving the pleading must also serve with it a copy of any such document together with an English translation of any foreign language text, certified as being accurate.]

Commencement   3 September 1990.
Amendments   See the note to Order 48A, r 1.

[Order 48A, r 6 Interrogatories and Notices to Admit Facts

(1)   (a) Interrogatories under Order 14, rule 11, and
        (b) a notice to admit facts under Order 20, rule 2,

may not be served without the leave of the court unless (in the case of a notice to admit facts) it is served within 14 days of the close of pleadings; and accordingly those provisions of Order 14, rule 11 (and of the RSC which are applied by that rule) which relate only to interrogatories without order shall not apply to proceedings under this Order.

(2)   An application for leave to serve interrogatories or a notice to admit facts may only be made on notice at the preliminary consideration under rule 8.]

Commencement   3 September 1990.
Amendments   See the note to Order 48A, r 1.

[Order 48A, r 7 Scientific Advisers, Assessors and Patent Office Reports

(1)   The court may at any time, on or without the application of any party:—
  (a)   appoint scientific advisers or assessors to assist the court; or
  (b)   order the Patent Office to inquire into and report on any question of fact or opinion.

(2)   RSC Order 104, rule 15 shall apply to the appointment of a scientific adviser under this rule.

(3)   Where the court appoints an assessor under this rule without the application of a party, paragraphs (3) and (6) of Order 13, rule 11 shall apply, and paragraph (4) of that rule shall apply with the omission of the words from "the applicant shall" to "and thereupon" inclusive.]

Commencement   3 September 1990.
Amendments   See the note to Order 48A, r 1.
Cross references   See RSC Order 104, r 15.

[Order 48A, r 8 Preliminary Consideration

(1)   Within fourteen days of the close of pleadings, all parties shall file and serve an application for directions, signed by the person settling it.

(2)   Each application for directions shall:
  (a)   summarise the outstanding issues in the proceedings;
  (b)   summarise the further steps necessary to prove the applicant's contentions in the proceedings and prepare his case for a hearing;
  (c)   give full particulars of any experiments the applicant intends to conduct, stating the facts which he intends to prove by them and the date by which he will submit a written report of the results; and
  (d)   set out all orders and directions the applicant will ask for at the preliminary consideration of the action.

(3)   As soon as is practicable after receipt of each party's application for directions, the proper officer shall set a date for the preliminary consideration.

(4)   On the preliminary consideration the judge may, with or without the application of any party and either after a consideration of the papers or having adjudicated upon a point of law strike out any point raised in the proceedings.

(5)   On the preliminary consideration, the judge shall give such directions as are necessary to prepare the proceedings for hearing and in particular shall consider and (where appropriate) give directions in respect of each or any of the following matters, namely:—

(a) the witnesses who may be called;

(b) whether their evidence should be given orally or in writing or any combination of the two;

(c) the exchange of witness statements;

(d) the provision of Patent Office Reports;

(e) the use of assessors at the hearing;

(f) transfer to the High Court;

(g) reference to the Court of Justice of the European Communities;

(h) applications for discovery and inspection;

(i) applications for leave under rule 6 above; and

(j) written reports of the results of any experiments of which particulars have been given under rule 8(2)(c).]

Commencement   3 September 1990.
Amendments   See the note to Order 48A, r 1.
Cross references   See RSC Order 104, r 14.

[Order 48A, r 9 General Modification of County Court Rules

In their application to proceedings to which this Order applies, county court rules shall be subject to the following modifications:—

(a) Order 3 rules 3(1) and (2)(c) shall have effect as if for the words "particulars of claim" there are substituted the words "statement of case".

(b) in Order 3, rule 3(2)(a), the words from "and in the case" to "return day" inclusive shall be omitted;

(c) Order 3, rule 3(3) shall not apply;

(d) Order 6, rule 7 shall not apply;

(e) Order 9 shall not apply, with the exception of Order 9 rule 19, which shall apply to every defence or counterclaim delivered under rule 4(6) above as it applies to those delivered under Order 9 rule 2.]

Commencement   3 September 1990.
Amendments   See the note to Order 48A, r 1.

[Order 48A, r 10 Application of Rules of the Supreme Court

(1)   RSC Order 104, rule 3 shall apply to applications by a patentee or the proprietor of a patent intending to apply under section 30 of the Patents Act 1949 or section 75 of the Patents Act 1977 for leave to amend his specification, save that references therein to an application by motion shall be construed, for the purposes of an application to a patents county court, as an application on notice to the patents judge.

(2)   RSC Order 104, rule 17 shall apply to actions to which this Order applies, with the omission of the words "by originating summons".

(3)   RSC Order 104, rule 16(3), rule 20 and rule 23 shall apply to actions to which this Order applies.]

Commencement   3 September 1990.
Amendments   See the note to Order 48A, r 1.

[ORDER 48B
ENFORCEMENT OF PARKING PENALTIES UNDER
THE ROAD TRAFFIC ACT 1991

Order 48B, r 1 Application and interpretation

(1)   This Order applies for the recovery of—
   (a)   increased penalty charges provided for in parking charge certificates issued under paragraph 6 of Schedule 6 to the 1991 Act; and
   (b)   amounts payable by a person other than an authority under an adjudication of a parking adjudicator pursuant to section 73 of the 1991 Act.

(2)   In this Order, unless the context otherwise requires—
   "authority" means the London authority which served the charge certificate;
   "order" means an order made under paragraph 7 of Schedule 6 to the 1991 Act or, as the case may be, under section 73 of that Act;
   "the Order" means the Enforcement of Road Traffic Debts Order 1993 made under section 78 of the 1991 Act;
   "relevant period" means the period of 21 days allowed for serving a statutory declaration by paragraph 8(1) of Schedule 6 to the 1991 Act or, where a longer period has been allowed pursuant to paragraph 8(4) of the said Schedule, that period;
   "respondent" means the person on whom the charge certificate was served or, as the case may be, the person (other than an authority) by whom the amount due under an adjudication of a parking adjudicator is payable;
   "specified debts" means the Part II debts specified in article 2 of the Order;
   "statutory declaration" means a declaration in the appropriate form which complies with paragraph 8(2) of Schedule 6 to the 1991 Act;
   "the 1991 Act" means the Road Traffic Act 1991.

(3)   Unless the context otherwise requires, expressions which are used in the 1991 Act have the same meaning in this Order as they have in that Act.]

Commencement   1 September 1993.
Amendments   Order 48B was inserted by SI 1993/2150, r 3.

[Order 48B, r 2 Requests for orders

(1)   An authority which wishes to take proceedings under this Order shall give notice to the proper officer and, where the proper officer so allows, requests for orders may be made, and such orders may be enforced, in accordance with the following provisions of this Order.

(2)   An authority shall file a request for an order in the appropriate form scheduling the increased penalty charges in respect of which an order is sought and Order 50, rule 4A shall not apply to requests under this Order.

(3)   The authority shall in the request or in another manner approved by the proper officer—
   (a)   certify—
      (i)   that 14 days have elapsed since service of the charge certificate,
      (ii)   the amount due under the charge certificate and the date on which the charge certificate was served, and
      (iii) that the amount due remains unpaid;
   (b)   give the charge certificate number;

(c) specify (whether by reference to the appropriate code or otherwise) the grounds stated in the notice to owner on which the parking attendant who issued the penalty charge notice believed that a penalty charge was payable with respect to the vehicle;

(d) state—

(i) the name and address of the respondent and, where known, his title;

(ii) the registration number of the vehicle concerned;

(iii) (whether by reference to the appropriate charge certificate number or otherwise) the authority's address for service;

(iv) the court fee.

(4) If satisfied that the request is in order, the proper officer shall order that the increased charge (together with the court fee) may be recovered as if it were payable under a county court order by sealing the request and returning it to the authority.

(5) When the proper officer so orders and on receipt of the sealed request, the authority may draw up the order and shall annex to any such order a form of statutory declaration for the respondent's use.

(6) Within 14 days of receipt of the sealed request, the authority shall serve the order (and the form of statutory declaration) on the respondent by—

(a) delivering the order to the respondent personally; or

(b) sending it by first-class post to the respondent at the address given in the request,

and Order 7, rules 10(3), 13(1) to (3) and 14 shall apply, with the necessary modifications, as they apply to the service of a summons.

(7) Where an authority requests an order in respect of amounts payable by a person other than an authority under an adjudication of a parking adjudicator pursuant to section 73 of the 1991 Act, paragraphs (2) and (3) shall apply with the necessary modifications and in addition the authority shall—

(a) state the date on which the adjudication was made;

(b) provide details of the order made on the adjudication;

(c) certify the amount awarded by way of costs and that the amount remains unpaid.]

Commencement 1 September 1993.
Amendments See the note to Order 48B, r 1.
Definitions 1991 Act: Road Traffic Act 1991.

[Order 48B, r 3 Documents

(1) Where by or under these rules any document is required to be filed, that requirement shall be deemed to be satisfied if the information which would be contained in the document is delivered in computer-readable form but nothing in this paragraph shall be taken as enabling an authority to commence proceedings without supplying a written request in the appropriate form under rule 2(2).

(2) For the purposes of paragraph (1), information which would be contained in a document relating to one case may be combined with information of the same nature relating to another case.

(3) Where by or under these rules or by virtue of any order a document which contains information is required to be produced, that requirement shall be deemed to

be satisfied if a copy of the document is produced from the computer records kept for storing such information.]

Commencement   1 September 1993.
Amendments   See the note to Order 48B, r 1.

[Order 48B, r 4 Functions of proper officer

(1)   The functions of the district judge under paragraph 8(4) and (5)(d) of Schedule 6 to the 1991 Act (longer period for service of the statutory declaration and notice of effect of statutory declaration) may be exercised by the proper officer.

(2)   Where pursuant to paragraph 8(4) of Schedule 6 to the 1991 Act a longer period is allowed for service of the statutory declaration, the proper officer shall notify the authority and the respondent accordingly.]

Commencement   1 September 1993.
Amendments   See the note to Order 48B, r 1.
Definitions   1991 Act: Road Traffic Act 1991.

[Order 48B, r 5 Enforcement of orders

(1)   Subject to the Order and to this rule, the following provisions of Orders 25 to 27, 30 and 31 of these Rules shall apply for the enforcement of specified debts.
>   Order 25, rules 1, 2 (except paragraph (3)(b), (c) and (d)), 3, 5 (except
>   paragraph (1)(a) and (b)) and 9.
>   Order 26, rule 5.
>   Order 27, rules 1 to 7, 7A, 9 to 16 and 18 to 22.
>   Order 30, rules 1 to 3, 5 and 7 to 15.
>   Order 31, rules 1 to 4.

(2)   In proceedings under this Order, no order under Order 16, rule 1 (general power of transfer) may be made except under paragraph (d) of that rule.

(3)   An authority desiring to issue a warrant of execution shall file a request in that behalf in the appropriate form or in another manner approved by the proper officer—
>   (a)   certifying the amount remaining due under the order,
>   (b)   specifying the date of service of the order on the respondent, and
>   (c)   certifying that the relevant period has elapsed.

(4)   The proper officer shall seal the request and return it to the authority which shall, within 7 days of the sealing of the request, prepare the warrant in the appropriate form.

(5)   No payment under a warrant shall be made to the court.

(6)   A warrant shall, for the purpose of execution, be valid for 12 months beginning with the date of its issue and nothing in this rule or in Order 26 shall authorise an authority to renew a warrant.

(7)   Where an order is deemed to have been revoked under paragraph 8(5) of Schedule 6 to the 1991 Act—
>   (a)   the proper officer shall serve a copy of the statutory declaration on the authority;
>   (b)   any execution issued on the order shall cease to have effect, and
>   (c)   on receipt of the proper officer's notice under paragraph 8(5)(d) of the said Schedule 6, the authority shall forthwith inform any bailiff instructed to levy execution of the withdrawal of the warrant.

(8)   In addition to the requirements of that rule, any application by an authority under Order 25, rule 2, shall—

    (a) where the authority has not attempted to enforce by execution, give the reasons why no such attempt was made;

    (b) certify that there has been no relevant return to the warrant of execution;

    (c) specify the date of service of the order on the respondent, and

    (d) certify that the relevant period has elapsed.

(9)   An application under Order 30, rule 2 and (unless provided pursuant to an application under Order 25, rule 2) any application by an authority under Order 25, rule 3, Order 27, rule 4(1) or Order 31, rule 1(2) shall, in addition to the requirements of those rules—

    (a) where the authority has not attempted to enforce by execution, give the reasons why no such attempt was made;

    (b) certify that there has been no relevant return to the warrant of execution;

    (c) specify the date of service of the order on the respondent, and

    (d) certify that the relevant period has elapsed.

(10)   In paragraphs (8) and (9) "no relevant return to the warrant" means that

    (i) the bailiff has been unable to seize goods because he has been denied access to the premises occupied by the respondent or because the goods have been removed from those premises;

    (ii) any goods seized under the warrant of execution are insufficient to satisfy the specified debt and the costs of execution; or

    (iii) the goods are insufficient to cover the cost of their removal and sale.

(11)   If the proper officer allows, an authority may combine information relating to one charge certificate with information concerning the same respondent in another charge certificate in any request made, or any application brought, under one of the provisions mentioned in paragraph (8) or (9) above.]

Commencement   1 September 1993.

Amendments   See the note to Order 48B, r 1.

Definitions   The Order: Enforcement of Road Traffic Debts Order 1993, SI 1993/2073. 1991 Act: Road Traffic Act 1991.

[ORDER 48C
THE CENTRAL LONDON COUNTY COURT BUSINESS LIST

Order 48C, r 1 Application and interpretation

(1)   This Order applies to business actions which are included in the Central London County Court Business List and, in their application to business actions, these rules shall have effect subject to the provisions of this Order.

(2)   In this Order, unless the context otherwise requires—
"action" includes actions and matters;
"business action" has the meaning given by rule 3;
"business list action" means an action included in the Central London County Court Business List;
"close of pleadings" shall be deemed to be 14 days after the service of points of defence or, where a counterclaim is served with the points of defence, 28 days after the service of points of defence;
"request for time for payment" has the meaning given by Order 9, rule 2(2);
"the business list" means the Central London County Court Business List; and
"the judge" means a judge having control of a business list action.]

Commencement   6 June 1994.
Amendments   Order 48C was inserted by SI 1994/1288, r 3.
Cross references   See RSC Order 72, r 1.

[Order 48C, r 2 Venue of business action

(1)   There shall be a list in the Central London County Court which shall be called "The Central London County Court Business List".

(2)   An action may be commenced in the Central London County Court for inclusion in the business list if it is a business action and has some connection with the South Eastern Circuit, for example, because—
(a)   the balance of convenience points to having the action tried in the Central London County Court; or
(b)   the cause of action arose, or one of the parties resides or carries on business, at a place in the South Eastern Circuit.

(3)   The provisions of Order 4 (Venue for bringing proceedings) shall not apply to a business action.]

Commencement   6 June 1994.
Amendments   See the note to Order 48C, r 1.
Cross references   See RSC Order 72, r 2.

[Order 48C, r 3 Meaning of business action

(1)   Whether or not an action is a business action shall be determined in accordance with the provisions of this rule.

(2)   The subject matter of a business action must relate to a commercial or business transaction and such an action may include (but shall not be limited to) an action which relates to—
(a)   a contract for the import and export of goods or the sale of goods other than a contract to which an individual consumer is a party;
(b)   the carriage of goods;
(c)   mercantile agency;

(d) insurance;

(e) banking, negotiable instruments, guarantees or other financial transactions;

(f) a contract relating to ships, shipping and aircraft;

(g) a dispute involving the construction of a commercial contract or relating to the customs and practices of particular trades, businesses or commercial organisations;

(h) proceedings to enforce an award under section 26 of the Arbitration Act 1950.

(3) No business action shall be brought concerning—

(a) an action to which Order 48A applies (proceedings in respect of which patents county courts have jurisdiction), or

(b) an action to which Order 19, rule 3 applies (automatic reference to arbitration of small claims).]

Commencement 6 June 1994.
Amendments See the note to Order 48C, r 1.
Cross references See RSC Order 72, r 1(2).

[Order 48C, r 4 Inclusion of action in the business list

(1) Subject to paragraph (2), a plaintiff may include an action in the business list by using the form of summons appropriate to a business list action or by marking in the top left hand corner of the originating process by which the action is to be begun the words "Business List".

(2) Where the value of an action (within the meaning of Order 1, rule 3) does not exceed £15,000, the action may be included in the business list only with the leave of the judge.

(3) Where the defendant to an action begun in accordance with paragraph (1) applies for the proceedings to be referred to arbitration under Order 19, the judge shall determine the application and, if the action is so referred, he shall transfer the action out of the business list.

(4) Where an action is included in the business list, the provisions of Order 9, rules 2(8) and 3(4) and (6) (automatic transfer to defendant's home court) shall not apply.]

Commencement 6 June 1994.
Amendments See the note to Order 48C, r 1.
Cross references See RSC Order 72, r 4.

[Order 48C, r 5 Documents in business list actions

Where an action has been included in the business list, every summons, notice, pleading, affidavit or other document relating to the action must be marked in the top left hand corner with the words "Business List".]

Commencement 6 June 1994.
Amendments See the note to Order 48C, r 1.

[Order 48C, r 6 Commencement of action

(1) The provisions of Order 3, rules 1, 2 and 3 (except paragraphs (5) to (8)) shall not apply to a business action.

(2) The summons in a business action shall be prepared by the plaintiff in the appropriate form and shall state the plaintiff's address for service.

(3) The plaintiff shall supply the proper officer with—
- (a) two copies of the completed summons;
- (b) two copies of the points of claim; and
- (c) where the summons is to be served out of England and Wales, a certificate that the conditions of Order 3, rule 3(6) are satisfied.

(4) On receipt of the documents mentioned in paragraph (3), the proper officer shall—
- (a) enter the action in the records of the court and allocate a case number;
- (b) seal both copies of the summons;
- (c) return the summons and one copy of the points of claim to the plaintiff; and
- (d) deliver to the plaintiff a notice of issue.

(5) One or more concurrent summonses may, at the request of the plaintiff, be issued at the time when the original summons was issued or at any time thereafter before the original summons ceases to be valid.]

Commencement   6 June 1994.
Amendments   See the note to Order 48C, r 1.

[Order 48C, r 7 Service

(1) Subject to paragraph (2), the summons in a business list action must be served personally on each defendant by the plaintiff.

(2) A summons for service on a defendant within England and Wales may be served—
- (a) by sending the summons by ordinary first-class post to the defendant at his usual or last-known address; or
- (b) if there is a letter box for that address, by inserting the summons, enclosed in a sealed envelope addressed to the defendant, through the letter box.

(3) Every summons for service on a defendant shall be sealed and shall be accompanied by—
- (a) a copy of the points of claim; and
- (b) a form of acknowledgment of service in the appropriate form on which the plaintiff has entered the title and number of the action.

(4) Where a summons is served by post under paragraph (2)—
- (a) Order 7, rule 10(3) and 10(4) and 13 and Order 37, rule 3 shall apply as if the summons had been served by an officer of the court;
- (b) Order 7, rules 6(1)(b) and 10(2) shall not apply; and
- (c) it shall be treated, for the purposes of these rules, as if it had been served by an officer of the court.

(5) This rule shall have effect subject to Order 7, rule 14 and to the provisions of any enactment which provides for the manner in which documents may be served on bodies corporate.]

Commencement   6 June 1994.
Amendments   See the note to Order 48C, r 1.

[Order 48C, r 8 Acknowledgment of service

(1) A defendant who wishes to defend a business list action must file an acknowledgment of service—
- (a) stating that he intends to defend the proceedings to which the acknowledgment relates; and
- (b) acknowledging service of the summons.

(2)   On receipt of an acknowledgment of service the proper officer shall—
    (a)   endorse on the acknowledgment the date he received it;
    (b)   record whether the defendant intends—
       (i)   to defend the proceedings; or
       (ii)   to make a request for time for payment; and
    (c)   send a copy of the acknowledgment to the plaintiff.

(3)   (a)   In the case of a summons served within England and Wales the time limited for acknowledging service of the summons shall be 14 days after service of the summons or, where that time has been extended under these rules, that time as so extended.
    (b)   An order granting leave to serve a summons out of England and Wales shall limit a time within which the defendant to be served must acknowledge service.

(4)   RSC Order 12, rules 6, 7, 8 and 8A shall apply to a business list action.]

Commencement   6 June 1994.
Amendments   See the note to Order 48C, r 1.

[Order 48C, r 9 Failure to give notice of intention to defend

(1)   Where the plaintiff's claim consists of or includes a liquidated demand, then, if the defendant fails to give notice of intention to defend within the time limited for acknowledging service, the plaintiff may on filing a request have judgment entered for the amount claimed and costs.

(2)   The provisions of Order 9, rule 6(1A) shall not apply but, unless the defendant has acknowledged service of the summons, the plaintiff must prove due service of the summons either by—
    (a)   filing an affidavit of service; or
    (b)   producing to the proper officer the defendant's solicitor's indorsement of acceptance of service.

(3)   Where the plaintiff's claim is for unliquidated damages, Order 9, rule 6(2) shall apply.

(4)   Paragraphs (5) to (7) shall apply where the defendant makes a request for time for payment and the provisions of Order 9, rule 3 shall not apply.

(5)   Where the defendant has filed an acknowledgment of service stating that, although he does not intend to defend the proceedings, he intends to make a request for time for payment, then no judgment shall be entered for a period of 14 days after filing the acknowledgment of service.

(6)   If within the period mentioned in paragraph (5), the defendant makes a request for time for payment, the application shall, unless the plaintiff accepts the defendant's proposal as to time of payment or the judge otherwise directs, be heard by the judge.

(7)   An application for time for payment shall be supported by an affidavit of means.]

Commencement   6 June 1994.
Amendments   See the note to Order 48C, r 1.

[Order 48C, r 10 Summary judgment and disposal of case on point of law

RSC Orders 14 and 14A shall apply to a business list action and Order 9, rule 14 of these rules shall not apply.]

Commencement   6 June 1994.
Amendments   See the note to Order 48C, r 1.

[Order 48C, r 11 Pleadings in business list actions

(1)   The pleadings in a business list action shall be in the form of points of claim or, as the case may be, points of defence, counterclaim, defence to counterclaim or reply.

(2)   Points of claim shall be served on the defendant when the summons is served on him.

(3)   Points of defence shall be served within 14 days after the time limited for acknowledging service.

(4)   In all other respects the pleadings in a business list action shall comply with RSC Order 18.

(5)   RSC Order 19 (Default of Pleadings) and RSC Order 20 (Amendment) shall apply to a business list action.]

Commencement   6 June 1994.
Amendments   See the note to Order 48C, r 1.
Cross references   See RSC Order 72, r 7.

[Order 48C, r 12 Discovery in business list actions

(1)   Unless the judge otherwise directs, there shall be discovery of documents within 14 days of close of pleadings and inspection within 7 days thereafter.

(2)   The provisions of RSC Order 24 (discovery and inspection of documents) shall apply to business list actions.]

Commencement   6 June 1994.
Amendments   See the note to Order 48C, r 1.

[Order 48C, r 13 Application for directions

(1)   The provisions of Order 3, rule 3(3) and Order 9, rule 5 (which require the proper officer to fix a day for the pre-trial review or for the hearing of an action) shall not apply to business list actions and RSC Order 25 shall apply, with the necessary modifications, to an application under this rule as it applies to a summons for directions.

(2)   Within one month after close of pleadings, the plaintiff must make an application, referred to in this rule as an application for directions.

(3)   The application for directions shall set out all orders and directions the applicant will ask for at the preliminary consideration of the action.

(4)   Notwithstanding paragraph (2) of this rule, any party may make an application for directions at any time after the defendant has served points of defence, or, if there are two or more defendants, at least one of them has served points of defence.

(5)   At the hearing of the application for directions, the judge shall consider the course of the proceedings and give all such directions as appear to be necessary or desirable for securing the just, expeditious and economical disposal of the action including (but not limited to)—
   (a)   whether the evidence of witnesses as to fact shall be given orally or in writing or any combination of the two;
   (b)   the exchange of witness statements and of experts' reports;
   (c)   the calling of, and meetings between, experts;

(d) the provision of skeleton or outline addresses, chronologies, lists of parties or witnesses or other summaries;

(e) the provision of plans, photographs, visual aids or computer facilities;

(f) the transfer of the action to the High Court or out of the business list;

(g) the date for the hearing of the matter; and

(h) the preparation of trial bundles.]

Commencement 6 June 1994.
Amendments See the note to Order 48C, r 1.
Cross references See RSC Order 72, r 8.

[Order 48C, r 14 Transfer to and from a business list

(1) At any stage of the proceedings, the judge may, on application or of his own motion, order—

(a) an action to be removed from the business list if he considers that it does not come within the terms of rule 3 or that it should be heard and determined other than in that list;

(b) an action to be transferred to another court if he considers that it could be more conveniently or fairly heard and determined in that court.

(2) Where an action is removed from the business list, directions taking effect under Order 17, rule 11 shall have effect subject to any directions given prior to the removal of the action from the business list.

(3) Where the judge or district judge of any court is satisfied that any action in that court could be more conveniently or fairly heard and determined as a business list action, he may (subject to Order 16, rule 3 (saving for statutory provisions)), order the action to be transferred to the business list.

(4) Subject to the provisions of this rule, the provisions of Order 16 (transfer of proceedings) shall apply with the necessary modifications to transfers to and from the business list.

(5) Nothing in rule 2(2) shall prevent the transfer of an action from the Commercial Court of the Queen's Bench Division to the business list.

(6) Subject to any order made under Order 25, rule 2 (transfer of proceedings for enforcement) an action shall be removed from the business list after final judgment has been entered on all matters in issue.]

Commencement 6 June 1994.
Amendments See the note to Order 48C, r 1.
Cross references See RSC Order 72, rr 5, 6.

[Order 48C, r 15 Jurisdiction of judge and district judge

(1) Subject to paragraph (2), unless the judge otherwise directs, interlocutory applications and trials relating to business list actions shall be heard by the judge.

(2) When an interlocutory matter needs to be dealt with urgently and the judge is not available, the matter may be dealt with by another judge.

(3) Where an action is transferred out of the business list, the judge may order it to be determined by a district judge where—

(a) the value of the action does not exceed £5,000; or

(b) judgment has been entered for damages to be assessed.]

Commencement 6 June 1994.
Amendments See the note to Order 48C, r 1.

ORDER 49
MISCELLANEOUS STATUTES

[Order 49, r 1 Access to Neighbouring Land Act 1992

(1)   In this rule, "the 1992 Act" means the Access to Neighbouring Land Act 1992, a section referred to by number means the section so numbered in the 1992 Act and expressions which are defined in the 1992 Act have the same meaning in this rule as they have in that Act.

(2)   An application for an access order under section 1 of the 1992 Act shall be made by originating application which shall be filed in the court for the district in which the dominant land is situated.

(3)   The application shall—
- (a)   identify the dominant land and the servient land and state whether the dominant land is or includes residential land;
- (b)   specify the works alleged to be necessary for the preservation of the whole or a part of the dominant land;
- (c)   state why entry upon the servient land is required and specify the area to which access is required by reference, if possible, to a plan annexed to the application;
- (d)   give the name of the person who will be carrying out the works if it is known at the time of the application;
- (e)   state the proposed date on which, or the dates between which, the works are to be started and their approximate duration, and
- (f)   state what (if any) provision has been made by way of insurance in the event of possible injury to persons or damage to property arising out of the proposed works.

(4)   The respondents shall be the owner and the occupier of the servient land and any respondent who wishes to be heard on the application shall file an answer within 14 days after the date of service of the application on him.

(5)   Order 24, rule 3 shall apply with the necessary modifications to service of the originating application under this rule.

(6)   The court may direct that notice of the application shall be given to any person who may be affected by the proposed entry and any such person may, within 14 days after service of the notice on him, apply to be made a respondent to the application.

(7)   The application may be heard and determined by the district judge and may, if the court thinks fit, be dealt with in chambers.]

Commencement   31 January 1993.

Amendments   Original Order 49, r 1 renumbered as Order 49, r 1A, and new Order 49, r 1 inserted, by SI 1992/3348, r 2.

Order 49, r [1A] Administration of Justice Act 1970

Any action by a mortgagee for possession of a dwelling-house, being an action to which section 36 of the Administration of Justice Act 1970 applies, shall be dealt with in chambers unless the court otherwise directs.

Commencement   1 September 1982.

Amendments   See the note to Order 49, r 1.

Order 49, r 2 Chancel Repairs Act 1932

(1)   A notice to repair under section 2 of the Chancel Repairs Act 1932 shall—
  (a) identify the responsible authority by whom it is given and the chancel alleged to be in need of repair;
  (b) state the repairs alleged to be necessary and the grounds on which the person to whom the notice is addressed is alleged to be liable to repair the chancel, and
  (c) call upon that person to put the chancel in proper repair,

and shall be served in accordance with Order 7, rule 1.

(2)   Proceedings to recover the sum required to put a chancel in proper repair shall be brought by action.

(3)   An application for the leave of the court under the proviso to subsection (2) of the said section 2 may be made in accordance with Order 13, rule 1.

(4)   If the court is satisfied that the defendant has a prima facie defence to the action on the merits, the court may, on an application made by the defendant in accordance with Order 13, rule 1, order the plaintiff to give security for the defendant's costs.

(5)   Where judgment is given for the payment of a sum of money in respect of repairs not yet executed, the court may order that the money be paid into court and dealt with in such manner as the court may direct for the purpose of ensuring that the money is spent in executing the repairs, but nothing in this paragraph shall prejudice a solicitor's lien for costs.

Commencement 1 September 1982.
Forms Notice to repair (N425).

Order 49, r 3 Companies Acts 1948 to [1981]

An application to a county court under the Companies Acts 1948 to [1981] shall be made by petition if a like application to the High Court would be made by petition.

Commencement 1 September 1982.
Amendments References to "1981" substituted by SI 1982/1140, r 7.
Cross references See RSC Order 102, r 4.

[Order 49, r 4 Consumer Credit Act 1974

(1)   In this rule "the Act" means the Consumer Credit Act 1974, a section referred to by number means the section so numbered in the Act and expressions which are defined in the Act have the same meaning in this rule as they have in the Act.

(2)   An action to recover possession of goods to which a regulated hire-purchase agreement relates shall be commenced in the court for the district in which the debtor resides or carries on business or resided or carried on business at the date when he last made a payment under the agreement.

(3)   Where in any action or matter relating to a regulated agreement the debtor or any surety has not been served with the originating process, the court may, on the ex parte application of the plaintiff made at or before the hearing of the action or matter, dispense with the requirement in section 141(5) that the debtor or surety, as the case may be, shall be made a party to the proceedings.

(4) Where an action or matter relating to a regulated agreement is brought by a person to whom a former creditor's rights and duties under the agreement have passed by assignment or by operation of law, the requirement in section 141(5) that all the parties to the agreement shall be made parties to the action shall not apply to the former creditor unless the court so directs.

(5) An application under section 129(1)(b) may be made by originating application and the application—

(a) shall be filed in the court for the district in which the applicant resides or carries on business; and

(b) shall state—

(i) the date of the agreement and the parties to it with the number of the agreement or sufficient particulars to enable the respondent to identify the agreement and details of any sureties;

(ii) if the respondent was not one of the original parties to the agreement, the name of the original party to the agreement;

(iii) the names and addresses of the persons intended to be served with the application;

(iv) the place where the agreement was signed by the applicant;

(v) details of the notice served by the respondent giving rise to the application;

(vi) the total unpaid balance admitted to be due under the agreement and the amount of any arrears (if known) together with the amount and frequency of the payments specified by the agreement;

(vii) the applicant's proposals as to payment of any arrears and of future instalments together with details of his means;

(viii) where the application relates to a breach of the agreement other than the non-payment of money, the applicant's proposals for remedying it.

(6) Any application under section 131 may be heard and determined by the judge or by the [district judge].

(7) In an action brought by the creditor to recover possession of goods comprised in an agreement to which section 90(1) applies, Order 9 shall have effect with the following modifications:—

(a) subject to sub-paragraph (b), rules 2 and 3(1) and 3(2) of the said Order shall apply, with the necessary modifications, in relation to a debtor who makes an offer as to conditions for the suspension of a return order under section 135(1)(b) as they apply in relation to a defendant in a default action who admits the whole or part of the plaintiff's claim and desires time for payment;

(b) where the plaintiff elects to accept such an offer as is mentioned in sub-paragraph (a) and a surety is a party to the action, judgment shall not be entered before the return day save with the consent of the surety;

(c) rule 4 of the said Order shall not apply where judgment is entered under rule 3(2) thereof;

(d) where such an offer as is mentioned in sub-paragraph (a) is made on the form appended to the summons but the plaintiff elects not to accept it, the court may, if the debtor does not attend on the return day, treat the form as evidence of the facts stated therein for the purposes of sections 129(2)(a) and 135(2).

(8) Where in relation to a regulated hire-purchase agreement the [district judge] has made a time order or an order for the return to the creditor of the goods suspended

under section 135(1)(b), any application under section 130(6), 133(6) or 135(4) may be heard and determined by the [district judge].

(9)   An application for an enforcement order may be made—
  (a) by originating application asking for leave to enforce the agreement in respect of which the order is sought, or
  (b) if, apart from the need to obtain an enforcement order, the creditor is entitled to payment of the money or possession of the goods or land to which the agreement relates, by fixed date action to recover the money, goods or land.

(10)   An originating application under paragraph (9)(a) and the particulars of claim in an action brought pursuant to paragraph (9)(b) shall state the circumstances rendering an enforcement order necessary.

(11)   Paragraph (9) shall apply to an order under section 86(2), 92(2) or 126 as it applies to an enforcement order, so however that in the case of an order under section 86(2) the personal representatives of the deceased debtor or hirer shall be made parties to the proceedings in which the order is sought, or, if no grant of representation has been made to his estate, the applicant shall, forthwith after commencing the proceedings, apply to the court for directions as to what persons, if any, shall be made parties to the proceedings as being affected or likely to be affected by the enforcement of the agreement.

(12)   Where by virtue of section 90(1) the creditor is not entitled to recover possession of the goods comprised in an agreement except on an order of the court, an application for such an order may be made only by action claiming possession of the goods.

(13)   An application for an order under section 92(1) entitling a creditor or owner to enter any premises to take possession of goods shall be made by originating application.

(14)   An application to a county court under section 139(1)(a) for a credit agreement to be reopened shall be made by originating application.

(15)   Where in any such proceedings in a county court as are mentioned in section 139(1)(b) or (c), the debtor or a surety desires to have a credit agreement reopened, he shall, within 14 days after the service of the originating process on him, give notice to that effect to the proper officer and to every other party to the proceedings and thereafter the debtor or surety, as the case may be, shall be treated as having delivered a defence or answer and accordingly, if the proceedings are a default action, no judgment shall be entered under Order 9, rule 6(1).]

Commencement   19 May 1985.
Amendments   This rule was substituted by SI 1985/566, r 7.
Cross references   See RSC Order 83.
Forms   Application for time order (N440).

[Order 49, r 4A Applications under section 114, 204 and 231 of the Copyright, Designs and Patents Act 1988

RSC Order 93, rule 24 shall apply with the necessary modifications to proceedings brought under sections 114(1), 204(1) and 231(1) of the Copyright, Designs and Patents Act 1988 in a county court.]

Commencement 1 November 1989.
Amendments This rule was inserted by SI 1989/1838, r 57.

Order 49, r 5 Fair Trading Act 1973

(1)   In this rule a section referred to by number means the section so numbered in the Fair Trading Act 1973 and "the Director" means the Director General of Fair Trading.

(2)   Proceedings in a county court under section 35, 38 or 40 shall be commenced by originating application.

(3)   The respondent shall file an answer.

(4)   Where in any proceedings under section 35 or 38 the Director intends to apply for a direction under section 40(2) that any order made against a body corporate (in this rule referred to as the "respondent body") which is a member of a group of interconnected bodies corporate shall be binding on all members of the group, he shall file notice of his intention together with as many copies of the originating application and of the notice as are required for the purposes of paragraph (5).

(5)   A copy of any notice under paragraph (4) shall be served on the respondent body and a copy of the notice together with a copy of the originating application and a notice of the return day shall be served on each of the bodies corporate specified in the notice under paragraph (4).

(6)   The respondent body may at any time serve on the Director a notice containing particulars of any interconnected body corporate not mentioned in a notice under paragraph (4).

(7)   With a view to deciding whether or in respect of which bodies notice should be given under paragraph (4) the Director may serve on the respondent body a notice requiring that body to give to him within 14 days after service of the notice particulars of any interconnected bodies corporate belonging to the same group as the respondent body and a copy of any such notice shall be filed.

(8)   An application under section 40(3) shall be made on notice to the respondent body and every interconnected body belonging to the same group.

Commencement 1 September 1982.

[Order 49, r 6 Housing Act 1988: assured tenancies

(1)   In this rule—
   "the 1988 Act" means the Housing Act 1988;
   "dwelling-house" has the same meaning as in Part I of the 1988 Act;
   a Ground referred to by number means the Ground so numbered in Schedule 2
       to the 1988 Act;
   "the requisite notice" means such a notice as is mentioned in any of those
       Grounds and
   "the relevant date" means the beginning of the tenancy.

(2)   This rule applies to proceedings brought by a landlord to recover possession of a dwelling-house which has been let on an assured tenancy in a case where all the conditions mentioned in paragraph (3) below are satisfied.

(3)   The conditions referred to in paragraph (2) are these.
   (a)   The tenancy and any agreement for the tenancy were entered into on or after 15th January 1989.
   (b)   The proceedings are brought
      (i)   on Ground 1 (landlord occupation),
      (ii)   on Ground 3 (former holiday occupation),
      (iii)   on Ground 4 (former student letting) or
      (iv)   on Ground 5 (occupation by a minister of religion).
   (c)   The only purpose of the proceedings is to recover possession of the dwelling-house and no other claim is made in the proceedings (such as for arrears of rent).
   (d)   The tenancy is an assured tenancy within the meaning of the 1988 Act (and consequently is not a protected, statutory or housing association tenancy under the Rent Act 1977) and
      (i)   is the subject of a written agreement, or
      (ii)   is on the same terms (though not necessarily as to rent) as a tenancy which was the subject of a written agreement and arises by virtue of section 5 of the 1988 Act, or
      (iii)   relates to the same or substantially the same premises which were let to the same tenant and is on the same terms (though not necessarily as to rent or duration) as a tenancy which was the subject of a written agreement.
      Where the tenancy in relation to which the proceedings are brought arises by virtue of section 5 of the 1988 Act but follows a tenancy which was the subject of an oral agreement, the condition mentioned in sub-paragraph (d)(ii) or (iii) above is not satisfied.
   (e)   The proceedings are brought against the tenant to whom the requisite notice was given.
   (f)   The tenant was given the requisite notice, not later than the relevant date.
   (g)   The tenant was given notice in accordance with section 8 of the 1988 Act that proceedings for possession would be brought.

(4)   Where the conditions mentioned in paragraph (3) of this rule are satisfied, the landlord may bring possession proceedings under this rule instead of making a claim in accordance with Order 6, rule 3 (action for recovery of land by summons).

(5)   The application must be made in the prescribed form and a copy of the application, with a copy for each defendant, must be filed in the court for the district in which the dwelling-house is situated.

(6)   The application shall include the following information and statements.
   (a)   A statement identifying the dwelling-house which is the subject matter of the proceedings.
   (b)   A statement identifying the nature of the tenancy, namely—
      (i)   whether it is the subject of a written agreement; or
      (ii)   whether the tenancy arises by virtue of section 5 of the 1988 Act, or
      (iii)   where it is the subject of an oral agreement whether the tenancy is periodic or for a fixed term and, if for a fixed term, the length of the term and the date of termination.
   (c)   A statement that the dwelling-house (or another dwelling-house) was not let to the tenant by the landlord (or any of his predecessors) before 15th January 1989.
   (d)   The date on which and the method by which the requisite notice was given to the tenant.

(e) A statement identifying the Ground on which possession is claimed giving sufficient particulars to substantiate the plaintiff's claim to be entitled to possession on that Ground.

(f) A statement that a notice was served on the tenant in accordance with section 8 of the 1988 Act,
   (i) specifying the date on which and the method by which the notice was served and
   (ii) confirming that the period of notice required by section 8 of the 1988 Act has been given.

(g) The amount of rent which is currently payable.

(7) Copies of the following documents shall be attached to the application—
   (i) the current (or most recent) written tenancy agreement,
   (ii) the requisite notice (referred to in paragraph (6)(d) above), and
   (iii) the notice served in accordance with section 8 of the 1988 Act,

together with any other documents necessary to prove the plaintiff's claim.

(8) The statements made in the application and any documents attached to the application shall be verified by the plaintiff on oath.

(9) Service of the application and of the attachments shall be effected by an officer of the court sending them by first-class post to the defendant at the address stated in the application and paragraphs (3) and (4) of Order 7, rule 10 (mode of service) and Order 7, rule 15 (service of summons for recovery of land) shall apply as they apply where service is effected under those rules.

(10) A defendant who wishes to oppose the plaintiff's application must, within 14 days after the service of the application on him, complete and deliver at the court office the form of reply which was attached to the application.

(11) On receipt of the defendant's reply the proper officer shall—
   (a) send a copy of it to the plaintiff;
   (b) refer the reply and the plaintiff's application to the judge,

and where a reply is received after the period mentioned in paragraph (10) but before a request is filed in accordance with paragraph (12) the reply shall be referred without delay to the judge.

(12) Where the period mentioned in paragraph (10) has expired without the defendant filing a reply, the plaintiff may file a written request for an order for possession and the proper officer shall without delay refer the plaintiff's application to the judge.

(13) After considering the application and the defendant's reply (if any), the judge shall either—
   (a) make an order for possession under paragraph (15) or
   (b) fix a day for a hearing under paragraph (14) and give directions regarding the steps to be taken before and at the hearing.

(14) The proper officer shall fix a day for the hearing of the application where the judge is not satisfied as to any of the following—
   (a) that the requisite notice was given before the relevant date,
   (b) that a notice was served in accordance with section 8 of the 1988 Act and that the time limits specified in the 1988 Act have been complied with,
   (c) that service of the application was duly effected, or
   (d) that the plaintiff has established that he is entitled to recover possession under the Ground relied on against the defendant.

(15) Except where paragraph (14) applies, the judge shall without delay make an order for possession without requiring the attendance of the parties.

(16) Where a hearing is fixed under paragraph (14)—
    (a) the proper officer shall give to all parties not less than 14 days' notice of the day so fixed;
    (b) the judge may give such directions regarding the steps to be taken before and at the hearing as may appear to him to be necessary or desirable.

(17) Without prejudice to Order 37, rule 3 (setting aside on failure of postal service), the court may, on application made on notice within 14 days of service of the order or of its own motion, set aside, vary or confirm any order made under paragraph (15).

(18) Without prejudice to Order 21, rule 5 and to Order 50, rule 3, a district judge shall have power to hear and determine an application to which this rule applies and references in this rule to the judge shall include references to the district judge.]

Commencement   1 November 1993.

Amendments   Original rule 6 revoked by SI 1985/566, r 8; new rule 6 inserted by SI 1992/793, r 11; that rule was renumbered as rule 7 and this rule was inserted by SI 1993/2175, r 18.

Forms   Application (N5A).

Reply (N11A).

Notice of issue/request (N206A).

Order (N26A).

[Order 49, r 6A Housing Act 1988: assured shorthold tenancies

(1) In this rule, "the 1988 Act" means the Housing Act 1988 and "dwelling-house" has the same meaning as in Part I of the 1988 Act.

(2) This rule applies to proceedings brought by a landlord under section 21 of the 1988 Act to recover possession of a dwelling-house let on an assured shorthold tenancy on the expiry or termination of that tenancy in a case where all the conditions mentioned in paragraph (3) below (or, as the case may be, paragraph (9)) are satisfied.

(3) The conditions referred to in paragraph (2) are these.
    (a) The tenancy and any agreement for the tenancy were entered into on or after 15th January 1989.
    (b) The only purpose of the proceedings is to recover possession of the dwelling-house and no other claim is made in the proceedings (such as for arrears of rent).
    (c) The tenancy—
       (i) was an assured shorthold tenancy and not a protected, statutory or housing association tenancy under the Rent Act 1977;
       (ii) did not immediately follow an assured tenancy which was not an assured shorthold tenancy;
       (iii) fulfilled the conditions mentioned in section 20(1)(a) to (c) of the 1988 Act, and
       (iv) was the subject of a written agreement.
    (d) A notice in writing was served on the tenant in accordance with section 20(2) of the 1988 Act and the proceedings are brought against the tenant on whom that notice was served.
    (e) A notice in accordance with section 21(1)(b) of the 1988 Act was given to the tenant in writing.

(4) Where the conditions mentioned in paragraph (3) or paragraph (9) of this rule are satisfied, the landlord may bring possession proceedings under this rule instead of making a claim in accordance with Order 6, rule 3 (action for recovery of land by summons).

(5) The application must be made in the prescribed form and a copy of the application, with a copy for each defendant, shall be filed in the court for the district in which the dwelling-house is situated.

(6) The application shall include the following information and statements.
    (a) A statement identifying the dwelling-house which is the subject matter of the proceedings.
    (b) A statement that the dwelling-house (or another dwelling-house) was not let to the tenant by the landlord (or any of his predecessors) before 15th January 1989.
    (c) A statement that possession is claimed on the expiry of an assured shorthold tenancy under section 21 of the 1988 Act giving sufficient particulars to substantiate the plaintiff's claim to be entitled to possession.
    (d) A statement that a written notice was served on the tenant in accordance with section 20(2) of the 1988 Act.
    (e) A statement that a notice in writing was given to the tenant in accordance with section 21(1) of the 1988 Act specifying the date on which, and the method by which, the notice was given.
    (f) In a case where the original fixed term tenancy has expired, a statement that no other assured tenancy is in existence other than an assured shorthold periodic tenancy (whether statutory or not).
    (g) A statement confirming that there is no power under the tenancy agreement for the landlord to determine the tenancy (within the meaning given for the purposes of Part I of the 1988 Act by section 45(4) of the 1988 Act) at a time earlier than six months from the beginning of the tenancy.
    (h) A statement that no notice under section 20(5) of the 1988 Act has been served.

(7) Copies of the following documents shall be attached to the application—
    (i) the written tenancy agreement (or, in a case to which paragraph (9) applies, the current (or most recent) written tenancy agreement),
    (ii) the written notice served in accordance with section 20(2) of the 1988 Act, and
    (iii) the notice in writing given in accordance with section 21 of the 1988 Act,

together with any other documents necessary to prove the plaintiff's claim.

(8) The statements made in the application and any documents attached to the application shall be verified by the plaintiff on oath.

(9) Where on the coming to an end of an assured shorthold tenancy (including a tenancy which was an assured shorthold but ceased to be assured before it came to an end) a new assured shorthold tenancy of the same or substantially the same premises (in this paragraph referred to as "the premises") comes into being under which the landlord and the tenant are the same as at the coming to an end of the earlier tenancy, then the provisions of this rule apply to that tenancy but with the following conditions instead of those in paragraph (3)—
    (a) The tenancy and any agreement for the tenancy were entered into on or after 15th January 1989.

(b) The only purpose of the proceedings is to recover possession of the dwelling-house and no other claim is made in the proceedings (such as for arrears of rent).

(c) The tenancy in relation to which the proceedings are brought—
   (i) is an assured shorthold tenancy within the meaning of section 20 of the 1988 Act and consequently is not a protected, statutory or housing association tenancy under the Rent Act 1977;
   (ii) did not immediately follow an assured tenancy which was not an assured shorthold tenancy, and
      (aa) is the subject of a written agreement, or
      (ab) is on the same terms (though not necessarily as to rent) as a tenancy which was the subject of a written agreement and arises by virtue of section 5 of the 1988 Act, or
      (ac) relates to the same or substantially the same premises which were let to the same tenant and is on the same terms (though not necessarily as to rent or duration) as a tenancy which was the subject of a written agreement.
   Where the tenancy in relation to which the proceedings are brought arises by virtue of section 5 of the 1988 Act but follows a tenancy which was the subject of an oral agreement, the conditions mentioned in sub-paragraph (c)(ii)(ab) or (ac) above is not satisfied.

(d) A written notice was served in accordance with section 20(2) of the 1988 Act on the tenant in relation to the first assured shorthold tenancy of the premises and the proceedings are brought against the tenant on whom that notice was served.

(e) A notice in writing was given to the tenant in accordance with section 21(4) of the 1988 Act.

(10) In a case to which paragraph (9) applies, the application shall include the following information and statements.

(a) A statement identifying the dwelling-house which is the subject matter of the proceedings.

(b) A statement identifying the nature of the tenancy, namely—
   (i) whether it is the subject of a written agreement;
   (ii) whether the tenancy arises by virtue of section 5 of the 1988 Act, or
   (iii) where it is the subject of an oral agreement whether the tenancy is periodic or for a fixed term and, if for a fixed term, the length of the term and date of termination.

(c) A statement that the dwelling-house (or another dwelling-house) was not let to the tenant by the landlord (or any of his predecessors) before 15th January 1989.

(d) A statement that possession is claimed under section 21 of the 1988 Act giving sufficient particulars to substantiate the plaintiff's claim to be entitled to possession.

(e) A statement that a written notice was served in accordance with section 20(2) of the 1988 Act in relation to the first assured shorthold tenancy of the premises on the tenant against whom the proceedings are brought.

(f) A statement that a notice in writing was given to the tenant in accordance with section 21(4) of the 1988 Act specifying the date on which, and the method by which, the notice was given.

(g) In a case where the tenancy is a fixed term tenancy which has expired, a statement that no other assured tenancy is in existence other than an assured shorthold periodic tenancy (whether statutory or not).

(h) A statement confirming that there was no power under the tenancy agreement for the landlord to determine (within the meaning given for the purposes of Part I of the 1988 Act by section 45(4) of the 1988 Act) the first assured shorthold tenancy of the premises to the tenant against whom the proceedings are brought at a time earlier than six months from the beginning of the tenancy.

(i) A statement that no notice under section 20(5) of the 1988 Act has been served.

(j) The amount of rent which is currently payable.

(11) Service of the application and of the attachments shall be effected by an officer of the court sending them by first-class post to the defendant at the address stated in the application and paragraphs (3) and (4) of Order 7, rule 10 (mode of service) and Order 7, rule 15 (service of summons for recovery of land) shall apply as they apply where service is effected under those rules.

(12) A defendant who wishes to oppose the plaintiff's application must, within 14 days after the service of the application on him, complete and deliver at the court office the form of reply which was attached to the application.

(13) On receipt of the defendant's reply the proper officer shall—
(a) send a copy of it to the plaintiff;
(b) refer the reply and the plaintiff's application to the judge

and where a reply is received after the period mentioned in paragraph (12) but before a request is filed in accordance with paragraph (14) the reply shall be referred without delay to the judge.

(14) Where the period mentioned in paragraph (12) has expired without the defendant filing a reply, the plaintiff may file a written request for an order for possession and the proper officer shall without delay refer any such request to the judge.

(15) After considering the application and the defendant's reply (if any), the judge shall either—
(a) make an order for possession under paragraph (17); or
(b) fix a day for a hearing under paragraph (16) and give directions regarding the steps to be taken before and at the hearing.

(16) The proper officer shall fix a day for the hearing of the application where the judge is not satisfied as to any of the following—
(a) that a written notice was served in accordance with section 20 of the 1988 Act,
(b) that a written notice was given in accordance with section 21 of the 1988 Act,
(c) that service of the application was duly effected, or
(d) that the plaintiff has established that he is entitled to recover possession under section 21 of the 1988 Act against the defendant.

(17) Except where paragraph (16) applies, the judge shall without delay make an order for possession without requiring the attendance of the parties.

(18) Where a hearing is fixed under paragraph (16)—
(a) the proper officer shall give to all parties not less than 14 days' notice of the day so fixed;
(b) the judge may give such directions regarding the steps to be taken before and at the hearing as may appear to him to be necessary or desirable.

(19) Without prejudice to Order 37, rule 3 (setting aside on failure of postal service), the court may, on application made on notice within 14 days of service of the order or of its own motion, set aside, vary or confirm any order made under paragraph (17).

(20) Without prejudice to Order 21, rule 5 and to Order 50, rule 3, a district judge shall have power to hear and determine an application to which this rule applies and references in this rule to the judge shall include references to the district judge.]

Commencement   1 November 1993.
Amendments   This rule was inserted by SI 1993/2175, r 18.
Forms   Application (N5A).
Reply (N11A).
Notice of issue/request (N206A).
Order (N26A).

[Order 49, r [7] Injunctions to prevent environmental harm: Town and Country Planning Act 1990 etc

(1)   An injunction under—
    (a)   section 187B or 214A of the Town and Country Planning Act 1990,
    (b)   section 44A of the Planning (Listed Buildings and Conservation Areas) Act 1990, or
    (c)   section 26AA of the Planning (Hazardous Substances) Act 1990,

may be granted against a person whose identity is unknown to the applicant; and in the following provisions of this rule such an injunction against such a person is referred to as "an injunction under paragraph (1)", and the person against whom it is sought is referred to as "the respondent".

(2)   An applicant for an injunction under paragraph (1) shall, instead of complying with Order 3, rule 4(2)(b), describe the respondent by reference to—
    (a)   a photograph,
    (b)   a thing belonging to or in the possession of the respondent, or
    (c)   any other evidence,

with sufficient particularity to enable service to be effected; and the form of originating application used shall be modified accordingly.

(3)   An applicant for an injunction under paragraph (1) shall, in addition to the documents referred to in Order 3, rule 4(3), also file evidence by affidavit—
    (a)   verifying that he was unable to ascertain, within the time reasonably available to him, the respondent's identity,
    (b)   setting out the action taken to ascertain the respondent's identity and
    (c)   verifying the means by which the respondent has been described in the originating application and that the description is the best that the applicant is able to provide.

(4)   Paragraph (2) is without prejudice to the power of the court to make an order for substituted service or dispensing with service.]

Commencement   1 June 1992 (para (1), in part); 1 April 1992 (remainder).
Amendments   Original rule 7 revoked by SI 1988/278, r 19; existing rule 6 (as inserted by SI 1992/793, r 11) renumbered as rule 7 by SI 1993/2175, r 18.

Order 49, r 8 Leasehold Reform Act 1967

(1)   In this rule a section referred to by number means the section so numbered in the Leasehold Reform Act 1967 and "Schedule 2" means Schedule 2 to that Act.

(2)   Where a tenant of a house and premises desires to pay money into court pursuant to section 11(4) or section 13(1) or (3)—
    (a)   he shall file in the office of the appropriate court an affidavit stating—
        (i)   the reasons for the payment into court,
        (ii)   the house and premises to which the payment relates and the name and address of the landlord, and
        (iii)   so far as they are known to the tenant, the name and address of every person who is or may be interested in or entitled to the money;
    (b)   on the filing of the affidavit the tenant shall pay the money into court and the proper officer shall enter the matter in the records of the court and send notice of the payment to the landlord and to every person whose name and address are given in the affidavit pursuant to sub-paragraph (a)(iii);
    (c)   any subsequent payment into court by the landlord pursuant to section 11(4) shall be made to the credit of the same account as the payment into court by the tenant and sub-paragraphs (a) and (b) shall apply as if for the references to the tenant and the landlord there were substituted references to the landlord and the tenant respectively;
    (d)   the appropriate court for the purposes of sub-paragraph (a) shall be the court for the district in which the property is situated or, if the payment into court is made by reason of a notice under section 13(3), any other county court specified in the notice.

(3)   Where the proceedings on an application are ordered to be transferred to a leasehold valuation tribunal under section 21(3), the proper officer shall—
    (a)   send notice of the transfer to all parties to the application and
    (b)   send to the leasehold valuation tribunal copies certified by the [district judge] of all entries in the records of the court relating to the application, together with the order of transfer and all documents filed in the proceedings.

(4)   Where an application is made under section 17 or 18 for an order for possession of a house and premises the respondent shall—
    (a)   forthwith after being served with the application, serve on every person in occupation of the property or part of it under an immediate or derivative sub-tenancy, a notice informing him of the proceedings and of his right under paragraph 3(4) of Schedule 2 to appear and be heard in the proceedings with the leave of the court, and
    (b)   within 14 days after being served with the application, file an answer stating the grounds, if any, on which he intends to oppose the application and giving particulars of every such sub-tenancy.

Commencement   1 September 1982.
Forms   Notice to respondent (N8(4)).
Notice of proceedings (N426).

[Order 49, r 9 Leasehold Reform, Housing and Urban Development Act 1993

(1)   In this rule—
    (a)   "the 1993 Act" means the Leasehold Reform, Housing and Urban Development Act 1993;

(b) a section or Schedule referred to by number means the section or Schedule so numbered in the 1993 Act; and

(c) expressions used in this rule have the same meaning as they have in the 1993 Act.

(2) Where an application is made under section 23(1) by a person other than the reversioner—

(a) on the issue of the application, the applicant shall send a copy of the application to the reversioner;

(b) the applicant shall promptly inform the reversioner either—

(i) of the court's decision; or

(ii) that the application has been withdrawn.

(3) Where an application is made under section 26(1) or (2) or section 50(1) or (2)—

(a) the application shall be made ex parte to the district judge, who may grant or refuse it or give directions for its future conduct, including the joinder as respondents of such persons as appear to have an interest in it; and

(b) the provisions of Order 3, rule 4(4)(b), (6) and (7) shall not apply.

(4) Where an application is made under section 26(3)—

(a) the applicants shall serve notice of the application on any person who they know or have reason to believe is a relevant landlord, giving particulars of the application and the return date and informing that person of his right to be joined as a party to the proceedings;

(b) the landlord whom it is sought to appoint as the reversioner shall be a respondent to the application, and shall file an answer;

(c) a person on whom notice is served under sub-paragraph (a) shall be joined as a respondent to the proceedings when he gives notice in writing to the proper officer of his wish so to be joined, and the proper officer shall notify all other parties of the joinder.

(5) Where a person wishes to pay money into court under section 27(3), section 51(3) or paragraph 4 of Schedule 8, rule 8(2) shall apply as it applies to payments into court made under the Leasehold Reform Act 1967, subject to the following modifications—

(a) references in rule 8 to the payment of money into court by a tenant shall be construed as references to the person or persons making a payment into court under the 1993 Act;

(b) the reference in rule 8(2)(a)(ii) to "house and premises" shall be construed as a reference to the interest or interests in the premises to which the payment into court relates, or, where the payment into court is made under section 51(3), to the flat to which it relates;

(c) the affidavit filed by the tenant under rule 8(2)(a) shall include details of any vesting order; and

(d) the appropriate court for the purposes of that sub-paragraph shall be—

(i) where a vesting order has been made, the court which made the vesting order; or

(ii) where no such order has been made, the court in whose district the premises are situated.

(6) Where an order is made under section 91(4), rule 8(3) (transfer to leasehold valuation tribunal) shall apply as it applies on the making of an order under section 21(3) of the Leasehold Reform Act 1967.

(7) Where a relevant landlord acts independently under Schedule 1, paragraph 7, he shall be entitled to require any party to proceedings under the 1993 Act (as

described in paragraph 7(1)(b) of Schedule 1) to supply him, on payment of the reasonable costs of copying, with copies of all documents which that party has served on the other parties to the proceedings.]

Commencement 17 January 1994.
Amendments Original rule 9 revoked by SI 1983/1716, r 12; new rule 9 inserted by SI 1993/3273, r 6.

Order 49, r 10 [Local Government Finance Act 1982]

(1) In this rule a section referred to by number means the section so numbered in the [Local Government Finance Act 1982].

(2) Proceedings in a county court [under section 19 or section 20] shall be commenced in the court for the district in which the principal office of the body to whose accounts the application relates (in this rule referred to as "the body concerned") is situated.

(3) An originating application for a declaration under [section 19(1)] shall state the facts on which the applicant intends to rely at the hearing of the application and the respondents to the application shall be the body concerned and any person against whom an order is sought under [section 19(2)].

(4) An appeal under [section 19(4) or section 20(3)] against a decision of [an auditor] shall be brought within 28 days of the receipt by the appellant of the [auditor's] statement of the reasons for his decision.

(5) The request for entry of an appeal to which paragraph (4) relates shall state—
    (a) the reasons stated by the [auditor] for his decision;
    (b) the date on which the appellant received the [auditor's] statement;
    (c) the facts on which the appellant intends to rely at the hearing of the appeal; and
    (d) in the case of a decision not to apply for a declaration, such facts within the appellant's knowledge as will enable the court to consider whether to exercise the powers conferred on it by [section 19(2)].

(6) The respondents to the appeal shall be:—
    (i) the [auditor] who for the time being has responsibility for the audit of the accounts of the body concerned;
    (ii) the body concerned; and
    (iii) in the case of an appeal against a decision not to certify under [section 20(1)] that a sum or amount is due from any person, that person.

(7) Without prejudice to its powers under Order 15, the court may at any stage of an application or appeal [under section 19 or section 20] direct that any officer or member of the body concerned be joined as a respondent.

Commencement 1 September 1982.
Amendments Rule heading: substituted by SI 1985/566, r 12(1).
Paras (1)–(7): words in square brackets substituted by SI 1985/566, rr 12, 13.

Order 49, r 11 Local Government (Miscellaneous Provisions) Act 1976

A person who appeals against a notice under section 21, 23 or 35 of the Local Government (Miscellaneous Provisions) Act 1976 shall state in his notice of appeal the grounds of the appeal and where one of those grounds is that it would have been fairer to serve the notice on another person or, as the case may be, that it would be reasonable for the whole or part of the expenses to which the notice relates to be paid by some other person, that person shall be made a respondent to the appeal, unless the court on the ex parte application of the appellant otherwise directs.

Commencement 1 September 1982.

Order 49, r 12 [Mental Health Act 1983]

(1) In this rule—

a section referred to by number means the section so numbered in the [Mental Health Act 1983] and "[Part II]" means [Part II] of that Act;

"place of residence" means, in relation to a patient who is receiving treatment as an in-patient in a hospital or other institution, that hospital or institution;

"hospital authority" means the managers of a hospital as defined in [section 145(1)].

(2) An application to a county court under [Part II] shall be made by originating application filed in the court for the district in which the patient's place of residence is situated or, in the case of an application made under [section 30] for the discharge or variation of an order made under [section 29], in that court or in the court which made the order.

(3) Where an application is made under [section 29] for an order that the functions of the nearest relative of the patient shall be exercisable by some other person—

(a) the nearest relative shall be made a respondent to the application unless the application is made on the ground set out in subsection (3)(a) of the said section or the court otherwise orders, and

(b) the court may order that any other person, not being the patient, shall be made a respondent.

(4) On the hearing of the application the court may accept as evidence of the facts stated therein any report made by a medical practitioner and any report made in the course of his official duties by—

(a) a probation officer, or

(b) an officer of a local authority or of a voluntary organisation exercising statutory functions on behalf of a local authority, or

(c) an officer of a hospital authority;

Provided that the respondent shall be told the substance of any part of the report bearing on his fitness or conduct which the judge considers to be material for the fair determination of the application.

(5) Unless otherwise ordered, an application under [Part II] shall be heard and determined in chambers.

(6) For the purpose of determining the application the judge may interview the patient either in the presence of or separately from the parties and either at the court or elsewhere, or may direct the [district judge] to interview the patient and report to the judge in writing.

Commencement 1 September 1982.
Amendments Rule heading: substituted by SI 1985/566, r 12(1).
Paras (1)–(3), (5): words in square brackets substituted by SI 1983/1716, r 13, Schedule.

[Order 49, r 13 Mobile Homes Act 1983

(1)   An application—
- (a)   under section 1 or 2 of the Mobile Homes Act 1983; or
- (b)   pursuant to paragraph 4, 5 or 6 of Part I of Schedule 1 to that Act; or
- (c)   with respect to any question arising under paragraph 8(1) or 9 of the same Part of that Schedule,

shall be made by originating application and the respondent shall file an answer.

(2)   Any application to which paragraph 1(b) applies may include an application for an order enforcing the rights mentioned in section 3(1)(b) of the Caravan Sites Act 1968.

(3)   Any application to which this rule applies may be heard and determined by the [district judge] and may, if the court thinks fit, be dealt with in chambers.]

Commencement   12 December 1983.
Amendments   This rule was substituted by SI 1983/1716, r 8.

Order 49, r 14   *(revoked by SI 1989/236)*

Order 49, r 15 Post Office Act 1969

(1)   An application under section 30(5) of the Post Office Act 1969 for leave to bring proceedings in the name of the sender or addressee of a postal packet or his personal representatives shall be made by originating application.

(2)   The respondents to the application shall be the Post Office and the person in whose name the applicant seeks to bring proceedings.

Commencement   1 September 1982.
Cross references   See RSC Order 77, r 17.

Order 49, r 16 Rentcharges Act 1977

Where for the purposes of section 9 of the Rentcharges Act 1977 the sum required to redeem a rentcharge is to be paid into the county court, it shall be paid into the court for the district in which the land affected by the rentcharge or any part thereof is situated.

Commencement   1 September 1982.

Order 49, r 17 Sex Discrimination Act 1975 and Race Relations Act 1976

(1)   In this rule—
- (a)   "the Act of 1975" and "the Act of 1976" mean respectively the Sex Discrimination Act 1975 and the Race Relations Act 1976;
- (b)   in relation to proceedings under either of those Acts expressions which are used in the Act concerned have the same meanings in this rule as they have in that Act;
- (c)   in relation to proceedings under the Act of 1976 "court" means a designated county court and "district" means the district assigned to such a court for the purposes of that Act.

(2)   A plaintiff who brings an action under section 66 of the Act of 1975 or section 57

of the Act of 1976 shall forthwith give notice to the Commission of the commencement of the proceedings and file a copy of the notice.

(3) Order 13, rule 11, shall have effect in relation to an assessor who is to be summoned in proceedings under section 66(1) of the Act of 1975, subject to the following modifications:—

> (a) whether or not the assessor is to be summoned pursuant to an application by one of the parties, paragraphs (4) and (8) of the said rule 11 shall be omitted;
> (b) paragraph (2) of the said rule 11 shall have effect where the judge decides to exercise his power to appoint an assessor without an application being made in that behalf as it has effect where the judge grants such an application.

(4) Proceedings under section 66, 71 or 72 of the Act of 1975 or section 57, 62 or 63 of the Act of 1976 may be commenced—

> (a) in the court for the district in which the defendant resides or carries on business, or
> (b) in the court for the district in which the act or any of the acts in respect of which the proceedings are brought took place.

(5) An appeal under section 68 of the Act of 1975 or section 59 of the Act of 1976 against a requirement of a non-discrimination notice shall be brought in the court for the district in which the acts to which the requirements relates were done.

(6) Where the plaintiff in any action alleging discrimination has questioned the defendant under section 74 of the Act of 1975 or section 66 of the Act of 1976—

> (a) either party may apply to the court under Order 13, rule 1, to determine whether the question or any reply is admissible under that section, and
> (b) Order 13, rule 5, shall apply to the question and any answer as it applies to any particulars of claim or defence.

(7) Where in any action the Commission claim a charge for expenses incurred by them in providing the plaintiff with assistance under section 75 of the Act of 1975 or section 66 of the Act of 1976—

> (a) the Commission shall, within 14 days after the determination of the action, give notice of the claim to the proper officer and the plaintiff and thereafter no money paid into court for the benefit of the plaintiff, so far as it relates to any costs or expenses, shall be paid out except in pursuance of an order of the court, and
> (b) the court may order the expenses incurred by the Commission to be taxed or assessed as if they were costs payable by the plaintiff to his own solicitor for work done in connection with the proceedings.

(8) Where an application is made for the removal or modification of any term of a contract to which section 77(2) of the Act of 1975 or section 72(2) of the Act of 1976 applies, all persons affected shall be made respondents to the application, unless in any particular case the court otherwise directs, and the proceedings may be commenced—

> (a) in the court for the district in which the respondent or any of the respondents resides or carries on business, or
> (b) in the court for the district in which the contract was made.

Commencement 1 September 1982.

Order 49, r 18 Solicitors Act 1974

Any application under Part III of the Solicitors Act 1974 may be heard and determined by the [district judge] and may, if the court thinks fit, be dealt with in chambers.

Commencement 1 September 1982.

[Order 49, r 18A Telecommunications Act 1984

(1)   Order 13, rule 11, shall have effect in relation to an assessor who is to be summoned in proceedings under paragraph 5 of Schedule 2 to the Telecommunications Act 1984 as if the judge had granted an application by the operator for the assessor to be summoned.

(2)   Any report made by the assessor pursuant to sub-paragraph (6)(a) of the said paragraph 5 shall be filed by the assessor, together with a copy for each party to the proceedings, and thereupon the proper officer shall send a copy to each party and shall, if the proceedings have not been adjourned to a day named, fix a day for the hearing and give notice thereof to all parties.]

Commencement 19 May 1985.
Amendments This rule was inserted by SI 1985/566, r 14.

[Order 49, r 18B Applications under section 58C of the Trade Marks Act 1938

RSC Order 100, rule 2(7) and (8) shall apply with the necessary modifications to proceedings brought under section 58C(1) of the Trade Marks Act 1938 in a county court.]

Commencement 1 November 1989.
Amendments This rule was inserted by SI 1989/1838, r 58.

Order 49, r 19 Trade Union Act 1913

(1)   Where a complainant desires to have an order of the Certification Officer under section 3 of the Trade Union Act 1913 recorded in the county court, he shall produce the order and a copy thereof to the proper officer of the court for the district in which he resides or the head or main office of the trade union is situate.

(2)   The order shall be recorded by filing it, and the copy shall be sealed and dated and returned to the complainant.

(3)   The sealed copy shall be treated as if it were the plaint note in an action begun by the complainant.

(4)   The costs, if any, allowed for recording the order shall be recoverable as if they were payable under the order.

(5)   The order shall not be enforced until proof is given to the satisfaction of the court that the order has not been obeyed and, if the order is for payment of money, of the amount remaining unpaid.

Commencement 1 September 1982.

Order 49, r 20 Trustee Act 1925, s 63

(1)   Any person wishing to make a payment into court under section 63 of the Trustee Act 1925 shall make and file in the office of the appropriate court an affidavit setting out—

(a) a brief description of the trust and of the instrument creating it or, as the case may be, of the circumstances in which the trust arose;

(b) so far as known to him, the names and addresses of the persons interested in or entitled to the money or securities to be paid into court;

(c) his submission to answer all such inquiries relating to the application of such money or securities as the court may make or direct;

(d) his place of residence, and

(e) an address where he may be served with any notice or application relating to such money or securities.

(2)   The appropriate court for the purposes of paragraph (1) shall be the court for the district in which the person or any of the persons making the payment into court resides.

(3)   The costs incurred in the payment into court shall be taxed and the amount of the taxed costs may be retained by the person making the payment into court.

(4)   The [district judge] may require, in addition to the affidavit, such evidence as he thinks proper with regard to the matter in respect of which the payment into court is made.

(5)   On the making of the payment into court the proper officer shall send notice thereof to each person mentioned in the affidavit pursuant to paragraph (1)(b).

(6)   An application for the investment or payment out of court of any money or securities paid into court under paragraph (1) may be made ex parte but on the hearing of the application the court may require notice to be served on such person as it thinks fit and fix a day for the further hearing.

(7)   No affidavit in support of the application shall be necessary in the first instance but the court may direct evidence to be adduced in such manner as it thinks fit.

(8)   The application may be heard and determined by the [district judge].

(9)   Paragraphs (6) to (8) are without prejudice to any provision of the County Court Funds Rules enabling or requiring the court to transfer money from a deposit to an investment account of its own motion.

Commencement 1 September 1982.
Forms Affidavit on payment in under Trustee Act 1925, s 63 (N432).

ORDER 50
General Provisions

Order 50, r 1 Practice directions

The Lord Chancellor may issue directions for the purpose of securing uniformity of practice in the county courts.

Commencement 1 September 1982.

Order 50, r 2 Powers of [district judge] when exercising his jurisdiction

(1)   Where the [district judge] is authorised by or under any Act or these rules to hear and determine any action or matter or to deal with any proceedings or to exercise any other jurisdiction, he shall, within the limits of that authority and subject to any right of appeal to or review by the judge, have all the powers of the judge.

(2)   Nothing in this rule shall authorise the [district judge] to commit any person to prison.

Commencement 1 September 1982.

Order 50, r 3 Distribution of business between judge and [district judge]

(1)   Where by or under any Act or these rules any jurisdiction or power may be exercised either by the judge or by the [district judge], its exercise by the [district judge] shall be subject to any arrangements made by the judge for the proper distribution of business between himself and the [district judge].

(2)   Where by or under any Act or these rules the leave of the judge is required for the exercise of any jurisdiction or power by the [district judge], such leave may be either general or special.

(3)   Where any proceedings are listed for hearing by the [district judge], he may refer to the judge any matter which he thinks should properly be decided by the judge and the judge may either dispose of the matter or refer it back to the [district judge] with such directions as he thinks fit.

Commencement 1 September 1982.

Order 50, r 4 Notices

Every notice required by these rules shall be in writing unless the court authorises it to be given orally.

Commencement 1 September 1982.

[Order 50, r 4A Preparation of documents

(1)   Without prejudice to Order 3, rule 3(1A), where by or under these rules a document is to be prepared by the court, that document may, if the proper officer so allows, be prepared by the plaintiff and, where a document is so produced—

(a) the plaintiff shall not be required also to file a request (provided that where by or under these rules a certificate as to any particular matter is to be given in the request the relevant information shall be given in the document produced to the court);

(b) the plaintiff shall provide a sufficient number of copies of the document for the court's use.

(2) Nothing in this rule shall—

(a) require the proper officer to accept a document which is illegible, has not been duly authorised or is for some other reason unsatisfactory;

(b) apply to documents to which Order 25, rule 5(3) (reissue of enforcement proceedings), Order 25, rule 8(5)(b) (reissue of warrant where condition upon which warrant was suspended not complied with) or Order 28, rule 11(1) (issue of warrant of committal) apply.

(3) In this rule "plaintiff" includes an applicant and a judgment creditor (within the meaning of Order 25, rule 1).]

Commencement 1 July 1991.
Amendments This rule was inserted by SI 1991/1126, r 27.
Cross references RSC Order 66, r 2.

Order 50, r 5 Change of solicitor etc

(1) Where a party to an action or matter for whom a solicitor has acted desires to change his solicitor, he or the new solicitor shall give notice of the change to the proper officer[, to the former solicitor,] and to every other party to the proceedings, stating the new solicitor's address for service, and unless and until such notice is given the former solicitor shall, subject to paragraph (5), be considered the solicitor of the party until the final conclusion of the action or matter.

[(1A) A notice to the proper officer under paragraph (1) or (3) shall contain a certificate by the party or his new solicitor that notice has also been given to the former solicitor and to every other party.]

(2) Where a party, after having sued or defended in person, appoints a solicitor to act on his behalf in the action or matter, except as advocate at the trial, he or the solicitor shall give notice of the appointment to the proper officer and to every other party to the proceedings, stating the solicitor's address for service.

(3) Where a party, after having sued or defended by a solicitor, intends to act in person, he shall give notice of his intention to the proper officer[, to the former solicitor,] and to every other party to the proceedings, stating the address for service of the party giving the notice.

(4) Where a solicitor who has acted for a party in an action or matter has ceased to act and no notice has been given of a change of solicitor or of the party's intention to act in person, the solicitor may apply to the court, on notice to the party for whom he has acted, for an order declaring that he has ceased to be the solicitor acting for that party in the action or matter, and a copy of any such order shall be served by the proper officer on every party to the action or matter; but unless and until the solicitor has obtained such an order and a copy has been served as aforesaid, he shall, subject to paragraph (5), be considered the solicitor of the party until the final conclusion of the action or matter.

(5)   Notwithstanding anything in this rule, where the certificate of an assisted person within the meaning of the [Civil Legal Aid (General) Regulations 1989] is revoked or discharged, the solicitor who acted for the assisted person shall cease to be the solicitor acting in the action or matter as soon as his retainer is determined under [regulation 83] of the said Regulations; and if the assisted person desires to proceed with the action or matter without legal aid and appoints that solicitor or another solicitor to act on his behalf, paragraph (2) shall apply as if that party had previously sued or defended in person.

Commencement   1 October 1991 (para (1A)); 1 September 1982 (remainder).
Amendments   Paras (1), (3): words ", to the former solicitor," added by SI 1991/1882, r 13(1).
Para (1A): added by SI 1991/1882, r 13(2).
Para (5): words "Civil Legal Aid (General) Regulations 1989" and "regulation 83" substituted by SI 1993/3273, r 8.
Cross references   See RSC Order 67, rr 1, 3, 4–6, 8.
Forms   Notice of change (N434, RSC PF144).
Notice of intention to act in person(RSC PF146).
Summons to remove solicitor from record (RSC PF147).
Order to remove solicitor from record (RSC PF148).

Order 50, r 6 Signing of pleadings settled by counsel

Every pleading or other document settled by counsel for the purpose of proceedings in a county court shall be signed by him and his name shall appear on every copy of the document used in the proceedings.

Commencement   1 September 1982.
Cross references   RSC Order 18, r 6(5).

[Order 50, r 6A Signature of documents by mechanical means

Where by or under these rules any document is required to bear a person's signature, that requirement shall be deemed to be satisfied if that person's name is printed by computer or other mechanical means.]

Commencement   1 December 1989.
Amendments   This rule was inserted by SI 1989/1838, r 53.

Order 50, r 7 Proper officer's obligations to be subject to payment of court fees

Any obligation imposed by these rules on the proper officer of a county court to do any act at the instance of a party to any proceeding in the court shall be subject to the payment of any fee required by a fees order to be paid on the proceeding.

Commencement   1 September 1982.

Order 50, r 8 Expense of advertisement

The expense of any advertisement in proceedings in a county court shall be borne in the first instance by such party as the court may direct and, if the advertisement is to be inserted by the proper officer, shall be paid before the advertisement is inserted.

Commencement   1 September 1982.

Order 50, r 9 Security for costs

Where by or under any Act or rule any person is required or authorised to give security for costs in relation to proceedings in a county court, then, subject to any express provision, the security shall be given in such manner, at such time and on such terms, if any, as the court may direct.

Commencement 1 September 1982.
Cross references RSC Order 23, r 2.

[Order 50, r 9A Misdirected documents

Where the defendant delivers to the plaintiff any document which by or under these rules is to be delivered to the court, the plaintiff shall forthwith file the document in the court office.]

Commencement 1 July 1991.
Amendments This rule was inserted by SI 1991/1126, r 37.

[Order 50, r [9B] Official shorthand note

RSC Order 68, rules 1(1) and (2), 2 and 8 shall apply to proceedings in a county court trial centre as they apply to proceedings in the High Court, but which the substitution for the words in rule 1(1) "unless the judge otherwise directs" of the words "if the judge so directs".]

Commencement 1 July 1991.
Amendments This rule was inserted as rule 9A by SI 1991/1328, r 12; it was subsequently renumbered as rule 9B by SI 1991/1882, r 12.

Order 50, r 10 Supply of documents from court records

(1)   Subject to payment of the prescribed fee, any party to proceedings in a county court may, on written application, be supplied from the records of the court with a copy of any document relating to those proceedings, but the proper officer may, before supplying a duplicate of any plaint note or other document issued to a party, require him to satisfy the [district judge], by affidavit or otherwise, of the loss or destruction of the document.

(2)   Without prejudice to Order 22, rule 8, no other person shall be supplied with a copy of any document from the records of the court except with the leave of the [district judge].

(3)   In this rule any reference to supplying a copy of a document includes examining a copy prepared by the applicant and marking it as an office copy.

Commencement 1 September 1982.

Order 50, r 11 Impounded documents

Documents impounded by order of the court shall not be delivered out of the custody of the court or inspected, except on an order made by the judge or, if the [district judge] ordered the document to be impounded, by the [district judge]:

Provided that where a Law Officer or the Director of Public Prosecutions makes a written request in that behalf, documents so impounded shall be delivered into his custody.

Commencement 1 September 1982.

Order 50, r 12 Payment out of small estate

Where a person entitled to a fund in court or a share of such a fund dies intestate and the court is satisfied that no grant of representation of his estate has been made and that the assets of his estate, including the fund or share, do not exceed in value the amount specified in any order for the time being in force under section 6 of the Administration of Estates (Small Payments) Act 1965 the court may order that the fund or share shall be paid, transferred or delivered to the person who, being a widower, widow, child, father, mother, brother or sister of the deceased, would be entitled to a grant of administration of the estate of the deceased.

Commencement 1 September 1982.

ORDER 51
REVOCATIONS AND TRANSITIONAL PROVISIONS

Order 51, r 1 Revocations *(revokes SR & O 1936/626)*

Order 51, r 2 Transitional Provisions

(1) These rules shall apply, so far as practicable, to any proceedings pending in a county court on the day on which these rules come into force and, where their application is excluded by virtue of the foregoing provision, the rules in force immediately before that day shall continue to apply to such proceedings.

(2) Nothing in paragraph (1) shall be taken as prejudicing the operation of the provisions of the Interpretation Act 1978 as respects the effect of repeals.

Commencement 1 September 1982.

APPENDIX A

HIGHER SCALES OF COSTS

(Order 38, rule 3(1))

		[Scale 1 *£* *100–3,000]*
Item *No*		

PART I
PREPARATION OF DOCUMENTS

The following items shall not apply to any action or matter to which Part II applies

1   *Institution of Proceedings:* Preparing, issuing, filing and service of particulars of claim or originating application, petition, or request for entry of appeal to a county court, or particulars of counterclaim, or third-party notice; preparing preliminary act or pleading in Admiralty action.   [7.75–31.50]

     Note 1   Except where item 14 or Note 2 below applies, no profit charges for service of any process are to be allowed.

     Note 2   Where a solicitor properly makes use of a process server, the process server's charges are to be shown as a disbursement.

2   *Interlocutory proceedings:* Preparing, issuing, filing and service of any documents in connection with interlocutory proceedings, including any application or notice of application or notice of interlocutory appeal.   [7.75–30.20]

     Note 1   This item applies to an arbitration, inquiry or reference.

     Note 2   Interpleader proceedings are to be treated as an application to which this item refers.

3   *Other Documents:* Preparing (including where necessary filing, serving or delivering to all parties) any document not otherwise provided for, including—

     (a)   any document to obtain an order for substituted service;

     (b)   pleadings (other than pleadings instituting proceedings), defence or counterclaim thereto, particulars of pleadings, requests for such particulars, interrogatories, affidavits and lists of documents, notice to produce, admit or inspect documents, and amendments to any documents;

     (c)   any other affidavit;

     (d)   any brief to counsel or case to counsel to advise in writing or in conference;

     (e)   any instructions to counsel to settle any document except where an allowance for the preparation of that document is recoverable under item 1, 2 or 3—

		[*Scale 1*
Item		£
No		*100–3,000*]

for first five A4 pages,	[5.45 per page (or proportionately)]
for each A4 page thereafter	[3.60 per page (or proportionately)]

Note 1 Items 1, 2, and 3 include engrossing and one copy for service and are only to be allowed where the document is signed by the solicitor or his clerk duly authorised in that behalf. Any additional copies required are to be charged under item 4. Item 3(d) and (e) include copy for counsel where counsel's fee is allowed. Preparation of proofs of evidence is to be charged under item 6 and not this item.

Note 2 Item 3 is not to be allowed for preparing a request for summons etc or a notice of acceptance or non-acceptance of an admission and proposal as to time of payment.

4   *Copy documents:*

(a)   Typed top copy—

A5 (quarto)	[0.70 per page]
A4 (foolscap)	[1.10 per page]
A3 (brief)	[1.50 per page]

(b)   Photographic, printed and carbon copies—

A5 and A4	[0.23 per page]
A3	[0.43 per page]

Note 1 Where the construction of documents is in issue, the costs of copies supplied for the use of the judge are to be allowed.

Note 2 Copy documents required to be exhibited to an affidavit are to be charged under item 4 and the collating time is to be charged under item 6, note 2(a)(ix).

PART II

5   BLOCK ALLOWANCE

In any action for damages for personal injuries, or for the cost of repairs to collision-damaged vehicles, and in any other action or matter as the party entitled to receive the costs may elect, a block allowance shall be made in place of the items prescribed in Part I unless, in any such case, the taxing officer otherwise directs.   [13.00–82.40]

Note 1 No profit charges for service of any process are to be allowed except (a) where item 14 applies or (b) where a solicitor properly makes use of a process server, in which case the process server's charges are to be shown as a disbursement.

Item
No

Note 2 In an action (other than one relating to personal injuries or collision-damage) where a party has elected to insert a block allowance, no application may be made on taxation for an allowance in excess of the permitted maximum.

Note 3 If an action for damages for personal injuries or for collision-damage is of such unusual weight that the block allowance would be wholly inappropriate, an application should be made to the taxing officer for leave to deliver an extended bill. This application may generally be made ex parte, and before the bill is drawn, by letter setting out the grounds, although the taxing officer may require the applicant to attend him before giving his decision. The lodging of a bill in extended form will in itself be accepted as an application for leave but there is no right of election in personal injuries and collision-damage cases and, should leave be refused, no extra costs will be allowed on taxation for drawing the rejected bill. Leave will normally be granted only where it is clearly shown that there are unusual circumstances which would make the use of the block allowance wholly inappropriate or unfair.

Note 4 In cases other than for personal injuries or collision-damage the lodging of a bill which includes a block allowance will generally be taken as a sufficient election. Since the taxing officer may of his own motion refuse to accept the election, with or without affording the elector the right to be heard, a preliminary application may, if so desired, be made to him ex parte by letter in any case of real doubt or difficulty.

PART III

6   PREPARATION FOR TRIAL

Instructions for trial or hearing of action or matter, whatever the mode of trial or hearing, or for the hearing of any appeal.

[such sum as is fair and reasonable not exceeding £1180]

Note 1 This item applies to an to an arbitration, inquiry or reference, but may only be allowed once in the same proceedings.

Note 2 This item is intended to cover—

(a)   the doing of any work not otherwise provided for and which was properly done in preparing for a trial, hearing or appeal, or before a settlement of the matters in dispute, including—

Item
No

(i) *The Client:* taking instruction to sue, defend, counterclaim, appeal or oppose etc; attending upon and corresponding with client;

(ii) *Witnesses:* interviewing and corresponding with witnesses and potential witnesses, taking and preparing proofs of evidence and, where appropriate, arranging attendance at court, including issue of witness summons;

(iii) *Expert evidence:* obtaining and considering reports or advice from experts and plans, photographs and models; where appropriate arranging their attendance at court, including issue of witness summons;

(iv) *Inspections:* inspecting any property or place material to the proceedings;

(v) *Searches and inquiries:* making searches in the Public Record Office and elsewhere for relevant documents; searches in the Companies Registration Office and similar matters;

(vi) *Special damages:* obtaining details of special damages and making or obtaining any relevant calculations;

(vii) *Other parties:* attending upon and corresponding with other parties or their solicitors;

(viii) *Discovery:* perusing, considering or collating documents for affidavit or list of documents; attending to inspect or produce for inspection any documents required to be produced or inspected by order of the court or otherwise;

(ix) *Documents:* consideration of pleadings, affidavits, cases and instructions to and advice from counsel, any law involved and any other relevant documents, including collating;

(x) *Negotiations:* work done in connection with negotiations with a view to settlement;

(xi) *Agency:* correspondence with and attendance upon or other work done by London or other agents;

(xii) *Notices:* preparation and service of miscellaneous notices, including notices to witnesses to attend court;

(b) the general care and conduct of the proceedings.

The sums sought under each sub-paragraph (i) to (xii) of paragraph (a) should be shown separately against each item followed by the total of all items under paragraph (a); the sum charged under paragraph (b) should be shown separately; and the total of the items under (a) and (b) should then follow.

Note 3 This item should be prefaced by a brief narrative indicating the issues, the status of the fee earners concerned and the expense rates claimed. The narrative should be followed by a statement in two parts—

(i) setting out the breakdown of the work done in relation to the relevant sub-paragraph of note 2(a); and

(ii) a statement in relation to care and conduct under note 2(b) referring to the relevant factors relied upon; the sum claimed for care and conduct should be expressed as a separate monetary amount as well as a percentage of the work figure.

Note 4 Telephone calls will be allowed as a time charge if, but only if, they stand in the place of an attendance whereby material progress has been made and the time has been recorded or can otherwise be established. A notional conversion into a time charge of letters and routine telephone calls will not be accepted.

Note 5 Where an action is settled before delivery of the brief, the costs of all work reasonably and properly (but not prematurely) done are allowable, and the taxing officer, having regard to the circumstances of each case, must decide whether the work was reasonable and proper and that the time for doing it had arrived.

Note to Parts III, IV and VI. Where in the opinion of the taxing officer, it would have been reasonable to employ a solicitor carrying on business nearer to any relevant place, he shall not allow under Parts III, IV and VI more than he would have allowed to such a solicitor.

PART IV
ATTENDANCES

7   *Lodging:* To lodge papers, when proceedings transferred to county court, including preparation of all necessary documents.   [7.75]

8   *Counsel:* Attending counsel in conference including attending to appoint the conference, for each half hour or part thereof.   [13.00]

	[Scale 1
Item	£
No	100–3,000]

9   *Interlocutory attendances etc.* Attending at court, or in
chambers, on an interlocutory or any other application
to judge or [district judge] in the course of or relating to
the proceedings including time travelling thereto—   [not exceeding

(a)   without counsel   95.00

(b)   with counsel   7.75–24.75]

Note 1 This term applies to further consideration
pursuant to Order 23, rule 3.

Note 2 This item applies to an arbitration, inquiry or
reference.

Note 3 Interpleader proceedings are to be treated as an
application to which this item refers.

10   *Examination:* On examination of witness under Order 25,
rule 3, or RSC Order 26, rule 5, as applied by Order 14,
rule 11, for each half-hour or part thereof.   [4.00–12.50]

Note. This item is allowable where any responsible
representative of the solicitor attends.

11   *Trial or hearing:* Attending the trial or hearing, or
hearing of an appeal from an interlocutory or final order
or judgment, or to hear a deferred judgment, or where
trial is adjourned for want of time on payment of costs
of the day, including time travelling thereto, per day or
part of a day   [not exceeding

(a)   without [counsel]   140.00

(b)   with counsel   7.75–69.50]

Note 1 An attendance on the examination of a witness
under Order 20, rule 13, is to be treated as an
attendance to which this item relates.

Note 2 This item applies to an arbitration, inquiry or
reference. If the reference or inquiry was
directed at the trial and began on the same day,
this item is only to be allowed once in respect of
that day.

Note to Part IV: Attendances in court or at chambers or
on counsel in conference should appear with a note of
the time engaged.

PART V
COUNSEL'S FEES

12   (a)   With brief on trial or on hearing   [33–272]

(b)   Where the trial or hearing is continued after the
first day or is adjourned for want of time, or on payment
of costs of the day or on examination of witness under
Order 20, rule 13, for each day or part of a day   [16.50–137]

Item	*[Scale 1*
No	*£*
	100–3,000]

(c) With brief on further consideration pursuant to Order 23, rule 3, or to hear a deferred judgment; with brief on application in the course of or relating to proceedings; with brief on examination of witness under Order 25, rule 3, or RSC Order 26, rule 5, as applied by Order 14, rule 11; with brief on hearing of judgment summons [or application for attachment of earnings order].   [13.00–67]

(d) Where there is no local Bar in the court town or within [40 kilometres] thereof, if in the opinion of the [district judge] the maximum fee allowable with the brief is insufficient, a further fee may be allowed, not exceeding for each day on which the trial or hearing takes place   [24.00]

Note 1 For the purpose of this sub-item there shall be deemed to be a local Bar only in such places as may from time to time be specified in a certificate of the General Council of the Bar published in their Annual Statement.

Note 2 This sub-item is not allowed in any court within [40 kilometres] of Charing Cross.

(e) On conference in chambers or elsewhere: for each half-hour or part thereof   [13.00]

and for leading counsel: [21.00]

(f) For settling any document including particulars of claim, defence, interrogatories and answer.   [7.70–34.00]

(g) For advising in writing including advising on liability and quantum   [4.70–40.75]

Note 3 Fees to counsel are not to be allowed unless the payment of them is vouched by the signature of counsel or the head of chambers.

Note 4 This item applies to an arbitration, inquiry or reference, but a fee reflecting preparation for trial is only to be allowed once in the same proceedings. If the reference or inquiry was directed at the trial and the reference or inquiry began on the same day, a fee for attending court or attending in chambers is only to be allowed once in respect of that day.

[(h) For advising in writing on liability, quantum and evidence   [8.75–67.50]]

PART VI
TAXATION OF COSTS

13   (a) *Taxation.* Preparing bill of costs and copies and attending to lodge; attending taxation; vouching and completing bill; paying taxing fee and lodging certificate or order   [9.00–67.50]

*Item
No*

(b) *Review.* Preparing and delivering objections to decision of taxing officer on taxation, or any answers to objections, including copies for service and lodging, considering opponent's objections or answers, if any; preparing for and attending hearing of review.

[9.00–24.25]

Note: This item includes travelling time.

PART VII
SERVICE OUT OF THE JURISDICTION

14 Service of process out of England and Wales, to include drawing, copying, attending to swear and file all affidavits and to obtain order and the fees paid for oaths, such sum as the [district judge] thinks reasonable.

Commencement 1 September 1982.
Amendments Sums in column 3 substituted by SI 1992/793, r 6.
Item 11: word "counsel" substituted by SI 1982/1140, r 2.
Item 12: in para (c) words "or application for attachment of earnings order" inserted by SI 1982/1794, r 13; in para (d), words "40 kilometres" substituted by SI 1991/1882, r 2(2); in note 2 thereto words "40 kilometres" substituted by SI 1991/1882, r 2(2); para (h) inserted by SI 1988/897, r 5.

APPENDIX B

FIXED COSTS

(Order 38, rule 18)

PART I

[DEFAULT AND FIXED DATE SUMMONSES AND GARNISHEE SUMMONSES]

Directions

1   The Tables in this Part of this Appendix show the amount to be entered on the summons (or garnishee order nisi) in respect of solicitors' charges—

    (a)   in an action for the recovery of a debt or liquidated demand (other than a rent action), for the purpose only of Order 11, rule 2(2) or 3(4), [Order 19, rule 4], and Part II of this Appendix; or

    (b)   in garnishee proceedings, for the purpose only of Order 30, rule 4, or

    (c)   in an action for the recovery of property, including land, with or without a claim for a sum of money, for the purpose of Part II of this Appendix or of fixing the amount which the plaintiff may receive in respect of solicitors' charges without taxation in the event of the defendant giving up possession and paying the amount claimed, if any, and costs; or

    (d)   ...

2   In addition to the amount entered in accordance with the relevant Table the appropriate court fees shall be entered on the summons.

3   In the Tables the expression "claim" means—

    (a)   the sum of money claimed, or

    (b)   in relation to an action for the recovery of land (with or without a claim for a sum of money), a sum exceeding £600 but not exceeding £2,000;

    (c)   in relation to an action for the recovery of property other than money or land, the value of the property claimed or, in the case of goods supplied under a hire-purchase agreement, the unpaid balance of the [total price].

4   The Tables do not apply where the summons is to be served out of England and Wales or where substituted service is ordered.

[TABLES OF FIXED COSTS

TABLE I
Where claim exceeds £25 but does not exceed £250

		Amount of charges
		£
(a)	Where service is not by solicitor	£24.75
(b)	Where service is by solicitor	£28.00

TABLE II
Where claim exceeds £250 but does not exceed £600

		Amount of charges £
(a)	Where service is not by solicitor	£33.00
(b)	Where service is by solicitor	£39.00

TABLE III
Where claim exceeds £600 but does not exceed £2,000

		Amount of charges £
(a)	Where service is not by solicitor	£56.00
(b)	Where service is by solicitor	£62.00

TABLE IV
Where claim exceeds £2,000

		Amount of charges £
(a)	Where service is not by solicitor	£61.00
(b)	Where service is by solicitor	£66.00]

Commencement 1 September 1982.
Amendments Part heading: substituted by SI 1982/1140, r 2.
Para 1: in sub-para (a) words "Order 19, rule 4" substituted by SI 1992/1965, r 16(d); sub-para (d) revoked by SI 1993/2175, r 17.
Para 3: words "total price" substituted by SI 1985/566, r 9.
Para 4: tables I–IV substituted by SI 1992/793, r 7.

PART II

JUDGMENTS

Directions

Where an amount in respect of solicitors' charges has been entered on the summons under Part I of this Appendix and judgment is entered or given in the circumstances mentioned in one of the paragraphs in column 1 of the following Table, the amount to be included in the judgment in respect of the plaintiff's solicitors' charges shall, subject to Order 38, rule 3(4), be the amount entered on the summons together with the amount shown in column 2 of the Table under the sum of money by reference to which the amount entered on the summons was fixed.

Where judgment is entered or given for a sum less than the amount claimed or for the delivery of goods of which the value or the balance of the [total price] is a sum less than the amount claimed, the foregoing paragraph shall, unless the court otherwise directs, have effect as if the amount entered on the summons had been fixed by reference to that sum.

[*Fixed Costs On Judgments*

	Column 2		
	Sum of Money		
Column 1	A *Exceeding* £25 *but not* *exceeding* £600	B *Exceeding* £600 *but not* *exceeding* £3,000	C *Exceeding* £3,000
	£	£	£
(a) Where judgment is entered in a default action in default of defence...	[8.75]	[16.50]	[18.25]
(b) Where judgment is entered on the defendant's admission and the plaintiff's acceptance of his proposal as to mode of payment	[15.50]	[32.50]	[38.00]
(c) Where judgment is entered on an admission delivered by the defendant and the court's decision is given as to the date of payment or instalments by which payment is to be made.................................	[21.00]	[41.50]	[49.00]

(d) Where judgment is given in a fixed date action for:—
 	
   (i) delivery of goods, or
 	
   (ii) possession of land suspended on payment of arrears of rent, whether claimed or not, in addition to current rent
 	
and the defendant has neither delivered a defence, admission or counter-claim, nor otherwise denied liability..
	[31.00]	[46.00]	[57.00]

	Exceeding £500 *but not exceeding* *£3,000*		*Exceeding £3,000*
(e) Where summary judgment is given under Order 9, rule 14..	[71.50]		[82.00]]

Commencement   1 September 1982.
Amendments   Words "total price" substituted by SI 1985/566, r 9.
Table: substituted by SI 1989/381, r 6; sums in column 2 substituted by SI 1992/793, r 8.

PART III

MISCELLANEOUS PROCEEDINGS

The following Table shows the amount to be allowed in respect of solicitors' charges in the circumstances mentioned.

	Amount to be allowed £
1 For making or opposing an application in the course of or relating to the proceedings where the costs are on lower scale.........	[10.00]
2 For making or opposing an application for a rehearing or to set aside a judgment where the costs are on lower scale........................	[10.00]
3 For filing a request for the issue of a warrant of execution for a sum exceeding £25..	[1.75]
4 For service of any document required to be served personally (other than an application for an attachment of earnings order or a judgment summons unless allowed under Order 27, rule 9(1)(a), or Order 28, rule 10(2)(a)(i)), including copy and preparation of certificate of service	[6.75]
5 For substituted service, including attendances, making appointments to serve summons, preparing and attending to swear and file affidavits and to obtain order, and the fees paid for oaths.....	[20.00]
6 For each attendance on the hearing of an application for an attachment of earnings order or a judgment summons where costs are allowed under Order 27, rule 9, or Order 28, rule 10..................	[6.75]
7 For the costs of the judgment creditor when allowed in garnishee proceedings or an application under Order 30, rule 12—	
[(a) where the money recovered [is less than £70.00]..........	[one half of the amount recovered]
[(b) where the money recovered [is not less than £70.00] ...	[£37.50]
8 For the costs of the judgment creditor when allowed on an application for a charging order..	[57.00]
9 For obtaining . . . a certificate of judgment [where costs allowed under Order 35, rule 5(3)(d)]...	[6.40]
[10 Where an order for possession is made under rule 6 or rule 6A of Order 49 without the attendance of the plaintiff, for preparing and filing the application, the documents attached to the application and the request for possession; the court fee to be allowed in addition as a disbursement	£64.00]

Commencement   1 September 1982.
Amendments   Items 1–6: sums in column 2 substituted by SI 1992/793, r 9.
Item 7: sub-paras (a), (b) and sums in column 2 substituted by SI 1992/793, r 9.
Item 9: in column 1 words omitted revoked and words "where costs allowed under Order 35, rule 5(3)(d)" substituted, by SI 1985/1269, r 12; sum in column 2 substituted by SI 1992/793, r 9.
Item 10: inserted by SI 1993/2175, r 19.

APPENDIX C

ASSESSMENT OF COSTS

(Order 38, r 19)

Directions

1   The following Table shows the amount which, pursuant to Order 38, rule 19, may be allowed where costs are to be assessed without taxation. The amount includes the fee for counsel where applicable.

2   In addition to the amount shown in the Table there may be allowed, where appropriate—
   (i)   court fees,
   (ii)   allowances to witnesses.

[*Column 1* *Scale 1*	*Column 2* *Amount of charges*
Lower Scale	46.00–71.50
£100–500	51.50–130.00
£500–3000	80.50–488.00]

Commencement   1 September 1982.
Amendments   Para (2): table substituted by SI 1992/793, r 10.

Table of amending Statutory Instruments

Rules of the Supreme Court

SI No

1966/559	Rules of the Supreme Court (Amendment) 1966
1966/1055	Rules of the Supreme Court (Amendment No 2) 1966
1966/1514	Rules of the Supreme Court (Amendment No 3) 1966
1967/829	Rules of the Supreme Court (Amendment No 1) 1967
1967/1809	Rules of the Supreme Court (Amendment No 2) 1967
1968/1244	Rules of the Supreme Court (Amendment No 1) 1968
1969/1105	Rules of the Supreme Court (Amendment) 1969
1969/1894	Rules of the Supreme Court (Amendment No 2) 1969
1970/671	Rules of the Supreme Court (Amendment) 1970
1970/944	Rules of the Supreme Court (Amendment No 2) 1970
1970/1208	Rules of the Supreme Court (Amendment No 3) 1970
1970/1861	Rules of the Supreme Court (Amendment No 4) 1970
1971/354	Rules of the Supreme Court (Amendment) 1971
1971/835	Rules of the Supreme Court (Amendment No 2) 1971
1971/1132	Rules of the Supreme Court (Amendment No 3) 1971
1971/1269	Rules of the Supreme Court (Amendment No 4) 1971
1971/1955	Rules of the Supreme Court (Amendment No 5) 1971
1972/813	Rules of the Supreme Court (Amendment) 1972
1972/1194	Rules of the Supreme Court (Amendment No 2) 1972
1972/1898	Rules of the Supreme Court (Amendment No 3) 1972
1973/1384	Rules of the Supreme Court (Amendment) 1973
1973/2046	Rules of the Supreme Court (Amendment No 2) 1973
1974/295	Rules of the Supreme Court (Amendment) 1974
1974/1115	Rules of the Supreme Court (Amendment No 2) 1974
1974/1360	Rules of the Supreme Court (Amendment No 3) 1974
1975/128	Rules of the Supreme Court (Amendment) 1975
1975/911	Rules of the Supreme Court (Amendment No 2) 1975
1976/337	Rules of the Supreme Court (Amendment) 1976
1976/1196	Rules of the Supreme Court (Amendment No 2) 1976
1976/2097	Rules of the Supreme Court (Amendment No 3) 1976
1977/532	Rules of the Supreme Court (Amendment) 1977
1977/960	Rules of the Supreme Court (Amendment No 2) 1977
1977/1955	Rules of the Supreme Court (Amendment No 3) 1977
1978/251	Rules of the Supreme Court (Amendment) (Bail) 1978
1978/359	Rules of the Supreme Court (Amendment No 2) 1978
1978/579	Rules of the Supreme Court (Amendment No 3) 1978
1978/1066	Rules of the Supreme Court (Amendment No 4) 1978
1979/35	Rules of the Supreme Court (Amendment) 1979
1979/402	Rules of the Supreme Court (Amendment No 2) 1979
1979/552	Rules of the Supreme Court (Amendment No 3) 1979
1979/1542	Rules of the Supreme Court (Amendment No 4) 1979
1979/1716	Rules of the Supreme Court (Writ and Appearance) 1979
1979/1725	Rules of the Supreme Court (Amendment No 5) 1979
1980/629	Rules of the Supreme Court (Amendment) 1980

SI No

1980/1010	Rules of the Supreme Court (Amendment No 2) 1980
1980/1908	Rules of the Supreme Court (Amendment No 3) 1980
1980/2000	Rules of the Supreme Court (Amendment No 4) 1980)
1981/652	Rules of the Supreme Court (Amendment) 1981
1981/1734	Rules of the Supreme Court (Amendment No 2) 1981
1982/375	Rules of the Supreme Court (Amendment) 1982
1982/1111	Rules of the Supreme Court (Amendment No 2) 1982
1982/1786	Rules of the Supreme Court (Amendment No 3) 1982
1983/531	Rules of the Supreme Court (Amendment) 1983
1983/1181	Rules of the Supreme Court (Amendment No 2) 1983
1984/1051	Rules of the Supreme Court (Amendment) 1984
1985/69	Rules of the Supreme Court (Amendment) 1985
1985/846	Rules of the Supreme Court (Amendment No 2) 1985
1985/1277	Rules of the Supreme Court (Amendment No 3) 1985
1986/632	Rules of the Supreme Court (Amendment) 1986
1986/1187	Rules of the Supreme Court (Amendment No 2) 1986
1986/2001	Insolvency (Amendment of Subordinate Legislation) Order 1986
1986/2289	Rules of the Supreme Court (Amendment No 3) 1986
1987/1423	Rules of the Supreme Court (Amendment) 1987
1988/298	Rules of the Supreme Court (Amendment) 1988
1988/1340	Rules of the Supreme Court (Amendment No 2) 1988
1989/177	Rules of the Supreme Court (Amendment) 1989
1989/386	Rules of the Supreme Court (Amendment No 2) 1989
1989/1307	Rules of the Supreme Court (Amendment No 3) 1989
1989/2427	Rules of the Supreme Court (Amendment No 4) 1989
1990/492	Rules of the Supreme Court (Amendment) 1990
1990/1689	Rules of the Supreme Court (Amendment No 2) 1990
1990/2599	Rules of the Supreme Court (Amendment No 3) 1990
1991/531	Rules of the Supreme Court (Amendment) 1991
1991/1329	Rules of the Supreme Court (Amendment No 2) 1991
1991/1884	Rules of the Supreme Court (Amendment No 3) 1991
1991/2671	Rules of the Supreme Court (Amendment No 4) 1991
1991/2684	Solicitors' Incorporated Practices Order 1991
1992/638	Rules of the Supreme Court (Amendment) 1992
1992/1907	Rules of the Supreme Court (Amendment No 2) 1992
1993/2133	Rules of the Supreme Court (Amendment) 1993
1993/2760	Rules of the Supreme Court (Amendment No 2) 1993

County Court Rules

SI No

1982/436	County Court Rules 1981 (Amendment) Rules 1982
1982/1140	County Court Rules 1981 (Amendment No 2) Rules 1982
1982/1794	County Court Rules 1981 (Amendment No 3) Rules 1982
1983/275	County Court (Amendment) Rules 1983
1983/1716	County Court (Amendment No 2) Rules 1983
1984/576	County Court (Amendment) Rules 1984
1984/878	County Court (Amendment No 2) Rules 1984
1985/566	County Court (Amendment) Rules 1985
1985/1269	County Court (Amendment No 2) Rules 1985

SI No

1986/636	County Court (Amendment) Rules 1986
1986/1189	County Court (Amendment No 2) Rules 1986
1986/2001	Insolvency (Amendment of Subordinate Legislation) Order 1986
1987/493	County Court (Amendment) Rules 1987
1987/1397	County Court (Amendment No 2) Rules 1987
1988/278	County Court (Amendment) Rules 1988
1988/897	County Court (Amendment No 2) Rules 1988
1989/236	County Court (Amendment) Rules 1989
1989/381	County Court (Amendment No 2) Rules 1989
1989/1838	County Court (Amendment No 3) Rules 1989
1989/2426	County Court (Amendment No 4) Rules 1989
1990/526	County Court (Amendment) Rules 1990
1990/1495	County Court (Amendment No 2) Rules 1990
1990/1764	County Court (Amendment No 3) Rules 1990
1991/525	County Court (Amendment) Rules 1991
1991/1126	County Court (Amendment No 2) Rules 1991
1991/1328	County Court (Amendment No 3) Rules 1991
1991/1882	County Court (Amendment No 4) Rules 1991
1991/2684	Solicitors' Incorporated Practices Order 1991
1992/793	County Court (Amendment) Rules 1992
1992/1965	County Court (Amendment No 2) Rules 1992
1992/3348	County Court (Amendment No 3) Rules 1992
1993/711	County Court (Amendment) Rules 1993
1993/2150	County Court (Amendment No 2) Rules 1993
1993/2175	County Court (Amendment No 3) Rules 1993
1993/3273	County Court (Amendment No 4) Rules 1993
1994/306	County Court (Amendment) Rules 1994
1994/1288	County Court (Amendment No 2) Rules 1994